Developmental Psychology

Second Canadian Edition

Developmental Psychology
Childhood and Adolescence

David R. Shaffer
University of Georgia

Eileen Wood
Wilfrid Laurier University

Teena Willoughby
Brock University

THOMSON

NELSON

Australia   Canada   Mexico   Singapore   Spain   United Kingdom   United States

THOMSON

NELSON

Developmental Psychology:
Childhood and Adolescence,
Second Canadian Edition

by David R. Shaffer, Eileen Wood, and
Teena Willoughby

**Associate Vice-President,
Editorial Director:**
Evelyn Veitch

Publisher:
Joanna Cotton

Senior Marketing Manager:
Murray Moman

Senior Developmental Editor:
Edward Ikeda

Photo Researcher:
Cindy Howard

Permissions Coordinator:
Cindy Howard

Production Editor:
Carrie McGregor

Copy Editor:
Gail Marsden

Proofreader:
Erin Moore

Indexer:
Andrew Little

Senior Production Coordinator:
Hedy Sellers

Creative Director:
Angela Cluer

Interior Design:
Gary Head

Interior Design Modifications:
Katherine Strain

Cover Design:
Katherine Strain

Cover Image:
© Brad Wilson/Photonica

Compositor:
Susan Calverley

Printer:
Courier Corp.

National Library of Canada Cataloguing in Publication Data

Shaffer, David R. (David Reed), 1946-
Developmental psychology: childhood and adolescence / David R. Shaffer, Eileen Wood, Teena Willoughby. — 2nd Canadian ed.

Includes bibliographical references and index.
ISBN 0-17-641674-9

1. Child psychology. 2. Adolescent psychology. I. Wood, Eileen, II. Willoughby, Teena, III. Title.

BF721.S4688 2004   155.4
C2004-903313-1

Brief Contents

Part I   *Theory and Research in the Developmental Sciences*

Chapter 1   Introduction to Developmental Psychology and Its Research Strategies 1

Chapter 2   Theories of Human Development 37

Part II   *Foundations of Development*

Chapter 3   Hereditary Influences on Development 70

Chapter 4   Prenatal Development, Birth, and Newborns' Readiness for Life 108

Chapter 5   The Physical Self: Development of the Brain, the Body, and Motor Skills 149

Part III   *Language, Learning, and Cognitive Development*

Chapter 6   Early Cognitive Foundations: Sensation, Perception, and Learning 183

Chapter 7   Cognitive Development: Piaget's Theory, Case's Neo-Piagetian Theory, and Vygotsky's Sociocultural Viewpoint 221

Chapter 8   Cognitive Development: Information-Processing Perspectives and Connectionism 264

Chapter 9   Intelligence: Measuring Mental Performance 311

Chapter 10   Development of Language and Communication Skills 350

Part IV   *Social and Personality Development*

Chapter 11   Emotional Development and the Establishment of Intimate Relationships 391

Chapter 12   Development of the Self and Social Cognition 434

Chapter 13   Sex Differences and Similarities, Gender-Role Development, and Sexual Behaviour 473

Chapter 14   Aggression, Altruism, and Moral Development 515

Part V   *The Ecology of Development*

Chapter 15   The Family 563

Chapter 16   Extrafamilial Influences: Television, Computers, Schools, and Peers 605

Contents

Part I Theory and Research in the Developmental Sciences

Chapter 1 Introduction to Developmental Psychology and Its Research Strategies 1

What Is Development? 2
What Causes Us to Develop? 2
What Goals Do Developmentalists Pursue? 3
Some Basic Observations about the Character of Development 4

Human Development in Historical Perspective 6
Childhood in Premodern Times 6
Toward Modern-Day Views on Childhood 7
Box 1.1 *On the "Invention" of Adolescence 8*
Development of Children's Rights in Canada 9
Origins of a Science of Development 10

Research Methods in Developmental Psychology 11
The Scientific Method 11
Gathering Data: Basic Fact-Finding Strategies 12

Detecting Relationships: Correlational and Experimental Designs 19
The Correlational Design 19
The Experimental Design 20
Box 1.2 *Assessing Causal Relationships in the Real World: The Field Experiment 22*
The Natural (or Quasi-) Experiment 23

Designs for Studying Development 24
The Cross-Sectional Design 24
The Longitudinal Design 26
The Sequential Design 28

Cross-Cultural Comparisons 29
Box 1.3 *A Cross-Cultural Comparison of Gender Roles 30*

Ethical Considerations in Developmental Research 31

Postscript: On Becoming a Wise Consumer of Developmental Research 33

Summary 34

Key Terms 36

Chapter 2   Theories of Human Development 37

The Nature of Scientific Theories 37

Questions and Controversies about Human Development 39
The Nature/Nurture Issue 39
The Active/Passive Issue 39
The Continuity/Discontinuity Issue 40

The Psychoanalytic Viewpoint 41
Freud's Psychosexual Theory 41
■ **Box 2.1** *Where Do You Stand on Major Developmental Issues? 42*
Contributions and Criticisms of Freud's Theory 43
Erikson's Theory of Psychosocial Development 44
Contributions and Criticisms of Erikson's Theory 45
Psychoanalytic Theory Today 46

The Learning Viewpoint 46
Watson's Behaviourism 47
Skinner's Operant Learning Theory (Radical Behaviourism) 47
Bandura's Cognitive Social Learning Theory 48
■ **Box 2.2** *An Example of No-Trial (Observational) Learning without Reinforcement 49*
Social Learning as Reciprocal Determinism 50
Contributions and Criticisms of Learning Theories 50

The Cognitive-Developmental Viewpoint 52
Piaget's View of Intelligence and Intellectual Growth 52
Contributions and Criticisms of Piaget's Viewpoint 54
Vygotsky's Sociocultural Perspective 55
Contributions and Criticisms of Vygotsky's Viewpoint 55

The Information-Processing Viewpoint 56
Contributions and Criticisms of the Information-Processing Viewpoint 56
■ **Box 2.3** *Helping Children to Correct Their Mistakes: An Information-Processing Approach 57*

The Ethological (or Evolutionary) Viewpoint 58
Assumptions of Classical Ethology 58
Ethology and Human Development 59
Contributions and Criticisms of the Ethological Viewpoint 60
■ **Box 2.4** *Is Altruism Part of Human Nature? 61*

The Ecological Systems Viewpoint 62
Bronfenbrenner's Contexts for Development 62
Contributions and Criticisms of the Ecological Systems Theory 64

Theories and World Views 65

Summary 68

Key Terms 69

Part II   Foundations of Development

Chapter 3   Hereditary Influences on Development 70

Principles of Hereditary Transmission 70
The Genetic Code 71

Growth of the Zygote and Production of Body Cells 71

The Germ (or Sex) Cells 71

Multiple Births 73

Male or Female? 74

What Do Genes Do? 75

How Are Genes Expressed? 76

■ **Box 3.1** *Examples of Dominant and Recessive Traits in Human Heredity 77*

Chromosomal and Genetic Abnormalities 80

Chromosomal Abnormalities 81

Genetic Abnormalities 83

Applications: Genetic Counselling, Prenatal Detection, and Treatment of Hereditary Disorders 85

Genetic Counselling 85

Prenatal Detection of Hereditary Abnormalities 85

Treating Hereditary Disorders 87

Hereditary Influences on Behaviour 88

■ **Box 3.2** *Ethical Issues Surrounding Treatments for Hereditary Disorders 89*

Methods of Studying Hereditary Influences 89

Hereditary Influences on Intellectual Performance 93

Hereditary Contributions to Personality 94

■ **Box 3.3** *Some Common Misconceptions about Heritability Estimates 95*

Hereditary Contributions to Behaviour Disorders and Mental Illness 97

Heredity and Environment as Developmental Co-Conspirators 98

The Canalization Principle 98

The Range-of-Reaction Principle 99

Genotype/Environment Correlations 100

Contributions and Criticisms of the Behavioural Genetics Approach 103

■ **Box 3.4** *Need Parenting Be "Good" or Simply "Good Enough"? 104*

Summary 105

Key Terms 107

Chapter 4 **Prenatal Development, Birth, and Newborns' Readiness for Life 108**

From Conception to Birth 108

The Germinal Period 109

The Period of the Embryo 110

The Period of the Fetus 111

Environmental Influences on Prenatal Development 114

Teratogens 114

■ **Box 4.1** *Teratogenic Effects of Sexually Transmitted Diseases 118*

■ **Box 4.2** *Peter A. Fried 121*

Maternal Characteristics 124

Prevention of Birth Defects 126

Childbirth and the Perinatal Environment 127

The Birth Process 127

The Baby's Experience 127

Labour and Delivery Medication 130

Approaches to Childbirth in Canada and Around the World 130

The Social Environment Surrounding Birth 133

Birth Complications 135

Anoxia 135

Low Birth Weight 136

Reproductive Risk and Capacity for Recovery 139

The Newborn's Readiness for Life 140

Newborn Reflexes 140

Infant States 142

Developmental Changes in Infant States 142

■ Box 4.3 *Sudden Infant Death Syndrome 144*

Summary 147

Key Terms 148

Chapter 5   The Physical Self: Development of the Brain, the Body, and Motor Skills 149

An Overview of Maturation and Growth 150

Changes in Height and Weight 150

Changes in Body Proportions 150

Skeletal Development 151

Muscular Development 152

Variations in Physical Development 152

Development of the Brain 153

Neural Development and Plasticity 153

Brain Differentiation and Growth 155

■ Box 5.1 *Bryan Kolb 155*

Motor Development 158

Basic Trends in Locomotor Development 158

■ Box 5.2 *Cultural Variations in Motor Development 161*

Fine Motor Development 162

Psychological Implications of Early Motor Development 164

Beyond Infancy: Motor Development in Childhood and Adolescence 165

Puberty: The Physical Transition from Child to Adult 166

The Adolescent Growth Spurt 166

■ Box 5.3 *Sport Participation and Self-Esteem among Adolescent Females 167*

Sexual Maturation 167

The Psychological Effects of Puberty 169

General Reactions to Physical Changes 169

Social Impacts of Pubertal Changes 170

■ Box 5.4 *Morton and Beverley Mendelson 170*

Does Timing of Puberty Matter? 171

Causes and Correlates of Physical Development 173

Biological Mechanisms 173

Environmental Influences 175

■ Box 5.5 *Two Serious Eating Disorders of Adolescence 177*

Summary 180

Key Terms 182

Part III Language, Learning, and Cognitive Development

Chapter 6 Early Cognitive Foundations: Sensation, Perception, and Learning 183

Early Controversies about Sensory and Perceptual Development 184
> Nature versus Nurture 184
> Enrichment versus Differentiation 184

"Making Sense" of the Infant's Sensory and Perceptual Experiences 185
> The Preference Method 185
> The Habituation Method 185
> Evoked Potentials 186
> High-Amplitude Sucking 186

Infant Sensory Capabilities 187
> Vision 187
> Hearing 188
> Taste and Smell 190
> Touch, Temperature, and Pain 190

Visual Perception in Infancy 191
> Perception of Patterns and Forms 192
> ■ Box 6.1 *When Do Babies "Perceive" Faces? 194*
> ■ Box 6.2 *Daphne Maurer 196*
> Perception of Three-Dimensional Space 196
> ■ Box 6.3 *Size Constancy in Newborns 198*

Intermodal Perception 200
> Are the Senses Integrated at Birth? 201
> Development of Intermodal Perception 201
> Explaining Intermodal Perception 202

Infant Perception in Perspective—and a Look Ahead 203
> Perceptual Learning in Childhood: Gibson's Differentiation Theory 203
> ■ Box 6.4 *How Do We Learn to Read? 205*
> Cultural Influences on Perception 206

Basic Learning Processes 207
> Habituation: Early Evidence of Information Processing and Memory 207
> Classical Conditioning 208
> Operant (or Instrumental) Conditioning 210
> ■ Box 6.5 *Punishment: Cultural Ideals and Alternatives 214*
> Observational Learning 215

Reflections on Perception and Learning 217

Summary 219

Key Terms 220

Chapter 7   Cognitive Development: Piaget's Theory, Case's Neo-Piagetian Theory, and Vygotsky's Sociocultural Viewpoint 221

Piaget's Theory of Cognitive Development 222

What Is Intelligence? 222

Cognitive Schemes: The Structure of Intelligence 223

How We Gain Knowledge: Piaget's Cognitive Processes 224

Piaget's Stages of Cognitive Development 226

The Sensorimotor Stage (Birth to 2 Years) 226

■ **Box 7.1** *Why Infants Know More about Objects Than Piaget Assumed 230*

The Preoperational Stage (2 to 7 Years) 233

■ **Box 7.2** *Play Is Serious Business 235*

The Concrete-Operational Stage (7 to 11 Years) 241

The Formal-Operational Stage (11 to 12 Years and Beyond) 243

■ **Box 7.3** *Piaget on Education 243*

■ **Box 7.4** *Children's Responses to a Hypothetical Proposition 244*

An Evaluation of Piaget's Theory 248

Piaget's Contributions 248

Challenges to Piaget 249

Case's Neo-Piagetian Theory 251

■ **Box 7.5** *Robbie Case 252*

Vygotsky's Sociocultural Perspective 252

The Role of Culture in Intellectual Development 253

The Social Origins of Early Cognitive Competencies 254

■ **Box 7.6** *Working in the Zone of Proximal Development in Different Cultures 257*

The Role of Language in Cognitive Development 259

Vygotsky in Perspective: Summary and Evaluation 260

Summary 262

Key Terms 263

Chapter 8   Cognitive Development: Information-Processing Perspectives and Connectionism 264

Information Flow and the Multistore Model 265

Developmental Differences in Information-Processing Capacity 266

Development of the Store-Term Store 266

Changes in Processing Speed 267

Developmental Differences in "Software": Strategies and Knowledge of "Thinking" 268

Production and Utilization Deficiences 268

Multiple- and Variable-Strategy Use 269

What Children Know about Thinking 270

Implicit Cognition, or Thought Without Awareness 271

Fuzzy-Trace Theory: An Alternative Viewpoint 272

■ **Box 8.1** *Can Age Changes in Inhibition Account for Changes in Cognitive Development? 274*

The Development of Attention 275

Changes in Attention Span 275

Development of Planful Attentional Strategies 275

Selective Attention: Ignoring Information That is Clearly Irrelevant 276

What Do Children Know about Attention? 276

Memory: Retaining and Retrieving Information 277

The Development of Memory Strategies 277

■ **Box 8.2** *Attention Deficit-Hyperactivity Disorder 278*

The Development of Event and Autobiographical Memory 284

■ **Box 8.3** *What Happened to Our Early Childhood Memories? 285*

■ **Box 8.4** *Carole Peterson 286*

Children as Eyewitnesses 289

■ **Box 8.5** *Anne McKeough 290*

Problem Solving and Reasoning 292

Learning to Use Rules 292

Analogical Reasoning 294

The Development of Number and Arithmetic Skills 297

Counting and Arithmetic Strategies 298

■ **Box 8.6** *Jeff Bisanz 299*

Cultural Influences on Mathematics Performance 300

Evaluating the Information-Processing Perspective 303

■ **Box 8.7** *Some Educational Implications of Research on Attention and Memory 304*

Connectionist Approaches to Cognitive Development 305

The Origins of Connectionism 306

How Are Networks Created? 306

How Connectionist Networks Work 306

Connectionism and Development 307

■ **Box 8.8** *Tom Shultz 308*

Summary 308

Key Terms 310

Chapter 9   Intelligence: Measuring Mental Performance 311

What Is Intelligence? 312

Psychometric Views of Intelligence 312

A Modern Information-Processing Viewpoint 316

Gardner's Theory of Multiple Intelligences 318

How Is Intelligence Measured? 319

The Stanford-Binet Intelligence Scale 319

■ **Box 9.1** *Making American Tests Valid in Canada 320*

The Wechsler Scales 321

■ **Box 9.2** *Donald H. Saklofske 321*

Distribution of IQ Scores 322

Group Tests of Mental Performance 322

Newer Approaches to Intelligence Testing 323

Assessing Infant Intelligence 323

Stability of IQ in Childhood and Adolescence 324

What Do Intelligence Tests Predict? 326

IQ as a Predictor of Scholastic Achievement 326

IQ as a Predictor of Vocational Outcomes 327

IQ as a Predictor of Health, Adjustment, and Life Satisfaction 327

■ **Box 9.3** *Mental Retardation: A Closer Look 329*

Factors That Influence IQ Scores 329

The Evidence for Heredity 330

The Evidence for Environment 331

Social and Cultural Correlates of Intellectual Performance 332

Home Environment and IQ 332

Social Class, Racial, and Ethnic Differences in IQ 335

Why Do Groups Differ in Intellectual Performance? 336

Box 9.4 *A Threat in the Air: How Social Sterotypes Can Influence Intellectual Performance 338*

Improving Cognitive Performance through Compensatory Education 340

Long-Term Follow-Ups 341

The Importance of Parental Involvement 341

The Importance of Intervening Early 342

Box 9.5 *An Effective Compensatory Intervention for Families 342*

Creativity and Special Talents 344

What Is Creativity? 344

The Psychometric Perspective 344

The Multicomponent (or Confluence) Perspective 345

Summary 348

Key Terms 349

Chapter 10 Development of Language and Communication Skills 350

Five Components of Language 351

Phonology 351

Morphology 352

Semantics 352

Syntax 352

Pragmatics 352

Theories of Language Development 353

The Learning (or Empiricist) Perspective 353

The Nativist Perspective 354

Box 10.1 *On the "Invention" of Language by Children 357*

The Interactionist Perspective 358

Before Language: The Prelinguistic Period 361

Early Reactions to Speech 361

Producing Sounds: The Infant's Prelinguistic Vocalizations 362

What Do Prelinguistic Infants Know about Language and Communication? 363

One Word at a Time: The Holophrastic Period 365

Early Semantics: Building a Vocabulary 365

Box 10.2 *Janet Werker 366*

Attaching Meaning to Words 367

When a Word Is More Than a Word 371

From Holophrases to Simple Sentences: The Telegraphic Period 371

A Semantic Analysis of Telegraphic Speech 372

The Pragmatics of Early Speech 372

Box 10.3 *Learning a Gestural Language 373*

Language Learning during the Preschool Period 374

Grammatical Development 375

Semantic Development 377

Development of Pragmatics and Communication Skills 378

Language Learning during Middle Childhood and Adolescence 379

Later Syntactic Development 380

Semantics and Metalinguistic Awareness 380

Further Development of Communication Skills 381

Learning More Than One Language: Bilingualism 383

■ **Box 10.4** *Fred Genesee 386*

■ **Box 10.5** *Ellen Bialystok 387*

Summary 388

Key Terms 389

Part IV   Social and Personality Development

Chapter 11   Emotional Development and the Establishment of Intimate Relationships 391

An Overview of Emotional Development 392

Displaying Emotions: The Development (and Control) of Emotional Expressions 392

Recognizing and Interpreting Emotions 396

Emotions and Early Social Development 397

Temperament and Development 398

Hereditary and Environmental Influences on Temperament 399

Stability of Temperament 399

Early Temperamental Profiles and Later Development 400

What Are Emotional Attachments? 402

Reciprocal Relationships 402

■ **Box 11.1** *Is Shyness a Social Disadvantage? It Depends on One's Culture 403*

Establishment of Interactional Synchrony 403

How Do Infants Become Attached? 404

The Growth of Primary Attachments 404

Theories of Attachment 405

Two Attachment-Related Fears of Infancy 409

■ **Box 11.2** *Combatting Stranger Anxiety: Some Helpful Hints for Doctors and Child-Care Professionals 410*

Individual Differences in Attachment Quality 412

Assessing Attachment Security 412

Cultural Variations in Attachment Classifications 414

Factors That Influence Attachment Security 415

Quality of Caregiving 415

Infant Characteristics 418

■ **Box 11.3** *Fathers as Attachment Objects 419*

Attachment and Later Development 420

■ **Box 11.4** *On the Intricate Interplay between Caregiving and Temperament in Shaping Infant Attachments 420*

Long-Term Correlates of Secure and Insecure Attachments 421

Why Might Attachment Quality Forecast Later Outcomes? 421

The Unattached Infant 424

Effects of Social Deprivation in Infancy and Childhood 424

Why Is Early Deprivation Harmful? 425

■ Box 11.5 *Lucy Le Mare 426*

Can Children Recover from Early Deprivation Effects? 427

Maternal Employment, Child Care, and Early Emotional Development 428

Quality of Alternative Care 428

Parenting and Parents' Attitudes about Work 430

Summary 431

Key Terms 433

Chapter 12 Development of the Self and Social Cognition 434

Development of the Self-Concept 435

The Emerging Self: Differentiation and Self-Recognition 435

Who Am I? Responses of Preschool Children 439

Children's Theory of Mind and Emergence of the Private Self 439

■ Box 12.1 *Chris Moore 440*

■ Box 12.2 *Is Theory of Mind Biologically Programmed? 442*

Conceptions of Self in Middle Childhood and Adolescence 443

■ Box 12.3 *Cultural Influences on the Self-Concept 445*

Self-Esteem: The Evaluative Component of Self 446

Origins and Development of Self-Esteem 446

■ Box 12.4 *Adolescent Suicide: The Tragic Destruction of Self 449*

Social Contributors to Self-Esteem 450

Development of Achievement Motivation and Academic Self-Concept 451

Early Origins of Achievement Motivation 451

Achievement Motivation during Middle Childhood and Adolescence 452

Beyond Achievement Motivation: Development of Achievement-Related Attributions 455

Who Am I to Be? Forging an Identity 459

Developmental Trends in Identity Formation 460

How Painful Is Identity Formation? 461

Influences on Identity Formation 461

The Other Side of Social Cognition: Knowing about Others 463

Age Trends in Person Perception 463

■ Box 12.5 *Ethnic Categorization and Prejudice in Young Children 464*

Theories of Social-Cognitive Development 465

Summary 470

Key Terms 472

Chapter 13 Sex Differences and Similarities, Gender-Role Development, and Sexual Behaviour 473

Categorizing Males and Females: Gender-Role Standards 474

Some Facts and Fictions about Sex Differences 474

Actual Psychological Differences between the Sexes 476

■ Box 13.1 *What Traits Characterize Males and Females? 476*

Cultural Myths 479

■ **Box 13.2** *Do Gender Stereotypes Colour Children's Interpretations of Counterstereotypic Information? 480*

Do Cultural Myths Contribute to Sex Differences in Ability (and Vocational Opportunity)? 481

Developmental Trends in Gender Typing 482

Development of the Gender Concept 483

Development of Gender-Role Stereotypes 484

■ **Box 13.3** *Lisa Serbin 484*

Development of Gender-Typed Behaviour 486

Theories of Gender Typing and Gender-Role Development 489

Money and Ehrhardt's Biosocial Theory 489

■ **Box 13.4** *Is Biology Destiny? 494*

Freud's Psychoanalytic Theory 495

Social Learning Theory 495

Kohlberg's Cognitive-Developmental Theory 497

Gender Schema Theory 498

An Integrative Theory 500

Psychological Androgyny: A Prescription for the Future? 501

Do Androgynous People Really Exist? 502

Are There Advantages to Being Androgynous? 502

Applications: On Changing Gender-Role Attitudes and Behaviour 503

■ **Box 13.5** *Combatting Gender Stereotypes with Cognitive Interventions 505*

Adolescent Sexuality 506

Cultural Influences on Sexuality 506

Sexual Attitudes and Behaviour 507

■ **Box 13.6** *On Sexual Orientation and the Origins of Homosexuality 508*

Personal and Social Consequences of Adolescent Sexual Activity 509

■ **Box 13.7** *Combatting Sexually Transmitted Diseases 511*

Summary 513

Key Terms 514

Chapter 14 Aggression, Altruism, and Moral Development 515

The Development of Aggression 516

Origins of Aggression in Infancy 516

Developmental Trends in Aggression 517

■ **Box 14.1** *How Girls Are More Aggressive Than Boys 519*

■ **Box 14.2** *Richard E. Tremblay 520*

Individual Differences in Aggressive Behaviour 520

Cultural and Subcultural Influences on Aggression 523

■ **Box 14.3** *Debra Pepler 523*

Coercive Home Environments: Breeding Grounds for Aggression and Delinquency 525

■ **Box 14.4** *Helping Children (and Parents) Who Are "Out of Control" 527*

Methods of Controlling Aggression and Antisocial Conduct 528

Altruism: Development of the Prosocial Self 530

Origins of Altruism 530

Developmental Trends in Altruism 531

Social-Cognitive and Affective Contributors to Altruism 532

Cultural and Social Influences on Altruism 535

■ **Box 14.5** *Cultural Differences in Thinking About Prosocial Conduct 536*

What Is Morality? 538

How Developmentalists Look at Morality 539

Psychoanalytic Explanations of Moral Development 539

Freud's Theory of Oedipal Morality 539

Evaluating Freud's Theory and Newer Psychoanalytic Ideas about Morality 540

Cognitive-Developmental Theory: The Child as Moral Philosopher 541

Piaget's Theory of Moral Development 541

An Evaluation of Piaget's Theory 543

Kohlberg's Theory of Moral Development 545

Support for Kohlberg's Theory 547

Criticisms of Kohlberg's Approach 550

■ **Box 14.6** *Cultural Differences in Moral Reasoning 551*

Morality as a Product of Social Learning (and Social Information Processing) 554

How Consistent Are Moral Conduct and Moral Character? 554

Learning to Resist Temptation 555

Who Raises Children Who Are Morally Mature? 557

■ **Box 14.7** *Temperament, Discipline, and Moral Internalization 559*

Summary 560

Key Terms 562

Part V The Ecology of Development

Chapter 15 The Family 563

Understanding the Family 563

The Family as a Social System 564

Direct and Indirect Influences 565

Families Are Developing Systems 566

Families Are Embedded Systems 567

A Changing Family System in a Changing World 567

Parental Socialization during Childhood and Adolescence 570

Two Major Dimensions of Parenting 570

Four Patterns of Parenting 571

Social Class and Ethnic Variations in Child-Rearing 574

The Quest for Autonomy: Renegotiating the Parent–Child Relationship during Adolescence 577

The Influence of Siblings and Sibling Relationships 578

■ **Box 15.1** *Michael Pratt 578*

■ **Box 15.2** *Does Part-Time Employment Foster a Healthy Sense of Autonomy (and Positive Developmental Outcomes)? 579*

Changes in the Family System When a New Baby Arrives 580

Sibling Relationships over the Course of Childhood 581

■ **Box 15.3** *Hildy Ross 582*

Contributions of Siblings to Development 582

Characteristics of Only Children 583

Diversity in Family Life 584

Adoptive Families 584

Gay and Lesbian Families 585

The Impacts of Family Conflict and Divorce 586

Remarriage and Blended Families 589

■ **Box 15.4** *Smoothing the Rocky Road to Recovery from a Divorce 590*

Maternal Employment 592

When Parenting Breaks Down: The Problem of Child Abuse 595

Who Are the Abusers? 595

Who Is Abused? 596

Social-Contextual Triggers: The Ecology of Child Abuse 596

Consequences of Abuse and Neglect 597

■ **Box 15.5** *Childhood Sexual Abuse 598*

How Might We Solve the Problem? 599

Reflections on the Family 601

Summary 602

Key Terms 604

Chapter 16 Extrafamilial Influences: Television, Computers, Schools, and Peers 605

Early Windows: Effects of Television and Computer Technologies on Children and Adolescents 605

Development of Television Literacy 606

Some Potentially Undesirable Effects of Television 607

Television as an Educational Tool 610

Child Development in the Computer Age 613

School as a Socialization Agent 616

■ **Box 16.1** *Should Preschoolers Attend School? 617*

Determinants of Effective (and Ineffective) Schooling 617

Do Our Schools Meet the Needs of All of Our Children? 621

■ **Box 16.2** *On the Difficult Transition to Secondary School 622*

■ **Box 16.3** *Gerald Adams 623*

How Well Educated Are Our Children? A Cross-Cultural Comparison 625

Peers as Agents of Socialization 628

Who or What Is a Peer, and What Functions Do Peers Serve? 629

The Development of Peer Sociability 632

Peer Acceptance and Popularity 637

■ **Box 16.4** *William Bukowski 640*

Children and Their Friends 641

■ **Box 16.5** *On Improving the Social Skills of Unpopular Children 642*

■ **Box 16.6** *Xinyin Chen 643*

■ **Box 16.7** *A Longitudinal Analysis of the Benefits of Chumships 645*

Parents and Peers as Influence Agents 646

Are Cross-Pressures a Problem? 647

■ **Box 16.8** *Nancy Galambos 647*

Summary 649

Key Terms 651

Appendix: Answers to Concept Checks A-1

Glossary G-1

References R-1

Name Index I-1

Subject Index I-

Credits C-1

This is the second Canadian edition of the already well-established textbook *Developmental Psychology*, by David R. Shaffer. In the first edition we were excited to have the opportunity to tailor a textbook that we both regard highly to the needs of our own students. We have used David Shaffer's textbook for years, because it is a rich and accurate source of information on many topics in developmental psychology. Like many other Canadians, however, we often wished the text contained information on issues we face in Canada. The text needed Canadian statistics, Canadian legislation, Canadian research, and Canadian perspectives. Writing the Canadian edition was our opportunity to address this issue. This second Canadian edition allowed us to further update, refine, and elaborate the information that we, and other Canadian instructors and students, wanted to see.

Like the previous edition, this text provides an overview of child and adolescent development that reflects the best theories, research, and practical advice that developmentalists have to offer. It is a substantive developmental text that we hope is interesting, accurate, up-to-date, and written in clear, concise language that introductory students can easily understand. We believe that a good text should talk to rather than at its readers. It should anticipate their interests, questions, and concerns. It should treat them as active participants in the learning process. It should stress the processes that underlie developmental change, so that students come away from the course with a firm understanding of the causes and complexities of development. We wanted this text to challenge students to think about the fascinating process of human development, to share in the excitement of our young and dynamic discipline, and to acquire a knowledge of developmental principles that will serve them well in their roles as parents, teachers, nurses, child-care workers, pediatricians, psychologists, or in any other capacity in which they may one day influence the lives of developing individuals.

PHILOSOPHY

Certain philosophical views underlie any systematic treatment of a field as broad as human development. The philosophy that guided the construction of this text can be summarized as follows:

WE BELIEVE IN THEORETICAL ECLECTICISM. Many theories have contributed to our knowledge about developing persons, and this theoretical diversity is a strength rather than a weakness. Some theories may do a better job than others of explaining particular aspects of development, but we see time and again *that different theories emphasize different aspects of development* and that knowledge of many theories is necessary to explain the course and complexities of human development. So this book does not attempt to convince its readers that any one theoretical viewpoint is best. The psychoanalytic, behaviouristic, cognitive-developmental, ecological, sociocultural, information-processing, ethological, and behavioural genetic viewpoints (as well as several less encompassing theories that address selected aspects of development) are all treated with respect.

The Best Information about Human Development Comes from Systematic Research.
To teach this course effectively, one must convince students of the value of theory and systematic research. Although there are many ways to achieve that objective, this text contrasts the modern developmental sciences with their "prescientific" versions and then discusses the many methodological approaches that researchers use to test their theories and answer questions about developing children and adolescents. Care has been taken to explain why there is no one best method for studying developing persons and why our most reliable findings are those that can be replicated using a variety of methods.

We Believe in a Strong Process Orientation. A shortcoming of many developmental texts (including some best-sellers) is that they describe human development without adequately explaining why it occurs. In recent years, investigators have become increasingly concerned about identifying and understanding developmental processes—the biological and environmental factors that cause us to change—and this book reflects that concern. We believe that students are more likely to remember what develops, and when, if they know and understand the reasons why these developments take place.

We Believe in a Strong Contextual Orientation. One important lesson that developmentalists have learned is that children and adolescents live in historical eras and sociocultural contexts that affect every aspect of their development. We have highlighted these contextual influences in three ways. First, *cross-cultural comparisons* are discussed throughout the text. Students enjoy learning about the development of people in other cultures and ethnically diverse subcultures, and cross-cultural research helps them see how human beings can be so much alike and, at the same time, so different from one another. In addition, the impacts of such immediate contextual influences as our families, neighbourhoods, schools, and peer groups are considered throughout the first 14 chapters, as we discuss each aspect of human development, and again in the final two chapters, as important topics in their own right.

Human Development Is a Holistic Process. Although individual researchers may concentrate on particular topics such as physical development, cognitive development, or the development of moral reasoning, development is not piecemeal but *holistic:* human beings are at once physical, cognitive, social, and emotional creatures, and each of these components of self depends, in part, on changes taking place in other areas of development. This holistic perspective is a central theme in the modern developmental sciences—and one that is emphasized throughout the text.

A Developmental Text Should Be a Resource Book for Students—One That Reflects Current Knowledge. This text cites many new studies—many are "hot-off-the press" (see the Inside Track research boxes)—to ensure that our coverage represents the most up-to-date understanding of topics in developmental psychology. However, we have avoided the tendency, common in textbooks, to ignore older research simply because it is older. Many of the classics of our discipline are featured prominently throughout the text to illustrate important breakthroughs and to show how our knowledge about developing persons builds on earlier findings and insights.

ORGANIZATION

There are two traditional ways of presenting human development. In the *chronological,* or "ages and stages," approach, the coverage begins at conception and proceeds through the life span, using ages or chronological periods as the organizing principle. By contrast, the *topical* approach is organized around areas of development and follows each from its origins to its mature forms. Each of these presentations has its advantages and disadvantages. On the one hand, a chronological focus highlights the holistic character of development but may obscure the links between early and later events within each developmental domain. On the other hand, a topical approach highlights developmental sequences and processes but at the risk of failing to convey that development is holistic in nature.

This book is organized topically to focus on developmental processes and to provide the student with an uninterrupted view of the sequences of change that children and adolescents experience within each developmental domain. In our opinion, this topical approach best allows the reader to appreciate the flow of development—the systematic, and often truly dramatic, transformations that take place over the course of childhood and adolescence, as well as the developmental continuities that make each individual a reflection of his or her past self. At the same time, we consider it essential to paint a holistic portrait of the developing person. To accomplish this aim, we have stressed the fundamental interplay among biological, cognitive, social, and cultural influences for *each and every aspect of development*. So even though this text is organized topically, students will not lose sight of the whole person and the holistic character of human development.

CONTENT

We made an effort to retain in this edition those qualities of the earlier edition that students and professors say they like. One such quality is the division of the book into five parts and 16 chapters.

- **Part I: Theory and Research in the Developmental Sciences.** This first part presents an orientation to the discipline and the tools of the trade, including a thorough discussion and illustration of *research methodologies* in **Chapter 1** and a succinct review of the *major theories of human development* in **Chapter 2**. These chapters illustrate why research methods and theories are important to an understanding of human development. The coverage also analyzes the contributions and the limitations of each research method and each major theory.
- **Part II: Foundations of Development.** Chapters 3–5 address foundations of development strongly influenced by biological factors. **Chapter 3** focuses on *hereditary contributions* to human development and illustrates how genes and environments interact to influence most human characteristics. **Chapter 4** focuses on *prenatal development* and on the many prenatal and perinatal environmental factors that influence a newborn's health and readiness for adapting to the world outside the womb. **Chapter 5** is devoted to *physical growth*, including the *development of the brain and motor skills*. Connections between physical growth and psychological development (particularly in adolescence) are emphasized.
- **Part III: Language, Learning, and Cognitive Development.** The five chapters of Part III address the many theories and the voluminous research pertaining to the development of language, learning capabilities, and intellectual development. **Chapter 6** begins exploring the growth of *perceptual* and *learning* capabilities—two crucial cognitive foundations for many other aspects of development. **Chapter 7** is devoted to three major viewpoints of intellectual growth: Piaget's *cognitive-developmental theory*, Case's *neo-Piagetian theory,* and Vygotsky's *sociocultural theory*. These theories are covered in detail, for each is important to understanding the social, emotional, and language developments that are covered in later chapters. **Chapter 8** explores perhaps the dominant model of intellect and development today—*the information-processing viewpoint*. In addition, the chapter highlights the more recent *connectionist models*. The application of information-processing researchers in applied

settings is presented in a summary of research related to the development of mathematical skills and knowledge. **Chapter 9** focuses on individual differences in intellectual performance. Here we review the *intelligence testing* movement, the many factors that influence children's IQ scores, and the merits of compensatory interventions designed to improve intellectual performance. The chapter concludes with a discussion of *creative abilities* and their development. **Chapter 10** explores the fascinating topic of *language development* and addresses a number of intriguing issues: Can apes acquire language? Do children acquire language easier than adults? Is sign language a true language? Does bilingualism promote or inhibit linguistic proficiency and cognitive development?

- **Part IV: Social and Personality Development.** The next four chapters focus on crucial aspects of social and personality development. **Chapter 11** examines the process of *emotional development,* the developmental significance of individual differences in temperament, and the growth and implications for later development of the *emotional attachments* that children form with their close companions. **Chapter 12,** on the *self,* traces the development of the *self-concept* and children's emerging sense of *self-esteem,* the establishment of an *interpersonal identity* (including a sense of ethnic identity) in adolescence, and the growth of *social cognition and interpersonal understanding.* **Chapter 13** focuses on *sex differences* and on how biological factors, social forces, and intellectual growth interact to steer males and females toward different gender roles. The chapter also examines the utility (or lack thereof) of traditional gender roles and discusses ways in which we might be more successful at *combating unfounded gender stereotypes.* Finally, the chapter examines sexuality. **Chapter 14** examines three interrelated aspects of social development that people often consider when making judgments about one's character: *aggression, altruism,* and *moral development.*

- **Part V: The Ecology of Development.** The final section of the text concentrates on the settings, or contexts, in which people develop—the ecology of development. **Chapter 15** is devoted to *family influences,* focusing on the functions that families serve, patterns of child rearing that foster adaptive or maladaptive outcomes, the impacts of siblings on developing children, and the effects of family diversities and family transitions on child and adolescent development. **Chapter 16** concludes the text with an in-depth examination of four extrafamilial influences on developing children and adolescents: *television, computer technology, schools,* and *the society of one's peers.*

NEW TO THE SECOND CANADIAN EDITION

One of the most challenging tasks we faced when writing the Canadian edition was coming to an understanding of what defines a Canadian text. What should a Canadian text in developmental psychology look like compared with the American texts we are accustomed to seeing? Although for the most part Canadian and American researchers investigate developmental psychology using the same theories, philosophies, designs, methods, and analyses, we acknowledge that there are differences—some obvious, some not—in how research is conducted. One of the obvious areas of difference between the two cultures is that of legal issues. Canadians and Americans have different legislation and therefore different expectations on such basic issues as parental leave, acceptable discipline, and the right to appropriate education. There are subtler differences, too, that also need to be addressed. For example, though both countries promote diversity, they do so in different ways. That Canadians embrace diversity is especially evident in the way we respond to questions of language. Like many other countries in the world, Canada supports more than one language. The study of language, second-language learning, and bilingualism in particular are areas of research in which Canadians are at the forefront. Throughout the text we present issues like these that are important to Canadians. The second edition in general includes (a) increased attention to cultural/subcultural/historical influences; (b) an even stronger focus on the intricate interplays among biological and environmental forces in shaping development; (c) greater emphasis on the importance of peer relations (and on the interplays between families and peers as social agents); and (d) expanded coverage of adolescent development. The empirical literature also has been extensively updated, including recent studies conducted by Canadian researchers.

Each chapter has been revised and updated to add the new topics that reflect current trends in our discipline. To make way for these additions, we have condensed or otherwise reorganized other topics or, in some cases, have eliminated coverage that the newer evidence has rendered obsolete. Here is a sampling of these changes:

- Expanded discussion of Bronfenbrenner's ecological systems (Chapter 2).
- Expanded discussion of the use of the new genetic technologies (Chapter 3).
- Inclusion of the latest research on smoking as a teratogen (Chapter 4).
- Inclusion of the latest research on the long-term correlates of low birth weight (Chapter 4).
- New findings of presumed contributors to and strategies for preventing sudden infant death syndrome (SIDS) (Chapter 4).
- Inclusion of the latest research on the importance of prenatal and infant experience on the architecture of the brain (Chapter 5).
- Resent research exploring the positive impacts of sporting activities on the self-esteem of adolescent girls (Chapter 5).
- Expanded coverage of infants' face perception (Chapter 6).
- New evidence on the interplays among perceptual skills, emergent literacy, and success at learning to read (Chapter 6).
- New interpretations of neonatal imitation (Chapter 6).
- Integration of Case's theoretical model (Chapter 7).
- Elaboration of neo-Nativist and "Theory" Theorists' challenges to Piaget's accounts of infant cognitive development (Chapter 7).
- Extended discussion of the fundamental components of the information–processing model (Chapter 8).
- New sections on the development of rule use and the growth of analogical reasoning (Chapter 8).
- Presentation of the Flynn effect as evidence for the malleability of intellectual performance (Chapter 9).
- More inclusive coverage of the components of language (Chapter 10).
- Dramatic new evidence from Nicaraguan Sign Language that children can create language-like communication systems (Chapter 10).
- Revised discussion of temperament and attachment (Chapter 11).
- A stronger focus on cultural variations in self-concepts (Chapter 12).
- Recent discoveries on how best to use praise to promote a mastery orientation to achievement challenges (Chapter 12).
- Evidence detailing some simple strategies that parents can use to delay the onset of adolescent sexual behaviour and promote safer sexual behaviours (Chapter 13).
- Expanded coverage of the psychobiosocial model of sex differences and gender typing (Chapter 13).
- Clear evidence for the intergenerational transmission of aggression and violence (Chapter 14).

- New research on the effectiveness of programs aimed at preventing aggression and violence at schools (Chapter 14).
- A closer look at variations in child and adolescent adjustment in *complex* vs. *simple* stepparent homes (Chapter 15).
- Expanded coverage of the role of the family in development (Chapter 15).
- Dramatic new data suggesting that violent video games may be a stronger instigator of aggression and violence than is violent television programming (Chapter 16).
- New data on the relation between peer rejection and aggression (Chapter 16).

Although this textbook is Canadian in its orientation, we felt it important to keep American data that provide insight into our understanding of developmental processes. Much of the work on cultural differences as a function of race is generated in the United States, and this research is valuable in highlighting critical issues that can affect development. We retained many of these studies and added related Canadian or international research to broaden the scope and provide the best available summary of these issues. Breadth of scope is an important feature of Canadian research, and in keeping with that expectation we tried to incorporate research from a range of countries to provide as complete a picture as possible.

 MARGIN ICONS. Also new to this edition are special icons to indicate topics that can also be found on the "Child and Adolescent Development" CD-ROM. See below for more details about this exciting supplement.

WRITING STYLE

Our goal has been to write a book that speaks directly to its readers and treats them as active participants in an ongoing discussion. We have tried to be relatively informal and down to earth in our writing style and to rely heavily on questions, thought problems, concept checks, and a number of other exercises to stimulate students' interest and involvement. We have attempted to prepare a manuscript that is substantive and challenging but that reads more like a dialogue or a story than like an encyclopedia.

SPECIAL FEATURES

Among the more important features that are included to encourage student interest and involvement and make the material easier to learn are the following:

- **Four-colour design.** An attractive four-colour design brightens the book and makes photographs, drawings, and other illustrations come alive.
- **Outlines and chapter summaries.** An outline and brief introductory section at the beginning of each chapter provide the student with a preview of what will be covered. Each chapter concludes with a comprehensive summary—organized according to the major subdivisions of each chapter and highlighting key terms—that allows one to quickly review the chapter's major themes.
- **Subheadings.** Subheadings are employed frequently to keep the material well organized and to divide the coverage into manageable bites.

- **Vocabulary/key terms.** Some 700 key terms appear in boldface type to alert the student that these are important concepts to learn.

- **Running glossary, key term lists, and comprehensive end-of-book glossary.** A running glossary provides on-the-spot definitions of boldface key terms as they appear in the text. At the end of each chapter is a list of key terms that appeared in the narrative, as well as the page number on which each term is defined. A complete glossary of key terms for the entire text appears at the end of the book.

- **Boxes.** Each chapter contains three to five or more boxes that highlight important ideas, processes, issues, or applications. The aim of these boxes is to permit a closer or more personal examination of selected topics while stimulating the reader to think about the questions, controversies, practices, and policies under discussion. The boxes fall into six categories: **Inside Track**, which highlights current Canadian research and researchers; **Cultural Influences**, which examines the impacts of culture, subcultures, or other social contexts on selected aspects of child/adolescent development; **Focus on Research**, which discusses a classic study or set of studies that have been influential in illuminating the causes of development; **Current Controversies**, which addresses hotly debated issues today; **Developmental Issues**, which permits a detailed examination of various developmentally significant topics or processes; and **Applying Developmental Research,** which focuses on applying what we know to optimize developmental outcomes. All of these boxes are carefully woven into the chapter narrative and were selected to reinforce central themes in the text.

- **The Inside Track Boxes**. One of the most exciting features in this Canadian edition is the Inside Track boxes. These boxes highlight one or two recent studies conducted by researchers at Canadian universities. In writing these features, we had the opportunity to communicate directly with almost all of the researchers represented, and the work summarized here represents their own choices of research projects to showcase. You will notice that the research presented is either hot off the press or *in* press, hence it captures the state-of-the-art work being conducted by Canadian researchers. Together, the Inside Track boxes identify the extraordinary array of research being conducted at Canadian universities. Nevertheless, these boxes feature only a few of the many individuals whose work is making an impact on our understanding of developmental issues. We would have liked to include many others but were limited, in some cases, by space restrictions and, in others, by the advanced level of research, which was beyond the scope of an introductory textbook. We have, however, integrated other important Canadian contributions throughout the body of the text. In many cases, university affiliations are provided with the researchers' names, to let students know where the researcher is located. Where affiliations are left out, we felt they impeded the flow of the text or compromised the clarity of the presentation. However, students can readily identify Canadian researchers by looking for the boldface entries in the name index, and, overall, students will have an opportunity to become acquainted with Canadian research and gain a better understanding of how it fits within the big picture in developmental psychology. In this second edition, we revisited each of the existing Inside Track boxes and revised and updated them, as well as adding four new researchers

- **Illustrations.** Photographs, tables, and figures are used extensively, and one noteworthy addition is the use of chronological tables to review important developmental milestones. Although the illustrations are designed, in part, to provide visual relief and to maintain student interest, they are not merely decorations. All visual aids, including the occasional cartoon, were selected to illustrate important principles and concepts and thereby enhance the educational goals of the text.

- **Concept Checks.** The Concept Checks are engaging and challenging features that permit an active assessment of one's mastery of important concepts and developmental processes. Answers to all Concept Checks can be found in the Appendix at the back of the book.

- **Critical thought questions.** The "What Do You Think?" feature—three thought questions per chapter—are designed to encourage students to think about current controversies and/or to apply what they have learned in formulating their own reasoned position on developmentally significant issues. Some of these questions address issues too new to have generated anything other than anecdotal evidence. Any and all of these questions may serve as excellent springboards for class discussion; in fact, that is where many of them came from, having been raised in class by students as we discussed topics pertaining in some way to these issues.

SUPPLEMENTARY AIDS

The supplemental support materials have been coordinated carefully, with learning objectives for each chapter made clear and consistent throughout.

INSTRUCTOR'S RESOURCE CD-ROM. The Instructor's Resource CD-ROM contains the Instructor's Manual, Test Bank, and Computerized Test Bank. See below for more details about each supplement.

INSTRUCTOR'S MANUAL. The Instructor's Manual provides chapter outlines, summaries and objectives, key terms, suggestions for class lectures and activities, and lists of particularly effective media materials. The manual also contains links to valuable Canadian Web sites where instructors can direct students to more information on material presented in the text as well as to international sites that feature Canadian research. Although many key researchers in Canada could not be highlighted in the textbook, for reasons explained above, we have highlighted some of these researchers in the Instructor's Manual and so provided an opportunity for instructors to use this research when planning more in-depth discussions in their classroom.

TEST BANK. The Test Bank for this edition is based on earlier test banks with new questions added to update the material and provide more choices for each topic. An extensive review and revision of the test bank was completed by Dr. Jacqueline Specht, a close colleague of the two Canadian authors. In addition, the Canadian authors developed questions to reflect the Canadian content. Over 100 multiple-choice questions are provided for each chapter, and all questions are classified by type—factual, definition, applied, or conceptual. Each question is cross-referenced to the learning objectives for each chapter and to its page location in the text.

COMPUTERIZED TEST BANK. Available only on the Instructor's Resource CD-ROM, all questions from the printed Test Items are available in Examview for Windows format. Examview allows instructors to create, deliver, and customize texts (both print and online) in minutes with this easy-to-use assessment and tutorial system.

MULTIMEDIA MANAGER FOR DEVELOPMENTAL PSYCHOLOGY. This CD-ROM presentation tool helps you put together PowerPoint lectures that include art, graphics, and video clips. The PowerPoint slides were created by Dr. Jennifer Sutton of the University of Western Ontario.

OBSERVING CHILDREN AND ADOLESCENTS CD-ROM AND WORKBOOK. *Observing Children and Adolescents* is a 180-minute program of narrated and unnarrated video segments that feature the highlights of infant, child, and adolescent development. Designed to deepen students' understanding of major developmental milestones from prenatal development through adolescence, the program focuses on concrete and observable behaviour, and features segments of participants interacting in naturalistic settings. *Observing Children and Adolescents* covers not only major developmental theories, but how these theories are exhibited in everyday behaviour. Also available on VHS for Instructor use.

CNN Today Videos: Developmental Psychology, Volumes 1, 2, and 3. Available to adopters of the text are videotapes of CNN stories on child development issues. Focusing on a range of topics from prenatal testing to adolescent concerns, these video segments have been selected to address important areas covered in the developmental psychology course.

Study Guide. Written for students who use this textbook, the Study Guide, adapted by Dr. Gillian Wark of Simon Fraser University, highlights the learning objectives for each chapter (which are consistent with the learning objectives in the Test Bank and the Instructor's Manual) and includes the following: a chapter outline with a summary of key points, a two-part vocabulary self-test, a set of short-answer study questions related to the learning objectives for each chapter, a 10–15-question multiple-choice self-test, and a set of activities and projects related to class material. Annotated answers are provided for the multiple-choice self-test, to explain why the indicated answer is correct and why the distracters are incorrect.

Child and Adolescent Development CD-ROM. Developed as a fully interactive guide to the major concepts and theories covered in child and adolescent development courses, this student CD-ROM is structured around three primary Learning Modules: Physical Development; Cognition, Language, and Learning; and Personality, Social-Emotional, and Moral Development. It features narrated concept overviews, video, animations, applications, games, quizzes, theorist biographies, and links to the Internet. Special margin icons in the text indicate where material from the CD-ROM is integrated with the text.

Developmental Psychology Study Centre on the World Wide Web. The dynamic Web site that accompanies this text can be found at www.developmentalpsych2e. nelson.com. The site gives students access to helpful learning resources such as practice quizzes, chapter-specific Web links, study tips, information on degrees and careers in psychology, and InfoTrac® links.

ACKNOWLEDGMENTS

As is always the case with projects as large as this one, there are many, many individuals whose assistance was invaluable in the planning and production of the book. The quality of any volume in human development depends to a large extent on the quality of the prepublication reviews from developmentalists around the world. Many colleagues (including several dozen or so interested and unpaid volunteers) have influenced this book by contributing constructive criticism, useful suggestions, references, and a whole lot of encouragement. Each of those experts has helped to make the final product a better one, and we thank them all.

The reviewers of the First Canadian Edition were Lilly Both, University of New Brunswick, Saint John; Elizabeth Bowering, Mount Saint Vincent University; Laura Melnyk Gribble, University of Western Ontario; Gretchen Hess, University of Alberta; Nina Howe, Concordia University; Jane Ledingham, University of Ottawa; Shelley Parlow, Carleton University; Carole Peterson, Memorial University of Newfoundland; Michael Pratt, Wilfrid Laurier University; Bruce Ryan, University of Guelph; Thomas Shultz, McGill University; Connie Varnhagen, University of Alberta; and Gillian Wark, Simon Fraser University. We thank them for their helpful comments.

The reviewers of the second Canadian Edition were Scott Adler, York University; Anne Bowker, Carleton University; Nancy Digdon, Grant MacEwan College; Helen Doan, York University; Darcy Hallet, University of British Columbia; Barbara Hodkin, Mount Saint Vincent University; William Roberts, University College of the Cariboo; and Thomas Shultz, McGill University. We would like to thank these reviewers for helping to guide some of the changes we made to the second edition.

Dr. Marc Joanisse of the University of Western Ontario deserves a special note of thanks for his assistance in constructing the section on connectionism in Chapter 8. This area of study is gaining more recognition among developmental psychologists but it is a relatively new addition to developmental textbooks. We appreciate Marc's ability to highlight the key information for students who may be becoming acquainted with connectionism for the first time.

We also thank Mustaq Khan for sharing his expertise and Jessica Gilbert for helping us to locate those hard-to-find articles.

We would also note the tremendous contributions of each Canadian researcher highlighted in this text. They not only took the time to identify their most important pieces of work and provide us with copies of their cutting-edge material most often summarized in the exact form it is presented in the text, but they also hunted down photographs so that we would be able to show you the person behind the research.

Many other people have contributed their professionalism and skills to the development and production of the second Canadian edition of this text. We are especially grateful to Joanna Cotton, the executive editor for this project; to Edward Ikeda, who served as developmental editor; to Carrie McGregor, the production editor; to Katherine Strain, who designed the book's cover; to Gail Marsden, for her skill, efficiency, and attention to detail in copy editing; to Erin Moore for proofreading; to Susan Calverley, for her page-formatting expertise; and to Murray Moman, the Senior Marketing Manager.

Introduction to Developmental Psychology and Its Research Strategies

PhotoDisc Collection/PhotoDisc.

Let's begin this book with a question: Why did you choose to enrol in a course on human development? For many of you majoring in psychology, family studies, elementary education, or nursing, this class is required and there is no way around it. Expectant parents may take the course in order to learn more about their babies. Occasionally, people choose the course seeking to answer specific questions about their own behaviour or that of a friend or family member. Whatever your reasons for taking this course, at one time or another you have probably been curious about one or more aspects of human development. For example:

- What does the world look like to newborn infants? Can they make any sense of their new surroundings?

- When do infants first recognize their mothers? their fathers? themselves (in a mirror)?

- Why do many 1-year-olds seem so attached to their mothers and wary of strangers?

- Foreign languages are difficult to follow if we merely listen to people conversing in them. Yet infants and toddlers pay close attention to conversations and will acquire their native language without any formal instruction. How is this possible? Is language learning easier for children than for adults? Is a child in a bilingual home at a disadvantage?

- Why do young children say that objects like the sun and clouds are alive?

- Why do you remember so little about the first two or three years of your life?

- Why are some people friendly and outgoing, while others are shy and reserved? Does the home environment influence one's personality? If so, why are children from the same family often so different from one another?

- What are the impacts on children of losing a parent (due to death or divorce) or gaining a stepparent?

- What roles do close friends play in a child's or an adolescent's development?

- Why is it that all humans turn out similar in many ways and, at the same time, so different from one another?

What Is Development?

Human Development in Historical Perspective

Research Methods in Developmental Psychology

Detecting Relationships: Correlational and Experimental Designs

Designs for Studying Development

Cross-Cultural Comparisons

Ethical Considerations in Developmental Research

Postscript: On Becoming a Wise Consumer of Developmental Research

Summary

Simply stated, the aim of this book is to seek answers for these and many other fascinating questions about developing persons by reviewing the theories, methods, discoveries, and many practical accomplishments of the modern developmental sciences. This introductory chapter lays the groundwork for the remainder of the book by addressing important issues about the nature of human development and how knowledge about development is gained. What does it mean to say that people "develop" over time? How is your experience of development different from that of developing persons in past eras or in other cultures? When were scientific studies of human development first conducted, and why are they necessary? What strategies or research methods do scientists use to study the development of children and adolescents? Let us begin by considering the nature of development.

WHAT IS DEVELOPMENT?

Development refers to systematic continuities and changes in the individual that occur between conception (when the father's sperm penetrates the mother's ovum, creating a new organism) and death. By describing *changes* as "systematic," we imply that they are orderly, patterned, and relatively enduring, so temporary mood swings and other transitory changes in our appearances, thoughts, and behaviours are excluded. We are also interested in **continuities** in development, ways in which we remain the same or continue to reflect our past.

If development represents the continuities and changes that an individual experiences from "womb to tomb," the science of development is the study of these phenomena. Actually, we might well speak of the sciences of development, for this area of study is truly a multidisciplinary enterprise. Although **developmental psychology** is the largest of these disciplines, many biologists, sociologists, anthropologists, educators, physicians, home economists, and even historians share an interest in developmental continuity and change and have contributed in important ways to our understanding of both human and animal development. Because the science of development is multidisciplinary, we use the term *developmentalist* to refer to any scholar—regardless of discipline—who seeks to understand the developmental process.

What Causes Us to Develop?

To grasp the meaning of development more fully, we must understand two important processes that underlie developmental change. One of these processes, **maturation**, refers to the biological unfolding of the individual according to a plan contained in the *genes*—the hereditary material passed from parents to their child at conception. Just as seeds become mature plants, assuming that they receive adequate moisture and nourishment, human beings grow within the womb. The human maturational program also calls for us to become capable of walking and uttering our first meaningful words at about 1 year of age, to reach sexual maturity at about age 11 to 15, and then to age and die on roughly similar schedules. Because the brain undergoes many maturational changes, maturation is partly responsible for psychological changes such as our increasing ability to concentrate, solve problems, and understand another person's thoughts or feelings. So one reason that we humans are similar in so many important respects is that our common "species heredity," or maturational blueprints, guide all of us through many of the same developmental changes at about the same points in our lives.

A second critical developmental process is **learning**—the process through which our *experiences* produce relatively permanent changes in our feelings, thoughts, and behaviours. Let's consider a simple example. Although a certain degree of physical maturation is necessary before an elementary-school child can become reasonably proficient at

development
systematic continuities and changes in an individual over the course of life

developmental continuities
ways in which we remain stable over time or continue to reflect our past

developmental psychology
branch of psychology devoted to identifying and explaining the continuities and changes that individuals display over time

maturation
developmental changes in the body or behaviour that result from the aging process rather than from learning, injury, illness, or some other life experience

learning
relatively permanent change in behaviour (or behavioural potential) that results from one's experiences or practice

skating, careful instruction and many hours of practice are essential if this child is ever to approximate the skating skills of athletes such as Wayne Gretzky. Most of our abilities and habits do not simply unfold as part of nature's grand plan; we often learn to feel, think, and behave in new ways from our observations of and interactions with parents, teachers, and other important people in our lives, as well as from events that we experience. Stated another way, we change in response to our *environments*—particularly in response to the actions and reactions of the people around us. Of course, most developmental changes are the product of *both* maturation and learning. And as we will see throughout this book, some of the more lively debates about human development are arguments about which of these processes contributes most to particular developmental changes.

Despite the common assumption that superstars are natural athletes, the special skills they display require an enormous amount of practice. Mike Weir worked hard to become such an accomplished golfer.

What Goals Do Developmentalists Pursue?

What objectives have developmentalists set for themselves? Three major goals stand out: to describe, to explain, and to optimize development (Baltes, Reese, & Lipsitt, 1980). In pursuing the goal of *description*, human developmentalists carefully observe the behaviour of people of different ages, seeking to specify how human beings change over time. Though there are typical pathways of development that virtually all people follow, researchers have discovered that no two people are exactly alike. Even when raised in the same home, children often display very different interests, values, abilities, and behaviours. Thus, to adequately describe development, it is necessary to focus both on typical patterns of change (or **normative development**) and on individual variations (or **ideographic development**), seeking to identify the important ways that developing humans resemble each other and how they are likely to differ as they proceed through life.

Adequate description provides us with the facts about development, but it is only the starting point. Ultimately, developmentalists seek to explain the changes they have observed. In pursuing this goal of *explanation*, researchers hope to determine *why* humans develop as they typically do and *why* some individuals turn out differently than others. Stated another way, explanation centres both on normative changes *within* individuals and variations in development *between* individuals. As we will see throughout the text, it is often easier to describe development than to conclusively explain why it occurs.

Finally, many researchers and practitioners hope to optimize development by applying what they have learned in attempts to help human beings develop in positive directions. This is clearly a practical side to the study of human development that has led to such breakthroughs as ways to

- Promote strong affectional ties between fussy, unresponsive infants and their frustrated parents.
- Assist children with learning difficulties to succeed at school.
- Help socially unskilled children and adolescents to prevent the emotional difficulties that could result from having no close friends and being rejected by peers.

Many believe that such *optimization* goals increasingly will influence research agendas in the 21st century (Fabes et al., 2000; Lerner, Fisher, & Weinberg, 2000) as developmentalists show greater interest in solving real problems and communicating the practical implications of their findings to the public and to policymakers (McCall & Groark, 2000). Yet this heavier focus on applied issues in no way implies that traditional descriptive and explanatory goals are any less important because optimization goals often cannot be achieved until researchers have adequately described normal and abnormal pathways of development and their causes (Schwebel, Plumert, & Pick, 2000).

normative development
developmental changes that characterize most or all members of a species; typical patterns of development

ideographic development
individual variations in the rate, extent, or direction of development

Some Basic Observations about the Character of Development

Now that we have defined development and talked briefly about the goals that developmentalists pursue, let's consider some of the conclusions they have drawn about the character of development.

A Continual and Cumulative Process

In his famous poem *Paradise Lost*, John Milton wrote: "Childhood shows the man as morning shows the day." This interesting analogy can be interpreted in at least two ways. It could be translated to mean that the events of childhood have little or no real impact on one's adult life, just as a sunny summer morning often fails to forecast an impending afternoon thundershower. Yet most people do not interpret Milton's statement that way. Instead, they take it to mean that the events of childhood play a very meaningful role in forecasting the future. Human developmentalists clearly favour this latter interpretation.

Although no one can specify precisely what adulthood holds in store from even the most meticulous examination of a person's childhood, developmentalists have learned that the first 12 years are an extremely important part of the life span that sets the stage for adolescence and adulthood. And yet how we perform on that stage also depends on the experiences we have later in life. Obviously, you are not the same person you were at age 10 or even at age 15. You have probably grown somewhat, acquired new academic skills, and developed very different interests and aspirations from those you had as a fifth-grader or a high school junior. And the path of such developmental change stretches ever onward, through middle age and beyond, culminating in the final change that occurs when we die. Altogether, human development is best described as a *continual* and *cumulative* process. The one constant is change, and the changes that occur at each major phase of life can have important implications for the future.

Table 1.1 presents a chronological overview of the life span as developmentalists see it. Our focus in this text is on development during the first five periods of life—the epochs known as childhood and adolescence. By examining how children develop from the moment they are conceived until they reach young adulthood, we will learn more about ourselves and the determinants of our behaviour. Our survey will also provide some insight as to why no two individuals are ever exactly alike, even when raised together in the same home. We won't promise that you will find answers to every impor-

TABLE 1.1   A Chronological Overview of Human Development

Period of life	Approximate age range
1.Prenatal period	Conception to birth
2. Infancy and toddler period*	First 2 years of life
3. Preschool period	2 to 6 years of age
4. Middle childhood	6 to 12 or so years of age (until the onset of puberty)
5. Adolescence	12 or so to 20 years of age (many developmentalists define the end of adolescence as the point at which the individual begins to work and is reasonably independent of parental sanctions)
6. Young adulthood	20 to 40 years of age
7. Middle age	40 to 65 years of age
8. Old age	65 years of age or older

*Some prefer to describe as "toddlers" children who have begun to walk and are approximately 1 to 2 years of age.

NOTE: The age ranges listed here are approximate and may not apply to any particular individual. For example, a few 10-year-olds have experienced puberty and are properly classified as adolescents. Some teenagers are fully self-supporting, with children of their own, and are best classified as young adults.

tant question you may have about developing children and adolescents, because the study of human development is still a relatively young discipline with many unresolved issues. But as we proceed, it should become clear that developmentalists of the past half-century have provided an enormous amount of practical information about younger people that can help us to become better educators, child and adolescent practitioners, and parents.

A Holistic Process

It was once fashionable to divide developmentalists into three camps: (1) those who studied *physical growth* and development, including bodily changes and the sequencing of motor skills; (2) those who studied *cognitive* aspects of development, including perception, language, learning, and thinking; and (3) those who concentrated on *psychosocial* aspects of development, including emotions, personality, and the growth of interpersonal relationships. Today we know that this classification is somewhat misleading, for researchers who work in any of these areas have found that changes in one aspect of development have important implications for other aspects. Let's consider an example.

What determines a person's popularity with peers? If you were to say that social skills are important, you would be right. Social skills such as warmth, friendliness, and willingness to cooperate are characteristics that popular children typically display. Yet there is much more to popularity than meets the eye. We now have some indication that the age at which a child reaches puberty, an important milestone in physical development, has an effect on social life. For example, boys who reach puberty early enjoy better relations with their peers than do boys who reach puberty later (Livson & Peskin, 1980). Children who do well in school also tend to be more popular with their peers than children who perform somewhat less admirably in the classroom.

We see, then, that popularity depends not only on the growth of social skills but also on various aspects of both cognitive and physical development. As this example illustrates, development is not piecemeal but **holistic**; humans are physical, cognitive, and social beings, and each of these components of self depends in part on changes taking place in other areas of development. The holistic perspective is perhaps the dominant theme of human development today, and we adopt this perspective in the organization of this book.

Plasticity

Plasticity refers to a capacity for change in response to positive or negative life experiences. Although we have described development as a continual and cumulative process and noted that past events often have implications for the future, developmentalists have known for some time that the course of development can change abruptly if important aspects of a person's life change. For example, sombre babies living in barren, understaffed orphanages often become quite cheerful and affectionate when placed in socially stimulating adoptive homes (Rutter, 1981). Highly aggressive children who are intensely disliked by their peers often improve their social status after learning and practising the social skills that popular children display (Mize & Ladd, 1990; Shure, 1989). It is indeed fortunate that human development is so plastic, for children who have horrible starts can often be helped to overcome their deficiencies.

Historical/Cultural Context

No single portrait of development is accurate for all cultures, social classes, or racial and ethnic groups. Each culture, subculture, and social class transmits a particular pattern of beliefs, values, customs, and skills to its younger generations, and the content of this cultural socialization has a strong influence on the attributes and competencies that individuals display. Development is also influenced by societal changes: historical events such as wars, technological breakthroughs such as the development of personal computer technology, and social causes such as the women's movement. Each generation

holistic perspective
unified view of the developmental process that emphasizes the important interrelationships among the physical, mental, social, and emotional aspects of human development

plasticity
capacity for change; a developmental state that has the potential to be shaped by experience

develops in its own way, and each generation changes the world for succeeding generations. So we should not automatically assume that developmental sequences observed in samples of North American or European children (the most heavily studied populations) are optimal, or even that they characterize people developing in other eras or cultural settings (Laboratory of Comparative Human Cognition, 1983). Only by adopting a historical/cultural perspective can we fully appreciate the richness and diversity of human development.

HUMAN DEVELOPMENT IN HISTORICAL PERSPECTIVE

Contemporary Western societies can be described as "child-centred": People often think of births as blessed events, spend a great deal of money to care for and educate their children, and excuse children from shouldering the full responsibilities of adulthood until attaining the legal age of 14 to 21 (depending on the society), when they have presumably gained the wisdom and skills to "pull their own weight." Yet childhood and adolescence were not always regarded as the very special, sensitive periods that we regard them as today. To understand how developmentalists think about and approach the study of children, it is necessary to see how the concept of childhood "developed" over time. You may be surprised just how recent our modern viewpoint really is. Of course, it was only after people came to view childhood as a very special period that they began to study children and the developmental process.

Childhood in Premodern Times

In the early days of recorded history, children had few if any rights, and their lives were not always valued by their elders. Archaeological research, for example, has shown that the ancient Carthaginians often killed children as religious sacrifices and embedded them in the walls of buildings to "strengthen" these structures (Bjorklund & Bjorklund, 1992). Until the fourth century A.D., Roman parents legally were entitled to kill their deformed, illegitimate, or otherwise unwanted infants. After this active infanticide was outlawed, unwanted babies were often left to die in the wilderness or were sold as servants or as objects for sexual exploitation on reaching middle childhood (deMause, 1974). Even wanted children were often treated harshly by today's standards. For example, boys in the city-state of Sparta were exposed to a strict regimen designed to train them for the grim task of serving a military state. As infants, they were given cold baths to "toughen" them. At age 7, when children in modern society are entering Grade 2, Spartan boys were taken from their homes and housed in public barracks, where they were often beaten or underfed to instil the discipline they would need to become able warriors (deMause, 1974; Despert, 1965).

Not all early societies treated their children as harshly as the citizens of Carthage, Rome, and Sparta. Yet for several centuries after the birth of Christ, children were viewed as family "possessions" who had no rights (Hart, 1991) and whom parents were free to exploit as they saw fit. In fact, it wasn't until the 12th century A.D. in Christian Europe that secular legislation equated infanticide with murder (deMause, 1974).

Currently, there is some debate about what childhood was like during the medieval era. Historian Philippe Aries (1962) analyzed documents and paintings from medieval Europe and concluded that European societies had *no* concept of childhood as we know it before 1600. Medieval children were not coddled or indulged to the extent that today's children are. They were often dressed in miniature versions of adult clothing and were depicted in artwork working alongside adults in the shop or the field or drinking and carousing with adults at parties. And except for exempting *very young children* from criminal culpability, medieval law generally made no distinctions between childhood and adult offences (Borstelmann, 1983; Kean, 1937).

But were medieval children really considered to be miniature adults? Probably not. More recent and extensive examinations of medieval history reveal that childhood was generally recognized as a distinct phase of life and that children were thought to have certain needs above and beyond those of adults (see Borstelmann, 1983; Kroll, 1977). Clearly, the experiences of children were different during medieval times than today, for many medieval children routinely performed economic activities that closely resemble adult work by today's standards. Yet it is certainly an overstatement to conclude that medieval societies had absolutely no concept of childhood and merely treated children as miniature adults (Cunningham, 1996).

Although medieval children dressed like their elders and often worked alongside them, it is doubtful that they were considered miniature adults.

Toward Modern-Day Views on Childhood

During the 17th and 18th centuries, attitudes toward children and child-rearing began to change. Religious leaders of that era stressed that children were innocent and helpless souls who should be shielded from the wild and reckless behaviour of adults. One method of accomplishing this objective was to send young people to school. Although the primary purpose of schooling was to provide a proper moral and religious education, it was now recognized that teaching important subsidiary skills such as reading and writing would transform the innocents into servants and workers who would provide society "with a good labor force" (Aries, 1962, p. 10; see also Box 1.1). Although children were still considered family possessions, parents were now discouraged from abusing their sons and daughters and were urged to treat them with more warmth and affection (Aries, 1962; Despert, 1965).

Early Philosophical Perspectives on Childhood

Why did attitudes toward children change so drastically in the 17th and 18th centuries? Although the historical record is not very clear on this point, it is likely that the thinking of influential social philosophers contributed meaningfully to the new look at children and child care. Lively speculation about human nature led these philosophers to carefully consider each of the following issues:

1. Are children inherently good or bad?
2. Are children driven by inborn motives and instincts, or rather, are they products of their environments?
3. Are children actively involved in shaping their characters, or are they passive creatures moulded by parents, teachers, and other agents of society?

original sin
idea that children are inherently negative creatures who must be taught to rechannel their selfish interests into socially acceptable outlets

innate purity
idea that infants are born with an intuitive sense of right and wrong that is often misdirected by the demands and restrictions of society

Debates about these philosophical questions produced quite different perspectives on children and child-rearing. For example, Thomas Hobbes's (1651/1904) doctrine of **original sin** held that children are inherently selfish egoists who must be restrained by society, whereas Jean Jacques Rousseau's (1762/1955) doctrine of **innate purity** maintained that children are born with an intuitive sense of right and wrong that society often corrupts. These two viewpoints clearly differ in their implications for child-rearing. Proponents of original sin argued that parents must actively control their egoistic offspring, while innate purists viewed children as "noble savages" who should be given freedom to follow their inherently positive inclinations.

CULTURAL INFLUENCES

1.1 On the "Invention" of Adolescence

Although modern-day concepts of childhood date to the 1700s, formal recognition of adolescence as a distinct phase of life came later, during the early years of the twentieth century (Hall, 1904). Ironically, the spread of industry in Western societies is probably the event most responsible for the "invention" of adolescence. As immigrants poured into industrialized nations and took jobs that had formerly been filled by children and teenagers, young people became economic liabilities rather than assets (or, as one person put it, "economically worthless but emotionally priceless") (Zelizer, cited in Remley, 1988). Moreover, the increasingly complex technology of industrial operations placed a premium on obtaining an educated labour force. So laws were passed in the late 19th century to restrict child labour and make schooling compulsory (Kett, 1977). Suddenly teens were spending much of their time surrounded by age-mates and separated from adults. As they hung out with friends and developed their own colourful "peer cultures," teenagers came to be viewed as a distinct class of individuals who had clearly emerged from the innocence of childhood but who were not yet ready to assume adult responsibilities (Hall, 1904).

After World War II, the adolescent experience broadened as increasing numbers of high-school graduates postponed marriages and careers to pursue college or university (and postgraduate) educations. Today, it is not at all unusual for young people to delay their entry into the workaday adult world until their mid- to late 20s (Hartung & Sweeney, 1991; Vobejda, 1991). And we might add that society condones this "extended adolescence" by requiring workers to obtain increasingly specialized training to pursue their chosen careers (Elder, Liker, & Cross, 1984).

Interestingly, many of the world's cultures have no concept of adolescence as a distinct phase of life. The St. Lawrence Inuit, for example, simply distinguish boys from men (or girls from women), following the tradition of many preliterate societies that passage to adulthood occurs at puberty (Keith, 1985). And yet, other cultures' depictions of the life span are much more intricate than our own. The Arasha of East Africa, for example, have at least six meaningful age strata for males: youths, junior warriors, senior warriors, junior elders, senior elders, and retired elders.

The fact that age does not have the same meaning in all eras or cultures reflects a basic truth that we have already touched on and will emphasize repeatedly throughout this book: The course of human development in one historical or cultural context is apt to differ, and to differ substantially, from that observed in other eras and cultural settings (Fry, 1996). Aside from our biological link to the human race, we are largely products of the times and places in which we live.

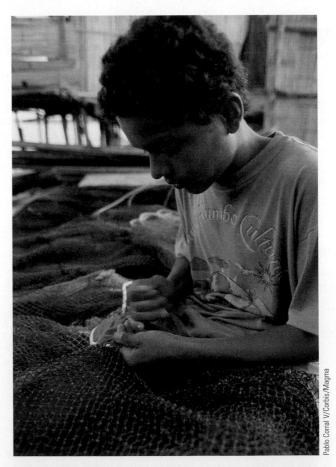

In some cultures, passage to adulthood occurs at puberty and adolescents are expected to assume adult responsibilities.

Another influential view on children and child-rearing was suggested by John Locke (1690/1913), who believed that the mind of an infant is a **tabula rasa**, or "blank slate," and that children have no inborn tendencies. In other words, children are neither inherently good nor inherently bad, and how they turn out depends entirely on their worldly experiences. Like Hobbes, Locke argued in favour of disciplined child-rearing to ensure that children would develop good habits and acquire few if any bad ones.

These philosophers also differed on the question of children's participation in their own development. Hobbes maintained that children must learn to rechannel their naturally selfish interests into socially acceptable outlets; in this sense, they are passive subjects to be molded by the more powerful elements of society—namely, parents. Locke, too, believed that the child's role is passive because the mind of an infant is a blank slate on which experience writes its lessons. But a strikingly different view was proposed by Rousseau, who believed that children are actively involved in the shaping of their own intellects and personalities. In Rousseau's words, the child is not a "passive recipient of the tutor's instruction" but a "busy, testing, motivated explorer. The active searching child, setting his own problems, stands in marked contrast to the receptive one ... on whom society fixes its stamp" (quoted in Kessen, 1965, p. 75).

Clearly, these philosophers had some interesting ideas about children and child-rearing. But how could anyone decide whether their views were correct? Unfortunately, the philosophers collected no objective data to back their pronouncements, and the few observations they did make were limited and unsystematic.

Children as Subjects: The Baby Biographies

The first glimmering of a systematic study of children can be traced to the late 19th century. This was a period in which investigators from a variety of academic backgrounds began to observe the development of their own children and to publish these data in works known as **baby biographies**.

Perhaps the most influential of the baby biographers was Charles Darwin, who made daily records of the early development of his son (Darwin, 1877; see also Charlesworth, 1992). Darwin's curiosity about child development stemmed from his earlier theory of evolution. Quite simply, he believed that young, untrained infants share many characteristics with their nonhuman ancestors, and he advanced the (now discredited) idea that the development of the individual child retraces the entire evolutionary history of the species, thereby illustrating the "descent of man." So Darwin and many of his contemporaries viewed the baby biography as a means of answering questions about our evolutionary past.

Baby biographies left much to be desired as works of science. Different baby biographers emphasized very different aspects of their children's behaviour, so different baby biographies were difficult to compare. Furthermore, parents are not entirely objective about their own children, and baby biographers like Darwin may also have let their assumptions about the nature of development bias their observations so that they only found what they were looking for. Finally, each baby biography was based on a single child—and often the child of a distinguished individual. Conclusions based on a single case may not hold true for other children.

Despite these shortcomings, baby biographies were a step in the right direction. The fact that eminent scientists such as Darwin were now writing about developing children implied that human development was a topic worthy of scientific scrutiny.

Development of Children's Rights in Canada

Issues regarding children's rights evolved to match the development of the concept of childhood. For example, societies had to struggle with defining who was responsible for children—society or parents—as well as defining how to protect children. Canadian public policy regarding the rights of children demonstrates the struggle that societies

Original sin

Innate purity

tabula rasa
idea that the mind of an infant is a "blank slate" and that all knowledge, abilities, behaviours, and motives are acquired through experience

baby biography
detailed record of an infant's growth and development over a period of time

Charles Darwin (1809–82) recorded baby biographies that stimulated interest in the study of development.

American psychologist G. Stanley Hall (1846–1924) is recognized as one of the founders of developmental psychology.

Sigmund Freud (1856–1939) developed one of the first theories to explain development.

faced in their efforts to cope with the evolving concept of childhood and the inherent changes in the responsibilities of parents and society. Brian Howe (1995), at the University College of Cape Breton, identifies three changes in Canadian policy that reflect the historical changes outlined above. Canadian children moved from being viewed as family property to dependants in need of state protection. Slowly this gave way to the recognition that children were semi-independent individuals with rights of their own. Now society is moving toward a recognition that children are entities in their own right and should be afforded the economic security guaranteed to other members of society.

Origins of a Science of Development

Introductory textbooks in most academic areas typically credit someone as the founder of the discipline. In developmental psychology, there were several influential pioneers who merit consideration for this honour. Still, the person who is most often cited as the founder of developmental psychology is G. Stanley Hall.

Well aware of the shortcomings of baby biographies, Hall set out in the late 19th century to collect more objective data on larger samples. Specifically, he was interested in children's thinking, and he developed a now familiar research tool—the *questionnaire*—to explore "the contents of children's minds" (Hall, 1891). By asking children questions about a range of topics, Hall discovered that children's understanding of the world grows rapidly during childhood and that the logic of young children is not very logical at all. Hall later wrote an influential book titled *Adolescence* (1904) that was the first work to call attention to adolescence as a unique phase of the human life span. His work was the first large-scale scientific investigation of developing youth, and it is on this basis that G. Stanley Hall merits consideration as the founder of developmental psychology (White, 1992).

At about the time Hall was using questionnaires to study children's minds, a young European neurologist was trying a different method of probing the mind and revealing its contents. The neurologist's approach was very fruitful, providing information that led him to propose a theory that revolutionized thinking about children and childhood. The neurologist was Sigmund Freud, and his ideas came to be known as *psychoanalytic theory*.

In many areas of science, new theories are often revisions or modifications of old theories. But in Freud's day, there were few "old" theories of human development to modify. Freud was truly a pioneer, formulating his psychoanalytic theory from the thousands of notes and observations he made while treating patients for various kinds of emotional disturbances.

Freud's highly creative and unorthodox theorizing soon attracted a lot of attention. Shortly after the publication of Freud's earliest theoretical monographs, the *International Journal of Psychoanalysis* was founded, and other researchers began to report their tests of Freud's thinking. By the mid-1930s, much of Freud's work had been translated into other languages, and the impact of psychoanalytic theory was felt around the world. Over the years, Freud's theory proved to be quite *heuristic*, meaning it continued to generate new research and to prompt other researchers to revise and extend Freud's thinking. Clearly, the field of developmental psychology was thriving by the time Freud died in 1939.

Freud's work—and other scientists' reactions to it—aptly illustrates the role that theories play in the science of human development. Although the word *theory* is an imposing term, theories are something that everybody has. If we were to ask you why males and females appear different as adults when they seem so very similar as infants, you probably would have some opinions on the issue. Your answer would state or at least reflect your own underlying theory of sex differences. So a **theory** is really nothing more than a set of concepts and propositions that allow the theorist to describe and explain some aspect of experience. In the field of psychology, theories help us to describe and explain various patterns of behaviour.

Good theories have another important feature: the ability to predict future events. These theoretical predictions, or **hypotheses**, are then tested by collecting additional data. The information we obtain when testing hypotheses not only provides some clues about the theory's ability to explain new observations but may also lead to new theoretical insights that extend our knowledge.

Today there are many theories that have contributed to our understanding of child and adolescent development, and in Chapter 2 we will examine several of the more influential of these viewpoints. Although it is natural for people reading about various theories to favour one, the scientist uses a rather stringent criterion to evaluate theories: He or she will formulate hypotheses and conduct research to determine whether the theory can adequately predict and explain new observations. Thus, there is no room for subjective bias when evaluating a theory. Theories in the developmental sciences are only as good as their ability to predict and explain important aspects of human development.

In the next section of the chapter, we will focus on the tools of the trade—that is, the research methods that developmentalists use to test their theories and gain a better understanding of child and adolescent development.

RESEARCH METHODS IN DEVELOPMENTAL PSYCHOLOGY

When detectives are assigned cases to solve, they first gather the facts, formulate hunches, and then sift through the clues or collect additional information until one of their hunches proves correct. Unravelling the mysteries of development is in many ways a similar endeavour. Investigators must carefully observe their subjects, analyze the information they collect, and use these data to draw conclusions about the ways people develop.

Our focus in this section is on the methods that researchers use to gather information about developing children and adolescents. Our first task is to understand why developmentalists consider it essential to collect all these facts. We will then discuss the advantages and disadvantages of five basic fact-finding strategies: self-report methodologies, systematic observation, case studies, ethnography, and psychophysiological methods. Finally, we will consider the ways developmentalists might design their research to detect and explain age-related changes in children's feelings, thoughts, abilities, and behaviours.

The Scientific Method

Modern developmental psychology is appropriately labelled a scientific enterprise because those who study developing organisms have adopted a value system we call the **scientific method** that guides their attempts at understanding. There is nothing mysterious about the scientific method. It is really more of an *attitude* or *value* than a method, one which dictates that, above all, investigators must be *objective* and must allow their observations (or data) to decide the merits of their thinking.

In earlier eras, when social philosophers such as Hobbes, Locke, and Rousseau were presenting their views on children and child-rearing, their largely unsubstantiated claims were often accepted as facts. People assumed that great minds always had great insights. Few individuals questioned the word of these well-known scholars because the scientific method was not yet a widely accepted criterion for evaluating knowledge.

theory
set of concepts and propositions designed to organize, describe, and explain an existing set of observations

hypothesis
theoretical prediction about some aspect of experience

scientific method
attitude or value about the pursuit of knowledge that dictates that investigators must be objective and must allow their data to decide the merits of their theorizing

?

WHAT DO YOU THINK?

What might you say to a person who rejects an established finding by saying "It didn't happen that way for my child"? If this parent's recollection is accurate, does this invalidate the finding?

The intent here is not to criticize the early social philosophers. In fact, today's developmentalists (and children) are deeply indebted to these thinkers for helping to modify the ways in which society regarded and treated its young. However, great minds may on occasion produce miserable ideas that can do a great deal of harm if their errors in thinking are uncritically accepted and influence the way human beings are treated. The scientific method, then, is a valuable safeguard that helps to protect the scientific community and society at large against flawed reasoning. Protection is provided by the practice of evaluating the merits of various theoretical pronouncements against the objective record, rather than simply relying on the academic, political, or social credibility of the theorist. Of course, this also means that the theorist whose ideas are being evaluated must be equally objective and, thus, willing to discard pet notions when there is evidence against them.

Gathering Data: Basic Fact-Finding Strategies

No matter what aspect of development we hope to study—be it the perceptual capabilities of newborn infants, the growth of friendships among elementary-school children, the relation between media violence and aggression, or the reasons some adolescents begin to use drugs—we must find ways to measure what interests us. Today researchers are fortunate in having many tried-and-true procedures that they might use to measure behaviour and to test their hypotheses about human development. But regardless of the technique one employs, scientifically useful measures must always display two important qualities: **reliability** and **validity**.

A measure is *reliable* if it yields consistent information over time and across observers. Suppose you go into a classroom and record the number of times each child behaves aggressively toward others, but your research assistant, using the same scheme to observe the same children, does not agree with your measurements; or you measure each child's aggressiveness one week but come up with very different aggressiveness scores while applying the same measure to the same children a week later. Clearly, your observational measure of aggression is unreliable because it yields highly inconsistent information. To be reliable and thus useful for scientific purposes, your measure would have to produce comparable estimates of children's aggression from independent observers (*interrater reliability*), and would yield similar scores for individual children from one testing to another shortly thereafter (*temporal stability*).

A measure is *valid* if it measures what it is supposed to measure. Obviously, an instrument must be reliable and measure consistently before it can possibly be valid. Yet reliability, by itself, does not guarantee validity (Miller, 1997). For example, a highly reliable observational scheme that is intended as a measure of children's aggression may provide grossly overinflated estimates of aggressive behaviour if the investigator simply classifies all acts of physical force as examples of aggression. What the researcher has failed to recognize is that much high-intensity behaviour simply may represent enjoyable forms of rough-and-tumble play without harmful or aggressive intent. Clearly, researchers must demonstrate that they are measuring the attribute they say they are measuring before we can have much faith in the data they collect or the conclusions they reach.

Keeping in mind the importance of establishing the reliability and validity of measures, let us consider some of the different ways in which aspects of human development might be measured.

reliability
extent to which a measuring instrument yields consistent results, both over time and across observers

validity
extent to which a measuring instrument accurately reflects what the researchers intended to measure

Self-Report Methodologies

Three common procedures that developmentalists use to gather information and test hypotheses are interviews, questionnaires (including psychological tests), and the clinical method. Although these approaches are similar in that each asks participants to answer questions posed by the investigator, they differ in the extent to which the investigator treats individual participants alike.

INTERVIEWS AND QUESTIONNAIRES. Researchers who opt for interview or questionnaire techniques ask the child (or the child's parents) a series of questions pertaining to such aspects of development as the child's conduct, feelings, beliefs, or characteristic methods of thinking. Collecting data via a questionnaire (and most psychological tests) simply involves putting questions on paper and asking participants to respond to them in writing, whereas interviews require participants to respond orally to the investigator's queries. If the procedure is a **structured interview** or **structured questionnaire**, all who participate in the study are asked the same questions in the same order. The purpose of this standardized or structured format is to treat each person alike so that the responses of different participants can be compared.

One interesting use of the interview technique is a project in which kindergarten, Grade 2, and Grade 4 children responded to 24 questions designed to assess their knowledge of social stereotypes about males and females (Williams, Bennett, & Best, 1975). Each question came in response to a different short story in which the central character was described by either stereotypically masculine adjectives (for example, *aggressive, forceful, tough*) or stereotypically feminine adjectives (for example, *emotional, excitable*). The child's task was to indicate whether the character in each story was male or female. Williams and his associates found that even kindergartners could usually tell whether the stories referred to boys or girls. In other words, these 5-year-olds were quite knowledgeable about gender stereotypes, although children's thinking became more stereotyped between kindergarten and Grade 2. One implication of these results is that stereotyping of the sexes must begin very early if kindergartners are already thinking along stereotyped lines.

Interviews and questionnaires have some very real shortcomings. First, neither approach can be used with very young children who cannot read or comprehend speech very well. Investigators also must hope that the answers they receive are honest and accurate and are not merely attempts by respondents to present themselves in a favourable or socially desirable way. Many adolescents, for example, may be unwilling to admit that they regularly masturbate, or that they smoke marijuana, or that they enjoy the risks of shoplifting. Clearly, inaccurate or untruthful responses lead to erroneous conclusions. Investigators must also be careful to ensure that participants of all ages interpret questions in the same way; otherwise, the age trends observed in the study may reflect differences in children's ability to comprehend and communicate rather than real underlying changes in their feelings, thoughts, or behaviours. Finally, researchers who interview both developing children and their parents (or teachers) may have trouble determining which set of reports is more accurate should the children's descriptions of their own behaviours differ from those of the other informants.

Despite these potential shortcomings, structured interviews and questionnaires can be excellent methods of obtaining large amounts of useful information in a short period of time. Both approaches are particularly useful when the investigator emphasizes to participants that their responses will be confidential and challenges them to report exactly what they know about an issue, thereby maximizing the likelihood of a truthful or accurate answer. In the gender stereotyping study, for example, the young participants probably considered each question a personal challenge or a puzzle to be solved and were thus motivated to answer accurately and to display exactly what they knew about males and females. Under the circumstances, then, the structured interview was an excellent method of assessing children's perceptions of the sexes.

THE CLINICAL METHOD. The **clinical method** is a very close relative of the interview technique. The investigator usually is interested in testing a hypothesis by presenting the research participant with a task or stimulus of some sort and then inviting a response. After the participant responds, the investigator typically asks a second question or introduces a new task to clarify the participant's original answer. Although subjects are often asked the same questions initially, each participant's answer determines what he or she is asked next. Thus, the clinical method is a flexible approach that considers each subject to be unique.

structured interview or structured questionnaire
technique in which all participants are asked the same questions in precisely the same order so that the responses of different participants can be compared

clinical method
type of interview in which a participant's response to each successive question (or problem) determines what the investigator will ask next

Jean Piaget, a famous Swiss psychologist, relied extensively on the clinical method to study children's moral reasoning and intellectual development. The data from Piaget's research are largely protocol records of his interactions with individual children. Here is a small sample from Piaget's work (1932/1965, p. 140) on the development of moral reasoning, which shows that this young child thinks about lying in a very different way than adults do:

> Do you know what a lie is?—*It's when you say what isn't true.*—Is 2 + 2 = 5 a lie?—
> *Yes, it's a lie.*—Why?—*Because it isn't right.*—Did the boy who said 2 + 2 = 5 know
> it wasn't right or did he make a mistake?—*He made a mistake.*—Then if he made
> a mistake, did he tell a lie or not?—*Yes, he told a lie.*

Like structured interviews, clinical methods are often useful for gathering large amounts of information in relatively brief periods. Proponents of this approach also cite its flexibility as an advantage: By asking follow-up questions that are tailored to the participant's original answers (as Piaget did in the above example), it is often possible to obtain a rich understanding of the meaning of those answers. However, the flexibility of the clinical method is also a potential shortcoming. Consider that it may be difficult, if not impossible, to directly compare the answers of participants who are asked different questions. Furthermore, the practice of tailoring one's questions to the participant's responses raises the possibility that the examiner's pre-existing theoretical biases may affect the particular follow-up questions asked and the interpretations provided. Since conclusions drawn from the clinical method depend, in part, on the investigator's *subjective* interpretations, it is always desirable to verify these insights using other research techniques.

Observational Methodologies

Often researchers prefer to observe people's behaviour directly rather than asking them questions about it. One method that many developmentalists favour is **naturalistic observation**—observing people in their common (i.e., natural) surroundings (Pellegrini, 1996). To observe children, this usually means going into homes, schools, or public parks and playgrounds and carefully recording what they do. Rarely will the investigator try to record every event that occurs; they usually are testing a specific hypothesis about one type of behaviour, such as cooperation or aggression, and will focus exclusively on acts of this kind. One strength of naturalistic observation is the ease with which it can be applied to infants and toddlers, who often cannot be studied through methods that demand verbal skills. But perhaps the greatest advantage of naturalistic observation is that it illustrates how people actually behave in everyday life (Willems & Alexander, 1982).

naturalistic observation
method in which the scientist tests hypotheses by observing people as they engage in everyday activities in their natural habitats (for example, at home, at school, or on the playground)

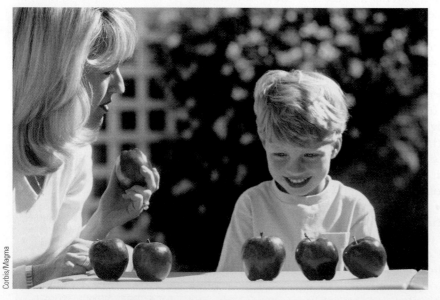

Investigators using the clinical method. All participants are asked the same questions at first, but each participant's answers to these initial questions determine what the researcher will ask next.

However, naturalistic observation also has its limitations. First, some behaviours occur so infrequently (for example, heroic rescues) or are so socially undesirable (for example, overt sex play or thievery) that they are unlikely to be witnessed by an unknown observer in the natural environment. Second, many events are usually happening at the same time in a natural setting, and any (or some combination) of them may affect people's behaviour. This makes it difficult to pinpoint the causes of participants' actions or of any developmental trends in behaviour. Finally, the mere presence of an observer sometimes makes people behave differently than they otherwise would. Children may ham it up when they have an audience, whereas parents may be on their best behaviour, showing a strong reluctance, for example, to spank a misbehaving child as they normally might. For these reasons, researchers often attempt to minimize **observer influence** by (1) videotaping their participants from a concealed location or (2) spending time in the setting before collecting their "real" data so that the individuals they are observing will grow accustomed to their presence and behave more naturally.

Several years ago, Mary Haskett and Janet Kistner (1991) conducted an excellent piece of naturalistic observation to compare the social behaviours of nonabused preschoolers with those of daycare classmates identified by child protection agencies as having been physically abused by their parents. The investigators first defined examples of the behaviours they wished to record—both *desirable* behaviours such as appropriate social initiations and positive play, and *undesirable* behaviours such as aggression and negative verbalizations. They then monitored 14 abused and 14 nonabused preschool children as they mingled with peers in a play area of a daycare facility. Observations were made according to a **time-sampling** procedure: each child was observed during three 10-minute play sessions on three different days. To minimize their influence on the play activities, observers stood outside the play area while making their observations.

The results were disturbing. As shown in Figure 1.1, abused children initiated fewer social interactions than their nonabused classmates and were somewhat socially withdrawn. And when they did interact with playmates, the abused youngsters displayed more aggressive acts and other negative behaviours than did their nonabused companions. Indeed, nonabused children often blatantly ignored the positive social initiations of an abused child, as if they did not want to get involved with him or her.

In sum, Haskett and Kistner's observational study shows that abused children are unattractive playmates who are likely to be disliked and even rejected by peers. But as is almost always the case in naturalistic observational research, it is difficult to pinpoint the exact cause of these findings. Did the negative behaviours of abused children cause their peers to reject them? Or did peer rejection cause the abused children to display negative behaviours? Either possibility can account for Haskett and Kistner's results.

How might observational researchers study unusual or undesirable behaviours that they are unlikely to observe in the natural environment? One way is to conduct **structured observations** in the laboratory. In a structured observational study, each participant is exposed to a setting that might cue the behaviour in question, and is then surreptitiously observed (via a hidden camera or through a one-way mirror) to see if he or she performs the behaviour. For example, Leon Kuczynski (1983) got children to promise to help him with a boring task and then left them alone to work in a room where attractive toys were present. This procedure enabled Kuczynski to determine whether youngsters would break a promise to work (an undesirable act that many children displayed) when they thought there was no one present to observe their transgression.

Children's tendency to perform for observers is one of the problems that researchers must overcome when using the method of naturalistic observation.

Joanna Cotton

observer influence
tendency of participants to react to an observer's presence by behaving in unusual ways

time-sampling
procedure in which the investigator records the frequencies with which individuals display particular behaviours during the brief time intervals that each participant is observed

structured observation
observational method in which the investigator cues the behaviour of interest and observes participants' responses in a laboratory

Figure 1.1 *Social initiations and negative behaviours of abused and nonabused preschool children. Compared with their nonabused companions, abused youngsters initiate far fewer social interactions with peers and behave much more negatively toward them.*

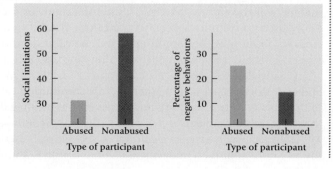

Aside from being a most feasible way of studying behaviours that occur infrequently or are not openly displayed in the natural environment, structured observations also ensure that every participant in the sample is exposed to the *same* eliciting stimuli and has an *equal opportunity* to perform the target behaviour—circumstances that are not always true in the natural environment. Of course, the major disadvantage of structured observations is that participants may not always respond in a contrived laboratory setting as they would in everyday life.

Case Studies

Any or all of the data collection methods we have discussed—structured interviews, questionnaires, clinical method, and behavioural observations—can be used to compile a detailed portrait of a single individual's development through the **case study** method. In preparing an individualized record, or case, the investigator typically seeks many kinds of information about the participant, such as his or her family background, socio-economic status, health records, academic or work history, and performance on psychological tests. Much of the information included in any case study comes from interviews with and observations of the individual, although the questions asked and observations made are typically not standardized and may vary considerably from case to case.

The baby biographies of the 19th and early 20th centuries are examples of case studies, and Sigmund Freud conducted many fascinating case studies of his clinical patients. In analyzing his cases, Freud noticed that different patients often described very similar events and experiences that had been noteworthy to them as they were growing up. He inferred from the observations that there must be important milestones in human development that all people share. As he continued to observe his patients and to listen to accounts of their lives, Freud concluded that each milestone in the life history of a patient was meaningfully related to earlier events. He then inferred that he had the data to construct a comprehensive explanation of human development—the account we know today as psychoanalytic theory.

Although Freud and many other developmentalists have used case studies to great advantage, there are major drawbacks to this approach. For example, it is often difficult to directly compare cases who have been asked different questions, taken different tests, and been observed under different circumstances. Case studies may also lack *generalizability*; that is, conclusions drawn from the experiences of the small number of individuals studied may simply not apply to most people. In fact, one recurring criticism of Freud's psychoanalytic theory is that it was formulated from the life histories of *emotionally disturbed patients*, who are hardly typical of the general population. For these reasons, any conclusions drawn from case studies should always be verified by using other research techniques.

Ethnography

Ethnography—a form of participant observation often used in the field of anthropology—is becoming increasingly popular among researchers who hope to understand the impacts of culture on developing children and adolescents. To collect their data, ethnographers often live within the cultural or subcultural community they are studying for periods of months or even years. The data they collect is typically diverse and extensive, consisting largely of naturalistic observations, notes made from conversations with members of the culture, and initial interpretations of these events. These data are eventually used to compile a detailed portrait of the cultural community and to draw conclusions about how the community's unique values and traditions influence one or more aspects of the development of its children and adolescents.

Clearly detailed ethnographic portraits of a culture or subculture that arise from close and enduring contact with members of the community can lead to a richer understanding of that community's traditions and values than is possible through a small number of visits, in which outsiders make limited observations and conduct a few interviews (LeVine et al., 1994). In fact, such extensive cultural or subcultural descriptions are particularly useful to investigators hoping to understand cultural conflicts and other developmental challenges

case study
research method in which the investigator gathers extensive information about the life of an individual and then tests developmental hypotheses by analyzing the events of the person's life history

ethnography
method in which the researcher seeks to understand the unique values, traditions, and social processes of a culture or subculture by living with its members and making extensive observations and notes

faced by minority children and adolescents in diverse multicultural societies (Segal, 1991; see also Patel, Power, & Bhavnagri, 1996). Despite these clear strengths, ethnography is a highly subjective method because researchers' own cultural values and theoretical biases can cause them to misinterpret what they have experienced. In addition, ethnographic conclusions pertain only to the culture or sub-culture studied and cannot be assumed to generalize to other contexts or social groups.

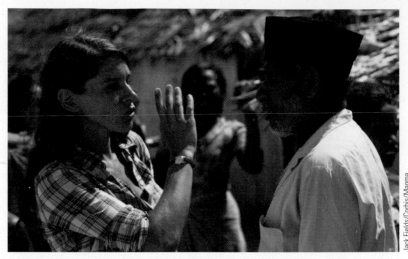

Ethnographic researchers attempt to understand cultural influences by living within the community and participating in all aspects of community life.

Psychophysiological Methods

In recent years, developmentalists have turned to **psychophysiological methods**—techniques that measure the relationship between physiological responses and behaviour—to explore the biological underpinnings of children's perceptual, cognitive, and emotional responses. Psychophysiological methods are particularly useful for interpreting the mental and emotional experiences of infants and toddlers who are unable to report such events (Bornstein, 1992).

Heart rate is an involuntary physiological response that is highly sensitive to one's psychological experiences. Compared with their normal resting, or *baseline*, levels, infants who are carefully attending to an interesting stimulus may show a *decrease* in heart rate, whereas those who are uninterested in it may show no heart rate change, and others, who are wary of or angered by the stimulus, may show a heart rate *increase* (Campos, Bertenthal, & Kermoian, 1992; Fox & Fitzgerald, 1990). Measures of brain function are also useful for assessing psychological state. For example, electroencephalogram (EEG) recordings of brain wave activity can be obtained by attaching electrodes to the scalp. Because different patterns of EEG activity characterize different arousal states, such as sleep, drowsiness, and alertness, investigators can track these patterns and determine how sleep cycles and other states of arousal change with age. Novel stimuli or events also produce short-term changes in EEG activity. So an investigator who hopes to test the limits of infant sensory capabilities can present novel sights and sounds and look for changes in brain waves (called *event-related potentials*, or *ERPs*) to determine whether these stimuli have been detected, or even discriminated, for two stimuli sensed as "different" will produce different patterns of brain activity (Bornstein, 1992). More recently, technological advances have made it possible to observe the brain "in action." Using MRI (Magnetic Resonance Imaging) and fMRI (functional Magnetic Resonance Imaging) technology, researchers can compare pictures before a subject engages in an activity and during the activity to see which areas of the brain were activated. The fMRI equipment, such as that found at the Robarts Institute at the University of Western Ontario and the London Health Sciences Centre, is allowing researchers to embark on new research.

Though very useful, psychophysiological responses are far from perfect indicators of psychological states. Even though an infant's heart rate or brain wave activity may indicate that he or she is attending to a stimulus, it is often difficult to determine exactly which aspect of that stimulus (shape, colour, etc.) has captured attention. Furthermore, changes in physiological responses often reflect mood swings, fatigue, hunger, or even negative reactions to the physiological recording equipment rather than a change in the infant's attention to a stimulus or emotional reactions to it. For these reasons, physiological responses are more likely to be valid indications of psychological experiences when participants (particularly very young ones) are initially calm, alert, and contented.

Newer technologies such as MRI and fMRI have two additional drawbacks. First, the machines used to generate the images are extremely expensive, so few machines are available. Those machines that are available, however, are often required for medical situations rather than for research purposes. When machines are available for research,

psychophysiological methods
methods that measure the relationships between physiological processes and aspects of children's physical, cognitive, social, or emotional behaviour and development

there can be very strict time frames in which the research can be conducted, which may not coincide with an infant's or child's ideal time for participation. The second concern is that the technology is invasive and has associated risks, which raises ethical issues, especially when young children are involved.

Table 1.2 provides a brief review of the data-gathering methods that we have examined thus far. In the sections that follow, we will consider how investigators might design their research to test hypotheses and detect developmental continuities and changes.

Concept Check 1.1
Matching Research Methods to Research Questions

Check your understanding of the uses and strengths of various research methods by figuring out which method is best suited for investigating each of the following questions. Choose from these methods: (a) structured interview, (b) ethnography, (c) naturalistic observation, (d) structured observation, (e) psychophysiological methods. Answers appear in the Appendix.

_____ 1. Will young elementary-school children break a solemn promise to watch a sick puppy when no one is around to detect their transgression?

_____ 2. Do 6-year-olds know any negative stereotypes about minority group members?

_____ 3. Can 6-month-old infants discriminate the colours red, green, blue, and yellow?

_____ 4. Are the aggressive actions that boy playmates display toward one another different from those that occur in girls' play groups?

_____ 5. How does life change for boys from the Sambia tribe once they have experienced tribal rites of puberty?

TABLE 1.2	Strengths and Limitations of Seven Common Research Methods	
Method	**Strengths**	**Limitations**
Self-reports		
Interviews and questionnaires	Relatively quick way to gather much information; standardized format allows the investigator to make direct comparisons between data provided by different participants.	Data collected may be inaccurate or less than completely honest, or may reflect variations in respondents' verbal skills and ability to understand questions.
Clinical method	Flexible methodology that treats subjects as unique individuals; freedom to probe can be an aid in ensuring that the participant understands the meaning of the questions asked.	Conclusions drawn may be unreliable in that participants are not all treated alike; flexible probes depend, in part, on the investigator's subjective interpretations of the participant's responses; can be used only with highly verbal participants.
Systematic observations		
Naturalistic observation	Allows study of behaviour as it actually occurs in the natural environment.	Observed behaviours may be influenced by observer's presence; unusual or undesirable behaviours are unlikely to be observed during the periods when observations are made.
Structured observation	Offers a standardized environment that provides every child an opportunity to perform target behaviour. Excellent way to observe infrequent or socially undesirable acts.	Contrived observations may not always capture the ways children behave in the natural environment.
Case studies	Very broad method that considers many sources of data when drawing inferences and conclusions about individual participants.	Kind of data collected often differs from case to case and may be inaccurate or less than honest; conclusions drawn from individual cases are subjective and may not apply to other people.
Ethnography	Provides a richer description of cultural beliefs, values, and traditions than is possible in brief observational or interview studies.	Conclusions may be biased by the investigator's values and theoretical viewpoints; results cannot be generalized beyond the groups and settings that were studied.
Psychophysiological methods	Useful for assessing biological underpinnings of development and identifying the perceptions, thoughts, and emotions of infants and toddlers who cannot report them verbally.	Cannot indicate with certainty what participants sense or feel; many factors other than the one being studied can produce a similar physiological response.

DETECTING RELATIONSHIPS: CORRELATIONAL AND EXPERIMENTAL DESIGNS

Once researchers have decided what they want to study, they must devise a research plan, or design, that permits them to identify relationships among events and behaviours and to specify the causes of these relationships. Here we consider the two general research designs that investigators might employ: correlational and experimental.

The Correlational Design

In a **correlational design**, the investigator gathers information to determine whether two or more variables of interest are meaningfully related. If the researcher is testing a specific hypothesis (rather than conducting preliminary descriptive or exploratory research), he or she will be checking to see whether these variables are related as the hypothesis specifies they should be. No attempts are made to structure or manipulate the participants' environment in any way. Instead, correlational researchers take people as they find them—already "manipulated" by natural life experiences—and try to determine whether variations in people's life experiences are associated with differences in their behaviours or patterns of development.

To illustrate the correlational approach to hypothesis testing, let's work with a simple theory specifying that youngsters learn a lot from watching television and are apt to imitate the actions of the characters they observe. One hypothesis we might derive from this theory is that the more frequently children observe TV characters who display violent and aggressive acts, the more inclined they will be to behave aggressively toward their own playmates. After selecting a sample of children to study, our next step in testing our hypothesis is to measure the two variables that we think are related. To assess children's exposure to violent themes on television, we might use the interview or naturalistic observational methods to determine what each child watches, and then count the number of aggressive acts that occur in this programming. To measure the frequency of the children's own aggressive behaviour toward peers, we could observe our sample on a playground and record how often each child behaves in a hostile, aggressive manner toward playmates. Having now gathered the data, it is time to evaluate our hypothesis.

The presence (or absence) of a relationship between variables can be determined by subjecting the data to a statistical procedure that yields a **correlation coefficient** (symbolized by an r). This statistic provides a numerical estimate of the strength and direction of the relationship between two variables. It can range in value from +1.00 to –1.00. The absolute value of r (disregarding its sign) tells us the *strength* of the relationship. Thus, correlation coefficients of –.70 and +.70 are of equal strength, and both are stronger than a moderate correlation of .50. An r of .00 indicates that the two variables are not systematically related. The sign of the correlation coefficient indicates the *direction* of the relationship. If the sign is positive, this means that as the variable increases, the other variable also increases. For example, height and weight are positively correlated: As children grow taller, they tend to get heavier (Tanner, 1990). Negative correlations, however, indicate inverse relationships; as one variable increases, the other *decreases*. Among elementary-school students, for example, aggression and popularity are negatively correlated: Children who behave more aggressively tend to be *less* popular with their peers (Crick, 1996).

correlational design
type of research design that indicates the strength of associations among variables; though correlated variables are systematically related, these relationships are not necessarily causal

correlation coefficient
numerical index (symbolized by an r), ranging from –1.00 to +1.00, of the strength and direction of the relationship between two variables

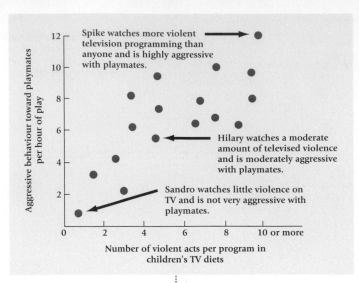

Spike watches more violent television programming than anyone and is highly aggressive with playmates.

Hilary watches a moderate amount of televised violence and is moderately aggressive with playmates.

Sandro watches little violence on TV and is not very aggressive with playmates.

Figure 1.2 *Plot of a hypothetical positive correlation between the amount of violence that children see on television and the number of aggressive responses they display. Each dot represents a specific child who views a particular level of televised violence (shown on the horizontal axis) and commits a particular number of aggressive acts (shown on the vertical axis). Although the correlation is less than perfect, we see that the more acts of violence a child watches on TV, the more inclined he or she is to behave aggressively toward peers.*

experimental design
research design in which the investigator introduces some change in the participant's environment and then measures the effect of that change on the participant's behaviour

independent variable
aspect of the environment that an experimenter modifies or manipulates in order to measure its impact on behaviour

dependent variable
aspect of behaviour that is measured in an experiment and assumed to be under the control of the independent variable

Now let's return to our hypothesized positive relationship between televised violence and children's aggressive behaviour. A number of investigators have conducted correlational studies similar to the one we have designed, and the results (reviewed in Liebert & Sprafkin, 1988) suggest a moderate positive correlation (between +.30 and +.50) between the two variables of interest: Children who watch a lot of violent television programming are more likely to behave aggressively toward playmates than are other children who watch little violent programming (see Figure 1.2 for a visual display).

Do these correlational studies establish that exposure to violent TV programming *causes* children to behave more aggressively? *No, they do not!* Although we have detected a relationship between exposure to televised violence and children's aggressive behaviour, the causal direction of the relationship is not at all clear. An equally plausible alternative explanation is that relatively aggressive children are more inclined to prefer violent programming. Another possibility is that the association between TV viewing and aggressive behaviour is actually caused by a third variable we have not measured. For example, perhaps parents who fight a lot at home (an unmeasured variable) cause their children to become more aggressive *and* to favour violent TV programming. If this were true, the latter two variables may be correlated, even though their relationship to each other is not one of cause and effect.

In conclusion, the correlational design is a versatile approach that can detect systematic relationships between any two or more variables that we might be interested in and capable of measuring. However, its major limitation is that *it cannot unambiguously indicate that one thing causes another.* How, then, might a researcher establish the underlying causes of various behaviours or other aspects of human development? One solution is to conduct experiments.

The Experimental Design

In contrast to correlational studies, **experimental designs** permit a precise assessment of the cause-and-effect relationship that may exist between two variables. Let's return to the issue of whether viewing violent television programming *causes* children to become more aggressively inclined. In conducting a laboratory experiment to test this (or any) hypothesis, we would bring participants to the lab, expose them to different treatments, and record their responses to these treatments as data.

The different treatments to which we expose our participants represent the **independent variable** of our experiment. To test the hypothesis we have proposed, our independent variable (or treatments) would be the type of television program that our participants observe. Half the children might view a program in which characters behave in a violent or otherwise aggressive manner toward others, whereas the other half would watch a program that contains little, if any, violence.

Children's reactions to the television shows would become the data, or **dependent variable**, in our experiment. Because our hypothesis centres on children's aggression, we would want to measure (as our dependent variable) how aggressively children behave after watching each type of television show. A variable is dependent because its value presumably depends on the independent variable. In the present case, we are hypothesizing that future aggression (our dependent variable) will be greater for children who watch violent programs (one level of the independent variable) than for those who watch nonviolent programs (the second level of the independent variable). If we are careful experimenters and exercise precise control over *all* other factors that may affect children's aggression, then the pattern of results that we have anticipated will allow us to draw a strong conclusion: Watching violent television programs *causes* children to behave more aggressively.

An experiment similar to the one we have proposed was actually conducted (Liebert & Baron, 1972). Half of the 5- to 9-year-olds in this study watched a violent three-minute clip from the *Untouchables*—one that contained two fistfights, two shootings, and a stabbing. The remaining children watched a three-minute film of a nonviolent but exciting track meet. So the *independent variable* was the type of program watched. Then each child was taken into another room and seated in front of a panel that had wires leading into an adjoining room. On the panel was a green button labelled HELP, a red button labelled HURT, and a white light between the buttons. The experimenter then told the child that another child in the adjoining room would soon be playing a handle-turning game that would illuminate the white light. The participant was told that by pushing the buttons when the light was on, he or she could either *help* the other child by making the handle easy to turn or *hurt* the child by making the handle become very hot. When it was clear that the participant understood the instructions, the experimenter left the room, and the light came on 20 times over the next several minutes. So each participant had 20 opportunities to help or hurt another child. The total amount of time each participant spent pushing the hurt button served as a measure of his or her aggression—the *dependent variable* in this study.

The results were clear: Despite the availability of an alternative, helping response, *both boys and girls were much more likely to press the HURT button if they had watched the violent television program.* So it appears that a mere 3-minute exposure to televised violence can *cause* children to behave more aggressively toward a peer, even though the aggressive acts they witnessed on television bore no resemblance to those they committed themselves.

?   WHAT DO YOU THINK?

Short of ridding all homes of televisions, what steps might concerned parents take to lessen the potentially harmful impacts of televised violence on young children? After formulating your plan, compare it to suggestions offered by the experts in Table 16.2 on page 610.

When students discuss this experiment in class, someone invariably challenges this interpretation of the results. For example, one student recently proposed an alternative explanation that "maybe the kids who watched the violent film were naturally more aggressive than those who watched the track meet." In other words, he was suggesting that a **confounding variable**—children's pre-existing levels of aggression—had determined their willingness to hurt a peer and that the independent variable (type of television program) had had no effect at all. Could this be correct? How do we know that the children in the two experimental conditions didn't differ in some important way that may have affected their willingness to hurt a peer?

This question brings us to the crucial issue of **experimental control**. In order to conclude that the independent variable is causally related to the dependent variable, the experimenter must ensure that all other confounding variables that could affect the dependent variable are *controlled*—that is, equivalent in each experimental condition. One way to equalize these extraneous factors is to do what Liebert and Baron (1972) did: randomly assign children to their experimental treatments. The concept of *randomization*, or **random assignment**, means that each research participant has an equal probability of being exposed to each experimental treatment or condition. Assignment of individual participants to a particular treatment is accomplished by an unbiased procedure such as the flip of a coin. If the assignment is truly random, there is only a very slim chance that participants in the two (or more) experimental conditions will differ on any characteristic that might affect their performance on the dependent variable; all of these confounding variables will have been randomly distributed within each condition and equalized across the different conditions. Because Liebert and Baron randomly assigned subjects to experimental conditions, they could be reasonably certain that children who watched the violent TV program were not naturally more aggressive than those who watched the nonviolent TV program. So it was reasonable for them to conclude that the former group of children were more aggressive *because* they had watched a TV program in which violence and aggression were central.

confounding variable
some factor other than the independent variable that, if not controlled by the experimenter, could explain any differences across treatment conditions in participants' performance on the dependent variable

experimental control
steps taken by an experimenter to ensure that all extraneous factors that could influence the dependent variable are roughly equivalent in each experimental condition; these precautions must be taken before an experimenter can be reasonably certain that observed changes in the dependent variable were caused by manipulating the independent variable

random assignment
control technique in which participants are assigned to experimental conditions through an unbiased procedure so that the members of the groups are not systematically different from one another

ecological validity
state of affairs in which the findings of one's research are an accurate representation of processes that occur in the natural environment

field experiment
experiment that takes place in a natural setting such as home, school, or playground

The greatest strength of the experimental method is its ability to establish unambiguously that one thing causes another. Yet critics of laboratory experimentation have argued that the tightly controlled laboratory environment is often contrived and artificial and that children are likely to behave differently in these surroundings than they would in a natural setting. Urie Bronfenbrenner (1977) has charged that a heavy reliance on laboratory experiments has made developmental psychology "the science of the strange behaviour of children in strange situations with strange adults" (p. 19). Similarly, Robert McCall (1977) notes that experiments tell us what *can* cause a developmental change but do not necessarily pinpoint the factors that *actually do* cause such changes in natural settings. Consequently, it is quite possible that conclusions drawn from laboratory experiments do not always apply to the real world. In Box 1.2, we consider a step that experimentalists can take to counter this criticism and assess the **ecological validity** of their laboratory findings.

1.2

FOCUS ON RESEARCH

Assessing Causal Relationships in the Real World: The Field Experiment

How can we be more certain that a conclusion drawn from a laboratory experiment also applies in the real world? One way is to seek converging evidence for that conclusion by conducting a similar experiment *in a natural setting*—that is, a **field experiment**. This approach combines all the advantages of naturalistic observation with the more rigorous control that experimentation allows. In addition, subjects are typically not apprehensive about participating in a "strange" experiment because all the activities they undertake are everyday activities. Indeed, they may not even be aware that they are being observed or participating in an experiment.

Let's consider a field experiment (Leyens et al., 1975) that sought to test the hypothesis that heavy exposure to media violence can cause viewers to become more aggressive. The subjects were Belgian delinquents who lived together in cottages at a minimum-security institution for adolescent boys. Before the experiment began, the experimenters observed each boy in their research sample to measure his characteristic level of aggression. These initial assessments served as a baseline against which future increases in aggression could be measured. The baseline observations suggested that the institution's four cottages could be divided into two subgroups consisting of two cottages populated by relatively aggressive inmates and two cottages populated by less aggressive peers. Then the experiment began. For a period of one week, violent movies (such as *Bonnie and Clyde* and *The Dirty Dozen*) were shown each evening to one of the two cottages in each subgroup, and neutral films (such as *Daddy's Fiancée* and *La Belle Américaine*) were shown to the other cottages. Instances of physical and verbal aggression among residents of each cottage were recorded twice daily (at lunchtime and in the evenings after the movie) during the movie week and once daily (at lunchtime) during a posttreatment week.

The most striking result of this field experiment was the significant increase in physical aggression that occurred in the evenings among residents of both cottages assigned to the violent-movie condition. Since the violent movies contained a large number of physically aggressive incidents, it

appears that they evoked similar responses from the boys who watched them. But as shown in the figure, violent movies prompted larger increases in aggression among boys who were already relatively high in aggression. Furthermore, exposure to the violent movies caused the highly aggressive boys to become more verbally aggressive as well—an effect that these boys continued to display through the movie week and the posttreatment week.

Clearly, the results of the Belgian field experiment are consistent with Liebert and Baron's (1972) laboratory study in suggesting that exposure to media violence does indeed instigate aggressive behaviour. Yet it also qualifies the laboratory findings by implying that the instigating effects of media violence in the natural environment are likely to be stronger and more enduring for the more aggressive members of the audience (see also Friedrich & Stein, 1973, for similar results with nursery-school children).

Mean physical aggression scores in the evening for highly aggressive (HA) and less aggressive (LA) boys under baseline conditions and after watching violent or neutral movies.
ADAPTED FROM LEYENS ET AL., 1975.

The Natural (or Quasi-) Experiment

There are many issues to which an experimental design either cannot be applied or should not be used for ethical reasons. Suppose, for example, that we want to study the effects of social deprivation in infancy on children's intellectual development. Clearly, we cannot ask one group of parents to lock their infants in an attic for two years so that we can collect the data we need. It is simply unethical to subject children to any experimental treatment that would adversely affect their physical or psychological well-being.

However, we might be able to accomplish our research objectives through a **natural** (or **quasi-**) **experiment** in which we observe the consequences of a natural event that subjects have experienced. So if we were able to locate a group of children who had been raised in impoverished institutions with limited contact with caregivers over the first two years, we could compare their intellectual development with that of children raised at home with their families. This comparison would provide valuable information about the likely impact of early social deprivation on children's intellectual development. (Indeed, precisely this kind of natural experiment is described in detail in Chapter 11.) The independent variable in a natural experiment is the event that subjects experience (in our example, the social deprivation experienced by institutionalized infants). The dependent variable is whatever outcome measure one chooses to study (in our example, intellectual development).

Let's note, however, that researchers conducting natural experiments do not control the independent variable, nor do they randomly assign participants to experimental conditions; instead, they merely observe and record the apparent outcomes of a natural happening or event. And in the absence of tight experimental control, it is often hard to determine precisely what factor is responsible for any group differences that are found. Suppose, for example, that our socially deprived institution children showed a poorer pattern of intellectual outcomes than children raised at home. Is the *social deprivation* that institutionalized children experienced the factor that accounts for this difference? Or is it that institutionalized children differed in other ways from family-reared children (for example, were more sickly as infants, were more poorly nourished, or simply had less intellectual potential) that might explain their poorer outcomes? Without randomly assigning participants to treatments and controlling other factors that may vary across treatments (for example, nutrition received), we simply cannot be certain that social deprivation is the factor responsible for the poor intellectual outcomes that institutionalized children display.

Despite its inability to make precise statements about cause and effect, the natural experiment is nonetheless useful because it can tell us whether a natural event could *possibly* have influenced those who experienced it and, thus, can provide some meaningful clues about cause and effect.

natural (or quasi-) experiment
study in which the investigator measures the impact of some naturally occurring event that is assumed to affect people's lives

Concept Check 1.2
Detecting Relationships

Check your understanding of the meaning of various relationships that developmentalists might detect as described in items 1 and 2. Answers appear in the Appendix.
1. Jo Brown finds that the better children feel about themselves (that is, the higher their *self-esteem* as reported in an interview), the higher their grades are at school. Check any *acceptable* conclusions based on these data.
_____ a. Low grades cause low self-esteem.
_____ b. Self-esteem and grades earned are positively correlated.
_____ c. Having high self-esteem causes children to earn good grades.

2. Ike Chang assigns 10 boys to a condition in which they receive positive feedback about their academic abilities, a manipulation that increases their self-esteem. Ten girls in the same class receive no such feedback. Chang then finds that the 10 boys earn higher grades over the course of the next year than the 10 girls do. He might conclude that
_____ a. Increases in self-esteem cause children to earn higher grades.
_____ b. Increases in self-esteem cause boys, but not girls, to earn higher grades.
_____ c. Neither of the above; Chang's experiment has failed to control for confounding variables (name one of these confounding variables if you choose this answer).

TABLE 1.3   Strengths and Limitations of General Research Designs

Design	Procedure	Strengths	Limitations
Correlational	Gathers information about two or more variables without researcher intervention.	Estimates the strength and direction of relationships among variables in the natural environment.	Does not permit determination of cause-and-effect relationships among variables.
Laboratory experiment	Manipulates some aspect of participants' environment (independent variable) and measures its impact on participants' behaviour (dependent variable).	Permits a determination of cause-and-effect relationships among variables.	Data obtained in artificial laboratory environment may lack generalizability to the real world.
Field experiment	Manipulates independent variable and measures its impact on the dependent variable in a natural setting.	Permits determination of cause-and-effect relationships and generalization of findings to the real world.	Experimental treatments may be less potent and harder to control when presented in the natural environment.
Natural (quasi-) experiment	Gathers information about the behaviour of people who experience a real-world (natural) manipulation of their environment.	Permits a study of the impact on natural events that would be difficult or impossible to simulate in an experiment; provides strong clues about cause-and-effect relationships.	Lack of precise control over natural events or the participants exposed to them prevents the investigator from establishing definitive cause-and-effect relationships.

Table 1.3 summarizes the strengths and limitations of each of the general research designs we have discussed. Now let's consider designs that focus more specifically on detecting developmental continuities and changes.

DESIGNS FOR STUDYING DEVELOPMENT

Developmentalists are not merely interested in examining people's progress at one particular phase of life; instead, they hope to determine how people's feelings, thoughts, abilities, and behaviours *develop* or *change* over time. How might we design research to chart these developmental trends? Let's briefly consider three approaches: the cross-sectional design, the longitudinal design, and the sequential design.

The Cross-Sectional Design

In a **cross-sectional design**, people who *differ in age* are studied at *the same point in time*. By comparing participants in the different age groups, investigators can often identify age-related changes in whatever aspect of development they happen to be studying.

An experiment by Brian Coates and Willard Hartup (1969) is an excellent example of a cross-sectional comparison. Coates and Hartup were interested in determining why preschool children are less proficient than Grade 1 or 2 children at learning new responses displayed by an adult model. Their hypothesis was that younger children do not spontaneously *describe* what they are observing, whereas older children produce verbal descriptions of the modelled sequence. When asked to perform the actions they have witnessed, the preschoolers are at a distinct disadvantage because they have no verbal "learning aids" that would help them to recall the model's behaviour.

cross-sectional design
research design in which subjects from different age groups are studied at the same point in time

To test this hypothesis, Coates and Hartup designed an interesting cross-sectional experiment. Children from two age groups—4- to 5-year-olds and 7- to 8-year-olds—watched a short film in which an adult model displayed 20 novel responses, such as throwing a beanbag between his legs, lassoing an inflatable toy with a Hula-Hoop, and so on. Some of the children from each age group were instructed to describe the model's actions, and they did so as they watched the film (induced-verbalization condition). Other children were not required to describe the model's actions as they observed them (passive-observation condition). When the show ended, each child was taken to a room that contained the same toys seen in the film and was asked to demonstrate what the model had done with these toys.

Figure 1.3 illustrates three interesting findings that emerged from this experiment. First, the 4- to 5-year-olds who were *not* told to describe what they had seen (that is, the passive observers) reproduced *fewer* of the model's responses than the 4- to 5-year-olds who described the model's behaviour (the induced verbalizers) or the 7- to 8-year-olds in either experimental condition. This finding suggests that 4- to 5-year-old children may not produce the verbal descriptions that would help them to learn unless they are explicitly instructed to do so. Second, the performance of younger and older children in the induced-verbalization condition was comparable. So younger children can learn just as much as older children by observing a social model *if the younger children are told to describe what they are observing*. Finally, 7- to 8-year-olds in the passive-observation condition reproduced about the same number of behaviours as 7- to 8-year-olds in the induced-verbalization condition. This finding suggests that instructions to describe the model's actions had little effect on 7- to 8-year-olds, who apparently describe what they have seen even when not told to. Taken together, the results imply that 4- to 5-year-olds may often learn less from social models because they, unlike older children, do not spontaneously produce the verbal descriptions that would help them to remember what they have observed.

An important advantage of the cross-sectional design is that the investigator can collect data from children of different ages over a short time. For example, Coates and Hartup did not have to wait three years for their 4- to 5-year-olds to become 7- to 8-year-olds in order to test their developmental hypotheses. They merely sampled from two age groups and tested both samples simultaneously. Yet there are two important limitations of cross-sectional research.

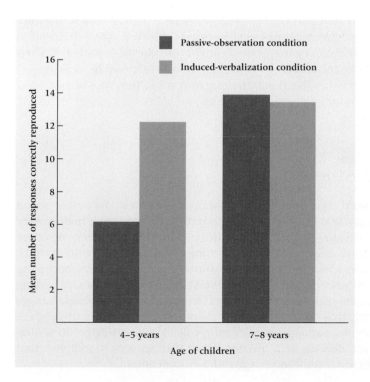

Figure 1.3 *Children's ability to reproduce the behaviour of a social model as a function of age and verbalization instructions.* ADAPTED FROM COATES & HARTUP, *1969.*

Cohort Effects

Notice that in cross-sectional research, participants at each age level are *different* people. That is, they come from different cohorts, where a *cohort* is defined as a group of people of the same age who are exposed to similar cultural environments and historical events as they are growing up. The fact that cross-sectional comparisons always involve different cohorts presents us with a thorny interpretive problem, for any age differences that are found in the study may not always be due to age or development but, rather, may reflect other cultural or historical factors that distinguish members of different cohorts. Stated another way, cross-sectional comparisons *confound age and cohort effects*.

An example should clarify the issue. For years, cross-sectional research consistently indicated that young adults score slightly higher on intelligence tests than middle-aged adults, who, in turn, score much higher than the elderly. But does intelligence decline with age, as these findings seem to indicate? Not necessarily! More recent research (Schaie, 1990) reveals that individuals' intelligence test scores remain relatively stable over the years and that the earlier studies were really measuring something quite different: age differences in education. The older adults in the cross-sectional studies had had less schooling and, therefore, scored lower on intelligence tests than the middle-aged and young adult samples. Their test scores had not declined but had always been lower than those of the younger adults with whom they were compared. So the earlier cross-sectional research had discovered a **cohort effect**, not a true developmental change.

Despite this important limitation, the cross-sectional comparison is still the design that developmentalists use most often. Why? Because it has the advantage of being quick and easy; we can go out this year, sample individuals of different ages, and be done with it. Moreover, this design is likely to yield valid conclusions when there is little reason to believe that the cohorts being studied have had widely different experiences while growing up. So if we compared 4- to 5-year-olds with 7- to 8-year-olds, as Coates and Hartup did, we might feel reasonably confident that history or the prevailing culture had not changed in any major way in the three years that separate these two cohorts. It is mainly in studies that attempt to make inferences about development over a span of many years that cohort effects present a serious problem.

Data on Individual Development

There is a second noteworthy limitation of the cross-sectional design: It tells us nothing about the development of *individuals* because each person is observed *at only one point in time*. So cross-sectional comparisons cannot provide answers to questions such as "When will *my* child become more independent?" or "Will aggressive 2-year-olds become aggressive 5-year-olds?" To address issues like these, investigators often turn to a second kind of developmental comparison, the longitudinal design.

The Longitudinal Design

In a **longitudinal design**, the same participants are observed repeatedly over a period of time. The time period may be relatively brief—six months to a year—or it may be very long, spanning a lifetime. Researchers may be studying one particular aspect of development, such as intelligence, or many. By repeatedly testing the same participants, investigators can assess the *stability* (continuity) of various attributes for each person in the sample. They can also identify normative developmental trends and processes by looking for commonalities, such as the point(s) at which most children undergo various changes and the experiences, if any, that children seem to share prior to reaching these milestones. Finally, tracking several participants over time will help investigators to understand *individual differences* in development, particularly if they are able to establish that different kinds of earlier experiences lead to very different outcomes.

cohort effect
age-related difference among cohorts that is attributable to cultural and historical differences in cohorts' growing-up experiences rather than to true developmental change

longitudinal design
research design in which one group of subjects is studied repeatedly over a period of months or years

Several very noteworthy longitudinal projects have followed children for decades and have assessed many aspects of development (see Kagan & Moss, 1962; Newman et al., 1997). However, most longitudinal studies are much more modest in direction and scope. For example, Carolee Howes and Catherine Matheson (1992) conducted a study in which the pretend play activities of a group of 1- to 2-year-olds were repeatedly observed at 6-month intervals over the next three years. Using a classification scheme that assessed the cognitive complexity of play, Howes and Matheson sought to determine (1) whether play did reliably become more complex with age, (2) whether children reliably differed in the complexity of their play, and (3) whether the complexity of a child's play reliably forecasted his or her social competencies with peers. Not surprisingly, all the children displayed increases in the complexity of their play over the three-year period, although there were reliable individual differences in play complexity at each observation point. In addition, there was a clear relationship between the complexity of a child's play and social competence with peers: Children who engaged in more complex forms of play at any given age were the ones who were rated as most outgoing and least aggressive at the next observation period six months later. So this longitudinal study shows that complexity of pretend play not only increases with age but is also a reliable predictor of children's future social competencies with peers.

Although we have portrayed the longitudinal design in a very favourable manner, this approach has several potential drawbacks as well. For example, longitudinal projects can be costly and time-consuming. These points are especially important in that the focus of theory and research in the developmental sciences is constantly changing, and longitudinal questions that seem exciting at the beginning of a 10- or 20-year project may seem rather trivial by the time the project ends. **Practice effects** can also threaten the validity of longitudinal studies: Participants who are repeatedly interviewed or tested may become test-wise or increasingly familiar with the content of the test itself, showing performance improvements that are unrelated to normal patterns of development. Longitudinal researchers may also have a problem with **selective attrition**: children may move away or become bored with participating, or they may have parents who, for one reason or another, will not allow them to continue in the study. The result is a smaller and potentially **nonrepresentative sample** that not only provides less information about the developmental issues in question but also may limit the conclusions of the study to those children who do not move away and who remain cooperative over the long run.

practice effects
changes in participants' natural responses as a result of repeated testing

selective attrition
nonrandom loss of participants during a study that results in a nonrepresentative sample

nonrepresentative sample
subgroup that differs in important ways from the larger group (or population) to which it belongs

Leisure activities of the 1930s (left) and the 2000s (right). As these photos illustrate, the kinds of experiences that children growing up in the 1930s had were very different from those of today's youth. Many believe that cross-generational changes in the environment may limit the results of a longitudinal study to the youngsters who were growing up while the research was in progress.

There is another shortcoming of long-term longitudinal studies that students often see right away—the **cross-generational problem**. Children in a longitudinal project are typically drawn from one cohort and are likely to have very different kinds of experiences than youngsters from other eras. Consider, for example, how the times have changed since the 1930s and 1940s, when children in some of the early long-term longitudinal studies were growing up. In this age of dual-career families, more youngsters are attending daycare centres and nursery schools than ever before. Modern families are smaller than those of years past, meaning that children now have fewer brothers and sisters. Families also move more frequently than they did in the 1930s and 1940s, so that many children from the modern era are exposed to a wider variety of people and places than was typical in years gone by. And no matter where they may be living, today's youngsters grow up in front of television sets and computers, influences that were not available during the 1930s and 1940s. So children of earlier eras lived in a very different world, and we cannot be certain that these youngsters developed in precisely the same way as today's children. Stated another way, cross-generational changes in the environment may limit the conclusions of a longitudinal project to those participants who were growing up while the study was in progress.

We have seen that the cross-sectional and the longitudinal designs each have distinct advantages and disadvantages. Might it be possible to combine the best features of both approaches? A third kind of developmental comparison—the sequential design—tries to do just that.

The Sequential Design

Sequential designs combine the best features of cross-sectional and longitudinal studies by selecting participants of different ages and following each of these cohorts over time. To illustrate, imagine that we wished to study the development of children's logical reasoning abilities between the ages of 6 and 12. We might begin in 2002 by testing the logical reasoning of a sample of 6-year-olds (the 1996 birth cohort) and a sample of 8-year-olds (the 1994 birth cohort). We could then retest the reasoning abilities of both groups in 2004 and 2006. Notice that the design calls for us to follow the 1996 cohort from ages 6 through 10 and the 1994 cohort from ages 8 through 12. A graphical representation of this research plan appears in Figure 1.4.

A major Canadian sequential study, called the National Longitudinal Survey of Children and Youth (NLSCY), has been collecting data on approximately 20 000 children since 1994. An initial cohort of about 15 000 children, aged 0–11 in 1994, is being followed every two years to age 25. Younger children are being added to the sample as the initial cohort ages. This younger cohort, which will eventually number over 20 000 children, will be followed through the transition into elementary school (Statistics Canada, 2003c). This survey is a joint project funded through Human Resources Development Canada and Statistics Canada.

cross-generational problem
fact that long-term changes in the environment may limit the conclusions of a longitudinal project to that generation of children who were growing up while the study was in progress

sequential design
research design in which subjects from different age groups are studied repeatedly over a period of months or years

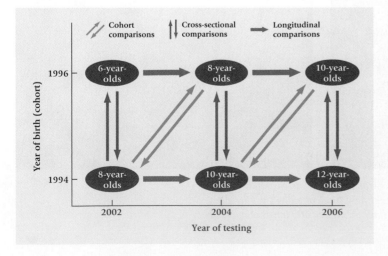

Figure 1.4 *Example of a sequential design. Two samples of children, one born in 1994 and one born in 1996, are observed longitudinally between the ages of 6 and 12. The design permits the investigator to assess cohort effects by comparing children of the same age who were born in different years. In the absence of cohort effects, the longitudinal and cross-sectional comparisons in this design also permit the researcher to make strong statements about the strength and direction of any developmental changes.*

Design	Procedure	Strengths	Limitations
Cross-sectional	Observes people of different ages (or cohorts) at one point in time.	Demonstrates age differences; hints at developmental trends; relatively inexpensive; takes little time to conduct.	Age trends may reflect extraneous differences between cohorts rather than true developmental change; provides no data on the development of individuals because each participant is observed at only one point in time.
Longitudinal	Observes people of one cohort repeatedly over time.	Provides data on the development of individuals; can reveal links between early experiences and later outcomes; indicates how individuals are alike and how they are different in the ways they change over time.	Relatively time-consuming and expensive; selective attrition may yield nonrepresentative sample that limits the generalizability of conclusions; cross-generational changes may limit one's conclusions to the cohort that was studied.
Sequential	Combines the cross-sectional and the longitudinal approaches by observing different cohorts repeatedly over time.	Discriminates true developmental trends from cohort effects; indicates whether developmental changes experienced by one cohort are similar to those experienced by other cohorts; often less costly and time-consuming than the longitudinal approach.	More costly and time-consuming than cross-sectional research; despite being the strongest design, may still leave questions about whether a developmental change is generalizable beyond the cohorts studied.

There are three major strengths of this sequential design. First, it allows us to determine whether cohort effects are influencing our results by comparing the logical reasoning of same-aged children who were born in different years. As shown in the figure, cohort effects are assessed by comparing the logical reasoning of the two samples at ages 8 and 10. If the samples do not differ, we can assume that cohort effects are not operating. Figure 1.4 also illustrates a second major advantage of our sequential design: It allows us to make both longitudinal and cross-sectional comparisons in the same study. If the age trends in logical reasoning are similar in both the longitudinal and the cross-sectional comparisons, we can be quite confident that they represent true developmental changes in logical reasoning abilities. Finally, sequential designs are often more efficient than standard longitudinal designs. In our example, we could trace the development of logical reasoning over a six-year age range, even though our study would take only four years to conduct. A standard longitudinal comparison that initially sampled 6-year-old participants would take six years to provide similar information. Clearly, this combination of the cross-sectional and longitudinal designs is a rather versatile alternative to either of these approaches.

To help you review and compare the three major developmental designs, Table 1.4 provides a brief description of each, along with its major strengths and weaknesses.

? WHAT DO YOU THINK?

Suppose you hoped to study the effects of famine on developing children. What research methods and designs would you choose to conduct your study?

CROSS-CULTURAL COMPARISONS

Developmentalists are often hesitant to publish a new finding or conclusion until they have studied enough people to determine that their discovery is reliable. However, their conclusions are frequently based on participants living at one point in time within one particular culture or subculture, and it is difficult to know whether these conclusions apply to future generations or even to youngsters currently growing up in other societies or subcultures (Lerner, 1991). Today, the generalizability of findings across samples and settings has become an important issue, for many theorists have implied that there are "universals" in human development—events and outcomes that all children share as they progress from infancy to adulthood.

Cross-cultural studies are those in which participants from different cultural or subcultural backgrounds are observed, tested, and compared on one or more aspects of development. Studies of this kind serve many purposes. For example, they allow the investigator to determine whether conclusions drawn about the development of children from one social context (such as middle-class, white youngsters in Canada) also characterize children growing up in other societies or even those from different ethnic or socioeconomic backgrounds within the same society (for example, Canadian children of Asian ancestry or those from economically disadvantaged homes). So the **cross-cultural comparison** guards against the overgeneralization of research findings and, indeed, is the only way to determine whether there are truly universals in human development.

However, many investigators who favour the cross-cultural approach are looking for *differences* rather than similarities. They recognize that human beings develop in societies that have very different ideas about issues such as the proper times and procedures for disciplining children, the activities that are most appropriate for boys and for girls, the time at which childhood ends and adulthood begins, the treatment of the aged, and countless other aspects of life (Fry, 1996). They have also learned that people from various cultures differ in the ways they perceive the world, express their emotions, think, and solve problems. Evidence of cultural differences is present even in our assumptions of how developmental research should be reported. Recently, two Canadian First Nations authors (Johnson & Cremo, 1995) highlighted their concerns regarding their ability to prepare a chapter for a book because they sensed a fundamental difference in the way First Nations and Western cultures define life. Beliefs of First Nations people support circularity rather than linearity in life. Western culture assumes that there is linearity

cross-cultural comparison
study that compares the behaviour or development of people from different cultural or subcultural backgrounds

---

CULTURAL INFLUENCES

1.3

A Cross-Cultural Comparison of Gender Roles

One of the greatest values of cross-cultural comparisons is that they can tell us whether a developmental phenomenon is or is not universal. Consider the roles that males and females play in our society. In our culture, playing the masculine role has traditionally required traits such as independence, assertiveness, and dominance. By contrast, females are expected to be more nurturant and sensitive to other people. Are these masculine and feminine roles universal? Could biological differences between the sexes lead inevitably to sex differences in behaviour?

Some years ago, anthropologist Margaret Mead (1935) compared the gender roles adopted by people in three tribal societies on the island of New Guinea, and her observations are certainly thought-provoking. In the Arapesh tribe, both men and women were taught to play what we would regard as a feminine role: They were cooperative, nonaggressive, and sensitive to the needs of others. By contrast, both men and women of the

Liba Taylor/Corbis/Magma

The roles assumed by men and women may vary dramatically from culture to culture.

Mundugumor tribe were brought up to be aggressive and emotionally unresponsive to other people—a masculine pattern of behaviour by Western standards. Finally, the Tchambuli displayed a pattern of gender-role development that was the direct opposite of the Western pattern: Males were passive, emotionally dependent, and socially sensitive, whereas females were dominant, independent, and assertive!

Mead's cross-cultural comparison suggests that cultural learning may have far more to do with the characteristic behaviour patterns of men and women than biological differences do. So we very much need cross-cultural comparisons such as Mead's. Without them, we might easily make the mistake of assuming that whatever holds true in our society holds true everywhere; with their help, we can begin to understand the contributions of biology and environment to human development.

Check your understanding of the uses and strengths of various developmental designs by selecting a design that seems most appropriate for each of the following research questions. Choose from the following designs: (a) cross-sectional, (b) longitudinal, (c) sequential, (d) cross-cultural. Answers appear in the Appendix.

_____ 1. A researcher wants to quickly assess whether 4-, 6-, and 8-year-olds differ in their willingness to donate part of their allowance to children less fortunate than themselves.

_____ 2. A researcher who has money for a six-week summer preschool education program wants to know whether the program will have greater long-term benefits for 2-year-olds than for 3- or 4-year-olds.

_____ 3. A developmentalist hopes to determine whether all children go through the same stages of intellectual development between infancy and adolescence.

_____ 4. A specialist in early childhood education hopes to learn whether especially bright 2-year-olds are likely to remain smarter than most peers by the time they are 6 years old.

between events (a movement from point a to point b). So apart from its focus on universals in development, the cross-cultural approach also illustrates that human development is heavily influenced by the cultural context in which it occurs (see Box 1.3 for a dramatic illustration of cultural diversity in gender roles).

Isn't it remarkable how many methods and designs developmentalists have at their disposal? This diversity of available procedures is a definite strength because findings gained through one procedure can then be checked and perhaps confirmed through other procedures. Indeed, providing such *converging evidence* serves a most important function by demonstrating that the conclusion a researcher draws is truly a discovery and not merely an artifact of the method or design used to collect the original data. So there is no best method for studying children and adolescents; each of the approaches we have considered has contributed substantially to our understanding of human development.

ETHICAL CONSIDERATIONS IN DEVELOPMENTAL RESEARCH

When designing and conducting research with humans, researchers may face thorny issues centring on *research ethics*—the standards of conduct that investigators are ethically bound to honour in order to protect their research participants from physical or psychological harm. Some ethical issues are easily resolved: One simply does *not* conduct experiments that will almost certainly cause physical or psychological damage, such as physical abuse, starvation, isolation for long periods, and the like. However, most ethical issues are far more subtle. Here are some of the dilemmas that developmentalists may have to resolve during their careers as researchers:

- Can children or adolescents be exposed to temptations that virtually guarantee that they will cheat or break other rules?

- Am I ever justified in deceiving participants, either by misinforming them about the purpose of my study or by telling them something untrue about themselves (for example, "You did poorly on this test")?

- Can I observe my participants in the natural setting without informing them that they are the subjects of a scientific investigation?

- Is it acceptable to tell children that their classmates think that an obviously incorrect answer is correct to see whether participants will conform to the judgments of their peers?

- Am I justified in using verbal disapproval as part of my research procedure?

Ethical considerations are especially complex when children participate in psychological research. Children are more vulnerable than adolescents and adults to physical and psychological harm. Moreover, young children may not always fully understand what they are committing themselves to when they agree to participate in a study. In order to protect children who participate in psychological research and to clarify the responsibilities of researchers who work with children, the Canadian Psychological Association (2000), the American Psychological Association (1992), and the Society for Research in Child Development (1993) have endorsed special ethical guidelines, the more important of which are as follows:

Protection from Harm*

The investigator may use no research operation that may harm the child either physically or psychologically. Psychological harm is difficult to define; nevertheless, its definition remains the responsibility of the investigator. When an investigator is in doubt about the possible harmful effects of the research operations, he or she must seek consultation from others. When harm seems possible, he or she is obligated to find other means of obtaining the information or abandon the research.

Informed Consent

The informed consent of parents as well as others who act on the child's behalf—teachers, superintendents of institutions, and so on—should be obtained, preferably in writing. Informed consent requires that the parent or other responsible adult be told all features of the research that may affect his or her willingness to allow the child to participate. Moreover, all children have the right to have explained to them, in understandable language, all aspects of the research that could affect their willingness to participate. Of course, children always have the right to choose not to participate or to discontinue

participation in research at any time. This provision is a tricky one, however: Even if they are told that they can stop participating in a study at any time, young children may not really grasp how to do so or may not really believe that they can stop without incurring a penalty of some kind. However, children are much more likely to understand their rights of assent and to exercise them if the researcher carefully explains that he or she would not be upset if the child chose not to participate or to stop participating (Abramovitch et al., 1995).

Confidentiality

Researchers must keep in confidence all information obtained from research participants. Children have the right to concealment of their identity on all data collected and reported, either in writing or informally. The one exception is that provinces have laws that require investigators to reveal the names of suspected victims of child abuse or neglect to provincial authorities (either police or agencies overseeing the protection of children). These laws are found under statutes governing child welfare—for example, Ontario's Child and Family Services Act (1990, section 72(2)).

Deception, Debriefing, and Knowledge of Results

Although children have the right to know the purposes of a study in advance, a particular project may necessitate concealment of information, or deception. Whenever concealment or deception is thought to be essential to the conduct of research, the investigator must satisfy a committee of peers that this judgment is correct. If deception or concealment is used, participants must later be debriefed—that is, told, in language they can understand, the true purpose of the study and why it was necessary to deceive them. Children also have the right to be informed, in language they can understand, of the results of the research in which they have participated.

*Ross Thompson (1990) has published an excellent essay on this topic. We recommend it to anyone who conducts (or plans to conduct) research with children.

---

informed consent
right of research participants to receive an explanation, in language they can understand, of all aspects of research that may affect their willingness to participate

benefits-to-risks ratio
comparison of the possible benefits of a study for advancing knowledge and optimizing life conditions versus its costs to participants in terms of inconvenience and possible harm

Before reading further, you may want to think about these issues and formulate your own opinions. Then read Table 1.5 and reconsider your viewpoints.

Have any of your opinions changed? It would not be terribly surprising if they hadn't. As you can see, the table guidelines are very general; they do not explicitly permit or prohibit specific operations or practices such as those described in the preceding dilemmas. In fact, any of these dilemmas mentioned above can be resolved in ways that permit an investigator to use the procedures in question and still remain well within current ethical guidelines. For example, it is generally considered permissible to observe young children in natural settings (for example, at school or in a park) without informing them that they are being studied if the investigator has previously obtained the **informed consent** (see Table 1.5) of the adults responsible for the children's care and safety in these settings. Ethical guidelines are just that: guidelines. The ultimate responsibility for treating children fairly and protecting them from harm falls squarely on the shoulders of the investigator.

How, then, do investigators decide whether to use a procedure that some may consider questionable on ethical grounds? They generally weigh the advantages and disadvantages of the research by carefully calculating its possible *benefits* (to humanity or to the participants) and comparing them with the potential *risks* that participants may face. If the **benefits-to-risks ratio** is favourable, and if there are no other less-risky procedures that could be used to produce these same benefits, the investigator will generally proceed. However, there are safeguards against overzealous researchers who underestimate the riskiness of their procedures. In Canada, for example, universities, research foundations, and government agencies that fund research with children have set up human-subjects review committees and procedures to provide second (and sometimes third) opinions on the ethical ramifications of all proposed research. The function of these review committees is to reconsider the potential risks and benefits of the proposed research and, more importantly, to help ensure that all possible steps are taken to protect the welfare of those who may choose to participate in the project.

Interestingly, clashes between the ethical provisions of **confidentiality** and **protection from harm** can pose serious ethical dilemmas for researchers who learn that the well-being of one or more participants (or their associates) may be seriously jeopardized by such life-threatening events as suicidal tendencies and untreated sexually transmitted diseases. These are risks that many investigators may feel ethically bound to report or to help the participant to self-report to the appropriate medical, social, or psychological services. Indeed, adolescents view reporting of these very serious risks (or, alternatively, helping the participant to self-report) in a very favourable way, and they may perceive inaction on the investigator's part as an indication that the problem is considered unimportant, that no services are available to assist them, or that knowledgeable adults cannot be depended on to help youngsters in need. (See Fisher et al., 1996, for an excellent discussion of the confidentiality dilemmas researchers may face and adolescents' views about appropriate courses of action for researchers to take.)

Of course, final approval of all one's safeguards and reporting procedures by a review committee does not absolve investigators of the need to reevaluate the benefits and costs of their projects, even while the research is in progress (Thompson, 1990). Suppose, for example, that a researcher studying children's aggression in a playground setting came to the conclusion that his subjects had (1) discovered his own fascination with aggressive behaviour and (2) begun to beat up on one another in order to attract his attention. At that point, the risks to participants would have escalated far beyond the researcher's initial estimates, and he would be ethically bound to stop the research immediately.

In the final analysis, guidelines and review committees do not guarantee that research participants will be treated responsibly; only investigators can do that by constantly reevaluating the consequences of their operations and by modifying or abandoning any procedure that may compromise the welfare or dignity of those who have volunteered to participate.

POSTSCRIPT: ON BECOMING A WISE CONSUMER OF DEVELOPMENTAL RESEARCH

At this point, you may be wondering, "Why do I need to know so much about the methods that developmentalists use to conduct research?" This is a reasonable question given that the vast majority of students who take this course will pursue other careers and will never conduct a scientific study of developing children or adolescents.

The answer is straightforward: Although survey courses such as this one are designed to provide a solid overview of theory and research in the discipline to which they pertain, they should also strive to help you evaluate the relevant information you may encounter in the years ahead. And you will encounter such information. Even if you don't read academic journals in your role as a teacher, school administrator, nurse, probation officer, social worker, or other professional who works with developing persons, you will certainly be exposed to such information through the popular media—television, newspapers, magazines, and the like. How can you know whether that seemingly dramatic and important new finding you've just read or heard about should be taken seriously?

confidentiality
right of participants to concealment of their identity with respect to the data that they provide

protection from harm
right of research participants to be protected from physical or psychological harm

This is an important issue, for new information about human development is often chronicled in the popular media several months or even years before the data on which the media reports are based finally make their appearance in professional journals. What's more, less than 30 percent of the findings that developmentalists submit are judged worthy of publication by reputable journals in our discipline. Many media reports of dramatic new findings are based on research that other scientists do not regard as very dramatic or even worth publishing.

Even if a media report is based on a published article, coverage of the research and its conclusions is often misleading. For example, one recent American TV news story reported on a published article, saying that there was clear evidence that "alcoholism is inherited." As we will see in Chapter 3, this is a far more dramatic conclusion than the authors actually drew. Another American newspaper report summarized a recent article from the prestigious journal *Developmental Psychology* with the headline "Day care harmful for children." What was never made clear in the newspaper article was the researcher's (Howes, 1990) conclusion that *very-low-quality* daycare may be harmful to the social and intellectual development of *some* preschool children but that most youngsters receiving good daycare suffer no adverse effects. The issue of daycare and its effects on developing children is explored in depth in Chapter 11.

We don't mean to imply that you can never trust what you read; rather, we caution you to be skeptical and to evaluate media (and journal) reports using the methodological information presented in this chapter. You might start by asking: How were the data gathered, and how was the study designed? Were appropriate conclusions drawn given the limitations of the method of data collection and the design (correlational versus experimental; cross-sectional versus longitudinal) that the investigators used? Were there proper control groups? Have the results of the study been reviewed by other experts in the field and published in a reputable academic journal? And please don't assume that published articles are beyond criticism. Many theses and dissertations in the developmental sciences are based on problems and shortcomings that students have identified in previously published research. So take the time to read and evaluate published reports that seem especially relevant to your profession or to your role as a parent. Not only will you have a better understanding of the research and its conclusions, but any lingering questions and doubts you may have can often be addressed through a letter, an e-mail message, or a phone call to the author of the article.

In sum, one must become a knowledgeable consumer in order to get the most out of what the field of human development has to offer. Our discussion of research methodology was undertaken with these objectives in mind, and a solid understanding of these methodological lessons should help you to properly evaluate the research you will encounter, not only throughout this text but also in many other sources in the years to come.

SUMMARY

What Is Development?

♦ **Developmental psychology** is the largest of many disciplines that study **development**—the systematic continuities and changes that individuals display over the course of their lives that reflect the influence of biological **maturation** and **learning**. **Normative developments** are typical developments characterizing all members of a species, whereas **ideographic developments** describe those that may vary across individuals. Developmentalists' goals are to describe, explain, and optimize development. Human devel-

opment is a continual and cumulative process that is **holistic**, highly **plastic**, and heavily influenced by the historical and cultural contexts in which it occurs.

Human Development in Historical Perspective

♦ In medieval times, children were afforded few of the rights and protections of today's youth. The 17th- and 18th-century philosophies of **original sin**, **innate purity**, and **tabula rasa** contributed to a more humane outlook on children, and shortly thereafter, some parents began to record the development of their infant sons and daughters in **baby biographies**. The scientific study of development did not emerge until nearly 1900, when G. Stanley Hall and Sigmund Freud began to collect data and formulate **theories** about human development. Soon, other researchers were deriving **hypotheses** and conducting research to evaluate and extend early theories.

Research Methods in Developmental Psychology

♦ Today's developmentalists, guided by the **scientific method**, use objective data to determine the viability of their theories. Acceptable research methods possess both **reliability** and **validity**. A method is reliable if it produces consistent, replicable results; it is valid if it accurately reflects what it was intended to measure.

♦ The most common methods of data collection in child and adolescent development are self-reports, observational methodologies, case studies, ethnography, and psychophysiological methods. Self-reports include standardized procedures, such as **structured interviews** or **structured questionnaires**, that allow direct comparisons among research participants, and flexible approaches like the **clinical method**, which yields an individualized portrait of each participant's feelings, thoughts, and behaviours.

♦ **Naturalistic observations** are obtained in the natural environments of children or adolescents, whereas **structured observations** take place in laboratories where the investigator cues the behaviour of interest.

♦ **Case studies** allow investigators to obtain an in-depth understanding of individual children or adolescents by collecting data based on interviews, observations, and test scores, as well as information from such knowledgeable sources as teachers and parents.

♦ **Ethnography**, used originally by anthropologists, is a descriptive procedure in which the researcher becomes a participant observer within a cultural or subcultural context. He or she carefully observes community members, makes notes from conversations, and compiles information into a detailed portrait of the group's values and traditions and their effects on developing children and adolescents.

♦ **Psychophysiological methods** measure the relationship between physiological responses and behaviour. They are often used to reveal the biological underpinnings of development and to interpret children's perceptual, cognitive, or emotional responses.

Detecting Relationships: Correlational and Experimental Designs

♦ Two general research designs permit researchers to identify relationships among variables that interest them. **Correlational designs** examine relationships as they naturally occur, without any intervention. The **correlation coefficient** is used to estimate the strength and magnitude of the association between variables. However, correlational studies cannot specify whether correlated variables are causally related.

♦ The **experimental design** points to cause-and-effect relationships. The experimenter manipulates one or more **independent variables**, exercises **experimental control** over all other **confounding variables** (often by **random assignment** of participants to treatments), and observes the effect(s) of the manipulation(s) on the **dependent variable**. Experiments may be performed in the laboratory or in the natural environment (that is, a **field experiment**), thereby increasing the **ecological validity** of the results. The impact of events that researchers cannot manipulate or control can be studied in **natural (quasi-) experiments**. However, lack of control over natural events prevents the quasi-experimenter from drawing definitive conclusions about cause and effect.

Designs for Studying Development

♦ Cross-sectional, longitudinal, and sequential designs are employed to detect developmental change. The **cross-sectional design**, which compares different age groups at a single point in time, is easy to conduct, but it cannot tell us how individuals develop, and its results may be misleading if the age trends observed are actually due to **cohort effects** rather than to true developmental change.

♦ The **longitudinal design** detects developmental change by repeatedly examining the same participants as they grow older. Though it identifies developmental continuities and changes and individual differences in development, the longitudinal design is subject to such problems as **practice effects** and **selective attrition**, which results in **nonrepresentative samples**. Moreover, the **cross-generational problem** of long-term longitudinal studies implies that results may be limited to the particular cohort studied.

♦ The **sequential design**, a combination of the cross-sectional and longitudinal designs, offers researchers the advantages of both approaches and allows them to discriminate true developmental trends from troublesome cohort effects.

Cross-Cultural Comparisons

♦ **Cross-cultural comparisons**, in which participants from different cultures and subcultures are compared on one or more aspects of development, are becoming increasingly important. Only by comparing people from many cultures can we identify universal patterns of development and, at the same time, demonstrate that other aspects of development are heavily influenced by the social context in which they occur.

Ethical Considerations in Developmental Research

♦ Research conducted with children and adolescents raises some challenging ethical issues. The benefits to be gained from the research should always exceed the risks to participants. But no matter how positive this **benefits-to-risks ratio**, participants have the rights to **protection from harm**, give **informed consent** to participate (or to stop participating), have their data treated with **confidentiality**, and receive explanations for any deception that may have been necessary to collect their data.

KEY TERMS

development, 2
developmental continuities, 2
developmental psychology, 2
maturation, 2
learning, 2
normative development, 3
ideographic development, 3
holistic perspective, 5
plasticity, 5
original sin, 8
innate purity, 8
tabula rasa, 9
baby biography, 9

theory, 11
hypothesis, 11
scientific method, 11
reliability, 12
validity, 12
structured interview or
    structured questionnaire, 13
clinical method, 13
naturalistic observation, 14
observer influence, 15
time-sampling, 15
structured observation, 15
case study, 16

ethnography, 16
psychophysiological methods, 17
correlational design, 19
correlation coefficient, 19
experimental design, 20
independent variable, 20
dependent variable, 20
confounding variable, 21
experimental control, 21
random assignment, 21
ecological validity, 22
field experiment, 22
natural (or quasi-) experiment, 23

cross-sectional design, 24
cohort effect, 26
longitudinal design, 26
practice effects, 27
selective attrition, 27
nonrepresentative sample, 27
cross-generational problem, 28
sequential design, 28
cross-cultural comparison, 30
informed consent, 32
benefits-to-risks ratio, 32
confidentiality, 33
protection from harm, 33

 You can find further information on the topics covered in this chapter by visiting:

www.developmentalpsych2e.nelson.com

 For additional reading, go to InfoTrac College Edition, your on-line research library, at:

infotrac.thomsonlearning.com

2

Theories of Human Development

That's only true in theory, not in practice!

ANONYMOUS

There is nothing as practical as a good theory.

KURT LEWIN

The authors of this book find "people watching" a fascinating activity. When we see interesting exchanges or events we ask ourselves, "Why would that be true?" and we often try to generate explanations based on the research we have read. Then we try to predict what might happen next. Even in this simple activity we are engaged in an elementary form of devising a theory. In some cases these naturally occurring events have served as the basis for some of our own research. For example, we (Eileen Wood and Teena Willoughby) noticed that a lot of elderly and very young people experience difficulties using computer technology. When we watched these two populations, we wondered whether part of their difficulties might be due to a lack of familiarity with computers and to their shared motor challenges (arthritis and slower reflexes for the elderly, and limited hand coordination skills in children). Our knowledge of existing research told us that when people have greater prior knowledge and familiarity with tasks, they perform better and have less anxiety. We also knew that these two groups faced special motor challenges and that they might prefer equipment such as touchscreens, where the direct relationship between action and product is obvious. We were then able to generate a research question, which involved determining whether the two groups performed differently and preferred different devices as a function of their motor and spatial skills.

THE NATURE OF SCIENTIFIC THEORIES

A scientific **theory** is nothing more than a set of concepts and propositions that describe, organize, and explain a set of observations. Some theories in the developmental sciences are broad in scope, seeking to explain the development of global domains, such as personality or cognition, whereas others are limited to

The Nature of Scientific Theories

Questions and Controversies about Human Development

The Psychoanalytic Viewpoint

The Learning Viewpoint

The Cognitive-Developmental Viewpoint

The Information-Processing Viewpoint

The Ethological (or Evolutionary) Viewpoint

The Ecological Systems Viewpoint

Theories and World Views

Summary

theory
set of concepts and propositions that describe, organize, and explain a set of observations

a specific issue, such as the impact of different computer devices on adult and child use of computer technology. But the beauty of all scientific theories is that they help us to organize our thinking about the aspects of experience that interest us. Imagine what life might be like for a researcher who plugs away at collecting data and cataloguing fact after fact without organizing this information around a set of concepts and propositions. Chances are that this person would eventually be swamped by seemingly unconnected facts, thus qualifying as a trivia expert who lacks a big picture. So theories are of critical importance to the developmental sciences (or any other scientific discipline), for each of them provides us with a lens through which we can interpret any number of specific observations about developing individuals.

What are the characteristics of a good theory? Ideally, it should be concise, or **parsimonious**, and yet be able to explain a broad range of phenomena. A theory with few principles that accounts for a large number of empirical observations is far more useful than a second theory that requires many more principles and assumptions to explain the same number of (or a lesser number of) observations. In addition, good theories are **falsifiable**—that is, capable of making explicit predictions about future events so that the theory can be supported or disconfirmed. And as the falsifiability criterion implies, good theories do not limit themselves to that which is already known. Instead, they are **heuristic**—meaning that they build on existing knowledge by continuing to generate testable hypotheses that, if confirmed by future research, will lead to a much richer understanding of the phenomenon of interest (see Figure 2.1).

Clearly, a theory that simply explains a set of observations without making any new predictions is neither falsifiable nor heuristic and is of limited scientific value. And even if a theory is parsimonious, falsifiable, and sufficiently heuristic to formulate a hypothesis, it may still be inaccurate or *invalid*, and may have to be discarded altogether if its predictions are consistently disconfirmed. So it may seem at times that some theoretical pronouncements *are* true only in theory, not in practice. However, there is clearly another side to this issue. Even theories that are later disconfirmed may have served a useful purpose by stimulating the new knowledge that led to their demise. We might also note that good theories survive because they continue to generate new knowledge, much of which may have practical implications that truly benefit humanity. In this sense, there is nothing quite so practical as a *good* theory.

In this chapter, we will examine the basic premises of six broad theoretical traditions that have had major impacts on the science of human development: the *psychoanalytic* viewpoint, the *learning* viewpoint, the *cognitive-developmental* viewpoint, the *information-processing* viewpoint, the *evolutionary* viewpoint, and the *ecological systems* viewpoint. Although these theories are central to our discipline and could be characterized as the con-

parsimony
criterion for evaluating the scientific merit of theories; a parsimonious theory is one that uses relatively few explanatory principles to explain a broad set of observations

falsifiability
criterion for evaluating the scientific merit of theories; a theory is falsifiable when it is capable of generating predictions that could be disconfirmed

heuristic value
criterion for evaluating the scientific merit of theories; a heuristic theory is one that continues to stimulate new research and discoveries

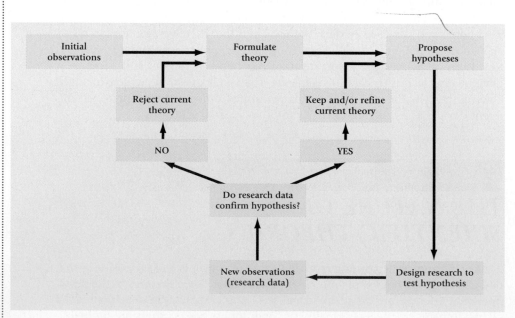

Figure 2.1 *The role of theory in scientific investigation*

ceptual bedrock of developmental psychology, there are many other recent viewpoints that have emerged as extensions of or complements to "the grand theories," and we will consider the strengths and weaknesses of these alternative approaches throughout the text. For example, exciting new theories of *behavioural genetics* are introduced in Chapter 3, where we concentrate on hereditary influences on human development.

As we will see in our upcoming review, different theories emphasize different areas or aspects of development. In addition, each theory makes a particular set of assumptions about human nature and the causes of development. So before reviewing the content of our grand theories, it may be helpful to consider some of the more basic issues on which they differ.

QUESTIONS AND CONTROVERSIES ABOUT HUMAN DEVELOPMENT

What are developing humans like? What causes development? What courses does it follow? Let us look at three major issues on which developmental theories often disagree.

The Nature/Nurture Issue

Is human development primarily the result of nature (biological forces) or nurture (environmental forces)? Perhaps no theoretical controversy has been more heated than this **nature/nurture issue**. Here are two opposing viewpoints:

> Heredity and not environment is the chief maker of people.... Nearly all of the misery and nearly all of the happiness in the world are due not to environment.... The differences among people are due to differences in germ cells with which they were born. (Wiggam, 1923, p. 42)

> Give me a dozen healthy infants, well formed, and my own specified world to bring them up in, and I'll guarantee to take any one at random and train them to become any type of specialist I might select—doctor, lawyer, artist, merchant, chief, and yes, even beggar and thief, regardless of his talents, penchants, tendencies, abilities, vocations, and race of their ancestors. There is no such thing as an inheritance of capacity, talent, temperament, mental constitution, and behavioral characteristics. (Watson, 1925, p. 82)

Of course, there is a middle ground that is endorsed by many contemporary researchers who believe that the relative contributions of nature and nurture depend on the aspect of development in question. However, they stress that all complex human attributes such as intelligence, temperament, and personality are the end products of a long and involved interplay between biological predispositions and environmental forces (see Plomin, 1990). Their advice to us then, is to think less about nature *versus* nurture and more about how these two sets of influences combine or *interact* to produce developmental change.

The Active/Passive Issue

Another topic of theoretical debate is the **activity/passivity issue**. Are children curious, active creatures who largely determine how agents of society treat them? Or are they passive souls on whom society fixes its stamp? Consider the implications of these opposing

nature/nurture issue
debate among developmental theorists about the relative importance of biological predispositions (nature) and environmental influences (nurture) as determinants of human development

active/passive issue
debate among developmental theorists about whether children are active contributors to their own development or, rather, passive recipients of environmental influence

viewpoints. If we could show that children are extremely malleable—literally at the mercy of those who raise them—then perhaps individuals who turned out to be less than productive would be justified in suing their overseers for malfeasance. Indeed, one troubled young man in the United States used this logic to bring a suit against his parents for failing in their parenting duties. Perhaps you can anticipate the defence that the parents' lawyer offered: Counsel argued that the parents had tried many strategies in an attempt to raise their child right but that he responded favourably to none of them. The implication is that this young man played an *active* role in determining how his parents treated him and is largely responsible for creating the climate in which he was raised. Recent debates in Canada about who is financially responsible for acts of vandalism perpetrated by children echo the theoretical active/passive debates. Some have argued that parents should pay restitution. The assumption is that the parents have "control" and are responsible for their child's behaviour. Others argue that the child acts independently and is responsible for his or her own actions.

Which of these perspectives do you consider more reasonable? Think about it, for very soon you will have an opportunity to state your views on this and other topics of theoretical debate.

The Continuity/Discontinuity Issue

Think for a moment about developmental change. Do you think that the changes we experience occur very gradually? Or would you say that these changes are rather abrupt?

On one side of this **continuity/discontinuity issue** are continuity theorists, who view human development as an additive process that occurs gradually and continuously, without sudden changes. They might represent the course of developmental change with a smooth growth curve like the one in Figure 2.2(a). By contrast, discontinuity theorists, such as Robbie Case at the University of Toronto, describe the road to maturity as a series of abrupt changes, each of which elevates the child to a new and presumably more advanced level of functioning. These levels, or stages, are represented by the steps of the discontinuous growth curve in Figure 2.2(b). Case (1992) refers to these steps as similar to a "staircase," with each step representing a leap from the step that preceded it (see Chapter 7 for more discussion of Case's work).

A second aspect of the continuity/discontinuity issue centres on whether developmental changes are quantitative or qualitative in nature. **Quantitative changes** are changes in *degree*. For example, children grow taller and run a little faster with each passing year, and they acquire more and more knowledge about the world around them. By contrast, **qualitative changes** are changes in *kind*—changes that make the individual

continuity/discontinuity issue
debate among theorists about whether developmental changes are quantitative and continuous or qualitative and discontinuous (i.e., stagelike)

quantitative change
incremental change in degree without sudden transformations; for example, some view the small yearly increases in height and weight that 2- to 11-year-olds display as quantitative developmental changes

qualitative change
changes in kind that make individuals fundamentally different than they were before; the transformation of a prelinguistic infant into a language user is viewed by many as a qualitative change in communication skills

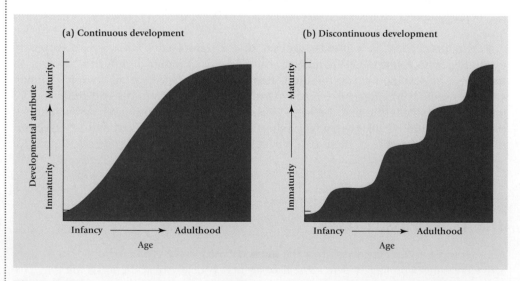

Figure 2.2 *The course of development as described by continuity and discontinuity (stage) theorists*

fundamentally different in some way than he or she was earlier. The transformation of a tadpole into a frog is a qualitative change. Similarly, an infant who lacks language may be qualitatively different from a preschooler who speaks well, and an adolescent who is sexually mature may be fundamentally different from a classmate who has yet to reach puberty. Continuity theorists generally think that developmental changes are basically quantitative in nature, whereas discontinuity theorists tend to portray development as a sequence of qualitative changes. Indeed, discontinuity theorists are the ones who claim that we progress through **developmental stages**, each of which is a distinct phase of life characterized by a particular set of abilities, emotions, motives, or behaviours that form a coherent pattern.

Interestingly, societies may take different positions on the continuity/discontinuity issue. Some Pacific and East Asian cultures, for example, have words for infant qualities that are never used to describe adults, and adult terms such as *intelligent* or *angry* are never used to characterize infants (Kagan, 1991). People in these cultures view personality development as discontinuous, and infants are regarded as so fundamentally different from adults that they cannot be judged on the same personality dimensions. By contrast, North Americans and Northern Europeans are more inclined to assume that personality development is a continuous process and to search for the seeds of adult personality in babies' temperaments.

These, then, are the major developmental controversies that theories resolve in different ways. You may wish to clarify your own stand on these issues by completing the brief questionnaire in Box 2.1. At the end of the chapter, Table 2.4 summarizes how the major developmental theories address these questions so you can compare their assumptions about human development with your own.

Now let's begin our survey of the theories, starting with Freud's psychoanalytic approach.

THE PSYCHOANALYTIC VIEWPOINT

It is difficult to think of a theorist who has had a greater impact on Western thought than Sigmund Freud, the Viennese physician who lived from 1856 to 1939. This revolutionary thinker challenged prevailing notions about human nature by proposing that we are driven by motives and conflicts of which we are largely unaware and that our personalities are shaped by our early life experiences. In this section, we will first consider Freud's early **psychosexual theory** of human development and then compare Freud's theory with that of his best-known follower, Erik Erikson.

Freud's Psychosexual Theory

Freud was a practising neurologist who formulated his theory of human development from his analyses of his emotionally disturbed patients' life histories. Seeking to relieve their nervous symptoms and anxieties, he relied heavily on such methods as hypnosis, free

developmental stage
distinct phase within a larger sequence of development; a period characterized by a particular set of abilities, motives, behaviours, or emotions that occur together and form a coherent pattern

psychosexual theory
Freud's theory that states that maturation of the sex instinct underlies stages of personality development, and that the manner in which parents manage children's instinctual impulses determines the traits that children display

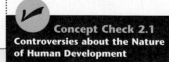

Concept Check 2.1
Controversies about the Nature of Human Development

Check your understanding of conceptual controversies about the nature of human development by identifying the following spokesperson's position on the nature/nurture issue, the active/passive issue, and the continuity/discontinuity issue. Answers appear in the Appendix.

Children the world over go through the same distinct phases of intellectual development. Yet, there are clear

individual differences. Very bright parents have the brightest youngsters; even when these children are cared for by undereducated nannies, their brightness will show through as long as they have many puzzles to solve and other challenges to master on their own.

2.1 Where Do You Stand on Major Developmental Issues?

1. Biological influences (heredity, maturational forces) and environmental influences (culture, neighbourhoods, parenting styles, educational experiences) both contribute to development. Overall,
   a. biological factors contribute more than environmental factors
   b. biological and environmental factors are equally important
   c. environmental factors contribute more than biological factors

2. Children and adolescents are
   a. active beings who play a major role in determining their own developmental outcomes
   b. passive beings whose developmental outcomes largely reflect the influences of other people and circumstances beyond their control

3. Development proceeds
   a. through distinct stages, so that the individual changes abruptly into a quite different kind of person than he or she was in an earlier stage
   b. continuously, in small increments without abrupt changes

4. A good analogy for a developing human being might be
   a. a complex machine that becomes ever more complex as its parts (behaviours, emotions, abilities) grow more numerous and sophisticated
   b. an entity that cannot be likened to a collection of parts and that blossoms with age, much as a simple seed evolves into a blooming rose

	Questions			
	1	2	3	4
Your Answers	____	____	____	____

---

association (a quick spelling out of one's thoughts), and dream analysis because they gave some indication of **unconscious motives** that patients had **repressed** (that is, forced out of their conscious awareness). By analyzing these motives and the events that caused their suppression, Freud concluded that human development is a conflictual process: As biological creatures, we have basic sexual and aggressive **instincts** that *must* be served; yet society dictates that many of these drives are undesirable and *must* be restrained. According to Freud, the ways in which parents manage these sexual and aggressive urges in the first few years of life play a major role in shaping their children's conduct and character.

Three Components of Personality

Freud's psychosexual theory specifies that three components of personality—id, ego, and superego—develop and gradually become integrated in a series of five psychosexual stages. The **id** is all that is present at birth. Its sole function is to satisfy inborn biological instincts, and it will try to do so immediately. Indeed, young infants often do seem to be "all id." When hungry or wet, they simply fuss and cry until their needs are met, and they are not known for their patience.

The **ego** is the conscious, rational component of the personality that reflects the child's emerging abilities to perceive, learn, remember, and reason. Its function is to find realistic means of gratifying instincts, as when a hungry toddler, remembering how she gets food, seeks out mom and says "cookie." As their egos mature, children become better at controlling their irrational ids and finding realistic ways to gratify needs on their own.

However, realistic solutions to needs are not always acceptable, as a hungry 3-year-old who is caught sneaking cookies between meals may soon discover. The final component of personality, or **superego**, is the seat of the conscience. It arises between the ages of 3 and 6 as children *internalize* (take on as their own) the moral values and standards of their parents (Freud, 1933). Once the superego emerges, children do not need an adult to tell them they have been good or bad; they are now aware of their own transgressions and will feel guilty or ashamed about their unethical conduct. So the superego is truly an internal censor: It insists that the ego find socially acceptable outlets for the id's undesirable impulses.

Obviously, these three components of personality inevitably conflict (Freud, 1940/1964). In the mature, healthy personality, a dynamic balance operates: The id communicates basic needs, the ego restrains the impulsive id long enough to find realistic

unconscious motives
Freud's term for feelings, experiences, and conflicts that influence a person's thinking and behaviour, but lie outside the person's awareness

repression
type of motivated forgetting in which anxiety-provoking thoughts and conflicts are forced out of conscious awareness

instinct
inborn biological force that motivates a particular response or class of responses

id
psychoanalytic term for the inborn component of the personality that is driven by the instincts

ego
psychoanalytic term for the rational component of the personality

superego
psychoanalytic term for the component of personality that consists of one's internalized moral standards

methods of satisfying these needs, and the superego decides whether the ego's problem-solving strategies are morally acceptable. The ego is clearly in the middle; it must serve two harsh masters by striking a balance between the opposing demands of the id and the superego, all the while accommodating the realities of the external world.

Stages of Psychological Development

Freud thought that sex was the most important instinct because he discovered that his patients' mental disturbances often revolved around childhood sexual conflicts that they had repressed. But are young children really sexual beings? Yes, said Freud (1940/1964), whose view of sex was very broad, encompassing such activities as thumbsucking and urinating that we would not consider erotic. Freud believed that, as the sex instinct matured, its focus shifted from one part of the body to another, and that each shift brought on a new stage of psychosexual development. Table 2.1 briefly describes each of Freud's five stages of psychosexual development.

Freud believed that parents must walk a fine line with their children at each psychosexual stage. He thought that permitting either too much or too little gratification of sexual needs might cause the child to become obsessed with whatever activity was strongly encouraged or discouraged. The child might then **fixate** on that activity (that is, display arrested development) and retain some aspect of it throughout life. For example, an infant who was strongly punished for and thus conflicted about sucking her thumb might express this oral fixation through such substitute activities as chain smoking or oral sex as an adult. Note the implication here: Freud claimed that early childhood experiences and conflicts can live on to influence our adult interests, activities, and personalities.

Contributions and Criticisms of Freud's Theory

How plausible do you think Freud's ideas are? Do you think that we are driven relentlessly by sexual and aggressive instincts? Or might the sexual conflicts that Freud thought so important merely have been reflections of the sexually repressive Victorian era in which he and his patients lived?

fixation
arrested development at a particular psychosexual stage that can prevent movement to higher stages

TABLE 2.1	Freud's Stages of Psychosexual Development	

Psychosexual stage	Age	Description
Oral	Birth–1 year	The sex instinct centres on the mouth because infants derive pleasure from such oral activities as sucking, chewing, and biting. Feeding activities are particularly important. For example, an infant weaned too early or abruptly may later crave close contact and become overdependent on a spouse.
Anal	1–3 years	Voluntary urination and defecation become the primary methods of gratifying the sex instinct. Toilet training produces major conflicts between children and parents. The emotional climate that parents create can have lasting effects. For example, children who are punished for toileting "accidents" may become inhibited, messy, or wasteful.
Phallic	3–6 years	Pleasure is now derived from genital stimulation. Children develop an incestuous desire for the opposite-sex parent (called the Oedipus complex for boys and the Electra complex for girls). Anxiety stemming from this conflict causes children to internalize the sex-role characteristics and moral standards of their same-sex parental rival.
Latency	6–11 years	Traumas of the phallic stage cause sexual conflicts to be repressed and sexual urges to be rechannelled into schoolwork and vigorous play. The ego and superego continue to develop as the child gains more problem-solving abilities at school and internalizes societal values.
Genital	Age 12 onward	Puberty triggers a reawakening of sexual urges. Adolescents must now learn how to express these urges in socially acceptable ways. If development has been healthy, the mature sex instinct is satisfied by marriage and raising children.

Bettman/Corbis/Magma

Erik Erikson (1902–94) empha-
sized the sociocultural determi-
nants of personality in his theory
of psychosocial development.

Few developmentalists today are strong proponents of Freud's theory. There is not much evidence that any of the early oral, anal, and genital conflicts that Freud stressed reliably predict adult personality (see, for example, Bem, 1989; Crews, 1996). One reason for this may be that Freud's account of human development was based on the recollections of a relatively small number of emotionally disturbed adults whose experiences may not apply to most people.

Yet we should not reject all of Freud's ideas simply because some of them may seem a bit outlandish. Perhaps Freud's greatest contribution was his concept of *unconscious motivation*. When psychology came into being in the mid-19th century, investigators were concerned with understanding isolated aspects of *conscious* experience, such as sensory processes and perceptual illusions. It was Freud who first proclaimed that the vast majority of psychic experience lay below the level of conscious awareness. Freud also deserves considerable credit for focusing attention on the influence of early experience on later development. Debates continue about exactly how critical early experiences are, but few developmentalists today doubt that some early experiences *can* have lasting effects. Finally, we might thank Freud for studying the emotional side of human development—the loves, fears, anxieties, and other powerful emotions that play important roles in our lives. These aspects of life have often been overlooked by developmentalists who have tended to concentrate on observable behaviours or on rational thought processes. In sum, Freud was truly a great pioneer who dared to navigate murky, uncharted waters that his predecessors had not even thought to explore. In the process, he changed our views of humankind.

Erikson's Theory of Psychosocial Development

As Freud became widely read, he attracted many followers. However, Freud's pupils did not always agree with him, and eventually they began to modify some of his ideas and became important theorists in their own right. Among the best known of these *neo-Freudian* scholars was Erik Erikson.

Comparing Erikson with Freud

Although Erikson (1963; 1982) accepted many of Freud's ideas, he differed from Freud in two important respects. First, Erikson (1963) stressed that children are *active*, curious explorers who seek to adapt to their environments, rather than passive slaves to biological urges who are moulded by their parents. Erikson has been labelled an "ego" psychologist because he believed that, at each stage of life, people must cope with social *realities* (in ego function) in order to adapt successfully and display a normal pattern of development. So in Erikson's theory, the ego is far more than a simple arbiter of the opposing demands of the id and superego.

A second critical difference between Erikson and Freud is that Erikson places much less emphasis on sexual urges and far more emphasis on cultural influences than Freud did. Clearly, Erikson's thinking was shaped by his own varied experiences. He was born in Denmark and raised in Germany, and spent much of his adolescence wandering throughout Europe. After receiving his professional training, Erikson came to the United States, where he studied college students, combat soldiers, civil rights workers in the South, and Native Americans. Having observed many similarities and differences in development across these diverse social groups, it is hardly surprising that Erikson emphasized *social* and *cultural* aspects of development in his own **psychosocial theory**.

psychosocial theory
Erikson's revision of Freud's theory that emphasizes sociocultural (rather than sexual) determinants of development and posits a series of eight psychosocial conflicts that people must resolve successfully to display healthy psychological adjustment

Eight Life Crises

Erikson believed that human beings face eight major crises or conflicts during the course of their lives. Each conflict emerges at a distinct time dictated by both biological maturation and social demands that developing people experience at particular points in life. Each crisis must be resolved successfully in order to prepare for a satisfactory resolution of the next life crisis. Table 2.2 briefly describes each of Erikson's eight crises (or psychosocial stages) and lists the Freudian psychosexual stage to which it corresponds. Notice that Erikson's developmental stages do not end at adolescence or young adulthood as Freud's do. Erikson believed that the problems of adolescents and young adults are very different from those faced by parents who are raising children or by the elderly who may be grappling with retirement, a sense of uselessness, and impending death. Most contemporary developmentalists agree.

Contributions and Criticisms of Erikson's Theory

Many people prefer Erikson's theory to Freud's because they simply refuse to believe that human beings are dominated by sexual instincts. An analyst like Erikson, who stresses

Approximate age	Erikson's stage or "psychosocial" crisis	Erikson's viewpoint: Significant events and social influences	Corresponding Freudian stage
Birth–1 year	Basic trust versus mistrust	Infants must learn to trust others to care for their basic needs. If caregivers are rejecting or inconsistent, the infant may view the world as a dangerous place filled with untrustworthy or unreliable people. The primary caregiver is the key social agent.	Oral
1–3 years	Autonomy versus shame and doubt	Children must learn to be "autonomous"—to feed and dress themselves, to look after their own hygiene, and so on. Failure to achieve this independence may force the child to doubt his or her own abilities and feel shameful. Parents are the key social agents.	Anal
3–6 years	Initiative versus guilt	Children attempt to act grown up and will try to accept responsibilities that are beyond their capacity to handle. They sometimes undertake goals or activities that conflict with those of parents and other family members, and these conflicts may make them feel guilty. Successful resolution of this crisis requires a balance: The child must retain a sense of initiative and yet learn not to impinge on the rights, privileges, or goals of others. The family is the key social agent.	Phallic
6–12 years	Industry versus inferiority	Children must master important social and academic skills. This is a period when the child compares him- or herself with peers. If sufficiently industrious, children acquire the social and academic skills to feel self-assured. Failure to acquire these important attributes leads to feelings of inferiority. Significant social agents are teachers and peers.	Latency
12–20 years	Identity versus role confusion	This is the crossroad between childhood and maturity. The adolescent grapples with the question "Who am I?" Adolescents must establish basic social and occupational identities, or they will remain confused about the roles they should play as adults. The key social agent is the society of peers.	Early genital (adolescence)
20–40 years (young adulthood)	Intimacy versus isolation	The primary task at this stage is to form strong friendships and to achieve a sense of love and companionship (or a shared identity) with another person. Feelings of loneliness or isolation are likely to result from an inability to form friendships or an intimate relationship. Key social agents are lovers, spouses, and close friends (of both sexes).	Genital
40–65 years (middle adulthood)	Generativity versus stagnation	At this stage, adults face the tasks of becoming productive in their work and raising their families or otherwise looking after the needs of young people. These standards of "generativity" are defined by one's culture. Those who are unable or unwilling to assume these responsibilities become stagnant and self-centred. Significant social agents are the spouse, children, and cultural norms.	Genital
Old age	Ego integrity versus despair	The older adult looks back at life, viewing it as either a meaningful, productive, and happy experience or a major disappointment full of unfulfilled promises and unrealized goals. One's life experiences, particularly social experiences, determine the outcome of this final life crisis.	Genital

TABLE 2.2 Erikson's and Freud's Stages of Development

our rational, adaptive nature, is much easier to accept. In addition, Erikson emphasizes many of the social conflicts and personal dilemmas that people may remember, are currently experiencing, or can easily anticipate or observe in people they know.

Erikson does seem to have captured many of the central issues of life in his eight psychosocial stages. Indeed, we will discuss his ideas on such topics as the emotional development of infants in Chapter 11, the growth of the self-concept in childhood and the identity issues facing adolescents in Chapter 12, and the influence of friends and playmates on social development in Chapter 16. (See also Sigelman, 1999, for a discussion of Erikson's contributions to the field of adult development.) On the other hand, Erikson's theory can be criticized for being vague about the *causes* of development. What kinds of experiences must people have to cope with and successfully resolve various psychosocial conflicts? How exactly does the outcome of one psychosocial stage influence personality at a later stage? Unfortunately, Erikson is not very explicit about these important issues. So his theory is really a descriptive overview of human social and emotional development that does not adequately explain how or why this development takes place.

Psychoanalytic Theory Today

Freud and Erikson are only two of many psychoanalysts who have had a meaningful influence on the study of human development (Tyson & Tyson, 1990). For example, Karen Horney (1967) has challenged Freud's ideas about sex differences in development and is now widely credited as a founder of the discipline we know today as the psychology of women. Alfred Adler (1929/1964), a contemporary of Freud's, was among the first to suggest that *siblings* (and sibling rivalries) are important contributors to social and personality development, a proposition we will explore in detail in Chapter 15. And American psychoanalyst Harry Stack Sullivan (1953) wrote extensively about how close, same-sex friendships during middle childhood set the stage for intimate love relationships later in life (see Chapter 16 for a discussion of this and other contributions that friends may make to social and personality development). Although their theories differ in focus, all of these *neo-Freudians* place much more emphasis on *social* influences on development and much less emphasis on the role of sexual instincts than Freud did.

Despite the important contributions that Freud and the neo-Freudians have made, many contemporary developmentalists have largely rejected the psychoanalytic perspective because its propositions are very difficult to either falsify or confirm. Suppose, for example, that we wanted to test a basic Freudian hypothesis that the healthy personality is one in which the id, ego, and superego are roughly equal in strength. How could we do it? There are objective tests that we could use to select mentally healthy persons, but we have no instrument that measures the relative strengths of the id, ego, and superego. The point is that many psychoanalytic hypotheses are untestable by any method other than the interview or a clinical approach; unfortunately, these techniques are time-consuming, expensive, and among the least objective of all methods used to study human development.

However, the main reason that so many developmentalists have abandoned the psychoanalytic perspective is that other theories seem more compelling. One perspective favoured by many is the learning approach, to which we now turn.

Karen Horney (1915–57) was the founder of the psychology of women.

THE LEARNING VIEWPOINT

Earlier in the text, we encountered a developmentalist who claimed that he could take a dozen healthy infants and train them to be whatever he chose—doctor, lawyer, beggar, and so on—regardless of their background or ancestry. What a bold statement! It implies that nurture is everything and that nature, or hereditary endowment, counts for nothing. The statement was made by John B. Watson, a strong proponent of the importance of learning in human development and the father of a school of thought known as **behaviourism** (Horowitz, 1992).

Watson's Behaviourism

A basic premise of Watson's (1913) behaviourism is that conclusions about human development should be based on observations of overt behaviour rather than on speculations about unconscious motives or cognitive processes that are unobservable. Moreover, Watson believed that well-*learned* associations between external stimuli and observable responses (**habits**) are the building blocks of human development. Like John Locke, Watson viewed the infant as a tabula rasa (blank slate) to be written on by experience. Children have no inborn tendencies; how they turn out depends entirely on their rearing environments and the ways in which their parents and other significant people in their lives treat them. According to a behavioural perspective, then, it is a mistake to assume that children progress through a series of distinct stages dictated by biological maturation, as Freud (and others) have argued. Instead, development is viewed as a continuous process of behavioural change that is shaped by a person's unique environment and may differ dramatically from person to person.

John B. Watson (1878–1958) was the founder of behaviourism and the first social learning theorist.

To prove just how malleable children are, Watson set out to demonstrate that infantile fears and other emotional reactions are acquired rather than inborn. In one demonstration, for example, Watson and Rosalie Raynor (1920) presented a gentle white rat to a 9-month-old named Albert. Albert's initial reactions were positive; he crawled toward the rat and played with it as he had previously with a dog and a rabbit. Then, two months later, Watson attempted to instil a fear response. Every time Albert reached for the white rat, Watson would slip behind him and bang a steel rod with a hammer. Did little Albert eventually associate the white rat with the loud noise and come to fear his furry playmate? Indeed, he did, thus illustrating that fears are easily learned.

Watson's belief that children are shaped by their environments carried a stern message for parents: They were largely responsible for what their children would become. Watson (1928, pp. 81–82) cautioned parents that they should begin to train their children at birth and cut back on the coddling if they hoped to instil good habits. Treat them, he said

> … as though they were young adults…. Let your behavior always be objective and kindly firm. Never hug and kiss them, never let them sit on your lap…. Shake hands with them in the morning. Give them a pat on the head if they have made an extraordinarily good job of a difficult task…. In a week's time, you will find how easy it is to be perfectly objective … [yet] kindly. You will be utterly ashamed at the mawkish, sentimental way you have been handling [your child] (pp. 81–82).

Since Watson's day, several theories have been proposed to explain how we learn from our social experiences and form the habits that Watson viewed as "bricks in the edifice of human development." Perhaps the theorist who did more than anyone to advance the behaviourist approach was B.F. Skinner.

Skinner's Operant Learning Theory (Radical Behaviourism)

Through his research with animals, Skinner (1953) came to understand a very important form of learning that he believed is the basis for most habits. Quite simply, Skinner proposed that both animals and humans repeat acts that lead to favourable outcomes and suppress those that produce unfavourable outcomes. So a rat that presses a bar and receives a tasty food pellet is apt to perform that response again. In the language of Skinner's theory, the freely emitted bar-pressing response is called an *operant*, and the

behaviourism
school of thinking in psychology that holds that conclusions about human development should be based on controlled observations of overt behaviour rather than speculation about unconscious motives or other unobservable phenomena; the philosophical underpinning for the early theories of learning

habits
well-learned associations between stimuli and responses that represent the stable aspects of one's personality

Associated Press

B.F. Skinner (1904–1990) proposed a learning theory that emphasized the role of external stimuli in controlling human behaviour.

Courtesy Albert Bandura

Albert Bandura (1925–   ) has emphasized the cognitive aspects of learning in his social learning theory.

reinforcer
any desirable consequence of an act that increases the probability that the act will recur

punisher
any consequence of an act that suppresses that act or decreases the probability that it will recur

operant learning
form of learning in which voluntary acts (or operants) become either more or less probable depending on the consequences they produce

observational learning
learning that results from observing the behaviour of others

food pellet that strengthens this response (by making it more probable in the future) is called a **reinforcer**. Similarly, a young girl may form a long-term habit of showing compassion toward distressed playmates if her parents consistently reinforce her kindly behaviour with praise, or a teenage boy may become more studious if his efforts are rewarded by higher grades. **Punishers**, on the other hand, are consequences that suppress a response and decrease the likelihood that it will occur in the future. If the rat who had been reinforced for bar pressing was suddenly given a painful shock each time it pressed the bar, the bar-pressing habit would begin to disappear. Similarly, a teenage girl who is grounded every time she stays out beyond her curfew is apt to become more concerned about being home on time.

In sum, Skinner believed that habits develop as a result of unique **operant learning** experiences. One boy's aggressive behaviour may increase over time because his playmates give in to (reinforce) his forceful tactics. Another boy may become relatively nonaggressive because his peers actively suppress (punish) aggressive conduct by fighting back. The two boys may develop in entirely different directions based on their different histories of reinforcement and punishment. According to Skinner, there is no "aggressive stage" in child development or "aggressive instinct" in human beings. Instead, he claimed that the majority of habits that children acquire—the very responses that comprise their unique personalities—are freely emitted operants that have been shaped by their consequences. So Skinner's *operant learning theory* claims that the directions in which we develop depend on *external* stimuli (reinforcers and punishers) rather than on internal forces such as instincts, drives, or biological maturation.

Today's developmentalists appreciate that human behaviour can take many forms and that habits can emerge and disappear over a lifetime depending on whether they have positive or negative consequences (Gewirtz & Pelaez-Nogueras, 1992). Yet many believe that Skinner placed far too much emphasis on operant behaviours shaped by *external* stimuli (reinforcers and punishers), while ignoring important *cognitive* contributors to social learning. One such critic is Albert Bandura, who has proposed a cognitive social learning theory of human development that is widely respected today.

Bandura's Cognitive Social Learning Theory

Can human social learning be explained on the basis of research with animals? Bandura (1977, 1986, 1992) doesn't think so. He agrees with Skinner that operant conditioning is an important type of learning, particularly for animals; however, Bandura stresses that humans are *cognitive* beings—active information processors—who, unlike animals, are likely to think about the relationships between their behaviour and its consequences. Therefore, they are often more affected by what they *believe* will happen than by the events they actually experience. Consider your own situation as a student. Your education is costly and time-consuming and may impose many stressful demands. Yet you tolerate the cost and toil because you may *anticipate* greater rewards after you obtain your degree. Your behaviour is not shaped by immediate consequences; if it were, few students would ever make it through the trials and tribulations of university. Instead, you persist as a student because you have *thought about* the long-term benefits of obtaining an education and have decided that they outweigh the short-term costs you must endure.

Nowhere is Bandura's cognitive emphasis clearer than in his decision to highlight **observational learning** as a central developmental process. Observational learning is simply learning that results from observing the behaviour of other people (called *models*). A 2-year-old may learn how to approach and pet the family dog by simply watching his older sister do it. An 8-year-old may acquire a very negative attitude toward a minority after hearing her parents talk about this group in a disparaging way. Observational learning simply could not occur unless cognitive processes were at work. We must *attend* carefully to a model's behaviour; actively digest (or *encode)* what we observe; and then *store* this information in memory (as an image or a verbal label) in order to imitate what we have observed at a later time. Indeed, as we will see in Box 2.2, children need not be reinforced in order to learn this way.

Why does Bandura stress observational learning in his cognitive social learning theory? Simply because this active, cognitive form of learning permits young children to quickly acquire literally thousands of new responses in a variety of settings where their models are simply pursuing their own interests and are not trying to teach them anything. In fact, many of the behaviours that children observe, remember, and may imitate are actions that models display but would like to discourage—practices such as swearing, smoking, or eating between meals. So Bandura claims children are continually learning both desirable and undesirable responses by "keeping their eyes (and ears) open," and he is not at all surprised that human development proceeds so rapidly along so many different paths.

FOCUS ON RESEARCH

2.2

An Example of No-Trial (Observational) Learning without Reinforcement

In 1965, Bandura made what was then considered a radical statement: Children can learn by merely observing the behaviour of a social model, *even without first performing the responses themselves or receiving any reinforcement for performing them*. Clearly, this "no-trial" learning is inconsistent with Skinner's theory, which claims that one must perform a response and then be reinforced in order to have learned that response.

Bandura (1965) then conducted a now-classic experiment to prove his point. Nursery-school children each watched a short film in which an adult model directed an unusual sequence of aggressive responses toward an inflatable Bobo doll, hitting the doll with a mallet while shouting "sockeroo," throwing rubber balls while shouting "bang, bang," and so on. There were three experimental conditions:

1. Children in the *model-rewarded* condition saw a second adult give the aggressive model candy and soda for a "championship performance."

2. Children in the *no-consequence* condition simply saw the model behave aggressively.

3. Children in the *model-punished* condition saw a second adult scold and spank the model for beating up Bobo.

When the film ended, each child was left alone in a playroom that contained a Bobo doll and the props that the model had used to beat up Bobo. Hidden observers then recorded all instances in which the child imitated one or more of the model's aggressive acts. These observations revealed how willing children were to perform the responses they had witnessed. The results of this "performance" test appear on the left-hand side of the figure. Notice that children in the model-rewarded and no-consequences conditions imitated more of the model's aggressive acts than those who had seen the model punished for aggressive behaviour. Clearly, this looks very much like the kind of no-trial observational learning that Bandura had proposed.

But an important question remained: Had children in the first two conditions actually learned more from observing the model than those who had seen the model punished? To find out, Bandura devised a test to see just how much they had learned. Each child was now offered

trinkets and fruit juice for reproducing all of the model's behaviours that he or she could recall. As we see in the right-hand side of the figure, this "learning test" revealed that children in each of the three conditions had learned about the same amount by observing the model. Apparently, children in the model-punished condition had imitated fewer of the model's responses on the initial performance test because they felt that they too might be punished for striking Bobo. But when offered a reward, they showed that they had learned much more than their initial performances had implied.

In sum, it is important to distinguish what children learn by observation from their willingness to perform these responses. Clearly, reinforcement is not necessary for observational learning—that is, for the formation of images or verbal descriptions that would enable the observer to imitate the model's acts. However, the reinforcing or punishing consequences that the model received may well affect the observer's tendency to perform what he or she has already learned by observation.

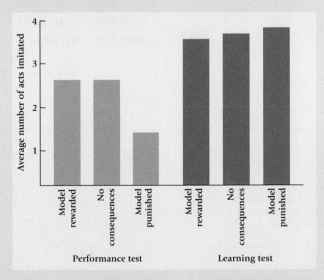

Average number of aggressive responses imitated during the performance test and the learning test for children who had seen a model rewarded, punished, or receive no consequences for his actions. ADAPTED FROM BANDURA, 1965.

Social Learning as Reciprocal Determinism

Early versions of learning theory were largely tributes to Watson's doctrine of **environmental determinism**: Young, unknowing children were viewed as passive recipients of environmental influence—they would become whatever parents, teachers, and other agents of society groomed them to be. Bandura (1986; 1989) takes strong exception to this point of view, stressing that children and adolescents are active, thinking beings who contribute in many ways to their own development. Observational learning, for example, requires the observer to *actively* attend to, encode, and retain the behaviours displayed by social models. And children are often free to choose the models to whom they will attend, so they have some say about *what* they will learn from others.

Bandura (1986) has proposed the concept of **reciprocal determinism** to describe his view that human development reflects an interaction among an "active" person (P), the person's behaviour (B), and the environment (E) (see Figure 2.3). Unlike Watson and Skinner, who maintained that the environment (E) shaped a child's personality and her behaviour, Bandura and others (most notably Richard Bell, 1979) propose that links among people, behaviours, and environments are *bidirectional*. Thus, a child can influence his environment by virtue of his own conduct. Consider an example.

Suppose that a 4-year-old discovers that he can gain control over desirable toys by assaulting his playmates. In this case, control over the desired toy is a favourable outcome that reinforces the child's aggressive behaviour. But note that the reinforcer here is produced by the child himself through his aggressive actions. Not only has bullying behaviour been reinforced (by obtaining the toy), but *the character of the play environment has changed*. Playmates who were victimized may be more inclined to give in to the bully, which in turn may make him more likely to pick on these same children in the future (Patterson, Littman, & Bricker, 1967).

In sum, cognitive learning theorists believe that human development is best described as a continuous *reciprocal interaction* between children and their environments. The situation or "environment" that a child experiences surely affects her, but her behaviour is thought to affect the environment as well. The implication is that children are actively involved in shaping the very environments that influence their growth and development.

Contributions and Criticisms of Learning Theories

Perhaps the major contribution of the learning viewpoint is the wealth of information it has provided about developing children and adolescents. Learning theories are very precise and testable (Horowitz, 1992). And by conducting tightly controlled experiments to

environmental determinism
the notion that children are passive creatures who are moulded by their environments

reciprocal determinism
the notion that the flow of influence between children and their environments is a two-way street; the environment may affect the child, but the child's behaviour also influences the environment

Figure 2.3 Bandura's model of reciprocal determinism. ADAPTED FROM BANDURA, 1977.

determine how their participants react to various environmental influences, learning theorists have begun to understand how and why developing people form emotional attachments, adopt gender roles, make friends, learn to abide by moral rules, and change in countless other ways over the course of childhood and adolescence. As we will see throughout the text, the learning perspective has contributed substantially to our knowledge of many aspects of human development (see also Gewirtz & Pelaez-Nogueras, 1992; Grusec, 1992).

Learning theory's emphasis on the immediate causes of overt behaviours also has produced important clinical insights and practical applications. For example, many problem behaviours can now be quickly eliminated by behavioural modification techniques in which the therapist identifies the reinforcers that sustain unacceptable habits and eliminates them while modeling or reinforcing alternative behaviours that are more desirable. Thus, distressing antics such as bullying or name-calling can often be eliminated in a matter of weeks with behaviour-modification techniques, whereas psychoanalysts might require months to probe the child's unconscious, searching for a conflict that may underlie these hostilities.

Despite its strengths, however, many view the learning approach as a grossly oversimplified account of human development. Consider what learning theorists have to say about individual differences. Presumably, people follow unique developmental paths because no two people grow up in precisely the same environment. Yet critics are quick to point out that each person is born with a unique genetic endowment that provides an equally plausible explanation for his or her individuality. So learning theorists may have badly oversimplified the issue of individual differences in development by downplaying the contribution of important biological influences.

Yet another group of critics, whose viewpoint we will soon examine, can agree with the behaviourists that development depends very heavily on the contexts in which it occurs. However, these *ecological systems theorists* argue that the environment that so powerfully influences development is really a series of social systems (for example, families, communities, and cultures). These social systems interact with each other and with the individual in complex ways that are impossible to simulate in a laboratory. Their conclusion is that only by studying children and adolescents in their natural settings are we likely to understand how environments truly influence development.

There is one final point. Despite the popularity of recent cognitively oriented learning theories that stress the child's active role in the developmental process, some critics maintain that learning theorists give too little attention to *cognitive* influences on development. Proponents of this "cognitive-developmental" viewpoint believe that a child's mental abilities change in ways that behaviourists completely ignore. Further, they argue that a child's impressions of and reactions to the environment depend largely on his or her level of **cognitive development**. Let's now turn to this viewpoint and see what it has to offer.

cognitive development
age-related changes that occur in mental activities such as attending, perceiving, learning, thinking, and remembering

---

Concept Check 2.2
Understanding the Positions of Four Major Theorists: Freud, Erikson, Skinner, and Bandura

Check your understanding of the implications of four of the major theories reviewed in this chapter by indicating who is likely to have made each statement quoted below. Choose from the following: (a) Sigmund Freud, (b) Erik Erikson, (c) B.F. Skinner, (d) Albert Bandura. Answers appear in the Appendix.

_____ 1. "Growing is ... differentiation during a sequence of critical periods. In personality growth, it is a task of the ego and of the social processes together [so that] at all times a human being is an ego and a member of society."

_____ 2. "Cognition has causal influence on behavior. A theory that denies that thoughts can regulate actions does not lend itself ... to the explanation of complex human behavior."

_____ 3. "In the traditional view, a person is free.... He can therefore be held responsible for what he does and justly punished if he offends. That view must be reexamined when a scientific analysis reveals unsuspected controlling relations between behavior and environment."

_____ 4. "The task of making conscious the most hidden recesses of the mind is one which ... is quite possible to accomplish."

Bettman/Corbis/Magma

*In his cognitive-developmental
theory, Swiss scholar Jean Piaget
(1896–1980) focused on the
growth of children's knowledge
and reasoning skills.*

scheme
organized pattern of thought or
action that a child constructs to
make sense of some aspect of his
or her experience; Piaget
sometimes used the term *cognitive
structures* as a synonym for
schemes

THE COGNITIVE-DEVELOPMENTAL VIEWPOINT

No theorist has contributed more to our understanding of children's thinking than Jean Piaget (1896–1980), a Swiss scholar who began to study intellectual development during the 1920s. Piaget was truly a remarkable individual. At age 10, he published his first scientific article about the behaviour of a rare albino sparrow. His early interest in the ways that animals adapt to their environments eventually led him to pursue a doctoral degree in zoology, which he completed in 1918. Piaget's secondary interest was *epistemology* (the branch of philosophy concerned with the origins of knowledge), and he hoped to be able to integrate his two interests. Thinking that psychology was the answer, Piaget journeyed to Paris, where he accepted a position at the Alfred Binet laboratories, working on the first standardized intelligence test. His experiences in this position had a profound influence on his career.

In testing mental ability, an estimate is made of the person's intelligence based on the number and kinds of questions that he or she answers correctly. However, Piaget soon found that he was more interested in children's *incorrect* answers than their correct ones. He first noticed that children of about the same age produced the same kinds of wrong answers. But why? As he questioned children about their misconceptions, using the clinical method he had learned while working in a psychiatric clinic, he began to realize that young children are not simply less intelligent than older children; rather, their thought processes are completely different. Piaget then set up his own laboratory and spent 60 years charting the course of intellectual growth and attempting to determine how children progress from one mode (or stage) of thinking to another.

Piaget's View of Intelligence and Intellectual Growth

Influenced by his background in biology, Piaget (1950) defined intelligence as a basic life process that helps an organism *adapt* to its environment. By adapting, Piaget means that the organism is able to cope with the demands of its immediate situation. For example, the hungry infant who grasps a bottle and brings it to her mouth is behaving adaptively, as is the adolescent who successfully interprets a road map while travelling. As children mature, they acquire ever more complex "cognitive structures" that aid them in adapting to their environments.

A cognitive structure—or what Piaget called a **scheme**—is an organized pattern of thought or action that is used to cope with or explain some aspect of experience. For example, many 3-year-olds insist that the sun is alive because it comes up in the morning and goes down at night. According to Piaget, these children are operating on the basis of a simple cognitive scheme that things that move are alive. The earliest schemes, formed in infancy, are motor habits such as rocking, grasping, and lifting that prove to be adaptive indeed. For example, a curious infant who combines the responses of extending an arm (reaching) and grasping with the hand is suddenly capable of satisfying her curiosity by exploring almost any interesting object that is no more than an arm's length away. Simple as these behavioural schemes may be, they permit infants to operate toys, to turn dials, to open cabinets, and to otherwise master their environments. Later in childhood, cognitive schemes take the form of "actions of the head" (for example, mental addition or subtraction) that allow children to manipulate information and think logically about the issues and problems they encounter in everyday life. At any age, children rely on their current cognitive structures to understand the world around them. And because cognitive structures take different forms at different ages, younger and older children may often interpret and respond to the same objects and events in very different ways.

How do children grow intellectually? Piaget claimed that infants have no inborn knowledge or ideas about reality, as some philosophers have claimed. Nor are children simply given information or taught how to think by adults. Instead, they *actively construct* new understandings of the world based on their own experiences. Children watch what goes on around them; they experiment with objects they encounter; they make connections or associations between events; and they are puzzled when their current understandings (or schemes) fail to explain what they have experienced.

To illustrate, let's return for a moment to the 3-year-old who believes that the sun is alive. Surely this idea is not something the child learned from an adult; it was apparently constructed by the child on the basis of her own worldly experiences. After all, many things that move *are* alive. So long as the child clings to this understanding, she may regard any new moving object as alive; that is, new experiences will be interpreted in terms of her current cognitive structures, a process Piaget called **assimilation**. Eventually, however, this child will encounter moving objects that almost certainly couldn't be alive, such as a paper airplane that was nothing more than a sheet of newsprint before dad folded it, or a wind-up toy that invariably stops moving until she winds it again. Now here are contradictions (or what Piaget termed **disequilibriums**) between the child's understanding and the facts. It becomes clear to the child that her "objects-that-move-are-alive" scheme needs to be revised. She is prompted by these disconfirming experiences to **accommodate**—that is, to alter her existing schemes so that they provide a better explanation of the distinction between animate and inanimate objects (perhaps by concluding that only things that move under their own power are alive).

Piaget believed that we continually rely on the complementary processes of assimilation and accommodation to adapt to our environments. Initially, we attempt to understand new experiences or solve problems using our current cognitive schemes (assimilation). But we often find that our existing schemes are inadequate for these tasks, which then prompts us to revise them (through accommodation) so that they provide a better "fit" with reality (Piaget, 1952). Biological maturation also plays an important role: As the brain and nervous system mature, children become capable of increasingly complex cognitive activities that help them to construct better understandings of what they have experienced (Piaget, 1970). Eventually, curious, active children, who are always forming new schemes and reorganizing their knowledge, progress enough to think about old issues in entirely new ways; that is, they pass from one stage of cognitive development to the next higher stage.

Four Stages of Cognitive Development

Piaget proposed four major periods (or stages) of cognitive development: the *sensorimotor* stage (birth to age 2), the *preoperational* stage (ages 2 to 7), the *concrete-operational* stage (ages 7 to 11 or 12), and the *formal-operational* stage (ages 11 to 12 and beyond). These stages form what Piaget called an **invariant developmental sequence**—that is, all children progress through the stages in exactly the order in which they are listed. They cannot skip stages because each successive stage builds on the previous stage and represents a more complex way of thinking.

Table 2.3 summarizes the key features of Piaget's four cognitive stages. Each of these periods of intellectual growth will be discussed in much greater detail when we return to the topic of cognitive development in Chapter 7.

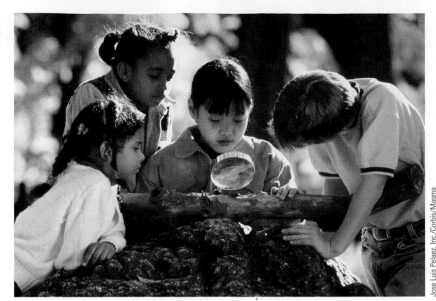

Jose Luis Pelaez, Inc./Corbis/Magma

Piaget believed that children are naturally curious explorers who are constantly trying to make sense of their surroundings.

assimilation
Piaget's term for the process by which children interpret new experiences by incorporating them into their existing schemes

disequilibriums
imbalances or contradictions between one's thought processes and environmental events. By contrast, *equilibrium* refers to a balanced, harmonious relationship between one's cognitive structures and the environment

accommodation
Piaget's term for the process by which children modify their existing schemes in order to incorporate or adapt to new experiences

invariant developmental sequence
series of developments that occur in one particular order because each development in the sequence is a prerequisite for the next

TABLE 2.3   Piaget's Stages of Cognitive Development

Approximate age	Stage	Primary schemes or methods of representing experience	Major developments
Birth–2 years	Sensorimotor	Infants use sensory and motor capabilities to explore and gain a basic understanding of the environment. At birth, they have only innate reflexes with which to engage the world. By the end of the sensorimotor period, they are capable of complex sensorimotor coordinations.	Infants acquire a primitive sense of "self" and "others," learn that objects continue to exist when they are out of sight (object permanence), and begin to internalize behavioural schemes to produce images or mental schemes.
2–7 years	Preoperational	Children use symbolism (images and language) to represent and understand various aspects of the environment. They respond to objects and events according to the way things appear to be. Thought is egocentric, meaning that children think everyone sees the world in much the same way that they do.	Children become imaginative in their play activities. They gradually begin to recognize that other people may not always perceive the world as they do.
7–11 years	Concrete operations	Children acquire and use cognitive operations (mental activities that are components of logical thought).	Children are no longer fooled by appearances. By relying on cognitive operations, they understand the basic properties of and relations among objects and events in the everyday world. They are becoming much more proficient at inferring motives by observing others' behaviour and the circumstances in which it occurs.
11 years and beyond	Formal operations	Adolescents' cognitive operations are reorganized in a way that permits them to operate on operations (think about thinking). Thought is now systematic and abstract.	Logical thinking is no longer limited to the concrete or the observable. Adolescents enjoy pondering hypothetical issues and, as a result, may become rather idealistic. They are capable of systematic, deductive reasoning that permits them to consider many possible solutions to a problem and to pick the correct answer.

Contributions and Criticisms of Piaget's Viewpoint

Like Freud and Watson, Piaget was an innovative renegade. He was unpopular with psychometricians because he claimed that their intelligence tests only measure what children know and tell us nothing about the most important aspect of intellect—how children think. In addition, Piaget dared to study an unobservable, mentalistic concept—"cognition"—that had fallen from favour among psychologists from the behaviourist tradition (Beilin, 1992).

By the 1960s, the times had clearly changed. Not only had Piaget's early theorizing and research legitimized the study of children's thinking, but also his early work linking moral development to cognitive development (see Chapter 14) contributed immensely to a whole new area of developmental research—*social cognition*. Recent social-cognitive theorists such as Lawrence Kohlberg and Robert Selman have found that the same mind that gradually constructs increasingly sophisticated understandings of the physical world also comes, with age, to form more complex ideas about sex differences, moral values, the significance of human emotions, the meaning and obligations of friendship, and countless other aspects of social life. The development of social cognition is a primary focus of Chapter 12, and the links between one's social-cognitive abilities and various aspects of social and personality development are discussed throughout the text.

Piaget's theory has also had a strong impact on education. For example, popular *discovery-based* educational programs are based on the premise that young children do not think like adults and learn best by having hands-on educational experiences with familiar aspects of their environment. So a preschool teacher in a Piagetian classroom might introduce the difficult concept of *number* by presenting her pupils with different numbers of objects to stack, colour, or arrange. Presumably, new concepts like number are best transmitted by methods in which curious, active children can apply their existing schemes and make the critical "discoveries" for themselves.

Although Piaget's pioneering efforts have left a deep and lasting imprint on our thinking about human development (see Beilin, 1992), many of his ideas have been challenged. It appears that Piaget regularly underestimated the intellectual capabilities of infants, preschoolers, and elementary-school children, all of whom show much greater problem-solving skills when presented with simplified tasks that are more familiar and thereby allow them to display their competencies (Bjorklund, 2000). Other investigators have noted that performance on Piagetian problems can be improved dramatically through training programs, which would seem to challenge Piaget's assumption that individualized discovery learning, rather than direct instruction, is the best way to promote intellectual growth.

Vygotsky's Sociocultural Perspective

One of the important challenges to Piaget's theory came from Russian developmentalist, Lev Vygotsky (1896–1934), a Russian psychologist who emphasized the role of culture and context on intellectual development (1934/1962). In his own **sociocultural theory**, Vygotsky focused on how *culture*—the beliefs, values, traditions, and skills of a social group—is transmitted from generation to generation. Rather than depicting children as independent explorers who make critical discoveries on their own, Vygotsky viewed cognitive growth as a *socially mediated activity*—one in which children gradually acquire new ways of thinking and behaving through cooperative dialogues with more knowledgeable members of society (Duncan, 1995). He argued that it was the verbal dialogue with these more knowledgeable members of society, in particular, that was the key to the development of thought.

According to Vygotsky, a child learns first through social interactions with others, and only gradually does learning come under the child's control. Children learn best when instruction is geared to match their **zone of proximal development**—the difference between what a child can do independently and what she or he can do with assistance. For example, competent adults or peers can adjust task demands to ensure that the child is operating in the zone that will allow her or him cognitive growth.

Vygotsky also rejected the notion that all children progress through the same stages of cognitive growth. Why? Because the new skills that children master through their interactions with more competent associates are often specific to their culture rather than universal cognitive structures. So from Vygotsky's perspective (which we will explore in more depth in Chapter 7), Piaget was too limited in his examination of important social and cultural influences on human development.

Contributions and Criticisms of Vygotsky's Viewpoint

Vygotsky's attention to social and cultural aspects of development has been a vital addition to our understanding of cognitive development. Unlike Piaget, who emphasized universal aspects of development, Vygotsky's theory suggests that cognitive development varies across cultures depending on their specific experiences.

Although Vygotsky's work was originally published at the beginning of the 20th century, it wasn't until 1962 that his work was translated into English. Therefore, criticisms of his theory are only now coming forward. For example, Vygotsky's theory has been criticized for its heavy emphasis on the role of verbal dialogue in instruction (Rogoff, 1990, 1998).

A dramatically different perspective on cognitive development is presented by the *information-processing* theorists. Let's examine the most important assumptions of this interesting and influential perspective.

sociocultural theory
Vygotsky's perspective on development, in which children acquire their culture's values, beliefs, and problem-solving strategies through collaborative dialogues with more knowledgeable members of society

zone of proximal development
Vygotsky's term for the range of tasks that are too complex to be mastered alone but can be accomplished with guidance and encouragement from a more skillful partner

THE INFORMATION-PROCESSING VIEWPOINT

By 1970, many developmentalists, disenchanted with the narrow, antimentalistic bias of behaviourism and the problems they saw in Piaget's theory, turned to such fields as cognitive psychology and computer science, seeking new insights into children's thinking. Digital computers, which rely on mathematically specified programs to operate on input (information) and generate solutions to problems, provided the framework for a new **information-processing theory** of cognitive growth. According to information-processing theory, the human mind is like a computer into which information flows, is operated on, and is converted into output—that is, answers, inferences, or solutions to problems (Klahr, 1992; Siegler, 1996a, b, c). Continuing to use the computer analogy, information-processing theorists view cognitive development as age-related changes that occur in the mind's *hardware* (that is, the brain and the peripheral nervous system) and *software* (mental processes such as attention, perception, memory, and problem-solving strategies).

Like Piaget, information-processing theorists acknowledge that biological maturation is an important contributor to cognitive growth. But unlike Piaget, who was vague about the connections between biological and cognitive development, information-processing theorists contend that maturation of the brain and nervous system enables children and adolescents to process information faster (Kail, 1992). As a result, developing persons become better at sustaining attention, recognizing and storing task-relevant information, and executing mental programs that allow them to operate on what they have stored so as to answer questions and solve problems. Yet information-processing theorists are also keenly aware that the strategies that children develop for attending to and processing information are greatly influenced by their *experiences*—that is, by the kinds of problems presented to them, by the kinds of instruction they receive at home and at school, and even by the skills that their culture or subculture specifies that they must master.

In what is perhaps their biggest break with Piaget, information-processing theorists insist that cognitive development is a *continuous* process that is not at all stagelike. Presumably, the strategies we use to gather, store, retrieve, and operate on information evolve gradually over the course of childhood and adolescence. So cognitive development from an information-processing perspective involves small *quantitative* rather than large qualitative changes.

Contributions and Criticisms of the Information-Processing Viewpoint

Clearly, this new perspective on cognitive development is changing the ways that developmentalists (and educators) view children's thinking. As we will see in Chapter 8, information-processing theorists have provided a host of new insights on the growth of many cognitive abilities that Piaget did not emphasize, and their research has also filled in many of the gaps in Piaget's earlier theory. Furthermore, the rigorous and intensive research methods favoured by information-processing researchers have enabled them to identify how children and adolescents approach various problems and why they may make logical errors (see Box 2.3). Educators have seen the practical use of this research: If teachers understand exactly *why* children are having difficulties with their reading, math, or science lessons, it becomes easier to suggest alternative strategies to improve student performances (Siegler & Munakata, 1993).

Despite its many strengths, information-processing theory is subject to criticism. Some question the utility of a theory based on the thinking that children display in artificial laboratory studies, arguing that it may not accurately reflect their thinking in everyday life. Others contend that the computer model on which information-processing theory is based seriously underestimates the richness and diversity of human cognition.

information-processing theory
perspective that views the human mind as a continuously developing symbol-manipulating system, similar to a computer, into which information flows, is operated on, and is converted into output (answers, inferences, or solutions to problems)

2.3

Helping Children to Correct Their Mistakes: An Information-Processing Approach

At any age, children and adolescents may make logical errors if they don't attend to or use all of the information that would help them solve the problems they face. Imagine that 6-year-old John and 10-year-old Jorge are presented with the balance-scale problem illustrated in the figure and are asked to predict what will happen (will the arms remain balanced? will the left arm go up? down?) when a brake that holds the arms motionless is released.

Clearly, two aspects of balance-scale problems are important: the number of weights on each arm and the distance of the weights from the fulcrum. For us, the problem shown in the figure is easy. We recognize that, although each arm has the same number of weights, the left arm will still drop because the weights are farther from the fulcrum. Although Jorge correctly answers that the left arm will drop, John says the arms will remain balanced. As shown in the figure, John and Jorge rely on difficult strategies to derive their answers. John is using a simple weight-only rule: If one arm has more weight on it than the other, it will drop; otherwise the arms remain balanced. He does not consider distance information and may not even encode it. By contrast, Jorge considers both the number of weights on each arm and their distances from the fulcrum. He then concludes that, because the weight is equalized, the arm with weights farthest from the fulcrum will drop.

How might we help John to solve similar balance-scale problems? According to Robert Siegler (1976), the answer depends on whether John had attended to and encoded the distance information. This might be assessed by memory tests that indicate whether John can remember the numbers and locations of weights he had seen on a balance scale when the scale is no longer visible. If John accurately recalls both the weight and the distance information, then a few demonstrations with different balance-scale problems should be sufficient to illustrate that the distance information he had encoded is important and should be considered when formulating answers. But if John has only encoded the number-of-weights information, simple demonstrations may not be enough to convince him to attend to, encode, retain, and use the distance information that he routinely ignores (Siegler, 1976). Under the circumstances, we would first have to persuade John to pay attention to distance information before he would likely discover its relevance to solving balance-scale problems.

Perhaps you can see the practical benefits of this approach. By carefully examining the information-processing strategies that children and adolescents use to attack scientific reasoning tasks, math problems, and even reading comprehension exercises, educators can often pinpoint the reasons that their pupils are failing and devise effective interventions to improve their performances (Siegler & Crowley, 1992; Siegler & Munakata, 1993).

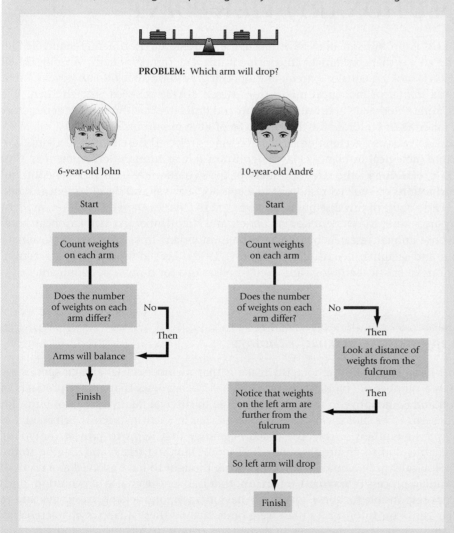

PROBLEM: Which arm will drop?

Information-processing flow chart showing the steps that a 6-year-old and a 10-year-old might take to answer a simple physics problem. Jorge's solution is correct, whereas John's leads to an incorrect answer.

After all, humans (but not computers) can dream, create, and reflect on their own and others' states of consciousness, and information-processing theory does not adequately explain these cognitive activities. Although there is some merit to both criticisms, information-processing researchers are now addressing them by studying children's memories for everyday events and activities, the reasoning they display in conversations with parents and peers, and the strategies they use in processing social information to form impressions of themselves and other people in their natural environments (see Hayden, Haine, & Fivush, 1997; Heyman & Gelman, 1999).

You may have noticed that both Piaget and the information-processing theorists contend that intellectual development is heavily influenced by the forces of nature (biological maturation) *and* nurture (that is, the environments that children and adolescents experience, which provide the input that they operate on to construct knowledge and develop problem-solving strategies). We will examine two additional theoretical perspectives, both of which concede that nature *and* nurture make important contributions to human development. However, one of these theories, *ethology*, emphasizes the biological side of development, while the other, *ecological systems theory*, stresses the crucial role that *contexts* play in influencing developmental outcomes. Let's first consider the ethological viewpoint.

THE ETHOLOGICAL (OR EVOLUTIONARY) VIEWPOINT

Behaviourist John Watson may have taken the extreme environmental stand he did partly because other prominent theorists of his era, most notably Arnold Gesell (1880–1961), took an equally extreme but opposing position that human development is largely a matter of biological maturation. Gesell (1933) believed that children, like plants, simply "bloomed," following a pattern and timetable laid out in their genes; how parents raised their children was thought to be of little importance.

Although today's developmentalists have largely rejected Gesell's radical claims, the notion that biological influences play a significant role in human development is alive and well in **ethology**—the scientific study of the evolutionary basis of behaviour and the contributions of evolved responses to a species' survival and development (Archer, 1992b). The origins of this discipline can be traced to Charles Darwin; however, modern ethology arose from the work of Konrad Lorenz and Niko Tinbergen, two European zoologists whose animal research highlighted some important links between evolutionary processes and adaptive behaviours (Dewsbury, 1992). Let's now examine the central assumptions of classical ethology and their implications for human development.

Assumptions of Classical Ethology

The most basic assumption ethologists make is that members of all animal species are born with a number of "biologically programmed" behaviours that are (1) products of evolution and (2) adaptive in that they contribute to survival. Many species of birds, for example, seem to be biologically prepared to engage in such instinctual behaviours as following their mothers (a response called *imprinting* that helps to protect the young from predators and to ensure that they find food), building nests, and singing songs. These biologically programmed characteristics are thought to have evolved as a result of the Darwinian process of **natural selection**; that is, over the course of evolution, birds with genes responsible for these adaptive behaviours were more likely to survive and to pass their genes on to offspring than were birds lacking these adaptive characteristics. Over many generations, the genes underlying the most adaptive behaviours became widespread in the species, characterizing nearly all individuals.

ethology
study of the bioevolutionary bases of behaviour and development

natural selection
evolutionary process, proposed by Charles Darwin, stating that individuals with characteristics that promote adaptation to the environment will survive, reproduce, and pass these adaptive characteristics to offspring; those lacking these adaptive characteristics will eventually die out

So ethologists focus on inborn or instinctual responses that (1) members of a species share and (2) may steer individuals along similar developmental paths. Where might one search for these adaptive behaviours and study their developmental implications? Ethologists have always preferred to study their subjects in the natural environment. Why? Simply because they believe that the inborn behaviours that shape human (or animal) development are most easily identified and understood if observed in the settings where they evolved and have proven to be adaptive (Hinde, 1989).

Ethology and Human Development

Instinctual responses that seem to promote survival are relatively easy to spot in animals. But do humans really display such behaviours? And if they do, how might these preprogrammed responses influence their development?

Human ethologists such as John Bowlby (1969; 1973) not only believe that children display a wide variety of preprogrammed behaviours but they also claim that each of these responses promotes a particular kind of experience that will help the individual to survive and develop normally. For example, the cry of a human infant is thought to be a biologically programmed distress signal that attracts the attention of caregivers. Not only are infants said to be biologically programmed to convey their distress with loud, lusty cries, but ethologists also believe that caregivers are biologically predisposed to respond to such signals. So the adaptive significance of an infant's crying ensures that (1) the infant's basic needs (for example, hunger, thirst, safety) are met and (2) the infant has sufficient contact with other human beings to form primary emotional attachments (Bowlby, 1973).

Although ethologists are especially critical of learning theorists for largely ignoring the biological bases of human development, they are well aware that development could not progress very far without learning. For example, the infant's cries may be an innate signal that promotes the human contact from which emotional attachments emerge. However, these emotional attachments do not happen automatically. The infant must first *learn* to discriminate familiar faces from those of strangers before showing any evidence of being emotionally attached to a regular companion. Presumably, the adaptive significance of this discriminatory learning goes back to a period in evolutionary history when humans travelled in nomadic tribes and braved the elements. In those days, it was crucial that an infant become attached to familiar companions and wary of strangers for failure to stay close to caregivers and to cry in response to a strange face might make the infant easy prey for a predatory animal.

Now consider the opposite side of the argument: Some caregivers who suffer from various life stresses of their own (for example, prolonged illness, depression, unhappy marriage) may be routinely inattentive or neglectful, so an infant's cries rarely promote any contact with them. Such an infant will probably not form secure emotional attachments to her caregivers and may become rather shy and emotionally unresponsive to other people for years to come (Ainsworth, 1979; 1989). What this infant has learned from her early experiences is that her closest companions are undependable and are not to be trusted. Consequently, she may become ambivalent or wary around her caregivers and may later assume that other regular associates, such as teachers and peers, are equally untrustworthy individuals who should be avoided whenever possible.

How important are an individual's early experiences? Like Freud, ethologists believe that early experiences are *very* important. In fact, they have

The cry is a distress signal that attracts the attention of caregivers.

PhotoDisc, Inc.

argued that there may be "critical periods" for the development of many attributes. A *critical period* is a limited time span during which developing organisms are biologically prepared to display adaptive patterns of development, provided they receive the appropriate input; outside this period, the same environmental events or influences are thought to have no lasting effects. Although this concept of critical period does seem to explain certain aspects of animal development, such as imprinting in young fowl, many human ethologists think that the term "sensitive period" is a more accurate description of human development. A **sensitive period** refers to a time that is optimal for the emergence of particular competencies or behaviours and in which the individual is particularly sensitive to environmental influences. The time frames of sensitive periods are less rigid or well-defined than those of critical periods. It is possible for development to occur outside a sensitive period, but is much more difficult to foster.

To illustrate, some ethologists believe that the first three years of life are a sensitive period for the development of social and emotional responsiveness in human beings (Bowlby, 1973). Presumably, we are most uniquely susceptible to forming close emotional ties during the first three years; and should we have little or no opportunity to do so during this period, we would find it much more difficult to make close friends or to enter into intimate emotional relationships with others later in life. Clearly, this is a most interesting and provocative claim about the emotional lives of human beings, which we will examine carefully when we discuss early social and emotional development in Chapter 11.

In sum, ethologists clearly acknowledge that we are heavily influenced by our experiences (Gottlieb, 1996), yet they emphasize that humans are inherently biological creatures whose inborn characteristics affect the kinds of learning experiences they are likely to have.

Contributions and Criticisms of the Ethological Viewpoint

If this text had been written 35 years ago, it would not have included a section on ethological theory. Although ethology came into its own in the 1960s, the early ethologists studied animal behaviour. Only within the past 20 years have ethologists made a serious attempt to specify evolutionary contributors to human development, and many of their hypotheses may still be considered speculative (Lerner & von Eye, 1992). Nevertheless, human ethologists have already made important contributions to our discipline by reminding us that every child is a biological creature who comes equipped with a number of adaptive, genetically programmed characteristics—attributes that influence other people's reactions to the child and thus the course that his development is likely to take. In addition, ethologists have made a major methodological contribution by showing us the value of (1) studying human development in everyday settings and (2) comparing human development with that of other species.

One intriguing ethological notion that we will discuss in detail in Chapter 11 is that infants are inherently sociable creatures who are quite capable of promoting and sustaining social interactions from the day they are born. This viewpoint contrasts sharply with that of behaviourists, who portray the newborn as a tabula rasa, and with Piaget's "asocial" infant, who enters the world equipped only with a few basic reflexes. Ethologists also believe that humans have evolved in ways that predispose us to develop and display prosocial motives such as **altruism** that contribute to the common good, permitting us to live and work together in harmony. Box 2.4 describes some observations suggesting that there may be a biological basis for certain aspects of altruism.

By way of criticism, evolutionary approaches are like psychoanalytic theory in being very hard to test. How does one prove that various motives, mannerisms, and behaviours are inborn, adaptive, or products of evolutionary history? Such claims are often difficult to confirm. Ethological theory has also been criticized as a *retrospective*, or post-hoc, explanation of development. One can easily apply evolutionary concepts to explain what has already happened, but can the theory *predict* what is likely to happen in the future? Many developmentalists believe that it cannot.

sensitive period
period of time that is optimal for the development of particular capacities or behaviours and in which the individual is particularly sensitive to environmental influences that foster these attributes

altruism
selfless concern for the welfare of others that is expressed through such prosocial acts as sharing, cooperating, and helping

Finally, proponents of other viewpoints (most notably, learning theory) have argued that, even if there is a biological basis for certain human motives or behaviours, these predispositions will soon become so modified by learning that it may not be helpful to spend much time wondering about their prior evolutionary significance. Even strong, genetically influenced attributes can be modified by experience. Consider, for example, that young mallard ducklings clearly prefer mallards' vocal calls to those of other birds—a behaviour that ethologists claim is innate and adaptive as a product of mallard evolution. Yet Gilbert Gottlieb (1991a) found that duckling embryos that were exposed to chicken calls before hatching preferred the call of a chicken to that of their mallard mother! In this case, the ducklings' *prenatal experiences* overrode a genetic predisposition. Of course, human beings have a much greater capacity for learning than ducklings do, leading many critics to argue that cultural learning experiences quickly overshadow innate evolutionary mechanisms in shaping human conduct and character.

Despite these criticisms, the evolutionary perspective remains a valuable addition to the developmental sciences. Not only has it provided a healthy balance to the heavy environmental emphasis of learning theories by identifying important biological contributions to human development, but it has also reinforced a crucial premise of our final theory: There is much to be learned about the process of development by studying children and adolescents in their everyday environments.

> **? WHAT DO YOU THINK?**
>
> What human attributes and behaviours would you say are part of the human genetic code through natural selection? Does your list include language, morality, love, and aggression, as some have claimed? Why or why not?

empathy
ability to experience the same emotions that someone else is experiencing

FOCUS ON RESEARCH

2.4 Is Altruism Part of Human Nature?

Darwin's notion of survival of the fittest seems to argue against altruism as an inborn motive. Many have interpreted Darwin's idea to mean that powerful, self-serving individuals who place their own needs ahead of others' are the ones who are most likely to survive. If this were so, evolution would favour the development of selfishness and egoism—not altruism—as basic components of human nature.

Martin Hoffman (1981; 1993) has challenged this point of view, listing several reasons why the concept of survival of the fittest actually implies altruism. His arguments hinge on the assumption that human beings are more likely to receive protection from natural enemies, satisfy all of their basic needs, and successfully reproduce if they live together in cooperative social units. If this assumption is correct, cooperative, altruistic individuals would be the ones who are most likely to survive long enough to pass along their "altruistic genes" to their offspring; individualists who go it alone would probably succumb to famine, predators, or some other natural disaster that they could not cope with by themselves. So, over thousands of generations, natural selection would favour the development of innate social motives such as altruism. Presumably, the tremendous survival value of being "social" makes altruism, cooperation, and other social motives much more plausible as components of human nature than competition, selfishness, and the like.

It is obviously absurd to argue that infants routinely help other people. However, Hoffman believes that even newborn babies are capable of recognizing and experiencing the emotion of others. This ability, known as **empathy**, is thought to be an important contributor to altruism, for a person must recognize that others are distressed in some way before he or she is likely to help. So Hoffman is suggesting that at least one aspect of altruism—empathy—is present at birth.

Hoffman's claim is based on an experiment (Sagi & Hoffman, 1976) in which infants less than 36 hours old listened to (1) another infant's cries, (2) an equally loud computer simulation of a crying infant, or (3) no sounds at all (silence). The infants who heard a real infant crying soon began to cry themselves, to display physical signs of agitation such as kicking, and to grimace. Infants exposed to the simulated cry or to silence cried much less and seemed not to be very discomforted. (A second study by Martin & Clark, 1982, confirmed these observations.) Moreover, Zahn-Waxler, Radke-Yarrow, Wagner & Chapman (1992) found that infants' crying and discomfort in response to another person's distress begins to be replaced by prosocial interventions (e.g., helping, sharing, comforting) during the second year of life. (See Chapter 14 for more discussion of studies examining altruism.)

Hoffman argues that there is something quite distinctive about the human cry. His contention is that infants listen to and experience the distress of another crying infant and become distressed themselves. Of course, this finding does not conclusively demonstrate that humans are altruistic by nature. But it does imply that the capacity for empathy may be present at birth and thus may serve as a biological basis for the eventual development of altruistic behaviour.

Chris Hildreth/Cornell University

*In his ecological systems theory,
Urie Bronfenbrenner (born 1917)
describes how multiple levels of
the surrounding environment
influence child and adolescent
development.*

THE ECOLOGICAL SYSTEMS VIEWPOINT

American psychologist Urie Bronfenbrenner offers an exciting new perspective on child and adolescent development that addresses many of the shortcomings of earlier environmentalist approaches. Behaviourists John Watson and B.F. Skinner had defined *environment* as any and all external focuses that shape the individual's development. Although modern learning theorists such as Bandura (1986, 1989) have backed away from this extremely mechanistic view by acknowledging that environments both influence and *are influenced by* developing individuals, they continue to provide only vague descriptions of the environmental contexts in which development takes place.

By contrast, Bronfenbrenner's **ecological systems theory** (1979; 1989; 1993) provides a detailed analysis of environmental influences. And because it also concedes that a person's biologically influenced characteristics interact with environmental forces to shape development, it is probably more accurate to describe this perspective as a *bioecological* theory (Bronfenbrenner, 1995).

Bronfenbrenner (1979) begins by assuming that *natural* environments are the major source of influence on developing persons—and one that is often overlooked (or simply ignored) by researchers who choose to study development in the highly artificial context of the laboratory. He proceeds to define environment (or the natural ecology) as "a set of nested structures, each inside the next, like a set of Russian dolls" (p. 22). In other words, the developing person is said to be at the centre of and embedded in several environmental systems, ranging from immediate settings such as the family to more remote contexts such as the broader culture (see Figure 2.4). Each of these systems is thought to interact with the others and with the individual to influence development in important ways. Let us take a closer look.

Bronfenbrenner's Contexts for Development

The Microsystem

Bronfenbrenner's innermost environmental layer, or **microsystem**, refers to the activities and interactions that occur in the person's immediate surroundings. For most young infants, the microsystem may be limited to the family. Yet this system eventually becomes much more complex as children are exposed to daycare, preschool classes, youth groups, and neighbourhood playmates. Not only are children influenced by the people in their microsystems, but also their own biologically and socially influenced characteristics—their habits, temperaments, physical characteristics, and capabilities—influence the behaviour of companions as well. For example, a temperamentally difficult infant can alienate her parents or even create friction between them that may be sufficient to impair their marital relationship (Belsky, Rosenberger, & Crnic, 1995). And interactions between any two individuals in microsystems are likely to be influenced by third parties. Fathers, for example, clearly influence mother–infant interactions: Happily married mothers who have close supportive relationships with their husbands tend to interact much more patiently and sensitively with their infants than mothers who experience marital tension, little support from their spouses, and feel that they are raising their children on their own (Cox et al., 1989; 1992). So microsystems are truly dynamic contexts for development in which each person influences and is influenced by all other persons in the system.

ecological systems theory
Bronfenbrenner's model emphasizing that the developing person is embedded in a series of environmental systems that interact with one another and with the person to influence development

microsystem
immediate settings (including role relationships and activities) that the person actually encounters; the innermost of Bronfenbrenner's environmental layers or contexts

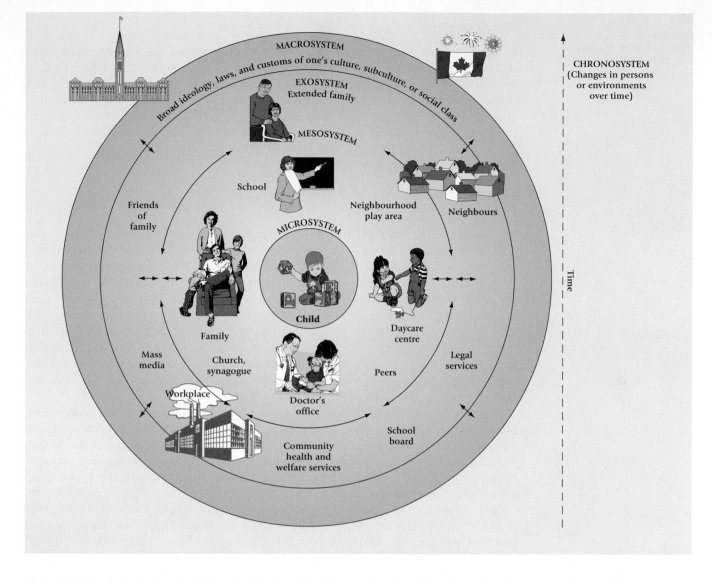

Figure 2.4 *Bronfenbrenner's ecological model of the environment as a series of nested structures. The microsystem refers to relations between the child and the immediate environment, the mesosystem to connections among the child's immediate settings, the exosystem to social settings that affect but do not contain the child, and the macrosystem to the overarching ideology of the culture.* BASED ON BRONFENBRENNER, 1979.

The Mesosystem

The second of Bronfenbrenner's environmental layers, or the **mesosystem**, refers to the connections or interrelationships among such microsystems as homes, schools, and peer groups. Bronfenbrenner believes that development is likely to be optimized by strong, supportive links between microsystems. For example, youngsters who have established secure and harmonious relationships with parents are especially inclined to be accepted by peers and to enjoy close, supportive friendships during childhood and adolescence (Clark & Ladd, 2000; Hodges, Finnegan, & Perry, 1999). A child's ability to master lessons at school depends not only on the quality of instruction that his teachers provide, but also on the extent to which parents value these scholastic activities and consult or cooperate with teachers (Gottfried, Fleming, & Gottfried, 1998; Luster & McAdoo, 1996). On the other hand, nonsupportive links between microsystems can spell trouble. For example, when peer groups devalue academics, they often undermine an adolescent's scholastic performance, despite the best efforts of parents and teachers to encourage academic achievement (Steinberg, Dornbusch, & Brown, 1992).

mesosystem
interconnections among an individual's immediate settings or microsystems; the second of Bronfenbrenner's environmental layers or contexts

The Exosystem

Bronfenbrenner's third environmental layer, or **exosystem**, consists of contexts that children and adolescents are not a part of but that may nevertheless influence their development. For example, parents' work environments are an exosystem influence, and children's emotional relationships at home may be influenced considerably by whether or not their parents enjoy their work (Greenberger, O'Neil, & Nagel, 1994). Similarly, children's experiences in school may be affected by their exosystem—by a social integration plan adopted by the school board, or by a factory closing in their community that results in a decline in the school's revenue.

The Macrosystem

Bronfenbrenner also stresses that development occurs in a **macrosystem**—that is, a cultural, subcultural, or social class context in which microsystems, mesosystems, and exosystems are imbedded. The macrosystem is really a broad ideology that dictates (among other things) how children should be treated, what they should be taught, and the goals for which they should strive. Of course, these values differ across cultures (and subcultures and social classes) and can greatly influence the kinds of experiences children have in their homes, neighbourhoods, schools, and all other contexts that affect them, directly or indirectly. To cite one example, the incidence of child abuse in families (a microsystem experience) is much lower in those cultures (or macrosystems) that discourage physical punishment of children and advocate nonviolent ways of resolving interpersonal conflict (Belsky, 1993; Levinson, 1989).

Finally, Bronfenbrenner's model includes a temporal dimension, or **chronosystem**, which emphasizes that changes *in the child* or in any of the ecological contexts of development can affect the direction that development is likely to take. Cognitive and biological changes that occur at puberty, for example, seem to contribute to increased conflict between young adolescents and their parents (Paikoff & Brooks-Gunn, 1991; Steinberg, 1996). And the impacts of environmental changes also depend on another chronological variable—the age of the child. For example, even though a divorce hits hard at youngsters of all ages, adolescents are less likely than younger children to experience the guilty sense that *they* were the cause of the breakup (Hetherington & Clingempeel, 1992).

Contributions and Criticisms of the Ecological Systems Theory

Though we have touched briefly on the ecological perspective here and will explore its propositions through the text, perhaps you can already see that it provides a much richer description of environment (and environmental influences) than anything offered by learning theorists. Each of us functions in particular microsystems that are linked by a mesosystem and embedded in the larger contexts of an exosystem and a macrosystem. It makes little sense to ecological theorists to try to study environmental influences in contrived laboratory contexts. Instead, they argue that only by observing transactions between developing persons and their ever-changing *natural* settings will we understand how individuals influence and are influenced by their environments.

Bronfenbrenner's detailed analysis of environmental influences has suggested many ways in which the development of children and adolescents might be optimized. To illustrate, imagine a working parent who is having a tough time establishing a pleasant relationship with a temperamentally difficult infant. At the level of the microsystem, a successful intervention might assist the other parent to become a more sensitive companion who assumes more of the daily child-care responsibilities and encourages more responsiveness and patience of the first parent with their baby (Howes & Markman, 1989). At the level of the exosystem, parents can often be helped to improve their relationships with their children if their community has parenting classes or groups where parents can express their

exosystem
social systems that children and adolescents do not directly experience but that may nonetheless influence their development; the third of Bronfenbrenner's environmental layers or contexts

macrosystem
larger cultural or subcultural context in which development occurs; Bronfenbrenner's outermost environmental layer or context

chronosystem
in ecological systems theory, changes in the individual or the environment that occur over time and influence the direction of development

concerns, enlist others' emotional support, and learn from each other how to elicit more favourable reactions from their children (Lyons-Ruth et al., 1990). And at the level of the macrosystem, a social policy guaranteeing parents the right to take paid or unpaid leave from their jobs to attend to family matters may be an especially important intervention, allowing distressed parents more time to resolve difficulties that arise with their children (Clark et al., 1997) and conveying an attitude that society views the resolution of family problems as important to society's well-being (Bronfenbrenner & Neville, 1995).

Despite its strengths, ecological systems theory falls far short of being a complete account of human development. Though Bronfenbrenner characterizes the theory as a bioecological model, it really has very little to say about specific biological contributors to development. Furthermore, Bronfenbrenner's emphasis on complex transactions between developing persons and their ever-changing environments is both a strength and a weakness of ecological systems theory (Dixon & Lerner, 1992). Where are the normative patterns of development? Must we formulate different theories for persons from different environments—one for Thai women born in the 1940s and another for Aboriginal women born in the 1970s? If unique individuals influence and are influenced by their unique environments, is each life span unique? In sum, the ecological systems theory may focus too heavily on ideographic aspects of change to ever provide a coherent normative portrait of human development; for this reason, it quantifies as an important complement to rather than a replacement for other developmental theories.

THEORIES AND WORLD VIEWS

Now that we have completed our survey of the major theories of human development, how might we compare them? One way is to group the theories into even grander categories, for each is grounded in a broader set of philosophical assumptions or *world view*. By examining the fundamental assumptions that underlie different theories, we can perhaps better appreciate just how deeply some of their disagreements run.

Early developmental theories adopted either of two broad world views (Overton, 1984). The **mechanistic model** likens human beings to machines by viewing them as (1) a collection of parts (behaviours) that can be decomposed, much as machines can be taken apart piece by piece; (2) passive, changing mostly in response to outside influences (much as machines depend on external energy sources to operate); and (3) changing gradually or continuously as their parts (specific behaviour patterns) are added or subtracted. By contrast, the **organismic model** compares humans with other living organisms by viewing them as (1) whole beings who cannot be understood as a simple collection of parts; (2); active in the developmental process, changing under the guidance of internal forces (such as instincts or maturation); and (3) evolving through distinct (discontinuous) stages as they mature.

Which theorists have adopted which model? Clearly, learning theorists such as Watson and Skinner favour the mechanistic world view, for they see human beings as passively shaped by environmental events and they analyze human behaviour response by response. Bandura's social learning theory is primarily mechanistic, yet it reflects the important organismic assumption that human beings are active creatures who both influence and are influenced by their environments. By contrast, psychoanalytic theorists such as Freud and Erikson and cognitive-developmentalists from the Piagetian tradition all base theories primarily on the organismic model: Given some nourishment from their surroundings, human beings will progress through discontinuous steps or stages, directed largely by forces lying within themselves (much as seeds evolve into blooming plants).

Another broad world view, the **contextual model**, has recently emerged as the perspective that many developmentalists favour (Lerner, 1996). The contextual model views development as the product of a dynamic interplay between person and environment. People are assumed to be active in the developmental process (as in the organismic model), *and* the environment is active as well (as in the mechanistic model). Development may have both universal aspects *and* aspects peculiar to certain cultures,

mechanistic model
view of children as passive entities whose developmental paths are primarily determined by external (environmental) influences

organismic model
view of children as active entities whose developmental paths are primarily determined by forces from within themselves

contextual model
view of children as active entities whose developmental paths represent a continuous, dynamic interplay between internal forces (nature) and external influences (nurture)

times, or individuals. The potential exists for both qualitative and quantitative change, and development may proceed along many different paths depending on the intricate interplay between internal forces (nature) and external influences (environment).

Although none of the theories we've reviewed provides a pure example of the contextual world view, four come reasonably close. Information-processing theorists describe children and adolescents as active processors of environmental input whose capabilities are heavily influenced by maturation and by the kinds of social and cultural experiences they encounter. Vygotsky's sociocultural theory makes the same assumption. Although they view development as basically continuous rather than stagelike, many information-processing theorists concede that changes that occur within particular intellectual domains may be uneven and that qualitative leaps in one's intellectual performance are possible.

Ethologists also seem to favour a contextual world view. They clearly make the organismic assumptions that humans are active beings who are born genetically equipped to display certain behaviours that promote adaptive developmental outcomes. However, they recognize that biological predispositions by themselves do not guarantee healthy development and that a child's outcomes depend critically on the environment he or she experiences. In addition, ethologists claim that we are continuously developing adaptive behaviours over the course of our lives (a mechanistic premise), although they stress that change can be abrupt, or discontinuous, as when a new, adaptive response emerges during its sensitive period for development.

Bronfenbrenner's ecological systems theory also adopts a contextual world view. Bronfenbrenner does make the mechanistic assumption that humans are heavily influenced by many environmental contexts, ranging from home settings to the wider society in which they live. Yet he is clearly aware that children and adolescents are active biological beings who change as they mature and whose behaviours and biologically influenced attributes influence the very environments that are influencing their development. So development is viewed as the product of a truly dynamic interplay between an active person and an ever-changing active environment, and it is on this basis that the ecological systems approach qualifies as a contextual theory.

Table 2.4 summarizes the philosophical assumptions and world views underlying each of the broad theoretical perspectives that we have reviewed. As you compare the viewpoints you expressed in Box 2.1 with those of the theorists, see if you can clearly determine your own world views on human nature and the character of human development.

In case you're wondering, we don't expect you to choose one of these theories as a favourite and reject the others. Indeed, because different theories emphasize different aspects of development, one may be more relevant to a particular issue or to a particular age group than another. Today, many developmentalists are theoretical **eclectics**: individuals who rely on many theories, recognizing that none of the grand theories can

---

?

WHAT DO YOU THINK?

After a divorce, children fare much better if their divorced parents can agree on how their children should be raised and support each other's parenting efforts. Which developmental theory seems best suited to explaining this finding, and how might it do so?

---

eclectics
those who borrow from many theories in their attempt to predict and explain human development

---

Concept Check 2.3
Understanding Theoretical Propositions

Check your understanding of some of the propositions of five developmental theories by noting the theory that best exemplifies each proposition below. Choose from the following options: (a) Piaget's cognitive-developmental theory, (b) information-processing theory, (c) ethology, (d) ecological systems theory, and (e) Vygotsky's sociocultural theory. Answers appear in the Appendix.

_____ 1. Theory claiming that children are "prepared" to display adaptive patterns of development, provided they receive appropriate kinds of environmental inputs at the most appropriate times.

_____ 2. Theory claiming that children actively construct knowledge and which has stimulated discovery-based educational programs.

_____ 3. Theory claiming that the natural environment that influences a developing child is a complex interlocking set of contexts that influence and are influenced by the child.

_____ 4. Theory claiming that the developing human mind is a system that operates on stimulus input to convert it to output—inferences, solutions, etc.

_____ 5. Theory claiming that cognitive growth is socially mediated and that there are no universal cognitive stages.

_____ 6. Theory(ies) claiming that children are active agents who influence the character of their own developmental outcomes. (Note all those that apply.)

explain all aspects of development and that each makes some contribution to our under-standing. For the remainder of this book, we will borrow from many theories to integrate their contributions into a unified, holistic portrait of the developing person. Yet we will also continue to explore theoretical controversies, which often produce some of the most exciting breakthroughs in the field. Join us now in examining not just the specific facts about human development, but also the broader theoretical insights that have helped to generate these facts and give them a larger meaning.

TABLE 2.4	A Summary of the Philosophies Underlying Six Major Development Perspectives			
Theory	**Active vs. passive person**	**Continuous vs. discontinuous development**	**Nature vs. nurture**	**World view**
Psychoanalytic perspective	*Active:* Children are driven by inborn instincts that are channelled (with the assistance of others) into socially desirable outlets.	*Discontinuous:* Emphasis is on stages of psychosexual development (Freud) or psychosocial development (Erikson).	*Both nature and nurture:* Biological forces (instincts, maturation) precipitate psychosexual stages and psychosocial crises; parental child-rearing practices influence the outcomes of these stages.	Organismic
Learning perspective	*Passive:* Children are moulded by their environments (although Bandura claims that developing persons also influence these environments).	*Continuous:* Emphasizes the gradual addition of learned responses (habits) that make up one's personality.	*Nurture most important:* Environmental input, rather than biological influences, is what determines the course of development.	Mechanistic
Piaget's cognitive-developmental theory	*Active:* Children actively construct more sophisticated understandings of the self, others, and the environment to which they adapt.	*Discontinuous:* Emphasizes an invariant sequence of qualitatively distinct cognitive stages.	*Both nature and nurture:* Children have an inborn need to adapt to the environment, which is in turn nurtured by a stimulating environment that provides many adaptive challenges.	Organismic
Vygotsky's sociocultural theory	*Active:* Children actively construct knowledge through verbal dialogues with others in their environment.	*Continuous:* Emphasizes the gradual acquisition of culturally valuable information.	*Both nature and nurture:* Emphasizes the active nature of children as learners and the importance of the culture and context for predicting what they will learn.	Contextual
Information-processing perspective	*Active:* Children actively process environmental information to answer questions, solve problems, or otherwise master challenges.	*Continuous:* Emphasizes gradual quantitative changes in attention, perception, memory, and problem-solving skills.	*Both nature and nurture:* Active processing capabilities that develop are heavily influenced by maturation and by social/cultural/educational influences.	Contextual
Ethological perspective	*Active:* Humans are born with biologically programmed behaviours that promote adaptive developments.	*Both:* Emphasizes that adaptive behaviours are added continuously, but adds that some adaptive capabilities emerge abruptly (or fail to emerge) during sensitive periods for their development.	*Nature:* Biologically programmed adaptive behaviours are stressed, although an appropriate environment is necessary for successful adaptation.	Contextual
Ecological systems perspective	*Both:* Humans actively influence the environmental contexts that influence their development.	*Both:* Emphasizes that transactions between ever-changing individuals and ever-changing environments lead to quantitative developmental changes. However, discontinuous personal or environmental events (for example, reaching puberty, parents' divorce) can produce abrupt qualitative changes.	*Nurture:* Impacts of environmental contexts on development are most clearly emphasized, although children's biologically influenced attributes can affect their environments.	Contextual
My viewpoint: (Review Box 2.1)				

SUMMARY

The Nature of Scientific Theories

◆ A **theory** is a set of concepts and propositions that describe and explain observations. Theories are particularly useful if they are concise, or **parsimonious**, and yet applicable to a wide range of phenomena. Good theories are also **falsifiable** and have **heuristic value**, which means that they build on existing knowledge by continuing to generate testable hypotheses leading to new discoveries and important practical applications.

Questions and Controversies about Human Development

◆ Theories of human development differ with respect to three fundamental issues: (1) Is development primarily determined by **nature** or **nurture**? (2) Are humans **actively** or **passively** involved in their development? and (3) Is development a quantitative and **continuous** process, or does it proceed in a **discontinuous** fashion through a series of qualitatively distinct **developmental stages**? Some theories take an intermediate position on one or more of these issues.

The Psychoanalytic Viewpoint

◆ The psychoanalytic perspective originated with Sigmund Freud's **psychosexual theory**, which claimed that humans are driven by inborn sexual and aggressive instincts that must be controlled. Much of human behaviour was said to reflect **unconscious motives** that people **repress**. Freud proposed five stages of psychosexual development—oral, anal, phallic, latency, and genital—in which three components of personality—the **id**, **ego**, and **superego**—emerge and become closely integrated.

◆ Erik Erikson's **psychosocial theory** revises and extends Freud's theory by concentrating less on the sex instinct and more on important sociocultural determinants of human development. According to Erikson, people progress through a series of eight psychosocial conflicts, beginning with "trust versus mistrust" in infancy and concluding with "integrity versus despair" in old age. Each conflict must be resolved in favour of the positive trait (trust, for example) if development is to be healthy.

The Learning Viewpoint

◆ The learning viewpoint, or **behaviourism**, originated with John B. Watson, who argued that infants are tabula rasae who develop **habits** as a result of their learning experiences. Development was viewed as a continuous process that could proceed in many different directions, depending on the kinds of environments to which a person is exposed. B.F. Skinner, who extended Watson's theory, claimed that development reflects the **operant** conditioning of children who are passively shaped by the **reinforcers** and **punishments** that accompany their behaviours. By contrast, Albert Bandura's cognitive social learning theory views children as *active* information processors who quickly develop many new habits through **observational learning**. Bandura rejects Watson's **environmental determinism**, proposing instead that children have a hand in creating the environments that influence their development (**reciprocal determinism**).

The Cognitive-Developmental Viewpoint

◆ The cognitive-developmental viewpoint of Jean Piaget depicts children as active explorers who construct cognitive **schemes**, through the processes of **assimilation** and **accommodation**, that enable them to resolve **disequilibriums** and adapt successfully to their environments. Piaget described **cognitive development** as an **invariant developmental sequence** of four stages: sensorimotor, preoperational, concrete-operational, and formal-operational. According to Piaget, the person's stage of cognitive development determines how she will interpret various events and, thus, what she can learn from her experiences.

◆ Lev Vygotsky's **sociocultural theory** argues that cognitive growth is largely a *socially mediated* activity, heavily influenced by culture. Children also more easily master tasks that are within the children's **zone of proximal development**.

The Information-Processing Viewpoint

◆ The information-processing theory views the mind as a complex symbol-manipulating system into which information flows and is operated on and converted to output (answers, inferences, and solutions). Cognitive development is said to be continuous rather than stagelike as children and adolescents gradually become better at attending to information, remembering and retrieving it, and formulating strategies to solve the problems they face.

The Ethological (or Evolutionary) Viewpoint

◆ The evolutionary viewpoint, as expressed in **ethology**, is that humans are born with a number of adaptive attributes that have evolved through **natural selection** and channel development in ways that promote survival. Ethologists recognize that humans are influenced by their experiences and even claim that certain adaptive characteristics are most likely to develop during **sensitive periods**, provided that the environment fosters this development. However, they remind us that humans' biologically influenced attributes affect the kind of learning experiences they are likely to have.

The Ecological Systems Viewpoint

♦ Urie Bronfenbrenner's **ecological systems theory** views development as the product of transactions between an ever-changing person and an ever-changing environment. Bronfenbrenner proposes that the natural environment actually consists of interacting contexts or systems—**microsystem, mesosystem, exosystem,** and **macrosystem**—each of which is also influenced by the **chronosystem**—that is, by changes that occur over time in the individual or in other environmental contexts. This detailed analysis of person–environment interactions has stimulated many new interventions to optimize development.

Theories and World Views

♦ Theories can be grouped according to the world views that underlie them. As developmentalists have come to appreciate the incredible complexity and diversity of human development, more of them favour a **contextual model** over the **mechanistic model** that guides learning theories or the **organismic model** that underlies stage theories. In addition, most contemporary developmentalists are theoretically **eclectic**, recognizing that no single theory offers a totally adequate account of human development but that each contributes importantly to our understanding of developing persons.

KEY TERMS

theory, 37
parsimony, 38
falsifiability, 38
heuristic value, 38
nature/nurture issue, 39
active/passive issue, 39
continuity/discontinuity issue, 40
quantitative change, 40
qualitative change, 40
developmental stage, 41
psychosexual theory, 41
unconscious motives, 42
repression, 42

instinct, 42
id, 42
ego, 42
superego, 42
fixation, 43
psychosocial theory, 44
behaviourism, 47
habits, 47
reinforcer, 48
punisher, 48
operant learning, 48
observational learning, 48
environmental determinism, 50
reciprocal determinism, 50

cognitive development, 51
scheme, 52
assimilation, 53
disequilibriums, 53
accommodation, 53
invariant developmental sequence, 53
sociocultural theory, 55
zone of proximal development, 55
information-processing theory, 56
ethology, 58
natural selection, 58

sensitive period, 60
altruism, 60
empathy, 61
ecological systems theory, 62
microsystem, 62
mesosystem, 63
exosystem, 64
macrosystem, 64
chronosystem, 64
mechanistic model, 65
organismic model, 65
contextual model, 65
eclectics, 66

 You can find further information on the topics covered in this chapter by visiting:

www.developmentalpsych2e.nelson.com

 For additional reading, go to InfoTrac College Edition, your on-line research library, at:

infotrac.thomsonlearning.com

3

Dr. Yorgos Nikas/Science Photo Library

Hereditary Influences on Development

Principles of Hereditary Transmission

Chromosomal and Genetic Abnormalities

Applications: Genetic Counselling, Prenatal Detection, and Treatment of Hereditary Disorders

Hereditary Influences on Behaviour

Heredity and Environment as Developmental Co-Conspirators

Contributions and Criticisms of the Behavioural Genetics Approach

Summary

genotype
genetic endowment that an individual inherits

C an you remember when you were first introduced to the concept of heredity? Although the idea of heredity may seem straightforward, this concept is sometimes a difficult one to understand. The challenges in presenting this information in a clear way became evident when one of us tried to explain it to her 4-year-old. How would you explain genetics to a 4-year-old? What worked was telling the child that all of us have "instructions" that make our bodies work and that these "instructions" are given to us from our parents. Unfortunately, providing such a simple explanation worked against the mother when the child asked, "What's wrong with your instructions?" when she made a mistake!

This chapter approaches human development from a hereditary perspective, seeking to determine how one's **genotype** (the **genes** that one inherits) is expressed as a **phenotype** (one's observable or measurable characteristics). We first will explore how hereditary information is transmitted from parents to their offspring and why the workings of heredity conspire to make us unique individuals. We then will review the evidence for hereditary contributions to such important psychological attributes as intelligence, personality, and even our inclinations toward displaying mentally healthy (or unhealthy) patterns of behaviour. Indeed, this evidence implies that many (and some would say all) of our most noteworthy phenotypic characteristics are influenced by the genes passed to us by our parents. Yet, the biggest lesson from this chapter is that genes, by themselves, determine less than you might imagine and that the expression "hereditary constraint" is something of a misnomer. As we will see, most complex human attributes are the result of a long and involved interplay between the forces of nature (heredity) and nurture (environment) (Plomin et al., 1997).

PRINCIPLES OF HEREDITARY TRANSMISSION

To understand the workings of heredity, we must start at **conception**, the moment when an ovum released by a woman's ovary and on its way to the uterus via the fallopian

The Genetic Code

The very first development that occurs after conception is protective: When a sperm cell penetrates the lining of the ovum, a biochemical reaction repels other sperm, thus preventing them from repeating the fertilization process. Within a few hours, the sperm cell begins to disintegrate, releasing its genetic material. The ovum also releases its genetic material, and a new cell nucleus forms around the hereditary information provided by the father's sperm and the mother's ovum. This new cell, called a **zygote**, is only 1/20th the size of the head of a pin. Yet this tiny cell contains the code, or biochemical recipe, for the zygote's development from a single cell into a recognizable human being.

What hereditary material is present in a human zygote? The new cell nucleus contains 46 elongated, threadlike bodies called **chromosomes**, each of which consists of thousands of chemical segments, or *genes*—the basic units of heredity. With one exception, which we will soon discuss, chromosomes come in matching pairs. Each member of a pair corresponds to the other in size, shape, and the hereditary functions it serves. One member of each chromosome pair comes from the mother's ovum and the other from the father's sperm cell. Thus each parent contributes 23 chromosomes to each of his or her children.

The genes on each chromosome also function as pairs, the two members of each gene pair being located at the same sites on their corresponding chromosomes. Genes are actually stretches of **deoxyribonucleic acid, or DNA**, a complex "double-helix" molecule that resembles a twisted ladder and provides the chemical "code" for development (see Figure 3.1). A unique feature of DNA is that it can duplicate itself. The rungs of this ladderlike molecule split in the middle, opening somewhat like a zipper. Then each remaining half of the molecule guides the replication of its missing parts. This special ability of DNA to replicate itself is what makes it possible for a one-celled zygote to develop into a marvellously complex human being.

Figure 3.1 *An illustration of the DNA double helix.*

Growth of the Zygote and Production of Body Cells

As the zygote moves through the fallopian tube toward its prenatal home in the uterus, it begins to reproduce itself through the process of **mitosis**. At first, the zygote divides into two cells, but the two soon become four, four become eight, eight become sixteen, and so on. Just before each division, the cell duplicates its 46 chromosomes, and these duplicate sets move in opposite directions. The division of the cell then proceeds, resulting in two "daughter" cells, each of which has the identical 23 pairs of chromosomes (46 in all) and thus the same genetic code as the original parent cell. This remarkable process is illustrated in Figure 3.2.

By the time a child is born, he or she consists of billions of cells, created through mitosis, that make up muscles, bones, organs, and other bodily structures. Mitosis continues throughout life, generating new cells that enable growth and replacing old ones that are damaged. With each division, the hereditary blueprint is duplicated, so that every new cell contains an exact copy of the 46 chromosomes we inherited at conception.

The Germ (or Sex) Cells

We have learned that a sperm and an egg combine to form a zygote that has 46 chromosomes (23 from each parent). But if cells normally contain 46 chromosomes each, why don't we start life with 92 chromosomes, 46 coming from the father's sperm cell and 46 from the mother's ovum? The answer is relatively simple.

genes
hereditary blueprints for development that are transmitted unchanged from generation to generation

phenotype
ways in which a person's genotype is expressed in observable or measurable characteristics

conception
moment of fertilization, when a sperm penetrates an ovum, forming a zygote

zygote
single cell formed at conception from the union of a sperm and an ovum

chromosome
threadlike structure made up of genes; in humans there are 46 chromosomes in the nucleus of each body cell

deoxyribonucleic acid (DNA)
long, double-stranded molecules that make up chromosomes

mitosis
process in which a cell duplicates its chromosomes and then divides into two genetically identical daughter cells

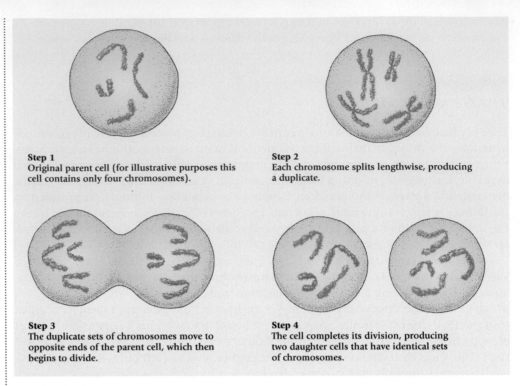

Step 1
Original parent cell (for illustrative purposes this cell contains only four chromosomes).

Step 2
Each chromosome splits lengthwise, producing a duplicate.

Step 3
The duplicate sets of chromosomes move to opposite ends of the parent cell, which then begins to divide.

Step 4
The cell completes its division, producing two daughter cells that have identical sets of chromosomes.

Figure 3.2 *Mitosis: the way that cells reproduce themselves.*

Production of Gametes through Meiosis

In addition to body cells, human beings have *germ* cells that serve one special hereditary function—to produce *gametes* (sperm in males and ova in females). When male germ cells in the testes and female germ cells in the ovaries produce sperm and ova, they do so through a process called **meiosis**, which is illustrated in Figure 3.3. The germ cell first duplicates its 46 chromosomes. Then an event called **crossing-over** often takes place: Adjacent chromosomes cross and break at one or more points along their length, exchanging segments of genetic material, much as if you were to exchange a couple of fingers with a friend after a handshake. Notice, then, that this transfer of genes during crossing-over creates new and unique hereditary combinations. Next, pairs of duplicated chromosomes (some of which have been altered by crossing-over) segregate into two parent cells that each contain 46 chromosomes. Finally, the parent cells divide so that each of their daughter cells (or gametes) contains 23 single, or *unpaired*, chromosomes. At conception, then, a sperm with 23 chromosomes unites with an ovum with 23 chromosomes, producing a zygote with a full complement of 46 chromosomes.

Brothers and sisters who have the same mother and father inherit 23 chromosomes from each of these parents. Why is it, then, that offspring of the same parents sometimes barely resemble one another? The reason is that meiosis conspires to make us genetically unique.

Hereditary Uniqueness

When a pair of chromosomes segregates during meiosis, it is a matter of chance which of the two chromosomes will end up in a particular parent cell. Because each chromosome pair segregates independently of all other pairs according to the principle of **independent assortment**, many different combinations of chromosomes could result from the meiosis of a single germ cell. Because human germ cells contain 23 chromosome pairs, each of which is segregating independently of the others, the laws of probability tell us that each parent can produce 2^{23} (more than 8 million) different genetic combinations in his or her sperm or ova. If a father can produce 8 million combinations of 23

meiosis
process in which a germ cell divides, producing gametes (sperm or ova) that each contain half of the parent cell's original complement of chromosomes; in humans, the products of meiosis contain 23 chromosomes

crossing-over
process in which genetic material is exchanged between pairs of chromosomes during meiosis

independent assortment
principle stating that each pair of chromosomes segregates independently of all other chromosome pairs during meiosis

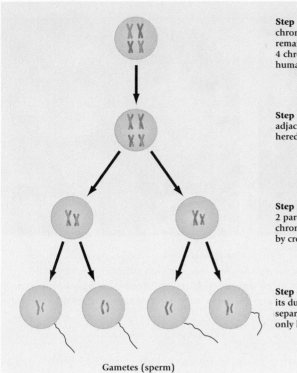

Step 1. Each of the germ cell's original chromosomes duplicates itself, and the duplicate remains attached. (To simplify, we show only 4 chromosomes and their duplicates. In human germ cells, there are 46 chromosomes.)

Step 2. Crossing-over takes place among adjacent chromosomes, thus creating new hereditary combinations.

Step 3. The original cell now divides to form 2 parent cells, each of which has 23 duplicated chromosomes (some of which have been altered by crossing over).

Step 4. Finally, each chromosome and its duplicate now split and segregate into separate gametes. Thus, each gamete has only half the chromosomes of its parent cell.

Gametes (sperm)

Figure 3.3 *Diagram of the meiosis of a male germ cell.*

chromosomes and a mother can produce 8 million, any couple could theoretically have 64 *trillion* babies without producing two children who inherited precisely the same set of genes! In fact, the odds of exact genetic replication in two siblings are even smaller than 1 in 64 trillion. Why? Because the *crossing-over* process, which occurs during the earlier phases of meiosis, actually alters the genetic composition of chromosomes and thereby increases the number of possible variations in an individual's gametes far beyond the 8 million that could occur if chromosomes segregated cleanly, without exchanging genetic information.

Of course, brothers and sisters resemble one another to some extent because their genes are drawn from a gene pool provided by the same two parents. Each brother or sister inherits half of each parent's genes, although two siblings never inherit the same half, owing to the random process by which parental chromosomes (and genes) segregate into the sperm and ovum that combine to produce each offspring. Thus, each individual is genetically unique. From an evolutionary perspective, the genetic variability produced by meiosis is highly adaptive because it increases the likelihood that some members of each species would survive any catastrophic changes in the environment (Strachan & Read, 1996).

Multiple Births

There is one circumstance under which two people will share a genotype. Occasionally, a zygote that has begun to duplicate will split into separate but identical cells, which then become two individuals. These are called **monozygotic** (or **identical**) **twins** because they have developed from a *single* zygote and have *identical* genes. Identical twins occur in about 1 of every 250 births around the world (Plomin, 1990). Because they are genetically identical, monozygotic twins should show very similar developmental progress if genes have much effect on human development.

monozygotic (or identical) twins
twins who develop from a single zygote that later divides to form two genetically identical individuals

Figure 3.4 Identical, or monozygotic, twins (left) develop from a single zygote. Because they have inherited identical sets of genes, they look alike, are the same sex, and share all other inherited characteristics. Fraternal, or dizygotic, twins (right) develop from separate zygotes and have no more genes in common than siblings born at different times. Consequently, they may not look alike (as we see in this photo) and may not even be the same sex.

More common, however (occurring in approximately 1 of every 125 births and as often as 1 in 20 births to women using fertility drugs), are **dizygotic,** or **fraternal, twins**—pairs that result when a mother releases *two* ova at the same time and each is fertilized by a *different* sperm (Brockington, 1996). So even though fraternal twins are born together, they have no more genes in common than any other pair of siblings. As illustrated in Figure 3.4, fraternal twins often differ considerably in appearance and need not even be the same sex.

In Canada and other developed countries, the incidence of multiple births involving three or more infants has increased dramatically. For example, births in Canada involving three or more infants have nearly tripled between 1979 and 1999, while the total number of births has decreased 7.7% (Best Start, 2002). The increase is often attributed to the use of assisted reproductive technologies, which include fertility drugs, artificial insemination, and in vitro fertilization, among others (Society of Obstetricians and Gynaecologists of Canada, 2000). Most of these multiple births involve siblings that are fraternal, not identical.

Male or Female?

A hereditary basis for sex differences becomes clear if we examine the chromosomes of normal men and women. These chromosomal portraits, or *karyotypes*, reveal that 22 of the 23 pairs of human chromosomes (called *autosomes*) are similar in males and females. Sex is determined by the 23rd pair. In males, the 23rd pair consists of one elongated body known as an **X chromosome** and a short, stubby companion called a **Y chromosome**. In females, both of these sex chromosomes are Xs (see Figure 3.5).

Throughout history, mothers have often been belittled, tortured, divorced, and even beheaded for failing to bear their husbands a male heir! This is both a social and a biological injustice in that fathers determine the sex of their offspring. When the sex chromosomes of a genetic (XY) male segregate into gametes during meiosis, half of the sperm produced will contain an X chromosome and half will contain a Y chromosome. By contrast, the ova produced by a genetic (XX) female all carry an X chromosome. Thus a child's sex is determined by whether an X-bearing or a Y-bearing *sperm* fertilizes the ovum. Located on the Y chromosome is a single "sex gene" that is responsible for male sexual development (Milunsky, 1992). If this gene is absent, the individual that develops is a female.

dizygotic (or fraternal) twins
twins that result when a mother releases two ova at roughly the same time and each is fertilized by a different sperm, producing two zygotes that are genetically different

X chromosome
The longer of the two sex chromosomes; normal females have two X chromosomes, whereas normal males have but one

Y chromosome
The shorter of the two sex chromosomes; normal males have one Y chromosome whereas females have none

Figure 3.5 *These karyotypes of a male (left) and a female (right) have been arranged so that the chromosomes could be displayed in pairs. Note that the 23rd pair of chromosomes for the male consists of one elongated X chromosome and a Y chromosome that is noticeably smaller, whereas the 23rd pair for the female consists of two X chromosomes.*

So far, so good: We have a genetically unique boy or girl who has inherited about 50 000 genes in all on his or her 46 chromosomes (Lemonick, 2001). Now an important question: How do genes regulate development and influence a person's phenotypic characteristics?

What Do Genes Do?

How do genes promote development? At the most basic, biochemical level, they call for the production of amino acids, which form enzymes and other proteins that are necessary for the formation and functioning of new cells (Mehlman & Botkin, 1998). Genes, for example, regulate the production of a pigment called melanin in the iris of the eye. People with brown eyes have genes that call for much of this pigment, whereas people with lighter (blue or green) eyes have genes that call for less pigmentation. Genes also guide cell differentiation, ensuring that some cells become the brain and central nervous system, some become the circulatory system, some become the bones, some become the skin, and so on. Genes influence and are influenced by the biochemical environment surrounding them during development. For example, a particular cell might become part of an eyeball or part of an elbow depending on what cells surround it during early embryonic development. However, no one completely understands the remarkable process that transforms a single-celled zygote into a remarkably complex, living, breathing human being.

Some genes are responsible for *regulating* the pace and timing of development. That is, specific genes with specific developmental blueprints are "turned on" or "turned off" by other regulatory genes at different points in the life span (Plomin et al., 1997). Regulatory genes, for example, might turn on the genes responsible for the growth spurt we experience as adolescents and then shut these growth genes down in adulthood.

Finally, here is an important point: *Environmental factors clearly influence how messages coded in the genes are carried out* (Gottlieb, 1996). Consider, for example, that a child who inherits genes for tall stature may or may not be tall as an adult. Should the child experience very poor nutrition for a prolonged period early in life, he or she could end up being only average or even below average in height, despite having the genetic potential for exceptional stature. Hence, environmental influences combine with genetic influences to determine how a genotype is translated into a particular phenotype—the way one looks, feels, thinks, and behaves.

Another way to approach the riddle of how genes influence development is to consider the major patterns of genetic inheritance: the ways in which parents' genes are expressed in their children's phenotypes.

How Are Genes Expressed?

There are five main patterns of genetic expression: simple dominant-recessive inheritance, codominance, sex-linked inheritance, genetic imprinting, and polygenic (or multiple gene) inheritance.

Simple Dominant-Recessive Inheritance

Many human characteristics are influenced by only one pair of genes (called **alleles**): one from the mother and one from the father. Although he knew nothing of genes, a 19th-century monk named Gregor Mendel contributed greatly to our knowledge of single gene-pair inheritance by cross-breeding different strains of peas and observing the outcomes. His major discovery was a predictable pattern to the way in which two alternative characteristics (for example, smooth seeds vs. wrinkled seeds, green pods vs. yellow pods) appeared in the offspring of cross-breedings. He called some characteristics (for example, smooth seeds) "dominant" because they appeared more often in later generations than their opposite traits, which he called "recessive" traits. Among peas and among humans, an offspring's phenotype often is not simply a blend of the characteristics of mother and father. Instead, one of the parental genes often dominates the other, and the child resembles the parent who contributed the dominant gene.

To illustrate the principles of **simple dominant-recessive inheritance**, consider the fact that about three-fourths of us have the ability to see distant objects clearly (that is, normal vision) whereas the remaining one-fourth of us cannot and are myopic (nearsighted). It happens that the gene associated with normal vision is a **dominant allele**. A weaker gene calling for nearsightedness is said to be a **recessive allele**. Therefore a person who inherits one allele for normal vision and one allele for myopia would display a phenotype of normal vision because the normal-vision gene overpowers (i.e., dominates) the nearsightedness gene.

Because a normal-vision allele dominates a nearsightedness allele, we represent the normal-vision gene with a capital *N* and the nearsightedness gene with a lowercase *n*. Perhaps you can see that there are three possible genotypes for this visual characteristic: (1) two normal-vision alleles (*NN*), (2) two nearsightedness alleles (*nn*), and (3) one of each (*Nn*). People whose genotype for an attribute consists of two alleles of the same kind are said to be **homozygous** for that attribute. Thus, an *NN* individual is homozygous for normal vision and will pass only genes for normal vision to his or her offspring. An *nn* individual is homozygous for nearsightedness (the only way one can actually be nearsighted is to inherit two of these recessive alleles) and will pass nearsightedness genes to his or her offspring. Finally, an *Nn* individual is said to be **heterozygous** for this visual trait because he or she has inherited alternative forms of the allele. This person will have normal vision because the *N* allele is dominant. What kind of allele will the heterozygous person pass along to his or her offspring? Either a normal-vision gene or a nearsightedness gene! Even though a heterozygous person has normal vision, exactly half the gametes produced by this individual will carry a gene for normal vision, and half will carry a gene for nearsightedness.

Can two individuals with normal vision ever produce a nearsighted child? The answer is yes—if each parent is heterozygous for normal vision and is a **carrier** of the recessive allele for nearsightedness. In Figure 3.6, the genotype of a carrier father appears at the head of the columns and that of a carrier mother appears at the left of the rows. What kind of vision will their children have? The various possibilities appear in the four quadrants of the chart. If a sperm bearing an *N* allele unites with an ovum carrying an *N* allele, the result is an *NN* zygote, or a child who is homozygous for normal vision. If a sperm bearing an *N* gene fertilizes an ovum carrying an *n* gene, or if an *n* sperm fertilizes

alleles
alternative forms of a gene that can appear at a particular site on a chromosome

simple dominant-recessive inheritance
pattern of inheritance in which one allele dominates another so that only its phenotype is expressed

dominant allele
relatively powerful gene that is expressed phenotypically and masks the effect of a less powerful gene

recessive allele
less powerful gene that is not expressed phenotypically when paired with a dominant allele

homozygous
having inherited two alleles for an attribute that are identical in their effects

heterozygous
having inherited two alleles for an attribute that have different effects

carrier
heterozygous individual who displays no sign of a recessive allele in his or her own phenotype but can pass this gene to offspring

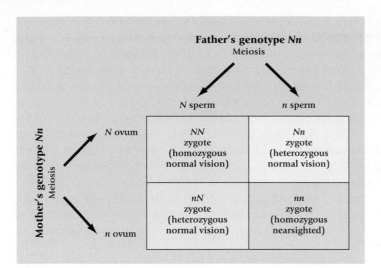

Figure 3.6 *Possible genotypes and phenotypes resulting from a mating of two heterozygotes for normal vision.*

an *N* ovum, the result is a heterozygous child with normal vision. Finally, if both sperm and ovum carry an *n* gene, the child will be nearsighted. Because each of these four combinations is equally likely in any given mating, the odds are 1 in 4 that a child of two *Nn* parents will be nearsighted.

The normal-vision/nearsightedness trait is but one of more than 5000 human attributes determined by a single gene pair in which one particular allele dominates another (Connor, 1995). Box 3.1 lists a number of other common dominant and recessive characteristics that people can display.

Codominance

Alternative forms of a gene do not always follow the simple dominant/recessive pattern described by Gregor Mendel. Instead, some are **codominant**: The phenotype they produce is a compromise between the two genes. For example, the alleles for human blood types A and B are equally expressive, and neither dominates the other. A heterozygous person who inherits an allele for blood type A and one for blood type B has equal proportions of A-antigens and B-antigens in his or her blood. So if your blood type is AB, you illustrate this principle of genetic codominance.

codominance
condition in which two heterozygous but equally powerful alleles produce a phenotype in which genes are both fully and equally expressed

---

Examples of Dominant and Recessive Traits in Human Heredity

Our discussion of dominant and recessive genes has centred on two particular alleles, a gene for normal vision and a gene for nearsightedness. Listed here are a number of other dominant and recessive characteristics in human heredity (Connor, 1995; McKusick, 1995).

A quick glance through the list reveals that most of the undesirable or maladaptive attributes are recessive. For this we can be thankful; otherwise, genetically linked diseases and defects might become widespread and eventually decimate the species.

One important genetic disease produced by a dominant gene is Huntington's disease, a condition that causes a gradual deterioration of the nervous system, leading to a progressive decline in physical and mental abilities and ultimately to death. Although some victims of Huntington's disease die in young adulthood, the disease normally appears much later, usually after age 40. Fortunately, the dominant allele that is responsible for this lethal condition is very rare.

Dominant Traits	Recessive Traits
Dark hair	Blond hair
Full head of hair	Pattern baldness
Curly hair	Straight hair
Facial dimples	No dimples
Farsightedness	Normal vision
Normal vision	Colour blindness*
Extra digits	Five digits
Pigmented skin	Albinism
Type A blood	Type O blood
Type B blood	Type O blood
Normal blood clotting	Hemophilia*
Huntington's disease	Normal physiology
Normal blood cells	Sickle-cell anemia*
Normal physiology	Cystic fibrosis*
Normal physiology	Phenylketonuria*
Normal physiology	Tay-Sachs disease*

*These conditions are discussed elsewhere in the chapter.

Another type of codominance occurs when one of two heterozygous alleles is stronger than the other but fails to mask all of its effects. The *sickle cell* trait is a noteworthy example of this incomplete dominance. Sickle-cell anemia is most prevalent among Blacks of African descent but is also found among certain populations in the Mediterranean basin and India (College of Physicians and Surgeons of Manitoba, 2001; Williams-Murphy et al., 1998). In Canada and the United States, about 1 in every 9 or 10 Blacks of African ancestry are heterozygous for this attribute, carrying a recessive "sickle-cell" allele (Camp Jumoke, 2001; Schulman & Black, 1993). The presence of this one sickle cell gene causes some of the person's red blood cells to assume an unusual crescent, or sickle, shape (see Figure 3.7). Sickled cells can be a problem because they tend to cluster together, distributing less oxygen throughout the circulatory system. Yet overt symptoms of circulatory distress, such as painful swelling of the joints and fatigue, are rarely experienced by these sickle cell carriers unless they experience oxygen deprivation, as they might after physical exertion at high altitudes or while under anesthesia (Strachan & Read, 1996).

The consequences are much more severe for those individuals who inherit *two* recessive sickle cell genes. They will develop a severe blood disorder, called **sickle cell anemia**, that causes massive sickling of red blood cells and inefficient distribution of oxygen at all times. Many who suffer from this painful disease die from heart or kidney failure or respiratory diseases during childhood (Institute of Medicine, 1999).

Sex-Linked Inheritance

Some traits are called **sex-linked characteristics** because they are determined by genes located on the sex chromosomes. In fact, the vast majority of these sex-linked attributes are produced by recessive genes that are found only on X chromosomes. Who do you suppose is more likely to inherit these recessive X-linked traits, males or females?

The answer is males, a point we can easily illustrate with a common sex-linked characteristic, *red/green colour blindness*. Many people cannot distinguish red from green, an inability caused by a recessive gene that appears only on X chromosomes. Recall that a normal (XY) male has only one X chromosome—the one he inherited from his mother. If this X chromosome carries a recessive gene for colour blindness, the male will be colour-blind. Why? This is because there is no corresponding gene on his Y chromosome that might counteract the effect of this colour-blind allele. By contrast, a genetic female who inherits only one gene for colour blindness will not be colour-blind because the

sickle-cell anemia
genetic blood disease that causes red blood cells to assume an unusual sickled shape and to become inefficient at distributing oxygen

sex-linked characteristic
attribute determined by a recessive gene that appears on the X chromosome; more likely to characterize males

Bettmann/Corbis/Magma

Figure 3.7 *Normal (round) and "sickled" (elongated) red blood cells from a person with sickle-cell anemia.*

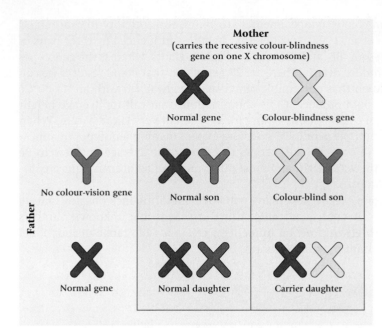

Mother
(carries the recessive colour-blindness gene on one X chromosome)

Normal gene · Colour-blindness gene

Father

No colour-vision gene · Normal son · Colour-blind son

Normal gene · Normal daughter · Carrier daughter

Figure 3.8 Sex-linked inheritance of red/green colour blindness. In the example here, the mother can distinguish reds from greens but is a carrier because one of her X chromosomes contains a colour-blind allele. Notice that her sons have a 50 percent chance of inheriting the colour-blind allele and being colour-blind, whereas none of her daughters would display that trait. A girl can be colour-blind only if her father is colour-blind and her mother is at least a carrier of the colour-blindness gene.

colour-normal gene on her second X chromosome will dominate the colour-blind gene, enabling her to distinguish red from green (see Figure 3.8). So a female cannot be colour-blind unless *both* of her X chromosomes contain a recessive gene for colour blindness.

Immediately, we have reason to suspect that more males than females will be colour-blind. Indeed, roughly 8 males in 100 cannot distinguish red from green. This finding suggests that the ratio of colour-blind to colour-normal genes in the gene pool is approximately 1:12. Since the odds are only 1 in 12 that any single X chromosome will contain a gene for colour blindness, the likelihood that a White female will inherit two of these genes (and be colour-blind) is 1/12 times 1/12, or only 1 in 144 (Burns & Bottino, 1989).

There are more than 100 sex-linked characteristics other than colour blindness, and most of them are disabling (Plomin et al., 1997). These include hemophilia (a disease in which the blood does not clot), two kinds of muscular dystrophy, degeneration of the optic nerve, and certain forms of deafness and night blindness. Because these disorders are determined by recessive genes on X chromosomes, males are much more likely than females to suffer their harmful effects.

Genetic Imprinting

Until recently, geneticists were confused about the distribution of certain traits that were known to be influenced by a single pair of alleles but followed none of the patterns of inheritance we have discussed. For example, children are more likely to develop diabetes if their fathers rather than their mothers have this disease, whereas *Angelman syndrome*, a disorder characterized by jerky movements, inappropriate laughter, and severe mental retardation, is typically transmitted by one's mother rather than ones's father (Plomin et al., 1997). Today we know that these parent-specific patterns of inheritance are a result of **genetic imprinting**—a process in which particular gene pairs are biochemically marked so that only one parent's allele (either the mother's or the father's) is expressed, regardless of its composition. Only a small number of alleles are subject to genetic imprinting, and it apparently does not occur in all individuals (Strachan & Read, 1996). At present the causes of genetic imprinting are poorly understood and its evolutionary significance, if any, is unknown.

Polygenic Inheritance

To this point, we have considered only those traits that are influenced by a single pair of alleles. However, most important human characteristics are influenced by many pairs of alleles and are called **polygenic traits**. Examples of polygenic traits include height,

genetic imprinting
pattern of inheritance in which a pair of alleles is biochemically marked so that only one parent's allele is expressed, regardless of its composition

polygenic trait
characteristic that is influenced by the action of many genes rather than a single pair

weight, intelligence, skin colour, temperamental attributes, susceptibility to cancer, and a host of others (Plomin et al., 1997). Imagine that height is influenced by three pairs of genes, and that the alleles AA, BB, and CC tend to produce giants, whereas the genotypes aa, bb, and cc tend to produce dwarfs. There are 27 genotypes that could result if we calculated all possible children that one couple of average height (each with an Aa Bb Cc genotype, for example) could produce. Gene combinations that call for average height would be more likely than combinations calling for very tall or very short stature. When a trait is influenced by multiple genes, we therefore expect many phenotypes to appear in the population, and we expect many people to be near the average and few to be extreme. This is exactly the way height and most other measurable human traits are distributed in large populations.

To date, nobody knows exactly how many pairs of alleles influence physical stature (height), intelligence, or other polygenic traits. All we can say is that unknown numbers of genes, interacting with environmental influences, create a wide range of individual differences in most important human attributes.

CHROMOSOMAL AND GENETIC ABNORMALITIES

Although the vast majority of newborn infants are pronounced healthy at birth, approximately 5 of every 100 have a congenital problem of some kind (Schulman & Black, 1993). By definition, **congenital defects** are those that are present at birth, although many of these conditions are not detectable when the child is born. For example, the gene that produces **Huntington's disease** is present from the moment of conception. As we learned in Box 3.1, the gradual deterioration of the nervous system associated with this condition is not apparent at birth and will not ordinarily appear until much later— usually after age 40. Researchers at the University of British Columbia have demonstrated that DNA testing for the disorder is 98.8 percent accurate (Huq & Hayden, 1998) and that fetal DNA tests (from amniocentesis or chorionic villus sampling, explained later in this chapter) can be performed for early detection.

In Chapter 4, we will consider a variety of congenital defects that are likely to result from abnormalities in the birth process or from harmful conditions to which children are exposed while developing within the womb. Here we will look only at those problems that are caused by abnormal genes and chromosomes.

congenital defect
problem that is present (though not necessarily apparent) at birth; such defects may stem from genetic and prenatal influences or from complications of the birth process

Huntington's disease
genetic disease caused by a dominant allele, that typically appears later in life and causes the nervous system to degenerate (see Box 3.1)

Concept Check 3.1
Understanding Principles of Hereditary Transmission

Check your understanding of the principles of hereditary transmission by answering each of the following questions. Answers appear in the Appendix.

1. You are a monozygotic (identical) twin. The odds that you and your twin are the same sex (that is, two boys or two girls) are
   (a) 100 percent (b) 50 percent (c) impossible to calculate

2. Most people can curl their tongues—a simple dominant-recessive trait that is determined by a dominant gene. Your father can curl his tongue, but neither your mother nor your sister can. The odds that you can curl your tongue are

   (a) 100 percent (b) 75 percent
   (c) 50 percent (d) 25 percent

3. If both *biological* parents cannot curl their tongues, then the odds that their child will be *unable* to curl his or her tongue are
   (a) 100 percent (b) 50 percent (c) 0 percent

4. A colour-blind mother and a colour-blind father have a son and a daughter. What is the probability that the boy will be colour-blind? The girl will be colour-blind?

Chromosomal Abnormalities

When a germ cell divides during meiosis, the distribution of its 46 chromosomes into sperm or ova is sometimes uneven. In other words, one of the resulting gametes may have too many chromosomes, while the other has too few. The vast majority of these chromosomal abnormalities are *lethal*, meaning that a zygote formed from the union of an abnormal and a normal gamete will fail to develop or will be spontaneously aborted. However, some chromosomal abnormalities are not lethal, as illustrated by the finding that approximately 1 child in 200 is born with either one chromosome too many or one too few (Plomin et al., 1997).

Abnormalities of the Sex Chromosomes

Many chromosomal abnormalities involve the 23rd pair—the sex chromosomes. Occasionally, males are born with an extra X or Y chromosome, producing the genotype XXY or XYY, and females may survive if they inherit a single X chromosome (XO) or even three (XXX), four (XXXX), or five (XXXXX) X chromosomes. Each of these conditions has somewhat different developmental implications, as we will see in examining four of the more common sex chromosome abnormalities in Table 3.1.

In addition to the abnormalities described in Table 3.1, about 1 individual in 1000 has an X chromosome that is brittle in places and may even have separated into two or more pieces—a condition known as the **Fragile-X syndrome** (Hagerman & Cronister, 1996). This condition is second only to Down syndrome (which we will soon discuss) as a genetic cause of mental retardation, and recent research suggests that it may contribute to some cases of *infantile autism*, a serious emotional disorder of early childhood characterized by extreme self-involvement, repetitive self-stimulating behaviours, and delayed (or absent) language and social skills. About 75 percent of fragile-X males show some degree of mental retardation (ranging from mild to severe), whereas a majority of females with a fragile-X chromosome are either intellectually normal or display only mild cognitive impairments (Hagerman, 1996). Investigators have located the gene responsible for this chromosomal abnormality—an abnormal gene on the X chromosome (Plomin et al., 1997). Research indicates that the defective allele at the fragile site is much more likely to produce mental retardation in daughters when the gene is passed from mother to child (Hagerman, 1996).

Autosomal Abnormalities

Several hereditary abnormalities are attributable to the **autosomes**—that is, the 22 pairs of chromosomes that are similar in males and females. The most common type of autosomal abnormality occurs when an abnormal sperm or ovum carrying an extra autosome combines with a normal gamete to form a zygote that has 47 chromosomes (2 sex chromosomes and 45 autosomes). In these cases, the extra chromosome appears along with 1 of the 22 pairs of autosomes to yield 3 chromosomes of that type, or a *trisomy*.

By far the most frequent of all autosomal abnormalities (in Canada, occurrence is about 1 in 900 births; Wyatt, 2000), is **Down syndrome**, or *trisomy 21*, a condition in which the child inherits all or part of an extra 21st chromosome. Children with Down syndrome are mentally retarded, with IQs that average 55 (the average IQ among normal children is 100). They may also have congenital eye, ear, and heart defects and are usually characterized by a number of distinctive physical features, including a sloping forehead, protruding tongue, short stubby limbs, slightly flattened nose, and almond-shaped eyes (see Figure 3.9). Although intellectually impaired, these youngsters reach many of the same developmental milestones as normal children, but at a slower pace (Carr, 1995; Evans & Gray, 2000). Most of these youngsters learn to care for their basic needs, and some have even learned to read and write (Carr, 1995; Gibson & Harris, 1988). Developmental progress appears to be best when parents and other care providers strive to include Down syndrome children in most family activities, are patient and work hard

Fragile-X syndrome
abnormality of the X chromosome caused by a defective gene and associated with mild to severe mental retardation, particularly when the defective gene is passed from mother to child

autosomes
the 22 pairs of human chromosomes that are identical in males and females

Down syndrome
chromosomal abnormality (also known as the presence of an extra 21st chromosome; people with this syndrome have a distinctive physical appearance and are moderately to severely retarded

TABLE 3.1   Four Common Sex Chromosome Abnormalities

Name/genotype(s)	Incidence	Developmental implications
Female abnormalities Turner's syndrome; XO	1 in 2500 female births	*Appearance:* Phenotypically female but small in stature with stubby fingers and toes, a webbed neck, a broad chest, and small, underdeveloped breasts. Normal sexual development lacking at puberty, although Turner females can assume a more "womanly" appearance by taking the female hormone estrogen. *Fertility:* Sterile. *Intellectual characteristics:* Normal verbal intelligence but frequently score below average on tests of spatial abilities such as puzzle assembly or the mental rotation of figures.
Poly-X or "superfemale" syndrome; XXX, XXXX, or XXXXX	1 in 1000 female births	*Appearance:* Phenotypically female and normal in appearance. *Fertility:* Fertile; produce children with the usual number of sex chromosomes. *Intellectual characteristics:* Score somewhat below average in intelligence, with greatest deficits on tests of verbal reasoning. Developmental delays and intellectual deficits become more pronounced with an increase in the number of extra X chromosomes inherited.
Male abnormalities Klinefelter's syndrome; XXY or XXXY	1 in 750 male births	*Appearance:* Phenotypically male, with the emergence of some female secondary sex characteristics (enlargement of the hips and breasts) at puberty. Significantly taller than normal (XY) males. In the past Klinefelter males from Eastern-bloc countries may have competed as females in athletic events, leading to the current practice of administering sex tests to all female Olympic athletes. *Fertility:* Have underdeveloped testes and are sterile. *Intellectual characteristics:* About 20 to 30% of Klinefelter males are deficient in verbal intelligence, and their deficiencies become more pronounced with an increase in the number of extra X chromosomes inherited.
Supermale syndrome; XYY, XYYY, or XYYYY	1 in 1000 male births	*Appearance:* Phenotypic males who are significantly taller than normal (XY) males, have large teeth, and often develop severe acne during adolescence. *Fertility:* Typically fertile, although many of these men have abnormally low sperm counts. *Intellectual characteristics:* Although once thought to be subnormal intellectually and prone to violence and aggression, these assumptions have been proven wrong by research. IQs of supermales span the full range of those observed in normal (XY) males. Moreover, careful studies of large numbers of XYYs indicate that they are no more violent or aggressive than normal males, and are sometimes shy and retiring.

Sources: Robinson et al., 1992; Plomin et al., 1997; Shafer & Kuller, 1996.

Figure 3.9 *Children with Down syndrome can lead happy lives if they receive affection and encouragement from their companions.*

to properly stimulate them, and provide them with lots of emotional support (Atkinson et al., 1995; Hauser-Cram et al., 1999). However, they may spend many of their adult years in group homes or supervised community settings, with some institutionalized because their developmental handicaps usually prevent them from becoming economically self-sufficient.

Causes of Chromosomal Abnormalities

Clearly, most chromosomal abnormalities result from the *uneven segregation of chromosomes* during the meiosis of male and female germ cells. However, errors of meiosis are not the only contributors to chromosomal abnormalities.

As shown in Table 3.2, the likelihood of Down syndrome and other chromosomal abnormalities increases dramatically among older mothers. Notice also that mothers who have already given birth to a child with Down syndrome are much more likely to have another child with Down syndrome, should they give birth again, than are other women of the same age.

Why are older mothers at higher risk for bearing children with chromosomal abnormalities? One common explanation is the **aging-ova hypothesis**. Although sexually mature males produce sperm throughout life, a female is born with all her ova already present in her ovaries. So a 45-year-old woman's ova are more than 45 years old and may simply have deteriorated either because of aging or because of increased exposure to environmental hazards such as radiation and toxic chemicals.

In addition, recent research from the U.S. Food and Drug Administration reveals that mothers of any age who have a common genetic condition that hinders metabolism of *folic acid*—a B vitamin found in leafy green vegetables, beans, tuna, and eggs—show an elevated risk of delivering a Down syndrome baby (James et al., 1999). The risk is greatest for women who have the genetic condition *and* maintain diets low in folic acid. As a precaution, all women who hope to conceive have been advised to eat more substances rich in this essential vitamin. (This advice is extended to *all* women of childbearing age because, as we will see in Chapter 4, diets rich in folic acid also protect against birth defects of the central nervous system.) Interestingly, the risk of chromosomal abnormalities is not as closely linked to paternal age or diet (Shafer & Kuller, 1996) although fathers can contribute to abnormal outcomes in other ways. Even though most cases of Down syndrome can be traced to mothers' abnormal ova, about one-fourth of these children receive their extra 21st chromosome from their fathers rather than their mothers (Magenis et al., 1977). The risk of chromosomal abnormalities is also greater if a father smokes or drinks heavily or has been exposed to such environmental hazards as repeated abdominal x-rays (radiation) (Merewood, 2000; Strigini et al., 1990). Furthermore, it appears that perhaps 80 percent of girls with Turner's syndrome (see Table 3.1) develop from a normal (X) ovum that has been fertilized by an abnormal *sperm*—one that contains neither an X nor a Y chromosome (Tolmie, 1995). Only the XYY (or supermale) syndrome is always attributable to one parent—in this case the father—because mothers have no Y chromosomes to transmit to their offspring.

Genetic Abnormalities

Parents who are themselves healthy are often amazed to learn that their child could have a hereditary defect. Their surprise is certainly understandable, because most genetic problems are recessive traits that few if any close relatives may have had. In addition, these problems will not appear unless *both* parents carry the harmful allele *and* the child inherits this particular gene from each parent. The exceptions to this rule are sex-linked defects that a *male* child will display if the recessive alleles for these traits appear on his X chromosome that he inherited from his mother.

TABLE 3.2	Risk of Down Syndrome and Other Chromosomal Abnormalities as a Function of Mother's Age		
	Probability that child will have Down syndrome		
Age of mother	**At any pregnancy**	**After birth of a child with Down syndrome**	**Probability of any chromosomal abnormality at birth**
<29	<1 in 1000	1 in 100	1 in 450
30–34	1 in 700	1 in 100	1 in 350
35–39	1 in 220	1 in 100	1 in 125
40–44	1 in 65	1 in 25	1 in 40
45–49	1 in 25	1 in 15	1 in 12

Source: Adapted from Shafer & Kuller, 1996.

aging-ova hypothesis
hypothesis that an older mother is more likely to have children with chromosomal abnormalities because her ova are degenerating as she nears the end of her reproductive years

Earlier in the chapter we discussed two recessive hereditary defects, one that is sex-linked (colour blindness) and one that is not (sickle cell anemia). Table 3.3 describes a number of additional debilitating or fatal diseases that are attributable to a single pair of recessive alleles.

Genetic abnormalities may also result from **mutations**—that is, changes in the chemical structure of one or more genes that produce a new phenotype. Many mutations occur spontaneously and are harmful or even fatal. Mutations can also be induced by environmental hazards such as toxic industrial waste, radiation, agricultural chemicals that enter the food supply, and possibly even some of the additives and preservatives in processed foods (Burns & Bottino, 1989).

Might mutations ever be beneficial? Evolutionary theorists think so. Presumably, any mutation that is induced by stressors present in the natural environment may provide an adaptive advantage to those who inherit the mutant genes, thus enabling these individuals to survive. The sickle cell gene, for example, is a mutation that originated in Africa, Southeast Asia, and other tropical areas where malaria is widespread. Heterozygous children who inherit a single sickle cell allele are well adapted to these environments because the mutant gene makes them more resistant to malarial infection and thus more likely to survive (Plomin et al., 1997). Of course, the mutant sickle cell gene is not advantageous in environments where malaria is not a problem.

mutation
change in the chemical structure or arrangement of one or more genes that has the effect of producing a new phenotype

TABLE 3.3	Brief Descriptions of Major Recessive Hereditary Diseases			
Disease	**Description**	**Incidence**	**Treatment**	**Prenatal detection**
Cystic fibrosis (CF)	Child lacks enzyme that prevents mucus from obstructing the lungs and digestive tract. Many who have CF die in childhood or adolescence, although advances in treatment have enabled some to live well into adulthood.	1 in 2500 Caucasian births; 1 in 15 000 births of North American Blacks of African descent	Bronchial drainage; dietary control; gene replacement therapy	Yes
Diabetes	Individual lacks a hormone that would enable him or her to metabolize sugar properly. Produces symptoms such as excessive thirst and urination. Can be fatal if untreated.	1 in 2500 births; 3 to 5 times higher in Canada's First Nations and Inuit populations	Dietary control; insulin therapy	Yes
Duchenne-type muscular dystrophy	Sex-linked disorder that attacks the muscles and eventually produces such symptoms as slurred speech and loss of motor capabilities.	1 in 3500 male births; rare in females	None. Death from weakening of heart muscle or respiratory infection often occurs between ages 7 and 14	Yes
Hemophilia	A sex-linked condition sometimes called "bleeder's disease." Child lacks a substance that causes the blood to clot. Could bleed to death if scraped or cut.	1 in 3000 male births; rare in females	Blood transfusions; precautions to prevent cuts and scrapes	Yes
Phenyl-ketonuria (PKU)	Child lacks an enzyme to digest foods (including milk) containing the amino acid phenylalanine. Disease attacks nervous system, producing hyperactivity and severe mental retardation.	1 in 10 000 Caucasian births; rare in children of African or Asian ancestry	Dietary control	Yes
Sickle-cell anemia	Abnormal sickling of red blood cells causes inefficient distribution of oxygen, pain, swelling, organ damage, and susceptibility to respiratory diseases.	1 in 600 births of North American Blacks of African descent; even higher incidence in Africa and Southeast Asia	Blood transfusions; painkillers; drug to treat respiratory infections; bone marrow transplantation (if suitable donor is found)	Yes
Tay-Sachs disease	Causes degeneration of the central nervous system starting in the first year. Victims usually die by age 4.	1 in 3600 births to Jews of European descent and French Canadians	None	Yes

SOURCES: Camp Jumoke, 2001; Kuller, Cheschier, & Cefalo, 1996; Strachan & Read, 1996.

APPLICATIONS: GENETIC COUNSELLING, PRENATAL DETECTION, AND TREATMENT OF HEREDITARY DISORDERS

In the past, many couples whose relatives were affected by hereditary disorders were reluctant to have children, fearing that they too would bear an abnormal child. Today, services such as genetic counselling, prenatal diagnosis, and even treatments to correct some hereditary defects before a baby is born allow these parents to make reasoned decisions about conceiving a child or carrying a pregnancy to term.

Genetic Counselling

Genetic counselling is a service that helps prospective parents assess the likelihood that their children will be free of hereditary defects. Genetic counsellors are trained in genetics, the interpretation of family histories, and counselling procedures. They may be geneticists, medical researchers, or practitioners, such as pediatricians. Although any couple who hope to have children might wish to talk with a genetic counsellor about the hereditary risks their children may face, genetic counselling is particularly helpful for couples who either have relatives with hereditary disorders or have already borne a child with a disorder.

Genetic counsellors normally begin by obtaining a complete family history, or *pedigree*, from each prospective parent to identify relatives affected by hereditary disorders. These pedigrees are used to estimate the likelihood that the couple would bear a child with a genetic disorder; in fact, pedigrees are the only basis for determining whether children are likely to be affected by certain disorders (one type of diabetes and some forms of muscular dystrophy, for example). Yet a pedigree analysis *cannot* guarantee that a child will be healthy, even when no genetic disorders are found among blood relatives. Fortunately, blood tests and DNA analyses can now determine whether *parents* carry genes for many serious hereditary disorders, including all those listed in Table 3.3, and Huntington's disease and the Fragile-X syndrome (Strachan & Read, 1996).

Once all the information and test results are in, the genetic counsellor helps the couple consider the options available to them, such as screening procedures. Screening procedures cannot reverse any defects that are found, but they allow expectant parents to decide whether to terminate a pregnancy rather than give birth to an abnormal child.

Prenatal Detection of Hereditary Abnormalities

Because the overall rate of chromosomal abnormalities dramatically increases after age 35, older mothers often undergo a prenatal screening known as **amniocentesis**. A large, hollow needle is inserted into the mother's abdomen to withdraw a sample of the amniotic fluid that surrounds the fetus. Fetal cells in this fluid can then be tested to determine the sex of the fetus and the presence of chromosomal abnormalities such as Down syndrome. In addition, more than 100 genetic disorders—including Tay-Sachs disease, cystic fibrosis, one type of diabetes, Duchenne muscular dystrophy, sickle cell anemia, and hemophilia—can now be diagnosed by analyzing fetal cells in amniotic fluid (Whittle & Connor, 1995). Although amniocentesis is considered a very safe procedure (Cabaniss, 1996), it triggers a miscarriage in a very small percentage of cases (currently about

genetic counselling
service designed to inform prospective parents about genetic diseases and to help them determine the likelihood that they would transmit such disorders to their children

amniocentesis
method of extracting amniotic fluid from a pregnant woman so that fetal body cells in the fluid can be tested for chromosomal abnormalities and other genetic defects

1 chance in 150). In fact, Canadian researchers in Toronto and British Columbia have followed children exposed to mid-trimester amniocentesis for seven (Finegan et al., 1996) to 18 years (Baird, Yee & Sadovnick, 1994), with no adverse effects reported.

A number of researchers, including those at the University of Toronto (Johnson et al., 1999), have found that amniocentesis is less risky when performed after the 13th week of pregnancy, when amniotic fluid becomes sufficiently plentiful to withdraw for analysis (Kuller, 1996). Because the results of the tests will not come back for another two weeks, parents have little time to consider a second-trimester abortion if the fetus has a serious defect and abortion is their choice. However, an alternative procedure known as **chorionic villus sampling (CVS)** collects tissue for the same tests as amniocentesis and can be performed during the eighth or ninth week of pregnancy (Kuller, 1996). As shown in Figure 3.10, there are two approaches to CVS. Either a catheter is inserted through the woman's vagina and cervix, or a needle is inserted through her abdomen, into a membrane called the *chorion* that surrounds the fetus. Fetal cells are then extracted and tested for hereditary abnormalities, with the results typically available within 24 hours. CVS often allows parents to know whether their fetus bears a suspected abnormality very early on, leaving them more time to carefully consider the pros and cons of continuing the pregnancy in the event that the fetus is abnormal. But despite its advantages, CVS is currently recommended only to parents at very high risk of conceiving an abnormal child because it entails a greater chance of miscarriage (about 1 chance in 50) than does amniocentesis, and its use, in rare instances, has been linked to limb deformities in the fetus (Kuller, 1996). Fortunately, a much safer early screening technique may be widely available within the next 10 years (Springen, 2001). The procedure involves DNA analysis of fetal cells that begin to enter the mother's bloodstream early in pregnancy and that, when isolated from the mother's cells, can be tested to determine whether the fetus carries any gene known to scientists. DNA screening will almost surely become more common once scientists are better able to locate and test fetal cells in the mother's bloodstream with absolutely no risk to the fetus.

Another common and safe prenatal diagnostic technique is **ultrasound** (sonar), a method of scanning the womb with sound waves that is most useful after the 14th week of pregnancy (Cheschier, 1996). Ultrasound provides the attending physician with an outline of the fetus in much the same way that sonar reveals outlines of the fish beneath

chorionic villus sampling (CVS)
an alternative to amniocentesis in which fetal cells are extracted from the chorion for prenatal tests. CVS can be performed earlier in pregnancy than is possible with amniocentesis

ultrasound
method of detecting gross physical abnormalities by scanning the womb with sound waves, thereby producing a visual outline of the fetus

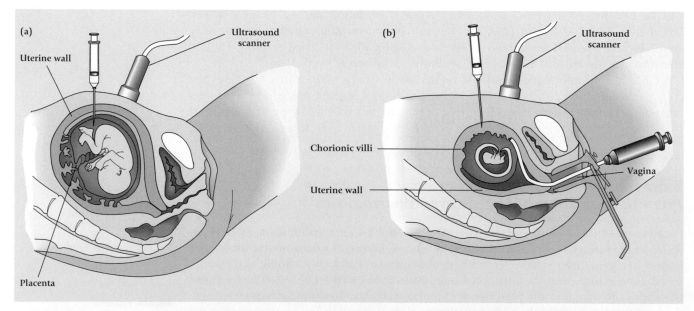

Figure 3.10 *Amniocentesis and chorionic villus sampling. (a) In amniocentesis, a needle is inserted through the abdominal wall into the uterus. Fluid is withdrawn and fetal cells are cultured, a process that takes about three weeks. (b) Chorionic villus sampling can be performed much earlier in pregnancy, and results are available within 24 hours. Two approaches to obtaining a sample of chorionic villi are shown here: inserting a thin tube through the vagina into the uterus or a needle through the abdominal wall. In either of these methods, ultrasound is used for guidance.* ADAPTED FROM MOORE & PERSAUD, 1993.

a fishing boat. It is particularly helpful for detecting multiple pregnancies, gross physical defects, and the age and sex of the fetus. It is also used to guide practitioners as they perform amniocentesis and CVS (see Figure 3.10). Ultrasound is even a pleasant experience for many parents, who seem to enjoy seeing their baby.

Treating Hereditary Disorders

Prenatal detection of a hereditary disorder leaves many couples in a quandary, particularly if their religious background or personal beliefs are opposed to abortion. If the disease in question is invariably fatal, such as Tay-Sachs, the couple must decide either to violate their moral principles and terminate the pregnancy or to have a baby who will appear normal and healthy but will rapidly decline and die young.

Might this quandary someday become a thing of the past? Very possibly. Less than 40 years ago, medical science could do little for children with another degenerative disease of the nervous system—**phenylketonuria (PKU)**. Like Tay-Sachs disease, PKU is a metabolic disorder. Affected children lack a critical enzyme that would allow them to metabolize phenylalanine, a component of many foods, including milk. As phenylalanine accumulates in the body, it is converted into a harmful substance, phenylpyruvic acid, that attacks the nervous system. In the past the majority of children who inherited this disorder soon became hyperactive and severely retarded.

The major breakthroughs came in the mid-1950s when scientists developed a diet low in phenylalanine, and in 1961, when they developed a simple blood test that could determine if a child had PKU within a few days after birth. Newborn infants are now routinely screened for PKU, and affected children are immediately placed on a low-phenylalanine diet. The outcome of this therapeutic intervention is a happy one: Children who remain on the diet throughout middle childhood suffer few if any of the harmful consequences of this formerly incurable disease. Outcomes are best when affected individuals remain on the special diet *for life*. This is particularly true of PKU women who hope to have children of their own; if they abandon the diet and their phenylalanine levels are high, they face great risk of either miscarrying or bearing a mentally deficient child (Verp, 1993b).

Today, the potentially devastating effects of many other hereditary abnormalities can be minimized or controlled. For example, new medical and surgical techniques, performed on *fetuses in the uterus*, have made it possible to treat some hereditary disorders by delivering drugs or hormones to the unborn organism (Hunter & Yankowitz, 1996), performing bone marrow transplants (Golbus & Fries, 1993), or surgically repairing some genetically transmitted defects of the heart, neural tube, urinary tract, and respiratory system (Yankowitz, 1996). In addition, children born with either Turner's syndrome or Klinefelter's syndrome can be placed on hormone therapy to make them more normal in appearance. Diabetes can be controlled by a low-sugar diet and by periodic doses of insulin, which help the patient to metabolize sugar. And youngsters who have such blood disorders as hemophilia or sickle cell anemia may now receive periodic transfusions to provide them with the clotting agents or the normal red blood cells they lack.

Advances in the treatment of *cystic fibrosis* (CF) illustrate the remarkable rate at which researchers are gaining the knowledge to combat genetic diseases. Only 15 years ago, about all that could be done for CF patients was to administer antibiotics to lessen the discomfort of their chronic lung obstructions and infections. But in 1989 researchers located the CF gene, and only one year later two research teams succeeded at neutralizing the damaging effects of this gene in the laboratory (Denning et al., 1991). Soon thereafter came the development and testing of a *gene replacement therapy* that involves inserting normal genes, carried by genetically engineered cold viruses, into the noses and lungs of patients with cystic fibrosis in the hope that these imported genes will override the effects of the CF genes. A similar genetic therapy has been attempted for *adenosine*

> **?** | **WHAT DO YOU THINK?**
>
> Because Huntington's disease is caused by a dominant gene, chances are 1 in 2 (or 50 percent) that a child of a parent with Huntington's disease will eventually display this disorder. A test to detect the gene that causes this disease is now available. Would you take this test to learn your fate if your mother or father had Huntington's disease? Why or why not?

phenylketonuria (PKU)
genetic disease in which the child is unable to metabolize phenylalanine; if left untreated, it soon causes hyperactivity and mental retardation

deaminese deficiency, an inherited disorder of the immune system. Although both approaches have had some limited success, they produce their benefits by lessening the patients' symptoms rather than by curing the disorders and must be repeated frequently to remain effective (Mehlman & Botkin, 1998).

Finally, advances in *genetic engineering* are raising the spectre of **germline gene therapy**—a process by which harmful genes are altered or replaced with healthy ones in the early embryonic stage, thereby permanently correcting a genetic defect. This approach has been used successfully to correct certain genetic disorders in animals (Strachan & Read, 1996), but the kinds of ethical issues raised in Box 3.2 may keep it from being sanctioned for use with humans for some time to come.

In sum, many abnormal children can lead normal lives if their hereditary disorders are detected and treated before serious harm has been done. Inspired by recent successes in fetal medicine, genetic mapping, and gene replacement therapy, geneticists and medical practitioners are hopeful that many untreatable genetic defects will become treatable, or even curable, in the near future (Mehlman & Botkin, 1998; Nesmith & McKenna, 2000).

> **? WHAT DO YOU THINK?**
>
> The Human Genome Project (HGP) is a publicly funded international research effort to sequence and map all of the human genes. A major goal of this project is to better diagnose, treat, and prevent disease. To date, the HGP has provided a rough road map of the approximately 30 000 genes that make up the human genetic code (see www.nhgri.nih.gov), but scientists are far from understanding what most genes do or how they interact (Lemonick, 2001). A recent Time/CNN poll of 1200 Americans, however, revealed that 75 percent of them did not want their individual genotypes available in a data bank. Why the caution? How do you feel about this issue and why?

HEREDITARY INFLUENCES ON BEHAVIOUR

We have seen that genes play a major role in determining our physical appearance and many of our metabolic characteristics. But to what extent does heredity affect such characteristics as intelligence? Can a strong case be made for genetic contributions to personality or mental health?

In recent years, investigators from the fields of genetics, zoology, population biology, and psychology have asked the question, "Are there certain abilities, traits, and patterns of behaviour that depend very heavily on the particular combination of genes that an individual inherits, and if so, are these attributes likely to be modified by one's experiences?" Those who focus on these issues in their research are known as *behavioural geneticists*.

Before we take a closer look at the field of **behavioural genetics**, it is necessary to dispel a common myth. Although behavioural geneticists view development as the process through which one's *genotype* (the set of genes one inherits) is expressed in one's *phenotype* (observable characteristics and behaviours), they are not strict hereditarians. They recognize, for example, that even physical characteristics such as height depend to some extent on environmental variables, such as the adequacy of one's diet (Plomin, 1990). They acknowledge that the long-term effects of inherited metabolic disorders such as PKU and diabetes also depend on one's environment—namely, the availability of medical facilities to detect and to treat these conditions. In other words, the behavioural geneticist is well aware that even attributes that have a strong hereditary component are often modified in important ways by environmental influences.

How, then, do behavioural geneticists differ from ethologists, who are also interested in the biological bases of development? The answer is relatively simple. Ethologists study inherited attributes that characterize *all* members of a species and conspire to make them *alike* (that is, attributes that contribute to *common* developmental outcomes). By contrast, behavioural geneticists focus on the biological bases for *variation* among members of a species. They are concerned with determining how the unique combination of genes that each of us inherits might be implicated in making us *different* from one another. Let's now consider the methods they use to approach this task.

germline gene therapy
a procedure, not yet perfected or approved for use with humans, in which harmful genes would be repaired or replaced with healthy ones, thereby permanently correcting a genetic defect

behavioural genetics
scientific study of how genotype interacts with environment to determine behavioural attributes such as intelligence, personality, and mental health

Ethical Issues Surrounding Treatments for Hereditary Disorders

Although many children and adolescents with hereditary disorders have clearly benefited from new treatments only recently introduced, scientists and society at large are now grappling with thorny ethical issues that have arisen from the rapid progress being made. Here is a small sampling of these concerns.

Issues surrounding fetal surgery

Most fetal surgical procedures are still experimental and often induce miscarriages and other harmful consequences. Consider that the risk of fetal death in urinary tract surgery is about 5 to 10 percent from the surgery itself, with another 20 to 30 percent suffering serious complications from the operation, and urinary tract surgery is safer than most other surgical procedures performed on fetuses (Yankowitz, 1996). Is it really in a fetus's best interests to undergo an operation that may end its life or produce birth defects? Should parents be held legally responsible if they choose to continue a pregnancy while refusing a fetal surgical procedure that might prevent their child from suffering from a serious handicap? Think about these questions, for they are some of the very issues that medical and legal practitioners are now debating.

Issues surrounding gene replacement therapy

All current gene replacement therapies for humans involve insertion of normal genes into patients' somatic (body) tissues to relieve the *symptoms* of genetic disorders. Are there major ethical problems here? Most observers think not (Strachan & Read, 1996). Clearly, investigators and practitioners are ethically bound to ensure the safety of their patients, because the techniques of somatic gene therapies are experimental and can have side effects. Yet, by limiting treatment to the patient's body cells, any consequences of the procedure are confined to the patient, who is usually suffering from a debilitating and even life-threatening disease for which no other effective therapy is available (Mehlman & Botkin, 1998). Thus, the benefits of somatic gene therapy are likely to greatly outweigh its costs. Many view this kind of treatment as analogous to (and at least as acceptable as) other medical procedures such as organ transplants. Some would even consider it *unethical* were parents to withhold somatic gene therapy from a seriously ill child who might benefit from the procedure.

Issues surrounding germline gene therapy

The hottest debates about new genetic technologies centre around the prospect of *germline gene therapy*, in which attempts would be made to repair or replace abnormal genes at the early embryonic stage and thereby cure genetic defects. This technology, which could be widely available by 2040 (Nesmith & McKenna, 2000), would bring us to the edge of a slippery slope where human beings will be capable of altering genotypes. This prospect seems perfectly acceptable to many observers, provided it is limited to correcting diagnosed genetic defects (Begley, 2000). However, others point out that permanent modification of a patient's genotype has consequences not only for the patient, but also for all individuals who inherit the modified gene in the future. Germline gene therapy would therefore deny the rights of these descendants to have any choice about whether their genetic make-up should have been modified in the first place, a state of affairs that some view as ethically unacceptable (see Strachan & Read, 1996).

Other critics have argued that approval of germline gene therapy for use with humans will inevitably put us on the path toward positive eugenics—that is, toward genetic enhancement programs that could involve artificial selection for genes thought to confer advantageous traits. This possibility is frightening to many. Who would decide which traits are advantageous and should be selected? Some have argued that parents who have produced many embryos via in vitro fertilization will begin to play God, using DNA screening and germline gene therapy to create what they judge to be the most perfect baby they can produce (Begley, 2000; 2001). Even if the motives of those who would alter genotypes were beyond reproach, would they really be any better at engineering a hardy human race than nature already has through the process of natural selection? Of course, the biggest concern that many people have about germline genetic engineering is its potential for political and social abuse. In the words of two molecular geneticists (Strachan & Read, 1996, p. 586):

> The horrifying nature of *negative eugenics* programs (most recently in Nazi Germany and in many states in the USA where compulsory sterilization of [feeble-minded] individuals was practiced well into the recent century) serves as a reminder ... of the potential Pandora's box of ills that could be released if ever human germline gene therapy were to be attempted.

Methods of Studying Hereditary Influences

Behavioural geneticists use two major strategies to assess hereditary contributions to behaviour: *selective breeding* and *family studies*. Each of these approaches attempts to specify the **heritability** of various attributes—that is, the amount of variation in a trait or a class of behaviour that is attributable to hereditary factors.

heritability
amount of variability in a trait that is attributable to hereditary influence

selective breeding experiment
method of studying genetic influences by determining whether traits can be bred in animals through selective mating

kinship
extent to which two individuals have genes in common

twin design (or twin study)
study in which sets of twins that differ in zygosity (kinship) are compared to determine the heritability of an attribute

adoption design
study in which adoptees are compared with their biological relatives and their adoptive relatives to estimate the heritability of an attribute, or attributes

Selective Breeding

Deliberately manipulating the genetic makeup of animals to study hereditary influences on behaviour is much like what Gregor Mendel did to discover the workings of heredity in plants. A classic example of such a **selective breeding experiment** is Tryon's (1940) attempt to show that maze-learning ability is a heritable attribute in rats. Tryon first tested a large number of rats for the ability to run a complex maze. Rats that made few errors were labelled "maze-bright"; those that made many errors were termed "maze-dull." Then, across several generations, Tryon mated bright rats with other bright rats and dull rats with dull rats. He also controlled the environments to which the rats were exposed to rule out their contribution to differences in maze-learning performance. As Figure 3.11 shows, differences across generations in the maze-learning performances of the maze-bright and maze-dull groups became progressively greater. Clearly, Tryon showed that maze-learning ability in rats is influenced by their genetic makeup. Other investigators have used this same selective breeding technique to show that genes contribute to such attributes as activity level, emotionality, aggressiveness, and sex drive in rats, mice, and chickens (Plomin et al., 1997).

Family Studies

Because people don't take kindly to the idea of being selectively bred by experimenters, human behavioural genetics relies on an alternative methodology known as the *family study*. In a typical family study, persons who live together are compared to see how similar they are on one or more attributes. If the attributes in question are heritable, then the similarity between any two pairs of individuals who live in the same environment should increase as a function of their **kinship**—the extent to which they have the same genes.

Two kinds of family (or kinship) studies are common today. The first is the **twin design**, or twin study, which asks the question, "Are pairs of identical twins reared together more similar to each other on various attributes than pairs of fraternal twins reared together?" If genes affect the attribute(s) in question, identical twins should be more similar because they have 100 percent of their genes in common (kinship = 1.00), whereas fraternal twins share only 50 percent (kinship = .50).

The second common family study, or **adoption design**, focuses on adoptees who are genetically unrelated to other members of their adoptive families. A researcher searching for hereditary influences would ask, "Are adopted children similar

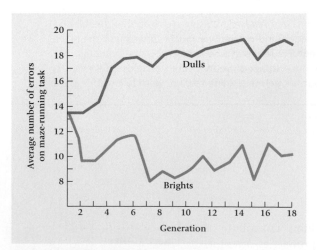

Figure 3.11 *Maze-running performance by inbred maze-bright and maze-dull rats over 18 generations.* FROM PLOMIN ET AL., 1997.

to their biological parents, whose *genes* they share (kinship = .50), or are they similar to their adoptive parents, whose *environment* they share?" If adoptees resemble their biological parents in intelligence or personality, even though these parents did not raise them, then genes must be influential in determining these attributes.

Family studies can also help us to estimate the extent to which various abilities and behaviours are influenced by the environment. To illustrate, consider a case in which two genetically unrelated adopted children are raised in the same home. Their degree of kinship with each other and with their adoptive parents is .00. Consequently, there is no reason to suspect that these children will resemble each other or their adoptive parents unless their common environment plays some part in determining their standing on the attribute in question. Another way the effects of environment can be inferred is to compare identical twins raised in the same environment with identical twins raised in different environments. The kinship of all pairs of identical twins, reared together or apart, is 1.00. So if identical twins reared together are more alike on an attribute than identical twins reared apart, we can infer that the environment plays a role in determining that attribute.

Estimating the Contribution of Genes and Environment

Behavioural geneticists rely on some simple and some not so simple mathematical calculations (1) to determine whether or not a trait is genetically influenced and (2) to estimate the degree to which heredity *and* environment account for individual differences in that trait. When studying traits that a person either does or does not display (for example, a drug habit or clinical depression), researchers calculate and compare **concordance rates**—the percentages of pairs of people (for example, identical twins, fraternal twins, parents and their adoptive children) in which *both* members of the pair display the trait if one member has it. Suppose that you are interested in determining whether homosexuality in men is genetically influenced. You might locate gay men who have twins, either identical or fraternal, and then track down their twin siblings to determine whether they too are gay. As Figure 3.12 shows, the concordance rate for identical twins in one such study was much higher (29 of the 56 co-twins of gay men were also gay) than the concordance rate for fraternal twins (12 of the 54 co-twins were also gay). This suggests that genotype does contribute to a man's sexual orientation. But because identical twins are not perfectly concordant for sexual orientation, we can also conclude that their *experiences* (that is, environmental influences) must also influence their sexual orientations—48 percent of the identical twin pairs had *different* sexual orientations, despite their identical genes.

For continuous traits that can assume many values (for example, height or intelligence), behavioural geneticists estimate hereditary contributions by calculating *correlation coefficients* rather than concordance rates. In a study of IQ scores, for example, a correlation coefficient would indicate whether the IQ scores of twins are systematically

Figure 3.12 *Concordance rates for homosexuality in 110 male twin pairs. From the higher concordance for identical twin pairs, we can infer that genes influence one's sexual orientation.* Based on Bailey & Pillard, 1991.

Table 3.4	Average Correlation Coefficients for Intelligence-Test Scores from Family Studies Involving Persons at Four Levels of Kinship	
Genetic relationship (kinship)	**Reared together (in same home)**	**Reared apart (in different homes)**
Unrelated siblings (kinship = .00)	+.34	–.01*
Adoptive parent/adoptive offspring (kinship = .00)	+.19	–
Half-siblings (kinship = .25)	+.31	–
Biological parent/child (kinship = .50)	+.42	+.22
Siblings (kinship = .50)	+.47	+.24
Twins		
Fraternal (kinship = .50)	+.60	+.52
Identical (kinship = 1.00)	+.86	+.72

*This is the correlation obtained from random pairings of unrelated people living apart.
Source: Bouchard & McGue, 1981.

concordance rate
percentage of cases in which a particular attribute is present for one member of a twin pair if it is present for the other

related to the IQ scores of their co-twins. Larger correlations indicate closer resemblances in IQ, thus implying that if one twin is bright, the other is bright too, and if one twin is dull, the other is probably dull as well.

As we noted earlier, behavioural genetics studies always tell us about *both* genetic and environmental influences on development. This point is easily illustrated by considering a review of family studies of intellectual performance (IQ) based on 113 942 pairs of children, adolescents, or adults, the results of which appear in Table 3.4. Here we will focus on the twin correlations (identical and fraternal) to show how behavioural geneticists can estimate the contributions of three factors to individual differences in intellectual performance (IQ).

Gene Influences

Genetic influences on IQ are clearly evident in Table 3.4. The correlations become higher when pairs of people are more closely related genetically and are highest when the pairs are identical twins. But just how strong is the hereditary influence?

Behavioural geneticists use statistical techniques to estimate the amount of variation in a trait that is attributable to hereditary factors. This index, called a **heritability coefficient**, is calculated as follows from twin data:

$H = (r$ identical twins $- r$ fraternal twins$) \times 2$

In words, the equation reads: Heritability of an attribute equals the correlation between identical twins minus the correlation between fraternal twins, all multiplied by a factor of 2 (Plomin, 1990).

Now we can estimate the contribution that genes make to individual differences in intellectual performance. If we focus on sets of twins raised together from Table 3.4, our estimate becomes

$H = (.86 - .60) \times 2 = .52$

The resulting heritability estimate for IQ is .52, which, on a scale ranging from 0 (not at all heritable) to 1.00 (totally heritable) is moderate at best. We might conclude that, within the populations from which our twins reared together came, IQ is influenced to a moderate extent by hereditary factors. However, it appears that much of the variability among people on this trait is attributable to nonhereditary factors—that is, to environmental influences and to errors we may have made in measuring the trait (no measure is perfect).

Interestingly, the data in Table 3.4 also allow us to estimate the contributions of *two* sources of environmental influence: nonshared environmental influences and shared environmental influences.

Nonshared environmental influences (NSE) are experiences that are unique to the individual—experiences that are *not* shared by other members of the family and thus make family members *different* from each other (Rowe & Plomin, 1981; Rowe, 1994). Where is evidence of nonshared environmental influence in Table 3.4? Notice that identical twins raised together are not perfectly similar in IQ, even though they share 100 percent of their genes and the same family environment: A correlation of +.86, though substantial, is less than a perfect correlation of +1.00. Because identical twins share the same genes and family environment, any *differences* between twins raised together necessarily must result from differences in their *experiences*. Perhaps they were treated differently by friends, or perhaps one twin favours puzzles and other intellectual games more than the other twin does. Because the only factors that can make identical twins raised together any *different* from each other are experiences they do *not* share, we can estimate the influence of nonshared environmental influences by the following formula (Rowe & Plomin, 1981):

$NSE = 1 - r$ (identical twins reared together)

heritability coefficient
numerical estimate, ranging from .00 to +1.00, of the amount of variation in an attribute that is attributable to hereditary factors

nonshared environmental influence (NSE)
environmental influence that people living together do not share that should make these individuals different from one another

So, the contribution of nonshared environmental influences to individual differences in IQ performance (that is, 1 – .86 = .14) is small, but detectable. As we will see, nonshared environmental influences make a bigger contribution to other attributes, most notably personality traits.

Shared environmental influences (SE) are experiences that individuals living in the same home environment share and that conspire to make them *similar* to each other. As you can see in Table 3.4, both identical and fraternal twins (and, indeed, biological siblings and pairs of unrelated individuals) show a greater intellectual resemblance if they live together than if they live apart. One reason that growing up in the same home may increase children's degree of intellectual similarity is that parents model similar interests for *all* their children and tend to rely on similar strategies to foster their intellectual growth (Hoffman, 1991; Lewin et al., 1993).

How do we estimate the contribution of shared environmental influence (SE) to a trait? One rough estimate can be made as follows:

$$SE = 1 - (H + NSE)$$

Translated, the equation reads: Shared environmental influences on a trait equal 1 (the total variation for that trait) minus the variation attributable to genes (*H*) *and* nonshared environmental influences (NSE). Previously, we found that the heritability of IQ in our twins-reared-together sample was .52, and the contribution of nonshared environment was .14. So, the contribution of shared environmental influences to individual differences in IQ (that is, SE = 1 – [.52 + .14] = .34) is moderate and meaningful.

One final note: Although heritability coefficients are useful for estimating whether genes make any meaningful contribution to various human attributes, these statistics are poorly understood and often misinterpreted. Box 3.3 takes a closer look at what heritability estimates *can* and *cannot* tell us.

Hereditary Influences on Intellectual Performance

As we have seen from data presented in Table 3.4, IQ is a moderately heritable attribute; genes account for about half the total variation in people's IQ scores. But because the correlations presented in Table 3.4 are based on studies of children *and* adults, they do not tell us whether the contributions of genes and environment to individual differences in intellectual performance might change over time. Might genes be more important early in life, whereas differences in our home and school experiences increasingly account for the variations we show in intellectual performance as we get older? Sensible as this idea may sound, it seems to be wrong. As children mature, genes actually seem to contribute *more* (rather than less) to individual differences in their IQs (Plomin et al., 1997).

Consider a longitudinal study of the intellectual development of twins reported by Ronald Wilson (1978, 1983). Wilson found that identical twins were no more similar than fraternal twins on tests of infant mental development during the first year of life. By age 18 months, however, genetic influences were already detectable. Not only did identical twins show a greater resemblance in test performance than fraternal twins did, but *changes* in test scores from one testing to the next also became more similar for identical twins than for fraternal twins. If one identical twin had a big spurt in mental development between 18 and 24 months of age, the other twin was likely to show a similar spurt at the same time. So it seemed as if genes were now influencing both the *course* and the *extent* of infants' mental development.

Figure 3.13 shows what happened as these twins continued to develop. Identical twins remained highly similar in their intellectual performance (average *r* = +.85) from age 3 through age 15. By contrast, fraternal twins were most similar intellectually at age

shared environmental influence (SE)
environmental influence that people living together share that should make these individuals similar to one another

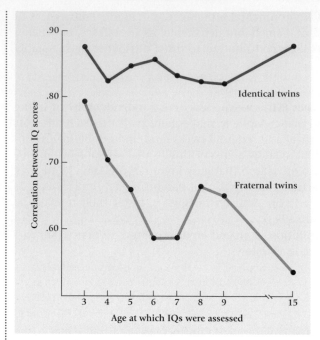

Figure 3.13 *Changes in the correlation between the IQ scores of identical and fraternal twins over childhood.* DATA FROM WILSON, 1983.

3 (*r* = +.79) and gradually became less similar over time. By age 15, they showed no greater intellectual resemblance (*r* = +.54) than pairs of nontwin siblings. Notice, then, that if we calculated heritability coefficients at each age shown in Figure 3.13, the heritability of IQ for these twin samples would actually increase from infancy to adolescence.

Adoption studies paint a similar picture. The IQs of adopted children are correlated with the intellectual performances of both their biological parents (suggesting a genetic influence) and their adoptive parents (indicating effects of shared family environment). By adolescence, the resemblance to biological parents is still apparent, but adoptees no longer resemble their adoptive parents intellectually (Scarr & Weinberg, 1978). What seems to be happening, in both the twin and the adoption studies, is that the influence of shared environment on intellectual performance declines with age, whereas the influence of both genes and nonshared environment become increasingly stronger. A very influential theory accounts for these changing patterns of influence on IQ scores (and on personality traits as well). But before we examine this theory, let's briefly review the evidence that suggests that our personalities are influenced by the genes we have inherited.

Hereditary Contributions to Personality

Although psychologists have typically assumed that the relatively stable habits and traits that make up our personalities are shaped by our environments, family studies and other longitudinal projects reveal that many core dimensions of personality are genetically influenced. For example, **introversion/extroversion**—the extent to which a person is shy, retiring, and uncomfortable around others versus outgoing and socially oriented— shows about the same moderate level of heritability as IQ does (Plomin et al., 1997). Another important attribute that is genetically influenced is **empathic concern**. A person high in empathy recognizes the needs of others and is concerned about their welfare. In Box 2.4 we saw that newborn infants react to the distress of another infant by becoming distressed themselves—a finding that implies to some investigators that the capacity for empathy may be innate. But are there any biological bases for *individual differences* in empathic concern?

Indeed there are. As early as 14 to 20 months of age, identical twin infants are already more similar in their levels of concern for distressed companions than fraternal twin infants are (Zahn-Waxler, Robinson, & Emde, 1992). And by middle age, identical

introversion/extroversion
opposite poles of a personality dimension: Introverts are shy, anxious around others, and tend to withdraw from social situations; extroverts are highly sociable and enjoy being with others

empathic concern
measure of the extent to which an individual recognizes the needs of others and is concerned about their welfare

Some Common Misconceptions about Heritability Estimates

Heritability coefficients are controversial statistics that are poorly understood and frequently misapplied. One of the biggest misconceptions that people hold is the notion that heritability coefficients can tell us whether we have inherited a trait. *This idea is simply incorrect.* When we talk about the heritability of an attribute, we are referring to the extent to which *differences* among individuals with that attribute are related to differences in the genes that they have inherited (Plomin, 1994). To illustrate that *heritable* means something other than *inherited*, consider that everyone inherits two eyes. Agreed? Yet the heritability of eyes is .00, simply because everyone has two and there are no individual differences in "eyeness" (except for those attributable to environmental events such as accidents).

In interpreting heritability coefficients, it is important to recognize that these estimates apply only to populations and *never to individuals*. So if you studied the heights of many pairs of 5-year-old twins and estimated the heritability of height to be .70, you could infer that a major reason that 5-year-olds *differ* in height is that they have different genes. But since heritability estimates say nothing about individuals, it is clearly inappropriate to conclude from an *H* of .70 that 70 percent of Shannon Jones's height is inherited, while the remaining 30 percent reflects the contribution of environment.

Let's also note that heritability estimates refer only to the particular trait in question as displayed by members of a *particular population* under *particular environmental circumstances*. Indeed, heritability coefficients may differ substantially for different research populations raised in different environments (Rowe, 1999). Suppose, for example, that we located a large number of identical and fraternal twin infants, each of whom was raised in an impoverished orphanage in which his or her crib was lined with sheets that prevented much visual or social contact with other infants or with adult caregivers. Previous research (which we will examine in Chapter 11) suggests that, if we measured

how sociable these infants are, we would find that they vary somewhat in sociability, but that virtually all of them are much less sociable than babies raised at home—a finding that we could reasonably attribute to their socially-depriving early environment. But because all these twins experienced the *same depriving environment*, the only reason that they might show any *differences* in sociability is the result of differences in their genetic predispositions. The heritability coefficient for sociability would actually approach 1.0 in this population—a far cry from the *H*s of .25 to .40 found in studies of other infants raised at home with parents (Plomin, 1994).

Finally, people have assumed that clearly heritable traits cannot be modified by environmental influences. *This, too, is a false assumption!* In Chapter 11, we will see that the depressed sociability of institutionalized infants can be improved substantially by placing them in socially-responsive adoptive homes. Similarly, in Chapter 9, we will see that children who score low on the heritable attribute of IQ can improve dramatically their intellectual and academic performances when exposed to intellectually-stimulating home and school environments. To assume that *heritable* means *unchangeable* (as some critics of compensatory education have done) is to commit a potentially grievous error based on a common misconception about the meaning of heritability coefficients.

In sum, the term *heritable* is not a synonym for *inherited*, and heritability estimates, which may vary widely across populations and environments, can tell us nothing about the development of individuals. And though heritability estimates are useful for helping us to determine whether there is any hereditary basis for the *differences* people display on any attribute we might care to study, they say nothing about children's capacity for change and should not be used to make public policy decisions that could constrain children's development or adversely affect their welfare.

---

twins who have lived apart for many years since leaving home still resemble each other on measures of empathic concern ($r = +.41$), whereas fraternal twins do not ($r = +.05$), thus suggesting that this attribute is a reasonably heritable trait (Matthews et al., 1981). In fact, the authors of this adult twin study noted that "If empathic concern … leads to altruistic motivation, [our] study provides evidence for a genetic basis for individual differences in altruism" (p. 246).

How Much Genetic Influence?

To what extent are our personalities influenced by the genes we have inherited? We get some idea by looking at personality resemblances among family members, as shown in Table 3.5. Note that identical twins are more similar to each other on this composite measure of personality than fraternal twins are. Were we to use the twin data to estimate the genetic contribution to personality, we might conclude that many personality traits are moderately heritable (i.e., $H = +.40$). Of course, one implication of a moderate heritability coefficient is that personality is heavily influenced by environmental factors.

TABLE 3.5	Personality Resemblances among Family Members at Three Levels of Kinship			
	Kinship			
	1.00 (identical twins)	**.50 (fraternal twins)**	**.50 (nontwin siblings)**	**.00 (unrelated children raised in the same household)**
Personality attributes (average correlations across several personality traits)	.50	.30	.20	.07

Sources: Loehlin, 1985; Loehlin and Nichols, 1976

Which Aspects of Environment Influence Personality?

Developmentalists have traditionally assumed that the home environment that individuals *share* is especially important in shaping their personalities. Now examine Table 3.5 again and see if you can find some problems with this logic. Notice, for example, that genetically unrelated individuals who live in the same home barely resemble each other on the composite personality measure (*r* = .07). Therefore, aspects of the home environment that all family members *share* must not contribute much to the development of personality.

How, then, does environment affect personality? According to behavioural geneticists David Rowe and Robert Plomin (Rowe & Plomin, 1981; Rowe, 1994) the aspects of environment that contribute most heavily to personality are *nonshared environmental influences*—influences that make individuals *different* from each other. And there are many sources of nonshared experience in a typical home. Parents, for example, often treat sons differently from daughters, or first-born children differently than later-born children. To the extent that siblings are not treated alike by parents, they will experience different environments, which will increase the likelihood that their personalities will differ in important ways. Interactions among siblings provide another source of nonshared environmental influence. For example, an older sibling who habitually dominates a younger one may become generally assertive and dominant as a result of these home experiences. But for the younger child, this home environment is a dominating environment that may foster the development of such personality traits as passivity, tolerance, and cooperation.

MEASURING THE EFFECTS OF NONSHARED ENVIRONMENTS. How could we ever measure the impact of something as broad as nonshared environments? One strategy used by Denise Daniels and her associates (Daniels, 1986; Daniels & Plomin, 1985) is simply to ask pairs of adolescent siblings whether they have been treated differently by parents and teachers or have experienced other important differences in their lives (for example, differences in their popularity with peers). Daniels finds that siblings do report such differences, and, more important, the greater the *differences* in parental treatment and other experiences that siblings report, the more dissimilar siblings are in their personalities. Although correlational studies of this sort do not conclusively establish that differences in experiences *cause* differences in personality, they do suggest that some of the most important environmental influences on development may be nonshared experiences unique to each member of the family (Dunn & Plomin, 1990).

DO SIBLINGS HAVE DIFFERENT EXPERIENCES BECAUSE THEY HAVE DIFFERENT GENES? Stated another way, isn't it possible that a child's genetically influenced attributes might affect how other people respond to him or her, so that a physically attractive youngster, for example, is apt to be treated very differently by parents and peers than a less attractive sibling would be? Although genes do contribute to some extent to the different experiences that siblings have (Pike et al., 1996; Plomin et al., 1994), there is ample reason to believe that our highly individualized, unique environments result not entirely from our having inherited different genes. How do we know this?

The most important clue comes from studies of identical twins. Because identical twins are perfectly matched from a genetic standpoint, any *differences* between them must necessarily reflect the contribution of environmental influences that they do *not* share. Clearly, these nonshared environmental influences cannot be attributed to the twins' different genes, because identical twins have identical genotypes! This is why the formula for estimating the contribution of nonshared environmental influences (that is, $1 - r$ [identical twins raised together]) makes sense, because the estimate it provides is based on environmental influences that are *not* in any way influenced by genes.

With these facts in mind, let's return to Table 3.5. Here we see that the average correlation for identical twins across many personality traits is only +.50, which implies that identical twins are similar in some respects and different in others. Applying the formula for estimating NSE $(1 - .50 = .50)$ tells us that nonshared environmental influences are very important contributors to personality—at least as important as genes are.

In sum, the family environment does make important contributions to personality, but not simply because it has a standard effect on all family members that makes them alike. True, there are some important areas of socialization for which parents do treat all their children alike and foster similarities among them. For example, parents often model and encourage the same moral, religious, social, and political interests and values in all their children. For these and many other psychological characteristics, *shared environmental influences* are often as important as, or even more important than, genes are in creating likenesses between brothers and sisters (Bussell et al., 1999; Hoffman, 1991, 1994). But when it comes to the shaping of many other basic personality traits, it is the *nonshared* experiences people have—in concert with genetic influences—that contribute most to their phenotypes (McGue, Sharma, & Benson, 1996; Pike et al., 1996; Plomin et al., 1997).

Hereditary Contributions to Behaviour Disorders and Mental Illness

Is there a hereditary basis for mental illness? Might some people be genetically predisposed to commit deviant or antisocial acts? Although these ideas seemed absurd 30 years ago, it now appears that the answer to both questions is a qualified yes.

Consider the evidence for **schizophrenia**—a serious mental illness, characterized by severe disturbances in logical thinking, emotional expression, and social behaviour, which typically emerges in late adolescence or early adulthood. A survey of several twin studies of schizophrenia suggests an average concordance rate of .48 for identical twins but only .17 for fraternal twins (Gottesman, 1991). In addition, children who have a biological parent who is schizophrenic are at increased risk of becoming schizophrenic themselves, even if they are adopted by another family early in life (Loehlin, 1992). These are strong indications that schizophrenia is genetically influenced.

In recent years, it has also become clear that heredity contributes to abnormal behaviours and conditions such as alcoholism, criminality, depression, hyperactivity, **manic-depressive** psychosis, and a number of **neurotic disorders** (Plomin et al., 1997; Rowe, 1994). Now, it is possible that you may have close relatives who were diagnosed as alcoholic, neurotic, manic depressive, or schizophrenic. Rest assured that this does *not* mean that you or your children will develop these problems. Only 9 percent of children who have one schizophrenic parent ever develop any symptoms that might be labelled schizophrenic (Plomin et al., 1997). Even if you are an identical twin whose co-

schizophrenia
serious form of mental illness characterized by disturbances in logical thinking, emotional expression, and interpersonal behaviour

manic depression
psychotic disorder characterized by extreme fluctuations in mood

neurotic disorder
irrational pattern of thinking or behaviour that a person may use to contend with stress or to avoid anxiety

twin has a serious psychiatric disorder, the odds are only between 1 in 2 (for schizophrenia) and 1 in 20 (for most other disorders) that you would ever experience anything that even approaches the problem that affects your twin.

Because identical twins are usually *discordant* (that is, not alike) with respect to mental illnesses and behaviour disorders, environment must be a very important contributor to these conditions. In other words, people do not inherit behavioural disorders; instead they inherit *predispositions* to develop certain illnesses or deviant patterns of behaviour. And even when a child's family history suggests that such a genetic predisposition may exist, it usually takes a number of very stressful experiences (for example, rejecting parents, a failure or series of failures at school, or a family breakup due to divorce) to trigger a mental illness (Plomin & Rende, 1991; Rutter, 1979). These findings provide some basis for optimism, in that it may someday be possible to prevent the onset of most genetically influenced disorders should we (1) learn more about the environmental triggers that precipitate these disturbances while (2) striving to develop interventions or therapeutic techniques that will help high-risk individuals to maintain their emotional stability in the face of environmental stress (Plomin & Rutter, 1998).

HEREDITY AND ENVIRONMENT AS DEVELOPMENTAL CO-CONSPIRATORS

Only 30 years ago, developmentalists were embroiled in the nature/nurture controversy: Was heredity or environment the primary determinant of human potential? Although this chapter has focused on biological influences, it should now be clear that *both* heredity and environment contribute importantly to development and that the often extreme positions taken by the hereditarians and environmentalists in the past are grossly oversimplified. Today, behavioural geneticists no longer think in terms of nature *versus* nurture; instead, they try to determine how these two important influences might combine or interact to promote developmental change.

The Canalization Principle

canalization
genetic restriction of phenotype to a small number of developmental outcomes; a highly canalized attribute is one for which genes channel development along predetermined pathways, so that the environment has little effect on the phenotype that emerges

Although both heredity and environment contribute to most human traits, our genes influence some attributes more than others. Many years ago, Conrad Waddington (1966) used the term **canalization** to refer to cases where genes limit or restrict development to a small number of outcomes. One example of a highly canalized human attribute is

Concept Check 3.3
Estimating Hereditary and Environmental Influences

A behavioural geneticist conducts a study of twins to try to determine whether heredity contributes in any meaningful way to the personality trait of creativity. She finds that the correlation between identical twins on this attribute is +.61, whereas the correlation between fraternal twins is +.50 (data from Plomin, 1990). Check your answers in the Appendix.

_____ 1. The hereditary contribution to creativity is best described as
(a) substantial (b) moderate (c) low

_____ 2. Do either shared environmental influences (SE) or nonshared environmental influences (NSE) contribute more than heredity does to individual differences in creativity?
(a) Both SE and NSE contribute more than heredity does.
(b) Only NSE contributes more than heredity does.
(c) Only SE contributes more than heredity does.
(d) Neither SE nor NSE contributes more than heredity does.

babbling in infancy. All infants, even deaf ones, babble in pretty much the same way over the first 8 to 10 months of life. The environment has little if any effect on this highly canalized attribute, which simply unfolds according to the maturational program in our genes. By contrast, less canalized attributes such as intelligence, temperament, and personality can be deflected away from their genetic pathways in any of several directions by a variety of life experiences.

Interestingly, we now know that potent *environmental* influences can also limit, or canalize, development. In Chapter 2, for example, we discussed Gilbert Gottlieb's (1991a) intriguing finding that duckling embryos exposed to chicken calls before hatching come to prefer the calls of chickens to those of their own mothers. In this case, the ducklings' prenatal *experiences* (environment) overrode the presumably canalized genetic predisposition to favour the vocalization of their own species. Environments may also canalize human development. For example, we will see in Chapters 5 and 9 that early environments in which nutrition and social stimulation are inadequate can permanently stunt children's growth and impair their intellectual development.

The canalization principle is a simple idea—yet a very useful one that illustrates that (1) there are multiple pathways along which an individual might develop, (2) nature and nurture combine to determine these pathways, and (3) either genes or environment may limit the extent to which the other factor can influence development. Irving Gottesman (1963) makes the same points about gene influences in a slightly different way in his own theory of genotype/environment interactions.

The Range-of-Reaction Principle

According to Gottesman (1963), genes typically do not rigidly canalize behaviour. Instead, an individual genotype establishes a range of possible responses to different kinds of life experiences: the so-called **range of reaction**. In other words, Gottesman claims that genotype sets boundaries on the range of possible phenotypes that one might display to different environments. An important corollary is that because people differ genetically, no two individuals should respond in precisely the same way to any particular environment.

The concept of reaction range, as applied to intellectual performance, is illustrated in Figure 3.14. Here we see the effects of varying degrees of environmental enrichment on the IQs of three children: Raj, who has high genetic potential for intellectual devel-

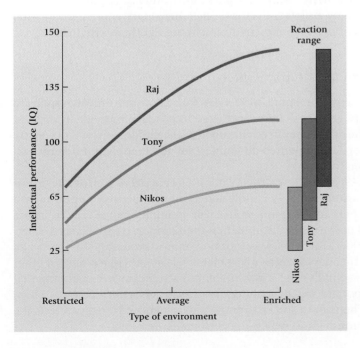

Figure 3.14 *Hypothetical reaction ranges for the intellectual performances of three children in restricted, average, and intellectually enriching environments.* ADAPTED FROM GOTTESMAN, *1963.*

range-of-reaction principle
idea that genotype sets limits on the range of possible phenotypes that a person might display in response to different environments

opment, Tony, whose genetic endowment for intelligence is average, and Nikos, whose potential for intellectual growth is far below average. Notice that under similar environmental conditions, Raj always outperforms the other two children. Raj also has the widest reaction range, in that his IQ might vary from well below average in a restricted environment to far above average in an enriched environment. By contrast, Nikos has a very limited reaction range; his potential for intellectual development is low and, as a result, he shows smaller variation in IQ across environments than do the other two children.

In sum, the range-of-reaction principle is a clear statement about the interplay between heredity and environment. Presumably, an individual's genotype sets a range of possible outcomes for any particular attribute, and the environment largely influences where, within that range, he or she will fall.

Genotype/Environment Correlations

Up until now, we have talked as if heredity and environment were *independent* sources of influence that somehow combine to determine our observable characteristics, or phenotypes. This view is probably much too simple. Many behavioural geneticists now believe that our genes may actually influence the kinds of environments that we are likely to experience (Plomin, DeFries, & Loehlin, 1977; Scarr & McCartney, 1983). This occurs in at least three ways.

Passive Genotype/Environment Correlations

According to Scarr and McCartney (1983), the kind of home environment that parents provide for their children is influenced, in part, by the parents' own genotypes. And because parents also provide their children with genes, it so happens that the rearing environments to which children are exposed are correlated with (and are likely to suit) their own genotypes.

The following example illustrates a developmental implication of these **passive genotype/environment correlations**. Parents who are genetically predisposed to be athletic may create a very athletic home environment by encouraging their children to play vigorously and take an interest in sporting activities. Besides being exposed to an athletic environment, the children may have inherited their parents' athletic genes, which might make them particularly responsive to that environment. So children of athletic parents may come to enjoy athletic pursuits for *both* hereditary and environmental reasons, and the influences of heredity and environment are tightly intertwined.

Evocative Genotype/Environment Correlations

Earlier, we noted that the environmental influences that contribute most heavily to many aspects of personality are nonshared experiences that make individuals *different* from one another. Might the differences in environments that children experience partly result from the fact that they have inherited different genes and may elicit different reactions from their companions?

Scarr and McCartney (1983) think so. Their notion of **evocative genotype/environment correlations** assumes that a child's genetically influenced attributes will affect the behaviour of others toward him or her. For example, happy, active babies receive more attention and positive social stimulation than moody, passive ones (Deater-Deckard & O'Connor, 2000). Educators may respond more favourably to physically attractive students than to their less attractive classmates. Clearly, these *reactions* of other people to the child (and the child's genetically influenced attributes) are environmental influences that play an important role in shaping that child's personality. So once again, we see an intermingling of hereditary and environmental influences: Heredity affects the character of the social environment in which the personality develops.

passive genotype/ environment correlations
notion that the rearing environments that biological parents provide are influenced by the parents' own genes, and hence are correlated with the child's own genotype

evocative genotype/ environment correlations
notion that our heritable attributes affect others' behaviour toward us and thus influence the social environment in which development takes place

Active Genotype/Environment Correlations

Finally, Scarr and McCartney (1983) propose that the environments that children prefer and seek out will be those that are most compatible with their genetic predispositions. For example, a child genetically predisposed to be extroverted is likely to invite friends to the house, to be an avid party-goer, and to generally prefer activities that are socially stimulating. By contrast, a child who is genetically predisposed to be shy and introverted may actively avoid large social gatherings and choose instead to pursue activities such as coin collecting that can be done alone. One implication of these **active genotype/environment correlations** is that people with different genotypes will *select* different environmental niches for themselves—niches that may then have a powerful effect on their future social, emotional, and intellectual development.

How Do Genotype/Environment Correlations Influence Development?

According to Scarr and McCartney (1983), the relative importance of active, passive, and evocative gene influences changes over the course of childhood. During the first few years infants and toddlers are not free to roam the neighbourhood, choosing friends and building environmental niches. Most of their time is spent at home in an environment that parents structure for them, so that passive genotype/environment correlations are particularly important early in life. But once children reach school age and venture away from home on a daily basis, they suddenly become much freer to select their own interests, activities, friends, and hangouts. So active, niche-building correlations should exert a greater influence on development as the child matures (see Figure 3.15). Finally, evocative genotype/environment correlations are always important; that is, a person's genetically influenced attributes and patterns of behaviour may influence the ways other people react to him or her throughout life.

If Scarr and McCartney's theory has any merit, virtually all siblings other than identical twins should become less similar over time as they emerge from the relatively similar rearing environments that parents impose during the early years and begin to actively select different environmental niches for themselves. Indeed, there is ample support for this idea. Pairs of genetically unrelated adoptees who live in the same home do show some definite similarities in conduct and in intellectual performance during early and middle childhood (Scarr & Weinberg, 1978). Because these adoptees share no genes with each other or with their adoptive parents, their resemblances must be a result of their common rearing environments. Yet, by late adolescence, genetically unrelated siblings barely resemble each other in intelligence, personality, or any other aspect of behaviour, presumably because they have selected very different environmental niches, which, in turn, have steered them along different developmental paths (Scarr, 1992; Scarr & McCartney, 1983). Even fraternal twins, who have 50 percent of their genes in

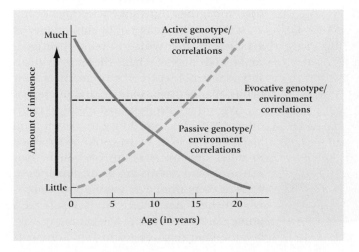

Figure 3.15 *Relative influence of passive, evocative, and active (niche-picking) genotype/environment correlations as a function of age.*

active genotype/ environment correlations notion that our genotypes affect the types of environments that we prefer and seek out common, are much less alike as adolescents or adults than they were as children (McCartney, Harris, & Bernieri, 1990; and recall the declining resemblance in fraternal twins' IQs over time as shown in Figure 3.13). Apparently the genes that fraternal twins do *not* share cause these individuals to select different environmental niches, which in turn, contribute to their declining resemblance over time.

By contrast, pairs of identical twins bear a close behavioural resemblance throughout childhood and adolescence. Why? For two reasons: (1) Not only do identical twins evoke similar reactions from other people, but (2) their identical genotypes predispose them to prefer and select very *similar* environments (that is, friends, interests, and activities), which will then exert comparable influences on these twin pairs and virtually guarantee that they will continue to resemble one another. Even identical twins raised apart should be similar in some respects, since their identical genes cause them to seek out and prefer similar activities and experiences. Let's take a closer look.

SEPARATED IDENTICAL TWINS. Thomas Bouchard and his associates (Bouchard et al., 1990; Neimark, 2000) have studied nearly 100 pairs of *separated identical twins*—people with identical genes who were raised in different home environments. One such pair was Oscar Stohr and Jack Yufe. Oscar was raised as a Catholic by his mother in Nazi-dominated Europe. He became involved in the Hitler Youth Movement during World War II and is now employed as a factory supervisor in Germany. Jack, a store owner, was raised as a Jew and came to loathe Nazis while growing up in a Caribbean country halfway around the world. Today, Jack is a political liberal, whereas Oscar is extremely conservative.

Like every pair of separated identical twins that Bouchard has studied, Oscar and Jack are different in some very noteworthy respects. One twin is usually more self-assured, outgoing, or aggressive than the other, or perhaps has a different religious or political philosophy (as Jack and Oscar do). Yet perhaps the more remarkable finding is that all these twin pairs also show a number of striking similarities. As young men, for example, Oscar and Jack both excelled at sports and had difficulty with math. They have similar mannerisms, and both tend to be absent minded. And then there are the little things, such as their common tastes for spicy foods and sweet liqueurs, their habit of storing rubber bands on their wrists, and their preference for flushing the toilet *before* and after using it.

How can separated identical twins be so different and, at the same time, so similar to each other? The concept of *active gene influences* helps explain the uncanny resemblances. When we learn that twins grow up in different environments, we tend to think of these settings as more dissimilar than they really are. In fact, identical twins raised apart are members of the same life cohort who are likely to be exposed to many of the same kinds of objects, activities, educational experiences, and historical events as they are growing up. So, if identical twins are genetically predisposed to select comparable aspects of the environment for special attention, and if their different environments provide them with reasonably similar sets of experiences from which to build their environmental niches, then these individuals should resemble each other in many of their habits, mannerisms, abilities, and interests.

Why, then, do separated identical twins often differ? According to Scarr and McCartney (1983), twins could be expected to differ on any attribute for which their rearing environments are so dissimilar as to prevent them from ever establishing comparable niches. Oscar Stohr and Jack Yufe are a prime example. They are alike in many ways because their separate rearing environments

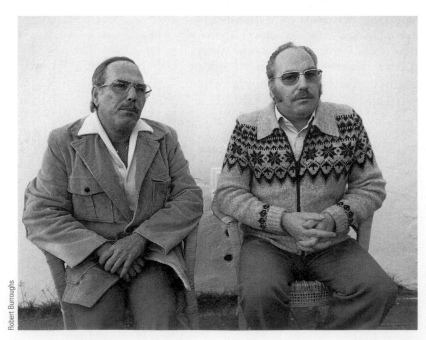

Jack Yufe (left) and Oscar Stohr (right)

Robert Burroughs

permitted them access to many of the same kinds of experiences (for example, sports, math classes, spicy foods, rubber bands), thereby enabling those genetically identical individuals to develop several similar habits, mannerisms, and interests. However, it was almost inevitable that they would differ in their political ideologies because their sociopolitical environments (Nazi-dominated Europe vs. the laid-back Caribbean) were so *dissimilar* as to prevent them from ever building the kinds of niches that would make them staunch political allies.

CONTRIBUTIONS AND CRITICISMS OF THE BEHAVIOURAL GENETICS APPROACH

Behavioural genetics is a relatively new discipline that is having a strong influence on the way scientists look at human development. We now know, for example, that many attributes previously thought to be shaped by environment are influenced, in part, by genes. As Scarr and McCartney put it, we are products of "cooperative efforts of the nature/nurture team, directed by the genetic quarterback" (1983, p. 433). In effect, genes may exert many of their influences on human development by affecting the experiences we have, which in turn influence our behaviour. And one very important implication of their viewpoint is that many of the environmental influences on development that have previously been identified may reflect, in part, the workings of heredity (Plomin et al., 1997).

Of course, not all developmentalists would agree that genetic endowment is the "quarterback" of the "nature/nurture team" (Gottlieb, 1996; Wachs, 1992; and see the debate about parenting in Box 3.4). Students often object to Scarr and McCartney's theory because they sometimes read it to mean that genes *determine* environments. But this is not what the theory implies. What Scarr and McCartney are saying is this:

1. People with different genotypes are likely to evoke different responses from others and to select different environmental niches for themselves.

2. However, the responses they evoke and the niches they select depend to no small extent on the particular individuals, settings, and circumstances they encounter. Although a child must be genetically predisposed to be outgoing and extroverted, for example, it would be difficult to act on this predisposition if she lived in the wilds of the Northwest Territories with a reclusive father. In fact, this youngster could well become rather shy and reserved when raised in such an asocial environment.

? WHAT DO YOU THINK?

Serbin, Peters, & Schwartzman (1996) at Concordia University followed the medical experiences of children born to mothers who were rated as aggressive, aggressive-withdrawn, or normal in their own childhood. The researchers assessed the number of emergency room visits as well as injuries, illnesses, and medical consultations that the children of these mothers experienced in their first four years of life. The sons of women who had been rated as aggressive and the sons and daughters of women who had been rated as aggressive-withdrawn had much higher levels of emergency room and other treatment issues. How would you use this information to support the interplay between environment and heredity?

In sum, genotypes and environments *interact* to produce developmental change and variations in developmental outcomes. True, genes exert some influence on those aspects of the environment that we are likely to experience. But the particular environments available to us limit the possible phenotypes that are likely to emerge from a particular genotype (Gottlieb, 1991b, 1996). Perhaps Donald Hebb (1980) was not far off when he said that behaviour is determined 100 percent by heredity and 100 percent by the environment, because it seems that these two sets of influences are complexly intertwined.

Interesting as these new ideas may be, critics argue that the behavioural genetics approach is merely a descriptive overview of how development might proceed rather than a well-articulated *explanation* of development. One reason for this sentiment is that we know so little about how genes exert their effects. Genes are coded to manufacture

Need Parenting Be "Good" or Simply "Good Enough"?

True or False? Within typical families, parenting practices have a major influence on children's development.

In Chapter 2, we saw that John Watson (1928) advised parents to take their role very seriously, for he believed that parents had the power to shape their children's destiny. Sandra Scarr (1992) disagrees with Watson, arguing that parents do not have the power to mold children in any way they see fit. Yet in some ways, Scarr's viewpoint is every bit as controversial as Watson's. She believes that human beings have evolved in ways that make them responsive to a wide range of environments and that:

1. Within the broad range of home environments that are typical of the human species, children display normal, adaptive patterns of development.

2. Particular child-rearing practices do not influence developmental outcomes to any great extent.

3. Only those home environments that fall far outside the normal range (for example, those in which parents are violent, abusive, or neglectful) are likely to seriously constrain development and produce maladaptive outcomes.

Of course, Scarr assumes that different children respond in somewhat different ways to the typical (or "average expectable") home environment, resulting in large part from the fact that they have different genes. However, Scarr also believes that a child's or an adolescent's development is so influenced by the reactions he or she evokes from people other than parents and by the environmental niches he or she constructs that parental child-rearing practices have little effect on development, provided that these practices are "good enough" (that is, within the range of what might be considered normal for human beings). So, in contrast to Watson, who advocated super parenting, Scarr states that parents need only provide an "average expectable environment" in order to foster healthy development and fulfil their own role as effective guardians. She states that:

> Children's outcomes do not depend on whether parents take (them) to a ball game or a museum so much as they depend on genetic transmission, on plentiful opportunities, and on having a *good enough* environment that supports children's development to become themselves. (Scarr, 1992, p. 15; emphasis added)

What do you think about Scarr's propositions? Many developmentalists were quick to criticize them. Diana Baumrind (1993), for example, points out that different child-rearing practices that fall well within what Scarr considers the range of "good enough" parenting produce *sizable differences* in children's and adolescents' developmental outcomes. In her own research, Baumrind consistently finds that "highly demanding–highly responsive" parents have children and adolescents who perform better academically and who show better social adjustment than do parents who are only moderately demanding or responsive but well within the "normal range" on these parenting dimensions. Baumrind also argues that just because children are active agents who, in part, shape their own environments in no way implies that parents are powerless to influence those environments in ways that might promote (or inhibit) adaptive outcomes. And recent, longitudinal research clearly supports Baumrind's position. Even after controlling for children's genetically-influenced (and other) characteristics, different patterns of parenting are reliably associated with different child outcomes (see Collins et al., 2000). Finally, Baumrind worries that telling parents they need only be "good enough" may cause them to become less invested in promoting children's competencies and quicker to absolve themselves of responsibility should their children founder. This would be unfortunate, in her view, because research consistently indicates that parents who feel personally responsible for fostering adaptive development typically have competent, well-adjusted sons and daughters, whereas those who are less personally involved tend to have children whose outcomes are less adaptive. For all those reasons, Baumrind concludes that Scarr's "good enough" parenting is simply *not* good enough.

Other critics (for example, Jackson, 1993) are concerned about the possible implications of Scarr's views for public policy were they to be accepted by those in power. Specifically, if we endorse Scarr's ideas that the "average expectable environment" is all children need to approximate their genetically influenced developmental potentials, then there would be little reason to intervene in an attempt to optimize the development of economically-disadvantaged children from homes that fall within the normal range of family environments. Yet Jackson (1993) notes that many such interventions promote cognitive and emotional development. Canadian public policy does not follow Scarr's position. In fact, the Canadian government has established a number of programs to foster healthy development, especially in the early years of life. For example, national programs such as "Growing Healthy Children," and "Aboriginal Head Start," and regional guidelines such as those found in Ontario's "Early Years Study" all actively promote physical, emotional, and cognitive intervention (Health Canada, Childhood and Youth Division, 1998; Growing Healthy Kids, 2001; Mustard, McCain & Bertrand, 2000; Ontario Children's Secretariat, 2001).

Clearly, this debate about the influence of parenting practices illustrates the very different perspectives on development taken by behavioural geneticists (Scarr) and environmentalists (Baumrind, Jackson). At this point, the debate is far from resolved, although we will see throughout the text that parenting does seem to have a meaningful effect on the developmental outcomes of children and adolescents and that many developmentalists would advise parents to strive to be much better than "good enough."

amino acids, not to produce such attributes as intelligence or sociability. Though we now suspect that genes affect behaviour *indirectly* by influencing the experiences we evoke from others or create for ourselves, we are still a long way from understanding how or why genes might impel us to prefer particular kinds of stimulation or to find certain activities especially satisfying (Plomin & Rutter, 1998). In addition, behavioural geneticists apply the term *environment* in a very global way, making few if any attempts to measure environmental influences directly or to specify *how* environments act on individuals to influence their behaviour. Perhaps you can see the problem: The critics contend that one has not *explained* development by merely postulating that *unspecified* environmental forces influenced in *unknown* ways by our genes will *somehow* shape our abilities, conduct, and character (Bronfenbrenner & Ceci, 1994; Gottlieb, 1996, 2003).

How exactly do environments influence people's abilities, conduct, and character? What environmental influences, at what ages, are particularly important? These are questions that we will be seeking to answer throughout the remainder of this text. We begin in our next chapter by examining how environmental events that occur even before a child is born combine with nature's scheme to influence the course of prenatal development and the characteristics of newborn infants.

SUMMARY

Principles of Hereditary Transmission

♦ Development begins at **conception**, when a sperm cell from the father penetrates an ovum from the mother, forming a **zygote**. A normal human zygote contains 46 **chromosomes** (23 from each parent), each of which consists of several thousand strands of **deoxyribonucleic acid** (or **DNA**) known as **genes**. Genes are the biological blueprint for the development of the zygote into a recognizable human being.

♦ Development of the zygote occurs through **mitosis**, a process by which new body cells are created as the 23 paired chromosomes in each cell duplicate themselves and separate into identical daughter cells. Specialized germ cells, which

also have 23 pairs of chromosomes, divide by a process known as **meiosis** to produce gametes (sperm or ova) that each contain 23 unpaired chromosomes. **Crossing-over** and the **independent assortment** of chromosomes ensure that each gamete receives a unique set of genes from each parent.

♦ **Monozygotic** (or **identical**) **twins** result when a single zygote divides to create two cells that develop independently. **Dizygotic** (or **fraternal**) twins result when two different ova are each fertilized by a different sperm cell.

♦ Human ova normally contain an unpaired **X chromosome**. Fathers determine the sex of their children. If the sperm that fertilizes an ovum bears a **Y chromosome**, the child will be a boy; if the sperm bears an X chromosome, the child will be a girl.

> ✔ **Concept Check 3.4**
> **Understanding Interplays between Genes and Environment**

Check your understanding of genotype-environmental interplays by matching each statement below with one of the following terms: (a) reaction range, (b) canalization, (c) evocative genotype-environment correlations, (d) active genotype-environmental correlations, or (e) passive genotype-environment correlations. Answers are in the Appendix.

_____1. Notion that our environments largely reflect our genetically-influenced interests and activity preferences.

_____2. Idea that our genetically-influenced attributes affect the ways in which people respond to us.

_____3. Idea that genes determine the range of phenotypes one might display in different environments.

_____4. Notion that children living with biological parents should experience environments that are often compatible with their genetic predispositions.

_____5. Idea that either genes or environments may limit the extent to which the other factor influences development.

♦ Among the developmental functions served by genes are the production of enzymes and other proteins that are necessary for the creation and functioning of new cells, and the regulation of the timing and pace of development. However, environmental factors influence how messages coded in genes are carried out.

♦ There are many ways in which one's **genotype** may affect **phenotype**—the way one looks, feels, thinks, or behaves. Some characteristics are determined by a single pair of **alleles**, one of which is inherited from each parent. In simple **dominant/recessive** traits, the individual displays the phenotype of the **dominant allele**. If a gene pair is **codominant**, the individual displays a phenotype in between those produced by the dominant and the **recessive alleles** (**sickle cell anemia** is an example of such a trait). **Sex-linked characteristics** are those caused by recessive genes on the X chromosome; they are more common in males, who have but one X chromosome and need only inherit one recessive gene to display these traits. Some traits arise because of **genetic imprinting**, in which only one parent's allele is expressed. Most complex human attributes, such as intelligence and personality traits, are **polygenic**, or influenced by many genes rather than a single pair.

Chromosomal and Genetic Abnormalities

♦ Occasionally, children inherit **congenital defects** (for example, **Huntington's disease**) that are caused by abnormal genes and chromosomes. In most cases of chromosomal abnormalities, the individual inherits too many or too few sex chromosomes. The **fragile-X syndrome**, a leading cause of mental retardation, is caused by an abnormal gene on the X chromosome that is more likely to be expressed when passed from mother to child.

♦ A major **autosomal** disorder is **Down syndrome**, in which the child inherits an extra 21st chromosome, displays a number of distinctive physical features, and is mentally retarded. Older mothers are at higher risk for bearing children with chromosomal abnormalities, but fathers contribute to many such abnormalities as well.

♦ Many genetic diseases may be passed to children by parents who are not affected but are carriers of the abnormal gene. Genetic abnormalities may also result from **mutations**—changes in the structure of one or more genes that can occur spontaneously or result from such environmental hazards as radiation or toxic chemicals.

Applications: Genetic Counselling, Prenatal Detection, and Treatment of Hereditary Disorders

♦ **Genetic counselling** is a service that informs prospective parents who are at risk of giving birth to a child with a hereditary defect about the odds of that happening from their family histories and from medical tests to determine whether they carry abnormal genes.

♦ A number of prenatal diagnostic methods, including **amniocentesis**, **chorionic villus sampling**, and **ultrasound**, make possible the early detection of many genetic and chromosomal abnormalities in offspring.

♦ Harmful effects of many heredity disorders (for example, **phenylketonuria[PKU]**) can now be minimized by such medical interventions as special diets, fetal surgery, drugs and

hormones, and gene replacement therapy. **Germline gene therapy**, in which abnormal genes may be repaired or replaced to cure hereditary defects, is on the horizon; however, it raises many ethical issues that will have to be resolved before it is likely to be approved.

Hereditary Influences on Behaviour

♦ **Behavioural genetics** is the study of how genes and environment contribute to individual variations in development. Although animals can be studied in **selective breeding experiments**, human behavioural geneticists must conduct family studies (often **twin designs** or **adoption designs**), estimating the **heritability** of various attributes from similarities and differences among family members who differ in **kinship**. Hereditary contributions to various attributes are estimated by evaluating **concordance rates** and **heritability coefficients**. Behavioural geneticists can also determine the amount of variability in a trait that is attributable to **nonshared environmental influences** and **shared environmental influences**.

♦ Family studies reveal that the genes people inherit influence their intellectual performances, such core dimensions of personality as **introversion/extroversion** and **empathic concern**, and even their predispositions to display such abnormalities as **schizophrenia**, **manic-depressive psychosis**, **neurotic disorders**, alcoholism, and criminality. However, none of these complex attributes are determined only genetically; all are heavily influenced by environment.

Heredity and Environment as Developmental Co-Conspirators

♦ Several theories have been proposed to explain how heredity and environment combine to produce developmental change. For example, the **canalization** principle implies that genes channel development along predetermined pathways that are sometimes difficult for the environment to alter. The **range-of-reaction principle** states that, for most human attributes, heredity sets a range of developmental potentials and the environment influences where in that range the individual will fall. A more recent theory proposes three avenues by which genes influence the environments we are likely to experience: through **passive genotype/environment correlations**, through **evocative genotype/environment correlations**, and through **active genotype/environment correlations**.

Contributions and Criticisms of the Behavioural Genetics Approach

♦ Behavioural genetics has had a strong influence on our outlook on human development by showing that many attributes previously thought to be environmentally determined are influenced, in part, by genes. It has also helped to defuse the nature versus nurture debate by showing that these two sources of influence are complexly intertwined.

♦ Behavioural genetics has been criticized as an incomplete theory of development that describes, but fails to *explain*, how either genes or environment influence our abilities, conduct, and character.

KEY TERMS

genotype, 70

genes, 71

phenotype, 71

conception, 71

zygote, 71

chromosome, 71

deoxyribonucleic acid (DNA), 71

mitosis, 71

meiosis, 72

crossing-over, 72

independent assortment, 72

monozygotic (or identical) twins, 73

dizygotic (or fraternal twins), 74

X chromosome, 74

Y chromosome, 74

alleles, 76

simple dominant-recessive inheritance, 76

dominant allele, 76

recessive allele, 76

homozygous, 76

heterozygous, 76

carrier, 76

codominance, 77

sickle-cell anemia, 78

sex-linked characteristic, 78

genetic imprinting, 79

polygenic trait, 79

congenital defect, 80

Huntington's disease, 80

Fragile-X syndrome, 81

autosomes, 81

Down syndrome, 81

aging-ova hypothesis, 83

mutation, 84

genetic counselling, 85

amniocentesis, 85

chorionic villus sampling (CVS), 86

ultrasound, 86

phenylketonuria (PKU), 87

germline gene therapy, 88

behavioural genetics, 88

heritability, 89

selective breeding experiment, 90

kinship, 90

twin design (or twin study), 90

adoption design, 90

concordance rate, 91

heritability coefficient, 92

nonshared environmental influence (NSE), 92

shared environmental influence (SE), 93

introversion/extroversion, 94

empathic concern, 94

schizophrenia, 97

manic depression, 97

neurotic disorder, 97

canalization, 98

range-of-reaction principle, 99

passive genotype/environment correlations, 100

evocative genotype/ environmental correlations, 100

active genotype/environment correlations, 101

 You can find further information on the topics covered in this chapter by visiting:

www.developmentalpsych2e.nelson.com

 For additional reading, go to InfoTrac College Edition, your on-line research library, at:

infotrac.thomsonlearning.com

Ryan McVay/Photodisc

4

Prenatal Development, Birth, and Newborns' Readiness for Life

From Conception to Birth

Environmental Influences on Prenatal Development

Childbirth and the Perinatal Environment

Birth Complications

The Newborn's Readiness for Life

Summary

prenatal development
development that occurs between the moment of conception and the beginning of the birth process

Take the quiz on page 109 entitled "The Beginnings of Life." The items are straightforward, but unless you have given a lot of thought to these issues or have had some personal experience, you may find them a little tricky.

The answer for all the items is "False." How well did you do? These questions challenge some of our everyday beliefs. While it is reassuring to think of the womb as a safe, protective place, the reality is that it is an environment, and like any environment, forces can act on it in a favourable or unfavourable way. Forces such as the mother's age and health, the food she eats, the drugs she takes, and the chemicals to which she is exposed all affect the environment during prenatal development.

Prenatal development—the development that occurs between the moment of conception and birth—signals the miraculous evolution of a one-celled zygote into a recognizable human being. Human growth and development, therefore, occurs most rapidly during the *prenatal period*, months before a child is born. Thus, the answer to question 3 is false. The answer to item 4 might best be summarized by the family physician who assisted at the delivery of one author's child. He said, "My job is just to catch." He explained that his assumption was that birth would occur at its own pace in its natural way and that his role was to sit back and let it happen. Finally, even though we study developmental psychology, we, like most new parents, were amazed by the incredible abilities of our own children as newborns, and we often talk about our initial introduction to their unique personalities.

FROM CONCEPTION TO BIRTH

In Chapter 3, we learned that development begins in the fallopian tube when a sperm penetrates the wall of an ovum, forming a zygote. From the moment of conception, it will take approximately 266 days for this tiny, one-celled zygote to become a fetus of some 200 billion cells that is ready to be born.

Prenatal development is often divided into three major phases. The first phase, called the **germinal period** (or the *period of the zygote*), lasts from conception through implantation, when the developing zygote becomes firmly attached to the wall of the uterus. The germinal period normally lasts about 14 days. The second phase of prenatal development, the **period of the embryo**, lasts from the beginning of the third week through the end of the eighth. This is the time when virtually all the major organs are formed and the heart begins to beat. The third phase, the **period of the fetus**, lasts from the ninth week of pregnancy until the child is born. During this phase, all the major organ systems begin to function, and the developing organism grows rapidly.

The Germinal Period

As the fertilized ovum, or zygote, moves down the fallopian tube toward the uterus, it divides by mitosis into two cells. These two cells and all their daughter cells continue to divide, forming a ball-shaped structure, or *blastocyst*, that will contain 60 to 80 cells within four days of conception (see Figure 4.1). Cell differentiation has already begun. The inner layer of the blastocyst, or *embryonic disk*, becomes the **embryo**, whereas the outer layer of cells develops into tissues that protect and nourish the embryo.

Within hours of conception, the fertilized ovum (zygote) divides, beginning a continuous process of cell differentiation.

Pascal Goetgheluck/Science Photo Library

Implantation

As the blastocyst approaches the uterus 6 to 10 days after conception, small, burrlike tendrils emerge from its outer surface. Upon reaching the uterine wall, these tendrils burrow inward, tapping the mother's blood supply. This is **implantation**. Once the blastocyst is implanted at 10 to 14 days after conception, it looks like a small translucent blister on the wall of the uterus (see Figure 4.1).

The Beginnings of Life
True or False?

1. A mother's womb is a protective haven that shields an unborn child from such external hazards as pollution and disease.

2. The environment first affects human development the moment a baby is born.

3. Human beings develop most rapidly between birth and 2 years of age.

4. Birth proceeds more smoothly with fewer complications when attended by a physician in a hospital.

5. Newborn human infants are asocial creatures who are poorly adapted for life.

germinal period
first phase of prenatal development, lasting from conception until the developing organism becomes firmly attached to the wall of the uterus (also called period of the zygote)

period of the embryo
second phase of prenatal development, lasting from the third through the eighth prenatal week, during which the major organs and anatomical structures take shape

period of the fetus
third phase of prenatal development, lasting from the ninth prenatal week until birth; during this period, all major organ systems begin to function and the fetus grows rapidly

embryo
name given to the prenatal organism from the third through the eighth week after conception

implantation
the burrowing of the blastocyst into the lining of the uterus

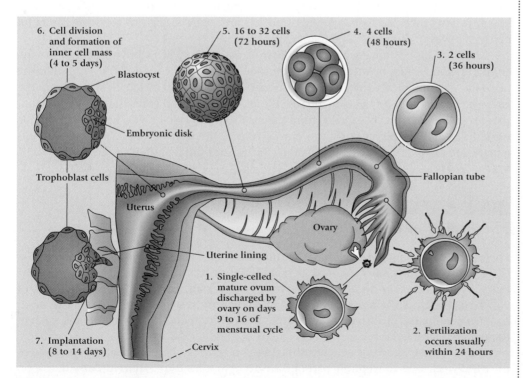

Figure 4.1 The germinal period.

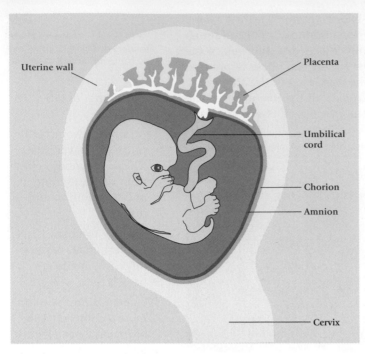

Uterine wall

Placenta

Umbilical cord

Chorion

Amnion

Cervix

Figure 4.2 *The embryo and its prenatal environment.*

Implantation is quite a development in itself. Only about half of all fertilized ova are firmly implanted; perhaps as many as half of all such implants are either genetically abnormal and fail to develop, or burrow into a site incapable of sustaining them and are miscarried (Moore & Persaud, 1993; Simpson, 1993). So it appears that nearly three zygotes out of four, including most of the abnormal ones, fail to survive the initial phase of prenatal development.

Development of Support Systems

Once implanted, the blastocyst's outer layer rapidly forms four major support structures that protect and nourish the developing organism (Sadler, 1996) (see Figure 4.2). One membrane, the **amnion**, is a watertight sac that fills with fluid from the mother's tissues. The purposes of this sac and its *amniotic fluid* are to cushion the developing organism against blows, regulate its temperature, and provide a weightless environment that will make it easier for the embryo to move. Floating in this watery environment is a balloon-shaped *yolk sac* that produces blood cells until the embryo is capable of producing its own. This yolk sac is attached to a third membrane, the **chorion**, which surrounds the amnion and eventually becomes the lining of the **placenta**—a multipurpose organ that we will discuss in detail. A fourth membrane, the *allantois*, forms the embryo's **umbilical cord**.

Purpose of the Placenta

Once developed, the placenta is fed by blood vessels from the mother and the embryo, although its hairlike villi act as a barrier that prevents these two bloodstreams from mixing. This placental barrier is semipermeable, meaning that it allows some substances to pass through, but not others. Gases such as oxygen and carbon dioxide, salts, and various nutrients such as sugars, proteins, and fats are small enough to cross the placental barrier. However, blood cells are too large.

Maternal blood flowing into the placenta delivers oxygen and nutrients into the embryo's bloodstream by means of the umbilical cord, which connects the embryo to the placenta. The umbilical cord also transports carbon dioxide and metabolic wastes from the embryo. These waste products then cross the placental barrier, enter the mother's bloodstream, and are eventually expelled from the mother's body along with her own metabolic wastes. Clearly, the placenta plays a crucial role in prenatal development, because this remarkable organ is the site of all metabolic transactions that sustain the embryo.

The Period of the Embryo

The period of the embryo lasts from the third through the eighth week of pregnancy. By the third week, the embryonic disk is rapidly differentiating into three cell layers. The outer layer, or *ectoderm*, becomes the nervous system, skin, and hair. The middle layer, or *mesoderm*, becomes the muscles, bones, and circulatory system. From the inner layer, or *endoderm*, come the digestive system, lungs, urinary tract, and other vital organs, such as the pancreas and liver.

Development proceeds at a breathtaking pace during the period of the embryo. In the third week after conception, part of the ectoderm folds into a **neural tube** that soon becomes the brain and spinal cord. By the end of the fourth week, the heart has not only formed but has already begun to beat. The eyes, ears, nose, and mouth are also beginning to form, and buds that will become arms and legs suddenly appear. Thirty days after conception, the embryo is only about 6 mm long, but already 10 000 times the size of the zygote from which it developed. At no time in the future will this organism ever grow as rapidly or change as much as it has during the first prenatal month.

The Second Month

During the second month, the embryo becomes much more human in appearance (see Figure 4.3) as it grows about 1 mm per day. A primitive tail appears, but it is soon enclosed by protective tissue and becomes the tip of the backbone, the coccyx. By the middle of the fifth week, the eyes have corneas and lenses. By the seventh week, the ears are well formed, and the embryo has a rudimentary skeleton. Limbs are now developing from the body outward; that is, the upper arms appear first, followed by the forearms, hands, and then fingers. The legs follow a similar pattern a few days later. The brain develops rapidly during the second month, and it directs the organism's first muscular contractions by the end of the embryonic period.

During the seventh and eighth prenatal weeks, the embryo's sexual development begins with the appearance of a genital ridge called the *indifferent gonad*. If the embryo is a male, a gene on its Y chromosome triggers a biochemical reaction that instructs the indifferent gonad to produce testes. If the embryo is a female, the indifferent gonad receives no such instructions and will produce ovaries. The embryo's circulatory system now functions on its own, for the liver and spleen have assumed the task of producing blood cells from the now-defunct yolk sac.

By the end of the second month, the embryo is slightly more than 2.5 cm long and weighs less than 7.0 g. Yet it is already a marvellously complex being: "All of the structures which will be present when the baby is born in seven more months have already formed, at least in beginning stages" (Apgar & Beck, 1974, p. 57).

Figure 4.3 *A human embryo at 40 days. The heart is now beating and the limbs are rapidly forming.*

At about 12 weeks after conception, the fetus is about 7.5 cm long and weighs almost 28.0 g. All major organ systems have formed and several are already functioning.

The Period of the Fetus

The last seven months of pregnancy, or period of the **fetus**, is a period of rapid growth (see Figure 4.4) and refinement of all organ systems.

The Third Month

During the third prenatal month, organ systems that were formed earlier continue their rapid growth and become interconnected. For example, coordination between the nervous and muscular systems allows the fetus to perform many interesting manoeuvres in its watery environment—kicking its legs, making fists, twisting its body—although these activities are far too subtle to be felt by the mother. The digestive and excretory systems are also working together, allowing the fetus to swallow, digest nutrients, and urinate. Sexual differentiation is progressing rapidly as the male testes secrete *testosterone*, the male sex hormone responsible for the development of a penis and scrotum; in the absence of testosterone, female genitalia form. By the end of the third month, the sex of a fetus can be detected by ultrasound, and its reproductive system already contains immature ova or sperm cells. All these detailed developments are present after 12 weeks even though the fetus is a mere 7.5 cm long and still weighs less than 28.0 g.

fetus
name given to the prenatal organism from the ninth week of pregnancy until birth

Age since fertilization in weeks

9 12 16 20   24   28   32   36   38

Figure 4.4 *Rate of body growth during the fetal period. Increase in size is especially dramatic from the ninth to the twentieth week.* ADAPTED FROM MOORE & PERSAUD, 1993.

The Second Trimester

Development continues at a rapid pace during the fourth, fifth, and sixth months of pregnancy, a period called the *second trimester*. At age 16 weeks, the fetus is approximately 20 to 25 cm long and weighs about 170 g. Its motor activity may include refined actions such as thumbsucking, as well as kicking that may be strong enough to be felt by the mother. The fetal heartbeat can be heard with a stethoscope, and the hardening skeleton can be detected by ultrasound. By the end of the fourth month, the fetus has assumed a distinctly human appearance, even though it stands virtually no chance of surviving outside the womb.

Lennart Nilsson/Albert Bonniers Forlag AB, *A Child Is Born*

Lennart Nilsson/Albert Bonniers Forlag AB, *A Child Is Born*

Left: This 24-week-old fetus has reached the age of viability and stands a slim chance of surviving outside the womb. From this point on, odds of survival in the event of a premature birth will increase with each day that passes.
Right: This 36-week-old fetus, covered with the cheese-like vernix that protects the skin against chapping, completely fills the uterus and is ready to be born within the next two weeks.

During the fifth and sixth months, the nails harden, the skin thickens, and eyebrows, eyelashes, and scalp hair suddenly appear. At 20 weeks, the sweat glands are functioning, and the fetal heartbeat is often strong enough to be heard by placing an ear on the mother's abdomen. The fetus is now covered with a white, cheesy substance called **vernix** and a fine layer of body hair called **lanugo**. Vernix protects fetal skin against chapping during its long exposure to amniotic fluid, and lanugo helps vernix stick to the skin.

By the end of the second trimester, the fetus's visual and auditory senses are clearly functional. We know this because preterm infants born only 25 weeks after conception become alert at the sound of a loud bell and blink in response to a bright light (Allen & Caputo, 1986). Six months after conception, the fetus is approximately 35 to 38 cm long and weighs just under 1 kg.

The Third Trimester

The last three months of pregnancy, or *third trimester*, is a "finishing phase" during which all organ systems mature rapidly, preparing the fetus for birth. Indeed, somewhere between 22 and 28 weeks after conception (usually in the seventh month), fetuses reach the **age of viability**, the point at which survival outside the uterus is possible (Moore & Persaud, 1993). Recent research using sophisticated fetal monitoring techniques reveals that the 28- to 32-week-old fetuses suddenly begin to show better-organized and more predictable cycles of heart rate activity, gross motor activity, and sleepiness/waking activity, findings that seem to indicate that their developing nervous systems are now sufficiently well organized to allow them to survive should their birth be premature (DiPietro et al., 1996; see also Groome et al., 1997). Nevertheless, many fetuses born this young still require oxygen assistance because the tiny *pulmonary alveoli* (air sacs) in their lungs are too immature to inflate and exchange oxygen for carbon dioxide on their own (Moore & Persaud, 1993).

By the end of the seventh month, the fetus weighs just over 1.8 kg and is about 40.0 to 43.0 cm long. One month later, it has grown to 46.0 cm and put on another 0.5 to 1.0 kg. Much of this weight comes from a padding of fat, deposited just beneath the skin, that later helps to insulate the newborn child from changes in temperature. By the middle of the ninth month, fetal activity slows and sleep increases (DiPietro et al., 1996; Sahni et al., 1995). The fetus is now so large that the most comfortable position within a restricted, pear-shaped uterus is likely to be a head-down posture at the base of the uterus, with the limbs curled up in the so-called fetal position. At irregular intervals over the last month of pregnancy, the mother's uterus contracts and then relaxes—a process that tones the uterine muscles, dilates the cervix, and helps to position the head of the fetus into the gap between the pelvic bones through which it will soon be pushed. As the uterine contractions become stronger, more frequent, and regular, the prenatal period draws to a close. The mother is now in the first stage of labour, and within a matter of hours she will give birth.

vernix
white, cheesy substance that covers the fetus to protect the skin from chapping

lanugo
fine hair covering the fetus's body that helps vernix stick to the skin

age of viability
point between the 22nd and 28th prenatal weeks when survival outside the uterus is possible

Concept Check 4.1
Understanding the Timing of Prenatal Milestones

For each of the following prenatal milestones, indicate the period (germinal, embryonic, or fetal) in which it occurs, the time span (in days, weeks, or months) during which the event occurs, and the term used to refer to the developing organism during this period. Answers appear in the Appendix.	*Event*	*Period*	*Time span*	*Name for organism*
	Implantation	_____	_____	_____
	Age of viability	_____	_____	_____
	First heartbeats	_____	_____	_____
	Kicks first felt by mother	_____	_____	_____
	Organs form	_____	_____	_____
	Sexual differentiation (external genitalia)	_____	_____	_____

ENVIRONMENTAL INFLUENCES ON PRENATAL DEVELOPMENT

Although the vast majority of newborn infants have followed the "normal" pattern of prenatal development just described (see Table 4.1), some encounter environmental obstacles that may channel their development along an abnormal path. In the following sections, we will consider a number of environmental factors that can harm developing embryos and fetuses, as well as interventions to prevent abnormal outcomes.

Teratogens

The term **teratogen** refers to any disease, drug, or other environmental agent that can harm a developing embryo or fetus by causing physical deformities, severely retarded growth, blindness, brain damage, and even death. The list of known and suspected teratogens has grown frighteningly long over the years, making many of today's parents quite concerned about the hazards their unborn children could face (Friedman & Polifka, 1996; Verp, 1993a, b). Before considering the effects of some of the major teratogens, let's emphasize that about 95 percent of newborn babies are perfectly normal and that many of those born with defects have mild, temporary, or reversible problems (Gosden, Nicolaides, & Whitting, 1994; Heinonen, Slone, & Shapiro, 1977). Let's also lay out a few generalizations about the effects of teratogens that will help us interpret the research that follows:

teratogens
external agents such as viruses, drugs, chemicals, and radiation that can harm a developing embryo or fetus

TABLE 4.1		A Brief Overview of Prenatal Development			
Trimester	**Period**	**Weeks**	**Size**		**Major developments**
First	Zygote	1			One-celled zygote divides and becomes a blastocyst.
		2			Blastocyst implants into uterine wall; structures that nourish and protect the organism—amnion, chorion, yolk sac, placenta, umbilical cord—begin to form.
	Embryo	3–4	0.65 cm		Brain, spinal cord, and heart form, as do the rudimentary structures that will become the eyes, ears, nose, mouth, and limbs.
		5–8	~2.5 cm 7.0 g		External body structures (eyes, ears, limbs) and internal organs form. Embryo produces its own blood and can now move.
	Fetus	9–12	~9.5 cm 28.0 g		Rapid growth and interconnections of all organ systems permit such new competencies as body and limb movements, swallowing, digestion of nutrients, urination. External genitalia form.
Second	Fetus	13–24	~35.0–38.0 cm ~0.9 kg		Fetus grows rapidly. Fetal movements are felt by the mother, and fetal heartbeat can be heard. Fetus is covered by vernix to prevent chapping; it also reacts to bright lights and loud sounds.
Third	Fetus	25–38	~48.0–53.0 cm ~3.2–3.6 kg		Growth continues and all organ systems mature in preparation for birth. Fetus reaches the age of viability and becomes more regular and predictable in its sleep cycles and motor activity. Layer of fat develops under the skin. Activity becomes less frequent and sleep more frequent during last 2 weeks before birth.

- The effects of a teratogen on a body part or organ system are worst during the period when that structure is forming and growing most rapidly.
- Not all embryos or fetuses are equally affected by a teratogen; susceptibility to harm is influenced by the genetic makeup of the mother and the embryo/fetus and the quality of the prenatal environment.
- The same defect can be caused by different teratogens.
- A variety of defects can result from a single teratogen.
- The longer the exposure to or higher the "dose" of a teratogen, the more likely it is that serious harm will be done.
- Embryos and fetuses can be affected by *fathers'* as well as by mothers' exposure to some teratogens.
- The long-term effects of a teratogen often depend on the quality of the *postnatal* environment.

Let's look more closely at the first generalization, because it is very important. Each major organ system or body part has a **sensitive period** when it is most susceptible to teratogenic agents—namely, the time when the particular part of the body is evolving and taking shape. Recall that most organs and body parts are rapidly forming during the period of the embryo (weeks three through eight of prenatal development). As we see in Figure 4.5, this is precisely the time—before a woman may even know that she is pregnant—that most organ systems are most vulnerable to damage. The most crucial period

sensitive period
period during which an organism is quite susceptible to certain environmental influences; outside this period, the same environmental influences must be much stronger to produce comparable effects

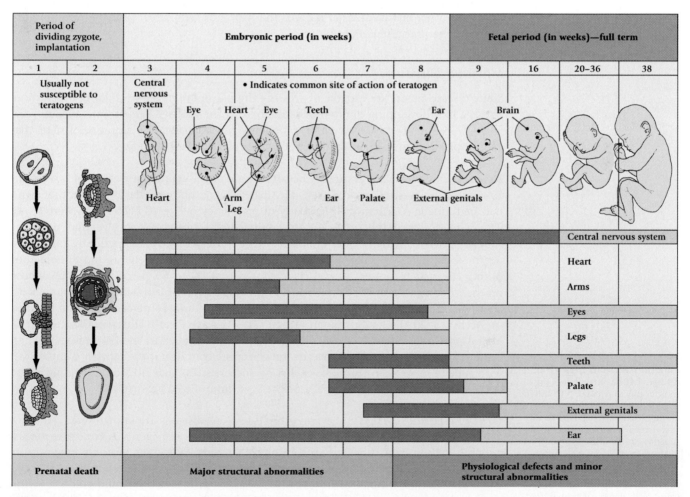

Figure 4.5 *The critical periods of prenatal development. Each organ or structure has a critical period when it is most sensitive to damage from teratogens. A dark band indicates the most sensitive periods. A light band indicates times that each organ or structure is somewhat less sensitive to teratogens, although damage may still occur.* ADAPTED FROM MOORE & PERSAUD, 1993.

for gross physical defects of the head and central nervous system is the third through the fifth prenatal weeks. The heart is particularly vulnerable from the middle of the third through the middle of the sixth prenatal week; the most vulnerable period for many other organs and body parts is the second prenatal month. Is it any wonder, then, that the period of the embryo is often called the critical phase of pregnancy?

Once an organ or body part is fully formed, it becomes somewhat less susceptible to damage. However, as Figure 4.5 also illustrates, some organ systems (particularly the eyes, genitals, and nervous system) can be damaged throughout pregnancy. Several years ago, Olli Heinonen and his associates (Heinonen et al., 1977) concluded that many of the birth defects found among the 50 282 children in their sample were *anytime malformations*—problems that could have been caused by teratogens at any point during the prenatal period. So it seems that the entire prenatal epoch could be considered a *sensitive period* for human development.

Finally, teratogens can have subtle effects on babies' behaviour that are not obvious at birth but nevertheless influence their psychological development. For example, we will see that babies whose mothers consumed as little as 30 mL of alcohol a day while pregnant usually display no obvious physical deformities; however, they are often slower to process information and may score lower on IQ tests and tests of cognitive skills later in childhood than children whose mothers did not drink (Jacobson & Jacobson, 1996; Kodituwakku, Kalberg, & May, 2001). These results may reflect subtle effects of alcohol on the development of the fetal brain. But there is another possibility: Caregivers may have been less inclined to stimulate a sluggish baby who was slow to respond to their bids for attention. And over time, those depressed levels of stimulation (rather than any effect of alcohol on the brain) may have stunted the child's intellectual development.

With these principles in mind, let's now consider some of the diseases, drugs, chemicals, and other environmental hazards that can adversely affect prenatal development or have other harmful consequences.

Maternal Diseases

Some disease agents are capable of crossing the placental barrier and doing much more damage to a developing embryo or fetus than to the mother herself. This makes sense when we remember that an embryo or fetus has an immature immune system that cannot produce enough antibodies to combat infections effectively.

Rubella. The medical community became aware of the teratogenic effect of diseases in 1941 when an Australian physician, McAllister Gregg, noticed that many mothers who had had rubella (German measles) early in pregnancy delivered babies who were blind. After Gregg alerted the medical community, doctors began to notice that pregnant rubella patients regularly bore children with a variety of defects, including blindness, deafness, cardiac abnormalities, and mental retardation. Rubella is most dangerous during the first trimester. Studies have shown that 60 to 85 percent of babies whose mothers had rubella in the first 8 weeks of pregnancy have birth defects, compared with about 50 percent of those infected in the third month and 16 percent of those infected in weeks 13–20 (Kelley-Buchanan, 1988). This disease clearly illustrates the sensitive period principle. The risk of eye and heart defects is greatest in the first 8 weeks (when these organs are forming), whereas deafness is more common if the mother comes down with rubella in weeks 6 through 13. Today, doctors stress that no woman should try to conceive unless she has had rubella or has been immunized against it.

Other Infectious Diseases. Several other infectious diseases are known teratogens (see Table 4.2 for examples). Among the more common of these agents is **toxoplasmosis**, which is caused by a parasite found in many animals. Expectant mothers may acquire the parasite by eating undercooked meat or by handling the feces of a family cat that has eaten an infected animal. Although toxoplasmosis produces only mild coldlike symptoms in adults, it can cause severe eye and brain damage if transmitted to the prenatal organism during the first trimester, and can induce a miscarriage if it strikes later in pregnancy (Carrington, 1995). Pregnant women can protect themselves against infection by

rubella (German measles)
disease that has little effect on a mother but may cause a number of serious birth defects in unborn children who are exposed in the first three to four months of pregnancy

toxoplasmosis
disease caused by a parasite found in raw meat and cat feces; can cause birth defects if transmitted to an embryo in the first trimester; can cause miscarriage later in pregnancy

cooking all meat until it is well-done, washing thoroughly any cooking implements that came in contact with raw meat, and avoiding the garden, a pet's litter box, or other locations where cat feces may be present.

Finally, no infections are more common and few are more hazardous than the *sexually transmitted diseases* examined in Box 4.1.

Drugs

People have long suspected that drugs taken by pregnant women could harm developing organisms. Even Aristotle thought as much when he noted that many drunken mothers had feeble-minded babies (Abel, 1981). Today, we know that these suspicions were often correct and that even mild drugs that have few if any lasting effects on a mother may prove extremely hazardous to a developing embryo or fetus. Unfortunately, the medical community learned this lesson the hard way.

THE THALIDOMIDE TRAGEDY. In 1960, a West German drug company began to market a mild tranquillizer, sold over the counter, that was said to alleviate the periodic nausea (morning sickness) that many women experience during the first trimester of pregnancy. Presumably, the drug was perfectly safe; in tests on pregnant rats, it had had no ill effects on mother or offspring. The drug was **thalidomide**.

What came to pass quickly illustrated that drugs that are harmless in tests with laboratory animals may turn out to be violent teratogens for human beings. Thousands of women who had used thalidomide during the first two months of pregnancy were suddenly giving birth to babies with horrible birth defects. Thalidomide babies often had badly deformed eyes, ears, noses, and hearts, and many displayed phocomelia—a structural abnormality in which all or parts of limbs are missing and the feet or hands may be attached directly to the torso, similar to flippers.

thalidomide
mild tranquillizer that, taken early in pregnancy, produced a variety of malformations of the limbs, eyes, ears, and heart of the baby

---

TABLE 4.2   Common Diseases That May Affect an Embryo, Fetus, or Newborn

		Effects		
Disease	**Miscarriage**	**Physical malformations**	**Mental impairment**	**Low birth weight/ premature delivery**
Sexually transmitted diseases (STDs)				
Acquired immune deficiency syndrome (AIDS)	?	?	?	+
Herpes simplex (genital herpes)	+	+	+	+
Syphilis	+	+	+	+
Other maternal diseases/conditions				
Chickenpox	0	+	+	+
Cholera	+	0	?	?
Cytomegalovirus	+	+	+	+
Diabetes	+	+	+	0
Influenza	+	+	?	?
Malaria	+	0	0	+
Mumps	+	0	0	0
Rubella	+	+	+	+
Toxemia	+	0	+	?
Toxoplasmosis	+	+	+	+
Tuberculosis	+	+	+	+
Urinary tract infection (bacterial)	+	0	0	+

NOTE: + = established finding; 0 = no clear evidence; ? = possible effect.
SOURCES: Carrington, 1995; Cates, 1995; Faden & Kass, 1996; Kelley-Buchanan, 1988.

Sexually transmitted diseases (STDs) can produce serious birth defects or otherwise compromise children's developmental outcomes (Cates, 1995). Three of these diseases—syphilis, genital herpes, and acquired immune deficiency syndrome (AIDS)—are especially hazardous.

Syphilis is most harmful in the middle and later stages of pregnancy, since syphilitic spirochetes (the microscopic organisms that transmit the disease) cannot cross the placental barrier until the 18th prenatal week. This is fortunate, because the disease is usually diagnosed with a blood test and treated with antibiotics long before it could harm a fetus. However, the mother who receives no treatment runs the risk of miscarrying or of giving birth to a child who has serious eye, ear, bone, heart, or brain damage (Carrington, 1995; Kelley-Buchanan, 1988).

The virus causing **genital herpes** (herpes simplex) can also cross the placental barrier, although most infections occur at birth as the newborn comes in contact with lesions on the mother's genitals (Gosden et al., 1994). Unfortunately, there is no cure for genital herpes, so mothers cannot be treated. And the consequences of a herpes infection can be severe: This incurable disease will kill about one-third of all infected newborns and cause such disabilities as blindness, brain damage, and other serious neurological disorders in another 25 to 30 percent (Ismail, 1993). For these reasons, mothers with active herpes infections are now routinely advised to undergo a **cesarean section** (a surgical birth in which the baby is delivered through an incision in the mother's abdomen) to avoid infecting their babies.

The STD of greatest concern today is **acquired immune deficiency syndrome (AIDS)**, a relatively new and incurable disease, caused by the HIV virus, that attacks the immune system and makes victims susceptible to a host of other opportunistic infections that will eventually kill them. Transfer of bodily fluids is necessary to spread the HIV virus; consequently, people are normally infected during sexual intercourse or by sharing needles while injecting illegal drugs. Worldwide, more than four million women of childbearing age carry the HIV virus and could transmit it to their offspring (Faden & Kass, 1996). Infected mothers may pass the virus (1) prenatally, through the placenta; (2) while giving birth, when there may be an exchange of blood between mother and child as the umbilical cord separates from the placenta; and (3) after birth, if the virus is passed through the mother's milk during breast-feeding (Eldred & Chaisson, 1996). Despite all of these possibilities, it appears that fewer than 30 percent of babies born to HIV-infected mothers are infected themselves. Prenatal transmission of the HIV virus is reduced by nearly 70 percent among mothers taking the antiviral drug ZDV (formerly known as AZT), with no indication that this drug (or the HIV virus) causes birth defects (Anderson, 1996; Friedman & Polifka, 1996; Institute of Medicine, 1999).

What are the prospects for babies born infected with HIV? Early reports were extremely depressing, claiming that the virus would devastate immature immune systems during the first year, causing most HIV-infected infants to develop full-blown AIDS and die by age 3 (Jones et al., 1992). However, several studies (reviewed in Hutton, 1996) find that more than half of all HIV-infected infants are living beyond age 6, with a fair percentage surviving well into adolescence. The antiviral drug ZDV, which interferes with HIV's ability to infect new cells, is now used to treat HIV-infected children, many of whom improve or remain stable for years if treatment is started early (Hutton, 1996). However, virtually all HIV-infected youngsters will eventually die from complications of their infection, while a much larger group of children who escaped HIV infection from their mothers will have to deal with the grief of losing their mothers to AIDS (Hutton, 1996; Wissow, Hutton, & McGraw, 1996).

Many experts believe that interventions aimed at modifying unsafe sexual practices and unsafe drug use may be about the only effective means to combat the HIV epidemic, because it may be many years before a cure for AIDS is found (Faden & Kass, 1996; Institute of Medicine, 1999).

This boy has no arms or hands—two of the birth defects that may be produced by thalidomide.

The kinds of birth defects produced by thalidomide depended on when the drug was taken. Babies of mothers who had taken the drug on or around the 21st day after conception were likely to be born without ears. Those whose mothers had used thalidomide on the 25th through the 27th day of pregnancy often had grossly deformed arms or no arms. If a mother had taken the drug between the 28th and 36th day, her child might have deformed legs or no legs. But if she had waited until the 40th day before using thalidomide, her baby was usually not affected (Apgar & Beck, 1974). However, most mothers who took thalidomide delivered babies with no apparent birth defects—a finding that illustrates the dramatic differences that individuals display in response to teratogens.

Other Common Drugs. Despite the lessons learned from the thalidomide tragedy, about 60 percent of pregnant women take at least one prescription or over-the-counter drug. Unfortunately, some of the most commonly used drugs are suspect. Heavy use of aspirin, for example, has been linked to fetal growth retardation, poor motor control, and even infant death (Barr et al., 1990; Kelley-Buchanan, 1988); although further research has failed to confirm these findings (Friedman & Polifka, 1996). The use of ibuprofen in the third trimester increases the risk of a prolonged delivery and pulmonary hypertension in newborns (Chomitz, Chung, & Lieberman, 2000). Some studies have linked heavy use of caffeine (that is, more than four soft drinks or cups of coffee per day) to such complications as miscarriage and low birth weight (Larroque, Kaminski, & Lelong, 1993; Leviton, 1993). However, the harmful outcomes attributed to caffeine may well have been caused by other drugs these mothers had used (Friedman & Polifka, 1996)—most notably, alcohol and nicotine, which we will soon discuss.

Several other prescription drugs pose a slight risk to developing embryos and fetuses. For example, antidepressants containing lithium can produce heart defects when taken in the first trimester (Friedman & Polifka, 1996). Medications containing sex hormones (or their active biochemical ingredients) can also affect a developing embryo or fetus. For example, oral contraceptives contain female sex hormones, and, if a woman takes the pill, not knowing that she is pregnant, her unborn child faces a slightly increased risk of heart defects and other minor malformations (Gosden et al., 1994; Heinonen et al., 1977).

One synthetic sex hormone that can have serious long-term effects is **diethylstilbestrol (DES)**, the active ingredient of a drug that was widely prescribed for the prevention of miscarriages between the mid-1940s and 1965. The drug seemed safe enough; newborns whose mothers had used DES appeared to be normal in every way. But in 1971 physicians clearly established that 17- to 21-year-old females whose mothers had used DES were at risk for developing abnormalities of the reproductive organs, including a rare form of cervical cancer. Clearly, the risk of cancer is not very great; fewer than 1 in 1000 DES daughters have developed the disease thus far (Friedman & Polifka, 1996). However, there are other complications. For example, DES daughters who themselves become pregnant are more likely than nonexposed women to miscarry or to deliver prematurely. What about DES sons? Although there is no conclusive evidence that prenatal exposure to DES causes cancer in sons, a small number of men who were exposed to DES before birth have developed minor genital-tract abnormalities that do not affect their fertility (Wilcox et al., 1995).

Clearly, the vast majority of pregnant women who take aspirin, caffeine, oral contraceptives, or DES deliver perfectly normal babies. And under proper medical supervision, use of medications to treat a mother's ailments is usually safe for mother and fetus (McMahon & Katz, 1996). Nevertheless, the fact that seemingly harmless drugs can produce congenital defects has convinced many mothers to restrict or eliminate their intake of all drugs during pregnancy.

ALCOHOL. Should a no-drug policy be extended to alcohol? Most contemporary researchers think so. Kenneth Jones and his colleagues (1973) described a **fetal alcohol syndrome (FAS)** that affects many children of alcoholic mothers. The most noticeable characteristics of fetal alcohol syndrome are defects such as microcephaly (small head) and malformations of the heart, limbs, joints, and face. FAS babies are likely to display excessive irritability, hyperactivity, seizures, and tremors. They are also smaller and lighter than normal, and their physical growth lags behind that of normal age-mates. Finally, the majority of the 1 to 2 in 1000 babies born with FAS in Canada each year (Health Canada, Canadian Perinatal Surveillance System, 2001a) score well below average in intelligence throughout childhood and adolescence, and over 90 percent of them display major adjustment problems as adolescents and young adults (Colburn, 1996; Stratton, Howe, & Battaglia, 1996).

How much can a mother drink without harming her baby? Perhaps a lot less than you might imagine. In keeping with the dosage principle of teratology, the symptoms of FAS are most severe when the "dose" of alcohol is highest—that is, when the mother is clearly an alcoholic. Yet even moderate "social drinking" (30 to 90 mg a day) can lead to less serious problems, called **fetal alcohol effects (FAE)**, in some babies. These effects include retarded physical growth and minor physical abnormalities, as well as such problems as poor motor skills, difficulty paying attention, and subnormal intellectual performance (Jacobson et al., 1993; Streissguth et al., 1993). Even a mother who drinks less than 30 mL of alcohol a day is more likely than a nondrinker to have an infant whose mental development is slightly below average (Jacobson & Jacobson, 1996). And there is no well-defined sensitive period for fetal alcohol effects; drinking late in pregnancy can

syphilis
common sexually transmitted disease that may cross the placental barrier in the middle and later stages of pregnancy, causing miscarriage or serious birth defects

genital herpes
sexually transmitted disease that can infect infants at birth, causing blindness, brain damage, or even death

cesarean section
surgical delivery of a baby through an incision made in the mother's abdomen and uterus

acquired immune deficiency syndrome (AIDS)
viral disease that can be transmitted from a mother to her fetus or neonate and that results in a weakening of the body's immune system and, ultimately, death

diethylstilbestrol (DES)
synthetic hormone, formerly prescribed to prevent miscarriage, that can produce cervical cancer in adolescent female offspring and genital-tract abnormalities in males

fetal alcohol syndrome (FAS)
group of serious congenital problems commonly observed in the children of mothers who abuse alcohol during pregnancy

fetal alcohol effects (FAE)
group of mild congenital problems that are sometimes observed in children of mothers who drink sparingly to moderately during pregnancy

David H. Wells/Corbis/Magma

This boy's widely spaced eyes, flattened nose, and underdeveloped upper lip are three of the common physical symptoms of fetal alcohol syndrome.

be just as risky as drinking soon after conception (Jacobson et al., 1993). Based on data collected through the National Longitudinal Survey of Children and Youth, it is estimated that approximately 17 percent of Canadian mothers reported consuming alcohol while pregnant in the 1996–97 year. Health Canada recommends that women not consume alcohol if they are pregnant or if they are planning to become pregnant (Health Canada, Canadian Perinatal Surveillance System, 2001b, p. 6).

CIGARETTE SMOKING. "In Canada, in 1996–1997, 21.3 percent of children under the age of 3 had mothers who reported smoking during their pregnancy. Among smokers, 90.9 percent reported smoking in the third trimester of pregnancy, when the negative effect on fetal health is the greatest" (Health Canada, 2001b, p. 3). Although there is little evidence that smoking causes physical defects (Friedman & Polifka, 1996; Verp, 1993a), one review of more than 200 studies concluded that smoking clearly retards the rate of fetal growth and increases the risk of spontaneous abortion or death shortly after birth in otherwise normal infants and is the leading contributor to fetal growth restriction and low-birth-weight babies (Chomitz et al., 2000). Smoking introduces nicotine and carbon monoxide into both the mother's and fetus's bloodstreams, which impairs the functioning of the placenta, especially the exchange of oxygen and nutrients to the fetus. And all of these events are clearly related in that the more cigarettes mothers smoke per day, the greater their risk of spontaneous abortion or of delivering a low-birth-weight baby who may struggle to survive (Carson, 1993). Newborn infants of fathers who smoke are also likely to be smaller than normal. Why? Because mothers who live with smokers become "passive smokers" who inhale nicotine and carbon monoxide that can dampen fetal growth (Friedman & Polifka, 1996).

The long-term effects of exposure to tobacco products are less clear. Some research has found that children whose mothers smoked during pregnancy or whose parents continue to smoke after they are born tend to be smaller on average and more susceptible to respiratory infections, and show slightly poorer cognitive performances early in childhood than do children of nonsmokers (Diaz, 1997; Chavkin, 1995). More recently, research conducted at Carleton University indicates that the negative impact of maternal smoking on cognitive performance may extend as far as 16 years of age (e.g., Fried & Watkinson, 2001; Fried, Watkinson, & Gray, 2003—see the Inside Track Box 4.2 for more details about these studies). On the other hand, differences between children of smokers and nonsmokers in some longer-term studies are very small, and often fail to find any differences at all (e.g., Chavkin, 1995; Lefkowitz, 1981). Nevertheless, the evidence is overwhelming that smoking during pregnancy can harm fetuses (not to mention, of course, the harmful long-term effects that this habit can have on parents). For these reasons, physicians today routinely advise pregnant women and their partners to stop smoking—if not forever, at least during pregnancy.

ILLICIT DRUGS. Use of recreational drugs, such as marijuana, cocaine, and heroin, has become so widespread that many infants are born each year having been exposed to one or more of these substances in the womb (Chavkin, 1995; Shearer, 1994). Marijuana, the most widely used of these drugs, produces few if any physical defects. However, mothers who report using the drug two or more times per week often deliver babies who display tremors, sleep disturbances, lack of interest in their surroundings over the first week or two of life (Brockington, 1996; Fried, 1993). These behavioural disturbances could place infants at risk for adverse outcomes later in childhood, such as was found in recent research demonstrating negative cognitive outcomes for the adolescent children of mothers who smoked marijuana (Fried & Watkinson, 2001).To discover more about the long-term implications of lighter and heavier use of marijuana see the Inside Track Box 4.2.

Peter A. Fried

Peter A. Fried works in the Department of Psychology at Carleton University in Ottawa. His research interests involve examining the impact of the social use of alcohol, cigarettes, and marijuana during pregnancy on the development and behaviour of offspring. June 2003 marked his 25th anniversary of involvement with the longitudinal research project known as the Ottawa Prenatal Prospective Study.

How far into the lives of developing children do the effects of cigarette and marijuana smoking extend? The answer to this question is beginning to unfold as a function of the work being conducted by a team of researchers in the psychology department at Carleton University. Dr. Peter Fried, and his colleagues, have followed a cohort of children (and their mothers) from their prenatal days to 20 years of age as part of the Ottawa Prenatal Prospective Study (OPPS). The sample of mothers includes non-smokers, light smokers, and heavy smokers of cigarettes (approximately one pack a day or more) and non-users, light users, and heavy users of marijuana (six or more joints a week). Although several studies have documented the developmental impact at earlier points in the lifespan, Fried and his colleagues' most recent published research examines cognitive implications among the teenage offspring in this cohort of mothers (Fried & Watkinson, 2001; Fried, Watkinson, & Gray 2003). Attention performance among the adolescent offspring differed as a function of whether the mothers had used cigarettes or marijuana while pregnant. Specifically, cigarette smoking reduced performance for attention tasks that examined how well the 13- to 16-year-olds were able to hold information while acquiring new information. The younger adolescents also performed more poorly on measures assessing impulsivity, although by 16 these latter effects were no longer evident (Fried & Watkinson, 2001). Marijuana exposure, on the other hand, reduced the stability of test performance. In a subsequent study (Fried, Watkinson, & Gray 2003), previous research linking lower overall IQ performance, and poorer performance on an auditory memory task among younger children of cigarette smokers, was extended to this adolescent group. Marijuana yielded poorer performance on tasks related to "visual memory, analysis and integration." Together, these studies show that teratogens introduced early in development may carry their effects well into the lives of the exposed children.

Although heroin, methadone, and other addictive narcotic agents do not appear to produce gross physical abnormalities, women who use these drugs are more likely than nonusers to miscarry, deliver prematurely, or have babies who die soon after birth (Brockington, 1996). The first month is often difficult for the 60 to 80 percent of these babies who are born addicted to the narcotic their mother has taken. When deprived of the drug after birth, addicted infants experience withdrawal symptoms such as vomiting, dehydration, convulsions, extreme irritability, weak sucking, and high-pitched crying. Symptoms such as restlessness, tremors, and sleep disturbances may persist for as long as three to four months. However, longer-term studies reveal that most heroin- or methadone-addicted infants show normal developmental progress by age 2, and that indifferent parenting, rather than early drug exposure, is the most likely contributor to the poor progress that some of these children display (Brockington, 1996).

Today, much concern centres on the risks associated with cocaine use, particularly the use of "crack" cocaine, a cheap form of the drug that delivers high doses through the lungs. In early research there were challenges in identifying the roles of cocaine for development because cocaine-using mothers are often malnourished and prone to using other teratogens such as alcohol (Friedman & Polifka, 1996). However, recent research, controlling for other teratogens, indicates that cocaine has an impact on physical and cognitive/neural development (e.g., Behnke et al., 2002; Mayes, 2002). Cocaine is known to constrict the blood vessels of both mother and fetus, thereby elevating fetal blood pressure and hampering the flow of nutrients and oxygen across the placenta (Chavkin, 1995; MacGregor & Chasnoff, 1993). As a result, babies of cocaine-using mothers, particularly mothers who use crack cocaine, are often miscarried or born prematurely. These babies are smaller, experience lower birth weights, have smaller head circumferences, and score lower on infant ability tests than non-exposed infants (e.g., Behnke et al., 2002; Singer et al., 2002), Like the babies of heroin or methadone users, they often display tremors, sleep disturbances, a sluggish inattention to the environment, and a tendency to become extremely irritable when aroused (Brockington, 1996; Lester et al., 1991).

Some investigators have suspected that the unpleasant demeanour that many cocaine babies display interferes with the emotional bonding that normally occurs between infants and their caregivers. Indeed, one study found that a majority of cocaine-exposed infants failed to establish secure emotional ties to their primary caregivers in the first year (Rodning, Beckwith, & Howard, 1991). Another study found that cocaine babies seem to derive less joy from learning than normal infants do, while showing much less concern (that is, anger or sadness) when their attempts to achieve a goal prove unsuccessful (Alessandri et al., 1993). By 18 months, these infants displayed clear decrements in their intellectual development (Alessandri, Bendersky, & Lewis, 1998). These poor outcomes stem from the babies' prior exposure to cocaine and, in addition, other variables may also contribute—such as their resulting negative emotional demeanour, their exposure to other teratogens (for example, alcohol and tobacco) commonly used by substance-abusing parents, or the less-than-adequate stimulation and care these babies may receive from drug-using parents (e.g., Frank, Brown, Johnson, & Cabral, 2002; Hans, 2002; Singer et al., 2002).

Table 4.3 catalogues a number of other drugs and their known or suspected effects on unborn children. What should we make of these findings? Assuming that our first priority is the welfare of unborn children, then perhaps Virginia Apgar has summarized it best: "A woman who is pregnant, or who thinks she could possibly be pregnant, should not take any drugs whatsoever unless absolutely essential—and then only when [approved] by a physician who is aware of the pregnancy" (Apgar & Beck, 1974, p. 445).

> **(?) WHAT DO YOU THINK?**
>
> Some people have argued that mothers who abuse alcohol or other teratogenic drugs while pregnant should be charged, if not with attempted murder, at least with child abuse. What is your view on this issue, and why? If you agree, is that also a basis for charging drug-abusing fathers?

Environmental Hazards

RADIATION. Soon after the atomic blasts of 1945 in Japan, scientists became painfully aware of the teratogenic effects of radiation. Not one pregnant woman who was within 0.8 km of these explosions gave birth to a live child. In addition, 75 percent of the pregnant women who were within 2 km of the blasts had seriously handicapped children who soon died, and the infants who did survive were often mentally retarded (Apgar & Beck, 1974; Vorhees & Mollnow, 1987).

Unfortunately, no one knows exactly how much radiation it takes to harm an embryo or fetus, and even if an exposed child appears normal at birth, the possibility of developing complications later in life cannot be dismissed. For these reasons, pregnant women are routinely advised to avoid X-rays, particularly of the pelvis and abdomen, unless they are crucial for the mother's own survival.

CHEMICALS AND POLLUTANTS. Pregnant women routinely come in contact with potentially toxic substances in their everyday environments, including organic dyes and colouring agents, food additives, artificial sweeteners, pesticides, and cosmetic products, some of which are known to have teratogenic effects in animals (Verp, 1993a). Unfortunately, the risks associated with a large number of these common chemical additives and treatments remain to be determined.

There are also pollutants in the air we breathe and the water we drink. For example, pregnant women may be exposed to concentrations of lead, zinc, mercury, or antimony discharged into the air or water by industrial operations or present in house paint and water pipes. These "heavy metals" are known to impair the physical health and mental abilities of adults and children and to have teratogenic effects (producing physical deformities and mental retardation) on developing embryos and fetuses. Polluting chemicals called PCBs (*polychlorinated biphenyls*), now outlawed but once widely used in plastics and carbon paper, represent another hazard. Joseph Jacobson and his colleagues (1984) found that even low-level exposure to PCBs, resulting from mothers eating contaminated fish from Lake Michigan, was enough to make newborns smaller on average and less responsive and neurologically mature than babies whose mothers did not eat polluted fish. At age 4, these children still performed poorly on tests of short-term memory and verbal

TABLE 4.3   Partial List of Drugs and Treatments Used by the Mother That Affect (or Are Thought to Affect) the Fetus or the Newborn

Maternal drug use	Effect on fetus/newborn
Alcohol	Small head, facial abnormalities, heart defects, low birth weight, and mental retardation (see text).

Amphetamines
   Dextroamphetamine
   Methamphetamine
	Premature delivery, stillbirth, irritability, and poor feeding among newborns.

Antibiotics
   Streptomycin
   Terramycin
   Tetracycline
	Heavy use of streptomycin by mothers can produce hearing loss in fetuses. Terramycin and tetracycline may be associated with premature delivery, retarded skeletal growth, cataracts, and staining of the baby's teeth

Aspirin	See text. (In clinical doses, ibuprofen and acetaminophen are very safe alternatives to aspirin.)
Barbiturates	All barbiturates taken by the mother cross the placental barrier. In clinical doses, they cause the fetus or newborn to be lethargic. In large doses, they may cause anoxia (oxygen starvation) and depress fetal growth. One barbiturate, primidone, is associated with malformations of the heart, face, and limbs.
Hallucinogens LSD	Lysergic and diethylamide (LSD) slightly increases the likelihood of limb deformities.
Marijuana	Heavy marijuana use during pregnancy is linked to behavioural abnormalities in newborns (see text).
Lithium	Heart defects, lethargic behaviour in newborns.

Narcotics
   Cocaine
   Heroin
   Methadone
	Maternal addiction increases the risk of premature delivery. Moreover, the fetus is often addicted to the narcotic agent, which results in a number of complications. Heavy cocaine use can seriously elevate fetal blood pressure and even induce strokes (see text).

Sex hormones
   Androgens
   Progestogens
   Estrogens
   DES (diethylstilbestrol)
	Sex hormones contained in birth control pills and drugs to prevent miscarriages taken by pregnant women can have a number of harmful effects on babies, including minor heart malformations, cervical cancer (in female offspring), and other anomalies (see text).

Tranquillizers (other than thalidomide)
   Chlorpromazine
   Reserpine
   Valium
	May produce respiratory distress in newborns. Valium may also produce poor muscle tone and lethargy.

Tobacco	Maternal cigarette smoking is known to retard fetal growth and to increase the risk of spontaneous abortion, stillbirth, and infant mortality (see text).
Vitamins	Excessive amounts of vitamin A taken by pregnant women can cause cleft palate, heart malformations, and other serious birth defects. The popular anti-acne drug Accutane, derived from vitamin A, is one of the most powerful teratogens, causing malformations of the eyes, limbs, heart, and central nervous system. Although teratogenic to animals (rabbits), vitamin D poses virtually no risk to humans, even if the mother takes 200 times the recommended daily dose.

SOURCES: Chavkin, 1995; Friedman & Polifka, 1996; Kelley-Buchanan, 1988.

reasoning ability, with the extent of their deficits corresponding to the "dose" of PCBs they received before birth (Jacobson, Jacobson, & Humphrey, 1990; Jacobson et al., 1992).

Even a father's exposure to environmental toxins can affect a couple's children. Studies of male doctors and dentists reveal that prolonged exposure to radiation, anesthetic gases, and other toxic substances can damage a father's chromosomes, increasing the likelihood of his child's being miscarried or having genetic defects (Gunderson & Sackett, 1982; Merewood, 2000; Strigini et al., 1990). And even when expectant mothers do *not* drink alcohol or use drugs, they are much more likely to deliver a low-birth-weight baby if the father is a heavy drinker or drug user (Merewood, 2000). Why? Possibly because certain substances (for example, cocaine and maybe even alcohol, PCBs, and other toxins) can apparently bind directly to live sperm or cause mutations in them, thereby altering prenatal development from the moment of conception (Merewood, 2000; Yazigi, Odem, & Polakoski, 1991). Taken together, these findings imply that (1) environmental toxins can affect the reproductive system of either parent so that (2) both mothers *and* fathers should limit their exposure to substances to known teratogens.

Maternal Characteristics

In addition to teratogens, a mother's nutrition, her emotional well-being, and even her age can affect the outcome of her pregnancy.

The Mother's Diet

Fifty years ago, doctors routinely advised mothers to gain no more than 1 kg a month while pregnant and believed that a total gain of about 7 to 8 kg was quite sufficient to ensure healthy prenatal development. Today, mothers are more often advised to eat a healthy, high-protein, high-calorie diet on which they gain about 1.0 to 2.0 kg during the first three months of pregnancy and about 0.5 kg a week thereafter, for a total increase of about 11.0 to 14.0 kg (Chomitz et al., 2000). Why has the advice changed? We now know that inadequate prenatal nutrition can be harmful.

Severe malnutrition, as often occurs during periods of famine, stunts prenatal growth and produces small, underweight babies (Susser & Stein, 1994). The precise effects of malnutrition depend on when it occurs. During the first trimester, malnutrition can disrupt the formation of the spinal cord and induce miscarriages. During the third trimester, malnutrition is more likely to result in low-birth-weight babies with small heads who may fail to survive the first year of life (Susser & Stein, 1994). (See Figure 4.6.) Indeed, autopsies of stillborn infants whose mothers were malnourished during the third trimester reveal fewer brain cells and lower brain weights than is typical among babies born to well-nourished mothers (Goldenberg, 1995; Winick, 1976).

Not surprisingly, then, babies born to malnourished mothers sometimes show cognitive deficits later in childhood. One contributor to these long-term problems is the babies' own behaviour. Malnourished babies whose diets *remain* inadequate after birth are often apathetic and quick to become irritated when aroused—qualities that can alienate their parents, who may fail to provide the kinds of playful stimulation and emotional support that would foster their social and intellectual development (Grantham-McGregor et al., 1994). Fortunately, dietary supplements, especially when combined with stimulating daycare and programs that help parents to become more sensitive, responsive caregivers, can significantly reduce or even eliminate the potentially damaging long-term effects of prenatal malnutrition (Grantham-McGregor et al., 1994; Super, Herrera, & Mora, 1990; Zeskind & Ramey, 1981).

In Canada, poor women are at risk for poor nutrition. To combat this problem, nutritional supplement programs have been established in some areas. For example, the Montreal Diet Dispensary Program was initiated in the 1960s to promote more positive pregnancy outcomes among socially disadvantaged urban women (see da Silva, 1994, for a brief review). Evaluation of this program indicates that mothers who had the dietary supplement had infants with higher birth weights compared with other siblings. Specifically, when supplements were provided during a second pregnancy, the birth weight for the second-born child was about 107 g higher than for first-borns who were not exposed to the supplements (da Silva, 1994).

Finally, it is important to note that expectant mothers who have plenty to eat may still fail to obtain all of the vitamins and minerals that help to ensure a healthy pregnancy. Adding small amounts of magnesium and zinc to a mother's diet improves the functioning of the placenta and reduces the incidence of many birth complications (Friedman & Polifka, 1996). And researchers around the world have discovered that diets rich in **folic acid**, a B-complex vitamin found in fresh fruits, liver, and green vegetables, help to prevent **spina bifida** and other defects of the neural tube (Cefalo, 1996; Chomitz et al., 2000; James et al., 1999). Most women consume less than half the recommended daily

folic acid
B-complex vitamin that helps to prevent defects of the central nervous system

spina bifida
bulging of the spinal cord through a gap in the spinal column

Figure 4.6 Incidence of infant mortality in the first 12 months for babies born to Dutch mothers who had experienced famine during World War II. ADAPTED FROM STEIN & SUSSER, 1976.

allowance of folic acid, and intensive campaigns are now underway to persuade all women of childbearing age to take vitamin-mineral supplements that provide them with at least 0.4 mg (but not more than 1.0 mg) of folic acid a day (Cefalo, 1996; Health Canada, 2003). Folic acid enrichment is particularly important from the time of conception through the first eight weeks of pregnancy, when the neural tube is forming (Friedman & Polifka, 1996). However, these supplementation campaigns are controversial. Many fear that some women encouraged to take vitamin-mineral supplements may assume that "more is better" and end up ingesting too much vitamin A, which in very high doses can produce birth defects (see Table 4.3). Yet, under proper medical supervision, use of these supplements is considered quite safe (Friedman & Polifka, 1996; Health Canada, 2003).

The Mother's Emotional Well-Being

Although most women are happy about conceiving a child, many pregnancies are unplanned and unintended. Does it matter how a mother feels about being pregnant or about her life while she is pregnant?

Indeed it may, at least in some cases. When a mother becomes emotionally aroused, her glands secrete powerful activating hormones such as adrenaline. These hormones may then cross the placental barrier, enter the fetus's bloodstream, and increase the fetus's motor activity. Temporarily stressful episodes such as a fall, a frightening experience, or an argument have few if any harmful consequences for a mother or her fetus (Brockington, 1996). However, *prolonged* and *severe* emotional stress is associated with stunted prenatal growth, premature delivery, low birth weight, and other birth complications (Lobel, 1994; Paarlberg et al., 1995). Others have found that babies of highly stressed mothers tend to be highly active, irritable, and irregular in their feeding, sleeping, and bowel habits (Sameroff & Chandler, 1975; Vaughn et al., 1987). Indeed, experiments with rhesus monkeys suggest a *causal* relationship between maternal stress and low birth weight/irregular infant demeanour (Schneider et al., 1999).

How might emotional stress stunt fetal growth and contribute to birth complications and newborn behavioural irregularities? A link between prolonged stress and growth retardation or low birth weight may reflect the influence of stress hormones, which divert blood flow to the large muscles and impede the flow of oxygen and nutrients to the fetus. Stress may also weaken the mother's immune system, making her (and her fetus) more susceptible to infectious diseases (Cohen & Williamson, 1991). Finally, emotionally stressed mothers may be inclined to eat poorly, smoke, or use alcohol and drugs, all of which are known to promote fetal growth retardation and low birth weight (Paarlberg et al., 1995). Of course, a mother whose source of stress *continues* after her baby is born may not make the most sensitive caregiver, which, coupled with a baby who is already irritable and unresponsive, can perpetuate the infant's difficult behavioural profile (Brockington, 1996; Vaughn et al., 1987).

Interestingly, not all highly stressed mothers experience the complications we have discussed. Why? Because it seems that the presence of objective stressors in a woman's life is far less important than her ability to manage such stress (McCubbin et al., 1996). Stress-related complications are much more likely when mothers (1) are ambivalent or negative about their marriages or their pregnancies and (2) have no friends or other bases of social support to turn to for comfort (Brockington, 1996). Counselling aimed at managing and reducing stress may help these mothers immensely. In one study, babies of stressed mothers who received such counselling weighed significantly more at birth than babies of stressed mothers who received no help (Rothberg & Lits, 1991).

The Mother's Age

The safest time to bear a child appears to be from about age 16 to age 35 (Amini et al., 1996; Dollberg et al., 1996). As shown in Figure 4.7, there is a relationship between a mother's age and the risk of death for her fetus or **neonate** (newborn). Compared with mothers in their 20s, mothers younger than 16 experience more birth complications and

neonate
newborn infant from birth to approximately 1 month old

are more likely to deliver prematurely and have low-birth-weight babies (Scholl, Hediger, & Belsky, 1994). Why are younger mothers and their offspring at risk? The major reason is simply that pregnant teenagers are often from economically impoverished family backgrounds (Gallant & Terrisse, 2001) characterized by poor nutrition and high levels of stress, and are less likely to access supervised prenatal care early in the pregnancy (Abma & Mott, 1991). Indeed, teenage mothers and their babies are usually *not* at risk when they receive good prenatal care and competent medical supervision during the birth process (Baker & Mednick, 1984; see also Seitz & Apfel, 1994a).

What risks do women face should they delay childbearing until after age 35? As Figure 4.7 indicates, there is an increased incidence of spontaneous abortion, due largely to the older woman's greater likelihood of conceiving children with chromosomal abnormalities (Verp, 1993b). (See Chapter 3.) The risks of other complications during pregnancy and delivery are also greater for older women, even when they receive adequate prenatal care (Dollberg et al., 1996). Even so, it is important to emphasize that the *vast majority* of older women—particularly those who are healthy and well-nourished and who receive adequate prenatal care—have normal pregnancies and healthy babies (Brockington, 1996).

Prevention of Birth Defects

Reading a chapter such as this one can be frightening to anyone who hopes to have a child. It is easy to come away with the impression that "life before birth" is a veritable minefield. After all, so many hereditary accidents are possible, and even a genetically normal embryo or fetus may encounter a large number of potential hazards while developing in the womb.

But clearly there is another side to this story. Recall that the majority of genetically abnormal embryos do not develop to term. And it appears that the prenatal environment is not so hazardous when we note that more than 95 percent of newborn babies are perfectly normal and that many of the remaining 5 percent have minor congenital problems that are only temporary or easily correctable (Gosden et al., 1994). Although there *is* reason for concern, prospective parents can reduce the odds that their babies will be abnormal by following some of the practical suggestions inherent in the material we have covered so far. For example, mothers should seek out appropriate health care (including inoculations against diseases such as rubella and treatment for STDs) before conception and follow through with this care throughout the pregnancy, mothers should eat nutritious food and monitor their diets, and mothers (and fathers) should avoid (or at least limit) exposure to teratogenic agents. Failure to abide by one or more of these suggestions will not necessarily mean that your child will be abnormal. Nor will exact compliance guarantee that a child will be healthy—accidents do happen. Following these recommendations may seem unnecessary to parents who have already given birth to healthy children. However, Apgar and Beck (1974, p. 452) remind us that "Each pregnancy is different. Each unborn child has a unique genetic make-up. The prenatal environment a mother provides is never quite the same for another baby. Thus, we believe no amount of effort is too great to increase the chances that a baby will be born normal, healthy, and without a handicapping birth defect."

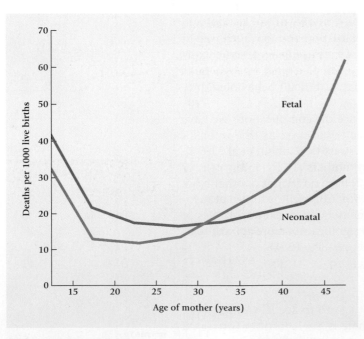

Figure 4.7 *Relationship between mother's age and risk of death for the fetus or neonate.* FROM KESSNER, *1973.*

CHILDBIRTH AND THE PERINATAL ENVIRONMENT

The *perinatal environment* is the environment surrounding birth; it includes influences such as drugs given to the mother during delivery, delivery practices, and the social environment shortly after the baby is born. As we will see, this perinatal environment is an important one that can affect a baby's well-being and the course of her or his future development.

The Birth Process

Childbirth is a three-stage process (see Figure 4.8). The **first stage of labour** begins as the mother experiences uterine contractions spaced at 10- to 15-minute intervals, and it ends when her cervix has fully dilated so that the fetus's head can pass through. This phase lasts an average of 8 to 14 hours for first-born children and 3 to 8 hours for later-borns. As labour proceeds, the uterus contracts more frequently and intensely. When the head of the fetus is positioned at the cervical opening, the second phase of labour is about to begin.

The **second stage of labour**, or *delivery*, begins as the fetus's head passes through the cervix into the vagina and ends when the baby emerges from the mother's body. This is the time when the mother may be told to bear down (push) with each contraction to assist her child through the birth canal. A quick delivery may take a half-hour, whereas a long one may last more than an hour and a half.

The **third stage of labour**, or *afterbirth*, takes only 5 to 10 minutes as the uterus once again contracts and expels the placenta from the mother's body.

The Baby's Experience

It was once thought that birth was an extremely hazardous and torturous ordeal for a contented fetus, who is suddenly expelled from a soft, warm uterus into a cold, bright world where, for the first time, it may experience chills, pain, hunger, and the startling rush of air into its lungs. Yet few people today would describe birth and birthing prac-

first stage of labour
period of the birth process lasting from the first regular uterine contractions until the cervix is fully dilated

second stage of labour
period of the birth process during which the fetus moves through the birth canal and emerges from the mother's body (also called *delivery*)

third stage of labour
expulsion of the placenta (afterbirth)

Concept Check 4.2
Understanding the Prenatal Environment

Check your understanding of environmental influences on prenatal development by matching each of the following influences with one of the statements below: (a) severe malnutrition, (b) toxoplasmosis, (c) diethylstilbestrol (DES), (d) rubella, (e) folic acid, (f) alcohol, and (g) syphilis. Answers appear in the Appendix.

_____ 1. disease that is most harmful to fetuses in the latter half of pregnancy

_____ 2. linked to cervical cancer in girls

_____ 3. teratogen for which father's use has been linked to low birth weight

_____ 4. disease that is a strong teratogen, even though mothers experience few symptoms

_____ 5. protects against spina bifida and defects of the neural tube

_____ 6. teratogenic effects of this disease are strongest during the first trimester

_____ 7. associated with stunted brain development if it occurs in the third trimester

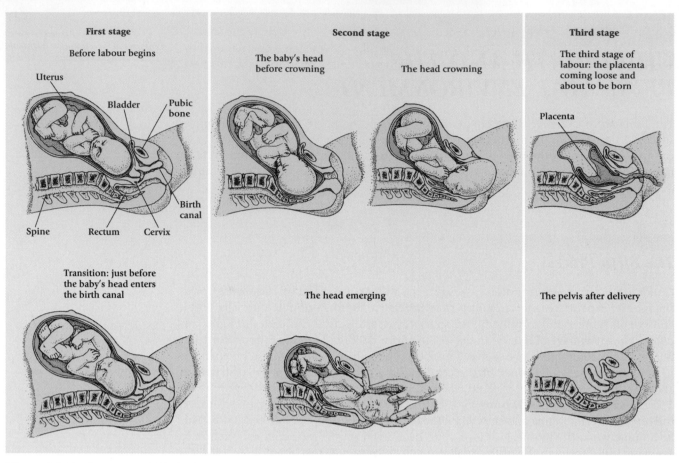

Figure 4.8 *The three stages of childbirth.*

tices as the "torture of the innocents" as French obstetrician Frederick Leboyer (1975) has. Fetuses *are* stressed by birth, but their own production of activating stress hormones is adaptive, helping them to withstand oxygen deprivation by increasing their heart rate and the flow of oxygenated blood to the brain (Nelson, 1995). Birth stress also helps to ensure that babies are born wide awake and ready to breathe. Aiden Macfarlane (1977) has carefully observed many newborn babies, noting that most of them quiet down and begin to adapt to their new surroundings within minutes of that first loud cry. So birth is a stressful ordeal, but hardly a torturous one.

The Baby's Appearance

To a casual observer, many newborns may not look especially attractive. Often born bluish in colour from oxygen deprivation during the birth process, babies' passage through the narrow cervix and birth canal may also leave them with flattened noses, misshapen foreheads, and an assortment of bumps and bruises. As the baby is weighed and measured, parents are likely to see a wrinkled, red-skinned little creature, about 50.0 cm long and weighing about 3.0 to 3.5 kg, with females weighing slightly less than males

Immediately after birth, babies are not particularly attractive, but their appearance improves dramatically over the first few weeks of life.

PhotoDisc Collection/PhotoDisc

(Committee on Nutritional Status during Pregnancy and Lactation, 1990), who is covered with a sticky substance. But even though newborns may hardly resemble the smiley, bouncing infants who appear in baby food commercials, most parents think that *their* baby is beautiful nevertheless and are usually eager to become acquainted with this new member of the family.

Assessing the Baby's Condition

In the very first minutes of life, a baby takes his or her first test. A nurse, midwife, or doctor checks the infant's physical condition by looking at five standard characteristics that are rated from 0 to 2, recorded on a chart, and totalled (see Table 4.4). A baby's score on this **Apgar test** (named for its developer, Dr. Virginia Apgar) can range from 0 to 10, with higher scores indicating a better condition. The test is often repeated five minutes later to measure improvements in the baby's condition. Infants who score 7 or higher on this second assessment are in good physical condition, whereas those who score 4 or lower are in trouble and often require immediate medical attention in order to survive.

Although useful as a quick method of detecting *severe* physical or neurological irregularities that require immediate attention, the Apgar test may miss less obvious complications. A second test, T. Berry Brazelton's **Neonatal Behavioral Assessment Scale (NBAS)**, is a more subtle measure of a baby's behavioural repertoire and neurological well-being (Brazelton, 1979). If the NBAS is administered, it is given a few days after birth. It assesses the strength of 20 inborn reflexes, as well as changes in the infant's state, and reactions to comforting and other social stimuli. One important value of this test is its early identification of babies who are slow to react to a variety of everyday experiences. If the infant is extremely unresponsive, the low NBAS score may indicate brain damage or other neurological problems. If the baby has good reflexes but is sluggish or irritable when responding to social stimuli, it is possible that he or she will not receive enough playful stimulation and comforting in the months ahead to develop secure emotional ties to caregivers. So a low NBAS score is a warning that problems could arise. Fortunately, the NBAS can also be used to help parents of these socially unresponsive infants get off to a good start with their babies. Several studies show that mothers and fathers who take part as the NBAS is administered often learn much about their baby's behavioural capabilities and how they might successfully quiet their fussy infant or elicit such pleasing responses as smiles and attentive gazes. When observed one month later, "NBAS trained" parents are generally more responsive toward and involved with their infants than are parents in control groups who received no training (Britt & Myers, 1994). Others have had similar success with filmed NBAS sessions (which illustrate newborns' social and perceptual capabilities) coupled with discussions, undertaken with the baby present, that stress the importance of affectionate handling and sensitive adaptation of one's caregiving to the baby's unique characteristics (Wendland-Carro, Piccinini, & Millar, 1999). So, NBAS training and other similar interventions appear to be highly effective at starting parents and their babies on the right foot. What's more, parents

TABLE 4.4	**The Apgar Test**		
	Score		
Characteristic	**0**	**1**	**2**
Heart rate	Absent	Slow (fewer than 100 beats per minute)	Over 100 beats per minute
Respiratory effort	Absent	Slow or irregular	Good; baby is crying
Muscle tone	Flaccid, limp	Weak, some flexion	Strong, active motion
Colour	Blue or pale	Body pink, extremities blue	Completely pink
Reflex irritability	No response	Frown, grimace, or weak cry	Vigorous cries, coughs, sneezes

Apgar test
quick assessment of the newborn's heart rate, respiration, muscle tone, colour, and reflexes that is used to gauge perinatal stress and to determine whether a neonate requires immediate medical assistance

Neonatal Behavioral Assessment Scale (NBAS)
test that assesses a neonate's neurological integrity and responsiveness to environmental stimuli

enjoy these simple, inexpensive programs, which seem especially well suited for (1) young, inexperienced caregivers who know little about babies, or (2) families with a baby who scores low on the NBAS and may otherwise frustrate parents with an irritable or unresponsive demeanour (Wendland-Carro et al., 1999).

Labour and Delivery Medication

The amount and kinds of drugs used during delivery have changed over time. The Canadian national guidelines for family-centred maternity and newborn care (Health Canada, 2001b) suggest that Canadian women who are expected to experience a normal delivery would require little or no drug intervention during the birth of their child. When drugs are used they may include one or more of analgesics and anesthetics to reduce pain, sedatives to relax the mother, and stimulants to induce or intensify uterine contractions. Obviously, these agents are administered in the hope of making the birth process easier for the mother, and their use is often essential to save a baby's life in a complicated delivery. However, a strong dose of birth medications can have some undesirable consequences.

Mothers who receive large amounts of anesthesia, for example, are often less sensitive to uterine contractions and do not push effectively during the delivery. As a result, their babies may have to be pulled from the birth canal with *obstetrical forceps* (a device that resembles a pair of salad tongs) or a *vacuum extractor* (a plastic suction cup attached to the baby's head). Unfortunately, in a small number of cases, applying these devices to a baby's soft skull can cause cranial bleeding and brain damage (Brockington, 1996).

Labour and delivery medications also cross the placenta and, in heavy doses, can make babies lethargic and inattentive. Infants of heavily medicated mothers smile infrequently, become irritable when aroused, and are difficult to feed or cuddle in the first weeks of life (Brackbill, McManus, & Woodward, 1985). Some researchers fear that parents could fail to become very involved with or attached to such a sluggish, irritable, and inattentive baby (Murray et al., 1981). Others have even claimed that some babies of heavily medicated mothers continue to show deficits in physical and mental development for at least a year after birth (Brackbill et al., 1985), although other researchers have not been able to replicate these long-term effects (Friedman & Polifka, 1996).

Access to drugs is important, especially for women at risk for birth complications, and also for those who experience difficult deliveries. In appropriate doses drugs can ease their discomfort without disrupting the delivery. In addition, doctors today use less toxic drugs in smaller doses at the safest times, so that taking medications is not as risky as it once was (Simpson & Creehan, 1996). Yet, in light of the uncertainties about the long-term consequences of obstetric medications for newborns, it is important to carefully weigh the pros and cons of their use and limit them whenever possible.

Anthro Photo

Childbirth is treated as a natural event in many cultures. Women may give birth in full view of others, wherever they may be at the moment.

Approaches to Childbirth in Canada and Around the World

Cultures clearly differ in the rituals surrounding birth (Steinberg, 1996). The majority of infants in many cultures are born at home, often with the mother in a vertical or squatting position, surrounded by family members and assisted by other women (Philpott, 1995; Mead & Newton,

Rankin Inlet). Traditional births in these northern Canadian communities take place in a variety of temporary dwellings (for example, snow houses and tents) and involve the support of a knowledgeable woman in the community (Canadian Association of Midwives, 2001). Among the Pokot people of Kenya, cultural rituals help to ensure strong social support of the birth mother (O'Dempsey, 1988). The whole community celebrates the coming birth, and the father-to-be must stop hunting and be available to support his wife. A midwife, assisted by female relatives, delivers the baby. The placenta is then ceremoniously buried in the goat enclosure, and the baby is given a tribal potion for its health. Mothers are secluded for a month to recover and are given three months, free of other chores, to devote themselves to their babies (Jeffery & Jeffery, 1993). By contrast, childbirth is viewed as shameful in Uttar Predesh in northern India. Babies are delivered by poorly paid attendants, who discourage a mother's cries of pain and offer little social support. The mother is isolated for days after a birth, and her "dirty" baby's head is shaved to avoid "polluting" others.

In contrast to many cultures in the world, the majority of Canadian births take place in hospitals, with a smaller but growing proportion taking place at home or in stand-alone birthing facilities (Wagner, 1998). Interestingly, hospital birthing is a relatively recent practice; before 1900, few babies were born in a hospital (Brockington, 1996; Wagner, 1998). This was followed by a period where mothers were heavily medicated and often gave birth lying flat on their backs with their legs in stirrups. Birth was viewed as a medically threatening condition to be managed with high technology (Brockington, 1996).

Recently, views regarding birth have moved away from a medical model toward understanding birth as a natural event that takes place within families, and Canadian women today now have considerably more freedom to give birth as they choose. This change in views has affected hospital procedures and birthing facilities. For example, procedures now encourage support personnel (nurses, doctors, and/or midwives) to provide continuity of care throughout the delivery, active planning and participation of the mother (and other support persons), and mobility and flexibility of birthing positions. In terms of facilities, current guidelines encourage the creation of "labour/birth/recovery (LBR)" rooms, or "LBRP" rooms where the mother labours, delivers, and experiences some or all of her postpartum care (Health Canada, 2001b).

Natural and Prepared Childbirth

The changing views toward childbirth in Canada continue to be heavily influenced by the philosophies behind **natural and prepared childbirth**. Natural and prepared childbirth are based on the idea that childbirth is a normal and natural part of life rather than a painful ordeal that women should fear. The natural childbirth movement arose from the work of Grantly Dick-Read in England, and prepared childbirth originated in Russia but was popularized by Fernand Lamaze in France. These two obstetricians claimed that most women could give birth quite comfortably without medication if they were taught to associate childbirth with pleasant feelings and to ready themselves for the process by practising exercises, breathing methods, and relaxation techniques that make childbirth easier (Dick-Read, 1933/1972; Lamaze, 1958). Mothers who have more knowledge, training, and confidence and less anxiety in their ability to navigate their delivery, require less medication, have fewer interventions (e.g., cesarean sections) and shorter labours (e.g., Bewley & Cockburn, 2002; Stockman & Altmaier, 2001).

Most Canadians have access to services that permit a prepared childbirth experience either at home or in a birthing centre or hospital. Parents usually attend classes for six to eight weeks before the delivery. They learn what to expect during labour and may even visit a delivery room (if they choose to deliver in a hospital) and become familiar with procedures used there as part of their preparation. They are also given a prescribed set of exercises and relaxation techniques to master. Typically, the father (or another companion) acts as a coach to assist the mother in toning her muscles and perfecting her breathing for labour. The birthing partner is also encouraged to support the mother during the delivery.

natural and prepared childbirth
delivery in which physical and psychological preparations for the birth are stressed and medical assistance is minimized

Research reveals that there are many benefits to natural and prepared childbirth, not the least of which is the important social support mothers receive from their partners and other close companions. When mothers attend childbirth classes regularly and have a companion present in the delivery room to assist and encourage them, they experience less pain during delivery, use less medication, and have more positive attitudes toward themselves, their babies, and the whole birth experience (Brockington, 1996; Wilcock, Kobayashi, & Murray, 1997). As a result, many more physicians now routinely recommend natural and prepared childbirth to their patients.

Home Births

A small but growing number of families are opting to deliver their babies at home with the aid of a certified midwife (who may or may not have a nursing background) trained in nonsurgical obstetrics. They believe that home deliveries will reduce the mother's fear and offer maximum social support by encouraging friends and family to be there, rather than a host of unfamiliar nurses, aides, and physicians. These families are also hoping to reduce their reliance on labour and delivery medications and other unnecessary and potentially harmful medical interventions. Indeed, it appears that the relaxed atmosphere and the social support available at a home delivery does have a calming effect on many mothers. Women who deliver at home have shorter labours and use less medication than those who deliver in hospitals (Beard & Chapple, 1995; Brackbill et al., 1985).

Are home births as safe as hospital deliveries? Childbirth statistics from many countries suggest that they are, as long as the mother is healthy, the pregnancy has gone smoothly, and the birth is attended by a well-trained midwife (Ackermann-Liebrich et al., 1996). There are also options for couples who seek a homelike birth environment but do not want to give birth at home. **Alternative birth centres** provide a homelike atmosphere but still make medical technology available. Sometimes these birth centres are free-standing and operate independently of hospitals, while others are attached to hospitals. Most employ a range of professionals, including obstetricians, certified midwives, and nurses (Beard & Chapple, 1995). Some delivering mothers also acquire the assistance of a doula—a woman experienced in childbirth—who provides additional support

alternative birth centre
hospital birthing room or other independent facility that provides a homelike atmosphere for childbirth but still makes medical technology available

Murray Moman

More women today are choosing to give birth at home or in alternative birth centres to share the joy of childbirth with family members. When assisted by a well-trained midwife, healthy women can give birth safely at home.

and advice. In birthing centres, spouses, friends, and often the couple's children can be present during labour, and healthy infants can remain in the same room with their mothers (room-in) rather than spend their first days in the hospital nursery. So far, the evidence suggests that giving birth in well-run alternative birth centres is no more risky to healthy mothers and their babies than hospital deliveries are (Fullerton & Severino, 1992; Harvey et al., 1996). However, mothers at risk for birth complications are always best advised to deliver in a hospital, where life-saving technologies are immediately available should they be needed.

In Canada, the resurgence in interest in midwife-assisted births is evident in the recent development of midwifery certification programs (such as the four-year Bachelor of Health Sciences in Midwifery degree program offered through McMaster, Ryerson, and Laurentian universities in Ontario) and through the development of governing bodies to regulate and legislate practising midwives. At present, midwifery is a regulated profession in Alberta, British Columbia, Manitoba, Ontario, Saskatchewan, the Northwest Territories, and Quebec (Canadian Association of Midwives, 2003). The availability of midwives varies by province/territory, and in some regions costs for midwives are covered publicly, whereas in others the user covers all costs. Canadian midwives practise in homes, birthing centres, and hospitals.

The Social Environment Surrounding Birth

Only 25 years ago, most hospitals barred fathers from delivery rooms and whisked babies away from their mothers to nurseries within minutes of delivery. However, times have changed, so that a birth today is much more likely to be a dramatic experience for both parents.

The Mother's Experience

The first few minutes after birth can be a special time for a mother to thoroughly enjoy her baby, provided she is given the opportunity. Marshall Klaus and John Kennell believe that the first 6 to 12 hours after birth are a *sensitive period* for **emotional bonding** when the mother is especially ready to respond to and develop a strong sense of affection for her baby (Kennell, Voos, & Klaus, 1979). In a study testing this hypothesis, Klaus and Kennell (1976) had half of a group of new mothers follow then-traditional hospital routine: They saw their babies briefly after delivery, visited with them 6 to 12 hours later, and had half-hour feeding sessions every four hours thereafter for the remainder of a three-day hospital stay. By contrast, mothers in an "extended-contact" group were permitted five extra hours a day to cuddle their babies, including an hour of skin-to-skin contact that took place within three hours of birth.

In a follow-up one month later, mothers who had had early extended contact with their babies appeared to be more involved with them and held them closer during feeding sessions than did mothers who had followed the traditional hospital routine. One year later, the extended-contact mothers were still the more highly involved group of caregivers, and their 1-year-olds outperformed those in the traditional-routine group on tests of physical and mental development. Apparently, extended early contact in the hospital fostered mothers' affection for their newborns, which in turn may have motivated those mothers to continue to interact in highly stimulating ways with their babies. In response to this and other similar studies, many hospitals have altered their routines to allow the kinds of early contact that can promote emotional bonding.

Does this mean that mothers who have no early contact with their newborns miss out on forming the strongest possible emotional ties to them? No! Later research has shown that early-contact effects are nowhere near as significant or long-lasting as Klaus and Kennell presumed (Eyer, 1992; Goldberg, 1983). Other research reveals that most adoptive parents, who rarely have any early contact with their infants, nevertheless develop strong emotional bonds with their adoptees that are just as secure, on average,

emotional bonding
term used to describe the strong affectionate ties that parents may feel toward their infant; some theorists believe that the strongest bonding occurs shortly after birth, during a sensitive period

as those seen in nonadoptive homes (Levy-Shiff, Goldschmidt, & Har-Even, 1991; Singer et al., 1985). So even though early contact can be a very pleasant experience that can help a mother *begin* to form an emotional bond with her child, she need not fear that problems will arise should something prevent her from having this experience.

POSTPARTUM DEPRESSION. Unfortunately, there is a downside to the birth experience for some mothers, who may find themselves depressed, tearful, irritable, and even resentful of their babies shortly after birth. Milder forms of this condition, called the *maternity blues*, may characterize as many as 40 to 60 percent of all new mothers (Kessel, 1995). This mild depression, which usually passes within a matter of a week or two, is probably linked to hormonal changes following childbirth and to stresses associated with the new responsibilities of parenthood (Hendrick & Altshuler, 1999; Wile & Arechiga, 1999).

By contrast, slightly more than 10 percent of new mothers don't bounce back so quickly, experiencing instead a more serious depressive reaction, called **postpartum depression**, that can last for months. Most victims of postpartum depression have a history of depressive episodes and are experiencing other life stresses beyond those associated with becoming a new mother (Brockington, 1996; Whiffen, 1992). Lack of social support—particularly a poor relationship with the father—dramatically increases the odds of postpartum depression (Field et al., 1985; Gotlib et al., 1991). Susan Campbell and her associates (1992) found that many of these depressed women did not want their infants in the first place and perceived them as difficult babies. They also interacted less positively with their infants and in some cases seemed downright hostile toward them. Other studies suggest that, when a mother remains chronically depressed, withdrawn, and unresponsive, the attachment that develops between her and her infant is likely to be insecure, and infants may develop depressive symptoms and behaviour problems of their own (Campbell, Cohn, & Myers, 1995; Murray, Fiori-Cowley, & Hooper, 1996). For their own sake and for the sake of their infants, then, mothers experiencing more than a mild case of the maternity blues should seek professional help.

A promising and innovative approach to lowering one contributor to postpartum depression, parenting stress, is presented in the work of Philip Dunham and his colleagues at Dalhousie University (Dunham et al., 1998). They designed a computer-mediated social support network to allow single young mothers to communicate with other single young mothers and access information about parenting issues. The computer network was offered for six months and was available for 24 hours a day. The 42 mothers involved accessed the network more than 16 670 times, with most messages providing emotional support. Participants who were regular and active users of the network reported a decrease in parenting stress.

postpartum depression
strong feelings of sadness, resentment, and despair that may affect the mother shortly after childbirth and that can linger for months

engrossment
paternal analogue of maternal emotional bonding; term used to describe fathers' fascination with their newborns, including their desire to touch, hold, caress, and talk to the newborn baby

Chrissie Rostek

This father displays a fascination with his newborn that is known as engrossment.

The Father's Experience

Fathers, like mothers, experience the birth process as a significant life event that involves a mix of positive and negative emotions. New fathers admitted that their fears mounted during labour, but said that they tried hard to appear calm nonetheless. Although they described childbirth as an agonizing and stressful ordeal, their negative emotions usually gave way to relief, pride, and joy when the baby finally arrived (Chandler & Field, 1997).

Like new mothers, new fathers often display a sense of **engrossment** with the baby—an intense fascination with and a strong desire to touch, hold, and caress this newest member of the family (Greenberg & Morris, 1974; Peterson, Mehl, & Liederman, 1979). One young father put it this way: "When I came up to see (my) wife … I go look at the kid and then I pick her up and put her down.... I keep going back to the kid. It's like a magnet. That's what I can't get over, the fact that I feel like that" (Greenberg & Morris, 1974, p. 524). Some studies find that fathers who have handled and helped to care for their babies in the hospital spend more time with them at home than fathers who have not had these early contacts with their newborns (Greenberg & Morris, 1974). Other studies have failed to find these long-term effects on father–infant interactions but suggest that early contact with a newborn can make fathers feel closer to their partners and more a part of the family (Palkovitz, 1985). So a father who is present at birth not only plays an important supportive role for the mother, but is just as likely as the mother to enjoy close contact with their newborn.

? **WHAT DO YOU THINK?**

Design the perfect birth experience for you and your baby. Where would you be? Who would be there? What would be done to make things as pleasant as possible for all participants in the process?

BIRTH COMPLICATIONS

Childbirth does not always proceed as smoothly as indicated in our earlier account of the "normal" delivery. Three birth complications that can adversely influence a baby's development are anoxia (oxygen deprivation), low birth weight, and a premature delivery.

Anoxia

Nearly 1 percent of babies are born showing signs of **anoxia**, or oxygen deprivation. In many cases, the child's supply of oxygen is interrupted because the umbilical cord has become tangled or squeezed during childbirth, as can easily happen when infants are lying in the **breech position** and are born feet or buttocks first. In fact, breech babies are often delivered by cesarean section to protect against anoxia (Lin, 1993a). Other cases of anoxia occur when the placenta separates prematurely, interrupting the supply of food and oxygen to the fetus. Anoxia can also occur after birth if sedatives given to the mother cross the placental barrier and interfere with the baby's breathing or if mucous ingested during childbirth becomes lodged in the baby's throat. Although newborns can tolerate oxygen deprivation far longer than older children and adults can, permanent brain damage can result if breathing is delayed for more than three to four minutes (Nelson, 1995).

Another potential cause of anoxia is a genetic incompatibility between an RH-positive fetus, who has a protein called **RH factor** in its blood, and an RH-negative mother, who lacks this substance. During labour and delivery, when the placenta is deteriorating, RH-negative mothers are often exposed to the blood of their RH-positive fetuses, and they begin to produce RH antibodies. If these antibodies enter a fetus's bloodstream, they can attack red blood cells, depleting oxygen and possibly producing brain damage and other birth defects. First-borns are usually not affected because an RH-negative mother has no RH antibodies until she gives birth to an RH-positive child. Fortunately, problems stemming from an RH incompatibility can now be prevented by administering a vaccine (e.g., *RhoGAM or WinRho SD*) after the delivery, which prevents the RH-negative mother from forming the RH antibodies that could harm her next RH-positive baby.

Children who experience mild anoxia are often irritable at birth and may score below average on tests of motor and mental development throughout the first three years (Sameroff & Chandler, 1975). However, these differences between mildly anoxic and normal children become smaller and smaller and are usually not detectable by age 7 (Corah et al., 1965). So even though *prolonged* oxygen deprivation can cause neurological damage and permanent disabilities, there is no compelling evidence that *mild* anoxia has any lasting effects on children's motor skills or intellectual development (Vaughn et al., 1984).

anoxia
lack of sufficient oxygen to the brain; may result in neurological damage or death

breech birth
delivery in which the baby emerges feet or buttocks first rather than head first

RH factor
blood protein that, when present in a fetus but not the mother, can cause the mother to produce antibodies; these antibodies may then attack the red blood cells of subsequent fetuses who have the protein in their blood

Low Birth Weight

Most babies in Canada are born between the 37th and 42nd weeks of pregnancy and are considered "timely." As we mentioned in the section about the appearance of the newborn, the average full-term, or "timely," infant is about 47.0 to 53.0 cm long and weighs about 3.0 to 3.5 kg.

About 6 percent of Canadian babies, however, weigh less than 2500 g at birth (da Silva, 1994; Austin & Moawad, 1993) and, until recently, were simply labelled "premature." Yet there are actually two kinds of low-birth-weight babies. Most are born more than three weeks before their due dates and are called **preterm infants**. Although small in size, the body weights of these babies are often appropriate for the amount of time they spent in the womb. Other low-birth-weight babies, called **small-for-date** or **small-for-gestational-age babies**, have experienced slow growth as fetuses and are seriously underweight, even when born close to their normal due dates (see Figure 4.9 for rates of small-for-gestational-age babies in each province except Ontario). Although both kinds of low-birth-weight babies are vulnerable and may have to struggle to survive, small-for-date infants are at greater risk of serious complications. For example, they are more likely to die during the first year or to show signs of brain damage. They are also more likely than preterm infants to remain small in stature throughout childhood, to experience learning difficulties and behaviour problems at school, and to perform poorly on IQ tests (Goldenberg, 1995; Lin, 1993b). Research at Laval University suggests that premature and low-birth-weight babies may also be less socially competent throughout their school-age years (Tessier et al., 1997).

What are the causes of low birth weight? We have already seen that mothers who smoke and drink heavily or use drugs or who are malnourished are likely to deliver undersized babies. Indeed, low-income women, especially from ethnic minority groups or those with disabilities, are particularly at risk, largely because their diets and the prenatal care they receive are often inadequate (Kopp & Kaler, 1989; Lin, 1993b; Morris, 2000). Although Canadians typically expect that women have ready access to appropriate medical care and sufficient funds to provide good nutrition, many Canadian women do not have these resources (Morris, 2000). Moreover, illnesses or accidents that impair the functioning of the placenta can retard fetal growth and result in a baby who is preterm or small-for-date. Yet another frequent contributor to undersized babies is multiple births. Multiple fetuses generally gain much less weight than a single fetus after the 29th week of pregnancy. And in addition to being small-for-date, triplets and quadruplets rarely develop to term in the uterus; in fact, they are often born five to eight weeks early (Papiernik, 1995).

preterm infants
infants born more than three weeks before their normal due dates

small-for-date, or small-for-gestational-age, babies
infants whose birth weight is far below normal, even when born close to their normal due dates

Figure 4.9 Rates for small-for-gestational-age infants, by province/territory, Canada (excluding Ontario), 1997. FROM: STATISTICS CANADA, CANADIAN VITAL STATISTICS SYSTEM, 1997, IN HEALTH CANADA, CANADIAN PERINATAL SURVEILLANCE SYSTEM (2001B, FIGURE 4.7).

*Ontario is excluded due to data quality concerns.
**Excludes live births with unknown gestational age and birth weight, and gestational age <20 weeks. CI: Confidence interval.

Short-Term Consequences of Low Birth Weight

The most trying task for a low-birth-weight baby is simply surviving the first few days of life. Although more of these infants are surviving each year, at least half of those who weigh less than 1000 g die at birth or shortly thereafter, even in the best hospitals. Small-for-date babies are often malformed, undernourished, or genetically abnormal—factors that will hinder them as they struggle to survive. Moreover, preterm infants are likely to experience a number of additional problems as a consequence of their general immaturity. Their most serious difficulty is breathing. A preterm infant often has very little *surfactin*, a substance that normally coats the lungs during the last three to four weeks of pregnancy to prevent them from collapsing. A deficiency of surfactin may result in **respiratory distress syndrome**, a serious respiratory ailment in which the affected child breathes very irregularly and may stop breathing altogether.

Preterm infants often spend their first few weeks of life in heated *isolettes* that maintain their body temperature and protect them from infection. Isolettes are aptly named because they do isolate; the infant is fed, cleaned, and changed through a hole in the device that is much too small to allow visiting parents to cuddle and love their baby in the usual way. Furthermore, preterm infants can try the patience of caregivers. Compared with full-term infants, they are slow to initiate social interactions and often respond to a parent's bids for attention by looking away or actively resisting such overtures (Lester, Hoffman, & Brazelton, 1985; Malatesta et al., 1986). Mothers of preterm infants often remark that their babies are "hard to read," and mothers are likely to become frustrated as their persistent attempts to carry on a social dialogue are apparently rebuffed by an aloof, fussy, squirming little companion (Lester et al., 1985). Indeed, preterm infants are at risk of forming less secure emotional ties to their caregivers than other babies do (Mangelsdorf et al., 1996; Wille, 1991), and although the vast majority of them are never mistreated, they are more likely than full-term infants to become targets of child abuse (Brockington, 1996).

Interventions for Preterm Infants

Twenty five years ago, hospitals permitted parents little if any contact with preterm infants for fear of harming these fragile little creatures. Today, parents are encouraged to visit their child often in the hospital and to become actively involved during their visits by touching, caressing, and talking to their baby. The objective of these early-acquaintance programs is to allow parents to get to know their child and to foster the development of positive emotional ties. But there may be important additional benefits, because babies in intensive care often become less irritable and more responsive and show quicker neurological and mental development if they are periodically rocked, stroked, massaged, or soothed by the sound of a mother's voice (Barnard & Bee, 1983; Scafidi et al., 1986, 1990).

Preterm and other low-birth-weight babies can also benefit from programs that teach their parents how to provide them with sensitive and responsive care at home. In one study, a pediatric nurse visited periodically with mothers and taught them how to read and respond appropriately to the atypical behaviours their preterm infants displayed. Although the intervention lasted only three months, the low-birth-weight infants whose mothers participated had caught up intellectually with normal-birth-weight peers by the age of 4 (Achenbach et al., 1990). In a recent Canadian study (Tessier et al., 2003), mothers (with relief provided by other caregivers) were encouraged to carry their children like a "kangaroo." As soon as infants were able to exist safely without interventions, they were carried on the mother's chest 24 hours a day. The infants had skin-to-skin contact, could view the care-provider continuously, and experienced the normal rhythms of movement and heartbeat, as well as the smells and sounds of their care-providers. In addition, mothers were encouraged to breast-feed (with sup-

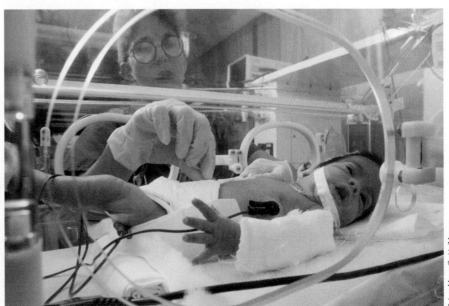

Isolettes do isolate. The holes in the apparatus allow parents and hospital staff to care for, talk to, and touch the baby, but close, tender cuddling is nearly impossible.

respiratory distress syndrome
serious condition in which a preterm infant breathes very irregularly and is at risk of dying (also called *hyaline membrane disease*)

plements added where necessary). This intervention lasted several days to several weeks after birth. The "kangaroo mother care" yielded positive mental gains for the infants and fostered more optimal parenting. And when combined with stimulating daycare programs, parental interventions not only foster the cognitive growth of low-birth-weight children but can also reduce the likelihood of their displaying behavioural disturbances (Brooks-Gunn et al., 1993; Spiker, Ferguson, & Brooks-Gunn, 1993). These interventions are most effective when they continue into the elementary-school years (Bradley et al., 1994; McCarton et al., 1997).

Of course, not all low-birth-weight infants (or their parents) have opportunities to participate in successful interventions. What happens to them?

Long-Term Consequences of Low Birth Weight

During the past 30 years, researchers reported that preterm and other low-birth-weight infants were likely to experience more learning difficulties later in childhood, score lower on IQ tests, and suffer more emotional problems than normal-birth-weight infants (Caputo & Mandell, 1970; Drillien, 1969; Saigal et al., 2000). Today, we know that these conclusions are overstated and that the long-term prognosis for low-birth-weight children depends largely on the environment in which they are raised. Outcomes are likely to be especially good when mothers are knowledgeable about the factors that promote healthy development. These mothers are likely to be highly involved with their children and to create a stimulating home environment that fosters cognitive and emotional growth (Benasich & Brooks-Gunn, 1996; Caughy, 1996). By contrast, low-birth-weight children from less stable or economically disadvantaged families are likely to remain smaller in stature than full-term children, experience more emotional problems, and show some long-term deficits in intellectual performance and academic achievement (Baker & Mednick, 1984; Kopp & Kaler, 1989; Rose & Feldman, 1996; Taylor et al., 2000).

Consider what Ronald Wilson (1985) found in his study of developing twins. Although twins are generally small for date and are often preterm, Wilson focused closely on twins who were especially small at birth (weighing under 1750 g). In Figure 4.10, we see that these preterm, low-birth-weight babies were indeed below average in mental performance throughout the first three years of life (a score of 100 on the test reflects average intellectual performance). Yet the figure also shows that low-birth-weight twins from middle-class (high SES) homes eventually made up their intellectual deficits, scoring average (or slightly above) on the tests by age 6, whereas their counterparts from low-income (low SES) backgrounds remained substantially below average in their intellectual performance. So the long-term prognosis for preterm and small-for-date children seems to depend critically on the *postnatal environment* in which they are raised.

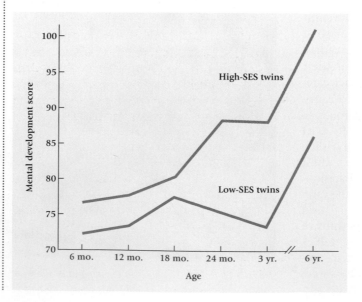

Figure 4.10 *Age trends in intellectual development for low-birth-weight twins from middle-class (high-SES) and lower socioeconomic (low-SES) backgrounds.* ADAPTED FROM WILSON, 1985.

Reproductive Risk and Capacity for Recovery

We have now discussed many examples of what can go wrong during the prenatal and perinatal periods, and some steps that expectant parents can take to try to prevent such outcomes. Once they occur, some of these damaging effects are irreversible; a baby blinded by rubella, for example, will never regain her sight, and a child who is mentally retarded due to fetal alcohol syndrome or severe anoxia will always be mentally retarded. And yet, there are many adults who turned out perfectly normal even though their mothers smoked, drank, or contracted harmful diseases while pregnant or received heavy doses of medication while in labour and childbirth. Why is this so? As we have already emphasized, not all embryos, fetuses, and newborns who are exposed to teratogens and other early hazards are affected by them. But what about those who are affected? Is it possible that many of these infants will eventually overcome their early handicaps later in life?

Indeed it is, and we now have some excellent longitudinal studies to tell us so. In 1955, Emmy Werner and Ruth Smith began to follow the development of all 670 babies born that year on the Hawaiian island of Kauai. At birth, 16 percent of these infants showed moderate to severe complications, another 31 percent showed mild complications, and 53 percent appeared normal and healthy. When the babies were reexamined at age 2, there was a clear relationship between severity of birth complications and developmental progress: The more severe their birth complications, the more likely children were to be lagging in their social and intellectual development. However, effects of the postnatal environment were already apparent. In homes rated high in emotional support and educational stimulation, children who had suffered severe birth complications scored slightly below average on tests of social and intellectual development. But in homes low in emotional support and educational stimulation, the intellectual performance of children who had experienced equally severe complications was *far* below average.

Werner and Smith then followed up on the children at ages 10 and 18, and again as young adults. What they found was striking. By age 10, early complications no longer predicted children's intellectual performance very well, but certain characteristics of the children's home environments did. Children from unstimulating and unresponsive home environments continued to perform very poorly on intelligence tests, whereas their counterparts from stimulating and supportive homes showed no marked deficiencies in intellectual performance. Clearly, children who had suffered the most severe early complications were the ones who were least likely to overcome their initial handicaps, even when raised in stimulating and supportive homes (see also Bendersky & Lewis, 1994; Saigal et al., 2000). But in summarizing the results of this study, Werner and Smith noted that long-term problems related to the effects of poor environments outnumbered those attributable to birth complications by a ratio of 10 to 1.

What, then, are we to conclude about the long-term implications of reproductive risk? First, we do know that prenatal and birth complications can leave lasting scars, particularly if these insults are severe. Yet the longitudinal data we have reviewed suggest ample reason for optimism should you ever give birth to a frail, irritable, unresponsive baby who is abnormal in appearance or behaviour. Given a supportive and stimulating home environment in which to grow, and the unconditional love of at least one caregiver, a majority of these children will display a strong "self-righting" tendency and eventually overcome their initial handicaps (Werner & Smith, 1992; Wyman et al., 1999).

Concept Check 4.3
Perinatal Influences

Check your understanding of some potentially important perinatal influences by matching the events listed below with the following *possible* consequences: (a) cranial bleeding, (b) emotional bonding/engrossment, (c) respiratory distress syndrome, (d) NBAS training, (e) RH incompatibility, (f) natural (or prepared) childbirth. Answers appear in the Appendix.

_____ 1. improvements in parent–infant interactions
_____ 2. delivery by obstetrical forceps
_____ 3. preterm delivery
_____ 4. anoxia in later-born children
_____ 5. can make the birth process easier
_____ 6. close contact with newborn

THE NEWBORN'S READINESS FOR LIFE

In the past, newborns were often characterized as fragile and helpless little organisms who were simply not very well-prepared for life outside the womb. This view may once have been highly adaptive, helping to ease parents' grief in earlier eras when medical procedures were rather primitive and a fair percentage of newborns did die. Even today, "many cultures in which the [newborn] death rate is high still institutionalize such practices as not speaking of the newborn as a [human] … or not naming him until he is 3 months old and more likely to survive" (Brazelton, 1979, p. 35).

Today, we know that newborns are much better prepared for life than many doctors, parents, and developmentalists had initially assumed. In Chapter 6, for example, we will see that all of a newborn's senses are in good working order and that he sees and hears well enough to detect what is happening around him and respond adaptively to many of these sensations. Very young infants are also quite capable of learning and can even remember some of the particularly vivid experiences they have had.

Two other indications that newborns are "organized" creatures who are quite well adapted for life are their repertoire of inborn reflexes and their predictable patterns, or cycles, of daily activity.

Newborn Reflexes

One of the neonate's greatest strengths is a full set of useful reflexes. A **reflex** is an involuntary and automatic response to a stimulus, as when the eye automatically blinks in response to a puff of air. Table 4.5 describes some reflexes that healthy newborns display. Some of these graceful and complex patterns of behaviour are called **survival reflexes** because they have clear adaptive value. Examples include the breathing reflex, the eye-blink reflex (which protects the eyes against bright lights or foreign particles), and the sucking and swallowing reflexes by which the infant takes in food. Also implicated in feeding is the *rooting* reflex: An infant who is touched on the cheek will turn in that direction and search for something to suck. When neonates are positioned with their mouths just touching their mother's nipple, they engage in bursts of suckling behaviours, and like other animals, they are able to attach for breast-feeding. Ann Bigelow and her colleagues at St. Francis Xavier University noted that newborns even engage in organized suckling routines that enable them to successfully attach to their food source (Koepke & Bigelow, 1997).

Not only do survival reflexes offer some protection against aversive stimulation and enable an infant to satisfy very basic needs, but they may also have a very positive impact on caregivers. Mothers, for example, may feel quite gratified and competent as caregivers when their hungry babies immediately stop fussing and suck easily and rhythmically at the nipple. And few parents can resist the feeling that their baby enjoys being close when he grasps their fingers tightly as his palm is touched. So these survival reflexes help to endear infants to older companions, who can protect them and attend to their needs (Bowlby, 1969, 1988).

Other so-called **primitive reflexes** in the table are not nearly as useful; in fact, many are believed to be remnants of our evolutionary history that have outlived their original purpose. The *Babinski reflex* is a good example. Why would it be adaptive for infants to fan their toes when the bottoms of their feet are stroked? We don't know. Other primitive reflexes may still have some adaptive value, at least in some cultures (Bowlby, 1969; Fentress & McLeod, 1986). The *swimming reflex*, for example, may help keep afloat an infant who is accidentally immersed in a pond or river. And the *grasping reflex* may help infants who are carried in slings or on their mothers' hips to hang on. Finally, other responses, such as the *stepping reflex*, may be forerunners of useful voluntary behaviours that develop later in infancy (Thelen, 1984).

reflex
unlearned and automatic response to a stimulus or class of stimuli

survival reflexes
inborn responses such as breathing, sucking, and swallowing that enable the newborn to adapt to the environment

primitive reflexes
reflexes controlled by subcortical areas of the brain that gradually disappear over the first year of life

TABLE 4.5   Major Reflexes Present in Full-Term Neonates

Name	Response	Development and course	Significance
Survival reflexes			
Breathing reflex	Repetitive inhalation and expiration.	Permanent.	Provides oxygen and expels carbon dioxide.
Eye-blink reflex	Closing or blinking the eyes.	Permanent.	Protects the eyes from bright light or foreign objects.
Pupillary reflex	Constriction of pupils to bright light; dilation to dark or dimly lit surroundings.	Permanent.	Protects against bright light; adapts the visual system to low illumination.
Rooting reflex	Turning the head in the direction of a tactile (touch) stimulus to the cheek.	Disappears over the first few weeks of life and is replaced by voluntary head turning.	Orients baby to the breast or bottle.
Sucking reflex	Sucking on objects placed (or taken) into the mouth.	Permanent.	Allows baby to take in nutrients.
Swallowing reflex	Swallowing.	Permanent.	Allows baby to take in nutrients.
Primitive reflexes			
Babinski reflex	Fanning and then curling the toes when the bottom of the foot is stroked.	Usually disappears within the first 8 months–1 year of life.	Its presence at birth and disappearance in the first year are an indication of normal neurological development.
Palmar grasping reflex	Curling the fingers around objects (such as a finger) that touch the baby's palm.	Disappears in first 3–4 months and is then replaced by a voluntary grasp.	Its presence at birth and later disappearance are an indication of normal neurological development.
Moro reflex	A loud noise or sudden change in the position of the baby's head causes the baby to throw his or her arms outward, arch the back, and then bring the arms toward each other as if to hold onto something.	The arm movements and arching of the back disappear over the first 4–6 months; however, the child continues to react to unexpected noises or a loss of bodily support by showing a startle reflex (which does not disappear).	Its presence at birth and later disappearance are an indication of normal neurological development.
Swimming reflex	An infant immersed in water will display active movements of the arms and legs and involuntarily hold his or her breath (thus giving the body buoyancy); this swimming reflex will keep an infant afloat for some time, allowing easy rescue.	Disappears in the first 4–6 months.	Its presence at birth and later disappearance are an indication of normal neurological development.
Stepping reflex	Infants held upright so that their feet touch a flat surface will step as if to walk.	Disappears in the first 8 weeks unless the infant has regular opportunities to practise this response.	Its presence at birth and later disappearance are an indication of normal neurological development.

NOTE: Preterm infants may show little or no evidence of primitive reflexes at birth, and their survival reflexes are likely to be weak. However, the missing primitive reflexes typically appear soon after birth and disappear a little later than they do among full-term infants.

Primitive reflexes normally disappear during the first few months of life. Why? Because they are controlled by the lower "subcortical" areas of the brain and are lost once the higher centres of the cerebral cortex mature and begin to guide voluntary behaviours. But even if many primitive reflexes are not very useful to infants, they are important diagnostic indicators to developmentalists. If these reflexes are *not* present at birth—or if they last too long in infancy—we have reason to suspect that something is wrong with a baby's nervous system.

In sum, a full complement of infant reflexes tells us that newborns are quite prepared to respond adaptively to a variety of life's challenges. And the timely disappearance of certain reflexes is one important sign that a baby's nervous system is developing normally.

Newborns' grasping reflex is quite strong, often allowing them to support their own weight.

This infant illustrates the rhythmic sucking, or sucking reflex, that neonates display when objects are placed into their mouths.

Infant States

Newborns also display organized patterns of daily activity that are predictable and foster healthy developmental outcomes. In a typical day (or night), a neonate moves in and out of six **infant states**, or levels of arousal, that are described in Table 4.6. During the first month, a baby may move rapidly from one state to another, as mothers will testify when their wide-awake babies suddenly nod off to sleep in the middle of a feeding. Neonates spend about 70 percent of their time (16 to 18 hours a day) sleeping and only two to three hours in the alert, inactive (attentive) state, when they are most receptive to external stimulation (Berg & Berg, 1987; Thoman, 1990). Sleep cycles are typically brief, lasting from 45 minutes to two hours. These frequent "naps" are separated by periods of drowsiness, alert or inalert activity, and crying, any of which may occur (as red-eyed parents well know) at all hours of the day and night.

The fact that neonates pass through a predictable pattern of states during a typical day suggests that their internal regulatory mechanisms are well-organized. Yet research on infant states also makes it clear that newborns show a great deal of individuality (Brown, 1964; Thoman & Whitney, 1989). For example, one newborn in one study was alert for only about 15 minutes a day, on average, whereas another was alert for more than eight hours a day (Brown, 1964). Similarly, one infant cried about 17 percent of the time, but another cried 39 percent of the time. These differences have some obvious implications for parents, who may find it far more pleasant to be with a bright-eyed baby who rarely cries than with one who is often fussy and inattentive (Columbo & Horowitz, 1987). The social implication of states is discussed more fully in Chapter 11 in the consideration of Temperament and Development. Here, we will focus on issues related to sleep and arousal.

Developmental Changes in Infant States

infant states
levels of sleep and wakefulness that young infants display

Two of the states in Table 4.6—sleep and crying—show regular patterns of change over the first year and provide important information about the progress a baby is making.

Changes in Sleep

As infants develop, they spend less time sleeping and more time awake, alert, and attending to their surroundings. By age 2 to 6 weeks, babies are sleeping only 14 to 16 hours a day; somewhere between 3 and 7 months of age, many infants reach a milestone that parents truly appreciate—they begin to sleep through the night and require only two or three shorter naps during the day (Berg & Berg, 1987; St. James-Roberts & Plewis, 1996).

From at least two weeks before they are born throughout the first month or two of life, babies spend at least half their sleeping hours in **REM sleep**, a state of active irregular sleep characterized by rapid eye movement (REM) under their closed eyelids and brain wave activity more typical of wakefulness than of regular (non-REM) sleep (Groome et al., 1997). However, REM sleep declines steadily after birth and accounts for only 25 to 30 percent of total sleep for a 6-month-old.

Why do fetuses and newborns spend so much time in REM sleep, and why does it decline so dramatically over the first few months? The most widely accepted theory is that this active REM sleep early in life provides fetuses and very young infants, who sleep *so* much, with enough internal stimulation to allow their nervous systems to develop properly. Consistent with this **autostimulation theory** is the finding that babies who are given lots of interesting visual stimuli to explore while awake spend less time in REM sleep than control infants who are denied these experiences (Boismier, 1977). Perhaps the reason REM sleep declines sharply over the first six months is that the infant's brain is rapidly maturing, she is becoming more alert, and there is simply less need for the stimulation provided by REM activity.

Few babies have problems establishing regular sleep cycles unless their nervous system is abnormal in some way. Yet one of the major causes of infant mortality is a very perplexing sleep-related disorder called crib death, or **sudden infant death syndrome (SIDS)**, which we will examine more carefully in Box 4.3.

The Functions and Course of Crying

A baby's earliest cries are unlearned and involuntary responses to discomfort—distress signals by which he makes caregivers aware of his needs. Most of a newborn's early cries are provoked by such physical discomforts as hunger, pain, or a wet diaper, although chills, loud noises, and even sudden changes in illumination (as when the light over a crib goes off) are often enough to make a baby cry.

REM sleep
state of active or irregular sleep in which the eyes move rapidly beneath the eyelids and brain wave activity is similar to the pattern displayed when awake

autostimulation theory
theory proposing that REM sleep in infancy is a form of self-stimulation that helps the central nervous system to develop

sudden infant death syndrome (SIDS)
unexplained death of a sleeping infant who suddenly stops breathing (also called *crib death*)

TABLE 4.6	**Infant States of Arousal**	
State	**Description**	**Daily duration in newborn (hours)**
Regular sleep	Baby is still, with eyes closed and unmoving. Breathing is slow and regular.	8–9
Irregular sleep	Baby's eyes are closed but can be observed to move under the closed eyelids (a phenomenon known as *rapid eye movement*, or REM). Baby may jerk or grimace in response to stimulation. Breathing may be irregular.	8–9
Drowsiness	Baby is falling asleep or waking up. Eyes open and close and have a glazed appearance when open. Breathing is regular but more rapid than in regular sleep.	1/2–3
Alert inactivity	Baby's eyes are wide open and bright, exploring some aspect of the environment. Breathing is even, and the body is relatively inactive.	2–3
Alert activity	Baby's eyes are open and breathing is irregular. May become fussy and display various bursts of diffuse motor activity.	1–3
Crying	Intense crying that may be difficult to stop and is accompanied by high levels of motor activity.	1–3

SOURCE: Wolff, 1966.

Sudden infant death syndrome (SIDS) occurs when seemingly healthy infants die in their sleep. These deaths are unexpected and unexplained. The incidence of SIDS in Canada has been declining (from 1.2 per 1000 births in 1980 to 0.5 per 1000 births in 1996); however, SIDS is still the leading cause of post-neonatal (after 27 days of age) death (Health Canada, Canadian Perinatal Surveillance System, 2001c). Approximately 26 percent of post-neonatal deaths are attributed to SIDS. Among Aboriginal populations, the incidence of SIDS is three to four times the Canadian rate (Smylie, 2001).

Although the exact cause of SIDS is not known, we do know that preterm and other low-birth-weight babies who had poor Apgar scores and experienced respiratory distress as newborns are most susceptible (Brockington, 1996; Frick, 1999). Mothers of SIDS victims are more likely to smoke; to have used illicit drugs; and to have received poor prenatal care (MacGregor & Chasnoff, 1993). Babies whose caregivers smoke even moderately (that is, 9 to 12 cigarettes a day) are two to six times more likely to die of SIDS than babies whose caregivers do not smoke (Frick, 1999). Even though few babies of smokers succumb to SIDS, the incidence of those tragic crib deaths can still be reduced by simply convincing parents and other caregivers not to smoke around their babies.

SIDS is most likely to occur during the winter months among infants who are 2 to 4 months old and who have a respiratory infection such as a cold. SIDS victims are likely to have been sleeping on their stomachs, and they are often wrapped tightly in clothing and blankets at the time of their death (Brockington, 1996; Dwyer et al., 1991). These findings have led some researchers to propose that factors that contribute to overheating the infant—more clothing or blankets and higher room temperatures—may seriously increase the risk of SIDS. Risks associated with overheating are particularly evident when infants also sleep on their stomachs (American Academy of Pediatrics, 2000). Intervention programs in Tasmania and England have found that SIDS rates can be reduced dramatically by simply instructing parents not to tightly bundle their babies or place them on their stomach to sleep (Brockington, 1996).

Many (but not all) SIDS victims have abnormalities in the *arcuate nucleus*, a portion of the brain that seems to be involved early in infancy in controlling breathing and waking during sleep (Kinney et al., 1995; Panigrahy et al.,

1997). Normally, a very young infant will sense inadequate oxygen intake while sleeping, and the brain will trigger waking, crying, and changes in heart rate to compensate for insufficient oxygen. However, abnormalities of the arcuate nucleus, which may stem from prenatal exposure to a toxic substance (e.g., illicit drugs or tobacco products), may prevent a young infant from becoming aroused when oxygen intake is inadequate (Franco et al., 1998; Frick, 1999). So, when babies with abnormalities in the lower brain centres are sleeping prone, are heavily bundled, or have a respiratory infection that may restrict breathing, they may not struggle sufficiently to breathe and succumb to SIDS. Nevertheless, it is important to note that (1) not all SIDS victims have identifiable brain abnormalities, and (2) researchers, as yet, have no good screening to predict which babies are at highest risk of SIDS.

Fortunately, there are some effective strategies for reducing the incidence of SIDS.

1. Do not place infants on their stomachs to sleep.

2. Do not place infants down to sleep on waterbeds, soft sofas, soft mattresses, or other soft surfaces.

3. Soft materials that may obstruct the infant's breathing (for example, unnecessary pillows, stuffed toys, comforters) should be kept away from the infant's sleeping environment.

4. Infants should be lightly clothed for sleep and the bedroom temperature kept comfortable for a lightly clothed adult so as to avoid infant overheating.

5. Create a smoke-free zone around the baby. Mothers should not smoke during pregnancy, and no one should smoke in the infant's presence.

6. Consider breast-feeding. There is some evidence that SIDS is less common in breast-fed infants.

Unfortunately, SIDS can still occur, even when caregivers follow these guidelines. SIDS has a devastating impact on most affected families. Parents often feel bitter or extremely guilty over their loss, and siblings may also grieve deeply over the death of a baby brother or sister and begin to display problem behaviours (Brockington, 1996). These families need social support, and, fortunately, parent support groups can often help them to cope with their loss.

An infant's cry is a complex vocal signal that may vary from a soft whimper to piercing shrieks and wails. Although it was once thought that neonates produced distinctive cries to communicate different needs and that "pain" cries were perceived by parents as the most serious and urgent (Wolff, 1969), later research has challenged this view. Experience clearly plays a role in helping adults to determine why an infant may be crying, because parents are better than nonparents at this kind of problem solving, and mothers (who typically have more contact with infants) are better at it than fathers are (Holden, 1988). Yet Philip Zeskind and his associates (1985) found that adults perceive the intense cries of hungry babies as just as arousing and urgent as equally intense "pain" cries. So crying probably conveys only one very general message—"Hey, I'm distressed"—and the effectiveness of this signal at eliciting attention depends more on the *amount* of distress it implies than on the *kind* of distress that the baby is experiencing (Gustafson & Harris, 1990; Zeskind et al., 1992).

DEVELOPMENTAL CHANGES IN CRYING. Babies around the world cry most often during the first three months of life (St. James-Roberts & Plewis, 1996). In fact, the declines we see early in life in both crying and REM sleep suggest that both these changes are meaningfully related to the maturation of a baby's brain and central nervous system (Halpern, MacLean, & Baumeister, 1995). And what role do parents play? Will those who are especially responsive to their infant's cries produce a spoiled baby who enslaves them with incessant demands for attention?

Probably not. Mary Ainsworth and her associates (1972) found that the babies of mothers who are relatively quick to respond to their cries come to cry *very little!* Is this because responsive mothers are especially effective at soothing distressed infants? Possibly, but Lewis & Ramsay (1999) found little evidence for this "soothing" hypothesis. Instead, they believe that sensitive, responsive parenting may result in a less fussy baby because a sensitive and attentive caregiver is more likely to *prevent* a baby from becoming highly distressed in the first place.

Pediatricians, midwives, and nurses are trained to listen carefully to the vocalizations of a newborn infant, because congenital problems are sometimes detectable from the way an infant cries. Preterm babies, for example, and those who are malnourished, brain-damaged, or born addicted to narcotics, often emit shrill, nonrhythmic cries that are perceived as much more "sickly" and aversive than those of healthy full-term infants (Frodi, 1985; Zeskind, 1980). In fact, Barry Lester (1984) reports that it is even possible to discriminate preterm infants who will develop normally from those who are likely to experience later deficiencies in cognitive development by analyzing their crying in the first few days and weeks of life. So the infant cry is not only an important communicative prompt for parents but is also a meaningful diagnostic tool.

Methods of Soothing a Fussy Baby

Although babies can be delightful companions when alert and attentive, they may irritate the most patient of caregivers when they fuss, cry, and are difficult to pacify. Many people think that a crying baby is either hungry, wet, or in pain, and if the infant has not eaten in some time, feeding may be a very effective method of pacification. Presenting a mild sucrose solution is particularly effective at calming distressed newborns (Smith & Blass, 1996; Blass, 1997), although even a nipplelike pacifier is often enough (Campos, 1989). Of course, the soothing effect of a pacifier may be short-lived if the baby really is hungry.

OTHER SOOTHING TECHNIQUES. When feeding or diaper changing doesn't work, rocking, humming, stroking, and other forms of continuous, rhythmic stimulation will often quiet restless babies (Rock, Trainor, & Addison, 1999). Swaddling (wrapping the infant snugly in a blanket) is also comforting because the wraps provide continuous tactile sensation all over the baby's body. Indeed, researchers at Queen's University have found that swaddling can calm infants even after the distress of the heel lance required for infant blood tests (Fearon et al., 1997). Perhaps the infant's nervous system is programmed to respond to soft, rhythmic stimulation, because studies have repeatedly shown that rocking, swaddling, and continuous rhythmic sounds have the effect of decreasing a baby's muscular activity and lowering heart and respiratory rates (Campos, 1989).

One particularly effective method of soothing crying infants is simply to pick them up. Whereas soft, rhythmic stimulation may put babies to sleep, lifting is likely to have the opposite effect (Korner, 1972), causing them to become visually alert, particularly if their caregivers place them against their shoulder—an excellent vantage point for visual scanning. Anneliese Korner (1972) believes that parents who often soothe their infants by picking them up may be doing them a favour, because the visual exploration that this technique allows helps babies to learn more about their environment.

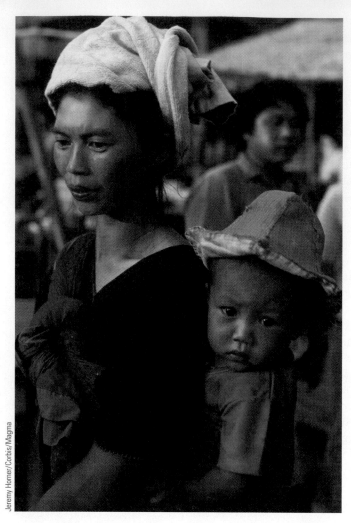

In many cultures, babies are kept quite contented through swaddling and having ample close contact with their mothers, who stand ready to nurse at the baby's first whimper.

?

WHAT DO YOU THINK?

What purposes might be served by each of the following stimuli in a newborn baby's environment: a rocker or a white noise machine, a mobile or other visual targets suspended over the crib, a caregiver who is responsive to the baby's cries?

INDIVIDUAL AND CULTURAL DIFFERENCES IN SOOTHABILITY.
Just as infants differ in their sleeping patterns and daily rhythms, they also differ in their irritability and ability to be soothed (Korner, 1996). Even in the first few days of life, some infants are easily distressed and difficult to soothe, whereas others are rarely perturbed and calm easily should they become overstimulated. There are also cultural differences in infant soothability: Caucasian babies tend to be much more restless and more difficult to calm than Chinese American, Native American, or Japanese infants (Freedman, 1979; Nugent, Lester, & Brazelton, 1989). These differential reactions to stress and soothing are present at birth and may be genetically influenced. Yet it is also clear that child-rearing practices can affect a baby's demeanour. Many Asian, South American, and Native American mothers, for example, are often successful at improving the dispositions of even their most irritable babies by swaddling them, carrying them around (in slings or pouches) as they do their chores, and nursing at the baby's first whimper (Nugent et al., 1989; Tronick, Thomas, & Daltabuit, 1994).

A baby who is not easily soothed can make a parent feel anxious, frustrated, or downright incompetent—reactions that may contribute to a poor parent–child relationship. For this reason, parents of difficult infants need to cast aside their preconceptions about the typical or "perfect" baby and learn how to adjust to the characteristics of their *own* child. Indeed, the NBAS training described earlier in this chapter was designed with just this objective in mind by (1) showing parents that even an irritable or unresponsive baby can react positively to them and (2) teaching the parents how to elicit these favourable responses.

Now that we have completed this chapter, please take a moment to reflect on just how much has happened since conception. A single-celled zygote evolves into a marvellously complex, organized human being who is ready to begin meeting life's demands and is usually strong enough to overcome many hazards and complications that he or she may encounter. So rather than thinking of newborns as "helpless babes," it is probably much more accurate to portray them as hardy and adaptive beings who are already hard at work writing a fascinating developmental story.

SUMMARY

From Conception to Birth

♦ **Prenatal development** is divided into three phases. The **germinal period** (or *period of the zygote*) lasts about two weeks, from conception until the *blastocyst* is firmly **implanted** in the wall of the uterus. The inner layer of the blastocyst will become the **embryo**; the outer layer forms the **amnion**, **chorion**, **placenta**, and **umbilical cord**—support structures that help to sustain the developing prenatal organism.

♦ The **period of the embryo** lasts from the beginning of the third through the eighth week of pregnancy. This is the period when all major organs are formed and some have begun to function.

♦ The **period of the fetus** lasts from the ninth prenatal week until birth. All organ systems become integrated in preparation for birth. Fetuses attain the **age of viability** at the beginning of the third trimester, usually between 22 to 28 weeks after conception.

Environmental Influences on Prenatal Development

♦ Many environmental agents can complicate prenatal development and the birth process. **Teratogens**—that is, diseases such as **rubella**, **toxoplasmosis**, **syphilis**, **genital herpes**, and **AIDS**; drugs such as **thalidomide** (which is no longer available for use in Canada), **diethylstilbestrol (DES)**, alcohol, and tobacco; and environmental hazards such as *radiation* and *toxic chemicals*—can attack a developing embryo or fetus, interfering with growth and causing birth defects. Teratogens are dangerous throughout pregnancy, but especially so during the first eight weeks when major organs and body parts are forming.

♦ Maternal characteristics can also influence prenatal development and birth outcomes. If a mother is malnourished, particularly during the third trimester, she runs the risk of delivering a preterm baby who may fail to survive. Supplementation of an otherwise normal diet with vitamins such as **folic acid** can help to prevent **spina bifida** and other birth defects. Malnourished babies are often irritable and unresponsive, which can contribute to poor social and intellectual development. Mothers under severe emotional stress are at increased risk of experiencing pregnancy complications. Complications are also more likely among mothers over 35 and younger teenage mothers who fail to obtain adequate prenatal care.

Childbirth and the Perinatal Environment

♦ Childbirth is a three-step process that begins with contractions that dilate the cervix (**first stage of labour**) so that the baby can be delivered (**second stage of labour**) and the afterbirth expelled (**third stage of labour**). The **Apgar test** is used to assess the newborn's condition immediately after birth, whereas the **Neonatal Behavioral Assessment Scale**

(NBAS), which is typically administered a few days later, is a more extensive measure of the baby's health and well-being. Labour and delivery medication given to mothers to ease pain can, in large doses, make babies lethargic and inattentive, which may interfere with the parent–infant relationship.

♦ Childbirth practices vary widely across cultures. **Natural and prepared childbirth**, now common in Western societies, can reduce maternal stress and medication. Home births, or those that take place in **alternative birth centres**, are just as safe as hospital deliveries, provided that the mother is healthy and is attended by a competent doctor or midwife.

♦ Many mothers feel exhilarated shortly after birth if they have close contact with their babies and begin the process of **emotional bonding**. Fathers, too, are often **engrossed** with their newborns, and the support of fathers during pregnancy and childbirth can make the birth experience easier and more pleasant for mothers. However, a lack of support from one's partner is a major contributor to **postpartum depression** and a poor mother–infant relationship.

Birth Complications

♦ **Anoxia** is a potentially serious birth complication that can cause brain damage (e.g., cerebral palsy) and other defects. Mild anoxia, however, usually has no long-term effects.

♦ Women who abuse alcohol and drugs, smoke heavily, or receive poor prenatal care are at risk for delivering preterm or low-birth-weight babies. **Small-for-date babies** usually have more severe and longer-lasting problems than do **preterm infants**. Interventions to stimulate these infants and to teach their parents how to respond appropriately to their sluggish or irritable demeanour can help to normalize their developmental progress.

♦ Fortunately, the problems stemming from both prenatal and birth complications are often overcome in time, provided that the child is not permanently brain damaged and has a stable and supportive postnatal environment in which to grow.

The Newborn's Readiness for Life

♦ Newborns are remarkably capable organisms who emerge from the womb prepared to begin life. Perhaps their greatest strength is their repertoire of **survival reflexes**, which helps them to adapt to their new surroundings and to satisfy basic needs. Other **primitive reflexes**, thought to be remnants of evolution, are not as useful; however, their disappearance in the first year is a sign that development is proceeding normally.

♦ Newborns also have a sleeping–waking cycle that becomes better organized over the first year. Although babies move into and out of six **infant states** in a typical day, they spend up to 70 percent of their time sleeping. One state, **REM sleep**, is characterized by twitches, jerks, and rapid eye movement.

Proponents of **autostimulation theory** believe that REM sleep's function is to provide very young infants with stimulation necessary for the development of the central nervous system. Unfortunately, **sudden infant death syndrome (SIDS)** is a leading cause of infant mortality.

◆ Crying is the state by which infants communicate distress. If a baby's cries are very shrill and nonrhythmic, he may be brain damaged. Crying normally diminishes over the first six months as the brain matures, caregivers become better at soothing, and infants learn to use other methods to communicate.

KEY TERMS

prenatal development, 108
germinal period, 109
period of the embryo, 109
period of the fetus, 109
embryo, 109
implantation, 109
amnion, 110
chorion, 110
placenta, 110
umbilical cord, 110
neural tube, 110
fetus, 111
vernix, 113
lanugo, 113
age of viability, 113

teratogens, 114
sensitive period, 115
rubella (German measles), 116
toxoplasmosis, 116
thalidomide, 117
syphilis, 119
genital herpes, 119
cesarean section, 119
acquired immune deficiency
    syndrome (AIDS), 119
diethylstilbestrol (DES), 119
fetal alcohol syndrome (FAS),
    119
fetal alcohol effects (FAE), 119
folic acid, 124

spina bifida, 124
neonate, 125
first stage of labour, 127
second stage of labour, 127
third stage of labour, 127
Apgar test, 129
Neonatal Behavioral Assessment
    Scale (NBAS), 129
natural and prepared childbirth,
    131
alternative birth centre, 132
emotional bonding, 133
postpartum depression, 134
engrossment, 134
anoxia, 135

breech birth, 135
RH factor, 135
preterm infants, 136
small-for-date (or small-for-
    gestational-age) babies, 136
respiratory distress syndrome,
    137
reflex, 140
survival reflexes, 140
primitive reflexes, 140
infant states, 142
REM sleep, 143
autostimulation theory, 143
sudden infant death syndrome
    (SIDS), 143

You can find further information on the topics covered in this chapter by visiting:

www.developmentalpsych2e.nelson.com

For additional reading, go to InfoTrac College Edition, your on-line research library, at:

infotrac.thomsonlearning.com

The Physical Self: Development of the Brain, the Body, and Motor Skills

PhotoDisc Collection/PhotoDisc

- "My, my, she's already walking! What a smart little girl!"
- "Look at you go. Oops, fall down, go boom!"
- "Get your rest, little guy. It will help you grow big and strong."
- "He's growing like a weed—and his arms are too long!"
- "Only 11 and she's got her period! What's the world coming to?"
- "All that girl thinks about is boys!"

Have you ever heard adults make these kinds of statements about developing children and adolescents? Few aspects of development are more interesting to the casual observer than the rapid transformation of a seemingly dependent and immobile little baby into a running, jumping bundle of energy who grows and changes at what may seem to be an astounding pace, and who may one day be taller than his or her parents. Those physical changes that many find so fascinating are the subject of this chapter.

We will begin by focusing on the changes that occur in the body, the brain, and motor skills throughout infancy and childhood. Then we will consider the impact of puberty—both the dramatic physical changes that adolescents experience and their social and psychological impacts. Finally, we will close by discussing the factors that influence physical growth and development throughout the first 20 years of life.

Having experienced most (if not all) of the changes covered in this chapter, you may assume that you know quite a bit about physical development. Yet students often discover that there is much they *don't* know. To check your own knowledge, take a minute to decide whether the following statements are true or false. Jot down your responses and we will see how you have fared on this "pretest" as we discuss these issues throughout the chapter. (The answers are at the bottom of the test.)

True or False?

1. Babies who walk early are inclined to be especially bright.
2. The average 2-year-old is already about half of his/her adult height.
3. Half the nerve cells (neurons) in the average baby's brain die (and are not replaced) over the first few years of life.
4. Most children walk when they are ready, and no amount of encouragement will enable a 6-month-old to walk alone.

An Overview of Maturation and Growth

Development of the Brain

Motor Development

Puberty: The Physical Transition from Child to Adult

The Psychological Effects of Puberty

Causes and Correlates of Physical Development

Summary

5. Hormones have little effect on human growth and development until puberty.

6. Emotional trauma can seriously impair the growth of young children, even those who are adequately nourished and free from illness, and who are not physically abused.

Answers to the pretest: 1 F; 2 T; 3 T; 4 T; 5 F; 6 T

AN OVERVIEW OF MATURATION AND GROWTH

Adults are often amazed at how quickly children grow. Even tiny babies don't remain tiny for long. In the first few months of life, they gain over 28.0 g each day and 2.5 cm each month. Yet the dramatic increases in height and weight that we see are accompanied by a number of important *internal* developments in the muscles, bones, and central nervous system that will largely determine the physical feats that children are capable of performing at different ages. In this section, we will briefly chart the course of physical development from birth through adolescence and see that there is a clear relationship between the external aspects of growth that are so noticeable and the internal changes that are much harder to detect.

Changes in Height and Weight

Babies grow very rapidly during the first two years, often doubling their birth weight by 4 to 6 months of age and tripling it (to about 9.5 to 10.0 kg) by the end of the first year. By age 2, infants are already half their eventual adult height and have quadrupled their birth weight to about 12 to 14 kg. If children continued to grow at this rapid pace until age 18, they would stand about 3.7 m and weigh several tonnes!

From age 2 until puberty children gain about 5.0 to 8.0 cm in height and about 3.0 kg in weight each year. During middle childhood (ages 6 to 11), children may seem to grow very little; over the course of an entire year, 5.0 cm and 3.0 kg gained are hard to detect on a child who stands 1.2 to 1.4 m tall and weighs 27.00 to 36.0 kg (Eichorn, 1979). But as shown in Figure 5.1, physical growth and development are once again obvious at puberty, when adolescents enter a two- to three-year "growth spurt," during which they may post an annual gain of about 4.5 to 7.0 kg and 5.0 to 10.0 cm in height. After this growth spurt, there are typically small increases in height until full adult height is attained in the mid to late teens (Tanner, 1990).

cephalocaudal development
sequence of physical maturation and growth that proceeds from the head (cephalic region) to the tail (or caudal region)

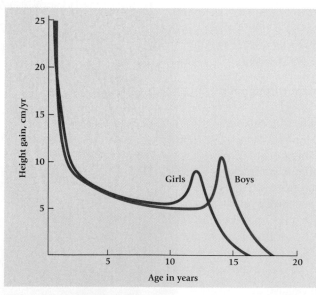

Figure 5.1 *Gain in height per year by males and females from birth through adolescence. At about age 10–12, girls begin their growth spurt. Boys follow some two and a half years later and grow faster than girls once their growth begins. BASED ON TANNER, WHITEHOUSE, & TAKAHISHI, 1966.*

Changes in Body Proportions

To a casual observer, neonates may appear to be "all head"—and for good reason. The newborn's head is already 70 percent of its eventual adult size and represents one-quarter of total body length, the same fraction as the legs.

As a child grows, body shape rapidly changes (see Figure 5.2). Development proceeds in a **cephalocaudal** (head downward) direction, and it is the trunk that grows fastest during the first year. At 1 year of age, a child's head now

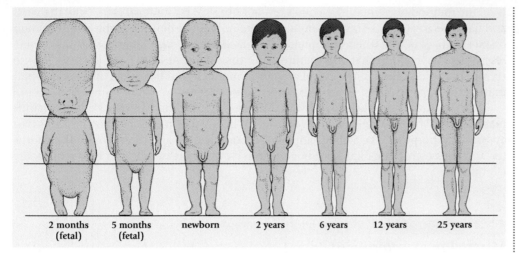

151

Chapter Five
The Physical Self:
Development of the Brain,
the Body, and Motor Skills

| 2 months (fetal) | 5 months (fetal) | newborn | 2 years | 6 years | 12 years | 25 years |

Figure 5.2 *Proportions of the human body from the fetal period through adulthood. The head represents 50 percent of body length at two months after conception, but only 12–13 percent of adult height. In contrast, the legs constitute about 12–13 percent of the total length of a 2-month-old fetus, but 50 percent of the height of a 25-year-old adult.*

accounts for only 20 percent of total body length. From the child's first birthday until the adolescent growth spurt, the legs grow rapidly, accounting for more than 60 percent of the increase in height (Eichorn, 1979). During adolescence the trunk once again becomes the fastest-growing segment of the body, although the legs are also growing rapidly at this time. When we reach our eventual adult height, our legs will account for 50 percent of total height and our heads only 12 percent.

While children grow upward, they are also growing outward according to a **proximodistal** (centre outward) formula. During prenatal development, for example, the chest and internal organs form first, followed by the arms and legs, and then the hands and feet. Throughout infancy and childhood, the arms and legs continue to grow faster than the hands and feet. However, this centre-outward growth pattern reverses just before puberty, when the hands and feet begin to grow rapidly and become the first body parts to reach adult proportions, followed by the arms and legs and finally the trunk. One reason teenagers often appear so clumsy or awkward is that their hands and feet (and later their arms and legs) may suddenly seem much too large for the rest of their bodies (Tanner, 1990).

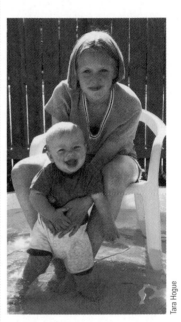

Body proportions change rapidly over the first few years as chubby toddlers become linear, long-legged children.

Skeletal Development

The skeletal structures that form during the prenatal period are initially soft cartilage that will gradually ossify (harden) into bony material. At birth, nearly all of the bones are a source of blood cells. During postnatal development the production of blood cells is limited to a few specific bones (Hill, 2003). At birth, most of the infant's bones are soft, pliable, and difficult to break. One reason that neonates cannot sit up or balance themselves when pulled to a standing position is that their bones are too small and too flexible.

Fortunately for both a mother and her baby, the neonate's skull consists of several soft bones that can be compressed to allow the child to pass through the cervix and the birth canal. These skull bones are separated by six soft spots, or *fontanelles*, that are gradually filled in by minerals to form a single skull by age 2, with pliable seams at the points where skull bones join. These seams, or sutures, allow the skull to expand as the brain grows larger.

Other parts of the body—namely, the ankles, feet, wrists, and hands—develop *more* (rather than fewer) bones as the child matures. In Figure 5.3, we see that the wrist and hand bones of a 1-year-old are both fewer and less well interconnected than the corresponding skeletal equipment of an adolescent.

proximodistal development sequence of physical maturation and growth that proceeds from the centre of the body (the proximal region) to the extremities (distal regions)

Tara Hogue

Figure 5.3 X-rays showing the amount of skeletal development seen in (a) the hand of an average male infant at 12 months or an average female infant at 10 months and (b) the hand of an average 13-year-old male or an average 10½-year-old female.

skeletal age
measure of physical maturation based on the child's level of skeletal development

One method of estimating a child's level of physical maturation is to X-ray the wrist and hand (as in Figure 5.3). The X-ray shows the number of bones and the extent of their ossification, which is then interpretable as a **skeletal age**. Using this technique, researchers have found that girls mature faster than boys. At birth, girls are only four to six weeks ahead of boys in their level of skeletal maturity, but by age 12 the gender "maturation gap" has widened to two full years (Tanner, 1990).

Not all parts of the skeleton grow and harden at the same rate. The skull and hands mature first, whereas the leg bones continue to develop until the mid to late teens. For all practical purposes, skeletal development is complete by age 18, although the widths (or thicknesses) of the skull, leg bones, and hands increase slightly throughout life (Tanner, 1990).

Muscular Development

Although one might think otherwise after listening to the claims of body builders, neonates are born with all the muscle fibres they will ever have (Tanner, 1990). At birth, muscle tissue is 35 percent water, and it accounts for no more than 18 to 24 percent of a baby's body weight (Marshall, 1977). However, muscle fibres soon begin to grow as the cellular fluid in muscle tissue is bolstered by the addition of protein and salts.

Muscular development proceeds in cephalocaudal and proximodistal directions, with muscles in the head and neck maturing before those in the trunk and limbs. Like many other aspects of physical development, the maturation of muscle tissue occurs very gradually over childhood and then accelerates during early adolescence. One consequence of this muscular growth spurt is that members of both sexes become noticeably stronger, although increases in both muscle mass and physical strength (as measured in tests of large-muscle activity) are more dramatic for boys than for girls (Malina, 1990). By the mid-20s, skeletal muscle accounts for 40 percent of the body weight of an average male, compared with 24 percent for the average female.

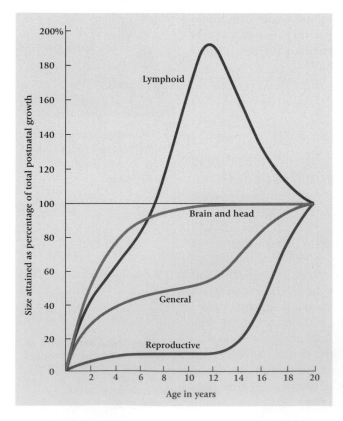

Variations in Physical Development

To this point, we have been discussing *sequences* of physical growth that all humans display. However, physical development is a very uneven process in which different bodily systems display unique growth patterns. As we see in Figure 5.4, the brain and head actually grow much faster and are quicker to reach adult proportions than the rest of the body is, whereas the genitals and other reproductive organs grow very slowly throughout childhood and develop rapidly in adolescence. Notice also that growth of the lymph tissues—which make up part of the immune system and help children fight off infections—actually overshoots adult levels late in childhood, before *declining* rapidly in adolescence.

Figure 5.4 Growth curves for different body systems. Each curve plots the size of a group of organs or body parts as a percentage of their size at age 20 (which is the 100 percent level on the vertical scale). The "general" curve describes changes in the body's size as well as the growth of respiratory and digestive organs and musculature. The brain and head grow more rapidly than the body in general, and the reproductive organs are the slowest to reach adult size. (The lymph nodes and other parts of the lymphoid system, which function as part of the immune system, also grow rapidly and actually exceed adult size during late childhood and adolescence.) FROM TANNER, 1962.

Individual Variations

Not only is the development of body systems an uneven or asynchronous process, but there are also sizable individual variations in the rates at which individuals grow. Look carefully at the photo here. These two boys are the same age, although one has already reached puberty and looks much older. As we will see later in the chapter, two elementary-school chums might begin the pubertal transition from child to adult as much as five years apart! Individual differences in the rate of maturation not only result in visible differences in physical features such as height, but they also contribute to differences in other areas of development, such as cognition. For example, Warren Eaton and colleagues at the University of Manitoba noted that maturational differences also predicted the speed with which children would be able to engage in cognitive tasks. Faster processing speed was found in early maturers, especially among boys (Eaton & Ritchot, 1995).

Cultural Variations

Finally, there are meaningful cultural and subcultural variations in physical growth and development. As a rule, people from Asia, South America, and Africa tend to be smaller than North Americans, Northern Europeans, and Australians. In addition, there are cultural differences in the *rate* of physical growth. Asian- and African-American children, for example, tend to mature faster than European-American and European children (Berkey et al., 1994; Herman-Giddens et al., 1997).

What accounts for all these variations in growth? Current thinking is that asynchronies in the maturation of different body systems are built into our species heredity—that is, the common maturational program that all humans share (Tanner, 1990). And later in the chapter, we will see that heredity—in concert with such environmental factors as the food people eat, the diseases they may encounter, and even the emotional climate in which they live—can produce significant variations in the rates at which they grow and the heights they attain.

There are large individual variations in the timing of the adolescent growth spurt, as we see in comparing the height of these two boys of the same age.

DEVELOPMENT OF THE BRAIN

The brain grows at an astounding rate early in life, increasing from 25 percent of its eventual adult weight at birth to 75 percent of adult weight by age 2. Indeed, the last three prenatal months and the first two years after birth have been termed the period of the **brain growth spurt** because more than half of one's adult brain weight is added at this time. Between the seventh prenatal month and a child's first birthday, the brain increases in weight by about 1.7 g a day, or more than a milligram per minute.

However, an increase in brain weight is a rather gross index that tells us very little about how or when various parts of the brain mature and affect other aspects of development. Let's take a closer look at the internal organization and development of the brain.

Neural Development and Plasticity

The human brain and nervous system consists of more than a trillion highly specialized cells that work together to transmit electrical and chemical signals across many trillions of

brain growth spurt
period between the seventh prenatal month and 2 years of age when more than half of the child's eventual brain weight is added

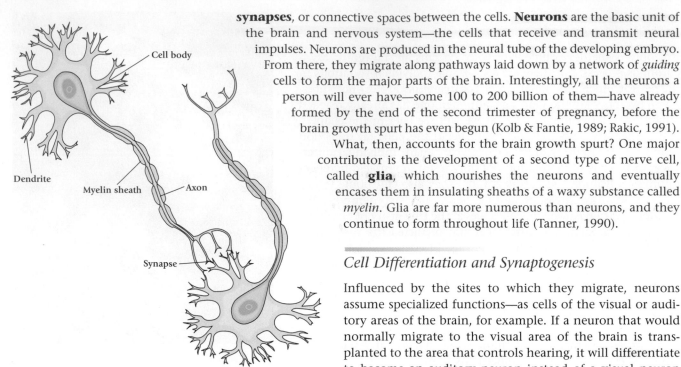

synapses, or connective spaces between the cells. **Neurons** are the basic unit of the brain and nervous system—the cells that receive and transmit neural impulses. Neurons are produced in the neural tube of the developing embryo. From there, they migrate along pathways laid down by a network of *guiding* cells to form the major parts of the brain. Interestingly, all the neurons a person will ever have—some 100 to 200 billion of them—have already formed by the end of the second trimester of pregnancy, before the brain growth spurt has even begun (Kolb & Fantie, 1989; Rakic, 1991).

What, then, accounts for the brain growth spurt? One major contributor is the development of a second type of nerve cell, called **glia**, which nourishes the neurons and eventually encases them in insulating sheaths of a waxy substance called *myelin*. Glia are far more numerous than neurons, and they continue to form throughout life (Tanner, 1990).

Figure 5.5 Two neurons forming a synapse. A synapse between neurons links the axon of one to the dendrites of the other. When the first neuron is activated, it releases neurotransmitters that stimulate (or inhibit) electrical activity in the second neuron. FROM JANOWSKY & CARPER, 1996.

Cell Differentiation and Synaptogenesis

Influenced by the sites to which they migrate, neurons assume specialized functions—as cells of the visual or auditory areas of the brain, for example. If a neuron that would normally migrate to the visual area of the brain is transplanted to the area that controls hearing, it will differentiate to become an auditory neuron instead of a visual neuron (Johnson, 1997). So individual neurons have the potential to serve any neural function, and the functions each serves depend on where it ends up.

Meanwhile, the process of **synaptogenesis**—the formation of synaptic connections among neurons—proceeds rapidly during the brain growth spurt. This brings us to one of the more interesting facts about the developing nervous system: The average infant has far more neurons and neural connections than adults do. The reason is that neurons that successfully interconnect with other neurons crowd out those that don't, making a more efficient system (Janowsky & Finlay, 1986; Thompson & Nelson, 2001). In all, about half the neurons produced early in life also die early in life (Janowsky & Finlay, 1986). Meanwhile, surviving neurons form hundreds of synapses, many of which also disappear if the neuron is not properly stimulated (Huttenlocher, 1994). If we likened the developing brain to a house under construction, we might imagine a builder who merrily constructs many more rooms and hallways than is needed, and then later goes back and knocks about half of them out!

What is happening here reflects the remarkable **plasticity** of the young infant's brain—the fact that its cells are highly responsive to the effects of experience. As William Greenough and his colleagues (1987) explain, the brain has evolved so that it produces an excess of neurons and synapses in preparation for receiving any and all kinds of sensory and motor stimulation that a human being could conceivably experience. Of course, no human being has this broad a range of experiences, so much of one's neural circuitry remains unused. Presumably, then, neurons and synapses that are most often stimulated continue to function. Other surviving neurons that are stimulated less often lose their synapses (a process called *synaptic pruning*) and stand in reserve to compensate for brain injuries or to support new skills (Huttenlocher, 1994). Note the implication then: The development of the brain early in life is not due entirely to the unfolding of a maturational program. It is the result of both a biological program and early experience (Greenough, Black, & Wallace, 1987; Johnson, 1998; Thompson & Nelson, 2001).

The Role of Experience

How do we know that early experience plays such a dramatic role in the development of the brain and central nervous system? The first clue came from research by Austin Riesen and his associates (Riesen, 1947; Riesen et al., 1951). Riesen's subjects were infant chimpanzees that were reared in the dark for periods ranging up to 16 months. His results

synapse
connective space (juncture) between one nerve cell (neuron) and another

neurons
nerve cells that receive and transmit neural impulses

glia
nerve cells that nourish neurons and encase them in insulating sheaths of myelin

synaptogenesis
formation of connections (synapses) among neurons

plasticity
capacity or change; a developmental state that has the potential to be shaped by experience

155

Chapter Five
The Physical Self:
Development of the Brain,
the Body, and Motor Skills

were striking. Dark-reared chimps experienced atrophy of the retina and the neurons that make up the optic nerve. This atrophy was reversible if the animal's visual deprivation did not exceed seven months, but was irreversible and often led to total blindness if the deprivation lasted longer than a year. So neurons that are not properly stimulated degenerate—a dramatic illustration of the "use it or lose it" principle.

Might we then foster the neural development of an immature, plastic brain by exposing participants to enriched environments that provide a wide variety of stimulation? Yes, indeed. Animals raised with lots of companions and many toys to play with have brains that are heavier and display more extensive networks of neural connections than those of litter-mates raised under standard laboratory conditions (Greenough & Black, 1992; Rosenzweig, 1984). Conversely, the brains of animals raised in stimulating environments lose some of their complexity if the animals are moved to less stimulating quarters (Thompson, 1993). Thus, even though genes may provide rough guidelines on how the brain should be configured, early experience largely determines the brain's specific architecture. Similarly, experiences later in life also affect the architecture of the brain (Thompson & Nelson, 2001). For example, research by Bryan Kolb and his colleagues (2003), at the University of Lethbridge, has demonstrated quantitative and qualitative differences in synaptic organization as a function of age (for more details see the Inside Track Box 5.1).

Brain Differentiation and Growth

Not all parts of the brain develop at the same rate. At birth, the most highly developed areas are the *brain stem* and the *midbrain*, which control states of consciousness, inborn reflexes, and vital biological functions such as digestion, respiration, and elimination.

THE INSIDE TRACK

5.1

Bryan Kolb

Bryan Kolb is a Professor of Psychology and Neuroscience at the Canadian Centre for Behavioural Neuroscience located at the University of Lethbridge in Alberta.

If you wanted to look for evidence of plasticity in the brain, where would you look? Kolb and his colleagues at the University of Lethbridge in Alberta would suggest that the "logical place to look for plastic changes [would be] at the junctions between neurons, that is, at synapses" (Kolb, Gibb, & Robinson, 2003, p. 1) because both reductions and increases in synapses indicate change. Given the overwhelming number of synapses in the human brain, measuring individual synapses is not feasible. However, one way to estimate the number of synapses is by looking at the length of dendrites because about 95 percent of cell synapses are found on their dendrites. Kolb and his colleagues use changes in dendritic length and changes in the density of synapses to signify whether synaptic change has occurred.

In a recent study, Kolb and his associates demonstrated that plastic changes can be both quantitative and qualitative depending on the age of the subject. When groups of juvenile, adult, and old animals were exposed to complex, stimulating environments, all the groups showed the expected increases in dendritic length, hence demonstrating a quantitative change. This was consistent with previous research. Among the adult and old animals the density of synapses showed an increase. However, this was not true of the juveniles. The juveniles shared the increase in dendritic length but showed a decrease in density. Thus, the same environmental experiences yielded qualitatively different outcomes (Kolb, Gibb, & Gorny, 2003). Such findings support the important role of experience and highlight how plastic changes in the brain may vary across the life span.

Kolb's work opens the door for many new questions. For example, the presence of changes occurring throughout the life span raises the question of whether plastic changes are permanent. Given the number of situations where behavioural change has been associated with plastic changes (such as the differing experiences outlined above, or changes following drug use or hormonal variation), it would be important to understand whether there are limits to what changes can occur and when, during the life span, changes can occur (Kolb et al., 2003). Understanding more about plasticity is critical for enhancing our understanding of the brain's development and behaviour.

Surrounding the midbrain are the *cerebrum* and *cerebral cortex*, the areas most directly implicated in voluntary bodily movements, perception, and higher intellectual activities such as learning, thinking, and production of language. The first areas of the cerebrum to mature are the *primary motor areas* (which control simple motor activities such as waving the arms) and the *primary sensory areas* (which control sensory processes such as vision, hearing, smelling, and tasting). Thus, human neonates are reflexive, "sensory-motor" beings because only the sensory and motor areas of the cortex are functioning well at birth. By 6 months of age, the primary motor areas of the cerebral cortex have developed to the point that they now direct most of the infant's movements. Inborn responses such as the Palmar grasp and the Babinski reflex should have disappeared by now, thus indicating that the higher cortical centres are assuming proper control over the more primitive "subcortical" areas of the brain.

Myelinization

As brain cells proliferate and grow, some of the glia begin to produce a waxy substance called *myelin*, which forms a sheath around individual neurons. This myelin sheath acts like an insulator to speed the transmission of neural impulses, thus allowing the brain to communicate more efficiently with different parts of the body.

Myelinization follows a definite chronological sequence that parallels the maturation of the nervous system. At birth or shortly thereafter, the pathways between the sense organs and the brain are reasonably well-myelinated. As a result, the neonate's sensory equipment is in good working order. As neural pathways between the brain and the skeletal muscles myelinate (in a cephalocaudal and proximodistal pattern), the child becomes capable of increasingly complex motor activities such as lifting the head and chest, reaching with the arms and hands, rolling over, sitting, standing, and eventually walking and running. Although myelinization proceeds very rapidly over the first few years of life, some areas of the brain are not completely myelinated until the mid to late teens or early adulthood (Fischer & Rose, 1995). For example, the *reticular formation* and the *frontal cortex*—parts of the brain that allow us to concentrate on a subject for lengthy periods—are not fully myelinated at puberty (Tanner, 1990). This may be one reason that the attention spans of infants, toddlers, and school-age children are much shorter than those of adolescents and adults.

Cerebral Lateralization

The highest brain centre, the **cerebrum**, consists of two halves (or *hemispheres*) connected by a band of fibres called the **corpus callosum**. Each of the hemispheres is covered by a **cerebral cortex**—an outer layer of grey matter that controls sensory and motor processes, perception, and intellectual functioning. Although identical in appearance, the left and the right cerebral hemispheres serve different functions and control different areas of the body. The left cerebral hemisphere controls the right side of the body, and, as illustrated in Figure 5.6, it contains centres for speech, hearing, verbal memory, decision making, language processing, and expression of positive emotions. By contrast, the right cerebral hemisphere controls the left side of the body and contains centres for processing visual–spatial information, nonlinguistic sounds such as music, tactile (touch) sensations, and expressing negative emotions (Fox et al., 1995). Thus, the brain is a *lateralized* organ. **Cerebral lateralization** also involves a preference for using one hand or one side of the body more than the other. About 90 percent of adults rely on their right hands (or left hemispheres) to write, eat, and perform other motor functions, whereas these same activities are under the control of the right hemisphere among most people who are left-handed. However, the fact that the brain is a lateralized organ does not mean that each hemisphere is totally independent of the other; the corpus callosum, which connects the hemispheres, plays an important role in integrating their respective functions.

When do the two cerebral hemispheres begin to "divide the work" and become lateralized? It was once thought that lateralization took place gradually throughout childhood and was not complete until adolescence (Lenneberg, 1967). Now, however, it is

myelinization
process by which neurons are enclosed in waxy myelin sheaths that will facilitate the transmission of neural impulses

cerebrum
highest brain centre; includes both hemispheres of the brain and the fibres that connect them

corpus callosum
bundle of neural fibres that connects the two hemispheres of the brain and transmits information from one hemisphere to the other

cerebral cortex
outer layer of the brain's cerebrum that is involved in voluntary body movements, perception, and higher intellectual functions such as learning, thinking, and speaking

cerebral lateralization
specialization of brain functions in the left and the right cerebral hemispheres

157

Chapter Five
The Physical Self:
Development of the Brain,
the Body, and Motor Skills

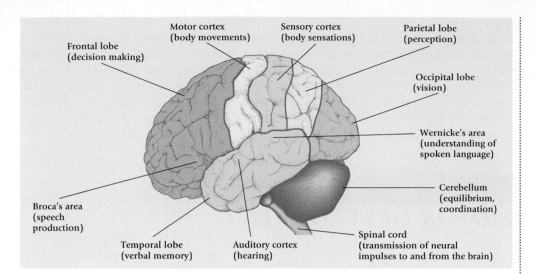

Figure 5.6 *Lateral view of the left cerebral cortex and some of the functions that it controls. Although the cerebellum and spinal cord are not part of the cerebral cortex, they serve important functions of their own.*

thought that brain lateralization may originate during the prenatal period and be well under way at birth (Kinsbourne, 1989). For example, about two-thirds of all fetuses end up positioned in the womb with their right ears facing outward, and it is thought that this gives them a right-ear advantage and illustrates the left hemisphere's specialization in language processing (Previc, 1991). From the first day of life, speech sounds stimulate more electrical activity in the left side of the cerebral cortex than in the right (Molfese, 1977). In addition, most newborns turn to the right rather than to the left when they lie on their backs, and these same babies later tend to reach for objects with their right hands (Kinsbourne, 1989). So it seems that the two cerebral hemispheres may be biologically programmed to assume different functions and have already begun to "divide the labour" by the time a baby is born (Kinsbourne, 1989; Witelson, 1987).

However, the brain is not completely specialized at birth; throughout childhood, we come to rely more and more on one particular hemisphere or the other to serve particular functions. Consider, for example, that even though left- or right-handedness is apparent early and is reasonably well-established by age 2, lateral preferences become stronger with age. In one experiment, preschoolers and adolescents were asked to pick up a crayon, kick a ball, look into a small, opaque bottle, and place an ear to a box to hear a sound. Only 32 percent of the preschoolers, but more than half of the adolescents, showed a consistent lateral preference by relying exclusively on one side of the body to perform all four tasks (Coren, Porac, & Duncan, 1981).

Because the immature brain is not completely specialized, young children often show a remarkable ability to bounce back from traumatic brain injuries as neural circuits that might otherwise have been lost assume the functions of those that have died (Kolb & Fantie, 1989; Rakic, 1991). Although adolescents and adults who suffer brain damage often regain a substantial portion of the functions they have lost, especially with the proper therapy, their recoveries are rarely as rapid or as complete as those of younger children (Kolb & Fantie, 1989). So the remarkable recuperative power of the human brain (that is, plasticity) is greatest early in life, before cerebral lateralization is complete.

Development of the Brain during Adolescence

Through the ages, adults have noticed that teenagers suddenly begin to ask hypothetical "What if" questions and to ponder weighty abstractions such as truth and justice. Are these changes in thinking tied to late developments in the brain?

Many researchers believe that they are (Case, 1992; Somsen et al., 1997). For example, myelinization of the higher brain centres, which continues well into adolescence, may not only increase adolescents' attention spans, but also explain why they process information much faster than elementary-school children do (Kail, 1991).

Furthermore, we now know that the brain retains at least some of its plasticity well beyond puberty (Nelson & Bloom, 1997; Nelson et al., 2002), and that reorganizations of the neural circuitry of the *prefrontal cortex*, which is involved in such higher-level cognitive activities as strategic planning, continues until at least age 20 (Spreen, Risser, & Edgell, 1995; Stuss, 1992). So even though changes in the brain during adolescence are less dramatic than those earlier in life, it is likely that some of the cognitive advances that teenagers display become possible only after their brains undergo a process of reorganization and fine-tuning.

MOTOR DEVELOPMENT

One of the more dramatic developments of the first year of life is the remarkable progress that infants make in controlling their movements and perfecting motor skills. Writers are fond of describing newborns as "helpless babes"—a characterization that largely stems from the neonates' inability to move about on their own. Clearly, human infants are disadvantaged when compared with the young of many species, who can follow their mothers to food (and then feed themselves) very soon after birth.

However, babies do not remain immobile for long. By the end of the first month, the brain and neck muscles have matured enough to permit most infants to reach the first milestone in locomotor development—lifting their chins while lying flat on their stomachs. Soon after, children lift their chests as well, reaching for objects, rolling over, and sitting up if someone supports them. Investigators who have charted motor development over the first two years of life find that motor skills evolve in a definite sequence, which appears in Table 5.1. Although the ages at which these skills first appear vary considerably from child to child, infants who are quick to proceed through this motor sequence are not necessarily any brighter or otherwise advantaged compared with those whose rates of motor development are average or slightly below average. So even though the age norms in Table 5.1 are a useful standard for gauging an infant's progress as he or she begins to sit, stand, and take those first tentative steps, that rate of motor development really tells us very little about *future* developmental outcomes.

Basic Trends in Locomotor Development

The two fundamental "laws" that describe muscular development and myelinization also hold true for motor development during the first few years. Motor development proceeds in a *cephalocaudal* (head-downward) direction, with activities involving the head, neck, and upper extremities preceding those involving the legs and lower extremities. At the same time, development is *proximodistal* (centre-outward), with activities involving the trunk and shoulders appearing before those involving the hands and fingers.

159

Chapter Five
The Physical Self:
Development of the Brain,
the Body, and Motor Skills

How do we explain the sequencing and timing of early motor development? Let's briefly consider three possibilities: the *maturational viewpoint*, the *experiential* (or practice) *hypothesis*, and a newer *dynamical systems theory* that views motor development as a product of a complex transaction among the child's physical capabilities, goals, and the experiences she or he has had (Thelen, 1995; Thelen, Fisher, Ridley-Johnson, 2002).

The Maturational Viewpoint

The maturational viewpoint (Shirley, 1933) describes motor development as the unfolding of a genetically programmed sequence of events where the nerves and muscles mature in a *downward* and *outward* direction. As a result, children gradually gain more control over the lower and peripheral parts of their bodies, displaying motor skills in the sequence shown in Table 5.1.

One clue that maturation plays a prominent role in motor development comes from cross-cultural research. Despite their very different early experiences, infants from around the world progress through roughly the same *sequence* of motor milestones. In addition, early studies in which one identical twin was allowed to practise motor skills (such as climbing stairs or stacking blocks) while the co-twin was denied these experiences suggested that practice had little effect on motor development. When finally allowed to perform, the unpractised twin soon matched the skills of the co-twin who had had many opportunities to practise (Gesell & Thompson, 1929; McGraw, 1935). Taken together, these findings seemed to imply that maturation underlies motor development and that practice merely allows a child to perfect those skills that maturation has made possible.

The Experiential (or Practice) Hypothesis

Although no one denies that maturation contributes to motor development, proponents of the experiential viewpoint believe that opportunities to practise motor skills are also important. Consider what Wayne Dennis (1960) found when he studied two groups of institutionalized orphans in Iran who had spent most of their first two years lying flat on their backs in their cribs. These infants were never placed in a sitting position, were rarely played with, and were even fed in their cribs with their bottles propped on pillows. Was their motor development affected by these depriving early experiences? Indeed it was! None of the 1- to 2-year-olds could walk, and less than half of them could even sit unaided. In fact, only 15 percent of the 3- to 4-year-olds could walk well alone! So Dennis concluded that maturation is *necessary but not sufficient* for the development of motor skills. In other words, infants who are physically capable of sitting, crawling, or walking will not be very proficient at these activities unless they have opportunities to practise them.

Not only does a lack of practice inhibit motor development, but the cross-cultural research in Box 5.2 also illustrates that a variety of enriching experiences can accelerate the process.

Motor Skills as Dynamic, Goal-Directed Systems

Although they would certainly agree that both maturation and experience contribute to motor development, proponents of an exciting new perspective—**dynamical systems theory**—differ from earlier theorists in two important ways. First, they do not view motor skills as genetically programmed responses that simply "unfold" as dictated by maturation and opportunities to practise. Instead, they view each new skill as a *construction* that emerges as infants *actively* reorganize existing motor capabilities into a new and more complex action system (Savelsbergh, van der Kamp, & Rosengren, 2002). At first, these new motor configurations are likely to be tentative, inefficient, and uncoordinated. New walkers, for example, spend a fair amount of time on their backsides and are called "toddlers" for a reason. But over a period of time, these new motor patterns are modified and refined until all components mesh and become smooth, coordinated actions such as bouncing, crawling, walking, running, and jumping (Thelen, 1995; Whitall & Getchell, 1995).

dynamical systems theory
theory that views motor skills as active reorganizations of previously mastered capabilities that are undertaken to find more effective ways of exploring the environment or satisfying other objectives

	Skill	Month when 50% of infants have mastered the skill	Month when 90% of infants have mastered the skill
1	Lifts head 90° while lying on stomach (1)	2.2	3.2
2	Rolls over (2)	2.8	4.7
3	Sits propped up (3)	2.9	4.2
4	Sits without support (4)	5.5	7.8
5	Stands holding on (5)	5.8	10.0
6	Crawls (6)	7.0	9.0
7	Walks holding on (7)	9.2	12.7
8	Plays pat-a-cake (8)	9.3	15.0
9	Stands alone momentarily (9)	9.8	13.0
10	Stands well alone (10)	11.5	13.9
11	Walks well (11)	12.1	14.3
12	Builds tower of two cubes (12)	13.8	19.0
13	Walks up steps (13)	17.0	22.0
14	Kicks ball forward (14)	20.0	24.0

SOURCES: Bayley, 1969; Frankenberg & Dodds, 1967.

Cross-cultural studies tell us that the ages at which infants attain major motor milestones are heavily influenced by parenting practices. The Kipsigis of Kenya, for example, work to promote motor skills. By their eighth week, infants are already practising their "walking" as parents grasp them by the armpits and propel them forward. And throughout the first few months, infants are seated in shallow holes, dug so that the sides support their backs and maintain an upright posture. Given these experiences, it is perhaps not surprising that Kipsigi infants sit unassisted about five weeks earlier and walk unaided about a month earlier than Western infants do.

Similarly, Brian Hopkins (1991) has compared the motor development of Black infants whose families emigrated to England from Jamaica with that of White infants in England. As in several other comparisons of Black and White infants, the Black infants displayed such important motor skills as sitting, crawling, and walking at earlier ages. Do these findings reflect genetic differences between Blacks and Whites? Probably not, because Black babies were likely to acquire motor skills early only if their mothers had followed traditional Jamaican routines for handling infants and nurturing motor development. These routines include massaging infants, stretching their limbs, and holding them by the arms while gently shaking them up and down. Jamaican mothers expect early motor development, work to promote it, and get it.

Dovetailing nicely with the cross-cultural work are experiments conducted by Philip Zelazo and his associates (1972, 1993), at McGill University, with North American infants. Zelazo found that 2- to 8-week-old babies who were regularly held in an upright posture and encouraged to practise their stepping reflex showed a strengthening of this response (which usually disappears early in life). They also walked at an earlier age than did infants in a control group who did not receive this training.

Why might having one's limbs stretched or being held (or sat) in an upright posture hasten motor development? Esther Thelen's (1986; Thelen & Fisher, 1982) view is that babies who are often placed in an upright position develop strength in the neck, trunk, and legs (an acceleration of muscular growth), which in turn promotes the early development of such motor skills as standing and walking. So it seems that both maturation and experience are important contributors to motor development. Maturation does place some limits on the age at which the child will first be capable of sitting, standing, and walking. Yet experiences such as upright posturing and various forms of practice may influence the age at which important maturational capabilities are achieved and translated into action.

But why would infants work so hard to acquire new motor skills? Unlike earlier theories that did not address this issue, dynamical systems theory offers a straightforward answer: Infants hope to acquire and perfect new motor skills that will help them to get to interesting objects they hope to explore or to accomplish other goals they may have in mind (Thelen, 1995). Consider what Eugene Goldfield (1989) learned in studying infants' emerging ability to crawl. Goldfield found that 7- to 8-month-old infants began to crawl only after they (1) regularly turned and raised their heads toward interesting sights and sounds in the environment, (2) had developed a distinct hand/arm preference when reaching for such stimuli, and (3) had begun to thrust (kick) with the leg opposite to the outstretched arm. Apparently, visual orientation *motivates* infants to approach interesting stimuli they can't reach, reaching steers the body in the right direction, and kicking with the opposite leg propels the body forward. So far from being a preprogrammed skill that simply unfolds according to a maturational plan, crawling (and virtually all other motor skills) actually represents an active and intricate *reorganization* of *several existing capabilities* that is undertaken by a curious, active infant who has a particular *goal* in mind.

Why, then, do all infants proceed through the same sequence of locomotor milestones? Partly because of their human maturational programming, which sets the stage for various accomplishments, and partly because each successive motor skill must necessarily build on specific component activities that have developed earlier. How does experience fit in? According to the dynamical systems theory, a world of interesting objects and events provides infants with many reasons to want to reach out or to sit up, crawl, walk, and run—that is, with *purposes* and *motives* that might be served by actively reorganizing their existing skills into new and more complex action systems. Of course, no two infants have exactly the same set of experiences (or goals), which may help to explain why each infant coordinates the component activities of an emerging motor skill in a slightly different way (Thelen et al., 1993).

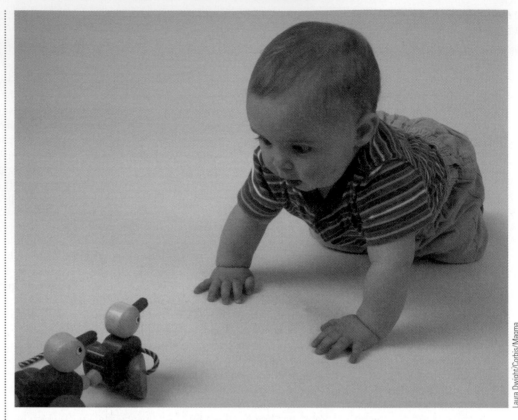

According to dynamical systems theory, new motor skills emerge as curious infants reorganize their existing capabilities in order to achieve important objectives.

In sum, the development of motor skills is far more interesting and complex than earlier theories assumed. Though maturation plays a very important role, the basic motor skills of the first two years do not simply unfold as part of nature's grand plan. Rather, they emerge largely because goal-driven infants are constantly recombining actions they can perform into new and more complex action systems that will help them to achieve their objectives.

Fine Motor Development

Two other aspects of motor development play especially important roles in helping infants to explore and adapt to their surroundings: *voluntary reaching* and *manipulatory* (or hand) *skills*.

Development of Voluntary Reaching

An infant's ability to reach out and manipulate objects changes dramatically over the first year. Recall that newborns come equipped with a grasping reflex. They are also inclined to reach for things, although these primitive thrusts (or *prereaches*) are really little more than uncoordinated swipes at objects in the visual field. Prereaching is truly a hit-or-miss proposition (Bower, 1982). By 2 months of age, infants' reaching and grasping skills may even seem to deteriorate. The reflexive Palmar grasp disappears and prereaching occurs much less often (Bower, 1982). However, these apparent regressions set the stage for the appearance of *voluntary* reaching. Babies 3 months of age and older display this new competency as they extend their arms and make in-flight corrections, gradually improving in accuracy until they can reliably grasp their objectives (Hofsten, 1984; Thelen et al., 1993). Infants clearly differ in how they reach for objects. Some

163

Chapter Five
The Physical Self:
Development of the Brain,
the Body, and Motor Skills

infants flap their arms at first and must learn to dampen their enthusiasm, whereas others reach tentatively and soon learn that they must supply more power to grasp their objectives (Thelen et al., 1993). So, here again, we see that reaching is a motor skill that does not simply "unfold"; instead, babies reach in different ways and take their own unique pathways to refining this important skill.

It was once thought that early reaching required visual guidance of the hand and arm for infants to locate their target. Yet recent research indicates that infants only 3 months old are just as successful at reaching for and grasping objects they can only hear (in the dark) as they are at grabbing those they can see (Clifton et al., 1993). And by 5 months, infants are becoming proficient at reaching for and touching (1) stationary illuminated objects that suddenly darken to become invisible as they begin their reaches (McCarty & Ashmead, 1999) and (2) glowing objects that *move* in the dark—even though these young reachers cannot see what their hands are doing (Robin, Berthier, & Clifton, 1996). So, far from being totally controlled by vision, early reaches are also dependent on **proprioceptive information** from the muscles, tendons, and joints that help infants guide their arms and hands to any interesting objects within arm's length.

Development of Manipulatory Skills

Once infants are able to sit well and to reach inward, across their body midline, at about age 4 to 5 months, they begin to grasp interesting objects with *both* hands and their exploratory activities forever change. Rather than merely batting or palming objects, they are now apt to transfer them from hand to hand or to hold them with one hand and finger them with the other (Rochat, 1989; Rochat & Goubet, 1995). Indeed, this fingering activity may be the primary method by which 4- to 6-month-olds gain information about objects, for their unimanual (one-handed) grasping skills are poorly developed. The reflexive palmar grasp has already disappeared by this age, and the **ulnar grasp** that replaces it is itself a rather clumsy, clawlike grip that permits little tactile exploration of objects by touch.

During the latter half of the first year, fingering skills improve and infants become much more proficient at tailoring all their exploratory activities to the properties of objects they are investigating (Palmer, 1989). Now, wheeled toys are likely to be scooted rather than banged, spongy objects are squeezed rather than scooted, and so on. The next major step in the growth of hand skills occurs near the end of the first year as infants use their thumbs and forefingers to lift and explore objects (Halverson, 1931). This **pincer grasp** transforms children from little fumblers into skillful manipulators who may soon begin to capture crawling bugs and to turn knobs, dials, and rheostats, thereby discovering that they can use their newly acquired hand skills to produce any number of interesting results.

Throughout the second year, infants are becoming much more proficient with their hands. At 16 months of age, they can scribble with a crayon, and by the end of the second year, they can copy a simple horizontal or vertical line and even build towers of five or more blocks. What is happening is

proprioceptive information
sensory information from the muscles, tendons, and joints that help one to locate the position of one's body (or body parts) in space

ulnar grasp
early manipulatory skill in which an infant grasps objects by pressing the fingers against the palm

pincer grasp
grasp in which the thumb is used in opposition to the fingers, enabling an infant to become more dexterous at lifting and fondling objects

The pincer grasp is a crucial motor milestone that underlies the development of many coordinated manual activities.

Comstock Images

quite consistent with dynamical systems theory: Infants are gaining control over simple movements and then integrating these skills into increasingly complex, coordinated systems (Fentress & McLeod, 1986). Building a tower, for example, requires the child to first gain control over the thumb and the forefinger and then use the pincer grip as part of a larger action sequence that involves reaching for a block, snatching it, laying it squarely on top of another block, and then delicately releasing it. But despite their ability to combine simple motor activities into increasingly complex sequences, even 2- to 3-year-olds are not very good at catching and throwing a ball, cutting food with utensils, or colouring within the lines of their colouring books. These skills will emerge later in childhood as the muscles mature and children become more proficient at using visual information to help them coordinate their actions.

? **WHAT DO YOU THINK?**

Can you identify a common thread between recent changes in thinking about how (1) the brain's normal circuitry is fine-tuned and (2) the emergence of motor skills? What are the implications of these new viewpoints for the nature versus nurture debate?

Psychological Implications of Early Motor Development

Life changes dramatically for both parents and infants once a baby is able to reach out and grasp interesting objects, especially after he can crawl or walk to explore these treasures. Suddenly, parents find they have to childproof their homes or limit access to certain areas, or else run the risk of experiencing a seemingly endless string of disasters,

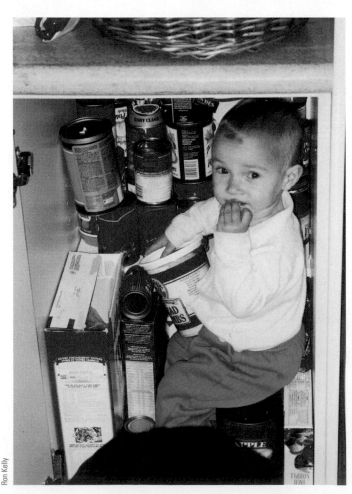

Ron Kelly

Life becomes more challenging for parents as infants perfect their motor skills.

including torn books, overturned vases, unravelled rolls of toilet paper, and irritable pets whose tails the little explorer has pulled. Placing limits on explorations often precipitates conflicts and a "testing of the wills" between infants and their caregivers (Biringen et al., 1995). Nevertheless, parents are often thrilled by their infant's emerging motor skills, which not only provide clear evidence that development is proceeding normally, but also permit such pleasurable forms of social interaction as pat-a-cake, chase, and hide-and-seek.

Aside from the entertainment value it provides, an infant's increasing control over bodily movements has important cognitive and social consequences. Mobile infants may feel much more bold, for example, about meeting people and seeking challenges if they know that they can retreat to their caregivers for comfort should they feel insecure (Ainsworth, 1979). Achieving various motor milestones may also foster perceptual development. For example, crawlers are better able to search for and find hidden objects than infants of the same age who are not mobile (Kermoian & Campos, 1988). The same outcomes were found for noncrawlers who were given access to special walkers and, hence, were made mobile. (Note, however, that there has been a voluntary ban on the sale of baby walkers in Canada since 1989 following large numbers of head injuries from infants falling down stairs while in walkers [Health Canada, 2000].) The self-produced movement of crawling and walking also makes infants more aware of *optical flow* (sensations that objects move as the infant does), which in turn helps them to orient themselves in space, improve their postures, and crawl or walk more efficiently (Higgins, Campos, & Kermoian, 1996). And as we will see in Chapter 6, crawling and walking both contribute to an understanding of distance relationships and a healthy fear of heights (Adolph, Eppler, & Gibson, 1993; Campos, Bertenthal, & Kermoian, 1992). So once again, we see that human development is a *holistic* enterprise: changes in motor skills have clear implications for other aspects of development.

165

Chapter Five
*The Physical Self:
Development of the Brain,
the Body, and Motor Skills*

Beyond Infancy: Motor Development in Childhood and Adolescence

The term *toddler* aptly describes most 1- to 2-year-olds, who often fall down or trip over stationary objects when they try to get somewhere in a hurry. But as children mature, their locomotor skills increase by leaps and bounds. By age 3, children can walk or run in a straight line and leap off the floor with both feet, although they can clear only very small (20 to 25 cm) objects in a single bound and cannot easily turn or stop while running. Four-year-olds can skip, hop on one foot, catch a large ball with both hands, and run much farther and faster than they could one year earlier (Corbin, 1973). By age 5, children are becoming rather graceful: like adults, they pump their arms when they run, and their balance has improved to the point that some of them can learn to ride a bicycle. Despite (or perhaps because of) the rapid progress they are making, young children often overestimate the physical feats they can perform, and the bolder ones may end up with bruises, burns, cuts, scrapes, and an assortment of other injuries (Schwebel & Plumert, 1999).

With each passing year, school-age children can run a little faster, jump a little higher, and throw a ball a little farther (Herkowitz, 1978; Keough & Sugden, 1985). Part of the reason that children are improving at these large-muscle activities is that they are growing larger and stronger. But they are also fine-tuning their motor skills. As shown in Figure 5.7, young children throw only with the arm, whereas adolescents are usually able to coordinate shoulder, arm, and leg movements to put the force of their bodies behind their throws. So older children and adolescents can throw farther than younger children can, not only because they are bigger and stronger, but also because they use more refined and efficient techniques of movement (Gallahue, 1989).

At the same time, eye–hand coordination and control of the small muscles are improving rapidly so that children can make more sophisticated use of their hands. Three-year-olds find it difficult to button their shirts, tie their shoes, or copy simple designs. By age 5, children can accomplish all of these feats and can even cut a straight line with scissors or copy letters and numbers with a crayon. By age 8 or 9, they can use household tools such as screwdrivers and have become skilled performers at games such as jacks and Nintendo that require eye–hand coordination. Finally, older children display quicker *reaction times* than younger children do (Williams et al., 1999), which helps to explain why they usually beat younger playmates at "action" games such as dodge ball or table tennis.

Boys and girls are nearly equal in physical abilities until puberty, when boys continue to post gains on tests of large-muscle activities, whereas girls level off or decline (Thomas & French, 1985). These sex differences are, in part, attributable to biology: Adolescent boys have more muscle and less fat than adolescent girls and might be expected to outperform them on tests of physical strength (Tanner, 1990). Yet biological developments do not account for all the difference in large-muscle performance between boys and girls (Smoll & Schutz, 1990), nor do they adequately explain the *declining* performance of girls, who continue to grow taller and heavier, between ages 12 and 17. Jacqueline Herkowitz (1978) believes that the apparent physical decline of

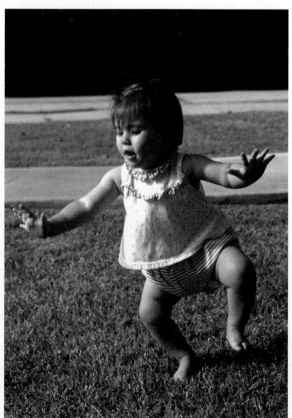

Top-heavy toddlers often lose their balance when they try to move very quickly.

Figure 5.7 *As these initial tosses and mature throws illustrate, large-muscle activities become more refined and efficient with age.*

adolescent girls is a product of gender-role socialization: With their widening hips and developing breasts, girls are often encouraged to become less tomboyish and more interested in traditionally feminine (and less athletic) activities.

There is clearly an element of truth to this notion in that female *athletes* show no apparent decline in large-muscle performance over time. Furthermore, as gender roles have changed in the past few decades, female athletes have been steadily improving their performances, and the male–female gap in physical performance has narrowed dramatically (Dyer, 1977; Whipp & Ward, 1992). So it seems that adolescent girls would almost certainly continue to improve on tests of large-muscle activity if they chose to remain physically active. And as we see in Box 5.3, they may experience important psychological benefits as well as remaining physically active throughout the teenage years.

PUBERTY: THE PHYSICAL TRANSITION FROM CHILD TO ADULT

The onset of adolescence is heralded by two significant changes in physical development. First, children change dramatically in size and shape as they enter the **adolescent growth spurt.** They also reach **puberty** (from the Latin word *pubertas*, meaning "to grow hairy"), the point in life when an individual reaches sexual maturity and becomes capable of producing a child.

adolescent growth spurt
rapid increase in physical growth that marks the beginning of adolescence

puberty
point at which a person reaches sexual maturity and is physically capable of fathering or conceiving a child

The Adolescent Growth Spurt

The term *growth spurt* describes the rapid acceleration in height and weight that marks the beginning of adolescence. Girls typically enter the growth spurt by age 10½, reach a peak growth rate by age 12, and return to a slower rate of growth by age 13 to 13½

Sport Participation and Self-Esteem among Adolescent Females

Over the past few years, developmentalists have begun to consider the benefits of **physical activity play,** speculating that it serves as a mechanism for building muscle strength and endurance and possibly for reducing levels of fat in children's growing bodies (Pellegrini & Smith, 1998). Physical activity play typically peaks in early to middle childhood and declines thereafter. This reduction in vigorous physical activity is much more apparent for girls than for boys, which undoubtedly helps to explain the decline in large-muscle strength often seen among girls during the adolescent years.

Interestingly, over the past 30 years our society has become much more supportive of one kind of physical activity for girls—participation in competitive and non-competitive sports. One proposed benefit of this change was an enhanced sense of self-worth (self-esteem) among female athletes. Is there any basis supporting such a benefit? To find out, Erin Richman and David Shaffer (2000) constructed an elaborate questionnaire to measure both the breadth and depth of female university students' participation in formal and informal sporting activities during their high school years. In addition, these women completed measures assessing their current levels of self-esteem, feelings of physical competence, assertiveness, and a healthy sense of competition.

The results provided some support for the notion of enhanced self-esteem from participation in sports. First, there was a clear relation between the young women's participation in sports during high school and their later self-esteem—those who had participated to a greater extent in high school sports enjoyed higher levels of general self-worth as college students. Further analysis revealed that the positive relation between sports participation and self-esteem reflected the findings that (1) sports participation was associated with increases in perceived physical competencies, development of a more favourable body image, and acquisition of attributes (such as assertiveness), and (2) all these developments, in turn, were positively correlated with (and apparently fostered) participants' self-esteem while at university.

In sum, it appears that girls' participation in sporting activities in the adolescent years may well contribute to an enhanced sense of self-worth—but this answer is overly simple and does not take into account the other related benefits from participating in sports, such as fostering physical competencies, more favourable body images, and assertiveness. These findings together imply that gym classes and formal team sports might be more beneficial to a larger number of girls if educators and coaches were to emphasize the physical gains and psychological benefits of formal and informal sporting activities, while concentrating less on the outcomes of competitive sports or the physical deficiencies of the less athletically competent girls under their tutelage.

(Tanner, 1981). Boys lag behind girls by two to three years. They typically begin their growth spurt by age 13, peak at age 14, and return to a more gradual rate of growth by age 16. Because girls mature much earlier than boys, it is not at all uncommon for females to be the tallest two or three students in a Grade 9 classroom.

In addition to growing taller and heavier, the body assumes an adultlike appearance during the adolescent growth spurt. Perhaps the most noticeable changes are a widening of the hips for girls and a broadening of the shoulders for boys. Facial features also assume adult proportions as the forehead protrudes, the nose and jaw become more prominent, and the lips enlarge.

Sexual Maturation

Maturation of the reproductive system occurs at roughly the same time as the adolescent growth spurt and follows a predictable sequence for girls and boys.

Sexual Development in Girls

For most girls, sexual maturation begins at about age 9 or 10 as fatty tissue accumulates around their nipples, forming small "breast buds" (Herman-Giddens et al., 1997). Usually pubic hair begins to appear a little later, although as many as one-third of all girls develop some pubic hair before the breasts begin to develop (Tanner, 1990).

As a girl enters her height spurt, the breasts grow rapidly and the sex organs begin to mature. Internally, the vagina becomes larger, and the walls of the uterus develop a powerful set of muscles that may one day be used to accommodate a fetus during pregnancy and to push it through the cervix and vagina during the birth process. Externally,

physical activity play
moderate to vigorous play activities such as running, jumping, climbing, play fighting, or game playing that raise a child's metabolic rate far above resting levels.

the mons pubis (the soft tissue covering the pubic bone), the labia (the fleshy lips surrounding the vaginal opening), and the clitoris all increase in size and become more sensitive to touch (Tanner, 1990).

At about age 12½, the average girl in Western societies reaches **menarche**—the time of her first menstruation. Though it is generally assumed that a girl becomes fertile at menarche, young girls often menstruate without ovulating and *may* remain unable to reproduce for 12 to 18 months after menarche (Tanner, 1978). In the year following menarche, female sexual development concludes as the breasts complete their development and axillary (underarm) hair appears.

Sexual Development in Boys

For boys, sexual maturation begins at about age 11 to 12 with an enlargement of the testes. The growth of the testes is often accompanied or soon followed by the appearance of unpigmented pubic hair. The male equivalent of menarche, *spermarche*, occurs between approximately 11½ and 15½ years (median age is just over 13 years). Spermarche refers to the onset of the production of spermatozoa—the male sex cells, and is evidenced by the boy's first ejaculation (Kulin et al., 1989; Nielson et al., 1986, 2003). By the time the penis is fully developed at age 14½ to 15, most boys will have reached puberty and are now capable of fathering a child (Tanner, 1990).

Somewhat later, boys begin to sprout facial hair, first at the corners of the upper lip and finally on the chin and jawline. Body hair also grows on the arms and legs, although signs of a hairy chest may not appear until the late teens or early 20s, if at all. Another hallmark of male sexual maturity is a lowering of the voice as the larynx grows and the vocal cords lengthen. In fact, many men may laugh (years later) about their voices "cracking" up and down between a squeaky soprano and a deep baritone, sometimes within a single sentence.

Individual Differences in Physical and Sexual Maturation

So far, we have been describing developmental norms, or the average ages when adolescent changes take place. But as Figure 5.8 indicates, there are great individual differences in the timing of physical and sexual maturation. An early-maturing girl who develops breast buds at age 8, starts her growth spurt at age 9½, and reaches menarche at age 10½

menarche
first occurrence of menstruation

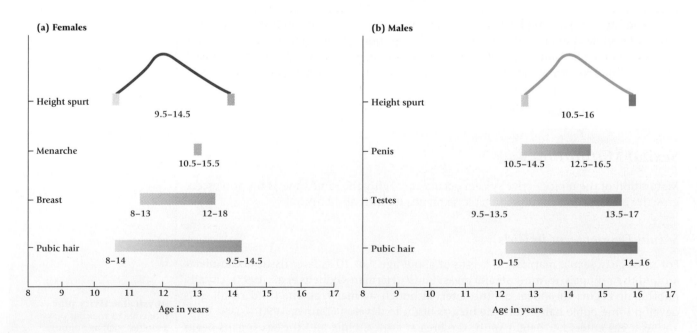

Figure 5.8 Milestones in the sexual maturation of (a) girls and (b) boys. The numbers represent the variation among individuals in the ages at which each aspect of sexual maturation begins or ends. For example, we see that the growth of the penis may begin as early as age 10½ or as late as age 14½. FROM TANNER, 1990.

may nearly complete her growth and pubertal development before the late-developing girls in her class have even begun. Individual differences among boys are at least as great. Some boys reach sexual maturity by age 12½ and are as tall as they will ever be by age 13, whereas others begin growing later than that and do not reach puberty until their late teens. This perfectly normal biological variation may be observed in any Grade 9 classroom, where one will find a wide assortment of bodies, ranging from those that are entirely childlike to those that are very adultlike.

169

Chapter Five
The Physical Self:
Development of the Brain,
the Body, and Motor Skills

Secular Trends: Are We Maturing Earlier?

About 20 years ago, women in one family were surprised when a sixth grade student began to menstruate shortly after her 12th birthday. The inevitable comparisons soon began, as the girl learned that neither of her great-grandmothers had reached this milestone until age 15 and that her grandmother had been nearly 14 and her mother 13. At this point, the girl casually replied, "Big deal! Lots of girls in my class have got their periods."

As it turns out, this young woman was simply "telling it like it is." In 1900, when her great-grandmother was born, the average age of first menstruation was 14 to 15. By 1950, most girls were reaching menarche between 13½ and 14, and today's norms have dropped even further, to age 12½ (Tanner, 1990). This **secular trend** toward earlier maturation started more than 100 years ago in the industrialized nations of the world, and now it is happening in the more prosperous nonindustrialized countries as well. Among industrialized nations the secular change continues but at a much slower rate (Fredriks et al., 2000). In addition, people in industrialized nations have been growing taller and heavier over the past century.

What explains these secular trends? Better nutrition and hygiene along with smaller families and advances in medical care seem to be most responsible (Fredriks et al., 2000; Tanner, 1990). Today's children are more likely than their parents or grandparents to reach their genetic potentials for maturation and growth because they are better fed and less likely to experience growth-retarding illnesses. Even within our own relatively affluent society, poorly nourished adolescents mature later than well-nourished ones do and in some cases do not meet their genetic potential (Lantzouni et al., 2002). Girls who are tall and overweight as children tend to mature early (Graber et al., 1994), whereas many dancers, gymnasts, and other girls who engage regularly in strenuous physical activity may begin menstruating very late or stop menstruating after they have begun (Hopwood et al., 1990). Here, then, are strong clues that nature and nurture interact to influence the timing of pubertal events.

> **?** **WHAT DO YOU THINK?**
>
> Although no Canadian research describes race differences for the onset of puberty, recent research in the United States (Herman-Giddens et al., 1997) reveals that nearly half of African-American girls have begun to develop breasts, pubic hair, or both by age 8, whereas only 15 percent of European-American girls show such early signs of pubertal change. How would you account for this race difference in female sexual maturation?

THE PSYCHOLOGICAL EFFECTS OF PUBERTY

General Reactions to Physical Changes

What do adolescents think about the dramatic physical changes they are experiencing? In Western cultures, girls typically become quite concerned about their appearance and worry about how other people will respond to them (Cauffman & Steinberg, 1996; Greif & Ulman, 1982). In general, teenage girls hope to be perceived as attractive, and changes that are congruent with the "feminine ideal" of slimness are often welcomed. However,

secular trend
trend in industrialized societies toward earlier maturation and greater body size now than in the past

they are often concerned that they are growing too tall or too fat (Swarr & Richards, 1996; Wichstrom, 1999), and their body images become increasingly negative from early to late adolescence (Rosenblum & Lewis, 1999). Even well-proportioned teenage girls may try to compensate for perceived physical faults by slouching, wearing flat shoes, or trying endless fad diets (Rosen, Tracey, & Howell, 1990). Girls who perceive that they are fat or who have poor body esteem are likely to have less positive views about themselves. Morton and Beverley Mendelson of McGill University and Vanier College, respectively, have examined the relationship between body esteem and body mass. Their results are highlighted in Box 5.4. (For examples of what can happen if a girl becomes overly pre-occupied with her weight, see Box 5.5, page 177.)

Girls' reactions to menarche are mixed (Greif & Ulman, 1982). They are often excited but somewhat confused as well, especially if they mature very early or have not been told what to expect (Brooks-Gunn, 1988). Few girls today are traumatized by menarche, but at the same time, few are overjoyed about becoming a woman (Koff & Rierdan, 1995; Moore, 1995).

Boys' body images are more positive than those of girls (Rosenblum & Lewis, 1999), and they are much more likely than girls to welcome their weight gains (Richards et al., 1990). Teenage boys also hope to be tall, hairy, and handsome, and they may become preoccupied with the aspects of body image that centre on physical and athletic prowess (Simmons & Blyth, 1987). Whereas menarche is a memorable event for girls, boys are often only dimly aware of the physical changes they are experiencing (Zani, 1991). They rarely tell anyone about their first ejaculation, often were not prepared for it, and like girls, express mixed reactions to becoming sexually mature (Gaddis & Brooks-Gunn, 1985; Stein & Reiser, 1994).

Social Impacts of Pubertal Changes

rites of passage
rituals that signify the passage from one period of life to another (for example, puberty rites)

Adolescents who are maturing physically and sexually not only come to feel differently about themselves but come to be viewed and treated differently by other people. In many nonindustrialized societies, rituals called **rites of passage** inform the whole com-

---

THE INSIDE TRACK

5.4

Morton and Beverley Mendelson

Morton and Beverley Mendelson collaborate together in their research on body mass, body esteem, and self-esteem. Morton Mendelson is a professor in the Department of Psychology at McGill University. Beverley Mendelson teaches psychology at Vanier College and conducts research at the Université de Montréal.

Morton and Beverley Mendelson and their colleagues (Mendelson, Mendelson, & Andrews, 2000; Mendelson, Mendelson, & White, 2001) have devised and tested the Body-Esteem Scale for adolescents and adults. The scale measures individuals' evaluations of their body through three subscales: general feelings about appearance, weight satisfaction, and how individuals think other people view their body and appearance.

Body esteem can be understood as a global term that is comprised of a number of smaller domains. For example, a person's evaluation of her or his weight can be distinguished from feelings about her or his appearance. In one study, the scale was tested to determine how effectively it measured the three components and how these items were related to other variables such as self-esteem (Mendelson et al., 2001). Several points became clear. Females were found to have lower body esteem regarding their weight and their appearance than did males; overweight individuals, especially females, were dissatisfied with their weight; and the appearance subscale predicted self-esteem. In another investigation with adolescents, these findings were confirmed and elaborated. For example, individuals who rated weight as important tended to rate weight satisfaction and their appearance low, and they had lower self-esteem (Mendelson et al., 2000). Especially for women, there was also a relation between higher weight (measured using the Body Mass Index, where weight is adjusted with respect to height) and lower evaluations for romantic confidence, appearance, and perceptions of others.

These findings support claims that adolescents' perceptions about their bodies and their weight might be one mechanism for understanding self-esteem.

171

Chapter Five
The Physical Self:
Development of the Brain,
the Body, and Motor Skills

munity that a child has become an adult (Schlegel & Barry, 1991). Among the Kaguru of eastern Africa, for example, pubertal boys are led into the bush, stripped, and shaved of all hair, which symbolizes losing their status as children (Beidelman, 1971). They then undergo the painful experience of circumcision without anesthesia, learn about tribal sexual practices, and are taught ritual songs and riddles that instruct them in the ways of manhood. Finally, they are "anointed" with red earth to mark their new status and led back to the village for celebrations and feasts. The Kaguru girl is initiated by herself whenever she experiences her first menstruation. Her genital area is cut as a mark of her new status, and she is instructed in the ways of womanhood, usually by her grandmother, before being welcomed back into society as an adult.

Although our society has no universal rites of passage to mark the transition from childhood to adolescence, or from adolescence to adulthood, pubertal changes may nonetheless have social consequences. Lawrence Steinberg (1981, 1988) reports that around ages 11 to 13, when pubertal changes are peaking, European-American adolescents become more independent and feel less close to their parents, with whom they often argue (see also Paikoff & Brooks-Gunn, 1991). These standoffs usually involve squabbles about unmade beds, late hours, and loud music rather than arguments about core values, but they can be unpleasant nonetheless. Hormonal changes in early adolescence may contribute to these conflicts, as well as to moodiness, bouts of depression, and restlessness (Buchanan, Eccles, & Becker, 1992; Udry, 1990). However, none of these experiences is inevitable. In fact, Mexican-American boys and their parents appear to become *closer* rather than more distant as puberty arrives, suggesting that cultural beliefs about the family or about the significance of becoming more adultlike can influence parent–child relations during adolescence (Molina & Chassin, 1996).

Even when parent–child relations are disrupted early in adolescence, they typically become warmer again later in adolescence, once the pubertal transition is over (Greenberger & Chen, 1996; Larson et al., 1996). Parents can help their children adjust successfully to puberty by maintaining close relationships, being patient, and helping adolescents to accept themselves and all the physical and social changes they are experiencing (Booth et al., 2003; Swarr & Richards, 1996). Clearly, the early teenage years are a period when biological changes interact with changes in the social environment to influence how adolescence is experienced (Magnusson, 1995; Paikoff & Brooks-Gunn, 1991).

Does Timing of Puberty Matter?

Think back for a moment to your own adolescence when you first realized that you were rapidly becoming a man or a woman. Did this happen to you earlier than to your friends, or later? Do you think that the timing of these events could have influenced your personality or social life?

Timing of puberty does have some meaningful implications, although its impact differs somewhat for boys and girls.

Possible Impacts on Boys

Longitudinal research conducted at the University of California suggests that boys who mature early enjoy a number of social advantages over boys who mature late. One study followed the development of 16 early-maturing and 16 late-maturing male adolescents over a six-year period and found late maturers to be more eager, anxious, and attention-seeking (and also rated by teachers as less masculine and less physically attractive) than early maturers (Jones & Bayley, 1950). Early maturers tended to be poised and confident in social settings and were more likely to win athletic honours and election to student offices. Although this study was based on only 32 boys, other researchers have found that late-maturing males do tend to feel somewhat socially inadequate and inferior (Duke et al., 1982; Livson & Peskin, 1980). Late-maturing boys also have lower educational aspirations than early maturers do, and they even score lower on school achievement tests early in adolescence (Dubas, Graber, & Petersen, 1991).

Early-maturing males tend to be poised and confident in social settings and popular with their peers.

Why is the early-maturing boy so advantaged? One reason may be that his greater size and strength often make him a more capable athlete, which in turn is apt to bring social recognition from adults and peers (Simmons & Blyth, 1987). The early maturer's adultlike appearance may also prompt others to overestimate his competencies and to grant him privileges and responsibilities normally reserved for older individuals. Indeed, parents hold higher educational and achievement aspirations for early-maturing than for late-maturing sons (Duke et al., 1982), and they have fewer conflicts with early maturers about issues such as acceptable curfews and the boy's choice of friends (Savin-Williams & Small, 1986). Perhaps you can see how this generally positive, harmonious atmosphere might promote the poise or self-confidence that enables early maturers to become popular and to assume positions of leadership within the peer group.

Do these differences between early and late maturers persist into adulthood? In general, they fade over time. By Grade 12, for example, differences in academic performance between early and late maturers have already disappeared (Dubas et al., 1991). However, Jones (1965) found that early-maturing boys from the longitudinal study were still somewhat more sociable, confident, and responsible in their 30s than their peers who had matured later. So, some of the advantages of early maturation may carry over into adulthood.

Possible Effects on Girls

For girls, maturing early may be somewhat of a *disadvantage*. Although early breast development is associated with a favourable body image and increased *self-confidence* (Brooks-Gunn & Warren, 1988), several studies find that early-maturing girls are somewhat *less* outgoing and *less* popular than their prepubertal classmates (Aro & Taipale, 1987; Clausen, 1975; Faust, 1960) and are likely to report more symptoms of anxiety and depression as well (Ge, Conger, & Elder, 1996; Hayward et al., 1997; Wichstrom, 1999). Intuitively, these findings make some sense. A girl who matures very early may look very different from female classmates, who

---

✓ Concept Check 5.2
Psychological Aspects of Physical and Motor Devlopment

Check your understanding of some of the psychological aspects of physical and motor development by matching one or more of the following developments with its psychological correlates as listed in items 1–8. The developments are (a) early maturation, (b) late maturation, (c) on-time maturation, (d) peak of pubertal changes, (e) locomotor skills, (f) sex-role socialization, (g) menarche/ejaculation. Answers appear in the Appendix.

_____ 1. decline in girl's large muscle strength

_____ 2. increase in parent–child conflict

_____ 3. improves likelihood of good social adjustment in boys

_____ 4. presents risk of adjustment difficulties for girls early in adolescence

_____ 5. likely to be met with mixed feelings by adolescents of each sex

_____ 6. may increase one's boldness and willingness to seek new challenges

_____ 7. presents risk of promoting low self-confidence and lower social status in boys

_____ 8. often associated with favourable peer status for girls early in adolescence may tease her. She will look older than boys in the class, who will not mature for two to three years and are not yet all that enthused about an early maturer's more womanly attributes (Caspi et al., 1993). As a result, early-maturing girls often seek (or are sought out by) older companions, particularly boys, who often steer them away from academic pursuits and into more adultlike, undesirable activities, such as smoking, drinking, drug use, and sex, that they are not yet prepared to handle (Caspi et al., 1993; Dick et al., 2000). Indeed, risks of psychological distress among early-maturing girls are much higher when they attend coed schools and have lots of boys as friends (Caspi et al., 1993; Ge, Conger, & Elder, 1996).

Some of the curses of early maturity can be long-lasting. One Swedish study, for example, found that early-maturing girls continued to perform less well at school and were more likely to drop out than their late-maturing or on-time classmates (Stattin & Magnusson, 1990). Yet most early-maturing girls fare better over time. Not only are they often admired later in junior high, once the female peer group discovers that early-maturing girls tend to be popular with boys (Faust, 1960), but as young adults, women who matured early are no less well-adjusted than their late-maturing peers (Stattin & Magnusson, 1990).

Overall, then, both the advantages of maturing early and the disadvantages of maturing late are greater for boys than for girls. But even though late-maturing boys and early-maturing girls are more likely to be distressed, the psychological differences between early and late maturers become smaller and more mixed in nature by adulthood. Finally, let's note that the differences between early and late maturers are not large and that many factors other than timing of puberty influence whether this period of life goes smoothly or not.

CAUSES AND CORRELATES OF PHYSICAL DEVELOPMENT

Although we have now charted the course of physical development from birth through adolescence, we've touched only briefly on the factors that influence growth. What *really* causes children to grow in the first place? And why do their bodies change so dramatically at adolescence, when growth accelerates? As we will see in the pages that follow, physical development results from a complex and continuous interplay between the forces of nature and nurture.

Biological Mechanisms

Clearly, biological factors play a major role in the growth process. Although children do not all grow at the same rate, we have seen that the *sequencing* of both physical maturation and motor development is reasonably consistent from child to child. Apparently, these regular maturational sequences that all humans share are species-specific attributes—products of our common genetic heritage.

Effects of Individual Genotypes

Aside from our common genetic ties to the human race, we have each inherited a unique combination of genes that influence our physical growth and development. For example, family studies clearly indicate that height is a heritable attribute: Identical twins are much more similar in height than fraternal twins, whether the measurements are taken during the first year of life, at 4 years of age, or in early adulthood (Tanner, 1990). *Rate of maturation* is also genetically influenced. James Tanner (1990) reports that female identical twins reach menarche within two to three months of each other, whereas fraternal twin sisters are typically about 10 months apart. Similar genetic influences hold for milestones in skeletal growth and even for the appearance of teeth in infants.

173

Chapter Five
The Physical Self:
Development of the Brain,
the Body, and Motor Skills

How does genotype influence growth? We are not completely certain, although it appears that our genes regulate the production of hormones, which have major effects on physical growth and development.

Hormonal Influences—The Endocrinology of Growth

Hormones begin to influence development long before a child is born. As we learned in Chapter 3, a male fetus assumes a male-like appearance because (1) a gene on his Y chromosome triggers the development of testes, which (2) secrete a male hormone (testosterone) that is necessary for the development of a male reproductive system. By the fourth prenatal month, the thyroid gland has formed and begins to produce **thyroxine**, a hormone that is essential if the brain and nervous system are to develop properly. Babies born with a thyroid deficiency soon become mentally handicapped if this condition goes undiagnosed and untreated (Tanner, 1990). Those who develop a thyroid deficiency later in childhood will not suffer brain damage because their brain growth spurt is over. However, they will begin to grow very slowly, a finding that indicates that a certain level of thyroxine is necessary for normal growth and development.

The most critical of the *endocrine* (hormone-secreting) glands is the **pituitary**, a "master gland" located at the base of the brain that triggers the release of hormones from all other endocrine glands. In addition to regulating the endocrine system, the pituitary produces a **growth hormone (GH)** that stimulates the rapid growth and development of body cells. Growth hormone is released in small amounts several times a day. When parents tell their children that lots of sleep will help them to grow big and strong, they are right: GH is normally secreted into the bloodstream about 60 to 90 minutes after a child falls asleep (Tanner, 1990). And GH is essential for *normal* growth and development. Children who lack this hormone do grow, and they are usually well-proportioned as adults. However, they will stand only about 130 cm tall (Tanner, 1990).

During infancy and childhood, physical growth seems to be regulated by thyroxine and the pituitary growth hormone. What, then, triggers the adolescent growth spurt and other pubertal changes?

Research (reviewed in Tanner, 1990) has clarified the endocrinology of adolescence far beyond what we knew only 10 to 15 years ago. Long before any noticeable physical changes occur, pituitary secretions stimulate a girl's ovaries to produce more **estrogen** and a boy's testes to produce more **testosterone**. Once these sex hormones reach a critical level, the hypothalamus (a part of the brain) instructs the pituitary to secrete more growth hormone (GH). This increase in GH seems to be wholly responsible for the adolescent growth spurt in girls and is primarily responsible for boys' growth spurt. As for sexual maturation, the female hormone estrogen triggers the growth of a girl's breasts, uterus, vagina, pubic and underarm hair, and the widening of her hips. In boys, testosterone is responsible for growth of the penis and prostate, voice changes, and the development of facial and body hair. And although GH may be the primary contributor to the male growth spurt, testosterone exerts its own independent effects on the growth of a boy's muscles, the broadening of his shoulders, and the extension of his backbone. So it seems that adolescent boys experience larger growth spurts than adolescent girls do simply because testosterone promotes muscular and bone growth in ways that estrogen does not. Finally, androgen secreted by *adrenal glands* plays a secondary role in promoting the maturation of muscles and bones in both sexes (Tanner, 1990).

What causes the pituitary to activate the endocrine glands and precipitate the dramatic physical changes of adolescence? No one can say for sure. We know that skeletal maturity, which seems to be genetically controlled, is an excellent predictor of when menarche will occur (Tanner, 1990). Yet any simple "genetic clock" theory that focuses on a singular precipitating factor is probably oversimplified, because the timing of breast growth, testicular development, and many other pubertal events are not closely synchronized with skeletal age (or with one another). So we have learned a great deal about *how* hormones affect human growth and development (see Figure 5.9 for a brief review). However, the events responsible for the timing and regulation of these hormonal influences remain unclear.

thyroxine
hormone produced by the thyroid gland; essential for normal growth of the brain and the body

pituitary
"master gland" located at the base of the brain that regulates the endocrine glands and produces growth hormone

growth hormone (GH)
pituitary hormone that stimulates the rapid growth and development of body cells; primarily responsible for the adolescent growth spurt

estrogen
female sex hormone, produced by the ovaries, that is responsible for female sexual maturation

testosterone
male sex hormone, produced by the testes, that is responsible for male sexual maturation

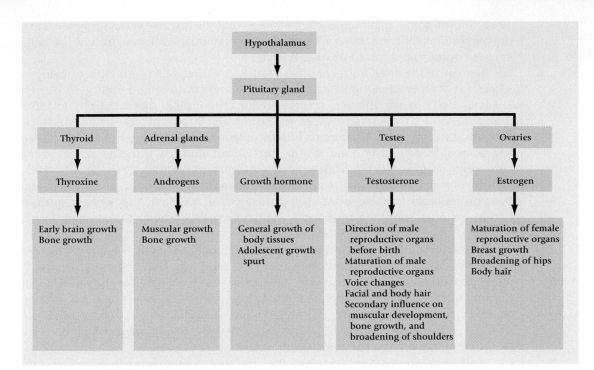

Figure 5.9
Hormonal influences on physical development.

Environmental Influences

Three kinds of environmental influence can have a major effect on physical growth and development: nutrition and eating behaviours, illnesses, and the quality of care that children receive.

Nutrition

Diet is perhaps the most potent environmental influence on human growth and development. As you might expect, children who are inadequately nourished grow very slowly, if at all. The dramatic effect of malnutrition on physical development can be seen by comparing the heights of children before and during wartime periods when food is scarce. In Figure 5.10, we see that the average heights of schoolchildren in Oslo, Norway, increased between 1920 and 1940—the period between the two world wars. However, this secular trend was clearly reversed during World War II, when it was not always possible to satisfy children's nutritional needs.

PROBLEMS OF UNDERNUTRITION. If undernutrition is neither prolonged nor especially severe, children will usually recover from any growth deficits by growing much faster than normal once their diet becomes adequate. James Tanner (1990) views this **catch-up growth** as a basic principle of physical development. Presumably, children who have experienced short-term growth deficits because of malnutrition grow very rapidly in order to regain (or catch up to) their genetically programmed growth trajectory.

However, prolonged undernutrition has a more serious impact, especially during the first five years of life: Brain growth may be seriously retarded, and children may remain relatively small in stature (Barrett & Frank, 1987; Tanner,

catch-up growth
period of accelerated growth in which children who have experienced growth deficits grow very rapidly to "catch up" to the growth trajectory that they are genetically programmed to follow

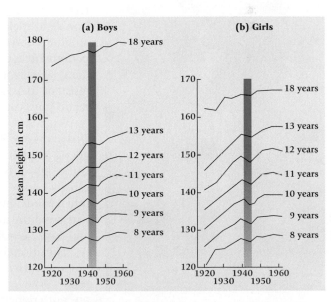

Figure 5.10 *The effect of malnutrition on growth. These graphs show the average heights of Oslo schoolchildren aged 8–18 between 1920 and 1960. Notice the trend toward increasing height (in all age groups) between 1920 and 1940, the period between the two world wars. This secular trend was dramatically reversed during World War II (the shaded section of the graphs), when nutrition was often inadequate. FROM TANNER, 1990.*

marasmus
growth-retarding disease that affects infants who receive insufficient protein and too few calories

kwashiorkor
growth-retarding disease that affects children who receive enough calories but little if any protein

vitamin/mineral deficiency
form of malnutrition in which the diet provides sufficient protein and calories but is lacking in one or more substances that promote normal growth

iron deficiency anemia
listlessness caused by too little iron in the diet that makes children inattentive and may retard physical and intellectual development

This child's swollen stomach and otherwise emaciated appearance are symptoms of kwashiorkor. Without adequate protein in the diet, children with kwashiorkor are more susceptible to many diseases and may die from illnesses that well-nourished children can easily overcome.

1990). These findings make sense when we recall that the first five years is a period when the brain normally gains about 65 percent of its eventual adult weight and the body grows to nearly two-thirds of its adult height.

In many of the developing countries of Africa, Asia, and Latin America, as many as 85 percent of all children under age 5 experience some form of undernutrition (Barrett & Frank, 1987). When children are severely undernourished, they are likely to suffer from either of two nutritional diseases—marasmus and kwashiorkor—each of which has a slightly different cause. **Marasmus** affects babies who get insufficient protein and too few calories, as can easily occur if a mother is malnourished and does not have the resources to provide her child with a nutritious commercial substitute for mother's milk. A victim of marasmus becomes very frail and wrinkled in appearance as growth stops and body tissues begin to waste away. Even if these children survive, they remain small in stature and often suffer impaired social and intellectual development (Barrett & Frank, 1987).

Kwashiorkor affects children who get enough calories but little if any protein. As the disease progresses, the child's hair thins; the face, legs, and abdomen swell with water; and severe skin lesions may develop. In many poor countries of the world, about the only high-quality source of protein readily available to children is mother's milk. So breast-fed infants do not ordinarily suffer from marasmus unless their mothers are severely malnourished; however, infants may develop kwashiorkor when they are weaned from the breast and denied their primary source of protein.

In Western industrialized countries, the preschool children who do experience protein/calorie deficiencies are rarely so malnourished as to develop marasmus or kwashiorkor. However, **vitamin and mineral deficiencies** affect children from lower socioeconomic backgrounds (Pollitt, 1994). Especially common among infants and toddlers are iron and zinc deficiencies that occur because rapid growth early in life requires more of these minerals than a young child's diet normally provides. Thus, children whose diets are deficient in zinc grow very slowly (Pollitt et al., 1996). And prolonged iron deficiency causes **iron deficiency anemia**, which not only makes children inattentive and listless, but also retards their growth rates and is associated with poor performances on tests of motor skills and intellectual development. Unfortunately, these motor and intellectual deficiencies are hard to completely overcome, even after the anemia is corrected by supplementing the child's diet (Lozoff, 1989; Pollitt et al., 1996). So iron deficiencies are a major health problem in Canada, the United States, and around the world. Even mild cases later in childhood are associated with poor performances on school achievement tests (Watkins & Pollitt, 1999), and children who experience prolonged vitamin/mineral deficiencies are also less resistant to a variety of illnesses that can affect intellectual performance and retard physical growth.

INTERVENTION STRATEGIES. Recall from Chapter 4 that malnutrition can cause young children to be lethargic, inattentive, irritable, and intolerant of stressful situations—a behavioural profile that places them at risk of alienating their caregivers and thereby receiving little social or intellectual stimulation. In other words, many of the long-term effects of undernutrition may stem, in part, from the unstimulating environments that malnourished children live in and have helped to create (Barrett & Frank, 1987; Valenzuela, 1990, 1997).

Nutritional supplements for malnourished children can make them much more receptive to social/intellectual stimulation (Pollitt et al., 1996). Yet the results of several intervention studies indicate that dietary supplements alone are not enough. Malnourished children are least likely to display long-term deficits in physical growth and social/intellectual development when (1) their diets are supplemented *and* (2) they receive ample social and intellectual stimulation, either through high-quality daycare (Zeskind & Ramey, 1981) or through a home visitation program that teaches caregivers about the importance of such stimulation and shows them how to provide it (Grantham-McGregor et al., 1994; Super, Herrera, & Mora, 1990).

5.5 Two Serious Eating Disorders of Adolescence

Anorexia nervosa is a potentially fatal eating disorder with no known organic cause. The Canadian Paediatric Society (1998) indicated that the incidence of anorexia nervosa has increased dramatically over the past three decades, reaching a rate as high as 5 percent among adolescent girls (compared to 1 in 2000 for adolescent boys or women). Somewhat lower incidence statistics are reported by the Canadian National Eating Disorder Information Centre, which estimates that between 1 and 2 percent of young women experience anorexia nervosa (Health Canada, 2001a). Anorexia is a significant problem for many young women whereas, young men account for only 5 percent of all reported cases (Health Canada, 2001a).

Anorexics have a morbid fear of becoming obese and will do whatever they can to purge their bodies of fat. The typical anorexic is a quiet, obedient teenage girl from a middle-class or affluent family who has reached puberty earlier than her peers and who suddenly begins to starve herself (Graber et al., 1994; Hsu, 1990; Reijonen et al., 2003). The process seems harmless at first as the young woman sets a modest goal and diets to the desired weight. But once she reaches her target, she continues to diet, eating less and less. After she loses 20 to 30 percent of her body weight, secondary sex characteristics (breasts and hips) may be scarcely noticeable, and menstruation often stops. And although she may resemble a walking skeleton, the 27 to 30 kg anorexic often insists that she is well-nourished and feels she could stand to lose a few more kilos (Hsu, 1990). Among men, a "reverse anorexia" may occur, such that these men have substantial muscle mass from excessive exercise and dieting, yet they perceive that their bodies are underdeveloped (Harvey & Robinson, 2003).

Why do relatively few girls become anorexic, even though nearly all of them experience social pressure to be thin? Genetic factors may predispose some individuals to develop the disorder. Anorexia runs in families (Hsu, 1990; Klump et al., 2000). Yet eating disorders rarely emerge unless a susceptible girl also experiences disturbed family relationships (Polivy & Herman, 2002; Swarr & Richards, 1996). According to Salvador Minuchin and his associates (1978), most anorexics have trouble making decisions and forming a personal identity. Why? One suggestion is that their parents may be firm, overprotective guardians who tolerate little dissent or negative emotionality (see also Pike & Rodin, 1991; Polivy & Herman, 2002). The result may be a young woman who can't seem to break free of her parents and who hopes to establish some sense of control over her life, by rigidly controlling her diet and body image (Smolak & Levine, 1993). The media has also been implicated as portraying unrealistic images for young women and men (Harvey & Robinson, 2003).

Family therapy seems to be an effective treatment. Treatment may begin by hospitalizing the patient to tube-feed her (if her life is in danger) or to apply behavioural modification techniques (i.e., rewarding her with praise and privileges for gaining weight) to change her eating habits. Once the patient begins to eat, family therapy begins. The purpose of the therapy is to persuade parents to exert less control over their child's activities while convincing the anorexic that she can achieve autonomy and higher self-esteem through means other than self-starvation. Unfortunately, fewer than half of treated anorexics recover completely (Zerbe, 1993). The prognosis is best for younger patients who have been ill less than three years (Russell et al., 1987). By contrast, only 25 to 30 percent of untreated anorexics show any improvement, and as many as 5 to 10 percent commit suicide or starve themselves to death (Hsu, 1990).

Bulimia is another serious eating disorder. Bulimia is present in approximately 2 to 3 percent of young Canadian women (Health Canada, 2001a) and is most common among university-age populations where as many as 3 percent of women (and less than 1 percent of men) partake in this "binge/purge" syndrome (McGilley & Pryor, 1998). Bulimics are binge eaters who may consume several times their normal daily caloric intake in a single sitting and then purge themselves of this feast by vomiting or taking laxatives, or rigid fasting and exercise (Fairburn et al., 1999). Although anorexics are often bulimics, most who suffer from bulimia are of normal weight or are slightly overweight. Like anorexics, bulimic individuals tend to have poor body images and are overly concerned about getting fat. Bulimics differ from anorexics in that they are often extroverted and impulsive rather than quiet and reserved, and they are more likely to experience open conflict and a lack of affection in their homes (Fairburn et al., 1999; Smolak & Levine, 1993). Teasing is also related to body dissatisfaction in both women and men (see Barker & Galambos, 2003).

Like anorexia, bulimia can have very serious side effects. Laxatives and diuretics can deplete the body of potassium and induce cardiac arrhythmia and heart attacks. Regular induction of vomiting can produce hernias, and bulimics have even drowned in their own vomit. Finally, binge eating is hardly a constructive approach to problems, particularly for someone who is concerned about getting fat. So it is perhaps understandable that many bulimics are depressed and that some turn to suicide as a solution to their problems.

Treatment for bulimia includes individual and family psychotherapy designed to help the patient understand the causes and control of binging, and antidepressant medication for those with clinical depression (McGilley & Pryor, 1998; Seabrook, 1997). Although most bulimics respond favourably to treatment (see Hsu, 1990, for a review), it has been estimated that up to 40 percent never recognize that they have a potentially serious problem and may continue to binge, sometimes displaying this maladaptive behaviour for the rest of their lives (McGilley & Pryor, 1998).

CP Picture Archive/Colin McConnell

Canadian singer Anne Murray brought national attention to the concerns and prevalence of anorexia nervosa and bulimia when she let the public know about her daughter's fight with this disorder.

Nutrition and diet also are a concern among some adolescents when they engage in eating behaviours that compromise their health and threaten their lives. See Box 5.5 for details about two eating disorders, anorexia nervosa and bulimia, that threaten the lives of some Canadian youth.

PROBLEMS OF OVERNUTRITION. Dietary excess (eating too much) is yet another form of poor nutrition that is increasing in Western societies and can have several long-term consequences (Galuska et al., 1996). The most immediate effect of overnutrition is that children may become **obese** and face added risk of diabetes, high blood pressure, and heart, liver, or kidney disease. Obese children may also find it difficult to make friends with age-mates, who are apt to tease them about their size and shape. Indeed, obese youngsters are often among the least popular students in elementary-school classrooms (Sigelman, Miller, & Whitworth, 1986; Staffieri, 1967). A recent study indicates that the body mass of Canadian children has been increasing steadily from 1981 (Tremblay & Willms, 2000). The prevalence of overweight boys and girls increased from 15.0 percent in 1981 to 28.8 percent for boys and 23.6 percent for girls by 1996. Obesity in children more than doubled from 5.0 percent to 13.5 percent for boys and 11.8 percent for girls during that same time period.

Is a plump baby likely to become an obese adolescent or adult? Not necessarily, because there is only a slight correlation between chubbiness in infancy and obesity later in life (Roche, 1981). However, obese grade-school children and adolescents are much more likely than their thinner peers to be obese later in adolescence and adulthood (Cowley, 2001). Heredity definitely contributes to these trends, because identical twins—even those raised apart—have very similar body weights, whereas the body weights of same-sex fraternal twins may differ dramatically (Stunkard et al., 1990). Yet a genetic predisposition does not guarantee obesity. Highest levels of obesity are found among children who eat a high-fat diet and who do not get sufficient exercise to burn the calories they've consumed (Cowley, 2001; Fisher & Birch, 1995).

Bad eating habits that can lead to obesity are often established early in life (Birch, 1990). Some parents overfeed infants because they almost always infer that a fussy baby must be hungry. Other parents use food, especially high-fat and high-calorie foods, to reinforce desirable behaviours (for example, "Clean your room and you can have some ice cream"), or they bribe their children to eat foods they do not want ("No dessert until you eat your peas") (Olvera-Ezzell, Power, & Cousins, 1990; Smith, 1997). These behaviours may lead children to attach a special significance to eating other than being a way to reduce hunger. Moreover, using high-fat foods as rewards may convince young children that the healthier foods that they are being "bribed" to eat must really be yucky stuff after all (Birch, Marlin, & Rotter, 1984).

anorexia nervosa
life-threatening eating disorder characterized by self-starvation and a compulsive fear of getting fat

bulimia
life-threatening eating disorder characterized by recurrent eating binges followed by such purging activities as heavy use of laxatives or vomiting

obese
medical term describing individuals who are at least 20 percent above the ideal weight for their height, age, and sex

In addition to their poor eating habits, obese children are less active than normal-weight peers. Of course, their inactivity may both contribute to obesity (obese children burn fewer calories) and be a consequence of their overweight condition. Lifestyle choices that promote sedentary behaviours, such as watching TV, have been implicated as part of the problem in increasing levels of obesity in Canadian children (Tremblay & Willms, 2000). Indeed, the amount of time children spend in the sedentary activity of watching television is one of the best predictors of *future* obesity (Anderson et al., 2001; Cowley, 2001; Tremblay & Willms, 2000). Television viewing may also promote poor eating habits. Not only do children tend to snack while passively watching TV, but the foods they see advertised are mostly high-calorie products containing lots of fat and sugar and few beneficial nutrients (Tinsley, 1992).

Crash diets for obese children are often counterproductive. Severe dietary restrictions can interfere with the development of the brain, muscles, and bones early in life, and older children on restrictive diets may feel deprived, rejected,

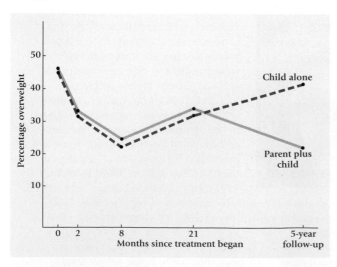

Figure 5.11 *Average percentage of excess body weight for obese children who participated in a weight-loss program with and without a parent. ADAPTED FROM EPSTEIN ET AL., 1987.*

and inclined to partake in binge eating should the opportunity arise (Kolata, 1986). To date, the most effective treatments for childhood obesity have been behavioural approaches that involve obese youngsters *and* their parents. In one particularly effective program (Epstein et al., 1987, 1990), parents and their obese children were taught to revise their eating and exercise habits, carefully monitor their own behaviour to ensure compliance with the regimen, and encourage other family members to exercise more and eat healthier foods. In addition, children entered into contracts with their parents whereby they could earn rewards for losing weight. As shown in Figure 5.11, obese children who received this intensive family therapy not only lost weight, but had also kept it off when observed during a follow-up five years later. By contrast, obese youngsters who had participated in the same program without their parents were unable to maintain the weight loss they had initially achieved. Here, then, is a strong indication that childhood obesity is a *family* problem that is most likely to be overcome when family members *work together* to change a home environment that has permitted children to become obese.

Illnesses

Among children who are adequately nourished, common childhood illnesses such as measles, chicken pox, or even pneumonia have little if any effect on physical growth and development. Major illnesses that keep a child in bed for weeks may temporarily retard growth, but after recovering, the child ordinarily shows a growth spurt (catch-up growth) that makes up for the progress lost while he or she was sick (Tanner, 1990).

Yet diseases are likely to permanently stunt the growth of children who are moderately to severely undernourished. A poor diet weakens the immune system, so that childhood diseases strike an undernourished child sooner and harder (Pollitt et al., 1996). Not only does malnutrition increase one's susceptibility to disease, but diseases also contribute to malnutrition by suppressing a child's appetite and limiting the body's ability to absorb and use nutrients (Pollitt, 1994). In developing countries where gastrointestinal infections and upper respiratory illnesses are common, young school-age children who have been relatively disease-free are already 2.5 to 5.0 cm taller and about 1.5 to 2.0 kg heavier on average than their more "sickly" peers (Martorell, 1980; Roland, Cole, & Whitehead, 1977) and are outperforming them on a variety of cognitive tests as well (Pollitt, 1994).

Emotional Stress and Lack of Affection

Otherwise healthy children who experience too much stress and too little affection are likely to lag far behind their age-mates in physical growth and motor development. This *failure-to-thrive* syndrome may characterize as many as 6 percent of preschool children in the United States and up to 5 percent of all patients admitted to pediatric hospitals in the United States (Lozoff, 1989).

Nonorganic failure to thrive is a growth disorder that appears early, usually by 18 months of age. Babies who display it stop growing and appear to be wasting away, in much the same way that malnourished infants with marasmus do. These infants do not have an obvious illness, and no other biological cause for their condition is apparent. Affected babies often have trouble feeding and, in many cases, their growth retardation is undoubtedly attributable to poor nutrition (Brockington, 1996; Lozoff, 1989). Of course, a major question is why would an otherwise healthy baby have trouble feeding?

One clue comes from these babies' behaviours around caregivers. They are generally apathetic and withdrawn, often watch their caregivers closely, but are unlikely to smile or cuddle when they are picked up. Why? Because their caregivers are typically cool and aloof, impatient with them, and sometimes even physically abusive (Brockington, 1996). So even though caregivers offer enough food for those babies to thrive, their impatience and hostility causes babies to withdraw and to become aloof themselves to the point of feeding poorly and displaying few, if any, positive social responses.

Deprivation dwarfism is a second growth-related disorder that stems from emotional deprivation and a lack of affection. It appears later, usually between 2 and 15 years of age, and is characterized by small stature and dramatically reduced rates of growth, even though children who display this disorder do not look especially malnourished and

179

Chapter Five
*The Physical Self:
Development of the Brain,
the Body, and Motor Skills*

nonorganic failure to thrive
infant growth disorder, caused by lack of attention and affection, that causes growth to slow dramatically or stop

deprivation dwarfism
childhood growth disorder that is triggered by emotional deprivation and characterized by decreased production of GH, slow growth, and small stature

usually receive adequate nutrition and physical care. What seems to be lacking in their lives is a positive involvement with other people, namely with their primary caregivers, who themselves are likely to be depressed by an unhappy marriage, economic hardships, or some other personal problem (Brockington, 1996; Roithmaier et al., 1988). It appears that deprivation dwarfs grow very slowly because their emotional deprivation depresses the endocrine system and inhibits the production of growth hormone. Indeed, when these youngsters are removed from their homes and begin to receive attention and affection, secretion of GH quickly resumes, and they display catch-up growth on the *same diet* on which they formerly failed to thrive (Brockington, 1996; Gardner, 1972).

The prognoses for children affected by nonorganic failure to thrive and deprivation dwarfism is very good if the caregiving problems responsible for these disorders are corrected by individual or family therapy, or if the affected child is placed with caring foster parents (Brockington, 1996). However, if nonorganic failure to thrive is not identified and corrected in the first two years, or if the emotional neglect that underlies deprivation dwarfism persists for several years, affected children may remain smaller than normal and display long-term emotional problems and intellectual deficiencies as well (Drotar, 1992; Lozoff, 1989).

In sum, failure to thrive provides yet another indication that children require love and responsive caregiving if they are to develop normally. Fortunately, there is hope for preventing these deprivation-related disorders if parents whose children are at risk can be identified early. And often they can be. Even before giving birth, women whose children may fail to thrive are more likely than other mothers to feel unloved by their parents, to reject their own mothers as a model, and to say that their own childhoods were unhappy. Within days of giving birth, these mothers are already having more problems feeding and soothing their babies than other mothers are (Lozoff, 1989). Clearly, these families need help and would almost certainly benefit from early interventions that teach parents how to be more sensitive and responsive caregivers.

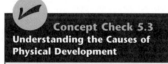

Concept Check 5.3
Understanding the Causes of Physical Development

Check your understanding of some of the causes of physical development by matching each of the consequences listed opposite with one or more of the following *causes/correlates* of that condition: (a) increases in GH production during adolescence, (b) malnutrition, (c) increase in testosterone/estrogen production during adolescence, (d) stress-induced inhibition of GH, (e) insensitive or abusive caregiving, (f) sedentary lifestyle. Answers appear in the Appendix.

_____ 1. lethargic, inattentive, irritable demeanour
_____ 2. adolescent growth spurt
_____ 3. deprivation dwarfism
_____ 4. obesity
_____ 5. sexual maturation at puberty
_____ 6. failure to thrive

SUMMARY

An Overview of Maturation and Growth

♦ The body is constantly changing between infancy and adulthood. Height and weight increase rapidly during the first two years. Growth then becomes more gradual until early adolescence, when there is a rapid "growth spurt."

♦ The shape of the body and body proportions also change because various body parts grow at different rates. Physical development follows a **cephalocaudal** (head-downward) and a **proximodistal** (centre-onward) formula in which structures in the upper and central regions of the body mature before those in the lower and peripheral regions.

♦ Skeletal and muscular development parallel the changes occurring in height and weight. The bones become longer and thicker and gradually harden, completing their growth and development by the late teens. **Skeletal age** is an excellent measure of physical maturation. Muscles increase in density and size, particularly during the growth spurt of early adolescence.

♦ Physical growth is quite uneven, or asynchronous, because the brain, the reproductive system, and the lymph tissues mature at different rates. There are also sizable individual and cultural variations in physical growth and development.

Development of the Brain

♦ A **brain growth spurt** occurs during the last three months of the prenatal period and the first two years of life. **Neurons** form **synapses** with other neurons; **glia** form to nourish the neurons and encase them in myelin—a waxy material that speeds the transmission of neural impulses. Many more neurons and synapses are formed than are needed, and those that are used often survive. Other neurons that are stimulated less often either die or lose their synapses and stand in reserve to compensate for brain injuries. Up until puberty, the brain shows a great deal of **plasticity**, which allows it to change in response to experience and to recover from many injuries.

♦ The highest brain centre, or **cerebrum**, consists of two hemispheres connected by the **corpus callosum**. Each hemisphere is covered by a **cerebral cortex**. Although the brain may be **lateralized** at birth so that the two hemispheres assume different functions, children come to rely increasingly on one particular hemisphere or the other to perform each function. **Myelinization** and reorganization of the neural circuitry of the cerebral cortex continue throughout adolescence.

Motor Development

♦ Like the physical structures of the body, motor development proceeds in a cephalocaudal and proximodistal direction. As a result, motor skills evolve in a definite sequence: Infants gain control over their heads, necks, and upper arms before they become proficient with their legs, feet, and hands. Yet the increasingly complex motor skills that infants display do not simply unfold according to a maturational timetable. Experience plays a crucial role, as shown by the retarded motor development of institutionalized children who have few opportunities to practise motor skills, and by cross-cultural research showing that motor development can be accelerated. According to **dynamical systems theory**, each new motor skill represents an active and intricate reorganization of several existing capabilities that infants undertake to achieve important objectives.

♦ Fine motor skills improve dramatically in the first year. Prereaching is replaced by voluntary reaching, and the claw-like **ulnar grasp** is replaced by the **pincer grasp**. These reaching and grasping skills transform infants into skillful manipulators who are soon reorganizing their existing capabilities to copy lines and build towers of blocks.

♦ Emerging motor skills often thrill parents and allow new forms of play. They also support other aspects of perceptual, cognitive, and social development.

♦ With each passing year, children's motor skills improve. Boys become notably stronger than girls early in adolescence, owing to their greater muscular development and the fact that girls are less encouraged by society to remain physically active.

Puberty: The Physical Transition from Child to Adult

♦ At about age 10½ for females and age 13 for males, the adolescent growth spurt begins. In addition to growing taller and heavier, the body assumes a more adultlike appearance.

♦ Sexual maturation begins about the same time as the adolescent growth spurt and follows a predictable sequence. For girls, **puberty** begins with the onset of breast and pubic-hair development and follows with a widening of the hips, enlarging of the uterus and vagina, **menarche** (first menstruation), and completion of breast and pubic-hair growth. For boys, development of the testes and scrotum is followed by the emergence of pubic hair, the growth of the penis, the ability to ejaculate, the appearance of facial hair, and a lowering of the voice. Because of improved nutrition and health care, people in industrialized societies have shown a **secular trend** to grow taller and heavier, and they are reaching sexual maturity earlier than was true in the past. Yet there are wide individual variations in the timing of sexual maturation and growth.

The Psychological Effects of Puberty

♦ Girls react to their changing body images by hoping to be attractive and worrying about their weight. Their reactions to menarche are mixed. Boys have better body images than girls do and are somewhat more positive about their first ejaculation than girls are about menarche.

♦ Many nonindustrialized societies take pubertal changes as a sign that a child has become an adult, marking this transition with formal **rites of passage**. In other societies, parent–child conflicts often heighten at puberty and usually decline later in adolescence.

♦ Timing of puberty can have personal and social consequences. Early-maturing boys and on-time and late-maturing girls have better body images, feel more self-confident, and display better social adjustment than late-maturing boys and early-maturing girls. However, these effects do not hold for all individuals and tend to fade over time.

Causes and Correlates of Physical Development

♦ Physical development results from a complex interplay between biological and environmental forces. Individual genotypes set limits for height, shape, and schedule of growth. Growth is also heavily influenced by hormones released by the endocrine glands as regulated by the **pituitary**. **Growth hormone (GH)** and **thyroxine** regulate growth throughout childhood. At adolescence, other endocrine glands secrete hormones, most notably **estrogen** from the ovaries, which triggers sexual development in girls, and **testosterone** from the testes, which instigates sexual development in boys.

♦ Adequate nutrition in the form of total calories, protein, and vitamins and minerals is necessary for children to reach their growth potentials. **Marasmus, kwashiorkor**, and **iron deficiency anemia** are three growth-retarding diseases that stem from undernutrition. In industrialized countries, **obesity** is a nutritional problem that has many physical and psychological consequences. **Anorexia nervosa** and **bulimia** are potentially fatal eating disorders.

♦ Chronic infectious diseases can combine with poor nutrition to stunt physical and intellectual growth. **Nonorganic failure to thrive** and **deprivation dwarfism** illustrate that affection and sensitive, responsive caregiving are important to ensuring normal growth.

KEY TERMS

cephalocaudal development, 150

proximodistal development, 151

skeletal age, 152

brain growth spurt, 153

synapse, 154

neurons, 154

glia, 154

synaptogenesis, 154

plasticity, 154

myelinization, 156

cerebrum, 156

corpus callosum, 156

cerebral cortex, 156

cerebral lateralization, 156

dynamical systems theory, 159

proprioceptive information, 163

ulnar grasp, 163

pincer grasp, 163

adolescent growth spurt, 166

puberty, 166

physical activity play, 167

menarche, 168

secular trend, 169

rites of passage, 170

thyroxine, 174

pituitary, 174

growth hormone (GH), 174

estrogen, 174

testosterone, 174

catch-up growth, 175

marasmus, 176

kwashiorkor, 176

vitamin/mineral deficiency, 176

iron deficiency anemia, 176

anorexia nervosa, 178

bulimia, 178

obese, 178

nonorganic failure to thrive, 179

deprivation dwarfism, 179

 You can find further information on the topics covered in this chapter by visiting:

www.developmentalpsych2e.nelson.com

 For additional reading, go to InfoTrac College Edition, your on-line research library, at:

infotrac.thomsonlearning.com

Early Cognitive Foundations: Sensation, Perception, and Learning

Linnea Nord

Imagine that you are a neonate, only 5 to 10 minutes old, who has just been sponged, swaddled, and handed to your mother. As your eyes meet hers, she smiles and says, "Hi there, sweetie" in a high-pitched voice as she moves her head closer and gently strokes your cheek. What would you make of all this sensory input? How would you interpret these experiences?

Developmentalists are careful to distinguish between sensation and perception. **Sensation** is the process by which sensory receptor neurons detect information and transmit it to the brain. Clearly, neonates "sense" the environment. They gaze at interesting sights, react to sounds, tastes, and odours, and are likely to cry up a storm when poked by a needle for a blood test. But do they "make sense" of these sensations? **Perception** is the interpretation of sensory input: recognizing what you see, understanding what is said to you, or knowing that the odour you've detected is fresh-baked bread. Are newborns capable of drawing any such inferences? Do they perceive the world, or merely sense it?

We might also wonder whether very young infants can associate their sensations with particular outcomes. When, for example, might a baby first associate his or her mother's breast with milk and come to view mom as a valuable commodity who eliminates hunger and other kinds of distress? Are infants capable of modifying their behaviour to persuade mom to attend to them? These are questions of *learning*—the process by which our behaviours change as a result of experience.

Maybe we should start with a more practical question: Why should we concern ourselves with the development of sensation, perception, and learning? Perhaps because these three processes are at the heart of human functioning. Virtually everything we do depends on our interpretations of and reactions to sensory input—the things we experience. So the study of early sensory, perceptual, and learning capabilities can provide some fundamental clues about how we gain knowledge of reality.

Early Controversies about Sensory and Perceptual Development

"Making Sense" of the Infant's Sensory and Perceptual Experiences

Infant Sensory Capabilities

Visual Perception in Infancy

Intermodal Perception

Infant Perception in Perspective—and a Look Ahead

Basic Learning Processes

Reflections on Perception and Learning

Summary

EARLY CONTROVERSIES ABOUT SENSORY AND PERCEPTUAL DEVELOPMENT

Nature versus Nurture

Long before anyone conducted any experiments to decide the issue, philosophers were already debating what newborns might sense and perceive. *Empiricist* philosophers believed that an infant was a tabula rasa (blank slate) who must learn to interpret sensations. In fact, William James (1890) argued that all senses are integrated at birth, so that sights, sounds, and other sensory inputs combine to present the newborn with a "blooming, buzzing confusion."

By contrast, *nativist* philosophers such as René Descartes (1638/1965) and Immanuel Kant (1781/1958) took the nature side of the nature/nurture issue, arguing that many basic perceptual abilities are innate. For example, they believed that we are born with an understanding of spatial relations. Presumably, infants do not need to learn that receding objects appear smaller or that approaching objects seem to increase in size; these were said to be adaptive perceptual understandings that were built into the human nervous system over the course of evolution.

Today's developmentalists take less extreme stands on this nature/nurture issue. Although most would concede that babies see some order in their surroundings from day 1, they recognize that the perceptual world of a human neonate is rather limited and that *both* maturational processes and experience contribute to the growth of perceptual awareness (Smith & Katz, 1996).

Enrichment versus Differentiation

sensation
detection of stimuli by the sensory receptors and transmission of this information to the brain

perception
process by which we categorize and interpret sensory input

enrichment theory
theory specifying that we must add to sensory stimulation by drawing on stored knowledge in order to perceive a meaningful world

differentiation theory
theory specifying that perception involves detecting distinctive features or cues that are contained in the sensory stimulation we receive

distinctive features
characteristics of a stimulus that remain constant; dimensions on which two or more objects differ and can be discriminated (sometimes called invariances or invariant features)

Now consider a second issue that early philosophers debated: Is the coherent reality that we experience through the senses simply "out there" to be detected? Or rather, do we construct our own interpretations of that reality based on our experiences? This issue is hotly contested in two modern theories of perceptual development: enrichment theory and differentiation theory.

Both these theories argue that there is an objective reality out there to which we respond. However, **enrichment theory** (Piaget, 1954, 1960) claims that sensory stimulation is often fragmented or confusing. To interpret such ambiguous input, we must use our available cognitive schemes to add to or enrich it. You have probably heard radio contests in which people call in to identify a song after hearing only a note or two. According to enrichment theory, contest winners can answer correctly because they draw on their memory of musical passages to add to what they have just heard and infer what the song must be. In sum, the enrichment position is that cognition *enriches* sensory experience. Our knowledge helps us construct meaning from the sensory stimulation we receive (see Figure 6.1).

By contrast, Eleanor Gibson's (1969, 1987, 1992) **differentiation theory** argues that sensory stimulation provides all we need to interpret our experiences. Our task as fledgling perceivers is simply to *detect* the differentiating information, or **distinctive features**, that enable us to discriminate one form of experience from another. Consider that many 2-year-olds are apt to say "doggie" whenever they see a dog, a cat, or some other small, furry animal. They have not yet noticed the critical differences in sizes, shapes, mannerisms, or sounds that enable us to discriminate these creatures. Once children master this perceptual learning, however, their continuing quest for differentiating information may soon enable them to discriminate long-nosed collies from pug-faced boxers or spotted Dalmatians, although they understand that all these animals are properly labelled dogs. Gibson's point is that the information needed to make these finer distinctions was always there in the animals themselves, and that the children's perceptual capabilities blossom as they *detect* these distinctive features.

So which theory is correct? Maybe both of them are. The research we will review in this chapter provides ample support for Gibson's view: Children do get better at detecting information already contained in their sensory inputs. Yet Piaget's view that existing knowledge provides a basis for interpreting our sensations is also well-documented, as we will see in examining Piaget's theory of cognitive development in Chapter 7.

"MAKING SENSE" OF THE INFANT'S SENSORY AND PERCEPTUAL EXPERIENCES

As recently as the early 1900s, many medical texts claimed that human infants were functionally blind, deaf, and impervious to pain for several days after birth; that is, babies were believed to be unprepared to extract any meaning from the world around them. Today, we know otherwise. Why the change in views? It is not that babies have become any more capable or any smarter. Instead, researchers have gotten smarter, having developed some ingenious methods of persuading nonverbal infants to tell us what they can sense and perceive. Let's briefly discuss four of these techniques.

Figure 6.1 *Expectations affect perception. If told to name the animal in this drawing, you would likely see a rat with large ears and its tail circling in front of the body. Yet, if you saw the drawing amid other drawings of faces, you would likely perceive an elderly bald man with glasses (see him?). So, as Piaget and other enrichment theorists have argued, cognition does affect our interpretation of sensory stimulation.* ADAPTED FROM REESE, 1963.

The Preference Method

The **preference method** is a simple procedure in which at least two stimuli are presented simultaneously to see whether infants will attend more to one of them than the other(s). This approach became popular during the early 1960s after Robert Fantz used it to determine whether very young infants could discriminate visual patterns (for example, faces, concentric circles, newsprint, and unpatterned disks). Babies were placed on their backs in a *looking chamber* (see Figure 6.2) and shown two or more stimuli. An observer located above the looking chamber recorded the amount of time the infant gazed at each of the visual patterns. If the infant looked longer at one target than the other, it was assumed that he preferred that pattern.

Fantz's early results were clear. Newborns could easily discriminate visual forms, and they preferred to look at patterned stimuli such as faces or concentric circles rather than at unpatterned disks. Apparently, the ability to detect and discriminate patterns is innate (Fantz, 1963).

The preference method has one major shortcoming. If an infant shows no preferences among the target stimuli, it is not clear whether he or she failed to discriminate them or simply found them equally interesting. Fortunately, each of the methods described below can resolve this ambiguity.

The Habituation Method

Perhaps the most popular strategy for measuring infant sensory and perceptual capabilities is the habituation method. **Habituation** is the process whereby a repetitive stimulus becomes so familiar that responses initially associated with it (for example, head or eye

preference method
method used to gain information about infants' perceptual abilities by presenting two (or more) stimuli and observing which stimulus the infant prefers

habituation
decrease in one's response to a stimulus that has become familiar through repetition

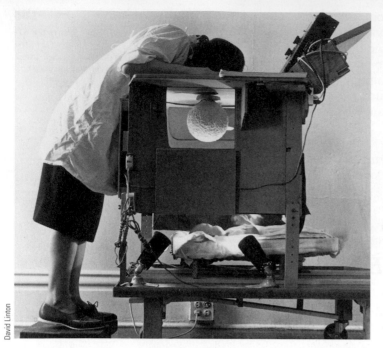

Figure 6.2 The looking chamber that Fantz used to study infants' visual preferences

movements, changes in respiration or heart rate) no longer occur. Thus, habituation is a simple form of learning. As infants stop responding to familiar stimuli, they are telling us that they recognize them as old hat—something that they have experienced before.

To test an infant's ability to discriminate two stimuli that differ in some way, the investigator first presents one of the stimuli until the infant stops attending or otherwise responding to it (habituates). Then the second stimulus is presented. If the infant discriminates this second stimulus from the first, he or she will **dishabituate**—that is, attend closely to it while showing a change in respiration or heart rate. Should the infant fail to react, it is assumed that the differences between the two stimuli were too subtle for him or her to detect. Because babies habituate and dishabituate to so many different kinds of stimulation—sights, sounds, odours, tastes, and touches—the habituation method is very useful for assessing their sensory and perceptual capabilities.

Evoked Potentials

Another way of determining what infants can sense (or perceive) is to present them with a stimulus and record their brain waves. Electrodes are placed on the infant's scalp above those brain centres that process the kind of sensory information that the investigator is presenting. This means that responses to visual stimuli are recorded from the back of the head, at a site above the occipital lobe, whereas responses to sounds are recorded from the side of the head, above the temporal lobe. If the infant detects (senses) the particular stimulus that we present, he or she will show a change in the patterning of his brain waves, or **evoked potential**. Stimuli that are not detected will produce no changes in the brain's electrical activity. This evoked potential procedure can even tell us whether infants can discriminate various sights or sounds, because two stimuli that are sensed as "different" produce different patterns of electrical activity.

High-Amplitude Sucking

dishabituation
increase in responsiveness that occurs when stimulation changes

evoked potential
change in patterning of the brain waves that indicates that an individual detects (senses) a stimulus

high-amplitude sucking method
method of assessing infants' perceptual capabilities that capitalizes on the ability of infants to make interesting events last by varying the rate at which they suck on a special pacifier

Finally, most infants can exert enough control over their sucking behaviour to tell us what they can sense and to give us some idea of their likes and dislikes. The **high-amplitude sucking method** provides infants with a special pacifier containing electrical circuitry that enables them to exert some control over the sensory environment. After the researcher establishes an infant's baseline sucking rate, the procedure begins. Whenever the infant sucks faster or harder than he or she did during the baseline observations (high-amplitude sucking), the infant trips the electrical circuit in the pacifier, thereby activating a slide projector or tape recorder that introduces some kind of sensory stimulation. Should the infant detect this stimulation and find it interesting, he or she can make it last by displaying bursts of high-amplitude sucking. But once the infant's interest wanes and her sucking returns to the baseline level, the stimulation ceases. If the investigator then introduces a second stimulus that elicits a dramatic increase in high-amplitude sucking, he or she could conclude that the infant has discriminated the second stimulus from the first. This procedure can even be modified to let the infant tell us which of two stimuli is preferred. If we wanted to determine whether babies prefer marches to lullabies, we could adjust the circuitry in the pacifier so that high-amplitude sucking activates one kind of music and low-amplitude (or no) sucking activates the other. By then noting what the baby does, we could draw some inferences about which of these musical compositions is preferred. Clearly, this high-amplitude sucking method is a clever and versatile technique!

Let us now see what these creative methods have taught us about babies' sensory and perceptual capabilities.

INFANT SENSORY CAPABILITIES

How well do newborns sense their environments? Better, perhaps, than you might imagine. Let's begin our exploration of infants' sensory world by examining their visual capabilities.

Vision

Although most of us tend to think of vision as our most indispensable sense, it may be the *least* mature of the newborn's sensory capabilities. Changes in brightness will elicit a subcortical *pupillary reflex*, which indicates that the neonate is sensitive to light (Pratt, 1954). Babies can also detect movement in the visual field and are likely to track a visual stimulus with their eyes as long as the target moves slowly (Banks & Salapatek, 1983). Newborn infants are more likely to track faces (or facelike stimuli) than other patterns (Johnson et al., 1991), although this preference for faces disappears within one or two months. Why do babies display it? One intriguing idea is that it represents an adaptive remnant of our evolutionary history—a *reflex*, controlled by subcortical areas of the brain, that serves to orient babies to their caregivers and promote social interactions (Johnson et al., 1991).

Using the habituation method, Russell Adams and Mary Courage of Memorial University of Newfoundland (1998) have found that neonates see the world in colour, but they have trouble discriminating blues, greens, and yellows from whites (Adams & Courage, 1998). However, rapid development of the visual brain centres and sensory

Sotographs/Gamma-Liaison

(a) Newborn's view

(b) Adult's view

The newborn's limited powers of accommodation and poor visual acuity make the mother's face look fuzzy (photo A) rather than clear (photo B); even when viewed from close up. (Try it yourself, by moving the photos to within 6–8 inches of your face.)

pathways allows their colour vision to improve quickly. By 2 to 3 months, babies can discriminate all the basic colours (Brown, 1990; Matlin & Foley, 1997), and by 4 months they are grouping colours of slightly different shades into the same basic categories—the reds, greens, blues, and yellows—that adults do (Bornstein, Kessen, & Weiskopf, 1976).

Despite these impressive capabilities, very young infants do not resolve fine detail very well (Kellman & Banks, 1998). Studies of **visual acuity** suggest that a neonate's distance vision is about 20/600, which means that one sees at 6 m what an adult with excellent vision sees at 183 m. What's more, objects at any distance look rather blurry to a very young infant, who has trouble accommodating—that is, changing the shape of the lens of the eye to bring visual stimuli into focus. Given these limitations, it is perhaps not surprising that many patterns and forms are difficult for a very young infant to detect; they simply require sharper **visual contrasts** to see them than adults do (Kellman & Banks, 1998). However, acuity improves rapidly during the first few months (Courage & Adams, 1996). By age 6 months, babies' visual acuities are about 20/100 and by age 12 months, they see about as well as adults do (Kellman & Banks, 1998).

In sum, the young infant's visual system is not operating at peak efficiency, but it is certainly working. Even newborns can sense movement, colours, changes in brightness, and a variety of visual patterns as long as these patterned stimuli are not too finely detailed and have a sufficient amount of light/dark contrast.

Hearing

Using the evoked potential method, researchers have found that soft sounds that adults hear must be made noticeably louder before a neonate can detect them (Aslin, Pisoni, & Jusczyk, 1983). In the first few hours of life, infants may hear about as well as an adult with a head cold. Their insensitivity to softer sounds could be due, in part, to fluids that have seeped into the inner ear during the birth process. Despite this minor limitation, habituation studies indicate that neonates are capable of discriminating sounds that differ in loudness, duration, direction, and frequency (Bower, 1982). They hear rather well indeed.

Reactions to Voices

Young infants are particularly attentive to voices, especially high-pitched feminine voices. But can they recognize their mother's voice?

Many people would undoubtedly chuckle if a mother were to claim that her week-old baby already recognized her voice. Yet the mother might have the last laugh because research by Anthony DeCasper and his associates (DeCasper & Fifer, 1980; DeCasper & Spence, 1986, 1991) reveals that newborns suck faster on a nipple to hear a recording of their mother's voice than a recording of another woman. In fact, when mothers were instructed to recite a passage (for example, portions of Dr. Seuss's *The Cat in the Hat*) many times during the last six weeks of their pregnancies, their newborns sucked faster and harder to hear *those particular stories* than to hear other samples of their mother's speech. Might these preferences reflect the experiences a baby had before birth, as he or she listened to the mother's muffled voice through the uterine wall? Probably so, and this special responsiveness to mother's voice may even be highly adaptive if it encourages the mother to talk to him or her and to provide the attention and affection that foster healthy social, emotional, and intellectual development.

The relative importance of infants' attention to social information provided through visual information from faces versus auditory information from voices was tested by Barbara D'Entremont of the University of Manitoba and Darwin Muir of Queen's University (1999). Adults interacted with children and provided combinations of facial expressions and/or vocal information to indicate either a happy state or a sad state. Although infants looked more when vocal expressions were available, they smiled much more when there were happy facial responses regardless of whether there were any vocal expressions. The results suggest that infants may need to see facial expressions to help them distinguish adult emotional states.

visual acuity
person's ability to see small objects and fine detail

visual contrast
amount of light/dark transition in a visual stimulus

Reactions to Language

Not only do babies attend closely to voices, but they are also able to discriminate basic speech sounds—called **phonemes**—very early in life. Peter Eimas (1975b, 1985) pioneered research in this area by demonstrating that infants 2 to 3 months old could distinguish consonant sounds that are very similar (for example, *ba* and *pa*). In fact, infants less than 1 week old can tell the difference between the vowels *a* and *i* (Clarkson & Berg, 1983) and can even segment words into discrete syllables (Bijeljac-Babic, Bertoncini, & Mehler, 1993). Just as babies divide the spectrum of light into basic colour categories, they seem to divide speech sounds into categories corresponding to the basic sound units of language (Miller & Eimas, 1996). In fact, 3- to 6-month-old infants are actually better than adults are at perceiving certain phonemes that are *not* a part of the language their companions speak (Jusczyk, 1995; Werker & Desjardins, 1995). These are impressive accomplishments indeed!

Finally, babies soon learn to recognize words that they hear often. By 4½ months, for example, they will reliably turn their head to hear their *own* name but not to hear other names, even when these other names share the same stress pattern as their own (Abbey vs. Johnny, for example) (Mandel, Jusczyk & Pisoni, 1995). Babies this young may not know that the word for their name refers to *them*, but they are able to recognize such frequently heard words very early in life.

Clearly, hearing is more highly developed at birth than vision is. The work of Sandra Trehub and her colleagues at York University indicates that although a baby's hearing improves over the first 4 to 6 months of life, even newborns are remarkably well prepared for such significant achievements as (1) using voices to identify and discriminate their companions and (2) segmenting speech into smaller units—the building blocks of language (Trehub et al., 1991).

Consequences of Hearing Loss

How important is hearing to human development? We gain some insight on this issue from the progress made by otherwise healthy youngsters whose hearing is impaired by a common childhood infection.

Otitis media, a bacterial infection of the middle ear, is the most frequently diagnosed disease among infants and preschool children. Almost all children are infected at least once, with up to one-third of them experiencing recurring infections despite receiving adequate medical care (Vernon-Feagans, Manlove, & Volling, 1996). Antibiotics can eliminate the bacteria that cause this disease but will do nothing to reduce the buildup of fluid in the middle ear, which often persists without any symptoms of pain or discomfort. Unfortunately, this fluid may produce mild to moderate hearing loss that can last for months after an infection has been detected and treated (Vernon-Feagans et al., 1996).

Otitis media strikes hardest between 6 months and 3 years. As a result, developmentalists have feared that youngsters with recurring infections may have difficulty understanding others' speech, which could hamper their language development and other cognitive and social skills that normally emerge early in childhood. And there is reason for concern. Children who have had recurring ear infections early in life do show delays in language development. For example, Susan Rvachew and colleagues (Rvachew et al., 1999) at McGill University demonstrated that infants with early-onset otitis media do not produce speech-like babble at the expected age. In addition, those with recurring infections show poorer academic perfor-

phonemes
smallest meaningful sound units that make up a spoken language

otitis media
common bacterial infection of the middle ear that produces mild to moderate hearing loss

Very young infants are particularly responsive to the sound of human voices.

mance early in elementary school than peers whose bouts with the disease were less prolonged (Friel-Patti & Finitzo, 1990; Teele et al., 1990). Another study found that 3-year-olds with chronic otitis media may be at risk of developing poor social skills because they spend more time playing alone and they have fewer positive contacts with daycare classmates than other children do (Vernon-Feagans et al., 1996). Although ongitudinal research is needed to determine whether the problems associated with chronic otitis media will persist later in childhood and adolescence, the early returns clearly imply that young children with mild to moderate hearing loss are likely to be developmentally disadvantaged and that otitis media, a major contributor to early hearing loss, needs to be detected early and treated aggressively.

Taste and Smell

Infants are born with some very definite taste preferences. For example, they apparently come equipped with something of a sweet tooth, because both full-term and premature babies suck faster and longer for sweet liquids than for bitter, sour, salty, or neutral (water) solutions (Crook, 1978; Smith & Blass, 1996). Different tastes also elicit different facial expressions from newborns. Sweets reduce crying and produce smiles and smacking of the lips, whereas sour substances cause infants to wrinkle their noses and purse their lips, and bitter solutions often elicit expressions of disgust—a downturning of the corners of the mouth, tongue protrusions, and even spitting (Blass & Ciaramitaro, 1994; Ganchrow, Steiner, & Daher, 1983). Furthermore, these facial expressions become more pronounced as solutions become sweeter, more sour, or more bitter, suggesting that newborns can discriminate different concentrations of a particular taste.

Newborns are also capable of detecting a variety of odours, and they react vigorously by turning away and displaying expressions of disgust in response to unpleasant smells such as vinegar, ammonia, or rotten eggs (Rieser, Yonas, & Wilkner, 1976; Steiner, 1979). During the first four days after birth, babies already prefer the odour of milk to that of amniotic fluid, in which they have been living for nine months (Marlier, Schall, & Soussignan, 1998) and a 1- to 2-week-old breast-fed infant can already recognize his or her mother (and discriminate her from other women) by the smell of her breasts and underarms (Cernoch & Porter, 1985; Porter et al., 1992). Like it or not, each of us has a unique olfactory signature—a characteristic that babies can use as an early means of identifying their closest companions.

Touch, Temperature, and Pain

Receptors in the skin are sensitive to touch, temperature, and pain. We learned in Chapter 4 that newborn infants reliably display a variety of *reflexes* if they are touched in the appropriate areas. Even while sleeping, neonates habituate to stroking at one locale but respond again if the tactile stimulation shifts to a new spot—from the ear to the chin, for example (Kisilevsky & Muir, 1984).

Sensitivity to touch clearly enhances infants' responsiveness to their environments. In Chapter 4, we learned that premature infants show better developmental progress when they are periodically stroked and massaged in their isolettes. The therapeutic effect of touch is due, in part, to the fact that gentle stroking and massaging arouses inattentive infants and calms agitated ones, often causing them to smile at and become more involved with their companions (Field et al., 1986; Stack & Muir, 1992). Later in the first year, babies begin to use their sense of touch to explore objects—first with their lips and mouths, and later with

? WHAT DO YOU THINK?

Based on what you now know about newborn sensory capabilities, prepare a brief description of what a newborn might sense as he or she gazes at his or her attentive mother and father. Can you think of any reason why the baby might be quicker to orient to one parent than the other? If so, which parent, and why?

their hands. So touch is a primary means by which infants acquire knowledge about their environment, which contributes so critically to their early cognitive development (Piaget, 1960).

Newborns are also quite sensitive to warmth, cold, and changes in temperature. They refuse to suck if the milk in their bottles is too hot, and they try to maintain their body heat by becoming more active should the temperature of a room suddenly drop (Pratt, 1954).

Do babies experience much pain? Apparently so, for even 1-day-old infants cry lustily when pricked with a needle for a blood test. In fact, very young infants show greater distress upon receiving an inoculation than 5- to 11-month-olds do (Axia, Bonichini, & Benini, 1999).

Male babies are highly stressed by circumcision, an elective operation that is usually done without anesthesia because giving these pain-killing drugs to infants is itself very risky (Hill, 1997). While the surgery is in progress, infants emit high-pitched wails that are similar to the cries of premature babies or those who are brain damaged (Porter, Porges, & Marshall, 1988). Moreover, plasma cortisol, a physiological indicator of stress, is significantly higher just after a circumcision than just before the surgery (Gunnar et al., 1985). Fortunately, researchers have found that babies treated with a mild topical anesthetic before circumcision and given a sugary solution to suck afterward are less stressed by the operation and are able to sleep more peacefully (Hill, 1997). Findings such as these, however, challenge the medical wisdom of treating infants as if they are insensitive to pain. In fact, the Canadian Pediatric Society in 1996 suggested that the procedure is largely unneccesary. Currently, most provincial health insurance plans in Canada no longer pay for this procedure.

In sum, each of the major senses is functioning at birth (see Table 6.1 for a review) so that even neonates are well-prepared to sense their environments. But do they interpret this input? Can they perceive?

VISUAL PERCEPTION IN INFANCY

Although newborn infants see well enough to detect and even discriminate some patterns, we might wonder what they see when looking at these stimuli. If we show them a □, do they see a square, or must they learn to construct a square from an assortment of lines and angles? When do they interpret faces as meaningful social stimuli or begin to distinguish the faces of close companions from those of strangers? Can neonates perceive depth? Do they think receding objects shrink, or do they know that these objects remain the same size and only look smaller when moved away? These are precisely the kinds of questions that have motivated curious investigators to find ways of persuading non-verbal infants to tell us what they see.

TABLE 6.1	The Newborn's Sensory Capabilities
Sense	**Newborn capabilities**
Vision	Least well-developed sense; accommodation and visual acuity limited; is sensitive to brightness; can discriminate some colours; tracks moving targets.
Hearing	Turns in direction of sounds; less sensitive to soft sounds that an adult would be but can discriminate sounds that differ in such dimensions as loudness, direction, and frequency; particularly responsive to speech; recognizes mother's voice.
Taste	Prefers sweet solutions; can discriminate sweet, salty, sour, and bitter tastes.
Smell	Detects a variety of odours; turns away from unpleasant ones; if breast-fed, can identify mother by the odour of her breast and underarm area.
Touch	Responsive to touch, temperature change, and pain.

Perception of Patterns and Forms

Recall Robert Fantz's observations of infants in his looking chamber: babies only 2 days old could easily discriminate visual patterns. In fact, of all the targets that Fantz presented, the most preferred stimulus was a face! Does this imply that newborns already interpret faces as a meaningful pattern? Might the nativists be correct in assuming that *form perception* is innate?

Early Pattern Perception (0 to 2 Months)

Other research implies that neonates' ability to perceive faces as a "meaningful" configuration may be more illusory than real. When Fantz (1961) presented young infants with a face, a stimulus consisting of scrambled facial features, and a simpler stimulus that contained the same amount of light and dark shading as the facelike and scrambled face drawings, the infants were just as interested in the scrambled face as the normal one (see Figure 6.3).

Later research revealed that very young infants prefer to look at *high-contrast* patterns with many sharp boundaries between light and dark areas, and at moderately complex patterns that have curvilinear features (Kellman & Banks, 1998). So faces and scrambled faces may have been equally interesting to Fantz's young subjects because these targets had the same amount of contrast, curvature, and complexity.

By analyzing the characteristics of stimuli that very young infants will or will not look at, we can estimate *what* they see. Figure 6.4, for example, indicates that babies less than 2 months old see only a dark blob when looking at a *highly complex* checkerboard, probably because their immature eyes don't accommodate well enough to resolve the fine detail. By contrast, infants see a definite pattern when gazing at the *moderately complex* checkerboard (Banks & Salapatek, 1983). Martin Banks and his associates have summarized the looking preferences of very young infants quite succinctly: *Babies prefer to look at whatever they see well* (Banks & Ginsburg, 1985), and the things they see best are moderately complex, high-contrast targets, particularly those that capture their attention by moving.

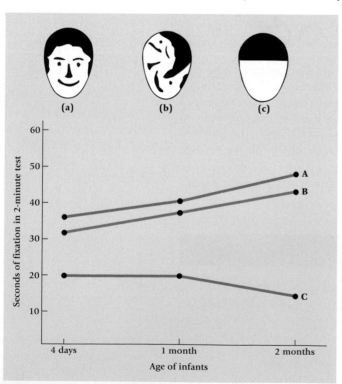

Figure 6.3 *Fantz's test of young infants' pattern preferences. Infants preferred to look at complex stimuli rather than at a simpler black-and-white oval. However, the infants did not prefer the facelike figure to the scrambled face.* ADAPTED FROM FANTZ, 1961.

Clearly very young infants can detect and discriminate different patterns. But can they perceive forms? If shown a triangle, do they see the △ that we do? Or rather, do they detect only pieces of lines and maybe an angle (such as ∠)? Although the answers to these questions are by no means established, most researchers believe that 1- to 2-month-old infants detect few *if any* forms because they see so poorly and they scan visual stimuli in a very limited way (see Figure 6.5). So unless the form is very small, they are unlikely to see all of it, much less put all this information together to perceive a unified whole.

Later Form Perception (2 Months to 1 Year)

Between 2 and 12 months of age, the infant's visual system is rapidly maturing. He or she now sees better and is capable of making increasingly complex visual discriminations. The infant is also organizing what he or she sees to perceive visual forms.

The most basic task in perceiving a form is to discriminate that object from its surrounding context (that is, other objects and the general background). How do you suppose an infant eventually recognizes that a bottle of milk in front of a centrepiece on the dining-room table is not just a part of the centrepiece? What information does the infant use to perceive forms, and when does he or she begin to do so?

Philip Kellman and Elizabeth Spelke (1983; Kellman, Spelke, & Short, 1986) were among the first to explore these issues. Infants were presented with a display consisting of a rod partially hidden by a block in front of it (see Figure 6.6*a* and *b*). Would they perceive the rod as a whole object, although part of it was not available for inspection, or would they act as though they had seen two short and separate rods?

To find out, 4-month-olds were presented with either display *a* (a stationary hidden rod) or display *b* (a moving hidden rod) and allowed to look at it until they habituated and were no longer interested. Then infants were shown displays *c* (a whole rod) and *d* (two rod segments), and their looking preferences were recorded. Infants who had habituated to the *stationary* hidden rod (display *a*) showed no clear preference for display *c* or display *d* in the later test. They were apparently not able to use available cues, such as the two identical rod tips oriented along the same

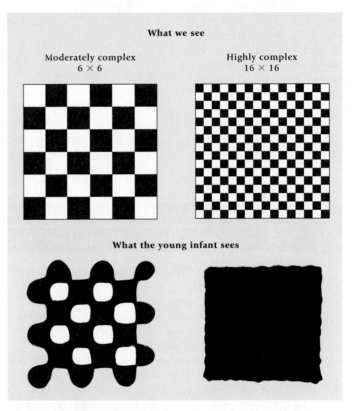

Figure 6.4 *What patterns look like to the young eye. By the time these two checkerboards are processed by eyes with poor vision, only the checkerboard on the left may have any pattern left to it. Poor vision in early infancy helps to explain a preference for moderately complex rather than highly complex stimuli.* ADAPTED FROM BANKS & SALAPATEK, 1983.

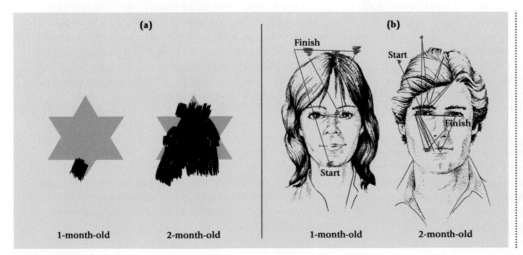

Figure 6.5 *By photographing eye movements, researchers can determine what babies are looking at when scanning a visual stimulus. Although very young infants rarely scan an entire form, 1-month-olds scan much less thoroughly than 2-month-olds do, concentrating most on specific outer edges or boundaries and least on internal features.* ADAPTED FROM SALAPATEK, 1975.

Figure 6.6 *Perceiving objects as wholes. An infant is habituated to a rod partially hidden by the block in front of it. The rod is either stationary (a) or moving (b). When tested afterward, does the infant treat the whole rod (c) as "old hat"? We certainly would, for we could readily interpret cues that tell us that there is one long rod behind the block, and would therefore regard the whole rod as familiar. But if the infant shows more interest in the whole rod (c) than in the two rod segments (d), he or she has apparently not been able to use available cues to perceive the whole rod.* ADAPTED FROM KELLMAN & SPELKE, 1983.

line, to perceive a whole rod when part of the rod was hidden. By contrast, infants *did* apparently perceive the *moving* rod (display *b*) as "whole," because after habituating to this stimulus they much preferred to look at the two short rods (display *d*) than at a whole rod (display *c*, which they now treated as old hat). It seems that these latter infants inferred the rod's wholeness from its synchronized movement—the fact that its parts moved in the same direction at the same time. So infants rely heavily on kinetic (motion) cues to identify distinct forms. (See Box 6.1 for an in-depth examination of infants' perception of facial forms.)

CURRENT CONTROVERSIES
6.1 When Do Babies "Perceive" Faces?

Human faces are a "form" that babies encounter often and that contain many of the features—high contrast, complexity, curvature, and movement—that are likely to capture their attention. So when do infants first respond to faces as if they were meaningful forms?

The answer to this question has been hotly debated over the years. Some researchers believe that babies have an inborn scheme for "facedness" as illustrated by occasional reports that even newborns prefer to look at well-formed facial stimuli rather than scrambled facial features (Valenza et al., 1996) and prefer to track facelike stimuli rather than other moving objects (Johnson et al., 1991). Yet this early preference for faces may simply reflect the elegant symmetry (or other attractive aspects) of facial stimuli rather than newborns' interpretation of faces as a meaningful form. As noted earlier, a newborn's attention to faces may even be an innate reflex, controlled by subcortical areas of the brain, that serves to orient babies to their caregivers and that typically disappears in a matter of weeks (Johnson, 1997). In fact, infants younger than 8 weeks attend mostly to the high-contrast outer boundaries of facial stimuli and spend very little time scanning internal features (noses, mouths, and lips) that are likely to define a face as a coherent and meaningful form (Bronson, 1991; Johnson & Gilmore, 1996) (and see Figure 6.5).

Somewhere between 2 and 3 months, infants begin to respond to faces as if they were meaningful configurations. Now they smile at familiar faces as if they recognize them and appreciate their significance (Johnson, 1997). Three-month-old infants can readily discriminate their own mothers' faces rather than those of other women who are similar in appearance (Barrera & Maurer, 1981). And all strangers don't look alike, because 3- to 6-month-olds prefer to gaze at adults with attractive rather than unattractive faces (Langlois et al., 1987; Rubenstein, Kalakanis, & Langlois, 1999). Interestingly, attractive faces are really kind of average—they tend to reflect the average range of facial features (for example, average nose length, average chin size, average spacing between the eyes) for both men and women and, as such, may be preferred because they match the infant's emerging general scheme for faces better than unattractive faces do (Rubenstein et al., 1999). And research using the evoked potential method reveals that by 6 months, facial stimuli are processed quicker and elicit different patterns of electrical activity in the brain than other familiar nonfacial objects do—a strong physiological cue that faces represent a unique category of experience for a 6-month-old (de Haan & Nelson, 1999; Johnson, 2000).

Clearly, there is more to be learned about early perception of faces. The data available at present seem to imply that a face is merely an interesting pattern that will capture attention in the early weeks of life. But as their visual systems mature and they have more experience with faces, 2- to 3-month olds reach a point at which they begin to develop a general scheme for facedness and variations on that theme, which enables them to quickly recognize their close companions and to discriminate one stranger from another. By 8 to 10 months of age, infants can even *interpret* some of the emotional expressions in their mothers' faces and to respond adaptively to this information (Feinman, 1992). Although this *social referencing* ability will be discussed later in Chapter 11 as a social and emotional milestone, it illustrates that an infant's response to social situations depends, in part, on his or her ability to "read" faces.

Interestingly, this impressive ability to use object movement to perceive form is apparently not present at birth (Slater et al., 1990b) but has developed by 2 months (Johnson & Aslin, 1995). By 3 to 4 months, infants can even perceive form in some stationary scenes that capture their attention. Look carefully at Figure 6.7. Do you see a square in this display? So do 3- to 4-month-olds (Ghim, 1990) This is a remarkable achievement indeed because the boundary of this "square" is a *subjective contour* that must be constructed mentally rather than simply detected by the visual system.

Further strides in form perception occur later in the first year as infants come to detect more and more structural configurations from the barest of cues (Craton, 1996). By 9 months, infants exposed to the moving point-light displays shown in Figure 6.8 pay much more attention to display (a) than to displays (b) and (c), as if they were interpreting this stimulus as a representation of the human form, just as adults do (Bertenthal et al., 1987). Twelve-month-old infants are even better at constructing form from limited information. After seeing a single point of light move so as to trace a complex shape such as a ☆, 12-month-olds (but not 8- or 10-month-olds) prefer to look at actual objects with *different* shapes. This preference for novelty on the part of the 12-month-olds indicates that they have perceived the form traced earlier by the light and now find it less interesting than other novel forms (Rose, 1988; Skouteris, McKenzie, & Day, 1992).

Understanding facial information and being able to discriminate faces are important perceptual and social accomplishments. When do we become fully able to process and discriminate critical information about faces? Research by Daphne Maurer at McMaster University suggests that some aspects of face recognition are not developed until the mid-teen years or later. Read Box 6.2 to find out more about the development of the skills needed to recognize faces.

Explaining Form Perception

You may have noticed from reading Box 6.1 that the development of face perception follows the same general course as the perception of other forms. Newborns are biologically prepared to seek visual stimulation and make visual discriminations. These early visual *experiences* are important because they keep the visual neurons firing and contribute to the *maturation* of the visual centres of the brain (Nelson, 1995). In fact, recent work at McMaster University demonstrates that visual input right after birth is necessary to set up the neural architecture that will be refined over the next 14 or more years (Le Grand et al., 2001).

Figure 6.7 *By 3 months of age, infants are perceiving subjective contours such as the "square" shown here. ADAPTED FROM BERTENTHAL, CAMPOS, & HAITH, 1980.*

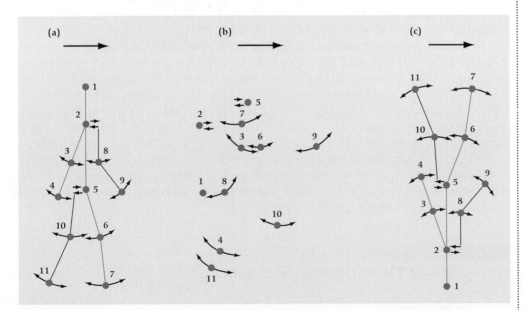

Figure 6.8 *The three point-light displays used in Bertenthal's research. FROM BERTENTHAL, PROFFITT, & CUTTING, 1984.*

6.2

Daphne Maurer

Daphne Maurer works in the Department of Psychology at McMaster University. Her research involves investigating the development of vision in human infants. She studies vision development in children with normal vision and children who have been treated for cataracts.

As adults, we are "experts" in face processing. We can recognize thousands of individual faces quickly and accurately. Three important pieces of information that we have to be able to process are the shape, or *contours*, of the individual's head (e.g., Jean Chrétien's jaw line); the shapes of individual *features* (e.g., the curl of Tony Blair's mouth); and the spacing among the features (e.g., the distance between George W. Bush's eyes). Sensitivity to the spacing of features—called *configural processing*—underlies our ability to recognize upright faces even under poor conditions such as brief exposure, low lighting, or a new angle of view. Although precursors of these skills are already evident at birth, even 14-year-olds make more errors than adults do (Carey, Diamond, & Woods, 1980).

In a recent study, Daphne Maurer and her colleagues at McMaster University (Mondloch, LeGrand, & Maurer, 2002) examined the reasons for the slow development in face recognition. They used photography and computer software to create the face of an imaginary female (called Jane) and the faces of her imaginary "sisters." The sisters were just like Jane except for one critical feature, such as the shape of the external contour (contour set), the shape of the eyes and mouth (featural set), or the spacing of the eyes and mouth (spacing set). Participants saw two faces in sequence and indicated whether they were the same or different. By age 6, children were as accurate as adults at discriminating the faces that had different external contours. By age 10, children were as accurate as adults in recognizing faces that had different features. But for the spacing set, although improvements continued until 14 years of age, the accuracy of children was still not as high as that of adults. Discriminating faces is clearly a complex task that develops over time (Mondloch, Geldart, Maurer, & Le Grand, 2003; Mondloch et al., 2002).

Recall that after birth the infant's visual acuity limits input to large objects with high contrast. How were the researchers able to determine that this period was critical? They compared normally developing children with children who had missed visual input during the first few months of life because they had dense cataracts in both eyes. Although the children treated for cataracts developed normal skills in differentiating the shapes of faces (e.g., jaw line) and individual features (e.g., mouth), they showed deficits in their ability to discriminate among faces that differed in the spacing of features (e.g., eye spacing). Because the cataracts were present at birth and treated shortly after, the researchers were able to conclude that the visual input from large objects with high contrast in infancy appears to "reserve the neural tissue for later refinement" (Geldart, Mondloch, Maurer, de Schonen, & Brent, 2002; LeGrand, Mondloch, Maurer, & Brent, 2001).

By about 2 to 3 months of age, maturation has progressed to the point of allowing an infant to see more detail, scan more systematically, and begin to construct visual forms, including one for faces in general as well as more specific configurations that represent the faces of familiar companions. All the while, infants are continuing their visual explorations and gaining knowledge that will permit them to make even finer distinctions among visual stimuli, and to draw some general inferences about the significance of such forms as an elongated toy that rattles when shaken or a gleeful look on a father's face.

Notice, then, that the growth of form perception results from a continuous interplay, or *interaction*, among the baby's inborn equipment (a working, but immature, visual sense), biological maturation, and visual experiences (or learning). Let's see if this same interactive model holds for spatial perception as well.

Perception of Three-Dimensional Space

Because we adults easily perceive depth and the third dimension, it is tempting to conclude that newborns can too. However, empiricists have argued that poor visual acuity and an inability to bring objects into sharp focus (that is, to accommodate) prevent the neonate from making accurate spatial inferences. In addition, infants younger than 2 to 3 months of age do not exhibit any **stereopsis**—a convergence of the visual images of the two eyes to produce a singular, non-overlapping image that has depth (Birch, 1993). All these limitations may make it difficult for newborns to perceive depth and to locate objects in space.

However, nativists argue that several cues to depth and distance are *monocular*—that is, detectable with only one eye. Movement of objects (such as the mother's head) toward and away from the face may be one such cue that newborns can detect. And artists make good use of other **pictorial** (or **perspective**) **cues** to create the illusion of three-dimensionality on a two-dimensional surface. Examples are *linear perspective* (making linear objects converge as they recede toward the horizon), *texture gradients* (showing more detail in nearby objects than in distant ones), *sizing cues* (drawing distant objects smaller than nearby ones), *interposition* (drawing a near figure to partly obscure one farther away), and *shading* (varying the lighting across an object's surface to create the impression of depth). If neonates can detect these monocular depth cues, then their world may be three-dimensional from the very beginning.

So when are infants capable of perceiving depth and making reasonably accurate inferences about size and spatial relations? We'll briefly consider three programs of research designed to answer these questions.

Size Constancy

Very young infants have shown some intriguing abilities to interpret movement across the third dimension. For example, a 1-month-old reacts defensively by blinking his or her eyes as a looming object approaches the face (called **visual looming**) (Nanez & Yonas, 1994). But do very young infants display **size constancy**, recognizing that an object remains the same size when its image on the retina becomes larger as it moves closer or smaller as it moves further away?

Until recently, researchers claimed that size constancy could not emerge until 3 to 5 months of age, after infants had developed good binocular vision (stereopsis) that would help them to make accurate spatial inferences. But as Box 6.3 illustrates, even newborns know something about an object's real size.

However, the finding that neonates display some size constancy does not mean that this ability is fully developed. Apparently, binocular vision does contribute to its development, for the 4-month-olds who show greater evidence of size constancy are those whose binocular capabilities are most mature (Aslin, 1987). **Kinetic cues** also contribute; inferences about real size among 4-month-olds are more likely to be accurate if the infants have watched an object approach and recede (Day & McKenzie, 1981). Size constancy steadily improves throughout the first year; however, this ability is not fully mature until 10 to 11 years of age (Day, 1987).

Use of Pictorial Cues

Albert Yonas and his associates have studied infants' reactions to monocular depth cues—the tricks artists and photographers use to portray depth and distance on a two-dimensional surface. In the earliest of these studies (Yonas, Cleaves, & Pettersen, 1978), infants were exposed to a photograph of a bank of windows taken at a 45 degree angle. As we see in Figure 6.9, the windows on the right appear (to us at least) to be much closer than those on the left. So if infants perceive pictorial depth cues, they might be fooled into thinking that the windows on the right are closer and they should reach to the right. But if they are insensitive to pictorial cues, they should reach out with one hand about as often as they do with the other.

What Yonas and colleagues found is that 7-month-olds reliably reached toward the windows that appeared nearest, whereas 5-month-olds displayed no such reaching preferences. In later research, Yonas and colleagues found that 7-month-olds are also sensitive to pictorial cues such as interposition (see Figure 6.10), relative size and shading cues, texture gradients, and linear perspective, whereas 5-month-olds are not (Arterberry, Yonas, & Bensen, 1989; Yonas, Arterberry, & Granrud, 1987).

Figure 6.9 *This bank of windows is actually a large photograph taken at a 45° angle, and the two edges of this stimulus are in fact equidistant from an infant seated directly in front of it. If infants are influenced by pictorial cues to depth, they should perceive the right edge of the photo to be nearer to them and indicate as much by reaching out to touch this edge rather than the more "distant" edge to their left.* ADAPTED FROM YONAS, CLEAVES, & PETTERSEN, 1978.

stereopsis
fusion of two flat images to produce a single image that has depth

pictorial (perspective) cues
depth and distance cues (including linear perspective, texture gradients, sizing, interposition, and shading) that are monocular—that is, detectable with only one eye

visual looming
expansion of the image of an object to take up the entire visual field as it draws very close to the face

Figure 6.10 *If infants are sensitive to the pictorial cue of interposition, they should reliably reach for the "closest" area of a visual display (left side in this example). Seven-month-olds show this reaching preference, whereas 5-month-olds do not.*
FROM GRANRUD & YONAS, 1984.

size constancy
tendency to perceive an object as
the same size from different
distances despite changes in the
size of its retinal image

kinetic cues
cues created by movements of
objects or movements of the
body; provide important
information for the perception of
forms and spatial relations

visual cliff
elevated platform that creates an
illusion of depth; used to test the
depth perception of infants

In sum, infants become sensitive to different spatial cues at different ages. From a limited capacity for size constancy at birth, babies extract spatial information from kinetic cues (that is, from looming and other moving objects) between 1 and 3 months, binocular cues at 3 to 5 months, and monocular (pictorial) cues by 6 to 7 months. Do these impressive accomplishments imply that a 6- to 7-month-old infant perceives depth and knows enough to avoid crawling off the edge of a sofa or a staircase? Let's see what researchers have learned from their attempts to answer these questions.

Development of Depth Perception

Eleanor Gibson and Richard Walk (1960) developed an apparatus they called the **visual cliff** to determine whether infants can perceive depth. The visual cliff (see Figure 6.11) consists of an elevated glass platform divided into two sections by a centre board. On the "shallow" side, a checkerboard pattern is placed directly under the glass. On the "deep" side, the pattern is placed several feet below the glass, creating the illusion of a sharp drop-off, or "visual cliff." The investigator tests an infant for depth perception by placing the child on the centre board and then asking the child's mother to try to coax the infant to cross both the shallow and the deep sides. Testing infants 6½ months and older,

---

Size Constancy in Newborns

Alan Slater and his associates (Slater, Mattock, & Brown, 1990) designed a clever experiment to see whether newborn babies can perceive an object's real size across changes in distance. Each of their 2-day-old subjects was given ample opportunity to gaze at either a small (5.1 cm) cube or a large (10.2 cm) cube that was presented at six different distances (although none of the babies actually saw their cube move). The purpose of these six "familiarization" trials was to expose infants to changes in the size of the retinal image of the cube in the hope that this might direct their attention to the cube's real (unchanging) size.

After the six familiarization trials came the test for size constancy. Each infant now saw two cubes: the small one at a distance of 30.5 cm and the large one at 61.0 cm. At

these distances, the two cubes cast retinal images of exactly the same size (see figure). How should a baby now respond if he perceives that the real size of the "familiar" cube was constant, despite changes in the size of its retinal image? He should quickly determine that whichever cube (large or small) that he had looked at before was still the "same old cube" and should now prefer to examine the novel cube.

This is precisely what 11 of Slater's 12 newborns did, spending more than 83 percent of their time gazing at whichever cube (large or small) they had not previously seen. So newborn infants were able to perceive the "real" size of the cube they had examined in the familiarization trials. In other words, they displayed clear evidence of size constancy in the first two days of life (see also Granrud, 1987).

The test trial from the Slater, Mattock, & Brown (1990) experiment. As shown at the left, babies viewed a small cube at a distance of 30.5 cm and a cube twice as large at twice that distance, or 61.0 cm. At these distances, the two cubes cast the same-size retinal image. The illustration at the right shows what the baby saw on this test trial.

Gibson and Walk (1960) found that 90 percent of them would cross the shallow side but fewer than 10 percent would cross the deep side. Apparently, most infants of crawling age clearly perceive depth and are afraid of drop-offs.

Might children who are too young to crawl also perceive depth? To find out, Joseph Campos and his associates (1970) recorded changes in infants' heart rates when they were lowered face down over the shallow and deep sides of the apparatus. Babies as young as 2 months of age showed a *decrease* in heart rate when over the deep side but no change in heart rate on the shallow side. Why a decrease in heart rate? When we are afraid, our hearts beat faster, not slower. A decrease in heart rate is a sign of interest. So 2-month-old infants *detect a difference* between the deep and shallow sides, but they have not learned to *fear* drop-offs.

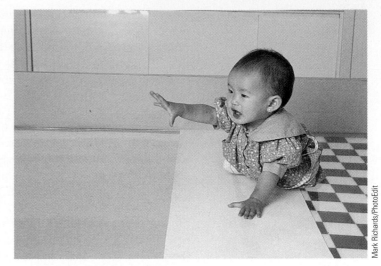

Figure 6.11 *An infant at the edge of the visual cliff.*

MOTOR DEVELOPMENT AND DEPTH PERCEPTION. One reason that many 6- to 7-month-olds come to fear drop-offs is that they are more sensitive to kinetic, binocular, and monocular depth cues than younger infants are. Yet this fear also depends very heavily on the experiences infants have creeping and crawling about and perhaps falling now and then. Joseph Campos and his associates (1992) find that infants who have crawled for a couple of weeks are much more afraid of drop-offs than infants of the same age who are not yet crawling. In fact, precrawlers quickly develop a healthy fear of heights when given special walkers that allow them to move about on their own. So motor development provides experiences that change infants' interpretation of the meaning of depth. And as we saw in Chapter 5, infants who have begun to move about on their own are better than those who haven't at solving other spatial tasks, such as finding hidden objects.

Why does self-produced movement make such a difference? Probably because young creepers and crawlers have discovered that the visual environment changes when they move, so that they are more inclined to use a *spatial landmark* to help them define where they (and hidden objects) are in relation to the larger spatial layout. A study by Dina Bai and Bennett Bertenthal (1992) nicely supports this interpretation. Seven- to 8-month-old creepers and pre-creepers saw a toy put into one of two different-coloured containers on a table. Next, either the infant or the table was rotated 180 degrees (see Figure 6.12) and the infant was allowed to search for the toy. The results were clear. *When the table had been rotated* (and the infant did not move), both creepers and pre-creepers tracked the movement *of the containers* and were equally proficient at finding the hidden toy. But when the infant had been rotated (and the containers did not move), creepers were much better at finding the hidden toy than pre-creepers were. Why? Because

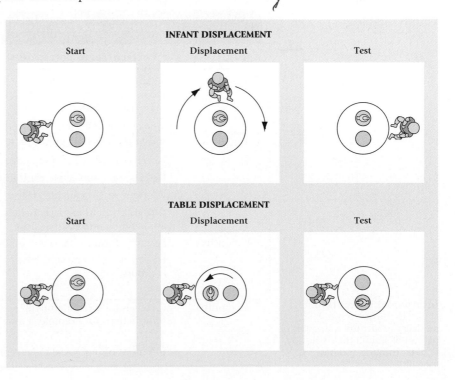

Figure 6.12 *Test trials for the Bai and Bertenthal (1992) experiment. Infants were allowed to search for a hidden toy after they had moved (top row) or the table had rotated, causing the hidden object to move (bottom row).* ADAPTED FROM BAI & BERTENTHAL, 1992.

creepers were more inclined to use the colour of the correct container as a spatial landmark to tell them where to search after their own position in space had changed. Self-produced movement also makes an infant more sensitive to *optical flow*—the sensation that other objects move when he or she does—which may promote the development of new neural pathways in the sensory and motor areas of the brain that underlie improvements in both motor skills and spatial perception (Bertenthal & Campos, 1987; Higgins et al., 1996; Schmuckler & Tsang-Tong, 2000).

Perhaps you have already inferred by now that the *interactive* model that best explains the growth of form perception applies equally well to the development of spatial abilities. Maturation of the visual sense enables infants to see better and to detect a greater variety of depth cues, while also contributing to the growth of motor skills. Yet experience is equally important: The first year is a time when curious infants are constantly making new and exciting discoveries about depth and distance relations as they become ever more skilled at reaching for and manipulating objects and at moving about to explore stairs, sloped surfaces, and other visual cliffs in the natural environment (Bertenthal, 1993; Bushnell & Boudreau, 1993).

Table 6.2 summarizes the remarkable changes in visual perception that occur during the first year of life. Now let's consider how infants come to integrate information from more than one sense to make perceptual inferences.

INTERMODAL PERCEPTION

Suppose you are playing a game in which you are blindfolded and are trying to identify objects by touch. A friend places a small, spherical object in your hand. As you finger it, you determine that it is about 3 cm in diameter, that it weighs a few grams, and that it is very hard and covered with many small dimples. You then say "Aha!" and conclude that the object is a _____.

A colleague who conducts this exercise in class reports that most students easily identify the object as a golf ball—even if they have never touched a golf ball in their lives. This is an example of **intermodal perception**—the ability to recognize by one

intermodal perception
ability to use one sensory modality to identify a stimulus or pattern of stimuli that is already familiar through another modality

TABLE 6.2	Milestones in Infant Visual Perception	
Age	**Pattern/form perception**	**Spatial perception**
Birth–1 month	Seeks visual input; prefers moderately complex stimuli with high visual contrast. Scans boundaries of visual targets.	Displays some size constancy. Responds to looming objects and kinetic depth lines.
2–4 months	Visual scanning of entire stimulus. Perceives forms from their motion. Detects some subjective contours. Prefers faces to scrambled faces. Recognizes mother's face; prefers attractive to unattractive faces.	Detects depth cues on the visual cliff. Becomes sensitive to binocular depth cues.
5–8 months	Perceives form in stationary objects. Detects more subtle subjective contours.	Size constancy improves. Becomes sensitive to pictorial (monocular) depth cues. Fears drop-offs.
9–12 months	Perceives form from limited information (for example, a moving light). Interprets others' facial expressions.	All aspects of spatial perception become more refined.

sensory modality (in this case, touch) an object that is familiar through another (vision). As adults, we can make many inferences of this kind. When do babies first display these abilities?

Are the Senses Integrated at Birth?

It would be obviously useful for an infant who is attempting to understand the world to be able to integrate information gained by viewing, fingering, sniffing, or otherwise exploring objects. Do the senses function in an integrative way early in life?

Suppose that you captured a baby's attention by floating a soap bubble in front of his or her face. Would he or she reach for it? If so, how do you think he or she would react when the bubble pops at his slightest touch?

Thomas Bower and his associates (Bower, Broughton, & Moore, 1970) exposed neonates to a situation similar to the soap-bubble scenario. The subjects were 8- to 31-day-old infants who could see an object well within reaching distance while they were wearing special goggles. Actually, this *virtual object* was an illusion created by a shadow caster. If the infant reached for it, his or her hand would feel nothing at all. Bower and colleagues (1970) found that the infants did reach for the virtual object and that they often became frustrated to tears when they failed to touch it. These results suggest that vision and touch are integrated: Infants expect to feel objects that they can see and reach, and an incongruity between vision and the tactile sense is discomforting.

Other research on auditory–visual incongruities (Aronson & Rosenbloom, 1971) reveals that 1- to 2-month-olds often become distressed when they *see* their talking mothers behind a soundproof screen but *hear* their mothers' voices through a speaker off to the side. Their discomfort implies that vision and audition are integrated; a baby who sees his mother expects to hear her voice coming from the general direction of her mouth.

In sum, the senses are apparently integrated early in life. Nevertheless, infants' negative emotional responses to confusing sensory stimulation says very little about their ability to use one sense to recognize objects and experiences that are already familiar through another sense.

Development of Intermodal Perception

Although intermodal perception has never been observed in newborns, it seems that babies only 1 month old have the ability to recognize by sight at least some of the objects they have previously sucked. In one study, Eleanor Gibson and Arlene Walker (1984) allowed 1-month-old infants to suck either a rigid cylinder or a spongy, pliable one. Then the two objects were displayed visually to illustrate that the spongy cylinder would bend and the rigid one would not. The results were clear: Infants who had sucked on a spongy object preferred to look at the rigid cylinder, whereas those who had sucked on a rigid cylinder now gazed more at the pliable one. Apparently, these infants could visualize the object they had sucked and now considered it less interesting than the other stimulus, which was new to them.

Because 30-day-old infants have had lots of experience sucking on both spongy objects (nipples) and rigid ones (their own thumbs), we cannot necessarily conclude that intermodal perception is innate. And before we get too carried away with the remarkable proficiencies of 1-month-olds, let's note that (1) oral-to-visual perception is the only cross-modal skill that has ever been observed in infants this young, and (2) this ability is weak, at best, in very young infants and improves dramatically over the first year (Rose, Gottfried, & Bridger, 1981). Even the seemingly related ability to match tactile sensations (from grasping) with visual ones does not appear until 4 to 6 months (Rose et al., 1981; Streri & Spelke, 1988), largely because infants younger than this cannot grasp objects well (Bushnell & Boudreau, 1993). In fact, researchers such as Daphne Maurer and her colleagues have tested touch-to-vision perception in 1-month-old infants and have shown that transfer is very tenuous and may be affected greatly by small experimental manipulations such as preferences for one stimulus over another (Maurer, Stager, and Mondloch, 1999).

Intermodal matching between vision and hearing emerges at about 4 months—precisely the time that infants begin to *voluntarily* turn their heads in the direction of sounds (Bahrick, Netto, & Hernandez-Reif, 1998). By age 4 months, infants can even match visual and auditory cues for distance. So if they are listening to a sound track in which engine noise is becoming softer, they prefer to watch a film of a train moving away rather than one showing a train approaching (Walker-Andrews & Lennon, 1985; Pickens, 1994). Clearly, 4-month-olds know what sights jibe with many sounds, and this auditory/visual matching continues to improve over the next several months.

Explaining Intermodal Perception

The findings that the senses are integrated at birth and that at least some intermodal matching is possible in the first few months seems most consistent with the *differentiation* theory of perception we discussed early in this chapter. Differentiation theorists projected that the *distinctive features* that characterize sensory input (shape, texture, etc.) are detectable by more than one sensory channel. Thus if the senses are integrated at birth (rather than independent, as *enrichment* theorists claim), infants may quickly detect these features in different sensory channels and display intermodal perception very early in life

Indeed, infants do quickly integrate *novel* sensory information to make accurate intermodal inferences. For example, 3-month-olds who have but 1 minute's experience with watching the rotation of each of the two cylinders in Figure 6.13 can later match corresponding sights with sounds. That is, when they see both cylinders being rotated *at the same time*, infants who hear the tape-recorded impact of only one object look appropriately at the cylinder to the right, whereas those who hear the impact of many objects look at the cylinder to the left (Bahrick, 1988). Apparently, differentiation theorists were correct: Matching of novel information across modalities occurs almost simultaneously, as long as infants are able to detect this input in each sensory channel.

Courtesy of Lorraine Bahrick, Intermodal Learning in Infancy

Figure 6.13 *Three-month-olds who briefly watched each cylinder rotate independently later saw both rotate at the same time as they listened to a tape of either one object or many objects hitting the bottom of a cylinder. As expected by differentiation theory, the infants immediately matched sights with sounds, looking to the right upon hearing the impact of one object, but to the left upon hearing the impact of many objects. FROM BAHRICK, 1988.*

Why, then, do intermodal judgments become more accurate over time? Probably because as each sense continues to develop, it becomes a more effective means of detecting the defining features of novel stimuli. But the fact that even young infants can match sensations across modalities is very significant, for this capacity helps them to organize and interpret a bewildering array of stimuli in the natural environment and keeps their world from becoming a "blooming, buzzing confusion." Indeed, learning about novel aspects of the environment occurs much quicker when infants have information available from more than one sense (Bahrick & Lickliter, 2000). And infants who were especially skilled at integrating their sensory experiences will later tend to perform well at age 11 on IQ tests, thus suggesting that intermodal perceptual ability is an early indicator of future intellectual performance (Rose & Feldman, 1995).

INFANT PERCEPTION IN PERSPECTIVE—AND A LOOK AHEAD

What remarkable perceptual competencies infants display! All their senses are functioning reasonably well at birth, and babies immediately put them to work, searching for stimuli to explore and identifying similarities and differences among these sensory inputs. Within the first few months, infants are becoming accomplished perceivers: They detect forms, react to depth and distance cues, recognize definite patterns in the language they hear, and regularly combine information from different sensory modalities to achieve a richer understanding of the natural environment.

We have concentrated heavily on the perceptual skills of infants because infancy is the period when most basic perceptual competencies emerge (Bornstein, 1992). In fact, many researchers believe that advances in perception beyond the first year stem primarily from children's increasing ability to focus their *attention* on sensory inputs and draw meaningful *inferences* from them—milestones that reflect advances in information processing and might be properly labelled *cognitive* developments. Before closing the book on perception, however, let's take note of one very influential theory of perceptual development that helps to explain why younger children may require much more information to recognize common objects than older ones do, why preschool children may have some difficulty trying to learn to read, and why people in different cultures might perceive the world in somewhat different ways.

> **?** **WHAT DO YOU THINK?**
>
> Learning to read is a complex intermodal task. Can you think of at least two intermodal integrations that underlie reading skills? You can check your reasoning in Box 6.4.

Perceptual Learning in Childhood: Gibson's Differentiation Theory

According to Gibson (1969, 1987, 1992), **perceptual learning** occurs when we actively explore objects in our environment and detect their *distinctive (or invariant) features*. As we have noted, a distinctive feature is any cue that *differentiates* one stimulus from all others. A 3-year-old may initially confuse rabbits and cats because both are furry animals of about the same size. However, the child will eventually discover that rabbits have long ears—a distinctive feature that differentiates them from cats, rats, squirrels, and all other small, furry animals. Gibson believes that the motivation for perceptual learning is inborn; from birth, humans are active information seekers who search for order and stability (invariants) in the natural environment.

perceptual learning
changes in one's ability to extract information from sensory stimulation that occur as a result of experience

Of course, some invariants are easier to detect than others. Even a 4-year-old whose attentional strategies are relatively immature soon notices large distinctive features such as an elephant's trunk or a rabbit's long ears. However, a 4-year-old may not easily differentiate *b* from *d* because the distinctive feature that discriminates these letters (the direction of curvature) is subtle and not very meaningful.

Gibson and her colleagues have conducted an experiment to study the ability of young children to distinguish different letterlike forms (Gibson, Gibson, Pick, & Osser, 1962). Children ages 4 to 8 were shown a standard letterlike stimulus and several transformations of this standard form (examples appear in Figure 6.14). Their task was to pick out the stimuli that were identical to the standard. The 4- and 5-year-olds had difficulties with all the transformations; they often judged these stimuli to be identical to the standard. However, 6- to 8-year-olds were generally able to detect the distinctive features that differentiated the transformations from the standard stimulus.

Perhaps you can see the relevance of Gibson's work for elementary education, particularly reading education. Clearly, the ability to discriminate and categorize letters of the alphabet is a major perceptual milestone that is necessary before children can hope to decode words and become proficient readers. Although preschool training in letter recognition (at home, at nursery school, and on educational television programs such as *Sesame Street*) helps children to recognize many letters and even a few written words (such as their own names), preschoolers younger than 5 to 5½ continue to confuse letters such as *b*, *h*, and *d*, or *m* and *w*, that have similar perceptual characteristics (Chall, 1983). By contrast, Gibson's subjects were beginning to detect and appreciate subtle differences in *unfamiliar* letterlike forms at precisely the time (age 6) that serious reading instruction begins at school. As it turns out, learning to read is a very complex task—one that deserves a closer look. Box 6.4 describes some of the major perceptual hurdles that children must overcome to make sense of all those funny little squiggles on the printed page.

In sum, Gibson is a *differentiation* theorist. She believes that young children are constantly extracting new and more subtle information from the environment and thereby discovering the properties, patterns, and distinctive features that will enable them to differentiate objects and events. As this differentiation continues, a child grows perceptually and becomes increasingly accurate at interpreting the broad array of stimuli that impinge on the sensory receptors.

However, other researchers believe that Gibson's theory is incomplete and that children do far more when making sense of their experiences than simply detecting distinctive features. Their point is that children also use their existing knowledge to *enrich* their sensory experiences and *construct* new interpretations. Indeed, unless infants used existing knowledge to *impose meaning* on ambiguous stimuli, it is hard to see how they could ever interpret the moving light display in Figure 6.8—a stimulus with few distinctive features—as an upright human form. So as we noted in opening this chapter, both the differentiation and the enrichment perspectives have some merit and have contributed substantially to our understanding of early perceptual (and cognitive) developments.

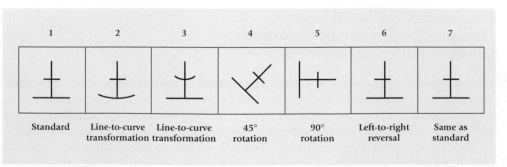

Figure 6.14 Examples of figures used to test children's ability to detect the distinctive features of letterlike forms. Stimulus 1 is the standard. The child's task is to examine each of the comparison stimuli (stimuli 2–7) and pick out those that are the same as the standard. ADAPTED FROM GIBSON ET AL., 1962.

How Do We Learn to Read?

One of the most challenging perceptual tasks that most children face is learning to read. How do they discover that the print on the page represents spoken words? How do they learn to translate print into spoken language?

Although most children learn to read at school, they first learn *about* reading at home as they acquire crucial **emergent literacy** skills (Whitehurst & Lonigan, 1998). One of the first such skills is *emergent reading*—children equate reading with storytelling, picking up storybooks and reading sensible sentences that have little relation to the words on the page. Later, preschoolers recognize that the squiggles on the printed page represent words. They may then try to match the spoken words of a familiar story to the symbols on the page but their matches are not correct. This kind of activity sets the stage for learning the letters and that each letter is related to a particular sound and that combinations of letters (and sounds) make up printed words (Crain-Thoreson & Dale, 1992). Knowledge of letters is a most important emergent literacy skill; in fact, the ability that 4- and 5-year-olds display at letter naming is a major predictor of their future reading achievement scores (Lonigan, Burgess, & Anthony, 2000; Schneider & Naslund, 1999). Finally, true reading begins as children become more skilled at decoding letters; they can "sound out" novel printed words by breaking them into individual sounds or syllables.

Perhaps you can see that reading is a complex *intermodal* task. Aspiring readers must learn to recognize the distinctive visual features of different letters, a skill that most children acquire by about 6 years (see text). Yet they must also learn which letters correspond to which sounds—a skill that depends very heavily on *phonological awareness*, the realization that *spoken* words can be decomposed into basic sound units, or phonemes. Most 4- and 5-year-olds perform poorly on phonological awareness tasks (such as breaking simple words like "cat" into its 3 phonemes), although 6-year-olds perform much better (Bjorklund, 2000). Phonological awareness is a very good predictor of later reading achievement (Lonigan et al., 2000; Muter et al., 1998), and research indicates that explicit instruction in phonological skills improves the subsequent reading ability of beginning readers (Schneider et al., 1997).

What does all this research imply about optimal reading instruction? The merits of two broad approaches to reading instruction have been hotly debated. The phonics or code-oriented approach is consistent with the differentiation theory of perception. It teaches children letter–sound correspondence rules that they can use to decode novel words by breaking them into their component sounds. By contrast, the whole-language approach is more consistent with an *enrichment* theory of perception. It teaches children to recognize whole words by sight and to use their knowledge of the context in which the words appear to figure out their meaning. This whole-language approach assumes that the parts of printed words (letters and phonemes) are not as meaningful as the whole words and that children can learn to read whole words as effortlessly as they learn to understand speech.

Clearly, both approaches have some strengths. Yet research indicates that children must somehow learn what the phonics approach teaches them if they are ever to read well (Whitehurst & Lonigan, 1998). As we have noted, explicitly teaching phonological awareness pays off in better reading skills. However, children eventually read for *meaning* rather than continuing to view reading as a decoding activity, and many scholars see the advantages of combining the phonics and whole-language approaches. In fact, meaning is so important that experts caution educators that a truly effective reading curriculum must maximize children's *motivation* to read. How? One approach favoured by experts is to expose young readers to stories that relate much more closely to their interests and cultural experiences than most children's readers do (Adams, Treiman, & Pressey, 1998; Loupe, 1997; Tharp, 1994).

How can we facilitate children's acquisition of the skills they need to read? Although parents are often told that they should read aloud to their children, there is little evidence supporting a direct link between shared reading and the child's reading development (Whitehurst & Lonigan, 1998). In two recent Canadian studies of children in primary grades (Evans, Shaw, & Bell, 2000; Sénéchal et al., 1998), book reading had a minimal impact on children's knowledge of vocabulary, reading, spelling skills, and phonological awareness. Does that mean that shared reading is not important? No. These studies examined the amount of shared reading, not the content of the shared reading activity. When parents engage in activities that foster phonetic awareness (such as those mentioned above), vocabulary building, and other activities that support reading skills, shared reading can promote reading and the motivation to read (see, for example, Evans et al., 2000).

Ryan McVay/Photodisc

Perceiving the distinctive features of letters and the correspondence between letters and sounds are tough tasks for preschool children.

Cultural Influences on Perception

How is perception influenced by one's culture and cultural traditions? Although people in different cultures rarely differ in such basic perceptual capabilities as the ability to discriminate forms, patterns, and degrees of brightness or loudness (Berry et al., 1992), culture can have some subtle but important effects on perception.

For example, we noted earlier that there are some phonemic discriminations that an infant can make better than adults can (Werker & Desjardins, 1995). Each of us begins life biologically prepared to acquire any language that humans speak. But as we are exposed to a particular language, we become especially sensitive to the sound patterns that are important to that language (that is, to its distinctive features) and less sensitive to auditory distinctions our language deems irrelevant. So all infants easily discriminate the consonants *r* and *l* (Eimas, 1975a). So can you if your native language is English, French, Spanish, or German. However, Chinese and Japanese make no distinction between *r* and *l*, and adult native speakers of these languages cannot make this auditory discrimination as well as infants can (Miyawaki et al., 1975).

Music is another cultural tool that influences our auditory perception. Michael Lynch and his associates (1990) had 6-month-old infants and American adults listen to melodies in either the Western major/minor scale or the Javanese pelog scale, which sounds a bit strange to Western adults. Inserted within the melodies was an occasional "mistuned" note that violated the musical scale. Remarkably, 6-month-old infants often detected these mistuned notes, regardless of whether they violated a Western or a Javanese melody. Apparently, babies are born with the potential to perceive "musicality" and to discriminate good music from bad music in a variety of musical scales. By contrast, American adults were much less sensitive to bad notes in the unfamiliar Javanese musical system than to mistuned notes in their native Western scale, suggesting that their years of experience with the Western musical system had shaped their perceptions of music.

These findings illustrate two general principles of development that are very important. First, the growth of perceptual abilities, like so many other aspects of development, is not simply a matter of adding new skills; it is also a matter of *losing* unnecessary ones. Second, our culture largely determines which sensory inputs are distinctive and how they should be interpreted. We *learn* not to hear certain phonemes if they are not distinctive to the language we speak. We Westerners *learn* to view rats and snakes as loathsome nonfood items, whereas people in many other cultures perceive them to be tasty delicacies. So the way we perceive the world depends not only on the detection of the objective aspects in our sensory inputs (*perceptual* learning) but also on *cultural* learning experiences that provide a framework for interpreting these inputs.

Let's now take a closer look at learning and see if we can determine why many developmentalists include it (along with maturation and perception) among the most fundamental developmental processes.

emergent literacy
skills, knowledge, and attitudes that precede and seem to promote conventional forms of reading and writing

Concept Check 6.2
Infant Perceptual Development

Check your understanding of selected aspects of early perceptual development by matching one of the following alternatives to the descriptions below: (a) intermodal perception, (b) depth cues, (c) face perception, (d) kinetic (motion) cues, (e) phonological awareness, (f) pictorial cues, (g) maturation of the brain's visual centres, (h) size constancy, (i) depth perception. The answers appear in the Appendix.

_____ 1. type of early stimulation that sensitizes infants to forms and spatial relations

_____ 2. spatial cues that may distress a 7-month-old but interest a 2-month-old

_____ 3. spatial ability present in a rudimentary form at birth

_____ 4. spatial cues that 7-month-olds are sensitive to but 5-month-olds are not

_____ 5. early visual stimulation promotes this process, which furthers visual perception

_____ 6. locomotor skills promote this development

_____ 7. perceptual skill that predicts later intellectual performance

_____ 8. important achievement in form perception that infants display at 2 to 3 months

_____ 9. crucial perceptual activity that predicts later reading achievement

BASIC LEARNING PROCESSES

Learning is one of those deceptively simple terms that are actually quite complex. Most psychologists think of learning as a change in behaviour (or behaviour potential) that meets the following three requirements (Domjan, 1993):

1. The individual now thinks, perceives, or reacts to the environment in a new way.

2. This change is clearly the result of a person's *experiences*—that is, attributable to repetition, study, practice, or the observations the person has made, rather than to hereditary or maturational processes or to physiological damage resulting from injury.

3. The change is relatively permanent. Facts, thoughts, and behaviours that are acquired and immediately forgotten have not really been learned; and temporary changes caused by fatigue, illness, or drugs do not qualify as learned responses.

Let's now consider four fundamental ways in which children learn: habituation, classical conditioning, operant conditioning, and observational learning.

Habituation: Early Evidence of Information Processing and Memory

Earlier, we touched on one very simple and often overlooked form of learning called *habituation*—the process by which we stop attending or responding to a stimulus that is repeated. Habituation can be thought of as learning to become disinterested in stimuli that are recognized as old hat and nothing to get excited about. It can occur even before a baby is born: 27- to 36-week-old fetuses initially become quite active when a vibrator is placed on the mother's abdomen, but soon stop moving (that is, habituate), as if they process these vibrations as a familiar sensation that is no longer worthy of attention (Madison et al., 1986).

How do we know that an infant is not merely fatigued when he or she stops responding to a familiar stimulus? We know because when a baby has habituated to one stimulus, he or she often *dishabituates*—that is, attends to or even reacts vigorously to a slightly different stimulus. Dishabituation, then, indicates that the baby's sensory receptors are not simply tired and that he or she can discriminate the familiar from the unfamiliar.

> **?** **WHAT DO YOU THINK?**
>
> In a debate, your opponent claims that all humans share a uniquely human nervous system that causes them to perceive the world in pretty much the same way. Do you agree? If not, how might you respond to your opponent?

Developmental Trends

Habituation improves dramatically throughout the first year. Infants less than 4 months old may require long exposures to a stimulus before they habituate; by contrast, 5- to 12-month-olds may recognize the same stimulus as familiar after a few seconds of sustained attention and are likely to retain this knowledge for days or even weeks (Fagan, 1984; Richards, 1997). This trend toward rapid habituation is undoubtedly related to the maturation of the sensory areas of the cerebral cortex. As the brain and the senses continue to mature, infants process information faster and detect more about a stimulus during any given exposure (Richards, 1997; Rovee-Collier, 1987).

Individual Differences

Infants reliably differ in the rate at which they habituate. Some are highly efficient information processors: They quickly recognize repetitive sensory inputs and are very slow to forget what they have experienced. Others are less efficient: They require longer expo-

learning
relatively permanent change in behaviour (or behavioural potential) that results from one's experiences or practice

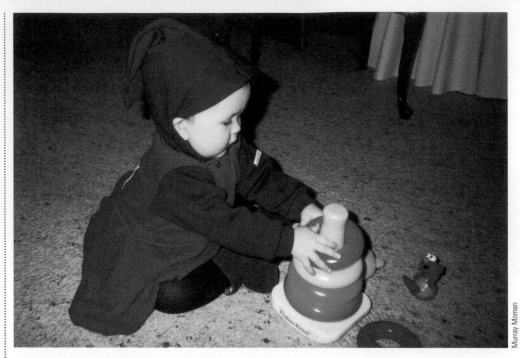

By 6 months of age, infants are quick to discriminate novel objects and events from familiar ones, and once they brand a stimulus as familiar, they may retain this knowledge for months.

sures to brand a stimulus as familiar and may soon forget what they have learned. Might these early individual differences in learning and memory have any implications for later development?

Apparently so. Infants who habituate rapidly during the first 6 to 8 months of life are quicker to understand and use language during the second year (Tamis-LeMonda & Bornstein, 1989) and reliably outscore their slower-habituating age-mates on standardized intelligence tests later in childhood (McCall & Carriger, 1993; Rose & Feldman, 1995). Why? Probably because rate of habituation measures the speed at which information is processed, attention, memory, and preferences for novelty, all of which underlie the complex mental activities and problem-solving skills normally measured on IQ tests (Rose & Feldman, 1995, 1996).

Classical Conditioning

A second way that young children learn is through **classical conditioning**. In classical conditioning, a neutral stimulus that initially has no effect on the child eventually elicits a response of some sort by virtue of its association with a second stimulus that always elicits the response. Russian physiologist Ivan Pavlov originally discovered this form of learning while studying digestive processes in dogs. Specifically, Pavlov noted that his dogs would often salivate at the appearance of the caretaker who had come to feed them. He then speculated that the dogs had probably associated the caretaker (an initially neutral stimulus) with food, a nonneutral stimulus that ordinarily makes dogs salivate (an unlearned, or reflexive, response to food). In other words, salivation at the sight of the caretaker was said to be a learned response that the dogs acquired as they made a connection between the caretaker and the presentation of food.

Pavlov then designed a simple experiment to test his hypothesis. Dogs first listened to a bell, a neutral stimulus in that bells do not ordinarily make them salivate. This neutral stimulus was sounded just before the dogs were fed. Of course, food normally elicits salivation: In the language of classical conditioning, food is an **unconditioned stimulus (UCS)**, and salivation is an unlearned or **unconditioned response (UCR)** to food. After the bell and the food had been paired several times, Pavlov then sounded the bell, with-

classical conditioning
type of learning in which an initially neutral stimulus is repeatedly paired with a meaningful nonneutral stimulus so that the neutral stimulus comes to elicit the response originally made only to the nonneutral stimulus

unconditioned stimulus (UCS)
stimulus that elicits a particular response without any prior learning

unconditioned response (UCR)
unlearned response elicited by an unconditioned stimulus

held the food, and observed that the dogs now salivated to the sound of the bell alone. Clearly, their behaviour had changed as a result of their experiences. In the terminology of classical conditioning, the dogs were now emitting a **conditioned response (CR)**, salivation, to an initially neutral or **conditioned stimulus (CS)**, the bell (see Figure 6.15).

Pavlov also discovered that a classically conditioned response would persist for long periods as long as the CS that elicited it was occasionally paired with the UCS to maintain their association. But if the CS (the bell) was presented alone enough times without being paired with the UCS (food), the CR (salivation) diminished in strength and eventually disappeared—a process known as **extinction**.

Classical Conditioning of Emotions

Although the salivary responses that Pavlov conditioned may seem rather mundane, it is quite likely that every one of us has learned many, many things through classical conditioning, including some of our fears, phobias, and attitudes. Consider the plight of little Albert (Watson & Raynor, 1920), the 11-month-old we met in Chapter 2, who had learned to fear a white rat because every time he reached for it, he heard a loud, startling bang behind him (the experimenter striking a rod with a hammer). In this case, the loud banging noise was the unconditioned stimulus (UCS) because it elicited fearful behaviour (the UCR) without any learning having taken place. And as the noise and the rat (an initially neutral stimulus) were repeatedly paired, Albert soon detected their association, coming to *fear* his furry companion (the CR). By today's standards, this experiment would be considered unethical, but Watson had made his point: Emotional responses can be acquired through classical conditioning.

Of course, classical conditioning may produce favourable attitudes or behavioural responses as well (Staats, 1975). Consider what Mary Cover Jones (1924) found when she tried to treat a young boy's existing phobia through **counterconditioning**—a therapeutic intervention based on classical conditioning procedures. Her patient was a 2-year-old named Peter who, like little Albert, had acquired a strong fear of furry objects. While Peter was eating some of his favourite foods (a UCS for pleasant feelings), he was exposed to a dreaded rabbit (for him, a strong CS for fear). The rabbit was gradually moved closer and closer until (after several sessions) Peter was able to hold it on his lap. Thus, by pairing the rabbit with *pleasurable stimuli*, Jones eliminated Peter's conditioned fear and replaced it with a more desirable response (playing with the rabbit).

Can Newborns Be Classically Conditioned?

Though it is extremely difficult and was once thought impossible, even newborns can be classically conditioned. Lewis Lipsitt and Herbert Kaye (1964), for example, paired

conditioned response (CR) learned response to a stimulus that was not originally capable of producing the response

conditioned stimulus (CS) initially neutral stimulus that comes to elicit a particular response after being paired with a UCS that always elicits the response

extinction gradual weakening and disappearance of a learned response that occurs because the CS is no longer paired with the UCS (in classical conditioning) or the response is no longer reinforced (in operant conditioning)

counterconditioning treatment based on classical conditioning in which the goal is to extinguish an undesirable response and replace it with a new and more adaptive one

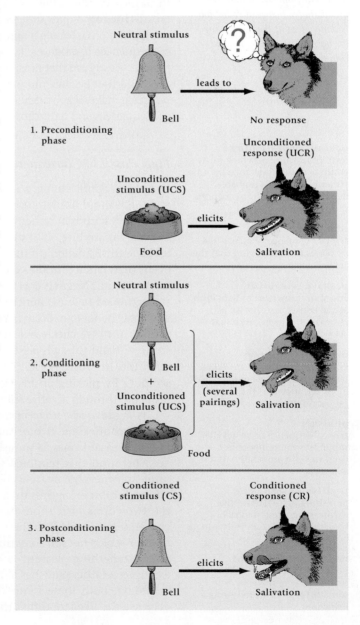

Figure 6.15 *The three phases of classical conditioning. In the preconditioning phase, the unconditioned stimulus (UCS) always elicits an unconditioned response (UCR), whereas the conditioned stimulus (CS) never does. During the conditioning phase, the CS and UCS are paired repeatedly and eventually associated. At this point, the learner passes into the postconditioning phase, in which the CS alone elicits the original response (now called a conditioned response, or CR).*

a neutral tone (the CS) with the presentation of a nipple (a UCS that elicits sucking) to infants 2 to 3 days old. After several of these conditioning trials, the infants began to make sucking motions at the sound of the tone, before the nipple was presented. Clearly, their sucking qualified as a classically conditioned response because it was now elicited by a stimulus (the tone) that does not normally elicit sucking behaviour.

Yet there are important limitations on classical conditioning in the first few weeks of life. Conditioning is likely to be successful only for biologically programmed reflexes, such as sucking, that have survival value. Furthermore, neonates process information very slowly and require more time than an older participant to associate the conditioned and unconditioned stimuli in classical conditioning experiments (Little, Lipsitt, & Rovee-Collier, 1984). But despite these early limitations in information processing, classical conditioning is almost certainly one of the ways in which very young infants recognize that certain events occur together in the natural environment and learn other important lessons, such as that bottles or breasts give milk, or that other people (notably caregivers) signify warmth and comfort.

First haircuts are fearful events for many young children. With gentle treatment from the hairdresser— and perhaps a treat after the job is done—fear of the barbershop (or hair salon) will be lessened by counterconditioning.

Operant (or Instrumental) Conditioning

In classical conditioning, learned responses are *elicited* by a conditioned stimulus. **Operant conditioning** is quite different: The learner first *emits* a response of some sort (that is, *operates* on the environment) and then associates this action with the pleasant or unpleasant consequences it produces. It was B.F. Skinner (1953) who made this form of conditioning famous. He argued that most human behaviours are those we emit voluntarily (that is, *operants*) and that become more or less probable, depending on their consequences. This basic principle makes a good deal of sense. We do tend to repeat behaviours that have favourable consequences and limit those that produce unfavourable outcomes (see Figure 6.16).

Four Possible Consequences of Operant Responses

In operant conditioning, a **reinforcer** is any consequence that *strengthens* a response by making it more likely to occur in the future. If a toddler smiles at his or her father, who then plays with him or her, the playful attention will probably serve as a **positive reinforcer** for smiling, as shown in Figure 6.16. *Positive* here means that something has *added to* this situation (in this case, playful stimulation), so a positive reinforcement is an event that, when introduced following a behaviour, makes that behaviour more probable in the future. **Negative reinforcers** also strengthen behaviours, but the behaviour is strengthened because something unpleasant is *removed* from the situation (or avoided) after the behaviour occurs. We have all been in cars in which an obnoxious buzzer sounds until we buckle our seat belts. The idea here is that "buckling up" will become a stronger habit through *negative reinforcement*; we learn to fasten the belt because this act ends the irritating noise. Similarly, if a child finds that he can prevent an aversive scolding by picking up his crayons after using them, tidying up should become more probable through *negative reinforcement*, avoiding something unpleasant.

Is *negative reinforcement* merely a fancy name for punishment? *No, it is not!* People tend to confuse the two because they generally think of pleasant stimuli as reinforcers and unpleasant ones as punishments. This source or confusion can be overcome if we keep in mind that reinforcers and punishers are defined not by their pleasantness or unpleasantness but by their *effects*: Reinforcers always *strengthen* responses, whereas **punishers** inhibit or *suppress* them. There are actually two forms of punishment that parallel the two forms of reinforcement. **Positive punishment** occurs when an unpleasant consequence is *added* to the situation following a behaviour (as in Figure 6.16 where a mother scolds her son for writing on the wall), whereas **negative punishment** occurs when something pleasant is *removed from* the situation following the behaviour (for example, a father punishes a daughter's hitting by suspending her trip to the movies on Saturday). Both these forms of punishment are intended to suppress behaviours and decrease the likelihood that they will recur.

operant conditioning
form of learning in which freely emitted acts (or operants) become either more or less probable depending on the consequences they produce

reinforcer
any consequence of an act that increases the probability that the act will recur

positive reinforcer
any stimulus whose presentation, as the consequence of an act, increases the probability that the act will recur

negative reinforcer
any stimulus whose removal or termination, as the consequence of an act, increases the probability that the act will recur

punisher
any consequence of an act that suppresses the response and decreases the probability that it will recur

positive punishment
punishing consequence that involves the presentation of something unpleasant following a behaviour

negative punishment
punishing consequence that involves the removal of something pleasant following a behaviour

Figure 6.16
Basic principles of operant conditioning.

Response		Consequence		Result
Child emits a response	which produces →	An outcome or consequence	which →	Affects the likelihood that the response will be repeated

1. Infant smiles when adult enters the room → which produces → Attention and playful gestures from a caregiver → which → Increases the likelihood that the infant will smile again to attract attention

2. Child writes on wall with crayons → which produces → A scolding and banishment to the bedroom → which → Fails to strengthen and will probably suppress the act of writing on the wall

These four possible consequences of a behaviour are summarized in Table 6.3. Which of these outcomes is most likely to encourage desirable habits? Skinner (1953) and other behavioural theorists emphasize the power of reinforcement, particularly *positive* reinforcement. They argue that punishment is less effective at producing desirable changes in behaviour because it merely suppresses ongoing or established responses without really teaching anything new. For example, a toddler who is scolded for grabbing food with his or her hands is likely to stop eating altogether rather than to learn to use a spoon. A much simpler way to promote the use of silverware is to positively reinforce this desirable response with lots of attention and praise (Skinner, 1953).

Operant Conditioning in Infancy

Even babies born prematurely are susceptible to operant conditioning (Thoman & Ingersoll, 1993). However, successful conditioning in very young infants is generally limited to the few biologically significant behaviours (for example, sucking, head turning) that they can control (Rovee-Collier, 1987). Newborns are also very inefficient information processors who learn very slowly. So if you hoped to teach 2-day-old infants to turn their heads to the right and offered them a nippleful of milk every time they did, you would find that they took about 200 trials, on average, to acquire this simple habit (Papousek, 1967). Older infants learn much faster. A 3-month-old requires only about 40 trials to display a conditioned head-turning response, and 5-month-olds acquire this habit in fewer than 30 trials. Apparently, older infants are quicker to associate their

TABLE 6.3   Four Common Consequences of an Operant Behaviour

Julio comes into the TV room and sees his father joking with his sister Rita as the two watch a gymnastics meet. Soon Julio begins to whine, louder and louder, that he wants to use the TV set to play Nintendo. Here are four possible consequences of Julio's whining behaviour.

	Positive stimulus (pleasant)	**Negative stimulus (unpleasant)**
Administered	*Positive reinforcement (strengthens the response)* Dad gives in to the whining and lets Julio use the TV, making whining more likely in the future.	*Positive punishment (weakens the response)* Dad calls Julio a "crybaby," which violates Julio's image of himself as a "big boy" and makes him less inclined to whine in the future.
Withdrawn	*Negative punishment (weakens the response)* Dad confiscates Julio's treasured Nintendo game to discourage such whining in the future.	*Negative reinforcement (strengthens the response)* Dad stops joking with Rita when Julio's whining becomes rather obvious. Since Julio gets jealous when Dad attends to Rita, his whining has enabled him to bring this unpleasant state of affairs to an end (and is thus reinforced).

behaviour (in this case, head turning) with its consequences (a tasty treat)—an advance in information processing that seems to explain infants' increasing susceptibility to operant conditioning over the first few months of life.

CAN INFANTS REMEMBER WHAT THEY HAVE LEARNED? Earlier, we noted that very young infants seem to have very short memories. Minutes after they have habituated to a stimulus, they may begin to respond once again to that stimulus as if they no longer recognize it as familiar. Yet the simple act of recognizing a stimulus as familiar may not be terribly meaningful to a neonate, or even a 2-month-old. Might young infants be better at remembering behaviours they have performed that have proven to be reinforcing in the past?

Yes indeed, and a program of research by Carolyn Rovee-Collier (1995, 1997; Hayne & Rovee-Collier, 1995) makes this point quite clearly. Rovee-Collier's procedure was to place an attractive mobile over the cribs of 2- to 3-month-old infants and to run a ribbon from the mobile to the infants' ankles (see Figure 6.17). Within a matter of minutes, these young participants discovered that they could make the mobile move by kicking their legs, and they took great pleasure in doing so. But would they remember how to make the mobile move a week later? To succeed at this memory task, the infant not only had to *recognize* the mobile but also had to *recall* that it moves and that kicking was the way to get it to move.

The standard procedure for testing an infant's memory was to put the child back in the crib to see whether kicking occurred when he or she saw the mobile. Rovee-Collier and her associates found that 2-month-old infants remembered how to make the mobile move for up to 3 days after the original learning, whereas 3-month-olds recalled this kicking response for more than a week. Clearly, a very young infant's memory is much more impressive than habituation studies would have us believe.

Why do infants eventually forget how to make the mobile move? It is not that their previous learning has been lost, because even *2 to 4 weeks after the original training* infants who were "reminded" of their previous learning by merely seeing the mobile move looked briefly at it and then kicked up a storm as soon as the

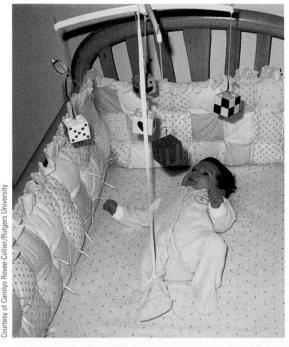

Figure 6.17 When ribbons are attached to their ankles, 2- to 3-month-old infants soon learn to make a mobile move by kicking their legs. But do they remember how to make the mobile move when tested days or weeks after the original learning? These are the questions that Rovee-Collier has explored in her fascinating research on infant memory.

Courtesy of Carolyn Rovee-Collier/Rutgers University

ribbon was attached to their ankles (Rovee-Collier, 1987). By contrast, infants who received no reminder did not try to make the mobile move when given an opportunity. So even 2- to 3-month-old infants can *retain* meaningful information for weeks, if not longer. However, they find it hard to retrieve what they have learned from memory unless they are given explicit reminders. Interestingly, these early memories are highly *context-dependent*: If young infants are not tested under the same conditions in which the original learning occurred (that is, with the same or a highly similar mobile), they show little retention of previously learned responses (Hayne & Rovee-Collier, 1995; Howe & Courage, 1993). So a baby's earliest memories can be relatively fragile.

THE SOCIAL SIGNIFICANCE OF EARLY OPERANT LEARNING. Because even newborns are capable of associating their behaviours with its outcomes, they should soon learn that they can elicit favourable responses from other people. For example, babies may come to display such sociable gestures as smiling or babbling because they discover that those responses often attract attention and affection from caregivers. At the same time, caregivers learn how to elicit favourable reactions from their baby, so that their social interactions gradually become smoother and more satisfying for both the infant and his or her companions. It is fortunate, then, that babies can learn, because in doing so they are likely to become ever more responsive to other people, who, in turn become more responsive to them. As we will see in Chapter 11, these positive reciprocal interactions provide a foundation for the strong emotional attachments that often develop between babies and their closest companions.

Punishment as a Tactic for Controlling Behaviour

Should parents use punishment to suppress their children's undesirable conduct? Most parents occasionally resort to punishment as a control tactic (Hoffman, 1988), and some learning theorists have argued that there is a case to be made for its use, particularly if the prohibited act is something dangerous like playing with matches or probing electrical sockets with metal objects. However, other theorists believe that punishment is a two-edged sword that may prove counterproductive and even harmful in the long run.

Operant theorists are among the strongest critics of punitive controls. They believe that punishment merely suppresses an undesirable response without teaching anything new. They also stress that punishment may engender anger, hostility, or resentment, and, at best, a *temporary* suppression of the behaviour it is designed to eliminate. Finally, they contend that a fear of aversive consequences can never be a totally effective deterrent because the child may simply inhibit unacceptable conduct until it is unlikely to be detected and punished.

Some theorists who adopt an information-processing approach suggest that in some cases where punishment is *properly applied* it can be an effective method of controlling undesirable behaviour. Turn first to Box 6.5, which presents the issue of punishment in Canada and other cultures, as well as some guidelines for using punishment effectively. We will then discuss why these findings make sense from a modern, information-processing perspective.

When researchers first began to study the effects of punishment, they generally favoured a *conditioning viewpoint*. Presumably, punishment produces fear or anxiety, which becomes associated with the punished act. Once this conditioning occurs, the child should resist temptation to repeat the prohibited act, either to avoid the anxiety she has come to associate with it or to avoid further punishment (Parke, 1972). Thus, conditioning theorists viewed punitive suppression as nothing more than a conditioned avoidance response.

The finding that all forms of punishment become more effective when accompanied by a good cognitive rationale, eventually led many researchers to reject the conditioning viewpoint in favour of an *information-processing model* of punishment. Information-processing theorists agree that punishment can make children anxious or emotionally aroused. However, they argue that it is not the amount of anxiety or apprehension that the child experiences that determines whether he or she will inhibit a punished act. Rather, the most critical determinant of a child's future conduct is his or her *interpreta-*

Although operant researchers emphasize the use of positive reinforcement to shape children's conduct, most parents use punishment at least occasionally to suppress undesirable behaviours. In a Canadian study, 72 percent of mothers indicated that they had spanked their preschoolers and over half of these mothers believed that parents should have the right to use physical punishment (Durrant & Rose-Krasnor, 1995). In Sweden, attitudes toward punishment changed following legislation in 1979 that banned corporal punishment, resulting in a decrease in its acceptance and use (Statistics Sweden, 1996).

Further work by Durrant, Rose-Krasnor, and colleagues suggests that cultural influences may affect North Americans' acceptance of corporal punishment (Durrant, Broberg, & Rose-Krasnor, 1999). They argue that physical punishment of children may be supported by a general tolerance of violence, combined with a lack of recognition of children as individuals who have rights of their own. There seems to be some conflict regarding the acceptance of corporal punishment in Canadian society. For example, whereas the Canadian government has signed the UN Convention on Children's Rights, which requires the government to work toward abolishing physical punishment against children, the Canadian Criminal Code still explicitly gives parents and other adults acting as parents the right to hit children (Durrant, Broberg, & Rose-Krasnor, 1999).

Given that corporal punishment has been associated with a variety of negative outcomes in young children, including severe temper tantrums (Needlman, Stevenson, & Zuckerman, 1991), lower compliance (Power & Chapieski, 1986), and aggression toward siblings, peers, and parents (Strassberg et al., 1994; Strauss, Sugarman, & Giles-Sims, 1997; Weiss et al., 1992), alternative techniques are desirable.

For example, parents who explain the consequences of the child's behaviours, firmly enforce age-appropriate rules, consider the child's perspective, clearly communicate expectations, and support the child's positive behaviours have children who are more socially, behaviourally, and academically competent than parents who either use rigid control or are permissive (Baumrind, 1967, 1971).

Other alternatives to physical punishment include taking away desirable things or privileges that the child already has (for example, candy) or would ordinarily receive in the future (a movie next Saturday). "Time out" is an effective procedure in which the adult removes children from the situation in which their misbehaviour is positively reinforced. A boy who thoroughly enjoys dominating his little sister might be sent to a quiet room where he is cut off from the pleasure he receives from his bullying behaviour. When misbehaviour is no longer reinforced, it weakens through extinction.

It is important to reinforce alternative appropriate behaviours. Since punishment alone tells a child what not to do, but not what to do, it makes sense to strengthen acceptable alternatives to the misbehaviour. The parent who does not want a toddler to play with an expensive vase might punish that behaviour but also reinforce play with an unbreakable plastic pot.

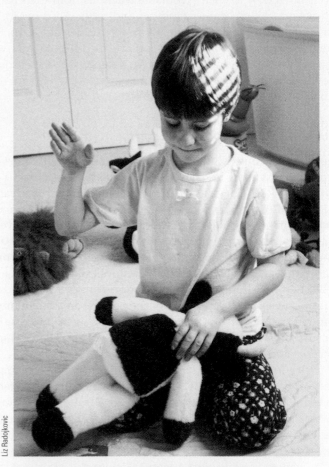

Liz Radojkovic

Improperly applied, physical punishment can have many undesirable side effects, including an increase in the child's aggressiveness.

tion of the uneasiness he or she is experiencing—a cognitive process that depends on the kind of rationale he or she has heard for modifying one's conduct. To illustrate, imagine a child who is given no rationale with her punishment or, alternatively, hears a rationale that focuses his or her attention on negative consequences (for example, "I'll blister your rear if I catch you again"). If this child interprets uneasiness as a fear of getting caught or a fear of the disciplinarian, he or she may well inhibit the punished act in the presence of authority figures but feel quite free to perform it when there is no one else around to detect these antics (see Figure 6.18).

By contrast, a second child who hears rationales specifying why a punished act is wrong and why *he or she* should feel bad for having performed it may be just as upset by the punishment received. But there is different information to process. The child may now feel rather immature and even ashamed for even contemplating this harmful act and thus be *internally* motivated to inhibit it in the future, even when there is no one else around to monitor one's conduct.

In sum, punitive episodes provide children with a rich array of information to process, and it is the child's *interpretation* of this input, rather than the sheer amount of anxiety he or she experiences, that determines the effectiveness of punitive controls (Hoffman, 1988; Parke, 1972).

Observational Learning

The last form of basic learning we will consider is **observational learning**, which results from observing the behaviour of other people. Almost anything can be learned by watching (or listening to) others. For example, a child may learn how to speak a language and tackle math problems, swear, snack between meals, and smoke, by imitating one's parents. As we saw in Chapter 2, observational learning takes centre stage in Albert Bandura's (1977, 1989) social learning theory. Recall that new responses acquired by observation need not be reinforced or even performed before they are learned (review Box 2.2). Instead, this *cognitive* form of learning occurs as the observer attends carefully to the model and constructs *symbolic representations* (for example, images or verbal summaries) of the model's behaviour. These mental symbols are then stored in memory and retrieved later to guide the observer's performance of what he or she has observed.

Of course, successful observational learning not only requires the capacity to imitate others, but also the ability to **encode** a model's behaviour and rely on mental symbols to reproduce what one has witnessed. When do these abilities first emerge?

Newborn Imitation

Researchers once believed that infants were unable to imitate the actions of another person until the latter half of the first year (Piaget, 1951). But beginning in the late 1970s, a number of studies began to report that babies less than 7 days old were apparently able to imitate a number of adult facial gestures, including sticking out their tongues, opening and closing their mouths, protruding their lower lips (as if they were sad), and even displaying happiness (Field et al., 1982; Meltzoff & Moore, 1977). (See also Figure 6.19.)

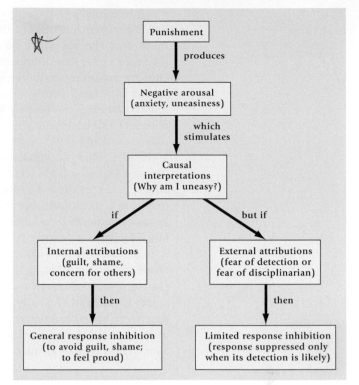

Figure 6.18 *An information-processing model of the suppressive effects of punishment.*

observational learning
learning that results from observing the behaviour of others

encoding
process by which external stimulation is converted to a mental representation

Figure 6.19 *Sample photographs from videotaped recordings of 2- and 3-week-old infants imitating tongue protrusion, mouth opening, and lip protrusion.*

Interestingly, these early imitative displays become much harder to elicit over the first 3 to 4 months of life (Abravanel & Sigafoos, 1984). Some have interpreted this to mean that the neonate's limited capacity for mimicry may be a largely involuntary *reflexive* scheme that disappears with age (as many other reflexes do), only to be replaced later by voluntary imitative responses (Kaitz et al., 1988; Vinter, 1986). Others have argued that these imitative displays are reliably confined only to tongue protrusions and mouth openings, both of which simply reflect an innate releasing mechanism, i.e., the release of a fixed-action pattern (e.g., tongue protrusion) in response to a particular stimulus (Anisfield, 1996; Heimann & Ullstadius, 1999; Heyes, 2001). However, Andrew Meltzoff (1990b) contends that these early expressive displays are *voluntary, imitative* responses because babies will often match an adult's facial expression after a short delay although the model is no longer posing that expression. Meltzoff's view is that neonatal imitation is simply another example of *intermodal* perception, one in which babies match facial movements they can see in the model's face to those they can feel in their own faces (Meltzoff & Moore, 1992). However, critics contend that if neonatal imitation represented an infant's *voluntary* intermodal matching, it should get stronger with age, rather than disappearing (Bjorklund, 2000). So the underlying cause of these early matching facial displays remains a topic of debate, although the innate releasing mechanism hypothesis currently has the most support (Heyes, 2001). But regardless of what we choose to call it, a newborn's responsiveness to facial gestures serves a useful function in that it is likely to warm the hearts of caregivers and help ensure that they and their baby get off to a good start.

deferred imitation
ability to reproduce a modelled activity that has been witnessed at some point in the past

Advances in Imitation and Observational Learning

An infant's capacity to imitate *novel* responses that are not a part of his or her behavioural repertoire becomes much more obvious and more reliable between 8 and 12 months of age (Piaget, 1951). At first, the model must be present and must continue to perform the new response before the child is able to imitate. But by age 9 months, some infants can imitate very simple acts (such as closing a wooden flap) up to 24 hours after they first observe them (Meltzoff, 1988c). This **deferred imitation**—the ability to reproduce the actions of a model at some point in the future—develops rapidly during the second year. By age 14 months, nearly half the infants in one study imitated the simple actions of a *televised* model after a 24-hour delay (Meltzoff, 1988a). And this study probably *underestimates* their imitative capabilities because 12- to 15-month-olds are much more inclined to recall and later imitate the actions of *live* rather than televised models (Barr & Hayne, 1999). Indeed, nearly all the 14-month-olds in one experiment were able to imitate at least three (of six) novel behaviours displayed by a live model *after a delay of one week* (Meltzoff, 1988b). What's more, 2-year-olds are able to reproduce the behaviour of absent models, even when the materials available to them differ somewhat from those that the model used (Herbert & Hayne, 2000).

Clearly, deferred imitation is an important developmental milestone—one indicating that children are not only constructing symbolic representations of their experiences, but can also retrieve this information from memory to guide their reproduction of past events. So 14- to 24-month-olds should now be prepared to learn a great deal by observing the behaviour of their companions. But do they take advantage of this newly acquired ability?

Yes indeed! Leon Kuczynski and his associates (1987) asked mothers to record the immediate and the delayed reactions of their 16- and 29-month-old toddlers to the behaviour

By age 2, toddlers are already acquiring important personal and social skills by imitating the adaptive acts of social models.

Image Source Limited/Index Stock Imagery

of parental and peer models. The results were quite interesting. All the children imitated their models a fair percentage of the time, but there were age differences in the content of these imitations. The 16-month-olds were more inclined to imitate emotional displays, such as laughing and cheering, and other high-intensity antics such as jumping, shaking the head to and fro, and pounding their fists on the table. By contrast, older toddlers more often imitated *instrumental* behaviours, such as household tasks and self-care routines, and their imitations had more of a self-instructional quality to them, as if the older children were now making an active attempt to (1) acquire skills their models had displayed or (2) understand the events they had witnessed. When imitating disciplinary encounters, for example, 16-month-olds simply repeated verbal prohibitions and physical actions such as hand slapping, usually directing these responses to themselves. However, older toddlers tended to reenact the entire scenario, including the social influence strategies the disciplinarian had used, and they usually directed these responses to another person, an animal, or a doll. So not only do older toddlers make use of their imitative capabilities, but it appears that observational learning is already an important means by which they acquire basic personal and social competencies and gain a richer understanding of the routines and regulations that they are expected to follow (see also Want & Harris, 2001).

Finally, elementary-school children become even better at learning from social models because they are less likely than toddlers and preschoolers to rely solely on imagery to represent what they have witnessed. Instead, they *verbally describe* the model's behaviour to themselves, and these verbal codes are much easier to store and retrieve than are visual or auditory images (Bandura, 1989; Coates & Hartup, 1969).

In sum, children can learn any number of new responses by merely attending to others' behaviour and retaining mental representations of what they have witnessed. Because observational learning requires neither formal instruction nor reinforcement, it probably occurs daily, even when models are simply pursuing their own interests and are not trying to teach anything in particular. Bandura (1977, 1986, 1989) reminds us that all developing children learn from a variety of social models and that no two children are exposed to exactly the same set of modelling influences. So children should never be expected to emerge as carbon copies of their parents, their siblings, or the child next door. Individual differences are an inevitable consequence of observational learning.

WHAT DO YOU THINK?

Why is it that after carefully attending to the *same sequence of actions* as they watch their dad open his combination safe, a 10-year-old may quickly succeed at this "safe-cracking" challenge whereas a 4-year-old sibling usually will not?

REFLECTIONS ON PERCEPTION AND LEARNING

Now that we have considered the growth of basic perceptual abilities and the means by which people learn from their experiences, we might reflect for a moment on the issue: Just how important are perception and learning to the process of human development?

Perhaps we can now agree that perceptual development is the growth of *interpretive* skills—a complex process that depends on the maturation of the brain and the sensory receptors, the kinds of sensory experiences the child has available to analyze and interpret, his or her emerging motor skills, and even the social and cultural context in which one is raised. Although we have focused heavily on perceptual growth in this chapter, we should remember that development is a *holistic* enterprise and that a child's maturing perceptual abilities influence all aspects of development. Take intellectual development, for example. As we will see in Chapter 7, Jean Piaget argued that all the intellectual advances of the first two years spring from the infant's sensory and motor activities. How else, Piaget asked, could infants ever come to understand the properties of objects without being able to see, hear, or smell them, fondle them, or pop them into their mouths? How could infants ever use language without first perceiving meaningful regularities in the speech they hear? So Piaget (and many others) claim that perception is central to everything—there is nothing we do (consciously, at least) that is not influenced by our interpretation of the world around us.

Of course, we not only interpret (perceive) the stimuli we encounter; our behaviour changes in response to these experiences. Simply stated, many of the behavioural changes that occur as we develop are the result of learning. We learn not to dwell too long on stimuli that are already familiar (habituation). We may come to like, dislike, or fear almost anything if our encounters with these objects and events have occurred under pleasant or unpleasant circumstances (classical conditioning). We form habits, some good and some bad, by associating various actions with their reinforcing and punishing consequences (operant conditioning). We acquire new attitudes, values, and patterns of conduct by observing the behaviours and listening to the pronouncements of social models (observational learning). Clearly, learning is an important developmental process. And when we recall that even newborns are capable of learning and change in response to their experiences, it is easy to see how behaviourists of the past might have championed learning as the fundamental developmental process—the mechanism by which we become like other human beings and, at the same time, develop our own idiosyncrasies.

Let's also note that human learning is most often an *active cognitive* process. Habituation and observational learning, for example, require participants to actively *attend* to the environment, to *encode* what they have witnessed, and to *retain* this information before showing any evidence of learning. And recall from Box 2.2 that reinforcement (or the promise of reinforcement) may make observers more inclined to *perform* responses that they have already learned by observation, but reinforcement is *not* necessary for this learning to occur in the first place. Even in operant learning, responses are not merely "stamped in" or "stamped out" by their reinforcing or punitive consequences. Instead, children treat reinforcers and punitive events as bits of information that they *interpret* when deciding whether or not to repeat various acts.

In sum, it is important to understand the growth of perceptual skills and the ways in which humans learn because perception and learning are *crucial cognitive foundations* that are truly at the heart of human development.

Concept Check 6.3
Basic Learning Processes

Check your understanding of some basic learning processes by completing the table below. For each vignette, decide what kind of learning is involved and identify the factor or type of consequence (if any) that is responsible for this learning. The answers appear in the Appendix.

Vignette	Kind of learning	Consequence responsible for learning
1. The "Scumbags," a rock group, receive little response from their audience when they play new material. Consequently, they gradually begin to rely on their old "hits," which bring cheers from their fans.	_____	_____
2. Whenever Geri walks her dog, she puts on a yellow jacket. Soon she notices her dog becoming excited whenever he sees this jacket.	_____	_____
3. Having overheard a group of strangers agree that politicians are dishonest, Fred comes to look for the ulterior motive in every statement he hears a politician make.	_____	_____
4. Mosquitoes consistently attack Jo in the outdoors until she applies insect repellent. Eventually, she comes to apply repellent before leaving the house.	_____	_____
5. After a week of work, Jim no longer notices the aromas that seemed so apparent when he first took his job at a bakery.	_____	_____

SUMMARY

Early Controversies about Sensory and Perceptual Development

♦ **Sensation** refers to the detection of sensory stimulation, whereas **perception** is the interpretation of what is sensed. Philosophers and developmentalists have debated whether basic perceptual skills are innate (the *nativist* position) or acquired (the *empiricist* position) and whether perception involves detection of the **distinctive features** of sensory input (**differentiation theory**) or the cognitive embellishment of sensations (**enrichment theory**). Today, most researchers favour an *interactionist* perspective, and many believe that both detection and embellishment of sensory information contribute to perceptual development.

"Making Sense" of the Infant's Sensory and Perceptual Experiences

♦ Researchers have devised several creative methods of persuading infants to tell us what they might be sensing or perceiving. Among the more useful of these approaches are the **preference method**, the **habituation method**, the **method of evoked potentials**, and the **high-amplitude sucking method**.

Infant Sensory Capabilities

♦ Babies sense their environments reasonably well. Newborns can see patterns and colours and can detect changes in brightness. Their **visual acuity** is poor by adult standards but improves rapidly over the first six months. Young infants can hear very well; even newborns can discriminate sounds that differ in loudness, direction, duration, and frequency. They already prefer their mother's voice to that of another woman, and are quite sensitive to **phonemic** contrasts in the speech they hear. Even mild hearing losses, such as those associated with **otitis media**, may have adverse developmental effects. Babies are also born with definite taste preferences, favouring sweet over sour, bitter, or salty substances. They avoid unpleasant smells and soon come to recognize their mothers by odour alone if they are breast-fed. Newborns are also quite sensitive to touch, temperature, and pain.

Visual Perception in Infancy

♦ Visual perception develops rapidly in the first year. For the first two months, babies are "stimulus seekers" who prefer to look at moderately complex, high-contrast targets, particularly those that move. Between 2 and 6 months of age, infants begin to explore visual targets more systematically, become increasingly sensitive to movement, and begin to perceive visual forms and recognize familiar faces. By 9 to 12 months, infants can construct forms from the barest of cues.

♦ Although newborns display some **size constancy**, they lack **stereopsis** and are insensitive to **pictorial cues** to depth; consequently, their spatial perception is immature. By the end of the first month, they are becoming more sensitive to **kinetic cues** and are responding to looming objects (**visual looming**). Their developing sensitivities to binocular cues (by 3 to 5 months) and pictorial cues (at 6 to 7 months), in conjunction with important motor developments and the experiences they provide, help explain why older infants come to fear heights (as on the **visual cliff**) and to make more accurate judgments about size constancy and other spatial relations.

Intermodal Perception

♦ Apparently, the senses are integrated at birth, because neonates look in the direction of sound-producing sources, reach for objects they can see, and expect to see the source of sounds or to feel objects for which they are reaching. As soon as sensory information is readily detectable through two or more senses, infants display **intermodal perception**—the ability to recognize by one sensory modality an object or experience that is already familiar through another modality.

Infant Perception in Perspective—and a Look Ahead

♦ Although infancy is the period when most basic perceptual competencies emerge, much **perceptual learning** occurs later as children continue to explore objects in their environment and to detect distinctive (invariant) features. These finer perceptual discriminations underlie many new competencies, including children's readiness to read.

♦ Cultural influences affect perceptual capabilities. Some of these influences involve losing the ability to attend to and detect sensory input that has little sociocultural significance.

Basic Learning Processes

♦ **Learning** is a relatively permanent change in behaviour that results from experience (repetition, practice, study, or observations) rather than from heredity, maturation, or physiological change resulting from injury.

♦ The simplest form of learning is habituation—a process in which infants come to recognize and cease responding to stimuli that are presented repeatedly. Although habituation may be possible even before birth, this early form of learning improves dramatically over the first few months of life.

♦ In **classical conditioning,** a neutral **conditioned stimulus (CS)** is repeatedly paired with an **unconditioned stimulus (UCS)** that always produces an **unconditioned response (UCR)**. After several such pairings, the CS alone comes to elicit the response, which is now called a **conditioned response (CR)**. Although newborns can be classically conditioned if the UCS and UCR have survival value, they process information very slowly and are less susceptible to this kind of learning than older infants are.

♦ In **operant conditioning**, the subject first emits a response and then associates this action with a particular outcome. **Positive** and **negative reinforcers** are outcomes that increase the probability that a response will be repeated; **positive** and **negative punishments** are outcomes that suppress an act and decrease the likelihood that it will be repeated.

♦ Punishment, properly applied, can be an effective means of suppressing undesirable conduct. Factors that influence the effectiveness of punishment include its timing, intensity, consistency, and underlying rationale and the relationship between the subject and the punitive agent. When applied improperly, punishment may produce a number of undesirable side effects that limit its usefulness.

♦ **Observational learning** occurs as the observer attends to a model and constructs symbolic representations of the model's behaviour. These symbolic codes are then stored in memory and may be retrieved at a later date to guide the child's attempts to imitate the behaviour he or she has witnessed. Infants become better at imitating the novel responses of social models and may even display **deferred imitation** by the end of the first year. Children's capacity for observational learning continues to improve, enabling them to rapidly acquire many new habits by attending to social models.

Reflections on Perception and Learning

♦ It is important to understand the growth of perceptual skills and the ways in which humans learn because perception and learning are fundamental cognitive processes that are central to human development.

KEY TERMS

sensation, 184

perception, 184

enrichment theory, 184

differentiation theory, 184

distinctive features, 184

preference method, 185

habituation, 185

dishabituation, 186

evoked potential, 186

high-amplitude sucking method, 186

visual acuity, 188

visual contrast, 188

phonemes, 189

otitis media, 189

stereopsis, 197

pictorial (perspective) cues, 197

visual looming, 197

size constancy, 198

kinetic cues, 198

visual cliff, 198

intermodal perception, 200

perceptual learning, 203

emergent literacy, 206

learning, 207

classical conditioning, 208

unconditioned stimulus (UCS), 208

unconditioned response (UCR), 208

conditioned response (CR), 209

conditioned stimulus (CS), 209

extinction, 209

counterconditioning, 209

operant conditioning, 210

reinforcer, 210

positive reinforcer, 210

negative reinforcer, 210

punisher, 210

positive punishment, 210

negative punishment, 210

observational learning, 215

encoding, 215

deferred imitation, 216

 You can find further information on the topics covered in this chapter by visiting:

www.developmentalpsych2e.nelson.com

 For additional reading, go to InfoTrac College Edition, your on-line research library, at:

infotrac.thomsonlearning.com

Cognitive Development: Piaget's Theory, Case's Neo-Piagetian Theory, and Vygotsky's Sociocultural Viewpoint

PhotoDisc, Inc.

Piaget's Theory of Cognitive Development

Piaget's Stages of Cognitive Development

An Evaluation of Piaget's Theory

Case's Neo-Piagetian Theory

Vygotsky's Sociocultural Perspective

Summary

TEACHER (TO A CLASS OF 9-YEAR-OLDS): For artwork today, I'd like each of you to draw me a picture of a person who has three eyes.

BILLY: How? Nobody has three eyes!

If you were asked to account for the reaction of this 9-year-old, you might be tempted to conclude that he either lacks imagination or is being sarcastic. Actually, Billy's feelings about the art assignment may be rather typical (see Box 7.4 on page 244) because 9-year-olds think differently than adults do, and they often find it extremely difficult to reflect on hypothetical propositions that have no basis in reality.

Our next three chapters examine the growth of **cognition**—a term psychologists use to refer to the activity of knowing and the mental processes by which human beings acquire and use knowledge to solve problems. The cognitive processes that help us to "understand" and to adapt to the environment include attending, perceiving, learning, thinking, and remembering—in short, the unobservable events and undertakings that characterize the human mind (Bjorklund, 2000).

The study of **cognitive development**—the changes that occur in children's mental skills and abilities over the course of their lives—is one of the more diverse and exciting topics in all of the developmental sciences. In this chapter, we begin our exploration of the developing mind, focusing first on the many important contributions of Swiss psychologist Jean Piaget, who charted what he (and others) believed to be a *universal* pattern of intellectual growth that unfolds during infancy, childhood, and adolescence. We will then examine Robert Case's neo-Piagetian theory, which builds on Piaget's original theories. Finally, we will compare and contrast Piaget's theory with Lev Vygotsky's *sociocultural* viewpoint—a theory that claims that cognitive growth is socially transmitted and heavily influenced by one's culture, and may be nowhere near as universal as Piaget and his followers assumed (Wertsch & Tulviste, 1992).

cognition
the activity of knowing and the processes through which knowledge is acquired

cognitive development
changes that occur in mental activities such as attending, perceiving, learning, thinking, and remembering

Chapter 8 introduces another influential perspective on the developing mind: *information processing*, a viewpoint that arose, in part, from questions left unanswered by Piaget's earlier work. Our attention will then shift to the *psychometric*, or intelligence testing, approach in Chapter 9, where we will discuss the many factors that contribute to individual differences in children's intellectual performance.

PIAGET'S THEORY OF COGNITIVE DEVELOPMENT

You were introduced to Piaget in Chapter 2. By far the most influential theorist in the history of child development, Jean Piaget combined his earlier interests in zoology and *epistemology* (the branch of philosophy concerned with the origins of knowledge) to develop a new science that he termed **genetic epistemology**, the experimental study of the origin of knowledge. (Piaget used the term *genetic* in an older sense, meaning essentially developmental.)

Piaget studied large samples of children through the *clinical method*, a flexible question-and-answer technique he used to discover how children of different ages thought about topics ranging from the rules of games to the laws of physics. Piaget also carefully observed his own three children as infants: how they explored new toys, solved simple problems that he arranged for them, and generally came to understand themselves and their world. From these observations, Piaget formulated his *cognitive-developmental* theory of intellectual growth.

What Is Intelligence?

Piaget's background in zoology is apparent in his definition of **intelligence** as a *basic life function* that helps the organism adapt to its environment. We observe such adaptation as we watch a toddler figure out how to turn on the TV, a school-aged child decide how to divide candies among friends, or an adolescent struggle at solving a tough geometry problem. Piaget proposed that intelligence is "a form of *equilibrium* toward which all cognitive structures tend" (1950, p. 6). His point was simply that all intellectual activity is undertaken with one goal in mind: to produce a balanced, or harmonious, relationship between one's thought processes and the environment (such a balanced state of affairs is called **cognitive equilibrium**, and the process of achieving it is called *equilibration*). Piaget stressed that children are active and curious explorers who are constantly challenged by many novel stimuli and events that are not immediately understood. He believed that these imbalances (or *cognitive disequilibria*) between the children's modes of thinking and environmental events prompt them to make mental adjustments that enable them to cope with puzzling new experiences and thereby restore cognitive equilibrium. So we see that Piaget's view of intelligence is an "interactionist" model that implies that mismatches between one's internal mental schemes (existing knowledge) and the external environment stimulate cognitive activity and intellectual growth.

A very important assumption underlies Piaget's view of intelligence: If children are to know something, they must *construct* that knowledge themselves. Indeed, Piaget described the child as a **constructivist**—an organism that acts on novel objects and events and thereby gains some understanding of their essential features. Children's constructions of reality (that is, interpretations of objects and events) depend on the knowledge available to them at that point in time: The more immature the child's cognitive system, the more limited his or her interpretation of an event. Consider the following example (from Cowan, 1978, p. 11):

genetic epistemology
the experimental study of the development of knowledge, developed by Piaget

intelligence
in Piaget's theory, a basic life function that enables an organism to adapt to its environment

cognitive equilibrium
Piaget's term for the state of affairs in which there is a balanced, or harmonious, relationship between one's thought processes and the environment

constructivist
one who gains knowledge by acting or otherwise operating on objects and events to discover their properties

223

Chapter Seven
*Cognitive Devlopment: Piaget's
Theory, Case's Neo-Piagetian
Theory, and Vygotsky's
Sociocultural Viewpoint*

A four-year-old child and his father are watching the setting sun. "Look Daddy. It's hiding behind the mountain. Why is it going away? Is it angry?" The father grasps the opportunity to explain to his son how the world works. "Well, Mark, the sun doesn't really feel things. And it doesn't really move. It's the earth that's moving. It turns on its axis so that the mountain moves in front of the sun...." The father goes on to other explanations of relative motion, interplanetary bodies, and such. The boy firmly and definitely responds, "But we're not moving. It is. Look, it's going down."

This child is making an important assumption that dominates his attempt at understanding—namely, that the way he sees things must correspond to the way they are. Obviously, it is the sun that is moving, ducking behind the mountain as if it were a live being who was expressing some feeling or serving a definite purpose by hiding. However, the father knows the characteristics that distinguish animate from inanimate objects (and a little about astronomy as well), so that he is able to construct a very different interpretation of the "reality" that he and his son have witnessed.

Cognitive Schemes: The Structure of Intelligence

Piaget used the term **schemes** to describe the models, or mental structures, that we create to represent, organize, and interpret our experiences. A scheme (sometimes called a *schema* in the singular, *schemata* in the plural) is a pattern of thought or action that is similar in some respects to what the layperson calls a strategy or concept. Piaget (1952, 1977) described three kinds of intellectual structures: behavioural (or sensorimotor) schemes, symbolic schemes, and operational schemes.

Behavioural (or Sensorimotor) Schemes

A **behavioural scheme** is an organized pattern of behaviour that the child uses to represent and respond to an object or experience. These are the first intellectual structures to emerge, and for much of the first two years of life, an infant's knowledge of objects and events is limited to that which she can represent through overt actions. So, for a 9-month-old infant, a ball is not conceptualized as a round toy that has a formal name; instead, a ball is simply an object that she and her companions can bounce and roll.

scheme
organized pattern of thought or action that one constructs to interpret some aspect of one's experience (also called *cognitive structure*)

behavioural schemes
organized patterns of behaviour that are used to represent and respond to objects and experiences

symbolic schemes
internal mental symbols (such as images or verbal codes) that one uses to represent aspects of experience

Symbolic Schemes

During the second year, children reach a point at which they can solve problems and think about objects and events without having acted on them. In other words, they are now capable of representing experiences mentally and using these mental symbols, or **symbolic schemes**, to satisfy their objectives. Consider the following observation of the antics of Jacqueline, Piaget's 16-month-old daughter:

> Jacqueline had a visit from a little boy (18 months of age) who, in the course of the afternoon got into a terrible temper. He screamed as he tried to get out of a playpen and pushed it backward, stamping his feet. Jacqueline stood watching him in amazement, never having witnessed such a scene before. The next day, she herself screamed in

Infants develop a broad range of behavioural schemes that they can use to explore and "understand" new objects and to solve simple problems.

her playpen and tried to move, stamping her foot ... several times in succession. (Piaget, 1951, p. 63)

Clearly, Jacqueline was imitating the responses of her absent playmate, even though she had not performed those actions at the time they were modelled. It appears that she must have formed a mental representation, or image, of the boy's tantrum that preserved this scene and guided her later imitation.

Operational Schemes

According to Piaget, the thinking of children aged 7 and older is characterized by *operational schemes*. A **cognitive operation** is an internal mental activity that a person performs to reach a logical conclusion. To illustrate, an 8-year-old who flattens a ball of Play-Doh into a disk is not fooled into thinking that he now has more Play-Doh as a result of spreading it out. Why? Because he can easily *reverse* this transformation in his head, thereby recognizing that the Play-Doh would become the same ball if it were rolled up once again. By contrast, 5-year-olds, who cannot "operate" on their objects of thought, are constrained to make judgments largely on the basis of overt appearances. So if they were to witness the ball-to-disk transformation, they would generally assume that the disk has more dough, because it now covers more area than the ball did. And even though they can imagine (with a little prompting) that the dough can be rolled up again, they do not yet recognize the logical consequences of doing so; that is, they continue to think that there is more dough in the disk.

According to Piaget, the most common cognitive operations are the mental activities implied by mathematical symbols such as +, −, ×, ÷, <, and >. Notice that each of these mental operations is a *reversible* activity (Figure 7.1); mental additions, for example, can quickly be undone by mental subtractions. Piaget believed that these fluid operational abilities permit elementary-school children and adolescents to construct rather elaborate intellectual schemes that enable them to think logically and systematically, first about their actual experiences and eventually about abstract or hypothetical events.

Figure 7.1 *Reversibility is an important cognitive operation that develops during middle childhood.*

How We Gain Knowledge: Piaget's Cognitive Processes

How do children construct and modify their intellectual schemes? Piaget believed that all schemes, all forms of understanding, are created through the workings of two inborn intellectual processes that he called *organization* and *adaptation*.

Organization is the process by which children combine existing schemes into new and more complex intellectual structures. For example, a young infant who has "gazing," "reaching," and "grasping" reflexes soon organizes these initially unrelated schemes into a more complex structure—*visually directed reaching*—that enables her to reach out and discover the characteristics of many interesting objects in the environment. Although intellectual schemes may assume radically different forms at different phases of development, the process of organization is unchanging. Piaget believed that children are constantly organizing whatever schemes they have into more complex and adaptive structures.

The goal of organization is to promote **adaptation**, the process of adjusting to the demands of the environment. According to Piaget, adaptation occurs through two complementary activities: *assimilation* and *accommodation*.

Assimilation is the process by which children try to interpret new experiences in terms of their existing models of the world, the schemes that they already possess. The young child who sees a horse for the first time may try to assimilate it into one of her existing schemes for four-legged animals and thus may think of this creature as a "doggie." In other words, the child is trying to adapt to this novel stimulus by construing it as something familiar.

cognitive operation
internal mental activity that one performs on objects of thought

organization
an inborn tendency to combine and integrate available schemes into coherent systems or bodies of knowledge

adaptation
an inborn tendency to adjust to the demands of the environment

assimilation
Piaget's term for the process by which children interpret new experiences by incorporating them into their existing schemes

TABLE 7.1   A Small Sample of Cognitive Growth from Piaget's Perspective

	Piagetian concept	Definition	Example
Start	Equilibrium	Harmony between one's schemes and one's experience	Toddler who has never seen anything fly but birds thinks that all flying objects are "birdies."
	Assimilation	Tries to adapt to new experience by interpreting it in terms of existing schemes	Seeing an airplane in the sky prompts child to call the flying object a birdie.
	Accommodation	Modifies existing schemes to better account for puzzling new experience	Toddler experiences conflict or disequilibrium upon noticing that the new birdie has no feathers and doesn't flap its wings. Concludes it is not a bird and invents a new name for it (or asks, "What dat?"). Successful accommodation restores equilibrium—for the moment, at least.
Finish	Organization	Rearranges existing schemes into new and more complex structures	Forms hierarchical scheme consisting of a superordinate class (flying objects) and two subordinate classes (birdies and airplanes).

NOTE: As an exercise, you may want to apply Piaget's concept to chart the further elaborations of the child's schemes upon encountering a butterfly and a Frisbee.

However, truly novel objects, events, and experiences may be difficult to interpret in terms of one's existing schemes. For example, our young child may soon notice that this big animal she is labelling a doggie has funny-looking feet and a most peculiar bark, and she may be inclined to seek a better understanding of the observations she has made. **Accommodation**, the complement of assimilation, is the process of modifying existing structures to account for new experiences. So the child who recognizes that a horse is not a dog may invent a name for this new creature or perhaps ask, "What dat?" and adopt the label that her companions use. In doing so, she has modified (accommodated) her scheme for four-legged animals to include a new category of experience—horses.

Piaget believed that assimilation and accommodation work together to promote cognitive growth. They do not always occur equally as in the preceding example, but assimilations of experiences that do not quite jibe with existing schemes eventually introduce cognitive conflict and prompt accommodations to those experiences. And the end result is adaptation, a state of equilibrium between one's cognitive structures and the environment.

Table 7.1 provides one example of how cognitive growth might proceed from Piaget's point of view—a perspective that stresses that cognitive development is an *active* process in which children are regularly seeking and *assimilating* new experiences, *accommodating* their cognitive structures to these experiences, and *organizing* what they know into new and more complex schemes. So two inborn activities—adaptation and organization—make it possible for children to construct progressively greater understandings of the world in which they live.

accommodation
Piaget's term for the process by which children modify their existing schemes in order to incorporate or adapt to new experiences

Concept Check 7.1
Understanding Piagetian Assumptions and Concepts

Check your understanding of some of Piaget's basic assumptions about cognitive development by indicating which of the following terms best describes each of the observations listed below. Choose from the following terms: (a) organization, (b) assimilation, (c) accommodation, (d) reversibility, (e) disequilibrium. The answers appear in the Appendix.

_____ 1. Thinking that objects fall when dropped, Josie is flabbergasted when a helium balloon rises, thus illustrating what Piaget calls _____.

_____ 2. Given a choice, Kai prefers a cookie that has dropped and broken over a whole one, because "Three little cookies are better than one big one." Kai lacks _____.

_____ 3. Josie's construction of an explanation for the fact that helium-filled balloons rise involves the process of _____.

_____ 4. Ten-month-old Sammie lifts a pillow to grab a toy his father has placed there. Sammie's coordination of his "lifting" and "grasping" schemes to achieve his goal is an example of _____.

_____ 5. Freda exclaims, "Oh, look at big kitty cat," upon seeing her first tiger at the circus. Freda's response illustrates _____.

PIAGET'S STAGES OF COGNITIVE DEVELOPMENT

Piaget identified four major periods of cognitive development: the *sensorimotor stage* (birth to 2 years), the *preoperational* stage (2 to 7 years), the stage of *concrete operations* (7 to 11 years), and the stage of *formal operations* (11 years and beyond). These stages of intellectual growth represent *qualitatively* different levels of cognitive functioning and form what Piaget calls an **invariant developmental sequence**; that is, all children progress through the stages in precisely the same order. Piaget further argued that stages can never be skipped because each successive stage builds on the accomplishments of previous stages.

Although Piaget believed that the sequencing of intellectual stages is invariant, he recognized that there are tremendous individual differences in the ages at which children enter or emerge from any particular stage. In fact, his view was that cultural factors and other environmental influences may either accelerate or retard a child's rate of intellectual growth, and he considered the age norms that accompany his stages (and substages) only rough approximations at best.

The Sensorimotor Stage (Birth to 2 Years)

During the **sensorimotor stage**, infants coordinate their *sensory* inputs and *motor* capabilities, forming behavioural schemes that permit them to "act on" and to get to "know" their environment. How much can they really understand by relying on overt actions to generate knowledge? More than you might imagine. During the first two years, infants develop from *reflexive* creatures with very limited knowledge into planful problem solvers who have already learned a great deal about themselves, their close companions, and the objects and events in their everyday world. So drastic is the infant's cognitive growth that Piaget divided the sensorimotor period into six substages that describe the child's gradual transition from a *reflexive* to a *reflective* being (see Table 7.2 on page 231). Our review will focus on three important aspects of sensorimotor development: *problem-solving skills* (or means/ends activities), *imitation*, and the growth of the *object concept*.

Development of Problem-Solving Skills

REFLEX ACTIVITY. Piaget characterized the first month of life as a stage of **reflex activity**—a period when an infant's actions are pretty much confined to exercising innate reflexes, assimilating new objects into these reflexive schemes (for example, sucking on blankets and toys as well as on nipples), and accommodating their reflexes to these novel objects. Granted, this is not high intellect, but these primitive adaptations represent the beginning of cognitive growth.

PRIMARY CIRCULAR REACTIONS (1–4 MONTHS). The first nonreflexive schemes emerge at 1 to 4 months of age as infants discover by chance that various responses that they can emit and control (for example, sucking their thumbs, making cooing sounds) are satisfying and, thus, worthy of repetition. These simple repetitive acts, called **primary circular reactions**, are always centred on the infant's own body. They are called "primary" because they are the first motor habits to appear, and "circular" because they are repetitive.

SECONDARY CIRCULAR REACTIONS (4–8 MONTHS). Between 4 and 8 months of age, infants are discovering (again by chance) that they can make interesting things happen to objects beyond their own bodies, such as making a rubber duck quack by squeezing it.

AN INFANT ACCOMMODATING HIS MOUTH TO THE SHAPE OF AN OBJECT

invariant developmental sequence
series of developments that occur in one particular order because each development in the sequence is a prerequisite for those appearing later

sensorimotor stage
Piaget's first intellectual stage, from birth to 2 years, when infants are relying on behavioural schemes as a means of exploring and understanding the environment

reflex activity
first substage of Piaget's sensorimotor stage; infants' actions are confined to exercising innate reflexes, assimilating new objects into these reflexive schemes, and accommodating their reflexes to these novel objects

primary circular reactions
second substage of Piaget's sensorimotor stage; a pleasurable response, centred on the infant's own body, that is discovered by chance and performed over and over.

These new schemes, called **secondary circular reactions**, are also repeated for the pleasure they bring. According to Piaget, 4- to 8-month-olds' sudden interest in external objects indicates that they have begun to differentiate themselves from objects they can control in the surrounding environment.

Is an infant who delights in such repetitive actions as swatting a brightly coloured mobile or making a toy duck quack engaging in *planful* or *intentional* behaviour? Piaget said no: The secondary circular reaction is not a fully intentional response, because the interesting result it produces was discovered by chance and was not a purposeful goal the first time the action was performed.

Coordination of Secondary Schemes (8–12 Months).

Truly planful responding first appears between 8 and 12 months of age, during the substage of the **coordination of secondary circular reactions**, as infants begin to coordinate two or more actions to achieve simple objectives. For example, if you were to place an attractive toy under a cushion, a 9-month-old might lift the cushion with one hand while using the other to grab the toy. In this case, the act of lifting the cushion is not a pleasurable response in itself, *nor is it emitted by chance*. Rather, it is part of a larger *intentional* scheme in which two initially unrelated responses—lifting and grasping—are coordinated as *a means to an end*. Piaget believed that these simple coordinations of secondary schemes represent the earliest form of *goal-directed behaviour*, and thus true problem solving.

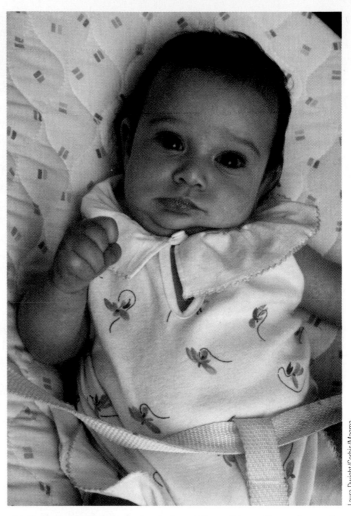

Laura Dwight/Corbis/Magma

Blowing bubbles is an accommodation of the sucking reflex and one of the infant's earliest primary circular reactions.

Tertiary Circular Reactions (12–18 Months).

Between 12 and 18 months of age, toddlers begin to actively experiment with objects and try to invent new methods of solving problems or reproducing interesting results. For example, an infant who had originally squeezed a rubber duck to make it quack may now decide to drop it, step on it, and crush it with a pillow to see whether these actions have the same or different effects on the toy. Or she may learn from her explorations that flinging is more efficient than spitting as a means of getting food to stick to the wall. Although parents may be less than thrilled by this exciting new cognitive advance, these trial-and-error exploratory schemes, called **tertiary circular reactions**, reflect an infant's active *curiosity*—her strong motivation to learn about the way things work.

Symbolic Problem Solving (18–24 Months).

The crowning achievement of the sensorimotor stage occurs as toddlers begin to internalize their behavioural schemes to construct mental symbols, or images, that they can then use to guide future conduct. Now the infant can experiment *mentally* and may show a kind of "insight" as to how to solve a problem. Piaget's son Laurent nicely illustrates this symbolic problem solving, or **inner experimentation**:

> Laurent is seated before a table and I place a bread crust in front of him, out of reach. Also, to the right ... I place a stick, about 25 cm. long. At first, Laurent tries to grasp the bread ... and then he gives up.... Laurent again looks at the bread, and without moving, looks very briefly at the stick, then suddenly grasps it and directs it toward the bread ... [he then] draws the bread to him. (Piaget, 1952, p. 335)

secondary circular reactions
third substage of Piaget's sensorimotor stage; a pleasurable response, centred on an external object, that is discovered by chance and performed over and over

coordination of secondary circular reactions
fourth substage of Piaget's sensorimotor stage; infants begin to coordinate two or more actions to achieve simple objectives

tertiary circular reactions
fifth substage of Piaget's sensorimotor stage; an exploratory scheme in which the infant devises a new method of acting on objects to reproduce interesting results

inner experimentation
in the sixth substage of Piaget's sensorimotor stage, the ability to solve simple problems on a mental, or symbolic, level without having to rely on trial-and-error experimentation

Clearly, this is not trial-and-error experimentation. Instead, Laurent's problem solving occurred at an internal, symbolic level as he visualized the stick being used as an extension of his arm to obtain a distant object.

Development of Imitation

Piaget recognized the adaptive significance of imitation, and he was very interested in its development. His own observations led him to believe that infants are incapable of imitating *novel* responses displayed by a model until 8 to 12 months of age (the same age at which they show some evidence of intentionality in their behaviour). However, the imitative schemes of infants this young are rather imprecise. Were you to bend and straighten your finger, the infant might mimic you by opening and closing her entire hand (Piaget, 1951). Indeed, precise imitations of even the simplest responses may take days (or even weeks) of practice (Kaye & Marcus, 1981), and literally hundreds of demonstrations may be required before an 8- to 12-month-old will catch on and begin to enjoy sensorimotor games such as peekaboo or pat-a-cake.

Voluntary imitation becomes much more precise at age 12 to 18 months, as we see in the following example:

> At [1 year and 16 days of age, Jacqueline] discovered her forehead. When I touched the middle of mine, she first rubbed her eye, then felt above it and touched her hair, after which she brought her hand down a little and finally put her finger on her forehead. (Piaget, 1951, p. 56)

According to Piaget, **deferred imitation**—the ability to reproduce the behaviour of an *absent* model—first appears at 18 to 24 months of age. When discussing symbolic schemes, we noted an example of deferred imitation—Jacqueline's reproduction of her playmate's temper tantrum 24 hours later. Piaget believed that older infants are capable of deferred imitation because they can now construct mental symbols, or images, of a model's behaviour that are stored in memory and retrieved later to guide the child's re-creation of the modelled sequence.

Other investigators disagree with Piaget, arguing that deferred imitation, and thus symbolic representation, begins much earlier. For example, researchers have found that 9-month-olds are able to imitate very simple acts (for example, button-pressing to activate a noise-making toy) days after observing them (Carver & Bauer, 1999; Meltzoff, 1988c), and toddlers have been shown to imitate particularly memorable events up to 12 months after first witnessing them (Bauer & Wewerka, 1995; Mandler & McDonough, 1995; Meltzoff, 1995b). So a capacity for deferred imitation—imitation requiring the infant to construct, store, and then retrieve mental symbols—is present much earlier than Piaget thought (Schneider & Bjorklund, 1998).

Development of Object Permanence

One of the more notable achievements of the sensorimotor period is the development of **object permanence**—the idea that objects continue to exist when they are no longer visible or detectable through the other senses. If you removed your watch and covered it with a mug, you would still be aware that the watch continues to exist. But because very young infants rely so heavily on their senses and their motor skills to "understand" an object, they seem to operate as if objects exist only if they can be sensed or acted upon. Indeed, Piaget (1954) and others have found that 1- to 4-month-olds will not search for attractive objects that are hidden from view. If a watch that interests them is covered by a mug, they soon lose interest, almost as if they believe that the watch no longer exists or has been transformed into a mug. At age 4 to 8 months, infants will retrieve toys that are partially concealed or placed beneath a semitransparent cover; but their continuing failure to search for objects that are *completely* concealed suggested to Piaget that, from the infant's perspective, disappearing objects no longer exist.

Clearer signs of an emerging object concept appear by 8 to 12 months of age. However, object permanence is far from complete, as we see in Piaget's demonstration with his 10-month-old daughter:

deferred imitation
ability to reproduce a modelled activity that has been witnessed at some point in the past

object permanence
realization that objects continue to exist when they are no longer visible or detectable through the other senses

Jacqueline is seated on a mattress without anything to ... distract her ... I take her [toy] parrot from her hands and hide it twice ... under the mattress, on her left [point A]. Both times Jacqueline looks for the object immediately and grabs it. Then I take it from her hands and move it very slowly *before her eyes* to the corresponding place on her right, under the mattress [point B]. Jacqueline watches this movement ... but at the moment when the parrot disappears [at point B] she turns to her left and looks where it was before [at point A]. (1954, p. 51; italics added)

Jacqueline's response is typical of 8- to 12-month-olds, who will search for a hidden object *where they found it previously* rather than where they saw it last (Marcovitch & Zelazo, 1999). Piaget's account of this **A-not-B error** was straightforward: Jacqueline acted as if her *behaviour* determines where the object will be found; consequently, she does not treat the object as if it exists independent of her own activity.

Between 12 and 18 months of age, the object concept improves. Toddlers now track the visible movements of objects and search

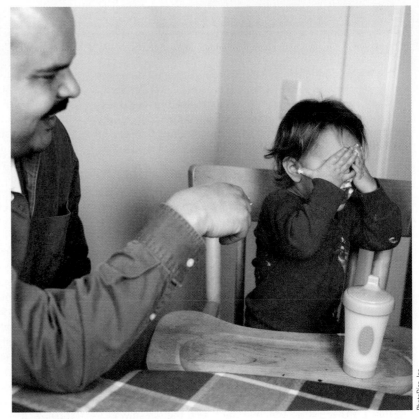

Playing peekaboo is an exciting activity for infants who are acquiring object permanence.

for them *where they were last seen*. However, object permanence is not complete, because the child cannot make the mental inferences necessary to understand *invisible displacements*. So if you conceal a toy in your hand, put your hand behind a barrier and deposit the toy there, remove your hand, and then ask the child to find the toy, 12- to 18-month-olds will search *where the toy was last seen*—in your hand—rather than looking behind the barrier.

By 18 to 24 months of age, toddlers are capable of *mentally representing* such invisible displacements and using these mental inferences to guide their search for objects that have disappeared. At this point, they fully understand that objects have a "permanence" about them and take great pride at locating their objectives in sophisticated games of hide and seek.

Challenges to Piaget's Account of Sensorimotor Development: Neo-Nativism and "Theory" Theories

Piaget was an amazing observer of infants, and at the level of describing the kinds of infant problem solving that most people (including parents) actually see, Piaget's account of infant development is generally accurate, although somewhat incomplete (Bjorklund, 2000). (See Table 7.2 for a summary and some updates.) Yet Piaget generally underestimated infants' cognitive capabilities, and many researchers today believe that new theories are needed to completely capture the richness of infant intelligence.

NEO-NATIVISM. The most articulate criticism of Piaget's infancy theory comes from **neo-nativism**. *Neo-nativists* are theorists who believe that infants are born with substantial knowledge about the nature of the physical world (Gelman & Williams, 1998; Mandler, 1998; Spelke & Newport, 1998). This perspective is nicely illustrated by the work of Renee Baillargeon (1987), described in Box 7.1, which suggests that infants know something about the permanency of objects very early on; such knowledge does not have to be "constructed" as Piaget proposed, but is part of an infant's genetic heritage. This does not mean that there is no development or that no experience is necessary for the mature

A-not-B error
tendency of 8- to 12-month-olds to search for a hidden object where they previously found it even after they have seen it moved to a new location

neo-nativism
idea that much cognitive knowledge, such as the object concept, is innate, requiring little in the way of specific experiences to be expressed, and that there are biological constraints in that the mind/brain is designed to process certain types of information in certain ways

Do young infants really believe that vanishing objects cease to exist? Renee Baillargeon (1987) doubts it, and her research illustrates a theme that has been echoed by many contemporary researchers: Young infants know more about objects than Piaget claimed they did; in fact, they may never be totally ignorant about the permanence of objects.

The trick in demonstrating what very young infants know is to conduct tests appropriate to their developmental level. Unfortunately, 3- to 4-month-old infants have limited motor skills, so their inability to search for things (Piaget's tests) really says very little about their knowledge of objects.

Baillargeon (1987; Baillargeon & De Vos, 1991) used the habituation/dishabituation paradigm to assess what 3½- to 4½-month-old infants may know about objects and their properties. Baillargeon (1987) first habituated each infant to a screen that moved 180°, from being flat with its leading edge facing the infant, rising continuously through an arc until it rested in the box with its leading edge farthest away from the infant (see panel [a] of figure). Once habituated to this event, infants were shown a colourful wooden block with a clown face painted on it, placed to the rear of the flat screen. (Actually, the block was an illusion created by a mirror.) Then, as illustrated in the figure, the screen was rotated to produce either a possible event (the screen would stop as if stopped by the block, see panel [b]), or an impossible event (the screen rotated 180°, passing through the block, see panel [c]). Baillargeon reasoned that if babies thought the block still existed, even when hidden by the screen, they would stare longer at the screen and be more surprised when it appeared to pass through the solid block (impossible event) than when it bumped the block and stopped its forward motion (possible event). That is exactly what most of the 4½-month-old and many of the 3½-month-old infants did, taking great interest in the impossible event.

Infants' performance in the "impossible event" condition reflects not only a knowledge of the permanence of objects, but also a knowledge that one solid object cannot pass through another. Elizabeth Spelke (1991; Spelke et al., 1992) has similarly demonstrated in a series of experiments that infants as young as 2½ months of age have a knowledge of the solidity and the continuity of objects (the fact that a moving object continues on its path); and more recent research by Baillargeon and her colleagues has illustrated young infants' understanding of support (an object must be supported or it falls), collisions (an object that is hit by another object moves) (Baillargeon, Kotovsky, & Needham, 1995), and containment (a larger object cannot fit into a smaller object) (Aguiar & Baillargeon, 1998).

It was once thought that memory deficits explained the *A-not-B error* that 8- to 12-month-olds display. But we know now that infants this old have reasonably good memories and are actually quite surprised if a hidden object turns out *not* to be where they have last seen it (at point B) (Baillargeon & Graber, 1988). So 8- to 12-month-olds who commit A-not-B errors will often remember that an object has been hidden at new location B; what they may lack is the ability to *inhibit* the tendency to search where they have previously found the object. Indeed, Adele Diamond (1985) claims that some infants who search inappropriately for hidden objects at point A hardly look there at all, as if they realize this is not the right place to search but simply cannot stop themselves. Diamond (1985) tested 25 infants in the A-not-B task, beginning at about 7½ months and continuing until 12 months of age. She reported that the delay between hiding and searching that was necessary to produce an A-not-B error increased with age at a rate of about 2 seconds per month. That is, 7½-month-old infants searched for the hidden object at the erroneous A position after only a 2-second delay. By 12 months of age, infants made the error only if 10 seconds had passed between the hiding of the object and the beginning of the search.

Based on these and other data, Diamond (1991, 1995) believes that maturational changes in the frontal lobes of the cerebral cortex during the second six months of life permit infants to gain more control over their motor responses, thus allowing them to inhibit an impulse to search for hidden objects at locations they know are incorrect. And she may be right. Using the evoked-potential method, Martha Bell and Nathan Fox (1992) found that 7- to 12-month-olds who *avoid* making A-not-B errors show far more frontal lobe electrical activity while performing the task than their age-mates who search less appropriately.

Though we've considered only a portion of the evidence, it is clear that Piaget's reliance on active search procedures caused him (1) to badly underestimate what very young infants know about objects and (2) to misinterpret why infants display the A-not-B error.

(a) Habituation event

(b) Possible event

(c) Impossible event

Representations of the habituation stimulus and the possible and impossible events shown to young infants in Baillargeon's (1987) experiment. Babies took great interest in the "impossible" event, thus suggesting that they knew that the box continues to exist and that the screen shouldn't have passed through it. BASED ON BAILLARGEON, 1987.

expression of an ability, but rather that babies enter the world with substantial knowledge and are prepared by evolution to make sense of certain aspects of their physical world (such as the permanency of objects or, as we learned in Box 6.3, size constancy).

Similarly, others argue that from the very earliest months of life, infants are symbolic beings, a perspective that is very different from Piaget's viewpoint (Meltzoff, 1990b). Research on deferred imitation (and neonatal imitation discussed in Chapter 6) is consistent with this position, and caused Andrew Meltzoff (1990b, p. 20) to argue that "in a very real sense, there may be no such thing as a purely 'sensorimotor period' in the normal human infant."

The early display of symbolic ability is illustrated in innovative research by Karen Wynn (1992), who used techniques similar to those of Baillargeon (1987) presented in Box 7.1 to assess simple *arithmetic* judgments in infants. In Wynn's experiment, 5-month-old infants were shown a sequence of events that involved the addition or subtraction of elements. Two of these sequences are shown in Figure 7.2. One sequence (the "possible outcome") led to the conclusion that 1 + 1 = 2; the other sequence (the "impossible outcome") led to the conclusion that 1 + 1 = 1. If infants have some primitive concept of addition, they should be surprised and thus spend more time looking at the "impossible outcome." This was exactly what occurred, both for the addition problem shown in Figure 7.2 and for a simple subtraction problem (2 – 1 = 1), and these findings have now been replicated by other researchers (Simon, Hespos, & Rochat, 1995; Uller et al., 1999).

Notice that infants are not simply making a perceptual discrimination between two arrays (that is, telling the difference between an array with one item in it and another with two). Rather, when they watch as one item is added to another behind a screen, they *expect* to see two items when the screen is dropped. This requires a certain level of object permanence and memory, but also some rudimentary ideas about addition. They must infer that the second object was added to the first, without actually seeing that this was done (recall that the screen blocked their vision). This line of work suggests that even 5-month-olds have much more quantitative (symbolic) knowledge than Piaget proposed, although it does not establish that babies are born knowing basic arithmetic or that infants and toddlers should be able to learn complicated mathematics.

231

Chapter Seven
Cognitive Devlopment: Piaget's Theory, Case's Neo-Piagetian Theory, and Vygotsky's Sociocultural Viewpoint

TABLE 7.2	Summary of Piaget's Account of Sensorimotor Development		
Substage	**Methods of solving problems or producing interesting outcomes**	**Imitation**	**Object concept**
1. Reflex activity (0–1 month)	Exercising and accommodation of inborn reflexes	Some reflective imitation of motor responses[1]	Tracks moving object but ignores its disappearance
2. Primary circular reactions (1–4 months)	Repeating interesting acts that are centred on one's own body	Repetition of own behaviour that is mimicked by a companion	Looks intently at the spot where an object disappeared[2]
3. Secondary circular reactions (4–8 months)	Repeating interesting acts that are directed toward external objects	Same as in substage 2	Searches for partly concealed object
4. Coordination of secondary schemes (8–12 months)	Combining actions to solve simple problems (first evidence of intentionality)	Gradual imitation of novel responses; deferred imitation of very simple motor acts after a brief delay	Clear signs of emerging object concept; searches for and finds concealed object that has not been visibly displaced
5. Tertiary circular reactions (12–18 months)	Experimenting to find new ways to solve problems or reproduce interesting outcomes	Systematic imitation of novel responses; deferred imitation of simple motor acts after a long delay	Searches for and finds object that has been *visibly* displaced
6. Invention of new means through mental combinations (18–24 months)	First evidence of insight as the child solves problems at an internal, symbolic level	Deferred imitation of complex behavioural sequences	Object concept is complete; searches for and finds objects that have been hidden through *invisible* displacements

[1]Imitation of simple motor acts (such as tongue protrusions, head movements, and the opening and closing of one's lips or hands) is apparently an inborn, reflexlike ability that bears little relation to the voluntary imitation that appears later in the first year.

[2]Many researchers now believe that object permanence may be present very early and that Piaget's reliance on search procedures badly underestimated what young infants know about objects (see Box 7.1).

1. Object placed in case   2. Screen comes up   3. Second object added   4. Hand leaves empty

Then either possible outcome ...   or impossible outcome
5. Screen drops ...   ... revealing 2 objects   5. Screen drops ...   ... revealing 1 object

Figure 7.2 *Sequence of events for the 1 + 1 = 2 (possible) outcome and the 1 + 1 = 1 (impossible) outcome from the experiment by Wynn (1992). FROM BJORKLUND, 2000.*

Neo-nativism theory, however, has recently come under criticism. For example, a number of theorists argue that there are simpler explanations for many of the results in nativist experiments (see Cohen & Cashon, 2003). According to Bogartz, Shinskey, and Schilling (2000) and Cashon and Cohen (2000), infants look longer at the "impossible" event (see Baillargeon's study in Box 7.1) because of a novelty and familiarity preference, not because the event was impossible. In fact, these authors suggest that findings reported by neo-nativists should not be interpreted as evidence for object permanence.

"THEORY" THEORIES. There are other theorists who concede that infants come into the world with more knowledge than Piaget proposed, but also believe that, beyond the very early stages of sensorimotor development, Piaget's constructivist account is generally close to the truth. These are the *"theory" theorists*, who combine aspects of neo-nativism with Piagetian constructivism (Gopnik & Meltzoff, 1997; Karmiloff-Smith, 1992). The basic idea behind **"theory" theories** is that infants are prepared from birth to make sense of certain classes of information (about objects and speech sounds, for example), much as neo-nativists propose; but that such innate knowledge is incomplete and requires substantial experience for infants to *construct* reality, much as Piaget proposed. Infants do this by devising ideas, or "theories," about how the world works and then testing and modifying their theories, much as scientists do, until their mental models resemble the way the world is structured. Developmental change is similar to that described by Piaget. According to Alison Gopnik and Andrew Meltzoff (1997, p. 63), "We will typically see a pattern in which the child holds to a particular set of predictions and interpretations for some time; the child has a particular theory. Then we may expect a period of disorganization, in which the theory is in crisis. And finally, we should see a new, equally coherent and stable theory emerge." This is reminiscent of Piaget's concept of equilibration.

Why, then, do infant "theorists" from diverse cultural backgrounds construct very *similar* theories about the physical (and early social) realities over the first two years? "Theory" theorists answer by noting that all infants start life with the same inborn knowledge. They then construct similar theories early on because they have so many similar experiences to adapt to, at about the same ages, throughout infancy and toddlerhood.

"theory" theories
theories of cognitive development that combine neo-nativism and constructivism, proposing that cognitive development progresses by children generating, testing, and changing theories about the physical and social world

Summing Up

Piaget's theory of infant cognitive development has been one of the most influential ever proposed. It uncovered previously unknown phenomena (for example, object permanence) and generated nearly a century of research. However, it has become obvious in recent decades that new theories are necessary to account for the very rich cognitive abilities that infants have been shown to possess. Yet as new research accumulates, it has also become clear that we do not want to throw out Piaget with the baby's bath water. Many of Piaget's ideas, particularly *constructivism*, have been shown to have staying power and have been incorporated into newer theories of infant development.

233

Chapter Seven
Cognitive Devlopment: Piaget's Theory, Case's Neo-Piagetian Theory, and Vygotsky's Sociocultural Viewpoint

The Preoperational Stage (2 to 7 Years)

As children enter Piaget's **preoperational stage**, we see a drastic increase in their use of mental symbols (words and images) to represent the objects and events they encounter. Basically, a *symbol* is something that stands for something else, as the word "dog" stands for a four-legged, medium-size, domesticated mammal. Judy DeLoache (1987, 2000) has referred to the knowledge that an entity can stand for something other than itself as **representational insight**.

The most obvious evidence of symbol use for Piaget was language. Other examples of symbol use in young children are deferred imitation, drawing, mental imagery, and symbolic play (for example, pretending a shoe is a telephone, or feeding imaginary cereal to a doll). Each of these forms of symbolism is available to most 2-year-olds, although how they use these symbols improves substantially over the next 10 to 12 years.

But despite this important new strength, Piaget's descriptions of preoperational intelligence focus mainly on the limitations, or deficiencies, in children's thinking. Indeed, he calls this period "preoperational" because he believed that preschool children have not yet acquired the operational schemes that enable them to think logically.

Piaget divided the preoperational period into two substages: the *preconceptual period* (2 to 4 years of age) and the *intuitive period* (4 to 7 years).

The Preconceptual Period

EMERGENCE OF SYMBOLIC THOUGHT. The **preconceptual period** is marked by the appearance of the **symbolic function**: the ability to make one thing, such as a word or an object, stand for, or represent, something else. This transition from the curious hands-on-everything toddler to the contemplative, symbolic preschool child is remarkable indeed. Consider, for example, that because 2- to 3-year-olds can use words and images to represent their experiences, they are now quite capable of reconstructing the past and thinking about or even comparing objects that are no longer present. And just how much does the ability to construct mental symbols transform a child's thinking? David Bjorklund (2000) answers by noting that the average, symbolic 3-year-old probably has more in common intellectually with a 21-year-old adult than with a 12-month-old

preoperational stage
Piaget's second stage of cognitive development, lasting from about age 2 to age 7, when children think at a symbolic level but do not yet use cognitive operations

representational insight
knowledge that an entity can stand for (represent) something other than itself

preconceptual period
early substage of preoperations, from age 2 to age 4, characterized by the appearance of primitive ideas, concepts, and methods of reasoning

symbolic function
ability to use symbols (for example, images and words) to represent objects and experiences

Concept Check 7.2
Understanding Infant Intelligence

Check your understanding of Piaget's work and the viewpoint of more recent theorists by matching each of the following activities/theoretical viewpoints with one of the following descriptive statements below. Choose from the following terms: (a) primary circular reaction; (b) secondary circular reaction; (c) tertiary circular reaction; (d) inner experimentation; (e) deferred imitation; (f) A-not-B error; (g) Piaget; (h) neo-nativist theorists; (i) "theory" theorists. The answers appear in the Appendix.

_____ 1. According to _____, all knowledge is constructed.

_____ 2. According to _____, much basic knowledge is inborn rather than constructed.

_____ 3. Billy delights at bouncing a ball over and over.

_____ 4. After seeing his brother throw a ball behind the sofa, Sammy looks for it in his toy box.

_____ 5. Juanita repeatedly coos to herself when placed in her crib after a feeding.

_____ 6. According to _____, some basic knowledge is inborn but is further elaborated with experience.

_____ 7. When her Dad finishes shaving and leaves the room, Ruth picks up his razor and tries to shave.

_____ 8. Seeing a duster on the couch, Susan assumes that she can use it to reach her balloon atop the bookcase.

_____ 9. Chang delights at discovering which foods fly farthest when he uses a chopstick to fling them.

infant. Although a 3-year-old's thinking will change in many ways over the next several years, it is similar to an adult's in that both preschool children and adults think by manipulating mental symbols.

Language is perhaps the most obvious form of symbolism that young children display. Although most infants utter their first meaningful word by the end of the first year, it is not until about 18 months of age—the point at which they show other signs of symbolism such as inner experimentation—that they combine two (or more) words to form simple sentences. Does the use of language promote cognitive development? Piaget says no, arguing instead that language merely reflects what the child *already knows* and contributes little to new knowledge. In other words, he believed that cognitive development promotes language development, not vice versa. (As we will see later in the chapter, Lev Vygotsky strongly disagrees with Piaget on this point.)

A second major hallmark of the early preconceptual period is the blossoming of **symbolic (or pretend) play**. Toddlers often pretend to be people they are not (mommies, superheroes), and they may play these roles with props such as a shoe box or a stick that symbolize other role-relevant objects such as a baby's crib or a gun. Although some parents are concerned when their preschool children immerse themselves in a world of make-believe and begin to invent imaginary playmates, Piaget felt that these are basically healthy activities, a viewpoint held by contemporary researchers (Gleason, Sebanc, & Hartup, 2000). In Box 7.2, we focus briefly on children's play and see how these "pretend" activities may contribute in a positive way to the child's social, emotional, and intellectual development.

NEW VIEWS ON SYMBOLISM. Piaget's emphasis on the symbolic nature of preoperational children's thought has captured the attention of developmentalists. Judy DeLoache and her colleagues, for example, have explored preschool children's abilities to use scale models and pictures as symbols (DeLoache, 1987, 2000; Uttal, Schreiber, & DeLoache, 1995). In DeLoache's studies, children are asked to find a toy hidden in a room. Before searching for the toys, children are shown a scale model of the room, with the experimenter hiding a miniature toy (Snoopy) behind a small chair in the model. The miniature toy and small chair symbolize the large Snoopy and real chair in the adjoining "real" room. Children are then asked to find the toy in the real room (Retrieval 1). After searching for the toy in the real room, they return to the model and are asked to find where the miniature toy was hidden (Retrieval 2). If children cannot find the large toy in the real room (Retrieval 1) but can find the miniature toy in the scale model (Retrieval 2), their failure to find the large toy cannot be due to forgetting where the miniature toy was hidden. A better interpretation would be that the children have no representational insight and cannot use the model in a symbolic fashion to guide their search.

The results of one such experiment with 2½- and 3-year-old children are shown in Figure 7.3. As we see, 3-year-olds performed well in *both* retrieval tasks, indicating that they remembered where the miniature toy was hidden and used the information from the scale model to find the large toy in the real room. The 2½-year-olds showed good memory for where the miniature toy had been hidden (Retrieval 2 in the figure), but performed very poorly when trying to find the large toy in the real room (Retrieval 1 in the figure). Apparently, 2½-year-olds failed to recognize that the scale model was a symbolic representation of the large room.

It is not that 2½-year-olds have no representational insight. If given a *photo* that shows Snoopy's hiding place in the real room, 2½-year-olds (but not 2-year-olds) can find him there when given the opportunity. Why do they do better with a two-dimensional photo than with an actual three-dimensional scale model? DeLoache believes that scale models are harder to use as symbols because 2½-year-olds lack **dual representation**—the ability to think about an

symbolic (or pretend) play
play in which one object, action, or actor symbolizes or stands for another

dual representation (dual encoding; dual orientation)
ability to represent an object simultaneously as an object itself and as a representation of something else

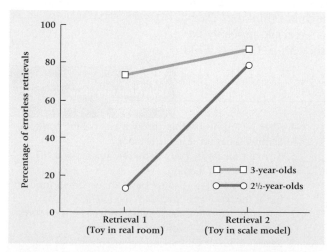

Figure 7.3 *The number of errorless retrievals (correctly locating the hidden toy) for 2½- (younger) and 3-year-olds (older) on a model task. Retrieval 1 involved locating the real toy in the real room; Retrieval 2 involved locating the miniature toy in the model. FROM DELOACHE, 1987.*

Play is an intrinsically satisfying activity—something young children do for the sheer fun of it (Rubin, Fein, & Vandenberg, 1983). In contrast to earlier views that childhood play activities were a frivolous waste of time, Piaget (1951) was fascinated by the young child's play. He believed that play provides a glimpse of the child's emerging cognitive schemes in action while allowing young players to practise and strengthen whatever competencies they possesses.

Sensorimotor play begins very early and develops in much the same way in all cultures (Pellegrini & Smith, 1998; Sigman & Sena, 1993). Infants progress from playing with their own bodies (for example, sucking their thumbs), to manipulating external objects such as rattles and stuffed animals, to fully *functional play*—using objects to serve the functions they normally serve—which appears by the end of the first year. So a 12-month-old is more inclined to push the buttons on a toy phone rather than merely sucking on or banging the toy.

Perhaps the most exciting breakthrough in play activities is the emergence of *symbolic (or pretend) play* at 11 to 13 months of age. The earliest "pretend" episodes are simple ones in which infants pretend to engage in familiar activities such as eating, drinking, or sleeping. But by 18 to 24 months of age, toddlers have progressed to a point where they pretend to perform multiple acts in a meaningful sequence; they can also coordinate their actions with those of a play partner, making social games of imitating each other and sometimes even cooperating to achieve a goal (Brownell & Carriger, 1990; Howes & Matheson, 1992). Parents can foster this development by providing toddlers with a secure base of affection and by playing along with their child's little dramas (O'Reilly & Bornstein, 1993; Slade, 1987).

Symbolic play truly blossoms during Piaget's preoperational period. By age 2, toddlers can use one object (a block) to symbolize another (a car) and are now using language in inventive ways to create rich fantasy worlds for themselves. They clearly understand pretence. If you hand them a towel and suggest that they wipe up the imaginary tea you just spilled, they will do it (Harris, Kavanaugh, & Meredith, 1994). Think about this: Because there is no tea in sight, the child's willingness to clean it up suggests that he can construct a mental representation of someone else's pretend event and then act according to this representation. Pretend play becomes increasingly social and complex between ages 2 and 5. More important, children combine their capacity for increasingly social play and their capacity for understanding pretence to cooperate with each other at *planning* their pretend activities. They name and assign roles that each player will enact, propose play scripts, and may even stop playing to modify the script if necessary (Howes & Matheson, 1992). Indeed, play episodes are among the most complex social interactions that preschoolers have (Pellegrini, 2002).

What good is play? Intellectually, play provides a context for using language to communicate and using the mind to fantasize, plan strategies, and solve problems. Children often show more advanced intellectual skills during pretend play than they do when performing other activities, suggesting that play fosters cognitive development (Lillard, 1993). Indeed, preschool children who engage in a great deal of pretend play (or who are trained to do so) perform better on tests of Piagetian cognitive development, language skills, and creativity than children who "pretend" less often (Fisher, 1992; Johnsen, 1991).

Preschool pretend activities may also promote social development. To be successful at social pretend play, children must adopt different roles, coordinate their activities, and resolve any disputes that may arise. Children may also learn about and prepare for adult roles by "playing house" or "playing school" and stepping into the shoes of their mothers, fathers, or nursery-school teachers (Gleason et al., 2000; Pellegrini, 2002). Perhaps because of the social skills they acquire (for example, an ability to cooperate) and the role-taking experiences they have, preschool children who participate in a lot of *social* pretend play tend to be more socially mature and more popular with peers than agemates who often play without partners (Connolly & Doyle, 1984; Howes & Matheson, 1992).

Finally, play may foster healthy emotional development by allowing children to express feelings that bother them or to resolve emotional conflicts (Fein, 1986). If Jennie, for example, has been scolded at lunch for failing to eat her peas, she may gain control of the situation at play as she scolds her doll for picky eating or persuades the doll to "eat healthy" and consume the peas. Indeed, playful resolutions of such emotional conflicts may even be an important contributor to children's understanding of authority and the rationales that underlie all those rules they must follow (Piaget & Inhelder, 1969).

Let it never be said, then, that play is useless. Although children play because it is fun, not because it sharpens their skills, players indirectly contribute to their own social, emotional, and intellectual development, enjoying themselves all the while. In this sense, play truly is the child's work—and is serious business indeed!

The reciprocal roles children enact during pretend play promote the growth of social skills and interpersonal understanding.

object in two different ways at the same time. Dual representation is not required with photos because the primary purpose of a photo is to represent something else. But a scale model is an interesting object in its own right, and 2½-year-olds may not recognize that it is also a representation of the larger room. If DeLoache is right, then anything that induces young children to pay less attention to the scale model as an object should persuade them to use it as a symbol and thereby improve their search for the hidden toy. Indeed, DeLoache (1991, 2000) reports that 2½-year-olds who are not allowed to play with the scale model but only to look through its windows do focus less on the interesting qualities of the scale model itself, treating it more like a symbol that helps them to find the hidden toy in the real room.

Although representational insight and dual-representational abilities improve drastically between 2½ and 3 years of age, they remain rather tentative and are easily disrupted. Consider, for example, that when 3-year-olds must wait five minutes after seeing a toy hidden in the scale model to make their initial search, they are typically unsuccessful at finding the toy in the larger room. It is not that they forget where the toy was hidden in the scale model. Instead they don't seem to remember over a five-minute delay that the scale model is a symbolic representation of the real room (Uttal et al., 1995). So dual representation is rather fragile in 3-year-olds but improves substantially over the preschool years (Deloache et al., 1999; Marzolf & DeLoache, 1994).

animism
attributing life and lifelike qualities to inanimate objects

egocentrism
tendency to view the world from one's own perspective while failing to recognize that others may have different points of view

Deficits in Preconceptual Reasoning. Piaget called 2- to 4-year-olds "preconceptual" because he believed that their ideas, concepts, and cognitive processes are rather primitive by adult standards. He claimed, for example, that young children often display **animism**—a willingness to attribute life and lifelike qualities (for example, motives and intentions) to inanimate objects. The 4-year-old who believed that the setting sun was alive, angry, and hiding behind the mountain provides a clear example of the animistic logic that children are likely to display during the preconceptual period.

According to Piaget, the most striking deficiency in children's preoperational reasoning—a deficiency that contributes immensely to the other intellectual shortcomings they display—is their **egocentrism**, a tendency to view the world from one's own perspective and to have difficulty recognizing another person's point of view. Piaget demonstrated this by first familiarizing children with an asymmetrical mountain scene (see Figure 7.4) and then asking them what an observer would see as he gazed at the scene from a vantage point other than their own. Often, 3- and 4-year-olds said the other person would see exactly what they saw, thus failing to consider the other's different perspective. Other examples of this self-centred thinking appear in the statements young children make. Here is a sample conversation in which the egocentrism of a 4-year-old named Sandy comes through as she describes an event she has witnessed.

Figure 7.4 *Piaget's three-mountain problem. Young preoperational children are egocentric. They cannot easily assume another person's perspective and often say that another child viewing the mountain from a different vantage point sees exactly what they see from their own location.*

SANDY: Uncle David, it got on your car and scratched it.

ADULT: What did?

SANDY: Come, I'll show you. (She takes her uncle outside and shows him a scratch on the hood of his new car.)

ADULT: Sandy, what made the scratch?

SANDY: Not me!

ADULT (laughing): I know, Sandy, but how did the scratch get there?

SANDY: It got on the car and scratched it with his claws.

ADULT: What did?

SANDY (looking around): There! (She points to a cat that is walking across the street.)

ADULT: Oh, a cat! Why didn't you tell me that in the first place?

SANDY: I did!

In this case, Sandy assumed that her uncle shared her perspective and must already know what had caused the scratch on his car. Consequently, her speech is not adapted to the needs of her listener, reflecting instead her egocentric point of view.

Finally, Piaget claimed that the young child's egocentric focus on the way things appear to be makes it nearly impossible for her to distinguish appearances from reality. Consider Rheta DeVries's (1969) classic study of the **appearance/reality distinction**. Children 3 to 6 years of age were first introduced to a cat named Maynard. After the children had petted Maynard, DeVries hid Maynard's head and shoulders behind a screen while she strapped a realistic mask of a dog's face onto Maynard's head (see Figure 7.5). The children were then asked such questions about Maynard's identity as "What kind of animal is it now?" and "Does it bark or meow?" Even though Maynard's back half and tail remained in full view during the transformation, nearly all the 3-year-olds focused on Maynard's new appearance and concluded that he really was a dog. By contrast, most 6-year-olds could distinguish appearances from reality, correctly noting that Maynard the cat now merely looked like a dog.

Why do 3-year-olds fail to distinguish between the misleading visual appearance of an object and its actual identity? Their problem, according to John Flavell and his associates (1986), is that they are not yet proficient at *dual encoding*—at representing an object in more than one way at a time. Just as young children have difficulty representing a scale model as both an *object* and a *symbol* (DeLoache, 2000), they struggle to construct simultaneous mental representations of an object that looks like something other than what it really is.

To illustrate, Flavell and his colleagues (1983, 1987, 1989) found that 3-year-olds who were shown a toy sponge that looked like a rock were apt to say that, not only did it look like a rock, but it "really and truly is a rock." Their representation of the object's identity was based on its single most salient feature—its deceptive appearance. Yet when 3-year-old children are persuaded to play a trick on someone (e.g., "Let's trick Sally and

237

Chapter Seven
Cognitive Devlopment: Piaget's Theory, Case's Neo-Piagetian Theory, and Vygotsky's Sociocultural Viewpoint

appearance/reality distinction
ability to keep the true properties or characteristics of an object in mind despite the deceptive appearance that the object has assumed; often lacking among young children during the preconceptual period.

Courtesy of Rheta de Vries

Figure 7.5 *Maynard the cat, without and with a dog mask. Three-year-olds who met Maynard before his change in appearance nonetheless believed that he had become a dog.*

make her think that this sponge really is a rock, and not just a sponge that looks like one"), or when they are asked to select an object that could wipe up some spilled water, many 3-year-olds are capable of forming dual representations of this object as a sponge (reality) that only looks like a rock (appearance) (Rice et al., 1997; Sapp, Lee, & Muir, 2000). Clearly, symbolic play activities, in which children pretend that objects (such as a large cardboard box) are something other than they really are (e.g., a fort) are an important contributor to dual representation and to children's gradually emerging abilities to distinguish misleading appearances from reality (Golomb & Galasso, 1995). But, as we'll see in the next section, these abilities develop gradually over the preschool period.

The Intuitive Period

Piaget called the phase between ages 4 and 7 the **intuitive period**. Intuitive thought is little more than an extension of preconceptual thought, although children are now somewhat less egocentric and much more proficient at classifying objects on the basis of shared perceptual attributes such as size, shape, and colour. The child's thinking is called "intuitive" because his understanding of objects and events is still largely based, or "**centred**," on their single most salient perceptual feature—the way things appear to be—rather than on logical or rational thought processes.

The most frequently cited examples of children's intuitive reasoning come from Piaget's famous conservation studies (Flavell, 1963). One of these experiments begins with the child adjusting the volumes of liquid in two identical containers until each is said to have "the same amount to drink." Next the child sees the experimenter pour the liquid from one of these tall, thin containers into a short, broad container. He is then asked whether the remaining tall, thin container and the shorter, broader container have the same amount of liquid (see Figure 7.6 for an illustration of the procedure). Children younger than 6 or 7 will usually say that the tall, thin receptacle contains *more* liquid than the short, broad one. The child's thinking about liquids is apparently *centred* on one perceptual feature—the relative heights of the columns (tall column = more liquid). In Piaget's terminology, preoperational children are incapable of **conservation**: they do not yet realize that certain properties of objects (such as volume, mass, or number) remain unchanged when the objects' appearances are altered in some superficial way.

Why do preschool children fail to conserve? The answer, according to Piaget, is that these *pre*operational children lack both of the cognitive operations that would help them to overcome their perceptually based intuitive reasoning. The first of these operations is **decentration**—the ability to concentrate on more than one aspect of a problem at the same time. Children at the intuitive stage are unable to attend *simultaneously* to both height and width when trying to solve the conservation of liquid problem. They centre their attention either on the difference in height or width and make their decisions on differences in that single dimension. Consequently, they fail to recognize that increases in the width of a column of liquid compensate for decreases in its height to preserve its absolute amount. Preschoolers also lack **reversibility**—the ability to mentally undo or negate an action. So an intuitive 5-year-old faced with the conservation-of-liquids problem is unable to mentally reverse what he has seen to conclude that the liquid in the short, broad beaker is still the same water and would attain its former height if it were poured back into its original container.

Does Piaget Underestimate the Preoperational Child?

Are preschool children really as intuitive, illogical, and egocentric as Piaget assumed? Can a child who has no understanding of cognitive operations be taught to conserve? Let's see what later research can tell us.

NEW EVIDENCE ON EGOCENTRISM. Numerous experiments indicate that Piaget underestimated the ability of preschool children to recognize and appreciate another person's point of view. For example, Piaget and Inhelder's three-mountain task has been criticized as being unusually difficult, and more recent research has shown that children look much less egocentric when provided with less complicated visual displays (Gzesh & Surber, 1985;

intuitive period
later substage of preoperations, from age 4 to age 7, when the child's thinking about objects and events is dominated by salient perceptual features

centration
in Piaget's theory, the tendency of preoperational children to attend to one aspect of a situation to the exclusion of others; contrasts with *decentration*

conservation
recognition that the properties of an object or substance do not change when its appearance is altered in some superficial way

decentration
in Piaget's theory, the ability of concrete-operational children to consider multiple aspects of a stimulus or situation; contrasts with *centration*

reversibility
ability to reverse or negate an action by mentally performing the opposite action (negation)

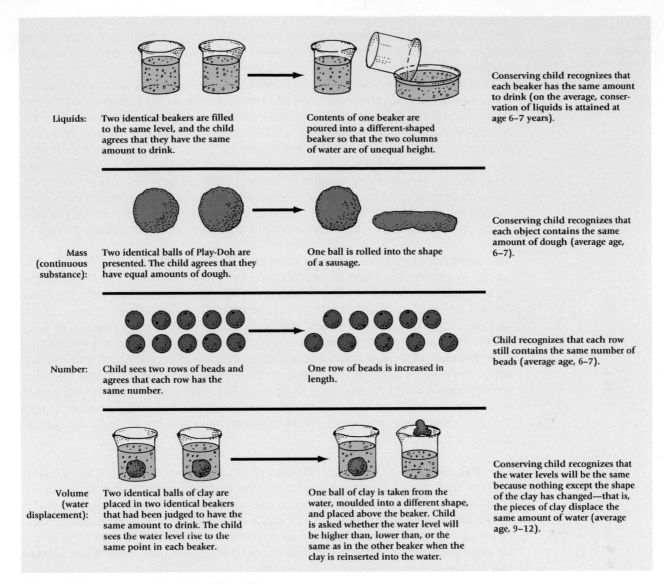

Liquids: Two identical beakers are filled to the same level, and the child agrees that they have the same amount to drink.

Contents of one beaker are poured into a different-shaped beaker so that the two columns of water are of unequal height.

Conserving child recognizes that each beaker has the same amount to drink (on the average, conservation of liquids is attained at age 6–7 years).

Mass (continuous substance): Two identical balls of Play-Doh are presented. The child agrees that they have equal amounts of dough.

One ball is rolled into the shape of a sausage.

Conserving child recognizes that each object contains the same amount of dough (average age, 6–7).

Number: Child sees two rows of beads and agrees that each row has the same number.

One row of beads is increased in length.

Child recognizes that each row still contains the same number of beads (average age, 6–7).

Volume (water displacement): Two identical balls of clay are placed in two identical beakers that had been judged to have the same amount to drink. The child sees the water level rise to the same point in each beaker.

One ball of clay is taken from the water, moulded into a different shape, and placed above the beaker. Child is asked whether the water level will be higher than, lower than, or the same as in the other beaker when the clay is reinserted into the water.

Conserving child recognizes that the water levels will be the same because nothing except the shape of the clay has changed—that is, the pieces of clay displace the same amount of water (average age, 9–12).

Figure 7.6 *Some common tests of the child's ability to conserve.*

Newcombe & Huttenlocher, 1992). John Flavell and his associates (1981), for example, showed 3-year-olds a card with a dog on one side and a cat on the other. The card was then held vertically between the child (who could see the dog) and the experimenter (who could see the cat), and the child was asked which animal the experimenter could see. The 3-year-olds performed flawlessly, indicating that they could assume the experimenter's perspective and infer that he must see the cat rather than the animal they could see.

Flavell's study investigated young children's *perceptual* perspective-taking—that is, the ability to make correct inferences about what another person can see or hear. Can preoperational children engage in *conceptual* perspective-taking by making correct inferences about what another person may be thinking or feeling when these mental states differ from their own? The answer is a qualified yes. In one study, conducted by Suzanne Hala from the University of Calgary and Michael Chandler from the University of British Columbia (1996), 3-year-olds were asked to play a trick on a person (Lisa) by moving some biscuits from their distinctive biscuit jar to a hiding place, so that Lisa would be fooled. When later asked where Lisa would look for the biscuits and where she would think the biscuits are, children who helped plan the deception performed quite well, saying that Lisa would look in the biscuit jar. By contrast, children who merely observed the experimenter planning the deception did not perform so well. Rather, they were more likely to answer this *false-belief task* erroneously, stating that Lisa would look for the biscuits in the new hiding place. In other words, when they planned to deceive someone,

3-year-olds were later able to take the perspective of that person. When they were not actively involved in the deceit, however, they performed egocentrically, stating that the unsuspecting person would look for the biscuits where they knew them to be (see also Carlson, Moses, & Hix, 1998).

Clearly, preoperational children are not nearly as egocentric as Piaget thought. Nevertheless, according to Ted Ruffman and David Olson from the University of Toronto, Piaget was right in claiming that young children often rely on their own perspectives and thus fail to make accurate judgments about other people's motives, desires, and intentions, and they do often assume that if they know something, others will too (1989; Ruffman et al., 1993). Today, researchers believe that children gradually become less egocentric and better able to appreciate others' points of view as they learn more and more—particularly about other people and the causes of their behaviour. In other words, perspective-taking abilities are not totally absent at one stage and suddenly present at another; they develop slowly and become more refined from early in life into adulthood (Bjorklund, 2000).

ANOTHER LOOK AT CHILDREN'S CAUSAL REASONING. Piaget was quite correct in stating that preschool children are likely to provide animistic answers to many questions and to make logical errors when thinking about cause-and-effect relationships. However, Susan Gelman and Gail Gottfried (1996) find that 3-year-olds do *not* routinely attribute life or lifelike qualities to inanimate objects, even such inanimates as a robot that can be made to move. In addition, most 4-year-olds recognize that plants and animals grow and will heal after an injury, whereas inanimate objects (for example, a table with a broken leg) will not (Backschneider, Shatz, & Gelman, 1993). Although preschool children do occasionally display animistic responses, these judgments stem not so much from a general belief that moving inanimates have lifelike qualities (Piaget's position) as from the (typically accurate) presumption that *unfamiliar* objects that appear to move *on their own* are alive (Dolgin & Behrend, 1984).

CAN PREOPERATIONAL CHILDREN CONSERVE? According to Piaget (1970), children younger than 6 or 7 cannot solve conservation problems because they have not yet acquired the operation of reversibility or decentration—the cognitive operations that would enable them to discover the constancy of attributes such as mass and volume. Piaget also argued that one cannot teach conservation to subjects younger than 6 or 7, for these *pre*operational children are much too intellectually immature to understand and use logical operations such as reversibility.

However, many researchers have demonstrated that nonconservers as young as 4 years of age, and even children with mental retardation, can be *trained* to conserve by a variety of techniques (Gelman, 1969; Hendler & Weisberg, 1992). One approach that has proved particularly effective is **identity training**—teaching children to recognize that the object or substance transformed in a conservation task is still the same object or substance, regardless of its new appearance. For example, a child being trained to recognize identities on a conservation-of-liquids task might be told "It may look like less water when we pour it from a tall, thin glass into this shorter one, but it is the same water, and there has to be the same amount to drink." Dorothy Field (1981) has shown that 4-year-olds who received this training not only conserved on the training task but could also use their new knowledge about identities to solve at least three (out of five) new conservation problems that were presented to them 2½ to 5 months after their training had ended. So contrary to Piaget's viewpoint, many preoperational children can learn to conserve, and their initial understanding of this law of nature seems to depend more on their ability to recognize identities than on their use of reversibility and decentration.

SUMMING UP. Taken together, the evidence we have reviewed suggests that preschool children are not nearly as illogical or egocentric as Piaget assumed. Today many researchers believe that Piaget underestimated the abilities of preschool children because his problems were too complex to allow them to demonstrate what they actually knew. If I were to ask you "What do quarks do?" you probably couldn't tell me unless you were a physics major. Surely, this is an unfair test of your "causal logic," just as Piaget's tests were when he questioned preschool children about phenomena that were equally unfamiliar to them

identity training
attempt to promote conservation by teaching nonconservers to recognize that a transformed object or substance is the same object or substance, regardless of its new appearance

(e.g., "What causes the wind?"). Even when they were thinking about familiar concepts, Piaget required children to verbally justify their answers—to state rationales that these young, relatively inarticulate preschoolers were often incapable of providing (to Piaget's satisfaction, at least). Yet later research consistently indicates that Piaget's participants may have had a reasonably good understanding of many ideas that they couldn't articulate (for example, class inclusion; distinctions between animates and inanimates) and would easily have displayed such knowledge if asked different questions or been given nonverbal tests of the same concepts (Bullock, 1985; Waxman & Hatch, 1992).

Clearly, Piaget was right in arguing that preschool children are more intuitive, egocentric, and illogical than older elementary-school children. Yet it is now equally clear that (1) preschoolers are capable of reasoning logically about simple problems or concepts that are familiar to them, and (2) a number of factors other than lack of cognitive operations may account for their poor performances on Piaget's cognitive tests.

241

Chapter Seven
Cognitive Devlopment: Piaget's Theory, Case's Neo-Piagetian Theory, and Vygotsky's Sociocultural Viewpoint

The Concrete-Operational Stage (7 to 11 Years)

During Piaget's **concrete-operational** period, children rapidly acquire cognitive operations and apply these important new skills when thinking about objects and events that they have experienced. Recall from our earlier discussion that a cognitive operation is an internal mental activity that enables the child to modify and reorganize her images and symbols to reach a logical conclusion (Flavell et al., 1993). With these powerful new operations in their cognitive arsenal, elementary-school children progress far beyond the static and centred thinking of the preoperational stage. For every limitation of the preoperational child, we can see a corresponding strength in the concrete operator (see Table 7.3).

Some Examples of Operational Thought

CONSERVATION. Concrete-operational children can easily solve several of Piaget's conservation problems. Faced with the conservation-of-liquids puzzle, for example, a 7-year-old concrete operator can *decentre* by focusing simultaneously on both the height and width of the two containers. She also displays *reversibility*—the ability to mentally undo the pouring process and imagine the liquid in its original container. Armed with these cogni-

concrete operations
Piaget's third stage of cognitive development, lasting from about age 7 to age 11, when children acquire cognitive operations and think more logically about real objects and experiences

TABLE 7.3	A Comparison of Preoperational and Concrete-Operational Thought	
Concept	**Preoperational thought**	**Concrete-operational thought**
Egocentrism	Children typically assume that others share their point of view.	Children may respond egocentrically at times but are now much more aware of others' divergent perspectives.
Animism	Children are likely to assume that unfamiliar objects that move on their own have lifelike qualities.	Children are more aware of the biological bases of life and do not attribute lifelike qualities to inanimates.
Perception-bound thought/concentration	Children make judgments based on perceptual appearances and focus on a single aspect of a situation when seeking answers to a problem.	Children can ignore misleading appearances and focus on more than one aspect of a situation when seeking answers to a problem (compensation).
Irreversibility/reversibility	Children cannot mentally undo an action they have witnessed. They cannot think back to the way an object or situation was before the object or situation changed.	Children can mentally negate changes they have witnessed to make before/after comparisons and consider how changes have altered the situation.
Performance on Piagetian tests of logical reasoning	Their egocentrism and their perception-bound, centred reasoning means that children often fail conservation tasks, have difficulty grouping objects into hierarchies of classes and subclasses, and display little ability to order objects mentally along such quantitative dimensions as height or length.	Their declining egocentrism and acquisition of reversible cognitive operations permit concrete-operational children to conserve, correctly classify objects on several dimensions, and *mentally* order objects on quantitative dimensions. Conclusions are now based on logic (the way things *must* necessarily be) rather than on the way they appear to be.

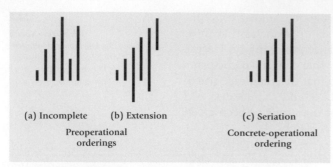

(a) Incomplete   (b) Extension

Preoperational
orderings

(c) Seriation

Concrete-operational
ordering

Figure 7.7 *Children's performance on a simple seriation task. If asked to arrange a series of sticks from shortest to longest, preoperational children often (a) line up one end of the sticks and create an incomplete ordering or (b) order them so the top of each successive stick extends higher than the preceding stick. Concrete operators, by contrast, can use the inverse cognitive operations greater than (>) and less than (<) to quickly make successive comparisons and create a correct serial ordering.*

mental seriation
cognitive operation that allows one to mentally order a set of stimuli along a quantifiable dimension such as height or weight

transitivity
ability to recognize relations among elements in a serial order (for example, if A is more than B and B is more than C, then A is more than C)

horizontal décalage
Piaget's term for a child's uneven cognitive performance; an inability to solve certain problems even though one can solve similar problems requiring the same mental operations

tive operations, then, she now *knows* that the two different containers each have the same amount of liquid; she uses *logic*, not misleading appearances, to reach her conclusion.

RELATIONAL LOGIC. An important hallmark of concrete-operational thinking is a better understanding of quantitative relations and relational logic. Do you remember an occasion when your gym teacher said, "Line up by height from tallest to shortest"? Carrying out such an order is really quite easy for concrete operators, who are now capable of **mental seriation**—the ability to mentally arrange items along a quantifiable dimension such as height or weight. By contrast, preoperational youngsters perform poorly on many seriation tasks (see Figure 7.7) and would struggle to comply with the gym teacher's request.

Concrete-operational thinkers also have mastered the related concept of **transitivity**, which describes the necessary relations among elements in a series. If, for example, John is taller than Mark, and Mark is taller than Miguel, who is taller, John or Miguel? It follows *logically* that John must be taller than Miguel, and the concrete operator grasps the transitivity of these size relationships. Lacking the concept of transitivity, the preoperational child relies on perceptions to answer the question and might insist that John and Miguel stand next to each other so that she can determine who is taller. Preoperational children probably have a better understanding of such transitive relations than Piaget gave them credit for (Gelman, 1978; Trabasso, 1975); but according to Markovits and Dumas from the Université du Québec à Montréal (1999), they still have difficulty grasping the logical necessity of transitivity (see also Chapman & Lindenberger, 1988).

The Sequencing of Concrete Operations

While examining Figure 7.6, you may have noticed that some forms of conservation (for example, mass) are understood much sooner than others (volume). Piaget was aware of this and other developmental inconsistencies, and he coined the term **horizontal décalage** (décalage is French for "discrepancy") to describe them.

Why does the child display different levels of understanding on conservation tasks that seem to require the same mental operations? According to Piaget, horizontal décalage occurs because problems that appear quite similar may actually differ in complexity. For example, conservation of volume (see Figure 7.6) is not attained until ages 9 to 12 because it is a complex task that requires the child to simultaneously consider the operations involved in the conservation of both liquids and mass *and* then to determine whether there are any meaningful relationships between these two phenomena. Although we have talked as if concrete operations were a set of skills that appeared rather abruptly over a brief period, this was not Piaget's view. Piaget always maintained that operational abilities evolve gradually and sequentially as the simpler skills that appear first are consolidated, combined, and reorganized into increasingly complex mental structures.

After reviewing some of the intellectual accomplishments of the concrete-operational period, we can see why many societies begin to formally educate their children at 6 to 7 years of age. According to Piaget, this is precisely the time when children are decentring from perceptual illusions and acquiring the cognitive operations that enable them to comprehend arithmetic; think about language and its properties; classify animals, people, objects, and events; and understand the relations between upper- and lowercase letters, letters and the printed word, and words and sentences. Although Piaget was a basic scientist, not an educator, we will see in Box 7.3 that he had some very interesting ideas about the kinds of education young children should receive.

243

Chapter Seven
Cognitive Devlopment: Piaget's
Theory, Case's Neo-Piagetian
Theory, and Vygotsky's
Sociocultural Viewpoint

The Formal-Operational Stage (11 to 12 Years and Beyond)

According to Piaget, the impressive thinking of concrete-operational children is limited because he believed they could apply their operational schemes only to objects, situations, or events that are real or imaginable. The transitive inferences of concrete operators, for example, are likely to be accurate only for real objects that are (or have been) *physically present*. Seven- to 11-year-olds cannot yet apply this relational logic to *abstract* signifiers such as the Xs, Ys, and Zs that we use in algebra. By contrast, **formal operations**, first seen between 11 and 13 years of age, are mental actions performed on *ideas* and *propositions*. No longer is thinking tied to the factual or observable, because formal operators can reason quite logically about hypothetical processes and events that may have no basis in reality.

formal operations
Piaget's fourth and final stage of cognitive development, from age 11 or 12 and beyond, when the individual begins to think more rationally and systematically about abstract concepts and hypothetical events

Hypothetico-Deductive Reasoning

The benchmark of formal operations is what Piaget referred to as **hypothetico-deductive reasoning** (Inhelder & Piaget, 1958). *Deductive reasoning*, which entails reasoning from the general to the specific, is not, in itself, a formal operational ability. Concrete-operational children can arrive at a correct conclusion if they are provided with the

hypothetico-deductive reasoning
in Piaget's theory, a formal operational ability to think hypothetically

---

7.3

APPLYING DEVELOPMENTAL RESEARCH

Piaget on Education

Late in his career, Piaget (1971; 1976) wrote about education, offering several suggestions for change that impressed educators and had a major impact on preschool and early-elementary-school curricula (Gallagher & Easley, 1978; Ginsburg & Opper, 1988). Among the more widely accepted of Piaget's ideas are the following:

1. *Tailor education to children's readiness to learn.* Appropriate learning experiences build on existing schemes. Piaget stressed that children profit most from *moderately novel* educational experiences that pique their curiosity, challenge their current understandings, and force them to reevaluate what they already know. If the experiences are too complex, students are unable to assimilate (much less accommodate to) them, and no new learning will occur.

2. *Be sensitive to individual differences.* Because children differ in their rates of intellectual development, they are not all ready to learn precisely the same lessons. In a Piagetian-based curriculum, these individual differences are accepted by teachers, who plan activities for individual students or small groups rather than the whole class (Ginsburg & Opper, 1988).

3. *Promote discovery-based education.* Piaget criticized traditional educational programs for relying much too heavily on passive, verbal forms of instruction that emphasize rote learning. He believed that young children are naturally inquisitive souls who learn best when they act directly on their environments, probing objects and participating in situations that allow them to *construct* new knowledge for themselves.

Based on these principles, Piaget advised educators against lecturing or demonstrating to students sitting passively; instead, he argued that children should be encouraged to explore a variety of educational props—storybooks, arts and crafts, puzzles, and games—that enable them to learn by doing. According to Piaget, "Children should be able to do their own experimenting and their own research. Teachers, of course, can guide them by providing appropriate materials, but the essential thing is that in order for a child to understand something, he must construct it for himself; he must reinvent it" (Piaget, 1972). Piaget insisted that even formal lessons can be structured to promote active learning. For example, he believed that basic arithmetic operations are best illustrated by having children add and subtract buttons rather than showing them how to solve problems on a blackboard. He advocated teaching the concepts of space and distance by allowing children to measure their heights or the widths of their desks, as opposed to lecturing them on the relations among millimetres, centimetres, and metres. In other words, Piaget stressed that the teacher's job is not so much to transmit facts and concepts or to actively reinforce correct answers as to provide the setting, materials, and guidance that will enable curious children to experience the *intrinsic* satisfaction of *discovering* this knowledge for themselves. Piaget saw a "discovery-based" education as critical because he believed that "the principal goal of education is to create [adults] who are capable of doing new things, not simply of repeating what other generations have done—[people] who are creative, inventive, discoverers" (Piaget, as cited in Elkind, 1977, p. 171).

proper concrete "facts" as evidence. Formal-operational children, on the other hand, are not restricted to thinking about previously acquired facts, but can generate hypotheses; what is possible is more important to them than what is real. In Box 7.4, we can see the differences between concrete-operational and formal-operational thinking as children consider a hypothetical proposition presented in the form of an art assignment.

Hypothetical thinking is also critical for most forms of mathematics beyond simple arithmetic. If $2x + 5 = 15$, what does x equal? The problem does not deal with concrete entities such as apples or oranges, only with numbers and letters. It is an arbitrary, *hypothetical* problem that can be answered only if approached abstractly, using a symbol system that does not require concrete referents.

FOCUS ON RESEARCH

7.4 Children's Responses to a Hypothetical Proposition

Piaget (Hall, 1970) argued that the thinking of concrete operators is reality-bound. Presumably, most 9-year-olds would have a difficult time thinking about objects that don't exist or events that could never happen. By contrast, children entering the stage of formal operations were said to be quite capable of considering hypothetical propositions and carrying them to a logical conclusion. Indeed, Piaget suspected that many formal operators would even enjoy this type of cognitive challenge.

Several years ago, a group of concrete operators (9-year-old Grade 4 students) and a group of children who were at or rapidly approaching formal operations (11- to 12-year-old Grade 6 students) completed the following assignment:

> Suppose that you were given a third eye and that you could choose to place this eye anywhere on your body. Draw me a picture to show where you would place your extra eye, and then tell me why you would put it there.

All the 9-year-olds placed the third eye on the forehead between their two natural eyes. It seems as if these children called on their concrete experiences to complete their assignment: Eyes are found somewhere around the middle of the face in all people. One 9-year-old boy remarked that the third eye should go between the other two because "that's where a cyclops has his eye." The rationales for this eye placement were rather unimaginative. Consider the following examples:

> JIM (age 9½): I would like an eye beside my two other eyes so that if one eye went out, I could still see with two.

> VICKIE (age 9): I want an extra eye so I can see you three times.

> TANYA (age 9½): I want a third eye so I could see better.

In contrast, the older, formal-operational children gave a wide variety of responses that were not at all dependent on what they had seen before. Furthermore, these children thought out the advantages of this hypothetical situation and provided rather imaginative rationales for placing the extra eye in unique locations. Here are some sample responses:

> KEN (age 11½): (draws the extra eye on top of a tuft of hair) I could revolve the eye to look in all directions.

> JOHN (age 11½): (draws his extra eye in the palm of his left hand) I could see around corners and see what kind of cookie I'll get out of the cookie jar.

> TONY (age 11): (draws a close-up of a third eye in his mouth) I want a third eye in my mouth because I want to see what I am eating.

When asked their opinions of the three-eye assignment, many of the younger children considered it rather silly and uninteresting. One 9-year-old remarked, "This is stupid. Nobody has three eyes." However, the 11- to 12-year-olds enjoyed the task and continued to pester their teacher for "fun" art assignments "like the eye problem" for the remainder of the school year (Shaffer, 1973).

So the results of this demonstration are generally consistent with Piaget's theory. Older children who are at or rapidly approaching the stage of formal operations are more likely than younger, concrete operators to generate logical and creative responses to a hypothetical proposition and to enjoy this type of reasoning.

Tanya's, Ken's, and John's responses to the "third eye" assignment

245

Chapter Seven
*Cognitive Devlopment: Piaget's
Theory, Case's Neo-Piagetian
Theory, and Vygotsky's
Sociocultural Viewpoint*

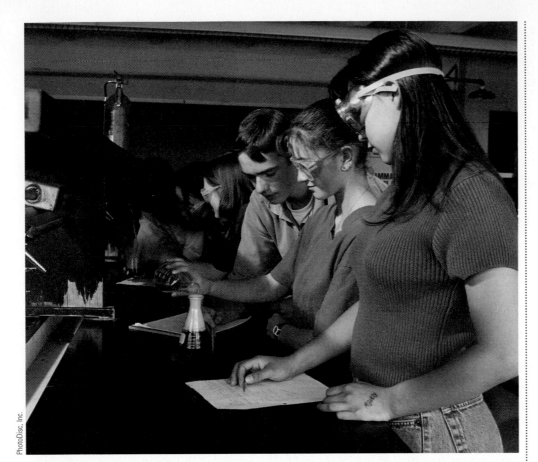

PhotoDisc, Inc.

A systematic approach to problem solving is one of the characteristics of formal-operational thinking.

Thinking Like a Scientist

In addition to the development of deductive reasoning abilities, formal-operational children are hypothesized to be able to think inductively, going from specific observations to broad generalizations. *Inductive reasoning* is the type of thinking that scientists display, where hypotheses are generated and then systematically tested in experiments.

Inhelder and Piaget (1958) used a series of tasks to assess *scientific reasoning*, one of which was the *pendulum problem*. Given strings of different lengths, objects of different weights to attach to one end of the strings, and a hook on which to hang the other end, the child's task is to discover which factor or factors influence how fast the string pendulum oscillates (that is, swings back and forth during a set time period). Is it the length of the string that matters? The heaviness of the weight? The force with which the weight is pushed? The height from which the weight is released? Or might two or more of these variables be important?

The key to solving this problem is to first identify the four factors that might control the pendulum's oscillation and to then systematically test each of these hypotheses, varying one factor at a time while holding all the other factors constant. Each successive hypothesis is tested in an if–then fashion: "*If* the weight on the string matters, *then* I should see a difference in oscillation when I compare a string with a heavy weight with a same-length string with a light weight, while holding other factors constant." Formal operators, who rely on this systematic approach to hypothesis generation and testing, eventually discover that the "weight hypothesis" is wrong and that the pendulum's oscillation depends on only one factor: the length of the string.

By contrast, 9- to 10-year-old concrete operators are not able to generate and systematically test the full range of possibilities that would permit them to draw the appropriate conclusion. They often begin with a reasonable hypothesis ("Maybe string length matters"), but they cannot isolate the effects of each variable. For example, they may test the string-length hypothesis without holding weight constant; should they find that a short string with a heavy weight oscillates faster than a longer one with a lighter weight, they are likely to erroneously conclude that both string length and weight control the pendulum's oscillation. Although subsequent research has not always supported all of Piaget's observations, it is generally agreed that scientific reasoning is a late-developing ability that even many adults fail to master (Kuhn, Amsel, & O'Loughlin, 1988; Moshman, 1998). Older concrete operators can be trained to reason more like formal operators when thinking about hypothetical but untrue propositions or when seeking solutions to problems (Adey & Shayer, 1992; Morris, 2000), but they are unable to generate these rational and methodical problem-solving strategies on their own. Even elementary-school children have been trained to use scientific reasoning with explicit instructions, but transfer of these trained strategies to new problems is limited to older preadolescents only (Chen & Klahr, 1999).

In sum, formal-operational thinking is rational, systematic, and abstract. The formal operator can now think planfully about thinking and can operate on ideas and hypothetical concepts, including those that contradict reality.

Personal and Social Implications of Formal Thought

Formal-operational thinking is a powerful tool that may change adolescents in many ways—some good and some not so good. First the good news: As we will see in Chapter 12, formal operations may pave the way for thinking about what is possible in one's life, forming a stable identity, and achieving a much richer understanding of other people's psychological perspectives and the causes of their behaviour. The formal-operational thinker is also better equipped to make difficult personal decisions that involve weighing alternative courses of action and their probable consequences for herself and other people (see Chapter 14, for example, on the development of moral reasoning). So advances in cognitive growth help to lay the groundwork for changes in many other aspects of development.

Now the bad news: Formal operations may also be related to some of the more painful aspects of the adolescent experience. Unlike younger children, who tend to accept the world as it is and to heed the dictates of authority figures, formal operators, who can imagine hypothetical alternatives to present realities, may begin to question everything from their parents' authority to impose strict curfews to the government's need to spend billions of dollars on weapons and the exploration of outer space when so many people are hungry and homeless. Indeed, the more logical inconsistencies and other flaws that adolescents detect in the real world, the more confused they become and the more inclined they are to become frustrated with or even to display rebellious anger toward the agents (for example, parents, the government) thought to be responsible for these imperfect states of affairs. Piaget viewed this idealistic fascination with the way things "ought to be" as a perfectly normal outgrowth of the adolescent's newly acquired abstract reasoning abilities, and he thus proclaimed formal operations the primary cause of the "generation gap."

Does Everyone Reach Formal Operations?

Piaget (1970) believed that the transition from concrete-operational to formal-operational reasoning takes place very gradually. For example, 11- to 13-year-olds who are entering formal operations are able to consider simple hypothetical propositions such as the three-eye problem mentioned in Box 7.4. However, they are not yet proficient at generating and testing hypotheses, and it may be another three to four years before they are capable of the planful, systematic reasoning that is necessary to deduce what determines how fast a pendulum will swing. Piaget never identified a stage of reasoning beyond formal operations, and he believed that most people show at least some signs of this highest level of intellect by ages 15 to 18.

Other investigators find that adolescents are much slower to acquire formal operations than Piaget had thought. In fact, Edith Neimark's (1979) review of the literature suggests that a sizable percentage of American adults do not often reason at the formal

247

Chapter Seven
*Cognitive Devlopment: Piaget's
Theory, Case's Neo-Piagetian
Theory, and Vygotsky's
Sociocultural Viewpoint*

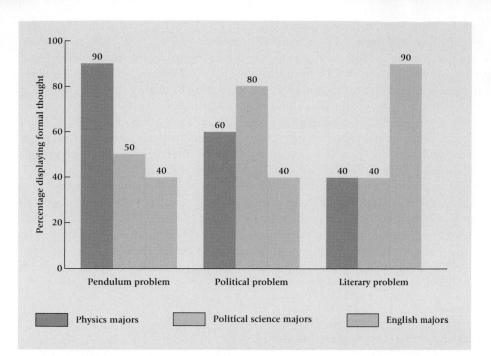

Figure 7.8 *Expertise and formal operations. University students show the greatest command of formal-operational thought in the subject area most related to their major.* ADAPTED FROM DE LISI & STAUDT, 1980.

level, and apparently there are some cultures—particularly those where formal schooling is rare or nonexistent—in which no one solves Piaget's formal-operational problems. Why do some people fail to attain formal operations? Cross-cultural research provides one clue: They may not have had sufficient exposure to the kinds of schooling that stress logic, mathematics, and science—experiences that Piaget believed help the child to reason at the formal level (Cole, 1990; Dasen, 1977).

In the later stages of his career, Piaget (1972) suggested another possibility: Perhaps nearly all adults are capable of reasoning at the formal level, but do so only on problems that hold their interest or are of vital importance to them. Indeed, Tulkin and Konner (1973) found that preliterate Bushman hunters who fail Piaget's test problems often do reason at the formal level on at least one task: tracking prey. Clearly, this is an activity of great importance to them that requires the systematic testing of inferences and hypotheses. A similar phenomenon has been observed among high-school and university students. Not only do twelfth-graders reason more abstractly about relevant everyday issues with which they are already familiar (Overton et al., 1987; Ward & Overton, 1990), but as we see in Figure 7.8, physics, political science, and English majors are all more likely to perform at the formal level on problems that fall within their own academic domains (De Lisi & Staudt, 1980).

Concept Check 7.3
Understanding Deficiencies and Milestones in Children's Thinking

Check your understanding of various aspects of children's thinking. First, match each scenario below with one of the following cognitive phenomena: (a) reversibility, (b) failure to conserve, (c) seriation, (d) dual representation, (e) animism, (f) hypothetico-deductive reasoning, (g) hypothetical reasoning. Then indicate the Piagetian stage in which each phenomenon allegedly emerges. The answers appear in the Appendix.

_____ 1. Enrico successfully arranges his many seashells from smallest to largest.

_____ 2. "You killed him!" Ben sobs when his mother destroys a clay pigeon while trap shooting.

_____ 3. Sarah flattens her Play-Doh into the shape of a pancake and says: "Look! Now I have more clay."

_____ 4. Knowing his sister will be surprised, Dimitri points a chocolate pistol at her and then takes a bite out of its muzzle.

_____ 5. Semareh blissfully contemplates how nice things would be if there were no racial prejudice.

_____ 6. Dexter anticipates all possible moves his chess opponent might make before selecting his "best move."

_____ 7. Akiko drops a vase and decides she'll glue it back together, hoping no one will notice.

It seems likely, then, that each person has an optimal, or "highest," level of cognitive performance that will show itself in familiar or well-trained content domains (Fischer, 1980; Fischer, Kenny, & Pipp, 1990). However, according to Zopito Marini from Brock University and the late Robbie Case from the University of Toronto, performance is likely to be inconsistent across domains unless the person has had a chance to build knowledge and to practise reasoning in all these content areas (Marini & Case, 1994). So we must be careful not to underestimate the cognitive capabilities of adolescents and adults who fail Piaget's formal-operational tests, for their less-than-optimal performances on these physical science problems may simply reflect either a lack of interest or a lack of experience with the subject matter rather than an inability to reason at the formal level.

One very interesting recent finding is that today's adolescents seem to acquire formal operations faster than their counterparts from the past. For example, tests of formal-operational abilities given to French adolescents between 1967 and 1996 reveal significantly higher scores for the more recent cohorts (Flieller, 1999). Is this an artifact? Probably not, because IQ tests scores around the world also have increased over the past 60 years (Flynn, 1987)—the so-called *Flynn effect*, which we will explore in more detail in Chapter 9.

AN EVALUATION OF PIAGET'S THEORY

We have already pointed to some shortcomings of Piaget's theory earlier in the chapter. Now it is time to take a broader view of this monumental theory. Let's start by giving credit where credit is due before considering the challenges to Piaget's viewpoint.

Piaget's Contributions

Piaget is a giant in the field of human development. As one anonymous scholar quoted by Harry Beilin (1992) put it, "assessing the impact of Piaget on developmental psychology is like assessing the impact of Shakespeare on English literature or Aristotle on philosophy—impossible" (p. 191). It is hard to imagine that we would know even a fraction of what we know about intellectual development had Piaget pursued his early interests in zoology and never worked with developing children.

So what exactly has Piaget contributed to the field of human development? The following list is a brief assessment of Piaget's major contributions made by several prominent researchers in honour of the 100th anniversary of Piaget's birth (Brainerd, 1996; Elkind, 1996; Fischer & Hencke, 1996; Flavell, 1996; Gopnik, 1996; Kessen, 1996; Siegler & Ellis, 1996):

1. Piaget founded the discipline we know today as cognitive development. His interest in children's thinking ensured that this field would be "developmental" and would not merely apply to children the ideas and methods from the study of adult thinking.

2. Piaget convinced us that children are curious, active explorers who play an important role in their own development. Although his assumptions that children actively construct their own knowledge may seem obvious today, this viewpoint was innovative and counter to the thinking of his time.

3. Piaget's theory was one of the first to try to *explain*, and not just *describe*, the process of development. Largely prompted by his theory, many theorists today, including Juan Pascual-Leone of York University, have taken seriously the need to explain transitions in children's thinking (Fischer, 1980; Fischer & Bidell, 1998; Nelson, 1996; Pascual-Leone, 1987; Siegler, 1996a, b, c).

249

Chapter Seven
Cognitive Devlopment: Piaget's Theory, Case's Neo-Piagetian Theory, and Vygotsky's Sociocultural Viewpoint

4. Piaget's description of broad *sequences* of intellectual development provides a reasonably accurate overview of how children of different ages think. He may have been wrong about some of the specifics, but as Robert Siegler (1991) notes, "His descriptions feel right.... The general trends ... appeal to our intuitions and our memories of childhood." (p. 18)

5. Piaget's ideas have had a major influence on thinking about social and emotional development as well as many practical implications for educators.

6. Finally, Piaget asked important questions and drew literally thousands of researchers to the study of cognitive development. And as often happens when heuristic theories such as Piaget's are repeatedly scrutinized, some of his research led to new insights while pointing to problems with his original ideas.

Challenges to Piaget

Over the past 30 years, critics have pointed to several apparent shortcomings of Piaget's theory. We will briefly consider four of these criticisms.

Piaget Failed to Distinguish Competence from Performance

We have commented repeatedly that Piaget underestimated the cognitive capabilities of infants, toddlers, and preschool children. Why? One reason is that Piaget was concerned with identifying the underlying *competencies*, or cognitive structures, that presumably determine how children perform on various cognitive tasks. He tended to assume that a child who failed one of his problems simply lacked the underlying concepts, or thought structures, he was testing.

We now know that this assumption is not valid because many factors other than a lack of critical competencies might undermine one's performance on a cognitive test. We've seen, for example, that 4- and 5-year-olds who seem to know the differences between animates and inanimates failed Piaget's tests, largely because Piaget required them to explain principles they understood (critical competency) but could not articulate. His tendency to equate task performances with competencies (and to ignore motivation, task familiarity, and all other factors that influence performance) is a major reason that his age norms for various cognitive milestones were often so far off target.

Does Cognitive Development Really Occur in Stages?

Piaget maintained that his stages of intellectual development are *holistic structures*—that is, coherent modes of thinking that are applied across a broad range of tasks. To say that a child is concrete-operational, for example, implies that he relies on cognitive operations and thinks logically about the vast majority of intellectual problems that he encounters.

Recently this holistic-structures assumption has been challenged by researchers, who question whether cognitive development is at all stagelike (Bjorklund, 2000; Siegler, 1996a). From their perspective, a "stage" of cognitive development implies that abrupt changes in intellectual functioning occur as the child acquires several new competencies over a relatively brief period. Yet we've seen that cognitive growth typically doesn't happen that way. Major transitions in intellect often occur quite gradually, and there is frequently very little consistency in the child's performance on tasks that presumably measure the abilities that define a given stage. For example, it may be years before a 7-year-old who can seriate or conserve number will be able to conserve volume (see Figure 7.6). Furthermore, it now appears that different concrete- and formal-operational problems are mastered in different orders by different children, a finding that suggests that there is a lot less consistency and coherence to cognitive growth than Piaget assumed (Case, 1985; Kuhn, 1992; Larivèe, Normandeau, & Parent, 2000).

So is cognitive development truly stagelike? The issue is still hotly debated and far from being resolved. Some theorists insist that cognitive development is coherent and does progress through a series of stages, though not necessarily through the same stages that Piaget proposed (Case, 1992; Case & Okamoto, 1996). However, many other theorists believe that intellectual development is a complex, multifaceted process in which children gradually acquire skills in many different content areas such as deductive reasoning, mathematics, visual–spatial reasoning, verbal skills, and moral reasoning, to name a few (Bjorklund, 2000; Fischer et al. 1990). Although development within each of these domains may occur in small, orderly steps, there is no assumption of consistency across domains. Thus, a 10-year-old who enjoys solving word puzzles and playing verbal games might outperform most age-mates on tests of verbal reasoning but function at a much lower level in less familiar domains, such as hypothesis testing or mathematical reasoning.

In sum, many aspects of cognitive development are orderly and coherent (and some would say stagelike) *within particular intellectual domains*. Yet there is very little evidence for strong consistencies in development across domains or for broad, holistic cognitive stages of the kind Piaget described.

Does Piaget Explain Cognitive Development?

Even those researchers who claim that cognitive growth is stagelike are bothered by Piaget's account of how children move from one stage of intellect to the next. Recall Piaget's interactionist viewpoint: Presumably children are (1) constantly assimilating new experiences in ways that their level of maturation allows, (2) accommodating their thinking to these experiences, and (3) reorganizing their structures into increasingly complex mental schemes that enable them to reestablish cognitive equilibrium with novel aspects of the environment. As children continue to mature, assimilate more complex information, and alter and reorganize their schemes, they eventually come to view familiar objects and events in new ways and move from one stage of intellect to the next.

This rather vague explanation of cognitive growth raises more questions than it answers. What maturational changes are necessary before children can progress from sensorimotor to preoperational intellect or from concrete operations to formal operations? What kinds of experiences must a child have before he will construct mental symbols, use cognitive operations, or operate on ideas and think about hypotheticals? Piaget was simply not very clear about these or any other mechanisms that might enable a child to move to a higher stage of intellect. As a result, a growing number of researchers now look on his theory as an elaborate description of cognitive development that has limited explanatory power (Gelman & Baillargeon, 1983; Kuhn, 1992).

Piaget Devoted Too Little Attention to Social and Cultural Influences

Children live in very different social and cultural contexts that affect the way their world is structured. Although Piaget admitted that cultural factors may influence the rate of cognitive growth, developmentalists now know that culture influences *how* children think as well (Rogoff, 1990, 1998). Piaget also paid too little attention to the ways that children's minds develop through their *social interactions* with more competent individuals. It would be an overstatement to say that Piaget ignored social influences on cognitive development. As we will see in Chapters 12 and 14, Piaget felt that conflict among peers was a major contributor to cognitive disequilibrium and intellectual growth, particularly the growth of perspective-taking skills and moral reasoning. Nevertheless, Piaget's descriptions emphasize the *self-directed* character of cognitive growth, almost as if the child was an isolated scientist exploring the world and making critical discoveries largely on her own. Today, we know that children develop many of their most basic (and not so basic) competencies by collaborating with parents, teachers, older siblings, and peers.

251

Chapter Seven
*Cognitive Devlopment: Piaget's
Theory, Case's Neo-Piagetian
Theory, and Vygotsky's
Sociocultural Viewpoint*

CASE'S NEO-PIAGETIAN THEORY

As we have seen, Piaget's theory has not gone unchallenged. Yet Piagetian theory revolutionized the way developmental psychologists view children. It also inspired many researchers who accepted the core principles in Piaget's theory to expand and develop the theory. These researchers became known as neo-Piagetians. A prominent neo-Piagetian is Juan Pascual-Leone from York University, who was the first to create a program of research into information-processing capacity (or M-space) as an explanation for cognitive development (Halford, 2002; Pascual-Leone, 1987). He found that the M-space demands of cognitive tasks predicted the age at which children were able to respond to the tasks correctly. See Chapter 8 for further discussion of information-processing capacity.

One of the best known neo-Piagetians is Robbie Case, who conducted his work at the Ontario Institute for Studies in Education (OISE) at the University of Toronto. Case agreed with the general concepts of accommodation and assimilation but refined these general concepts to explain how the processes occur. For example, he believed that accommodation occurs through exploration and problem solving. As children explore their environment and engage in problem solving, they expand their existing cognitive structures. Case explained assimilation through the concepts of *consolidation* and *automatization*. To acquire new concepts, children first have to consolidate existing knowledge—that is, establish firm links among bits of information that form a concept. Children also need to have an opportunity for repeated practice, because it is through practice that existing knowledge is automatized and thus readily accessed.

By viewing accommodation as exploration and problem solving, and assimilation as consolidation and automatization, Case allowed for related skills to be acquired at different times. Although he agreed with Piaget that many tasks are accomplished in a fairly universal sequence, Case argued that acquisition across tasks is similar only if the problems have a similar level of complexity and problem-solving procedures (Case & Okamoto, 1996; Case et al., 1992; Marini & Case, 1994; McKeough, 1992). If they differ, generalization to other tasks will not occur at the same time. For example, children acquire conservation of volume later than conservation of mass (see Figure 7.6) because the volume problem is more complex. Interestingly, Case also argued that children must progress through the same number and same sequence of steps for each of the concepts. For example, the general sequence of problem-solving processes needed to acquire conservation of mass would also be necessary to acquire conservation of volume—and concepts outside the logico-mathematico domain as well, such as social cognition.

Case also suggested that processing capacity and biological factors are important predictors of cognitive growth (Case, 1985). His focus on capacity applied Piagetian theory to an emerging area of cognition called *information processing* (which we will explore in Chapter 8). Children's capacity to attend to information, or "working memory," is cited as one of the major constraining factors, or upper limits, on their developing cognition. Case held that specific biological factors determine the upper limits on working memory—factors such as *myelinization* (Case, 1985). As noted in Chapter 5, myelinization involves the development of myelin sheaths that facilitate transmission of neural impulses. See Box 7.5 for further information on Case's theory.

Finally, Case was sensitive to the role of experience and cultural variations in cognition (Case, 1992, 1998; Case & Okamoto, 1996). He argued that the overarching symbolic logic proposed by Piaget was not sensitive to cultural differences. Instead, Case proposed that cognitive structures can be specific to a culture and not universal. For example, the formal structures of Western science and math involve segmenting problems into small enough units that they can be systematically manipulated and controlled. Other cultures engage in equally sophisticated processing but may not use this particular method. In fact, Case suggested that cultural experience is a vital component of children's ability to master new skills. Although processing capacity may be similar across children, their experiences differ. This focus on experience highlights the role of the family and the larger culture on development, a perspective that many critics feel

Robbie Case

Robbie Case

Robbie Case (1944–2000) was affiliated with the University of Toronto until his sudden death. His research was motivated by his fascination with the developing mind and his lifelong commitment to supporting and enhancing development in educational contexts. His deep love and respect for children inspired and encouraged him to seek ways to transform developmental theory into something that could help children and teachers.

Why do young children fail to coordinate and integrate the same information that their older peers use with relative ease? For example, very young children faced with the task of deciding which end of a balance beam will go down typically consider only one dimension—the number of weights on each side—when generating an answer. Older children consider two dimensions and integrate them: the number of weights on each side as well as the distance of the weights from the centre of the balance beam. Robbie Case believed that these developmental differences could be explained through a construct he called *central-processing structures* (Case 1992; Case & Griffin, 1990; Case & McKeough, 1990; Case et al., 1993; Case & Sandieson, 1988).

Central-processing structures are similar to the general cognitive structures that Piaget proposed. Recall that Piaget suggested that general structures are overarching and cross over vast domains. Case proposed that, although central-processing structures may have broad application (they cross over some domains), they are limited and do not cross over as many domains as Piaget's general structures. Case also suggested that a working-memory or processing-capacity component is critical for this structure. These two constraints help to explain developmental differences in children's abilities to solve problems like the balance-beam scenario.

Case defined the central-processing structures as "central" in at least three different ways. First, they form the conceptual "centre" of children's understanding of a broad array of situations, both within and across culturally defined disciplines or content areas. Second, they form the core elements out of which more elaborate structures will be constructed in the future. In effect, central-processing structures constitute the conceptual kernel on which children's future cognitive growth will depend. Third, they are the product of children's central-processing or working-memory capacity. When children are asked to solve tasks such as the balance-beam problem, the content of information used in working memory is domain-specific (that is, the properties of the balance beam). However, the limitations associated with working-memory or information-processing capacity are system-wide. Younger children fail to solve the balance-beam problem because they do not have the processing resources to manage more than one dimension at a time.

Case's construct allows us to understand why young children generally perform more poorly than their older peers, and explains why these outcomes may not be consistent across domains.

---

that Piaget did not highlight enough. Indeed, the belief that social interaction contributes importantly to cognitive growth is a cornerstone of the *sociocultural perspective* on cognitive development offered by one of Piaget's contemporaries, Lev Vygotsky.

VYGOTSKY'S SOCIOCULTURAL PERSPECTIVE

sociocultural theory
Vygotsky's perspective on cognitive development, in which children acquire their culture's values, beliefs, and problem-solving strategies through collaborative dialogues with more knowledgeable members of society

In order to view Piaget's work from a new vantage point, let's consider a perspective on cognitive development that has been arousing a great deal of interest lately—the **sociocultural theory** of Lev Vygotsky (1934/1962; 1930–35/1978; see also Rogoff, 1990, 1998; Wertsch & Tulviste, 1992). This Russian developmentalist was an active scholar in the 1920s and 1930s when Piaget was formulating his theory. Unfortunately, Vygotsky died at the age of 38 before his work was complete. Nevertheless, he left us with much food for thought by insisting that (1) cognitive growth occurs in a sociocultural context that influences the form it takes, and (2) many of a child's most noteworthy cognitive skills evolve from social interactions with parents, teachers, and other more competent associates.

253

Chapter Seven
*Cognitive Development: Piaget's
Theory, Case's Neo-Piagetian
Theory, and Vygotsky's
Sociocultural Viewpoint*

The Role of Culture in Intellectual Development

Four Interrelated Levels of Analysis

Vygotsky proposed that we should evaluate human development from four interrelated perspectives: ontogenetic, microgenetic, phylogenetic, and sociohistorical. **Ontogenetic development**, development of the individual over his or her lifetime, is the topic of this book and the level of analysis for nearly all developmental psychologists. **Microgenetic development** refers to changes that occur over relatively brief periods of time, such as those one may see in a child solving addition problems every week for 11 consecutive weeks (Siegler & Jenkins, 1989), or even the changes in children's use of memory strategies over five different trials in the course of a 20-minute session (Coyle & Bjorklund, 1997). This is obviously a finer-grained analysis than that afforded by the traditional ontogenetic perspective. **Phylogenetic development** refers to changes over evolutionary time, measured in thousands and even millions of years. Here, Vygotsky anticipated the current evolutionary psychology perspective, believing that an understanding of the species' history can provide insight into child development (Geary & Bjorklund, 2000; Bjorklund & Pellegrini, 2000). Finally, **sociohistorical development** refers to the changes that have occurred in one's culture and the values, norms, and technologies such a history has generated. It is this sociohistorical perspective that modern-day researchers have emphasized most about Vygotsky's ideas, particularly his belief that human cognition, even when carried out in isolation, is inherently *sociocultural*—affected by the beliefs, values, and tools of intellectual adaptation passed to individuals by their culture. And because these values and intellectual tools may vary substantially from culture to culture, Vygotsky believed that neither the course nor the content of intellectual growth is as universal as Piaget assumed.

The sociocultural theory of Lev Vygotsky (1896–1934) views cognitive development as a socially mediated process that may vary from culture to culture.

Tools of Intellectual Adaptation

Vygotsky proposed that infants are born with a few *elementary mental functions*—attention, sensation, perception, and memory—that are eventually transformed by the culture into new and more sophisticated mental processes he called *higher mental functions*. Take memory, for example. Young children's early memorial capabilities are limited by biological constraints to the images and impressions they can produce. However, each culture provides its children with **tools of intellectual adaptation** that permit them to use their basic mental functions more adaptively. So children in information-age societies may enhance their memory by taking notes, whereas their age-mates in preliterate societies represent each object they must remember by tying a knot in a string. Such socially transmitted memory strategies and other cultural tools teach children how to use their minds—in short, *how* to think. And since each culture also transmits specific beliefs and values, it teaches children *what* to think as well.

One subtle difference in cultural tools of intellectual adaptation that can make a noticeable difference in children's cognitive functioning is how a language names its numbers. For example, in all languages, the first 10 digits must be learned by rote. However, after that, some languages take advantage of the base-10 number system and name numbers accordingly. English does this beginning at 20 ("twenty-one," "twenty-two," and so on). However, the teen numbers in English are not so easily represented. Rather, 11 and 12 also must be memorized. Not until 13 does a base-10 system begin (three + ten = "thirteen"), and even then, several of the number names do not correspond to the formula digit + ten. "Fourteen," "sixteen," "seventeen," "eighteen," and "nineteen" do, but the number names for "thirteen" and "fifteen" are not as straightforward (i.e., they are not expressed as "threeteen" and "fiveteen"). What's more, the teen numbers state the digit unit first ("*four*teen," "*six*teen"), whereas the higher numbers state the decade number first ("*twenty*-one," "*thirty*-two"). Thus the number system becomes regular in English beginning with number 20.

ontogenetic development
development of the individual over his or her lifetime

microgenetic development
changes that occur over relatively brief periods of time—in seconds, minutes, or days—as opposed to larger-scale changes, as conventionally studied in ontogenetic development

phylogenetic development
development over evolutionary time

sociohistorical development
changes that have occurred in one's culture and the values, norms, and technologies such a history has generated

tools of intellectual adaptation
Vygotsky's term for methods of thinking and problem-solving strategies that children internalize from their interactions with more competent members of society

Other languages, such as Chinese, have a more systematic number-naming system. In Chinese, as in English, the first 10 digits must be memorized. However, from this point, the Chinese number-naming system follows a base-10 logic, with the name for 11 translating as "ten one," the name for 12 translating as "ten two," and so on. Kevin Miller and his colleagues (1995) reasoned that differences in the number-naming systems between English and Chinese might be associated with early mathematical competence, specifically counting. They tested 3- through 5-year-old children in Champaign-Urbana, Illinois, and Beijing, China. They asked each child to count as high as possible. There were no cultural differences for the 3-year-olds, but the Chinese children began to show a counting advantage by age 4, and this advantage was even larger at age 5. Further analyses indicated that cultural differences were centred on the teens: Although more than 90 percent of children could count to 10, only 48 percent of American children could count to 20, compared to 74 percent of the Chinese children. These findings indicate how differences in the number-naming system of a language (a tool of intellectual adaptation) can contribute to an early difference in mathematical competence—one that might well contribute to the later differences in mathematical abilities that have been observed between Chinese and American children (Stevenson & Lee, 1990).

The Social Origins of Early Cognitive Competencies

Vygotsky agreed with Piaget that young children are curious explorers who are actively involved in learning and discovering new principles. However, unlike Piaget, Vygotsky believed that many of the truly important "discoveries" that children make result not from solitary explorations; instead, they occur within the context of cooperative, or collaborative, *dialogues* between a skillful tutor, who models the activity and transmits verbal instructions, and a novice pupil, who first seeks to understand the tutor's instruction and eventually internalizes this information, using it to regulate his or her own performance.

To illustrate collaborative (or guided) learning as Vygotsky viewed it, let's imagine that Annie, a 4-year-old, has just received her first jigsaw puzzle as a birthday present. She attempts to work the puzzle but gets nowhere until her father comes along, sits down beside her, and gives her some tips. He suggests that it would be a good idea to put together the corners first, points to the pink area at the edge of one corner piece and says, "Let's look for another pink piece." When Annie seems frustrated, he places two interlocking pieces near each other so that she will notice them, and when Annie succeeds, he offers words of encouragement. As Annie gradually gets the hang of it, he steps back and lets her work more and more independently.

The Zone of Proximal Development

How do collaborative dialogues foster cognitive growth? First, Vygotsky would say that Annie and her father are operating in what he called the **zone of proximal development**—the difference between what a learner can accomplish independently and what he or she can accomplish with the guidance and encouragement of a more skilled partner. It is this zone in which sensitive instruction should be aimed and in which new cognitive growth can be expected to occur. Annie obviously becomes a more compe-

zone of proximal development
Vygotsky's term for the range of tasks that are too complex to be mastered alone but can be accomplished with guidance and encouragement from a more skilled partner

According to Vygotsky, new skills are often easier to acquire if children receive guidance and encouragement from a more competent associate.

255

Chapter Seven
Cognitive Devlopment: Piaget's Theory, Case's Neo-Piagetian Theory, and Vygotsky's Sociocultural Viewpoint

tent puzzle-solver with her father's help than without it. More importantly, she will internalize the problem-solving techniques that she uses in collaboration with him and will ultimately use them on her own, rising to a new level of independent mastery.

One feature of social collaboration that fosters cognitive growth is **scaffolding**, the tendency of more expert participants to carefully tailor the support they provide to the novice learner's current situation so that he can profit from that support and increase his understanding of a problem (Wood et. al., 1976). It occurs not just in formal educational settings, but any time a more expert person adjusts her input to guide a child to a level near the limits of his capabilities. The behaviour of Annie's father in the preceding example reflects not only working in the zone of proximal development, but also scaffolding.

Consider another example of effective scaffolding observed by Michael Pratt and colleagues at Wilfrid Laurier University (Pratt et al., 1992). In an observational study of parent tutoring of Grade 5 students' long-division math homework, parents were more likely to provide tutorial support to children who had poorer initial skills on solving long-division problems. In addition, greater parental support was offered, on average, when the children experienced failure at solving the problems, while less support was offered following success, consistent with a scaffolding approach. Decreasing the level of support after success allows the child to take greater responsibility for the task. Children whose parents adjusted their tutorial support according to their child's level of expertise were also more likely to be successful in solving long-division problems in an independent session following the tutoring (see also Pratt & Savoy-Levine, 1998).

All the responsibility for determining the extent of adult involvement is not on the adult. Both adults and children jointly determine the degree to which children can function independently. For example, children who are less able to solve problems on their own will elicit more support from adults than will more capable children. More skilled children need less adult support, or scaffolding, to solve a problem (Plumert & Nichols-Whitehead, 1996). Similarly, Tara Callaghan from St. Francis Xavier University found that young children aged 3 and 4 who received scaffolding produced better drawings than children who did not (Callaghan & Rankin, 2002).

Apprenticeship in Thinking and Guided Participation

In many cultures, children do not learn by going to school with other children, nor do their parents formally teach such lessons as weaving and hunting. Instead, they learn through **guided participation**—by actively *participating* in culturally relevant activities alongside more skilled partners who provide necessary aid and encouragement (Rogoff, 1998; Rogoff et al., 1993). Guided participation is an informal "apprenticeship in thinking" in which children's cognitions are shaped as they partake, alongside adults or other more skillful associates, in such everyday culturally relevant tasks as preparing food, tracking prey, harvesting crops, or simply conversing about the world around them. Barbara Rogoff believes that cognitive growth is shaped as much or more by these informal adult–child transactions as it is by more formal teaching or educational experiences.

The idea of an apprenticeship or guided participation may seem reasonable in cultures where children are integrated early into the daily activities of adult life, such as the agrarian Mayans of Guatemala and Mexico, or the !Kung of Africa, whose hunting-and-gathering lifestyle has remained virtually unchanged for thousands of years. But this idea may seem less relevant for a culture such as our own, because many aspects of cognitive development in Western culture have shifted from parents to professional educators, whose job it is to teach important cultural knowledge and skills to children. Nevertheless, learning certainly occurs at home in modern societies, particularly during the preschool years. And in many ways, these home learning experiences prepare children for the schooling that will follow. For example, formal education in Canada, Europe, and the United States involves children responding to adults' questions when the adults already know the answers. It also involves learning and discussing things that have no immediate relevance—knowledge for knowledge's sake. Such **context-independent learning**, foreign to so many cultures, is fostered from infancy and early childhood in our own culture (Rogoff, 1990). Consider the following interchange between 19-month-old Brittany and her mother:

scaffolding
process by which an expert, when instructing a novice, responds contingently to the novice's behaviour in a learning situation, so that the novice gradually increases his or her understanding of a problem

guided participation
adult–child interactions in which children's cognitions and modes of thinking are shaped as they participate with or observe adults engaged in culturally relevant activities

context-independent learning
learning that has no immediate relevance to the present context, as is done in modern schools; acquiring knowledge for knowledge's sake

MOTHER: Brittany, what's at the park?

BRITTANY: Babyswing.

MOTHER: That's right, the babyswing. And what else?

BRITTANY: (shrugs)

MOTHER: A slide?

BRITTANY: (smiling, nods yes)

MOTHER: And what else is at the park?

BRITTANY: (shrugs)

MOTHER: A see …

BRITTANY: Seesaw!

MOTHER: That's right, a seesaw.

This type of conversation is typical for a Canadian mother and her child, and it is a good example of Vygotsky's zone of proximal development. Brittany, in this case, was not only learning to recall specific objects with her mother's help, but was also learning the importance of remembering information *out of context* (mother and daughter were in their living room at the time, far from the park). Brittany was learning that she could be called upon to state facts to her mother that her mother already knew. She was also learning that she could depend on her mother to help provide answers when she was unable to generate them herself. Yet, as Box 7.6 explains, the guided participation that children in traditional cultures experience is often much less verbal and less directive than that which is typical of Western societies.

Another important behaviour that is often guided by older, more expert associates is children's play activity. Investigators have found that toddlers are more likely to engage in symbolic play when they play with someone else rather than alone, and that mothers, in particular, stimulate high levels of symbolic play from young children (Bornstein et al., 1996; Youngblade & Dunn, 1995). Close examinations of play episodes between mothers and their 21-month-old toddlers reveal that many mothers adjust their level of play to that of their child. What's more, mothers who know the most about the development of play provide the most challenging play interactions by adjusting their own playful behaviours to a level just beyond the child's own (Damast, Tamis-LeMonda, & Bornstein, 1996). So, consistent with Vygotsky's idea of a zone of proximal development and Rogoff's idea of guided participation, children who play with more skilled partners become more proficient players than those who lack this social support.

Similar guidance of children's play activities occurs in most cultures, although there are cultural differences in the form that this guidance takes. Chinese children, for example, pretend more with caregivers than with other children, whereas Irish-American children show the opposite pattern (Haight et al., 1999). Argentine mothers are more likely than American mothers to involve their 20-month-old toddlers in symbolic play, but are less likely than American mothers to foster *exploratory* play (Bornstein et al., 1999). Much remains to be determined about how these cultural variations in play styles influence child development. Yet we do know that it is important to facilitate children's play, because according to Astington and Jenkins (1995) from the University of Toronto, the amount of cooperative social pretend play that preschoolers display (usually with siblings or parents) is a good predictor of their later understanding of other people's feelings and beliefs (see also Youngblade & Dunn, 1995). Indeed, an understanding that others can have thoughts, emotions, and beliefs that differ from one's own (and that account for much of their behaviour) represents what has been called a *theory of mind*—a development we will discuss in Chapter 12 that is thought to provide the foundation for all complex social cognitive abilities that humans display. Viewed in this way, the scaffolding of pretend play by parents and other more competent associates seems to be a most important guided participation indeed.

It is easy to think of cognitive development as something that "just happens" exactly the same way for children worldwide. After all, evolution has provided all humans with a uniquely human nervous system, and virtually no one would deny that

Although the process of guided participation may be universal, how it is carried out varies from culture to culture. Rogoff and her colleagues (1993) have classified cultures into two general types: (1) cultures such as ours, where, beginning in the preschool years, children are often segregated from adults and receive much culturally important information in school; and (2) cultures where children are in close contact most of the day with adults, observing and interacting with them while they perform culturally important activities. Rogoff then observed 14 families with toddlers in each of four communities, two where culturally important information is transmitted mainly "out of context," through formal schooling (Salt Lake City, in the United States, and Kecioren, a middle-class community in Turkey), and two where culturally important information is transmitted mainly in context (the Guatemalan Mayan town of San Pedro and Dhol-Ki-Patti, a tribal village in India). Toddlers and their caregivers were observed while performing routine activities (for example, feeding, dressing), playing social games (for example, peekaboo), and playing with novel objects (for example, an embroidery hoop, a jumping jack—a marionette that kicks its legs). The following excerpts are two examples of guided participation, one from the middle-class United States community in Salt Lake City, and the other from the tribal Indian village of Dhol-Ki-Patti.

Salt Lake City: A 21-month-old boy and his mother exploring a glass jar that contains a peewee doll.

Sandy's mother held the jar up and chirped excitedly, "What is it? What's inside?" and then pointed to the peewee doll inside. "Is that a little person?" When Sandy pulled down on the jar, she suggested, "Can you take the lid off?"

Sandy inspected the round knob on top and said, "Da ball."

"Da ball, yeah," his mother confirmed. "Pull the lid," she encouraged, and demonstrated pulling on the knob. "Can you pull?" Sandy put his hand on hers, and they pulled the lid off together triumphantly. "What's inside?" asked his mother, and took the peewee out. "Who is that?"

Sandy reached for the lid, and mother provided running commentary. "OK you put the lid back on." And when Sandy exclaimed "Oh!" his mother repeated "Oh!" after him. When Sandy lost interest, his mother asked with mock disappointment, "Oh, you don't want to play anymore?" and suggested, "We could make him play peekaboo."

When Sandy took the peewee out, she asked "Where did he go?" and sang, "There, he's all gone," as she covered the peewee with her hands, "Aaall gone." (Rogoff et al., 1993, p. 81)

Dhol-Ki-Patti, India: An 18-month-old girl and her mother playing with a jumping jack.

Roopa was not holding the top and bottom strings taut enough to cause the jumping jack to jump, so her mother took Roopa's hand in her own, grasped the bottom string with both hands, and pulled on the string twice, saying, "Pull here, pull here," as she demonstrated. She then released her hold of Roopa's hand to enable Roopa to do it on her own.

But the jumping jack fell to the ground because Roopa was not holding it tight. The mother, quick to help, lifted the jumping jack as Roopa reached for it. Twice again, she pulled on the bottom string with her left hand, repeating, "Pull it here." Then she released her hold, letting Roopa take the object. She held her hands close to (but not touching) Roopa's, ready to help if necessary. (Rogoff et al., 1993, p. 114)

Although toddlers and caregivers in all communities interacted in ways permitting all participants to develop an understanding of the task at hand, there were important differences between the middle-class and more traditional communities. As illustrated in these examples, parents in Salt Lake City (and the Turkish town) placed a far greater emphasis on verbal than nonverbal instruction, with the adults providing a good deal of structure to foster children's involvement in learning, including praise and other techniques to motivate their charges. By contrast, parents in the Mayan and Indian villages used more explicit *nonverbal* communication and only occasionally instructed their children in a particular task. In these communities, children are around adults most of the day, and they can observe competent adult behaviour and interact with adults while they perform the important tasks of their society. Rogoff and her colleagues concluded that children's observation skills are more important and better developed in traditional than in middle-class communities, with children in the traditional communities being better at learning by attending to adult behaviour.

Rogoff's findings make it clear that there is not one single path to becoming an effective member of society, and that different forms of guided participation are likely to be used, depending on the requirements culture places on adults and children. One form is not necessarily better than another—it depends on how a competent adult in a society is expected to behave and on what skills a competent child is expected to acquire.

the centre of our flexible intelligence is the brain. Yet intelligence is also rooted in the environment, particularly in the culture. Understanding how cultural beliefs and technological tools influence cognitive development through child-rearing practices helps us better comprehend the process of development and our role as guides in fostering that process.

Implications for Education

Vygotsky's theory has some rather obvious implications for education. Like Piaget, Vygotsky stressed active rather than passive learning and took great care to assess what the learner already knew, thereby estimating what he was capable of learning. The major difference in approaches concerns the role of the instructor. Whereas students in Piaget's classroom would spend more time in independent, discovery-based activities, teachers in Vygotsky's classroom would favour guided participations in which they structure the learning activity, provide helpful hints or instructions that are carefully tailored to the child's current abilities, and then monitor the learner's progress, gradually turning over more of the mental activity to their pupils. Teachers may also arrange *cooperative learning exercises* in which students are encouraged to assist one another; the idea here is that the less competent members of the team are likely to benefit from the instruction they receive from their more skillful peers, who also benefit by playing the role of teacher (Palinscar, Brown, & Campione, 1993).

Is there any evidence that Vygotsky's collaborative-learning approach might be a particularly effective educational strategy? Consider what Lisa Freund (1990) found when she had 3- to 5-year-olds help a puppet decide which furnishings (for example, sofas, beds, bathtubs, and stoves) should be placed in each of six rooms of a dollhouse that the puppet was moving into. First, children were tested to determine what they already knew about proper furniture placement. Then each child worked at a similar task, either alone (as might be the case in Piaget's discovery-based classroom) or with his or her mother (Vygotsky's guided learning). Then to assess what they had learned, children performed a final, rather complex, furniture-sorting task. The results were clear: Children who had sorted furniture with help from their mothers showed dramatic improvements in sorting ability, whereas those who had practised on their own showed little improvement at all, even though they had received some corrective feedback from the experimenter (see also Diaz, Neal, & Vachio, 1991; Rogoff, 1998).

Similar advances in problem-solving skills have been reported when children collaborate with peers, as opposed to working alone (Azmitia, 1992; Gauvain & Rogoff, 1989; Johnson & Johnson, 1987), and the youngsters who gain the most from these collaborations are those who were initially much less competent than their partners (Azmitia, 1988; Tudge, 1992). Johnson and Johnson (1987) conducted an analysis of 378 studies that compared the achievement of people working alone versus cooperatively and found that cooperative learning resulted in superior performance in more than half of the studies; by contrast, working alone resulted in improved performance in fewer than 10 percent of the studies.

There appear to be at least three reasons why cooperative learning is effective. First, children are often more motivated when working on problems together (Johnson & Johnson, 1989). Second, cooperative learning requires children to explain their ideas to one another and to resolve conflicts. These activities help young collaborators to examine their own ideas more closely and to become better at articulating them so that they can be understood. Finally, children are more likely to use high-quality cognitive strategies while working together—strategies that often lead to ideas and solutions that no one in the group would likely have generated alone (Johnson & Johnson, 1989).

As with other aspects of sociocultural theory, the effectiveness of collaborative learning varies by culture. North American children, accustomed to competitive "do your own work" classrooms, sometimes find it difficult to adjust to the shared decision making found in cooperative learning (see Rogoff, 1998), although they get better at cooperative decision making with practice (Socha & Socha, 1994). As the structure of schools changes to support peer collaboration, with teachers' roles being that of active participants in the children's learning experiences and not simply directors of it, the benefits of cooperative learning are sure to increase (Rogoff, 1998).

259

Chapter Seven
*Cognitive Development: Piaget's
Theory, Case's Neo-Piagetian
Theory, and Vygotsky's
Sociocultural Viewpoint*

The Role of Language in Cognitive Development

From Vygotsky's viewpoint, language plays two critical roles in cognitive development by (1) serving as the primary vehicle through which adults pass culturally valued modes of thinking and problem solving on to their children, and (2) eventually becoming one of the more powerful "tools" of intellectual adaptation in its own right. As it turns out, Vygotsky's perspective on language and thinking contrasts sharply with that of Piaget.

Piaget's Theory of Language and Thought

Piaget was very interested in children's language, and he observed that infants' first words were typically centred on objects and activities that they already understood through nonverbal sensorimotor processes. He then concluded that language clearly illustrates the child's *existing* schemes but plays no meaningful role in shaping thought or helping the child to construct new knowledge.

As Piaget (1926) recorded the chatterings of preschool children, he noticed that they often talked *to themselves* as they went about their daily activities, almost as if they were play-by-play announcers ("Put the big piece in the corner. Not that one, the pink one"). Indeed, two preschool children playing close to each other sometimes carried on their own separate monologues rather than truly conversing. Piaget called these self-directed utterances **egocentric speech**—talk not addressed to anyone in particular and not adapted in any meaningful way so that a companion might understand it.

What part might such speech play in a child's cognitive development? Very little, according to Piaget, who saw egocentric speech as merely reflecting the child's ongoing mental activity. However, he did observe that speech becomes progressively more social and less egocentric toward the end of the preoperational stage, which he attributed to the child's increasing ability to assume the perspective of others and thus adapt her speech so that listeners might understand. So here was another example of how cognitive development (a decline in egocentrism) was said to promote language development (a shift from egocentric to communicative speech), rather than the other way around.

> **?** ────────────── **WHAT DO YOU THINK?**
>
> Starting at a pupil's current level of mastery, many computer-assisted instructional programs present increasingly difficult problems, often diagnosing errors and intervening with hints of clues when progress has broken down. Why might both Piaget and Vygotsky see some merit in supplementing traditional classroom instruction with these computer-assisted learning activities?

Vygotsky's Theory of Language and Thought

Vygotsky agreed with Piaget that the child's earliest thinking is prelinguistic and that early language often reflects what the child already knows. However, he argued that thought and language eventually merge and that many of the nonsocial utterances that Piaget called "egocentric" actually illustrate the transition from prelinguistic to verbal reasoning.

According to Vygotsky, a preschool child's self-directed monologues occur more often in some contexts than in others. Specifically, Vygotsky observed that children are more likely to talk to themselves as they attempt to solve problems or achieve important goals, and he claimed that this nonsocial speech increased dramatically whenever these young problem solvers encountered obstacles in pursuing their objectives. He then concluded that nonsocial speech is not egocentric but communicative; it is "speech for self," or **private speech**, that helps young children to plan strategies and regulate their behaviour so that they are more likely to accomplish their goals. Viewed through this theoretical lens, language may thus play a critical role in cognitive development by making children more organized and efficient problem solvers! Vygotsky also claimed that private speech becomes more abbreviated with age, progressing from the whole phrases that 4-year-olds produce, to single words, to simple lip movements that are more common among 7- to 9-year-olds. His view was that private speech never completely disappears; it serves as a **cognitive self-guidance system** and then goes "underground," becoming silent or *inner speech*—the covert verbal thought that we use to organize and regulate our everyday activities.

egocentric speech
Piaget's term for the subset of a young child's utterances that are nonsocial—that is, neither directed to others nor expressed in ways that listeners might understand

private speech
Vygotsky's term for the subset of a child's verbal utterances that serve a self-communicative function and guide the child's thinking

cognitive self-guidance system
in Vygotsky's theory, the use of private speech to guide problem-solving behaviour

Which Viewpoint Should We Endorse?

Contemporary research sides squarely with Vygotsky's theory over that of Piaget (see Berk, 1992). It seems that the *social speech* that occurs during guided learning episodes (for example, the conversation between Annie and her father as they worked jointly on a puzzle) gives rise to much of the *private speech* (Annie's talking aloud as she tries to work the puzzle on her own) that preschool children display. Also consistent with Vygotsky's claims, children rely more heavily on private speech when facing difficult rather than easy tasks. For example, Robert Duncan of Sir Francis Xavier University and Michael Pratt of Wilfrid Laurier University asked preschoolers to carry out paper-folding and story-sequencing tasks over three sessions. They found that a greater percentage of preschoolers' private speech occurred when they were presented with difficult or novel items compared to easy or familiar items (Duncan & Pratt, 1997). Children also often use private speech when deciding how to proceed after making errors (Berk, 1992), and their performance often improves after using self-instruction (Behrend, Rosengren, & Perlmutter, 1989; Berk & Spuhl, 1995). Furthermore, it is the brighter preschool children who rely most heavily on private speech, a finding that links this "self-talk" to cognitive *competence* rather than the cognitive immaturity (egocentrism) that Piaget claimed it represents (Berk, 1992; Kohlberg, Yaeger, & Hjertholm, 1968). Finally, private speech does eventually go underground, progressing from words and phrases to whispers and mutterings, to inner speech (Bivens & Berk, 1990), and this internalization process occurs earlier among the brighter members of an elementary-school class (Berk & Landau, 1993; Kohlberg et al., 1968).

So private speech does appear to be an important tool of intellectual adaptation—a means by which children plan and regulate their mental activities to solve problems and make new discoveries (Vygotsky, 1934/1962).

Vygotsky in Perspective: Summary and Evaluation

Vygotsky's sociocultural theory offers a new lens through which to view cognitive development by stressing the importance of specific social processes that Piaget (and others) largely overlooked. According to Vygotsky, children's minds develop as they (1) take part in cooperative dialogues with skilled partners on tasks that are within their zone of proximal development, and (2) incorporate what skillful tutors say to them into what they say to themselves. As social speech is translated into private speech and then inner speech, the culture's preferred methods of thinking and problem solving—or tools of intellectual adaptation—work their way from the language of competent tutors into the child's own thinking.

Unlike Piaget, who stressed *universal* sequences of cognitive growth, Vygotsky's theory leads us to expect wide variations in cognitive development across cultures that reflect differences in children's cultural experiences. So children in Western cultures acquire context-independent memory and reasoning skills that prepare them for highly structured Western classrooms, whereas children of Australian and African Bushmen hunters acquire elaborate spatial reasoning skills that prepare them to successfully track the prey on which their lives absolutely depend. Neither set of cognitive capacities is necessarily any more "advanced" than the other; instead, they represent alternative forms of reasoning, or "tools of adaptation," that have evolved because they enable children to adapt successfully to cultural values and traditions (Rogoff, 1998; Vygotsky, 1978).

As we see in Table 7.4, Vygotsky's theory challenges many of Piaget's most basic assumptions and has attracted a lot of attention lately among Western developmentalists, whose own research efforts tend to support his ideas. Yet many of Vygotsky's writ-

261

Chapter Seven
Cognitive Development: Piaget's
Theory, Case's Neo-Piagetian
Theory, and Vygotsky's
Sociocultural Viewpoint

TABLE 7.4	Comparing Vygotsky's and Piaget's Theories of Cognitive Development	
Vygotsky's sociocultural theory	**Piaget's cognitive-developmental theory**	
1. Cognitive development varies across cultures.	Cognitive development is mostly universal across cultures.	
2. Cognitive growth stems from social interactions (from guided learning within the zone of proximal development as children and their partners "co-construct" knowledge).	Cognitive development stems largely from independent explorations in which children construct knowledge on their own.	
3. Social processes become individual–psychological processes (for example, social speech becomes private speech and, eventually, inner speech).	Individual (egocentric) processes become social processes (for example, egocentric speech is adapted in ways to allow more effective communication).	
4. Adults are especially important as change agents (by transmitting their culture's tools of intellectual adaptation that children internalize).	Peers are especially important as change agents (because peer contacts promote social perspective taking, a topic we will explore in detail in Chapter 12).	

ings are only now being translated from Russian to other languages (Wertsch & Tulviste, 1992), and his theory has not received the intense scrutiny that Piaget's theory has. Nevertheless, at least some of his ideas have already been challenged. Barbara Rogoff (1990, 1998), for example, argues that guided participations that rely heavily on the kinds of verbal instruction that Vygotsky emphasized may be less adaptive in some cultures or less useful for some forms of learning than for others. A young child learning to stalk prey in Australia's outback or to plant, care for, and harvest rice in Southeast Asia may profit more from observation and practice than from verbal instruction and encouragement (see also Rogoff et al., 1993). Other investigators are finding that collaborative problem solving among peers does not always benefit the collaborators and may actually *undermine* task performance if the more competent collaborator is not very confident about what he knows or fails to adapt his instruction to a partner's level of understanding (Levin & Druyan, 1993; Tudge, 1992). Robert Duncan suggests that private speech is used with considerable frequency by adults, challenging Vygotsky's claims that this speech form is peculiar to childhood (2000). But despite whatever criticism his theory may generate in the years ahead, Vygotsky has provided a valuable service by reminding us that cognitive growth, like all other aspects of development, is best understood when studied in the cultural and social contexts in which it occurs.

✔
Concept Check 7.4
Understanding Vygotsky's
Sociocultural Theory

Check your understanding of some of the basic premises of Vygotsky's theory by matching each of the following concepts with the descriptions listed below: (a) tools of intellectual adaptation, (b) private speech, (c) zone of proximal development, (d) elementary mental functions, (e) guided participation, (f) cooperative learning exercises, (g) scaffolding. The answers appear in the Appendix.

_____ 1. important means of planning and self-regulation
_____ 2. problems children cannot master alone but will master with skillful guidance

_____ 3. informal means by which culturally significant cognitive processes are transferred across generations
_____ 4. sensitive tailoring of guidance to a novice learner's capabilities
_____ 5. that which is transformed in the context of collaborative activities with more skillful associates
_____ 6. culturally significant cognitive processes and methods of problem solving
_____ 7. mechanism by which peers can become significant contributors to cognitive development

SUMMARY

♦ This and the following two chapters are devoted to an examination of **cognition**, the mental processes by which humans acquire and use knowledge, and to **cognitive development**.

Piaget's Theory of Cognitive Development

♦ Piaget's theory of **genetic epistemology** (cognitive development) defines **intelligence** as a basic life function that helps the child to adapt to the environment. Piaget described children as active explorers who **construct** three kinds of **schemes** (**behavioural, symbolic, and operational**) to establish **cognitive equilibrium** between their thinking and their experiences. Schemes are constructed and modified through the processes of **organization** and **adaptation**. Adaptation consists of two complementary activities: **assimilation** (attempts to fit new experiences to existing schemes) and **accommodation** (modifying existing schemes in response to new experiences). Cognitive growth results as assimilations stimulate accommodations, which induce the reorganization of schemes, permitting further assimilations, and so on.

Piaget's Stages of Cognitive Development

♦ Piaget claimed that intellectual growth proceeds through an **invariant developmental sequence** of stages that can be summarized as follows:

♦ **Sensorimotor stage** (0 to 2 years). From basic **reflex activity**, infants over the first two years come to know and understand objects and events by acting on them, constructing **primary, secondary**, and **tertiary circular reactions**. These behavioural schemes are eventually internalized to form mental symbols that support such achievements as **inner experimentation**. Although Piaget's general sequences of sensorimotor development have been confirmed, recent evidence indicates that Piaget's explanation of **A-not-B errors** was incorrect and that infants achieve such milestones as **deferred imitation** and **object permanence** earlier than Piaget thought. Alternative approaches, such as **neonativism** and **"theory" theories**, assume, counter to Piaget, that infants possess innate knowledge that directs their early development.

♦ **Preoperational stage** (roughly 2 to 7 years). Symbolic reasoning increases dramatically as children in the **preconceptual period** rely on **symbolic function** and display **representational insight**. Symbolism gradually becomes more sophisticated as children acquire a capacity for **dual representation**. However, Piaget described the thinking of 2- to 7-year-olds as **animistic** and **egocentric**, characterized by **centration**. Although preoperational children often fail to make **appearance/reality distinctions**, recent research indicates that they are much more logical and less egocentric when thinking about familiar issues or about simplified versions of Piaget's tests. Furthermore, procedures such as **identity training** enable preoperational children to solve complex problems such as Piaget's **conservation** tasks. So preschool children possess an early capacity for logical reasoning that Piaget overlooked.

♦ **Concrete-operational stage** (7 to 11 years). During concrete operations, children acquire such cognitive operations as **decentration** and **reversibility** that enable them to think logically and systematically about tangible objects, events, and experiences. Becoming operational in their thinking permits children to conserve, **seriate**, and display **transitivity**. However, concrete operators can apply their logic only to real or tangible aspects of experience and cannot reason abstractly.

♦ **Formal-operational stage** (11 or 12 and beyond). Formal-operational reasoning is rational, abstract, and much like the **hypothetico-deductive reasoning** of a scientist. Attainment of formal operations may sometimes contribute to confusion and idealism. Formal operations may elude those adolescents and adults who have not been exposed to educational experiences that foster this reasoning. And even at this highest level, performance is uneven: Adults are most likely to display formal operations in areas of special interest or expertise.

An Evaluation of Piaget's Theory

♦ Piaget founded the field of cognitive development and provided the first theory that purported to explain and not simply describe cognitive growth. Many important principles about developing children were discovered by Piaget, who influenced thousands of researchers in psychology and related fields.

♦ Although Piaget seems to have adequately described general sequences of intellectual development, his tendency to infer underlying competencies from intellectual performances often led him to underestimate children's cognitive capabilities. Some investigators have challenged Piaget's assumption that development occurs in stages, and others have criticized his theory for failing to specify how children progress from one stage of intellect to the next, and for underestimating social and cultural influences on intellectual development.

Case's Neo-Piagetian Theory

♦ Robbie Case agreed with Piaget's constructs of accommodation and assimilation, but he refined our understanding of how these processes take place. Specifically, accommodation occurs through problem solving and exploration; assimilation occurs through consolidation and automatization.

Vygotsky's Sociocultural Perspective

♦ Vygotsky's **sociocultural theory** emphasizes social and cultural influences on intellectual growth. He proposed that we should evaluate development from the perspective of four interrelated levels in interaction with children's environments: **ontogenetic**, **microgenetic**, **phylogenetic**, and **sociohistorical**. Each culture transmits beliefs, values, and preferred methods of thinking or problem solving—its **tools of intellectual adaptation**—to each successive generation. Thus, culture teaches children what to think and how to go about it.

♦ Children acquire cultural beliefs, values, and problem-solving strategies in the context of collaborative dialogues with more skillful partners as they gradually internalize their tutor's instructions to master tasks within their **zone of proximal development.** Learning occurs best when more skillful associates properly **scaffold** their intervention. Much of what children acquire from more skillful associates occurs through **guided participation**, a process that may involve highly **context-independent learning** (in Western cultures) or may occur in the context of day-to-day activities (as is most common in traditional cultures).

♦ Unlike Piaget, who argued that children's self-talk, or **egocentric speech**, plays little if any role in constructing new knowledge, Vygotsky claimed that a child's **private speech** becomes a **cognitive self-guidance system** that regulates problem-solving activities and is eventually internalized to become covert, verbal thought. Recent research favours Vygotsky's position over Piaget's, suggesting that language plays a most important role in children's intellectual development.

♦ Vygotsky has provided a valuable service by reminding us that cognitive growth is best understood when studied in the social and cultural contexts in which it occurs. Although this theory has fared well to date, it has yet to receive the intense scrutiny that Piaget's theory has.

KEY TERMS

cognition, 221
cognitive development, 221
genetic epistemology, 222
intelligence, 222
cognitive equilibrium, 222
constructivist, 222
scheme, 223
behavioural schemes, 223
symbolic schemes, 223
cognitive operation, 224
organization, 224
adaptation, 224
assimilation, 224
accommodation, 225
invariant developmental
    sequence, 226
sensorimotor stage, 226
reflex activity, 226
primary circular reactions, 226

secondary circular reactions,
    227
coordination of secondary
    circular reactions, 227
tertiary circular reactions, 227
inner experimentation, 227
deferred imitation, 228
object permanence, 228
A-not-B error, 229
neo-nativism, 229
"theory" theories, 232
preoperational stage, 233
representational insight, 233
preconceptual period, 233
symbolic function, 233
symbolic (or pretend) play, 234
dual representation (dual
    encoding; dual orientation),
    234

animism, 236
egocentrism, 236
appearance/reality distinction,
    237
intuitive period, 238
centration, 238
conservation, 238
decentration, 238
reversibility, 238
identity training, 240
concrete operations, 241
mental seriation, 242
transitivity, 242
horizontal décalage, 242
formal operations, 243
hypothetico-deductive
    reasoning, 243
sociocultural theory, 252
ontogenetic development, 253

microgenetic development,
    253
phylogenetic development,
    253
sociohistorical development,
    253
tools of intellectual adaptation,
    253
zone of proximal development,
    254
scaffolding, 255
guided participation, 255
context-independent learning,
    255
egocentric speech, 259
private speech, 259
cognitive self-guidance system,
    259

You can find further information on the topics covered in this chapter by visiting:

www.developmentalpsych2e.nelson.com

For additional reading, go to InfoTrac College Edition, your on-line research library, at:

infotrac.thomsonlearning.com

Kevin Leigh/Index Stock Imagery

8

Cognitive Development: Information-Processing Perspectives and Connectionism

Information Flow and the Multistore Model

Developmental Differences in Information-Processing Capacity

Developmental Differences in "Software": Strategies and Knowledge of "Thinking"

Fuzzy-Trace Theory: An Alternative Viewpoint

The Development of Attention

Memory: Retaining and Retrieving Information

Problem Solving and Reasoning

The Development of Number and Arithmetic Skills

Evaluating the Information-Processing Perspective

Connectionist Approaches to Cognitive Development

Summary

Piaget's and Vygotsky's theories have had a profound influence on our current understanding of cognitive development. Piaget saw children as active agents in their own development, always constructing knowledge and changing their cognitive structures to better understand the world. Vygotsky saw children as active participants in collaborative arrangements with others, acquiring the tools of thought appropriate for their culture. Yet, the shortcomings of those approaches led many cognitive scholars to believe that a fresh outlook on human cognition was necessary.

Then came the digital computer—a wondrous new invention that intrigued many scientists with its capacity for rapidly and systematically converting input (or information) into output (answers and solutions). Might the operations of a computer be similar in certain respects to the workings of the human mind? Proponents of a third influential viewpoint on cognitive development—the *information-processing perspective*—certainly thought so (Klahr & MacWhinney, 1998; Newell & Simon, 1961).

How is the human mind similar to a computer? One way is that both the mind and a computer have a *limited capacity* for processing information associated with their hardware and software. Computer *hardware* is the machine itself—its keyboard (or input system), storage capacity, and logic units. The mind's "hardware" is the nervous system, including the brain, the sensory receptors, and their neural connections. The computer's *software* consists of the programs used to store and manipulate information—word processing, statistics programs, and the like. The mind, too, has its "software"—rules, strategies, and other "mental programs" that specify how information is registered, interpreted, stored, retrieved, and analyzed. As children's brains and nervous systems mature (hardware improvements) and as they adopt new strategies for attending to information, interpreting it, remembering what they have experienced, and monitoring their mental activities (software improvements), they are able to perform increasingly complex cognitive feats with greater speed and accuracy (Bjorklund, 2000). (Of course, information-processing theorists offer the mind-computer analogy as a metaphor rather than a representation of reality.

INFORMATION FLOW AND THE MULTISTORE MODEL

There is no single information-processing theory of cognition or cognitive development. Yet, central to all information-processing perspectives is the idea that people use a variety of cognitive operations, or strategies, to process information through a limited-capacity system. More than 30 years ago, Richard Atkinson and Richard Shiffrin (1968) developed a **multistore model** of the information-processing system, and this model continues to be a useful guide for understanding how people think. A slightly modified and updated version of their important and influential model appears in Figure 8.1.

As we see in the figure, the first of these components is the **sensory store** (or **sensory register**). This is the system's log-in unit; it simply holds raw sensory input as a kind of "afterimage" (or echo) of what you have sensed. There are separate sensory registers for each sense modality, and presumably they can hold large quantities of information, but only for very brief periods of time (milliseconds in the case of vision). The contents of sensory stores are thus extremely volatile and soon disappear without further processing.

Should you attend to this information, however, it passes into the **short-term store (STS)**, a processing unit that can store a limited amount of information (perhaps five to nine pieces) for several seconds. Thus, the capacity of the short-term store is sufficient to allow you to retain a telephone number for about as long as it takes you to dial it. But unless this information is rehearsed or otherwise operated on, it too is soon lost. The short-term store has also been referred to as the *primary memory*, or *working memory*, because all conscious intellectual activity is thought to take place here. So short-term, or "working," memory has two functions: (1) to store information temporarily so that (2) you can do something with it.

Finally, new information that is operated on while in the short-term store passes into the **long-term store (LTS)**—a vast and relatively permanent storehouse of information that includes your knowledge of the world, your impressions of past experiences and events, and the strategies that you use to process information and solve problems.

This brief description may give the impression that the person plays a relatively passive role in information processing. This is not the case. People must decide what information to attend to, and which, if any, strategies to execute in order to move

multistore model
information-processing model that depicts information as flowing through three processing units (or stores): the sensory store, the short-term store (STS), and the long-term store (LTS)

sensory store (or sensory register)
first information-processing store, in which stimuli are noticed and are briefly available for further processing

short-term store (STS)
second information-processing store, in which stimuli are retained for several seconds and operated upon (also called *working memory*)

long-term store (LTS)
third information-processing store, in which information that has been examined and interpreted is permanently stored for future use

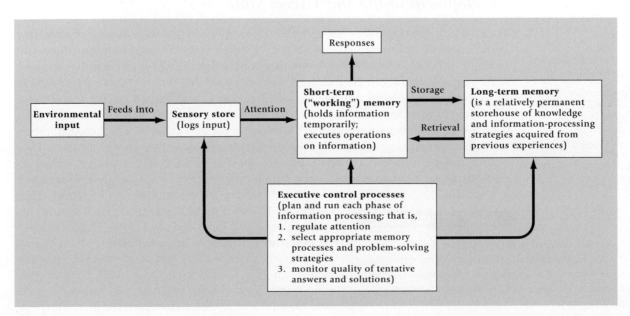

Figure 8.1 *A schematic model of the human information-processing system.* ADAPTED FROM ATKINSON & SHIFFRIN, *1968.*

information through the system. So, information does not simply flow on its own through the various stores, or processing units, of the system; instead, we actively channel the input. This is why most information-processing models include **executive control processes**—the processes involved in planning and monitoring what you attend to and what you do with this input. We sometimes refer to such executive control processes as **metacognition**—knowledge of one's cognitive abilities and processes related to thinking.

Our executive control processes are thought to be largely under voluntary control and are, in fact, what most clearly distinguish human information processors from computers. Unlike computers, we humans must initiate, organize, and monitor our own cognitive activities. We decide what to attend to; we select our own strategies for retaining and retrieving this input; we call up our own programs for solving problems; and last but not least, we are often free to choose the very problems we attempt to solve. Clearly we humans are rather versatile information processors.

In this chapter we will examine developmental differences in several important aspects of children's thinking that have been analyzed from an information-processing perspective. However, we will first look at aspects of children's information processing that influences all types of thinking. Two of these are examples of hardware: the capacity of short-term store and speed of processing. Two others can be considered as forms of software: Children's use of strategies and children's understanding of what it means to think, which is closely related to metacognition, or executive functioning. As we discuss different domains of children's thinking, you will notice that these four aspects of information processing are repeatedly involved in describing and explaining differences in how children think. A fifth factor that is related to the other four and that influences nearly all forms of children's thinking is knowledge base, what children know about the things they are thinking about.

executive control processes
the processes involved in regulating attention and determining what to do with the information just gathered or retrieved from long-term memory

metacognition
one's knowledge about cognition and about the regulation of cognitive activities

knowledge base
one's existing information about a topic or content area

memory span
measure of the amount of information that can be held in the short-term store

span of apprehension
the number of items that people can keep in mind at any one time, or the amount of information that people can attend to at a single time without operating mentally to store this information

DEVELOPMENTAL DIFFERENCES IN INFORMATION-PROCESSING CAPACITY

Development of the Short-Term Store

Traditionally, the capacity of the short-term store has been assessed by tests of **memory span**. Memory span refers to the number of *rapidly presented* and *unrelated* items (for example, digits) that can be recalled in exact order. Age differences in memory span are highly reliable (see Figure 8.2). In fact, they are so reliable that memory span is used as one indication of general intelligence on the two most widely used intelligence tests for children. However, critics of these memory span tests believe that they overestimate the *capacity* of the short-term store. Why? Because people may "chunk" or rehearse numbers presented successively, much as we do when trying to remember phone numbers. Thus developmental differences on traditional memory span tests may represent age differences in strategy use rather than age differences in the capacity of the short-term store.

Clearer evidence for developmental differences in the *capacity* of the short-term store comes from a study by Nelson Cowan and his colleagues (1999). Cowan assessed age differences in **span of apprehension**, a term used to refer to the number of items that people can keep in mind at any one time, or can attend to at once without operating mentally on this information. Does span of apprehension represent an absolute capacity of the short-term store, and does it increase with age? In the study by Cowan

? **WHAT DO YOU THINK?**

Information-processing theorists often point to similarities in the workings of human minds and digital computers. In what important ways might the human mind *differ* from a computer? What kinds of thinking might we humans do better than computers can?

and colleagues (1999), first-grade children, fourth-grade children, and adults played a computer game. Over earphones they also heard series of digits that they were to ignore. Occasionally and unexpectedly, however, they were signalled to recall, in exact order, the most recently presented set of digits they had heard. Because participants were not explicitly attending to the digits, making it unlikely that they were using any encoding strategies to remember them, performance on this task seems to be a fair test of span of apprehension—the capacity of the short-term store. Average span of apprehension was about 3.5 digits for adults, about 3 digits for fourth-grade children, and about 2.5 digits for first-grade children. Cowan and his colleagues interpreted these significant age differences as reflecting a true developmental difference in the capacity of short-term store—a difference that serves as the foundation for age differences on memory span tasks.

Despite these capacity differences in span of apprehension, individual and developmental differences in memory span are also influenced by children's *prior knowledge* of the material they are asked to remember. In one classic study (Chi, 1978), a group of graduate students were given two simple memory tests. The first was a digit-span task. On a second test, they were shown chess pieces on a chessboard (about one chess piece per second), then given the pieces and asked to place them at their previous positions on the board. Their performance on these tasks was compared with that of a group of 10-year-olds. But, in all fairness, these were not typical 10-year-olds; they were all chess experts—winners of local tournaments or members of chess clubs. If younger children simply have smaller short-term stores than adults, the graduate students should have outperformed the 10-year-olds on both memory tests. But this is not what Chi found. As we see in Figure 8.3, the child-experts clearly outperformed the adults when memory for chess pieces was tested. However, their remarkable performance was limited to what they knew well, because they performed much worse than adults when their memory for digits was tested (see also Schneider et al., 1993).

These findings indicate that having a detailed knowledge base for a particular domain (in this case, chess) facilitates memory performance for information from that domain but not necessarily for information from other areas. How does being an "expert" in a subject such as chess result in improved memory span? Although a number of possibilities have been suggested, the factor that seems to play the most crucial role is *ease of item identification*—how quickly the child identifies items to be remembered. Children who are experts in a domain can rapidly process information in that domain and thus have an advantage when it comes to memory span. Their speed of item identification is an indication of their *domain-specific* processing efficiency. Yet, in domains in which they are not experts, older children tend to process most types of information faster than younger children, and faster processing contributes to larger memory spans (Chuah & Maybery, 1999).

Changes in Processing Speed

It is not just identifying items on memory-span tasks that shows age-related improvements in speed of processing. Robert Kail (1992, 1997) finds that general developmental changes in processing speed are similar across a variety of different problems, ranging from simple tasks in which participants must determine whether the objects in two pictures have the same name (for example, are they both pictures of bananas?) to complex mental arithmetic (see also Miller & Vernon, 1997). Kail concedes that our past experiences (such as being a chess expert) can influence speed of processing within a particular domain, but he believes that maturationally based factors are primarily responsible for broad age-related differences in speed of information processing.

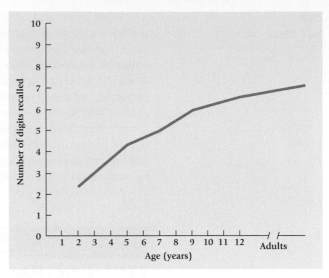

Figure 8.2 *Children's memory span for digits (digit span) shows regular increases with age.* FROM DEMPSTER, 1981.

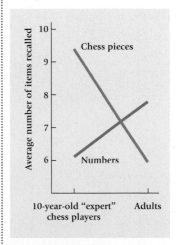

Figure 8.3 *Knowledge base affects memory. Children who are chess "experts" recall more about locations of chess pieces than "novice" adults do. However, adults recall more about numbers than children do, a finding Chi attributes to adults' greater familiarity with (or knowledge of) numbers.* ADAPTED FROM CHI, 1978.

What maturational developments might underlie age-related changes in processing speed? Increased myelinization of neurons in the associative ("thinking") areas of the brain and the elimination of unnecessary (or excess) neural synapses that could interfere with efficient information processing are two possible candidates. As we noted in Chapter 5, myelin is a fatty substance that surrounds nerves and facilitates transmission of nerve impulses. Whereas myelinization of most sensory and motor areas of the brain is accomplished within the first several years of life, myelinization of the associative area is not complete until adolescence or young adulthood. Many theorists have proposed that age differences in myelinization are directly responsible for age differences in speed of information processing, and, ultimately, for age differences in the efficient use of one's limited mental capacity (Bjorklund & Harnishfeger, 1990; Case, 1985; Kail & Salthouse, 1994).

DEVELOPMENTAL DIFFERENCES IN "SOFTWARE": STRATEGIES AND KNOWLEDGE OF "THINKING"

Age differences in information-processing hardware—how much a child can hold in mind at one time and how quickly she can process information—will clearly influence how effectively that child can "think." Yet central to the information-processing perspective is the idea that people possess a variety of cognitive operations that they apply to information, and that both the quantity and quality of these operations change with age.

Cognitive processes vary along a number of dimensions. Some processes are executed automatically, so that you may not even be aware that you are thinking. When you look at a drawing, for example, you effortlessly "see" the images without having to consciously concentrate on converting the light waves into coherent patterns. And if you tried to analyze how you performed such a complicated feat, you probably couldn't do it. Other cognitive processes are more effortful ones, of which we are quite aware. If, when looking at that same picture, for example, you were searching for a particular detail ("Find Waldo"), you would need to use more effortful and planful cognitive processes to perform the task. It is these latter types of processes, called *strategies*, that change substantially with age.

Strategies are usually defined as deliberately implemented, goal-directed operations used to aid task performance (Harnishfeger & Bjorklund, 1990; Schneider & Pressley, 1997). Much of our conscious thinking is guided by strategies, and even young children may discover or invent strategies when they encounter problems in everyday life. Yet, many strategies that children living in information-age societies find so useful are explicitly taught in school (Moely, Santulli, & Obach, 1995). These include strategies involved in mathematics, reading, memory, and scientific problem solving.

Age differences in strategy use account for a substantial part of the age-related differences we see in children's cognitive performance. Generally speaking, younger children use fewer strategies and use them far less effectively than older children do. Yet, the development of cognitive strategies is much more complex than this statement implies, for even young children can use some strategies effectively, and the more sophisticated strategies that older children choose do not always help them as much as one might expect.

Production and Utilization Deficiencies

strategies
goal-directed and deliberately implemented mental operations used to facilitate task performance

Developmentalists once believed that preschool children were *astrategic*; that is, they didn't use any strategies when approaching most problems. Later research has seriously questioned these assumptions. Consider that even 18- to 36-month-olds rely on simple strategies to locate hidden objects in hide-and-seek games. If instructed to remember where a stuffed animal (Big Bird) has been hidden so that they can later wake him up from his nap, these young children strategically remind themselves where the toy is by repeatedly looking at or pointing to its hiding place (DeLoache, 1986). More recently, Michael Cohen (1996) asked 3- and 4-year-olds to play "store," a game in which they had to fill customers' vegetable orders by relying on such strategies as adding, subtracting, or making no changes in the number of objects (for example, tomatoes) in an existing display. These young children used a variety of possible strategies and became more efficient (that is, made fewer moves to fill an order) with practice. Clearly, preschool children can be strategic in their thinking and problem solving, although the strategies they devise for themselves tend to be simple and to increase in efficiency with age.

Do younger children lack the cognitive capacity to execute and benefit from the more effective strategies on which older children rely? One way to find out is to try to teach them these new strategies and see if their cognitive performances improve. Dozens of training studies of this kind have been conducted, and their findings are reasonably consistent: Children who do not use a strategy on their own can be trained to do so and often benefit from its use (Bjorklund & Douglas, 1997; Harnishfeger & Bjorklund, 1990). So rather than being astrategic or lacking cognitive capacity, younger children often display **production deficiencies**; they merely fail to produce effective strategies, even though they are often quite capable of putting those strategies to good use.

Nevertheless, acquiring a new and more sophisticated strategy does not always lead to dramatic improvements in task performance or problem solving. Instead, children who spontaneously generate and use such strategies often display what Patricia Miller (1990, 2000) calls a **utilization deficiency**; they do not benefit as much from strategy use as equally strategic older children do, and they may often revert to using a less effective strategy (or no strategy). Utilization deficiencies are commonly found as children acquire new memory strategies (Coyle & Bjorklund, 1996), reading strategies (Gaultney, 1995), attentional strategies (Miller, Woody-Ramsey, & Aloise, 1991), and strategies for reasoning by analogy (Muir-Broaddus, 1995). Even when children are trained to use a new strategy at school or in the laboratory, they often display utilization deficiencies by failing to benefit immediately from its use (Bjorklund et al., 1997).

Why do children display utilization deficiencies if the new and more sophisticated strategies that they are acquiring are generally better ways to approach the problems they face? Information-processing theorists suggest three possible reasons. First, executing a novel strategy may require so much mental effort that children have few cognitive resources left to gather and store information relevant to the problems they face (Bjorklund et al., 1997; Miller & Seier, 1994). Second, new strategies are often intrinsically interesting to children. Much as Piaget proposed that children use a scheme just for the sheer joy of having it, children may use a strategy for the novelty of trying something different (Siegler, 1996c). Third, younger children, in particular, may know less about how to monitor their cognitive activities and may not even be aware that they are failing to benefit from using a new strategy. However, this poor metacognition may actually be beneficial if it prompts children to practise the effortful new strategy until it can be executed much quicker and becomes a truly effective aid to problem solving (Bjorklund et al., 1997).

Clearly, the fact that children display both production deficiencies and utilization deficiencies implies that the growth of strategic thinking is a slow and uneven process. In fact, Robert Siegler's recent studies of children's problem-solving strategies show just how uneven the process can be (see below).

Young children devise simple strategies for dealing with the problems they face.

production deficiency
failure to spontaneously generate and use known strategies that could improve learning and memory

utilization deficiency
failure to benefit from effective strategies that one has spontaneously produced; thought to occur in the early phases of strategy acquisition when executing the strategy requires much mental effort

Multiple- and Variable-Strategy Use

Children's strategies do not develop in a stagelike fashion, with earlier strategies being replaced by more complicated and effective strategies. Rather, children of all ages have a variety of strategies available to them and select among those strategies when trying to solve a problem.

Consider what Robert Siegler and his colleagues (1996a, b, c; Siegler & Jenkins, 1989) found when researching young children's arithmetic strategies. In learning to add, young children frequently use a *sum* strategy that involves counting both numbers out loud (for example, for 5 + 3 = ?, saying "1, 2, 3, 4, 5 [pause], 6, 7, 8"). A more sophisticated strategy is to begin with the larger number (in this case, 5) and count up from there (for example, saying "5 [pause], 6, 7, 8"). This is called the *min* strategy. A more sophisticated strategy still, known as *fact retrieval*, is "just knowing" the answer, and retrieving it directly from long-term memory without having to count at all (for example, simply saying "8" to the question "How much is 5 + 3?"). When looking at cross-sectional data across age groups, one gets the impression that children progress from using the sum strategy to using the min strategy to using fact retrieval. Yet closer examination reveals that individual children use a variety of these strategies at any given time, and the frequency with which each strategy is used varies with age, with older children using more sophisticated strategies more often (see Alibali, 1999; Bjorklund & Rosenblum, 2001). Multiple- and variable-strategy use has been found in other cognitive domains as well, including serial-recall (remembering a list of digits in exact order) (McGilly & Siegler, 1990); simple same-different tasks (Blöte et al., 1999); free recall (Coyle & Bjorklund, 1997); tic-tac-toe (Crowley & Siegler, 1993), and scientific reasoning (Schauble, 1990).

Siegler and his colleagues (1996a, b, c; Crowley, Shrager, & Siegler, 1997) have formulated an **adaptive strategy choice model** to describe children's multiple strategy use and how strategies change over time. Basically, Siegler believes that children's multiple strategies compete with one another for use on problems for which they are relevant. Sometimes one strategy will "win" the mental competition (the min strategy, for example) and sometimes another strategy will win (fact retrieval, for example). With age, experience, and improved information-processing abilities, more sophisticated strategies are apt to win, so that min, on average, replaces sum as a preferred strategy, and later on fact retrieval replaces min. But for new problems or problems with which children are less familiar, the older fallback strategies often come up as the winners. So from Seigler's perspective, strategy development is not the simple matter of abandoning older, less sophisticated strategies for newer, more powerful ones. Rather, multiple strategies reside side by side in a child's mind, and old strategies never die; they simply lie in wait for a chance to be used when a newer, more preferred strategy doesn't quite fit or fails to produce the correct answer. So, Siegler does not see strategies developing in a steplike fashion, but rather as a series of overlapping waves, as illustrated in Figure 8.4.

adaptive strategy choice model

Siegler's model to describe how strategies change over time; the view that multiple strategies exist within a child's cognitive repertoire at any one time, with these strategies competing with one another for use

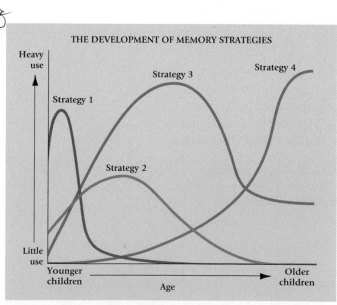

THE DEVELOPMENT OF MEMORY STRATEGIES

Figure 8.4 *Siegler's adaptive strategy choice model of development. Change in strategy use is seen as a series of overlapping waves, with different strategies being used more frequently at different ages. FROM SIEGLER, 1996C.*

As the work of Siegler and others makes clear, the issue facing cognitive developmentalists today is not whether young children can be strategic—they are from an early age. Rather, developmentalists must now determine what combination of strategies children employ within different cognitive domains. They must explain why the simpler strategies that younger children prefer gradually give way to the more sophisticated and effective strategies used by older children, adolescents, and adults, and how variations in strategy use might be related to cognitive performance and development (Coyle, 2001).

What Children Know about Thinking

Four-year-old Joshua had pushed his father's patience too far. "Joshua," said his father, "I want you to go over to that corner and just *think* about all this for a while." Instead of following his father's orders, Joshua stood where he was, not defiantly, but with a confused look and quivering lips, as if he were trying to say something but was afraid to. "What's the matter now?" his father asked, his irritation still showing. "But, Daddy," Joshua said, "I don't know *how* to think." Obviously 4-year-old Joshua did know how to think. He just did not know that he did.

You don't necessarily have to know what you are doing to do a good job of it, at least when it comes to thinking. Much of our day-to-day cognition is **implicit**, or unconscious. For example, despite the fact that we are all highly proficient speakers of our mother tongue, very few of us can consciously enumerate all the linguistic rules that underlie our language. Of course, much of the richness of cognition—both children's and adults'—comes from the type of thought that is conscious, or **explicit.** Aspects of explicit cognition become especially important when we consider executive functions. To a large extent, in order to regulate our thinking, it helps to understand what thinking is. It seems obvious that Joshua lacked knowledge about what it means to think, and we should not be surprised if his cognition were limited by his lack of understanding.

Preschool children often confuse various forms of thinking. For example, they seem not to be aware of the differences between remembering, knowing, and guessing (Johnson & Wellman, 1980; Schwanenflugel et al., 1998). Young children also think they have greater control of their thoughts than they really do. For example, John Flavell, Frances Green, and Eleanor Flavell (1998) asked 5-, 9-, and 13-year-old children and adults a series of questions related to mental uncontrollability. Will a child who hears a strange noise automatically wonder what the noise is, even if he or she doesn't want to? Is it possible to go for three days without thinking about anything? Adults and older children understood that the mind "has a mind of its own" better than younger children did. That is, they understood that the mind will sometimes think about things even if the person has no interest in thinking about it (the source of an unexpected noise, for example), and that one cannot avoid thinking for an extended period of time. Yet younger children are much less likely to make these claims than adolescents and adults are (Flavell & Green, 1999).

John Flavell and his colleagues have shown that children's awareness of their own thoughts and the distinction between consciousness and unconsciousness develop gradually during childhood (Flavell et al., 1999, 2000). For example, many 5- and some 7- and 8-year-old children believe that people continue to wish, pretend, think, and hear things while still sound asleep and not dreaming (Flavell et al., 1999). In other research, 5- and 8-year-olds said that, try as they might, thinking of nothing was not possible. By contrast, most 5-year-olds claimed that they were able to keep *all* thoughts from their minds and were unaware of the stream of consciousness that seemingly runs through every waking person's mind. This and other research (see Flavell, 1999) indicates that children have a lot to learn about thinking.

Knowledge of one's thought processes, termed *metacognition,* is important for many aspects of higher-order thinking and problem solving. Although we do perform some complicated cognitive tasks unconsciously (or implicitly), many learning and memory tasks are best accomplished when we are consciously aware of the mental processes involved. The benefits of good metacognition for several cognitive challenges will become clear later in this chapter. But first, we will take a brief look at the other side of the coin, cognition without awareness, and see that young children are often as good as adults at certain implicit cognitive tasks.

Implicit Cognition, or Thought Without Awareness

We previously defined *implicit cognition* as thought without awareness. Annette Karmiloff-Smith (1992) has developed a theory that postulates that most of infants' and young children's knowledge is implicit. For example, young infants' knowledge of physical objects or young children's (and adults') knowledge of language would be represented implicitly. This knowledge, impressive as it may be, is similar to the knowledge a spider has about making a web, a blue jay has about building a nest, or a newborn goat has about avoiding falling off cliffs.

implicit cognition
thought that occurs without awareness that one is thinking

explicit cognition
thinking and thought processes of which we are consciously aware

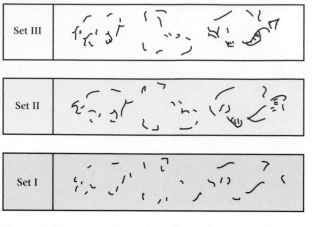

Figure 8.5 *Incomplete drawings similar to these are used in studies of implicit memory.* FROM E.S. GOLLIN, 1962.

Related to this is the idea that *implicit learning* (acquiring new knowledge without explicit awareness) is an early-developing ability. Recent research has shown that 6- and 10-year-old children learn serial sequences of responses (i.e., learning which of several responses follows one another) as well as adults do, despite having no explicit (verbalizable) knowledge of what they have learned (Meulemans, Van der Linden, & Perruchet, 1998; Vinter & Perruchet, 2000). Similarly, implicit memory (memory without awareness) has also been proposed to be an early-developing ability that shows little improvement across childhood. For example, one procedure used to assess implicit memory in children involves the use of fragmented pictures such as those shown in Figure 8.5. A fragmented (incomplete) picture is presented, and children are asked to identify it. This is very difficult to do initially, but as more of the picture is completed, it becomes increasingly easier to identify the object. In experiments using this task, children are shown the series of degraded pictures and later given another task involving those degraded pictures. Do children perform this second task better (faster or more accurately) for pictures they had previously seen than for those they hadn't seen, despite the fact that they do not remember seeing any of the pictures before? The answer is generally yes, and more importantly, there are few age differences in magnitude of this "implicit memory" effect (Drummey & Newcombe, 1995; Hayes & Hennessy, 1996).

Although there has been relatively little developmental research on implicit learning and memory, what research there is presents a consistent picture. Substantial age differences are found on tests of *explicit* learning and memorization and on children's understanding of what it means to think; but few age differences are found on tests of *implicit* learning or memory (Ausley & Guttentag, 1993; Perez, Peynircioglu, & Blaxton, 1998). Both implicit and explicit cognition can be thought of in terms of information-processing mechanisms; yet the very different developmental patterns they display indicate that cognitive development is multifaceted and does not follow a single course for all types of thinking.

FUZZY-TRACE THEORY: AN ALTERNATIVE VIEWPOINT

Most traditional accounts of human information processing assume that we solve problems by encoding discrete pieces of information and then reasoning about those items. So to solve the problem "How much is 27 + 46?" one must encode both numbers precisely and perform the proper mental operations to arrive at a correct answer. Not all of our thinking requires such precision. In fact, most of our thinking about everyday issues may actually be *hindered* somewhat by trying to rely on verbatim information. Instead, we also encode much of what we encounter in very general terms ("The stereo was cheaper at Canadian Tire than at Future Shop") and solve problems using this less-than-exact information ("I'll buy the stereo at Canadian Tire").

Charles Brainerd's and Valerie Reyna's (2001; Reyna & Brainerd, 1995) **fuzzy-trace theory** takes this fact of mental life into account, proposing that there are important developmental differences in how children represent information to solve problems. At the core of fuzzy-trace theory is the idea that memory representations (or *memory traces*) exist on a continuum from literal verbatim representations to vague, fuzzy representations called **gists** that preserve the essential content without all of the precise details.

fuzzy-trace theory
theory proposed by Brainerd and Reyna that postulates that people encode experiences on a continuum from literal, verbatim traces to fuzzy, gistlike traces

gist
fuzzy representation of information that preserves the central content but few precise details

The theory also assumes that gistlike representations, or fuzzy traces, are not merely degraded forms of our verbatim representations. Indeed, we encode both verbatim and fuzzy, gistlike representations of the information we encounter and use whichever representation is easier or more appropriate for the problem we are trying to solve.

Fuzzy and verbatim traces differ in important ways. Compared with verbatim traces, fuzzy traces are more easily accessed and generally require less effort to use. Also, verbatim traces are more susceptible to interference and forgetting than fuzzy traces are. For example, when comparing the price of two sweaters at two stores, you may quickly forget the exact prices of the sweaters. More resistant to forgetting, however, will be the information that the sweater at The Bay was cheaper than the comparable sweater at Le Chateau. If your problem is to decide which sweater is the better buy, you can rely on the gistlike knowledge of the relative price of the two sweaters. If, however, you are trying to decide whether you have enough money to buy either of the sweaters, you will need the verbatim information.

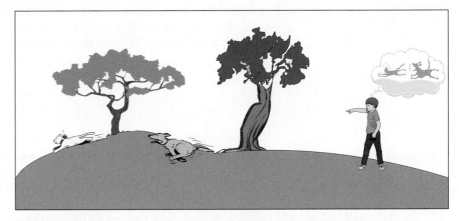

A gistlike representation, or fuzzy trace, preserves the central content of a scene or an event without all the precise details. This boy may remember that he saw a dog chasing a cat without recalling the colour of the animals or the fact that the cat wore a red collar.

Although people generally find it easier and actually prefer to reason using fuzzy traces rather than verbatim representations of information, this varies with age. Before age 6 or 7, children seem to be biased toward encoding and remembering verbatim traces of the information they encounter; whereas older children, like adults, are more inclined to encode and remember fuzzy, gistlike traces (Brainerd & Gordon, 1994; Marx & Henderson, 1996). Brainerd and Gordon (1994), for example, gave preschool and Grade 2 children simple numerical problems to solve, based on the following background information:

> Farmer Brown owns many animals. He owns 3 dogs, 5 sheep, 7 chickens, 9 horses, and 11 cows.

They were then asked a series of questions, some requiring verbatim knowledge for their correct answer, such as

> How many cows does Farmer Brown own: 11 or 9?

and others requiring only gist information, such as

> Which of Farmer Brown's animals are the most: cows or horses?

They found that preschoolers performed better on the verbatim questions than on gist-based ones, whereas Grade 2 students performed better on gist-based questions than on verbatim items. The Grade 2 students performed just as well as preschoolers on the verbatim questions. The only age difference was that preschoolers were not as good as the older children at solving gist-based problems.

Fuzzy-trace theory has been useful for describing developmental changes in the ways that children encode information and use it to solve problems. Relying on gist information is easier than trying to retrieve verbatim details and is just as effective (or more so) for solving a large number of problems that children face. Some tasks, such as mental arithmetic, do require verbatim representations. But a major reason that young children may think more slowly and less efficiently than older children do is that they often get bogged down with processing unnecessary verbatim detail that consumes much of their limited cognitive resources and interferes with effective problem solving.

inhibition
the ability to prevent ourselves
from executing some cognitive or
behavioural response

Other alternatives to traditional information-processing models also help to explain age differences in children's thinking. One such approach is recent research on children's **inhibition**, which is discussed in Box 8.1.

We have described the basic premises of information-processing theory and have discussed the development of processing hardware and software in a general way. Now we will trace the development of four critical information-processing attributes—attention, memory, problem solving, and arithmetic skills—and will comment on the practical and theoretical importance of these developments.

8.1 DEVELOPMENTAL ISSUES

Can Age Changes in Inhibition Account for Changes in Cognitive Development?

Researchers have proposed that age changes in children's abilities to *inhibit* preferred or well-established responses may play an important role in cognitive development (Diamond & Taylor, 1996; Harnishfeger, 1995). Where traditional information-processing theories have emphasized the *activation* of operations and knowledge, these new accounts propose that *inhibiting* an operation or preventing some piece of knowledge from getting into consciousness may be equally important for cognitive development (see also Dempster, 1993).

Deficits in inhibition are thought to influence cognition both in infancy and childhood. Recall from Chapter 7 that infants solving Piaget's A-not-B problems often reach for a hidden object at location A, even after seeing it hidden at location B. They cannot inhibit their tendency to search where they had previously found the object (at point A) despite seemingly "knowing" better.

Age-related changes in inhibitory processes have also been noted for a number of other cognitive challenges that older children face. For example, children's ability to selectively forget unimportant information is affected by their ability to keep the to-be-forgotten information out of mind. Older elementary-school children are simply better able to execute these inhibitory processes than younger children are (Lehman et al., 1997; Pope & Kipp, 1998). In general, young children have a difficult time executing anything other than their preferred or predominant response. Children's ability to regulate their conduct (which involves inhibiting unacceptable responses as well as performing more desirable acts) also improves with age (Kochanska et al., 1996; Luria, 1961).

What factors contribute to the development of inhibitory control? Neurological maturation seems to contribute. In Chapter 7, we learned that infants' ability to inhibit inappropriate responses in A-not-B search problems is related to maturation of the frontal lobes of the cerebral cortex. Furthermore, both preschool children and adults with lesions of the frontal lobes show the same difficulties at performing tasks in which verbal instructions require them to inhibit a dominant response. So if told to tap a pencil one more time (or one less time) than an experimenter does, both young children and brain-damaged adults have trouble inhibiting their preferred tendency to imitate the number of taps the experimenter displays (Diamond & Taylor, 1996). Taken together, these findings imply that maturation of the frontal lobes plays a major role in permitting us to inhibit various thoughts and behaviours.

Katherine Kipp Harnishfeger and David Bjorklund (Bjorklund & Harnishfeger, 1990; Harnishfeger, 1995; Harnishfeger & Bjorklund, 1994) have proposed a model of "inefficient inhibition" to account for the influence of inhibitory mechanisms on cognitive development. The central idea in their model is that age differences in the ability to keep task-inappropriate information out of working memory influences task performance. Young children may not only have difficulty ignoring task-irrelevant input from the environment, but they also have a difficult time suppressing task-irrelevant "thoughts." This greater amount of task-irrelevant information in working memory thus results in "cognitive clutter," which effectively reduces functional working-memory space and prevents the successful execution of other cognitive strategies (Lorsbach, Katz, & Cupak, 1998).

Recognizing that inhibitory processes play an important role in cognitive development seems to be an important step forward in helping us understand children's thinking. Yet, the inhibitory perspective should be seen as supplementing information-processing views of development and not replacing them. Age changes in inhibition may permit certain other abilities to be expressed, but they do not cause them to develop in the first place. Stated another way, improvements in inhibitory control may promote cognitive growth by reducing cognitive clutter, thereby allowing more advanced information-processing abilities to emerge.

THE DEVELOPMENT OF ATTENTION

Clearly, a person must first detect and *attend* to information before it can be encoded, retained, or used to solve problems. Although even young infants attend to a variety of sensory inputs, their attention is often "captured" by objects and events: A 1-month-old baby does not choose to attend to a face; instead, faces attract his attention. Similarly, preschoolers who seem totally immersed in one activity can quickly lose interest and just as quickly get caught up in another activity. But as children grow older, they become better able to sustain their attention and more selective in what they attend to, and they acquire the ability to formulate and carry out systematic plans for gathering information necessary to accomplish their goals.

Changes in Attention Span

Visit a nursery school and you will see that teachers are likely to switch classroom activities every 15 to 20 minutes. Why? Because young children have very short **attention spans**; they rarely concentrate on any single activity for very long. Even when doing things they like, such as playing with toys or watching TV, 2- and 3-year-olds often look away, move about, and direct their attention elsewhere, spending far less time on the activity at hand than older children do (Ridderinkhoff & van der Molen, 1995; Ruff, Capozzolli, & Weisberg, 1998). Part of the younger child's problem in trying to "concentrate" is that her attention is easily captured by distractions and she is often unable to inhibit the intrusion of task-irrelevant thoughts (Dempster, 1993; Harnishfeger, 1995).

The capacity for sustained attention gradually improves throughout childhood and early adolescence, and these improvements may be due, in part, to maturational changes in the central nervous system. For example, the **reticular formation**, an area of the brain responsible for regulating attention, is not fully *myelinated* until puberty. Perhaps this neurological development helps to explain why adolescents and young adults are suddenly able to spend hours on end cramming for upcoming exams or typing furiously to make morning deadlines on term papers.

Another reason that attention capabilities increase with age is that older children use more effective strategies to regulate their attention.

Development of Planful Attentional Strategies

With age, children become increasingly planful and systematic in their gathering of information. In a series of classic studies (Vurpillot, 1968; Vurpillot & Ball, 1979), 4- to 10-year-olds were asked to search pictures of two houses and to judge whether the contents of the windows of the houses were identical or different. As shown in Figure 8.6, 4- and 5-year-olds were not very planful; they searched only a few windows and often reached the wrong conclusion. By contrast, children older than 6½ were highly systematic. Their planned searches involved checking each window in one house with the corresponding window in the other house, pair by pair, until they arrived at a judgment (which was likely to be correct). Older children are also more likely than younger children to formulate a systematic plan for searching the environment for a lost toy, often limiting their search to areas between where the toy was last seen and where they discovered it missing rather than wandering the yard aimlessly looking for it (Wellman, 1985). So, the planful gathering of information that helps children solve problems develops gradually over the course of childhood.

attention span
capacity for sustaining attention to a particular stimulus or activity

reticular formation
area of the brain that activates the organism and is thought to be important in regulating attention

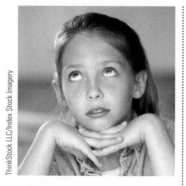

| 5-year-old: "The same" | 8-year-old: "Not the same" |

Figure 8.6 *Are the houses in each pair exactly the same or different? Preschool children often guess incorrectly because they do not systematically compare all the pairs of windows as school-aged children do.* BASED ON VURPILLOT, 1968.

Although the ability to concentrate improves dramatically during middle childhood, elementary-school students are not always successful at overcoming distractions.

Selective Attention: Ignoring Information That is Clearly Irrelevant

Would young children perform as well as older children if they were told in advance which information is most relevant to the tasks they face and did not have to be so planful? Probably not, because younger children demonstrate little ability to display **selective attention**—to concentrate only on task-relevant stimuli and not be distracted by other "noise" in the environment. Consider what Patricia Miller and Michael Weiss (1981) found when they told 7-, 10-, and 13-year-olds to remember the locations of a number of *animals*, each of which was hidden behind a different cloth flap. When each flap was lifted to reveal an animal, the children could also see a household object positioned either above or below the animal. Here, then, is a learning task that requires the child to attend selectively to certain information (the animals) while ignoring other potentially distracting input (the household objects). When the children were tested to see whether they had learned where each animal was located, the 13-year-olds outperformed the 10-year-olds, who in turn performed slightly better than the 7-year-olds. Miller and Weiss then tested to see whether children had attended to the incidental (irrelevant) information by asking them to recall which household object had been paired with each animal. They found exactly the opposite pattern on this incidental-learning test: 13-year-olds recalled *less* about the household objects than either 7- or 10-year-olds. In fact, both of the younger groups recalled as much about the irrelevant objects as about the locations of the animals. Taken together, these findings indicate that older children are much better than younger ones at concentrating on relevant information and filtering out extraneous input that may interfere with task performance.

What Do Children Know about Attention?

Do young children know more about attentional processes than their behaviour might indicate? Indeed, they do. Even though 4-year-olds generally cannot overcome distractions when performing selective-attention tasks, they are apparently aware that distractions can be a problem, because they realize that two stories will be harder to understand if the storytellers speak simultaneously rather than taking turns (Pillow, 1988). Yet, when

selective attention
capacity to focus on task-relevant aspects of experience while ignoring irrelevant or distracting information

4-year-olds are told that a woman is examining a set of decorative pins to select one as a gift, they are largely unaware that she would be thinking primarily about the pins and would not have other things on her mind (Flavell, Green, & Flavell, 1995). It is as if these preschoolers simply do not realize what is involved in selective attention, even though they know something about distractions.

In other research, Miller & Weiss (1982) asked 5-, 7-, and 9-year-olds to answer a series of questions about factors known to affect performance on an incidental-learning task (that is, a task like the "animals and objects" test described earlier). Although knowledge about attentional processes generally increased with age, even the 5-year-olds realized that they should at least *look first* at task-relevant stimuli and then *label* these objects as an aid to remembering them. The 7- and 9-year-olds further understood that they must *attend selectively* to task-relevant stimuli and *ignore* irrelevant information in order to do well on these problems.

In sum, the development of attention is apparently a lengthy process in which a child first learns to translate what she knows into appropriate actions and then gradually comes to rely on these strategies as they become more routine and effective means of gathering information to achieve her objectives.

Despite these normal trends, a fair number of elementary-school children find it nearly impossible to sustain their attention for long or develop planful attentional strategies. In Box 8.2, we will take a closer look at this **attention deficit-hyperactivity disorder** and its implications for children's academic, social, and emotional development.

MEMORY: RETAINING AND RETRIEVING INFORMATION

Once children have attended to information of some kind, they must find a way to retain it if they are to learn from their experiences or use this input to solve a problem. Thus, the development of *memory*—the processes by which we store and retrieve information— is central to information-processing theories of intellectual development.

In the pages that follow, we will trace the development of two general kinds of memory: *strategic memory* and *event memory*. **Strategic memory** refers to the processes involved when we *consciously try* to retain or retrieve such information as a telephone number, the route to a theatre across town, or the words to "O Canada" for the beginning of a basketball game. Information-processing researchers have investigated a variety of **memory strategies**, or **mnemonics**, that might promote academic performance, and we will examine the development of several such strategies and some of the factors that influence their development. By contrast, **event memory** refers to stored memories of such events as what you ate for breakfast this morning, The Bare Naked Ladies' opening number at the concert you attended last year, or the joy your mother displayed when your baby brother was born. Memory for events, which includes **autobiographical memories** of events that happened *to you*, is what most people think of as "natural" memory, and it rarely requires use of any strategies. We will examine the growth of event memory and look at recent research examining children's memory for events when serving as eyewitnesses.

The Development of Memory Strategies

Researchers have studied a variety of memory strategies, and, not surprisingly, they find that the number of such strategies and their effectiveness increase with age (Bjorklund & Douglas, 1997). However, as is the case with cognitive strategies in general, children at any age use a variety of different strategies, although the sophistication of the "average" strategy that children use increases with age (Coyle & Bjorklund, 1997; Coyle et al., 1999).

attention deficit-hyperactivity disorder (ADHD)
attentional disorder involving distractibility, hyperactivity, and impulsive behaviour that often leads to academic difficulties, poor self-esteem, and social/emotional problems

strategic memory
processes involved as one consciously attempts to retain or retrieve information

mnemonics (memory strategies)
effortful techniques used to improve memory, including rehearsal, organization, and elaboration

event memory
long-term memory for events

autobiographical memory
memory for important experiences or events that have happened to us

They can't sit still; they don't pay attention to the teacher; they mess around and get into trouble; they try to get others into trouble; they are rude; they get mad when they don't get their way.... (Henker & Whalen, 1989, p. 216)

These and other similar descriptions are widely endorsed by classmates of those elementary-school children (mostly boys) diagnosed as having attention deficit-hyperactivity disorder (ADHD). The comparative prevalence rates of ADHD in Canada, Germany, New Zealand, the United Kingdom, and the United States range from 1.7 to 16.1 percent (U.S. Department of Health and Human Services, 1999). ADHD youngsters display three major symptoms: (1) They are highly impulsive, often acting before thinking and blurting out whatever is on their minds; (2) they are inattentive, frequently failing to listen and displaying an inability to concentrate or to finish tasks; and (3) they are hyperactive, as they constantly fidget, squirm, or move about (American Psychiatric Association, 1994). As you might expect, these youngsters perform miserably on tests of sustained and selective attention (Landau, Milich, & Lorch, 1992). They also do poorly in school and often alienate both teachers and classmates by their failure to comply with requests and their disruptive and aggressive behaviour (Henker & Whalen, 1989; Hinshaw & Melnick, 1995).

It was once believed that hyperactive children simply outgrew their problems after reaching puberty. Although they generally become less fidgety and overactive during the teenage years, many people diagnosed in childhood as having ADHD continue to display serious adjustment problems later in life. For example, attention-disordered adolescents are likely to struggle both socially and academically, and they frequently drop out of high school or impulsively commit reckless, delinquent acts without thinking about the consequences (Wender, 1995). The picture is somewhat more positive by early adulthood, as about half of all ADHD individuals seem to be functioning well in their jobs (Wender, 1995). But for many with ADHD, young adulthood is characterized by above-average rates of job changes (or dismissals), marital disruptions, traffic accidents, legal infractions, and other personality problems or emotional disorders (Green et al., 1997; Mannuzza et al., 1993).

What causes ADHD? Unfortunately, we do not yet have a clear answer. Some people may be genetically predisposed to develop the disorder, in that one identical twin is likely to have it if the other does (Levy et al., 1997). Environment also matters. The incidence of ADHD is higher among children who were exposed prenatally to alcohol, drugs, and the disease rubella (Millberger et al., 1996; Silver, 1992), and a harsh, highly controlling style of parenting may also

contribute to, or at least aggravate, the problem in some cases (Jacobvitz & Sroufe, 1987; Sroufe, 1997). However, earlier theories linking the syndrome to food additives, excessive dietary intake of sugar, lead poisoning, and brain damage have received little support (Henker & Whalen, 1989; Silver, 1992).

What can be done to help children with ADHD? One treatment that seems to help 70 percent of them is to administer stimulant drugs such as Ritalin (Cantwell, 1996; Lore, 2000). Although it may seem odd to give overactive children drugs that increase their heart rates and respiratory levels, stimulants work because they also make ADHD children better able to focus their attention and less distractible and disruptive (Gillberg et al., 1997). Important benefits of this increased attentional focusing is that both academic performance and peer relations are likely to improve (Pelham et al., 1993). However, critics of this approach argue that stimulants do little more than suppress ADHD symptoms while possibly producing such serious side-effects as curbing appetites, disrupting sleep cycles, and reducing children's desire to play and acquire any number of important skills that are not taught at school (Panksepp, 1998; Schachar et al., 1997).

Gains in scholastic performance have also been achieved through cognitive-behavioural programs that teach ADHD children how to set academic goals that require sustained attention, while allowing these youngsters to reinforce their successes with tokens that can be exchanged for prizes. Indeed, ADHD children seem to benefit most from a combination of drug and behaviour therapies (Cantwell, 1996). And recently, researchers have found that if parents can remain warm and supportive but firm in their demands, their hyperactive sons exhibit fewer problem behaviours and are much better accepted by peers (Hinshaw & Melnick, 1995; Hinshaw et al., 1997). So, family therapies aimed at teaching often-exasperated parents to be more patient and to effectively manage the antics of a child with ADHD are likely to enhance the effectiveness of existing drug and behavioural interventions (Hinshaw et al., 1997).

A final note: Although therapeutic interventions do improve the self-esteem, social behaviours, and academic performance of ADHD children, many of these "treated" individuals are no better adjusted as adults than hyperactive peers who received no therapy (Hart et al., 1995; Wilens & Biederman, 1992). Undoubtedly, the long-term prognosis will improve as we learn more about this disorder. At present, we can say that the many problems associated with ADHD clearly illustrate just how important the regulation of attention is—not only to cognitive development and academic performance, but to one's social and emotional development as well.

---

rehearsal
strategy for remembering that involves repeating the items one is trying to retain

Rehearsal

One very simple yet *effective* strategy that people use to retain new information is **rehearsal**—repeating it over and over until we think we will remember it.

When instructed to try to remember a group of toys they have been shown, 3- to 4-year-olds look very carefully at the objects and often label them (once), but they rarely rehearse (Baker-Ward, Ornstein, & Holden, 1984; Oyen & Bebko, 1996). By contrast, 7- to 10-year-olds rehearse more efficiently than younger children do, and the more they rehearse, the more they remember (Flavell, Beach, & Chinsky, 1966). Older children also rehearse *differently* than younger children. If asked to recall a list of words presented one at a time, 5- to 8-year-olds usually rehearse each word in just that way—one at a time. By contrast, 12-year-olds are more likely to rehearse word *clusters*, repeating the earlier items over and over again as they rehearse each successive word. As a result, they remember more words than children who rehearse just one item at a time (Guttentag, Ornstein, & Siemans, 1987; Ornstein, Naus, & Liberty, 1975).

Why don't young children rehearse more efficiently? Possibly because their attempts to execute the more complex clustering strategy require so much of their limited working-memory capacity that they are unable to *retrieve* enough information to form useful clusters. A study by Peter Ornstein and his associates (1985) supports this interpretation. Ornstein and his colleagues tried to teach 7-year-olds to use the "clustering" rehearsal strategy and found that the children did so *only if earlier items on the list remained visible.* So when these younger children were able to form item clusters without having to expend mental effort retrieving the items, they could execute the complex clustering strategy. By contrast, 12-year-olds relied on the clustering strategy *regardless of whether earlier items were visually displayed.* Apparently, this efficient rehearsal technique has become so automatized for most 12-year-olds that they implement it almost effortlessly, thus leaving themselves ample space in working memory for retrieving items to rehearse.

Organization

Although rehearsal can be a very effective strategy, in one sense, it is a rather unimaginative memory device. If a rehearser merely repeats the names of items to be remembered, he or she may fail to notice certain meaningful relations among the stimuli that should make them easier to recall. Consider the following example:

List 1: boat, match, hammer, coat, grass, nose, pencil, dog, cup, flower

List 2: knife, shirt, car, fork, boat, pants, sock, truck, spoon, plate

Richard T. Nowitz/Corbis/Magma

Few naturalistic experiences may contribute more to the development of effective memory skills than playing strategic games with a more competent opponent.

Figure 8.7 *An example of an elaborative image that one might create to associate pato (pronounced "pot-o"), the Spanish word "duck," with its English translation.*

Although these 10-item lists should be equally difficult to recall if one simply rehearses them, the second list is actually much easier for many people. The reason is that its items can be grouped into three semantically distinct categories (eating utensils, clothes, and vehicles) that can serve as cues for storage and retrieval. Until about age 9 to 10, children are not any better at recalling items that can be **semantically organized** (such as List 2) than those that are difficult to categorize (such as List 1) (Hasselhorn, 1992). This finding suggests that young children make few attempts to organize information for later recall.

How do children learn to organize materials in ways that could help them to remember? If we think back to Vygotsky's perspective on how many new skills are socially mediated, we might suspect that organizational strategies evolve from experiences children have had (1) categorizing highly related objects and events under a teacher's direction at school, or (2) watching as the teacher presents materials in a highly organized fashion. Interestingly, elementary-school instructors in the United States spend little time teaching children explicit memory strategies, although those who provide more strategic suggestions do have students who tend to rely more on organizational strategies and perform better on recall tests (Moely et al., 1995).

Yet, important as schooling experience may be, memory strategies may also be fostered at home through collaborative or guided learning experiences that children have with their parents. For example, Martha Carr and her associates (1989) found that 8- to 9-year-olds who rely heavily on organizational strategies and perform well on recall tests tend to have parents who often (1) play strategy-related games with them, and (2) show them how to be planful and strategic when completing and checking their homework. So it seems that such pleasurable and strategic pursuits as chess, card games, Concentration, and the like are not only effective ways of promoting togetherness and passing leisure time, but are likely to contribute to a youngster's intellectual growth as well!

Elaboration

Another effective strategy for improving recall is to add to, or *elaborate* on, the information that we hope to remember (Kee, 1994; Schneider & Pressley, 1997). **Elaboration** is particularly useful whenever our task is to associate two or more stimuli, such as a foreign word and its English equivalent. For example, one way to remember the Spanish word for duck, *pato* (pronounced "pot-o"), is to elaborate on the word *pato* by creating an image of a pot that is in some way linked to a duck (see Figure 8.7 for an example).

However, elaboration is a "latecomer to the memorizer's bag of tricks" that is rarely seen before adolescence (Schneider & Pressley, 1997). Why? Possibly because adolescents simply have a larger knowledge base than younger children do and are better able to imagine how any two (or more) stimuli might be linked (Bjorklund, 1987). As we will see, there is now ample evidence that a person's knowledge base does indeed affect his or her performance on many memory tasks.

Retrieval Processes

Once information has entered the long-term store, it is of little use unless we can get it out, or **retrieve** it. Young children are notoriously bad at retrieving information on their own. This is where the distinction between **free recall** and **cued recall** becomes important. In free recall, children are given a general prompt for information, such as "Tell me what happened at school today." When these kinds of general prompts are provided, young children have a difficult time retrieving much information. However, if more focused cued-recall questions are asked, prompting younger children to retrieve more specific information, they often remember things rather well. When one 5-year-old boy who had spent the afternoon with his grandparents seeing his first play, "Little Shop of Horrors," was asked by his mother, "Well, how was your afternoon?" the child replied "OK." The mother persisted with a second general prompt: "Well, did you have a good time?" The child said, "Yeah." However, when cued by his grandmother to "Tell about Audrey II, the plant," he provided extensive details, telling how the plant ate some of the main characters, talked, and sang, and how it took three people underneath it to make it move. The child had a wealth of information, but it could only be retrieved when specific cues were provided.

semantic organization
strategy for remembering that involves grouping or classifying stimuli into meaningful (or manageable) clusters that are easier to retain

elaboration
strategy for remembering that involves adding something to (or creating meaningful links between) the bits of information one is trying to retain

retrieval
class of strategies aimed at getting information out of the long-term store

free recall
recollection that is not prompted by specific cues or prompts

cued recall
recollection that is prompted by a cue associated with the setting in which the recalled event originally occurred

Young children can be instructed in the use of rehearsal, organization, and retrieval strategies, and their memory performance typically increases (Bjorklund & Douglas, 1997). However, when given the opportunity to use their newly learned strategy on a new set of materials, children frequently revert back to their nonstrategic ways. Why do they fail to make good use of a strategy they have just used successfully? One gets the feeling that younger children simply know less about memory aids and the circumstances under which it is appropriate to use them. They also know less in general than older children do, and their limited knowledge may hinder their attempts to categorize or elaborate on materials they are trying to remember. Let's see what researchers have learned in attempting to evaluate these hypotheses.

Metamemory and Memory Performance

Earlier we used the term *metacognition* to refer to knowledge of the workings of one's mind, including one's mental strong and weak points. One important aspect of metacognition is **metamemory**—one's knowledge of memory and memory processes. Children display metamemory if they recognize, for example, that there are limits to what they can remember, that some things are easier to remember than others, or that certain strategies are more effective than others at helping them to remember (Schneider & Bjorklund, 1998, 2001).

How do we know what children know about their memories? One straightforward way of finding out is simply to ask them. Julia O'Sullivan at Lakehead University conducted interview studies of this kind that reveal that even 3- and 4-year-olds have some idea that the mind has a limited capacity and that some materials will be easier to learn and retain than others (O'Sullivan, 1997). For example, preschoolers realize that remembering many items is more difficult than remembering a few (Yussen & Bird, 1979) and that, the longer they study materials, the more likely they are to retain them (Kreutzer, Leonard, & Flavell, 1975). Yet, they usually overestimate how much they will remember and know very little about *forgetting*, even saying that it is just as easy to remember something (like a phone number) over a long period of time as over a short period (Kreutzer et al., 1975; Lyon & Flavell, 1993). It is almost as if young preschool children view information they have retained as a "mental copy" of reality that is filed away in one of the mind's drawers and will be available for use when they need it.

Knowledge about memory increases dramatically between ages 4 and 12 as children come to regard the mind as an active, constructive agent that stores only *interpretations* (rather than copies) of reality. Many 5-year-olds, for example, now know that items such as phone numbers are quickly forgotten unless they write them down, thus displaying an awareness that external cues can help them to remember (Kreutzer et al., 1975). Yet, knowledge about memory strategies develops very gradually. Children younger than 7 are often unaware that such strategies as rehearsal and organization may be useful to

metamemory
one's knowledge about memory and memory processes

Concept Check 8.1
Modelling Human Information Processing

Check your understanding of information-processing models and assumptions by matching each descriptive statement below to one of the following ideas or concepts: (a) gist, (b) long-term store, (c) short-term store/working memory, (d) adaptive strategy choice model, (e) implicit learning/memory, (f) increase in processing speed, (g) development of strategies, (h) production deficiency, (i) utilization deficiency, (j) span of apprehension, (k) executive control processes. Answers appear in the Appendix.

_____ 1. vast storehouse of acquired information
_____ 2. failure to benefit from the strategies one generates
_____ 3. method of assessing information-processing capacity
_____ 4. means by which we monitor information processing

_____ 5. fuzzy representation of information one has encountered
_____ 6. site of all conscious intellectual activity
_____ 7. aspect of information processing that does not improve much with age
_____ 8. failure to generate effective information-processing strategies
_____ 9. hardware improvement that contributes to age-related increases in information-processing capacity
_____ 10. claims that even young children have alternative strategies for processing information
_____ 11. software improvement that contributes to age-related increases in information-processing ability

them (Justice et al., 1997), and even if they realize that related items are easier to remember than unrelated items, they often cannot say why this is so (O'Sullivan, 1996). And although 7- and 9-year-olds now realize that rehearsing and categorizing are more effective strategies than merely looking at items or labelling them once, not until age 11 do children recognize that organization is more effective than rehearsal (Justice et al., 1997).

Does a person's metamemory influence how well he or she will perform on memory tasks? The evidence is mixed. Two reviews of the literature found only low to moderate positive correlations between memory and metamemory, thus implying that *good metamemory is not always necessary for good recall* (Cavanaugh & Perlmutter, 1982; Schneider & Pressley, 1997). Nevertheless, studies that have trained children to use memory strategies are often more successful when training includes a metamemory component, such as making children aware that being strategic has improved their memory performance (Ghatala et al., 1986; Melot, 1998).

These findings dovetail nicely with studies that have attempted to help children improve their reading comprehension by training them to use effective memory aids and other metacognitive strategies (for example, identifying the most important information in a passage, evaluating the text for clarity, and monitoring how well the material has been understood). Briefly, training studies show that merely teaching strategies is not enough; to be effective, the training must also inform the child on *why* each strategy is better than others she might use and *when* it is advantageous to use it. Children who receive this informed training when learning ways to extract and retain more information from their reading materials soon rely on the strategies they have learned and usually show distinct improvements in reading comprehension (a measure of retention) and other academic skills (Brown & Campione, 1990; Paris, 1988).

So a child's understanding of how or why memory strategies work seems to be the best metacognitive predictor of his use of these techniques. Indeed, the finding that measures of metamemory and memory are often more highly correlated among children 10 years of age and older (Schneider & Pressley, 1997) undoubtedly reflects the fact that older children have had more time to discover *why* various memory strategies make remembering easier.

Knowledge Base and Memory Development

As we noted earlier, children who are experts in a particular domain, such as chess, have longer memory spans when tested on information from their area of expertise (Chi, 1978). Consider an implication of this finding. Since older children generally know more about the world than younger ones do, they are relative experts on most topics. Thus, age differences in recall memory could be due as much to increases in children's **knowledge base** as to increases in their use of strategies (Bjorklund, 1987; Schneider & Bjorklund, 2001).

Consider what David and Barbara Bjorklund (1985) found when testing elementary-school children's memory for one area in which they have some expertise: the identities of their classmates. Some students were given a specific strategy for performing this task (recall names row by row), whereas others were left to their own devices. Nearly all the children using the efficient row-by-row strategy listed the names they recalled in perfect row-by-row order, yet they left out (forgot) just as many classmates as did children using other schemes, even those who professed to use no strategy. In other words, use of the row-by-row strategy did not gain these children anything in the way of greater memory performance, presumably because they were all experts when it came to their current classmates, making the row-by-row strategy unnecessary.

This is not to say that strategy use is unimportant to knowledgeable individuals. In their own areas of expertise, whether the topic is math, chess, dinosaurs, or soccer, children seem to develop highly specialized strategies for processing information that make learning and remembering new information about that topic much easier (Bjorklund, 1987; Hasselhorn, 1995). Think about the difference between reading about a topic that you already know well and reading about an unfamiliar topic. In the first case, you can process the information quickly by linking it to existing knowledge. That is, you already

Liz Radojkovic

Metamemory improves dramatically in middle childhood. This 8-year-old is now aware that writing down a phone number is an effective strategy for ensuring that she retains this information.

knowledge base
one's existing information about a topic or content area

have a scheme for organizing or elaborating new input. However, learning and retaining information about an unfamiliar topic is much more effortful because you have no existing conceptual pegs to hang it on.

Just how important is one's knowledge base to memory performance? In one study of Grades 3, 5, and 7 soccer experts and nonexperts conducted in Germany, children's ability to recall information about a soccer-related story was influenced more by their knowledge about soccer than by their general intellectual aptitude! As we see in Figure 8.8, experts recalled more than novices, even when the experts were of low general aptitude and the novices were high in general mental ability (Schneider et al., 1989). Although low-ability experts do not always outperform high-ability novices on all tasks, experts generally recall far more new information about their area of expertise than do novices of the same intellectual level (Schneider, Bjorklund, & Maier-Bruckner, 1996).

Although adolescents and adults know more, and can use their knowledge to help them learn more efficiently, their memory performance can be enhanced when they use strategies that encourage them to use their existing knowledge. Wood, Willoughby, and their colleagues in Ontario have demonstrated the potency of an elaboration strategy called *elaborative interrogation* for helping learners to use their prior knowledge to learn factual material (Wood, Pressley, & Winne, 1990; Willoughby, Wood, & Khan, 1994). Elaborative interrogation involves asking learners to answer the question "Why would that fact be true?" when they

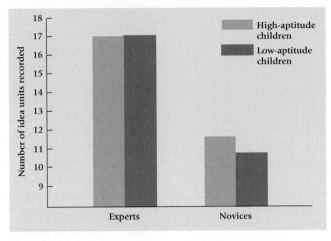

Figure 8.8 *Number of idea units remembered about a soccer story for high- and low-aptitude soccer experts and soccer novices. In this case, being an expert eliminated any effect of academic aptitude (IQ) on performance.* ADAPTED FROM DATA PRESENTED IN SCHNEIDER, KÖRKEL, & WEINERT, 1989.

encounter factual material for which they have some level of familiarity. By answering the question, the learner creates an association between the novel fact and existing knowledge, and this association facilitates retrieval of the information. In general, this strategy enhances memory performance in populations ranging from very young children to adults.

In sum, knowledge is power, and the more one knows about a topic, the more one can learn and remember. Detailed general knowledge may result in improved memory performance because the better established the information is in one's mind, the more easily it can be activated, or brought to consciousness (Bjorklund, 1987; Kee, 1994). And because older children usually know more than younger children about most subjects, they expend less mental effort to activate what they know, leaving them with more mental capacity to encode, classify, and execute other cognitive operations on the new material they encounter.

Culture and Memory Strategies

Cultures clearly differ in the extent to which they support and encourage particular memory strategies (Kurtz, 1990; Mistry, 1997). Rehearsal, organization, and elaboration, for example, are especially helpful to children from Western industrialized societies, whose school activities involve a great deal of rote memorization and list learning. Yet, these same strategies may not be so useful to unschooled children from nonindustrialized societies, whose most important memory tasks might involve recalling the location of objects (water, game animals) in a natural setting or remembering instructions passed along in the context of proverbs or stories. In list-learning experiments, Western children rely heavily on strategies acquired at school and clearly outperform their unschooled peers from nonindustrialized societies (Cole & Scribner, 1977; Rogoff & Waddell, 1982). Yet, their superior performance does not extend to other kinds of memory tasks. Unschooled Australian Aborigine children, for example, are better than their Anglo-Australian peers at remembering the location of objects in natural settings (Kearins, 1981), and African adolescents display better recall for orally transmitted stories than American adolescents (Dube, 1982). Indeed, Western children actually remember less if they try to rehearse or organize information in these latter kinds of memory tasks (Rogoff, 1990).

These findings make perfectly good sense when viewed through the lens of Vygotsky's *sociocultural theory:* Cognitive development always occurs within a particular cultural context, which not only defines the kinds of problems that children must solve, but also dictates the strategies (or tools of intellectual adaptation) that enable them to master these challenges.

Summing Up

How might we briefly summarize the ground we have covered? One way is to review Table 8.1, which describes four general conclusions about the development of strategic memory that have each gained widespread support.

Let's also note that these four aspects of development *interact* with one another rather than evolving independently. For example, automatization of certain information processes may leave the child with enough working-memory space to use effective memory strategies that were just too mentally demanding earlier in childhood (Case, 1985; Kee, 1994; Miller et al. 1991). Or a child's expanding knowledge base may permit faster information processing and suggest ways that information can be categorized and elaborated (Bjorklund, 2000). So there is no one "best" explanation for the growth of memorial skills. All the developments that we have discussed contribute in important ways to the dramatic improvements that occur in children's strategic memory.

The Development of Event and Autobiographical Memory

Although the growth of strategic memory is clearly an important aspect of cognitive development, most of what children and adolescents remember are episodes, or events, particularly those that happened to them. *Event memory* in general, and our memory for particularly important personal experiences, or *autobiographical memory*, are rarely as intentional as strategic memory is. Although we may sometimes try very hard to recon- struct a past experience, rarely do we deliberately organize or rehearse such events to ensure that we will remember them. Instead, we will see that event and autobiographical memories are closely tied to language skills and to our ability to represent our experi- ences in storylike narratives (Nelson, 1996).

Origins of Event Memory

In Chapter 6, we learned that the ability to *recognize* the familiar is apparently inborn, for newborns who habituate to a repetitive stimulus are telling us that they remember this object or event as something they have experienced before. When are infants

TABLE 8.1	Four Major Contributors to the Development of Learning and Memory
Contributor	**Developmental trends**
1. Working-memory capacity	Older children have greater information-processing *capacity* than younger children do, particularly in the sense that they process information faster (and more efficiently), leaving more of their limited working-memory space for storage and other cognitive processes.
2. Memory strategies	Older children use more effective *memory strategies* for encoding, storing, and retrieving information.
3. Metamemory	Older children know more about memory processes, and their greater *metamemory* allows them to select the most appropriate strategies for the task at hand and to carefully monitor their progress.
4. Knowledge base	Older children know more in general, and their greater *knowledge base* improves their ability to learn and remember.

What Happened to Our Early Childhood Memories?

avid and Barbara Bjorklund (1992, p. 206) recount the following story:

> We received a letter from a woman … who was worried because her 10-year-old son could remember very little from his preschool days. She said that she and her husband had always tried to be good parents but thought that her son's inability to remember things from early childhood was an indication that either they hadn't done a very good job after all, or they had done a truly terrible job and her son was repressing this painful period of his life. We assured her that her son's inability to remember events much before his fourth birthday is quite normal, and is certainly not an indication that those events were unimportant.

Though infants are quite capable of remembering, many adults recall almost nothing that happened to them before the age of 3, or, if they do have memories, many turn out to be pure fiction. JoNell Usher and Ulric Neisser (1993) studied this lack of memory for the early years, or *infantile amnesia*, by questioning college students about experiences they had had early in life, such as the birth of a younger sibling, a stay in the hospital, a family move, or the death of a family member. To assess recall, a series of questions was asked about each event that the participant had experienced (for example, "Who told you your mother was going to the hospital to give birth? What were you doing when she left? Where were you when you first saw the new baby?") As we see in the accompanying figure, the percentage of questions that college students could answer increased substantially the older the person was when he or she had experienced the event. Usher and Neisser concluded that the earliest age of any meaningful recall was about age 2 for the birth of a sibling or a hospitalization, and age 3 for the death of a family member or a family move. Even 9- and 10-year-olds who are shown photographs of their daycare classmates from six or seven years earlier have difficulty discriminating these youngsters, who were once very familiar to them, from other young daycare children they have never seen before (Newcombe & Fox, 1994). More recently, Carole Peterson and Nikki Whalen (2001) also asked children to remember their hospitalization and confirmed that these episodes could be recalled after a five-year lag among children who were as young as 2 years of age when they were hospitalized. (For specific details about this research, see Box 8.4.) So infants can remember their experiences, and it appears that for some significant events, like hospitalization, older children and adults have some early memories. Why is it, then, that elementary-school children and adults often report that they remember very little about what their lives were like as infants and toddlers?

Sigmund Freud thought infantile amnesia simply reflected our tendency to repress the emotional conflicts of early childhood. However, contemporary researchers have rejected Freud's view in favour of more cognitive explanations. For example, infants do not use language and adults do, so it is possible that early memories are stored in some nonverbal code that we cannot retrieve once we become language users (Sheingold & Tenney, 1982). Even slightly older children, who can talk, may not represent their experiences in the same way as older children and adults. It is not until 2 to 3 years of age that most children easily encode and remember their experiences in terms of narratives (stories about their lives) (Peterson, 1999; 2002)—usually with much help from adults. It is only after being guided by adults that children learn to code memories and realize that language can be used to share memories with others (Nelson, 1996). Mark Howe at Lakehead University and his colleague Mary Courage at Memorial University (1993, 1997) suggest yet another interesting possibility to explain limited early memories: Maybe what is lacking in infancy is not cognitive or language ability, but a sense of self around which personal experiences can be organized. Once an infant gains a firm sense of self (to be discussed in Chapter 12) at about 18 to 24 months of age, events may become more memorable when encoded as "things that happened to *me.*" Interestingly, recent research implies that both the development of a sense of self and adult assistance in constructing personal narratives help young preschool children to remember past events that happened to them (Harley & Reese, 1999). So, our lack of both linguistic proficiency and a concept of "selfhood" for the first 18 to 24 months help explain why our early life experiences remain a blank for most of us.

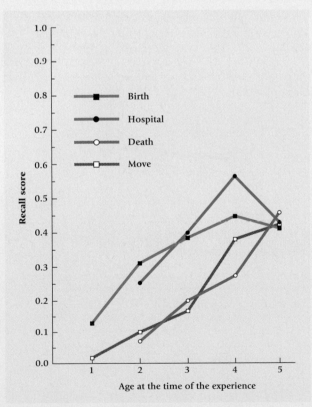

College students' recall of early life events increases as a function of their age at the time of the event. From Usher & Neisser, 1993.

capable of *pure recall*—of actively retrieving information from memory when no cues are present to remind them of their experiences? A big breakthrough occurs at age 8 to 12 months (Nelson, 1996). This is when infants begin to search for and find hidden toys in object permanence tests, thereby illustrating that they *recall* that the object exists. Other early evidence of event memory is *deferred imitation*. Many 9-month-olds are able to recall and imitate the novel actions of an adult model (for example, pushing a button to produce a beep) after a 24-hour delay (Meltzoff, 1988c). And infants less than 2 years old appear to be capable of reconstructing a noteworthy sequence of actions they observed *8 months earlier* (Bauer, 1997).

If infants and toddlers can recall events that happened months ago, then why is it that when you ask adults to remember things that happened to them during their first few years, they are often unable to remember anything that happened prior to 3 or 4 years of age—something we call **infantile amnesia**? Although initial studies suggested that infantile amnesia was a robust phenomenon, more recent research questions the earliest age at which adults can retrieve memories. It seems that, for some types of events, we can recall things that happen at or after 2 years of age. For a review of this new research, see Box 8.3 and Box 8.4. Let's look at this fascinating memory issue more closely.

infantile amnesia
lack of memory for the early years of one's life

script
general representation of the typical sequencing of events (that is, what occurs and when) in some familiar context

Development of Scripted Memory

What events do toddlers and preschool children remember best? The things they tend to recall very well are recurring events that typically happen in familiar contexts. Katherine Nelson and her colleagues (1996) find that young children organize familiar routines into **scripts**—that is, schemes for certain experiences that preserve the ordering and

---

THE INSIDE TRACK

8.4

Carole Peterson

Carole Peterson works in the Department of Psychology at Memorial University of Newfoundland. Her area of expertise is child psychology, with specialization in issues related to eyewitness testimony (for example, children's accounts of traumatic injury) and children's autobiographical stories.

under the right circumstances, young children's memories may serve as a reliable source of information (Peterson, 2002).

Just how early do our memories go? Carole Peterson and her colleagues (2001) have followed a group of children who were admitted to hospital for various injuries (broken bones, cuts requiring stitches, dog bites, and burns). These children ranged in age from 2 to 13 when they were injured. They were interviewed about their injury about one week, six months, two years, and, most recently, five years after their injury. Even after five years the children (now 7 to 18 years of age) demonstrated very good memory for the details surrounding their injury (how the injury occurred, who was the first to help them, etc.). Their memory for the details of the hospital treatment, however, was not as complete. Although older children remembered more than younger children, even those who were as young as 2 at the time of their injury recalled many of the details about the event—even after a five-year delay (see the table). These data suggest that even very early memories can be recalled. In a recent review (Peterson, 2002), the implications of this research for eyewitness testimony suggests that,

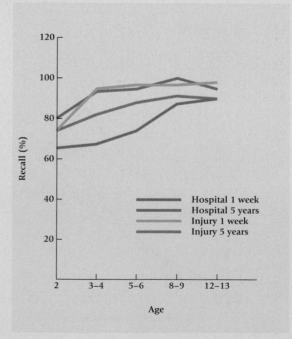

Percentage of central information for both injury and hospitalization events among children one week after an injury and five years later. ADAPTED FROM PETERSON & WHALEN (2001).

causal relations among the events that unfold. For example, a 3-year-old describing her fast-food restaurant script might say, "You drive there, go in, get in line, get hamburgers and fries, eat, and go home." Even 2-year-olds can organize information in a scriptlike fashion (Bauer, 1997; Fivush, Kuebli, & Clubb, 1992). And although scripted knowledge may become more elaborate with age, preschool children continue to learn and remember what usually happens at snack time at school, birthday parties, fast-food restaurants, and bedtime at home, and in a variety of other familiar settings (Fivush, 1997; Nelson, 1996).

Forming scripts thus appears to be a means by which young children organize and interpret their experiences and make predictions about what they can expect on similar occasions in the future. Yet, young children's organization of events into scripts has its costs, for it results in their tending *not* to remember much in the way of novel, atypical (or nonscript) information. In one study (Fivush & Hamond, 1990), 2½-year-olds were questioned about such recent "noteworthy" events as a trip to the beach, a camping trip, or a ride on an airplane. Rather than recalling the novel aspects of these special events, children were more likely to focus on what adults would consider to be routine information. So when describing a camping trip, one child first recalled sleeping outside, which is unusual, but then mostly remembered very mundane activities (Fivush & Hamond, 1990, p. 231):

INTERVIEWER: You slept outside in a tent? Wow, that sounds like a lot of fun.

CHILD: And then we waked up and eat dinner. First we eat dinner, then go to bed, and then wake up and eat breakfast.

INTERVIEWER: What else did you do when you went camping? What did you do when you got up, after breakfast?

CHILD: Umm, in the night, and went to sleep.

It may seem strange that a young child would talk about such routine events as waking up, eating, and going to bed when so many new and exciting things must have happened on a camping trip. But the younger the child, the more he or she may need to embed novel events into familiar routines. According to Fivush and Hamond, everything is new to 2-year-olds, who are most concerned with making some sense of the events they experience.

As children grow older, they eventually remember more specific and atypical information over extended periods, especially if the event sequence they experienced is highly unusual and particularly noteworthy. For example, Hamond and Fivush (1991) interviewed 3- and 4-year-olds six or 18 months after they had gone to Disney World. All children recalled a great deal of information about their trip, even after 18 months. The 4-year-olds recalled more details and required fewer prompts to describe them than the 3-year-olds did. Nevertheless, recall for this single, special experience was quite good, perhaps because it deviated so far from, and could not easily be assimilated into, a familiar, scriptlike routine.

The Social Construction of Autobiographical Memories

One interesting aspect of Hamond and Fivush's (1991) study was that children who talked more with their parents about the Disney World trip recalled more about the trip. This implies that parents play an important role in the growth of autobiographical memory, a point recently made by several theorists (Farrant & Reese, 2000; Harley & Reese, 1999). Judith Hudson (1990), for example, proposes that memory for events begins as a joint activity in which children talk about past events, guided by adults who expand on their skimpy recollections. In most families, Hudson proposes, parents begin talking about the past by asking such contextual questions as "Where did we go this morning?" "What did we see?" "Who went with us?" and "What else did we see?" Here is one example of a conversation in which a mother prompted her 19-month-old daughter to recall details of their morning trip to a zoo:

MOTHER: Allison, what did we see at the zoo?

ALLISON: Elephunts.

MOTHER: That's right! We saw elephants. And what else?

ALLISON: (shrugs)

MOTHER: Panda bear? Did we see a panda bear?

ALLISON: (smiles and nods)

MOTHER: Can you say "panda bear?"

ALLISON: Panda bear.

MOTHER: Good! Elephants and panda bears. What else?

ALLISON: Elephunts.

MOTHER: That's right, elephants. And also a gorilla.

ALLISON: Go-rilla!

From these interchanges, children learn that the important facts to remember about events are the whos, whens, and wheres of their experiences. And when parents request this information in ways that reconstruct the temporal order and causal sequences among events and ask children to *evaluate* these happenings (what was *your* favourite part?), they are helping youngsters to organize their experiences into storylike *narratives* and to recall them as events that have *personal* significance—as "things that happened to me" (Farrant & Reese, 2000; Hayden, Haine, & Fivush, 1997). Clearly, these joint reconstructions of past experiences should remind us of Vygotsky's ideas about the social construction of knowledge and Rogoff's ideas about guided or collaborative learning. Indeed, 2- to 3½-year-olds whose parents have often collaborated with them by asking questions about past events recall more autobiographical experiences one to two years later than do age-mates whose parents have rarely questioned them about the past (Harley & Reese, 1999; Reese, Hayden, & Fivush, 1993).

? WHAT DO YOU THINK?

To what extent do you think each of the following experiences might prompt or inhibit the development of autobiographical memory, and why: (a) watching children's shows such as *Sesame Street,* (b) watching rock videos on MuchMusic, (c) participating in "show and tell" in nursery school?

By encouraging children to reconstruct past events in which they have participated, parents foster the development of autobiographical memory.

Interestingly, parents' co-constructions of past events become increasingly detailed as their children develop more competent language and narrative skills (Hayden et al., 1997). The development of narrative skills may also reflect a change in the *way* children of different ages think, with older children being better at generating more complex narratives than their younger peers (e.g., McKeough, 2000; McKeough & Genereux, 2003; see Box 8.5 for more information about the development of narrative thought). So over the preschool years, autobiographical memory appears and blossoms as children, guided by their parents, learn to construct increasingly detailed personal narratives in which they place their experiences in the larger context of their own lives.

Children as Eyewitnesses

One topic related to event memory that has attracted a lot of attention lately concerns the reliability of children as eyewitnesses. Not surprisingly, much of the recent interest has come about because of children's increasing participation in the legal system, either as victims or as witnesses to purported crimes (Ceci & Bruck, 1998). Issues of interest both to psychologists and to the legal profession include the following:

How much do children of different ages remember of events they witnessed?

How long do these memories last?

How accurate are their memories?

How susceptible are children to suggestion?

Age Differences in Eyewitness Memory

Eyewitness memory is really not different from event memory, except that some misdeed or traumatic experience is usually embedded in the witnessed event. Research in which children observe and are later asked to recall such events yields the typical developmental differences in event memory, with older children remembering far more than younger children (Ornstein, Gordon, & Larus, 1992; Poole & Lindsay, 1995). But even though preschool (and young elementary-school) children recall few precise details, what they do remember is generally accurate and central to the event (Bjorklund, Brown, & Bjorklund, 2001; Poole & White, 1995). In a video involving a boy and a girl in which the boy steals a bike, for example, young children typically recall the bike theft but are much less likely than older children or adults to describe the participants, characteristics of the bike, or details of the setting (Cassel & Bjorklund, 1995). When children are prompted with more specific cues (for example, "Tell me what the girl looked like"), they recall more information. However, in addition to remembering more *correct* facts, they also tend to relate some *incorrect* "facts" as well, reducing the overall accuracy of their recall (Bjorklund et al., 1998; Goodman et al., 1994). And unfortunately, these *false memories* often persist and may be as resistant as or more resistant to forgetting than true memories are (Brainerd & Poole, 1997; Brainerd, Reyna, & Poole, 2000).

How Suggestible Are Child Witnesses?

The fact that children sometimes report and retain false memories implies that their recall of witnessed or experienced events may be highly susceptible to suggestion. Research has shown that people of all ages report more inaccurate information if asked leading questions that suggest inaccurate facts or events (for example, "He touched your penis, didn't he?"). And most of the available evidence implies that children younger than 8 or 9 are far more susceptible to such memory distortions than older children, adolescents, and adults are (Ceci & Bruck, 1998; Lindberg, Keiffer, & Thomas, 1999; Quas et al., 1999; Templeton & Wilcox, 2000).

Anne McKeough

Anne McKeough works in the Faculty of Education at the University of Calgary. Her research interests in narratives are complemented by interests in cognitive development as well as the evaluation and design of instruction and assessment approaches that are developmentally appropriate.

Anne McKeough

ACTION-BASED: She walked to the front door.

INTENTIONAL: She walked to the front door because she *wanted* to get in. (The word *wanted* signifies the intent.)

INTERPRETIVE: She walked to the front door because she wanted to get in because she *knew* her friend was in there. (The word *knew* indicates "why" the action occurred.)

Narratives tell us what children and adolescents can remember about their lives, and they can also be used to understand how children and adolescents think and how their thinking changes over time. Narrative thought underlies our social knowledge; that is, we use narrative thought when we think about the nature, causes, and consequences of human actions and human interactions (McKeough, 2000; McKeough & Genereux, 2003). What can we say about children's thoughts from our study of their narratives? A common developmental observation is that children's narratives become more and more complex as they get older. This observation has prompted developmental theorists to suggest a model of narrative thought that describes the changes in narrative thought as progressing from an action-based understanding in early childhood, to an intentional structure during middle childhood, to an interpretive model in adolescence (see McKeough et al., 2000; McKeough & Genereux, 2003). The following sentences demonstrate this progression:

The model assumes that as children develop, working-memory resources increase. The increase in capacity, along with greater domain-specific knowledge, allows the learner to coordinate greater amounts of information—which is evident in more complex social understanding of situations and more structurally complex stories. Recent tests of this developmental model were conducted by Anne McKeough and her colleagues at the University of Calgary. They asked 9- to 18-year-olds to compose stories (McKeough, 2000; McKeough et al., 2000; McKeough & Genereux, 2003). The stories were evaluated for their structural complexity as well as for their social-psychological content. From early to late adolescence, stories increased in structural complexity and in interpretiveness (McKeough & Genereux, 2003). In addition, the outcomes provided clear support for the model: Developmental change in narrative thought appears to be a product of both increases in processing capacity (or working-memory resources) and increases in domain-specific knowledge.

Don't misunderstand: False memories of this kind can be induced in people of all ages (Lindberg et al., 1999; Loftus & Pickrell, 1995; Oakes & Hyman, 2000). Nevertheless, it is much easier to create them in preschool and young elementary-school children, even when the memories address events that allegedly happened *to them* and the children initially *deny* the experiences. Stephen Ceci and his associates (1994), for example,

Concept Check 8.2
Development of Attention and Memory

Check your understanding of the development of attention and memory by matching each descriptive statement below to one of the following ideas or concepts: (a) rehearsal, (b) knowledge base, (c) elaboration, (d) false memories, (e) storylike narratives, (f) scripts, (g) metamemory, (h) sustained attention, (i) retrieval, (j) autobiographical memory. Answers appear in the Appendix.

_____ 1. one's increasing capacity for _____ depends, in part, on maturation of the reticular formation

_____ 2. strategic memory strategy that rarely appears before adolescence

_____ 3. early memory device by which children organize and represent their experiences

_____ 4. excellent performance of child experts illustrates the role of _____ in facilitating strategic memory

_____ 5. memory that infants and toddlers lack

_____ 6. memory process aided greatly by cued-recall prompts

_____ 7. representations that contribute greatly to the development of autobiographical memory

_____ 8. easily created in young children by asking leading questions

_____ 9. executive control process that can promote memory performance

_____ 10. memory strategy that involves repeating materials to be remembered asked preschool children and 6-year-olds if they could ever remember having experienced such events as catching a finger in a mousetrap. Although almost no one admitted to recalling these *fictional* events in the initial interviews, after repeated questioning, more than 50 percent of the younger preschool children and about 40 percent of the 5- and 6-year-olds said that these events had happened to them and often provided vivid accounts of their experiences! Furthermore, many children continued to believe that these events actually happened even after being told by the interviewers and their parents that the events were just made up and had never taken place.

Plausibility is an important factor here. Even though getting one's finger caught in a mousetrap might be an event that few children have ever actually experienced, it is one that could happen in many households. Kathy Pezdek and Danielle Hodge (1999) demonstrated that about one third of 5- to 7-year-old children "remembered" being lost in a mall (which they had not been) whereas only 1 of 19 children (about 5 percent) "remembered" being given an enema (see also Connolly & Lindsay, 2001). Although most of these children knew what an enema was, the event was implausible. If such an embarrassing and invasive thing had happened to them, they certainly would have remembered. Pezdek and Hodge also found that children reported more details for true memories than false ones. So even though there is no "Pinocchio test" for determining whether a memory is true or not, on average, children's recollections of events that actually did happen to them tend to be clearer and more detailed than their recollections of planted, or false, memories (Pezdek & Taylor, 2000).

In sum, it is often possible to convince young children to confirm an interviewer's allegations by falsely recalling information or experiences that never happened, particularly when the suggestions and accusations are strong, persistent, and plausible. Why are younger children so suggestible? Such social factors as a young child's desire to please adults or to comply with their requests almost certainly contribute to their heightened suggestibility. So, too, does a young child's preference for encoding and reporting exact details (which they are more prone to forgetting) rather than gist information, which is easier to remember over the long run (Brainerd et al., 2000). So when an interviewer suggests a fact that they haven't encoded or can't recall (for example, "The man who touched your sister had a scar on his face, didn't he?"), younger children, who are especially motivated to recall details, may answer "Yes" and remain convinced that this is what they really saw.

Implications for Legal Testimony

Although children aged 5 or under are rarely asked to testify in court, 6- to 10-year-olds are often called as witnesses. What steps might legal practitioners take to help ensure that testimony provided by child-witnesses is accurate and not tainted by false memories?

According to Kim Roberts from Wilfrid Laurier University, an important step to lessen the likelihood of suggestibility might be to place sensible limitations on the ways children are interviewed (Roberts, 2002; Roberts & Powell, 2001). This can be accomplished by asking questions in nonleading ways, by limiting the number of times children are interviewed, and by cautioning children that it is better to say "I don't remember" or admit to not knowing an answer than it is to guess or go along with what an interviewer is implying (Ceci & Bruck, 1993). Remaining friendly and patient with a child, rather than stern and adversarial, also seems to lessen the probability that children will report inaccurate details or construct false memories.

Other procedures have been used to spare children the trauma of having to face an abusive parent in court or to answer pointed questions about uncomfortable issues, such as sexual abuse, that they may not understand and can easily misreport. For example, young children are sometimes asked to "act out" with dolls what they have experienced, or to answer questions about sensitive issues posed by a puppet with whom they feel more comfortable. Yet, these methods are controversial, for they may not improve the accuracy of children's testimony (Greenhoot et al., 1999) and can even induce some young witnesses to imply the occurrence of inappropriate physical and sexual contact that never happened (Bruck et al., 1995b). Other children are spared the discomfort of facing family members in the emotionally charged atmosphere of the courtroom by testifying on videotape, which is later entered as evidence during the trial. Although this procedure can lessen children's emotional concerns (that is, anxiety, fear of punishment) and increase reporting accuracy, it is important that the interrogators be impartial and question children in nonleading ways that are unlikely to promote false memories (Bruck, Ceci, & Hembrooke, 1998).

PROBLEM SOLVING AND REASONING

Life is full of problems, and learning how to solve them is a major task of childhood. We say that someone is solving a problem when there is a specific goal in mind that cannot be attained immediately because of the presence of one or more obstacles. Much of what we have studied in this and the previous chapter has been concerned with problem solving. Finding the sum of two numbers is problem solving, as is finding a solution to the pendulum problem, or the behaviour of infants as they try to retrieve an object hidden under a cloth. Information-processing approaches have much to contribute to the understanding of problem solving and its development. Recall, we examined Robert Siegler's general approach to problem solving when we discussed his *adaptive strategy choice* model earlier in this chapter, proposing that children have a variety of different strategies available to them at any one time and that these strategies compete with one another for use.

In this section we will look at two additional aspects of problem solving. First we will consider how children learn to use *rules* to solve simple problems; then we will examine children's use of *analogical reasoning*, a seemingly advanced form of problem solving, but one that, in some form, may be present in early infancy.

Learning to Use Rules

Rules specify relations between two or more variables and are usually thought of in terms of "if...then" statements (If condition A exists, make response X; if condition B exists, make response Y.") (Zelazo & Jacques, 1997). When do children induce, or discover, rules as a result of experience, and how do they use these rules to solve problems?

When Can Children Induce Rules?

One simple task that requires the discovery of a rule is an oddity problem. This will be familiar to any readers who grew up watching *Sesame Street* and the game "One of these things is not like the other." In this game, and in oddity problems in general, people must figure out which object is different, or odd, relative to the others in the set. These problems can be very simple, based on perceptual similarity (e.g., £ £ β), or more complex, based on *conceptual similarity* (e.g., shirt, hat, table; or Susan, Joan, David).

Oddity tasks can even be administered to preverbal children and animals. In these cases, participants are shown a series of problems and receive a reward when they select the correct (odd) item. William Overman and his colleagues (1996) used such an oddity task, showing participants ranging from 16-month-old toddlers to adults a series of three objects, two of which were the same. Selection of the odd object always earned participants a reward. This was a difficult task for toddlers (16 to 31 months), even more difficult for the preschoolers (32 to 60 months), but relatively trivial for participants 6 years and older. Yet, most of the younger children did eventually learn the oddity rule although it took them several hundred trials, and most children of all ages quickly solved the problems in the second experiment when given verbal instructions to "pick the one that's different."

It is interesting that the lack of verbal instructions (i.e., performing the task using nonverbal procedures as is done when testing animals) was particularly detrimental for 2½- to 5-year-olds. It appears that these preschool children's overreliance on verbal instructions made inducing a nonverbal rule very difficult, whereas the problem was simple enough for older children and adults to figure out without being told explicitly what to do. But the fact that preschoolers were able to solve the problem easily as soon as they were told the rule ("Pick the one that's different.") indicates that they can apply this rule across different problems, and simply have a difficult time inducing a rule based on nonverbal information alone.

Selecting Appropriate Rules: The Importance of Inhibitory and Cognitive Controls

Although Overman's research illustrates that even 2- and 3-year-olds are able to induce and follow a simple rule (especially when given verbal instructions), they struggle to solve many problems in contexts where more than one rule could apply. This is quite clear in experiments using a *dimensional card-sorting task* developed by Philip Zelazo, Douglas Frye, and Tanja Rapus (1996). In this task children are shown sets of cards that vary on two dimensions, such as colour and shape. Figure 8.9 shows two such target cards, a yellow van and a green flower. When playing the colour game, children are told that all the yellow cards they'll see go with the yellow van and all the green cards go with the green flower. Children then are given a series of test cards (for instance, yellow flowers and green cars) and are asked to sort them by colour. This most children do easily. Then children are told they are going to play a new game, called the shape game. Now they are to place cars in the box with the yellow van and flowers in the box with the green flower. These are called *switch trials because* the rules have been switched (from sorting on the basis of colour to shape). Suddenly, most 3-year-old children fail, continuing to sort the cards according to the original dimension (colour). Yet, when asked what the new rule is, most can easily and correctly tell the experimenter. That is, 3-year-olds can verbalize the new rule but cannot follow it! By 4 years, most children do fine on both tasks.

Why do 3-year-olds have difficulties on these tasks? What develops to enable 4- and 5-year-olds to select and follow the appropriate rule when more than one might be available? One clue comes from the type of errors children make. Three-year-olds tend to persist making responses they had learned earlier, termed *perseverative errors* (Zelazo et al., 1995, 1996), and this suggests that one source of their problem is poor inhibitory control (Harnishfeger, 1995). That is, children have learned one response in this context and have a difficult time not making that same dominant response (sort by colour) when the rules change (now sort by shape). Yet Zelazo and Frye (1997) believe that there is more involved. Specifically, they contend that a major factor governing young children's use of rules is the complexity of rule systems they can represent mentally. With age, children gain increasing *conscious control* over their problem solving; they are increasingly able to reflect on the multiple rules that might apply to a problem, deliberately selecting which rules are most appropriate for which situation. This is one example of *explicit* cognition that we discussed earlier in the chapter and that gradually develops from late in the preschool period through adolescence. When children lack such higher-order cognition, they will perseverate on whichever lower-order rule seems most compelling. Thus age-related changes in children's ability to consciously (explicitly) represent information, and the resulting executive control that such self-aware representation allows, result in improved use of rules and better problem solving.

Target Cards

Test Cards

Figure 8.9 *Dimensional card-sorting task. Children are to sort cards initially by one dimension (colour) and later by a second dimension (shape).* FROM ZELAZO, FRYE & RAPUS, 1996.

Analogical Reasoning

Reasoning is a special type of problem solving, one that usually requires that one make an *inference*. That is, to reason, one must go beyond the information given. It is not enough just to figure out the rules associated with some game. In reasoning one must take the evidence presented and arrive at a *new conclusion* based on that evidence. The result is often new knowledge (DeLoache et al., 1998).

Perhaps the type of reasoning that people are most familiar with is **analogical reasoning**. Analogical reasoning involves using something you already know to help you understand something you don't know yet. Classical analogical reasoning problems are stated A:B::C:? For example, *dog* is to *puppy* as *cat* is to? The answer here, of course, is *kitten*. By knowing the relation between the first two elements in the problem (a *puppy* is a baby *dog*), one can use that knowledge to complete the analogy for the new item (*cat*). Analogies are thus based on *similarity relations*. One must understand the similarity between dogs and cats and puppies and kittens if one is to solve the analogy.

Analogical reasoning is a tremendously important ability that can help a person to quickly acquire new knowledge as long as she understands the base relation and can apply it appropriately to new contexts. You can probably remember examples from your own education in which analogies were used to help you learn or solve problems. I can remember achieving a better understanding of the configurations of molecular components in chemistry by comparing (and contrasting) them with interplanetary bodies (a sun, planets, and comets). Can young children reason by analogy? If so, can they use these skills to infer rules that they can use to solve novel problems?

Analogical reasoning is often assessed on intelligence tests, and gifted children show a sizable advantage over their normal peers in reasoning by analogy (Muir-Broaddus, 1995). This suggests to some researchers that analogical reasoning is a complex skill that is not well developed before adolescence (Inhelder & Piaget, 1958). Others, however, have proposed that analogical thinking serves as the basis for many other reasoning and problem-solving skills and *might be present at birth* (Goswami, 1996)!

How can there be such divergence of opinion about when analogical reasoning emerges? Part of the problem lies in the nature of the problems children are asked to solve. In cases when successful problem solving is not seen until late childhood or adolescence, the problems often involve objects or concepts with which children are unfamiliar. Perhaps more than any other factor, knowledge about the objects and relations among objects in analogical reasoning problems is critical in determining whether a child will solve or fail to solve a problem. Other factors also contribute to a child's success on analogical-reasoning problems, including memory for the premises and metacognitive knowledge (DeLoache et al., 1998). In the following sections we will review age trends in children's ability to solve analogical-reasoning problems and look at some of the factors that contribute to these cognitive developments.

Analogical Reasoning in Young Children

Counter to Piaget's account of analogical reasoning, Usha Goswami (1996) has proposed the **relational primacy hypothesis,** proposing that analogical reasoning is available early in infancy. In one of the few experiments to assess analogical reasoning in infancy, Zhe Chen, Rebecca Sanchez, and Tammy Campbell (1997) tested 1-year-old infants (Experiment 1). The basic task involved placing a desirable toy out of reach of the infant, with a barrier between the baby and the toy. Two strings, one attached to the toy and one not, were also out of the infant's reach, but each string was on a cloth that *was* within reach. To get the toy, the infants had to pull the cloth toward them and then pull the string attached to the toy. There were three similar tasks although the toy, the barrier, and the colour of the cloth varied across the three tasks. These are illustrated in Figure 8.10. If infants did not solve the problems after 100 seconds, their parents modelled the correct solution. The primary research question was: After solving an initial

reasoning
a particular type of problem solving that involves making inferences

analogical reasoning
reasoning that involves using something one knows already to help reason about something not known yet

relational primacy hypothesis
the hypothesis that analogical reasoning is available in infancy

Figure 8.10 *The configuration of the three problems 1-year-olds solve to test their reasoning by analogy.* FROM CHEN, SANCHEZ, & CAMPBELL, 1997.

problem, either with or without parental modelling, would the infants see the similarity with the later problems and be more apt to solve them? That is, would infants use analogical reasoning?

Few infants solved the first problem spontaneously (most required modelling by a parent). However, the percentage of infants solving the problems increased from 29 percent for the first problem, to 43 percent for the second, to 67 percent for the third.

So it seems that 1-year-olds are able to use analogical reasoning to solve simple problems. However, these perceptual analogies are very different from the classic problems used in research: Often the similarity between objects is *relational* rather than *perceptual*. Consider a study by Usha Goswami and Ann Brown (1990), who showed 4-, 5-, and 9-year-old children sets of pictures of the A:B::C? type. Children were given four alternatives and had to choose which of the four best completed the analogy. An example of a problem used in this study is shown in Figure 8.11. In this problem children must dis-

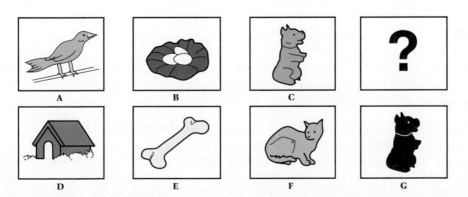

Figure 8.11 *Example of problem used in Goswami & Brown. Children must select from set of pictures in bottom row (picture D through G) the one that best completes the visual analogy on the top row (the correct answer is D).* FROM GOSWAMI & BROWN, 1990.

cover the relation between bird and nest (a bird lives in a nest) and make the analogous inference for *dog* (i.e., dog house). Children of all ages performed far better than expected by chance (59 percent, 66 percent, and 94 percent correct for the 4-, 5-, and 9-year-olds, respectively, with chance = 25 percent). Note that children are not solving the problems based on *perceptual similarity.* The bird and dog look nothing alike, nor do the nest and the dog house. To solve this problem, they must do so on the basis of *relational similarity*—the relation between the A and B terms (bird and nest) is used to find the best match for the C term (dog). This is clearly a more advanced form of analogical reasoning than that demonstrated by the 1-year-old infants in the Chen and colleagues (1997) study.

The Role of Knowledge in Children's Analogical Reasoning

One factor that affects whether children will use relational similarity to solve an analogical-reasoning problem is their knowledge, or familiarity, with the underlying relations used to make the analogy. Remember, the function of analogical reasoning is to use something you *know* to help you understand something you *don't know*. From this perspective, analogical reasoning can only make sense if a child is familiar with the base relation. You might get a better understanding of the human nervous system, for example, if you see it as analogous to electrical circuits. But if you know nothing about electrical circuits, it won't help you understand the nervous system at all, no matter how well developed your analogical reasoning abilities are.

The role of familiarity is illustrated in a study by Goswami (1995) that used a familiar children's story, *Goldilocks and the Three Bears* ("The Daddy Bear has all the big things, the Mummy Bear has all the medium-sized things, and the Baby Bear has all the tiny things," to help children make *transitive mappings*. As we learned in Chapter 7, a transitive relation involves relations among at least three objects. If object A is longer than object B, and object B is longer than object C, then object A must be longer than object C (i.e., A>B>C). Can young children use the transitive relation on one dimension (e.g., Daddy Bear, Mummy Bear, and Baby Bear) as an analogy for mapping transitive relations on another dimension, such as size or loudness, for example?

In Goswami's (1995) study, 3- and 4-year-old children were asked to use the relation in the Goldilocks story (Daddy Bear>Mummy Bear>Baby Bear) to classify objects that differed in quantity (a lot versus a medium amount versus a little pizza, candy, or lemonade), or to rank order (three levels) certain phenomena on the basis of loudness (of footsteps), pitch (of voices), temperature (of porridge), saltiness (of porridge), width (of beds), or height (of mirrors). Four-year-olds generally performed well on all these tasks, using the Three Bears analogy to map onto other dimensions. Three-year-olds did less well although they performed above chance levels on most tasks.

Goswami's findings are really quite remarkable. Recall that Piaget claimed that children cannot make transitive inferences until age 6 to 7, when they enter his concrete-operational stage of cognitive development. Yet Goswami's 3- and 4-year-old were quite capable of transitivity by analogy, *as long as the basis for the analogy* (in this case, the Three Bears story) *was familiar to them.*

The Role of Metacognition in Children's Analogical Reasoning

To what extent is *explicit* awareness of the relations between entities on analogical reasoning tasks important in solving problems? Can children think analogically but be unable to articulate what they are doing? Might such knowledge be *implicit*, and unavailable to consciousness? It certainly appears that the knowledge that the infants in the Chen and colleagues (1997) study had must have been implicit. These preverbal children's metacognitive understanding of the problem and their solutions to the problem were likely nonexistent. How important is metacognitive knowledge for analogical reasoning during childhood?

Apparently, metacognitive knowledge is very important. Successful training of analogical reasoning in preschool children is best accomplished when children receive explicit instruction about the rationale that underlies the analogy (Brown & Kane, 1988; Chen & Daehler, 1989). Consider a program of research by Ann Brown and her associates (Brown & Kane, 1988; Brown, Kane, & Long, 1989) who assessed preschool children's **learning to learn** by analogy.

In Brown and Kane's studies preschool children were given a series of problems in which they had to move some gumballs in one bowl on a table to another, out-of-reach bowl, without leaving their chair. They had various objects available to them that they could use to solve the problem, including scissors, an aluminum cane, tape, string, and a sheet of paper. Before solving the problem, children heard a story about a genie who had a similar problem of moving some jewels from one bottle within his reach to another bottle, out of his reach. If children in the experimental condition did not "solve" the problem, they were told that the genie could roll his carpet into a tube that could be used to transport the jewels. They were then given a similar problem (the Easter Bunny needing to transport eggs by using a rolled-up blanket), and then a third (a farmer transporting cherries using a rolled-up rug). Children receiving this series of problems, and who were made aware of the solution to the first problem when they failed, showed a large learning-to-learn effect. For the "rolling" solution, 46 percent of the children used analogical reasoning to solve the second problem, and 98 percent of the children did so for the third task. By contrast, control children who received the three sets of rolling problems but who did not receive the hints performed far worse: only 20 percent solved the first novel problem and 30 percent solved the second. So it seems that metacognitive awareness really does improve analogical problem solving. After solving the first two rolling problems, one 4-year-old commented at the beginning of the third problem; "And all you need to do is get this thing rolled up? I betcha!" Brown and Kane (1988) commented that the "aware" children had developed a mind-set to look for analogies, expecting to extract some general rule to solve problems and to be able to use knowledge they acquired in new contexts.

In sum, analogical reasoning, which seems to be present in a simple implicit form in *infancy*, gradually develops and becomes more explicit throughout childhood. This is an important finding that has clear education implications: Even preschool children can use analogies to acquire new information and become better problem solvers as long as they (1) understand the base relation from which inferences might be drawn, and (2) are (or are made) aware of the value of reasoning by analogy.

THE DEVELOPMENT OF NUMBER AND ARITHMETIC SKILLS

Another kind of reasoning that is heavily emphasized and almost essential to children growing up in today's information-age societies is quantitative or arithmetic reasoning. When are human beings first capable of processing quantitative information?

Remarkable as it may seem, this may be an innate ability (Geary, 1995). Very young infants can easily discriminate visual displays containing different numbers of objects and, by age 5 months, can learn that a particular numerical cue (for example, two objects rather than one or three) presented to their left means that an interesting stimulus will soon appear to their right (Canfield & Smith, 1996). By age 16 to 18 months, toddlers have even acquired a rudimentary sense of *ordinal* relationships, recognizing, for example, that three objects are *more than* two (Strauss & Curtis, 1981). These early understandings, coupled with the acquisition and use of such quantitative labels as *big, lots, small, and little*, reveal that toddlers are quite well-prepared for such feats as learning to count and to think about quantities.

learning to learn
improvements in performance on novel problems as a result of acquiring a new rule or strategy from the earlier solution of similar problems

Counting and Arithmetic Strategies

Counting

Counting normally begins shortly after children begin to talk. However, early counting strategies are very imprecise, often consisting of no more than uttering a few number words (for example, "one, three, four, six") while pointing to objects that a companion has counted (Fuson, 1988). By age 3 to 4, most children can count "accurately," establishing a one-to-one correspondence between number words and the items they represent (Gallistel & Gelman, 1992). And by age 4½ to 5, most children have acquired the principle of **cardinality**—the knowledge that the last word in a counting sequence (for example, "one, two, three, four, *five*") represents the number of items in a set (Bermejo, 1996). These developments in counting are especially important because they pave the way for the emergence of simple arithmetic strategies.

Early Arithmetic Strategies

cardinality
principle specifying that the last number in a counting sequence specifies the number of items in a set

Children's earliest arithmetic strategies are based on counting, at first out loud, and often using such props as fingers. The *sum* strategy we discussed earlier is perhaps the simplest method of adding numbers. Given the problem "What is 2 + 3?" the child begins by counting out the first number ("1, 2") and then counts out the second, starting from the cardinal value of the first (... 3, 4, **5**). Although this sum strategy is quite accurate, it takes a considerable amount of time to execute and is not very effective for problems where larger numbers (for example, 22 + 8) are involved.

More sophisticated addition strategies take short-cuts in counting. For example, a 6-year-old using the *min* strategy performs the minimum number of counts. Asked for the sum of 8 + 3, this child would start with the cardinal value of the larger number and count up from there (for example, "8 ... 9, 10, **11**"). Although preschoolers may use rules other than the sum and min strategies to add (and subtract) numbers, their approaches almost always involve counting out by ones the concrete objects to be added or subtracted (Carpenter & Moser, 1982).

Development of Mental Arithmetic

At some point during the early school years, children's solutions to simple arithmetic problems become more covert. They no longer rely on counting objects on their fingers because they can perform arithmetic operations in their heads. The earliest mental arithmetic strategies may still be such counting strategies as covert sum or min solutions. However, the many experiences they have in adding and subtracting numbers, coupled with knowledge about number systems that is often taught at school, soon permit elementary-school children to employ other, more efficient arithmetic strategies. For example, knowledge of the base-10 number system underlies decomposition strategies, in which children transform an original problem into two simpler prob-

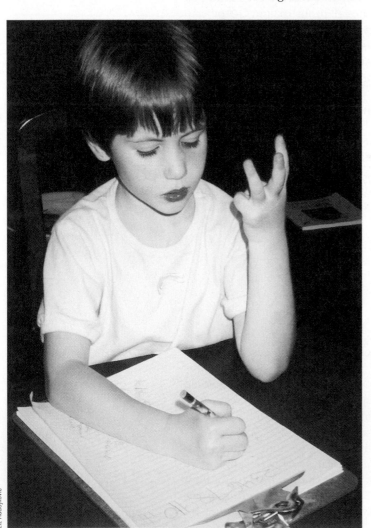

Liz Radojkovic

Counting on one's fingers is an early strategy that children use to solve arithmetic problems, one that is used less frequently as they develop more mathematical knowledge.

lems. Given 13 + 3 = ? for example, a child might think "13 is 10 + 3, 3 + 3 = 6, 10 + 6 = 16, so the answer is 16." Initially, use of a decomposition strategy may be slower than use of a min strategy, particularly for simple problems where not many "counts" are involved. But as children become practised at decomposing numbers into base-10 components, they solve problems faster by decomposition, particularly if they are working with larger numbers (for example, 26 + 17) for which counting strategies are laborious (Siegler, 1996a, b, c). Finally, children come to solve many simple arithmetic problems by fact retrieval—they simply know the correct answer (that is, 8 + 6 = 14) and retrieve it from long-term memory.

Once children begin to perform arithmetic computations "in their heads," knowing precisely what they are doing becomes more difficult. However, it is possible to infer their arithmetic strategies from the time it takes for them to arrive at a correct answer. If children are using a min strategy, for example, their reaction times for addition problems should increase as the size of the smaller of the two numbers (that is, the number of counts it requires) increases. If children are using fact retrieval, by contrast, they should answer very quickly, regardless of the numbers involved.

The arithmetic strategies children use increase in sophistication with age, but they do not follow a stagelike pattern. As we discussed earlier in this chapter when introducing Robert Siegler's (1996a, b) adaptive choice model, children have multiple strategies available to them that compete with one another for use. Thus, although preschool children rarely use fact retrieval, they do occasionally, particularly for simple problems such as those involving doubles (2 + 2 =?) (Bjorklund & Rosenblum, 2001). Likewise, older children and adults typically use more sophisticated strategies such as fact retrieval to solve most problems, but will fall back to use counting strategies such as min on occasion (Bisanz & LeFevre, 1990). Jeff Bisanz and Jo-Anne LeFevre (Carleton University) and their colleagues suggest that information-processing demands and poorer conceptual understanding explain preschoolers' poor arithmetic performance and help to account for some developmental increases in performance (e.g., Bisanz & LeFevre, 1992; LeFevre, Sadesky, & Bisanz, 1996; Mabbott & Bisanz, 2003). For more details on this intriguing argument, see Box 8.6.

8.6

THE INSIDE TRACK

Jeff Bisanz

Jeff Bisanz

Jeff Bisanz is the director of the Community–University Partnership for the Study of Children, Youth, and Families at the University of Alberta. He is well known for his research in cognitive development, including problem solving, reasoning, and memory in math and science.

His current research involves the study of mathematical cognition.

As noted in the chapter, a common finding reported in the study of early arithmetic skills is that children get better as they get older. What accounts for this developmental increase in arithmetic performance? In the text we have reviewed the acquisition and use of arithmetic strategies, which explains, in part, why older children outperform their younger peers. However, work by Jeff Bisanz and his colleagues suggests that information-processing demands—specifically demands in working memory—combined with some conceptual shortcomings may limit young children's performance (Bisanz & LeFevre, 1990; Klein & Bisanz, 2000). In one study, 48 4-year-olds were presented with nonverbal two- and three-term arithmetic problems

(e.g., 4 + 1 = , 3 + 2 – 2 =). When children represent objects in working memory, it is assumed that they represent each object as a discrete unit. When a set of four objects is presented, for example, the child represents each object internally and the *representational set size* is four. The researchers found a strong relationship between children's ability to answer simple, two-term problems and the representational set size required to solve these problems. This suggests that as working-memory demands increase, performance decreases. Among the three-term problems, earlier research suggests that children may not use conceptual shortcuts to help them solve problems (e.g., using inversion, which in the example above would mean recognizing that adding and subtracting the 2 would cancel each other out, and hence would require no computation). However, recent research suggests that even among Grade 1 and preschool children there is evidence of the spontaneous use of inversion (Klein & Bisanz, 2000; Rasmussen, Ho, & Bisanz, 2003) and children with greater visual-spatial working memory appear to be more likely to use inversion. Clearly, information-processing and conceptual skills are important factors in understanding the development of mathematical cognition.

Complex Computations

Obviously, not all mathematical proficiencies rest on our ability to retrieve numerical facts or perform computations in our heads. Children in schooled societies are explicitly taught a number of computational procedures, such as the carrying and borrowing rules that enable them to solve multidigit addition and subtraction problems, multiply large numbers, and perform long division. Many pupils have trouble learning and applying these rules, and often educators can quickly correct these deficiencies if they have carefully analyzed the requirements of the problems they present and have inferred what a child is doing wrong from the kinds of errors he makes (see Box 8.7 for other educational implications of information-processing research). If Johnny, for example, is presented with 350 − 131 and answers 221 rather than 219, he is using a faulty strategy that says "when subtracting from 0, enter the bottom digit." He will require different instruction from Tamar, who works the same problem and comes up with an answer of 119. Can you diagnose the faulty strategy Tamar is using? (If not, see the answer at the bottom of the page.)

Cultural Influences on Mathematics Performance

One of the major claims that Vygotsky made in his *sociocultural* theory was that cognitive development always occurs in a cultural context that influences the way one thinks and one solves problems. Can this important principle possibly hold for a rule-bound domain such as arithmetic? Let's see if it does.

Arithmetic Competencies of Unschooled Children

Although children in most cultures learn to count and acquire some very simple arithmetic strategies during the preschool years, the computational procedures on which higher mathematics are based are typically taught at school. Does this imply that children who receive minimal or no schooling are hopelessly incompetent in math?

One might answer "yes" if math competencies are assessed by the paper-and-pencil tests so often used to assess arithmetic and other quantitative skills in Western societies. However, these tests often badly underestimate the skills that unschooled children display.

T.N. Carraher and associates (1985), for example, examined the mathematical competencies of unschooled 9- and 15-year-old street vendors in Brazil. They found that problems embedded in real-life contexts (for example, "If a large coconut costs 76 cruzeiros, and a small one costs 50, how much do the two cost together?") were solved correctly *98 percent of the time*. By contrast, the same problems presented in a standard, out-of-context way ("How much is 76 + 50?") were answered correctly only 37 percent of the time. Street vendors can quickly and accurately add and subtract currency values *in their heads*, just as they must when conducting street transactions, where mistakes can have economic consequences. By contrast, the same numerical problems presented in out-of-context paper-and-pencil format have little practical application, and unschooled participants are apparently less motivated to expend the effort necessary to solve them. Other unschooled participants, such as bricklayers and lottery bookies, also develop flexible arithmetic competencies that they use with great skill in their own work (Schliemann, 1992).

$$\begin{array}{r} 3\overset{4}{5}0 \\ -\ 131 \\ \hline 119 \end{array}$$

Tamar uses an inappropriate borrowing rule. She thinks that whenever she needs to borrow, she must borrow from every column—that is,

Although unschooled street vendors may often fail at paper-and-pencil math problems, they display sophisticated arithmetic skills by quickly and accurately making change during sales transactions.

These findings are clearly consistent with Vygotsky's most basic sociocultural premise: Children acquire the skills they need within their own cultural context. Parents of unschooled Brazilian children, for example, construct arithmetic tasks for them (such as buying things at local stores with currency) that are appropriate for their current developmental level and contribute to a brand of arithmetic reasoning that is functional in their daily lives (Guberman, 1996).

Cultural Variations in Arithmetic among Schooled Children

Much has been written, both in the popular and the scholarly presses, about the fact that East Asian youngsters from China, Taiwan, and Japan typically outperform North American children in certain academic subjects, most notably mathematics. Specifically, American children performed much worse than age-mates from the two Asian cultures, even in Grade 1, and this cultural difference in math performance becomes more apparent with age (Baker, 1992; Stevenson, Chen, & Lee, 1993; Stevenson & Lee, 1990).

In attempting to explain these findings, researchers quickly ruled out the possibility that East Asian students are inherently smarter than Americans, because Grade 1 students in all three cultures do equally well on standardized intelligence tests (Stevenson et al., 1985). Yet, East Asian Grade 1 students already rely on a more sophisticated mix of basic arithmetic strategies than American Grade 1 students do, including the relatively sophisticated (for Grade 1 children) decomposition and fact-retrieval strategies (Geary, Fan, & Bow-Thomas, 1992). And later research reveals that the math-strategy advantage that East Asian children display is already apparent during the *preschool* period (Geary et al., 1993).

A critic might ask, "So what?" We are talking here about the most basic of arithmetic strategies that children clearly master by the end of elementary school. Yet, David Geary and his colleagues have shown that the sophistication of early arithmetic strategies and speed of fact retrieval predict later performance in more complex forms of mathematics (Geary & Burlingham-Dubre, 1989; Geary & Widaman, 1992). So if early mastery of basic skills promotes more complex mathematical competencies, it may not be surprising that East Asian students display a consistent mathematical advantage over their North American peers at all levels of schooling.

Now the obvious question becomes "Why are young East Asians so advantaged in acquiring basic mathematical skills?" Let's briefly consider some linguistic and instructional supports for acquiring mathematical concepts that are available to East Asian children but not to their North American counterparts.

LINGUISTIC SUPPORTS. Basic differences in how the Chinese (and Japanese and Korean) versus the English languages represent numbers seems to contribute to some of the early differences in arithmetic proficiency. Recall from Chapter 7 that the number words in Chinese for 11, 12, and 13 are translated as "ten-one," "ten-two," and "ten-three," which helps children to learn to count sooner than North American children, who must use the more idiosyncratic number words of eleven, twelve, and thirteen (Miller et al., 1995). The Chinese number-naming system also helps children to understand that the 1 in 13 has a place value of 10 (rather than 1). By contrast, English words for two-digit numbers in the teens are irregular and do not convey the idea of tens and ones. In one study, Korean second- and third-grade children had an excellent understanding of the meaning of digits in multidigit numbers, knowing that the 1 in 186 stands for "hundreds" and the eight stands for "eight-tens." Consequently, they performed very well on three-digit addition and subtraction problems ("What is 142 + 318?"), even though they had not yet received any formal instruction on adding or subtracting numbers this large (Fuson & Kwon, 1992). By contrast, the irregular form of many English multidigit numbers makes the meaning of larger numbers less intuitive and may even contribute to the problems English-speaking children experience with the borrowing and carrying rules they must acquire to perform multidigit addition and subtraction.

Recent research has suggested that language may also play a role in understanding more complicated arithmetic, specifically fractions. Irene Miura and her colleagues (1999) studied 6- and 7-year-old Croatian, Korean and American children's understanding of fractions and reported significantly greater understanding for the East Asian than for the Western children. They then looked at the way fractions are expressed in the Korean versus the English and Croatian languages. In Western languages the fraction 1/3 is expressed as "one-third." In Korean, one-third is spoken as *sam bun ui il* which is literally translated as "of three parts one." Miura and her colleagues argue that the intuitively clear way fractions are expressed in Korean helps children better understand the concept of the whole divided into parts and is primarily responsible for the early superiority of Korean children's understanding of fractions.

The finding that children's early arithmetic abilities differ as a function of their culture's language is consistent with Vygotsky's ideas about the importance of a culture's *tools of intellectual adaptation* for influencing thought. Cultures affect thinking not only in obvious ways, such as the provision of formal versus informal education, but also in less obvious ways, such as how the language describes and organizes important concepts.

INSTRUCTIONAL SUPPORTS. Finally, several East Asian instructional practices support the rapid learning of math facts and computational procedures involved in multidigit addition and subtraction. East Asian students practise computational procedures more than American students do (Stevenson, Lee, et al., 1990), and practice of this sort fosters the retrieval of math facts from memory (Geary et al., 1992). And the type of instruction provided seems to matter. For example, East Asian teachers instructing students how to carry a sum from one column of a multidigit number to the next higher will say to "bring up" the sum instead of "carrying" it. The term "bring up" (rather than "carry") may help children learning multidigit addition to remember that each digit to the left in a multidigit number is a base-10 increment of the cardinal value of that digit (that is, the 5 in 350 represents "50" rather than "5," and the 3 represents "300"). Furthermore, Asian math texts help children to avoid confusing place values by having different colour codes for the "hundreds," "tens," and "ones" column of multidigit numbers (Fuson, 1992).

How much do these linguistic and instructional supports contribute to the superior math performance of East Asian students? They almost certainly matter, but are hardly the sole contributors. Consider that East Asian students have always had the linguistic advantages over their

Figure 8.12 Performance of Grade 5 children from the U.S., Taiwan, and Japan on a mathematics test in 1980, 1984, 1990. FROM STEVENSON, CHEN, & LEE, 1993.

Linguistic supports, instructional supports, and a lot of practice help to explain the high proficiency that East Asian students display in mathematics.

American counterparts, yet American children who received their elementary-school education during the 1930s were quicker to acquire basic mathematical competencies than today's American students are, showing a proficiency for mathematics that rivals today's East Asian students (Geary, Salthouse, Chen, & Fan, 1996). So differences in mathematical competencies between East Asian and American students seem to be a relatively recent phenomenon that undoubtedly reflects broader cultural differences in educational philosophies and supports for education, as well as the differences in linguistic and instructional supports for mathematics learning that we have discussed here. Indeed, we will see just how true this speculation is in Chapter 16, where we will examine the many roles that schooling plays in the social, emotional, and intellectual lives of developing children and adolescents.

EVALUATING THE INFORMATION-PROCESSING PERSPECTIVE

Today, the information-processing perspective has become the dominant approach to the study of children's intellectual development, and justifiably so. Simply stated, information-processing researchers have provided a reasonably detailed description of how such cognitive processes as attention, memory, and metacognition—processes that Piaget did not emphasize—change with age and influence children's thinking. Furthermore, the detailed examination of certain domain-specific academic skills that information-processing theorists have undertaken has led to important instructional changes that enhance scholastic performances.

Despite these obvious strengths, the information-processing approach has several drawbacks that render it woefully incomplete as an explanation of cognitive development. Some of the stronger challenges have come from the developing field of cognitive neuroscience, which is concerned with identifying evolutionary and neurological contributors to cognition and intellectual growth. Research on the neural correlates of inhibition that we reviewed in Box 8.1 is one small step in this direction. Other researchers are looking seriously at the relations between brain and cognitive development in

PhotoDisc, Inc.

Recall that Piaget offered educators two important suggestions for helping their pupils to learn. First, teachers should view children as naturally inquisitive beings who learn best by *constructing* knowledge from *moderately novel* aspects of experience—that is, from information that challenges their current understanding and forces them to reevaluate what they already know. Second, Piaget stressed that a teacher's job is not so much to transmit facts or to reinforce correct answers as to provide the climate, setting, and materials that will allow curious children the personal satisfaction of *discovering* important concepts for themselves.

Information-processing theorists can agree with Piaget that children are active and curious explorers who learn best by constructing knowledge from experiences that are just beyond current levels of understanding. However, their own guidelines for effective instruction are much more explicit than Piaget's and come closer to the views of Lev Vygotsky (1978), implying that teachers (and parents or other more competent associates) should take a more *active, directive* role than Piaget had envisioned. The following six implications for instruction flow directly from the research we have reviewed on the development of attention, strategic memory, and problem solving:

1. *Analyze the requirements of problems that you present to your pupils.* Know what information must be encoded and what mental operations must be performed to arrive at a correct answer or to otherwise grasp the lesson to be learned. Without such knowledge, it may be difficult to tell why students are making errors or help them overcome their mistakes.

2. *Reduce short-term memory demands to a bare minimum.* Problems that require young elementary-school children to encode more than three or four bits of information are likely to overload their short-term storage capacity and prevent them from thinking logically about this input. The simplest possible version of a new problem or concept is what teachers should strive to present. If a problem involves several steps, students might be encouraged to break it down into parts (or subroutines) and perhaps to record the solutions to these parts in their notes in order to reduce the demands on their short-term storage. Once children grasp a concept and their information processing becomes more "automatized," they will have the short-term storage capacity to succeed at more complex versions of these same problems (Case, 1992).

3. *Encourage children to have fun using their memories.* Strategic games such as 20 Questions or Concentration are not only enjoyable to elementary-school children but also help them to appreciate the advantages of being able to retain information and retrieve it for a meaningful purpose.

4. *Provide opportunities to learn effective memory strategies.* A teacher can do this by grouping materials into distinct categories as she talks about them or by giving children easily categorizable sets of items to sort and classify (Bjorklund, 1987). Question-and-answer games of the form "Tell me why leopards, lions, and house cats are alike" or "How do dragonflies and hummingbirds differ from helicopters and jets?" are challenging to young children and make them aware of conceptual similarities and differences on which organizational strategies depend.

5. *Provide opportunities for analogical reasoning.* Creative use of analogical puzzles and games encourages children to use what they know to reason and master novel challenges (Goswami, 1995). Proficiency at analogical reasoning may be particularly useful for helping children and adolescents grasp unfamiliar or unobservable concepts. Inducing students to think about concrete models that they can see or easily imagine (e.g., the arc of a spark across a spark plug, or the operation of a digital computer) should help those who are practised at reasoning by analogy to grasp more abstract or less tangible phenomena (such as transmission of neural impulses across a synapse, or the workings of the human mind).

6. *Structure lessons so that children are likely to acquire metacognitive knowledge and to understand why they should plan, monitor, and control their cognitive activities.* Simply teaching appropriate information-processing strategies does not guarantee that your pupils will use them. If these skills are to transfer to settings other than the training task, it is important that children understand *why* these strategies will help them to achieve their objectives and *when* it is appropriate to use them. As an instructor, you can help by making your own metacognitive knowledge more explicit ("I'll have to read this page more than once to understand it"), offering suggestions to the child ("You might find it easier to remember the months of the year if you group them according to seasons. Summer includes …"), or asking questions that remind children of strategies already taught ("Why is it important to summarize what you've read?" "Why do you need to double-check your answer?"). All these approaches have proven quite successful at furthering children's metacognitive skills and persuading them to apply this knowledge to the intellectual challenges they face (Brown & Campione, 1990; Paris, 1988).

---

infancy and childhood and developing new theories that integrate these different levels of organization (Byrnes & Fox, 1998; Johnson, 2000). In fact Byrnes and Fox (1998) propose that research in developmental cognitive neuroscience has placed us on the threshold of a new revolution, equivalent to the cognitive revolution of 40 years ago that replaced behavioural perspectives of how children learn and think.

Still other critics point out that information-processing theorists have paid little attention to important social and cultural influences on cognition that Vygotsky and others (e.g., Rogoff, 1998) have emphasized. And, those who favour the elegant coherence of Piaget's stage model question what they see as the "fragmented" approach of information-processing theorists, who focus on specific cognitive processes and view development as the gradual acquisition of skills in many different domains. These critics contend that information-processing researchers have succeeded in breaking cognition into pieces, but haven't been able to put it back together into a broad, comprehensive theory of intellectual development. Although this criticism has some merit, information-processing theorists would reply by noting that it was the many, many problems with Piaget's broad-brush account of cognitive development that helped to stimulate their work in the first place.

Even some of the central assumptions on which information-processing theory rests have been assailed in some quarters. For example, the classic assumption that all cognitive activities take place in a single, limited-capacity working-memory store has now been challenged. Charles Brainerd and Johannas Kingma (1985), for example, propose that working memory should be viewed as a series of independent stores, each with its own resources and each performing such specific operations as information encoding, information retrieval, and execution of strategies. Of course, we have already discussed another alternative to traditional information-processing models—*fuzzy-trace theory*—which claims that we process information at more than one level rather than merely making verbatim mental copies of what we experience.

In sum, the information-processing approach is itself a developing theory that has greatly advanced our understanding of children's intellectual growth while experiencing some very real "growing pains" of its own. We like to think of this model as a necessary complement to, rather than a replacement for, Piaget's earlier framework. And our guess is that this new look at cognitive development will continue to evolve, aided by advances in cognitive neuroscience and other complementary perspectives (see Fischer & Bidell, 1998), eventually filling in many of the gaps that remain in its own framework and that of Piaget, and thereby contributing to a comprehensive theory of intellectual growth that retains the best features of both approaches.

CONNECTIONIST APPROACHES TO COGNITIVE DEVELOPMENT[1]

The introduction of computers not only yielded the information-processing approach but also led to another theoretical approach called **connectionism**. Connectionism attempts to parallel the neural activity that occurs in the brain. Computers are used to construct artificial neural networks, and simulations are conducted using these networks to see if the network can generate the expected cognitive outcome. This differs from the information-processing model, which uses the computer as a metaphor for understanding how information is handled. An important distinction is made between cognitive *hardware* (the brain) and *software* (the mind). Connectionists argue that this metaphor does not capture how the human brain is constructed or how the human brain learns. Humans, after all, are physiologically very different from computers. Instead of being split into different components (like a CPU, RAM, and hard drive), the human brain is a single processing unit that accomplishes all of our mental tasks. Realizing this, researchers in the 1980s began taking a different view of cognition to more closely parallel how the brain actually computes information.

connectionism
field of cognitive science that seeks to understand mental processes as resulting from assemblies (or groups) of real or artificial neurons

---

[1] Dr. Marc Joanisse at the University of Western Ontario provided substantial guidance and written support in the construction of this section.

Connectionists believe that cognitive processes are the product of many simple processing units that are massively interconnected. The processing units are roughly similar to brain neurons, and the connections among them are similar to brain synapses. When they work together, the processing units and connections form a network.

The Origins of Connectionism

Modern connectionism emerged in the 1980s with the advent of fast computers capable of modelling cognitive tasks within large artificial neural networks. One of the best known of the new approaches is called parallel distributed processing, or PDP (McClelland & Rumelhart, 1986). The word "parallel" in PDP assumes that many things are being processed at the same time. This is similar to the brain, which is made up of millions of simple neurons that are working simultaneously. The term "distributed" refers to the fact that information is being encoded across the neurons in the brain instead of using discrete elements (like the files and folders on a computer).

How Are Networks Created?

Similar to the human brain, the networks that are created to perform each task involve varying numbers of processing units (neurons), and varying strength of the connections among the processing units. The number of processing units depends on the type of cognitive task that is being performed—some tasks require more units than others. Stronger connections are present when processing units work closely together, and weaker connections represent processing units that are more peripheral to the task at hand. Networks are derived from theories about how cognitive tasks are conducted. Based on the expectations set out by the theory, connectionists can specify the number of processing units and the relative strengths of the connections. A computer simulation is run, and the researcher looks at the output that is generated. The network can be modified and refined, if necessary, by changing the number of processing units or the strength of the connections. Simulations that generate the anticipated output or "cognitive performance" can be used to explain how human processing occurs.

How Connectionist Networks Work

To understand how networks work, let's look at a simulation designed to explain how people learn to read words aloud. This cognitive task was studied by Mark Seidenberg while he was at McGill University and James McClelland at Carnegie Mellon University (1989). To simulate this task, the network was given the written form of a word, such as the word "gave," as an input, and it had to learn to produce the sound of the word (its phonological form) as the output. As you may already know, this task is not as easy as it seems, since English spelling is inconsistent. For example, regular English words have a predictable relationship between the sound of the word (phonology) and the spelling (e.g., gave, mint, plain), while irregular words do not have such a predictable match (e.g., have, pint, plaid). Nevertheless, the network learned to read all types of English words by encoding spelling-to-sound regularities—and exceptional cases—within its connections. Earlier models of reading had suggested that reading required two separate pathways: one for reading regular words, and one for reading irregular words (Coltheart, 1978). The simulation suggested that only one pathway was required.

Connectionism and Development

One reason connectionist networks are appealing to developmental psychologists is that they challenge our usual assumptions about the types of information that a child is using to acquire a cognitive ability. As you have seen throughout this book, children do not always learn in a linear fashion. A famous case of this in language learning is how English-speaking children acquire past tense verbs. Most English past tense verbs are created by adding the "-ed" sound (known as the past tense *morpheme*) to a verb (bake → baked, step → stepped, grate → grated).[2] However, there are a number of exceptions to this rule—for example, take → took, sleep → slept, go → went, and ring → rang.

Child language researchers have observed that children appear to pass through three distinct stages as they acquire irregular past tenses (Marcus et al., 1992). Early on, children use several irregular past tenses correctly. For example, they correctly use words such as went and took. Later, they begin to overuse the "-ed" past tense rule and apply it in all cases, even for irregular verbs that they may have used correctly before (e.g., goed and taked). At the third stage of acquisition, the correct past tense for irregular verbs reappears, and children continue to use the correct past tense for regular verbs. When a connectionist model generated a similar pattern of learning, the researchers were able to offer a novel explanation for the appearance, disappearance, and then reappearance of the correct use of the past tense for irregular verbs (Rumelhart & McClelland, 1986): They suggested that, like children, the network first attempted to memorize each past tense form, but because the network had a limited capacity, it eventually needed to learn a rule to derive past tenses. As a result, it began overgeneralizing the "-ed" form to irregular past tenses. Eventually, the network learned when to suppress this rule and generated correct performance for both regular and irregular verbs.

Connectionist models offer great insights into the underpinnings of cognitive development and have both challenged and supported interpretations offered through other cognitive theories (see Thomas & Karmiloff-Smith, 2002). However, the models have also come under criticism. For example, Steven Pinker (1994) argued that the early models, like the one used to describe the acquisition of past tense verbs, tended to produce behaviours that we never see in children, such as irregularization errors (ding→dang instead of ding → dinged). In response, more recent models have been designed that address some of these problems, while other concerns remain to be addressed (see Plunkett, 2000). Nevertheless, more and more developmental researchers are turning to the growing number of neural-based theories of learning to better understand the mechanisms underlying learning and cognition. Tom Shultz of McGill University has investigated the development of a number of cognitive skills, including traditional Piagetian tasks, using connectionist simulations. To find out more about his work, see Box 8.8.

---

2 If you listen carefully, you'll notice that there are three past tense endings in English—the "t," "d," and "ed" sounds. Each is used in a specific context based on the last sound at the end of the present tense verb. Because the alternatives are determined systematically, linguists usually treat this as a single grammatical rule that is realized in three slightly different ways.

Tom Shultz

Tom Shultz is in the Department of Psychology at McGill University. He has research interests in the areas of cognitive science, connectionism, reasoning, and cognitive development.

Connectionist simulations provide a novel view of how knowledge is represented in children (as a network's weighted connections) and a detailed, compelling picture of how and why developmental changes in knowledge occur (through learning and growth). One of the most useful connectionist techniques is called cascade-correlation. This technique allows networks to grow as they learn by adding new units as needed, a process that corresponds roughly to the formation of new neurons and new synapses in the brain. Such networks were trained on Piaget's conservation of number problems and were able to simulate many of the psychological phenomena found with children. For example, there were the typical sudden jumps in performance as conservation was acquired.

Recall the Piagetian task where two rows of marbles are laid out and in one row the marbles are placed close together, while in the other the marbles are spaced farther apart. Nonconservers typically indicate that the longer row has more marbles even though the number of marbles is equal. The networks also demonstrated this length bias. In addition, small number problems were easier than large number problems (Shultz, 1998). Analysis of how the network arrived at its solutions showed how perceptual and cognitive information, although initially in conflict, are eventually integrated.

Piaget designed his conservation problems so that how things look conflict with reasoning about how they must be. Similar to children, networks started out by focusing on how the rows of items looked, in terms of their length and density, and ended by focusing on the nature of the transformation that was applied to one of the rows. Shultz also has generated other simulations to determine how children navigate problems such as Piaget's balance-scale problem, as well as examining issues related to the concept of stages (see Shultz, 2003). Networks such as these enhance theoretical precision and help to clarify theoretical debates surrounding cognitive development.

SUMMARY

Information Flow and the Multistore Model

♦ Information-processing theorists approach the topic of intellectual growth by charting the development of cognitive skills such as attention, memory, metacognition, and academic skills. Many analogies are drawn between human minds and computers. The mind, like a computer, is thought to be a *limited-capacity* system composed of mental "hardware" and "software." The **multistore model** depicts the human information-processing system as consisting of a **sensory store** to detect, or "log in" input; a **short-term store (STS)**, where information is stored temporarily until we can operate on it; and a "permanent," or **long-term store (LTS)**. Also included in most information-processing models is a concept of **executive control processes**, or **metacognition**, which include processes by which we plan, monitor, and control all phases of information processing.

Developmental Differences in Information-Processing Capacity

♦ Age differences in information-processing hardware have been examined by assessing **memory span** and **span of apprehension** to evaluate capacity of STS. Although sub-

stantial age differences in the STS have been found, many developmental differences in memory can be attributed to increases in **knowledge base** and how quickly children can process information.

Developmental Differences in "Software": Strategies and Knowledge of "Thinking"

♦ Research on developmental changes in information-processing software has focused mainly on **strategies**—goal directed operations used to aid task performance. Frequent findings include **production deficiencies**, in which children fail to produce a strategy spontaneously but can do so when instructed, and **utilization deficiencies**, in which children experience little or no benefit when they use a new strategy. Children of all ages have been found to use multiple and variable strategies in solving problems, a phenomenon that is explained by Robert Siegler's **adaptive strategy choice model.**

♦ Children's understanding of what it means to think increases over the preschool and early school years. By contrast, few or no developmental differences are observed for **implicit cognition**, cognition that is performed without conscious awareness.

Fuzzy Trace Theory: An Alternative Viewpoint

♦ Recent alternatives to the multistore model of information processing is **fuzzy-trace theory**, which claims that we process information at both a **gist** and a verbatim level and accounts for some age differences in memory and problem solving; and theories that emphasize the role of **inhibition** in children's intellectual development.

The Development of Attention

♦ With age, the **attention spans** of children and adolescents increase dramatically, owing in part to increasing myelinization of the central nervous system.

♦ Attention also becomes more planful and more **selective** with age as children and adolescents steadily improve in their ability to seek and concentrate on task-relevant stimuli and to not be distracted by other "noise" in the environment. **Attention deficit-hyperactivity disorder (ADHD)** describes children who find it nearly impossible to sustain their attention for long or to develop planful attentional strategies.

Memory: Retaining and Retrieving Information

♦ The effective use of **strategic memory** strategies, or **mnemonics**, increases with age. Frequently used memory strategies include **rehearsal**, **semantic organization**, **elaboration,** and **retrieval**. Memory strategies are usually assessed on either **free-recall** or **cued-recall** tasks, the latter of which provide specific cues, or prompts, to aid retrieval. The particular memory strategies that one acquires are heavily influenced by culture and the kinds of information that children are expected to remember.

♦ **Metamemory** (or knowledge of the workings of memory) increases with age and contributes to developmental and individual differences in strategic memory.

♦ **Event memory** in general, and our memory for personal experiences, or **autobiographical memory**, are rarely as intentional as strategic memory. Although infants can recall events that happened earlier in time, most of us display **infantile amnesia**—an inability to recall much about the first few years of life.

♦ Early autobiographical memory is based on **scripts**, or schematic organizations of recurring real-world events organized in terms of their causal and temporal sequences. Even very young children organize their experiences in terms of scripts, which become more detailed with age.

♦ Autobiographical memory expands dramatically during the preschool years. Parents play an important role in the growth of autobiographical memories by discussing past events, providing clues about what information is important to remember, and helping children to recall their experiences in rich personal narratives.

♦ One aspect of autobiographical memory that has received much attention is age differences in eyewitness memory and suggestibility. As in general episodic memory, the accuracy of children's eyewitness memory increases with age. Young children are generally more susceptible to suggestion than older children and are more likely to form false memories. Steps to increase the accuracy of children's eyewitness testimony in legal proceedings include limiting the number of times child witnesses are interrogated, asking questions in nonleading ways, and cautioning the child against guessing or providing answers merely to satisfy the interrogator.

Problem Solving and Reasoning

♦ Problem solving involves having a goal, obstacles to the goal, strategies for overcoming the obstacles, and an evaluation of the results. Zelazo and his colleagues have focused on children's ability to follow rules and report that young children often fail to use a rule even though they can demonstrate knowledge of the rule.

♦ **Reasoning** is a special type of problem solving that requires that one make an inference. **Analogical reasoning** involves applying what one knows about one set of elements to infer relations about different elements. The **relational primacy hypothesis** proposes that analogical reasoning is available as early as infancy. Many factors affect children's analogical reasoning—two important ones are *metacognition,* or a conscious awareness of the basis on which one is solving a problem, and knowledge of the relations on which the analogy is based.

Development of Number and Arithmetic Skills

♦ Even infants are capable of processing and using quantitative information, and toddlers have already acquired a rudimentary understanding of ordinal relationships. Counting begins once children begin to talk, and preschoolers gradually construct such basic mathematical understandings as the principle of **cardinality**. Early arithmetic strategies usually involve counting out loud, but eventually children perform simple arithmetic operations in their heads using increasingly sophisticated arithmetic strategies. Yet, children of any age actually use a variety of strategies to solve math problems, as described by Siegler's *adaptive strategy choice model.*

♦ There are sizable cultural variations in mathematics performance and the use of arithmetic strategies. Unschooled children develop arithmetic strategies that they apply quite skillfully to the practical problems they encounter. Among those who are taught arithmetic strategies at school, East Asian children consistently outperform their North American age-mates, owing in part to the structure of their languages and to instructional practices that help them retrieve math facts and acquire computational skills and other mathematical knowledge.

Evaluating the Information-Processing Perspective

♦ Despite its many strengths, the information-processing perspective has been criticized for largely ignoring neurological, evolutionary, and sociocultural influences on cognitive growth; for failing to provide a broad, integrative theory of children's intelligence; and for underestimating the richness and diversity of human cognitive activities.

Connectionist Approaches to Cognitive Development

♦ **Connectionism** involves using computational modelling to simulate how the brain processes information. The models contain networks comprised of processing units and connections where the processing units are roughly similar to neurons and the connections are similar to synapses. Simulations have provided a precise means of understanding and explaining how cognitive development occurs. One crit-

icism is that the models also generate outcomes that are not seen in human development.

KEY TERMS

multistore model, 265

sensory store (or sensory register), 265

short-term store (STS), 265

long-term store (LTS), 265

executive control processes, 266

metacognition, 266

knowledge base, 266

memory span, 266

span of apprehension, 266

strategies, 268

production deficiency, 269

utilization deficiency, 269

adaptive strategy choice model, 270

implicit cognition, 271

explicit cognition, 271

fuzzy-trace theory, 272

gist, 272

inhibition, 274

attention span, 275

reticular formation, 275

selective attention, 276

attention deficit-hyperactivity disorder (ADHD), 277

strategic memory, 277

mnemonics (memory strategies), 277

event memory, 277

autobiographical memory, 277

rehearsal, 278

semantic organization, 280

elaboration, 280

retrieval, 280

free recall, 280

cued recall, 280

metamemory, 281

knowledge base, 282

infantile amnesia, 286

script, 286

reasoning, 294

analogical reasoning, 294

relational primacy hypothesis, 294

learning to learn, 297

cardinality, 298

connectionism, 305

 You can find further information on the topics covered in this chapter by visiting:

www.developmentalpsych2e.nelson.com

 For additional reading, go to InfoTrac College Edition, your on-line research library, at:

infotrac.thomsonlearning.com

9

Intelligence: Measuring Mental Performance

PhotoDisc, Inc.

"**W**hen he was 3 years old, the 19th-century philosopher John Stuart Mill began to study Greek under his father's direction. At age 6½ he wrote a history of Rome. He tackled Latin at age 8 [when] he also began his study of geometry and algebra. Mill's IQ score has been estimated at 190, on a scale on which 100 is average" (Cox, 1926).

At age 27, Susan lives in an institution for the mentally retarded. She has been labelled profoundly retarded, has an IQ of 37, and usually responds to people with smiles. She cannot read, write, feed, or dress herself. Yet, remarkably, she can flawlessly recite just about any poem after hearing it only once.

As these examples indicate, the range of human cognitive potentials is immense. So far, our explorations of cognitive development have focused mainly on what human minds have in common. Piaget, after all, was interested in identifying *universal* stages in the way thinking is organized or structured. Similarly, information-processing theorists have been primarily concerned with understanding the basic cognitive processes on which all people rely to learn, remember, and solve problems.

In this chapter, we continue our exploration of how the human mind changes over the course of childhood and adolescence, but with a greater emphasis on *individual differences* in cognitive performance. We will begin by introducing yet another perspective on intellectual development—the *psychometric* approach—which has led to the creation and widespread use of intelligence tests. Unlike the Piagetian and information-processing approaches, which focus on cognitive *processes*, psychometricians are more *product oriented*. They seek to determine how many and what kinds of questions children can answer *correctly* at different ages and whether this index of intellectual performance can predict such developmental outcomes as scholastic achievement, occupational attainments, and even health and life satisfaction.

There may be some surprises ahead as we consider what a person's score on an intelligence test implies about his or her ability to learn, to perform in academic settings, or to succeed at a job. Perhaps the biggest surprise for many people is learning that intelligence test scores, which can vary dramatically over the course of one's life, are assessments of intellectual *performance* rather than innate potential or intellectual *capacity*. True, heredity does affect intellectual performance. But so do a variety of environmental factors that we will examine, including one's cultural and socioeconomic background, the character of one's home environment, the schooling one receives, and even social and emotional factors surrounding the testing situation itself. We will then evaluate the merits of educational interventions designed to promote the scholastic performances of

What is Intelligence?

How is Intelligence Measured?

What Do Intelligence Tests Predict?

Factors that Influence IQ Scores

Social and Cultural Correlates of Intellectual Performance

Improving Cognitive Performance through Compensatory Education

Creativity and Special Talents

Summary

children who are at risk, or who perform poorly on intelligence tests. Finally, we will conclude by exploring the growth of highly valued *creative* talents that are not adequately represented on our current intelligence tests.

WHAT IS INTELLIGENCE?

Ask five people to summarize in a single sentence what intelligence means to them and then to list up to five attributes that characterize highly intelligent people. Chances are their summary sentences will state that intelligence is how "smart" someone is compared with other people, or perhaps that it represents one's capacity for learning or problem solving. However, you can almost bet that your five interviewees will show some meaningful differences in the attributes they view as characterizing highly intelligent individuals. Simply stated, intelligence does not mean the same thing to all people (Neisser et al., 1996).

And so it goes with behavioural scientists. Even today there is no clear consensus about what intelligence is (e.g., Richardson, 2002). Clearest agreement comes in "one-sentence" characterizations. Piaget (1970), for example, defined intelligence as "adaptive thinking or action." And in a recent survey, 24 experts provided somewhat different one-sentence definitions of what intelligence meant to them, but virtually all these definitions centred in some way on the ability to think abstractly or to solve problems effectively (Sternberg, 1997).

? WHAT DO YOU THINK?

Before reading further, list five attributes that you think characterize people you would consider "highly intelligent" and say why these attributes define intelligence for you. As you read the section entitled "What Is Intelligence?" think about whose views of intelligence are most compatible with your own.

So why is there still no singular definition of intelligence? Simply because different theorists have very different ideas about which attributes (and how many of them) are core aspects of this construct they call intelligence. Let's now consider some of the more influential viewpoints on the nature of intelligence, beginning with the psychometric perspective.

Psychometric Views of Intelligence

The research tradition that spawned the development of standardized intelligence tests is the **psychometric approach** (Thorndike, 1997). According to psychometric theorists, intelligence is a trait or a set of traits that characterizes some people to a greater extent than others. The goal of psychometric theorists, then, was to identify precisely what those traits might be and to *measure* them so that intellectual differences among individuals could be described. But from the start, psychometricians could not agree on the *structure* of intelligence. Was it a single ability that influenced how people performed on all cognitive tests, or was intelligence best described as many distinct abilities?

Alfred Binet's Singular Component Approach

Alfred Binet and a colleague, Theodore Simon, produced the forerunner of modern intelligence tests. In 1904, Binet and Simon were commissioned by the French government to construct a test that would identify "dull" children who might profit from remedial instruction. They then devised a large battery of tasks measuring skills presumed to be necessary for classroom learning: attention, perception, memory, numerical reasoning, verbal comprehension, and so on. Items that successfully discriminated normal children from those described by teachers as dull or slow were kept in the final test.

In 1908, the Binet-Simon test was revised, and all test items were age-graded. For example, problems that were passed by most 6-year-olds but few 5-year-olds were assumed to reflect the mental performance of a typical 6-year-old; those passed by most

psychometric approach
theoretical perspective that portrays intelligence as a trait (or set of traits) on which individuals differ; psychometric theorists are responsible for the development of standardized intelligence tests

12-year-olds but few 11-year-olds were said to measure the intellectual skills of an average 12-year-old, and so on. This age-grading of test items for ages 3 to 13 allowed a more precise assessment of a child's level of intellectual functioning. A child who passed all items at the 5-year-old level but none at the 6-year-old level was said to have a **mental age (MA)** of 5 years. A child who passed all items at the 10-year-old level and half of those at the 11-year-old level would have an MA of 10½ years.

In sum, Binet had created a test that enabled him to identify slow learners and to estimate their levels of intellectual development. This information proved particularly useful to school administrators, who began to use children's mental ages as a guideline for planning curricula for both typical and retarded students.

Factor Analysis and the Multicomponent View of Intelligence

Other psychometric theorists were quick to challenge the notion that a single score, such as mental age, adequately represents human intellectual performance. Their point was that intelligence tests (even Binet's earliest versions) require people to perform a variety of tasks such as defining words or concepts, extracting meaning from written passages, answering general information questions, reproducing geometric designs with blocks, and solving arithmetic puzzles (see Figure 9.1 for some sample items). Couldn't these different subtests be measuring a number of distinct mental abilities rather than a single, overarching ability?

One way of determining whether intelligence is a single attribute or many different attributes is to ask participants to perform a large number of mental tasks and then analyze their performances using a statistical procedure called **factor analysis**. This technique identifies clusters of tasks, or test items, called *factors* that are highly correlated with one another and unrelated to other items on the test. Each factor (if more than one are found) presumably represents a distinct mental ability. Suppose, for example, we found that examinees performed very similarly on four items that require verbal skills and on three items that require mathematical skills, but that their verbal-skill score was not correlated with their score on the math items. Under these circumstances, we might conclude that verbal ability and mathematical ability are distinct intellectual factors. But if subjects' verbal and math scores were highly correlated with each other and with scores for all other kinds of mental problems on the test, we might conclude that intelligence is a singular attribute rather than a number of distinct mental abilities.

EARLY APPLICATIONS OF FACTOR ANALYSIS. Charles Spearman (1927) was among the first to use factor analysis to try to determine whether intelligence was one or many abilities. He found that a child's scores across a variety of cognitive tests were moderately correlated and thus inferred that there must be a *general mental factor*, which he called **g**, that affects one's performance on most cognitive tasks. However, he also noticed that intellectual performance was often inconsistent. A student who excelled at most tasks, for example, might perform poorly on a particular test, such as verbal analogies or musical aptitude. So Spearman proposed that intellectual performance has two aspects: **g**, or general ability, and **s**, or special abilities, each of which is specific to a particular test.

Louis Thurstone (1938) took issue with Spearman's theory. When he factor-analyzed 50 mental tests administered to Grade 8 and college students, Thurstone came up with *seven* factors that he called **primary mental abilities**: spatial ability, perceptual speed (quick processing of visual information), numerical reasoning, verbal meaning (defining words), word fluency (speed at recognizing words), memory, and inductive reasoning (forming a rule that describes a set of observations). He then concluded that Spearman's *g* really consists of seven distinct mental abilities.

LATER FACTOR-ANALYTIC MODELS. Spearman's and Thurstone's early work implied that a relatively small number of basic mental abilities make up what we call "intelligence." J.P. Guilford (1967, 1988) disagreed, proposing instead that there may be as many as 180 basic mental abilities. He arrived at this figure by first classifying cognitive tasks along three major dimensions: (1) *content* (what the person must think about), (2) *operations*

Alfred Binet (1857–1911), the father of intelligence testing

mental age (MA)
measure of intellectual development that reflects the level of age-graded problems a child is able to solve

factor analysis
statistical procedure for identifying clusters of tests or test items (called *factors*) that are highly correlated with one another and unrelated to other test items

g
Spearman's abbreviation for *neogenesis*, which, roughly translated, means one's ability to understand relations (or one's general mental ability)

s
Spearman's term for mental abilities that are specific to particular tests

primary mental abilities
seven mental abilities, identified by factor analysis, that Thurstone believed to represent the structure of intelligence

Item Type	Typical Verbal Items
Vocabulary	What does "telephone" mean?
Verbal analogies	A metre is short; a kilometre is____.
Verbal reasoning	What is wrong with this story? "One day we saw several icebergs that had been entirely melted by the warmth of the Gulf Stream."
General information	How many centimetres make a metre? In what month of the year does New Year's Day fall?
Number series	Which number comes next in the series 5 7 6 9 8 ___ ?
Arithmetic reasoning	If I buy 6 cents' worth of candy and give the clerk 25 cents, I will get _____ back in change.

Typical nonverbal/performance items

Picture oddities — Which picture does not belong with the others?

Puzzle completions — Put these pieces together so that they make a bicycle.

Picture series — Arrange these pictures in the right order so that they make sense.

Figure 9.1 Items similar but not identical to those appearing on intelligence tests for children.

(what kind of thinking the person is asked to perform), and (3) *products* (what kind of answer is required). Guilford argued that there are five kinds of intellectual contents, six kinds of mental operations, and six kinds of intellectual products. Thus, his **structure-of-intellect model** allows for as many as 180 primary mental abilities, based on all the possible combinations of the various intellectual contents, operations, and products (that is, $5 \times 6 \times 6 = 180$).

Guilford then set out to construct tests to measure each of his 180 mental abilities. For example, the test of social intelligence illustrated in Figure 9.2 measures the mental ability that requires the test taker to act on a *behavioural* content (the figure's facial expression) using a particular operation, *cognition*, to produce a particular product—the probable *implication* of that expression. To date, tests have been constructed to assess more than 100 of the 180 mental abilities in Guilford's model of intellect. However, the scores that people obtain on these presumably independent intellectual factors are often correlated, suggesting that these abilities are not nearly as independent as Guilford has assumed (Brody, 1992).

structure-of-intellect model
Guilford's factor-analytic model of intelligence, which proposes that there are 180 distinct mental abilities

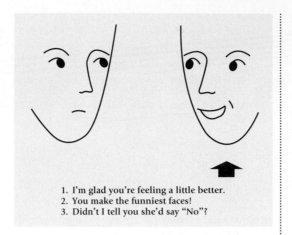

Figure 9.2 *An item from one of Guilford's tests of social intelligence. The task is to read the characters' expressions and to decide what the person marked by the arrow is most probably saying to the other person. You may want to try this yourself (the correct answer appears below).* ADAPTED FROM GUILFORD, 1967.

1. I'm glad you're feeling a little better.
2. You make the funniest faces!
3. Didn't I tell you she'd say "No"?

Finally, Raymond Cattell and John Horn have influenced current thinking about intelligence by proposing that Spearman's *g* and Thurstone's primary mental abilities can be reduced to two major dimensions of intellect: *fluid intelligence* and *crystallized intelligence* (Cattell, 1963; Horn & Noll, 1997). **Fluid intelligence** refers to one's ability to solve novel and abstract problems of the sort that are not taught and are relatively free of cultural influences. Examples of the kinds of problems that tap fluid intelligence are the verbal analogies and number series tests from Figure 9.1, as well as tests of one's ability to recognize relationships among otherwise meaningless geometric figures (see Figure 9.9 on page 336 for an example). By contrast, **crystallized intelligence** is the ability to solve problems that depend on knowledge acquired as a result of schooling and other life experiences. Tests of general information ("At what temperature does water boil?"), word comprehension ("What is the meaning of *duplicate*?"), and numerical abilities are all measures of crystallized intelligence.

A MORE RECENT HIERARCHICAL MODEL. So what have we learned from factor-analytic studies of intelligence? Perhaps that Spearman, Thurstone, and Cattell and Horn were all partially correct. Indeed, many psychometricians today favour **hierarchical models of intellect** in which intelligence is viewed as consisting of (1) a general ability factor at the top of the hierarchy, which influences one's performance on many cognitive tests, and (2) a number of specialized ability factors (something similar to Thurstone's primary mental abilities) that influence how well one performs in particular intellectual domains (for example, on tests of numerical reasoning or tests of spatial skills). The most elaborate of these hierarchical models, based on analyses of hundreds of studies of mental abilities conducted over the past 50 years, is John Carroll's **three-stratum theory of intelligence**. As shown in Figure 9.3, Carroll (1993) represents intelligence as a pyramid, with *g* at the top and eight broad intellectual abilities at the second level. This model implies that each of us may have particular intellectual strengths or weaknesses depending on the patterns of second-stratum intellectual abilities we display. It also explains how a person of below-average general ability (*g*) might actually excel in a narrow third-stratum domain (for example, reciting poems heard only once) if she displays an unusually high second-stratum ability (general memory) that fosters good performance in that domain.

So hierarchical models depict intelligence as *both* an overarching general mental ability *and* a number of more specific abilities that each pertain to a particular intellectual domain. Are we now closer to a consensus on the definition of intelligence? No, because a growing number of researchers believe that no psychometric theory of intelligence fully captures what it means to be intelligent (Neisser et al., 1996). Let's now examine two alternative viewpoints that should help us to appreciate some of the limitations of today's intelligence tests.

fluid intelligence
ability to perceive relationships and solve relational problems of the type that are not taught and are relatively free of cultural influences

crystallized intelligence
ability to understand relations or solve problems that depend on knowledge acquired from schooling and other cultural influences

hierarchical model of intelligence
model of the structure of intelligence in which a broad, general ability factor is at the top of the hierarchy, with a number of specialized ability factors nested underneath

three-stratum theory of intelligence
Carroll's hierarchical model of intelligence with *g* at the top of the hierarchy, eight broad abilities at the second level, or stratum, and narrower domains of each second-stratum ability at the third stratum

Answer to Figure 9.2: 3.

Figure 9.3 *John Carroll's three-stratum hierarchical model of intelligence. Second-stratum abilities are arranged from left to right in terms of their decreasing correlation with g. So fluid intelligence and the reasoning it supports (for example, quantitative reasoning) are more closely associated with general mental ability g than are auditory perception, cognitive speed, and the third-stratum skills that these abilities support.* FROM CARROLL, 1993.

A Modern Information-Processing Viewpoint

One recurring criticism of psychometric definitions of intelligence is that they are very narrow, focusing primarily on intellectual content, or what a person knows, rather than on the processes by which this knowledge is acquired, retained, and used to solve problems. Furthermore, traditional intelligence tests measure one's proficiency at mathematical, verbal, and spatial reasoning while ignoring other attributes that people commonly think of as indications of intelligence, such as common sense, social and interpersonal skills, and the talents that underlie creative accomplishments in music, drama, and athletics (Gardner, 1983).

Robert Sternberg (1985, 1991) proposed a **triarchic theory** of intelligence that emphasizes three aspects, or components, of intelligent behaviour: *context*, *experience*, and *information-processing* skills (see Figure 9.4). As we will see in reviewing this model, Sternberg's view of intelligence is much, much broader than that of psychometric theorists.

Context

First, Sternberg argues that what qualifies as intelligent behaviour will depend in large part on the context in which it is displayed. According to Sternberg, intelligent people are those who can successfully adapt to their environments or who are successful at shaping their environments to suit them better. These people display practical intelligence or "street smarts." Psychologists, Sternberg believes, must begin to understand intelligence as adaptive *real-world* behaviour, not as behaviour in taking tests (Sternberg, 1997).

triarchic theory
recent information-processing theory of intelligence that emphasizes three aspects of intelligent behaviour not normally tapped by IQ tests: the *context* of the action, the person's *experience* with the task (or situation), and the *information-processing strategies* the person applies to the task (or situation)

Figure 9.4 *Sternberg's triarchic theory of intelligence.*

From a contextual perspective, what is meant by intelligent behaviour may vary from one culture or subculture to another, from one historical epoch to another, and from one period of the life span to another. Sternberg describes an occasion when he attended a conference in Venezuela and showed up on time, at 8:00 A.M., only to find that he and four other North Americans were the only ones there. In North American society, it is considered smart to be punctual for important engagements. However, strict punctuality is not so adaptive in Latin cultures, where people are more relaxed (by our standards, at least) about being on time. History can also have an impact on assessments of intelligence. Thirty years ago, it was considered quite intelligent to be able to perform arithmetic operations quickly and accurately. However, an individual who spends countless hours perfecting these same skills today might be considered somewhat less than intelligent given that computers and calculators can perform these computations much faster.

Cameramann/The Image Works

The sophisticated ability that this child displays is considered intelligent in his culture, but is not measured by traditional IQ tests.

The Experiential Component

According to Sternberg, one's experience with a task helps to determine whether one's performance qualifies as intelligent behaviour. He believes that relatively novel tasks require active and conscious information processing and are the best measures of one's reasoning abilities, as long as these tasks are not so foreign that the person is unable to apply what he may know (as would be the case if geometry problems were presented to 5-year-olds). So responses to *novel* challenges are an indication of the person's ability to generate good ideas or fresh insights.

In daily life, however, people also perform more or less intelligently on familiar tasks (such as driving, balancing a chequebook, or quickly extracting the most important content from a newspaper). This second kind of experiential intelligence reflects *automatization*, or increasing efficiency of information processing with practice. According to Sternberg, it is a sign of intelligence when we develop automatized routines or "programs of the mind" for performing everyday tasks accurately and efficiently, so that we don't have to waste much time thinking about how to accomplish them.

The experiential component of Sternberg's theory has a most important implication for intelligence testers: It is crucial to know how familiar test items are to examinees in order to assess examinees' intelligence fairly. For example, if the items on an intelligence test are generally familiar to members of one cultural group but unfamiliar to members of another, the second group will perform much worse than the first, thereby reflecting a **cultural bias** in the test itself. A valid comparison of the intellectual performances of people from diverse cultural backgrounds requires the test items to be equally familiar (or unfamiliar) to all test takers.

The Componential (or Information-Processing) Component

Sternberg's major criticism of psychometric theorists is that they estimate a person's intelligence from the quality, or correctness, of her answers while completely ignoring *how* she produces intelligent responses. Sternberg is an information-processing theorist who believes that we must focus on the componential aspects of intelligent behaviour— that is, the cognitive processes by which we size up the requirements of problems, formulate strategies to solve them, and then monitor our cognitive activities until we've accomplished our goals. He argues that some people process information faster and more efficiently than others and that our cognitive tests could be improved considerably were they to measure these differences and treat them as important aspects of intelligence.

cultural bias
situation that arises when one cultural or subcultural group is more familiar with test items than another group and therefore has an unfair advantage

In sum, Sternberg's triarchic theory provides us with a very rich view of the nature of intelligence. It suggests that if you want to know how intelligent people are, you have to consider (1) the *context* in which they are performing (that is, the culture and historical period in which they live; their ages), (2) their *experience* with the tasks and whether their behaviour qualifies as responses to novel or automatized processes, and (3) the *information-processing skills* that reflect how each person is approaching these tasks. Unfortunately, the most widely used intelligence tests are not based on such a broad and sophisticated view of intellectual processes.

Gardner's Theory of Multiple Intelligences

Howard Gardner (1983, 1999) is another theorist who criticizes the psychometricians for trying to describe a person's intelligence with a single score. In his book *Frames of Mind*, Gardner (1983) outlines his **theory of multiple intelligences**, proposing that humans display at least seven distinctive kinds of intelligence, which are described in Table 9.1.

Gardner (1999) does not claim that these seven abilities represent the universe of intelligences. But he makes the case that each ability is distinct, is linked to a specific area of the brain, and follows a different developmental course. As support for these ideas, Gardner points out that injury to a particular area of the brain usually influences only one ability (linguistic or spatial, for example), leaving others unaffected.

As further evidence of the independence of these abilities, Gardner notes that some individuals are truly exceptional in one ability but poor in others. This is dramatically clear in cases of the *savant syndrome*—mentally retarded people with an extraordinary talent. Leslie Lemke is one such individual. He is blind, has cerebral palsy, and is mentally retarded, and he could not talk until he was an adult. Yet he can hear a musical piece once

theory of multiple intelligences
Gardner's theory that humans display at least seven distinct kinds of intelligence, each linked to a particular area of the brain, several of which are not measured by IQ tests

TABLE 9.1	Gardner's Multiple Intelligences	
Type of intelligence	**Intellectual processes**	**Vocational end-states**
Linguistic	Sensitivity to the meaning and sounds of words, to the structure of language, and to the many ways language can be used	Poet, novelist, journalist
Spatial	Ability to perceive visual–spatial relationships accurately, to transform these perceptions, and to re-create aspects of one's visual experience in the absence of the pertinent stimuli	Engineer, sculptor, cartographer
Logical-mathematical	Ability to operate on and to perceive relationships in abstract symbol systems and to think logically and systematically in evaluating one's ideas	Mathematician, scientist
Musical	Sensitivity to pitch, melody; ability to combine tones and musical phrases into larger rhythms; understanding of the emotional aspects of music	Musician, composer
Body-kinesthetic	Ability to use the body skillfully to express oneself or achieve goals; ability to handle objects skillfully	Dancer, athlete
Interpersonal	Ability to detect and respond appropriately to the mood, temperaments, motives, and intentions of others	Therapist, public relations specialist
Intrapersonal	Sensitivity to one's own inner states; recognition of personal strengths and weaknesses and ability to use information about the self to behave adaptively	Contributes to success in almost any walk of life
Naturalist	Sensitivity to the factors influencing, and influenced by, organisms (fauna and flora) in the natural environments	Biologist, naturalist
Spiritual/existential (speculative at this point)	Sensitivity to issues related to the meaning of life, death, and other aspects of the human condition	Philosopher, theologian

SOURCE: Adapted from Gardner, 1983, 1999.

and play it flawlessly on the piano or imitate songs in German or Italian perfectly even though his native language is still primitive. And despite their abysmal performance on intelligence tests, other mentally retarded individuals with savant skills can draw well enough to gain admittance to art school or calculate almost instantaneously what day of the week January 16, 1909 was (O'Connor & Hermelin, 1991). Finally, Gardner notes that different intelligences mature at different times. Many of the great composers and athletes, for example, begin to display their immense talents in childhood (e.g., Mozart and Gretzky), whereas logical-mathematical intelligence often shows up much later in life.

Gardner's ideas have had an impact, particularly on investigators who study the development of creativity and special talents—a topic we will explore later in this chapter. Nevertheless, critics have argued that even though such talents as musical or athletic prowess are important human characteristics, they are not the same kind of *mentalistic* activities as those most people view as the core of intelligence (Bjorklund, 2000). And although children gifted in the visual arts or athletics are often notably better in these areas than in Gardner's other intelligences (see Winner, 2000), current intelligence tests do tap Gardner's linguistic, spatial, and logical-mathematical intelligences, which are moderately correlated rather than highly distinct (Jensen, 1998). Perhaps it is too early, then, to totally reject the concept of *g*, or general mental ability. Yet Gardner is almost certainly correct in arguing that we surely misrepresent and underestimate the talents of many individuals by trying to characterize their intelligence with a single test score.

HOW IS INTELLIGENCE MEASURED?

When psychometricians began to construct intelligence tests at the beginning of this century, their concern was not with defining the nature of intelligence but with the more practical goals of determining which schoolchildren were likely to be slow learners. Recall that Binet and Simon produced a test that accomplished this goal and characterized each child's intellectual development with a single score, or *mental age*. Among the more popular of our contemporary intelligence tests for children is a direct descendant of Binet and Simon's early test.

The Stanford-Binet Intelligence Scale

In 1916, Lewis Terman of Stanford University translated and published a revised version of the Binet scale for use with American children. This test came to be known as the **Stanford-Binet Intelligence Scale**.

Stanford-Binet Intelligence Scale
modern descendant of the first successful intelligence test; measures general intelligence and four factors: verbal reasoning, quantitative reasoning, spatial reasoning, and short-term memory

Concept Check 9.1
Recognizing Different Perspectives on Intelligence

Check your understanding of various theories on the nature of intelligence by matching the names of their originators with brief descriptions of the theories' main themes that appear below. Choose from among the following theorists: (a) Raymond Cattell/John Horn, (b) Howard Gardner, (c) J.P. Guilford, (d) Charles Spearman, (e) Robert Sternberg, (f) Louis Thurstone. Answers appear in the Appendix.

_____ 1. This theorist proposes that there may be as many as 180 distinct mental abilities.

_____ 2. This theorist claims that intelligence consists of a general mental factor, or *g*, and a number of special abilities, *s*, each of which is specific to a particular kind of reasoning.

_____ 3. This theorist thinks that there are seven distinctive kinds of intelligence, several of which (for example, musical intelligence) are not measured on intelligence tests.

_____ 4. This psychometrician also claims that there are seven forms of intelligence, which he identified through factor analysis and called *primary mental abilities*.

_____ 5. This theory claims that *g*, or general mental ability, and the so-called primary mental abilities can be divided into two kinds of intelligence: *fluid* and *crystallized*.

_____ 6. This person's theory emphasizes three aspects of intelligence: the *contextual*, *experiential*, and *componential* (or information-processing) components.

Like Binet's scale, the original version of the Stanford-Binet consisted of age-graded tasks designed to measure the average intellectual performance of children aged 3 through 13. Terman first gave his test to a sample of about 1000 middle-class American schoolchildren in order to establish performance norms against which an individual child could be compared. But unlike Binet, who classified children according to mental age, Terman used a ratio measure of intelligence, developed by Stern (1912), that came to be known as an **intelligence quotient**, or **IQ**. The child's IQ, which was said to be a measure of his brightness or rate of intellectual development, was calculated by dividing his mental age by his chronological age and then multiplying by 100:

$$IQ = MA/CA \times 100$$

Notice that an IQ of 100 indicates average intelligence; it means that a child's *mental age is exactly equal to her chronological age*. An IQ greater than 100 indicates that the child's performance is comparable to that of people older than she is, whereas an IQ less than 100 means that her intellectual performance matches that of children somewhat younger than herself.

A revised version of the Stanford-Binet is still in use (Thorndike, Hagen, & Sattler, 1986). Its **test norms** are now based on representative samples of people (6-year-olds through adults) from many socioeconomic and ethnic backgrounds rather than merely reflecting the performance of White middle-class schoolchildren. The revised test continues to measure abilities thought to be important to academic success: verbal reasoning, quantitative reasoning, visual–spatial reasoning, and short-term memory. However, the concept of mental age is no longer used to calculate IQ on the Stanford-Binet or any other modern intelligence test. Instead, individuals receive IQ scores that reflect how well or poorly they do *compared with others of the same age*. An IQ of 100 is still average, and the higher (or lower) the IQ score an individual attains, the better (or worse) her performance is compared with age-mates.

intelligence quotient (IQ)
numerical measure of a person's performance on an intelligence test relative to the performance of other examinees

test norms
standards of normal performance on psychometric instruments that are based on the average scores and the range of scores obtained by a large, representative sample of test takers

---

CULTURAL INFLUENCES
9.1
Making American Tests Valid in Canada

Although the United States is Canada's next-door neighbour, the two countries and the two cultures differ in a number of ways. As a result, many researchers have called for "Canadianized" tests and "Canadianized" norms to reflect our cultural differences (Saklofske, 2003). For example, consider the following two cultural issues as important considerations when standardizing American tests for Canadian populations. The first involves simple differences between our two countries that reflect our social, educational, life, and, to some extent, socioeconomic experiences. The second issue involves differences in language. To address the first difference, specific items on tests can be altered if they do not apply and/or Canadian norms can be devised by testing large numbers of Canadian individuals. Norms are based on representative samples of Canadians so that other Canadians taking the tests can be compared against this norm. Canadian researchers have conducted many studies to assess the validity of original and adapted tests. These psychometric comparisons (statistical comparisons) can be used to see whether a test is equally appropriate for different cultural groups, whether the test has to be altered or adapted, or whether some components of the test are appropriate while others need to be interpreted more cautiously. (See Box 9.2 for more details about this Canadian research.)

For the most part, the Wechsler tests are appropriate IQ tests for Canadian populations (Roid & Worrall, 1997;

Hildebrand & Saklofske, 1996). However, one study conducted at Mount Saint Vincent University found that, although children performed equally on the full WPPSI test, Canadian children showed greater variability on some of the subtests. The researchers concluded that these subtests should be interpreted more cautiously for Canadian populations (French, French, & Rutherford, 1999). In an effort to reduce the time taken to administer the WISC, a shortened version of the test called the General Ability Index is often used. This shorter test has also proven effective for Canadian populations (Weiss et al., 1999).

The second major cultural difference between Canadians and Americans involves language. Canada has two official languages, a number of Aboriginal languages, and many other languages consistent with our multicultural diversity. Tests devised in the United States are prepared in English. A partial solution to this problem has been to translate tests like the WISC into French and to test them among French-speaking populations. The indications are that the translated versions are reliable and valid (Facon & Facon-Bollengier, 1999; Gregoire, Penhouet, & Boy, 1996). However, this still does not solve the problem for the many other language groups in Canada. When testing people who belong to other language groups, there must be sensitivity in interpreting outcomes, especially if an individual is tested in his or her second language.

The Wechsler Scales

David Wechsler has constructed two intelligence tests for children, both of which are widely used. The **Wechsler Intelligence Scale for Children—III (WISC-III)** is appropriate for schoolchildren aged 6 to 16, whereas the *Wechsler Preschool and Primary Scale of Intelligence— Revised (WPPSI-R)*, is designed for children between ages 3 and 8 (Wechsler, 1989, 1991).

One reason Wechsler constructed his own intelligence tests is that he believed that earlier versions of the Stanford-Binet were overloaded with items that require verbal skills. Specifically, he felt that this heavy bias toward verbal intelligence discriminated against children who have certain language handicaps—for example, those for whom English is a second language or those who have reading difficulties or are hard of hearing. To overcome this problem, Wechsler's scales contain verbal subtests similar to those on the Stanford-Binet as well as *nonverbal,* or "performance" subtests. Items on the performance subtests are designed to measure such predominantly nonverbal skills as the ability to assemble puzzles, solve mazes, reproduce geometric designs with coloured blocks, and rearrange sets of pictures so that they tell a meaningful story. Test takers receive three scores: a *verbal IQ,* a *performance IQ,* and a *full-scale IQ* based on a combination of the verbal and performance measures.

The Wechsler scales soon became quite popular. Not only did the new performance subscales allow children from all backgrounds to display their intellectual strengths, but the tests were also sensitive to inconsistencies in mental skills that may be early signs of neurological problems or learning disorders. For example, children who display reading disorders often do much worse on the verbal component of the WISC.

The WISC and WPPSI scales were originally standardized with American children. These tests have been assessed using Canadian samples, and Canadian norms have been developed to ensure that the test interpretation generalizes across these two cultures. Why do we need to develop Canadian norms and compare test performance among Canadians with the data from the United States? To find out, read Box 9.1. See also Box 9.2, which highlights research in this area.

Wechsler Intelligence Scale for Children—III (WISC-III) widely used individual intelligence test that includes a measure of general intelligence and both verbal and performance intelligence

---

THE INSIDE TRACK

9.2

Donald H. Saklofske

Donald Saklofske works in the Department of Educational Psychology and Special Education at the University of Saskatchewan. He is also an associate member of the Department of Psychology. Among his research and clinical interests are personality, intelligence, individual differences, psychological assessment, and school and applied psychology practices.

Dr. Don Saklofske and his colleagues have examined IQ tests to determine whether Canadian children and adults perform in a similar way to Americans, and to assess whether the underlying structures of the IQ tests remain constant across the two cultures. In other words, the goal was to determine "How well the [tests] travelled?" (Saklofske, 2003, p. 61). In one study, it was found that the Wechsler Abbreviated Scale of Intelligence (WASI) could be used to assess Canadians (Saklofske, Caravan, & Schwartz, 2000). In another study, Saklofske and his colleagues wanted to see if Canadian data would produce the same underlying dimensions or structures that are typically found for the Weschler Adult Intelligence Scale—III (WAIS-III) when American samples are tested (Saklofske, Hildebrand, & Gorsuch, 2000). These underlying structures (called factors) describe the abilities

tapped by the various items on the WAIS-III. After 718 Canadian adults completed the WAIS-III, statistical techniques (called factor analyses) were used to assess whether the underlying dimensions or structures were replicated. Indeed, all four factors appeared: verbal comprehension, perceptual organization, working memory, and processing speed. These data suggest that the WAIS-III measures similar cognitive factors in Canadian and American populations. However, a final sample of 1105 Canadian adults showed that the WAIS-III scores were different for Canadian adults, requiring the publication of Canadian norms in the WAIS-III Canadian Technical Manual (Psychological Corporation, 2001) for which Dr. Saklofske served as project director. Similarly, an earlier standardization study of Canadian children tested on the WISC-III demonstrated the need for separate Canadian norms and the importance of having testers who are sensitive to the cultural and social contexts of the "testee" (Saklofske, 2003). The robustness of the WISC-III factor structure across 14 countries was recently supported (Georgas, Weiss, van de Vijver, & Saklofske, 2003). However, once again, differences reflected the importance of cultural and linguistic factors when using these tests to assess the intellectual and cognitive abilities of children. More recently, Dr. Saklofske has collaborated on studies of the structure of intelligence and memory in adults (Tulsky, Saklofske, et al., 2003) and emotional intelligence (e.g., Saklofske, Austin & Minski, 2003).

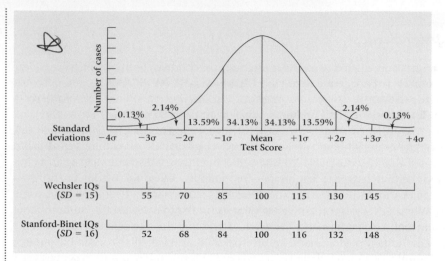

Figure 9.5 *The approximate distribution of IQ scores people make on contemporary intelligence tests. These tests are constructed so that the average score made by examinees in each age group is equivalent to an IQ of 100. Note that more than two-thirds of all examinees score within 15 points of this average (that is, IQs of 85–115) and that 95 percent of the population scores within 30 points of the average (IQs of 70–130). ADAPTED FROM SATTLER, 2001.*

Distribution of IQ Scores

If a young girl scores 130 on the Stanford-Binet or the WISC, we know that her IQ is above average. But how bright is she? To find out, we would have to know something about the way IQs are distributed in the population at large.

One interesting feature of all modern IQ tests is that people's scores are **normally distributed** around an IQ of 100 (see Figure 9.5). This patterning of scores is hardly an accident. By definition, the average score made by examinees from each age group is set at 100, and this is the most common score that people obtain (Neisser et al., 1996). Note that approximately half the population scores below 100 and half above. Moreover, roughly equal numbers of examinees obtain IQs of 85 and 115 (15 points from the average) or 70 and 130 (30 points from average). To determine the meaning of an IQ of 130, we can consider what percentage of the population a person outperforms by scoring at that level. An IQ of 130 equals or exceeds the IQs of 97 percent of the population; it is a very high IQ indeed. Similarly, fewer than 3 percent of all test takers obtain IQs below 70, a cutoff that is commonly used today to define mental retardation.

Group Tests of Mental Performance

Because the Stanford-Binet and the Wechsler scales must be administered individually by a professional examiner and it can take more than an hour to assess each person's IQ, psychometricians soon saw the need for more cost-effective, paper-and-pencil measures—tests that could be group-administered to quickly assess the intellectual performance of large numbers of army recruits, job applicants, and students. Indeed, you have almost certainly taken a *group test* of intelligence (or scholastic aptitude) at some point in your life. Among the more widely used of these tests are the *Canadian Cognitive Abilities Test*, the *Canadian Achievement Test—2*, and the *Lorge-Thorndike Test*, which are designed for elementary- and high-school students, and the *Graduate Record Examination* (*GRE*), which is often required of applicants to graduate school. These instruments are sometimes called "achievement" tests because they call for specific information that the examinee has learned at school (i.e., crystallized intelligence) and are designed to predict future academic achievement.

normal distribution
symmetrical, bell-shaped curve that describes the variability of certain characteristics within a population; most people fall at or near the average score, with relatively few at the extremes of the distribution

Newer Approaches to Intelligence Testing

Although traditional IQ tests are still heavily used, new tests are constantly being developed. For example, there are intelligence scales based on Piagetian concepts and developmental milestones (see Humphreys, Rich, & Davey, 1985). The **Kaufman Assessment Battery for Children (K-ABC)** is another recent test that is based on modern information-processing theory. The test is heavily nonverbal in content, primarily measuring what Cattell and Horn call fluid intelligence (Kaufman & Kaufman, 1983).

Other investigators, disenchanted with the ways in which intelligence has been defined and measured, have developed entirely new approaches to intellectual assessment. One promising approach called **dynamic assessment** attempts to evaluate how well children actually learn new material when an examiner provides them with competent instruction (Campione et al., 1984; Lidz, 1997). Reuven Feuerstein and his colleagues (1997), for example, have argued that, even though intelligence is often defined as a *potential* to learn from experience, IQ tests typically assess what has been learned, not what *can be* learned. Thus, the traditional psychometric approach may be biased against children from culturally diverse or economically disadvantaged backgrounds who lack opportunities to learn what the tests measure. Feuerstein's *Learning Potential Assessment Device* asks children to learn new things with the guidance of an adult who provides increasingly helpful hints—precisely the kind of collaborative learning that Vygotsky emphasized in his sociocultural theory. This test interprets intelligence as the ability to learn quickly with minimal guidance. Robert Sternberg (1985, 1991) used a similar approach in a test he constructed based on his triarchic theory of intelligence. To better understand the information processes involved in verbal comprehension, for example, Sternberg does not ask people to define words they learned in the past, as IQ testers so often do. Instead, he places an unfamiliar word in a set of sentences and asks people to learn, from its *context*, what the new word means, just as they must do in real life.

In sum, modern perspectives on intelligence are now beginning to be reflected in the content of intelligence tests (Sternberg, 1997; Sternberg & Grigorenko, 2002). However, these new tests and testing procedures have a very short history, and it remains to be seen whether they will eventually replace more traditional assessments of mental performance such as the WISC and the Stanford-Binet.

Assessing Infant Intelligence

None of the standard intelligence tests can be used with children much younger than 2½ because the test items require verbal skills and attention spans that infants do not have. However, attempts have been made to measure infant "intelligence" by assessing the rate at which babies achieve important developmental milestones. Perhaps the best known and most widely used of the infant tests is the *Bayley Scales of Infant Development* (Bayley, 1969, 1993). This instrument, designed for infants aged 1 to 42 months, has three parts:

1. the *motor* scale (which assesses such motor capabilities as grasping a cube, throwing a ball, or drinking from a cup)

2. the *mental* scale (which includes adaptive behaviours such as categorizing objects, searching for a hidden toy, and following directions)

3. the *Infant Behavioural Record* (a rating of the child's behaviour on dimensions such as goal directedness, fearfulness, and social responsivity)

On the basis of the first two scores, the infant is given a **developmental quotient**, or **DQ**, rather than an IQ. The DQ summarizes how well or poorly the infant performs in comparison with a large group of infants of the same age.

Kaufman Assessment Battery for Children (K-ABC)
individual intelligence test for children; grounded heavily in information-processing theory

dynamic assessment
approach to assessing intelligence that evaluates how well individuals learn new material when an examiner provides them with competent instruction

developmental quotient (DQ)
numerical measure of an infant's performance on a developmental schedule relative to the performance of other infants of the same age

Do DQs Predict Later IQs?

Infant scales are very useful for charting babies' developmental progress and for diagnosing neurological disorders and other signs of mental retardation, even when these conditions are fairly mild and difficult to detect in a standard neurological exam (Columbo, 1993; Honzik, 1983). Yet these instruments generally fail to predict a child's later IQ or scholastic achievements (Honzik, 1983; Rose et al., 1989) except in the case of children with mental deficits. Among typical infants, a DQ measured early in infancy may not predict the child's DQ later in infancy!

Why do infant tests do such a poor job of predicting children's later IQs? Perhaps the main reason is that infant tests and IQ tests tap very different kinds of abilities. Infant scales are designed to measure sensory, motor, language, and social skills, whereas standardized IQ tests such as the WISC and the Stanford-Binet emphasize more abstract abilities such as verbal reasoning, concept formation, and problem solving. So to expect an infant test to predict the later results of an IQ test is like expecting a measuring tape to tell us how much someone weighs. There may be some correspondence between the two measures (a measuring tape indicates height, which is correlated with weight; DQ indicates developmental progress, which is related to IQ), but the relationship is not very great.

Evidence for Continuity in Intellectual Performance

Is it foolish, then, to think that we might ever accurately forecast a child's later IQ from his or her behaviour during infancy? Maybe not. As we learned in Chapter 6, information-processing theorists have discovered that certain measures of infant attention and memory are much better at predicting IQ during the preschool and elementary-school years than are the Bayley scales or other measures of infant development. Three attributes appear especially promising: how quickly infants look when presented with a visual target (*visual reaction time*), the rate at which they *habituate* to repetitive stimuli, and the extent to which they prefer novel stimuli to familiar ones (*preference for novelty*). Measures of these information-processing skills obtained during the first four to eight months of life have an average correlation of .45 with IQ in childhood, with visual reaction time corresponding more closely to later measures of performance IQ, and the other measures predicting better for verbal IQ (Dougherty & Haith, 1997; McCall & Carriger, 1993).

So there is some continuity between infant intelligence and childhood intelligence after all. Perhaps we can now characterize the "smart" infant as one who prefers and seeks out novel experiences and who soaks up new information quickly—in short, a speedy and efficient information processor (Rose, Feldman, & Jankowski, 2001).

Stability of IQ in Childhood and Adolescence

It was once assumed that a person's IQ reflected his or her genetically determined intellectual *capacity* and remained quite stable over time. In other words, a child with an IQ of 120 at age 5 was expected to obtain a similar IQ at age 10, 15, or 20.

How much support is there for this idea? As we have seen, infant DQs do not predict later IQ test scores very well at all. But starting at about age 4, there is a meaningful relationship between early and later IQs (Sameroff et al., 1993), and the relationship grows even stronger during middle childhood. Table 9.2 summarizes the results of a longitudinal study of more than 250 children conducted at the University of California (Honzik, Macfarlane, & Allen, 1948). In examining these data, we see that the shorter the interval between two testings, the higher the correlations between children's IQ scores. But even after a number of years have passed, IQ seems to be a reasonably stable attribute. After all, the scores that children obtain at age 8 are still clearly related to those they obtain 10 years later at age 18.

TABLE 9.2	Correlation of IQs Measured during the Preschool Years and Middle Childhood, with IQs Measured at Ages 10 and 18	
Age of child	**Correlation with IQ at age 10**	**Correlation with IQ at age 18**
4	.66	.42
6	.76	.61
8	.88	.70
10	—	.76
12	.87	.76

Source: Adapted from Honzik, Macfarlane, & Allen, 1948.

There is something that these correlations are not telling us, however. Each of them is based on a large group of children, and they do not necessarily mean that the IQs of *individual children* remain stable over time. Robert McCall and his associates (1973) looked at the IQ scores of 140 children who had taken intelligence tests at regular intervals between age 2½ and 17. Their findings were remarkable. More than half of these individuals displayed meaningful fluctuations in IQ over time, and the average range of variation in the IQ scores of these fluctuators was more than 20 points (see also Gottfried et al., 1994).

So it seems that IQ is more stable for some children than for others. Clearly, these findings challenge the notion that IQ is a reflection of one's absolute potential for learning or intellectual capacity; if it were, the intellectual profiles of virtually all children would be highly stable, showing only minor variations due to errors of measurement (Simpson et al., 2002).

What, then, does an IQ represent, if not one's intellectual competence or ability? Today, many experts believe that an IQ score is merely an estimate of the examinee's intellectual *performance* at one particular point in time—an estimate that may or may not be a good indication of the examinee's intellectual capacity.

Interestingly, children whose IQs change the most usually do not fluctuate randomly; their scores tend to either increase or decrease over time. Who are the gainers and who are the losers? Gainers typically come from homes in which parents are interested in their intellectual accomplishments, urge them to achieve, and are neither too strict nor too lax in their child-rearing practices (Honzik et al., 1948; McCall et al., 1973). On the other hand, meaningful declines in IQ often occur among children who live in poverty, especially when that poverty is prolonged rather than temporary (Duncan & Brooks-Gunn, 1997). Otto Klineberg (1963) proposed a **cumulative-deficit hypothesis** to explain this: Presumably, impoverished environments dampen intellectual growth, and these inhibiting effects accumulate over time. Consequently, the longer children remain in a barren intellectual environment, the worse they perform on IQ tests.

Support for such a cumulative-deficits effect comes from a study of the intellectual performance of Romanian children adopted into middle-class English homes after spending varying amounts of time in understaffed, poverty-stricken Romanian institutions (O'Connor et al., 2000). As we see in

cumulative-deficit hypothesis
notion that impoverished environments inhibit intellectual growth and that these inhibiting effects accumulate over time

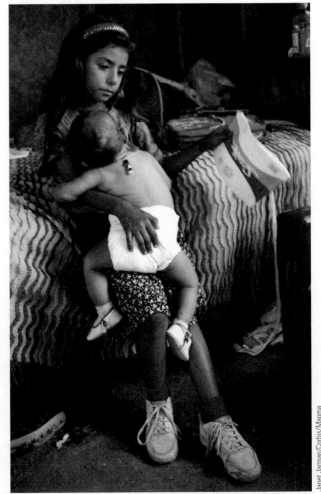

Impoverished environments dampen intellectual growth, leading to a progressive decline in children's IQ scores.

Janet Jarman/Corbis/Magma

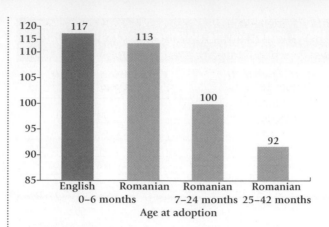

Figure 9.6 *Mental performance at age 6 years for early-adopted English children and Romanian orphans adopted at different ages. Notice that the longer the Romanian children had lived in the barren institutional environment, the lower their cognitive performances at age 6—a finding that supports the cumulative-deficit hypothesis.* ADAPTED FROM O'CONNOR ET AL., *2000.*

Figure 9.6, the 6-year-old mental performance scores of Romanian children adopted in the first six months of life were comparable to those of English children adopted within their first six months. By contrast, Romanian children adopted later showed lingering cognitive deficits at age 6, with children who had spent more time in the poverty-stricken orphanages posting the lowest scores (or larger deficits).

WHAT DO INTELLIGENCE TESTS PREDICT?

We have seen that IQ tests measure intellectual performance rather than capacity and that a person's IQ may vary considerably over time. Given these qualifications, it seems reasonable to ask whether IQ scores can tell anything very meaningful about the people who are tested. For example, does IQ predict future academic accomplishments? Is it in any way related to a person's health, occupational status, or general life satisfaction? Let's first consider the relationship between IQ and academic achievement.

IQ as a Predictor of Scholastic Achievement

Since the original purpose of IQ testing was to estimate how well children would perform at school, it should come as no surprise that modern intelligence tests do predict academic achievement. The average correlation between children's IQ scores and their current and future grades at school is about .50 (Neisser et al., 1996).

Not only do children with high IQs tend to do better in school, but they stay there longer (Brody, 1997); that is, they are less likely to drop out of high school and more likely than other high-school graduates to attempt and to complete university.

Some have argued that IQ tests predict scholastic performance because both measures depend on the abstract reasoning abilities that make up Spearman's *g*, or general mental ability (Jensen, 1998). However, critics of this viewpoint argue that both IQ tests and measures of scholastic achievement reflect knowledge and reasoning skills that are culturally valued. One line of evidence consistent with this viewpoint is that schooling, which largely reflects cultural values, actually *improves* IQ test performance (Ceci & Williams, 1997). How? By transmitting factual knowledge pertinent to test questions, promoting memory strategies and categorization skills that are measured on IQ tests, and encouraging attitudes and behaviours, such as trying hard and working under pressure, that foster successful test-taking skills (Ceci, 1991; Huttenlocher, Levine, & Vevea, 1998). Viewed from this perspective, then, IQ tests could almost be considered tests of academic achievement.

Finally, let's keep in mind that the moderate correlations between IQ and scholastic performance are based on *group* trends and that the IQ score of any individual student may not accurately reflect his or her current or future academic accomplishments. Clearly, academic performance also depends very heavily on such factors as a student's work habits, interests, and motivation to succeed (Neisser et al., 1996). So even though IQ (and aptitude) tests predict academic achievement better than *any other type of test*, judgments about a student's prospects for future success *should never be based on a test score alone*. Indeed, studies have consistently shown that the best single predictor of a student's future grades is not an IQ or aptitude score but, rather, the grades the student has previously earned (Minton & Schneider, 1980).

WHAT DO YOU THINK?

The correlation between IQ scores and future university grades is approximately +.50, which means that these tests account for about 25 percent of the variability in students' grade-point averages (that is, variance accounted for = r2, or .50 × .50 = .25). Does this imply to you that admissions offices may be putting too much emphasis on standardized test scores? Why or why not?

IQ as a Predictor of Vocational Outcomes

Do people with higher IQs land better jobs? Are they more successful in their chosen occupations than coworkers who test lower in intelligence?

There is a clear relationship between IQ and occupational status. Figure 9.7 shows that (1) professional and other white-collar businesspeople consistently score higher in IQ than blue-collar, or manual, workers, and (2) the IQ gap across occupations is smaller for recent cohorts than for earlier ones, perhaps due to improvements over time in educational opportunities for the less wealthy (Weakliem, McQuillan, & Schauer, 1995). Generally, the average IQ for an occupation increases as the prestige of the occupation increases. And one contributor to this relationship is the link between IQ and education: It undoubtedly takes more intellectual ability to complete law school and become a lawyer than it does to become a farmhand (Brody, 1997). Yet IQs vary considerably in every occupational group, and many people in low-status jobs have high IQs.

Does IQ predict job *performance*? Are bright lawyers, electricians, or farmhands more successful or productive than their less intelligent colleagues? The answer here is also yes. The correlations between mental test scores and such indications of job performance as ratings from supervisors average about +.50—about as high as IQ correlates with academic achievement (Hunter & Hunter, 1984; Neisser et al., 1996). However, an astute manager or personnel officer would never rely exclusively on an IQ score to decide whom to hire or promote. One reason for looking beyond IQ is that people differ in **tacit (or practical) intelligence**—the ability to size up everyday problems and take steps to solve them—which is not closely related to IQ, but predicts job performance rather well (Sternberg et al., 1995). In addition, variables such as prior job performance, interpersonal skills, and motivation to succeed may be as important or even more important than IQ as predictors of future job performance (Neisser et al., 1996).

tacit (or practical) intelligence
ability to size up everyday problems and solve them; only modestly related to IQ

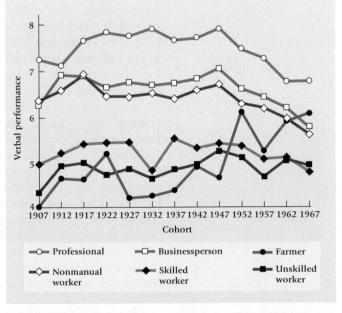

Figure 9.7 *Mean verbal ability scores differ across occupational groups, but the size of the gap seems to be narrower for people born in the 1960s than for people born early in the century. FROM WEAKLIEM, MCQUILLAN, & SCHAUER, 1995.*

IQ as a Predictor of Health, Adjustment, and Life Satisfaction

Are bright people any healthier, happier, or better adjusted than those of average or below-average intelligence? Let's see what researchers have learned by considering the life outcomes of people at opposite ends of the IQ continuum: the *intellectually gifted* and the *mentally retarded*.

In 1922, Lewis Terman began an interesting longitudinal study of more than 1500 Californian schoolchildren who had IQs of 140 or higher—a study that continues today. The purpose of the project was to collect as much information as possible about the abilities and personal characteristics of these gifted children and to follow up on them every few years for the rest of their lives to see what they were accomplishing.

It soon became clear that these children were exceptional in many respects other than intelligence. For example, they had learned to walk and talk much sooner than most toddlers, and their general health, as determined from physicians' reports, was much better than average. The gifted children were rated by teachers as better adjusted emotionally and more morally mature than their less intelligent peers. And although they were no more popular, on average, than their classmates, the gifted children were quicker to take charge and assume positions of leadership. Taken together, these findings demolish the stereotype of child prodigies as frail, sickly youngsters who are socially inadequate and emotionally immature.

Yet it is inappropriate to conclude that intellectually gifted children are immune to adjustment problems. Other studies find that very-high-IQ children are about twice as likely as non-gifted peers to feel socially isolated and depressed, and they may even try to hide their abilities in the hope of becoming more popular (Winner, 2000). Intellectually gifted youngsters who display these adjustment problems may profit from skipping grades or otherwise having their education accelerated so that they are challenged academically and exposed to peers who think as complexly as they do. However, a decision to accelerate the education of gifted children should always be made on an individual basis because some accelerated children become anxious and depressed at being so far behind their older classmates both socially and emotionally (Winner, 1997).

What becomes of gifted children as adults? Most of Terman's gifted sample remained remarkable in many respects. Fewer than 5 percent were rated as seriously maladjusted, and the incidence of problems such as ill health, alcoholism, and delinquent behaviour was only a fraction of that normally observed in the general population (Terman, 1954). The occupational attainments of the gifted men were impressive. The vast majority were working in professional or semiprofessional jobs by age 40. As a group they had taken out more than 200 patents and written some 2000 scientific reports, 100 books, 375 plays or short stories, and more than 300 essays, sketches, magazine articles, and critiques. The achievements of the gifted women are more difficult to discern because most of the women invested their energies in raising families (Schuster, 1990; Tomlinson-Keasey & Little, 1990). Consistent with societal changes with respect to work outside the home, recent cohorts of gifted women are pursuing careers more vigorously and seem to have a greater sense of well-being than Terman's gifted women did (Schuster, 1990; Subotnik, Karp, & Morgan, 1989).

In short, most of Terman's participants were well-adjusted people living happy, healthy, and highly productive lives. Nevertheless, approximately 15 percent of the sample were not particularly happy or successful as middle-aged adults (Shurkin, 1992; Terman, 1954). In their analysis of factors that predicted the paths these adults' lives took over a 40-year period, Carolyn Tomlinson-Keasey and Todd Little (1990) found that the most well-adjusted and successful participants had highly educated parents who offered them lots of love and intellectual stimulation; by contrast, the least successful of the group were likely to have experienced disruption of family ties due to their parents' divorce and less social support and encouragement (see also Friedman et al., 1995). So a high IQ, by itself, does not guarantee health, happiness, or success. Even among a select sample of children with superior IQs, the quality of the home environment contributes substantially to future outcomes and accomplishments.

mental retardation
significant below-average intellectual functioning associated with impairments in adaptive behaviour in everyday life

What about the other end of the IQ continuum? Do mentally retarded individuals have much hope of succeeding in life or achieving happiness? Although our stereotypes about **mental retardation** might persuade us to say "no," the research presented in Box 9.3 suggests a very different conclusion.

Mental Retardation: A Closer Look

In a recent Canadian study, the prevalence of mental retardation in an adolescent population was estimated at 7.18 cases per 1000. As many as 3 percent of school-age children are classified as mentally retarded (Bradley, Thompson & Bryson, 2002)—that is, these individuals met the criteria that defines them as significantly below average in intellectual functioning, with limitations in such adaptive behaviours as self-care and social skills (Roeleveld, Zielhuis, & Gabreels, 1997). Although many labels have been (and are currently) used to identify individuals with intellectual challenges, in an attempt to minimize stigmatization (e.g., designations like "developmental delay," "mentally challenged," etc.), the term "mental retardation" continues to be the formal label used as a diagnosis by psychologists and medical practitioners (see Diagnostic and Statistical Manual of Mental Disorders or DSM-IV). Individuals with mental retardation differ greatly in their levels of functioning. Severely retarded individuals with IQs lower than 55 are often affected by organic retardation—deficits caused by such identifiable causes as Down syndrome, diseases, or injuries. These individuals may require basic care throughout life, often in institutions. More common, however, are mildly retarded individuals (IQs 55 to 70), who usually display cultural-familial retardation—deficits reflecting a combination of low genetic potential and an unstimulating rearing environment (Simonoff, Bolton, & Rutter, 1996). Mildly retarded individuals can learn both academic and practical lessons at school, and they can often work and live independently or with occasional help as adults.

What kinds of life outcomes do mildly retarded individuals display? We gain some clues from a follow-up study of men and women (average IQ = 67) who had been placed in special education classes for the mentally retarded during the 1920s and 1930s (Ross et al., 1985). Nearly 40 years later, their life outcomes were compared with those of siblings and nonrelated peers, and with the highly favourable attainments of Terman's gifted sample.

Generally, the mentally retarded adults had less favourable life outcomes in middle age than the nonretarded groups (see also Schalock et al., 1992). As we see in the table, about 80 percent of the retarded men were employed, but they usually held semiskilled or unskilled jobs that required little education or intellectual ability. (Retarded women usually married and did not work outside of the home.) Compared with nonretarded peers, retarded men and women had lower incomes, less adequate housing, poorer social skills, and a greater dependency on others.

Yet the authors of this study still found grounds for optimism. After all, the vast majority of these mildly retarded individuals had worked and married, and they were generally satisfied with their accomplishments. In fact, only one in five reported having any need for public assistance in the 10 years before they were interviewed. Clearly, they were faring much better than common stereotypes about the mentally retarded would lead us to believe.

So this study, like others before it, reveals that many individuals labelled mildly retarded in school, and who do indeed have some difficulty mastering academic lessons, often "vanish" into the adult population after they leave school. Apparently, they adapt to the demands of adult life, displaying a fair amount of the practical intelligence or "street smarts" that Sternberg (1997) talks about—and that is not measured by standardized IQ tests. As the authors put it, "It does not take as many IQ points as most people believe to be productive ... and self-fulfilled" (Ross et al., 1985, p. 149).

Midlife Occupations of Mentally Retarded, Nonretarded, and Gifted Males

Occupational classification	Mentally retarded participants (n = 54), %	Nonretarded siblings (n = 31), %	Nonretarded peers (n = 33), %	Terman's gifted sample (n = 757), %
Professional, managerial	1.9	29.1	36.4	86.3
Retail business, skilled trade, agricultural	29.6	32.3	39.4	12.5
Semiskilled, miner or business, clerical	50.0	25.8	15.2	1.2
Slightly skilled, unskilled	18.5	13.0	9.4	0.0

SOURCE: Adapted from Ross et al., 1985.

FACTORS THAT INFLUENCE IQ SCORES

Why do people differ so dramatically in their IQ scores? In addressing this issue, we will briefly review the evidence for hereditary and environmental influences and then take a closer look at several important social and cultural correlates of intellectual performance.

The Evidence for Heredity

In Chapter 3, we reviewed two major lines of evidence indicating that heredity affects intellectual performance and that about half the variation in IQ scores within a particular population of test takers is due to genetic differences among these individuals.

Twin Studies

The intellectual resemblance between pairs of individuals living in the same home increases as a function of their kinship (that is, genetic similarity). For example, the IQ correlation for identical twins, who inherit identical genes, is substantially higher than the IQ correlations for fraternal twins and normal siblings, who have half their genes in common.

Adoption Studies

Adopted children's IQs are more highly correlated with the IQs of their biological parents than with those of their adoptive parents. This finding can be interpreted as evidence for a genetic influence on IQ, because adoptees share genes with their biological parents but not with their adoptive caregivers.

We also learned in Chapter 3 that a person's genotype may influence the type of environment that he or she is likely to experience. Indeed, Scarr and McCartney (1983) have proposed that people seek out environments that are compatible with their genetic predispositions, so that identical twins (who share identical genes) select and experience more similar environments than fraternal twins or ordinary siblings do. This is a major reason that identical twins resemble each other intellectually throughout life, whereas the intellectual resemblances between fraternal twins or ordinary siblings become progressively smaller over time (McCartney, Harris, & Bernieri, 1990).

Do these observations imply that a person's genotype *determines* his environment and exerts the primary influence on his intellectual development? *No, they do not!* A child who has a genetic predisposition to seek out intellectual challenges could hardly be expected to develop a high IQ if she is raised in a barren environment that offers few such challenges for her to meet. Alternatively, a child who does not gravitate toward intellectual activities might nevertheless obtain an average or above-average IQ if raised in a stimulating environment that continually provides him with cognitive challenges that he must master. Let's now take a closer look at how environment might influence intellectual performance.

✔ Concept Check 9.2
On the Character and Predictive Power of Assessments of Mental Performance

Check your understanding of the character and usefulness of various assessments of mental performance by matching each of the following alternatives to a statement that appears below: (a) Wechsler Intelligence Scale for Children—III (WISC-III), (b) Stanford-Binet Intelligence Scale, (c) cumulative deficit, (d) dynamic assessment, (e) grades previously earned, (f) tacit (or practical) intelligence, (g) developmental quotient (DQ), (h) habituation rate. Answers appear in the Appendix.

_____ 1. assessment of how well children learn from competent instruction

_____ 2. measure of infant functioning that does *not* forecast childhood IQ

_____ 3. IQ test designed to overcome the heavily verbal bias of earlier tests

_____ 4. concept explaining how IQs might decline over time

_____ 5. measure of infant functioning that forecasts childhood IQs moderately well

_____ 6. although not closely related to IQ, attribute that predicts future job performance rather well

_____ 7. first American IQ test

_____ 8. predicts future academic success as well or better than IQ scores

The Evidence for Environment

The evidence for environmental effects on intelligence comes from a variety of sources. For example, we learned in Chapter 3 that there is a small to moderate intellectual resemblance between pairs of *genetically unrelated* children who live in the same household—a resemblance that can only be attributable to their common rearing environment since they share no genes. And earlier in this chapter, we noted that children from impoverished backgrounds show a progressive decline (or cumulative deficit) in IQ as they grow older, thus implying that economic disadvantage inhibits intellectual growth.

Might we then promote intellectual development and improve children's IQs by enriching the environments in which they live? Indeed we can, and at least two lines of evidence tell us so.

A Secular Trend: The Flynn Effect

People have been getting smarter throughout the twentieth century. Average IQs in all countries studied have increased about 3 points per decade since 1940, a phenomenon called the **Flynn effect** after its discoverer, James Flynn (1987, 1996). An increase this large that occurs this quickly cannot be caused by evolution and must therefore have *environmental* causes. So what might be responsible for improving IQ scores?

Worldwide improvements in education could increase IQs in three ways, helping people to become more "testwise," more knowledgeable in general, and more likely to rely on sophisticated problem-solving strategies (Flieller, 1999; Flynn, 1996). Yet, improved education is probably not the sole contributor because the Flynn effect is much clearer on measures of fluid intelligence, even though one might expect crystallized intelligence to benefit most from educational enrichment. Twentieth-century improvements in nutrition and health care are two other potent environmental factors that many believe to have contributed to improved intellectual performance by helping to optimize the development of growing brains and nervous systems (Flynn, 1996; Flieller, 1999; Flynn, 1996).

Adoption Studies

Other investigators have charted the intellectual growth of adopted children who left disadvantaged family backgrounds and were placed with highly educated adoptive parents (Scarr & Weinberg, 1983; Skodak & Skeels, 1949). By the time these adoptees were 4 to 7 years old, they were scoring well above average on standardized IQ tests (about 110 in Scarr and Weinberg's study and 112 in Skodak and Skeels's). Interestingly, the IQ scores of these adoptees were still correlated with the IQs of their *biological* mothers, thus reflecting the influence of heredity on intellectual performance. And yet, the *absolute* IQs these adoptees attained were considerably *higher* (by 10 to 20 points) than one would expect on the basis of the IQs and educational levels of their biological parents, and their levels of academic achievement remained slightly above the national norm well into adolescence (Weinberg, Scarr, & Waldman, 1992; Waldman, Weinberg, & Scarr, 1994). So the *phenotype* that one displays on a genetically influenced attribute like intelligence is clearly influenced by one's environment. Since the adopting parents in these studies were themselves highly educated and above average in intelligence, it seems reasonable to assume that they were providing enriched, intellectually stimulating home environments that fostered the cognitive development of their adoptees.

So environment is truly a powerful force that may either promote or inhibit intellectual growth. Yet our use of the term *environment* here is very global, and the evidence that we have reviewed does not really tell us which of the many life experiences that children have are most likely to affect their intellectual development. In the next section, we will look more closely at environmental influences and see that a child's performance on IQ tests depends to some extent on parental attitudes and child-rearing practices, the structure and socioeconomic status of the family, and even the sociocultural group to which the family belongs.

Flynn effect
systematic increase in IQ scores
observed over the 20th century

SOCIAL AND CULTURAL CORRELATES OF INTELLECTUAL PERFORMANCE

Home Environment and IQ

Earlier, we implied that the quality or character of the home environment may play an important role in determining children's intellectual performance and eventual life outcomes. Arnold Sameroff and his colleagues (1993) listed 10 environmental factors that place children at risk of displaying low IQ scores, 9 of which were characteristics of children's homes and families (or family members). These researchers measured each of the IQ risk factors listed in Table 9.3 at age 4, and again when the children in their sample were 13 years old. Every one of these risk factors was related to IQ at age 4, and most also predicted IQ at age 13. In addition, the greater the number of these risk factors affecting a child, the lower his or her IQ; which particular risk factors a child experienced were less important than how many he or she experienced. It is clearly not conducive to intellectual development to grow up in an economically disadvantaged home with highly stressed or poorly educated parents who are unable to provide much intellectual stimulation.

Assessing the Character of the Home Environment

Exactly how do parents influence a child's intellectual development? In an attempt to find out, Bettye Caldwell and Robert Bradley have developed a widely used instrument, called the **HOME inventory** (**H**ome **O**bservation for **M**easurement of the **E**nvironment), that allows an interviewer/observer to visit an infant, preschooler, or school-age child at home and determine how intellectually stimulating (or impoverished) that home environment is (Caldwell & Bradley, 1984). The infant version of the HOME inventory, for example, consists of 45 statements, each of which is scored yes (the statement is true of this family) or no (the statement is not true of this family). To gather the information necessary to complete the inventory, the researcher (1) asks the child's

HOME inventory
measure of the amount and type of intellectual stimulation provided by a child's home environment

TABLE 9.3	Environmental Risk Factors Associated with Low IQ and Mean IQs at Age 4 of Children Who Did or Did Not Experience Each Risk Factor

	Mean IQ at age 4	
Risk factor	**Child experienced risk factor**	**Child did not experience risk factor**
Child is member of minority group	90	110
Head of household is unemployed or low-skilled worker	90	108
Mother did not complete high school	92	109
Family has four or more children	94	105
Father is absent from family	95	106
Family experienced many stressful life events	97	105
Parents have rigid child-rearing values	92	107
Mother is highly anxious/distressed	97	107
Mother has poor mental health/diagnosed disorder	99	107
Mother shows little positive affect toward child	88	107

SOURCE: Data and descriptions compiled from Sameroff et al., 1993.

parent (usually the mother) to describe her daily routine and child-rearing practices, (2) carefully observes the parent as she interacts with her child, and (3) notes the kinds of play materials that the parent makes available to the child. The 45 bits of information collected are then grouped into the six subscales in Table 9.4. The home then receives a score on each subscale. The higher the scores across all six subscales, the more intellectually stimulating the home environment.

Does the HOME Inventory Predict IQ?

Research conducted in the United States consistently indicates that the scores that homes obtain on the HOME inventory do predict the intellectual performances of toddlers, preschoolers, and elementary-school children, regardless of their social class or ethnic backgrounds (Gottfried, Fleming, & Gottfried, 1998; Jackson et al., 2000; Luster & Dubow, 1992). Similar results have been obtained in other cultures. For example, when the HOME inventory was used to assess infants and their families in Costa Rica, the measure provided modest predictive power for the infants' IQ (measured by the WPPSI) when they were 5 years old (Lozoff et al., 1995). However, the HOME inventory did not predict performance on the Bayley Scales of Infant Development. Among American samples, gains in IQ from age 1 to age 3 are likely to occur among children from stimulating homes, whereas children from families with low HOME scores often experience 10- to 20-point declines in IQ over the same period (Bradley et al., 1989).

WHICH ASPECTS OF THE HOME ENVIRONMENT MATTER MOST? Although all of the HOME subscales are moderately correlated with children's IQ scores, some are better predictors of intellectual performance than others. During infancy, HOME subscales measuring *parental involvement* with the child, provision of *age-appropriate play materials*, and opportunities for *variety in daily stimulation* are the best predictors of children's later IQs and scholastic achievement (Bradley, Caldwell, & Rock, 1988; Gottfried et al., 1994). And preschool measures of *parental warmth*, *stimulation of language*, and *academic behaviours* are also closely associated with children's future intellectual performances (Bradley & Caldwell, 1982; Bradley et al., 1988).

TABLE 9.4	Subscales and Sample Items for the HOME Inventory (Infant Version)

Subscale 1: Emotional and verbal responsivity of parent (11 items)
Sample items: Parent responds verbally to child's vocalizations or verbalizations.
Parent's speech is distinct, clear, and audible.
Parent caresses or kisses child at least once.

Subscale 2: Avoidance of restriction and punishment (8 items)
Sample items: Parent neither slaps nor spanks child during visit.
Parent does not scold or criticize child during visit.
Parent does not interfere with or restrict child more than three times during visit.

Subscale 3: Organization of physical and temporal environment (6 items)
Sample items: Child gets out of house at least four times a week.
Child's play environment is safe.

Subscale 4: Provision of appropriate play materials (9 items)
Sample items: Child has a push or pull toy.
Parent provides learning facilitators appropriate to age:
mobile, table, and chairs, highchair, playpen, and so on.
Parent provides toys for child to play with during visit.

Subscale 5: Parental involvement with child (6 items)
Sample items Parent talks to child while doing household work.
Parent structures child's play periods.

Subscale 6: Opportunities for variety in daily stimulation (5 items)
Sample items: Father provides some care daily.
Child has three or more books of his or her own.

SOURCE: Adapted from Caldwell & Bradley, 1984.

What these findings imply, then, is that an intellectually stimulating home is one in which parents are warm, verbally engaging, and eager to be involved with their child (Fagot & Gauvain, 1997; Hart & Risley, 1995; MacPhee, Ramey, & Yeates, 1984). These parents describe new objects, concepts, and experiences clearly and accurately, and they provide the child with a variety of challenges that are appropriate for her age or developmental level. They encourage the child to ask questions, solve problems, and think about what she is learning. As the child matures and enters school, they stress the importance of academic achievement and expect her to get good grades (Luster & Dubow, 1992). When you stop and think about it, it is not at all surprising that children from these "enriched" home settings often have high IQs; after all, their parents are obviously concerned about their cognitive development and have spent several years encouraging them to acquire new information and to practise many of the cognitive skills that are measured on intelligence tests.

A Hidden Genetic Effect? It turns out that brighter parents are likely to provide more intellectually stimulating home environments (Coon et al., 1990). Is it possible, then, that any correlation between the quality of the home environment and children's IQ scores simply reflects the fact that bright parents transmit genes for high intelligence to their children?

There is some support for this idea in that correlations between HOME scores and IQ scores are higher for biological children, who share genes with their parents, than for adopted children, who are genetically unrelated to other members of their family (Braungart, Fulker, & Plomin, 1992). So does the quality of the home environment have any effect on children's intellectual development that does not reflect the influence of genes?

The answer is yes, and two lines of evidence tell us so. First, adopted children's IQ scores rise considerably when they are moved from less stimulating to more stimulating homes (Turkheimer, 1991). Clearly, this change in IQs has to be an *environmental* effect because adoptees share no genes with their adoptive parents. Equally revealing are the results of a longitudinal study of 112 mothers and their 2- to 4-year-old children conducted by Keith Yeates and his associates (1983). These investigators measured the mothers' IQs; the IQ of each child at ages 2, 3, and 4; and the quality of the families' home environments (as assessed by the HOME). The best predictor of a child's IQ at age 2 was the mother's IQ, just as a genetic hypothesis would suggest. But the picture had changed by the time children were 4 years old; now the quality of the home environment was a strong predictor of children's IQs, even *after* the influence of mothers' IQs was taken into account.

Orderly home environments in which family members are warm, responsive, and eager to be involved with one another are precisely the kind of setting that promotes children's intellectual development.

PhotoDisc, Inc.

So it appears that the quality of the home environment is truly an important contributor to a child's intellectual development that becomes more apparent later in the preschool period, when IQ becomes a more stable attribute (Sameroff et al., 1993; Yeates et al., 1983). However, let's also note that the relationship between HOME scores and children's IQs does decline somewhat during the elementary-school years (Luster & Dubow, 1992), probably because older children are away from home more often and are exposed to other people, such as teachers, who also influence their intellectual development (Bjorklund, 2000).

Social Class, Racial, and Ethnic Differences in IQ

One of the most reliable findings in the intelligence literature is a social class effect: Children from lower- and working-class homes average some 10 to 15 points below their middle-class age-mates on standardized IQ tests (Helms, 1997). Infants are apparently the only exception to this rule, as there are no reliable social class differences on infant information-processing measures of habituation and preference for novelty that predict later IQ scores (McCall & Carriger, 1993) or in the developmental quotients (DQs) that infants obtain on infant "intelligence" tests (Golden et al., 1971).

There are also racial and ethnic differences in intellectual performance. You may recall the tremendous publicity surrounding the publication of a Canadian researcher's theory in the early 1990s that argued that there were fundamental IQ differences among races (Rushton, 1992). Although his theory has since been discredited, one of its founding features concerned a fairly common outcome in IQ tests; that is, on average, individuals of Asian ancestry typically outperform Whites, who in turn typically outperform Blacks on IQ tests (Rushton, 1992). Additional research generally finds that Whites tend to obtain higher IQ scores than members of First Nations groups (Dolan, 1999). There is a similar pattern in the United States, with European-Americans scoring about 12 to 15 points higher than individuals of African-American and Native-American ancestry (Flynn, 1991; Neisser et al., 1996). In addition, different subcultural groups sometimes display distinctive ability profiles. African-American children, for example, often perform better on verbal tests than on other subtests, whereas Native-American children sometimes do particularly well on nonverbal items that assess spatial abilities (Neisser et al., 1996; Suzuki & Valencia, 1997).

Before we try to interpret these social class, racial, and ethnic differences, an important truth is worth stating here—one that is often overlooked when people discover that Asian children outperform their Black or White classmates, or that White children outperform their Black classmates on IQ tests. The fact is that we cannot predict anything about the IQ or the future accomplishments of an *individual* on the basis of his or her ethnicity or skin colour. As we see in Figure 9.8, the IQ distributions for samples of

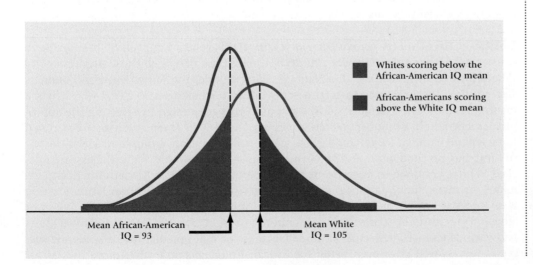

■ Whites scoring below the African-American IQ mean

■ African-Americans scoring above the White IQ mean

Mean African-American IQ = 93

Mean White IQ = 105

Figure 9.8 *Approximate distributions of IQ scores for African-American and White children reared by their biological parents. BASED ON BRODY, 1992; NEISSER ET AL., 1996.*

African Americans and White Americans overlap considerably. So, even though the average IQ scores of African Americans are somewhat lower than those of Whites, the overlapping distributions mean that many African-American children obtain higher IQ scores than many White children. In fact, approximately 15 to 25 percent of the African-American population score higher—in many cases, substantially higher—than most of the White population.

Why Do Groups Differ in Intellectual Performance?

Over the years, developmentalists have proposed three general hypotheses to account for racial, ethnic, and social class differences in IQ: (1) a *cultural test bias* hypothesis that standardized IQ tests and the ways they are administered are geared toward White, middle-class cultural experiences and seriously underestimate the intellectual capabilities of economically disadvantaged children, especially those from minority subcultures; (2) a *genetic* hypothesis that group differences in IQ are hereditary; and (3) an *environmental* hypothesis that the groups scoring lower in IQ come from intellectually impoverished backgrounds—that is, neighbourhoods and home environments that are not very conducive to intellectual growth.

The Cultural Test Bias Hypothesis

Those who favour the **cultural test bias hypothesis** believe that group differences in IQ are an artifact of our tests and testing procedures (Helms, 1992). To illustrate, they point out that IQ tests currently in use were designed to measure cognitive skills (for example, assembling puzzles) and general information (for example, "What is a 747?") that White, middle-class children are more likely to have acquired. They note that subtests measuring vocabulary and word usage may be harder for African Americans and Latinos, who often speak a different English dialect from that of the White middle class. Also, as we discussed earlier in Box 9.1, language is an important cultural obstacle that must be taken into account when interpreting the validity of IQ tests. Even the way language is used varies across ethnic groups. For example, White parents ask a lot of "knowledge-training" questions ("What does a doggie say?" "Where do the Inuit live?") that require brief answers and are similar to the kinds of questions asked on IQ tests. By contrast, African-American parents are more inclined to ask *real questions* (for example, "Why didn't you come right home after school?") that they may not know the answer to—questions that often require elaborate, story-type responses that are quite unlike those called for at school or when taking an IQ test (Heath, 1989). So if IQ tests assess proficiency in the White culture, as many critics contend, minority children are bound to appear deficient (Helms, 1992).

DOES TEST BIAS EXPLAIN GROUP DIFFERENCES IN IQ? Several attempts have been made to construct **culture-fair IQ tests** that do not place poor people or those from minority subcultures at an immediate disadvantage. For example, the *Raven Progressive Matrices Test* requires the examinee to scan a series of abstract designs, each of which has a missing section. The examinee's task is to complete each design by selecting the appropriate section from a number of alternatives (see Figure 9.9). These problems are assumed to be equally familiar (or unfamiliar) to people from all ethnic groups and social classes, the test has no time limit, and the instructions are very simple. Nevertheless, middle-class Whites continue to outperform their lower-income and/or African-American age-mates on these culture-fair measures of intelligence (Jensen, 1980). Translating existing tests into the English dialect spoken by urban African-American children also does not appear to increase the scores that these children make (Quay, 1971). And finally, IQ tests and various tests of intellectual aptitude (such as the GRE) predict future academic successes just as well as or even better for African Americans and other minorities as for

cultural test bias hypothesis notion that IQ tests and testing procedures have a built-in, middle-class bias that explains the substandard performance of children from lower-class and minority subcultures

culture-fair IQ tests intelligence tests constructed to minimize any irrelevant cultural biases in test content that could influence test performance

Figure 9.9 *An item similar to those appearing in the Raven Progressive Matrices Test.*

Whites (Neisser et al., 1996). Taken together, these findings imply that group differences in IQ scores are not solely attributable to biases in the *content* of our tests or the dialect in which they are administered. But another possibility remains.

MOTIVATIONAL FACTORS. Critics have argued that many minority children and adolescents are not inclined to do their best in formal testing situations (Moore, 1986; Ogbu, 1994; Steele, 1997). They may be wary of unfamiliar examiners (most of whom are White) or testing procedures, and they may see little point in trying to do well, often appearing more interested in answering quickly (rather than correctly) to get the unpleasant testing experience over with (Boykin, 1994; Moore, 1986).

Changes in testing procedures to make minority examinees more comfortable and less threatened can make a big difference. When minority children are allowed to warm up to a friendly examiner who is patient and supportive, they score several points higher on IQ tests than they normally would when tested in the traditional way by a strange examiner (Kaufman, Kamphaus, & Kaufman, 1985; Zigler et al., 1982). Even minority youngsters from *middle-class* homes may benefit from these procedural changes because they are often much less comfortable in testing situations than middle-class Whites are (Moore, 1986).

IMPACTS OF NEGATIVE STEREOTYPES. John Ogbu (1994) believes that negative stereotypes about their intellectual abilities may cause some minority youngsters to feel that their life prospects will be restricted by prejudice and discrimination. Consequently, they may reject certain behaviours sanctioned by the majority culture, such as excelling in school or on tests, as less relevant to them or as "acting White." What's more, the research presented in Box 9.4 points to a more subtle way that negative stereotypes can undermine the intellectual performance of minority students—even talented students who are highly motivated to achieve.

The Genetic Hypothesis

Controversy surrounding the causes of racial and ethnic differences in IQ scores was fuelled by the publication of Richard Herrnstein and Charles Murray's book, *The Bell Curve*, in 1994. These authors argued that ethnic differences in average IQ scores were largely the result of genetic differences between the ethnicities. Many Canadian researchers disagreed with the work of Herrnstein and Murray. In fact, a special issue of one Canadian journal was devoted to examining the flaws in the work on philosophical (Barrow, 1995), statistical (Krishnan, 1995), educational (Kirby, 1995), and logical grounds (Bateson, 1995; Siegel, 1995), with some of these arguments outlined below.

On the other hand, Arthur Jensen (1980, 1985) agrees with the **genetic hypothesis**. He claims that two broad classes of intellectual abilities are equally heritable among different racial and ethnic groups. **Level I abilities** include attentional processes, short-term memory, and associative skills that are important for simple kinds of rote learning. **Level II abilities** allow one to reason abstractly and to manipulate words and symbols to form concepts and solve problems. According to Jensen, Level II abilities are highly correlated with school achievement, whereas Level I abilities are not. Of course, it is predominantly Level II abilities that are measured on IQ tests.

Jensen (1985) finds that Level I tasks are performed equally well by children from all races, ethnic groups, and social classes. However, middle-class and White children outperform lower-income and African-American children on the more advanced Level II tasks. Since Level I and Level II tasks are equally heritable *within* each social class and ethnic group, Jensen proposes that the IQ differences *between* groups must be hereditary.

CRITICISMS OF THE GENETIC HYPOTHESIS. Although Jensen's arguments may sound convincing, there are reasons to suspect that genetic influences do not explain group differences in IQ. For example, Jensen's critics have noted that within-group heritability estimates imply absolutely nothing about between-group differences in an attribute (Lewontin, 1976). Richard Lewontin (1976) makes this point quite clearly with an analogy. Suppose that corn seeds with different genetic makeups are randomly drawn

genetic hypothesis
notion that group differences in IQ are hereditary

Level I abilities
Jensen's term for lower-level intellectual abilities (such as attention and short-term memory) that are important for simple association learning

Level II abilities
Jensen's term for higher-level cognitive skills that are involved in abstract reasoning and problem solving

A Threat in the Air: How Social Stereotypes Can Influence Intellectual Performance

Two students, one Black and the other White, sit next to each other in a first-year English class. Both are from middle-class families and attended top-flight high schools, where they earned good grades. Yet the Black student is now flunking out whereas the White student is not. Why is their performance so different?

Claude Steele (1997) believes that the answer may have little to do with ethnic differences in genetics, parenting, social-class, or family dysfunction. Instead, he argues that any member of an ethnic group characterized by such negative stereotypes as "Blacks are less intelligent" or "Natives are lazy" often experience **stereotype threat** in testing situations—an underlying suspicion that the stereotypes about his social group could be true and a fear that he will be judged to have traits associated with the negative stereotype. Once aroused, this stereotype threat creates a disruptive anxiety that impairs the student's ability to do his best in testing situations. So, according to Steele, a minority group member might still be influenced by a negative stereotype even if he has publicly proclaimed it to be false.

To test his theory, Steele and Joshua Aronson (1995) administered a very difficult verbal-skills test to older adolescent females after telling them that these problems were either (1) designed to assess their abilities (which might trigger stereotype threat among stigmatized minorities) or (2) simply of interest to the researchers (no stereotype threat). As the figure indicates, African Americans performed poorly when they thought their abilities were being assessed, but performed much better—in fact, just as well as White students did—when the test was portrayed as a nonevaluative exercise. In a second study, Steele and Aronson found that simply having Black students indicate their ethnicity on the test booklet is sufficient to trigger stereotype threat and undermine test performance.

So it appears that stereotype threat can handicap affected minority students and contribute most importantly to ethnic differences in intellectual and academic performance. And there is more. Joshua Aronson and colleagues (in press; see also Major & Schmader, 1998) find that students who experience stereotype threat can become extremely frustrated and actually disidentify with school or with those domains of schooling to which the stereotypes apply, coming to view them as less important to their own

life outcomes. This disidentification may thus close the door on many career options and even contribute to a decision to drop out of school. How might these vulnerabilities to negative stereotypes be overcome?

One approach that Steele favours is a program in which Blacks and Whites regularly study together, discussing personal and social issues, as well as participating in mastery workshops in their academic subjects. By avoiding self-segregation, these cross-race collaborative programs can help minority students see that students from all racial and ethnic backgrounds must often struggle to master their lessons and that members of no ethnicity are inherently inferior intellectually to any other—perceptions that should surely go a long way toward defusing stereotype threat. Interestingly, both Black and White college students who have participated in such programs show increases in their grade-point averages, with the improvement being especially striking for Black students (Steele, as cited in Woo, 1995). Steele also claims that schools might further reduce stereotype threat by (1) ending remedial programs that set only minimal goals and (2) relying less on those kinds of affirmative-action efforts that, in subtle ways, send minorities the message that they can't compete or succeed without assistance. If there is one single principle, Steele says, it is to "challenge (minorities), don't remediate them. Challenge conveys faith in their (own) potential" (as cited in Woo, 1995)

Average performance on a difficult verbal test as a function of race and test characterization. African-American students perform poorly on tests of mental abilities when they think they are taking a test that may result in their being stereotyped as unintelligent. ADAPTED FROM STEELE & ARONSON, 1995.

---

stereotype threat
fear that one will be judged to have traits associated with negative social stereotypes about his or her racial or ethnic group

from a bag and planted in two fields—one that is barren and one that has fertile soil. Because all plants within each field were grown in the *same* soil, any differences in height among the plants within a field would have to be caused by differences in genetic makeup. But if the plants grown in the fertile soil are taller, on average, than those grown in the barren soil (see Figure 9.10), this *between-field* difference is almost certainly the result of environment—the quality of soil in which the plants grew. Similarly, even though genes partially explain individual differences in IQ *within* Black groups and White groups, the average difference in IQ between the two ethnicities may represent nothing more than differences in the environments they typically experience.

Data available on mixed-race children also fails to support the genetic hypothesis. Eyferth (as cited in Loehlin, Lindzey, & Spuhler, 1975) obtained the IQ scores of German children fathered by African-American soldiers and compared these mixed-race children to a group of German children fathered by White-American soldiers. Clearly, the mixed-race group should have scored lower than their White age-mates if their African-American fathers had had fewer IQ-enhancing genes to pass along to them. However, Eyferth found that these two groups of children did not differ in IQ. Similarly, extremely bright African-American children have no higher percentage of White ancestors than is typical of the African-American population as a whole (Scarr et al., 1977).

Despite this negative evidence, the genetic hypothesis lives on. T. Edward Reed (1997), for example, points to methodological problems with existing studies of mixed-race children that, in his opinion, call their findings into question. Other investigators claim that race differences in head and brain size (with Whites having larger heads and brains than Blacks) provide strong evidence that race differences in IQ are largely hereditary (Lynn, 1997; Rushton, 1999). Are these *physical* differences between Blacks and Whites truly evidence that *genes* are responsible for Black/White differences in IQ? Ulric Neisser (1997) certainly doesn't think so. He points out that both head and brain size are heavily influenced by such factors as adequacy of prenatal care and nutrition—*environmental* variables that differ across racial and ethnic groups and can strongly affect children's intellectual performances. So even though IQ is a genetically influenced attribute within all racial and ethnic groups, conclusions drawn in *The Bell Curve* are badly overstated. Simply stated, there is no evidence to conclusively demonstrate that *group differences* in IQ are genetically determined (Neisser et al., 1996).

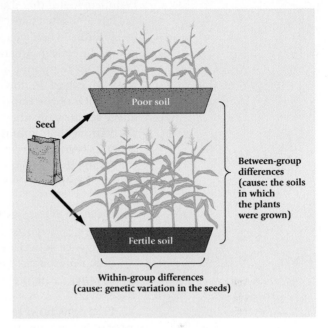

Figure 9.10 *Why within-group differences do not necessarily imply anything about between-group differences. Here we see that the difference in the heights of the plants within each field reflects the genetic variation in the seeds that were planted there, whereas the difference in the average heights of the plants across the fields is attributable to an environmental factor: the soils in which they were grown. ADAPTED FROM GLEITMAN, 1991.*

The Environmental Hypothesis

A third explanation for group differences in IQ is the **environmental hypothesis** that poor people and members of various minority groups tend to grow up in environments that are much less conducive to intellectual development than those experienced by most Whites and other members of the middle class.

Recently, developmentalists have carefully considered how a low-income or poverty-stricken lifestyle is likely to influence a family's children, and several of these findings bear directly on the issue of children's intellectual development (Duncan & Brooks-Gunn, 2000; Garrett, Ng'andu, & Ferron, 1994; McLoyd, 1998). Consider, for example, that a family's poverty status and lack of adequate income may mean that some children from low-income families are undernourished, which may inhibit brain growth and make them listless and inattentive (Pollitt, 1994). Furthermore, economic hardship creates psychological distress—a strong dissatisfaction with life's conditions that makes lower-income adults edgy and irritable and reduces their capacity to be sensitive, supportive, and highly involved in their children's learning activities (McLoyd, 1990, 1998). Finally, low-income parents are often poorly educated themselves and may have neither the knowledge nor the money to provide their children with age-appropriate books, toys, or other experiences that contribute to an intellectually stimulating home environment (Klebanov et al., 1998). Scores on the HOME inventory are consistently lower in low-income than in middle-class homes (Bradley et al., 1989; Duncan & Brooks-Gunn, 2000). And children who have always lived in poverty and whose parents have the fewest financial resources are the ones who experience the least stimulating home environments (Garrett et al., 1994). So there are ample reasons for suspecting that social class differences in intellectual performance are largely *environmental* in origin.

environmental hypothesis notion that groups differ in IQ because the environments in which they are raised are not equally conducive to intellectual growth

Carefully conducted transracial adoption studies lead to a similar conclusion. Sandra Scarr and Richard Weinberg (1983; Waldman et al., 1994; Weinberg et al., 1992) have studied more than 100 African-American (or interracial) children who were adopted by White, middle-class families. The adoptive parents were well above average in IQ and highly educated, and many had biological children of their own. Although Scarr and Weinberg found that the childhood IQs of the adoptees were about six points lower than the IQs of White children of these same families, this small racial difference seems rather insignificant when we look at the *absolute* performance of the transracial adoptees. As a group, the African-American adoptees obtained an average IQ of 106—6 points above the average for the population as a whole and 15 to 20 points above comparable children who are raised in low-income African-American communities. Ten years later, the average IQs of the transracial adoptees had declined somewhat (average = 97), although direct comparisons may be misleading since the IQ test used in the follow-up was different from that administered in childhood. Nevertheless, these transracial adolescent adoptees remained well above the average IQ obtained by low-income African-American youth, and they scored slightly higher than the national norm in academic achievement. Scarr and Weinberg (1983, p. 261; italics added) concluded that

> the high IQ scores for the black and interracial [adoptees] ... mean that (a) genetic differences do not account for a major portion of the IQ performance difference between racial groups, and (b) African-American and interracial children *reared in the* [*middle class*] *culture of the tests and the schools* perform as well as other ... children in similar families.

Let's note, however, that Scarr and her associates are not suggesting that White parents are better parents or that disadvantaged children would be better off if they were routinely placed in middle-class homes. In fact, the researchers caution that debates about who might make better parents only distract us from the more important message of the transracial adoption study—namely, that much of the intellectual and academic discrepancies that have been attributed to race or ethnicity may largely reflect *ethnic differences in socioeconomic status*. Indeed, Charlotte Patterson and her associates (1990) found that variation in family income is a better predictor of the academic competencies of Black and White schoolchildren than is ethnicity (see also Greenberg et al., 1999).

IMPROVING COGNITIVE PERFORMANCE THROUGH COMPENSATORY EDUCATION

compensatory interventions
special educational programs designed to further the cognitive growth and scholastic achievements of disadvantaged children

Head Start
large-scale preschool educational program designed to provide children from low-income families with a variety of social and intellectual experiences that might better prepare them for school

A variety of preschool education programs have been created to enrich the learning experiences of economically disadvantaged children. Project Head Start is perhaps the best known of these **compensatory interventions**. This program originated in the United States, but recent Canadian correlates have begun to appear. For example, in 1995, a four-year pilot project called Aboriginal Head Start was initiated, with many of the same objectives defined by the original Head Start program (Health Canada, Childhood and Youth Division, 2001).

The original goal of **Head Start** (and similar programs) was to provide disadvantaged children with the kinds of educational experiences that middle-class youngsters were presumably getting in their homes and nursery-school classrooms. It was hoped that these early interventions would compensate for the disadvantages that these children may have already experienced and would place them on a roughly equal footing with their middle-class peers by the time they entered Grade 1.

The earliest reports suggested that Head Start and comparable programs were a smashing success. Program participants were posting an average gain of about 10 points on IQ tests, whereas the IQs of nonparticipants from similar social backgrounds remained unchanged. However, this initial optimism soon began to wane. When program participants were reexamined after completing a year or two of elementary school, the gains they had made on IQ tests had largely disappeared (Gray & Klaus, 1970). In other words, few if any lasting intellectual benefits seemed to be associated with these interventions, thus prompting Arthur Jensen (1969, p. 2) to conclude that "compensatory education has been tried and it apparently has failed."

However, many developmentalists were reluctant to accept this conclusion. They felt that it was shortsighted to put so much emphasis on IQ scores as an index of program effectiveness. After all, the ultimate goal of compensatory education is not so much to boost IQ as to improve children's academic performance. Others have argued that the impact of these early interventions might be cumulative, so that it may be several years before the full benefits of compensatory education are apparent.

Long-Term Follow-Ups

As it turns out, Jensen's critics may have been right on both counts. In 1982 Irving Lazar and Richard Darlington reported on the long-term effects of 11 high-quality, university-based early intervention programs initiated during the 1960s. The program participants were disadvantaged preschool children. At regular intervals throughout the elementary-school years, the investigators examined the participants' scholastic records and administered IQ and achievement tests. The participants and their mothers were also interviewed to determine the children's feelings of self-worth, attitudes toward school and scholastic achievement, and vocational aspirations, as well as mothers' aspirations for their children and their feelings about their children's progress at school. Other longitudinal follow-ups of these or similar high-quality interventions have been conducted since 1982 (Barnett, 1995; Berrueta-Clement et al., 1984; Darlington, 1991). Together, these longitudinal studies suggest that program participants score higher in IQ than nonparticipants for two to three years after the interventions are over, but that their IQ scores eventually decline. Did the program fail then?

No, indeed! Children who participated in the interventions were much more likely to meet their school's basic requirements than nonparticipants were. They were less likely to be assigned to special education classes or to be retained in a grade, and they were more likely than nonparticipants to complete high school. Program participants had more positive attitudes about school and (later) about job-related successes than nonparticipants did, and their mothers were more satisfied with their academic performances and held higher occupational aspirations for them as well. There was even some evidence that teenagers who had participated in these high-quality interventions earlier in life were less likely to become pregnant or to be involved in delinquent activities and were more likely to be employed than were nonparticipants.

Can we expect to do better than this in the future? Many believe that we can if compensatory education begins earlier in life and lasts longer, and if ways are found to help parents become more involved in their children's learning activities (Ramey & Ramey, 1998).

The Importance of Parental Involvement

Comparisons of the impact of early intervention programs suggest that the most effective ones almost always involve parents in one way or another. For example, Joan Sprigle and Lyn Schaefer (1985) evaluated the long-term benefits of two preschool interventions, Head Start and Learning to Learn (LTL), a program that educated parents about its goals, provided them with informational updates about their children's progress, and repeatedly emphasized that a partnership between home and school was necessary to ensure the program's success. When the disadvantaged students who participated in these interventions were later observed in Grades 4, 5, and 6, the outcomes consistently favoured the LTL program, in which parents had been heavily involved. Although LTL students did not necessarily outperform those from Head Start on IQ tests, they were making better grades in basic academic subjects (such as reading) and were less likely to have failed a grade in school or to have been placed in costly special education classes for the learning disabled.

Other investigators favour **two-generation interventions** that not only provide children with high-quality preschool education, but also provide disadvantaged parents with social support and the educational and vocational training they need to lift themselves out of poverty (Ramey & Ramey, 1998). The research described in Box 9.5 suggests that this kind of family intervention is likely to improve parents' psychological well-being, which may translate into more effective patterns of parenting and, ultimately, into long-term gains in children's intellectual performances.

The Importance of Intervening Early

two-generation intervention
interventions with goals to both stimulate children's intellectual development through preschool daycare/education and to assist parents to move out of poverty

Critics of Head Start have argued that it begins too late (often after age 3) and is simply too brief to have any lasting impact. Might interventions that begin *in infancy* and *last for several years* produce more enduring gains in the IQs and academic performances of disadvantaged children?

APPLYING DEVELOPMENTAL RESEARCH

9.5

An Effective Compensatory Intervention for Families

In Chapters 5 and 13, we learn that disadvantaged children of teenage mothers are at risk of displaying poor cognitive development and of becoming academic underachievers throughout childhood and adolescence. Victoria Seitz and Nancy Apfel (1994b; Seitz, Rosenbaum, & Apfel, 1985) described a two-generation family intervention that looks very promising as a means of preventing these outcomes.

Seitz and Apfel's family intervention was a 30-month program targeting poverty-stricken mothers who had recently delivered healthy first-born children. It provided pediatric care, developmental evaluations, and monthly home visits by a psychologist, nurse, or social worker, who gave mothers social support, information about child-rearing and other family matters, and assistance in obtaining education or vocational training needed to land a job (or a better-paying job). The children received stimulating, high-quality daycare from a provider who met frequently with mothers to discuss their children's developmental progress and to help them deal constructively with any child-rearing problems they had encountered. Other mothers and their first-borns from the same socioeconomic backgrounds received no intervention and served as a control group.

Ten years later, Seitz and her associates (1985) followed up on the first-born children of these families to assess their academic progress. They found that children who had received the intervention were doing well. They were much more likely than control children to be attending school regularly and making normal progress, and were much less likely to have been retained in a grade or to have required costly remedial services such as special education. Clearly, this intervention appeared to benefit the children who had participated.

But there was more—what might be called a *diffusion* effect. Specifically, the *younger* siblings of the "intervention" and the "control" participants displayed precisely the same differences in scholastic outcomes that the older children did, even though these younger brothers and sisters had not been born *until the intervention was over* (Seitz & Apfel, 1994b). Apparently, this family intervention had made disadvantaged mothers who participated more involved in their children's lives and more confident and effective in their parenting—a change that not only benefited their first-born child who received stimulating daycare, but *all of their subsequent children* as well. It was an effective intervention indeed!

Two-generation family interventions that target disadvantaged children and their parents lead to changes in parenting that benefit all children in the family

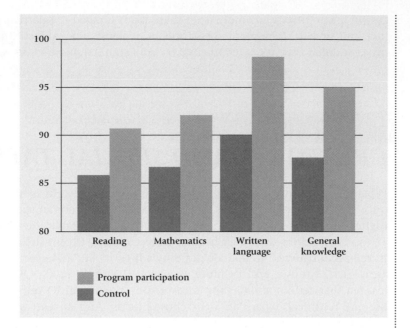

Figure 9.11 *Average academic achievement scores at age 12 for Abecedarian preschool program participants and control children.* ADAPTED FROM CAMPBELL & RAMEY, *1994.*

The Carolina Abecedarian Project (Campbell & Ramey, 1994, 1995; Campbell et al., 2001) is a particularly ambitious early intervention that was designed to answer these questions. Program participants were selected from families considered to be at risk for producing mildly retarded children. These families were all on welfare, and most were headed by a single parent, the mother, who had scored well below average on a standardized IQ test (obtaining an IQ of 70 to 85). The project began when the participating children were only 6 to 12 weeks old, and it continued for the next five years. Half of the high-risk children took part in a special daycare program designed to promote their intellectual development. The program was truly a full-time endeavour, running from 7:15 A.M. to 5:15 P.M. five days a week for 50 weeks each year, until the child entered school. The remaining control children received exactly the same dietary supplements, social services, and pediatric care given to their age-mates in the experimental group, but they did not attend daycare. At regular intervals over the next 21 years, the progress of these two groups of high-risk children was assessed by administering IQ tests. Periodic tests of academic achievement were also given at school.

Figure 9.11 summarizes the achievement scores at age 12. The high-risk daycare children began to outperform their counterparts in the control group by 18 months of age, and they *maintained* this IQ advantage over the long run (now through age 21). Here, then, is evidence that high-quality preschool education that begins very early can have *lasting* intellectual benefits. It can have lasting educational benefits, too, because the daycare children outperformed the control group in all areas of academic achievement from the third year of school onward (Campbell et al., 2001).

Programs such as the family intervention described in Box 9.5 and the Abecedarian Project are expensive to administer, and critics claim that they would not be worth the high cost of providing them to all disadvantaged families. However, such an attitude may be "penny wise and pound foolish," because Victoria Seitz and her associates (1985) found that extensive two-generation interventions emphasizing quality daycare often pay for themselves by (1) allowing more parents freedom from full-time child care to work, thereby reducing their need for public assistance, and (2) providing the foundation for cognitive growth that enables most disadvantaged children to avoid special education in school—a savings that, by itself, would justify the expense of extensive compensatory interventions (Karoly et al., 1998). And when we consider the long-term economic benefits that could accrue later in life, when gainfully employed adult graduates of highly suc-

? WHAT DO YOU THINK?

How do you feel about providing two-generation interventions on a large scale to economically disadvantaged populations? Do the demonstrated benefits justify the expenditures (which may be high)? Why or why not?

cessful interventions pay more taxes than disadvantaged nonparticipants, need less welfare, and are less often maintained at public expense in penal institutions, the net return on each dollar invested in compensatory education could be impressive indeed.

CREATIVITY AND SPECIAL TALENTS

giftedness
possession of unusually high intellectual potential or other special talent (or talents)

creativity
ability to generate novel ideas or works that are useful and valued by others

convergent thinking
thinking that requires one to come up with a single correct answer to a problem; what IQ tests measure

divergent thinking
thinking that requires a variety of ideas or solutions to a problem when there is no one correct answer

What do we mean when we say that a child or an adolescent is "gifted"? This term was once limited to people such as those in Terman's longitudinal study with IQs of 140 or higher. Yet despite their lofty IQs and generally favourable life outcomes, not one of Terman's gifted children ever became truly eminent. Recent definitions of **giftedness** have been broadened to include not only a high IQ but also special talents in particular areas such as music, art, literature, or science (Winner, 2000). Over the years, we have learned that certain abilities not measured by traditional IQ tests help some people to become technical experts in their chosen fields. And at least a few of these experts become truly innovative creators.

What Is Creativity?

Creativity may be more important than a high IQ in permitting a Mozart, an Einstein, or a Piaget to break new ground. What is creativity? Debates about the meaning of this construct have provoked nearly as much controversy as those about the meaning of intelligence (Mumford & Gustafson, 1988). Yet almost everyone agrees that **creativity** represents an ability to generate novel ideas and innovative solutions—products that are not merely new and unusual but are also appropriate in context and *valued* by others (Simonton, 2000; Sternberg & Lubart, 1996). Creativity is important *to individuals*, who must solve challenging problems on the job and in daily life, as well as *to society*, when it underlies new inventions, new scientific discoveries, and innovations in social programs or the humanities that enrich our lives. Nevertheless, creativity received little attention from the scientific community until the 1960s and 1970s, when psychometricians began to construct tests to try to measure it.

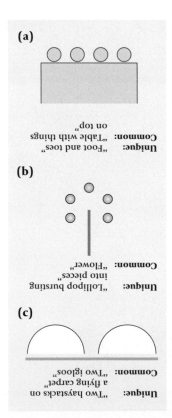

(a)

Common: "Table with things on top"
Unique: "Foot and toes"

(b)

Common: "Flower"
Unique: "Lollipop bursting into pieces"

(c)

Common: "Two igloos"
Unique: "Two haystacks on a flying carpet"

Figure 9.12 *Are you creative? Indicate what you see in each of the three drawings. Below each drawing you will find examples of unique and common responses drawn from a study of creativity in children.* ADAPTED FROM WALLACH & KOGAN, *1965.*

The Psychometric Perspective

In his structure-of-intellect model, J.P. Guilford (1967, 1988) proposed that creativity represents divergent rather than convergent thinking. **Convergent thinking** requires individuals to generate the one best answer to a problem and is precisely what IQ tests measure. By contrast, **divergent thinking** requires individuals to generate a variety of solutions to problems for which there is no one right answer. Figure 9.12 presents a *figural* measure of divergent thinking, whereas a *verbal* measure might ask respondents to list all words that can be made from the letters in the word *baseball*, and a *"real-world" problem* measure might ask them to devise as many practical uses as possible for common objects such as a clothespin or cork (Runco, 1992; Torrance, 1988).

Interestingly, divergent thinking is only modestly correlated with IQ (Wallach, 1985; Sternberg & Lubart, 1996) and seems to be more heavily influenced by children's home environments than by their genes (Plomin, 1990). Specifically, children who score high in divergent thinking have parents who encourage their intellectual curiosity and grant them a great deal of freedom to select their own interests and explore them in depth (Getzels & Jackson, 1962; Harrington, Block, & Block, 1987; Runco, 1992). So divergent thinking is a cognitive skill that is distinct from general intelligence and can be nurtured.

However, many researchers became disenchanted with the psychometric approach to creativity once it became rather obvious that the scores people make on tests of divergent thinking during childhood and adolescence are, at best, only modestly related to their creative accomplishments later in life (Feldhusen & Goh, 1995; Runco, 1992). Clearly, divergent thinking may foster creative solutions; but, by itself, it is a woefully incomplete account of what it means to be creative (Amabile, 1983; Simonton, 2000).

The Multicomponent (or Confluence) Perspective

Think for a moment about the characteristics of people you consider creative. Chances are you view them as reasonably intelligent, but it is also likely that they display such characteristics as being highly inquisitive and flexible individuals who love their work, make connections between ideas that others don't, and may be a bit unorthodox and nonconforming. This creativity syndrome may be no accident, for researchers today generally believe that creativity results from a *convergence* of many personal and situational factors (Gardner, 1993; Simonton, 2000; Sternberg & Lubart, 1996).

If creativity truly reflects *all* of the attributes above, then it is perhaps understandable why many people with high IQs are not particularly creative or why so few are truly eminent (Winner, 2000). Yet Robert Sternberg and Todd Lubart (1996) have argued that most people have the potential to be creative and will be, at least to some degree, if they can marshal the *resources* that foster creativity and can invest themselves in the right kinds of goals. Let's briefly consider this new but influential **investment theory of creativity** and its implications for promoting the creative potential of children and adolescents.

Sternberg and Lubart's Investment Theory

According to Sternberg and Lubart (1996), creative people are willing to "buy low and sell high" in the realm of ideas. "Buying low" means that they invest themselves in ideas or projects that are novel (or out of favour) and may initially encounter resistance. But by persisting in the face of such skepticism, a creative individual generates a product that is highly valued, and can now "sell high" and move on to the next novel or unpopular idea that has growth potential.

Jose Luis Pelaez, Inc./ Corbis/Magma

Parents of creative children encourage their intellectual curiosity and allow them to explore their interests in depth.

investment theory of creativity
recent theory specifying that the ability to invest in innovative projects and to generate creative solutions depends on a convergence of creative resources—namely, background knowledge, intellectual abilities, personality characteristics, motivation, and environmental support/encouragement

What factors determine whether an individual will invest in an original project and bring it to a creative end? Sternberg and Lubart believe that creativity depends on a convergence, or confluence, of six distinct but interrelated sets of resources. Let's briefly consider these components of creativity and how we might seek to promote them.

1. *Intellectual resources*. Sternberg and Lubart (1996) believe that three intellectual abilities are particularly important to creativity. One is the ability to *find new problems* to solve or see old problems in new ways. Another is the ability to *evaluate* one's ideas to determine which are worth pursuing. Finally, one must be able to *sell others* on the value of new ideas in order to gain the support that may be necessary to fully develop them. All three abilities are important. If one cannot evaluate new ideas one has generated or sell others on their value, they are unlikely to ever blossom into creative accomplishments.

2. *Knowledge*. A child, an adolescent, or an adult must be familiar with the current state of the art in her chosen area if she is ever to advance or transform it as the groundbreaking artist, musician, or science-fair winner does. As Howard Gruber (1982) puts it, "Insight comes to the prepared mind" (p. 22).

3. *Cognitive style*. A *legislative cognitive style*—that is, a preference for thinking in novel and divergent ways of *one's own choosing*—is important to creativity. It also helps to think in broad, *global* terms—to be able to distinguish the forest from the trees—which will help in deciding which of one's ideas are truly novel and worth pursuing.

4. *Personality*. Previous research indicates that the personality variables most closely associated with high creativity are a willingness to take sensible risks, to persevere in the face of uncertainty or ambiguity, and to have the self-confidence to defy the crowd and pursue ideas that will eventually win recognition.

5. *Motivation*. People rarely do creative work in an area unless they have a passion for what they are trying to accomplish and focus on *the work itself* rather than its potential rewards (Amabile, 1983). The ground-breaking Olympic gymnast Olga Korbut put it well: "If gymnastics did not exist, I would have invented it" (Feldman, 1982, p. 35). This does not mean that the prospect of winning Olympic medals had nothing to do with Ms. Korbut's success, for prizes and other incentives indicate what goals are socially valued and encourage people to work on innovative projects. But creativity can truly suffer if children focus too much on the rewards and lose their intrinsic interest in the work they are pursuing (Simonton, 2000; Winner 2000).

6. *Supportive environment*. Several studies of children with special talents in such domains as chess, music, or mathematics reveal that these child prodigies are blessed with an environment that nurtured their talents and motivations and rewarded their accomplishments (Feldman & Goldsmith, 1991; Hennessey & Amabile, 1988; Monass & Engelhard, 1990). Parents of creative youngsters generally encourage intellectual activities and accept their children's idiosyncrasies (Albert, 1994; Runco, 1992). They are also quick to recognize unusual talents and help to foster their growth by soliciting the assistance of expert coaches or tutors. Furthermore, some societies value creativity more than others do and devote many financial and human resources to nurturing creative potential (Simonton, 1994, 2000). Indeed, Olga Korbut's brilliant talent might not have bloomed had gymnastics not been so highly valued in Russian society when she was growing up.

A Test of Investment Theory

If investment theory is sound, then people who have more creative resources at their disposal should generate more creative solutions to problems. Lubart and Sternberg (1995) tested this hypothesis in a study of adolescents and adults. A battery of questionnaires, cognitive tests, and personality measures was administered to measure five of the six sets of creative resources (environment was not assessed). Participants then worked at innovative problems in writing (for example, create a story about the octopus's sneakers), art (draw a picture to illustrate "hope"), advertising (create an ad for Brussels sprouts), and science (how might we detect extraterrestrials among us?). Their solutions were then rated for creativity by a panel of judges, who showed high levels of agreement in their ratings.

The results supported investment theory in that all five sets of creativity resources were moderately to highly correlated with the creativity ratings participants received, and participants whose solutions were rated most creative were those who had higher scores across all five kinds of creative resources. Apparently, creativity does reflect the convergence of many factors rather than the possession of a dominant cognitive attribute such as divergent thinking.

Promoting Creativity in the Classroom

How might educators foster creativity in the classroom? Most current programs for gifted students concentrate on enriching and accelerating traditional learning and may do little, beyond providing background knowledge, to promote creativity (Sternberg, 1995; Winner, 1997). Gardner's theory of multiple intelligences has been used as a framework for promoting the growth of intelligences that are not heavily stressed in school. These programs enrich the experiences of all pupils to foster such abilities as *spatial intelligence* (through sculpting or painting), *kinesthetic-body intelligence* (through dance or athletics), and *linguistic intelligence* (through storytelling). Whether these efforts truly foster creativity is not yet clear, although they have been successful at identifying special talents of children who are not at all exceptional in traditional academic subjects (Ramos-Ford & Gardner, 1997).

The investment theory of creativity suggests several possible means of fostering creative potential. Were teachers to allow students more freedom to design their own art projects or science experiments and to explore any unusual interests in depth, they would more closely approximate the kind of home environment that nurtures curiosity, risk taking, perseverance, intrinsic interest, and a concern with task performance (rather than with such performance outcomes as earning a passing grade). Less emphasis on memorizing facts and obtaining correct answers (convergent thinking) and more emphasis on discussing complex problems that have many possible answers may also help students to develop divergent thinking skills, tolerance for ambiguity, and a global analytic style that fosters creative solutions. Unfortunately, attempts to further the creative potential of children are in their infancy, and it is not yet clear which procedures work best. However, the research we have reviewed implies that parents and educators might try to be a bit more enthusiastic when youngsters display an unusual passion for an offbeat or otherwise nontraditional interest. By providing such support (and exposure to experts if any are available), we may be helping to nurture the creative potential of future innovators.

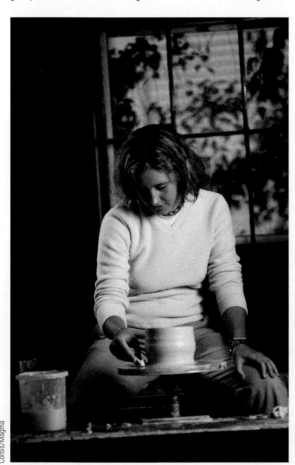

Corbis/Magma

Programs to encourage the development of "intelligences" not usually stressed at school often identify hidden talents and may foster creativity.

SUMMARY

What is Intelligence?

♦ The **psychometric** (or testing) **approach** defines intelligence as a trait (or set of traits) that allows some people to think and to solve problems more effectively than others. Alfred Binet developed the first successful intelligence test, which conceived of intelligence as a general mental ability. Yet researchers relying on **factor analysis** argue that intelligence is not a singular trait. Spearman viewed intelligence as a *general mental ability* (or *g*) and *special abilities* (or *s*), each of which was specific to a particular test. Thurstone claimed that intelligence consists of seven **primary mental abilities**. Guilford's **structure-of-intellect model** proposed that intelligence consists of 180 mental abilities, whereas Cattel and Horn make a distinction between **fluid intelligence** and **crystallized intelligence**. **Hierarchical models**, such as Carroll's **three-stratum theory of intelligence**, are the most elaborate psychometric classifications of mental abilities to date.

♦ New viewpoints on intelligence are becoming increasingly influential. Robert Sternberg's **triarchic theory** criticizes psychometric theories of intelligence for their failure to consider the *contexts* in which intelligent acts are displayed, the test taker's *experience* with test items, and the *information-processing strategies* on which people rely when thinking or solving problems.

♦ Gardner's **theory of multiple intelligences**, which is currently influencing research on creativity and special talents, contends that human beings display at least seven distinctive kinds of intelligence, several of which are not assessed by traditional intelligence tests.

How is Intelligence Measured?

♦ Today, there are literally hundreds of intelligence tests, and the **Stanford-Binet Intelligence Scale** and the **Wechsler Intelligence Scale for Children—III (WISC-III)** are widely used. Both scales compare children's performance against **test norms** for age-mates and assign them **intelligence quotients (IQs)**, which are normally distributed around the average score of 100. Many of these tests have been given to Canadian participants in order to generate Canadian norms. In addition, some have been translated into French to permit better access among francophones.

♦ New approaches to intelligence testing include the **Kaufman Assessment Battery for Children (K-ABC)**, which is grounded in information-processing theory, and **dynamic assessment**, which is compatible with Vygotsky's theory and Sternberg's triarchic theory.

♦ Infant intelligence tests, which tap perceptual and motor skills and assign **developmental quotient (DQ)** scores, are poor predictors of childhood IQs. Newer measures of infant information-processing capabilities are much better predictors of later intellectual performance.

♦ IQ is a relatively stable attribute for some individuals. However, many others will show wide variations in their IQ scores over the course of childhood. The fact that IQ can wander upward or downward over time suggests that IQ tests measure intellectual *performance* rather than an inborn capacity for thinking and problem solving. Children whose home environments are stable and stimulating often display IQ stability or increases over time, whereas children from impoverished backgrounds often display a **cumulative deficit** in IQ.

What Do Intelligence Tests Predict?

♦ When we consider trends for the population as a whole, IQ scores predict important outcomes such as future academic accomplishments, occupational status, and even health and happiness. But at the individual level, an IQ score is not always a reliable indicator of one's future health, happiness, or success. Besides IQ, one's family background, work habits, education, **tacit (or practical) intelligence**, and motivation to succeed are important contributors to the successes one attains.

Factors that Influence IQ Scores

♦ Both heredity and environment contribute heavily to intellectual performance. The evidence from twin studies and studies of adopted children indicates that about half the variation among individuals in IQ is attributable to hereditary factors. But regardless of one's genetic predispositions, barren intellectual environments clearly inhibit cognitive growth, whereas enriched, intellectually stimulating environments can clearly promote it as evidenced by the Flynn effect.

Social and Cultural Correlates of Intellectual Performance

♦ Research with the **HOME inventory** reveals that parents who create a stimulating home environment by becoming involved in their children's learning activities, explaining new concepts, and providing age-appropriate challenges and consistent encouragement are likely to have children who score relatively high in academic achievement and IQ.

♦ A common finding cited in both Canadian and American studies is that individuals of Asian ancestry outperform White and Black individuals, and that White individuals outperform First Nations individuals on IQ tests. Similarly, children from middle-class backgrounds tend to outperform those from lower-income backgrounds on IQ tests. Among American populations, these differences are still apparent on **culture-fair IQ tests**, and although some minority students may be less motivated in testing situations or may display the effects of **stereotype threat, cultural test bias** does not explain all the group differences in IQ. Nor is there any conclusive evidence for the **genetic hypothesis** (or the **Level I–Level II** distinction), which posits that group differences in IQ are hereditary. The best explanation for group differences in IQ is the **environmental hypothesis**: many poor people and minority group members score lower on IQ tests because they grow up in impoverished environments that are much less conducive to intellectual development than those of their middle-class age-mates.

Improving Cognitive Performance through Compensatory Education

♦ **Head Start** and other **compensatory interventions** for disadvantaged preschoolers rarely produce lasting gains in IQ. However, the best of these interventions do improve children's chances of succeeding in the classroom, and they help to prevent the progressive decline in intellectual performance and academic achievement so often observed among students from disadvantaged backgrounds.

♦ Compensatory education is most effective when it starts early, lasts through the preschool period, and involves children's parents. The **two-generation interventions** and those beginning early in infancy look especially promising.

Creativity and Special Talents

♦ Definitions of **giftedness** have been expanded to include not only a high IQ but also special talents, including **creativity**.

♦ Psychometricians distinguish IQ (which rests on **convergent thinking**) from creativity, or **divergent thinking**. Although divergent thinking is only modestly correlated with IQ, it also fails to predict future creativity very well.

♦ Recent multicomponent (or confluence) perspectives, such as the **investment theory of creativity**, specify that a variety of cognitive, personal, motivational, and environmental resources combine to foster creative problem solving. This theory looks very promising, both in terms of its existing empirical support and its suggestions for fostering creativity.

KEY TERMS

psychometric approach, 312

mental age (MA), 313

factor analysis, 313

g, 313

s, 313

primary mental abilities, 313

structure-of-intellect model, 314

fluid intelligence, 315

crystallized intelligence, 315

hierarchical model of intelligence, 315

three-stratum theory of intelligence, 315

triarchic theory, 316

cultural bias, 317

theory of multiple intelligences, 318

Stanford-Binet Intelligence Scale, 319

intelligence quotient (IQ), 320

test norms, 320

Wechsler Intelligence Scale for Children—III (WISC-III), 321

normal distribution, 322

Kaufman Assessment Battery for Children (K-ABC), 323

dynamic assessment, 323

developmental quotient (DQ), 323

cumulative-deficit hypothesis, 326

tacit (or practical) intelligence, 327

mental retardation, 328

Flynn effect, 331

HOME inventory, 332

cultural test bias hypothesis, 336

culture-fair IQ tests, 336

genetic hypothesis, 337

Level I abilities, 337

Level II abilities, 337

stereotype threat, 338

environmental hypothesis, 339

compensatory interventions, 340

Head Start, 340

two-generation intervention, 342

giftedness, 344

creativity, 344

convergent thinking, 344

divergent thinking, 344

investment theory of creativity, 345

 You can find further information on the topics covered in this chapter by visiting:

www.developmentalpsych2e.nelson.com

 For additional reading, go to InfoTrac College Edition, your on-line research library, at:

infotrac.thomsonlearning.com

10

Development of Language and Communication Skills

Five Components of Language

Theories of Language Development

Before Language: The Prelinguistic Period

One Word at a Time: The Holophrastic Period

From Holophrases to Simple Sentences: The Telegraphic Period

Language Learning during the Preschool Period

Language Learning during Middle Childhood and Adolescence

Learning More Than One Language: Bilingualism

Summary

"Rrrrrruh! Rrrrrruh!" exclaims 11-month-old Carlos as he sits in his exerciser looking out the window. "What are you saying, little man?" asks his aunt Maria. "He's saying daddy's car is in the driveway; he's home from work!" Carlos's mother replies.

"Oops! It broked. Fix it daggy." (18-month-old Ani responding to the arm that has come loose from her doll)

"I can see clearly now … I see all *icicles* in my way." (2½-year-old Todd singing his rendition of a popular song; the correct lyric is "obstacles")

One truly astounding achievement that sets humans apart from the rest of the animal kingdom is our creation and use of **language**. Although animals can **communicate** with one another, their limited number of calls and gestures are merely isolated signals that convey very specific messages (for example, a greeting, a threat, a summons to congregate) in much the same way that single words or stereotyped phrases do in a human language (Tomasello & Camaioni, 1997). By contrast, human languages are amazingly *flexible* and *productive*. From a small number of individually meaningless sounds, children come to generate thousands of meaningful auditory patterns (syllables, words, and even idiosyncratic vocables such as Carlos's "Rrrrrruh!") that are eventually combined according to a set of grammatical rules (with a few missteps, such as Ani's use of the word *broked*) to produce an infinite number of messages. Language is also an *inventive* tool with which we express our thoughts and interpretations (or in Todd's case, misinterpretations) of what we have seen, heard, or otherwise experienced. In singing the lyrics above, Todd was trying to faithfully reproduce what he had heard. However, most of what children say in any given situation is not merely a repetition of what they have said or heard before; speakers create many novel utterances on the spot, and the topics they talk about may have nothing to do with their current state or the stream of ongoing events. Yet creative as they may be in generating new messages, even 3- and 4-year-olds are generally able to converse quite well with each other as long as their statements adhere to the rules and social conventions of the language they are speaking.

Although language is one of the most abstract bodies of knowledge we ever acquire, children in all cultures come to understand and use this intricate form of communication very early in life. In fact, some infants are talking before they can walk. How is this possible? Are infants biologically programmed to acquire language?

What kinds of linguistic input must they receive in order to become language users? Is there any relation between a child's cooing, gesturing, or babbling and the later production of meaningful words? How do infants and toddlers come to attach meaning to words? Do all children pass through the same steps or stages as they acquire their native language? And what practical lessons must children learn to become truly effective communicators? These are only a few of the issues we will consider as we trace the development of children's linguistic skills and try to determine how youngsters become so proficient in using language at such an early age.

FIVE COMPONENTS OF LANGUAGE

Perhaps the most basic question that **psycholinguists** have tried to answer is the "what" question: What must children learn in order to master the intricacies of their native tongue? After many years and literally thousands of studies, researchers have concluded that five kinds of knowledge underlie the growth of linguistic proficiency: *phonology, morphology, semantics, syntax,* and *pragmatics.*

Phonology

Phonology refers to the basic units of sound, or **phonemes**, that are used in a language and the rules for combining these sounds (for example, in English, the sounds /p/ and /b/). Each language uses only a subset of sounds that humans are capable of generating, and no two languages have precisely the same phonologies, which explains why foreign languages may sound strange to us. Clearly, children must learn how to discriminate, produce, and combine the speechlike sounds of their native tongue in order to make sense of the speech they hear and to be understood when they try to speak.

Animals communicate through a series of calls and gestures that convey a limited number of very specific messages.

PhotoDisc, Inc.

language
small number of individually meaningless symbols (sounds, letters, gestures) that can be combined according to agreed-on rules to produce an infinite number of messages

communication
process by which one organism transmits information to and influences another

psycholinguists
those who study the structure and development of children's language

phonology
the sound system of a language and the rules for combining these sounds to produce meaningful units of speech

phonemes
basic units of sound that are used in a spoken language

Morphology

Rules of **morphology** specify how words are formed from sounds. In English these rules include the rule for forming past tenses of verbs by adding *–ed*, the rule for forming plurals by adding *–s*, rules for using other prefixes and suffixes, and rules that specify proper combinations of sounds to form meaningful words. We learn, for example, that *flow* (not *vlow*) is how to describe what the river is doing.

Semantics

Semantics refers to the *meanings* expressed in words and sentences. The smallest meaningful units of language are called **morphemes,** and there are two types. **Free morphemes** can stand alone as words (e.g., *dog*) whereas **bound morphemes** cannot stand alone but change meaning when attached to a free morpheme (e.g., adding the bound morpheme *–s* to the word *dog* means that the speaker is talking about more than one animal). Clearly, children must recognize that words and bound grammatical morphemes convey meaning—that they symbolize particular objects, actions, and relations and can be combined to form larger and more complex meanings (sentences)—before they can comprehend the speech of others or be understood when they speak.

Syntax

Language also involves **syntax**, or the rules that specify how words are to be combined to form meaningful phrases and sentences. Consider these three sentences:

1. Garfield Odie bit.
2. Garfield bit Odie.
3. Odie bit Garfield.

Even very young speakers of English recognize that the first sentence violates the rules of English sentence structure, although this word order would be perfectly acceptable in languages with a different syntax, such as French. The second and third sentences are grammatical English sentences that contain the same words but convey very different meanings. They also illustrate how word meanings (semantics) interact with sentence structure (word order) to give the entire sentence a meaning. Clearly, children must acquire a basic understanding of the syntactical features of their native tongue before they can become proficient at speaking or understanding that language.

Pragmatics

Language learners must also master the **pragmatics** of language—knowledge of how language might be used to *communicate effectively*. Imagine a 6-year-old who is trying to explain a new game to her 2-year-old brother. Clearly, she cannot speak to the toddler as if he were an adult or an age-mate; she has to adjust her speech to his linguistic capabilities if she hopes to be understood.

Pragmatics also involves **sociolinguistic knowledge**—culturally specified rules that dictate how language should be used in particular social contexts. A 3-year-old may not yet realize that the best way of getting a cookie from grandma is to say, "Grandma, may I please have a cookie?" rather than demanding "Gimme a cookie, grandma!" In order to communicate most effectively, children must become "social editors" and take into account where they are, with whom they are speaking, and what the listener already knows, needs, and wants to hear.

morphology
rules governing the formation of meaningful words from sounds

semantics
expressed meaning of words and sentences

morphemes
smallest meaningful language units

free morphemes
morphemes that can stand alone as a word (e.g., *cat, go, yellow*)

bound morphemes
morphemes that cannot stand alone but that modify the meaning of free morphemes (e.g., the *–ed* attached to English verbs to indicate past tense)

syntax
structure of a language; the rules specifying how words and grammatical markers are to be combined to produce meaningful sentences

pragmatics
principles that underlie the effective and appropriate use of language in social contexts

sociolinguistic knowledge
culturally specific rules specifying how language should be structured and used in particular social contexts

Finally, the task of becoming an effective communicator requires not only a knowledge of the five aspects of language but also an ability to properly interpret and use *nonverbal signals* (facial expressions, gestures, and so on) that often help to clarify the meaning of verbal messages and are important means of communicating in their own right. This brings us to a second basic question: *How* do young, cognitively immature toddlers and preschool children acquire all this knowledge so quickly?

THEORIES OF LANGUAGE DEVELOPMENT

As psycholinguists began to chart the course of language development, they were amazed that children could learn such a complex symbol system at such a breathtaking pace. After all, many infants are using arbitrary and *abstract signifiers* (words) to refer to objects and activities before they can walk. And by age 5, children already seem to know and use most of the syntactical structures of their native tongue, even though they have yet to receive their first formal lesson in grammar. How do they do it?

In addressing the "how" question, we will once again encounter a nativist/empiricist (nature/nurture) controversy. Learning theorists represent the empiricist point of view. From their perspective, language is obviously *learned*: after all, Japanese children acquire Japanese, French children acquire French, and profoundly deaf children of hearing parents may acquire few formal communication skills unless they receive instruction in sign language. However, other theorists point out that children the world over seem to display similar linguistic achievements at about the same age: They all babble by 4 to 6 months of age, utter their first meaningful word by age 12 to 13 months, begin to combine words by the end of the second year, and know the meanings of many thousands of words and are constructing a staggering array of grammatical sentences by the tender age of 4 or 5. These **linguistic universals** suggested to *nativists* that language acquisition is a *biologically programmed* activity that may even involve highly specialized linguistic processing capabilities that operate most efficiently early in childhood.

Of course, there is an intermediate point of view favoured by an increasing number of *interactionists*, who believe that language acquisition reflects a complex interplay among a child's biological predispositions, her cognitive development, and the characteristics of her unique linguistic environment.

The Learning (or Empiricist) Perspective

Ask most adults how children learn language and they are likely to say that children imitate what they hear, are reinforced when they use proper grammar, and are corrected when they say things wrong. Indeed, learning theorists have emphasized these same processes—imitation and reinforcement—in their own theories of language learning.

In 1957, B.F. Skinner published a book entitled *Verbal Behavior* in which he argued that children learn to speak appropriately because they are reinforced for grammatical speech. He believed that adults begin to shape a child's speech by selectively reinforcing those aspects of babbling that most resemble words, thereby increasing the probability that these sounds will be repeated. Once they have "shaped" sounds into words, adults then withhold further reinforcement (attention or approval) until the child begins combining words, first into primitive sentences and then into longer grammatical utterances. Other social-learning theorists (e.g., Bandura, 1971; Whitehurst & Vasta, 1975) add that children acquire much of their linguistic knowledge by carefully listening to and *imitating* the language of older companions. So according to the learning perspective, caregivers "teach" language by modelling and reinforcing grammatical speech.

linguistic universal
aspect of language development
that all children share

Rick Friedman/Corbis/Magma

*Noam Chomsky's nativist theory
dominated thinking about language development in the 1960s
and 1970s.*

**language acquisition device
(LAD)**
Chomsky's term for the innate
knowledge of grammar that
humans were said to possess,
which might enable young
children to infer the rules
governing others' speech and to
use these rules to produce
language

**language-making capacity
(LMC)**
hypothesized set of specialized
linguistic processing skills that
enable children to analyze speech
and to detect phonological,
semantic, and syntactical
relationships

Evaluation of the Learning Perspective

Imitation and reinforcement clearly play some part in early language development. Certainly, it is no accident that children end up speaking the same language their parents speak, down to the regional accent. In addition, young children are quicker to acquire and use the proper names for novel toys when reinforced for doing so by receiving the toys to play with (Whitehurst & Valdez-Menchaca, 1988). Finally, parents who frequently encourage conversations and who produce many novel and sophisticated words (e.g., *vehicle* rather than *car*) in the context of play, storybook reading, and other supportive interventions have children who are more advanced in their language development than age-mates whose parents converse less often or use a less diverse vocabulary (Bohannon & Bonvillain, 1997; Weizman & Snow, 2001).

Despite these observations, learning theorists have had little success accounting for the development of syntax. If parents really "shaped" grammar, as Skinner claimed, then they ought to reliably praise or otherwise reinforce the child's grammatical utterances. Yet careful analyses of conversations between mothers and young children reveal that a mother's approval or disapproval depends far more on the *truth value* (semantics) of what a child says than on the statement's grammatical correctness (Baron, 1992; Brown, Cazden, & Bellugi, 1969). So if a child gazing at a cow says, "Him cow" (truthful but grammatically incorrect), his mother is likely to approve ("That's right!"), yet if the child says, "There's a dog!" (grammatically correct, but untruthful), his mother would probably correct him ("No, that's a *cow!*"). Clearly, these findings cast doubt on the notion that parents shape syntax by directly reinforcing grammatical speech.

Nor is there much evidence that children acquire grammatical rules by imitating adult speech. Many of a child's earliest sentences are highly creative statements such as "Allgone cookie" or "It broked" that do not appear in adult speech and could not have been learned by imitation. And when young children do try to imitate an adult utterance such as "Look, the kitty is climbing the tree," they condense it to conform to their existing level of grammatical competence, saying something like "Kitty climb tree" (Baron, 1992; Bloom, Hood, & Lightbown, 1974).

How, then, might young children acquire grammatical knowledge if they do not directly imitate adult grammar and are not consistently reinforced for speaking grammatically? A number of psychologists have proposed a biological theory of language development—*nativism*—in an attempt to answer this question.

The Nativist Perspective

According to the nativists, human beings are biologically programmed to acquire language. Linguist Noam Chomsky (1959; 1968) has argued that the structure of even the simplest of languages is incredibly elaborate—far too complex, he believed, to be either taught by parents (as Skinner proposed) or discovered via simple trial-and-error processes by cognitively immature toddlers and preschool children. Instead, Chomsky proposed that we humans (and only humans) come equipped with a **language acquisition device (LAD)**—an inborn linguistic processor that is activated by verbal input. According to Chomsky, the LAD contains a *universal grammar*, or knowledge of universal rules common to all languages. So regardless of the language (or languages) a child has been listening to, the LAD should permit any child who has acquired a sufficient vocabulary to combine words into novel, rule-bound utterances and to understand much of what she hears.

Other nativists make similar claims. Dan Slobin (1985), for example, does not assume that children have any innate knowledge of language (as Chomsky did), but he thinks that they have an inborn **language-making capacity (LMC)**—a set of cognitive and perceptual abilities that are highly specialized for language learning. Presumably, these innate mechanisms (a LAD or LMC) enable young children to process linguistic input and to infer the phonological regularities, semantic relations, and rules of syntax that characterize whatever language they are listening to. These inferences about the meaning and structure of linguistic information represent a "theory" of language that children construct for themselves and use to guide their own attempts to communicate (see Figure 10.1). Of course, young children are likely to make some erroneous inferences because their linguistic database is very limited, but as they continue to process more and more input, their underlying theories of language become increasingly elaborate until they eventually approximate those used by adults. For the nativists, then, language acquisition is quite natural and almost automatic, as long as children have linguistic data to process.

Support for the Nativist Perspective

Are children biologically programmed to acquire language? Several observations seem to suggest that they are. For example, we've noted that children the world over reach certain linguistic milestones at about the same age, despite cultural differences in the structure of their languages. Nativists interpret these *linguistic universals* as clear evidence that language must be guided by some species-specific biological blueprint. Even some retarded children who perform very poorly on a broad range of cognitive tasks nevertheless acquire a near-normal knowledge of syntax and become quite adequate conversationalists (Flavell, Miller, & Miller, 1993; Pinker, 1991).

Also consistent with the nativist viewpoint is the observation that language is species-specific. Although animals can communicate with each other, no species has ever devised anything in the wild that closely resembles an abstract, rule-bound linguistic system. After years of training, apes can learn simple sign languages and other symbolic codes that enable the best of them to communicate with humans at a level comparable to that of a 2- to 2½-year-old child (Savage-Rumbaugh et al., 1993). Only humans spontaneously use language.

BRAIN SPECIALIZATION AND LANGUAGE. As we learned in Chapter 5, the brain is a lateralized organ with major language centres in the left cerebral hemisphere. Damage to one of these language areas typically results in *aphasia*—a loss of one or more language functions; the symptoms that an aphasic displays depend on the site and the extent of the injury. Injuries to **Broca's area**, near the frontal lobe of the left hemisphere, typically affect speech production rather than comprehension (Slobin, 1979). By contrast, patients who suffer an injury to **Wernicke's area**, on the temporal lobe of the left hemisphere, have difficulty understanding speech but may speak fluently albeit nonsensically.

Apparently, the left hemisphere is sensitive to some aspects of language from birth. In the first day of life, speech sounds already elicit more electrical activity from the left side of an infant's brain, while music and other nonspeech sounds produce greater activity from the right cerebral hemisphere (Molfese, 1977). Furthermore, we learned in Chapter 6 that infants are quite capable of discriminating important phonetic contrasts in the first few days and weeks of life (Miller & Eimas, 1996). These findings seem to imply that the neonate is "prewired" for speech perception and is prepared to analyze speechlike sounds.

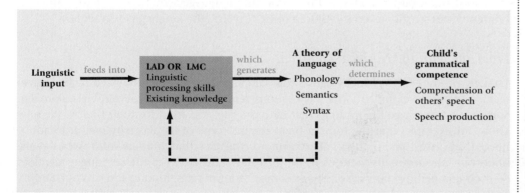

Figure 10.1 *A model of language acquisition proposed by nativists.*

Broca's area
structure located in the frontal lobe of the left hemisphere of the cerebral cortex that controls language production

Wernicke's area
structure located in the temporal lobe of the left hemisphere of the cerebral cortex that is responsible for interpreting speech

Figure 10.2 *As shown here, there is a clear relationship between the age at which immigrants arrived in the United States and their eventual adult performance in English grammar. Those who arrived early in childhood end up performing like native speakers of English, whereas those who arrived as teenagers or adults perform much more poorly.* ADAPTED FROM JOHNSON & NEWPORT, 1989.

sensitive-period hypothesis (of language acquisition)
notion that human beings are most proficient at language learning before they reach puberty

THE SENSITIVE-PERIOD HYPOTHESIS. Many years ago, nativist Erik Lenneberg (1967) proposed that languages should be most easily acquired between birth and puberty, the period when the lateralized human brain is becoming increasingly specialized for linguistic functions. This **sensitive-period hypothesis** for language development was prompted by observations that child aphasics often recover their lost language functions without special therapy, whereas adult aphasics usually require extensive therapeutic interventions to recover even part of their lost language skills. Lenneberg's explanation for this intriguing age difference was straightforward. Presumably, the right hemisphere of a child's relatively unspecialized brain can assume any linguistic functions lost when the left hemisphere is damaged. By contrast, the brain of a person who is past puberty is already fully specialized for language and other neurological duties. So aphasia may persist in adolescents and adults because the right hemisphere is no longer available to assume linguistic skills lost from a traumatic injury to the left side of the brain.

If language really is most easily acquired before puberty, then children who were largely deprived of a normal linguistic environment should find it difficult to acquire language later in life. Two excellent case studies reflect nicely on this idea. One is the case of Genie, a child who was locked away in a back room as an infant and was not discovered by the authorities until she was nearly 14 years old. While confined, Genie heard very little language; no one was permitted to talk to her, and she was beaten by an abusive father if she made any noise (Curtiss, 1977). Then there is Chelsea, a deaf woman who—because of her deafness and her family's isolation—was 32 years old before she was ever exposed to a formal language system. Extensive efforts were undertaken to teach these women language, and each made remarkable progress, learning the meaning of many words and even producing lengthy sentences that were rich in their semantic content. Yet neither woman has mastered the rules of syntax that virtually all children acquire without formal instruction (Curtiss, 1977; 1988), thus suggesting that learning a first language is easier early in life.

What about learning a second language? Is acquiring a foreign language a tougher task for a postpubertal adolescent whose sensitive period for language learning is over? Research by Jacqueline Johnson and Elissa Newport suggests that this may be the case. In one study (Johnson & Newport, 1989), native speakers of Korean or Chinese who had emigrated to the United States at different ages were tested as adults for mastery of English grammar. As we see in Figure 10.2, immigrants who began to learn English between 3 and 7 years of age were as proficient in English as native speakers are. By contrast, immigrants who arrived after puberty (particularly after age 15) performed rather poorly. Similarly, deaf adults show much better mastery of sign language if they were exposed to it as young children than if their training began later in life (Newport, 1991).

Finally, there are differences between early and late second language learners in the organization of the brain. Specifically, speaking either of their two languages activates the *same* area of the brain in bilinguals who acquired their second language in early childhood, whereas speaking two languages activates *different* areas of the brain in bilinguals who acquired their second language after puberty (Kim et al., 1997).

Taken together, these findings imply that language learning is easier (and may even occur differently) early in life, almost as if the cognitive system of the young child is especially well suited for this task. What's more, nativists interpret the research presented in Box 10.1 as a rather dramatic illustration that language acquisition is a fundamental human characteristic—even if children must "invent" the language they acquire.

Problems with the Nativist Approach

Though almost everyone today agrees that language learning is influenced by biological factors, many developmentalists have serious reservations about the nativist approach. Some have challenged the findings that nativists cite as support for their theory. We now know, for example, that the human brain retains some of its plasticity well into adulthood (Nelson & Bloom, 1997). Furthermore, the fact that human infants can make important phonemic distinctions in the first days and weeks of life no longer seems to be such compelling support for the existence of a uniquely human LAD. Why? Simply because the young of other species (for example, rhesus monkeys and chinchillas) show similar powers of auditory discrimination (Passingham, 1982).

On the "Invention" of Language by Children

Suppose that 10 children were raised in isolation by an adult caregiver who attended to their basic needs but never talked or even gestured to them in any way. Would these youngsters devise some method of communicating among themselves? No one can say for sure because children such as these have never been studied. However, the results of two programs of research suggest that our hypothetical children not only would learn to communicate but also might even invent their own language.

Transforming Pidgins into True Languages

When adults from different cultures migrate to the same area, they often begin to communicate in **pidgin**—a hybrid of their various languages that enables them to convey basic meanings and thus understand each other. In the 1870s, for example, large numbers of immigrants from China, Korea, Japan, the Philippines, Portugal, and Puerto Rico migrated to Hawaii to work in the sugar fields. What evolved from this influx was Hawaiian Pidgin English, a communication system with a small vocabulary and a few basic rules for combining words that enabled residents from different linguistic communities to communicate well enough to get by. Yet in the course of a generation, this pidgin was transformed into a **creole**—that is, a true language that evolves from a pidgin. Indeed, Hawaiian Creole English was a rich language with a vocabulary that sprang from the pidgin and its foreign language predecessors and had formal syntactical rules. How did this transformation from marginal pidgin to true language occur so rapidly?

Linguist Derek Bickerton (1983; 1984) claims that children of pidgin-speaking parents do not continue to speak pidgin. Instead, they spontaneously invent syntactical rules that creolize the pidgin to make it a true language that future generations in these multilingual communities will use. How did he decide that children were responsible? One clue was that whenever pidgins arise, they are quickly transformed into creoles, usually within a single generation. But the more important clue was that creole syntax closely resembles the (often inappropriate) sentences that young children construct when acquiring virtually any language. For example, questions of the form "Where he is going?"

and double negatives such as "I haven't got none" are perfectly acceptable in creole languages. Finally, the structure of different creoles is similar the world over—so similar that it cannot be attributed to chance. Bickerton believes that only a nativist model can account for these observations. He says: "The most cogent explanation of this similarity ... is that it derives from ... a species-specific program for language, genetically coded and expressed ... in the structures ... and operation of the human brain" (Bickerton, 1984, p. 173).

Unfortunately, no one has yet carefully observed the language development of children whose parents speak pidgins; thus it is not completely clear that children transform pidgins to creoles by themselves (as Bickerton claims), without adult assistance (Bohannon et al., 1990; Tomasello, 1995). So let's consider a second set of observations.

Creating a Sign Language

Deaf children often develop sets of gestures that symbolize objects and actions and allow them to communicate with their hearing parents (Goldin-Meadow & Mylander, 1984). Might deaf youngsters raised together create their own sign language?

Recent observations suggest that they may indeed. When the Sandinistas assumed power in Nicaragua in 1979, they established schools for deaf children, many of whom had never met another deaf person and who had relied on idiosyncratic gestures to communicate with hearing members of their families. Soon these pupils began to pool their individual gestures into a system, similar to a spoken pidgin, that allowed them to communicate. Yet, the more remarkable observation is that the second generation of deaf pupils has transformed this pidgin sign into a full-blown language—Nicaraguan Sign Language—complete with grammatical signs and rules that enable its users to express the same range of ideas and messages that are possible in spoken languages (Brownlee, 2001).

So it seems that children who lack a formal linguistic model—be they deaf or subjected to marginally linguistic pidgins—will create language-like codes to communicate with their companions. Apparently, they have some linguistic predispositions that serve them well.

Others have argued that nativists don't really *explain* language development by attributing it to a built-in language acquisition device. An explanation would require knowing *how* such an inborn processor sifts through linguistic input and infers the rules of language, yet nativists are not at all clear about how a LAD (or LMC) might operate (Moerk, 1989).[1] In some ways, attributing language development to the mysterious workings of a LAD or LMC is like saying that physical growth is biologically programmed—and then stopping there, failing to identify the underlying variables (nutrition, hormones, and so forth) that explain why growth follows the course that it takes. Clearly, the nativist approach is woefully incomplete; it is really more a description of language learning than a true explanation.

pidgins
structurally simple communication systems that arise when people who share no common language come into constant contact

creoles
languages that develop when pidgins are transformed into grammatically complex "true" languages

---

[1]Connectionists have created computer models that process linguistic input (Elman et al., 1996). These computer models do not assume that humans possess an inborn grammar module (or LAD) as nativists do, and they have achieved some success at estimating how young children might infer the meanings of individual words and some rules of syntax from regularities in the speech they hear. However, none of these artificial neural networks has come close to the linguistic computational powers of a typical 2½ to 3-year-old (Brownlee, 2001).

Finally, there are those who claim that nativists, who focus almost exclusively on biological mechanisms and on the deficiencies of learning theories, have simply overlooked the many ways in which a child's language environment promotes linguistic competencies. Let's now turn to a third theoretical viewpoint that claims that language development reflects an interaction of nature and nurture.

The Interactionist Perspective

Proponents of the **interactionist theory** believe that both learning theorists and nativists are partially correct: Language development results from a complex interplay among biological maturation, cognitive development, and an ever-changing linguistic environment that is heavily influenced by the child's desire to communicate with her companions (Bohannon & Bonvillian, 1997; Tomasello, 1995).

Biological and Cognitive Contributors

Clearly, the remarkable similarities that young children display when learning very different languages imply that biology contributes to language acquisition. But must we attribute language development to the mysterious workings of a LAD or LMC to explain these linguistic universals?

Apparently not. According to the interactionist viewpoint, young children the world over talk alike and display other linguistic universals because they are all members of the same species *who share many common experiences*. What is inborn is not any specialized linguistic knowledge or processing skills but rather a sophisticated brain that *matures* very slowly and predisposes children to develop similar ideas at about the same age— ideas that they are then motivated to express in their own speech (Bates, 1993; Tomasello, 1995). Indeed, there is ample support for links between general cognitive development and language development. For example, words are symbols, and infants speak their first meaningful words at about 12 months of age, shortly after they first display some capacity for symbolism in their *deferred imitation* of adult models (Meltzoff, 1988c). Furthermore, we will see that infants' first words centre heavily on objects they have manipulated or on actions they have performed—in short, on aspects of experience they can understand through their sensorimotor schemes (Pan & Gleason, 1997). Finally, words like *gone* and *oh oh* emerge during the second year, about the same time infants are mastering *object permanence* and are beginning to appraise the success or failure of their problem-solving activities (Gopnik & Meltzoff, 1987). So infants and toddlers often seem to talk about whatever cognitive understandings they are acquiring at the moment.

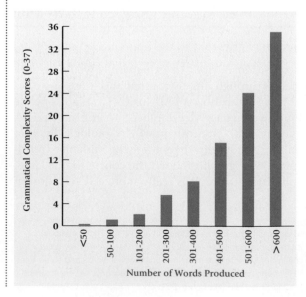

Figure 10.3 *Grammatical complexity increases as a function of the size of children's productive vocabulary.* FROM BATES, 1999.

interactionist theory
notion that biological factors and environmental influences interact to determine the course of language development

Like the nativists, then, interactionists believe that children are biologically prepared to acquire a language. However, the preparation consists *not* of a LAD or LMC but, rather, of a powerful human brain that slowly matures, allowing children to gain more and more knowledge, which gives them more to talk about. However, this does not mean that biological maturation and cognitive development totally explain language development. Elizabeth Bates (1999) believes that grammatical speech arises out of *social* necessity: As children's vocabularies increase beyond 100 to 200 words, they must find ways of organizing all this linguistic knowledge to produce utterances that others will understand. Consistent with Bates's idea, there is a strong relationship between the number of words young children have acquired and the grammatical complexity of their utterances (Robinson & Mervis, 1998) (Figure 10.3). But how might young children discover subtle points of grammar without the aid of a specialized linguistic processor? Here is where the linguistic environment comes into play.

Environmental Supports for Language Development

Interactionists stress that language is primarily a means of *communicating* that develops in the context of social interactions as children and their companions strive to get their messages across one way or another (Bohannon & Bonvillian, 1997; Tomasello, 1995). Over the years, psychologists have discovered that parents and older children have distinctive ways of talking to and interacting with infants and toddlers—that is, strategies for communicating with them that seem to foster language learning. Let's see what they have learned.

LESSONS FROM JOINT ACTIVITIES. Long before infants use words, their caregivers show them how to take turns in conversations, even if the only thing these young infants can contribute when their turn comes is to laugh or babble (Bruner, 1983). As adults converse with young children, they create a supportive learning environment (zone of proximal development) that helps the children grasp the regularities of language (Bruner, 1983; Harris, 1992). For example, parents may go through their children's favourite picture books at bedtime asking, "What's this?" or "What does the kitty say?" This gives their children repeated opportunities to learn that conversing involves taking turns, that things have names, and that there are proper ways to pose questions and give answers.

LESSONS FROM CHILD-DIRECTED SPEECH. Cross-cultural research points to a nearly universal tendency of parents and older siblings to address infants and toddlers with very short, simple sentences that psycholinguists call *child-directed speech*, or **motherese** (Gelman & Shatz, 1977; Kuhl et al., 1997; Pine, 1994). Typically, these utterances are spoken slowly in a high-pitched voice, are often repeated, and emphasize key words (usually words for objects and activities). For example, a mother trying to get her young son to throw a ball might say, "*Throw* the *ball*, Daniel! Not the rattle. See the *ball*? Yes, that's the *ball*; *throw* it!" From the earliest days of life, infants pay more attention to the high-pitched sounds and varied intonational patterns of motherese than to the "flatter" speech that adults use when communicating with each other (Cooper & Aslin, 1990; Pegg, Werker, & McLeod, 1992), and they process more information about objects introduced by infant-directed speech as well (Kaplan et al., 1996). Indeed, infants even seem to grasp certain messages carried in their parents' tone of voice (for example, "Pay attention!" or "That's good!") long before they can understand a word about what is being said (Fernald, 1989; 1993).

Interestingly, parents gradually increase both the length and the complexity of their simplified child-directed speech as their children's language becomes more elaborate (Shatz, 1983). And at any given point in time, a parent's sentences are slightly longer and slightly more complex than the child's (Bohannon & Bonvillian, 1997; Sokolov, 1993). Here then, is a situation that might seem ideal for language learning: The child is constantly exposed to new semantic relations and grammatical rules that appear in simple utterances that she will probably understand, particularly if older companions frequently repeat or paraphrase the ideas they are trying to communicate (Bjorklund & Schwartz, 1996; Harris, 1992). Clearly, this is a form of modelling by the parent. However, children do not acquire new

motherese
short, simple, high-pitched (and often repetitive) sentences that adults use when talking with young children (also called *child-directed speech*)

grammatical principles by mimicking them directly, nor do adults consciously attempt to teach these principles by illustration. Parents speak in motherese for one main reason—to *communicate effectively* with their children (Fernald & Morikawa, 1993; Penner, 1987).

LESSONS FROM NEGATIVE EVIDENCE. Although parents do not reliably attempt to reinforce correct grammar, they do provide the child with negative evidence; that is, they respond to ungrammatical speech in ways that subtly communicate that an error has been made and provide information that might be used to correct these errors (Bohannon & Bonvillian, 1997; Saxton, 1997). For example, if a child says, "Doggie go," an adult may respond with an **expansion**—a grammatically correct and enriched version of the child's ungrammatical statement ("Yes, the doggie is going away"). A slightly different form of expansion occurs when adults **recast** the child's sentences into new grammatical forms. For example, a child who says, "Doggie eat" might have his sentence recast as "What is the doggie eating?" or "Yes, the doggie is hungry." These recasts are moderately novel utterances that probably command the child's attention and thereby increase the likelihood that he will notice the new grammatical forms that appear in the adult's speech. Finally, parents are likely to respond to grammatically appropriate sentences by simply maintaining and extending the conversation (topic extension). By carrying on without revising the child's utterance, adults provide a strong clue that the utterance was grammatical (Bohannon & Stanowicz, 1988; Penner, 1987).

Do children profit from negative evidence? Apparently so, for adults who frequently expand, recast, or otherwise extend their children's speech have youngsters who are quicker to acquire grammatical rules and who score relatively high on tests of expressive language ability compared with children whose parents rely less on these conversational techniques (Bohannan et al., 1996; Valdez-Menchaca & Whitehurst, 1992).

THE IMPORTANCE OF CONVERSATION. Would young children learn language just as well by merely listening to others converse? Apparently not. Nativists, who claimed that all children need to acquire language is regular exposure to speech samples, have clearly underestimated the role of *social* interactions in language learning. Mere exposure to speech is simply not enough; children must be actively involved in using language (Locke, 1997). Catherine Snow and her associates, for example, found that a group of Dutch-speaking children, despite the fact that they watched a great deal of German television, did not acquire any German words or grammar (Snow et al., 1976). Furthermore, hearing children of profoundly deaf parents often show an approximately normal pattern of language development as long as they spend 5 to 10 hours a week in the company of a hearing/speaking adult who *converses* with them (Schiff-Myers, 1988). True, there are cultures (for example, the Katuli of New Guinea, the natives of American Samoa, and the Trackton people of the Piedmont Carolinas) in which children acquire language without noticeable delays, even though adults rarely restructure their primitive sentences or address them in motherese (Gordon, 1990; Ochs, 1982; Schieffelin, 1986). Yet even these youngsters regularly participate in *social* interactions in which language is used, and that is what seems to be most essential in mastering a language (Lieven, 1994).

SUMMING UP. From an interactionist perspective, then, language development is the product of a complex transaction between nature and nurture. Children are born with a powerful human brain that *matures* slowly and predisposes them to acquire new understandings that they are *motivated to share with others* (Bates, 1999; Tomasello, 1995). Yet interactionists emphasize—as Vygotsky (1978) did in his model of collaborative learning—how conversations with older companions foster cognitive and language development. As their nervous systems continue to mature and children grow intellectually, they express their new understandings in increasingly complex utterances that prompt close companions to increase the complexity of their replies (Bohannon & Bonvillian, 1997; Sokolov, 1993). As illustrated in Figure 10.4, the pattern of influence is clearly reciprocal: The child's early attempts to communicate influence the speech of older companions, which in turn provides information that the child can process to infer linguistic principles and speak more clearly, and to influence the speech of companions once again. Stated another way, the interactionists propose that the language of young children is heavily influenced by a rich, responsive, and ever

expansions
responding to a child's ungrammatical utterance with a grammatically improved form of that statement

recasts
responding to a child's ungrammatical utterance with a nonrepetitive statement that is grammatically correct

more complex linguistic environment that they have had a hand in creating (Bloom et al., 1996).

One final note: Although the interactionist perspective is the approach that many developmentalists favour, the question of how children acquire language is by no means resolved. We still know much more about *what* children acquire as they learn a language than about exactly *how* they acquire this knowledge. So let's now chart the course of language development, a process that is well under way long before children utter their first meaningful word.

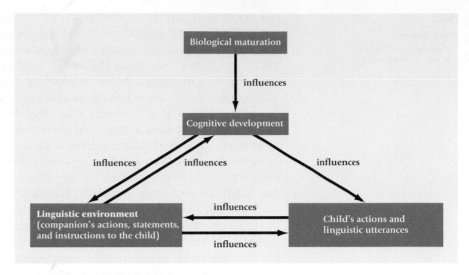

Figure 10.4 *An overview of the interactionist perspective on language development.*

BEFORE LANGUAGE: THE PRELINGUISTIC PERIOD

For the first 10 to 13 months of life, children are said to be in the **prelinguistic phase** of language development—the period before speaking their first meaningful words. But even though young infants are preverbal, they are quite responsive to language from the day they are born.

Early Reactions to Speech

In Chapter 6, we learned that newborns may be programmed to "tune in" to human speech. When spoken to, neonates often open their eyes, gaze at the speaker, and sometimes even vocalize themselves (Rheingold & Adams, 1980; Rosenthal, 1982). By 3 days of age, an infant already recognizes his or her mother's voice and clearly prefers it to the voice of a female stranger (DeCasper & Fifer, 1980), and newborns suck faster to hear recorded speech than to hear instrumental music or other rhythmic sounds (Butterfield & Siperstein, 1972). So babies can discriminate speech from other sound patterns, and they pay particularly close attention to speech from the very beginning.

prelinguistic phase
period before children utter their first meaningful words

Concept Check 10.1
Theories of Language Development

Check your understanding of theories of language development by matching each descriptive statement below with one of the following concepts or hypotheses: (a) appropriate grammar, (b) recasts, (c) language acquisition device, (d) sensitive-period hypothesis, (e) creolizing of pidgins by children, (f) universals in cognitive development, (g) conversations with language users, (h) appropriate semantics. Answers appear in the Appendix.

_____ 1. explains why adolescents might have a harder time acquiring foreign languages than children do

_____ 2. means by which companions introduce new linguistic forms to children

_____ 3. offered as support for the *nativist* perspective on language acquisition

_____ 4. aspect of early speech that parents are most likely to reinforce

_____ 5. essential input for mastering a language

_____ 6. mechanism that *interactionists* cite to explain linguistic universals

_____ 7. proposed inborn linguistic processor with a "universal" grammar common to all languages

_____ 8. aspect of early speech that *learning theorists* claim that parents reinforce

Do different samples of speech all sound alike to the very young infant? Apparently not. Within the first few days after birth, babies begin to discriminate different stress patterns, or rhythms, in two- and three-syllable words (Sansavini, Bertoncini, & Giovanelli, 1997), and they already prefer the sound pattern of the language their mother speaks to that of a foreign tongue (Moon, Cooper, & Fifer, 1993). As we noted in Chapter 6, 1-month-old infants are as capable as adults of discriminating consonant sounds such as *ba* and *da* and *ta*, and by 2 months of age even recognize that a particular vowel (an *a*, for example) is still the same sound when spoken at different pitches or intensities by different speakers (Jusczyk, 1995; Maye, Werker, & Gerken, 2002; Marean, Werner, & Kuhl, 1992). In fact, as Janet Werker and Renee Desjardins (1995) at the University of British Columbia point out, very young infants are actually able to discriminate a wider variety of phonemes than adults can, but as we learned in Chapter 6, we lose the ability to make phonemic distinctions that are not important in our native language (see also Werker & Tees, 2002).

It seems, then, that the abilities to discriminate speech from nonspeech and to differentiate a variety of speechlike sounds are either (1) innate or (2) acquired in the first few days and weeks of life. In either case, young infants are remarkably well prepared for the task of decoding the speech they hear.

The Importance of Intonational Cues

Earlier, we noted that adults typically speak to infants in a highly intonated motherese that attracts their attention. Furthermore, adults reliably vary their tone of voice when trying to communicate different "messages" to their preverbal infants (Fernald, 1989; Katz, Cohn, & Moore, 1996). Rising intonations (for example, "Look at mom^my") are used to recapture the attention of a baby who looks away, whereas falling intonations such as "HEY _there!" are often used to comfort or to *elicit positive affect* (smiles, bright eyes) from a somber baby. These intonational prompts are often successful at affecting a baby's mood or behaviour (Fernald, 1989, 1993), and 2- to 6-month-old infants frequently produce a vocalization in return that matches the intonation of what they have just heard (Masataka, 1992). So it is tempting to conclude that preverbal infants not only discriminate different intonational patterns but soon recognize that certain tones of voice have a particular meaning. In fact, some researchers believe that a 2- to 6-month-old's successful interpretation of intonational cues may provide some of the earliest evidence that speech is a *meaningful* enterprise—and is something she might try to perfect (Fernald, 1989, 1993).

During the second half of the first year, infants become increasingly attuned to the "rhythm" of a language, which helps them to segment what they hear, first into phrases and eventually into words. Phrase boundaries in infant-directed speech are characterized by long pauses that are preceded by very long vowel sounds—acoustic cues that provide ample information about where one phrase ends and another begins (Fisher & Tokura, 1996). By 7 months of age, infants can detect phrase units and clearly prefer to listen to speech that contains natural breaks and pauses to that in which pauses are inserted at unnatural places, such as the middle of a phrase (Hirsh-Pasek et al., 1987). By age 9 months, infants are becoming sensitive to smaller speech units. They now prefer to listen to speech samples that match the syllabic stress patterns and phonemic combinations of the language their caregivers speak (Jusczyk, Cutler, & Redanz, 1993), and they can even parse this information into two-syllable wordlike segments (Brownlee, 2001; Morgan & Saffran, 1995). So by the last quarter of the first year, infants' increasing familiarity with the phonological aspects of their native tongue provides important clues about which patterns in an ongoing stream of speech represent individual words.

Producing Sounds: The Infant's Prelinguistic Vocalizations

coos
vowel-like sounds that young infants repeat over and over during periods of contentment

The first vocal milestone other than crying occurs by 2 months of age as babies make vowel-like noises called **cooing**. These "ooooohs" and "aaaaahs" are likely to be heard after a feeding when the baby is awake, alert, dry, and otherwise content. By 4 to 6 months of age, infants have added consonant sounds to their vocal repertoires and are now **babbling**—that is, repeating vowel–consonant combinations such as "mamama" or "papapa" that may sound like words but convey no meaning. Interestingly, deaf infants whose parents are deaf and communicate in sign language will, themselves, babble manually, experimenting with gestures in much the same way that hearing infants experiment with sounds (Petito & Marentette, 1991).

For the first six months, infants the world over (even deaf ones) sound pretty much alike, a finding that suggests that early babbling is heavily influenced by maturation of the brain and the muscles controlling verbal articulation (Hoff-Ginsburg, 1997). Yet, the effects of experience soon come into play. Deaf infants, who hear no speech, begin to fall far behind hearing infants in their ability to produce well-formed, vocal, language-like phonemes (Eilers & Oller, 1994; Oller & Eilers, 1988). By contrast, hearing infants attend very carefully to others' speech. Researchers at York University (Blake & Boysson-Bardies, 1992) found that by the end of the first year, hearing infants match the intonation of their babbles to the tonal qualities of the language they hear, and they actually begin to sound as if they are speaking that language (see also Davis et al., 2000). Apparently, babies are learning the tune before the words (Bates, O'Connell, & Shore, 1987; Petitto et al., 2001).

As babbling progresses, 10- to 12-month-olds often reserve certain sounds for particular situations. For example, one infant began to use the *m* sound (*"mmmm"*) when making requests and various vowel sounds (*"aaaach"*) when manipulating objects (Blake & Boysson-Bardies, 1992). According to Charles Ferguson (1977), infants who produce these **vocables** are now aware that certain speech sounds have consistent meanings and are about ready to talk.

What Do Prelinguistic Infants Know about Language and Communication?

Do young infants know more about language than they can possibly tell? It now appears that they do and that one of the first things they learn about speech is a practical lesson. During the first six months, babies often coo or babble *while* their caregivers are speaking (Rosenthal, 1982). It is almost as if very young infants view "talking" as a game of noisemaking in which the object is to "harmonize" with their speaking companions. But by 7 to 8 months of age, infants are typically silent while a companion speaks and wait to respond with a vocalization when their partner stops talking. Apparently, they have learned their first rule in the *pragmatics* of language: Don't talk while someone else is speaking, because you'll soon have an opportunity to have your say.

Vocal turn-taking may come about because parents typically say something to the baby; wait for the baby to smile, cough, burp, coo, or babble; and address the baby again, thereby inviting another response (Snow & Ferguson, 1977). Of course, infants may also learn about the importance of turn-taking from other contexts in which they assume reversible roles with their companions (Bruner, 1983). Examples of these reciprocal exchanges might include bouts of nose touching, pat-a-cake, and toy sharing. By 4 months infants begin to respond more positively to organized than disorganized social games (Rochat, Querido & Striano, 1999). By 9 months of age, infants clearly understand the alternation rules of many games, and if such activities are interrupted by the adult's failure to take her turn, the infant is likely to vocalize, urge the adult to resume by offering her a toy, or wait for a second or two and take the adult's turn before looking once again at the adult (Ross & Lollis, 1987). So it seems that the ways caregivers structure interactions with an infant may indeed help the child to recognize that many forms of social discourse, including "talking," are patterned activities that follow a definite set of rules.

babbles
vowel–consonant combinations that infants begin to produce at about 4 to 6 months of age

vocables
unique patterns of sound that a prelinguistic infant uses to represent objects, actions, or events

Gestures and Nonverbal Responses

By 8 to 10 months of age, preverbal infants begin to use gestures and other nonverbal responses (for example, facial expressions) to communicate with their companions (Acredolo & Goodwyn, 1990). Two kinds of preverbal gestures are common: *declarative gestures*, in which the infant directs others' attention to an object by pointing at or touching it, and *imperative gestures*, in which the infant tries to convince others to grant his requests through such actions as pointing at candy he wants or tugging at a caregiver's pantleg when he hopes to be picked up. Eventually, some of these gestures become entirely representational and function like words. For example, a 1- to 2-year-old might raise her arms to signify that she wants to be picked up, hold her arms out to signify an airplane, or even pant heavily to represent the family dog (Acredolo & Goodwyn, 1990; Bates et al., 1989). Once children begin to speak, they often supplement their one- and two-word utterances with a gesture or an intonational cue to ensure that their messages are understood (Butcher & Goldin-Meadow, 2000; Ingram, 1989). And, contrary to popular belief, use of gestures to accompany speech actually increases as speech becomes more complex (Nicoladis, Mayberry, & Genesee, 1999), with some types of gestures most apparent for complex speech (Nicoladis, 2002). In fact, gestures so often accompany vocal communications at all ages (see Goldin-Meadow, 2000) that we might rename the spoken language system as the "speech-gesture" system.

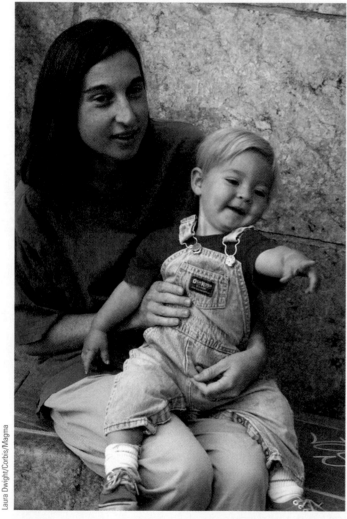

Laura Dwight/Corbis/Magma

Pointing is an early but very effective means of communication. By the end of the first year, children are calling attention to interesting objects and activities by pointing at them with the index finger.

WHAT DO YOU THINK?

Suppose three male and three female infants are raised on an isolated island and only have contact with one nonlinguistic adult who gives them love and cares for their basic needs. Would these children come to communicate with one another? Do you think they would devise a language? Why or why not?

Do Preverbal Infants Understand the Meaning of Words?

Although most babies do not utter their first meaningful words until the end of the first year, parents are often convinced that their preverbal infants can understand at least some of what is said to them. Yet well-controlled tests of word comprehension suggest that preverbal infants understand the meaning of few, if any, words. In one study, 11- and 13-month-olds were told by their mothers to look at an object that was familiar to them. Mothers were *out of sight* and could not use gestures or other nonverbal cues to direct the infants' attention. Clearly, the 13-month-olds did understand the meaning of the word that named this object, for they gazed intently at its referent when told to, and they looked very little at other distractor stimuli. By contrast, most 11-month-olds did *not* understand the meaning of this word, for they were as likely to gaze at distractor stimuli as at the word's referent (Thomas et al., 1981). By age 12 to 13 months, however, infants are beginning to realize that individual words have meaning. In fact, Sharon Oviatt (1980) found that 12- to 17-month-olds understand the meaning of many nouns and verbs long before they use them in their own speech. So infants seem to know much more about language than they can possibly say. Apparently, **receptive language** (comprehension) is ahead of **productive language** (expression) from the 12th or 13th month of life and possibly even sooner.

receptive language
that which the individual comprehends when listening to others' speech

productive language
that which the individual is capable of expressing (producing) in his or her own speech

ONE WORD AT A TIME: THE HOLOPHRASTIC PERIOD

In the first stage of meaningful speech, the **holophrastic period**, infants utter single words that often seem to represent an entire sentence's worth of meaning (that is, **holophrases**). At first, the child's productive vocabulary is constrained, in part, by the sounds she can pronounce, so that her very first words may be intelligible only to close companions—for example, "ba" (for "ball") or "awa" (for "I want," as the child points to a cookie) (Hura & Echols, 1996). Sounds that begin with consonants and end with vowels are easiest for infants, whose longer words are often repetitions of the syllables they can pronounce (for example, "mama," "bye-bye").

However, phonological development occurs very rapidly. By the middle of the second year, infants' cute and creative pronunciations are already guided by rules, or strategies, that enable them to produce simplified but more intelligible versions of adult words (Ingram, 1986; Vihman et al., 1994). For example, they often delete the unstressed syllable of a multisyllable word (saying "ghetti" for "spaghetti"), or replace an ending consonant syllable with a vowel (saying "appo" for "apple"). The fact that these early pronunciation errors are somewhat similar across languages and are resistant to adults' attempts to correct them implies that they stem, in part, from biological constraints— namely, an immature vocal tract. Yet there are tremendous individual differences: All toddlers do not sound alike, even if they have been exposed to the same language (Vihman et al., 1994). Why? Probably because articulating phonemes and combining them into words is a vocal-*motor* skill, which like all of the dynamic motor systems we discussed in Chapter 5, reflects the unique paths that individual children follow as they combine the sounds that *they* have been attending closely to and producing themselves into new and more complex patterns in an attempt to achieve a most important goal: communicating effectively with their companions (Thelen, 1995; Vihman et al., 1994). As the vocal tract matures during the preschool period, and children have more and more opportunities to decipher and produce the phonemic combinations in the speech of older models, their pronunciation errors become much less frequent. Indeed, most 4- to 5-year-olds already pronounce most words in pretty much the same way that adults do (Ingram, 1986).

A large percentage of children's first words are the names of objects that move or can be acted on.

Early Semantics: Building a Vocabulary

As infants begin to speak, the growth of their vocabularies literally proceeds one word at a time (Bloom, 1973). In fact, three to four months may pass before most children have a vocabulary of 10 words. Yet the pace of word learning quickens dramatically between 18 and 24 months of age, when infants may add anywhere from 10 to 20 new words a week (Reznick & Goldfield, 1992). This vocabulary spurt is sometimes called the **naming explosion**, because as most parents will attest, toddlers seem to arrive at the wonderful realization that everything has a name and they want to learn all the names they can (Reznick & Goldfield, 1992). A typical 2-year-old may now produce nearly 200 words (Nelson, 1973) and may comprehend a far greater number (Benedict, 1979).

Much work has been undertaken to try to explain how the dramatic shift in word learning ability occurs between younger, novice word learners and the more experienced 18- to 24-month-olds. As mentioned earlier in the chapter, even very young learners demonstrate skills that allow them to discriminate and produce the sounds of their own language (e.g., Best et al., 1995; Pegg & Werker, 1997), the stress patterns in their native language (Jusczyk, Cutler, & Redanz, 1993), and other phonological and prosodic information that allows them to discriminate individual words from a stream of speech (Jusczyk, 1999). Given all of these skills, it has been a challenge to determine what causes

holophrastic period
period when the child's speech consists of one-word utterances, some of which are thought to be holophrases

holophrase
single-word utterance that represents an entire sentence's worth of meaning

naming explosion
dramatic increase in the pace at which infants acquire new words in the latter half of the second year; so named because many of the new words acquired are the names of objects

Janet Werker

Janet Werker studies maturational and experiential factors that facilitate language acquisition, including the impact of speech perception and cognitive factors. She works in the Department of Psychology at the University of British Columbia.

Infants of 14 months have difficulty mapping similar-sounding words such as "bih" versus "dih" onto two different objects (Stager & Werker, 1997) even though they can easily do so with dissimilar words such as "lif" and "neem" (Werker et al., 1998) and can easily discriminate "bih" from "dih" in speech perception tasks. Werker, Fennell, Corcoran, & Stager (2002) compared infants of various ages learning similar-sounding words to try to determine why novice word learners typically fail at this task.

Infants aged 14, 17, and 20 months were tested in a simplified word-learning task called the "switch" design. Infants seated on their parent's lap were shown videos of

one or another object moving back and forth. The displays were accompanied by repetitions of a single nonsense word (one object paired with the word "bih" and the other with the word "dih"). Once infants habituated, they were given two test trials: a "same" trial in which the familiar word and object were shown in a familiar combination, and a "switch" trial in which the familiar word and object were presented in a new combination. Because infants show a preference for novelty, if they had learned the pairing they would show greater looking time for the "switch" than for the "same" trial. To assess a possible link to overall vocabulary size, infant vocabulary was measured through a parent report questionnaire.

The 17- and 20-month-old infants succeeded at learning minimally different words, while 14-month-olds as a group failed. However, the 14-month-olds with particularly large vocabularies succeeded. Werker et al. concluded that the task of linking words to objects is sufficiently challenging that until infants become more proficient word learners, they do not have the attentional resources available to listen closely to the sound shape of words.

---

or facilitates the sudden word learning ability of older infants. Janet Werker and her colleagues at the University of British Columbia have studied novice and more experienced word learners to see whether these differences in ability over time can be explained by children's knowledge of the sounds of words or whether other knowledge or resources available to children can explain this change in skill (Stager & Werker, 1997; Werker et al., 2002). Their work suggests that there are developmental differences in the ability to use perceptual information (specifically, phonetic information) that may be attributed to cognitive limitations such as attentional resources. The details of this research are featured in Box 10.2.

What do infants talk about? Katherine Nelson (1973) studied 18 infants as they learned their first 50 words and found that nearly two-thirds of these early words referred to *objects*, including familiar people (see Table 10.1). Furthermore, these objects were nearly all either manipulable by the child (for example, balls or shoes) or capable of moving themselves (for example, animals, vehicles); rarely do infants mention objects such as plates or chairs that simply sit there not doing anything. Toddlers' first words also include many references to familiar *actions* (Nelson, Hampson, & Shaw, 1993; see Table 10.1). In fact, recent research indicates that young infants are especially likely to under-

---

TABLE 10.1	Types of Words Used by Children with Productive Vocabularies of 50 Words	
Word category	**Description and examples**	**Percentage of utterances**
Object words	Words used to refer to classes of objects (*car, doggie, milk*) Words used to refer to unique objects (*mummy, Rover*)	65
Action words	Words used to describe or accompany actions or to demand attention (*bye-bye, up, go*)	13
Modifiers	Words that refer to properties or quantities of things (*big, hot, mine*)	9
Personal/social words	Words used to express feelings or to comment about social relationships (*please, thank you, no, ouch*)	8
Function words	Words that have a grammatical function (*what, where, is, to, for*)	4

SOURCE: Adapted from Nelson, 1973.

stand and use words introduced in **multimodal motherese**—that is, exaggerated utterances by an adult that are accompanied by some *action* that calls attention to the referents of these words (Gogate, Bahrick, & Watson, 2000). So it seems that infants talk mostly about those aspects of experience that they already understand through their sensorimotor activities.

Individual and Cultural Variations in Early Language

Nelson's (1973) early study revealed an interesting individual difference in the kinds of words infants produced. Most infants displayed what she called a **referential style**; their early vocabularies consisted mainly of words that referred to people or objects. By contrast, a smaller number of infants displayed an **expressive style**; their vocabularies were more diverse and contained a larger number of personal/social words such as *please*, *thank you*, *don't*, and *stop it*. Apparently, language serves somewhat different functions for these two groups of children. Referential children seem to think words are for naming objects, whereas expressive children use words to call attention to their own and others' feelings and to regulate their social interactions (Nelson, 1981).

Interestingly, a child's birth order seems to influence the linguistic environment in ways that could affect her language style. Most first-borns in Western cultures adopt a referential style, perhaps reflecting parents' willingness to label and to ask questions about interesting objects that have captured their attention (Nelson, 1973). By contrast, later-borns hear a great deal of speech directed to an older sibling that first-borns haven't heard (Pine, 1995). So later-borns may spend somewhat less time talking with parents about objects and more time listening to speech designed to control their own or their siblings' conduct. As a result, they are more likely than first-borns to conclude that the function of language is to regulate social interactions, prompting them to adopt an expressive language style (Nelson, 1973).

Culture also influences language styles. When talking about a stuffed animal, American mothers treat the interaction as an opportunity to teach the infant about objects ("It's a doggie! Look at its big ears"), thereby encouraging a referential style. Japanese mothers, by contrast, are more inclined to emphasize social routines and consideration for others ("Give the doggie love!") that seem to promote an expressive style (Fernald & Morikawa, 1993). Indeed, in Asian cultures such as Japan, China, and Korea that stress interpersonal harmony, children are much quicker to acquire verbs and personal/social words than American children are (Gopnik & Choi, 1995; Tardif, Gelman & Xu, 1999).

By emphasizing social routines and concern for others, Japanese mothers encourage their children to adopt an "expressive" language style.

Attaching Meaning to Words

How do toddlers figure out what words mean? In many cases, they seem to employ a **fast-mapping** process, quickly acquiring (and retaining) a word after hearing it applied to its referent on a small number of occasions. Apparently, even 13- to 15-month-olds can learn the meaning of new words by fast-mapping (Schaefer & Plummert, 1998; Woodward, Markman, & Fitzsimmons, 1994), although the names of objects are more easily acquired at this age than the names of actions or activities (Casasola & Cohen, 2000). Fast-mapping clearly improves with age. Eighteen- to 20-month-olds are likely to learn the meaning of novel words that a speaker introduces only if they and the speaker are *jointly attending* to the object that is labelled (Baldwin et al., 1996). Yet, by 24 to 30 months children are much better at inferring what speakers are talking about and will now fast-map a novel word to its referent, even if (1) they've merely overheard the word as the speaker addresses someone else (Akhktar, Jipson, & Callanan, 2001) or (2) other objects or events are competing for their attention (Moore, Angelopoulos, & Bennett, 1999).

If 13- to 15-month-olds can fast-map word meanings, why do you suppose that children this young produce so few words? One possibility is that fast-mapping allows these youngest language users to *comprehend* word meanings, but that they have trouble

Elizabeth Crews

multimodal motherese
older companion's use of information that is exaggerated and synchronized across two or more senses to call an infant's attention to the referent of a spoken word

referential style
early linguistic style in which toddlers use language mainly to label objects

expressive style
early linguistic style in which toddlers use language mainly to call attention to their own and others' feelings and to regulate social interactions

fast-mapping
process of linking a word with its referent after hearing the word once or twice

retrieving known words from memory when they try to talk. Consider a recent study in which 14- to 24-month-olds who knew the names of objects hidden in a box and who had seen the objects placed there were asked "What's inside the box?" (Dapretto & Bjork, 2000). Toddlers who had yet to enter the naming explosion generally could not retrieve words *they knew well* to answer correctly, whereas their counterparts who had already displayed a vocabulary spurt performed much better. So one important reason why productive vocabulary may be so far behind receptive vocabulary early in life is that 12- to 15-month-olds who are fast-mapping the meaning of many new words are often unable to retrieve these words from memory to talk about their referents.

Common Errors in Word Use

Despite their remarkable fast-mapping capabilities, toddlers often attach meanings to words that differ from those of adults (Pan & Gleason, 1997). One kind of error that they frequently make is to use a word to refer to a wider variety of objects or events than an adult would. This phenomenon, called **overextension**, is illustrated by a child's use of the term *doggie* to refer to all furry, four-legged animals. **Underextension**, the opposite of overextension, is the tendency to use a general word to refer to a smaller range of objects than an adult would—for example, applying the term *cookie* only to chocolate chip cookies. Why young children overextend or underextend particular words is not always clear, but it is likely that fast-mapping contributes to these errors. Suppose, for example, that a mother points to a collie and says "doggie," and then turns toward a fox terrier and says "Look, another doggie." Applying the same name to these perceptually discriminable objects will cause her toddler to mentally abstract their common features, forming a category (Samuelson & Smith, 2000). The child may note that the two things these two beasts have in common are four legs and a hairy exterior, thus leading him to fast-map the word *doggie* onto these perceptual attributes. And having done so, he may then be inclined to *overextend* the word *doggie* to other animals (opossums, raccoons) that share similar perceptual (semantic) features (Clark, 1973). Fast-mapping could lead to underextensions as well. If the only dog a toddler has ever seen is the family pet, which he has heard his mother refer to as "doggie" a couple of times, he may initially assume that *doggie* is the proper name of this particular companion and use the term only when referring to his pet.

Of course, deciphering the meaning of many new words is more difficult than these examples imply because it is often unclear exactly what new words refer to. For example, if mother sees a cat walking alongside a car and exclaims, "Oh, there's a kitty!", the child must first decide whether mum is referring to the car or to the animal. If he rules out the car, it is still not obvious whether the word *kitty* refers to four-legged animals, to this particular animal, or to the cat's pointed ears, leisurely gait, or even the meowing sound it makes. How does the child decide among these many possibilities, all of which may seem plausible to him?

Strategies for Inferring Word Meanings

Determining how young children figure out what new words mean when their referents are *not* immediately obvious (as in the *kitty* example) has proved to be a challenging task that is far from complete. Nameera Akhtar and associates (1996) believe that 2-year-olds are already especially sensitive to *social* and *contextual* cues that help them to determine what novel aspects of a companion's speech might mean. To illustrate this point, Akhtar and associates had 2-year-olds and two adults play with three *unnamed* objects that were unfamiliar to the children. Then one adult left the room, and a fourth unnamed object was added to the mix. Later, when the absent adult returned, she exclaimed, "Look, I see a gasser! A gasser!" without pointing at or displaying any other clue to indicate which of the four objects she was referring to. Even though *gasser* could have referred to any of the four unnamed objects, a substantial percentage of these 2-year-olds correctly inferred the speaker's referential intent, picking the novel object (which was novel *only for the speaker* and not for them) when asked to show a *gasser*. They realized that the second adult had not previously seen this fourth object and then assumed that she must be talking about whichever object was new to her.

overextension
young child's tendency to use relatively specific words to refer to a broader set of objects, actions, or events than adults do (for example, using *car* to refer to all motor vehicles)

underextension
young child's tendency to use general words to refer to a smaller set of objects, actions, or events than adults do (for example, using *candy* to refer only to mints)

In addition to using social or contextual cues to infer word meanings, 2-year-olds have a number of other cognitive strategies, or **processing constraints**, that help them narrow down what a new word might possibly mean (de Villiers & de Villiers, 1992; Golinkoff et al., 1996; Hall & Waxman, 1993; Littschwager & Markman, 1994). Several of the more basic constraints that seem to guide children's inferences about word meanings are described in Table 10.2.

Of course, these constraints may often work together to help children infer word meanings. For example, when 2-year-olds hear the words *horn* and *clip* applied to two very different objects, they assign each word correctly to a whole object rather than to its parts or attributes (**object scope constraint**), and they display **mutual exclusivity** by almost never calling the horn a *clip* (or vice versa) when tested later (Waxman & Senghas, 1992).

However, the mutual exclusivity constraint is not very helpful when adults use more than one word to refer to the same object (for example, "Oh, there is a *doggie*—a *cocker spaniel*"). Under these circumstances, 2-year-olds who already know the word *doggie* often apply the **lexical contrast constraint**, concluding that *cocker spaniel* must refer to a particular kind of dog that has the distinctive features (long floppy ears, heavy coat) that this one displays (Taylor & Gelman, 1988, 1989; Waxman & Hatch, 1992). Indeed, this tendency to contrast novel with familiar words may explain how children form hierarchical linguistic categories, eventually recognizing, for example, that a dog is also an animal and a mammal (superordinate designations) as well as a cocker spaniel who has a proper name such as Pokey (subordinate designations) (Mervis, Golinkoff, & Bertrand, 1994).

SYNTACTICAL CLUES TO WORD MEANING. Young language learners may often infer word meanings by paying close attention to the way the word is used in a sentence. For example, a 2-year-old who hears a new word, *zav*, used as a noun to refer to a toy ("This is a *zav*") is likely to conclude that this new word refers to the toy itself. However, a child who hears *zav* used as an adjective ("This is a *zav* one") is more likely to conclude that *zav* refers to some characteristic of the toy, such as its shape or colour (Taylor & Gelman, 1988; Waxman & Markow, 1998).

Notice, then, children infer word meanings from sentence structure, or *syntactical* clues. Indeed, this **syntactical bootstrapping** may be particularly important in helping them to decipher the meaning of new verbs (Gleitman, 1990). Consider the following two sentences:

1. The duck is gorping the bunny. (Gorping refers to a causative action.)
2. The duck and the bunny are gorping. (Gorping is a synchronized action.)

processing constraints
cognitive biases or tendencies that lead infants and toddlers to favour certain interpretations of the meaning of new words over other interpretations

object scope constraint
notion that young children assume that a new word applied to an object refers to the whole object rather than to parts of the object or to object attributes (for example, its colour)

mutual exclusivity constraint
notion that young children assume that each object has only one label and that different words refer to separate and not overlapping categories

lexical contrast constraint
notion that young children make inferences about word meanings by contrasting new words with words they already know

syntactical bootstrapping
notion that young children make inferences about the meaning of words by analyzing the way words are used in sentences and inferring whether they refer to objects (nouns), actions (verbs), or attributes (adjectives)

TABLE 10.2	Some Processing Strategies, or Constraints, that Guide Young Children's Inferences about the Meaning of New Words	
Constraint	**Description**	**Example**
Object scope constraint	The assumption that words refer to whole objects rather than to parts of the objects or to object attributes	The child concludes that the word *kitty* refers to the animal he sees rather than to the animal's ears, tail, meowing, or colour.
Taxonomic constraint	The assumption that words label categories of *similar* objects that share common perceptual features	The child concludes that the word *kitty* refers to the animal she has seen *and* to other small, furry, four-legged animals.
Lexical contrast constraint	The assumption that each word has a unique meaning	The child who already knows the meaning of *doggie* assumes that a label such as *Dalmatian* applied to a dog refers to that particular kind of dog (subordinate class).
Mutual exclusivity	The assumption that each object has one label and that different words refer to separate, nonoverlapping categories	The child who already knows the word for *doggie* assumes that the word *kitty* refers to the fleeing animal if he hears someone say, "Look at the doggie chasing the kitty."

When 2-year-olds hear one or the other of these sentences, they prefer to look at a video that matches what they have heard—for example, looking at a duck *causing* a rabbit to bend back after hearing sentence 1 (Naigles, 1990). Clearly the verb's syntax—the form that it takes in a sentence—provides important clues about what it means (Naigles & Hoff-Ginsberg, 1995).

Finally, 2-year-olds can use the meaning of a familiar verb to limit the possible referents of a novel noun. So if they know what eating means and hear the sentence "Daddy is eating cabbage," they will map this name onto the leafy substance that dad is consuming rather than wondering whether cabbage refers to the ham, bread, or other objects on the dining room table (Goodman, McDonough, & Brown, 1998). By age 3 children become so proficient at inferring word meanings from syntactical cues that they trust their understanding of *sentence structure* rather than other processing constraints when (1) the referent of a new word is unclear and (2) syntactical cues and other processing constraints would lead to different interpretations (Hall, Quantz, & Persoage, 2000).

Summing Up. Toddlers are remarkably well prepared for the task of figuring out what new words mean (Hollich, Hirsh-Pasek, & Golikoff, 2000). Their strong desire to share meaning with companions makes them especially sensitive to novel aspects of the speech they hear and highly motivated to use contextual cues and other available information to decode new words. By age 2, toddlers already produce nearly 200 words—a sufficient baseline for lexical contrast. And apparently they already understand enough about sentence structure (syntax) to determine whether many new words are nouns, verbs, or adjectives—a second important clue to word meaning. While it is true that toddlers make many semantic errors, they often seem to know much more about the meaning of words than their errors might indicate. For example, 2-year-olds who say "doggie" when they see a horse can usually discriminate dogs from other animals if they are given a set of animal pictures and asked to find a horse (Naigles & Gelman, 1995). Why, then, might they choose to call a horse a doggie when they can easily tell the animals apart?

One possibility is that toddlers who know relatively few words may use overextension as yet another strategy for learning the names of new objects and activities. A child who sees a horse may call it a *doggie* not because she believes it is a dog, but because she has no better word in her vocabulary to describe this animal and has learned from experience that an incorrect label is likely to elicit reactions such as "No, Jennie, that's a *horse*. Can you say *horsie*? C'mon, say *horsie*" (Baron, 1992; Ingram, 1989).

Syntactical bootstrapping. Young children can use the form of a verb to infer that the sentence "The duck is gorping the bunny" refers to the causative action in the first drawing, whereas the sentence "The duck and the bunny are gorping" refers to the synchronized action in the second drawing.

When a Word Is More Than a Word

Many psycholinguists characterize an infant's one-word utterances as *holophrases* because they often seem less like labels and more like attempts to convey an entire sentence's worth of meaning. These single-word "sentences" can serve different communication functions depending on how they are said and the context in which they are said (Greenfield & Smith, 1976). For example, 17-month-old Shelley used the word *ghetti* (spaghetti) three times over a five-minute period. First, she pointed to the pan on the stove and seemed to be *asking*, "Is that spaghetti?" Later, the function of her holophrase was to *name* the spaghetti when shown the contents of the pan, as in "It is spaghetti!" Finally, she left little question that she was *requesting* spaghetti when she tugged at her companion's sleeve as he was eating and used a whining tone.

Of course, there are limits to the amount of meaning that can be packed into a single word, but infants in the holophrastic phase of language development do seem to display such basic language functions as naming, questioning, requesting, and demanding—functions that will later serve to produce different kinds of sentences. They are also learning an important *pragmatic* lesson: that their one-word messages are often ambiguous and may require an accompanying gesture or intonational cue if they are to be understood (Ingram, 1989).

FROM HOLOPHRASES TO SIMPLE SENTENCES: THE TELEGRAPHIC PERIOD

At about 18 to 24 months of age, children begin to combine words into simple "sentences" such as "Daddy eat," "Kitty go," and "Mommy drink milk" that are remarkably similar across languages as diverse as English, Finnish, German, and Samoan (see Table 10.3). These early sentences have been called **telegraphic speech** because, like telegrams, they contain only critical content words—such as nouns, verbs, and adjectives—and leave out such frills as articles, prepositions, pronouns, and auxiliary verbs.

telegraphic speech
early sentences that consist of content words and omit the less meaningful parts of speech, such as articles, prepositions, pronouns, and auxiliary verbs

TABLE 10.3   Similarities in Children's Spontaneous Two-Word Sentences in Four Languages

Function of sentence	Language			
	English	**Finnish**	**German**	**Samoan**
To locate or name	There book	Tuossa Rina (there Rina)	Buch da (book there)	Keith lea (Keith there)
To demand	More milk Give candy	Annu Rina (give Rina)	Mehr milch (more milk)	Mai pepe (give doll)
To negate	No wet Not hungry	Ei susi (not wolf)	Nicht blasen (not blow)	Le'ai (not eat)
To indicate possession	My shoe Mama dress	Täti auto (aunt's car)	Mein ball (my ball) Mamas hut (Mama's hat)	Lole a'u (candy my)
To modify or qualify	Pretty dress Big boat	Rikki auto (broken car)	Armer wauwau (poor dog)	Fa'ali'i pepe (headstrong baby)
To question	Where ball	Missa pallo (where ball)	Wo ball (where ball)	Fea Punafu (where Punafu)

Source: Adapted from Slobin, 1979.

Why do young children stress nouns and verbs and omit many other parts of speech in their earliest sentences? Certainly not because the omitted words serve no function. Children clearly encode these words in others' speech, for they respond more appropriately to fully grammatical sentences (for example, "Get the ball") than to telegraphic (or otherwise ungrammatical) versions of the same idea (such as "Get ball" or "Point to gub ball") (Gerken & McIntosh, 1993; Petretic & Tweney, 1977). Current thinking is that telegraphic children omit words because of their own processing and production constraints. A child who can generate only very short utterances will choose to deemphasize smaller, less important words in favour of those heavily stressed nouns and verbs that are necessary for effective communication (Gerken, Landau, & Remez, 1990; Valian, Hoeffner, & Aubry, 1996).

Interestingly, telegraphic speech is not nearly as universal as earlier researchers had thought. Russian and Turkish children, for example, produce short but reasonably grammatical sentences from the very beginning. Why? Because their languages put more stress on small grammatical markers and have less rigid rules about word order than other languages do (de Villiers & de Villiers, 1992; Slobin, 1985). So it seems that whatever is most noticeable about the structure of a language is what children acquire first. And if content words and word-order rules are most heavily stressed (as in English), then young children will include this information and omit the lightly stressed articles, prepositions, and grammatical markers to produce what appear to be "telegraphic" utterances.

A Semantic Analysis of Telegraphic Speech

Psycholinguists have approached early child language as if it were a foreign language and have tried to describe the rules that young children use to form their sentences. Early attempts to specify the structural characteristics, or syntax, of telegraphic speech made it quite clear that many of children's earliest two-word sentences followed at least some grammatical rules. English-speaking children, for example, usually say "Mummy drink" rather than "Drink mummy" or "My ball" rather than "Ball my," thus suggesting that they already realize that some word orders are better than others for conveying meaning (de Villiers & de Villiers, 1992).

However, it soon became obvious that analyses of telegraphic speech based on syntax alone grossly underestimated the young child's linguistic capabilities. Why? Because young children often use the *same* two-word utterance to convey *different* meanings (or semantic relations) in different contexts. For example, one of Lois Bloom's (1970) young subjects said "Mummy sock" on two occasions during the same day—once when she picked up her mother's sock and once while her mother was putting a sock on the child's foot. In the first instance, "Mummy sock" seems to imply a possessive relationship—"Mummy's sock." But in the second instance, the child was apparently expressing a different idea, namely "Mummy is putting on my sock." So to properly interpret telegraphic statements, one must determine the child's *meaning* or *semantic intent* by considering not only the words that she generates but also the contexts in which these utterances take place.

The Pragmatics of Early Speech

Because early sentences are incomplete and their meanings are often ambiguous, children continue to supplement their words with gestures and intonational cues to ensure that their messages are understood (O'Neill, 1996). Although adults who are proficient with the spoken language may consider nonverbal gestures a rather limited and inefficient form of communication, such an attitude is extremely shortsighted. Indeed, many deaf children learn and use a rather sophisticated language that is based entirely on nonverbal signs and gestures (see Box 10.3).

Learning a Gestural Language

Children who are born deaf or who lose their hearing very early in childhood have a difficult time learning an oral language. Contrary to popular opinion, deaf people do not learn much from lip reading. In fact, many deaf children (especially those of hearing parents) may be delayed in their language development unless they are exposed early to an English gestural system such as American Sign Language (ASL) (Mayberry, 1994) or a French gestural system such as Langue des signes québécoise (LSQ).

Although sign languages such as ASL are produced by the hands rather than orally, they are a remarkably flexible medium (Bellugi, 1988). Some signs represent entire words; others stand for grammatical morphemes such as the progressive ending -*ing*, the past tense -*ed*, and auxiliaries. Each sign is constructed from a limited set of gestural components in much the same way that the spoken word is constructed from a finite number of distinctive sounds (phonemes). Syntactical rules specify how signs are to be combined to form declarative sentences, to ask questions, and to negate a proposition. And, like an oral language, ASL permits the user to sign plays on words (puns), metaphorical statements, and poetry. So people who are proficient in this gestural system can transmit and understand an infinite variety of highly creative messages. They are true language users!

Deaf children who are exposed early to ASL acquire it in much the same way that hearing children acquire an oral language (Bellugi, 1988; Locke, 1997). Indeed, signs are readily visible to the infant and grow from sensorimotor schemes, perhaps explaining why many children produce their first truly referential sign or gesture at about the same time or slightly before hearing children utter their first meaningful words (Folven & Bonvillian, 1991; Goodwyn & Acredolo, 1993). Deaf mothers support sign learning by signing to their infants in "motherese"—that is, signing slowly with exaggerated movements that are repeated often to ensure comprehension (Masataka, 1996). And the deaf child usually begins by "babbling" in sign, forming rough approximations of signs that parents use, before proceeding to one-word, or "holophrastic," phrases, in which a single sign is used to convey a number of different messages.

Furthermore, the linguistic advances of both deaf and hearing children are closely linked to advances in cognitive development; for example, putting signs or words together in sentences happens at about the same age that children put sequences of actions together in their play (Spencer, 1996). Deaf children become quite proficient at fast-mapping and using other processing constraints to expand their vocabularies (Lederberg, Prezbindowski, & Spencer, 2000), and when they begin to combine signs, their two-sign sentences are "telegraphic" statements that express the same set of semantic relations that appears in the early speech of hearing children.

Finally, the language areas of the brain develop much the same in deaf children exposed early to sign language as in hearing children exposed to speech. Helen Neville and her colleagues (1997) examined the brain activity of deaf ASL users and hearing individuals as they processed sentences in their respective languages. For the most part, reliance on areas of the left hemisphere of the cerebral cortex to process sentences was just as strong among participants who acquired ASL early in life as among hearing individuals who acquired English early in life. However, early learners of ASL also used their right hemisphere in responding to sentences, perhaps because spatial skills controlled by the right hemisphere come into play in interpreting the gestures of someone who is signing.

What do these striking parallels tell us about theories of language acquisition? They surely imply that language learning depends, to no small extent, on biological processes (Meier, 1991). What isn't clear, however, is whether the linguistic milestones and abilities that deaf children share with hearing children reflect (1) the operation of an inborn specialized linguistic knowledge (or LAD) that enables children to acquire any and all languages (nativist position), or (2) the gradual development of a highly plastic (i.e., changeable) human brain and achievement of cognitive understandings that children are then motivated to express in language-like ways to communicate more effectively with their companions (interactionist position).

Some signs in American Sign Language. FROM REIKEHOF, *1963.*

Toddlers are also becoming quite sensitive to many of the social and situational determinants of effective communication. For example, 2-year-olds are rather proficient at vocal turn-taking; they know that speakers "look up" at the listener when they are about to yield the floor, and they now use this same nonverbal cue to signal the end of their own utterances (Rutter & Durkin, 1987). By age 2 to 2½, children know that they must either stand close to a listener or compensate for distance by raising their voices if they are to communicate with that person (Johnson et al., 1981; Wellman & Lempers, 1977). And remarkably, 2- to 2½-year-olds are already considering what a partner knows (or doesn't know) when choosing a conversational topic or making a request. They much prefer to talk about events that their partners haven't shared with them or don't already know about (Shatz, 1994), and their requests for assistance in obtaining a toy that is out of reach are much more elaborate and more likely to include a gesture when they know that their partners are unaware of the toy's whereabouts (O'Neill, 1996). In fact, 2½-year-olds can even monitor others' *verbal* responses to their messages and clarify many utterances that an adult has misunderstood (Levy, 1999). So a child who requested a toy duck and hears an adult say "You asked for the sock" will often repair his failed message with a statement such as "I don't want that! Want duck!" (Shwe & Markman, 1997).

Finally, young children also learn certain sociolinguistic prescriptions, such as the need to be polite when making requests, and they begin to understand what is polite and what isn't in other people's speech (Baroni & Axia, 1989; Garton & Pratt, 1990). Although we have seen that parents do not intentionally teach grammar to their children, they *do* instruct them in etiquette (Flavell et al., 1993). Such common parental prompts as "What do you say?" or "Say the magic word and the cookie is yours" play an important part in this learning.

In sum, most 2- to 2½-year-olds have learned many pragmatic lessons about language and communication and are usually able to get their meaning across to conversational partners. But even though toddlers can converse with adults and older children, their communication skills pale in comparison with those of a 5-year-old, a 4-year-old, or even many 3-year-olds. Our next task is to determine what it is that preschool children acquire that enables them to become rather sophisticated users of language by the time they enter kindergarten.

LANGUAGE LEARNING DURING THE PRESCHOOL PERIOD

In the short period from age 2½ to 5, children learn to produce sentences that are remarkably complex and adultlike. Table 10.4 gives an inkling of how fast language progresses in the brief span of 7 to 10 months. What are children acquiring that accounts for this language explosion? Surely they are mastering basic morphology and syntax: As we see in Table 10.4, a child of 35 to 38 months is now inserting articles, auxiliary verbs, and grammatical markers (for example, *-ed*, *-ing*) that were previously omitted, as well as

---

Concept Check 10.2
Language Learning among Infants and Toddlers

Check your understanding of *selected aspects* of early language learning by matching each descriptive statement below with one of the following terms or concepts: (a) vocal turn-taking, (b) syntactical bootstrapping, (c) expressive style, (d) telegraphic speech, (e) holophrastic speech, (f) intonational cues, (g) overextension, (h) referential style, (i) object scope constraint. Answers appear in the Appendix.

_____ 1. early linguistic style more common among later-borns and children in Asian societies

_____ 2. very early clue that caregivers' speech conveys distinct meanings

_____ 3. term to describe children's one-word utterances

_____ 4. early linguistic style more common among first-borns and children in Western societies

_____ 5. first pragmatic rule that children learn

_____ 6. assumption that a new word refers to a whole object rather than to its parts

_____ 7. term characterizing a child's earliest sentences

_____ 8. inferring word meaning from the way the word is used in a sentence

_____ 9. semantic "error" that may promote vocabulary development by virtue of its impact on older companions

TABLE 10.4   Samples of One Boy's Speech at Three Ages

Age		
28 months (telegraphic speech)	**35 months**	**38 months**
Somebody pencil	No—I don't know	I like a racing car
Floor	What dat feeled like?	I broke my racing car
Where birdie go?	Lemme do again	It's broked
Read dat	Don't—don't hold with me	You got some beads
Hit hammer, mummy	I'm going to drop it—inne dump truck	Who put dust on my hair?
Yep, it fit	Why—cracker can't talk?	Mummy don't let me buy
Have screw	Those are mines	Why it's not working?

SOURCE: Adapted from McNeill, 1970.

negating propositions and occasionally asking a well-formed question (Hoff-Ginsberg, 1997). And although it is not as obvious from the table, we will see that preschool children are also beginning to understand much more about the pragmatics of language and communication.

Grammatical Development

Development of Grammatical Morphemes

Grammatical morphemes are modifiers that signify subtle changes in meaning in the sentences we construct. These meaning modifiers usually appear sometime during the third year as children begin to pluralize nouns by adding -*s*, to signify location with the prepositional morphemes *in* and *on*, to indicate verb tense with the present progressive -*ing* or the past tense -*ed*, and to describe possessive relations with the inflection '*s*.

TABLE 10.5   Order of Acquisition of English Grammatical Morphemes

Morpheme	Example
1. Present progressive: -*ing*	He is sit*ting* down.
2. Preposition: *in*	The mouse is *in* the box.
3. Preposition: *on*	The book is *on* the table.
4. Plural: -*s*	The dog*s* ran away.
5. Past irregular: for example, *went*	The boy *went* home.
6. Possessive: -'*s*	The girl'*s* dog is big.
7. Uncontractible copula *be*: for example, *are*, *was*	*Are* they boys or girls? *Was* that a dog?
8. Articles: *the*, *a*	He has *a* book.
9. Past regular: -*ed*	He jump*ed* the stream.
10. Third person regular: -*s*	She run*s* fast.
11. Third person irregular: for example, *has*, *does*	*Does* the dog bark?
12. Uncontractible auxiliary *be*: for example, *is*, *were*	*Is* he running? *Were* they at home?
13. Contractible copula *be*: for example, -'*s*, -'*re*	That'*s* a spaniel.
14. Contractible auxiliary *be*: for example, -'*s*, -'*re*	They'*re* running very slowly.

SOURCE: Adapted from Clark & Clark, 1977.

grammatical morphemes prefixes, suffixes, prepositions, and auxiliary verbs that modify the meaning of words and sentences

Roger Brown (1973) kept records on three children as they acquired 14 grammatical morphemes that frequently appear in English sentences. He found that these three children varied considerably with respect to (1) the age at which they began to use grammatical markers and (2) the amount of time it took them to master all 14 rules. However, all three children in this longitudinal study learned the 14 grammatical morphemes in the exact order in which they appear in Table 10.5, a finding confirmed in a cross-sectional study of 21 additional children (de Villiers & de Villiers, 1973).

Why do children who have very different vocabularies learn these 14 grammatical markers in one particular order? Brown (1973) soon rejected a frequency-of-mention hypothesis when he found that the grammatical morphemes learned first appear no more often in parents' speech than morphemes acquired later. What he did discover is that the morphemes acquired early are less semantically and syntactically complex than those acquired later. For example, the present progressive *-ing*, which describes an ongoing action, appears before the past regular *-ed*, which describes both action and a sense of "earlier in time." Moreover, *-ed*, which conveys two semantic features, is acquired earlier than the uncontractible forms of the verb *to be* (*is, are, was, were*), all of which are more syntactically complex and specify *three* semantic relations: number (singular or plural), tense (present or past), and action (ongoing process).

Once young children have acquired a new grammatical morpheme, they apply this rule to new as well as to familiar contexts. For example, if the child realizes that the way to pluralize a noun is to add the grammatical inflection *-s*, he or she has no problem solving the puzzle in Figure 10.5: These two funny-looking creatures are obviously wugs (Berko, 1958).

Overregularization. Interestingly, children occasionally overextend new grammatical morphemes to cases in which the adult form is irregular—a phenomenon known as **overregularization**. Statements such as "I brushed my *tooths*," "She *goed*," or "It *runned* away" are common examples of the kind of overregularization errors that 2½- to 3-year-olds make. Oddly enough, children have often used the correct forms of many irregular nouns and verbs (for example, "It *ran* away"; "My *feet* are cold") *before* they learn any grammatical morphemes (Brown, 1973; Mervis & Johnson, 1991). Even after acquiring a new rule, a child's overregularizations are relatively rare, occurring on only about 2.5 to 5 percent of those occasions in which irregular verbs are used (Marcus et al., 1992). So overregularization is not a serious grammatical defect that must be unlearned. Instead, most of the errors seem to occur because children occasionally fail to retrieve the irregular form of a noun or a verb from memory and must then apply their new morpheme (overregularize) to communicate the idea they are trying to express (Marcus et al., 1992).

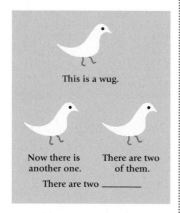

This is a wug.

Now there is another one.   There are two of them.

There are two _____

Figure 10.5 *A linguistic puzzle used to determine young children's understanding of the rule for forming plurals in English.* From Berko, 1958.

overregularization
overgeneralization of grammatical rules to irregular cases where the rules do not apply (for example, saying *mouses* rather than *mice*)

transformational grammar
rules of syntax that allow one to transform declarative statements into questions, negatives, imperatives, and other kinds of sentences

Mastering Transformational Rules

In addition to grammatical morphemes, each language has rules for creating variations of the basic declarative sentence. Applying these rules of **transformational grammar**, the declarative statement "I was eating pizza" can easily be modified to produce a *question* ("What was I eating?") or to generate *negative* sentences ("I was *not* eating pizza"), *imperatives* ("Eat the pizza!"), *relative clauses* ("I, who hate cheese, was eating pizza"), and *compound sentences* ("I was eating pizza, and Larissa was eating spaghetti").

Between the ages of 2 and 2½, most children begin to produce some variations of declarative sentences, many of which depend on their mastery of the auxiliary verb *to be* (de Villiers & de Villiers, 1992). However, children acquire transformational rules in a step-by-step fashion, so that their earliest transformations are very different from those of an adult. We can easily illustrate this point by considering the phases that children go through as they learn to ask questions, negate propositions, and generate complex sentences.

Asking Questions. Two kinds of questions are common to virtually all languages. *Yes/no questions*, the simpler form that is mastered first, ask whether particular declarative statements are true or false (for example, "Is that a doggie?"). By contrast, *wh- questions* call for responses other than a simple yes or no. These queries are called *wh-* questions because, in English, they almost always begin with a *wh-* word such as *who, what, where, when,* or *why.*

The child's earliest questions often consist of nothing more than a declarative sentence uttered with a rising intonation that transforms it into a yes/no question (for example, "See doggie?"). However, *wh-* words are occasionally placed at the beginning of telegraphic sentences to generate simple *wh-* questions such as "Where doggie?" or "What daddy eat?" During the second phase of question asking, children begin to use the proper auxiliary, or helping, verbs, but their questions are of the form "What daddy is eating?" or "Where doggie is going?" Finally, children learn the transformational rule that calls for moving the auxiliary verb ahead of the subject, and they begin to produce adultlike questions such as "What is daddy eating?"

PRODUCING NEGATIVE SENTENCES. Like questions, children's negative sentences develop in a steplike fashion. Children the world over initially express negations by simply placing a negative word in front of the word or statement they wish to negate, producing such utterances as "No mitten" or "No I go." Notice, however, that these first negatives are ambiguous: "No mitten"

Curious 3- to 5-year-olds display their knowledge of transformational grammar by asking many "who," "what," and "why" questions of their companions.

can convey *nonexistence* ("There's no mitten"), *rejection* ("I won't wear a mitten"), or *denial* ("That's not a mitten") (Bloom, 1970). This ambiguity is clarified once the child begins to insert the negative word inside the sentence, in front of the word that it modifies (for example, "I not wear mitten" or "That not mitten"). Finally, children learn to combine negative markers with the proper auxiliary verbs to negate sentences in much the same way adults do. Indeed, Peter and Jill de Villiers (1979) describe a delightful experiment in which young children were persuaded to argue with a talking puppet. Whenever the puppet made a declarative statement, such as "He likes bananas," the child's task was to negate the proposition (argue) in any way he or she could. Most 3- to 4-year-olds thoroughly enjoyed this escalating verbal warfare between themselves and the puppet. But more important, these young children were quite capable of using a wide variety of negative auxiliaries, including *wouldn't, wasn't, hasn't,* and *mustn't,* to properly negate almost any sentence the puppet produced.

PRODUCING COMPLEX SENTENCES. By age 3, most children have begun to produce complex sentences. Relative clauses that modify nouns (for example, "That's the box *that they put it in*") and conjunctions to join simple sentences ("He was stuck *and* I got him out") are usually the first to appear, followed by embedded sentences (for example, "The man *who fixed the fence* went home") and more intricate forms of questions as well (for example, "Matthew will come, won't he?" "Where did you say you put my doll?") (de Villiers & de Villiers, 1992). By the end of the preschool period, at age 5 to 6, children are using most of the grammatical rules of their language and speaking much like adults do, even though they have never had a formal lesson in grammar.

Semantic Development

Another reason that preschoolers' language becomes more complex is that 2- to 5-year-olds are beginning to understand and express relational contrasts such as big/little, tall/short, in/on, before/after, here/there, and I/you (de Villiers & de Villiers, 1979, 1992). *Big* and *little* are usually the first spatial adjectives to appear, and these terms are soon used to specify a variety of relations. By age 2 to 2½, for example, children can use *big* and *little* to draw proper *normative* conclusions (a 10 cm egg, viewed by itself, is "big" relative to other eggs the child remembers seeing) and *perceptual* inferences (a 10 cm egg placed next to an even bigger egg is "little") (Ebeling & Gelman, 1988; 1994). By age 3, children are even capable of using these terms to make appropriate *functional* judgments such as deciding that an oversized article of doll clothing, which is little relative to what the child wears, is nonetheless too "big" to fit the doll in question (Gelman & Ebeling, 1989).

Although preschoolers are becoming increasingly aware of a variety of meaningful relations and are rapidly learning how to express them in their own speech, their incomplete knowledge of syntax leads them to make some interesting semantic errors. Consider the following sentences:

1. The girl hit the boy.
2. The boy was hit by the girl.

Children younger than 4 or 5 frequently misinterpret *passive* constructions, such as sentence 2. They can easily understand the *active* version of the same idea—that is, sentence 1. But if asked to point to a picture that shows "The boy was hit by the girl," preschoolers usually select a drawing that shows a boy hitting a girl. What they have done is to assume that the first noun is the agent of the verb and that the second is the object; consequently, they interpret the passive construction as if it were an active sentence. Passive sentences based on mental-state verbs such as *like* and *know* (for example, "Goofy was liked by Donald") are particularly difficult and are not understood until later in elementary school (Sudhalter & Braine, 1985).

It's not that young children lack the cognitive capacity to understand the more syntactically complex passive sentence. Even 3-year-olds can correctly interpret *irreversible* passives such as "The candy was eaten by the girl" because it is nonsense to interpret this as an active sentence and assume that the candy was doing the eating (de Villiers & de Villiers, 1979). What's more, 3-year-olds learning new (nonsense) verbs can quickly learn to *produce* passive sentences if they have observed an action, heard a passive sentence to describe the action ("Yes, Big bird is meeking the car."), and are asked questions that focus attention on the object of the action (Question: "What happened to the car?" Common answer: "It got meeked.") (Brooks & Tomasello, 1999). Why then do preschoolers often misinterpret passives and rarely produce them? Probably because people speaking to them rarely use passives or ask questions that would encourage their use (Brooks & Tomasello, 1999). Indeed, Inuktitut and Zulu children, who hear many passive constructions in speech directed at them, come to understand and to produce passive sentences much earlier than Western children do (Allen & Crego, 1996).

Development of Pragmatics and Communication Skills

During the preschool period, children acquire a number of conversational skills that help them to communicate more effectively and accomplish their objectives. For example, 3-year-olds are already beginning to understand *illocutionary intent*—that the real underlying meaning of an utterance may not always correspond to the literal meaning of the words speakers use. Notice how the 3-year-old in the following example uses this knowledge to her advantage as she turns a declarative statement into a successful command (Reeder, 1981, p. 135):

SHEILA: Every night I get an ice cream.

BABYSITTER: That's nice, Sheila.

SHEILA: Even when there's a babysitter, I get an ice cream.

BABYSITTER (TO HIMSELF): Backed into a corner by a 3-year-old's grasp of language as a social tool!

Three- to five-year-olds are also learning that they must tailor their messages to their audience if they hope to communicate effectively. Marilyn Shatz and Rochel Gelman (1973) recorded the speech of several 4-year-olds as they introduced a new toy to either a 2-year-old or an adult. An analysis of the tapes revealed that 4-year-old children are already beginning to adjust their speech to their listener's level of understanding. When talking to a 2-year-old, the older children used short sentences and were careful to choose phrases such as "Watch," "Look, Perry," and "Look here" that would attract and maintain the toddler's attention. By contrast, 4-year-olds explaining how the toy worked to an adult used complex sentences and were generally more polite.

Referential Communication

An effective communicator is one who not only produces clear, unambiguous messages, but is also able to detect any ambiguities in others' speech and ask for clarification. These aspects of language are called **referential communication skills**.

It was once generally assumed that preschool children lacked the abilities to detect uninformative messages and resolve most problems in communication. Indeed, if asked to evaluate the quality of an ambiguous message such as "Look at *that* horse" when a number of horses are in view, preschool children are more likely than their elementary-school counterparts to say that this is an *informative* message. Apparently, they often fail to detect linguistic ambiguities because they are focusing on what they *think* the speaker means rather than on the (ambiguous) *literal* meaning of the message (Beal & Belgrad, 1990; Flavell et al., 1993). Why do preschoolers guess at the meaning of uninformative messages? Possibly because they are often quite successful at inferring the true meaning of ambiguous utterances from other contextual cues, such as their knowledge of a particular speaker's attitudes, preferences, and past behaviours (see, for example, Ackerman, Szymanski, & Silver, 1990). Four-year-olds are also less likely than 7-year-olds to detect and rephrase their own uninformative messages. In fact, they often assume that their own statements are perfectly informative and that failures to communicate should be blamed on their listeners (Flavell et al., 1993).

However, most 3- to 5-year-olds display better referential communication skills in the natural environment than on laboratory tasks, particularly when there are contextual cues to help them clarify an otherwise ambiguous message (Ackerman, 1993; Beal & Belgrad, 1990). Furthermore, even 3-year-olds know that they cannot carry out an unintelligible request made by a yawning adult, and they quickly realize that other impossible requests (such as "Bring me the refrigerator") are problematic as well (Revelle, Wellman, & Karabenick, 1985). These young children also know how they might resolve such breakdowns in communication, because they often say "What?" or "Huh?" to a yawning adult or ask "How? It's too heavy!" when told to retrieve a refrigerator.

In sum, 3- to 5-year-olds are not very good at detecting ambiguities in the *literal* meaning of oral messages. Nevertheless, they are better communicators than many laboratory studies of comprehension monitoring might suggest because they are often successful at inferring what an ambiguous message must mean from nonlinguistic contextual information.

LANGUAGE LEARNING DURING MIDDLE CHILDHOOD AND ADOLESCENCE

referential communication skills
abilities to generate clear verbal messages, recognize when others' messages are unclear, and clarify any unclear messages one transmits or receives

Although 5-year-olds have learned a great deal about language in a remarkably brief period, many important strides in linguistic competence are made from ages 6 to 14—

the elementary-school and junior high-school years. Not only do schoolchildren use bigger words and produce longer and more complex utterances, they also begin to think about and manipulate language in ways that were previously impossible.

Later Syntactic Development

During middle childhood, children correct many of their previous syntactical errors and begin to use a number of complex grammatical forms that did not appear in their earlier speech. For example, 5- to 8-year-olds are beginning to iron out the kinks in their use of personal pronouns, so that sentences such as "Him and her went" become much less frequent (Dale, 1976). By age 7 to 9, children understand and may occasionally even produce such complex *passive* sentences as "Goofy was liked by Donald" (Sudhalter & Braine, 1985) and *conditional sentences* such as "If Goofy had come, Donald would have been delighted" (Boloh & Champaud, 1993).

So middle childhood is a period of syntactical refinement. Children are learning subtle exceptions to grammatical rules and coming to grips with the more complex syntactical structures of their native tongue. However, this process of syntactic elaboration occurs very gradually, often continuing well into adolescence or young adulthood (Clark & Clark, 1977; Eisele & Lust, 1996).

Semantics and Metalinguistic Awareness

Children's knowledge of semantics and semantic relations continues to grow throughout the elementary-school years. Vocabulary development is particularly impressive. Work conducted at the University of Waterloo indicates that 6-year-olds already understand approximately 10 000 words and continue to expand their *receptive vocabularies* at the rate of about 20 words a day, until they comprehend some 40 000 words by age 10 (Anglin, 1993). Of course, elementary-school children do not use all these new words in their own speech and may not even have heard many of them before. What they have gained is **morphological knowledge**—knowledge of the meaning of morphemes that make up words—which enables them to analyze the structure of such unfamiliar words as "sourer," "custom-made," or "hopelessness" and to quickly figure out what they mean (Anglin, 1993). Finally, adolescents' capacity for formal-operational reasoning permits them to further expand their vocabularies, adding a host of abstract words (for example, "ironic," "eradicate") that they rarely heard (or didn't understand) during the elementary-school years (McGhee-Bidlack, 1991).

Elementary-school children are also becoming more proficient at *semantic integrations*—that is, at drawing linguistic inferences that enable them to understand more than is actually said. For example, if 6- to 8-year-olds hear "Sophie did not see the rock; the rock was in the path; Sophie fell," they are able to infer that Sophie must have tripped over the rock. Interestingly, however, 6- to 8-year-olds often assume that the story explicitly described Sophie tripping and are not consciously aware that they have drawn an inference (Beal, 1990). By age 9 to 11, children are better able to make these kinds of linguistic inferences and recognize them as *inferences* (Beal, 1990; Casteel, 1993), even when the two or more pieces of information that are necessary to draw the "appropriate" conclusion are separated by a number of intervening sentences (Johnson & Smith, 1981; van den Broek, 1989). And once children begin to integrate different kinds of linguistic information, they are able to detect *hidden* meanings that are not immediately obvious from the content of an utterance. For example, if a noisy 6-year-old hears her teacher quip "My, but you're quiet today," the child will probably note the contradiction between the literal meaning of the sentence and its satirical intonation or its context and thereby detect the *sarcasm* in her teacher's remark (Dews et al., 1996); although a true appreciation of the humour of the remark appears to develop later (Harris & Pexman, 2003).

morphological knowledge
one's knowledge of the meaning of morphemes that make up words

One reason that school-age children are able to go beyond the information given when making linguistic inferences is that they are rapidly developing **metalinguistic awareness**—an ability to think about language and to comment on its properties (Whitehurst & Lonigan, 1998). This reflective ability is present to some degree among preschoolers, particularly 4- to 5-year-olds, who are beginning to display much more *phonological awareness* (for example, if you take the *s* sound out of *scream*, what's left?) and *grammatical awareness* (for example, is "I be sick" the right or wrong way to say it?) than younger children do (de Villiers & de Villiers, 1979). Yet the metalinguistic competencies that 5-year-olds display are limited compared with those of a 9-year-old, a 7-year-old, or even a 6-year-old (Bialystok, 1986; Ferreira & Morrison, 1994).

By reading to young children, a parent can promote the development of reading skills.

An emerging awareness that language is an arbitrary and rule-bound system may have important educational implications. Specifically, 4- to 6-year-olds who score relatively high in such phonological skills as detecting phonemes, syllables, and rhymes learn to read much quicker and remain more proficient readers throughout the first few grades of school (Lonigan et al., 2000; Whitehurst & Lonigan, 1998). Indeed, this strong relationship between phonological awareness and reading achievement holds even after controlling for differences in young readers' intelligence, vocabulary, memory skills, and social class. Some theorists believe some degree of phonological awareness is necessary before a child can learn to read (Wagner et al., 1997), and interventions designed to foster children's phonemic awareness clearly promote children's reading and speaking skills (Schneider et al., 1997; Whitehurst & Lonigan, 1998). In fact one of the strongest arguments in favour of the phonics method of reading instruction (see Box 6.4) is that it promotes the very phonological skills that seem so necessary for young children to learn in order to read well.

Interestingly, research suggests that such home literacy experiences as shared story-book reading with parents does not promote children's phonological skills to any great extent (see Whitehurst & Lonigan, 1998 for a review). However, shared storybook reading experiences do promote such aspects of emergent literacy as vocabulary growth and letter recognition, and receptive language development, which also predict children's success at learning to read (Reese & Cox, 1999, Lonigan et al., 2000; Senechal & LeFevre, 2002)

Further Development of Communication Skills

Earlier, we examined a study (Shatz & Gelman, 1973) in which preschool children adjusted the style and content of their speech to a listener's level of understanding. Recall that the 4-year-olds in this study were face to face with their 2-year-old or adult companion and thus could see whether the listener was responding appropriately to their messages or following their instructions. Could children this young have communicated effectively with their partners if they had been asked to deliver their messages over a telephone?

Probably not. In one early study of children's referential communication skills, 4- to 10-year-olds were asked to describe blocks with unfamiliar graphic designs on them to a peer who was on the other side of an opaque screen so that the peer could identify them (Krauss & Glucksberg, 1977). As shown in Table 10.6, preschool children described these designs in highly idiosyncratic ways that neither communicated much to their listeners nor enabled them to identify which blocks the speaker was talking about. By contrast, 8- to 10-year-olds provided much more informative messages. They realized that their listener could not see what they were referring to, thus requiring them to somehow *differentiate* these objects and make each distinctive if their messages were to be understood.

metalinguistic awareness
a knowledge of language and its properties; an understanding that language can be used for purposes other than communication

Four- and five-year-olds perform much better on referential communication tasks that require them to describe the whereabouts of *real* (rather than abstract) objects that are hidden or missing (Plumert, Ewert, & Spear, 1995). But even so, their messages are more ambiguous than those of elementary-school children (Craton et al., 1990).

Dramatic improvements in referential communication skills during the early elementary-school years are due, in part, to the growth of cognitive skills and sociolinguistic understanding. Six- to seven-year-olds have learned from earlier miscommunications about the importance of generating more informative messages. This is also the age at which they are becoming notably less egocentric and acquiring some role-taking skills, two *cognitive developments* that help them to adapt their speech to the needs of their listeners in such highly demanding situations as talking on the phone (or participating in a referential communication experiment), where it may be difficult to tell whether one's message has been interpreted correctly (Hoff-Ginsberg, 1997). Furthermore, *sociolinguistic understanding* is required to make the right kinds of speech adjustments, because messages that are clear for one listener may not be for others. For example, a listener who is unfamiliar with the stimuli in a referential communication task may require more differentiating information and more message redundancy than a second person who is already familiar with these objects. Six- to ten-year-olds do provide longer messages to unfamiliar than to familiar listeners. Yet only the 9- and 10-year-olds among them adjusted the *content* of their communications to the listeners' needs by providing richer *differentiating* information to an unfamiliar listener (Sonnenschein, 1986, 1988).

> **?**
>
> **WHAT DO YOU THINK?**
>
> How would you try to improve 5-year-olds' referential communication skills? Might having them play games in which they must seek limiting information (for example, 20 Questions) be of any help? Why or why not?

What Role Do Siblings Play in the Growth of Communication Skills?

Most studies of social influences on language development have focused on mother–child pairs (usually mothers and their *first-born* children). Yet children with siblings spend a fair amount of time conversing with them or listening as a sibling converses with a parent (Barton & Tomasello, 1991). Might conversations involving siblings contribute in any meaningful way to the growth of communication skills?

TABLE 10.6   Typical Idiosyncratic Descriptions Offered by Preschool Children When Talking about Unfamiliar Graphic Designs in the Kraus and Glucksberg Communication Game

			Child		
Form	1	2	3	4	5
⌐	Man's legs	Airplane	Drapeholder	Zebra	Flying saucer
ᘯ	Mother's hat	Ring	Keyhold	Lion	Snake
⊔	Daddy's shirt	Milk jug	Shoe hold	Coffeepot	Dog

SOURCE: Adapted from Krauss & Glucksberg, 1977.

Indeed, it appears that interactions among linguistically immature siblings may actually *promote* effective communication. Consider, for example, that because older children are less likely than parents to adjust their speech to a younger sibling's ability to understand (Tomasello, Conti-Ramsden, & Ewert, 1990), the comprehension errors that a younger sibling displays may make older brothers and sisters more aware of listeners' needs and more inclined to monitor and repair their own ambiguous messages. And because older siblings are also less likely than parents are to correctly *interpret* a younger sibling's uninformative messages and grant her wishes, the younger sibling may learn from her failures to communicate and be prompted to speak in ways that are more widely understood (Perez-Granados & Callanan, 1997). So if children truly learn from breakdowns in communication, then opportunities to converse with relatively immature linguistic partners (siblings and peers) would seem to provide fertile ground for the growth of communication skills. In addition, Oshimo-Takane at McGill and her colleagues demonstrated that, having the opportunity to hear older siblings interact with careproviders, as well as having the older sibling talking to the younger sibling, promotes more advanced use of some aspects of language such as the use of pronouns (Oshimo-Takane, Goodz, & Derevensky, 1996).

In sum, the rapid pace at which cognitively immature children master the fundamentals of language and communication is truly awe-inspiring. Table 10.7 briefly summarizes the ground we have covered in tracing the evolution of young human beings from preverbal creatures, who are prepared for language learning and motivated to share meaning with their companions, to highly articulate adolescents, who can generate and comprehend an infinite number of messages.

LEARNING MORE THAN ONE LANGUAGE: BILINGUALISM

In many countries throughout the world, children are born into families or social environments where they are exposed to more than one language and, hence, have the opportunity to be **bilingual**—that is, to acquire two or more languages. The adoption of the Official Languages Act (1985) in the 1980s identified Canada as a bilingual nation where residents could expect and receive federal government services in either of the country's two official languages, French or English. Subsequent federal and

bilingual
fluent in two languages

Concept Check 10.3
Language Development from
Toddlerhood to Adolescence

Check your understanding of *selected aspects* of language development from the preschool period through early adolescence by matching each statement below with one of the following terms/concepts: (a) referential communication skills, (b) overregularization, (c) metalinguistic awareness, (d) transformational grammar, (e) phonological awareness, (f) morphological knowledge, (g) grammatical morphemes. Answers appear in the Appendix.

_____ 1. rules enabling children to produce variations of declarative sentences

_____ 2. enables children to reflect on language and its properties

_____ 3. enables children to expand their receptive vocabularies at a dramatic rate

_____ 4. helps speakers tailor messages to listeners' needs and characteristics

_____ 5. modifiers that give more precise meaning to sentences

_____ 6. grammatical "error" that reflects new linguistic understandings

_____ 7. especially good predictor of preschool children's future reading achievement

TABLE 10.7   Important Milestones in Language Development

Age (years)	Phonology	Semantics	Grammar/syntax	Pragmatics	Metalinguistic awareness
0–1	Receptivity to speech and discrimination of speech sounds Babbling begins to resemble the sounds of native language	Some interpretation of intonational cues in others' speech Preverbal gestures appear Vocables appear Little if any understanding of individual words	Preference for phrase structure and stress patterns of native language	Joint attention with caregiver to objects and events Turn-taking in games and vocalizations Appearance of preverbal gestures	None
1–2	Appearance of strategies to simplify word pronunciations	First words appear Rapid expansion of vocabulary after age 18 months Overextensions and underextensions of word meanings	Holophrases give way to two-word telegraphic speech Sentences express distinct semantic relations Acquisition of some grammatical morphemes	Use of gestures and intonational cues to clarify messages Richer understanding of vocal turn-taking rules First signs of etiquette in children's speech	None
3–5	Pronunciations improve	Vocabulary expands Understanding of spatial relations and use of spatial words in speech	Grammatical morphemes added in regular sequence Awareness of most rules of transformational grammar	Beginning understanding of illocutionary intent Some adjustment of speech to different audiences Some attempts at clarifying obviously ambiguous messages	Some phonemic and grammatical awareness
6–adolescence	Pronunciations become adultlike	Dramatic expansion of vocabulary, including abstract words during adolescence Appearance and refinement of semantic integrations	Acquisition of morphological knowledge Correction of earlier grammatical errors Acquisition of complex syntactical rules	Referential communication improves, especially the ability to detect and repair uninformative messages one sends and receives	Metalinguistic awareness blossoms and becomes more extensive with age

provincial/territorial statutes and proposed legislation recognizes the status of heritage languages, especially Aboriginal languages (e.g., British Columbia's First Peoples' Heritage, Language and Culture Act, 1996; Canadian Multiculturalism Act, 1995). These legislative acts provide the foundation for promoting and retaining languages, but how many Canadians are bilingual?

Sample data from the census suggests that most Canadians are monolingual—that is, speak only one language. In 1996, about 19 million individuals identified themselves as English and about 4 million as French speakers, while only about 5 million were bilingual in English and French (Statistics Canada, 2001d). These numbers, however, underestimate the number of bilingual people in Canada because they do not include those who speak languages other than the two official languages.

Many children have experience with another language through their families or cultural groups. As many as 50 other languages, in addition to one or both official languages, are spoken by Canadians (Statistics Canada, 1993). The diversity of languages available to young children in Canada appears to be shared by children around the world, with some researchers speculating that there are as many or more children growing up bilingual as those growing up monolingual (e.g., Tucker, 1998).

How does learning two or more languages simultaneously affect language development? Before 1960, many researchers suggested that young children who learned more than one language at a time would be at risk. These concerns were supported by studies in which bilingual children scored lower than their monolingual peers on tests of linguistic knowledge and general intelligence (Hakuta, 1988). The studies, however, were seriously flawed. The bilingual children were often first- or second-generation Canadians from immigrant families from lower socioeconomic backgrounds who were not very proficient in English. Furthermore, the tests they took were administered in English (rather than in their language of greatest proficiency), and their performances were compared with samples largely comprised of middle-class, English-speaking monolingual children (Diaz, 1983). No wonder the bilingual children performed so poorly!

Starting in the 1960s, researchers began to look more carefully at the process of becoming bilingual. The research findings are clear and consistent: Children exposed to more than one language early (before age 3) have little difficulty becoming proficient in each language. Early research indicated that, by age 3, children are well aware that the languages are independent systems and that each is associated with particular contexts in which it is to be spoken (Lanza, 1992; Reich, 1986). Later research suggests that even younger bilingual children have acquired these skills. For example, Genesee, Nicoladis, and Paradis (1995) observed French–English bilingual children in Montreal interacting with their parents. Each parent had a different native language, and both tended to use his or her own native language when interacting with the child. The parent, then, was the cue or context for the language that the child should speak. Even at 22 to 26 months of age, the children most often used the language that was native to the parent when interacting with that parent—that is, the children spoke French to the French-speaking parent and English to the English-speaking parent. Additional research demonstrates that young bilingual children can also tailor their language to meet the needs of monolingual strangers (Genesee, Boivin, & Nicoladis, 1996). Clearly even young bilingual children understand where and when to use their different languages. Research also demonstrates that by age 4 they display normal language proficiency in the language of their community and solid to excellent linguistic skills in the second language, depending on how much they are exposed to it. Even when preschool children acquire a second language *sequentially* (that is, after age 3, when they are already conversant in their native tongue), it often takes them no more than a year to achieve near-native abilities in that language (Reich, 1986).

One unique observation about bilingual toddlers is that they sometimes use elements from one language when speaking another language. These crossovers are referred to as "code-mixing." Some researchers argue that these errors are an indication that the child has not yet fully differentiated the separate languages and is not truly bilingual. Instead, children's language is perceived as being fused in a single unified system. This interpretation is known as the *unitary language system hypothesis* (a review of which is presented in Genesee, 2001). Others, such as Fred Genesee at McGill University, suggest that code-mixing is not an indication of the bilingual child's lack of competence or a problem in the acquisition of the language, but rather indicates the child's ability to use his or her knowledge of language strategically in order to enhance communication. Genesee's research regarding code-mixing is highlighted in Box 10.4.

What about the cognitive consequences of bilingualism? Recent, well-controlled studies that matched bilingual and monolingual individuals on important variables such as socioeconomic status have consistently found that there are cognitive *advantages* to bilingualism. Bilingual children score as high or higher than monolingual peers on tests of language proficiency, Piagetian conservation problems, and nonverbal intelligence (see for example Diaz, 1985; Ginsburg & McCoy, 1982). Canadian researchers have demonstrated that bilingual individuals outperform monolingual individuals on measures of metalinguistic awareness (e.g., Bialystok, 1988; Galambos & Goldin-Meadow, 1990)—particularly those that call for people to recognize the correspondence among letters, words, and their phonological components (Bialystok, 1997; Bialystok, Shenfield, & Codd, 2000). Recent research conducted by Ellen Bialystok and her colleagues, however, suggests that the bilingual advantage found for some areas of metalinguistic development, may not be present for phonemic awareness (Bialystok, Majmuder, & Martin, 2003). (For more information on this research see the Inside Track Box 10.5.)

Fred Genesee

Fred Genesee

Fred Genesee studies language, second-language learning and representation in bilingual and second-language populations. He works in the Department of Psychology at McGill University.

Young children in the process of learning two languages simultaneously often use elements from both languages in the same utterance or stretch of conversation when they begin to talk. This is called *code-mixing* or *code-switching*. The mixed elements can include different aspects of language, including sounds, words, morphosyntactic structures, or pragmatic patterns. Bilingual code-mixing has often been interpreted to mean that children have not yet differentiated between the two languages, at least during the initial stage of acquisition. If this were true, then we would expect to find that children's code-mixing within the same utterances would be random, and also that it would result in sentences that are grammatically incorrect from the point of view of one or both languages.

Genesee (2001) has examined code-mixing between sentences by English–French and English–Inuktitut bilingual children from 2 to 3½ years of age. He found that these children do not violate the grammatical constraints of either language when they code-mix. Additional research in Genesee's lab has also shown that young bilingual children tend to code-mix more when using their less-proficient language and when they do not know a word in the language they are speaking. Thus, mixing is a form of borrowing that allows these children to fill lexical gaps. In sum, far from being a sign of linguistic fusion or incompetence, code-mixing by young bilingual children is a communicative strategy they use to stretch their linguistic resources so that they can express themselves.

Bilingual children, however, also outperform monolinguals at *nonlinguistic* tasks that require selective attention to overcome distractions (Bialystok, 1999). Why is the bilingual mind advantaged? Ellen Bialystok and her associates (2000) suggest two reasons. The bilingual advantage at some metalinguistic tasks may stem from learning very early that linguistic representations are *arbitrary*. For example, English–French bilinguals learn that the same (canine) animal is symbolized in their two languages by the words "dog" and "chien," which neither look nor sound alike. And bilinguals' advantage at overcoming distractions may simply reflect the fact that they are well practised at monitoring their surroundings and producing the language understood by their immediate companions, while *inhibiting* the distracting second language that is irrelevant to that context.

Positive research findings such as those above, along with increased federal and provincial funding, have enhanced opportunities for Canadian children to receive their education in Canada's two official languages (e.g., Stern, 1998) and in some Aboriginal heritage languages (e.g., Canadian Heritage, 1999; Ignace, 1998). The two most common language instructional approaches in Canada are **core language** and **immersion** programs. In core instruction, the new language is taught as a course subject for one period on one or more days of the week (Lapkin, 1998). In immersion programs, instruction is entirely in the language that is to be learned. Immersion can occur for part or all of the school day, and it can be introduced at various points in the academic system, from early (starting in kindergarten or Grade 1), to middle (starting in Grade 4 or 5), to late (starting in Grade 6 or 7) immersion (see Johnson & Swain, 1997).

The relative benefits of these programs are difficult to assess given the differences in how they are implemented, but research indicates that the amount of time spent in the to-be-learned language is a critical factor (Calman & Daniel, 1998; Turnbull et al., 1998), with greater amounts of intense time yielding stronger language gains. In general, immersion programs result in higher proficiency than core programs, immersion programs do not negatively affect the development of the mother tongue, and total and early immersion leads to greater gains than partial or late immersion (see Hamers & Blanc, 2000, for a review).

Although highly controversial (Delcampo & Delcampo, 1998), some educators and researchers argue that all children should receive a bilingual education. Such an approach may not only promote broader linguistic proficiency and better academic per-

core language
involves explicit instruction in a second language, usually through a specific language course (e.g., French class); occasionally the explicit instruction is embedded within a particular curriculum area

immersion
involves instruction in a second language where all or most of the curriculum is provided in the second language

formance, but may also foster a greater appreciation of ethnic diversity and address our increasing societal need for a bilingually competent work force (Hakuta & Garcia, 1989; Sleek, 1994). Such claims must be considered cautiously. For example, the impact of some immersion programs has been detrimental for some Canadian minority groups.

Historically, Aboriginal Canadian children have been placed in immersion programs where their native language is discouraged in favour of one of Canada's official languages (Freeman, 1978). Recently, programs have been introduced where immersion involves both the culturally dominant language (English or French) and the native language, or, in a few cases, all instruction is in the native language. These latter two approaches appear to be important for enhancing self-esteem among Aboriginal children. Steven Wright at the University of California, in collaboration with Donald Taylor of McGill University (Wright & Taylor, 2001), assessed Inuit, White, and mixed-heritage kindergarten children after their first year in a heritage language program or a second-language program. When children were educated in their heritage language, there was an associated increase in individual self-esteem. In addition there was an increase in collective self-esteem among the minority-group Inuit children. For minority children, who often feel stigmatized in the majority culture, instruction in their native language may be critical for fostering positive regard for themselves and their community. Apart from the positive social outcomes, heritage language instruction promotes first-language skills and does not negatively affect academic achievement or the subsequent acquisition of a majority language (see Wright & Taylor, 2001).

? | **WHAT DO YOU THINK?**

What would your reaction be if the federal government mandated immersion education for all elementary-school children by the year 2007? How could this order be implemented given that most elementary-school teachers are monolingual and some classrooms have students from a variety of linguistic backgrounds, including some with limited skills in either French or English (for example, Chinese, Polish, Somali, etc.)?

THE INSIDE TRACK

10.5

Ellen Bialystok

Ellen Bialystok is in the Psychology Department of the Faculty of Arts at York University. Her research interests explore cognitive development, particularly issues related to the development of symbolic skills such as language, number and spatial cognition, and second-language acquisition.

Does being bilingual facilitate metalinguistic development? Indeed, research has supported just such a benefit for metalinguistic competencies related to word and syntactic awareness. However, the answer to this question may not be as simple as a straightforward yes. Ellen Bialystok and her colleagues recently investigated potential bilingual advantages for phonological awareness (Bialystok, Majmuder, & Martin, 2003). Specifically, Bialystok and her colleagues conducted a series of three studies. The first study investigated bilingual and monolingual children's performance on phonemic awareness tasks while also manipulating working memory demands (through the provision of, or absence of, verbal or pictorial cues). The purpose was to separate the demands of working memory from the demands associated with the phonemic awareness task. Overall, there were no differences between the bilingual (French–English) and monolingual (English) children in their ability to solve the phonological awareness problem, although there was

some tentative support suggesting that the children may have used different strategies to approach the problem. In addition, older children (Grades 1 and 2) performed better than those in kindergarten. In the second study, the methods were refined to allow for a more stringent assessment of working memory, and to test bilingual children in both languages. Again, the older children outperformed the younger children. When the effects of literacy instruction were taken into account, again, the performance of the monolinguals and bilinguals did not differ. In the third study, different forms of phonological awareness tasks were compared to see if different elements of phonological awareness would show an advantage for the bilingual children. Two bilingual groups (Spanish/English and Chinese/English) were compared with the English monolinguals. Interestingly, the groups performed differently on one of the phonemic tasks; however, the differences could not be attributed to a bilingual advantage because the two bilingual groups themselves were not the same—one achieved higher scores than the monolinguals and the other, lower scores. Instead the important factors were the two languages the children spoke and the language in which they were learning to read. Together, these studies suggest that, although bilinguals experience advantages in some metalinguistic awareness situations, that advantage is not present for phonemic awareness. It is important to note, however, that there was no bilingual "disadvantage"; that is, in general, bilingual children were equivalent to the monolingual children.

SUMMARY

Five Components of Language

♦ The five aspects of **language** that children must acquire to **communicate** effectively in their native tongue are **phonology**, a knowledge of the language's sound system; **morphology**, rules specifying how words are formed from sounds; **semantics**, an understanding of the meaning of **bound morphemes, free morphemes (**words), and sentences; **syntax**, the rules that specify how words are combined to produce sentences; and **pragmatics**, the principles governing how language is to be used in different social situations.

Theories of Language Development

♦ There are three major theoretical perspectives on language acquisition. Learning theorists propose that children acquire language as they imitate others' speech and are reinforced for grammatically correct utterances. However, research provides very little support for the notions that parents shape grammatical speech or that children acquire language by mimicking the sentences they hear. Adults speak in **motherese** to young children and reshape their primitive sentences with **expansions** and **recasts**, but as long as children have partners with whom to converse, they will acquire language even without these environmental supports.

♦ Nativists believe that human beings are innately endowed with linguistic processing capabilities (that is, a **language acquisition device** or **language-making capacity**) that function most efficiently before puberty. Presumably, children require nothing other than being exposed to speech in order to learn any and all languages. The identification of **linguistic universals** is consistent with the nativist viewpoint, as are the observations that language functions are served by **Broca's** and **Wernicke's areas** of the brain, and that deaf children of hearing parents and other children exposed to ungrammatical pidgins may create languages of their own. Furthermore, both first- and second-language learning seem to proceed more smoothly during the **sensitive period** before puberty. Yet many of these findings have been challenged, and unfortunately nativists are not very clear about how children sift through verbal input and make the crucial discoveries that further their linguistic competencies.

♦ Proponents of the **interactionist theory** acknowledge that children are biologically prepared to acquire language. However, they suggest that what may be innate is not any specialized linguistic processor but, rather, a nervous system that gradually matures and predisposes children to develop similar ideas at about the same age, which they are motivated to share with their companions. Thus, biological maturation is said to affect cognitive development, which in turn influences language development. However, interactionists stress that the environment plays a crucial role in language learning, for companions continually introduce new linguistic rules and concepts in engaging conversations that children can easily comprehend.

Before Language: The Prelinguistic Period

♦ Infants are well prepared for language learning. During the **prelinguistic phase** they easily discriminate speechlike sounds and are sensitive to a wider variety of phonemes than adults are. They are sensitive to intonational cues from the beginning and, by 7 to 10 months of age, are already segmenting others' speech with phrases and wordlike units.

♦ Infants begin **cooing** by age 2 months and start to **babble** by age 4 to 6 months. Later in the first year, infants match the intonation of their babbles to the tonal qualities of the language they hear and may produce their own **vocables** to signify meaning.

♦ Although infants less than 1 year old understand the meaning of few, if any, individual words, they have already learned that people take turns while vocalizing and that gestures can be used to communicate and share meaning with companions. Once infants begin to understand individual words, their **receptive language** is ahead of their **productive language**.

One Word at a Time: The Holophrastic Period

♦ During the one-word, or **holophrastic**, **period**, infants speak in **holophrases** and spend several months expanding their vocabularies one word at a time. They talk mostly about moving or manipulable objects that interest them and show a vocabulary spurt, or **naming explosion**, between 18 and 24 months of age. Most children in Western cultures develop a **referential style** of language; however, a smaller number of Western infants and a larger number from cultures emphasizing social harmony adopt an **expressive style** of language.

• Toddlers are quite adept at using social and contextual cues to **fast-map** words onto objects, actions, and attributes. Other strategies, or **processing constraints**, that help them to figure out what new words mean include the **object scope constraint**, the **mutual exclusivity constraint**, the **lexical contrast constraint**, and **syntactical bootstrapping**. Nevertheless, toddlers frequently make such semantic errors as **overextensions** and **underextensions**.

• Many psycholinguists call a toddler's one-word utterances *holophrases* because they often seem less like labels and more like attempts to communicate an entire sentence's worth of meaning.

From Holophrases to Simple Sentences: The Telegraphic Period

♦ At 18 to 24 months of age, toddlers begin to produce two- and three-word sentences known as **telegraphic speech** because they omit grammatical markers and smaller, less important words. Although telegraphic sentences are not grammatical by adult standards, they are far more than random word combinations. Not only do children follow certain rules of word order when combining words, but they also express the same categories of meaning (semantic relations) in their earliest sentences.

◆ Telegraphic toddlers are also becoming highly sensitive to pragmatic constraints, including the realization that speakers must be more directive and elaborate when a listener doesn't share their knowledge. Young children are also learning certain sociolinguistic prescriptions such as the need to be polite when making requests.

Language Learning during the Preschool Period

◆ During the preschool period (ages 2½ to 5), the child's language becomes much more similar to an adult's. As children produce longer utterances, they begin to add **grammatical morphemes** such as the *-s* for plurality, the *-ed* for past tense, the *-ing* for present progressive, and articles, prepositions, and auxiliary verbs. Although individual children acquire grammatical markers at different rates and occasionally **overregularize** them, there is a striking uniformity in the order in which these morphemes appear. The preschool period is also the time when a child learns rules of **transformational grammar** that will enable him or her to change declarative statements into questions, negations, imperatives, relative clauses, and compound sentences. By the time they enter school, children have mastered most of the syntactical rules of their native language and can produce a wide variety of sophisticated, adultlike messages.

◆ Another reason that language becomes increasingly complex during the preschool years is that youngsters are beginning to appreciate and use semantic and relational contrasts such as big/little, wide/narrow, more/less, and before/after.

◆ Preschool children are beginning to understand such pragmatic lessons as the need to tailor their messages to a listener's ability to comprehend if they hope to be understood. Children's **referential communication skills** are not well developed, although they have begun to detect at least some of the uninformative messages they receive and to ask for clarification.

Language Learning during Middle Childhood and Adolescence

◆ Middle childhood and early adolescence is a period of linguistic refinement. Children learn subtle exceptions to grammatical rules and begin to understand even the most complex syntactical structures of their native language. Vocabulary grows rapidly as children acquire **morphological knowledge** as well as **metalinguistic awareness**—an ability to think about language and to comment on its properties, which is a good predictor of reading achievement. School-age children also display much better referential communication skills because they attend more carefully to literal meanings of ambiguous utterances and are more likely to clarify the uninformative messages they send and receive. Cognitive development, the growth of sociolinguistic knowledge, and opportunities to communicate with linguistically immature siblings and peers all contribute to the development of communication skills.

Learning More Than One Language: Bilingualism

◆ **Bilingualism** is becoming increasingly common in Canada, and children exposed early and regularly to two languages can easily acquire them both. There are cognitive advantages to bilingualism, and recent bilingual education programs (**core language** instruction and **immersion**) appear to promote language skills and self-perceived academic and social competencies. The exception to these gains may be evident in minority groups whose primary language is not English or French.

KEY TERMS

language, 351
communication, 351
psycholinguists, 351
phonology, 351
phonemes, 351
morphology, 352
semantics, 352
morphemes, 352
free morphemes, 352
bound morphemes, 352
syntax, 352
pragmatics, 352
sociolinguistic knowledge, 352
linguistic universal, 353
language acquisition device
   (LAD), 354

language-making capacity
   (LMC), 354
Broca's area, 355
Wernicke's area, 355
sensitive-period hypothesis (of
   language acquisition), 356
pidgins, 357
creoles, 357
interactionist theory, 358
motherese, 359
expansions, 360
recasts, 360
prelinguistic phase, 361
coos, 362
babbles, 363
vocables, 363

receptive language, 364
productive language, 364
holophrastic period, 365
holophrase, 365
naming explosion, 365
multimodal motherese, 367
referential style, 367
expressive style, 367
fast-mapping, 367
overextension, 368
underextension, 368
processing constraints, 369
object scope constraint, 369
mutual exclusivity constraint,
   369
lexical contrast constraint, 369

syntactical bootstrapping, 369
telegraphic speech, 371
grammatical morphemes, 375
overregularization, 376
transformational grammar, 376
referential communication
   skills, 379
morphological knowledge, 380
metalinguistic awareness, 381
bilingual, 383
core language, 386
immersion, 386

You can find further information on the topics covered in this chapter by visiting:

www.developmentalpsych2e.nelson.com

 For additional reading, go to InfoTrac College Edition, your on-line research library, at:

infotrac.thomsonlearning.com

Emotional Development and the Establishment of Intimate Relationships

PhotoDisc, Inc.

Two 18-month-olds, Jean-Paul and Maya, are playing in Jean-Paul's living room when a delivery truck enters the driveway and backfires loudly. Jean-Paul, obviously startled and fearful, whimpers, stands, and moves nearer his mother on the sofa. Maya is more curious. She looks wide-eyed at her mother, who smiles and exclaims, "That truck went boom!" Maya then runs to the window and gazes out at the two delivery men, who are now unloading the washer and dryer that Jean-Paul's mother has ordered.

Clearly, these toddlers had very different emotional reactions to the startling event they experienced. Jean-Paul, noticeably upset, sought comfort from his mother, whereas Maya, more intrigued than scared, first looked to her mother for clarification before exploring the situation for herself. Why might these two children have reacted so differently to the same novel experience?

In this chapter, we will address this issue by turning to the literature on children's emotions and the development of emotional ties to parents and other close companions. We begin by charting age-related changes in children's displays and interpretations of emotions, and by considering some of the roles that emotions play in early social and personality development. We will then look at individual differences in emotional reactivity, or *temperament*, and see that the early temperamental attributes that so often explain why young children react differently to everyday events are now considered by many developmentalists to be important building blocks of adult personalities. We will then turn to emotional *attachments* and explore the processes by which infants and their closest companions establish these intimate affectional ties. Finally, we will review a rapidly expanding base of evidence suggesting that the kind of emotional attachments infants are able to establish can have important implications for their later social, emotional, and intellectual development.

An Overview of Emotional Development

Temperament and Development

What are Emotional Attachments?

How Do Infants Become Attached?

Individual Differences in Attachment Quality

Factors that Influence Attachment Security

Attachment and Later Development

The Unattached Infant

Maternal Employment, Child Care, and Early Emotional Development

Summary

AN OVERVIEW OF EMOTIONAL DEVELOPMENT

Do babies have feelings? Do they experience and display specific emotions such as happiness, sadness, fear, and anger the way older children and adults do? Most parents think so. In one study, more than half the mothers of 1-month-old infants said that their babies displayed at least five distinct emotional expressions: interest, surprise, joy, anger, and fear (Johnson et al., 1982). Although one might argue that this is simply a case of proud mothers reading much too much into the behaviour of their babies, there is now reliable evidence that even very young infants are emotional creatures.

Displaying Emotions: The Development (and Control) of Emotional Expressions

Carroll Izard and his colleagues at the University of Delaware have studied infants' emotional expressions by videotaping babies' responses to such events as grasping an ice cube, having a toy taken away, or seeing their mothers return after a separation (Izard, 1982, 1993). Izard's procedure is to ask raters, who are unaware of the events that an infant has experienced, to tell him what emotion the infant is experiencing from the facial expression the infant displays. These studies reveal that different adult raters observing the same expressions reliably see the same emotion in a baby's face (see Figure 11.1). Other investigators find that adults can usually tell what *positive* emotion a baby is experiencing (for example, interest versus joy) from facial expressions, but that negative emotions (fear versus anger, for example) are much more difficult to discriminate on the basis of facial cues alone (Izard et al., 1995; Matias & Cohn, 1993). Nevertheless, most researchers agree that babies communicate a variety of feelings through their facial expressions, and that each expression becomes a more recognizable sign of a particular emotion with age (Camras et al., 1992; Izard et al., 1995).

Interest: brows raised; mouth may be rounded; lips may be pursed.

Fear: mouth retracted; brows level and drawn up and in; eyelids lifted.

Disgust: tongue protruding; upper lip raised; nose wrinkled.

Joy: bright eyes; cheeks lifted; mouth forms a smile.

Sadness: corners of mouth turned down; inner portion of brows raised.

Anger: mouth squared at corners; brows drawn together and pointing down; eyes fixed straight ahead.

Figure 11.1 *Young infants display a variety of emotional expressions.*

Courtesy of Carol E. Izard, University of Delaware

Sequencing of Discrete Emotions

Various emotions appear at different times over the first two years. At birth, babies show interest, distress, disgust, and contentment (as indicated by a rudimentary smile). Other **primary (or basic) emotions** that emerge between 2 and 7 months are anger, sadness, joy, surprise, and fear (Izard et al., 1995). These so-called primary emotions may be biologically programmed because they emerge in all normal infants at roughly the same ages and are displayed and interpreted similarly in all cultures (Camras et al., 1992; Izard, 1982, 1993). Yet some learning (or cognitive development) may be necessary before babies express any emotion not present at birth. Indeed, one of the strongest elicitors of surprise and joy among 2- to 6-month-olds is their discovery that they can exert some control over objects and events. And disconfirmation of these *learned* expectancies (as when someone or something prevents them from exerting control) is likely to *anger* many 2- to 4-month-olds and may *sadden* 4- to 6-month-olds as well (Lewis, Alessandri, & Sullivan, 1990; Sullivan, Lewis, & Alessandri, 1992).

Later in the second year, infants begin to display such **secondary (or complex) emotions** as embarrassment, shame, guilt, envy, and pride. These feelings are sometimes called *self-conscious emotions* because each involves some damage to or enhancement of our sense of self. Michael Lewis and his associates (1989) believe that embarrassment, the simplest self-conscious emotion, will not emerge until the child can recognize herself in a mirror or photograph (a self-referential milestone that we will discuss in detail in Chapter 12), whereas *self-evaluative* emotions such as shame, guilt, and pride may require both self-recognition *and* an understanding of rules or standards for evaluating one's conduct.

Most of the available evidence is consistent with Lewis's theory. For example, the only toddlers who become noticeably embarrassed by lavish praise or by requests to show off for strangers are those who display self-recognition (Lewis, Sullivan, et al., 1989). By about age 3, when children are better able to evaluate their performances as good or bad, they begin to show clear signs of *pride* (smiling, applauding, or shouting "I did it!") when they succeed at a difficult task and *shame* (a downward gaze with a slumped posture, often accompanied by statements such as "I'm no good at this") should they fail at an easy task (Lewis, Alessandri, & Sullivan, 1992; Stipek, Recchia, & McClintic, 1992).

Of course, parents can clearly influence a child's experience and expression of self-evaluative emotions. In one study (Alessandri & Lewis, 1996), mothers' reactions were observed as their 4- to 5-year-olds succeeded or failed at a variety of puzzles. As expected, children generally showed some signs of pride over their successes and shame over their failures. Yet the amounts of pride and shame they displayed largely depended on their mothers' reactions to these outcomes. Mothers who accentuated the negative by being especially critical of failures tended to have children who displayed high levels of shame after a failure and little pride after successes. By contrast, mothers who were more inclined to react positively to successes had children who displayed more pride in their accomplishments and less shame on those occasions when they failed to achieve their objectives.

Interestingly, toddlers and young preschool children are likely to display self-evaluative emotions only when an adult is present to observe their conduct (Harter & Whitesell, 1989; Stipek et al., 1992). So it seems that young children's self-evaluative emotions may stem largely from the reactions they anticipate receiving from adult evaluators. In fact, it may be well into the elementary-school period before children fully internalize many rules or evaluative standards and come to feel especially prideful, shameful, or guilty about their conduct in the absence of external surveillance (Bussey, 1992; Harter & Whitesell, 1989).

Socialization of Emotions and Emotional Self-Regulation

Each society has a set of **emotional display rules** that specify the circumstances under which various emotions should or should not be expressed (Gross & Ballif, 1991; Harris, 1989). Children in North America, for example, learn that they are supposed to express happiness or gratitude when they receive a gift from grandma and, by all means, to sup-

primary (or basic) emotions
set of emotions present at birth or emerging early in the first year that some theorists believe to be biologically programmed

secondary (or complex) emotions
self-conscious or self-evaluative emotions that emerge in the second year and depend, in part, on cognitive development

emotional display rules
culturally defined rules specifying which emotions should or should not be expressed under which circumstances

press any disappointment they may feel should the gift turn out to be underwear. In some ways, these emotional codes of conduct are similar to the pragmatic rules of language: Children must acquire and use them in order to get along with other people and to maintain their approval. When does this learning begin?

Earlier than you might imagine! Consider that when mothers play with 7-month-old infants, they restrict themselves mainly to displays of joy, interest, and surprise, thus serving as models of positive emotions for their babies (Malatesta & Haviland, 1982). Mothers also respond selectively to their infants' emotions; over the first several months, they become increasingly attentive to babies' expressions of interest or surprise and less responsive to the infants' negative emotions (Malatesta et al., 1986). Through basic learning processes, then, babies are trained to display more pleasant faces and fewer unpleasant ones, and they do just that over time.

However, the emotions that are considered socially acceptable may be quite different from one culture to another. North American parents love to stimulate their babies until they reach peaks of delight. By contrast, caregivers among the Gusii and Aka people of central Africa hardly ever take part in face-to-face play with their babies, seeking instead to keep young infants as calm and contented as possible (Hewlett et al., 1998; LeVine et al., 1994). So North American babies learn that intense emotion is okay as long as it is positive, whereas Gusii and Aka babies learn to restrain both positive and negative emotions.

REGULATING EMOTIONS. To comply with these emotional lessons, however, babies must devise strategies for **regulating** and controlling their emotions. This is a difficult task for very young infants, who do manage to reduce at least some of their negative arousal by turning their bodies away from unpleasant stimuli or by sucking vigorously on objects (Mangelsdorf, Shapiro, & Marzolf, 1995). Interestingly, 6-month-old boys find it harder than 6-month-old girls to regulate unpleasant arousal and are more inclined than girls are to fuss and cry in an attempt to elicit regulatory support (soothing) from caregivers (Weinberg et al., 1999).

By the end of the first year, infants develop additional strategies for reducing negative arousal such as rocking themselves, chewing on objects, and moving away from people or events that upset them (Kopp, 1989; Mangelsdorf et al., 1995). And by age 18 to 24 months, toddlers are now more likely to try to control the actions of people or objects (for example, mechanical toys) that upset them (Mangelsdorf et al., 1995), and they are beginning to cope with frustrations of having to wait for snacks or gifts by talking to companions, playing with toys, or otherwise distracting themselves from the source of their disappointments (Grolnick, Bridges, & Connell, 1996). In fact, toddlers this young have even been observed to knit their brows or compress their lips as they actively attempt to suppress their anger or sadness (Malatesta et al., 1989). Yet, toddlers find it almost impossible to regulate *fear* (Buss & Goldsmith, 1998); instead, they develop methods of *expressing* fear that successfully attract the attention and comforting of caregivers (Bridges & Grolnick, 1995).

As young preschool children become more talkative and begin to discuss their feelings, parents and other close companions often help them to deal constructively with negative emotions by distracting them from the most distressing aspects of unpleasant situations (for example, telling a child who is about to receive an inoculation to look at a brightly coloured poster on the wall) or by otherwise helping them to understand frightening, frustrating, or disappointing experiences (Thompson, 1994; 1998). These supportive interventions are a form of guided instruction of the kind that Vygotsky wrote about—experiences that should help preschoolers to devise effective strategies for regulating their own emotions. Indeed, 2- to 6-year-olds do become better and better at coping with unpleasant emotional arousal by directing their attention away from frightening events ("I scared of the shark. Close my eyes"), by thinking pleasant thoughts to overcome unpleasant ones ("Mummy left me, but when she comes back, we're going to the movies") and by reinterpreting the cause of their distress in a more satisfying way ("He [story character] didn't *really* die ... it's just pretend") (Thompson, 1994). Unfortunately, youngsters who experience a good deal of negative emotionality but do not learn how to regulate it are likely to alienate both adults and peers when they act out their anger or frustrations (Belsky, Friedman, & Hsieh, 2001; Eisenberg et al., 1995, 1997).

emotional self-regulation
strategies for managing emotions or adjusting emotional arousal to an appropriate level of intensity

Interestingly, adaptive regulation of emotions may sometimes involve *maintaining* or *intensifying* one's feelings rather than suppressing them. For example, children may learn that *conveying* their anger helps them to stand up to a bully (Thompson, 1994). And as we will see in Chapter 14, parents often call attention to (and thereby seek to maintain) the uneasiness that young children experience after causing another person distress or breaking a rule. Why? Because they hope to persuade youngsters to *reinterpret* these feelings in ways that cause them to (1) *sympathize* with victims of distress and act on this concern, or (2) feel *guilty* about their transgressions and become less inclined to repeat them (Dunn, Brown, & Maguire, 1995; Kochanska, 1991). Another form of emotional arousal that parents may seek to maintain or enhance in children is *pride* in their accomplishments, an important contributor to a healthy sense of achievement motivation and to the development of a positive academic self-concept (see Chapter 12 for further discussion of this point). So effective regulation of emotions involves an ability to suppress, maintain, or even intensify our emotional arousal in order to remain productively engaged with the challenges we face or the people we encounter (Thompson, 1994).

Acquiring Emotional Display Rules. An ability to regulate emotions is only the first skill that children must acquire in order to comply with a culture's emotional display rules. Indeed, these prescriptions often dictate that we not only suppress whatever unacceptable emotions that we are actually experiencing, but also *replace* them (outwardly, at least) with whatever feeling that the display rule calls for in that situation (for example, acting happy rather than sad on receiving a disappointing gift).

By about age 3, children are beginning to show some limited ability to disguise their true feelings. Michael Lewis and his associates (Lewis, Stanger, & Sullivan, 1989), for example, found that 3-year-olds who had lied about peeking at a forbidden toy showed subtle signs of anguish (detectable on film played in slow motion); however, they were able to mask their feelings well enough to make it impossible for uninformed adult judges to discriminate them from other children who truthfully reported that they hadn't peeked. With each passing year, preschool children become a little better at posing outward expressions that differ from their inner feelings (Peskin, 1992; Ruffman et al., 1993). Yet, even 5-year-olds are not especially skilled at disguising their true emotions or at convincing others that their lies are true (Polak & Harris, 1999).

Throughout the elementary-school years, children become increasingly aware of socially sanctioned display rules, learning more about which emotions to express (and which to suppress) in particular social situations (Jones, Abbey, & Cumberland, 1998; Zeman & Shipman, 1997). Perhaps because parents place stronger pressure on girls to act nice in social situations, girls are both more motivated and more skilled at complying with display rules than boys are (Davis, 1995). Furthermore, mothers who emphasize positive emotions in their parent–child interactions tend to have children who are better able to mask disappointment and other negative feelings (Garner & Power, 1996). Yet even simple display rules take some time to fully master. As we see in Figure 11.2, many 7- to 9-year-olds (especially boys) are still unable to act thrilled and to mask all their disappointment on receiving an undesirable gift. And even many 12- to 13-year-olds fail to suppress all their anger when taunted by a peer (Underwood et al., 1999) or thwarted by a respected adult exercising authority (Underwood, Coie, & Herbsman, 1992).

Compliance with culturally specified rules for displaying emotions occurs earlier and is especially strong in communal peoples such as the Japanese or the Chhetri-Brehmin of Nepal that stress social harmony and place the needs of the social order over those of the individual (Cole & Tamang, 1998; Matsumoto, 1990). Clearly, this socialization of emotions works for the good of society: Even in an individualistic culture such as Canada or the United States, children's increasing compliance with emotional display rules is largely motivated by a desire to maintain social harmony and to avoid criticism (Saarni, 1990; Zeman & Garber, 1996); and children who have mastered these emotional codes of conduct are viewed as more likable and more competent by their teachers and peers (Jones et al., 1998).

Toddlers and preschool children are not very skilled at masking their true feelings.

Figure 11.2 With age, children are better able to display positive emotional reactions after receiving a disappointing gift. *Adapted from Saarni, 1984.*

Recognizing and Interpreting Emotions

Currently, there is some debate about when babies begin to recognize and interpret the emotional expressions that others display (Kahana-Kalman & Walker-Andrews, 2001). As we learned in Chapter 6, 3-month-olds can discriminate different emotions posed by adults in photos; however, these demonstrations may simply reflect their powers of visual discrimination and do not necessarily imply that infants this young *interpret* various expressions as happy, angry, or sad (Nelson, 1987).

Social Referencing

Infants' ability to reorganize and interpret particular emotional expressions become more obvious between 7 and 10 months (Soken & Pick, 1999)—the point at which they begin to monitor parents' emotional reactions to uncertain situations and to use this information to regulate their own behaviour (Feinman, 1992). This **social referencing** becomes more common with age (Walden & Baxter, 1989) and soon extends to people other than parents (Repacholi, 1998). By the end of the first year, for example, infants typically approach and play with unfamiliar toys if a nearby stranger is smiling, but are apt to avoid these objects if the stranger displays a fearful expression (Klinnert et al., 1986). A mother's *vocal* expressions of emotion seem to convey as much information for a 12-month-old infant as her facial expressions do (Mumme, Fernald, & Herrera, 1996), and some investigators have wondered whether these emotional signals might not best be interpreted as commands (for example, "don't touch") rather than as active information seeking on the infant's part (Baldwin & Moses, 1996). But during the second year, toddlers often look to their companions *after* they have appraised a new object or situation, thereby suggesting that they are now using others' emotional reactions as information to assess the accuracy of their *own* judgments (Hornik & Gunnar, 1988).

Conversations about Emotions

Once toddlers begin to talk about emotions at 18 to 24 months of age, family conversations that centre on emotional experiences can help them achieve a much richer understanding of their own and others' feelings. In fact, Judy Dunn and her associates (1991; Herrera & Dunn, 1997) found that the more often 3-year-olds had discussed emotional

social referencing
use of others' emotional expressions to infer the meaning of otherwise ambiguous situations

Conversations that focus on the emotional experiences that family members have had promote emotional understanding, empathy, and social competencies in young children.

experiences with other family members, the better they were at interpreting others' emotions and at settling disputes with friends three years later in elementary school. Of course, the ability to identify how others are feeling and to understand why they feel that way is a central aspect of social cognition that has important social consequences. We will see in Chapter 14, for example, that understanding the *causes* of others' emotions is an important contributor to **empathy**, which often motivates children to comfort or otherwise assist distressed companions. In fact, these prosocial inclinations may largely explain why children who score high on tests of emotional understanding tend to be rated high in social competence by teachers and enjoy especially good relations with their peers (Cassidy et al., 1992; Garner, Jones, & Miner, 1994; Oppenheim et al., 1997).

Later Milestones in Emotional Understanding. The ability to recognize and interpret others' emotional displays steadily improves throughout childhood. By age 4 to 5, children can correctly infer whether a person is happy, angry, or sad from his or her expressive body movements (Boone & Cunningham, 1998). What's more, they increasingly recognize that a person's current emotional state (particularly negative emotions) may stem not from current events but, rather, from her thinking about *past* events (Lagattuta & Wellman, 2001). As elementary-school children gradually begin to rely more on personal, situational, and historical information to interpret emotions, they achieve several important breakthroughs in emotional understanding. For example, they eventually recognize at about age 8 that many situations (for example, the approach of a big dog) elicit different emotional reactions (for example, fear versus joy) from different individuals (Gnepp & Klayman, 1992). Furthermore, 6- to 9-year-olds also begin to understand that a person can experience more than one emotion (for example, excitement and wariness) at the same time (Arsenio & Kramer, 1992; Brown & Dunn, 1996), and they display some ability to integrate contrasting facial, behavioural, and situational cues to infer what those emotions might be (Hoffner & Badzinski, 1989). According to Maxine Wintre and Denise Vallance from York University (1994), however, it is not until age 6 that children recognize that they could experience multiple emotions but of varying intensity, and not until age 8 that they predict that they could experience multiple emotions of varying intensity and different valence (scared and happy).

Notice that these latter advances in emotional understanding emerge at about the same age that children can integrate more than one piece of information (for example, height and width of a column of liquid) in Piagetian conservation tasks, and they may depend, in part, on the same underlying cognitive developments. However, social experiences are also important. Jane Brown and Judy Dunn (1996), for example, found that 6-year-olds who show an early understanding of conflicting emotions had often discussed the *causes* of emotions with their parents earlier in childhood. Apparently, these discussions prepared them to analyze mixed feelings that may have arisen from squabbles with siblings and peers.

Emotions and Early Social Development

What role do emotions play in early social development? Clearly, a baby's displays of emotion serve a *communicative* function that is likely to affect the behaviour of caregivers. For example, cries of distress summon close companions. Early suggestions of a smile or expressions of interest may convince caregivers that their baby is willing and even eager to strike up a social relationship with them. Later expressions of fear or sadness may indicate that the infant is insecure or feeling blue and needs some attention or comforting. Anger may imply that the infant wishes her companions to cease whatever they are doing that is upsetting her, whereas joy serves as a prompt for caregivers to prolong an ongoing interaction or perhaps signals the baby's willingness to accept new challenges. So infant emotions are adaptive in that they promote social contact and help caregivers to adjust their behaviour to the infant's needs and goals. Stated another way, the emotional expressions of infancy help infants and their close companions get to know each other (Tronick, 1989).

empathy
ability to experience the same emotions that someone else is experiencing

At the same time, the infant's emerging ability to recognize and interpret others' emotions is an important achievement that enables him to infer how he should be feeling or behaving in a variety of situations. The beauty of this social referencing is that children can quickly acquire *knowledge* in this way. For example, a sibling's joyful reaction to the family dog should indicate to a toddler that this ball of fur is a friend rather than an unspeakable monster. A mother's worried expression and accompanying vocal concern might immediately suggest that the knife in one's hand is an implement to be avoided. And given the frequency with which expressive caregivers direct an infant's attention to important aspects of the environment or display their feelings about an infant's appraisal of objects and events, it is likely that the information contained in their emotional displays contribute in a major way to the child's understanding of the world in which he lives (Rosen, Adamson, & Bakeman, 1992). (Table 11.1 provides a brief overview of emotional development.)

TEMPERAMENT AND DEVELOPMENT

As parents well know, every baby has a distinct personality. In trying to describe infant personality, researchers have focused on aspects of **temperament**—an individual's tendency to respond in predictable ways to environmental events that many believe to be the emotional and behavioural building blocks of the adult personality (Caspi & Silva, 1995; Goldsmith et al., 1987). Although different researchers do not always define or measure temperament in precisely the same ways, most would agree that the following five attributes are important components of temperament (Buss & Plomin, 1984; Goldsmith et al., 1987; Rothbart, 1981):

temperament
person's characteristic modes of responding emotionally and behaviourally to environmental events, including such attributes as activity level, irritability, fearfulness, and sociability

TABLE 11.1 An Overview of Emotional Development		
Age	**Emotional expressions/regulations**	**Emotional understandings**
Birth–6 months	All primary emotions appear. Displays of positive emotion are encouraged and become more commonplace. Attempts to regulate negative emotions by sucking or turning away are observed.	Children can discriminate such facial expressions as happiness, anger, and sadness.
7–12 months	Primary emotions such as anger, fear, and sadness become more apparent. Emotional self-regulation improves as infants rock themselves, chew on objects, or move away from distressing stimuli.	Recognition of others' primary emotions improves. Social referencing appears.
1–3 years	Secondary (self-conscious) emotions appear. Emotional regulation improves as toddlers distract themselves from or attempt to control stimuli that upset them.	Toddlers begin to talk about and play-act emotions. Sympathetic responding appears.
3–6 years	Cognitive strategies for regulating emotions appear and are refined. Some masking of emotions and compliance with simple display rules appear.	Children use expressive body movements to recognize emotions. Understanding of the external causes and consequences of emotions improves. Empathic responding becomes more common.
6–12 years	Compliance with display rules improves. Self-conscious emotions become more closely tied to internalized standards of "right" or "competent" behaviour. Self-regulation strategies (including those allowing one to intensify emotions when appropriate) become more varied and complex.	Children integrate internal and external cues to understand others' emotions. Empathic responding becomes stronger. Children become aware that people may differ in their emotional reactions to the same event. Understands that others may experience mixed emotions.

1. *Activity level*—typical pace or vigour of one's activities.
2. *Irritability/negative emotionality*—how easily or intensely upset one becomes over negative events.
3. *Soothability*—ease with which one calms after becoming upset.
4. *Fearfulness*—wariness of intense or highly unusual stimulation.
5. *Sociability*—receptiveness to social stimulation.

Hereditary and Environmental Influences on Temperament

Hereditary Influences

To many, the very term *temperament* implies a biological foundation for individual differences in behaviour, a foundation that is genetically influenced and stable over time. Behavioural geneticists have looked for hereditary influences by comparing the temperamental similarities of pairs of identical and fraternal twins. By the middle of the first year, identical twins are already more similar than fraternal twins are on most temperamental attributes, including activity level, demands for attention, irritability, and sociability (Braungart et al., 1992; Emde et al., 1992) (see Figure 11.3). Although the heritability coefficients for most temperamental attributes are moderate at best throughout infancy and the preschool period (Goldsmith, Buss, & Lemery, 1997), it seems that many important components of temperament are genetically influenced.

Environmental Influences

The fact that most temperamental attributes are only moderately heritable means that environment also influences children's temperaments. Which aspects of environment are most important? Recent research implies that the home environments that siblings share most clearly influence such *positively toned* aspects of temperament as smiling/sociability and soothability; yet shared environment contributes very little to children's activity levels and to *negatively* toned attributes such as irritability and fearfulness because siblings living together often barely resemble each other in these aspects of temperament (Goldsmith et al., 1997, 1999). Instead, negatively toned temperamental attributes are shaped more by *nonshared environmental influences*—those aspects of environment that siblings do not share and that conspire to make them temperamentally *dissimilar*. This can easily happen if parents notice early behavioural differences among their children and adjust their parenting to them. For example, if a mother observes that her infant son Jimmy is much more upset by strangers and unfamiliar settings than her 3-year-old daughter Jennifer was at Jimmy's age, she may allow Jimmy more freedom to avoid new experiences, thereby encouraging him to become ever more fearful of novel contexts he may later encounter, such as daycare (Park et al., 1997).

Stability of Temperament

How stable is early temperament over time? Is the fearful 8-month-old who is highly upset by a strange face likely to remain wary of strangers at 24 months and to shun new playmates as a 4-year-old? Longitudinal research indicates that several components of temperament—namely, activity level, irritability, sociability, and shyness—are moderately stable through infancy, childhood, and sometimes even into the early adult years (Caspi & Silva, 1995; Lemery et al., 1999; Pedlow et al., 1993). In

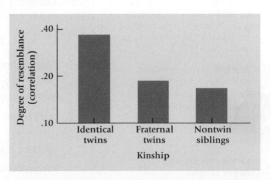

Figure 11.3 *Average correlations in infant temperament among identical twins, fraternal twins, and nontwin siblings born at different times.* BASED ON BRAUNGART ET AL., *1992;* EMDE ET AL., *1992.*

fact, one longitudinal study in New Zealand found that several components of temperament measured at age 3 were not only moderately stable between ages 3 and 18, but also predicted individual differences in participants' antisocial tendencies and the quality of their personal and family relationships at ages 18 to 21 (Caspi & Silva, 1995; Henry et al., 1996; Newman et al., 1997). Findings such as these illustrate why many developmentalists consider temperament to be the cornerstone of the adult personality. However, not all individuals are so temperamentally stable.

Consider what Jerome Kagan and his associates found while conducting longitudinal studies of a temperamental attribute they call **behavioural inhibition**, the tendency to withdraw from unfamiliar people or situations (Kagan, 1992; Snidman et al., 1995). At age 4 months, inhibited infants are already fussing and showing heightened motor activity to such novel objects as a brightly coloured mobile, and they often display intense physiological arousal (for example, high heart rates) to situations that barely phase uninhibited infants. When tested at 21 months, toddlers classified as inhibited were rather shy and sometimes even fearful when they encountered unfamiliar people, toys, or settings, whereas most uninhibited children responded quite adaptively to these events. And when retested at ages 4, 5½, and 7½, inhibited youngsters were still less sociable with strange adults and peers and more cautious than uninhibited children were about engaging in activities that involved an element of risk (for example, walking a balance beam).

So behavioural inhibition is a moderately stable attribute that may have deep biological roots. Indeed, researchers have been finding that infants easily upset by novelty show greater electrical activity in the right cerebral hemisphere of the brain (the centre for negative emotions) than in the left hemisphere, whereas infants who are less reactive show either the opposite pattern or no hemispheric differences in electrical activity (Fox et al., 2001; Fox, Bell, & Jones, 1992). In addition, family studies clearly indicate that behavioural inhibition is a genetically influenced attribute (DiLalla, Kagan, & Reznick, 1994; Robinson et al., 1992). Nevertheless, both Kagan and his associates (1998) and a research team in Sweden (Kerr et al., 1994) found that children at the *extremes* of the continuum—the most highly inhibited and most highly uninhibited youngsters—were most likely to display such long-term stability, with most other children showing considerable fluctuation in their levels of inhibition over time. What these observations imply is that genetically influenced aspects of temperament are often modified by environmental influences. Interestingly, a similar conclusion emerges from Alexander Thomas and Stella Chess's classic longitudinal research on the stability of *temperamental profiles* from infancy to adulthood.

Early Temperamental Profiles and Later Development

In their earliest reports, Thomas and Chess (1977; Thomas, Chess, & Birch, 1970) noted that certain aspects of infant temperament tend to cluster in predictable ways, forming broader temperamental profiles. In fact, the majority of the 141 infants in their *New York Longitudinal Study* could be placed into one of three temperamental profiles:

1. **Easy temperament** (40 percent of the sample). Easygoing children are even-tempered, are typically in a positive mood, and are quite open and adaptable to new experiences. Their habits are regular and predictable.

2. **Difficult temperament** (10 percent of the sample). Difficult children are active, irritable, and irregular in their habits. They often react very vigorously to changes in routine and are very slow to adapt to new people or situations.

3. **Slow-to-warm-up temperament** (15 percent of the sample). These children are quite inactive, somewhat moody, and can be slow to adapt to new people and situations. But, unlike difficult children, they typically respond to novelty in mildly, rather than intensely, negative ways. For example, they may resist cuddling by looking away rather than by kicking or screaming.

behavioural inhibition
temperamental attribute reflecting one's tendency to withdraw from unfamiliar people or situations

easy temperament
temperamental profile in which the child quickly establishes regular routines, is generally good-natured, and adapts easily to novelty

difficult temperament
temperamental profile in which the child is irregular in daily routines and adapts slowly to new experiences, often responding negatively and intensely

slow-to-warm-up temperament
temperamental profile in which the child is inactive and moody and displays mild passive resistance to new routines and experiences

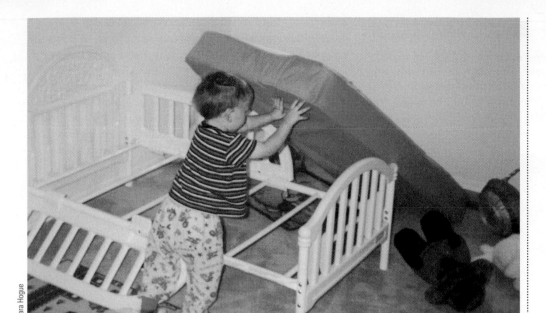

Difficult children are likely to retain their difficult temperaments if parents are impatient and forceful with them.

The remaining children fit none of these profiles, showing their own unique patterns of temperamental attributes.

Temperamental Profiles and Children's Adjustment

Apparently, these broader temperamental patterns may persist over time and influence a child's adjustment to a variety of settings later in life. For example, temperamentally difficult children are more likely than other children to have problems adjusting to school activities, and they are often irritable and aggressive in their interactions with siblings and peers (Lytton, 1990; Thomas, Chess, & Korn, 1982). By contrast, about half of all children who are slow to warm up show a different kind of adjustment problem because their hesitation to embrace new activities and challenges may cause them to be ignored or neglected by peers (Chess & Thomas, 1984).

Child-Rearing and Temperament

Do those observations imply that early temperamental profiles are difficult to alter and largely determine our personalities and social adjustment? No, they do not! Thomas and Chess (1986; Chess & Thomas, 1984) found that early temperamental characteristics *sometimes do* and *sometimes do not* carry over into later life. In other words, temperament can change, and one factor that often determines whether it does change is the **"goodness of fit"** between the child's temperamental style and patterns of child-rearing used by parents.

Let's first consider a good fit between temperament and child-rearing. Difficult infants and toddlers who fuss a lot and have trouble adapting to new routines often become less cranky and more adaptable over the long run if parents remain calm as they insist that their children comply with rules, while also exercising restraint and allowing them to respond to new routines at a more leisurely pace. Indeed, many difficult infants who experience such patient, sensitive, and yet demanding caregiving are no longer classifiable as temperamentally difficult or displaying problem behaviours later in childhood or adolescence (Bates et al., 1998; Chess & Thomas, 1984). Yet it is not always easy for parents to be patient and sensitive with a highly active, moody child who resists their bids for attention; in fact, many parents become irritable, impatient, demanding, and punitive with difficult children (van den Boom, 1995). Unfortunately, these attitudes and behaviours constitute a poor fit with a difficult child, who is apt to become all the

"goodness-of-fit" model
Thomas and Chess's notion that development is likely to be optimized when parents' child-rearing practices are sensitively adapted to the child's temperamental characteristics

From Lynn Wilson, Partnerships, 2nd ed. (Nelson Thomson Learning, 2001)

Young children and caregivers who are securely attached interact often and try to maintain proximity.

more fussy and resistant in response to the parents' forceful and punitive tactics. And true to form, difficult infants and toddlers are especially likely to remain difficult and to display behaviour problems later in life if their parents are often irritable, impatient, and forceful with them (Chess & Thomas, 1984; Rubin et al., 1998).

Finally, there is a great deal of variation across cultures in what qualifies as a desirable temperament and in the developmental outcomes that are associated with particular temperamental attributes. Box 11.1 briefly examines some cross-cultural differences in the developmental implications of childhood and adolescent shyness.

WHAT ARE EMOTIONAL ATTACHMENTS?

Although babies can communicate many of their feelings right from the start, their social lives change dramatically as they become emotionally attached to their caregivers. What is an emotional **attachment**? John Bowlby (1969) uses the term to describe the strong affectional ties that we feel for the special people in our lives. According to Bowlby (1969), people who are securely attached take pleasure in their interactions and feel comforted by their partner's presence in times of stress or uncertainty. So 10-month-old Michael may reflect the attachment relationship he shares with his mother by reserving his biggest grins for her and by crying out to her or crawling in her direction whenever he is upset, discomforted, or afraid.

attachment
close emotional relationship between two people, characterized by mutual affection and a desire to maintain proximity

Reciprocal Relationships

Bowlby (1969) also stressed that parent–infant attachments are *reciprocal* relationships: Infants become attached to parents, and parents become attached to infants. Parents clearly have an edge on infants when it comes to forming these intimate affectional ties. Even before their baby is born, they often display their readiness to become attached by

✔ **Concept Check 11.1**
Understanding Early Emotional Development

Check your understanding of selected aspects of temperament and early emotional development by matching each descriptive statement that follows with one of the following concepts: (a) goodness of fit; (b) emotional self-regulation; (c) self-recognition; (d) lack of inhibition (uninhibited); (e) social referencing; (f) disconfirmed expectancies; (g) shared environmental influence; (h) ability to interpret emotions (emotional understanding); (i) nonshared environmental influence; (j) infant emotional expressions; (k) shyness/behavioural inhibition. The answers appear in the Appendix.

_____ 1. thought to be necessary for the development of all complex emotions

_____ 2. communicative signals that affect the behaviour of caregivers

_____ 3. correlate of children's social competence/peer relations in elementary school

_____ 4. using others' emotional expressions to regulate one's conduct

_____ 5. may underlie early expressions of anger, surprise, and sadness

_____ 6. necessary to comply with emotional display rules

_____ 7. environmental influence that contributes most to *positively* toned temperamental attributes

_____ 8. environmental influence that contributes most to *negatively* toned temperamental attributes

_____ 9. temperamental attribute that is valued more highly in Asian than in Western societies (see Box 11.1)

_____ 10. adults whose parenting illustrates _____ have children who adapt well, despite their temperaments

_____ 11. temperamental attribute describing children who adapt well to unfamiliar people, settings, or toys

CULTURAL INFLUENCES

11.1

Is Shyness a Social Disadvantage? It Depends on One's Culture

In North America, children who are shy and reserved are at a social disadvantage. They run the risk of being neglected or even rejected by peers, which can lead to low self-esteem, depression, and a number of other adjustment problems that we will discuss in detail in Chapter 16. Furthermore, even if shy adolescents or young adults are otherwise well-adjusted, they often fail to act boldly or assertively enough to take advantage of many opportunities, and they typically lag far behind bolder peers in getting married, having children, and firmly establishing themselves in a career (Caspi et al., 1988).

By contrast, many Asian cultures *value* what North Americans would call a shy and somewhat inhibited demeanour. Xinyin Chen from the University of Western Ontario and his associates suggest that in China, for example, children who are shy and reserved are perceived as socially mature by their teachers (Chen, Rubin, & Li, 1995), and they are much more likely than active, assertive children to be popular with their peers—precisely the opposite pattern to what we see in Canada (Chen, Rubin, & Sun, 1992). And the boisterous classroom behaviours that many Western children display on occasion (and that Canadian teachers view as normal) are likely to be branded *conduct disorders* by teachers in Thailand, who expect their pupils to be reserved, respectful, and obedient (Weisz et al., 1995).

There are even differences among Western cultures in outcomes associated with shyness. Swedes, for example, view shyness somewhat more positively than Americans do and prefer shy, reserved behaviours to bold, assertive, or attention-seeking antics. Consequently, shyness is not really a disadvantage for Swedish men. Like shy American men, shy Swedish men marry and have children later than their less shy counterparts; however, shyness does not constrain their careers in the same way it does for American men (Kerr, Lambert, & Bem, 1996). What about Swedish women? Shyness poses no problems for them in establishing intimate relationships, because shy Swedish girls marry and have children at roughly the same age as their less shy peers. But unlike shy American women, who are generally well educated and marry successful men, shy Swedish women complete *fewer* years of education than their bolder counterparts and marry men who make less money, thus suggesting that shyness may place them at some risk of economic disadvantage. Why do shy Swedish girls receive less education than their less shy peers? Margaret Kerr and her associates (1996) speculate that Swedish teachers are more likely to encourage shy students to continue their education if the students are males. So, lacking the initiative to approach teachers and seek their guidance, shy Swedish girls end up having fewer educational opportunities than nonshy girls or shy boys do.

We see, then, that outcomes associated with shyness vary dramatically across cultures (and even within a culture, depending on one's gender). Clearly, some temperamental qualities provide better fits with a culture's specific values and traditions than others do. And because cultural traditions vary so widely, we can safely conclude that no one temperamental profile is most adaptive in all cultures.

---

talking blissfully about the baby, formulating grand plans for him or her, and expressing delight in such milestones as feeling the fetus kick or hearing his heart beat with the aid of a stethoscope (Grossman, Eichler, Winickoff, 1980). And as we learned in Chapter 4, close contact with a newborn in the first few hours after birth can intensify positive feelings parents already have for their baby (Klaus & Kennell, 1982), particularly if they are younger, economically disadvantaged, and know very little about babies or infant care (Eyer, 1992). Yet it is important to emphasize that genuine emotional *attachments* build slowly from parent–infant interactions that occur over the first several months and can become highly intimate, even when there is no early contact between parents and their newborn (Brockington, 1996).

Establishment of Interactional Synchrony

One important contributor to the growth of attachments is the **synchronized routines** that caregivers and infants often establish over the first few months of a baby's life (Stern, 1977; Tronick, 1989). These coordinated interactions, which have been likened to dances, are most likely to develop if the caregiver attends carefully to her baby's state, provides playful stimulation when the baby is alert and attentive, and avoids pushing things when an overexcited or tired infant is fussy and sending the message "Cool it! I just need a break from all this excitement." Edward Tronick (1989, p. 112) described one very synchronous interaction that unfolded as a mother played peekaboo with her infant:

synchronized routines generally harmonious interactions between two people in which participants adjust their behaviour in response to each other's actions

The infant abruptly turns away from his mother as the game reaches its peak of intensity and begins to suck on his thumb and stare into space with a dull facial expression. The mother stops playing and sits back watching.... After a few seconds the infant turns back to her with an inviting expression. The mother moves closer, smiles, and says in a high-pitched, exaggerated voice, "Oh, now you're back!" He smiles in response and vocalizes. As they finish crowing together, the infant reinserts his thumb and looks away. The mother again waits. [Soon] the infant turns ... to her and they greet each other with big smiles.

Notice that much information is exchanged in this simple but synchronous exchange. By turning away and sucking, the excited infant is saying, "Hey, I need to slow down and regulate my emotional state." His mother tells him she understands by patiently awaiting his return. As he returns, mom tells him she's glad he's back, and he acknowledges that signal with a smile and an excited blurt. And when the baby becomes overstimulated a minute or two later, his mother waits for him to calm once again, and he communicates his thanks by smiling wide for her when he turns back the second time. Clearly, this is a dyad that not only interacts smoothly but also quickly repairs any interactive errors.

Daniel Stern (1977) believes that synchronized interactions between infants and their caregivers may occur several times a day and are particularly important contributors to emotional attachments. As an infant continues to interact with a particular caregiver, she learns what this person is like and how she can regulate her attention (Keller et al., 1999). Of course, the caregiver should become better at interpreting the baby's signals and learn how to adjust her behaviour to successfully capture and maintain her attention. As the caregiver and the infant practise their routines and become better "dance partners," their relationship should become more satisfying for both parties and eventually blossom into a strong reciprocal attachment (Isabella, 1993; Isabella & Belsky, 1991).

HOW DO INFANTS BECOME ATTACHED?

Although many parents do find themselves emotionally drawn to their infant very soon after their baby is born, an infant requires some time before she is developmentally ready to form a genuine attachment to another human being. Many theories have been proposed to explain how and why infants become emotionally involved with the people around them. But before we consider these theories, we should briefly discuss the phases that babies go through in becoming attached to a close companion.

The Growth of Primary Attachments

Many years ago, Rudolph Schaffer and Peggy Emerson (1964) studied the development of emotional attachments by following a group of Scottish infants from early infancy to 18 months of age. Once a month, mothers were interviewed to determine (1) how the infant responded when separated from close companions in seven situations (for example, being left in a crib, being left in the presence of strangers) and (2) the people to whom the infant's separation responses were directed. A child was judged to be attached to someone if separation from that person reliably elicited a protest.

Schaffer and Emerson found that infants pass through the following phases as they develop close ties with their caregivers:

The Asocial Phase (0 to 6 Weeks)

The very young infant is somewhat "**asocial**" in that many kinds of social or nonsocial stimuli produce a favourable reaction, and few produce any kind of protest. By the end of this period, infants are beginning to show a preference for such social stimuli as a smiling face.

The Phase of Indiscriminate Attachments (6 Weeks to 6 to 7 Months)

Now infants clearly enjoy human company but tend to be somewhat **indiscriminate**. They smile more at people than at such other lifelike objects as talking puppets (Ellsworth, Muir, & Hains, 1993) and are likely to fuss whenever *any* adult puts them down. Although 3- to 6-month-olds reserve their biggest grins for familiar companions (Watson et al., 1979) and are more quickly soothed by a regular caregiver, they seem to enjoy the attention they receive from just about anyone (including strangers).

The Specific Attachment Phase (about 7 to 9 Months)

Between 7 and 9 months of age, infants begin to protest only when separated from one particular individual, usually the mother. Now able to crawl, infants often try to follow along behind their mother, stay close, and greet her warmly when she returns. They also become somewhat wary of strangers. According to Schaffer and Emerson (1964), these babies have established their first genuine attachments.

The formation of a strong attachment to a caregiver has another important consequence: It promotes the development of exploratory behaviour. Mary Ainsworth (1979) emphasizes that an attachment figure serves as a **secure base** for exploration, a point of safety from which an infant can feel free to venture away. Thus Luc, a securely attached infant visiting a neighbour's home with his mother, may be quite comfortable exploring the far corners of the living room so long as he can check back occasionally to see that mother is still seated on the couch. But should she disappear into the bathroom, Luc may become wary and reluctant to explore. Paradoxical as it may seem, then, infants apparently need to rely on another person in order to feel confident about acting independently.

The Phase of Multiple Attachments

Within weeks after forming their initial attachments, about half the infants in Schaffer and Emerson's study were becoming attached to other people such as fathers, siblings, grandparents, or perhaps even a regular babysitter. By 18 months of age, very few infants were attached to only one person, and some were attached to five or more.

Theories of Attachment

If you have ever had a kitten or a puppy, you may have noticed that pets often seem especially responsive and affectionate to the person who feeds them. Might the same be true of human infants? Developmentalists have long debated this very point, as we will see in examining four influential theories of attachment: psychoanalytic theory, learning theory, cognitive-developmental theory, and ethological theory.

asocial phase (of attachment)
approximately the first six weeks of life, in which infants respond in an equally favourable way to interesting social and nonsocial stimuli

phase of indiscriminate attachments
period between 6 weeks and 6 to 7 months of age in which infants prefer social to nonsocial stimulation and are likely to protest whenever any adult puts them down or leaves them alone

phase of specific attachment
period between 7 and 9 months of age when infants are attached to one close companion (usually the mother)

secure base
infant's use of a caregiver as a base from which to explore the environment and to which to return for emotional support

phase of multiple attachments
period when infants form attachments to companions other than their primary attachment object

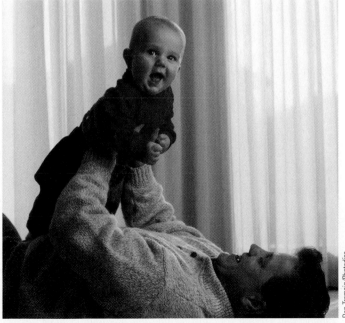

For many infants, fathers assume the role of special playmate.

Don Tremain/Photodisc

Psychoanalytic Theory: I Love You because You Feed Me

According to Freud, young infants are "oral" creatures who derive satisfaction from sucking and mouthing objects and should be attracted to any person who provides oral pleasure. Because it is usually mothers who pleasure oral infants by feeding them, it seemed logical to Freud that the mother would become the baby's primary object of security and affection, particularly if she was relaxed and generous in her feeding practices.

Erik Erikson also believed that a mother's feeding practices influence the strength or security of her infant's attachments. However, he claimed that a mother's *overall responsiveness* to her child's needs is more important than feeding itself. According to Erikson, a caregiver who consistently responds to all of an infant's needs fosters that infant's sense of *trust* in other people, whereas unresponsive or inconsistent caregiving breeds mistrust. He adds that children who have learned *not* to trust caregivers during infancy may come to avoid close mutual-trust relationships throughout life.

Before we examine the research on feeding practices and attachments, we need to consider another viewpoint that assumes that feeding is important: learning theory.

Learning Theory: Rewardingness Leads to Love

secondary reinforcer
initially neutral stimulus that acquires reinforcement value by virtue of its repeated association with other reinforcing stimuli

For quite different reasons, some learning theorists have also assumed that infants become attached to people who feed them and gratify their needs. Feeding was thought to be particularly important for two reasons (Sears, 1963). First, it should elicit positive responses from a contented infant (smiles, coos) that are likely to increase a caregiver's affection for the baby. Second, feeding is often an occasion when mothers can provide an infant with *many comforts*—food; warmth; tender touches; soft, reassuring vocalizations; changes in scenery; and even a dry diaper (if necessary)—*all in one sitting*. Over time, then, an infant should come to associate his mother with pleasant or pleasurable sensations, so that the mother herself becomes a valuable commodity. Once the mother (or any other caregiver) has attained this status as a **secondary reinforcer**, the infant is attached; he or she will now do whatever is necessary (smile, cry, coo, babble, or follow) in order to attract the caregiver's attention or to remain near this valuable and rewarding individual.

Just how important *is* feeding? In 1959, Harry Harlow and Robert Zimmerman reported the results of a study designed to compare the importance of feeding and tactile stimulation for the development of attachments in infant monkeys. The monkeys were separated from their mothers in the first day of life and reared for the next 165 days by two surrogate mothers. As you can see in the photograph, each surrogate mother had a face and well-proportioned body constructed of wire. However, the body of one surrogate (the "cloth mother") was wrapped in foam rubber and covered with terry cloth. Half the infants were always fed by this warm, comfortable cloth mother, the remaining half by the rather uncomfortable "wire mother."

The research question was simple: Would these infants become attached to the "mother" who fed them, or would they instead prefer the soft, cuddly "cloth mother"? It was no contest! Even if their food had come from the "wire mother," infants spent time with "her" *only while feeding* and ran directly to the *cloth* mother whenever they were upset or afraid. So all infants became attached to the cloth mother, thereby implying that *contact comfort* is a more powerful contributor to attachment in monkeys than feeding or the reduction of hunger.

Martin Rogers/Stock Boston

The wire and cloth "surrogate mothers" used in Harlow and Zimmerman's research. Infants became attached to the cloth mother even if it was the wire mother who fed them.

Apparently, feeding is no more important to human infants than to baby monkeys. When Schaffer and Emerson (1964) asked mothers about the feeding schedules (regular interval versus demand feeding) they had used and the age at which they had weaned their infants, they found that the generosity of a mother's feeding practices simply did not predict the quality of her infant's attachment to her. In fact, for 39 percent of these infants, the person who usually fed, bathed, and changed them (typically the mother) was not even the child's primary attachment object!

CURRENT VIEWPOINTS. Although it is now quite clear that feeding is not the primary contributor to attachments in either monkeys or humans, modern learning theorists continue to argue that *reinforcement* is the mechanism responsible for social attachments (Gewirtz & Petrovich, 1982). Their revised viewpoint, which is similar to that of Erik Erikson, is that infants are attracted to any individual who is quick to respond to all their needs and who provides them with a variety of pleasant or rewarding experiences. Indeed, Schaffer and Emerson (1964) found that the two aspects of a mother's behaviour that predicted the character of her infant's attachment to her were her *responsiveness* to the infant's behaviour and the *total amount of stimulation* that she provided. Mothers who responded reliably and appropriately to their infants' bids for attention and who often played with their babies had infants who were closely attached to them.

Cognitive-Developmental Theory: To Love You, I Must Know You Will Always Be There

Cognitive-developmental theory has little to say about which adults are most likely to appeal to infants, but it does remind us of the holistic character of development by suggesting that the ability to form attachments depends, in part, on the infant's level of intellectual development. Before an attachment can occur, the infant must be able to discriminate familiar companions from strangers. She must also recognize that familiar companions have a "permanence" about them (object permanence) because it would be difficult to form a stable relationship with a person who ceases to exist whenever she passes from view (Schaffer, 1971). So perhaps it is no accident that attachments first emerge at age 7 to 9 months—precisely the time when infants are entering Piaget's *fourth sensorimotor substage*, the point at which they first begin to search for and find objects that they've seen someone hide from them.

Barry Lester and his associates (1974) evaluated this hypothesis by giving 9-month-old infants a test of object permanence before exposing them to brief separations from their mothers, their fathers, and a stranger. They found that 9-month-olds who scored high (substage 4 or above) in object permanence only protested when separated from their mothers, whereas age-mates who scored lower (stage 3 or below) showed little evidence of *any* separation protest. So it seemed that only the cognitively advanced 9-month-olds had formed a primary attachment (to their mothers), which implies that the timing of this important emotional milestone depends, in part, on the infant's level of object permanence.

Ethological Theory: Perhaps I Was Born to Love

Ethologists have proposed a most interesting and influential explanation for emotional attachments that has strong evolutionary overtones. A major assumption of the ethological approach is that all species, including human beings, are born with a number of innate behavioural tendencies that have in some way contributed to the survival of the species over the course of evolution. Indeed, John Bowlby (1969, 1980), who was originally a psychoanalyst, came to believe that many of these built-in behaviours are specifically designed to promote attachments between infants and their caregivers. Even the attachment relationship itself is said to have adaptive significance, serving to protect the young from predators and other natural calamities and to ensure that their needs are met. Of course, ethologists would argue that the long-range purpose of the primary attachment is to permit members of each successive generation to live long enough to reproduce, thereby enabling the species to survive.

ORIGINS OF THE ETHOLOGICAL VIEWPOINT. Interestingly, the ethological theory of attachment was prompted by research with animals. In 1937, Konrad Lorenz reported that very young goslings followed almost any moving object—their mothers, a duck, or even a human being—a behaviour he labelled **imprinting**. Lorenz also noted that imprinting (1) is automatic—young fowl do not have to be taught to follow, (2) occurs only within a narrowly delimited *critical period* after the bird has hatched, and (3) is irreversible—once the bird begins to follow a particular object, it will remain attached to it.

Lorenz then concluded that imprinting was an adaptive response. Young birds generally survive if they follow their mothers so that they are led to food and afforded protection. Those that wander away may starve or be eaten by predators and thus fail to pass their genes to future generations. So over the course of many, many generations, then, the imprinting response eventually became an inborn, **preadapted characteristic** that attaches a young fowl to its mother, thereby increasing its chances of survival.

ATTACHMENT IN HUMANS. Although human infants do not imprint on their mothers in the same way that young fowl do, they seem to have inherited a number of attributes that help them to maintain contact with others and to elicit caregiving. Lorenz (1943),

for example, suggested that a baby's "**kewpie doll**" appearance (that is, large forehead, chubby cheeks, and soft, rounded features; see Figure 11.4) makes the infant appear cute or lovable to caregivers. Thomas Alley (1981) agrees. Alley found that adults judged line drawings of infant faces (and profiles) to be "adorable"—much cuter than those of 2-, 3-, and 4-year-old children. So babyish facial features may well help to elicit the kinds of positive attention from others that promote social attachments, and the more attractive the baby, the more favourably mothers and other companions respond to him or her (Barden et al., 1989; Langlois et al., 1995). Nevertheless, babies need not be adorable to foster close attachments, for a clear majority of unattractive infants end up securely attached to their caregivers (Speltz et al., 1997).

Not only do most infants have "cute" faces, but many of their inborn, reflexive responses may have an endearing quality about them (Bowlby, 1969). For example, the rooting, sucking, and grasping reflexes may lead parents to believe that their infant enjoys being close to them. Smiling, which is initially a reflexive response to almost any pleasing stimulus, is a particularly potent signal to caregivers, as are cooing, excited blurting, and spontaneous babbling (Keller & Scholmerich, 1987). In fact, an adult's typical response to a baby's smiles and positive vocalizations is to smile at (or vocalize to) the infant (Gewirtz & Petrovich, 1982; Keller & Scholmerich, 1987), and parents often interpret their baby's grins, laughs, and babbles as an indication that the child is contented and that they are effective caregivers. So a smiling or babbling infant can reinforce caregiving activities and thereby increase the likelihood that parents or other nearby companions will want to attend to this happy little person in the future.

Figure 11.4 *Infants of many species display the "kewpie-doll" effect that makes them appear lovable and elicits caregivers' attention.* ADAPTED FROM LORENZ, 1943.

imprinting
innate or instinctual form of learning in which the young of certain species follow and become attached to moving objects (usually their mothers)

preadapted characteristic
innate attribute that is a product of evolution and serves some function that increases the chances of survival for the individual and the species

kewpie doll effect
notion that infantile facial features are perceived as cute and lovable and elicit favourable responses from others

Finally, Bowlby insists that under normal circumstances, adults are just as biologically predisposed to respond favourably to a baby's signals as the baby is to emit them. It is difficult, he claims, for parents to ignore an urgent cry or to fail to warm up to a baby's big grin. In sum, human infants and their caregivers are said to have evolved in ways that predispose them to respond favourably to each other and to form close attachments, thus enabling infants (and ultimately, the species) to survive.

Does this mean that attachments are automatic? No, indeed! Bowlby claims that secure attachments develop gradually as parents become more proficient at reading and reacting appropriately to the baby's signals and the baby is *learning* what his parents are like and how he might regulate their behaviour. Yet the process can easily go awry, as illustrated by the finding that an infant's preprogrammed signals eventually wane if they fail to produce favourable reactions from an unresponsive companion, such as a depressed mother or an unhappily married father (Ainsworth et al., 1978). So while Bowlby believes that human beings are biologically *prepared* to form close attachments, he also stresses that secure emotional bonds will not develop unless each participant has *learned* how to respond appropriately to the behaviour of the other.

Comparing the Four Theoretical Approaches

Although the four theories we have reviewed differ in many respects, each has something to offer. Clearly, feeding practices are not as important to human attachments as psychoanalysts originally thought, but it was Freud who stressed that we need to know more about mother–infant interactions if we hope to understand how babies form attachments. Erik Erikson and the learning theorists pursued Freud's early leads and concluded that caregivers do play an important role in the infant's emotional development. Presumably, infants are likely to view a responsive companion who provides many comforts as a trustworthy and rewarding individual who is worthy of affection. Ethologists can agree with this point of view, but they add that infants are *active participants* in the attachment process who emit preprogrammed responses that enable them to promote the very interactions from which attachments are likely to develop. Finally, cognitive theorists have contributed by showing that the timing of emotional attachments is related to the infant's level of cognitive development. So it makes little sense to tag one of these theories as "correct" and to ignore the others, for each theory has helped us to understand how infants become attached to their most intimate companions.

Few signals attract as much attention as a baby's social smile.

Two Attachment-Related Fears of Infancy

At about the same time that infants are establishing close affectional ties to a caregiver, they often begin to display negative emotional reactions that may puzzle or even annoy their companions. In this section, we will briefly look at two of the common fears of infancy: *stranger anxiety* and *separation anxiety*.

Stranger Anxiety

Nine-month-old Katie is sitting on the floor in the den when her mother leads a strange person into the room. The stranger suddenly walks closer, bends over, and says "Hi, Katie! How are you?" If Katie is like many 9-month-olds, she may stare at the stranger for a moment and then turn away, whimper, and crawl toward her mother.

This wary reaction to a stranger, or **stranger anxiety**, stands in marked contrast to the smiling, babbling, and other positive greetings that infants often display when approached by a familiar companion. Most infants react positively to strangers until they form their first attachment, and then become apprehensive shortly thereafter (Schaffer & Emerson, 1964). Wary reactions to strangers, which are often mixed with signs of interest, peak at 8 to 10 months of age, and gradually decline in intensity over the second year (Sroufe, 1977). However, even an 8- to 10-month-old is not afraid of every strange face she sees and may occasionally react positively to strangers. In Box 11.2, we consider the circumstances under which stranger anxiety is most likely to occur and see how medical personnel and other child-care professionals might use this knowledge to head off fear and trembling in their offices.

Separation Anxiety

Many infants who have formed primary attachments also begin to display obvious signs of discomfort when separated from their mothers or other attachment objects. Ten-month-old Tony, for example, is likely to cry as he sees his mother put on a coat and pick up her purse as she prepares to go shopping, whereas 15-month-old Margit might even follow her mother to the door while whining and pleading not to be left at home. These reactions

stranger anxiety
wary or fretful reaction that infants and toddlers often display when approached by an unfamiliar person

Combatting Stranger Anxiety: Some Helpful Hints for Doctors and Child-Care Professionals

It is not unusual for toddlers visiting the doctor's office to cry and cling tenaciously to their parents. Some youngsters who may remember previous visits may be suffering from "shot anxiety" rather than stranger anxiety, but many are simply reacting fearfully to the approach of an intrusive physician who may poke and prod them in ways that are atypical and upsetting. Fortunately, there are steps that caregivers and medical personnel (or any other stranger) can take to make such encounters less terrifying for an infant or toddler. What can we suggest?

1. *Keep familiar companions available.* Infants react much more negatively to strangers when they are separated from their mothers or other close companions. Indeed, most 6- to 12-month-olds are not particularly wary of an approaching stranger if they are sitting on their mother's lap; however, they frequently whimper and cry at the stranger's approach if seated only a metre from their mother (Morgan & Ricciuti, 1969; and see Bohlin & Hagekull, 1993). Clearly, doctors and nurses can expect a more constructive response from their youngest patients if they can avoid separating them from their caregivers.

2. *Arrange for companions to respond positively to the stranger.* Stranger anxiety is less likely to occur if the caregiver issues a warm greeting to the stranger or uses a positive tone of voice when talking to the infant about the stranger (Feinman, 1992). These actions permit the child to engage in *social referencing* and to conclude that maybe the stranger really isn't all that scary. It might not hurt, then, for medical personnel to strike up a pleasant conversation with the caregiver before directing their attention to the child.

3. *Make the setting more "familiar."* Stranger anxiety occurs less frequently in familiar settings than in unfamiliar ones. For example, few 10-month-olds are especially wary of strangers at home, but most react negatively to strange companions when tested in an unfamiliar laboratory (Sroufe, Waters, & Matas, 1974). Physicians could make at least one of their examination rooms more home-like for young children, perhaps by placing an attractive mobile in one corner and posters of cartoon characters on the wall, or by having a stuffed toy available for the child to play with. The infant's familiarity with a strange setting also makes a difference: Whereas the vast majority (90 percent) of 10-month-olds become upset if a stranger approaches them within a minute after being placed in an unfamiliar room, only about half will react negatively to the stranger when they have had 10 minutes to grow accustomed to this setting (Sroufe et al., 1974). Trips to the doctor might become more tolerable for an infant or a toddler if medical personnel gave the child a few minutes to familiarize himself with the examination room before making their entrance.

4. *Be a sensitive, unobtrusive stranger.* Not surprisingly, an infant's response to a stranger depends on the stranger's behaviour (Sroufe, 1977). The meeting is likely to go best if the stranger initially keeps his or her distance and then approaches slowly while smiling, talking, and offering a familiar toy or suggesting a familiar activity (Bretherton, Stolberg, & Kreye, 1981; Sroufe, 1977). It also helps if the stranger, like any sensitive caregiver, takes his or her cues from the infant (Mangelsdorf, 1992). Babies prefer strangers they can control! Intrusive strangers who approach quickly and force themselves on the child (for example, by trying to pick infants up before they have time to adjust) probably get the response they deserve.

5. *Try looking a little less strange to the child.* Stranger anxiety depends, in part, on the stranger's physical appearance. Jerome Kagan (1972) has argued that infants form mental representations, or *schemas*, for the faces that they encounter in daily life, and are most likely to be afraid of people whose appearance is not easily assimilated into these existing schemas. So a doctor in a white lab coat with a stethoscope around her neck can make infants and toddlers wary! Pediatric professionals can and often do shed their strange instruments and white uniforms for more "normal" attire that will help their youngest patients recognize them as members of the human race. Babysitters with spiked hair or nose rings might also heed this advice if they hope to establish rapport with their young companions.

Most children respond favourably to a friendly stranger—even a doctor—who offers a toy.

reflect the children's **separation anxiety**. Separation anxiety normally appears at 6 to 8 months of age (at about the time infants are forming emotional attachments), peaks at 14 to 18 months, and gradually becomes less frequent and less intense throughout infancy and the preschool period (Kagan, Kearsley, & Zelazo, 1978; Weinraub & Lewis, 1977). However, elementary-school children and even adolescents may still show signs of anxiety and depression when separated for long periods from their loved ones (Thurber, 1995).

Why Do Infants Fear Strangers and Separations?

Why do infants who are just beginning to experience the pleasures of love suddenly become wary of strangers and anxious when separated from their objects of affection? Let's consider two views that have received some support.

THE ETHOLOGICAL VIEWPOINT. Ethologist John Bowlby (1973) claims that many situations that infants face qualify as *natural clues to danger*; they have been so frequently associated with danger throughout human evolutionary history that a fear or avoidance response has become "biologically programmed." Among the situations that infants may be programmed to fear, once they can readily discriminate familiar objects and events from unfamiliar ones, are strange faces (which, in earlier eras, may have been a predatory animal), strange settings, and the "strange circumstance" of being separated from familiar companions.

Consistent with this ethological viewpoint, infants show stronger reactions to strangers and separations in an unfamiliar laboratory than at home; presumably the "strangeness" of the laboratory magnifies the apprehension they ordinarily experience upon encountering a stranger or having to endure a separation. This ethological viewpoint also explains an interesting cross-cultural variation in separation anxiety: Infants from many nonindustrial societies, who sleep with their mothers and are nearly always in close contact with them, begin to protest separations about two to three months earlier than Western infants do. Why? Because those infants are so rarely apart from their caregivers that almost any separation is a very strange and fear-provoking event for them (Ainsworth, 1967).

Ethological theory also explains why stranger and separation anxieties decline during the second year. Once infants begin to walk and can use their attachment objects as *secure bases* for exploration, they actively initiate separations, becoming much more tolerant of them and much less wary of other novel stimuli (including friendly strangers) that had previously been a source of concern (Ainsworth, 1989; Posada et al., 1995).

THE COGNITIVE-DEVELOPMENTAL VIEWPOINT. Cognitive theorists view both stranger anxiety and separation anxiety as natural outgrowths of the infant's perceptual and cognitive development. Jerome Kagan (1972, 1976) suggests that 6- to 10-month-olds have finally developed stable schemes for (1) the faces of familiar companions and (2) these companions' probable whereabouts at home (if they are not present). Suddenly, a strange face that is discrepant with the infants' schemes for caregivers now upsets children because they can't *explain* who this is or what has become of familiar caregivers. Kagan also proposes that 7- to 10-month-olds will *not* protest most separations at home because they have a pretty good idea where a caregiver has gone should he leave them in the living room and proceed to a familiar area, such as the kitchen. But should a caregiver violate this "familiar faces in familiar places" scheme by picking up his briefcase and walking out the front door, an infant cannot easily account for his whereabouts and will probably cry.

Indeed, infants observed at home are more likely to protest when caregivers depart through an unfamiliar doorway (such as the entry to the cellar) than through a familiar one (Littenberg, Tulkin, & Kagan, 1971). And 9-month-old infants who have played quietly during a separation soon become extremely upset after looking for their mother and discovering that she is not where they thought she was, according to Carl Corter of the University of Toronto and his associates (Corter et al., 1980). Clearly, these observations support Kagan's theory: Infants are most likely to protest separations from a caregiver when they are uncertain about her whereabouts.

In sum, stranger anxiety and separation anxiety are relatively complex emotional responses that stem, in part, from an infant's *general apprehension of the unfamiliar* (the ethological viewpoint), and her inability to *explain* who a stranger may be or what has

separation anxiety
wary or fretful reaction that infants and toddlers often display when separated from the people to whom they are attached

become of familiar companions (cognitive-developmental viewpoint). Yet it is important to note that infants vary dramatically in their responses to separations and strangers: Some are almost indifferent to these events, whereas others act as if they are terrified. Why the variations? Developmentalists now believe that they often reflect individual differences in the quality, or security, of infants' attachment relationships.

INDIVIDUAL DIFFERENCES IN ATTACHMENT QUALITY

The attachment relationships that virtually all home-reared infants establish with their caregivers clearly differ in quality. Some infants are quite secure and relaxed around caregivers, whereas others seem highly anxious or uncertain about what to expect next. Why are some infants secure and others insecure in their attachment relationships? And does the security of a child's early attachments have any impact on later development? To answer these questions, researchers first had to find ways of measuring attachment quality.

Assessing Attachment Security

The most widely used technique for measuring the quality of attachments that 1- to 2-year-olds have established with their mothers or other caregivers is Mary Ainsworth's **strange situation** procedure (Ainsworth et al., 1978). The strange situation consists of a series of eight episodes (summarized in Table 11.2) that attempt to simulate (1) naturalistic caregiver–infant interactions in the presence of toys (to see if the infant uses the caregiver as a *secure base* from which to explore), (2) brief separations from the caregiver and encounters with strangers (which often stress the infant), and (3) reunion episodes (to determine whether a stressed infant derives any comfort and reassurance from the caregiver and can once again become involved with toys). By recording and analyzing an infant's responses to these episodes—that is, exploratory activities, reactions to strangers and to separations, and, in particular, behaviours when reunited with the close companion—it is usually possible to characterize her attachment to the caregiver in one of four ways.

	TABLE 11.2 The Eight Episodes of the Strange Situation	
Episode	**Events**	**Potential attachment behaviours noted**
1.	Experimenter introduces parent and baby to playroom and leaves.	
2.	Parent sits while baby plays.	Parent as a secure base
3.	Stranger enters, sits, and talks to parent.	Stranger anxiety
4.	Parent leaves, stranger offers comfort if the baby is upset.	Separation anxiety
5.	Parent returns, greets baby, and offers comfort if baby is upset. Stranger leaves.	Reunion behaviours
6.	Parent leaves room.	Separation anxiety
7.	Stranger enters and offers comfort.	Ability to be soothed by stranger
8.	Parent returns, greets baby, offers comfort if necessary, and tries to interest baby in toys.	Reunion behaviours

NOTE: All episodes, except the first, last three minutes; although separation episodes may be abbreviated and reunion episodes extended for babies who become extremely upset.

SOURCE: Based on Ainsworth et al., 1978.

strange situation
series of eight separation and reunion episodes to which infants are exposed in order to determine the quality of their attachments

Secure Attachment

About 65 percent of 1-year-old North American infants fall into this category. The **securely attached** infant actively explores while alone with the mother and may be visibly upset by separations. The infant *often greets the mother warmly when she returns and, if highly distressed, often seeks physical contact with her*, which helps to alleviate that distress. The child is outgoing with strangers while the mother is present.

Resistant Attachment

About 10 percent of 1-year-olds show this type of "insecure" attachment. These infants try to stay close to their mother but explore very little while she is present. They become very distressed as the mother departs. But when she returns, the infants are ambivalent: They *remain near her*, although they seem angry at her for having left them and are likely to *resist physical contact initiated by the mother*. **Resistant** infants are quite wary of strangers, even when their mother is present.

Avoidant Attachment

These infants (about 20 percent of 1-year-olds) also display an "insecure" attachment. They often show little distress when separated from the mother and generally *turn away from and may continue to ignore their mother, even when she tries to get their attention*. **Avoidant** infants are often rather sociable with strangers but may sometimes avoid or ignore them in much the same way that they avoid or ignore their mother.

Disorganized/Disoriented Attachment

This recently discovered attachment pattern characterizes the 5 to 10 percent of North American infants who are most stressed by the strange situation and who may be the most insecure (Hertsgaard et al., 1995). It appears to be a curious combination of the resistant and the avoidant patterns that reflects confusion about whether to approach or avoid the caregiver (Main & Solomon, 1990). When reunited with their mothers, these infants may act dazed and freeze, or they may move closer but then abruptly move away as the mother draws near, or they may show both patterns in different reunion episodes.

Unfortunately, the strange situation is not as useful for characterizing the attachments of children much older than 2, who are becoming accustomed to (and less stressed by) brief separations and encounters with strangers. Recently, an alternative assessment of attachment quality—the **Attachment Q-set (AQS)**—has become quite popular. Appropriate for use with 1- to 5-year-olds, the Attachment Q-set requires an observer—usually a parent or trained observer—to sort a set of 90 descriptors of attachment-related behaviours (for example, "Child looks to mother for reassurance when wary," "Child greets mother with big smiles") into categories ranging from "most like" to "least like" the

secure attachment
infant–caregiver bond in which the child welcomes contact with a close companion and uses this person as a secure base from which to explore the environment

resistant attachment
insecure infant–caregiver bond characterized by strong separation protest and a tendency of the child to remain near but resist contact initiated by the caregiver, particularly after a separation

avoidant attachment
insecure infant–caregiver bond characterized by little separation protest and a tendency of the child to avoid or ignore the caregiver

disorganized/disoriented attachment
insecure infant–caregiver bond, characterized by the infant's dazed appearance on reunion or a tendency to first seek and then abruptly avoid the caregiver

Attachment Q-set (AQS)
alternative method of assessing attachment security that is based on observing the child's attachment-related behaviours at home; can be used with infants, toddlers, and preschool children

---

✔ Concept Check 11.2
Understanding Theories of Attachment

Check your understanding of various theories of attachment by matching each descriptive statement below to one of the following theories or theorists: (a) Sigmund Freud, (b) Erik Erikson, (c) learning perspective, (d) John Bowlby, (e) Mary Ainsworth, (f) cognitive-developmental perspective. Answers appear in the Appendix.

_____ 1. believes that stranger/separation anxieties gradually decline as infants use their attachment objects as secure bases for exploration

_____ 2. proposes that infants are attached once the caregiver attains the status of a secondary reinforcer

_____ 3. claims that infants protest separations when they cannot account for the caregiver's whereabouts

_____ 4. proposes that caregivers' feeding practices determine the strength or character of infant attachments

_____ 5. thinks that strange faces and separations from attachment objects are natural clues to danger that infants are programmed to fear

_____ 6. emphasizes caregiver responsiveness and the infant's feelings of trust as the primary determinants of attachment security child's behaviour at home. The resulting profile represents how secure the child is with his or her caregiver (Waters et al., 1995). According to David Pederson and Greg Moran (1996) of the University of Western Ontario, trained observers' Q-set assessments for infants and toddlers are usually concordant with strange situation attachment classifications (see also Vaughn & Waters, 1990). In addition, Doug Symons of Acadia University and colleagues (Symons, Clark, Isaksen, & Marshall, 1998) found that Attachment Q-set security scores are relatively stable from age 2 to 5. And the ability to classify the attachment security of older preschool children *in their natural environments* makes the AQS a versatile alternative to the strange situation.

Cultural Variations in Attachment Classifications

The percentages of infants and toddlers who fall into the various attachment categories differ somewhat from culture to culture and seem to reflect cultural variations in child-rearing. For example, parents in northern Germany deliberately encourage their infants to be independent and tend to discourage clingy, close contact, perhaps explaining why more German than American babies show reunion behaviours characteristic of the avoidant attachment pattern (Grossmann et al., 1985). Furthermore, intense separation and stranger anxieties, which characterize resistant attachments, are much more common in cultures such as Japan, where caregivers rarely leave their infants with substitute caregivers, and Israel, where communally reared kibbutz children sleep in infant houses without their parents being accessible to them at night (Avierzer et al., 1999; Sagi et al., 1994).

Western researchers generally interpret these findings as evidence that the meanings of attachment relationships and attachment security are culturally universal, and that cultural variations in attachment classifications simply illustrate how different patterns of caregiving across cultures lead to varying percentages of securely or insecurely attached infants (van IJzendoorn & Sagi, 1999; Waters & Cummings, 2000). Yet other researchers strongly disagree, arguing that what qualifies as a secure (or an insecure) attachment varies from culture to culture.

In Japan, for example, mothers respond very differently to babies than Western mothers do (Rothbaum, Pott, et al., 2000; Rothbaum, Weisz, et al., 2000). Compared with Western mothers, Japanese mothers have much more close contact with their infants and strive to anticipate and satisfy all of their babies' needs, rather than react to their needy babies' cries. Japanese mothers emphasize social routines more and exploration less than Western mothers do, and they seek to promote the infant's **amae**—a state of total dependence on the mother and a presumption of mother love and indulgence. Given these child-rearing practices, it is hardly surprising that Japanese babies are upset by separations and will cling to their mother on reunion—behaviours that cause many of them to be classified as insecurely attached when tested in the strange situation. Yet the establishment of a healthy sense of amae is considered highly adaptive in Japan, a hallmark of attachment *security*, because it sets the stage for the development of a culturally valued communal orientation (or symbiotic harmony)—one in which Japanese children learn to become *interdependent* by accommodating to others' needs, cooperating, and

amae
Japanese concept; refers to an infant's feeling of total dependence on his or her mother and the presumption of mother's love and indulgence

Although child-rearing traditions vary dramatically across cultures, secure attachments are more common than insecure attachments around the world.

Corel

working toward the accomplishment of *group* goals (Rothbaum, Weisz, et al., 2000). By contrast, a secure attachment in Western societies is one in which infants have been encouraged to *separate* themselves from their watchful and protective caregivers to explore the environment, to become independent and autonomous, and to pursue mostly *individual* goals.

In sum, both the meaning and the long-range outcomes of secure attachments may vary from culture to culture and reflect important cultural values. What seems to be universal is that parents around the world prefer that their youngsters feel secure in their relationships with them, and most parents try to promote culturally valued forms of security (Posada et al., 1995, 1999; Rothbaum, Pott, et al., 2000). However, much of what we know about the origins of secure and insecure attachments comes from research conducted in European and North American cultures. With this limitation in mind, let's see what researchers have learned about how Western infants become securely or insecurely attached.

FACTORS THAT INFLUENCE ATTACHMENT SECURITY

Among the many factors that seem to influence the kinds of attachments that infants establish are the quality of caregiving they receive, the character or emotional climate of their homes, and their own health conditions and temperaments.

Quality of Caregiving

Mary Ainsworth (1979) believes that the quality of an infant's attachment to his mother (or any other close companion) depends largely on the kind of attention he has received. According to this **caregiving hypothesis**, mothers of *securely attached* infants are thought to be sensitive, responsive caregivers from the very beginning. And apparently they are. One recent review of 66 studies found that mothers who display the characteristics described in Table 11.3 tend to have infants who form secure attachments with them (De Wolff & van IJzendoorn, 1997). So if a caregiver has a positive attitude toward her baby, is usually sensitive to his needs, has established interactional synchrony with him, and provides ample stimulation and emotional support, the infant often derives comfort and pleasure from their interactions and is likely to become securely attached.

Babies who show a *resistant* rather than secure pattern of attachment sometimes have irritable and unresponsive temperaments (Cassidy & Berlin, 1994; Waters, Vaughn, & Egeland, 1980), but more often they have parents who are *inconsistent* in their care-

TABLE 11.3	Aspects of Caregiving That Promote Secure Mother–Infant Attachments
Characteristic	**Description**
Sensitivity	Responding promptly and appropriately to the infant's signals
Positive attitude	Expressing positive affect and affection for the infant
Synchrony	Structuring smooth, reciprocal interactions with the infant
Mutuality	Structuring interactions in which mother and infant attend to the same thing
Support	Attending closely to and providing emotional support for the infant's activities
Stimulation	Frequently directing actions toward the infant

NOTE: These six aspects of caregiving are moderately correlated with one another.
SOURCE: Based on data from De Wolff and van IJzendoorn, 1997.

caregiving hypothesis
Ainsworth's notion that the type of attachment that an infant develops with a particular caregiver depends primarily on the kind of caregiving he or she has received from that person

giving—reacting enthusiastically or indifferently depending on their moods and being unresponsive a good deal of the time (Ainsworth, 1979; Isabella, 1993; Isabella & Belsky, 1991). The infant copes with this inconsistent caregiving by trying desperately—through clinging, crying, and other attachment behaviours—to obtain emotional support and comfort and then becomes sad and resentful when these efforts often fail.

At least two patterns of caregiving place infants at risk of developing *avoidant* attachments. Ainsworth and others (for example, Isabella, 1993) find that some mothers of avoidant infants are often impatient with their babies and unresponsive to their signals, are likely to express negative feelings about their infants, and seem to derive little pleasure from close contact with them. Ainsworth (1979) believes that these mothers are rigid, self-centred people who are likely to *reject* their babies. In other cases, however, avoidant babies have overzealous parents who chatter endlessly and provide high levels of stimulation even when their babies do not want it (Belsky, Rovine, & Taylor, 1984; Isabella & Belsky, 1991). Infants may be responding quite adaptively by learning to avoid adults who seem to dislike their company or who bombard them with stimulation they cannot handle. Whereas resistant infants make vigorous attempts to gain emotional support, avoidant infants seem to have learned to do without it (Isabella, 1993).

Finally, Mary Main believes that infants who develop *disorganized/disoriented* attachments are often drawn to but also *fearful* of caregivers because of past episodes in which they were neglected or physically abused (Main & Solomon, 1990). Indeed, the infant's approach/avoidance (or totally dazed demeanour) at reunion is quite understandable if she has experienced cycles of acceptance and abuse (or neglect) and doesn't know whether to approach the caregiver for comfort or to retreat from her to safety. Available research supports Main's theorizing: Although disorganized/disoriented attachments are occasionally observed in research samples, they seem to be the *rule* rather than the exception among groups of abused infants (Carlson, 1998; Carlson et al., 1989). And this same curious mixture of approach and avoidance, coupled with sadness upon reunion, also characterizes many infants of severely depressed mothers, who may be inclined to mistreat or neglect their babies (Lyons-Ruth et al., 1990; Murray, Fiori-Cowley, & Hooper, 1996; Teti et al., 1995).

Who is at Risk of Becoming an Insensitive Caregiver?

Several personal characteristics place parents at risk of displaying the insensitive patterns of parenting that contribute to insecure attachments. For example, insecure attachments of one kind or the other are the *rule* rather than the exception when a child's primary caregiver has been diagnosed as clinically depressed (Radke-Yarrow et al., 1985; Teti et al., 1995). Depressed parents often ignore babies' social signals and generally fail to establish satisfying and synchronous relationships with them. And infants often become angry at these caregivers' lack of responsiveness and may soon begin to match their depressive symptoms, even when interacting with other *nondepressed* adults (Campbell, Cohn, & Myers, 1995; Field et al., 1988; Pickens & Field, 1993).

Another group of parents who are often insensitive caregivers are those who themselves felt unloved, neglected, or abused as children. These formerly mistreated caregivers often start out with the best intentions, vowing never to do to their children what was done to them, but they often expect their infants to be perfect and to love them right away. So when their babies are irritable, fussy, or inattentive (as all infants are at times), these emotionally insecure adults are likely to feel as if they are being rejected once again (Steele & Pollock, 1974). They may then back off or withdraw their own affection (Biringen, 1990; Crowell & Feldman, 1991), sometimes to the point of neglecting or even abusing their babies.

Finally, caregivers whose pregnancies were unplanned and their babies unwanted can be particularly insensitive caregivers whose children fare rather poorly in all aspects of development. In one longitudinal study in Czechoslovakia (Matejcek, Dytrych, & Schuller, 1979), mothers who had been denied permission to abort an unwanted pregnancy were judged to be less closely attached to their children than a group of same-aged mothers of similar marital and socioeconomic status who had not requested an abortion. Although both the wanted and the unwanted children were physically healthy at birth, over the next nine years, the unwanted children were more frequently hospitalized, made lower grades in school, had less stable family lives and poorer relations with peers, and were generally more irritable than the children whose parents had wanted them. Follow-up observations in young adulthood tell much the same story: Compared with their wanted peers, the formerly unwanted children were now much less satisfied with their marriages, jobs, friendships, and general mental health, having more often sought treatment for a variety of psychological disorders (David, 1992, 1994). Clearly, parents are unlikely to be very sensitive or to foster the development of children they do not care to raise.

Ecological Constraints on Caregiving Sensitivity

Of course, parent–child interactions always take place in a broader ecological context that may influence how caregivers respond to their children. Insensitive parenting, for example, is much more likely among caregivers who are experiencing health-related, legal, or financial problems, and it is hardly surprising that the incidence of insecure attachments is highest among poverty-stricken families that receive inadequate health care (Murray et al., 1996; NICHD Early Child Care Research Network, 1997).

The quality of a caregiver's relationship with his or her spouse can also have a dramatic effect on parent–infant interactions. Consider that parents who were unhappily married *before* the birth of their child (1) are less sensitive caregivers after the baby is born, (2) express less favourable attitudes about their infant and the parenting role, and (3) establish less secure ties with their infants and toddlers compared with other parents from similar socioeconomic backgrounds whose marriages are close and confiding (Cox et al., 1989; Howes & Markman, 1989). Happily married couples, on the other hand, usually support each other's parenting efforts, and this positive social support for parenting is especially important if the baby has already shown a tendency to be irritable and unresponsive. In fact, Jay Belsky (1981) found that newborns who are at risk for later emotional difficulties (as indicated by their poor performance on the Brazelton Neonatal Behavioral Assessment Scale) are likely to have nonsynchronous interactions with their parents *only when the parents are unhappily married*. So it seems that an unhappy marriage is a major environmental hazard that can hinder or even prevent the establishment of secure emotional ties between parents and their infants.

What Can Be Done to Assist Insensitive Caregivers?

Fortunately, there are ways of assisting at-risk parents to become more sensitive and responsive caregivers. In one intervention, depressed poverty-stricken mothers were visited regularly by a professional, who first established a friendly, supportive relationship, and then taught them how to elicit more favourable responses from their babies and encouraged their participation in weekly parenting groups. Toddlers whose mothers received this support later scored higher on intelligence tests and were much more likely to be securely attached than those of other depressed mothers who hadn't participated in an intervention (Lyons-Ruth et al., 1990).

In another intervention in Holland, economically disadvantaged mothers whose babies were *extremely irritable* received a three-month intervention designed to improve their sensitivity and responsiveness to their infants' social signals. Not only did those mothers become more sensitive

Insensitive parenting is more likely to occur in families experiencing health-related, financial, or marital distress.

Jonathan Nourok/PhotoEdit

caregivers, but their infants were also more likely than those of comparable mothers who received no intervention to be securely attached at age 12 months and to remain more secure with their mothers at age 3½ (van den Boom, 1995).

So the intervention studies clearly indicate that caregiving sensitivity can be fostered and that it promotes secure attachments. Unfortunately, most of the research conducted to date has focused exclusively on caregiving provided by mothers and has largely ignored fathers. In Box 11.3, we take a closer look at fathers as caregivers and at the contributions that fathers can make to their infants' social and emotional development.

Infant Characteristics

Thus far, we have talked as if parents are responsible for the kind of attachments that infants establish. But since it takes two people to form an attachment relationship, we might suspect that babies can also influence the quality of parent–infant emotional ties. Indeed, Jerome Kagan (1984, 1989) has argued that the strange situation really measures individual differences in infants' temperaments rather than the quality of their attachments. This idea grew from his observation that the percentages of 1-year-olds who have established secure, resistant, and avoidant attachments corresponds closely to the percentages of babies who fall into Thomas and Chess's easy, difficult, and slow-to-warm-up temperamental profiles (see Table 11.4). The linkages even make some sense: Kagan suggests that a temperamentally difficult infant who actively resists changes in routine and is upset by novelty may become so distressed by the strange situation that he is unable to respond constructively to his mother's comforting and is thus classified as resistant. By contrast, a friendly, easygoing child is apt to be classified as securely attached, whereas one who is shy or slow to warm up may appear distant or detached in the strange situation and will probably be classified as avoidant. So Kagan's **temperament hypothesis** implies that infants, not caregivers, are the primary architects of their attachment classifications. Presumably, the attachment behaviours that a child displays reflect his or her own temperament.

Does Temperament Explain Attachment Security?

Although such components of temperament as irritability and negative emotionality predict certain attachment behaviours (e.g., intensity of separation protests) and can certainly contribute to the quality of an infant's attachments (Goldsmith & Alansky, 1987; Seifer et al., 1996; Vaughn et al., 1992), most experts view Kagan's temperament hypothesis as far too extreme. Consider, for example, that many infants are securely attached to one close companion and insecurely attached to another—a pattern that we would not expect to see if attachment classifications were merely reflections of the child's relatively stable temperamental characteristics (Goossens & van IJzendoorn, 1990; Sroufe, 1985).

In addition, we have already seen that when mothers of *temperamentally difficult* Dutch infants are trained to be more sensitive, the vast majority of their babies establish secure rather than insecure attachments, which indicates that sensitive caregiving is causally related to attachment quality (van den Boom, 1995). Finally, one review of 34

temperament hypothesis
Kagan's view that the strange situation measures individual differences in infants' temperaments rather than the quality of their attachments

TABLE 11.4	Percentage of 1-Year-Olds Who Can Be Classified as Temperamentally "Easy," "Difficult," and "Slow to Warm Up" Who Have Established Secure, Resistant, and Avoidant Attachments with Their Mothers		
Temperamental profile	**Percentage of "classifiable" infants**	**Attachment classification**	**Percentage of 1-year-olds**
Easy	60	Secure	65
Difficult	15	Resistant	10
Slow to warm up	23	Avoidant	20

SOURCES: Ainsworth et al., 1978; Thomas & Chess, 1977.

11.3

Fathers as Attachment Objects

In 1975, Michael Lamb described fathers as the "forgotten contributors to child development." And he was right. Until the mid-1970s, fathers were treated as biological necessities who played only a minor role in the social and emotional development of their infants and toddlers. However, fathers appear to be as engrossed with their newborn infants as mothers are (Nichols, 1993), and they become increasingly involved with their babies over the first year of life, spending an average of nearly an hour a day interacting with their 9-month-olds (Ninio & Rinott, 1988). Fathers are most involved with their infants and hold more favourable attitudes about them when they are happily married (Belsky, 1996) and when their wives encourage them to become an important part of their babies' lives (DeLuccie, 1995; Palkovitz, 1984).

Many infants form secure attachments to their fathers during the latter half of the first year (Lamb, 1997), particularly if the father has a positive attitude about parenting, is extroverted and agreeable, spends a lot of time with them, and is a sensitive caregiver (Cox et al., 1992; van IJzendoorn & De Wolff, 1997). And how do fathers compare with mothers as companions? Research conducted in Australia, Israel, India, Italy, Japan, and the United States reveals that mothers and fathers in all these societies tend to play somewhat different roles in a baby's life. Mothers are more likely than fathers to hold their infants, to soothe and talk to them, to play traditional games such as peekaboo, and to care for their physical needs; fathers are more likely than mothers to provide playful physical stimulation and to initiate unusual or unpredictable games that infants often enjoy. Although most infants prefer their mothers' company when upset or afraid, fathers are often preferred as playmates (Lamb, 1997).

However, the playmate role is but one of many that modern fathers fulfill, particularly if their wives are working and they assume some caregiving responsibility (Grych & Clark, 1999). And what kinds of caregivers do fathers make? Many fathers are (or soon become) skillful at virtually all phases of routine care (including diapering, bathing, and soothing a distressed infant). Moreover, once fathers become objects of affection, they begin to serve as a secure base from which their babies will venture to explore the environment (Hwang, 1986; Lamb, 1997). So fathers are versatile companions who can assume any and all functions normally served by the other parent (of course, the same is true of mothers).

Although many infants form the same kind of attachment with their fathers that they have established with their mothers (Fox, Kimmerly, & Schafer, 1991), it is not at all unusual for a child to be securely attached to one parent and insecure with the other (van IJzendoorn & De Wolff, 1997). For example, when Mary Main and Donna Weston (1981) used the strange situation to measure the quality of 44 infants' attachments to their mothers and their fathers, they found that 12 infants were securely attached to both parents, 11 were secure with the mother but insecure with the father, 10 were insecure with the mother but secure with the father, and 11 were insecurely attached to both parents.

What does the father add to a child's social and emotional development? Main and Weston (1981) addressed this issue by exposing the 44 toddlers in their study to a friendly and animated stranger in a clown outfit and observing how appropriately responsive they were to the clown. As we see in the table, infants who were securely attached to *both* parents were most appropriately responsive (and least fearful) whereas those who were securely attached to either the mother or father were significantly more socially appropriate (and less fearful) than those who were insecurely attached to both parents. Other recent research has shown that, compared with children who are securely attached to only one or to neither parent, those who are secure with *both* parents are less anxious and withdrawn and make better adjustments to the challenges of attending school (Verschueren & Marcoen, 1999), while also displaying better emotional self-regulation, greater social competencies with peers, and lower levels of problem behaviours and delinquency throughout childhood and adolescence (Cabrera et al., 2000; Lieberman, Doyle, & Markiewicz, 1999). Indeed, the positive benefits of having a secure, supportive relationship with one's father often occur even when he may no longer be residing in the home (Black et al., 1999; Coley, 1998). So not only are fathers potentially important contributors to many (perhaps *all*) aspects of child development, but it seems that a secure attachment to the father may help compensate for the potentially negative effects of an insecure mother-child attachment relationship (Main & Weston, 1981; Verschueren & Marcoen, 1999).

Average Levels of Social Responsiveness and Emotional Conflict Shown by Infants Who Were Either Securely or Insecurely Attached to Their Mothers and Fathers

	Patterns of attachment			
Measure	Securely attached to both parents	Secure with mother, insecure with father	Insecure with mother, secure with father	Insecurely attached to both parents
Social responsiveness	6.04	4.87	3.30	2.45
Emotional conflict	1.17	1.00	1.80	2.50

NOTE: Social responsiveness ratings could vary from 1 (wary, distressed) to 9 (happy, responsive). Conflict ratings could vary from 1 (no conflict) to 5 (very conflicted).

SOURCE: Adapted from Main & Weston, 1981.

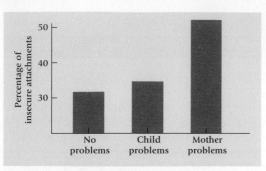

Figure 11.5 *Comparing the impact of maternal and child problem behaviours on the incidence of insecure attachments. Maternal problems were associated with a sharp increase in insecure attachments, whereas child problems were not.* BASED ON VAN IJZENDOORN ET AL., 1992.

studies revealed that maternal characteristics that often predict insensitive parenting, such as illness, depression, and child maltreatment, were associated with a sharp increase in insecure attachments (see Figure 11.5). However, child temperamental problems stemming from prematurity, illness, and other psychological disorders had virtually no impact on attachment quality (van IJzendoorn et al., 1992).

Although the findings just cited seem to favour Ainsworth's caregiving hypothesis over Kagan's temperamental model, look carefully at the research in Box 11.4. This study clearly illustrates the important link between sensitive caregiving and secure attachments while also demonstrating how child development can sometimes contribute to the kinds of attachments infants form.

ATTACHMENT AND LATER DEVELOPMENT

Both psychoanalytic theorists (Erikson, 1963; Freud, 1905/1930) and ethologists (Bowlby, 1969) believe that the feelings of warmth, trust, and security that infants gain from secure attachments set the stage for healthy psychological development later in life. Of course, one implication of this viewpoint is that insecure attachments may forecast less than optimal developmental outcomes in the years ahead.

CURRENT CONTROVERSIES

On the Intricate Interplay between Caregiving and Temperament in Shaping Infant Attachments

Recently, Grazyna Kochanska (1998) sought to test an integrative theory of infant–caregiver attachments—one specifying that (1) quality of caregiving is most important in determining whether an infant's emerging attachments are secure or insecure, but (2) infant temperament is the better predictor of the type of insecurity infants display should their attachments be insecure. Kochanska began by measuring quality of caregiving mothers provided (i.e., maternal responsiveness to the infant; the synchrony of positive emotions between mother and infant) when their babies were 8 to 10 and 13 to 15 months old. She also assessed the aspect of infant temperament known as fearfulness. Fearful children are prone to showing strong distress in new and uncertain situations and are similar to those children Kagan calls behaviourally *inhibited*. *Fearless* children, by contrast, are largely unperturbed by strange settings, people, or separations and are similar to those children Kagan refers to as behaviourally *uninhibited*. Finally, Kochanska used the strange situation to assess the quality of infants' attachments to their mothers at 13 to 15 months. Thus she had data allowing her to determine whether caregiving or temperament contributed more strongly to the security and specific type of attachments that infants display.

The study produced two particularly interesting sets of results. First, as anticipated by the integrative theory, quality of caregiving (but not infant temperament) clearly predicted whether infants established secure or insecure attachments with their mothers, with positive, responsive parenting being associated with secure attachments. However, quality of caregiving did not predict the type of insecurity that infants with insecure attachments displayed.

What, then, predicted *type* of insecurity? Infant temperament did! As anticipated by the integrative theory and a knowledge of the fearfulness–fearlessness dimension, temperamentally fearful children who had insecure attachments were prone to display *resistant* attachments, whereas insecure infants who were temperamentally fearless were more likely to display *avoidant* attachments.

Clearly, the findings imply that strong versions of both the caregiving hypothesis and the temperament hypothesis are overstatements. In fact, the data are actually quite consistent with Thomas and Chess's (1977) *goodness-of-fit model:* Secure attachments evolve from relationships in which there is a good fit between the caregiving that a baby receives and his or her own temperament, whereas insecure attachments are more likely to develop when highly stressed or otherwise inflexible caregivers fail to accommodate to their infants' temperamental qualities. Indeed, one reason caregiver sensitivity predicts attachment security is that the very notion of *sensitive* care implies an ability to tailor one's routines to whatever temperamental qualities a baby might display (van den Boom, 1995).

Long-Term Correlates of Secure and Insecure Attachments

Although the existing data are somewhat limited in that they focus almost exclusively on infants' attachments to their mothers, it seems that infants who have established secure primary attachments are likely to display more favourable developmental outcomes. For example, infants who were securely attached at age 12 to 18 months are better problem solvers as 2-year-olds (Frankel & Bates, 1990), are more complex and creative in their symbolic play (Pipp, Easterbrooks, & Harmon, 1992), display more positive and few negative emotions (Kochanska, 2001), and are more attractive to toddlers as playmates (Fagot, 1997; Jacobson & Wille, 1986) than children who were insecurely attached. In fact, infants whose primary attachments are disorganized/disoriented are at risk of becoming hostile and aggressive preschool and elementary-school children whom peers are likely to reject (Lyons-Ruth, Alpern, & Repacholi, 1993; Lyons-Ruth, Easterbrooks, & Cibelli, 1997).

Many longer-term studies of securely and insecurely attached children paint a similar picture. Everett Waters and his associates (1979), for example, first measured the quality of children's attachments at 15 months of age and then observed these children in a nursery-school setting at age 3½. Children who had been securely attached to their mothers at age 15 months were now social leaders in the nursery school: They often initiated play activities, were generally sensitive to the needs and feelings of other children, and were very popular with their peers. Observers described these children as curious, self-directed, and eager to learn. By contrast, children who had been insecurely attached at age 15 months were socially and emotionally withdrawn, were hesitant to engage other children in play activities, and were described by observers as less curious, less interested in learning, and much less forceful in pursuing their goals. A follow-up in a camp setting when these children were 11 to 12 and 15 to 16 years old revealed that those who had been securely attached still displayed better social skills, enjoyed better peer relations, and were more likely to have close friends than age-mates whose primary attachments had been insecure (Elicker, Englund, & Sroufe, 1992; Englund et al., 2000; Shulman, Elicker, & Sroufe, 1994). And recent studies with other samples—for example, a study conducted by Barry Schneider from the University of Ottawa, Leslie Atkinson from the Centre for Addiction and Mental Health, and Christine Tardif from Brock University (2001; see also Allen et al., 1998; Carlson, 1998; DeMulder et al., 2000)—reveal that youngsters whose attachments to parents were or are currently insecure are more likely than those with secure attachments to experience poor peer relations and fewer close relationships and to display deviant behaviours (e.g., disobedience at school) and other psychopathological symptoms throughout childhood and adolescence.

So it seems that children can be influenced by the quality of their early attachments for many years to come. This is due, in part, to the fact that attachments are often stable over time. In middle-class samples, most children (84 percent in one American sample and 82 percent in a German sample) experienced the same kind of attachment relationships with their parents during the elementary-school years that they did in infancy (Main & Cassidy, 1988; Wartner et al., 1994). In fact, a sizable majority of adolescents and young adults from stable family backgrounds continue to display the same kinds of attachments that they had established in infancy with their parents (Hamilton, 2000; Waters et al., 2000).

Why Might Attachment Quality Forecast Later Outcomes?

Why is the quality of one's early attachments so often stable over time? And how might attachments shape one's behaviour and influence the character of one's future interpersonal relationships?

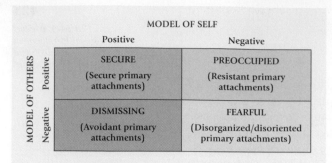

		MODEL OF SELF	
		Positive	Negative
MODEL OF OTHERS	Positive	SECURE (Secure primary attachments)	PREOCCUPIED (Resistant primary attachments)
	Negative	DISMISSING (Avoidant primary attachments)	FEARFUL (Disorganized/disoriented primary attachments)

Figure 11.6 *Four perspectives on close emotional relationships that evolve from the positive or negative "working models" of self and others that people construct from their experiences with intimate companions.* ADAPTED FROM BARTHOLOMEW & HOROWITZ, 1991.

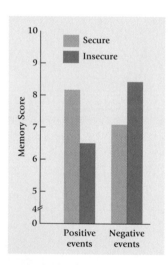

Figure 11.7 *Because of differences in their internal working models, securely attached children are biased to remember positive experiences and insecurely attached children to remember negative experiences.* BASED ON BELSKY, SPRITZ, & CRNIC, 1996.

internal working models cognitive representations of self, others, and relationships that infants construct from their interactions with caregivers

Attachments as Working Models of Self and Others

Ethologists John Bowlby (1980, 1988) and Inge Bretherton (1985, 1990) have proposed an interesting explanation for both the stability and the enduring effects of early attachment classifications. They believe that as infants continue to interact with primary caregivers, they develop **internal working models**—that is, cognitive representations of *themselves* and *other people*—that are used to interpret events and to form expectations about the character of human relationships. Sensitive, responsive caregiving should lead the child to conclude that people are dependable (positive working model of others), whereas insensitive, neglectful, or abusive caregiving may lead to insecurity and a lack of trust (negative working model of others). Although this sounds very similar to Erik Erikson's earlier ideas about the importance of trust, ethologists go one step further, arguing that infants also develop a working model of the *self* based largely on their ability to elicit attention and comfort *when they need it*. So an infant whose caregivers respond quickly and appropriately to her bids for attention is apt to believe that "I'm lovable" (positive working model of self), whereas one whose signals are ignored or misinterpreted may conclude that "I'm unworthy or unlovable" (negative working model of self). Presumably, these two models combine to influence the quality of the child's primary attachments and the expectations she has about future relationships. What kinds of expectations might she form?

A recent version of this working-models theory appears in Figure 11.6. As shown, infants who construct positive working models of themselves and their caregivers are the ones who should (1) form secure primary attachments, (2) have the *self*-confidence to approach and master new challenges, and (3) be inclined to establish secure, mutual-trust relationships with friends and spouses later in life (Waters & Cummings, 2000). By contrast, a positive model of self coupled with a negative model of others (as might result when infants can successfully attract the attention of an insensitive, overintrusive caregiver) is thought to predispose the infant to form *avoidant* attachments and to dismiss the importance of close emotional bonds. A negative model of self and a positive model of others (as might result when infants sometimes can but often cannot attract the attention they need) should be associated with *resistant* attachments and a preoccupation with establishing secure emotional ties. Finally, a negative working model of both the self and others is thought to underlie *disorganized/disoriented* attachments and an emerging fear of being hurt (either physically or emotionally) in intimate relationships (Bartholomew & Horowitz, 1991).

Recently, Jay Belsky and his associates (1996) demonstrated for the first time that children who were securely or insecurely attached as infants process information in ways that suggest that they have formed very different internal working models of self and others. Three-year-olds were treated to puppet shows dramatizing positive events such as getting a birthday present and negative events such as spilling juice. The researchers hypothesized that children who had been securely attached as infants would expect positive experiences in life and remember them especially well, whereas children with insecure attachment histories would expect and tend to recall the more negative events. Although the securely and insecurely attached children did not differ in their attention to positive and negative events, Figure 11.7 shows that the securely attached children did excel at remembering the positive events whereas insecurely attached children were better at remembering the negative ones.

Later research reveals that children with positive working models of both self and their caregivers are more likely than those whose working models are not so positive to display *self*-confidence and earn higher grades later in adolescence, develop better social skills and more positive representation of peers, and enjoy closer, more supportive friendships (Cassidy et al., 1996; Jacobsen & Hofmann, 1997; Verschueren & Marcoen, 1999). So Bowlby was on the right track in theorizing that differences in the internal working models that securely and insecurely attached people form may have important implications for later development (Waters & Cummings, 2000).

Parents' Working Models and Attachment

Interestingly, parents also have positive or negative working models of themselves and others based on their own life experiences. Several methods now exist to measure adults' working models, based either on a detailed analysis of their memories of childhood attachment experiences or on their current view of themselves, other people, and the character of interpersonal relationships (Bartholomew & Horowitz, 1991; Main & Goldwyn, 1994). Using these instruments, adults can be reliably cast into the classifications described earlier in Figure 11.6. Do their own working models influence the kinds of attachments that their babies form?

Indeed they do. Peter Fonagy and his associates (1991), for example, found that English mothers' working models of attachment relationships measured *before their babies were born* accurately predicted about 75 percent of the time whether their infants would establish secure or insecure attachments with them. Similar results have now been reported in studies conducted in Canada, Germany, the Netherlands, and the United States (Benoit & Parker, 1994; Das Eiden, Teti, & Corns, 1995; Steele, Steele, & Fonagy, 1996; van IJzendoorn, 1995), with an exact matching of working models occurring in 60 to 70 percent of the mother–infant dyads. One contributor to these working-model matches is that mothers with the more positive working models are more likely to provide the kind of sensitive, responsive, and nonintrusive caregiving that fosters secure infant attachment (Aviezer et al., 1999; Slade et al., 1999). Another contributor is that mothers with secure attachment representations derive more joy and pleasure from interacting with their infants than do those whose attachment representations are insecure (Slade et al., 1999), and according to David Pederson, Greg Moran, and colleagues from the University of Western Ontario (1998), it appears that these two factors may contribute *independently* to the kinds of attachment infants form (Pederson et al., 1998).

So it seems that cognitive representations of intimate relationships are often transmitted from generation to generation. Indeed, Bowlby (1988) proposed that once formed early in life, working models may stabilize, becoming an aspect of personality that continues to influence the character of one's close emotional ties throughout life.

Is Attachment History Destiny?

Although it appears that early working models can be long-lasting, and that there are some clear advantages to having formed secure emotional attachments early in life, the future is not always so bleak for infants who are insecurely attached. As we learned in Box 11.3, a secure relationship with another person such as the father (or perhaps a grandparent or daycare provider) can help to offset whatever undesirable consequences might otherwise result from an insecure attachment with the mother (Clarke-Stewart, 1989).

Let's also note that secure attachments sometimes become insecure should a mother return to work, deliver another baby that requires attention, or experience such life stresses as marital problems, a major illness, or financial woes that drastically alter the ways that she and her infant respond to each other (Holden & Miller, 1999; Weinfield, Sroufe, & Egeland, 2000). One reason Bowlby used the term *working* models was to underscore that a child's cognitive representations of self, others, and close emotional relationships are dynamic and can change (for better or for worse) if later experiences with caregivers, close friends, romantic partners, or spouses imply that a revision is necessary.

In sum, secure attachment histories are no guarantee of positive adjustment later in life, nor are insecure early attachments a certain indicator of poor life outcomes (Fagot & Kavanagh, 1990). Yet we should not underestimate the adaptive significance of secure early attachments, because children who have functioned adequately as infants but very poorly during the preschool period are more likely to recover and to display good social skills and self-confidence during the elementary-school years if their early attachment histories were secure rather than insecure (Sroufe, Egeland, & Kreutzer, 1990).

THE UNATTACHED INFANT

Some infants have very limited contacts with adults during the first year or two of life and do not appear to become attached to anyone. Occasionally, these socially deprived youngsters are reared at home by very abusive or neglectful caregivers, but most of them are found in understaffed institutions where they may see a caregiver only when it is time to be fed, changed, or bathed. Will these infants suffer as a result of their experiences?

Effects of Social Deprivation in Infancy and Childhood

In the 1940s, physicians and psychologists began to discover and study infants who were living under conditions of extreme social deprivation. For example, it was not uncommon for the impoverished institutions in which these infants lived to have only one caregiver for every 10 to 20 infants. Adult caregivers rarely interacted with the infants except to bathe and change them or to prop a bottle against their pillows at feeding time. Infants were often housed in separate cribs with sheets hung over the railings so that, in effect, they were isolated from the world around them. By today's standards, these babies were victims of extreme neglect (DeAngelis, 1997b).

Infants raised under these conditions appear quite normal for the first three to six months of life: They cry for attention, smile and babble at caregivers, and make the proper postural adjustments when they are about to be picked up. But in the second half of the first year, their behaviour changes. Now they seldom cry, coo, or babble; they become rigid and fail to accommodate to the handling of caregivers, and they often appear rather depressed and uninterested in social contact (Goldfarb, 1943; Provence & Lipton, 1962; Ribble, 1943; Spitz, 1945). Here is a description of one such infant:

> Outstanding were his soberness, his forlorn appearance, and lack of animation.... He did not turn to adults to relieve his distress.... He made no demands.... As one made active and persistent efforts at a social exchange he

Children raised in barren, understaffed institutions show many signs of developmental retardation.

H. Bradner/The Image Works

became somewhat more responsive, animated and ... active, but lapsed into his depressed ... appearance when the adult became less active.... If you crank his motor you can get him to go a little; but he can't start on his own. (Provence & Lipton, 1962, pp. 134–5)

What are these institutionalized infants like as schoolchildren and adolescents? The answer depends, in part, on how long they remain in the institution. William Goldfarb (1943, 1947) compared children who left an understaffed orphanage during the first year with similar children who spent their first three years at the orphanage before departing for foster homes. After interviewing, observing, and testing these children at ages 3½, 6½, 8½, and 12, Goldfarb found that youngsters who had spent three years in the institution lagged behind the early adoptees in virtually all aspects of development. They scored poorly on IQ tests, were socially immature, were remarkably dependent on adults, had poor language skills, and were prone to behaviour problems such as aggression and hyperactivity. By early adolescence, they were often loners who had a difficult time relating to peers or family members.

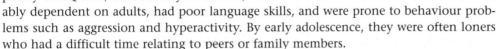

WHAT DO YOU THINK?

Imagine that you are a researcher who studies the developmental significance of infant emotions (both emotional expression and emotional understanding). Knowing what you do, how would you explain the sober, depressed behaviour of infants in understaffed institutions?

More recently, concerns have been expressed about serious developmental impairments found in some children from deprived institutions in Romania who were adopted into homes in Canada, the United States, and the United Kingdom after the fall of the Romanian government in 1989. These Romanian adoptees reportedly spent their infancies in orphanages with 20 to 30 children in a room and only one caregiver for every 10 to 20 children, most of the time rocking back and forth in their cribs with little human affection or bouts of play and virtually no synchronous routines with anyone (Fisher et al., 1997). Infants who spent 8 months or more in such orphanages displayed eating disorders and medical problems, and many were withdrawn and seemingly overwhelmed by later interactions with adoptive siblings and peers (Fisher et al., 1997). In one recent study the majority of late-adopted Romanian children were eventually able to establish attachment bonds with adoptive parents, although the incidence of insecure attachments was substantially higher in this sample than among age-mates raised with parents from birth (Chisholm, 1998). However, other investigators have found that a fair number of institutionalized Romanian adoptees display **reactive attachment disorder**, an inability to bond, securely or otherwise, to adoptive or foster parents, even when these new caregivers have secure working models of attachment relationships (DeAngelis, 1997b; Marcovitchet al., 1997). Indeed, the insecure attachments that these children form may help to explain why they are often restless and troubled and have few close friends later in childhood and adolescence.

Why Is Early Deprivation Harmful?

No one questions that early social deprivation can have lasting effects, but there is some disagreement about why this is so. Proponents of the **maternal deprivation hypothesis** (Bowlby, 1969; Spitz, 1965) think that neglected children and those in understaffed institutions develop abnormally because they lack the warm, loving attention of a single mother-figure to whom they can become attached. But despite its popularity, there are many observations that the maternal deprivation hypothesis cannot easily explain. Studies of adequately staffed institutions in Russia and Israel, for example, reveal that infants who are cared for by dozens of responsive caregivers appear quite normal and are as well adjusted later in childhood as those who are reared at home (Bronfenbrenner, 1970; Kessen, 1975; Oppenheim, Sagi, & Lamb, 1988). Similarly, Efe (Pygmy) infants in Zaire seem to thrive from birth on being cared for and even nursed by a variety of caregivers (Tronick, Morelli, & Ivey, 1992). So it seems that the impairments characterizing children in understaffed institutions probably reflect something other than their lack of an exclusive attachment to a singular mother figure.

reactive attachment disorder
inability to form secure attachment bonds with other people; characterizes many victims of early social deprivation and/or abuse

maternal deprivation hypothesis
notion that socially deprived infants develop abnormally because they have failed to establish attachments to a primary caregiver

Lucy Le Mare

Lucy Le Mare

Lucy Le Mare works in the Faculty of Education at Simon Fraser University. Her research interests lie in the area of children's social-emotional development, particularly as it relates to adjustment in the classroom, the peer group, and school life.

In the two years following the fall of the Ceaucescu dictatorship in 1989, more than 1400 children were adopted to Canada from Romania. Approximately half of these children came from orphanages. In 1991, Elinor Ames from Simon Fraser University began following the development of a group of children who were adopted from Romanian institutions by families living primarily in British Columbia. These 46 children were adopted between the ages of 8 and 68 months and, at the times of their adoptions, all had spent nearly their entire lives in an institution. To date, these children have been comprehensively assessed on three occasions: when they had been in their adoptive homes for 11 months (Time 1), when most were 4½ years old (Time 2), and most recently when the majority were 10½ years old (Time 3). The research at Times 1 and 2 was headed by Dr. Ames and at Time 3 by Lucy Le Mare, also of Simon Fraser University. The Romanian orphan (RO) children have been compared with a group of Canadian-born (CB) nonadopted children matched for age, sex, and family demographic factors. A second comparison group is comprised of 29 Romanian adoptees who were adopted before 4 months of age and who were matched in the same way to the 29 youngest children in the RO and CB groups. These early adopted (EA) children are similar to the RO children in terms of biological family background and pre- and perinatal care but do not share their extensive institutional experience.

At Times 2 and 3, the RO children showed a higher rate of insecure attachments than their CB and EA comparisons, who did not differ from each other (L. Le Mare, personal communication, March, 2004). One of the difficulties linked to attachment status within the RO group was indiscriminately friendly behaviour. At Time 3, the RO children displayed more indiscriminately friendly behaviour than both comparison groups and this behaviour remained relatively stable over the previous six years.

On the positive side, peers, teachers, and parents at Time 3 reported that the RO children were as well accepted by their peers as the CB and EA children. Moreover, the RO children perceived themselves to be as well accepted as children in the comparison groups. Despite this acceptance, however, the RO children reported having less social support from their peers than CB children, and parents of the RO children reported that their children engaged in less peer group activity than children in the other groups. RO children who displayed indiscriminately friendly behaviour at 4½ years of age reported feeling lonelier and less supported by a close friend, had fewer friends, engaged in less peer activity, and experienced more unreciprocated peer attraction at 10½ years than both comparison groups.

RO children also experienced deficits in intellectual functioning, which was related to poorer school performance than displayed by the comparison groups. Nevertheless, despite their relatively poor academic performance, the RO children felt equally positive about their academic abilities as the comparison children did. The intellectual functioning of the RO children was related to the length of time they spent in an orphanage prior to adoption, suggesting that the longer the children were in an institution, the lower their IQ.

RO children displayed more problems focusing attention and controlling impulses than the CB and EA children. Time 3 findings indicated a link between the early adoptive home environment and later attention difficulties within the RO group. Although all children in the study experienced positive home environments, those in more nurturing and stimulating homes were less likely to experience attention difficulties at Time 3.

Might socially deprived infants develop abnormally simply because they have little contact with anyone who responds to their social signals? Proponents of the **social stimulation hypothesis** think so, arguing that the normal development of Chinese, Russian, Israeli, and Efe infants raised by a multitude of caregivers implies that infants need *sustained* interactions with *responsive* companions—either one or several—in order to develop normally. Such stimulation may be particularly important because it often depends, in part, on the infant's own behaviour: People often attend to the infant *when* he or she cries, smiles, babbles, or gazes at them. This kind of association between one's own behaviour and the behaviour of caregivers may lead an infant to believe that she has some *control* over the social environment—an important contributor to a positive working model of self. And as she exerts this "control" and receives others' attention and affection, she develops a positive working model of others and becomes more outgoing.

Now consider the plight of socially deprived infants who may emit many signals and rarely receive a response from their overburdened or inattentive caregivers. What these children likely learn from their experiences is that *their* attempts to attract the attention

social stimulation hypothesis
notion that socially deprived infants develop abnormally because they have had little contact with companions who respond contingently to their social overtures

of others are useless (negative working model of self) because nothing they do seems to matter to anyone (negative working model of others). Consequently, they may develop a sense of **learned helplessness** and simply stop trying to elicit responses from other people (Finkelstein & Ramey, 1977). Here, then, is a very plausible reason why socially deprived infants are often passive, withdrawn, and apathetic.

Can Children Recover from Early Deprivation Effects?

Fortunately, socially deprived children can overcome many of their initial handicaps if placed in homes where they receive lots of attention from affectionate and responsive caregivers (Clarke & Clarke, 1976; O'Connor et al., 2000). Recovery seems to go especially well if children are deprived for less than two years, have not been physically abused, and are placed with *highly educated, relatively affluent* parents who, as we learned in Chapter 9, have the personal, social, and financial resources to foster adaptive development (DeAngelis, 1997b; Hodges & Tizard, 1989). Elinor Ames, Lucy Le Mare, and associates from Simon Fraser University (Le Mare et al., 2001; Morison, Ames, & Chisholm, 1995; Morison & Ellwood, 2000), for example, studied a group of Romanian orphans who had lived in institutions for at least eight months before coming to Canada. These institutions were impoverished environments, with many children spending their days lying or sitting in their cribs. But despite the lack of stimulation and responsiveness that they had endured, these children made remarkable progress. After only 11 months of being exposed to the stimulating environment of their adoptive homes, the children made substantial gains in achievement and cognitive development. Follow-up studies completed three and eight years after adoption, however, revealed that the longer children had been in the institution, the worse off they were postadoption (Le Mare et al., 2001; Le Mare, Warford, & Fernyhough, 2001; Morison & Ellwood, 2000). See Box 11.5 for a summary of current research findings from this population.

In sum, infants who have experienced social and emotional deprivation over the first two years often show a strong capacity for recovery when they are placed in a stimulating home environment and receive individualized attention from responsive caregivers. However, the lingering deficiencies and reactive attachment disorders that many abuse victims and late adoptees display suggest that infancy and toddlerhood may be a *sensitive period* for the establishment of *secure* affectional ties and other capacities that these ties may foster. Can they make complete recoveries? We don't really know yet (see O'Connor et al., 2000) although it is likely that especially severe or prolonged adversity may take longer to overcome and may require stronger interventions than merely placing these children in good homes. Fortunately, recently developed *attachment therapies*, specifically aimed at

learned helplessness
failure to learn how to respond appropriately in a situation because of previous exposures to uncontrollable events in the same or similar situations

Concept Check 11.3
Understanding Individual Differences in Attachment

Check your understanding of individual differences in attachment by matching each descriptive statement below with one of the following models/hypotheses: (a) Ainsworth's caregiving hypothesis, (b) Kagan's temperament hypothesis, (c) Thomas & Chess's goodness-of-fit model, (d) Kochanska's integrative theory, (e) Bowlby/ Bretherton internal working models hypothesis, (f) maternal deprivation hypothesis, (g) social stimulation hypothesis. Answers appear in the Appendix.

_____ 1. best summarizes how characteristics of infants and caregivers combine to influence attachment quality

_____ 2. has difficulty explaining why an infant might be securely attached to one parent and insecure with the other

_____ 3. easily explains why institutionalized infants show no developmental impairments when exposed to many responsive caregivers

_____ 4. claims that babies may be responding adaptively by forming avoidant attachments with unresponsive caregivers who seem to dislike their company

_____ 5. explains how early attachments can affect the character of one's interpersonal relationships later in life

_____ 6. now-discredited explanation for the developmental delays shown by children in understaffed institutions

_____ 7. claims that temperament influences attachment classification only when caregiving does not foster a secure attachment building emotional bridges to adoptive parents and at fostering more positive working models of others, look quite promising. One recent study found that 85 percent of children who had undergone attachment therapy eventually established secure bonds to their caregivers (although the success rate with *teenage* victims of reactive attachment disorder was very poor) (DeAngelis, 1997b). Treatment centres, such as the Hincks-Dellcrest Treatment Centre in Toronto, focus on a broad range of services, including prevention, early intervention, outpatient services, day treatment, and residential treatment (Hincks-Dellcrest Centre, 2001). So there is hope that new and improved interventions that begin as soon as children show signs of reactive attachment disorders will eventually enable victims of prolonged social adversity to put their lingering deficiencies behind them.

MATERNAL EMPLOYMENT, CHILD CARE, AND EARLY EMOTIONAL DEVELOPMENT

In recent years, an important question has arisen about the ways in which young children in our society spend their time. Should they be cared for at home by a parent, or can they pursue their developmental agendas just as well in a child-care centre? Now that more than 65 percent of all mothers with children aged 0–6 work outside the home at least part time (Pence & Benner, 2000), more and more young children are receiving alternative forms of care. According to a 1994 Canadian study, 32 percent of children aged 0 to 11 were cared for on a regular basis by someone other than their parents. Of those children, approximately 21.4 percent were cared for outside the home by other relatives, 14.2 percent were cared for at home by a nonrelative, 34.2 percent received care outside the home in the home of a nonrelative, 15.7 percent were enrolled in regulated child-care centres, 7.2 percent were cared for in a regulated home child-care setting, 4.0 percent were enrolled in a regulated before- or after-school program, and 2.5 percent were cared for by a sibling or in self-care (numbers do not add up to 100.0 percent because of rounding) (Ross, Scott, & Kelly, 1996; Statistics Canada, National Longitudinal Survey of Children and Youth, 1996).

Do infants who attend child-care homes or centres suffer in any way compared with those who stay at home with a parent? Research to date suggests that they usually do not (Clarke-Stewart, 1993; NICHD Early Child Research Network, 1997). In fact, we learned in Chapter 9 that high-quality child care promotes both the social responsiveness and the intellectual development of children from disadvantaged backgrounds, who are otherwise at risk of experiencing developmental delays (Burchinal et al., 1996; Campbell & Ramey, 1995; Ramey & Ramey, 1998). Furthermore, a large, well-controlled longitudinal study of 1153 children in alternative care revealed that neither the age at which children enter child-care centres nor the amount of child care they receive was related to the security of their attachments to their mothers or their emotional well-being (NICHD Early Child Care Research Network, 1997).

However, this broad generalization does not tell the full story. Let's briefly consider two factors that are likely to influence how an infant or toddler adjusts to maternal employment and child care.

Quality of Alternative Care

Table 11.5 lists what experts believe to be the most important characteristics of high-quality child care for infants and toddlers (Howe & Jacobs, 1995; Howes, Phillips, & Whitebrook, 1992; Zigler & Gilman, 1993). A recent study of 234 daycare centres across

TABLE 11.5	Characteristics of High-Quality Infant and Toddler Daycare
Physical setting	The indoor environment is clean, well-lit, and well-ventilated; outdoor play areas are fenced, spacious, and free of hazards and include age-appropriate equipment (slides, swings, sandbox, etc.).
Child:caregiver ratio	The ratio is no more than 3 infants or 4–6 toddlers per adult caregiver.
Caregiver characteristics/ qualifications	Caregivers have specialized, extensive training (2 years or more) in early childhood education at the postsecondary level, and are warm, emotionally expressive, and responsive to children's bids for attention. Teacher job satisfaction is high. Staff turnover rates are low so that infants and toddlers can form relationships (even attachment relationships) with their caregivers.
Toys/activities	Toys and activities are age-appropriate; infants and toddlers are always supervised, even during free play indoors.
Family links	Parents are always welcome, and caregivers confer freely with them about their child's progress.
Licensing	The child-care setting is licensed by the province.

Canada revealed that sensitive and engaged caregiver behaviour as well as physically safe environments are the norm in most centres (Goelman et al., 2000). A cause for concern, however, is that fewer than half of the preschool rooms (44.3 percent) and only 28.7 percent of the infant/toddler rooms also provided educationally stimulating activities or materials that would enhance children's social, language, and thinking skills. Similar results were found in regulated home child-care settings (Doherty et al., 2000).

In addition, access to child-care services varies widely across Canada's provinces and territories, with only a small minority of parents having access to the services that they require (Friendly, 2000). In general, however, government policies and monitoring of alternative care is much better in Canada than in the United States (Symons & Carr, 1995). The majority of provinces and territories have regulations concerning group sizes of children, teacher:child ratios, and training of teachers, although the regulations are often fragmented and uncoordinated (Jacobs, 2000).

How important is high-quality care? Apparently, there is far less risk that children will display insecure attachments (or any other adverse outcome) when they receive excellent child care—*even when that care begins very early.* Jerome Kagan and his associates (1978), for example, found that the vast majority of infants who entered a high-quality, American university–sponsored child-care program at age 3½ to 5½ months not only developed secure attachments to their mothers but were just as socially, emotionally, and intellectually mature over the first two years of life as children from similar backgrounds who had been cared for at home. Studies conducted in Sweden (where child care is government subsidized, closely monitored, and typically of high quality) report similar positive outcomes (Broberg et al., 1997), and it seems that the earlier that Swedish infants enter high-quality child care, the better their cognitive, social, and emotional development six to eight years later in elementary and junior high school (Andersson, 1989, 1992). Finally, studies of U.S. children in daycare centres of varying quality reveal that early entry into higher-quality daycare is a reasonably good predictor of favourable social, emotional, and intellectual outcomes throughout the first three years of life (Burchinal et al., 2000; Howes, 1997; NICHD Early Child Care Research Network, 2000), with low-quality care being associated with poor outcomes.

Unfortunately, children who receive the poorest and most unstable child care are often those whose parents are living complex, stressful lives of their own that may constrain their sensitivity as parents and their involvement in children's learning activities (Fuller, Holloway, & Liang, 1996; Howes, 1990). So a child's poor progress in daycare may often stem as much from a disordered home life, in which parents are not all that enthused about parenting, as from the less-than-optimal alternative care that the child receives (NICHD Early Child Care Research Network, 1997). Let's explore this idea further.

Parenting and Parents' Attitudes about Work

According to Lois Hoffman (1989), a mother's attitudes about working and child care may be as important to her child's social and emotional well-being as her actual employment status. Mothers tend to be much happier and more sensitive as caregivers when their employment status matches their attitudes about working (Crockenberg & Litman, 1991; Hock & DeMeis, 1990; NICHD Early Child Care Research Network, 1998b). So, if a woman wants to work, it may make little sense to pressure her into staying home to care for her child when she might be depressed, hostile, or otherwise unresponsive in that role.

Even when children receive less-than-optimal alternative care, their outcomes depend greatly on the parenting they receive (NICHD Early Child Care Research Network, 1997, 1998b). Outcomes are likely to be better if a working mother has positive attitudes *both* about working and about being a mother (Belsky & Rovine, 1988; Crockenberg & Litman, 1991). And it also helps immensely if her spouse approves of her working and supports her in her parenting role (Cabrera et al., 2000). Ultimately, parents' attitudes about parenting and the quality of care they provide at home have far more to do with an infant's development than the kind of alternative care he or she receives (Broberg et al., 1997; NICHD Early Child Care Research Network, 1997, 1998a).

What conclusions can we draw, then, about child care and children's emotional development? Considered together, the evidence suggests that (1) children who receive sensitive, responsive care at home are at little risk of poor emotional outcomes, and that (2) excellent child care helps buffer children against emotional insecurity (or other adverse outcomes) should the parenting they receive be far less than optimal. One way excellent child care may serve this protective function is by making children more socially and intellectually responsive, which may have the effect of making parents more sensitive and responsive to them (see Burchinal et al., 2000; NICHD Early Child Care Research Network, 1999). In the final analysis, it seems that child care is most likely to be associated with poor emotional (and other negative) outcomes should infants and toddlers face the *dual risk* of insensitive parenting and poor alternative care (NICHD Early Child Care Research Network, 1997).

What, then, might be done to help working parents to establish and maintain more secure ties with their infants and toddlers and to otherwise optimize their development? A national policy governing parental leave for child care is certainly one step in the right direction. Parental-leave policies in Canada have recently been extended to a maximum of 52 weeks and compare favourably with those of many other industrialized societies (see Table 11.6).

An early report on the impact of maternal leave reveals that longer leaves are more beneficial than shorter ones. Specifically, American mothers who took four-month leaves after the birth of their babies displayed less negative affect when interacting with their babies than did mothers whose leaves lasted only two months (Clark et al., 1997). The benefits of longer leaves were most noticeable among mothers who reported depressive symptoms or who had babies with difficult temperaments: These mothers were much more *positively* involved with their infants and more sensitive in their face-to-face interactions if their leave had lasted a full four months. Longer leaves may allow depressed mothers to become more confident as caregivers, while allowing more time for those with difficult infants to establish a "good fit" between their parenting and their babies' temperamental attributes.

A workable national policy governing daycare may be equally (or more) important. Recent debate in Canada has centred on whether quality child care should be universally accessible. At present, middle-class families are the ones caught most directly in a child-care squeeze. Upper-income families have the resources to purchase excellent child care, and the subsidized alternative care that many lower-income children receive is typically of higher quality than what middle-class parents can afford to purchase (Scarr, 1998).

? WHAT DO YOU THINK?

Assume that you live in a country in which parents can share leave benefits at half-pay for nine months after a baby is born. Should you and your spouse share these benefits, or should the mother take them all? How do you justify your point of view?

TABLE 11.6	Sample Parental-Leave Policies in Modern Industrialized Nations
Canada	Working mothers receive 17 to 18 weeks of maternity leave, and either parent can receive an additional 35 weeks for a total of up to 52 weeks. Of the 52 weeks, parents are covered by Employment Insurance benefits at 55% pay for up to 50 weeks.
Finland	Mothers receive 18 weeks of leave at 70% pay. Additional parental leave of 26 weeks at 70% pay is available to either parent.
Germany	Mothers receive 14 weeks at 100% pay and up to 2½ years of additional leave at partial pay.
Sweden	Mothers receive 14 weeks of leave at 80% pay; the mother or father may take an additional 38 weeks of parental leave at 60% pay, and may extend leave benefits for yet another 6 months, receiving a similar fraction of pay.
United Kingdom	Mothers receive 6 weeks of 90% pay and 12 additional weeks in which they receive a flat-rate monetary stipend. Thirteen weeks of additional unpaid leave can be taken by either parent.
United States	Either parent may take 12 weeks of unpaid leave in firms of 50 or more employees.

SOURCE: Kamerman, 2000.

Meanwhile, parents from all social backgrounds must often struggle to find and keep competent sitters or other high-quality child-care placements. Increasingly, employers are realizing that it is in their best interest to help workers obtain quality child care, and a few have even established daycare centres at the work site (Hymes, 1990). But until more options are available, working parents will continue to face the challenges of finding good alternative care at a cost they can afford.

SUMMARY

An Overview of Emotional Development

◆ Human infants are clearly emotional beings. At birth, babies reliably display interest, distress, disgust, and contentment (as indicated by their facial expressions), with the remaining **primary emotions** (that is, anger, sadness, surprise, and fear) normally appearing by the middle of the first year. Such **secondary emotions** as embarrassment, pride, guilt, and shame emerge in the second (or third) year, after children reach such cognitive milestones as self-recognition and have acquired standards for evaluating their conduct.

◆ The socialization of emotions and **emotional self-regulation** begin very early, as parents model positive emotions for their infants, attend carefully to and try to prolong their infants' pleasant feelings, and become less responsive to infants' negative emotional displays. By the end of the first year, infants develop simple strategies for regulating aversive arousal; soon thereafter, they make active attempts to suppress their sadness or anger. However, the ability to regulate and control emotions develops very slowly, and it may be well into the elementary-school years before children become proficient at complying with culturally defined **emotional display rules**.

◆ The infant's ability to recognize and interpret others' emotions improves dramatically over the first year. By 8 to 10 months of age, infants are capable of **social referencing**, and their ability to identify and interpret others' emotions continues to improve throughout childhood, aided, in part, by cognitive development and by family conversations centring on the causes of one's own and others' emotions.

◆ Emotions play at least two important roles in an infant's life. The child's emotional displays promote social contact with caregivers and help them to adjust their behaviours to her needs and goals. The infant's ability to recognize and interpret others' emotions serves an important *knowledge* function by helping the child to infer how she should feel, think, or behave in uncertain situations.

Temperament and Development

◆ Many components of **temperament,** a person's tendency to respond in predictable ways to environmental events, are genetically influenced. Environment also contributes heavily to temperament, with shared environmental influences having the larger impact on positively toned temperamental attributes and nonshared environmental influences having the larger impact on negatively toned aspects of temperament.

♦ Such components of temperament as activity level, irritability, sociability, and **behavioural inhibition** are moderately stable over time and forecast later variations in adult personality. Stability is greatest for individuals at the extremes of a temperamental dimension.

♦ Temperamental attributes often cluster in predictable patterns such as the **easy**, **difficult**, and **slow-to-warm-up** profiles. Although children with difficult and slow-to-warm-up temperaments are at greater risk of experiencing adjustment problems, whether they actually develop these problems depends on the **goodness of fit** between parenting and their own temperamental attributes.

What Are Emotional Attachments?

♦ Infants form affectional ties to their close companions during the first year of life. These **attachments** are reciprocal relationships, because an infant's **attachment objects** (parents and other intimate companions) will normally become attached to him. Parents' initial *bonding* with their infant builds in strength as they gear their behaviour to his social signals and establish **synchronized routines**. These exquisite interactions are pleasing for both parents and infants and are thought to contribute to strong reciprocal attachments.

How Do Infants Become Attached?

♦ Infants pass through an **asocial phase** and a **phase of indiscriminate attachment** before forming their first true attachments at 7 to 9 months of age during the **phase of specific attachment**. Attached infants become more curious, using their attachment object as a **secure base** for exploration. They eventually enter the **phase of multiple attachments**, forming affectional ties to more than one person.

♦ Early *psychoanalytic* and *learning* theories were largely discredited by the finding that feeding plays much less of a role in human attachments than these models expected. The *cognitive-developmental* notion that attachments depend, in part, on cognitive development has received some support. *Ethological* theory, which specifies that humans have **preadapted characteristics** that predispose them to form attachments, has become especially influential in recent years.

♦ At about the time infants are becoming attached to a close companion, they often begin to display **stranger anxiety** and **separation anxiety**. These two fears, which stem from infants' wariness of strange situations and their inability to explain who strangers are and the whereabouts of absent companions, usually decline dramatically in the second year as toddlers mature intellectually and venture away from their secure bases to explore.

Individual Differences in Attachment Quality

♦ Ainsworth's **strange situation** is most commonly used to assess the quality of attachments that 1- to 2-year-olds have formed, although the **Attachment Q-set** is a versatile alternative that is becoming quite popular. Four attachment classifications have been identified: **secure**, **resistant**, **avoidant**, and **disorganized/disoriented**.

♦ Although the distributions of various attachment classifications varies across cultures and often reflects cultural differences in child-rearing, more infants around the world establish secure attachments than any other pattern.

Factors that Influence Attachment Security

♦ Sensitive, responsive caregiving is associated with the development of secure attachments, whereas inconsistent, neglectful, overintrusive, and abusive caregiving predicts insecure attachments. Thus, there is ample support for the **caregiving hypothesis**.

♦ Infant characteristics and temperamental attributes may also influence attachment quality by affecting the character of caregiver–infant interactions. However, the **temperament hypothesis**—that attachments are merely reflections of infant temperament—is clearly an overstatement. Today, many favour an integrative viewpoint such as Kochanska's notion that caregiving determines whether attachments are secure or insecure and child temperament determines the kind of insecurity displayed by a child who receives insensitive caregiving.

Attachment and Later Development

♦ Secure attachment during infancy predicts intellectual curiosity and social competence later in childhood. One reason for this is that infants form **internal working models** of themselves and others that are often stable over time and influence their reactions to people and challenges for years to come. Parents' working models correspond closely with those of their children and contribute independently, along with caregiving sensitivity, to the attachments infants form. However, children's working models can change, so that a secure attachment history is no guarantee of positive adjustment later in life and insecure attachments are not a certain indication of poor life outcomes.

The Unattached Infant

♦ Infants who are socially deprived or abused are likely to be withdrawn and apathetic and may later display intellectual deficits, behaviour problems, and **reactive attachment disorders**. Their problems appear to stem more from their lack of responsive social stimulation (**social stimulation hypothesis**) than from failure to receive care from a singular mother figure (**maternal deprivation hypothesis**), and they often display a strong capacity for recovery, overcoming many of their initial handicaps. However, special interventions are needed for those whose early adversities were prolonged or severe.

Maternal Employment, Child Care, and Early Emotional Development

♦ It was once feared that regular separations from working parents and placement in daycare might prevent infants from establishing secure attachments. However, there is little evidence that either a mother's employment outside the home or alternative caregiving has such effects, provided that the care is of good quality and that parents are sensitive and responsive caregivers when they are at home.

KEY TERMS

primary (or basic) emotions, 393

secondary (or complex) emotions, 393

emotional display rules, 393

emotional self-regulation, 394

social referencing, 396

empathy, 397

temperament, 398

behavioural inhibition, 400

easy temperament, 400

difficult temperament, 400

slow-to-warm-up temperament, 400

"goodness-of-fit" model, 401

attachment, 402

synchronized routines, 403

asocial phase (of attachment), 405

phase of indiscriminate attachments, 405

phase of specific attachment, 405

secure base, 405

phase of multiple attachments, 405

secondary reinforcer, 406

imprinting, 408

preadapted characteristic, 408

kewpie doll effect, 408

stranger anxiety, 409

separation anxiety, 411

strange situation, 412

secure attachment, 413

resistant attachment, 413

avoidant attachment, 413

disorganized/disoriented attachment, 413

Attachment Q-set (AQS), 413

amae, 414

caregiving hypothesis, 415

temperament hypothesis, 418

internal working models, 422

reactive attachment disorder, 425

maternal deprivation hypothesis, 425

social stimulation hypothesis, 426

learned helplessness, 427

 You can find further information on the topics covered in this chapter by visiting:

www.developmentalpsych2e.nelson.com

 For additional reading, go to InfoTrac College Edition, your on-line research library, at:

infotrac.thomsonlearning.com

PhotoDisc, Inc.

Development of the Self and Social Cognition

Who am I?

I'm a person who says what I think . . . not [one] who's going to say one thing and do the other. I'm really lucky. I've never [drunk or] done drugs, but I'm always high. I love life. I've got a lot of different business interests . . . a construction company, oil wells, land . . . I'm trying everything. I travel a lot . . . it's difficult to be traveling and in school at the same time. [People] perceive me as being unusual . . . very mysterious, and I hope they see me as being a competitor, because I do all my talking on the field.

HERSCHEL WALKER, FORMER COLLEGE STUDENT, OLYMPIC BOBSLEDDER, AND PROFESSIONAL FOOTBALL STAR (AS QUOTED BY BLOUNT, 1986)

Development of the Self-Concept

Self-Esteem: The Evaluative Component of Self

Development of Achievement Motivation and Academic Self-Concept

Who Am I to Be? Forging an Identity

The Other Side of Social Cognition: Knowing about Others

Summary

self
combination of physical and psychological attributes that is unique to each individual

looking-glass self
idea that a person's self-concept is largely determined by the ways that other people respond to him or her

How would you answer the "Who am I?" question above? If you are like most adults, you would probably respond by mentioning some of your noteworthy personal characteristics (honesty, friendliness), some roles you play in life (student, volunteer), your religious or moral views, and perhaps your political leanings. In doing so, you would be describing that elusive concept that psychologists call the **self**.

Although no one else knows you as well as you do, it is a safe bet that much of what you know about yourself stems from your contacts and experiences with other people. When a university undergraduate says that he is a friendly, outgoing person who is active in his student association, the Young Liberals of Canada, and Big Brothers, he is telling us that his past experiences with others and the groups to which he belongs are important determinants of his personal identity. Many years ago, sociologists Charles Cooley (1902) and George Herbert Mead (1934) proposed that the self-concept evolves from social interactions and undergoes many changes over the course of a lifetime. Cooley used the term **looking-glass self** to emphasize that a person's understanding of self is a reflection of how other people react to her: The self-concept is the image cast by a social mirror.

Cooley and Mead believed that the self and social development are completely intertwined, that they emerge together and that neither can progress far without the other. Presumably, newborns experience people and events as simple "streams of impressions" and have absolutely no concept of "self" until they realize that they exist independent of the objects and individuals that they encounter regularly. Once infants make this important distinction between self and nonself, they establish interactive routines with close companions (that is, develop socially) and learn that their behaviour elicits predictable reactions from others. In other words, they are acquiring information about the "social self" based on the ways that people respond to them. Mead (1934) concluded that

> the self has a character that is different from that of the physiological organism proper. The self is something which ... is not initially there at birth but arises in the process of social development. That is, it develops in a given individual as a result of his relations to that process as a whole and to other individuals within the process.

Do babies really have no sense of self at birth? We explore this issue in the first section of the chapter as we trace the growth of the self-concept from infancy through adolescence. We will then consider how children and adolescents evaluate the self and construct a sense of self-esteem. Our focus next shifts to a very important contributor to self-esteem as we explore how children develop an interest (or disinterest) in achievement and form positive or negative academic self-concepts. We will then discuss a major developmental hurdle faced by adolescents: the need to establish a firm, future-oriented self-portrait, or *identity*, with which to approach the responsibilities of young adulthood. Finally, we will consider what developing children know about other people and interpersonal relationships and will see that this aspect of **social cognition**, which parallels the development of the self-concept, nicely illustrates Cooley's and Mead's point that personal (self) and social aspects of development are intertwined in complex ways.

Of course, we all develop conceptions of ourselves (and others) as males or females and as moral (or immoral) beings. Research on these topics is now so extensive that they merit chapters of their own (see Chapters 13 and 14). For now, let's return to the starting point and see how children come to know this entity we call the *self*.

DEVELOPMENT OF THE SELF-CONCEPT

When do infants first distinguish themselves from other people, objects, and environmental events? At what point do they sense their uniqueness and form self-images? What kinds of information do young children use to define the self? How do their self-images and feelings of self-worth change over time? These are some of the issues we will explore as we trace the development of the **self-concept** from infancy through adolescence.

The Emerging Self: Differentiation and Self-Recognition

Like Mead, many developmentalists believe that infants are born without a sense of self. Psychoanalyst Margaret Mahler (Mahler, Pine, & Bergman, 1975) likens the newborn to a "chick in an egg" who has no reason to differentiate the self from the surrounding environment. After all, every need that the child has is soon satisfied by his or her ever-present companions, who are simply "there" and have no identities of their own.

By contrast, other developmentalists (see Brown, 1998; Meltzoff, 1990a) claim that even newborns may have the capacity to distinguish themselves from their surrounding environment. For example, newborns become distressed at hearing a recording of another baby's cries but not on hearing a recording of their own cries, thus implying that a differentiation of self and others is possible at birth (Dondi, Simion, & Caltran, 1999). Furthermore, newborns anticipate the arrival of their own hands at their mouths, and as

social cognition
the thinking people display about the thoughts, feelings, motives, and behaviours of themselves and other people

self-concept
one's perceptions of one's unique attributes or traits

we noted in Chapter 6, newborns seem capable of using **proprioceptive feedback** from their own facial expressions to mimic at least some of the facial expressions their caregivers display. These kinds of observations suggested to Andrew Meltzoff (1990a) that "the young infant possesses an embryonic body scheme. [Although] this body scheme develops [over time], it is present as a psychological primitive right from the earliest phases of infancy" (p. 160).

Of course, these observations are subject to alternative interpretations (many believe them to be mere reflexes), and it is by no means an easy task to clearly establish when infants first become self-aware. Yet almost everyone agrees that the first glimmerings of this capacity can be seen in the first two or three months (Samuels, 1986; Stern, 1995). Recall Piaget's (and others') descriptions of cognitive development early in infancy. During the first two months, babies exercise their reflexive schemes and repeat pleasurable acts centred in their own bodies (for example, sucking their thumbs and waving their arms). In other words, they are becoming acquainted with their own physical capabilities. We also learned in Chapter 6 that infants only 2 to 3 months old delight at producing interesting sights and sounds by kicking their legs or pulling their arms when they are attached by strings to mobiles or to audiovisual machinery (Lewis, Alessandri, & Sullivan, 1990; Rovee-Collier, 1995). Even an 8-week-old infant can recall how to produce these interesting events for two or three days, and if the strings are disconnected so she can no longer exert any control, she may pull or kick all the harder and become distressed (Lewis et al., 1990; Sullivan, Lewis, & Alessandri, 1992). Thus it seems that 2-month-old infants may have some limited sense of **personal agency**, or understanding that *they* are responsible for at least some of the events that so fascinate them.

In sum, it is still an open question whether *newborns* can truly differentiate themselves from the surrounding environment. But even if they can't, it is likely that they learn the limits of their own bodies during the first month or two, and differentiate this physical self from the external objects that they can control shortly thereafter (Samuels, 1986). So if a 2- to 6-month-old could talk, he might answer the "Who am I?" question by saying "I am a looker, a chewer, a reacher, and a grabber who acts on objects and makes things happen."

?

WHAT DO YOU THINK?

Newborn babies distinguish their own cries from those of other babies (review Box 2.4 on page 61) and visually orient themselves to moving objects (Brown, 1998). Do you think these achievements imply that newborns differentiate the self from the environment? Why or why not?

Self-Recognition

Once infants know that they *are* (that they exist independent of other entities), they are in a position to find out *who* or *what* they are (Harter, 1983). When, for example, do infants recognize their own physical features and become able to tell themselves apart from other infants?

One way to answer these questions is to expose infants to a visual representation of the self (i.e., a videotape or mirror reflection) and see how they respond to these images. Research of this type reveals that infants only 5 months old seem to treat their own faces as familiar social stimuli. For example, Marie Legerstee and her associates (1998) found that 5-month-olds who viewed moving images of themselves and an age-mate (on videotape) could clearly discriminate their own image from that of the peer, as indicated by their preference to gaze at the peer's face (which was novel and interesting to them) rather than at their own (which was presumably familiar and, hence, less interesting). How might infants this young come to discriminate their own faces from those of other people? One explanation is that infants (in Western cultures, at least) often find themselves in front of mirrors, usually beside a caregiver who is playing a social game with them (Fogel, 1995; Stern, 1995). Such experiences may allow ample opportunity for infants to match their own movement-produced proprioceptive information with the actions of one of the figures in the mirror, thereby discriminating this self from an older social partner, whose movements do not correspond so closely with their own (Legerstee et al., 1998).

proprioceptive feedback
sensory information from the muscles, tendons, and joints that help one to locate the position of one's body (or body parts) in space

personal agency
recognition that one can be the cause of an event

Yet the remarkable feats that these young infants display may simply represent their powers of visual discrimination rather than any conscious awareness that the image in a mirror or on videotape is "me." How might we determine whether infants have truly constructed a firm *self*-image that is stable over time?

Michael Lewis and Jeanne Brooks-Gunn (1979) have studied the development of **self-recognition** by asking mothers to surreptitiously apply a spot of rouge to their infants' noses (under the pretext of wiping the infants' faces) and then place the infants in front of a mirror. If infants have a scheme for their own faces and recognize their mirror images as themselves, they should soon notice the new red spot and reach for or wipe their *own* noses. When infants 9 to 24 months old were given this *rouge* test, the younger ones showed no self-recognition. They seemed to treat the image in the mirror as if it were some other child. Signs of self-recognition were observed among a few of the 15- to 17-month-olds, but only among the 18- to 24-month-olds did a majority of infants touch their own noses, apparently realizing that they had a strange mark on their faces. They knew exactly who that child in the mirror was (see also Asendorpf, Warkentin, & Baudonniere, 1996)!

Interestingly, infants from nomadic tribes, who have no experience with mirrors, begin to display self-recognition on the rouge test at the same age as city-reared infants (Priel & deSchonen, 1986). And many 18- to 24-month-olds can even recognize themselves in current photographs and often use a personal pronoun ("me") or their own name to label their photographic image (Lewis & Brooks-Gunn, 1979). Yet children this young are not fully aware that the self is an entity that is stable over time. Not until age 3½ will they retrieve a brightly coloured sticker placed surreptitiously on their heads if their first glimpse of it comes after a two- to three-minute delay on videotape or in a photograph (Povinelli, Landau, & Perilloux, 1996). Apparently, 2- to 3-year-olds who display some self-recognition do not retrieve the sticker because their concept of self is limited to that of a **present self**, and they don't yet appreciate that events that occurred in the past have implications for them now. By contrast, 4- and 5-year-olds quickly retrieve the sticker after a *brief delay*, but will not retrieve it if the videotape depicts events that happened a week earlier. These older preschoolers have developed the concept of **extended self**: They recognize that the self is stable over time and that (1) events that happened very recently have implications for the present, but (2) the sticker they see a week later on film is not still on their heads because this event happened to them a long time ago (Povinelli et al., 1999; Povinelli & Simon, 1998).

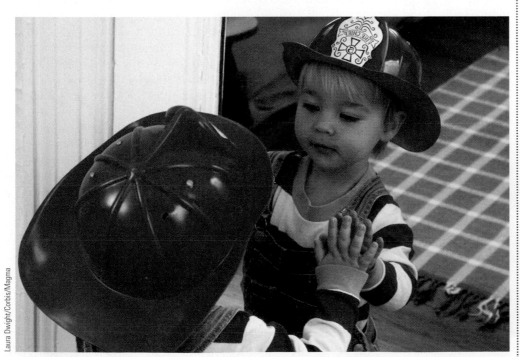

Laura Dwight/Corbis/Magma

Recognizing one's mirror image as "me" is a crucial milestone in the development of self.

self-recognition
ability to recognize oneself in a mirror or photograph

present self
early self-representation in which 2- and 3-year-olds recognize current representations of self but are unaware that past self-representations or self-relevant events have implications for the present

extended self
more mature self-representation, emerging between ages 3½ and 5 years, in which children are able to integrate past, current, and unknown future self-representations into a notion of a self that endures over time

Figure 12.1 *Average scores on a test of self-knowledge as a function of age and attachment quality.* ADAPTED FROM PIPP, EASTERBROOKS, & HARMON, 1992.

categorical self
person's classification of the self along socially significant dimensions such as age and sex

Contributors to Self-Recognition

Why do 18- to 24-month-olds reliably recognize themselves in a mirror? Recall that this is precisely the age when toddlers are said to internalize their sensorimotor schemes to form mental images, at least one of which may be an image of their own facial features. Even children with Down syndrome can recognize themselves in a mirror if they have attained a mental age of 18 to 20 months (Hill & Tomlin, 1981). And once 3½- to 4-year-olds begin to encode noteworthy experiences as autobiographical memories, as we discussed in Chapter 8, they now clearly realize that the self is a stable entity and that earlier events that they remember did indeed happen to *them* (Nelson, 1993; Povinelli et al., 1996).

Although a certain level of cognitive development may be necessary for self-recognition, social experiences are probably of equal importance. Gordon Gallup (1979) found that adolescent chimpanzees easily recognized themselves in a mirror (as shown by the rouge test) unless they had been reared in complete social isolation. In contrast to normal chimps, social isolates react to their mirror images as if they were looking at another animal! So the term *looking-glass self* may apply to chimpanzees as well as to humans: Reflections in a "social mirror" enable normal chimps to develop some self-awareness, whereas a chimpanzee that is denied these experiences fails to acquire a clear self-image.

One social experience that contributes to self-awareness in humans is a secure attachment to a primary caregiver. Sandra Pipp and her associates (1992) administered a complex test of self-knowledge to 2- and 3-year-olds—a test that assessed the child's awareness of his name and gender as well as tasks to assess self-recognition. As we see in Figure 12.1, securely attached 2-year-olds outperformed their insecurely attached age-mates on the test, and differences in self-knowledge between secure and insecure 3-year-olds were even greater.

Social and Emotional Consequences of Self-Recognition

The growth of self-recognition and an emerging awareness of oneself as a participant in *social* interactions pave the way for many new social and emotional competencies (Pipp-Siegel & Foltz, 1997). For example, we saw in Chapter 11 that the ability to experience *self-conscious* emotions such as embarrassment depends on self-recognition. Furthermore, toddlers who have reached this self-referential milestone soon become more outgoing and socially skilled. They now take great pleasure in imitating a playmate's activities (Asendorpf & Baudonniere, 1993; Asendorpf et al., 1996) and occasionally even *cooperate* (as illustrated by one child's operating a handle so that another can retrieve toys from a container) to achieve shared goals (Brownell & Carriger, 1990).

Once toddlers display self-recognition, they also become more sensitive to the ways in which people differ and begin to categorize themselves on these dimensions—a classification called the **categorical self** (Stipek, Gralinski, & Kopp, 1990). Age, sex, and evaluative dimensions are the first social categories that toddlers incorporate into their self-concepts, as illustrated by such statements as "I *big girl*, not a *baby*" or "Jennie *good girl*."

Interestingly, young children are even becoming aware of ethnic categories, although it may take a while before they can classify themselves correctly. For example, in an American study involving Native-American 3- to 5-year-olds, the children could

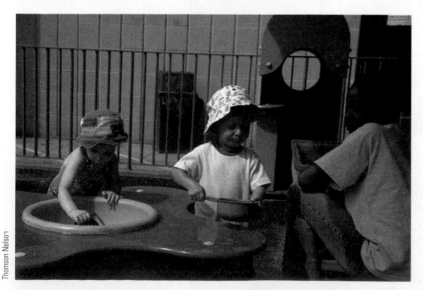

Toddlers who display self-recognition become much more socially skilled and can now cooperate to achieve shared goals.

easily discriminate Native Americans from Whites in photographs but were less often accurate in specifying which category they most resembled (Spencer & Markstrom-Adams, 1990). A similar "misidentification" phenomenon has been observed among First Nations kindergarten and Grade 1 children in Canada (Corenblum & Annis, 1987) and African Americans in the United States (Cross, 1985; Spencer, 1988). All of these children displayed a strong pro-White bias. The African-American preschoolers also associated fewer positive attributes with the colour black or with African-American people. However, these "misidentifications" and pro-White biases do not necessarily mean that minority youngsters are unaware of their own ethnicity. Instead, they may simply reflect the same early awareness of negative stereotypes about minorities that White children display (Bigler & Liben, 1993) and a desire to align themselves with what they believe to be the most socially desirable group (Spencer & Markstrom-Adams, 1990).

Who Am I? Responses of Preschool Children

Until very recently, developmentalists believed that the self-concepts of preschool children were concrete, based in physicality, and nearly devoid of any *psychological* self-awareness. Why? Because when 3- to 5-year-olds are asked to describe themselves, they talk mostly about their physical attributes ("I have blue eyes"), their possessions ("I have a new bike"), or about *actions* of which they feel especially proud, such as hitting a baseball or walking to nursery school on their own. By contrast, psychological descriptors such as "I'm happy," "I'm good at sports," or "I like people" are rarely used by children this young (Damon & Hart, 1988; Keller, Ford, & Meachum, 1978).

However, not everyone agrees that preschoolers' self-concepts are limited to observable characteristics. Rebecca Eder (1989, 1990) finds that when 3½- to 5-year-olds are asked to respond to contrasting forced-choice statements that require fewer verbal skills than open-ended "Who am I?" questions, they can quickly characterize themselves on *psychological* dimensions such as sociability (by choosing, for example, between such statements as "I like to play by myself" versus "I like to play with my friends"). Furthermore, they characterize themselves differently on different dimensions, and these self-characterizations are stable over time (Eder, 1990). Although preschool children may not be consciously aware of what it means to be "sociable" or "athletic" or to be an "achiever," Eder's research implies that they have rudimentary psychological conceptions of self long before they can express this knowledge in traitlike terminology (see also Flavell, Miller, & Miller, 1993).

Children's Theory of Mind and Emergence of the Private Self

When adults think about the self, they know that it consists of a **public self** (or **me**) that others can see and a **private self** (or **I**) that has an inner, reflective (thinking) character not available to others. Are young children aware of both the public and private aspects of self? Such a distinction implies that they have a **theory of mind**, an understanding of how the human mind works and a knowledge that humans are cognitive beings whose mental states are not always shared with or accessible to others.

Early Understandings of Mental States

The first steps toward acquiring a theory of mind are the realizations that oneself and other humans are animate (rather than inanimate) objects whose behaviours reflect goals and intentions. Remarkably, 2-month-old infants are making some progress—they are already more likely to repeat simple gestures displayed by a human rather than an inanimate object, thereby suggesting that they may already identify with human models (Legerstee, 1991). Darwin Muir and Sylvia Hains of Queen's University (1999) suggest

public self (or me)
those aspects of self that others can see or infer

private self (or I)
those inner, or subjective, aspects of self that are known only to the individual and are not available for public scrutiny

theory of mind
understanding that people are cognitive beings with mental states (beliefs, motives, feelings, and intentions) that are not always accessible to others and that often guide their behaviour

12.1

Chris Moore

Chris Moore works in the Department of Psychology at Dalhousie University. His main research interests are in the early development of social understanding. He has a secondary interest in evolutionary psychology.

During the years from about 1 to 5, children make great strides in understanding their social worlds and in understanding themselves. By the end of the first year, infants can use others' gaze direction and emotional expressions to find out about objects in the world. Chris Moore and his associates at Dalhousie University have been examining some of the social interaction phenomena of the second half of infancy, concentrating in particular on joint attention. Their main interest is in how infants start to follow the gaze of others in order to find out about objects in the environment. Among other things, the researchers have been looking at the cues that infants use to follow gaze (e.g., head movements versus eye movements) and the

mechanisms that allow infants to start to follow gaze (e.g., learning versus attention cuing). For example, infants from about 3 months of age will follow head turns when there are peripheral targets in the visual field. Until about 9 months of age, they will not follow gaze when no targets are visible, but from this age they will turn in response to head turns by the interactive partner, indicating that they know there is something potentially interesting to see. From 9 months old through the first half of the second year, gaze following to absent targets appears limited to head turn cues. Around 18 months of age, infants start to be able to use changes in eye direction of the interactive partner to achieve the same end. Chris Moore believes that the earliest gaze following depends more on reflexive responses and that it isn't until infants follow gaze to absent targets that we can suggest that they "understand" the meaning of the other's head-turning behaviour. In other words, when no target is visible, infants appear to understand that the head turn indicates the potential for a target in a particular location. These studies highlight the developing ability of infants to use other people to find out about the world.

---

that infants as young as 3 months of age are quite sophisticated in their knowledge of adult behaviour. Young infants appear to be quite sensitive to eye contact and adult eye direction, as well as contingency or responsiveness on the part of the adult (see also Bigelow, 1999, and Box 12.1 for current work by Chris Moore on infants' ability to follow gaze). By 6 months, infants perceive human actions as purposeful and know that humans behave differently toward people than they do toward inanimate objects. For example, if 6-month-olds see an actor *talking* to an unseen stimulus behind a screen, they expect a person to appear when the screen is removed and are surprised if an inanimate object appears. By contrast, if the actor *manipulated* the unseen stimulus, 6-month-olds expect to see an object and are surprised if a person appears (Legerstee, Barna, & DiAdamo, 2000). By 9 months, infants will often point or otherwise direct a companion's attention to objects or events, thus implying that they perceive a social partner as capable of understanding or sharing their own intentions (Tomasello, 1999). And by 18 months of age toddlers know that *desires* direct actions and can often reason accurately about other people's desires. So having seen a woman express disgust at the thought of eating crackers, they know that she would prefer vegetables to the crackers that they personally favour when offered a choice between these snacks (Repacholi & Gopnik, 1997).

Between ages 2 and 3, children often talk about such mental states as perceptions, feelings, and desires, and they even display some understanding of connections between different mental states. They know, for example, that a child who wants a cookie will *feel good* (happy) if she receives it and *feel bad* (angry, sad) if she doesn't (Moses, Coon, & Wusinich, 2000; Wellman, Phillips, & Rodriquez, 2000). According to Daniela O'Neill of the University of Waterloo, 2- to 3-year-olds are also aware that they may know something that others don't (O'Neill, 1996). In addition, they know that people cannot actually observe their thoughts (Flavell et al., 1993). Yet, even though 3-year-olds are mindful of the human mind and of an emerging private self, they still have a very primitive understanding of such constructive or interpretive mental activities as beliefs and inferences. In fact, they might be labelled **desire theorists** because they think that a person's actions generally reflect his *desires* and are much less inclined to assume that what a person *believes* might influence his behaviour (Cassidy, 1998; Wellman & Woolley, 1990).

desire theory
early theory of mind in which a person's actions are thought to be a reflection of her or his desires rather than other mental states such as belief

Between the ages of 3 and 4, children develop a **belief-desire theory** of mind in which they recognize, as we adults do, that beliefs and desires are different mental states and that either or both can influence one's conduct (Wellman, 1990). So, a 4-year-old who has broken a vase while roughhousing may try to overcome his mother's *desire* to punish him by trying to make her *believe* that his breaking the vase was unintentional ("I didn't mean to, mama. It was an accident!").

Origins of a Belief-Desire Theory

Very young children may view desire as the most important determinant of behaviour because their own actions are so often triggered by desires and they may assume that other people's conduct reflects similar motives. In addition, 3-year-olds have a very curious view of beliefs: They assume that beliefs are accurate reflections of reality that everyone shares. They don't seem to appreciate, as older children do, that beliefs are merely *interpretations* of reality that may differ from person to person and may be *inaccurate*. Consider children's reactions to the following story—a **false-belief task** that assesses the understanding that people can hold incorrect beliefs and be influenced by them, wrong though they may be:

> Sam puts some chocolate in a blue cupboard and goes out to play. In his absence, his mother moves the chocolate to the green cupboard. When Sam returns, he wants his chocolate. Where does he look for it?

Three-year-olds say "in the green cupboard." They know where the chocolate is, and because beliefs represent reality, they assume that the boy will be driven by his *desire* for chocolate to look in the right place. By contrast, 4- to 5-year-olds display a *belief-desire theory of mind:* They now understand that beliefs are merely mental representations of reality that may be inaccurate and that someone else may not share; thus, they know that the boy will look for his chocolate in the blue cupboard where he *believes* it is (beliefs determine behaviour, even if they are false) rather than in the green cupboard where they know it is (Wellman & Woolley, 1990).

Once children understand that people act on the basis of false beliefs, they may use this knowledge to their own advantage by lying or attempting other deceptive ploys. In Chapter 7 we noted that 4-year-olds (but not 3-year-olds) who are playing hide-the-object games will *spontaneously* generate false clues, trying to mislead their opponent about the object's true location (Sodian et al., 1991). Notice that 4-year-olds make a clear distinction between public and private self, because they recognize that their deceptive *public* behaviour will lead their opponent to adopt a belief that differs from their own *private* knowledge.

It's not that younger children haven't the capacity to recognize a false belief or its implications. For example, 3-year-olds can tell from thought-bubble depictions or from knowledge that a story character is just pretending that the incorrect beliefs that story characters express really do contradict reality (Cassidy, 1998; Wellman, Hollander, & Schult, 1996). And if they have collaborated with an adult in formulating a deceptive strategy in a hide-the-object game, their performance improves dramatically on other false-belief tasks (Hala & Chandler, 1996). Nevertheless, between ages 3 and 4 is when children normally achieve a much richer understanding of mental life and clearly discriminate the private self-as-knower from the public self that they present to others. How important are those developments? David Bjorklund (2000) answers by claiming that if developing children never learned to read minds and failed to recognize that public appearances do not necessarily reflect private realities, they would be largely incapable of drawing meaningful *psychological* inferences about their own or others' behaviour, and the intricate social interactions and cooperative activities that we humans display would be virtually impossible.

How Does a Theory of Mind Originate?

How do children manage to construct a theory of mind so early in life? Philip Zelazo of the University of Toronto and his American colleagues (Frye et al., 1996) suggest that the age differences found with theory-of-mind tasks may be related to the development of

belief-desire theory
theory of mind that develops between ages 3 and 4; the child now realizes that both beliefs and desires may determine behaviour and that people act on their beliefs, even if they are inaccurate

false-belief task
method of assessing one's understanding that people can hold inaccurate beliefs that can influence their conduct, wrong as these beliefs may be

Is Theory of Mind Biologically Programmed?

Some theorists claim that the capacities underlying self-consciousness and complex theories of mind are products of human evolution and are the basis for our social intelligence and the development of cultures (Baron-Cohen, 1995; Mitchell, 1997). Presumably, our ancestors would have found it highly adaptive to understand beliefs, desires, and other mental states because this ability to read minds allows for the evolution of cooperative divisions of labour that help ensure survival and more accurate assessments of the motives of rival groups that might threaten survival.

Simon Baron-Cohen (1995) has proposed that humans possess brain modules that are specialized for mind reading in much the same way that a language acquisition device is specialized for language learning. One such module is the *shared-attention mechanism* (SAM), which is said to develop between 9 and 18 months of age and allows two or more individuals to understand that they are attending to the same thing. Another such mechanism is the *theory of mind module* (TOMM), which allegedly develops between 18 and 48 months and permits children to eventually discriminate such mental states as beliefs, desires, and intentions.

Indeed, there is some evidence that development of a belief-desire theory of mind may reflect processing skills that are *domain specific*—that is, apart from normal intelligence. For example, about 85 percent of both 4-year-olds with normal intelligence and 4-year-olds with Down syndrome pass false-belief problems. Yet shared attention and understanding of false beliefs are lacking in young children with autism, even though these children may perform quite well on other intellectual tasks. Autism is a severe psychological disorder; affected children seem to be in a world of their own, and they have difficulties with most forms of social interaction. Baron-Cohen (1995) claims that individuals with autism lack a TOMM and display severe deficits in reading minds, or *mindblindness*. Imagine how confusing and fright-

ening it would be to interact with other humans if you lacked the capacity to understand their desires or recognize that they may try to deceive you. Temple Grandin, a woman with autism who is a professor of animal sciences, describes having to compensate for her lack of mind-reading skills by actively creating a memory bank of how people behave and what emotions they are likely to express in particular situations (Sacks, 1993). Although she can grasp simple emotions such as happiness, she never could quite understand what *Romeo and Juliet* was all about.

Baron-Cohen's nativist theory is new and interesting, and it will undoubtedly prove to be highly controversial, much as Chomsky's nativist theory of language has been. What is clear at this point is that not everyone believes that the mind-reading problems that children with autism experience are attributable to their lack of a specialized TOMM. They might also stem from deficits that children with autism show in shared attention (Leekam, Lopez, & Moore, 2000), or from more general problems they display at tying together related pieces of information to reach appropriate conclusions (Jarrold et al., 2000).

It is also clear that not all aspects of self-consciousness or theory of mind are uniquely human. Chimpanzees, for example, show self-recognition on the rouge test, and apes can share attention by following the gaze of another ape to an object, learn from one another socially, communicate by calls and gestures, and collaborate to obtain resources. Yet Josep Call and Michael Tomasello (1999) found that orangutans and chimpanzees could not pass a nonverbal false-belief problem—a task that 4- and 5-year-olds passed at about the same time they passed other false-belief problems that mark them as acquiring a belief-desire theory of mind. So it is conceivable that humans have something like a TOMM that helps to explain the rich social-cognitive abilities we display, although much more research will be necessary to properly evaluate this claim.

causal reasoning skills. Other tasks that have similar information-processing requirements show similar age differences (see Chapter 8 for a summary of the information-processing perspective). According to Andrew Meltzoff (1995a), however, human infants may be just as biologically prepared and as motivated to acquire information about mental states as they are to share meaning through language. As Box 12.2 explains, some even believe that theory of mind is a product of evolution and that the human brain has specialized modules that allow children to construct an understanding of mental activities.

But even if humans are biologically predisposed to develop a theory of mind, many social experiences foster its development. Pretend play, for example, is an activity that prompts children to think about mental states. As toddlers and preschool children conspire to make one object represent another or to enact pretend roles such as cops and robbers, they become increasingly aware of the creative potential of the human mind—an awareness that beliefs are merely mental constructions that can influence behaviour (Hughes & Dunn, 1998; Taylor & Carlson, 1997). Young children also have ample opportunity to learn how the mind works from family conversations centring on the discussion of motives, intentions, and other mental states (Sabbagh & Callanan, 1998), and on the resolution of conflicts among siblings as well as reasoning about moral issues (Dunn,

1994). Indeed, researchers such as Jennifer Jenkins and Janet Astington (1996) at the University of Toronto have found that preschoolers with siblings, especially those with two or more, do better on false-belief tasks than only children do (see also Lewis et al., 1996; Perner, Ruffman, & Leekam, 1994; Ruffman et al., 1998). Having siblings may provide more opportunities for pretend play, as well as more interactions involving deception or trickery—experiences that may illustrate the links between beliefs and behaviours. Nina Howe from Concordia University and Harriet Petrakos and Christina Rinaldi from McGill University (1998) found that siblings who engaged in frequent pretend play were more likely than siblings who engaged in infrequent pretend play to use internal state language (e.g., emotional states such as happy, scared, good; physiological states such as hungry or thirsty), especially during high-level negotiations, which may facilitate their understanding of the mental and emotional states of others. However, preschoolers who perform especially well on false-belief tasks also interact with a larger number of adults, which implies that children are apprentices to a variety of tutors as they acquire a theory of mind (Lewis et al., 1996).

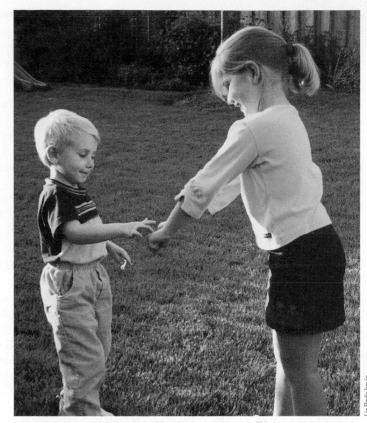

Sibling interactions involving deception or trickery contribute to the development of a theory of mind.

CULTURAL INFLUENCES. Do children in all cultures construct such a rich understanding of how the mind works during the preschool period? Apparently not. Even 8-year-olds among the Junin Quechua people of Peru have difficulty understanding that beliefs can be false (Vinden, 1996). Why? Probably because Junin Quechua speakers do not often talk about their own or others' mental states. Most of these people are subsistence farmers who work from dawn to dusk just to survive, and they do not often need to reflect on what they or others feel or believe in order to live productive lives. In fact, their language has few mental-state words, and references to mental states are largely absent from their folktales. So the appearance of a belief-desire theory of mind by age 4 is not universal and is likely to be delayed in cultures that lack the social supports for its emergence.

Conceptions of Self in Middle Childhood and Adolescence

Once children develop a theory of mind and clearly differentiate their public and private selves, their self-descriptions gradually evolve from listings of their physical, behavioural, and other "external" attributes to sketches of their enduring *inner* qualities—that is, their traits, values, beliefs, and ideologies (Damon & Hart, 1988; Livesley & Bromley, 1973). This developmental shift toward a more abstract or "psychological" portrayal of self can be seen in the following three responses to the "Who am I?" question (Montemayor & Eisen, 1977, pp. 317–8):

> *9-year-old:* My name is Bruce C. I have brown eyes. I have brown hair. I love! sports. I have seven people in my family. I have great! eye site. I have lots! of friends. I live at…. I have an uncle who is almost 7 feet tall. My teacher is Mrs. V. I play hockey! I'm almost the smartest boy in the class. I love! food…. I love! school.

11½-year-old: My name is A. I'm a human being ... a girl ... a truthful person. I'm not pretty. I do so-so in my studies. I'm a very good cellist. I'm a little tall for my age. I like several boys.... I'm old fashioned. I am a very good swimmer.... I try to be helpful.... Mostly I'm good, but I lose my temper. I'm not well liked by some girls and boys. I don't know if boys like me....

17-year-old: I am a human being ... a girl ... an individual ... I am a Pisces. I am a moody person ... an indecisive person ... an ambitious person. I am a big curious person.... I am lonely. I am an American (God help me). I am a Democrat. I am a liberal person. I am a radical. I am conservative. I am a pseudoliberal. I am an Atheist. I am not a classifiable person (i.e., I don't want to be).

In addition to using more psychological terms to describe the self than elementary-school children do, adolescents are also becoming much more aware that they are not the same person in all situations—a fact that may puzzle or even annoy them. Susan Harter and Ann Monsour (1992) asked 13-, 15-, and 17-year-olds to describe themselves when they are with (1) parents, (2) friends, (3) romantic partners, and (4) teachers and classmates. Then each participant was asked to sort through the four self-descriptions, picking out any inconsistencies and indicating how confusing or upsetting they were. As we see in Figure 12.2, 13-year-olds reported few inconsistencies and were not bothered much by those they did detect. By contrast, 15-year-olds listed many oppositional attributes and were often confused about them. One 15-year-old talked about her tendency to be happy with friends but depressed at home: "I really think of myself as happy—and want to be that way because I think that's my true self, but I get depressed with my family and it bugs me ..." (Harter & Monsour, 1992, p. 253). These 15-year-olds seemed to feel that there were several different selves inside them and were concerned about finding the "real me." Interestingly, adolescents who are most upset over inconsistencies in their self-portrayals are those who put on false fronts, acting out of character in an attempt to improve their image or win the approval of parents or peers. Unfortunately, those who most often display these **false-self behaviours** are the ones who feel least confident that they know who they truly are (Harter et al., 1996).

Inconsistent self-portrayals are somewhat less bothersome to older adolescents, who have often integrated them into a higher-order, more coherent view of themselves. A 17-year-old boy, for example, might conclude that it is perfectly understandable to be relaxed and confident in most situations but nervous on dates if one has not yet had much dating experience, or that *moodiness* can explain his being *cheerful* with friends on some occasions but *irritable* on others. Harter and Monsour believe that cognitive development—specifically the formal-operational ability to compare abstract traits like cheerful and irritable and to ultimately integrate them into more general concepts like moodiness—is behind this change in self-perception.

false-self behaviour
acting in ways that do not reflect one's true self or the "true me"

In sum, one's self-concept becomes more psychological and abstract, and more of a coherent, integrated self-portrait from childhood through adolescence. Truly, the adolescent becomes a sophisticated self-theorist who can reflect on and understand the workings of her personality.

One final point, but an important one: The overview of self-concept development presented here stems largely from research conducted in Western industrialized societies that value independence and view *personal* attributes as the hallmark of one's character. Yet, as we shall see in Box 12.3 this Eurocentric perspective on the meaning of self may not completely capture the experiences of people from many *collectivist* societies around the world.

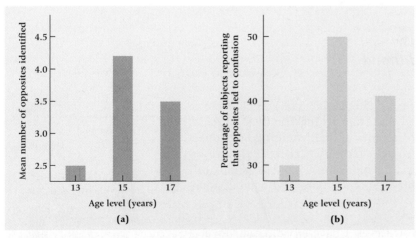

Figure 12.2 *Average number of oppositional attributes reported by (a) 13-, 15-, and 17-year-olds and (b) percentages of 13-, 15-, and 17-year-olds who said they were confused or "mixed up" by these inconsistencies in their self-portraits.* ADAPTED FROM HARTER & MONSOUR, 1992.

Indicate on the following scale the extent to which you agree or disagree with each of the following items:

1	2	3	4	5	6	7
Strongly Disagree						Strongly Agree

1. I have respect for authority figures with whom I interact.

2. I am comfortable with being singled out for praise or rewards.

3. My happiness depends on the happiness of those around me.

4. Speaking up in class is not a problem for me.

5. I should take my parents' advice into consideration when making my education/career plans.

6. My identity independent of others is very important to me.

What is considered desirable in the way of self-concept may vary dramatically across cultures. Western societies such as Canada, Australia, the United States, and the industrialized countries of Europe might be termed **individualistic societies**: They value competition and individual initiative and tend to emphasize ways in which people differ from each other. By contrast, many Asian cultures (e.g., India, Japan, and China) could be considered **collectivist (or communal) societies**: People are more cooperative and interdependent rather than competitive and independent, and their identities are closely tied to the groups to which they belong (e.g., families, religious organizations, and communities) rather than to their own accomplishments and personal characteristics (Triandis, 1995). In fact, people in East Asian cultures such as China, Korea, and Japan tend to value self-effacement and to view individuals who are preoccupied with personal concerns as somewhat abnormal and maladjusted (Marcus & Kitayama, 1994; Triandis, 1995).

Indeed, cross-cultural variations in the nature or content of people's self-concepts are quite clear in the responses of older Americans and Japanese adolescents to a Who am I? questionnaire. The questionnaire required them to first rate themselves on *personal/individualistic* attributes (e.g., "I am honest," "I am smart") and *social/relational* attributes (e.g., "I am a student," "I'm a good son"). Participants were then asked to place a check mark by the five responses they viewed as most self-descriptive and central to their self-concepts.

The results of the study were quite clear. As shown in the figure, the majority of American students' core self-descriptors (59 percent) were personal/individualistic attributes whereas these same attributes made up only

19 percent of the core self-descriptors of the Japanese students. By contrast, Japanese students were much more inclined than American students were to list social/relational attributes as especially noteworthy components of their self-concepts. In terms of developmental trends, older Japanese and Chinese adolescents are less inclined than preadolescents are to make distinctions among people on the basis of individualistic attributes, whereas American participants become more inclined to make such distinctions as they grow older (Crystal et al., 1998). Finally, research reveals that Asian-American adolescents, whose families often retain many collectivist values even after immigrating to the United States, tend to place more emphasis on their social identities and connections to other people than European-American adolescents do (see Brown, 1998).

Average percentages of personal/individualistic and social/relational attributes listed as core dimensions of the self-concept by American and Japanese students who responded to a "Who am I? questionnaire. ADAPTED FROM COUSINS, 1989.

Where do you stand on the individualistic-collectivist continuum? If you are like most people from individualistic societies, you probably indicated greater agreement with items 2, 4, and 6 (which tap independence and individualistic concerns), whereas people from collectivist societies usually find it easier to agree with items 1, 3, and 5 (which tap interdependence or communal concerns).

Clearly, the traditional values and benefits of one's culture can dramatically influence the kinds of self-concepts that emerge. And as we will see throughout the remainder of the text, the distinctions between individualistic and collectivist cultures and value systems are important ones that have implications for such aspects of self as the ways in which individuals look at and evaluate achievement behaviour, aggression, altruism, and moral development, to name just a few.

SELF-ESTEEM: THE EVALUATIVE COMPONENT OF SELF

As children develop, they not only understand more and more about themselves and construct more intricate self-portraits, but they also begin to *evaluate* the qualities that they perceive themselves as having. This evaluative aspect of self is called **self-esteem**. Children with high self-esteem are fundamentally satisfied with the type of person they are; they recognize their strong points, can acknowledge their weaknesses (often hoping to overcome them), and generally feel quite positive about the characteristics and competencies they display. By contrast, children with low self-esteem view the self in a less favourable light, often choosing to dwell on perceived inadequacies rather than on any strengths they may happen to display (Brown, 1998).

Origins and Development of Self-Esteem

Children's *evaluation* of themselves and their competencies is a most important aspect of self that can influence all aspects of their conduct and their psychological well-being. How does self-esteem originate, and when do children first establish a realistic sense of self-worth?

These questions are not easy to answer, but Bowlby's (1988) working-models theory that we discussed in Chapter 11 provides some meaningful clues. The theory predicts that securely attached children, who presumably construct a *positive* working model of

individualistic society
society that values personalism and individual accomplishments, which often take precedence over group goals. These societies tend to emphasize ways in which individuals differ from each other.

collectivist (or communal) society
Society that values cooperative interdependence, social harmony, and adherence to group norms. These societies generally hold that the group's well-being is more important than that of the individual.

self-esteem
one's evaluation of one's worth as a person based on an assessment of the qualities that make up the self-concept

In adolescence, the quality of one's friendships becomes one of the strongest determinants of self-esteem.

Ryan McVay/Photodisc

self, should soon begin to evaluate themselves more favourably than insecurely attached children, whose working models of self are not so positive. And apparently they do. In a Belgian study, 4- to 5-year-olds were asked questions about their worthiness, which they answered through a hand puppet (for example, "Do you [puppet] like to play with [this child]?"; "Is [this child] a good [bad] boy/girl?"). Children with secure ties to their mothers not only described themselves more favourably (through the puppet) than did children who were insecurely attached, but they were also rated as more competent and socially skilled by their preschool teachers (Verschueren, Marcoen, & Schoefs, 1996); what's more, the positivity (or negativity) of children's self-descriptions was highest for those children who were securely attached to both of their parents (Verschueren & Marcoen, 1999) and proved to be stable over time when reassessed at age 8 (Verschueren, Buyck, & Marcoen, 2001). So it seems that by age 4 or 5 (and possibly sooner), children have already established an early and meaningful sense of self-esteem that is influenced by their attachment history and is a reasonably accurate reflection of how teachers evaluate their competencies.

Components of Self-Esteem

When we adults think about self-esteem, a global appraisal of self comes to mind based on the strengths and weaknesses we display in several different life domains. The same is true for children, who first evaluate their competencies in many different areas and only later integrate these impressions into an overall self-evaluation.

Susan Harter (1982, 1999) has proposed a hierarchical model of childhood self-esteem that is shown in Figure 12.3. To test her model, she asks children to complete a Self-Perception Scale on which they evaluate themselves in five domains: *scholastic competence, social acceptance, physical appearance, athletic competence, and behavioural conduct*. They make these self-appraisals by indicating the extent to which statements such as "Some kids are good at figuring out answers at school" (scholastic competence) and "Some kids are always chosen for games" (athletic competence) are true of themselves.

According to Harter, 4- to 7-year-olds might be accused of having inflated egos because they tend to rate themselves positively in all domains. Some researchers think that these very positive assessments reflect a *desire* to be liked or to be good at various activities rather than a firm sense of self-worth (Eccles et al., 1993; Harter & Pike, 1984). However, the self-appraisals of 4- to 7-year-olds are not totally unrealistic because they are modestly correlated with ratings that teachers give them on the same competency domains (Measelle et al., 1998).

Starting at about age 8 children's own competency appraisals begin to more closely reflect other people's evaluations of them (Harter, 1982; Marsh, Craven, & Debus, 1998). For example, ratings of social self-esteem are now confirmed by peers who had been asked to rate their classmates' social competencies; and children with high athletic self-esteem are more frequently chosen for team sports and are rated higher in physical competence by gym teachers than are classmates who feel physically inadequate. Taken together, these findings suggest that both self-knowledge and self-esteem may depend to a large extent on the way that others perceive and react to our behaviour. This is precisely the point that Charles Cooley (1902) was making when he coined the term *looking-glass self* to explain how we construct a self-image.

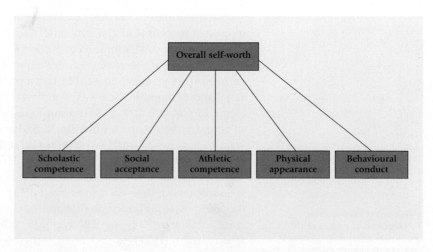

Figure 12.3 *A multidimensional and hierarchical model of self-esteem.* ADAPTED FROM *HARTER, 1996.*

By early adolescence one's perceptions of self-worth become increasingly centred on interpersonal relationships. Susan Harter and her associates (1998) coined the term **relational self-worth** to describe their finding that adolescents often begin to perceive their self-worth somewhat differently in different relational contexts (e.g., with parents, with teachers, with male classmates, and with female classmates). Clearly, all of these domains of relational self-worth contribute to one's global self-esteem, although the same domain may be much more important for some adolescents than for others. Thus one adolescent may enjoy high global self-esteem because he views himself as especially bright and as receiving ample support and admiration from his teachers, even though peers may consider him nerdy; another may enjoy equally high global self-esteem because she views her competencies with peers in a very favourable way, even though she feels much less efficacious in her relationships with parents and teachers. Here, then, is an indication that our self-esteem depends not only on how others might evaluate us but also on *how we choose to evaluate ourselves* (i.e., on the kinds of relationships and aspects of relational self-worth that we view as most central or important to our self-concepts).

Given the increasing importance of interpersonal relationships, it is hardly surprising that new relationship-oriented dimensions such as *romantic appeal* and *quality of close friendships* become very important contributors to an adolescent's global self-esteem (Masden et al., 1995; Richards et al., 1998), although they may influence the self-appraisal of boys and girls in somewhat different ways (Thorne & Michaelieu, 1996). Girls who enjoy high self-esteem have had *supportive* relationships with friends, whereas boys are more likely to derive high self-esteem from their ability to successfully *influence* their friends. Low self-esteem in girls is most strongly associated with a failure to win friends' approval, whereas a major contributor to low self-esteem in adolescent boys is a lack of romantic competence, as reflected by their failure to win or maintain the affection of girls.

Changes in Self-Esteem

How stable are one's feelings of self-worth? Is a child who enjoys high self-esteem as an 8-year-old likely to feel especially good about himself as an adolescent? Or is it more reasonable to assume that the stresses and strains of adolescence cause most teenagers to doubt themselves and their competencies, thereby undermining their self-esteem?

Erik Erikson (1963) favoured the latter point of view, arguing that young adolescents who experience the many physical, cognitive, and social changes associated with puberty often become confused and show at least some decline in self-esteem as they leave childhood behind and begin to search for stable adult identity. Indeed, according to Bonnie Leadbeater from the University of Victoria and colleagues (Leadbeater, Kuperminc, Blatt, & Herzog, 1999), some young adolescents, particularly girls, do experience meaningful declines in self-esteem as they leave elementary school as the oldest and most revered students, and enter junior high, where they are the youngest and least competent (see also Simmons et al., 1987). This dip in self-esteem is likely to be greatest when multiple stressors pile up—for example, when adolescents are not only making the transition to junior high school but also coping with pubertal changes, beginning to date, and perhaps dealing with family transitions, such as a divorce, all at the same time (Simmons et al., 1987). Furthermore, adolescents experience more daily hassles and other negative events, both at home and at school, than younger children do, and these stresses largely account for the increased sulkiness and other negative emotions that seventh- to ninth-graders display (Larson & Ham, 1993; Seidman et al., 1994). So early adolescence can be a somewhat painful experience that can even drive some teenagers to consider taking their own lives (see Box 12.4).

But before we conclude that adolescence is hazardous to our sense of self-worth, let's note that *most* 11- to 14-year-olds show no appreciable decline in self-esteem (Nottelmann, 1987). In fact, teenagers generally display gradual though modest *increases* in self-esteem over the course of adolescence (Leadbeater et al., 1999; Mullis, Mullis, & Normandin, 1992; Savin-Williams & Demo, 1984).

relational self-worth
feelings of self-esteem within a particular relationship context (e.g., with parents, with classmates); may differ across relationship contexts

12.4 Adolescent Suicide: The Tragic Destruction of Self

Surprising as it may seem to anyone who has never contemplated taking her own life, suicidal thoughts are shockingly common among adolescents and young adults (Group for the Advancement of Psychiatry, Committee on Adolescence, 1996). In one survey of Canadian adolescents, 5 to 10 percent of boys and 10 to 20 percent of girls aged 12 to 16 reported at least one instance of suicidal thinking or had attempted suicide within the previous six months (Joffe, Offord, & Boyle, 1988).

Suicide rates among 15- to 19-year-olds have been somewhat stable in Canada over the last 20 years, although they are double the rates of 30 years ago (Langlois & Morrison, 2002). Suicide was the second leading cause of death for this age group in the period 1989–91, ranking behind only motor vehicle accidents (Health Canada, Laboratory Centre for Disease Control, 1996). Among some Aboriginal communities, suicidal thoughts and behaviours are often even more widespread (Mao et al., 1992). Estimates of the suicide rate within Aboriginal communities average from 1.5 to 2.9 times the Canadian population rate (Statistics Canada, 2000b). However, according to Michael Chandler of the University of British Columbia and Christopher Lalonde of the University of Victoria (1998, Chandler, Lalonde, Sokol, Hallett, 2003), Aboriginal communities that have taken active steps to preserve and rehabilitate their own cultures have youth suicide rates that are dramatically lower. Overall, females *attempt* suicide more often than males do, but males are more often successful in their attempts by a ratio of about 3 to 1, a difference that holds up across most cultures studied (Girard, 1993). Males succeed more often simply because they shun slower-acting pills in favour of more abruptly lethal techniques such as hanging and guns.

Although teenagers *attempt* suicide more often than adults do, we see in the figure that adults are more likely to actually commit suicide. The suicide rate for women peaks in middle age, whereas it climbs for White males throughout adulthood. Because adolescents are far less successful than adults at killing themselves when they try, some researchers believe that their suicide attempts are often a desperate "cry for help." Unlike suicidal adults, who are often determined to end it all, many suicidal adolescents hope to improve their lives; they may see their suicide attempts as a way of forcing others to take their problems seriously, but by miscalculation or sudden impulse, they often die before they can be helped (Berman & Jobes, 1991; Rubenstein et al., 1989).

Unfortunately, there is no sure way to identify young people who will try to kill themselves. Suicidal adolescents come from all racial and ethnic groups and all social classes, and even popular adolescents of superior intelligence may take their own lives. Yet there are some telltale warning signs. Suicidal adolescents are often severely depressed, abusing drugs, or displaying other forms of antisocial conduct (Group for the Advancement of Psychiatry, Committee on Adolescence, 1996; Vannatta, 1996). They have often experienced deteriorating relationships with parents, peers, or romantic partners; suffered academic failures; and lost all interest in hobbies or other enjoyable activities as they sink into a state of hopelessness and despair and feel incapable of coping with their problems (Berman & Jobes, 1991; Wagner, 1997).

Friends and associates can play an important role in preventing adolescent suicide by recognizing the warning signs and encouraging their deeply depressed or suddenly hostile young companions to talk about their problems—a step that adults often fail to take, thinking that the teenager's unruly or depressed demeanour reflects the typical "storm and stress" of adolescence. Should a troubled youngster divulge suicidal thoughts, companions might try to convince him or her that there are ways other than suicide to cope with distress. But perhaps the most important thing friends and associates can do is to tell what they have learned to other people who are in a better position to help, such as the adolescent's parents, a teacher, or a school counsellor. Clearly, it is better to break a confidence than to let the person die.

As for parents, perhaps the best advice is to take *all* suicidal thinking seriously. And professional assistance is definitely called for after an unsuccessful suicide attempt, because adolescents who try once are at risk of succeeding in the future if they receive little help and continue to feel incapable of coping with their problems (Berman & Jobes, 1991).

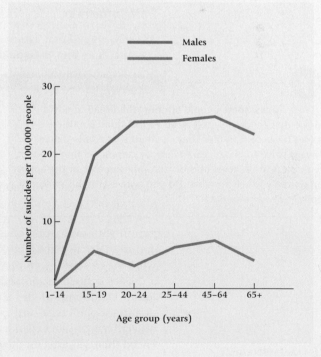

Suicides in Canada per 100 000 people by age and sex. DATA FROM STATISTICS CANADA, 1997.

The only contributor to perceived self-worth that reliably declines early in adolescence is girls' satisfaction with their bodies and physical appearance (Leadbeater et al., 1999; Rosenblum & Lewis, 1999)—a finding that helps explain why more boys than girls are likely to show gains in self-esteem during the adolescent years (Thorne & Michaelieu, 1996). But most youths emerge from adolescence with approximately the same level of global self-esteem that they displayed late in childhood (Block & Robins, 1993; Brown, 1998).

Social Contributors to Self-Esteem

Parenting Styles

Parents can play a crucial role in shaping a child's self-esteem. As we noted in Chapter 11, the sensitivity of parenting early in childhood clearly influences whether infants and toddlers construct positive or negative working models of self. Furthermore, elementary-school children and adolescents with high self-esteem tend to have parents who are warm and supportive, set clear standards for them to live up to, and allow them a voice in making decisions that affect them personally (Coopersmith, 1967; Isberg et al., 1989; Lamborn et al., 1991). The link between high self-esteem and this nurturing, democratic parental style is much the same in Taiwan and Australia as it is in Canada and the United States (Scott, Scott, & McCabe, 1991). Although these child-rearing studies are correlational and we cannot be sure that warm, supportive parenting *causes* high self-esteem, it is easy to imagine such a causal process at work. Certainly, sending a message that "You're a good kid whom I trust to follow rules and make good decisions" is apt to promote higher self-esteem than more aloof or more controlling styles in which parents may be saying, in effect, "Your inadequacies turn me off."

Peer Influences

As early as age 4 or 5, children begin to recognize differences among themselves and their classmates as they use **social comparison** information to tell them whether they perform better or worse in various domains than their peers (Butler, 1998; Pomerantz et al., 1995). For example, they glance at each others' papers and say "How many did you miss?" or will make such statements as "I'm faster than you" after winning a footrace (Frey & Ruble, 1985). This kind of comparison increases and becomes more subtle with age (Pomerantz et al., 1995) and plays an important role in shaping children's self-esteem—particularly in Western cultures where competition and individual accomplishments are stressed. Interestingly, this preoccupation with evaluating oneself in comparison with peers is not nearly as strong among communally reared kibbutz children in Israel, perhaps because cooperation and teamwork are so strongly emphasized there (Butler & Ruzany, 1993).

Peer influences on self-esteem become even more apparent during adolescence. Recall that some of the strongest contributions to adolescent self-appraisals are the quality of one's relationships with particularly close friends. In fact, when young adults reflect back on life experiences that were noteworthy to them and that may have influenced their self-esteem, they mention experiences with friends and romantic partners far more frequently than experiences with parents and family members (Thorne & Michaelieu, 1996).

One major aspect of self-esteem that has been studied in some depth is the development of children's academic self-concepts—a topic to which we now turn.

> ? **WHAT DO YOU THINK?**
>
> Today, some people offering child-rearing advice argue that children simply need to feel good about themselves to succeed in life. They contend that adults should always strive to boost self-esteem by complimenting children, regardless of the level of their accomplishments or the appropriateness of their conduct. Do you agree with this philosophy? Why or why not?

social comparison
process of defining and evaluating the self by comparing oneself with other people

DEVELOPMENT OF ACHIEVEMENT MOTIVATION AND ACADEMIC SELF-CONCEPT

In Chapter 9, we learned that even though IQ predicts academic achievement, the relationship is far from perfect. Why? Because children also differ in **achievement motivation**—their willingness to strive to succeed at challenging tasks and to meet high standards of accomplishment. Although the meaning of achievement varies somewhat from society to society, one survey conducted in 30 cultures revealed that people around the world value personal attributes such as self-reliance, responsibility, and a willingness to work hard to attain important objectives (Fyans et al., 1983).

Many years ago, psychoanalyst Robert White (1959) proposed that from infancy onward, human beings are intrinsically motivated to master their environments—to have an effect on or to cope successfully with a world of people and objects. We see this **mastery motive** in action as we watch infants struggle to turn knobs, open cabinets, and operate toys, and then notice their pleasure when they succeed (Mayes & Zigler, 1992). Even infants and toddlers who are mentally retarded actively seek out challenges just for the joy of mastering them (Hauser-Cram, 1996).

But even though all babies may be curious, mastery-oriented beings, it is obvious that some children try harder than others to master their school assignments, music lessons, or the positions they play on the neighbourhood softball team. How do we explain these individual differences? Let's begin by tracing the development of achievement motivation early in life and examining some of the factors that promote (or inhibit) its growth.

Early Origins of Achievement Motivation

How does a baby's mastery motivation evolve into an elementary-school child's achievement motivation? Deborah Stipek and her associates (Stipek, Recchia, & McClintic, 1992) have conducted a series of studies with 1- to 5-year-olds to find out when children develop the capacity to evaluate their accomplishments against performance standards—a capacity central to achievement motivation. In Stipek's research, children were observed as they undertook activities that had clear-cut achievement goals (for example, hammering pegs into pegboards, working puzzles, knocking down plastic pins with a

achievement motivation
willingness to strive to succeed at challenging tasks and to meet high standards of accomplishment

mastery motivation
inborn motive to explore, understand, and control one's environment

Concept Check 12.1
Development of the Self-Concept and Self-Esteem

Check your understanding of important processes and milestones in the development of the self by matching each descriptive statement below with one of the following concepts: (a) autism, (b) categorical self, (c) self-esteem, (d) looking-glass self, (e) self-assertion, (f) parental warmth/responsiveness, (g) belief-desire theory of mind, (h) pretend play, (i) social comparison, (j) self-recognition, (k) friendship quality, (l) private self. Answers appear in the Appendix.

_____ 1. evaluative component of the self that is influenced by attachment history

_____ 2. inner, reflective component of self

_____ 3. central component of the self-concepts of children from collectivist societies

_____ 4. self-portrait based on other's reactions to one's behaviours and attributes

_____ 5. condition associated with impaired theory of mind

_____ 6. early contributor to socially skilled play activities

_____ 7. early self-description along such socially significant dimensions as age and sex

_____ 8. appears to underlie successful use of deceptive ploys

_____ 9. strong contributor to self-esteem beginning in adolescence

_____ 10. important contributor to self-esteem in cultures that stress individual accomplishments

_____ 11. promotes high self-esteem in childhood

_____ 12. important social contributor to theory of mind

bowling ball). Tasks were structured so that children either could or could not master them in order to observe reactions to success or failure. Based on this research, Stipek and her colleagues suggest that children progress through three phases in learning to evaluate their performances in achievement situations, phases we will call *joy in mastery, approval-seeking,* and *use of standards.*

Phase 1: Joy in Mastery

Before the age of 2, infants are visibly pleased to master challenges, displaying the mastery motivation that White (1959) wrote about. However, they do not call other people's attention to their triumphs or otherwise seek recognition, and, rather than being bothered by failures, they simply shift goals and attempt to master other toys. They are not yet evaluating their outcomes in relation to performance standards that define success and failure.

Three-year-olds are highly motivated to master challenges and can take pride in their accomplishments.

Phase 2: Approval-Seeking

As they near age 2, toddlers begin to anticipate how others will evaluate their performances. They seek recognition when they master challenges and expect disapproval when they fail. For example, children as young as 2 who succeeded on a task often smiled, held their heads and chins up high, and made such statements as "I did it" as they called the experimenter's attention to their feats. Meanwhile, 2-year-olds who failed to master a challenge often turned away from the experimenter as though they hoped to avoid criticism. It seems, then, that 2-year-olds already appraise their outcomes as mastery successes or nonsuccesses and have already learned that they can expect approval after successes and disapproval after failures (see also Bullock & Lutkenhaus, 1990).

Phase 3: Use of Standards

An important breakthrough occurs around age 3 as children begin to react more independently to their successes and failures. They seem to have adopted objective standards for appraising their performance and are not as dependent on others to tell them when they have done well or poorly. These Phase 3 children seem capable of experiencing real *pride* (rather than mere pleasure) in their achievements and real *shame* (rather than mere disappointment) after failure.

In sum, infants are guided by a mastery motive and take pleasure in their everyday accomplishments; 2-year-olds begin to anticipate others' approval or disapproval of their performances; and children 3 and older evaluate their accomplishments against performance standards and are capable of experiencing pride or shame depending on how successfully they match those standards.

Achievement Motivation during Middle Childhood and Adolescence

In their pioneering studies of achievement motivation, David McClelland and his associates (1953) gave children and adolescents a series of four somewhat ambiguous pictures and asked them to write stories about them as part of a test of creative imagination. Assuming that people project their own motives into their stories, one can measure their achievement motivation by counting the number of achievement-related themes they mention. What kind of story would you tell about the scene portrayed in Figure 12.4? A person high in achievement motivation might respond by saying that the individual in the photo has been working for months on a new scientific breakthrough that will revolutionize the field of medicine, whereas a person who scores low might say that this worker is glad the day is over so that she can go home and relax. Early research revealed that children and adolescents who scored high in achievement motivation on this and other measures tended to receive better grades in school than those who scored low

(McClelland et al., 1953). These findings prompted investigators to look more closely at parent–child interactions to determine how the home setting influences achievement motivation.

Home Influences on Mastery Motivation and Achievement

Over the years, researchers have identified three especially potent home influences on children's mastery/achievement motivation and actual achievement behaviour: the quality of the child's attachments, the character of the home environment, and the child-rearing practices that parents use, which can either foster or inhibit a child's will to achieve.

Figure 12.4 *Scenes like this one were used by David McClelland and his associates to measure achievement motivation.*

QUALITY OF ATTACHMENT. In Chapter 11, we learned that children who were securely attached to primary caregivers at age 12 to 18 months were more likely than those who were insecurely attached to solve problems successfully as 2-year-olds and to display a strong sense of curiosity, self-reliance, and an eagerness to solve problems some three to five years later as they enter elementary school. And children whose attachments are secure on entering school tend to be more self-assured and do better in school than their insecurely attached peers throughout middle childhood and adolescence—even when other factors known to affect academic achievement, such as IQ and social class, are held constant (Jacobson & Hoffman, 1997). Interestingly, securely attached preschoolers are no more intellectually competent, on average, than their insecurely attached age-mates; instead they seem to be more *eager* to *apply* their competencies to the new challenges they encounter (Belsky, Garduque, & Hrncir, 1984). So children apparently need the secure base provided by a loving, responsive parent to feel comfortable about taking risks and *seeking* challenges.

THE HOME ENVIRONMENT. The young child's tendency to explore, acquire new skills, and solve problems will also depend on the kind of challenges the home environment provides. In one study (van Doorninck et al., 1981), researchers visited the homes of 50 12-month-old infants from lower-income families and used the *HOME inventory* (described in Chapter 9) to classify each child's early environment as intellectually stimulating or unstimulating. Five to nine years later, the research team followed up on these children by looking at their standardized achievement test scores and the grades they had earned at school. As we see in Table 12.1, the quality of the home environment at 12 months of age predicted children's academic achievement several years later. Two out of three children from stimulating homes were now performing quite well at school, whereas 70 percent of those from unstimulating homes were doing very poorly (see also Bradley, Caldwell, & Rock, 1988). Not only do stimulating home environments foster good grades among children from all ethnic groups and social classes, but they also promote an **intrinsic orientation to achievement**—a strong willingness to seek out and master challenges to satisfy *personal* needs for competence or mastery (Gottfried, Fleming, & Gottfried, 1998). So, even though the seeds of mastery motivation may well be innate, the joy of discovery and problem solving is most likely to blossom in an intellectually stimulating home environment that provides many age-appropriate challenges and the encouragement to master them.

CHILD-REARING AND ACHIEVEMENT. In their book The Achievement Motive, McClelland and his associates (1953) proposed that parents who stress independence training— doing things on one's own—and who warmly reinforce such self-reliant behaviour contribute in a positive way to achievement motivation. And research bears this out (Grolnick & Ryan, 1989; Winterbottom, 1958). However, it is important to note that successfully fostering autonomy and self-reliance requires far more than isolating a child to accomplish objectives alone. Consistent with Vygotsky's viewpoint on the importance of

intrinsic achievement orientation
a desire to achieve in order to satisfy one's *personal* needs for competence or mastery (as opposed to achieving for external incentives such as grades)

TABLE 12.1   Relation between Quality of Home Environment at 12 Months of Age and Children's Elementary-School Academic Achievement Five to Nine Years Later

Quality of home environment at age 12 months	Academic achievement	
	Average or high (top 70%)	Low (bottom 30%)
Stimulating	20 children	10 children
Unstimulating	6 children	14 children

SOURCE: Adapted from van Doorninck et al., 1981.

collaborative learning, one recent longitudinal study found that 2-year-olds whose parents had carefully scaffolded their efforts, thereby allowing them to eventually master challenges that would have been impossible without such gentle parental guidance, were the ones who felt most comfortable and most motivated in achievement contexts one year later, as 3-year-olds (Kelley, Brownell, & Campbell, 2000). What's more, direct achievement training—setting high standards and encouraging children to do things well—also fosters achievement motivation (Rosen & D'Andrade, 1959). Finally, patterns of praise (or punishment) that accompany the child's accomplishments are also important: Children who seek challenges and display high levels of achievement motivation have parents who praise their successes and are not overly critical of an occasional failure; by contrast, children who shy away from challenges and are low in achievement motivation have parents who are slow to acknowledge their successes (or who do so in a matter-of-fact way) and are inclined to criticize or punish failures (Burhans & Dweck, 1995; Kelley et al., 2000; Teeven & McGhee, 1972).

We see, then, that parents of youngsters high in achievement motivation possess three characteristics: (1) they are warm, accepting, and quick to praise the child's accomplishments; (2) they provide guidance and control by setting standards for the child to live up to and then monitoring her progress to ensure that she does; and (3) they permit the child some independence or autonomy, carefully scaffolding tasks for young children to allow them to succeed on their own and allowing older ones a say in deciding how best to master challenges and meet their expectations. Diana Baumrind calls this warm, firm, but democratic parenting an **authoritative parenting** style—a style that she and others have found to foster positive attitudes about achievement and considerable academic success among elementary-school children and adolescents, both in Western societies (Glasgow et al., 1997; Lamborn et al., 1991; Steinberg, Elmen, & Mounts, 1989) and in Asia (Lin & Fu, 1990). If children are encouraged and supported in a positive manner as they tackle their schoolwork, they are likely to enjoy new challenges and feel confident about mastering them (Connell, Spencer, & Aber, 1994). By contrast, parents can undermine a child's school performance and motivation to succeed if they (1) are uninvolved and offer little in the way of guidance or (2) are highly controlling and do such things as nag continually about homework, offer tangible bribes for good grades, or harp incessantly about bad ones (Ginsburg & Bronstein, 1993).

PEER GROUP INFLUENCES. Peers are also an important source of influence on elementary-school children and adolescents who may sometimes support and at other times undermine parents' efforts to encourage academic achievement. For example, researchers in the United States suggest that peer pressures that interfere with academic achievement may be especially acute for many lower-income African-American and Latino students and may help explain why they often lag behind Anglo-American and Asian-American students in school achievement (Slaughter-Defoe et al., 1990; Tharp, 1989). Lawrence Steinberg and his colleagues (Steinberg, Dornbusch, & Brown, 1992) found that the African-American and Latino peer cultures in many low-income areas actively discourage academic achievement, whereas European-American and Asian-American peer groups tend to value and encourage it. High-achieving African-American students in some

authoritative parenting
flexible, democratic style of parenting in which warm, accepting parents provide guidance and control while allowing the child some say in deciding how best to meet challenges and obligations

inner-city schools actually run the risk of being rejected by their African-American peers if their academic accomplishments cause them to be perceived as acting White (Ford & Harris, 1996; Fordham & Ogbu, 1986).

On the other hand, children whose parents value education highly and work hard to promote their achievement tend to associate with peers who share those values. In his recent study of Latino, East Asian, Filipino, and European immigrant families, Andrew Fuligni (1997) found that immigrant adolescents tend to make higher grades at school than native-born U.S. adolescents do, despite the fact that their parents are not highly educated and often speak little English at home. Why? Because the parents of these high achievers strongly endorsed the value of academics, a value that was clearly reinforced by their friends, who often studied together with them, shared class notes, and encouraged them to do well in school. This kind of peer support for parental values also fosters the academic achievement of talented African-American students (Ford & Harris, 1996) and preadolescents in Shanghai, China (Chen, Rubin, & Li, 1997), and is probably a strong contributor to the academic successes of students from any background. Clearly, it is easier to remain focused on academic goals if one is not receiving mixed messages about their value from parents and peers.

Beyond Achievement Motivation: Development of Achievement-Related Attributions

Many contemporary researchers acknowledge that the concept of achievement motivation has some value, but they believe it is naive to presume that this one global motive predicts behaviour in all achievement situations. Why? Because they have also discovered that children's achievement behaviour and academic self-concepts depend heavily on their **achievement attributions**, or how they *interpret* their successes and failures.

Types of Achievement Attributions

Bernard Weiner (1974, 1986) finds that adolescents and young adults tend to attribute their successes and failures to any of four possible causes: *ability* (or the lack thereof), *effort*, *task difficulty*, or *luck* (either good or bad). As shown in Table 12.2, two of these causes, ability and task difficulty, are *stable* causes, which foster strong **achievement expectancies**, whereas effort and luck are *unstable*, or highly variable from situation to situation, and promote weaker expectancies. To illustrate, if you do poorly on a test and attribute your failure to a *stable* cause like low ability, you should feel less confident of future success (strong negative expectancy) than if you attributed that failure to low effort, which you might overcome by studying harder next time. Notice also that two of the causes, ability and effort, are *internal* causes (characteristics of the individual), whereas the other two are *external* causes (characteristics of the situation). Weiner proposes that the internality–externality of our achievement attributions affects how much we *value* our achievement outcomes. So if we attribute an A on a test to an *internal* cause such as our high ability or hard work, we are more likely to value our success than if we attributed it to such external factors as blind luck or a ridiculously easy exam.

According to Weiner, it is adaptive to attribute our successes to high ability because this internal and stable attribution causes us to *value* what we have accomplished and leads us to *expect* that we can repeat our success. By contrast, it is more adaptive to attribute *failures* to low effort (rather than low ability) because effort is unstable and we are more likely to believe that we can do better in the future if we just try harder.

In sum, Weiner's attribution theory claims that two cognitive variables influence our willingness to work to achieve particular objectives within any given achievement domain. Presumably, the perceived *locus of causality* (i.e., internality or externality) of an outcome affects how much we value the outcome, whereas our attributions about the stability of the outcome affect our achievement expectancies. Together, these two cognitive judgments influence our willingness to undertake similar challenges in the future (see Figure 12.5 for an overview of Weiner's theory).

achievement attributions
causal explanations that one provides for his or her successes and failures

achievement expectancy
how well (or poorly) one expects to perform should she try to achieve a particular objective

TABLE 12.2	Weiner's Classification of the Causes of Achievement Outcomes (and Examples of How You Might Explain a Terrible Test Grade)	
	Locus of causality	
	Internal cause	**External cause**
Stable cause	*Ability* "I'm hopeless in math."	*Task difficulty* "That test was incredibly hard and much too long."
Unstable cause	*Effort* "I should have studied more instead of going out to the concert."	*Luck* "What luck! Every question seemed to be about information taught on the days of class I missed."

Age Differences in Achievement-Related Attributes

If it seems to you as if Weiner's theory sounds a little too cognitive and abstract to explain the achievement attributions that young children display, you would be right. Before age 7 or so, children tend to be unrealistic optimists who think they have the ability to succeed on almost any task, even those that they have repeatedly failed to master in the past (Stipek & Mac Iver, 1989). Preschool and primary-grade teachers may contribute to this rosy optimism by setting mastery goals and by praising children more for their efforts than for the quality of their work, thus leading them to believe that they can accomplish much and "be smart" by working hard (Rosenholtz & Simpson, 1984; Stipek & Mac Iver, 1989). Indeed, young children do seem to have an **incremental view of ability**: They believe that ability is changeable, not stable, and that they can get smarter or become more capable through increased effort and lots of practice (Droege & Stipek, 1993; Dweck & Leggett, 1988).

When do children begin to distinguish ability from effort? When do they move toward an **entity view of ability**—a perspective that ability is a fixed or stable trait that is not influenced much by effort or practice? It turns out that many 8- to 12-year-olds begin to distinguish effort from ability (Nicholls & Miller, 1984) due, in part, to the changing character of their experiences at school. Teachers gradually put more and more emphasis on *ability* appraisals; they assign grades that reflect the quality of work that students perform rather than the amount of effort expended, and these performance evaluations are supplemented by such competitive activities as science fairs and spelling bees, which also place a premium on the *quality* rather than the quantity of students' work.

incremental view of ability
belief that one's ability can be improved through increased effort and practice

entity view of ability
belief that one's ability is a highly stable trait that is not influenced much by effort or practice

Furthermore, older elementary-school children are often placed into ability groups based on the teacher's appraisal of their competencies (Rosenholtz & Simpson, 1984; Stipek & Mac Iver, 1989). So all of these practices, coupled with children's increased use of social comparison to appraise their outcomes (Pomerantz et al., 1995), help explain why older elementary-school students begin to distinguish effort from ability and make the kind of causal attributions for their successes and failures that Weiner's theory anticipates.

Interestingly, the late elementary-school period (fourth to sixth grades) is also the time when many students begin to value academic achievement less and to develop rather negative academic self-concepts, a

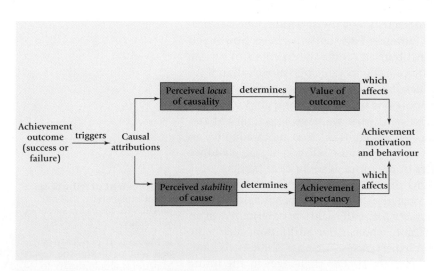

Figure 12.5 An overview of Weiner's attribution theory of achievement.

trend that becomes even stronger during the junior high school years (Butler, 1999; Eccles et al., 1993). And as we are about to see, children's tendency to distinguish ability and effort and to adopt an *entity view* of ability is a major contributor to these trends.

Dweck's Learned-Helplessness Theory

All children fail on occasion as they attempt to master challenges, but they don't all respond to failure in the same way. Building on Weiner's attribution theory, Carol Dweck and her colleagues have tried to understand why some children persist in the face of failure and ultimately achieve their objectives, whereas others who fail quickly give up. Their findings revealed that these two types of children explain their achievement outcomes in very different ways (Dweck & Elliott, 1983; Dweck & Leggett, 1988).

Some children are **mastery oriented**: They attribute their successes to their high ability but tend to externalize the blame for their failures ("That test was ambiguous and unfair") or to attribute them to *unstable* causes that they can easily overcome ("I'll do better if I try harder"). These students are called mastery oriented because they persist in the face of failure, believing that their increased effort will allow them to succeed. Although they see their ability as a reasonably stable attribute that doesn't fluctuate radically from day to day (which allows them to feel confident about repeating their successes), they still think that they can improve their competencies (an *incremental* viewpoint) by trying harder after a failure. So mastery-oriented youngsters are highly motivated to "master" new challenges, regardless of whether they have previously succeeded or failed at similar tasks (see Figure 12.6).

By contrast, other children often attribute their successes to the *unstable* factors of hard work or luck; they do not experience the pride and self-esteem that come from viewing themselves as highly competent. Yet they often attribute their failures to a stable and internal factor—namely, their *lack of ability*—which causes them to form low expectations of future successes and give up. It appeared to Dweck as if these youngsters were displaying a **learned-helplessness orientation**: If failures are attributed to a *stable* cause—lack of ability—that the child thinks he can do little about (an *entity view* of ability), he becomes frustrated and sees little reason to try to improve. So he stops trying

mastery orientation
tendency to persist at challenging tasks because of a belief that one has high ability and that earlier failures can be overcome by trying harder

learned-helplessness orientation
tendency to give up or stop trying after failing because these failures have been attributed to a lack of ability that one can do little about

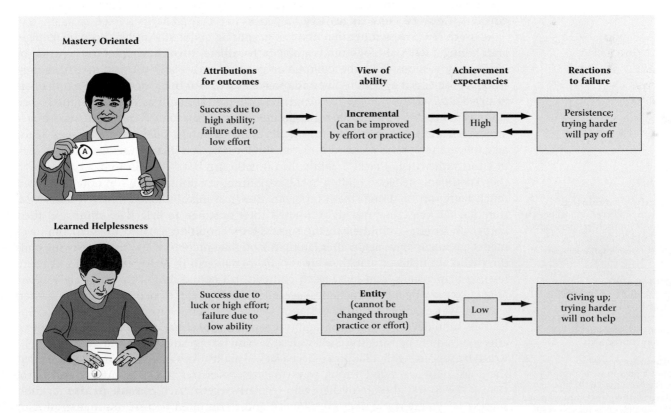

Figure 12.6 *Characteristics of the mastery-oriented and learned-helplessness achievement orientations.*

and acts helpless (see also Pomerantz & Ruble, 1997). Unfortunately, even talented students may adopt this unhealthy attributional style that, once established, tends to persist over time and eventually undermines their academic performances (Fincham, Hokoda, & Sanders, 1989; Phillips, 1984; Ziegert et al., 2001).

How Does Learned Helplessness Develop? According to Dweck (1978), parents and teachers may unwittingly foster the development of a helpless achievement orientation if they praise the child for *working hard* when she succeeds but criticize her *lack of ability* when she fails. Apparently, even 4- to 6-year-olds can begin to develop a helpless orientation if their failures are often punished or otherwise criticized in ways that cause them to doubt their self-worth (Burhans & Dweck, 1995; Ziegert et al., 2001). By contrast, if parents and teachers praise the child's *efforts at devising effective problem-seeking strategies* when she succeeds but emphasize her *lack of effort* when she fails, the child may conclude that she is certainly capable enough and could do much better if she tried harder—precisely the viewpoint adopted by mastery-oriented youngsters (Dweck, 2001). In one clever experiment, Dweck and her associates (1978) demonstrated that fifth-graders who received the *helplessness-producing* pattern of evaluation while working at unfamiliar problems began to attribute their failures to a lack of ability, whereas classmates who received the *mastery-oriented* evaluative pattern attributed their failures to a lack of effort, saying, in effect, "I need to try harder." These strikingly different attributional styles were created in less than one hour in this experiment, thus implying that similar patterns of evaluative feedback from parents or teachers, given consistently over a period of months or years, might well contribute to the development of the contrasting helpless and mastery orientations so often observed among elementary-school (and older) students.

On Helping the Helpless to Achieve. Obviously, giving up as soon as one begins to founder is not the kind of achievement orientation that adults hope to encourage. What can be done to help these "helpless" children to persist at tasks where they have failed? According to Dweck, one effective therapy might be a form of **attribution retraining** in which children with a learned-helplessness orientation are persuaded to attribute their failures to unstable causes—namely, insufficient effort—that they can do something about, rather than continuing to view the failures as stemming from their lack of ability, which is not so easy to change.

Dweck (1975) tested her hypothesis by exposing children who had become helpless after failing a series of tough math problems to either of two therapies. Over a period of 25 therapy sessions, half the children received a *success-only* therapy in which they worked problems they could solve and received tokens for their successes. The other half received *attribution retraining:* They experienced nearly as many successes over the 25 sessions as did the children in the other group but were also told after each of several prearranged failures that they had not worked fast enough and *should have tried harder*. Thus, an explicit attempt was made to convince these youngsters that failures can reflect a lack of effort rather than a lack of ability. Did this therapy work? Yes indeed! At the end of the experiment, helpless children in the attribution-retraining condition now performed much better on the tough math problems they had initially failed to solve, and when they did fail one, they usually attributed their outcome to a lack of effort and tried harder. By contrast, children in the success-only condition showed no such improvements, giving up once again after failing the original problems. So merely showing children who act helpless that they are capable of succeeding is not enough! To alleviate learned helplessness, one must teach children to respond more constructively to their *failures* by viewing these experiences as something they can overcome if they try harder.

Can we do better than this? Certainly we can: by taking steps to *prevent* learned helplessness from developing. Parents and teachers can play a major part in these preventive efforts by simply praising the child's successes and taking care not to undermine her self-worth by suggesting that failures reflect a lack of ability. And recent research suggests that there are right ways and wrong ways to praise successes. Claudia Mueller and Carol Dweck (1998) found that children who regularly receive such **person praise** for their success as "you're really *smart, intelligent,*" and so on often become more interested in **performance goals** than in new learning when faced with novel challenges, as they

attribution retraining
therapeutic intervention in which "helpless" children are persuaded to attribute failures to their lack of effort rather than a lack of ability

person praise
praise focusing on desirable personality traits such as intelligence; this praise fosters performance goals in achievement contexts

performance goal
state of affairs in which one's primary objective in an achievement context is to display one's competencies (or to avoid looking incompetent)

seek to *show how smart they are*. A failure quickly undermines this performance goal, causing the child to give up and act helpless. How, then, are adults to praise a child's successes? Melissa Kamins and Carol Dweck (1999) find that children who receive **process-oriented praise** when they succeed—feedback that praises the effort they have expended at finding or formulating *good problem-solving strategies*—tend to adopt **learning goals**. That is, they come to view task mastery rather than displaying their smarts as the most important objective when faced with new challenges. An initial failure at a new problem simply tells these youngsters that they need to devise a new strategy and keep working if they hope to achieve their learning goal, and they do just that rather than giving up and acting helpless (Kamins & Dweck, 1999).

So *process-oriented* rather than person-oriented praise for success appears to promote a mastery orientation and prevent learned helplessness. In addition, Dweck's distinction between adaptive *learning goals* and maladaptive *performance goals* implies that a little restructuring of classroom activities could go a long way toward preventing learned helplessness. For example, altering curricula to emphasize *individual mastery* and improving one's competencies should not only convince children to adopt learning goals (Dweck, 2001), but should be particularly helpful to slower learners who fare so poorly by comparison with their peers should they try to demonstrate their competencies through such competitive performance appraisals as grades (Butler, 1999; Stipek & Mac Iver, 1989). Such a focus on mastering new skills *for their own sake* should also persuade students to view initial failures as evidence that they need to change strategies and keep on working rather than treating such missteps as proof that they have little ability and simply cannot master their assignments.

WHO AM I TO BE? FORGING AN IDENTITY

According to Erik Erikson (1963), the major developmental hurdle that adolescents face is establishing an **identity**—a firm and coherent sense of who they are, where they are heading, and where they fit into society. Forging an identity involves grappling with many important choices: What kind of career do I want? What religious, moral, and political values should I adopt? Who am I as a man or a woman, and as a sexual being? Just where do I fit into society? All of this is, of course, a lot for teenagers to have on their minds, and Erikson used the term **identity crisis** to capture the sense of confusion, and even anxiety, that adolescents may feel as they think about who they are today and try to decide "What kind of self can (or should) I become?"

Can you recall a time during the teenage years when you were confused about who you were, what you should be, and what you were likely to become? Is it possible that you have not yet resolved these identity issues and are still seeking answers? If so, does that make you abnormal or maladjusted?

James Marcia (1980) of Simon Fraser University has developed a structured interview that allows researchers to classify adolescents into one of four *identity statuses—identity diffusion, foreclosure, moratorium,* and *identity achievement*—based on whether they have explored various alternatives and made firm commitments to an occupation, a religious ideology, a sexual orientation, and a set of political values. These identity statuses are as follows:

1. **Identity diffusion.** People classified as diffuse have not yet thought about or resolved identity issues and have failed to chart future life directions. *Example:* "I haven't really thought much about religion, and I guess I don't know exactly what I believe."

2. **Foreclosure.** People classified as foreclosed are committed to an identity but have made this commitment without experiencing the crisis of deciding what really suits them best. *Example:* "My parents are Baptists and so I'm a Baptist; it's just the way I grew up."

process-oriented praise
praise of effort expended to formulate good ideas and effective problem-solving strategies; this praise fosters learning goals in achievement contexts

learning goal
state of affairs in which one's primary objective in an achievement context is to increase one's skills or abilities

identity
mature self-definition; a sense of who one is, where one is going in life, and how one fits into society

identity crisis
Erikson's term for the uncertainty and discomfort that adolescents experience when they become confused about their present and future roles in life

identity diffusion
identity status characterizing individuals who are not questioning who they are and have not yet committed themselves to an identity

foreclosure
identity status characterizing individuals who have prematurely committed themselves to occupations or ideologies without really thinking about these commitments

3. **Moratorium.** People in this status are experiencing what Erikson called an *identity crisis* and are actively asking questions about life commitments and seeking answers. *Example:* "I'm evaluating my beliefs and hope that I will be able to decide what's right for me. I like many of the answers provided by my Catholic upbringing, but I'm skeptical about some teachings as well. I have been looking into Unitarianism to see if it might help me answer my questions."

4. **Identity achievement.** Identity-achieved individuals have solved identity issues by making *personal* commitments to particular goals, beliefs, and values. *Example:* "After a lot of soul-searching about my religion and other religions too, I finally know what I believe and what I don't."

moratorium
identity status characterizing individuals who are currently experiencing an identity crisis and are actively exploring occupational and ideological positions in which to invest themselves

identity achievement
identity status characterizing individuals who have carefully considered identity issues and have made firm commitments to an occupation and ideologies

Developmental Trends in Identity Formation

Although Erikson assumed that the identity crisis occurs in early adolescence and is often resolved by age 15 to 18, his age norms were overly optimistic. When Philip Meilman (1979) measured the identity statuses of males between the ages of 12 and 24, he observed a clear developmental progression. But as shown in Figure 12.7, the vast majority of 12- to 18-year-olds were identity diffuse or foreclosed, and not until age 21 or older had the majority of participants reached the moratorium status or achieved stable identities.

Is the identity formation process different for girls and women than it is for boys and men? In most respects, no (Archer, 1992a; Kroger, 1996). Girls make progress toward achieving a clear sense of identity at about the same ages that boys do (Streitmatter, 1993). However, one intriguing sex difference has been observed: Although today's university/college women are just as concerned about establishing a career identity as men are, they attach greater importance to the aspects of identity that centre on sexuality, gender roles, and the issue of how to balance career and family goals (Archer, 1992a; Kroger, 1996; Patterson, Sochting, & Marcia, 1992).

Judging from this research, identity formation takes quite a bit of time. Not until late adolescence—during the university/college years—do many young men and women move from the diffusion or foreclosure status into the moratorium status and then achieve a sense of identity (Waterman, 1982). But this is by no means the end of the identity formation process. Many adults are *still* struggling with identity issues or have reopened the question of who they are after thinking they had all the answers earlier in life (Waterman & Archer, 1990). A divorce, for example, may cause a homemaker to rethink what it means to be a woman and raise questions about other aspects of her identity as well.

The process of achieving identity is also quite uneven (Archer, 1982; Kroger, 1996). For example, Sally Archer (1982) assessed the identity statuses of sixth- to twelfth-graders in four domains: occupational choice, gender-role attitudes, religious beliefs, and political ideologies. Only 5 percent of her adolescents were in the same identity status in all four areas, with 95 percent being in two or even three statuses across the four domains. So adolescents can achieve a strong sense of identity in one area and still be searching in others.

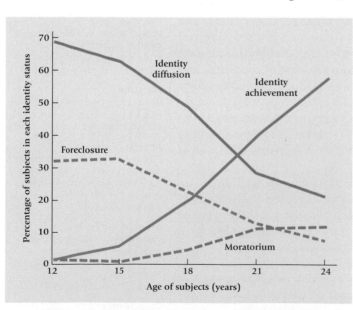

Figure 12.7 *Percentage of participants in each of Marcia's four identity statuses as a function of age. Note that resolution of the identity crisis occurs much later than Erikson assumed: Only 4 percent of the 15-year-olds and 20 percent of the 18-year-olds had achieved a stable identity.* FROM MEILMAN, 1979.

WHAT DO YOU THINK?

Adolescents are often encouraged to volunteer in community agencies or enrol in conferences such as those put on by the Students Commission in Toronto so that they can experience and discuss important issues facing Canadians. What identity status do you think involvement in these programs is encouraging youth to assume? To whom do you think this pitch is most likely to appeal, and why?

How Painful Is Identity Formation?

Perhaps it is unfortunate that Erikson used the term *crisis* to describe the adolescent's active search for an identity (or identities), because adolescents in the moratorium status do not appear all that "stressed out." In fact, James Marcia and his associates (1993) find that these active identity seekers feel much better about themselves and their futures than do age-mates in the diffusion and foreclosure statuses. Yet Gerald Adams of the University of Guelph and his American colleagues (Adams, Abraham, & Markstrom, 1987) suggest that Erikson was right in characterizing identity achievement as a very healthy and adaptive development, because identity achievers do enjoy higher self-esteem and are less self-conscious or preoccupied with personal concerns than their counterparts in the other three identity statuses (see also O'Connor, 1995).

What may be most painful or crisislike about identity seeking is a long-term failure to establish one. Erikson believed that individuals without a clear identity eventually become depressed and lacking in self-confidence as they drift aimlessly, trapped in the diffusion status. Or alternatively, they might heartily embrace what Erikson called a *negative identity*, becoming a "black sheep," "delinquent," or "loser." Why? Because for these foundering souls, it is better to become everything that one is not supposed to be than to have no identity at all (Erikson, 1963). Indeed, many adolescents who are stuck in the diffusion status are highly apathetic and express a sense of hopelessness about the future (Waterman & Archer, 1990). Others who enter high school with very low self-esteem often drift into delinquency and view their deviant self-image as having provided them with a boost in self-worth (Loeber & Stouthamer-Loeber, 1998; Wells, 1989). So it seems that a small minority of adolescents and young adults experience what might be termed an identity *crisis* after all.

Influences on Identity Formation

The adolescent's progress toward identity achievement is influenced by at least four factors: cognitive growth, parenting, schooling, and the broader sociocultural context.

Cognitive Influences

Cognitive development plays an important role in identity achievement. Adolescents who have achieved solid mastery of formal-operational thought and who can reason logically about hypotheticals are now better able to imagine and contemplate future identities. Consequently, they are more likely to raise and resolve identity issues than are age-mates who are less intellectually mature (Boyes & Chandler, 1992; Waterman, 1992).

Parenting Influences

The relationships that adolescents have with their parents can also affect their progress at forging an identity (Markstrom-Adams, 1992; Waterman, 1982). Adolescents in the diffusion status are more likely than those in other statuses to feel neglected or rejected by their parents and to be distant from them (Archer, 1994). Perhaps it is difficult to establish one's own identity without first having the opportunity to identify with respected parental figures and take on some of their desirable qualities. At the other extreme, adolescents in the identity foreclosure status are often extremely close to and sometimes fear rejection from relatively controlling parents (Kroger, 1995). Foreclosed adolescents may never question parental authority or feel any need to forge a separate identity.

By contrast, adolescents in the moratorium and identity achievement statuses appear to have a solid base of affection at home combined with considerable freedom to be individuals in their own right (Grotevant & Cooper, 1986). In family discussions, for example, these adolescents experience a sense of closeness and mutual respect while feeling free to disagree with their parents. So the same loving and democratic style of parenting that fosters academic achievement and helps children gain a strong sense of self-esteem is also associated with healthy and adaptive identity outcomes in adolescence.

Scholastic Influences

Does attending university/college help one to forge an identity? The answer is yes—and no. Attending university/college does seem to push people toward setting career goals and making stable occupational commitments (Waterman, 1982), but these students are often far behind their working peers in terms of establishing firm political and religious identities (Munro & Adams, 1977). In fact, some university/college students regress from identity achievement to the moratorium or even the diffusion status in certain areas, most notably religion. But let's not be too critical of the university/college environment, because, like university/college students, many adults later reopen the question of who they are if exposed to people or situations that challenge old viewpoints and offer new alternatives (Kroger, 1996).

Sociocultural Influences

Finally, identity formation is strongly influenced by the broader social and historical context in which it occurs—a point that Erikson himself emphasized. In fact, the very idea that adolescents should choose a personal identity after carefully exploring many options may well be peculiar to industrialized societies of the 20th century (Cote & Levine, 1988). As in past centuries, adolescents in many nonindustrialized societies today simply adopt the adult roles they are expected to adopt, without any soul-searching or experimentation: Children of farmers become farmers, children of fishers become (or perhaps marry) fishers, and so on. For many of the world's adolescents, then, what Marcia calls identity foreclosure is probably the most adaptive route to adulthood.

In sum, Western societies permit and expect adolescents to raise serious questions about the self and to answer them. And Erikson was right in claiming that the individual who achieves identity, regardless of the society in which he or she lives, is likely to be better off for it. Although Erikson recognized that identity issues can and do crop up later in life, even for people who forge positive identities as adolescents, he quite rightly identified adolescence as the key time of life for defining who we are (and will likely become).

✔ Concept Check 12.2
Establishing an Achievement Orientation and a Personal Identity

Check your understanding of identity formation and the development of achievement orientations by matching each descriptive statement below to one of the following concepts: (a) strong parental criticism of failures, (b) process-oriented praise, (c) negative peer influences, (d) stability of achievement attributions, (e) person praise, (f) children with a mastery orientation, (g) children with a learned-helplessness orientation, (h) identity crisis, (i) identity foreclosure, (j) identity diffusion, (k) identity achievement. Answers appear in the Appendix.

_____ 1. thought to be an adaptive route to identity formation in nonindustrialized societies

_____ 2. strong contributor to academic underachievement among disadvantaged minorities

_____ 3. attribute successes to high ability and failures to lack of effort

_____ 4. adolescents displaying this status often feel distant from their parents

_____ 5. attribute successes to high effort (or luck) and failures to lack of ability

_____ 6. solid mastery of formal operations promotes this status

_____ 7. correlate of low achievement motivation

_____ 8. predictor of future achievement expectancies

_____ 9. likely to promote adoption of learning goals (and a mastery orientation)

_____ 10. likely to promote adoption of performance goals (and a helpless orientation)

_____ 11. Erikson's use of this term overstates the case for most adolescents

THE OTHER SIDE OF SOCIAL COGNITION: KNOWING ABOUT OTHERS

Being appropriately social requires us to interact with other people, and these interactions are more likely to be harmonious if we know what our social partners are thinking or feeling and can predict how they are likely to behave (Heyman & Gelman, 1998). Children's development of a *belief-desire theory of mind* between ages 3 and 4 is a crucial step in understanding and appreciating the beliefs, motives, and intentions that underlie human behaviour. But their knowledge about other people—their descriptions of others' characteristics and the inferences they make about their companions' feelings, thoughts, and actions—become much more accurate with age (Bartsch & London, 2000; Flavell & Miller, 1998). What kinds of information do children use to form impressions of others? How do these impressions change over time? And what skills do children acquire that might explain such changes in person perception? These are the issues that we will now explore.

Age Trends in Person Perception

Children younger than 7 or 8 are likely to characterize people they know in the same concrete, observable terms that they use to describe the self (Livesley & Bromley, 1973; Ruble & Dweck, 1995). (See Box 12.5.) Five-year-old Chloë, for example, said, "My daddy is big. He has hairy legs and eats mustard. Yuck! My daddy likes dogs—do you?" Not much of a personality profile there! When young children do use a psychological term to describe others, it is typically a very general attribute such as "He's *nice*" or "She's *mean*" that they may use more as a label for the other person's recent behaviour than as a description of the person's enduring qualities (Rholes & Ruble, 1984; Ruble & Dweck, 1995).

It's not that preschoolers have *no* appreciation for the inner qualities that people display. As we noted earlier in the chapter, even 18-month-olds imitate the purposeful acts of humans but not of mechanical toys, thus reflecting an awareness that human behaviours are guided by intentions (Meltzoff, 1995a). By age 3 to 5, children are aware of how their closest peer companions typically behave in a variety of situations (Eder, 1989). And kindergartners already know that their classmates differ in academic competencies and social skills; furthermore, they reliably choose the smart ones as teammates for academic competitions and the socially skilled classmates as partners for play activities (Droege & Stipek, 1993). Not only are 5- to 6-year-olds becoming more aware of *behavioural consistencies* that their companions display, they are also beginning to make other kinds of trait-like inferences based on their emerging understanding of such subjective mental states as desires and motives that might *explain* other people's conduct. For example, 5-year-olds who hear stories about a child who has often shared and a second child who rarely shares can correctly infer that the first child will be *motivated* to share in the future and is generous (as opposed to selfish), whereas the second child will be *unmotivated* to share and is selfish (Yuill & Pearson, 1998). Thus, 5-year-olds assume that individual differences in past behaviours imply different motives and different traits. What's more, even 4-year-olds have some appreciation of traitlike labels and can use them to make appropriate psychological inferences. When told that a boy is shy, for example, they know that he would prefer to use the swimming pool when there are few people around and would be upset rather than pleased on encountering a lot of people there (Heyman & Gelman, 1999).

If 4- to 6-year-olds are capable of thinking about traits in psychologically meaningful ways, why do they use so few trait words to describe their companions? Probably because (1) they are less likely than older children to view traits as stable over time, thinking that they are subject to change (Heyman & Dweck, 1998), and (2) they are still using trait labels as adjectives to describe recent behaviours (e.g., "That was *mean*, Billy!") without fully understanding how to weave their emerging knowledge of traits into their everyday speech.

DEVELOPMENTAL ISSUES

12.5

Ethnic Categorization and Prejudice in Young Children

Because toddlers and preschool children tend to define others in terms of their observable characteristics and to place people into categories, it may come as no surprise to learn that even 3- and 4-year-olds have formed ethnic categories and can apply labels such as *Black* and *White* to different people or to photos of Blacks and Whites. Furthermore, studies conducted in Canada, Australia, and the United States reveal that by age 5, most White children have some knowledge of ethnic stereotypes (Bigler & Liben, 1993) and, according to Anna Beth Doyle of Concordia University and Frances Aboud of McGill University (1995), display at least some prejudicial attitudes toward Black people and Native Americans (see also Black-Gutman & Hickson, 1996).

Interestingly, parents often believe that their own children are largely oblivious to ethnic diversity, and that prejudicial attitudes and behaviours in other children arise when their bigoted parents pass their own intolerant views to them (Burnette, 1997). However, research suggests otherwise, because the ethnic attitudes of young children often bear little relation to those of their parents or their friends (Aboud, 1988; Burnette, 1997). So the origins of ethnic prejudice may be more *cognitive* than social, reflecting the tendency of egocentric youngsters to rigidly categorize people by skin colour (and other physical correlates of ethnicity) and to favour the group to which they belong.

As children enter concrete operations and become more flexible in their thinking, prejudicial attitudes often decline in strength. Doyle and Aboud (1995) found that the increased tolerance of 8- to 9-year-olds reflects their more realistic evaluation of ethnic groups, in which out-groups are viewed more favourably and their own group somewhat less favourably than was true during the preschool years. Nevertheless, social forces can obviously play a role in maintaining or even intensifying ethnic prejudice. Daisa Black-Gutman and Fay Hickson (1996) found that Euro-Australian children's prejudice toward Black Aborigines declined between ages 5 and 9, and then intensified at age 10 to 12, returning to the high levels displayed by 5- to 6-year-olds! Since the 10- to 12-year-olds were no longer constrained by the egocentrism and rigid categorization schemes of a 5- or 6-year-old, their increased prejudice apparently reflected the influence of adult attitudes—namely, the deep-seated animosity that many Euro-Australians feel toward Black Aborigines.

Of course, not all 10- to 12-year-olds show an intensification of stereotyping and prejudice. Sheri Levy and Carol Dweck (1999) recently found that children with an *entity view of personality*—those who believe most strongly that one's personality traits are stable or unchangeable—are the ones who are most inclined to endorse negative stereotypes about other groups. These children are quick to (1) blame the individual rather than situational factors for negative behaviours and (2) generalize these personal characteristics to all other members

of that individual's group. So the same entity perspective on human behaviour that fosters maladaptive achievement orientations is also implicated in the perpetuation and intensification of stereotyping and prejudice in middle childhood.

Developmentalists now believe that the best way to combat racism is for parents and teachers to talk openly about ethnic diversity, ideally beginning in the preschool period when prejudicial attitudes often take root (Burnette, 1997). One especially promising program in the public schools of western Massachusetts takes a three-pronged approach:

1. *Teacher training.* Teachers receive a four-month course that defines ethnic prejudice, explores how educators and children display it, and provides guidance for handling it at school.

2. *Youth groups.* Children of different ethnicities first meet for seven weeks with ethnic peers to discuss the values and traditions of their own subcultures. Then participants meet for seven more weeks in mixed-ethnicity groups to discuss their different perspectives and to devise strategies for getting along.

3. *Parent groups.* Once a month, parents of program participants attend classes to learn more about ethnic prejudice and about how to comfortably discuss diversity issues with their children.

This program is based on the proposition that the key to combatting ethnic prejudice is to be honest about it with children rather than shunning the topic or trying to cover it up. As developmentalist Vonnie McLoyd (cited in Burnette, 1997, p. 33) has noted, "Racism is so deeply rooted that [overcoming it] is going to take hard work by open, honest, fair-minded people who are not easily discouraged."

Mixed-ethnicity discussion groups can foster an appreciation of diverse subcultural traditions and combat the formation of prejudicial attitudes.

Between ages 7 and 16, children come to rely less and less on concrete attributes and more on psychological descriptors to characterize their friends and acquaintances. These changes are nicely illustrated in a program of research by Carl Barenboim (1981), who asked 6- to 11-year-olds to describe three people they knew well. Rather than simply listing the behaviours that close companions displayed, 6- to 8-year-olds often *compared* others on noteworthy behavioural dimensions, making such statements as "Narina *runs faster* than Jason" or "He *draws the best* pictures in our whole class." As shown in Figure 12.8, use of these **behavioural comparisons** increased between ages 6 and 8 and declined rapidly after age 9. One outgrowth of the behavioural comparison process is that children become increasingly aware of regularities in a companion's behaviour and eventually begin to attribute them to stable **psychological constructs**, or traits, that the person is now presumed to have. So a 10-year-old who formerly described one of her acquaintances as drawing better than anyone in her class may now convey the same impression by saying that the acquaintance is "very artistic." Notice in reexamining the figure that children's use of these psychological constructs increased rapidly between ages 8 and 11, the same period when behavioural comparisons became less common. Eventually, children begin to compare and contrast others on important psychological *dimensions*, making statements such as "Azim is more shy than Ted" or "Adrienne is the most artistic person in our class." Although few 11-year-olds generate these **psychological comparisons** when describing others (see Figure 12.8), the majority of 12- to 16-year-olds in Barenboim's second study actively compared their associates on noteworthy psychological dimensions.

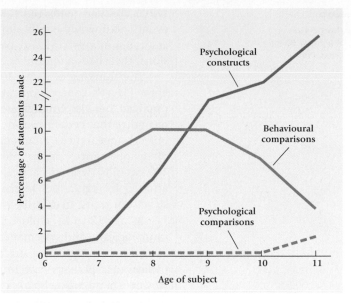

Figure 12.8 *Percentages of descriptive statements classified as behavioural comparisons, psychological (traitlike) constructs, and psychological comparisons for children between the ages of 6 and 11.* FROM BARENBOIM, 1981.

By age 14 to 16, adolescents are not only aware of the *dispositional* similarities and dissimilarities that characterize their acquaintances, but they are also beginning to recognize that any number of *situational* factors (e.g., illness, family strife) can cause a person to act "out of character" (Damon & Hart, 1988). So, by midadolescence, young people are becoming sophisticated "personality theorists" who are able to look both inside and outside a companion to explain her conduct and form coherent impressions of her character.

Why do children progress from behavioural comparisons to psychological constructs to psychological comparisons? Why do their own self-concepts and their impressions of others become increasingly abstract and coherent over time? In addressing these issues, we will first examine two cognitive points of view before considering how social forces might contribute, both directly and indirectly, to the growth of social cognition.

Theories of Social-Cognitive Development

Cognitive Theories of Social Cognition

The two cognitive theories that are most often used to explain developmental trends in social cognition are Piaget's cognitive-developmental approach and Robert Selman's role-taking analysis.

COGNITIVE-DEVELOPMENTAL THEORY. According to cognitive-developmental theorists, the ways that children think about the self and other people largely depend on their own levels of cognitive development. Recall that the thinking of 3- to 6-year-old preopera-

behavioural comparisons phase tendency to form impressions of others by comparing and contrasting their overt behaviours

psychological constructs phase tendency to base one's impressions of others on the stable traits that these individuals are presumed to have

psychological comparisons phase tendency to form impressions of others by comparing and contrasting these individuals on abstract psychological dimensions tional children tends to centre on the most salient perceptual aspects of stimuli and events. So it would hardly surprise a Piagetian to find that 3- to 6-year-olds describe their associates in very concrete, observable terms, mentioning their appearances and possessions, their likes and dislikes, and the actions that they can perform.

The thinking of 7- to 10-year-olds will change in many ways as these youngsters enter Piaget's concrete-operational stage. Not only is egocentrism becoming less pronounced, but also children are now *decentring* from perceptual illusions and beginning to recognize that certain properties of an object remain unchanged despite changes in the object's appearance (*conservation*). Clearly, these emerging abilities to look beyond immediate appearances and to infer underlying invariances might help to explain why 7- to 10-year-olds, who are actively comparing themselves with their peers, become more attuned to regularities in their own and others' conduct and use psychological constructs, or traits, to describe these patterns.

By age 12 to 14, children are entering formal operations and are now able to think more logically and systematically about abstractions. Although the concept of a psychological trait is itself an abstraction, it is one based on regularities in concrete, observable behaviours, perhaps explaining why *concrete* operators can think in these terms. However, a trait *dimension* is even more of a mental inference or abstraction that has few if any concrete referents. Thus, the ability to think in dimensional terms and to reliably order people along these continua (as is necessary in making psychological comparisons) implies that a person is able to operate on abstract concepts—a formal-operational ability (O'Mahoney, 1989).

Although children begin to make behavioural comparisons at ages 6 to 8 and psychological comparisons at age 12—precisely the times that Piaget's theory implies that they should—Robert Selman (1980) believes that one particular aspect of cognitive development underlies a mature understanding of the self and other people: the growth of **role-taking** skills.

SELMAN'S ROLE-TAKING THEORY. According to Selman (1980; Yeates & Selman, 1989), children gain much richer understandings of themselves and other people as they acquire the ability to discriminate their own perspectives from those of their companions and to see the relationships between these potentially discrepant points of view. Simply stated, Selman believes that in order to know a person, one must be able to assume his perspective and understand his thoughts, feelings, motives, and intentions—in short, the *internal* factors that account for his behaviour. If a child has not yet acquired these important role-taking skills, she may have little choice but to describe her acquaintances in terms of their external attributes—that is, their appearance, their activities, and the things they possess.

Selman has studied the development of role-taking skills by asking children to comment on a number of interpersonal dilemmas. Here is one example (from Selman, 1976, p. 302):

> Holly is an 8-year-old girl who likes to climb trees. She is the best tree climber in the neighborhood. One day while climbing down from a tall tree, she falls … but does not hurt herself. Her father sees her fall. He is upset and asks her to promise not to climb trees any more. Holly promises.

> Later that day, Holly and her friends meet Shawn. Shawn's kitten is caught in a tree and can't get down. Something has to be done right away or the kitten may fall. Holly is the only one who climbs trees well enough to reach the kitten and get it down but she remembers her promise to her father.

To assess how well a child understands the perspectives of Holly, her father, and Shawn, Selman asks: Does Holly know how Shawn feels about the kitten? How will Holly's father feel if he finds out she climbed the tree? What does Holly think her father will do if he finds out she climbed the tree? What would you do? Children's responses to these probes led Selman to conclude that role-taking skills develop in a stagelike manner, as shown in Table 12.3.

role taking
ability to assume another person's perspective and understand his or her thoughts, feelings, and behaviours

TABLE 12.3 Selman's Stages of Social Perspective Taking

Stage of role taking	Typical responses to the "Holly" dilemma
0. Egocentric or undifferentiated perspective (roughly 3–6 years) Children are unaware of any perspective other than their own. They assume that whatever they feel is right for Holly to do will be agreed on by others.	Children often assume that Holly will save the kitten. When asked how Holly's father will react to her transgression, these children think he will be "happy because he likes kittens." In other words, these children like kittens themselves, and they assume that Holly and her father also like kittens.
1. Social-informational role taking (roughly 6–8 years) Children now recognize that people have perspectives that differ from their own but believe that this happens *only* because these individuals have received different information.	When asked whether Holly's father will be angry because she climbed the tree, the child may say, "If he didn't know why she climbed the tree, he would be angry. But if he knew why she did it, he would realize that she had a good reason."
2. Self-reflective role taking (roughly 8–10 years) Children now know that their own and others' points of view may conflict even if they have received the same information. They are now able to consider the other person's viewpoint. They also recognize that the other person can put himself in their shoes, so that they are now able to anticipate the person's reactions to their behaviour. However, the child cannot consider her own perspective and that of another person at the same time.	If asked whether Holly will climb the tree, the child might say, "Yes. She knows that her father will understand why she did it." In doing so, the child is focusing on the father's consideration of Holly's perspective. But if asked whether the father would want Holly to climb the tree, the child usually says "No," thereby indicating that he is now assuming the father's perspective and considering the father's concern for Holly's safety.
3. Mutual role taking (roughly 10–12 years) The child can now simultaneously consider her own and another person's points of view and recognize that the other person can do the same. The child can also assume the perspective of a disinterested third party and anticipate how each participant (self and other) will react to the viewpoint of his or her partner.	At this stage, a child might describe the outcome of the "Holly" dilemma by taking the perspective of a disinterested third party and indicating that she knows that both Holly and her father are thinking about what each other is thinking. For example, one child remarked: "Holly wanted to get the kitten because she likes kittens, but she knew that she wasn't supposed to climb trees. Holly's father knew that Holly had been told not to climb trees, but he couldn't have known about [the kitten]."
4. Societal role taking (roughly 12–15 years and older) The adolescent now attempts to understand another person's perspective by comparing it with that of the social system in which he operates (that is, the view of the "generalized other"). In other words, the adolescent expects others to consider and typically assume perspectives on events that most people in their social group would take.	When asked if Holly should be punished for climbing the tree, the stage 4 adolescent is likely to say "No" and claim that the value of humane treatment of animals justifies Holly's act and that most fathers would recognize this point.

SOURCE: Adapted from Selman, 1976.

Notice in examining the table that children progress from largely egocentric beings, who may be unaware of any perspective other than their own (stage 0), to sophisticated social-cognitive theorists, who can keep several perspectives in mind and compare each with the viewpoint that "most people" would adopt (stage 4). Apparently, these role-taking skills represent a true developmental sequence, because 40 of 41 boys who were repeatedly tested over a five-year period showed a steady forward progression from stage to stage, with no skipping of stages (Gurucharri & Selman, 1982). Perhaps the reason that they develop in one particular order is that they are closely related to Piaget's invariant sequence of cognitive stages (Keating & Clark, 1980): Preoperational children are at Selman's first or second level of role taking (stage 0 or 1), whereas most concrete operators are at the third or fourth level (stage 2 or 3), and formal operators are about equally distributed between the fourth and fifth levels of role taking (stages 3 and 4).

ROLE-TAKING AND THINKING ABOUT RELATIONSHIPS. As children acquire role-taking skills, their understanding of the meaning and character of human relationships begins to change. Consider what children of different ages say about the meaning of *friendship.*

Preschoolers at Selman's egocentric (level 0) stage think that virtually any pleasant interactions between themselves and available playmates qualify those playmates as "friends." So 5-year-old Chang might describe Brian as a close friend simply because "He lives next door and plays games with me" (Damon, 1977).

Common activity continues to be the principal basis for friendship among 6- to 8-year-olds (Hartup, 1992). But because these youngsters have reached Selman's stage 1 and recognize that others may not always share their perspectives, they begin to view a friend as someone who *chooses* to "do nice things for me." Friendships are often one-way at this stage, for the child feels no strong pressure to reciprocate these considerations. And should a friend fail to serve the child's interests (for example, by spurning an invitation to camp out in the backyard), she may quickly become a nonfriend.

Later, at Selman's stage 2, 8- to 10-year-olds show increasing concern for the needs of a friend and begin to see friendships as reciprocal relationships, based on *mutual trust*, in which two people exchange respect, kindness, and affection (Selman, 1980). No longer are common activities sufficient to brand someone a friend; as children appreciate how their own interests and perspectives and those of their peers can be similar or different, they insist that their friends be *psychologically* similar to themselves.

By early adolescence, many children have reached Selman's stage 3 or 4. Although they still view friends as psychologically similar people who like, trust, and assist each other, they have expanded their notions of the obligations of friendship to emphasize the exchange of intimate thoughts and feelings (Berndt & Perry, 1990). They increasingly expect their friends to stick up for them and be *loyal*, standing ready to provide close emotional support whenever they may need it (Berndt & Perry, 1990; Buhrmester, 1990).

So, with the growth of role-taking skills, children's conceptions of friendship gradually change from the one-sided, self-centred view of friends as "people who benefit me" to a harmonious, reciprocal perspective in which each party truly understands the other, enjoys providing him or her with emotional support and other niceties, and expects these same considerations in return. Perhaps because they rest on a firmer basis of intimacy and interpersonal understanding, the close friendships of older children and adolescents are viewed as more important and are more stable, or long-lasting, than those of younger children (Berndt, 1989; Berndt & Hoyle, 1985; Furman & Buhrmester, 1992).

Table 12.4 briefly summarizes the changes in thinking about the self and others that we have discussed—changes that are clearly influenced by cognitive development. Yet, as we will see in concluding the chapter, the growth of *social* cognition is also heavily influenced by *social* interactions and experiences that children and adolescents have had.

Social Influences on Social-Cognitive Development

Many developmentalists have wondered whether the growth of children's self-awareness and their understanding of other people are as closely tied to cognitive development as cognitive theorists have assumed. Consider, for example, that even though children's role-taking abilities are related to their performances on Piagetian measures and IQ tests (Pellegrini, 1985), it is quite possible for a child to grow less egocentric and to mature intellectually without becoming an especially skillful role taker (Shantz, 1983). So other, *noncognitive* factors must contribute to the growth of role-taking skills and may even exert their own unique effects on children's social-cognitive development. Might social experiences play such a role? No less an authority than Jean Piaget thought so.

Disagreements among peers are important contributors to role-taking skills and the growth of interpersonal understanding.

TABLE 12.4   Milestones in the Development of Self and Social Cognition

Age (years)	Self-concept/Self-esteem	Self-control	Social cognition
0–1	Differentiation of self from the external environment Sense of personal agency emerges		Discriminates familiar from unfamiliar people Prefers familiar companions (attachment objects)
1–2	Self-recognition emerges Categorical self develops	Compliance emerges	Recognizes that others act on intentions Categorizes others on socially significant dimensions
3–5	Self-concept emphasizes actions Evaluation of accomplishments emerge Undifferentiated self-esteem emerges Belief-desire theory of mind and private self appear Achievement attributions reflect incremental view of ability	Compliance improves Can use adult-generated strategies to self-regulate and delay gratification	Impressions are based on other's actions and concrete attributes Knowledge of racial stereotypes and prejudicial attitudes emerge Friendships are based on shared activities
6–10	Self-concepts come to emphasize personality traits Self-esteem is based on one's academic, physical, and social competencies Achievement attributions progress toward an entity view of ability	Self-generated strategies for self-control appear Begins to value self-regulation/self-control	Impressions come to be based on the traits others display (psychological constructs) Prejudicial attitudes often decline in strength Friendships are based largely on psychological similarities and mutual trust
11 and beyond	Friendships, romantic appeal, and job competence become important to one's self-esteem Self-concepts now reflect one's values and ideologies and become more integrated and abstract Identity is achieved	Generates abstract strategies to regulate conduct and defer gratification Internalizes norms that stress the value of self-control	Impressions are now based on others' dispositional similarities and dissimilarities (psychological comparisons) Prejudicial attitudes may decline or intensify, depending on social influences Friendships are based on loyalty and sharing of intimacies

SOCIAL EXPERIENCE AS A CONTRIBUTOR TO ROLE TAKING. Many years ago, Piaget (1965) argued that playful interactions among elementary-school children promote the development of role-taking skills and mature social judgments. Piaget's view was that, by assuming different roles while playing together, young children become more aware of discrepancies between their own perspectives and those of their playmates. When conflicts arise in play, children must learn to coordinate their points of view with those of their companions (that is, compromise) in order for play to continue. So Piaget assumed that *equal-status contacts among peers* are an especially important contributor to social perspective taking and the growth of interpersonal understanding.

Not only has research consistently supported Piaget's viewpoint, but it also appears that some forms of peer contact may be better than others at fostering the growth of interpersonal understanding. Specifically, Janice Nelson and Francis Aboud (1985) of McGill University propose that disagreements among *friends* are particularly important because children tend to be more open and honest with their friends than with mere acquaintances and are more motivated to resolve disputes with friends. As a result, disagreeing friends should be more likely than disagreeing acquaintances to provide each other with the information needed to understand and appreciate their conflicting points of view. Indeed, when 8- to 10-year-olds discuss an interpersonal issue on which they disagree, pairs of friends are much more critical of their partners than pairs of acquaintances are, but friends are also more likely to fully explain the rationales for their own points of view. Furthermore, disagreeing friends display increases in social understanding after these discussions are over, whereas disagreeing acquaintances do not (Nelson & Aboud, 1985). So it seems that equal-status contacts among friends may be especially important for the growth of role-taking skills and interpersonal understanding.

SOCIAL EXPERIENCE AS A DIRECT CONTRIBUTOR TO PERSON PERCEPTION. Social contacts with peers not only contribute *indirectly* to person perception by fostering the development of role-taking skills, but they are also a form of *direct experience* by which children can learn what others are like. In other words, the more experience a child has with peers, the more *motivated* she should be to try to understand them and the more *practised* she should become at appraising the causes of their behaviour (Higgins & Parsons, 1983).

Popularity is a convenient measure of social experience; that is, according to Lucy LeMare of Simon Fraser University and Kenneth Rubin from University of Maryland (1987), popular children interact more often with a wider variety of peers than do their less popular age-mates. So, if the amount of direct experience that a child has with peers exerts its own unique influence on his or her social-cognitive judgments, then popular children should outperform less popular age-mates on tests of social understanding, *even when their role-taking skills are comparable*. This is precisely what Jackie Gnepp (1989) found when she tested the ability of popular and less popular 8-year-olds to make appropriate traitlike inferences about an unfamiliar child from a small sample of the child's previous behaviours. So it seems that both social experience (as indexed by popularity) and cognitive competence (role-taking skills) contribute in their own ways to the development of children's understanding of other people. Apparently, Cooley (1902) and Mead (1934) were quite correct in suggesting that social cognition and social experience are completely intertwined—that they develop together and are reciprocally related, and that neither can progress very far without the other.

✔ **Concept Check 12.3**
Understanding Social Cognition

Check your understanding of the growth of social-cognitive abilities by matching each descriptive statement below with one of the following terms: (a) loyalty/sharing of intimacies, (b) common activities, (c) psychological similarities, (d) entity perspective on personality; (e) role-taking skills, (f) behavioural comparisons, (g) belief-desire theory of mind; (h) psychological constructs, (i) psychological comparisons, (j) social experiences with peers. Answers appear in the Appendix.

_____ 1. principal basis for friendships among 9- to 12-year-olds

_____ 2. impressions derived by noting and comparing the *actions* of one's associates

_____ 3. principal basis for friendships among adolescents

_____ 4. impressions based on the *traits* that others are presumed to have

_____ 5. major contributor to children's thinking about the meaning of friendships

_____ 6. principal basis for friendship among 3- to 7-year-olds

_____ 7. contribute in two ways to the growth of social cognition

_____ 8. impressions stemming from dispositional similarities/ dissimilarities that others display

_____ 9. early cognitive prerequisite for understanding others' beliefs, motives, and intentions

_____ 10. associated with negative stereotyping and prejudicial attitudes

---

SUMMARY

◆ The **self** is thought to arise from social interactions and to largely reflect other people's reactions to us (that is, a **looking-glass self**). The development of **social cognition** deals with how children's understanding of the self and other people changes with age.

Development of the Self-Concept

◆ Most developmentalists believe that infants are born without a **self-concept** and gradually come to distinguish themselves from the external environment over the first two to six months of life, as they gain a sense of personal agency and learn (from their experiences before mirrors) to discriminate their faces from those of other people.

- By 18 to 24 months of age, toddlers display true **self-recognition**—a milestone that depends on cognitive development and social experiences with companions. Initial self-recognition provides evidence for toddlers' conception of a **present self**, which gradually evolves into a conception of **extended self**, or a self that is stable over time. Toddlers also classify themselves along socially significant dimensions such as age and sex, forming a **categorical self.**

- Although preschool children know how they typically behave in many situations and can classify themselves along psychological dimensions if asked to do so in ways that do not tax their verbal skills, the self-descriptions of 3- to 5-year-olds are typically very concrete, focusing mostly on their physical features and possessions and the activities they can perform.

- Between ages 3 and 4, children's **theory of mind** progresses from a **desire theory** to a **belief-desire theory** that more closely resembles adults' conception of how the mind works. Once children achieve this milestone, which is fostered by pretend play and conversations about mental states with siblings and adults, they more clearly distinguish their **private self** from their **public self** and are better prepared to make meaningful psychological inferences about their own and others' behaviour.

- By about age 8, children begin to describe themselves in terms of their inner and enduring psychological attributes. Adolescents have an even more integrated and abstract self-concept that includes not only their dispositional qualities (i.e., traits, beliefs, attitudes, and values) but also a knowledge of how these characteristics might interact with one another and with situational influences to affect their behaviour. However, frequent displays of **false-self behaviours** can leave adolescents confused about who they really are.

- Core aspects of self-concept tend to be personal characteristics among people in **individualistic societies** but social or relational attributes among people in **collectivist (or communal) societies**.

Self-Esteem: The Evaluative Component of Self

- **Self-esteem**, the judgments we make about our self-worth, begins to take shape early in life as infants form positive or negative working models of self from their interactions with caregivers. By age 8, children's self-evaluations become more accurate reflections of how others would evaluate their behavioural and social competencies. In adolescence, feelings of **relational self-worth** and romantic appeal and quality of close friendships also become important contributors to global self-esteem. Except for a temporary decline that some children experience with the transition to junior high school, self-esteem is reasonably stable over time and often increases throughout adolescence, particularly for boys.

- Warm, responsive, democratic parenting fosters self-esteem, whereas aloof or controlling parenting styles seem to undermine it. Peers influence one another's self-esteem through **social comparison** during the elementary-school years. For adolescents, some of the strongest determinants of self-worth are the quality of one's relationships with peers, particularly with close friends and prospective romantic partners.

Development of Achievement Motivation and Academic Self-Concept

- Although all infants display an inborn **mastery motive**, children come to differ in **achievement motivation**—their willingness to strive for success and to master new challenges (**mastery motivation**). Infants who are securely attached to responsive caregivers who provide them with a stimulating home environment are likely to become curious nursery-school children who will later do well at school. Parents may also foster the development of achievement motivation by encouraging their children to do things on their own and to do them well, and by reinforcing a child's successes without becoming overly distressed about an occasional failure. Parents who combine all of these practices into one parenting style (**authoritative parenting**) tend to raise children who seek challenges and achieve considerable academic success. However, peers may either foster or undermine parents' efforts to encourage academic achievement.

- Academic self-concepts also depend very heavily on children's **achievement attributions**. **Mastery-oriented** children and adolescents have very positive achievement expectancies. They attribute their successes to stable, internal causes (such as high ability) and their failures to unstable causes (lack of effort), and they adopt an **incremental view of ability**; consequently, they feel quite competent and will work hard to overcome failures. By contrast, **helpless children** often stop trying after a failure because they display an **entity view of ability** and attribute their failures to a lack of ability that they feel they can do little about. Children who are often criticized for their lack of ability and who feel pressured to adopt **performance goals** rather than **learning goals** are at risk of becoming helpless. Helpless children can become more mastery-oriented if they are taught (through **attribution retraining**) that their failures can and often should be attributed to unstable causes, such as a lack of effort, that they can overcome by trying harder.

Who Am I to Be? Forging an Identity

- One of the more challenging tasks of adolescence is that of resolving one's **identity crisis** and forming a stable **identity** (or identities) with which to embrace the responsibilities of young adulthood. From the **diffusion** and **foreclosure** statuses, many university/college-age youths progress to the **moratorium** status (where they are experimenting to find an identity) and ultimately to **identity achievement**. Identity formation is an uneven process that often continues well into adulthood.

- The process of seeking an identity is a lot less crisislike than Erik Erikson assumed. Identity achievement and moratorium are psychologically healthy statuses. If there is a crisis, it is a long-term failure to form an identity, because adolescents stuck in the diffusion status often assume a *negative identity* and display poor psychological adjustment.

- Healthy identity outcomes are fostered by cognitive development; by warm, supportive parents who encourage individual self-expression; and by a culture that permits and expects adolescents to find their own niches. For minority youth, achieving a positive *ethnic identity* fosters healthy identity outcomes.

The Other Side of Social Cognition: Knowing about Others

◆ Although children younger than 7 or 8 are not oblivious to other people's inner qualities and can make some accurate and appropriate traitlike inferences, they generally describe friends and acquaintances in the same concrete observable terms that they use to describe the self. As they compare themselves and others on noteworthy behavioural dimensions, elementary-school children become more attuned to regularities in their own and others' conduct (**behavioural comparisons phase**) and begin to rely on stable psychological constructs, or traits, to describe these patterns (**psychological constructs phase**). Young adolescents' impressions of others become even more abstract as they begin to make **psychological comparisons** among their friends and acquaintances. And by age 14 to 16, adolescents are becoming sophisticated personality theorists who know that any number of situational influences can cause a person to act out of character.

◆ The growth of children's social-cognitive abilities is related to cognitive development in general and to the emergence of **role-taking** skills in particular: To truly know a person, one must be able to assume her perspective and understand her thoughts, feelings, motives, and intentions. However, *social interactions*—particularly equal-status contacts with friends and peers—are crucial to social-cognitive development. They contribute indirectly by fostering the growth of role-taking skills and more directly by providing the experiences children need to learn what others are like.

KEY TERMS

self, 435

looking-glass self, 435

social cognition, 435

self-concept, 435

proprioceptive feedback, 436

personal agency, 436

self-recognition, 437

present self, 437

extended self, 437

categorical self, 438

public self (or me), 439

private self (or I), 439

theory of mind, 439

desire theory, 440

belief-desire theory, 441

false-belief task, 441

false-self behaviour, 444

individualistic society, 446

collectivistic (or communal society), 446

self-esteem, 446

relational self-worth, 448

social comparison, 450

achievement motivation, 451

mastery motivation, 451

intrinsic achievement orientation, 453

authoritative parenting, 454

achievement attributions, 455

achievement expectancy, 455

incremental view of ability, 456

entity view of ability, 456

mastery orientation, 457

learned-helplessness orientation, 457

attribution retraining, 458

person praise, 458

performance goal, 458

process-oriented praise, 459

learning goal, 459

identity, 459

identity crisis, 459

identity diffusion, 459

foreclosure, 459

moratorium, 460

identity achievement, 460

behavioural comparisons phase, 465

psychological constructs phase, 465

psychological comparisons phase, 465

role taking, 466

 You can find further information on the topics covered in this chapter by visiting:

www.developmentalpsych2e.nelson.com

 For additional reading, go to InfoTrac College Edition, your on-line research library, at:

infotrac.thomsonlearning.com

Sex Differences and Similarities, Gender-Role Development, and Sexual Behaviour

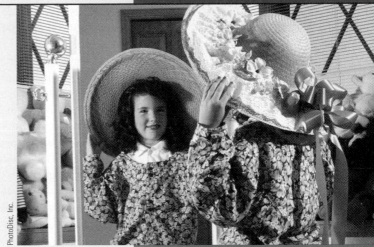

PhotoDisc, Inc.

How important is a child's gender to his or her development? Many people would say "Very important!" Often the first bit of information that parents receive about their child is his or her sex, and the question "Is it a boy or a girl?" is the very first one that most friends and relatives ask when proud new parents announce the birth of their baby (Intons-Peterson & Reddel, 1984). Indeed, the ramifications of this gender labelling are normally swift and direct. From day one, parents often call an infant son things like "big guy" or "tiger," and they are likely to comment on the vigour of his cries, kicks, or grasps. By contrast, infant daughters are more likely to be labelled "sugar" or "sweetie" and described as soft, cuddly, and adorable (Maccoby, 1980; MacFarlane, 1977). A newborn infant is usually blessed with a name that reflects his or her sex, and in many Western societies boys are immediately adorned in blue and girls in pink. Mavis Hetherington and Ross Parke (1975, pp. 354–5) describe the predicament of a developmental psychologist who did not want her observers to know whether they were watching boys or girls:

> Even in the first few days of life some infant girls were brought to the laboratory with pink bows tied to wisps of their hair or taped to their little bald heads.... When another attempt at concealment of sex was made by asking mothers to dress their infants in overalls, girls appeared in pink and boys in blue overalls, and "Would you believe overalls with ruffles?"

This gender indoctrination continues during the first year as parents and others provide their children with "gender-appropriate" clothing, toys, and hairstyles (Pomerleau et al., 1990). They also play differently with and expect different reactions from their young sons and daughters (Caldera, Huston, & O'Brien, 1989). So it is clear that a child's companions view gender as an important attribute that often determines how they respond to him or her.

Why do people react differently to males and females, especially *infant* males and females? One explanation centres on the biological differences between the sexes. Recall that fathers determine the sex of their offspring. A zygote that receives an X chromosome from each parent is a genetic (XX) female that develops into a baby girl, whereas a zygote that receives a Y chromosome

Categorizing Males and Females: Gender-Role Standards

Some Facts and Fictions about Sex Differences

Developmental Trends in Gender Typing

Theories of Gender Typing and Gender-Role Development

Psychological Androgyny: A Prescription for the Future?

Adolescent Sexuality

Summary

Tanny Strand

Sex-role socialization begins very early as parents provide their children with "gender-appropriate" clothing, toys, and hairstyles.

gender typing
process by which a child becomes aware of his or her gender and acquires motives, values, and behaviours considered appropriate for members of that sex

gender-role standard
behaviour, value, or motive that members of a society consider more typical or appropriate for members of one sex

expressive role
social prescription, usually directed toward females, that one should be cooperative, kind, nurturant, and sensitive to the needs of others

instrumental role
social prescription, usually directed toward males, that one should be dominant, independent, assertive, competitive, and goal-oriented

from the father is a genetic (XY) male that normally assumes the appearance of a baby boy. Could it be that this basic genetic difference between the sexes is ultimately responsible for *sex differences in behaviour* that might explain why parents often do not treat their sons and daughters alike? We will explore this interesting idea in some detail in a later section of the chapter.

However, there is more to sex differences than just biological heritage. Virtually all societies expect males and females to behave differently and to assume different roles. In order to conform to these expectations, the child must understand that he is a boy or that she is a girl and must incorporate this information into his or her self-concept. In this chapter, we will concentrate on the interesting and controversial topic of **gender typing**—the process by which children acquire not only a gender identity but also the motives, values, and behaviours considered appropriate in their culture for members of their biological sex.

We begin the chapter by summarizing what people generally believe to be true about sex differences in cognition, personality, and social behaviour. As it turns out, some of these beliefs have an element of truth to them, although many others are best described as fictions or fables that have no basis in fact. We will then look at developmental trends in gender typing and see that youngsters are often well aware of gender-role stereotypes and display gender-typed patterns of behaviour long before they are old enough to go to kindergarten. And how do children learn so much about the sexes and gender roles at such an early age? We will address this issue by reviewing several influential theories that specify how biological forces, social experiences, and cognitive development might combine or interact to influence the gender-typing process. And after examining a new perspective that asserts that traditional gender roles have outlived their usefulness in today's modern society, we will briefly consider how the constraining and potentially harmful effects of gender stereotypes might be reduced. Finally, we will end the chapter with a discussion on adolescent sexual activity.

CATEGORIZING MALES AND FEMALES: GENDER-ROLE STANDARDS

Most of us have learned a great deal about males and females by the time we enter university or college. In fact, if you and your classmates were asked to jot down 10 psychological dimensions on which men and women are thought to differ, it is likely that every member of the class could easily generate such a list. Here's a head start: Which gender is most likely to display emotions? to be tidy? to be competitive? to use harsh language?

A **gender-role standard** is a value, motive, or behaviour that is considered more appropriate for members of one sex than the other. Taken together, a society's gender-role standards describe how males and females are expected to behave and reflect the stereotypes by which we categorize and respond to members of each sex.

The female's role as childbearer is largely responsible for the gender-role standards and stereotypes that have prevailed in many societies, including our own. Girls have typically been encouraged to assume an **expressive role** that involves being kind, nurturant, cooperative, and sensitive to the needs of others (Parsons, 1955). These psychological traits, it was assumed, would prepare girls to play the wife and mother roles—to keep the family functioning and raise children successfully. By contrast, boys have been encouraged to adopt an **instrumental role**, because as a traditional husband and father a male would face the tasks of providing for the family and protecting it from harm. Thus, young boys are expected to become dominant, assertive, independent, and competitive. Similar norms and role prescriptions are found in many, though certainly not all, societies (Williams & Best, 1990). In one ambitious project, Herbert Barry, Margaret Bacon, and Irving Child (1957) analyzed the gender-typing practices of 110 nonindustrialized societies, looking for sex differences in the socialization of five attributes: nurturance, obedience, responsibility, achievement, and self-reliance. As shown in Table 13.1, achievement and self-reliance were more strongly encouraged in young boys, whereas young girls were encouraged to become nurturant, responsible, and obedient.

Children in modern industrialized societies also face strong gender-typing pressures, though not always to the same extent and in the same ways that children in nonindustrialized societies do. For example, parents in many Western societies put roughly equal emphasis on achievement for sons and for daughters (Lytton & Romney, 1991). Furthermore, the findings in Table 13.1 do not imply that self-reliance in girls is frowned on or that disobedience by young boys is acceptable. In fact, all five attributes that Barry et al. studied were encouraged in *both* boys and girls, but with different emphases on different attributes depending on the sex of the child (Zern, 1984). So it appears that the first goal of socialization is to encourage children to acquire those traits that will enable them to become well-behaved, contributing members of society. A second goal (but one that adults view as important nevertheless) is to "gender type" the child by stressing the importance of relationship-oriented (or expressive) attributes for girls and individualistic (or instrumental) attributes for boys.

Because cultural norms specify that girls should assume an expressive role and boys an instrumental role, we may be inclined to assume that girls and women actually display expressive traits and that boys and men possess instrumental traits (Broverman et al., 1972; Williams & Best, 1990). If you assume that these stereotypes have disappeared as attention to women's rights has increased and as more women have entered the labour force, think again. Although some change has occurred, adolescents and young adults still endorse many traditional stereotypes about men and women (Bergen & Williams, 1991; Twenge, 1997; and test yourself in Box 13.1). Might these beliefs about sex differences have any basis in fact? Let's see if they do.

SOME FACTS AND FICTIONS ABOUT SEX DIFFERENCES

The old French maxim "Vive la différence" reflects a fact we all know to be true: Males and females are anatomically different. Adult males are typically taller, heavier, and more muscular than adult females, while females may be hardier in the sense that they live longer. But although these physical variations are fairly obvious, the evidence for sex differences in psychological functioning is not as clear as most of us might think.

TABLE 13.1	**Sex Differences in the Socialization of Five Attributes in 110 Societies**	
	Percentage of societies in which socialization pressures were greater for:	
Attribute	**Boys**	**Girls**
Nurturance	0	82
Obedience	3	35
Responsibility	11	61
Achievement	87	3
Self-reliance	85	0

NOTE: The percentages for each attribute do not add up to 100 because some of the societies did not put differential pressures on boys and girls with respect to that attribute. For example, 18 percent of the societies for which pertinent data were available did not differentiate between the sexes in the socialization of nurturance.

SOURCE: Adapted from Barry, Bacon, & Child, 1957.

Actual Psychological Differences between the Sexes

In a classic review of more than 1500 studies comparing males and females, Eleanor Maccoby and Carol Jacklin (1974) concluded that few traditional gender stereotypes have any basis in fact. In fact, their review pointed to only four *small* but reliable differences between the sexes that were consistently supported by research. Here are their conclusions, with some updates and amendments.

Verbal Ability

Girls have greater verbal abilities than boys. Girls acquire language and develop verbal skills at an earlier age than boys and display a small but consistent verbal advantage on tests of reading comprehension and speech fluency throughout childhood and adolescence (Halpern, 1997; Hedges & Nowell, 1995).

Visual/Spatial Abilities

visual/spatial abilities
abilities to mentally manipulate or otherwise draw inferences about pictorial information

Boys outperform girls on tests of **visual/spatial abilities**—that is, the ability to draw inferences about or otherwise mentally manipulate pictorial information (see Figure 13.1 for two kinds of visual/spatial tasks on which sex differences have been found). The male advantage in spatial abilities is not large, although it is detectable by middle childhood and persists across the life span (Kerns & Berenbaum, 1991; Voyer, Voyer, & Bryden, 1995).

13.1 DEVELOPMENTAL ISSUES

What Traits Characterize Males and Females?

Several surveys have asked university students to respond to lists of various mannerisms and personal characteristics by saying which of these traits characterize the "typical" man or "typical" woman (or by judging which are clearly "masculine" or clearly "feminine" attributes). Although you may not agree with peer consensus, see if you can anticipate how students have responded by indicating whether each trait in the list below is more characteristic of men or of women. (The results of the survey are given at the bottom of the page.)

Trait	More characteristic of:	
	Men	**Women**
1. Active	____	____
2. Aware of others' feelings	____	____
3. Adventurous	____	____
4. Considerate	____	____
5. Aggressive	____	____
6. Creative	____	____
7. Ambitious	____	____
8. Cries easily	____	____
9. Competitive	____	____
10. Other-oriented	____	____
11. Dominant	____	____
12. Emotional	____	____

Trait	Men	Women
13. Independent	____	____
14. Artistic	____	____
15. Displays leadership	____	____
16. Excitable	____	____
17. Mathematical	____	____
18. Empathic	____	____
19. Makes decisions easily	____	____
20. Feelings hurt easily	____	____
21. Mechanical	____	____
22. Gentle	____	____
23. Outspoken	____	____
24. Kind	____	____
25. Persistent	____	____
26. Neat	____	____
27. Self-confident	____	____
28. Seeks approval	____	____
29. Skilled in business	____	____
30. Tactful	____	____
31. Takes a stand	____	____
32. Understanding	____	____

SOURCE OF TRAITS: Ruble, 1983.

Answers for Box 13.1: University students generally indicate that the even-numbered traits characterize women, whereas the odd-numbered ones are more characteristic of men.

Mathematical Ability

Beginning in adolescence, boys show a small but consistent advantage over girls on tests of *arithmetic reasoning* (Halpern, 1997; Hyde, Fennema, & Lamon, 1990; and see Figure 13.2). Girls actually exceed boys in computational skills, but boys have acquired more mathematical problem-solving strategies that enable them to outperform girls on complex word problems, geometry, and the mathematics section of the Scholastic Assessment Test (SAT) (Byrnes & Takahira, 1993; Casey, 1996). The male advantage in mathematical problem solving is most apparent among high math achievers; more males than females are exceptionally talented in math (Stumpf & Stanley, 1996). And it seems that sex differences in visual/spatial abilities and the problem-solving strategies they support contribute to sex differences in arithmetic reasoning (Casey, Nuttal, & Pezaris, 1997). However, researchers such as Jim Duffy at Memorial University of Newfoundland suggest that social forces also come into play (Duffy, Gunther, & Walters 1997; Walsh, Hickey, & Duffy, 1999). We will soon see that the messages boys and girls receive about these respective abilities can also influence their mathematical, verbal, and visual/spatial reasoning skills.

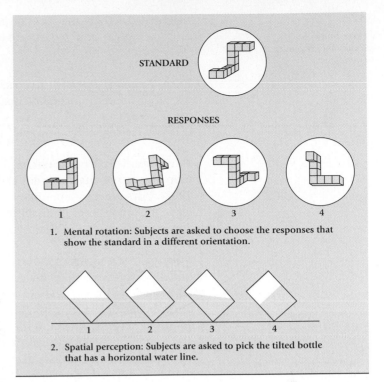

1. Mental rotation: Subjects are asked to choose the responses that show the standard in a different orientation.

2. Spatial perception: Subjects are asked to pick the tilted bottle that has a horizontal water line.

Figure 13.1 *Two spatial tasks for which sex differences in performance have been found.* FROM LINN & PETERSEN, 1985.

Aggression

Boys are more physically and verbally *aggressive* than girls, starting as early as age 2. Girls, however, are more likely than boys to display covert forms of hostility toward others by snubbing or ignoring them, or by trying to undermine their relationships or social status (Crick, Casas, & Mosher, 1997; Crick & Grotpeter, 1995). Throughout development, boys are more likely to engage in antisocial and violent behaviours than girls, and this is clearly evident in crime statistics. For example, male youths are identified as part of the increase in crimes from 1988 to 1998. These males showed increases in violent activity across development, peaking at age 17. Violence among females 14 to 15 years of age was fairly consistent across development (Statistics Canada, 1999f). Note that males are more often involved in serious acts of violence than their female counterparts both as youths and as adults (Correctional Service of Canada, 1995), and the number of males charged with violent crimes far exceeds the number of females charged. For example, for those charged with violent crimes in 1991, 88 percent were male and 12 percent were female (Correctional Service of Canada, 1995).

Other Possible Differences

Critics were quick to challenge Maccoby and Jacklin's review, claiming that the procedures they used to gather and tabulate their results led them to underestimate the number of sex differences that actually exist (Block, 1976; Huston, 1983). More recent research, which often combines the results of several studies and provides a better estimate of the reliability of sex-related differences, points to several additional sex differences in personality and social behaviour. For example:

ACTIVITY LEVEL. Even before they are born, boys are more physically active than girls (DiPietro et al., 1996), and they remain more active throughout childhood, especially when interacting with peers (Eaton & Enns, 1986; Eaton & Yu, 1989). In fact, the

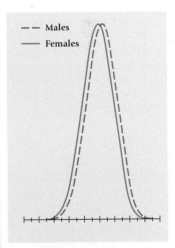

Figure 13.2 *These two distributions of scores—one for males, one for females—give some idea of the size of the gap between the sexes in abilities for which sex differences are consistently found. Despite a small difference in average performance, the scores of males and females overlap considerably.* ADAPTED FROM HYDE, FENNEMA, & LAMON, 1990.

heightened activity that boys display may help to explain why they are more likely than girls to initiate and be receptive to bouts of nonaggressive, rough-and-tumble play (Pellegrini & Smith, 1998).

FEAR, TIMIDITY, AND RISK TAKING. As early as the first year of life, girls appear to be more fearful or timid in uncertain situations than boys are. They are also more cautious and less assertive in these situations than boys are, taking far fewer risks than boys do (Christophersen, 1989; Feingold, 1994).

DEVELOPMENTAL VULNERABILITY. From conception, boys are more physically vulnerable than girls to prenatal and perinatal hazards and to the effects of disease (Raz et al., 1994; 1995). Boys are also more likely than girls to display a variety of developmental problems, including reading disabilities, speech defects, hyperactivity, emotional disorders, and mental retardation (Halpern, 1997; Henker & Whalen, 1989).

EMOTIONAL EXPRESSIVITY/SENSITIVITY. In some ways, females appear to be more emotionally expressive than males. Two-year-old girls are already using more emotion-related words than 2-year-old boys do (Cervantes & Callanan, 1998), and parents of preschoolers talk more with daughters than with sons about emotions and memorable emotional events (Kuebli, Butler, & Fivush, 1995; Reese & Fivush, 1993). Indeed, this social support for reflecting on their feelings may help to explain why girls and women characterize their emotions as deeper, or more intense, and feel freer to express them than boys and men do (Diener, Sandvik, & Larsen, 1985; Fuchs & Thelen, 1988; Saarni, 1999).

The evidence for sex differences in empathic sensitivities is mixed. Girls and women consistently *rate themselves* (and are described by others) as more nurturant and empathic than boys and men (Cohen & Strayer, 1996; Feingold, 1994). Yet boys often appear no

Rough-and-tumble play is more common among boys than among girls.

less empathic or compassionate than girls when studied in naturalistic settings (Fabes, Eisenberg, & Miller, 1990; Zahn-Waxler et al., 1992). For example, boys display at least as much affection toward and concern for the welfare of their pets and older relatives as girls do (Melson, Peet, & Sparks, 1991). Researchers such as Janet Strayer at Simon Fraser University have found that variables such as empathy, although evident in both males and females, may predict different social outcomes. For example, high levels of empathy in boys clearly predicts general prosocial behaviour, whereas for girls the relation between empathy and prosocial behaviours is restricted to friendship circles (Roberts & Strayer, 1996).

COMPLIANCE. From early in the preschool period, girls are more compliant than boys with the requests and demands of parents, teachers, and other authority figures (Feingold, 1994; Maccoby, 1998). And when trying to persuade others to comply with them, girls are more likely to rely on tact and polite suggestions; whereas boys, who are quite capable of and usually do collaborate amicably, are nevertheless more likely than girls to resort to demanding or controlling strategies (Leaper, Tennenbaum, & Shaffer, 1999; Strough & Berg, 2000).

In reviewing the evidence for "real" sex differences, we must keep in mind that the data reflect *group averages* that may or may not characterize the behaviour of any particular individual. For example, gender accounts for about 5 percent of the variation that children display in aggressive behaviour (Hyde, 1984), so the remaining 95 percent is due to differences between people other than their sex. Furthermore, the sex differences in verbal, spatial, and mathematical abilities that Maccoby and Jacklin identified are also small, are most apparent at the extreme (that is, very high or very low) ends of the ability distributions (Halpern, 1997), and may not be evident elsewhere (Stetsenko et al., 2000). For example, women do better on tests of mathematical ability, sometimes outperforming men, in societies like Israel, where women have excellent opportunities in technical training and technical occupations (Baker & Jones, 1992). Findings such as these imply that most sex differences are not biologically inevitable and that cultural and other social influences play an important role in the development of males and females (Halpern, 1997).

What, then, should we conclude about psychological differences between the sexes? Although contemporary scholars may quibble at times about which sex differences are real or meaningful (Eagly, 1995; Hyde & Plant, 1995), most developmentalists can agree on this: *Males and females are far more psychologically similar than they are different,* and even the most well-documented differences seem to be modest. So it is impossible to accurately predict the aggressiveness, mathematical skills, activity level, or emotional expressivity of any individual simply by knowing his or her gender. Only when group averages are computed do sex differences emerge.

Cultural Myths

Another conclusion that most developmentalists now endorse is Maccoby and Jacklin's (1974) proposition that many (perhaps most) gender-role stereotypes are "cultural myths" that have no basis in fact. Among the most widely accepted of these myths are the notions that females are more sociable, suggestible, and illogical, and less analytical and achievement oriented than males.

Why do these inaccuracies persist? Maccoby and Jacklin (1974, p. 355) propose that

a ... likely explanation for the perpetuation of "myths" is the fact that stereotypes are such powerful things. An ancient truth is worth restating here: if a generalization about a group of people is believed, whenever a member of the group behaves in the expected way the observer notes it and his belief is confirmed and strengthened; when a member of the group behaves in a way that is not consistent with the observer's expectations, the instance is likely to pass unnoticed, and the observer's generalized belief is protected from disconfirmation.... [This] well-documented [selective attention] ... process ... results in the perpetuation of myths that would otherwise die out under the impact of negative evidence.

> **? WHAT DO YOU THINK?**
>
> Imagine that you meet a 1-year-old named Pat who is dressed in gender-neutral clothing and is sporting a pudding-bowl hairstyle, so that you cannot tell whether Pat is a boy or a girl. How long would it be before you became curious about Pat's sex? How would you determine whether a 1-year-old like Pat is a boy or a girl?

In other words, gender-role stereotypes are well-ingrained cognitive schemes that we use to interpret and often distort the behaviour of males and females (Martin & Halverson, 1981; see Box 13.2). People even use these schemas to classify the behaviour of infants. In one study (Condry & Condry, 1976), university students watched a videotape of a 9-month-old child who was introduced as either a girl ("Dana") or a boy ("David"). As the students observed the child at play, they were asked to interpret his/her reactions to toys such as a teddy bear or a jack-in-the-box. The resulting impressions of the infant's behaviour clearly depended on his or her presumed sex. For example, a strong reaction to the jack-in-the-box was labelled "anger" when the child was presumed to be a boy and "fear" when the child was presumed to be a girl (see also Burnham & Harris, 1992).

As it turns out, the persistence of unfounded or inaccurate sex-role stereotypes has important consequences for both boys and girls. Some of the more negative implications of these cultural myths are discussed in the following section.

FOCUS ON RESEARCH

13.2

Do Gender Stereotypes Colour Children's Interpretations of Counterstereotypic Information?

Maccoby and Jacklin (1974) proposed that, once people learn gender stereotypes, they are more likely to attend to and remember events that are consistent with these beliefs than events that would disconfirm them. Carol Martin and Charles Halverson (1981) agree, arguing that gender stereotypes are well-ingrained schemes or naive theories that people use to organize and represent experience. Once established, these gender schemes should have at least two important effects on a child's (or an adult's) cognitive processes: (1) an *organizational* effect on memory, such that information consistent with the scheme will be easier to remember than counterstereotypic events, and (2) a *distortion* effect, such that counterstereotypic information will tend to be remembered as much more consistent with one's gender scheme than the information really is. For example, it should be easier for people to remember that they saw a girl at the stove cooking (gender-consistent information) than a boy doing the same (gender-inconsistent information). And if people were to witness the latter event, they might distort what they had seen to make it more consistent with their stereotypes—perhaps by remembering the actor as a girl rather than a boy or by reconstructing the boy's activities as *fixing* the stove rather than cooking.

Martin and Halverson (1983) tested their hypotheses in an interesting study with 5- and 6-year-olds. During the first session, each child was shown 16 pictures, half of which depicted a child performing *gender-consistent* activities (for example, a boy playing with a truck) and half showing children displaying *gender-inconsistent* behaviours (for example, a girl chopping wood). One week later, children's memory for what they had seen was assessed.

The results of this experiment were indeed interesting. Children easily recalled the sex of the actor for scenes in which actors had performed gender-consistent activities. But when the actor's behaviour was gender *inconsistent*, these youngsters often distorted the scene by saying that the actor's sex was consistent with the activity they recalled (for example, they were likely to say that it had been a boy rather than a girl who had chopped wood). As predicted, children's *confidence* about the sex of the actors was greater for gender-consistent scenes than for gender-inconsistent ones, suggesting that counterstereotypic information is harder to remember. But it was interesting to note that, when children actually distorted a gender-inconsistent scene, they were just as confident about the actor's sex (which they recalled *incorrectly*) as they were for the gender-consistent scenes in which they correctly recalled the actor's sex. So it seems that children are likely to distort counterstereotypic information to be more consistent with their stereotypes and that these memory distortions are as "real" to them as stereotypical information that has not been distorted.

Why, then, do inaccurate gender stereotypes persist? Because we find disconfirming evidence harder to recall and, in fact, often distort that information in ways that will confirm our initial (and inaccurate) beliefs.

Do Cultural Myths Contribute to Sex Differences in Ability (and Vocational Opportunity)?

In 1968 Phillip Goldberg asked university women to judge the merits of several scientific articles that were attributed to a male author ("John McKay") or to a female author ("Joan McKay"). Although these manuscripts were identical in every other respect, participants judged the articles written by the male to be of higher quality than those written by the female.

These young women were reflecting a belief, common to people in many societies, that girls and women lack the potential to excel in either math and science courses or in occupations that require this training. Kindergarten and Grade 1 girls already believe that they are not as good as boys in arithmetic, and throughout the elementary-school years, children increasingly come to regard reading, art, and music as girls' domains and mathematics, athletics, and mechanical subjects as boys' domains (Eccles, Jacobs, & Harold, 1990; Eccles et al., 1993; Entwisle & Baker, 1983). Furthermore, an examination of the percentages of male and female practitioners in various occupations reveals that women are overrepresented in fields that call for verbal ability (for example, library science, elementary education) and are seriously underrepresented in most other professions, particularly the sciences and other technical fields (for example, engineering) that require a math/science background (Smith, 2000). How do we explain these dramatic sex differences? Are the small sex-related differences in verbal, mathematical, and visual/spatial performances responsible? Or do gender-role stereotypes create a **self-fulfilling prophecy** that *promotes* sex differences in cognitive performance and steers boys and girls along different career paths? Today, many developmentalists favour the latter viewpoint. Let's take a closer look.

Home Influences

Parents may often contribute to sex differences in ability and self-perceptions by treating their sons and daughters differently. Jacquelynne Eccles and her colleagues (1990) have conducted a number of studies aimed at understanding why girls tend to shy away from math and science courses and are underrepresented in occupations that involve math and science. They find that parental expectations about sex differences in mathematical ability become self-fulfilling prophecies. The plot goes something like this:

1. Parents, influenced by gender stereotypes, expect their sons to outperform their daughters in math. Even before their children receive any formal math instruction, mothers in the United States, Japan, and Taiwan express a belief that boys have more mathematical ability than girls (Lummis & Stevenson, 1990; Stevenson, Chen, & Lee, 1993).

2. Parents attribute their sons' successes in math to ability but credit their daughters' successes to hard work (Parsons, Adler, & Kaczala, 1982). These attributions further reinforce the belief that girls lack mathematical talent and turn in respectable performances only through plodding effort.

3. Children begin to internalize their parents' views, so that boys feel self-confident whereas girls are somewhat more inclined to become anxious or depressed and to underestimate both their general academic abilities (Cole et al., 1999; Stetsenko et al., 2000) and, in particular, their proficiencies in math (Jacobs & Eccles, 1992).

4. Thinking they lack ability, girls become less interested in math, less likely to take math courses, and less likely than boys to pursue career possibilities that involve math after high school (Benbow & Arjimand, 1990; Environment Canada, 1999; U.S. Bureau of the Census, 1997).

In short, parents who expect their daughters to have trouble with numbers may get what they expect. In their research, Eccles and her colleagues have ruled out the possibility that parents (and girls themselves) expect less of girls because girls actually do worse in math

self-fulfilling prophecy
phenomenon whereby people cause others to act in accordance with the expectations they have about those others

than boys do. The negative effects of low parental expectancies on girls' self-perceptions are evident even when boys and girls perform *equally well* on tests of math aptitude and attain similar grades in math (Eccles et al., 1990). And the lower math expectancies that girls develop undoubtedly help explain why fewer girls than boys "bounce back" to show good math performance should they begin to underachieve in math (Kowaleski-Jones & Duncan, 1999). Parental beliefs that girls excel in English and that boys excel in sports contribute to sex differences in interests and competencies in these areas as well (Eccles et al., 1990).

Scholastic Influences

Teachers also have stereotyped beliefs about the relative abilities of boys and girls in particular subjects. Grade 6 math teachers, for example, believe that boys have more ability in math but that girls try harder at it (Jussim & Eccles, 1992). And even though these teachers often reward girls' greater efforts by assigning them equal or higher grades than they give to boys (Jussim & Eccles, 1992), their message that girls must try harder to succeed in math may nonetheless convince many girls that their talents might be best directed toward other nonquantitative achievement domains for which they are better suited—such as music or English.

In sum, unfounded beliefs about sex differences in cognitive abilities may indeed contribute to the small sex-related ability differences we have discussed and, ultimately, to the large underrepresentation of women in the sciences and other occupations requiring quantitative skills. Clearly, the chain of events that Eccles describes is not inevitable. In fact, girls whose parents are nontraditional in their gender-role attitudes and behaviours do not show the declines in math and science achievement that girls from more traditional families are likely to display (Updegraff, McHale, & Crouter, 1996). Yet, female underachievement in math and science remains a serious problem that has professionals from many disciplines calling for programs to educate parents, teachers, and counsellors about the subtle ways that gender stereotypes can undermine the educational and occupational aspirations of talented female students (Associated Press, 1994a; Benbow & Arjimand, 1990). Fortunately, there are some hopeful signs that times are changing.

Recent statistics suggest that 70 percent of employed women work in traditionally female-oriented occupations such as teaching, nursing, and so on. This percentage represents a decline in the number of women in these occupations since 1987 (Statistics Canada, 2000c). Even though fewer women are represented in traditionally female occupations, there are some traditionally male occupations where women remain highly underrepresented—at only about 20 percent, the 1987 rate—in the natural sciences, engineering, and mathematics (Environment Canada, 1999). On the other hand, by 1999 women represented nearly 50 percent of business and financial professionals, 47 percent of doctors and dentists, and 35 percent of managerial positions (Statistics Canada, 2000c).

Men have also started to show shifts in occupational domains. For example, at the University of British Columbia, a record number of men have enrolled in the traditionally female Bachelor of Science in Nursing program (University of British Columbia, 1996). So there is reason to suspect that many of the constraining stereotypes about women's and men's competencies will eventually crumble.

Now let's examine the gender-typing process to see why it is that boys and girls may come to view themselves so differently and often choose to assume different roles.

DEVELOPMENTAL TRENDS IN GENDER TYPING

gender identity
one's awareness of one's gender and its implications

Gender-typing research has traditionally focused on three separate but interrelated topics: (1) the development of **gender identity**, or the knowledge that one is either a boy or a girl and that gender is an unchanging attribute; (2) the development of *gender-*

role stereotypes, or ideas about what males and females are supposed to be like; and (3) the development of *gender-typed* patterns of *behaviour*—that is, the child's tendency to favour same-sex activities over those normally associated with the other sex.

Development of the Gender Concept

The first step in the development of a gender identity is to discriminate males from females and to put oneself into one of these categories. By 6 months of age, infants use differences in vocal pitch to discriminate female speech from male speech (Miller, 1983), and by the end of the first year, they can reliably discriminate photographs of men and women (women are the long-haired ones) and are beginning to match male and female voices with faces in tests of intermodal perception (Leinbach & Fagot, 1993; Poulin-Dubois et al., 1994). For example, in one set of experiments conducted by Canadian researchers, 18-month-olds were shown pictures of men's and women's faces that were paired with either a man's or a woman's voice, or a label such as man or lady (Poulin-Dubois, Serbin, & Derbyshire, 1998). In the first test, children spent more time looking at pictures where the voice matched the gender shown in the picture. In the second test, only girls were able to match the gender label (man or lady) with the appropriate face. When child voices and faces were used, the 18-month-olds could not perform the task well, but the term "boy" was understood even among these young children. This series of studies indicates that some awareness of gender labels is present very early in life.

Between ages 2 and 3, children begin to tell us what they know about gender as they acquire and correctly use such labels as "mommy" and "daddy" and (slightly later) "boy" and "girl" (Leinbach & Fagot, 1986). By age 2½ to 3, almost all children can accurately label themselves as either boys or girls (Thompson, 1975), although it takes longer for them to grasp the fact that gender is a permanent attribute. Many 3- to 5-year-olds, for example, think that boys could become mommies or girls daddies if they really wanted to, or that a person who changes clothing and hairstyles can become a member of the other sex (Fagot, 1985b; Szkrybalo & Ruble, 1999). Children normally begin to understand that sex is an unchanging attribute between the ages of 5 and 7, so that most youngsters have a firm, future-oriented identity as a boy or girl by the time they enter elementary school.

By age 2½ to 3, children know that boys and girls prefer different kinds of activities, and they have already begun to play in gender-stereotyped ways.

Development of Gender-Role Stereotypes

Remarkable as it may seem, toddlers begin to acquire gender-role stereotypes at about the same time that they become aware of their basic identities as boys or girls. Deanna Kuhn and her associates (1978) showed a male doll ("Michael") and a female doll ("Lisa") to 2½- to 3½-year-olds and then asked each child which of the two dolls would engage in sex-stereotyped activities such as cooking; sewing; playing with dolls, trucks, or trains; talking a lot; giving kisses; fighting; or climbing trees. Almost all the 2½-year-olds had some knowledge of gender-role stereotypes. For example, boys and girls agreed that girls talk a lot, never hit, often need help, like to play with dolls, and like to help their mothers with chores such as cooking and cleaning. By contrast, these young children felt that boys like to play with cars, help their fathers, and build things, and are apt to make statements such as "I can hit you." The 2- to 3-year-olds who know most about gender stereotypes are those who can correctly label photographs of other children as boys or girls (Fagot, Leinbach, & O'Boyle, 1992). So an understanding of gender labels seems to accelerate the process of gender stereotyping. Work by Lisa Serbin and her colleagues suggests even by their second birthday young toddlers may have acquired knowledge of gender-role stereotypes, especially for feminine activities (Serbin, Poulin-Dubois, & Eichstedt, 2002). See Box 13.3 for a summary.

Over the preschool and early elementary-school years, children learn more about the toys, activities, and achievement domains considered appropriate for boys and for girls (Serbin, Powlishta, & Gulko, 1993; Welch-Ross & Schmidt, 1996). Eventually, elementary-school children draw sharp distinctions between the sexes on *psychological* dimensions, learning first the positive traits that characterize their own gender and the negative traits associated with the other sex (Serbin et al., 1993). By age 10 to 11, children's stereotyping of personality traits begins to rival that of adults. In one well-known cross-cultural study, Deborah Best and her colleagues (1977) found that children aged 9 and 10 in England, Ireland, and the United States generally agreed that women are weak, emotional, soft-hearted, sophisticated, and affectionate; whereas men are ambitious, assertive, aggressive, dominating, and cruel.

Do children take gender stereotypes seriously and believe that they must conform to these prescriptions? Many 3- to 7-year-olds do; they often reason like little chauvinists, treating sex-role standards as blanket rules that are not to be violated (Biernat, 1991; Ruble & Martin 1998). Consider the reaction of one 6-year-old to a boy named George who likes to play with dolls:

THE INSIDE TRACK

13.3

Lisa Serbin

Lisa Serbin is the director for the Centre for Research in Human Development at Concordia University. Apart from her research on the development of gender concepts and stereotypes, she is actively involved in a longitudinal research program investigating the inter-generational transfer of health and developmental risk.

Pinpointing the point at which young children come to be aware of gender and are able to distinguish activities stereotyped as masculine or feminine is a challenging task. In a recent study, Lisa Serbin and her colleagues (2002) tested young toddlers to determine the point at which children become aware of gender-stereotyped activities. Specifically, 24-month-old toddlers viewed a series of nine pairs of photographs. Each pair showed a male and a female engaged in the same activity. The activities were either female gender-stereotyped (e.g., putting on makeup), male gender-stereotyped (e.g., hammering), or gender-neutral (e.g., reading). A preferential looking paradigm was used to record the amount of time children attended to each of the photographs in each pair. Interestingly, children spent much longer looking at men engaged in female stereotyped activities, than women engaged in these same activities. Children did not differ in their looking times when male stereotyped activities were being viewed. Serbin and colleagues (2002) suggest that these young toddlers have formed differential expectations for the behaviour of men and women, at least in regard to some very familiar and highly gender differentiated activities.

(*Why do you think people tell George not to play with dolls?*) Well, he should only play with things that boys play with. The things that he is playing with now is girls' stuff.... (*Can George play with Barbie dolls if he wants to?*) No sir!... (*What should George do?*) He should stop playing with girls' dolls and start playing with G.I. Joe. (*Why can a boy play with G.I. Joe and not a Barbie doll?*) Because if a boy is playing with a Barbie doll, then he's just going to get people teasing him ... and if he tries to play more, to get girls to like him, then the girls won't like him either (Damon, 1977, p. 255; italics added).

Why are young children so rigid and intolerant of sex-role transgressions? Possibly because gender-related issues are very important to them between ages 3 and 7: After all, this is the time when they are firmly classifying themselves as boys or girls and beginning to suspect that they will *always be* boys and girls. Thus, they may exaggerate gender-role stereotypes to "get them cognitively clear" so that they can live up to their self-images (Maccoby, 1998).

By age 8 to 9, however, children are becoming more flexible and less chauvinistic in their thinking about gender (Damon, 1977; Levy, Taylor, & Gelman, 1995; McHale et al., 2001). Notice how 9-year-old James makes a clear distinction between moral rules that people are obligated to obey and gender-role standards that are customary but *nonobligatory.*

(What do you think his parents should do?) They should ... get him trucks and stuff, and see if he will play with those. (What if ... he kept on playing with dolls? Do you think they would punish him?) No. (How come?) It's not really doing anything bad. (Why isn't it bad?) Because ... if he was breaking a window, and he kept on doing that, they could punish him because you're not supposed to break windows. But if you want to you can play with dolls. (What's the difference?...) Well, breaking windows you're not supposed to do. And if you play with dolls, you can, but boys usually don't (Damon, 1977, p. 263; italics added).

However, just because elementary-school children say that boys and girls can legitimately pursue cross-sex interests and activities does not necessarily imply that they *approve* of those who do. When asked about whether they could be friends with a boy who wears lipstick or a girl who plays football and to evaluate such gender-role transgressions, elementary-school children (and adults) were reasonably tolerant of violations by girls. However, participants (especially boys) came down hard on boys who behaved like girls, viewing these transgressions as almost as bad as violating a moral rule. Here, then, is an indication of the greater pressure put on boys to conform to gender roles (Levy et al., 1995).

Thinking about the traits that males and females might display and the hobbies and occupations they might pursue becomes increasingly flexible during early adolescence, as children make the transition from elementary school to junior high. But soon thereafter, gender-role prescriptions once again become less flexible, with both boys and girls showing a strong intolerance of cross-sex mannerisms displayed by either males or females (Alfieri, Ruble, & Higgins, 1996; Sigelman, Carr, & Begley, 1986; Signorella, Bigler, & Liben, 1993; and see Figure 13.3). How might we explain this second round of gender chauvinism?

Apparently, an adolescent's increasing intolerance of cross-sex mannerisms and behaviours is tied to a larger process of **gender intensification**—a magnification of sex differences that is associated with increased pressure

gender intensification
magnification of sex differences early in adolescence; associated with increased pressure to conform to traditional gender roles

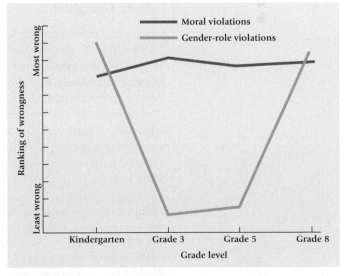

Figure 13.3 *Children's rankings of the wrongness of gender-role transgressions (such as pushing another child from a swing). Notice that children of all ages deplore immoral acts but only kindergartners and adolescents view gender-role violations as wrong. Elementary-school children come to think about gender-role standards in a more flexible way than they did earlier in life, but adolescents become concerned about the psychological implications of deviating from one's "proper" gender identity.* ADAPTED FROM STODDART & TURIEL, 1985.

to conform to gender roles as one reaches puberty (Boldizar, 1991; Galambos, Almeida, & Petersen, 1990; Hill & Lynch, 1983). Boys begin to see themselves as more masculine; girls emphasize their feminine side (McHale et al., 2001). Why might gender intensification occur? Parental influence is one contributor: As children enter adolescence, mothers become more involved in joint activities with daughters, and fathers become more involved with sons (Crouter, Manke, & McHale, 1995). However, peer influences may be even more important (Maccoby, 2002). For example, adolescents increasingly find that they must conform to traditional gender norms in order to succeed in the dating scene. A girl who was a tomboy and thought nothing of it may find during adolescence that she must dress and behave in more "feminine" ways to attract boys, and a boy may find that he is more popular if he projects a more "masculine" image (Burn, O'Neil, & Nederend, 1996; Katz, 1979). Social pressures on adolescents to conform to traditional roles may even help to explain why sex differences in cognitive abilities sometimes become more noticeable as children enter adolescence (Hill & Lynch, 1983; Roberts et al., 1990). Later in high school, teenagers become more comfortable with their identities as young men or women and more flexible once again in their thinking about gender (Urberg, 1979). Yet even adults may remain highly intolerant of males who blatantly disregard gender-role prescriptions (Levy et al., 1995).

Development of Gender-Typed Behaviour

The most common method of assessing the "gender-appropriateness" of children's behaviour is to observe whom and with what they like to play. Sex differences in toy preferences develop very early, even before the child has established a clear gender identity or can correctly label various toys as "boy things" or "girl things" (Blakemore, LaRue, & Olejnik, 1979; Fagot, Leinbach, & Hagan, 1986; Weinraub et al., 1984). Boys aged 14 to 22 months usually prefer trucks and cars to other objects, whereas girls of this age would rather play with dolls and soft toys (Smith & Daglish, 1977). In fact, 18- to 24-month-old toddlers often refuse to play with cross-sex toys, even when no other objects are available for them to play with (Caldera et al., 1989).

Gender Segregation

Children's preferences for same-sex playmates also develop very early. In nursery school, 2-year-old girls already prefer to play with other girls (La Freniere, Strayer, & Gauthier, 1984), and by age 3, boys reliably select boys rather than girls as companions. This **gender segregation**, which has been observed in a variety of cultures (Leaper, 1994; Whiting & Edwards, 1988), becomes progressively stronger with each passing year (Serbin et al., 1993). By age 6½, children spend more than 10 times as much time with same-sex as with opposite-sex companions (Maccoby, 1988). What's more, elementary and preadolescent children generally find cross-gender contacts less pleasing and are likely to behave more negatively toward opposite-sex than same-sex peers (Underwood, Schockner, & Hurley, 2001). Alan Sroufe and his colleagues (1993) find that those 10- to 11-year-olds who insist most strongly on maintaining clear gender boundaries and who avoid consorting with the "enemy" tend to be viewed as socially competent and popular, whereas children who violate gender segregation rules tend to be much less popular and less well-adjusted. In fact, children who display a *preference* for cross-sex friendships are likely to be *rejected* by their peers (Kovacs, Parker, & Hoffman, 1996). However, gender boundaries and biases against other-sex companions decline in adolescence when the social and physiological events of puberty trigger an interest in members of the opposite sex (Bukowski, Sippola, & Newcomb, 2000; Serbin et al., 1993).

Why does gender segregation occur? Eleanor Maccoby (1998) believes that it largely reflects differences between boys' and girls' play styles—an incompatibility that may stem from boys' heightened levels of androgen, which fosters active, rambunctious behaviour. In one study (Jacklin & Maccoby, 1978), an adult observer recorded how often pairs of same-sex and mixed-sex toddlers played together or alone when put in a play-

gender segregation
children's tendency to associate with same-sex playmates and to think of the other sex as an out-group

room with several interesting toys. As we see in Figure 13.4, boys directed far more social responses to boys than to girls, whereas girls were more sociable with girls than with boys. Interactions between playmates in the same-sex pairings were lively and positive in character. By contrast, girls tended to withdraw from boys in the mixed-sex pairs. Boys were simply too boisterous and domineering to suit the taste of many girls, who prefer less roughhousing and would rather rely on polite negotiations than demands or shows of force when settling disputes with their playmates (see also Alexander & Hines, 1994; Martin & Fabes, 2001; Moller & Serbin, 1996).

Cognitive and social-cognitive development also contribute to the increasing gender segregation children display. Once preschoolers label themselves as boys or girls and begin to acquire gender stereotypes, they come to favour the group to which they belong and eventually view the other sex as a homogeneous out-group with many negative characteristics (Martin, 1994; Powlishta, 1995). In fact, children who hold the more stereotyped views of the sexes are most likely to maintain gender segregation in their own play activities and to make few if any opposite-sex friends (Kovacs et al., 1996; Martin, 1994).

Sex Differences in Gender-Typed Behaviour

Many cultures, including our own, assign greater status to the male gender role (Turner & Gervai, 1995), and boys face stronger pressures than girls to adhere to gender-appropriate codes of conduct (Bussey & Bandura, 1992; Lobel & Menashri, 1993). Consider that fathers of baby girls are generally willing to offer a truck to their 12-month-old daughters, whereas fathers of baby boys are likely to withhold dolls from their sons (Snow, Jacklin, & Maccoby, 1983). And boys are quicker than girls to adopt gender-typed toy preferences (Blakemore et al., 1979). By age 3 to 5, boys (1) are much more likely than girls to say that they *dislike* opposite-sex toys (Bussey & Bandura, 1992; Eisenberg, Murray, & Hite, 1982) and (2) *may* even prefer a girl playmate who likes "boy" toys to a boy playmate who prefers girls' activities (Alexander & Hines, 1994).

Between the ages of 4 and 10, both boys and girls are becoming more aware of what is expected of them and conforming to these cultural prescriptions (Huston, 1983). Yet girls are more likely than boys to retain an interest in cross-sex toys, games, and activities (Ruble & Martin, 1998). Consider what John Richardson and Carl Simpson (1982) found when recording the toy preferences of 750 5- to 9-year-olds as expressed in their letters to Santa Claus. Although most requests were clearly gender-typed, we see in Table 13.2 that more girls than boys asked for "opposite-sex" items. With respect to their actual gender-role preferences, young girls often wish they were boys, and nearly half of today's university women claim that they were tomboys when they were young (Burn et al., 1996). Yet it is unusual for a boy to wish he were a girl (Martin, 1990).

There are probably several reasons that girls are drawn to male activities and the masculine role during middle childhood. For one thing, they are becoming increasingly aware that masculine behaviour is more highly valued, and perhaps it is only natural that girls would want to be what is "best" (or at least something other than a second-class citizen) (Frey & Ruble, 1992). Furthermore, girls are given much more leeway than boys are to partake in cross-sex activities; it is okay to be a "tomboy," but it is a sign of ridicule and rejection to label a boy a "sissy" (Martin, 1990). Finally, fast-moving masculine games and "action" toys may simply be more interesting than the familiar household playthings and pastimes (dolls, dollhouses, dish sets, cleaning and caretaking utensils) often imposed on girls to encourage them to adopt a nurturant, expressive orientation.

In spite of their earlier interest in masculine activities, most girls come to prefer (or at least to comply with) many of the prescriptions for the feminine role by early adolescence. Why? Probably for biological, cognitive, and social reasons. Once they reach puberty and their bodies assume a more womanly appearance (*biological growth*), girls often feel the need to become more "feminine" if they hope to be attractive to members of the other sex (Burn et al., 1996; Katz, 1979). These young adolescents are also attaining formal operations and advanced role-taking skills (*cognitive growth*), which may help to explain why they become (1) self-conscious about their changing body

Figure 13.4 *Two- to three-year-old toddlers already prefer playmates of their own sex. Boys are much more social with boys than with girls, whereas girls are more outgoing with girls than with boys.* ADAPTED FROM JACKLIN AND MACCOBY, 1978.

TABLE 13.2	Percentages of Boys and Girls Who Requested Popular "Masculine" and "Feminine" Items from Santa Claus	
	Percentage of boys requesting	**Percentage of girls requesting**
Masculine items		
Vehicles	43.5	8.2
Sports equipment	25.1	15.1
Spatial/temporal toys (construction sets, clocks, and so on)	24.5	15.6
Feminine items		
Dolls (adult female)	0.6	27.4
Dolls (babies)	0.6	23.4
Domestic accessories	1.7	21.7

SOURCE: Adapted from Richardson & Simpson, 1982.

images (Von Wright, 1989), (2) so concerned about other people's evaluation of them (Elkind, 1981), and thus (3) more inclined to conform to the *social* prescriptions of the female role.

In sum, gender-role development proceeds at a remarkable pace (Ruble & Martin, 1998) (see Table 13.3). By the time they enter school, children have long been aware of their basic gender identities, have acquired many stereotypes about how the sexes differ, and have come to prefer gender-appropriate activities and same-sex playmates. During middle childhood, their knowledge continues to expand as they learn more about gender-stereotyped *psychological* traits, and they become more flexible in their thinking about gender roles. Yet their *behaviour*, especially if they are boys, becomes even more gender-typed, and they segregate themselves even more from the other sex. Now the most intriguing question: How does all this happen so fast?

TABLE 13.3	An Overview of Gender Typing		
Age (years)	**Gender identity**	**Gender stereotyping**	**Gender-typed behaviour**
0–2½	Ability to discriminate males from females emerges and improves.		Gender-typed toy/activity preferences emerge.
	Child accurately labels the self as a boy or a girl.	Some gender stereotypes emerge.	Preferences for same-sex playmates emerge (gender segregation).
3–6	Conservation of gender (recognition that one's gender is unchanging) emerges.	Gender stereotyping of interests, activities, and occupations becomes quite rigid.	Gender-typed play/toy preferences become stronger, particularly for boys. Gender segregation intensifies.
7–11		Gender stereotyping of personality traits and achievement domains emerges.	Gender segregation continues to strengthen.
		Gender stereotyping becomes less rigid.	Gender-typed toy/activity preferences continue to strengthen for boys; girls develop (or retain) interest in some masculine activities.
12 and beyond	Gender identity becomes more salient, reflecting gender intensification pressures.	Intolerance of cross-sex mannerisms increases early in adolescence.	Conformity to gender-typed behaviours increases early in adolescence, reflecting gender intensification.
		Gender stereotyping becomes more flexible in most respects later in adolescence.	Gender segregation becomes less pronounced.

THEORIES OF GENDER TYPING AND GENDER-ROLE DEVELOPMENT

Several theories have been proposed to account for sex differences and the development of gender roles. Some theories emphasize the role of biological differences between the sexes, whereas others emphasize *social* influences on children. Some emphasize how society influences children, others the choices children make as they try to understand gender and all its implications. Let's briefly examine a biologically oriented theory and then consider the more "social" approaches offered by psychoanalytic theory, social learning theory, cognitive-developmental theory, and gender schema theory.

Money and Ehrhardt's Biosocial Theory

"Once there was a baby named Chris ... [who] went to live on a beautiful island ... [where] there were only boys and men; Chris was the only girl. Chris lived a very happy life on this island, but she never saw another girl or woman" (Taylor, 1996, p. 1559). What would Chris be like?

When Marianne Taylor (1996) asked 4- to 10-year-olds to indicate Chris's toy preferences, occupational aspirations, and personality traits, 4- to 8-year-olds assigned stereotypically feminine attributes to Chris despite the fact that she was raised in a masculinizing environment and never saw a girl or woman. In other words, preschool and young elementary-school children display an *essentialist bias*, assuming that Chris's biological status as a girl determines what she will become. Only the 9- to 10-year-olds in this study showed any awareness that Chris's masculinizing environment might influence her activities, aspirations, and personality characteristics.

Many scholars once displayed a similar essentialist bias by assuming that virtually all sex differences were largely attributable to biological variations between males and females. What biological differences might be so important? For one, males have a Y chromosome and therefore some genes that all females lack. For another, the sexes clearly differ in hormonal balance, with males having higher concentrations of androgens (including testosterone) and females having higher levels of estrogen. But do these biological *correlates* of gender and gender differences actually cause sex differences in behaviour? Do they predispose boys and girls to prefer and adopt different gender roles?

Today, even biologically oriented theorists take a more moderate stance, arguing that biological and social influences *interact* to determine a person's behaviours and role preferences. This interactive emphasis is quite apparent in a *biosocial theory* proposed by John

Concept Check 13.1
Understanding Sex Differences and Gender-Role Development

Check your understanding of sex differences and selected aspects of gender-role development by matching each descriptive statement below with one of the following terms: (a) achievement motivation, (b) gender identity, (c) gender intensification, (d) gender segregation, (e) reading comprehension, (f) self-fulfilling prophecy, (g) gender-role stereotypes, (h) visual/spatial ability, (i) gender-role standard. Answers appear in the Appendix.

_____ 1. attribute for which girls show a small but consistent advantage

_____ 2. knowledge about one's gender and its permanence

_____ 3. value, motive, or behaviour considered more appropriate for members of one sex than the other

_____ 4. process by which others' expectancies may promote sex differences in behaviour

_____ 5. attribute for which boys show a small but consistent advantage

_____ 6. affiliative preference that becomes stronger with age across childhood

_____ 7. attribute on which boys and girls *do not* differ

_____ 8. process that seems responsible for young teens' renewed intolerance of cross-sex mannerisms

_____ 9. can cause us to distort or misinterpret gender-atypical behaviours that we observe

Money and Anke Ehrhardt (1972). Although biosocial theory concentrates on biological forces that may channel and constrain the development of boys and girls, it also acknowledges that early biological developments affect other people's *reactions* to the child and suggests that these social forces play a major part in steering the child toward a particular gender role. Let's take a closer look at this influential theory.

A Biosocial Overview of Gender Differentiation and Development

Money and Ehrhardt (1972) propose that a number of critical episodes or events affect a person's eventual preference for the masculine or the feminine gender role. The first critical event occurs at conception as the child inherits either an X or a Y chromosome from the father. Over the next six weeks, the developing embryo has only an undifferentiated gonad, and the sex chromosomes determine whether this structure becomes the male testes or the female ovaries. If a Y chromosome is present, the embryo develops testes; otherwise, ovaries form.

These newly formed gonads then determine the outcome of episode 2. The testes of a male embryo secrete two hormones: *testosterone*, which stimulates the development of a male internal reproductive system, and *müllerian inhibiting substance (MIS)*, which inhibits the development of female organs. In the absence of these hormones, the embryo develops the internal reproductive system of a female.

At a third critical point, three to four months after conception, secretion of testosterone by the testes normally leads to the growth of a penis and scrotum. If testosterone is absent (as in normal females) or if the male fetus has inherited a rare recessive disorder, called **testicular feminization syndrome (TFS)**, that makes his body insensitive to male sex hormones, female external genitalia (labia and clitoris) form. Testosterone also alters the development of the brain and nervous system. For example, it signals the male brain to stop secreting hormones in a cyclical pattern so that males do not experience menstrual cycles at puberty.

Once a child is born, *social* factors immediately come into play. Parents and other people label and begin to react to the child based on the appearance of his or her genitals. If a child's genitals are abnormal, so that he or she is mislabelled as a member of the other sex, this incorrect label can affect the child's future development. For example, if a biological male was consistently labelled and treated as a girl (as a boy with TFS syndrome and female external genitalia might be), he would, by about age 2½ to 3, acquire the gender identity (though not the biological characteristics) of a girl.

Finally, biological factors enter the scene again at puberty when large quantities of hormones are released, stimulating the growth of the reproductive system, the appearance of secondary sex characteristics, and the development of sexual urges. These events, in combination with one's earlier self-concept as a male or a female, provide the basis for an adult gender identity and gender-role preference (see Figure 13.5). But how much is nature and how much is nurture?

Evidence for Biological Influences on Gender-Role Development

GENETIC INFLUENCES. Genetic factors may contribute to some sex differences in personality, cognitive abilities, and social behaviour. Corrine Hutt (1972), for example, suspects that several of the developmental disorders more commonly seen among boys may be X-linked recessive traits. (Recall from Chapter 3 that boys are more likely to display such traits because they have only one X chromosome and need inherit only one recessive gene to be affected.) Furthermore, timing of puberty, a biological variable regulated in part by our genotypes, has a slight effect on visual/spatial performances (the **timing-of-puberty effect**). Both boys and girls who mature *late* tend to outperform early maturers of their own sex on some visual/spatial tasks, allegedly because slow maturation promotes increasing specialization of the brain's right hemisphere, which serves spatial functions (see Newcombe & Dubas, 1987). However, later research indicates that the spa-

testicular feminization syndrome (TFS)
genetic anomaly in which a male fetus is insensitive to the effects of male sex hormones and develops female-like external genitalia

timing-of-puberty effect
finding that people who reach puberty late perform better on visual/spatial tasks than those who mature early

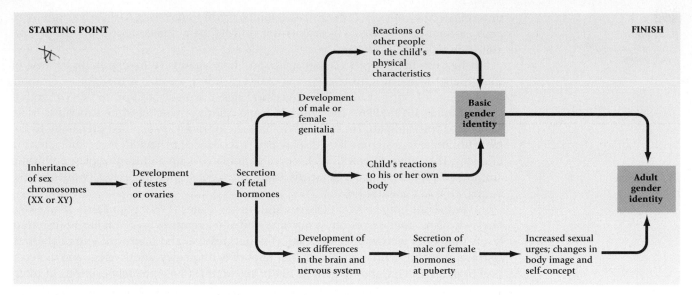

Figure 13.5 *Critical events in Money and Ehrhardt's biosocial theory of sex typing.* FROM MONEY & EHRHARDT, 1972.

tial performances of both boys and girls are more heavily influenced by their *previous involvement* in spatial activities and their *self-concepts* than by the timing of puberty (Levine et al., 1999; Newcombe & Dubas, 1992; Signorella, Jamison, & Krupa, 1989). Specifically, it appears that having a strong masculine self-concept and ample experience with spatial toys and activities fosters the growth of spatial skills in both boys and girls, whereas having restricted spatial experiences and a feminine self-concept seems to inhibit spatial abilities.

How closely are our masculine and feminine self-concepts related to the genes that we have inherited? Results from several behavioural genetics studies of adolescent twins suggest that genotype accounts for about 50 percent of the variability in people's masculine self-concepts but only 0 to 20 percent of the variability in their feminine self-concepts (Loehlin, 1992; Mitchell, Baker, & Jacklin, 1989). So even though genes determine our biological sex and may have some influence on the outcome of gender typing, it appears that at least half the variability in people's masculine and feminine self-concepts is attributable to environmental influences.

HORMONAL INFLUENCES. Biological influences on development are also evident in studies of children who have been exposed to the "wrong" hormones during the prenatal period (Ehrhardt & Baker, 1974; Gandelman, 1992; Money & Ehrhardt, 1972). Before the consequences were known, some mothers who had had problems carrying pregnancies to term were given drugs containing progestins, which are converted to the male hormone testosterone by the body. Other children with a condition known as **congenital adrenal hyperplasia (CAH)** have a genetic defect that causes their adrenal glands to produce unusually high levels of androgen from the prenatal period onward. These conditions usually have no effect on males, but female fetuses are often masculinized so that, despite their XX genetic endowment and female internal organs, they are born with external genitalia that resemble those of a boy (for example, a large clitoris that looks like a penis and fused labia that resemble a scrotum).

Money and Ehrhardt (1972; Ehrhardt & Baker, 1974) have followed several of these **androgenized females** whose external organs were surgically altered and who were then raised as girls. Compared with their sisters and other girls, many more androgenized girls were tomboys who often played with boys and who preferred boys' toys and activities to traditionally feminine pursuits (see also Berenbaum & Snyder, 1995; Hines & Kaufman, 1994). As adolescents, they began dating somewhat later than other girls and felt that marriage should be delayed until they had established their careers. A high proportion (37 percent) described themselves as homosexual or bisexual (Money, 1985; see also Dittman, Kappes, & Kappes, 1992). Androgenized females also perform better than

congenital adrenal hyperplasia (CAH)
genetic anomaly that causes one's adrenal glands to produce unusually high levels of androgen from the prenatal period onward; often has masculinizing effects on female fetuses

androgenized females
females who develop male-like external genitalia because of exposure to male sex hormones during the prenatal period

most girls and women on tests of spatial ability, further suggesting that early exposure to male hormones may have "masculinizing" effects on a female fetus's brain (Kimura, 1992; Resnick et al., 1986).

It has also been suggested that males are more aggressive than females because of their higher levels of testosterone—the male sex hormone that is thought to promote heightened activity, a readiness to anger, and hence a predisposition to behave aggressively (Archer, 1991, 1996). The evidence seems quite convincing when experiments are conducted with animals. For example, female rhesus monkeys exposed prenatally to the male hormone testosterone later display patterns of social behaviour more characteristic of males: They often threaten other monkeys, initiate rough-and-tumble play, and try to "mount" a partner as males do at the beginning of a sexual encounter (Wallen, 1996; Young, Goy, & Phoenix, 1964).

What about humans? Dan Olweus and his associates (1980) found that 16-year-old boys who label themselves physically and verbally aggressive have higher testosterone levels than boys who view themselves as nonaggressive, and men with extremely high testosterone levels tend to display higher rates of delinquency, abusiveness, and violence (Dabbs et al., 1995; Dabbs & Morris, 1990). Yet we must be extremely cautious in interpreting these correlational findings, because a person's hormonal level may depend on his or her experiences. To illustrate, Irwin Bernstein and his associates (Rose, Bernstein, & Gordon, 1975) found that the testosterone levels of male rhesus monkeys rose after they had won a fight but fell after they had been defeated. Similarly, human participants who beat opponents at competitive games show increases in testosterone whereas losers show a clear decline (Geen, 1998). What these findings imply is that higher concentrations of male sex hormones may be either a cause or an effect of oppositional behaviour, and it is difficult to establish conclusively that these hormones either *cause* one to act aggressively or explain sex differences in aggression (Archer, 1991).

Evidence for Social-Labelling Influences

Although biological forces may steer boys and girls toward different activities and interests, Money and Ehrhardt (1972) insist that social-labelling influences are also important—so important, in fact, that they can modify or even *reverse* biological predispositions. Indeed, some of the evidence for this provocative claim comes from Money's own work with androgenized girls.

In the past some androgenized girls were labelled boys at birth and raised as such until their abnormalities were detected. Money and Erhardt (1972) report that the discovery and correction of this condition (by surgery and gender reassignment) presents few if any adjustment problems, provided that the sex change occurs *before age 18 months*. But after age 3, gender reassignment is exceedingly difficult because these genetic females have experienced prolonged masculine gender typing and have already labelled themselves boys. These data led Money to conclude that there is a "critical period" between 18 months and 3 years of age for the establishment of gender identity. As illustrated in Box 13.4, it may be more accurate to call the first three years a *sensitive* period, because other investigators have claimed that it is possible to assume a new identity later in adolescence. Nevertheless, Money's findings indicate that early social labelling and gender-role socialization can play a very prominent role in determining a child's gender identity and role preferences.

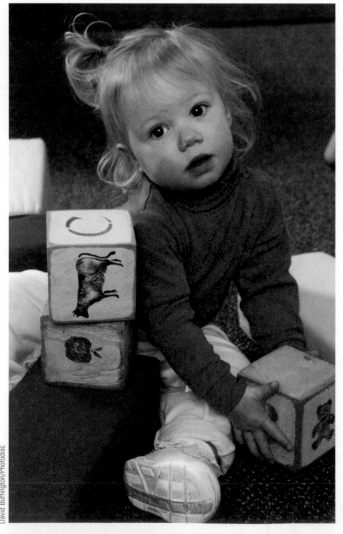

Girls who often play with visual/spatial toys tend to perform better on tests of spatial ability.

David Buffington/Photodisc

CULTURAL INFLUENCES. The fact that most societies promote instrumental traits in males and expressive traits in females has led some theorists to conclude that traditional gender roles are part of the natural order of things—a product of our bioevolutionary history (Archer, 1996; Buss, 1995). Yet there are sizable differences across cultures in what people expect of boys and girls (Whiting & Edwards, 1988). Consider Margaret Mead's (1935) classic study of three tribal societies in New Guinea. *Both* males and females among the Arapesh were taught to be cooperative, nonaggressive, and sensitive to the needs of others. This behavioural profile would be considered "expressive" or "feminine" in Western cultures. By contrast, *both* men and women of the Mundugumor tribe were expected to be assertive, aggressive, and emotionally unresponsive in their interpersonal relationships—a "masculine" pattern of behaviour by Western standards. Finally, the Tchambuli displayed a pattern of gender-role development opposite to that of Western societies: Males were passive, emotionally dependent, and socially sensitive, whereas females were dominant, independent, and assertive. So members of these three tribes developed in accordance with the gender roles that were *socially* prescribed by their culture, none of which matched the female/expressive—male/instrumental pattern seen in Western societies. Clearly, social forces contribute heavily to gender typing.

In sum, Money and Ehrhardt's biosocial theory stresses the importance of early biological developments that influence how parents and other social agents label a child at birth and that possibly also affect behaviour more directly. However, the theory also holds that whether children are socialized as boys or girls strongly influences their gender-role development—in short, that biological and social forces *interact*. But how, exactly, do they interact?

A PSYCHOBIOSOCIAL VIEWPOINT. Diane Halpern (1997) has recently proposed a *psychobiosocial model* to explain how nature and nurture might jointly influence the development of gender-typed attributes. According to the model, prenatal exposure to male or female hormones influences the organization of male and female brains in ways that might make boys, for example, somewhat more receptive to spatial activities and girls somewhat more susceptible to quiet verbal exchanges. These heightened sensitivities, in concert with others' beliefs about the kinds of experiences most appropriate for boys and for girls, means that boys are likely to (and actually do) receive a richer array of spatial experiences than girls do, whereas girls are exposed more often to verbal play activities (see Bornstein et al., 1999). Drawing on recent advances in the field of cognitive neuroscience, Halpern proposes that the different early experiences that boys and girls have will

Gender-role behaviours are often specific to one's culture. Like many Peruvian boys, this youngster routinely washes clothes and attends to other household tasks.

Rick Smolan/Stock Boston

When biological sex and social labelling conflict, which wins out? Consider the story of two male identical twins born in Winnipeg in 1967 (Colapinto, 2000). One of the twins, Bruce, suffered irreparable damage to his penis during a circumcision. After seeking medical advice and considering the alternatives, the parents agreed to a surgical procedure that made their 21-month-old son a girl anatomically. After the operation, the family began to actively gender-type this boy-turned-girl by changing her name (Brenda) and her hairstyle; dressing her in frilly blouses, dresses, and the like; purchasing feminine toys for her to play with; and teaching her such feminine behaviours as sitting to urinate. In addition, Brenda was regularly flown to Johns Hopkins Hospital, where she could be tested and observed and receive "treatment" from psychologist Dr. John Money to help her assume her female identity (Colapinto, 2000). By age 5, the "girl" twin was quite different from her genetically identical brother: She knew she was a girl and was far neater and daintier than her brother. Here, then, was a case in which assigned sex and gender-role socialization seemed to overcome biological predispositions. Or did they?

Milton Diamond and Keith Sigmundson (1997) followed up on this "Bruce" turned "Brenda" and found that the story was more than it appeared to be and had a twist ending. Over time, Brenda became quite uncomfortable with doll play and other traditionally feminine pursuits; she preferred to dress up in men's clothing, play with her twin brother's toys, and take things apart to see how they worked. Somewhere around the age of 10, she had the distinct feeling that she was not a girl: "I began to see how different I felt and was … I thought I was a freak or something … but I didn't want to admit it. I figured I didn't want to wind up opening a can of worms" (Diamond & Sigmundson, 1997, pp. 299–300). Being rejected by other children because of her masculine looks and feminine dress also took their toll, as did continued pressure from psychiatrists to behave in a more feminine manner. Finally, at age 14, after years of inner turmoil and suicidal thinking, Brenda had had it and simply refused to take female hormones and pretend to be a girl any longer. She then received male hormone shots, a mastectomy, and surgery to construct a

penis, and emerged as a quite handsome and popular young man who dated girls, married at age 25, and, after all of this struggle, appears to be comfortable with his hard-won identity as a man. (Note that his comfort in his present life does not negate the extraordinary emotional experiences this man has already grappled with and will continue to confront throughout his life.) Perhaps, then, we should back off from the conclusion that early gender-role socialization is all that matters; biology matters too.

A second source of evidence that biology matters is a study of 18 biological males in the Dominican Republic who had a genetic condition (testicular feminization syndrome [TFS] syndrome) that made them insensitive prenatally to the effects of male hormones (Imperato-McGinley et al., 1979). They had begun life with ambiguous genitals, and were labelled and raised as girls. But once their male hormones caused them to sprout beards and to look more masculine, 16 of these 18 individuals adopted masculine identities and heterosexual relationships with women. At face value, this study seems to challenge Money's critical period hypothesis and support the idea that gender identity and role preferences are determined more by hormones than by early socialization experiences.

Yet, the Dominican study is not conclusive (Ehrhardt, 1985). It is likely that Dominican parents, knowing that TFS is common in their society, treated these boys-who-look-like-girls differently from other girls when they were young. If so, these "girls" may have never fully committed themselves to being girls in early childhood. Nor should we assume that their later incorporation of the masculine role was a result of hormones. One study of TFS males raised as females among the Sambia of New Guinea found that *social pressures*—namely, the argument that they could not bear children—is what appeared most responsible for the gender switches that occurred after puberty (Herdt & Davidson, 1988).

What studies of individuals with genital abnormalities appear to teach us is this: We are predisposed by our biology to develop as males or females; the first three years of life are a *sensitive period* perhaps, but not a critical period, for gender-role development; and *neither* biology *nor* social labelling can fully account for gender-role development.

---

influence the neural pathways laid down in their immature and highly *plastic* (i.e., changeable) brains. Although the genetic code imposes some constraints on brain development, it does not provide specific "wiring" instructions, and the precise architecture of the brain is heavily influenced by the experiences one has (Johnson, 1998). So, according to Halpern (1997), boys who receive more early spatial experiences than girls do may develop a richer array of neural pathways in the areas of the brain's right cerebral hemisphere that serve spatial functions, which, in turn, may make them ever more receptive to spatial activities and to acquiring spatial skills. By contrast, girls may develop a richer array of neural interconnections in areas of the left cerebral hemisphere that serve verbal functions, thereby becoming ever more receptive to verbal activities and to acquiring verbal skills. From a psychobiosocial perspective, then, nature and nurture feed on each other and are a false dichotomy. In Halpern's words, "[B]iology and environment are as inseparable as conjoined twins who share a common heart" (Halpern, 1997, p. 1097).

What both biosocial theory and the psychobiosocial model do *not* do is to specify the precise social processes that contribute most heavily to children's emerging gender identities and gender-typed patterns of behaviour. Let's turn now to the social theories of gender typing, the first of which was Sigmund Freud's psychoanalytic approach.

? WHAT DO YOU THINK?

Do you think that an interactive model such as Halpern's *psychobiosocial approach* can explain the late conversion from female-to-male gender identities seen among the TFS males we discussed in Box 13.4? Why or why not?

Freud's Psychoanalytic Theory

Recall from Chapter 2 that Freud thought that sexuality (the sex instinct) was inborn. However, he believed that one's gender identity and preference for a gender role emerge during the **phallic stage** as children begin to emulate and **identify** with their same-sex parent. Specifically, Freud claimed that a 3- to 6-year-old boy internalizes masculine attributes and behaviours when he is forced to identify with his father as a means of renouncing his incestuous desire for his mother, reducing his **castration anxiety**, and thus resolving his **Oedipus complex**. However, Freud believed that gender typing is more difficult for a young girl, who lacks a penis, already feels castrated, and experiences no overriding fear that would compel her to identify with her mother and resolve her **Electra complex**. Why, then, would a girl ever develop a preference for the feminine role? Freud offered several suggestions, one of which was that the object of a girl's affection, her father, was likely to encourage her feminine behaviour—an act that increases the attractiveness of the mother, who serves as the girl's model of femininity. So by trying to please her father (or to prepare for relationships with other males after she recognizes the implausibility of possessing her father), a girl is motivated to incorporate her mother's feminine attributes and eventually becomes gender-typed (Freud, 1924/1961).

Although children are rapidly learning gender stereotypes and developing gender-typed playmate and activity preferences at roughly the ages Freud said they should, his psychoanalytic theory of gender typing has not fared well at all. Many 4- to 6-year-olds are so ignorant about differences between male and female genitalia that it is hard to see how most boys could fear castration or how most girls could feel castrated as Freud said they do (Bem, 1989; Katcher, 1955). Furthermore, Freud assumed that a boy's identification with his father is based on fear, but most researchers find that boys identify more strongly with fathers who are warm and nurturant rather than overly punitive and threatening (Hetherington & Frankie, 1967; Mussen & Rutherford, 1963). Finally, studies of parent–child resemblances reveal that school-age children and adolescents are not all that similar psychologically to either parent (Maccoby & Jacklin, 1974). Clearly, these findings are damaging to the Freudian notion that children acquire important personality traits by identifying with the same-sex parent.

Let's now consider the social learning interpretation of gender typing to see whether this approach looks any more promising.

Social Learning Theory

According to social learning theorists such as Albert Bandura (1989; Bussey & Bandura, 1999), children acquire their gender identities and gender-role preferences in two ways. First, through **direct tuition** (or *differential reinforcement*), children are encouraged and rewarded for gender-appropriate behaviours and are punished or otherwise discouraged for behaviours considered more appropriate for members of the other sex. Second, through *observational learning*, children adopt the attitudes and behaviours of a variety of same-sex models.

phallic stage
Freud's third stage of psychosexual development (from 3 to 6 years of age), in which children gratify the sex instinct by fondling their genitals and developing an incestuous desire for the parent of the other sex

identification
Freud's term for the child's tendency to emulate another person, usually the same-sex parent

castration anxiety
in Freud's theory, a young boy's fear that his father will castrate him as punishment for his rivalrous conduct

Oedipus complex
Freud's term for the conflict that 3- to 6-year-old boys were said to experience when they develop an incestuous desire for their mothers and a jealous and hostile rivalry with their fathers

Electra complex
female version of the Oedipus complex, in which a 3- to 6-year-old girl was thought to envy her father for possessing a penis and to choose him as a sex object in the hope that he would share with her this valuable organ that she lacked

direct tuition
teaching young children how to behave by reinforcing "appropriate" behaviours and by punishing or otherwise discouraging inappropriate conduct

According to Freud, children become appropriately "masculine" or "feminine" by identifying with the same-sex parent.

Direct Tuition of Gender Roles

Are parents actively involved in teaching boys how to be boys and girls how to be girls? Yes, indeed (Leaper, Anderson, & Sanders, 1998; Lytton & Romney, 1991), and their shaping of gender-typed behaviours begins early. Beverly Fagot and Mary Leinbach (1989), for example, found that parents are already encouraging gender-appropriate activities and discouraging cross-gender play during the second year of life, *before* children have acquired their basic gender identities or display clear preferences for male or female activities. By age 20 to 24 months, daughters are consistently reinforced for dancing, dressing up (as women), following parents around, asking for help, and playing with dolls, and they are generally discouraged from manipulating objects, running, jumping, and climbing. By contrast, sons are often reprimanded for such "feminine" behaviours as playing with dolls or seeking help and are actively encouraged to play with masculine items such as blocks, trucks, and push-and-pull toys that require large muscle activity (Fagot, 1978).

Are children influenced by the "gender curriculum" their parents provide? They certainly are! In fact, parents who show the clearest patterns of differential reinforcement have children who are relatively quick to (1) label themselves as boys or girls, (2) develop strong gender-typed toy and activity preferences, and (3) acquire an understanding of gender stereotypes (Fagot & Leinbach, 1989; Fagot, Leinbach, & O'Boyle, 1992). And fathers are even more likely than mothers to encourage "gender-typed" behaviours and to discourage behaviours considered more appropriate for the other sex (Leve & Fagot, 1997; Lytton & Romney, 1991). So it seems that a child's earliest preferences for gender-typed toys and activities may well result from their parents' (particularly fathers') successful attempts to reinforce these interests.

Throughout the preschool period, parents become less and less inclined to carefully monitor and differentially reinforce their children's gender-typed activities (Fagot & Hagan, 1991; Lytton & Romney, 1991). Why? Because many other factors conspire to maintain these interests, not the least of which is the behaviour of same-sex peers (Beal, 1994; McHale, Crouter, & Tucker, 1999). Peer influences are especially powerful: Even before they have established their basic gender identities, 2-year-old boys often belittle or disrupt each other for playing with "girl toys" or with girls, and 2-year-old girls are quite critical of other girls who choose to play with boys (Fagot, 1985a). So peers are beginning to differentially reinforce gender-typed attitudes and behaviours, and will continue to do so throughout childhood (Martin & Fabes, 2001), even as parents are becoming less likely to insist that their children pursue gender-typed interests and activities.

Observational Learning

According to Bandura (1989), children acquire many of their gender-typed attributes and interests by observing and imitating a variety of same-sex models. The assumption is that boys will see which toys, activities, and behaviours are "for boys" and girls will learn which activities and behaviours are "for girls" by selectively attending to and imitating a variety of *same-sex* models, including peers, teachers, older siblings, media personalities, and their mothers or their fathers.

Yet, there is some question about just how important *same-sex* modelling influences are during the preschool period because researchers often find that 3- to 6-year-olds learn much about typical patterns of both male and female behaviour by carefully observing models of each sex (Leaper, 2000; Ruble & Martin, 1998). What's more, John Masters and his associates (1979) found that preschool children are much more concerned about the sex-appropriateness of the *behaviour* they are observing than the sex of the model who displays it. Four- to 5-year-old boys, for example, will play with objects labelled "boys' toys" even after they have seen a girl playing with them. However, these youngsters are reluctant to play with "girls' toys" that boy models have played with earlier, and they think that other boys would also shun objects labelled girls' toys (Martin, Eisenbud, & Rose, 1995). So children's toy choices are affected more by the labels attached to the toys than by the sex of the child who served as a model. But once they recognize that gender is an unchanging aspect of their personalities (at age 5 to 7), children do begin to attend more selectively to same-sex models and are now likely to avoid toys and activities that other-sex models seem to enjoy (Frey & Ruble, 1992; Ruble, Balaban, & Cooper, 1981).

MEDIA INFLUENCES. Not only do children learn by observing other children and adult models with whom they interact, but they also learn about gender roles from reading stories (e.g., Clark et al., 2003) and watching television. Although sexism in children's books has declined over the past 50 years, male characters are still more likely than female characters to engage in active, instrumental pursuits such as riding bikes or making things; whereas female characters are often depicted as passive and dependent individuals who spend much of their time playing quietly indoors and "creating problems that require masculine solutions" (Kortenhaus & Demarest, 1993; Turner-Bowker, 1996). It is similar in the world of television: Males are usually featured as the central characters who work at professions, make important decisions, respond to emergencies, and assume positions of leadership; whereas females are often portrayed as relatively passive and emotional creatures who manage a home or work at "feminine" occupations such as waitressing or nursing (Liebert & Sprafkin, 1988).

Apparently, children are influenced by these highly sexist media portrayals, because those who watch a lot of television are more likely to prefer gender-typed activities and to hold highly stereotyped views of men and women than their classmates who watch little television (McGhee & Frueh, 1980; Signorielli & Lears, 1992).

In sum, there is a lot of evidence that differential reinforcement and observational learning contribute to gender-role development. However, social learning theorists have often portrayed children as *passive pawns* in the process: Parents, peers, and TV characters show them what to do and reinforce them for doing it. Might this perspective miss something—namely, the child's *own* contribution to gender-role socialization? Consider, for example, that children do not always receive gender-stereotyped presents because their sexist parents force these objects on them. Many parents who would rather buy gender-neutral or educational toys end up "giving in" to sons who beg for machine guns or daughters who want tea sets (Robinson & Morris, 1986).

Kohlberg's Cognitive-Developmental Theory

Lawrence Kohlberg (1966) has proposed a cognitive theory of gender typing that is quite different from the other theories we have considered and helps to explain why boys and girls adopt traditional gender roles even when their parents may not want them to. Kohlberg's major themes are as follows:

- Gender-role development depends on cognitive development; children must acquire certain understandings about gender before they will be influenced by their social experiences.

- Children *actively socialize themselves*; they are not merely passive pawns of social influence.

According to both psychoanalytic theory and social learning theory, children first learn to do "boy" or "girl" things because their parents encourage these activities, then they come to identify with or habitually imitate same-sex models, thereby acquiring a stable gender identity. By contrast, Kohlberg suggests that children *first* establish a stable gender identity and then *actively* seek out same-sex models and other information to learn how to act like a boy or a girl. To Kohlberg, it's not "I'm treated like a boy; therefore, I must be one" (social learning position). It's more like "Hey, I'm a boy; therefore, I'd better do everything I can to find out how to behave like one" (cognitive–self-socialization position).

Kohlberg believes that children pass through the following three stages as they acquire a mature understanding of what it means to be male or female:

1. **Basic gender identity.** By age 3, children have labelled themselves boys or girls.
2. **Gender stability.** Somewhat later, gender is perceived as *stable over time*. Boys invariably become men, and girls grow up to be women.
3. **Gender consistency.** The gender concept is complete when the child realizes that one's sex is also *stable across situations*. Five- to 7-year-olds who have reached this stage are no longer fooled by appearances. They know, for example, that one's gender cannot be altered by cross-dressing or taking up cross-sex activities.

When do children become motivated to socialize themselves—that is, to seek out same-sex models and learn how to act like males and females? According to Kohlberg, self-socialization begins only after children reach *gender consistency*. So for Kohlberg, a mature understanding of gender (1) instigates true sex typing and (2) is the *cause* rather than the consequence of attending to same-sex models.

Studies conducted in more than 20 different cultures reveal that preschool children do proceed through Kohlberg's three stages of gender identity in the sequence he describes and that attainment of gender consistency (or conservation of gender) is clearly associated with other relevant aspects of cognitive development, such as the conservation of liquids and mass (Marcus & Overton, 1978; Munroe, Shimmin, & Munroe, 1984). Furthermore, boys who have achieved gender consistency begin to pay more attention to male than to female characters on television (Luecke-Aleksa et al., 1995) and favour novel toys that male models prefer to those that female models like—even when the toys they don't want are the *more attractive objects* (Frey & Ruble, 1992). So children with a mature gender identity (especially boys) often play it safe and select the toy or activity that other members of their gender view as more appropriate for them.

Criticisms of Kohlberg's Theory

The major problem with Kohlberg's theory is that gender typing is well under way before the child acquires a mature gender identity. Recall that 2-year-old boys prefer masculine toys before they have achieved a basic gender identity, and that 3-year-olds of each sex have learned many gender-role stereotypes and already prefer same-sex activities and playmates long before they begin to attend more selectively to same-sex models. Furthermore, we've noted that gender reassignment is exceedingly difficult after children reach age 3 (Kohlberg's basic identity stage) and have *initially* categorized themselves as boys or girls. So Kohlberg badly overstates the case in arguing that a mature understanding of gender is necessary for gender typing to begin. As we are about to see, only a rudimentary understanding of gender permits children to acquire gender stereotypes and develop strong gender-typed toy and activity preferences.

basic gender identity
stage of gender identity in which the child first labels the self as a boy or a girl

gender stability
stage of gender identity in which the child recognizes that gender is stable over time

gender consistency
stage of gender identity in which the child recognizes that a person's gender is invariant despite changes in the person's activities or appearance (also known as *gender constancy*)

gender schemas
organized sets of beliefs and expectations about males and females that guide information processing

Gender Schema Theory

Carol Martin and Charles Halverson (1981, 1987) have proposed a somewhat different cognitive theory of gender typing (actually, an information-processing theory) that appears quite promising. Like Kohlberg, Martin and Halverson believe that children are intrinsically motivated to acquire interests, values, and behaviours that are consistent with their "boy" or "girl" self-images. But unlike Kohlberg, they argue that this self-socialization begins as soon as the child acquires a *basic gender identity* at age 2½ or 3 and is well under way by age 6 to 7 when the child achieves gender consistency.

According to Martin and Halverson's gender schema theory, establishment of a basic gender identity motivates a child to learn about the sexes and to incorporate this information into **gender schemas**—that is, organized sets of beliefs and expectations about males and females that influence the kinds of information he or she attends to, elaborates, and remembers. First, children acquire a simple **in-group/out-group schema** that allows them to classify some objects, behaviours, and roles as "for boys" and others as "for girls" (for example, trucks are for boys, girls can cry but boys should not, and so on). This is the kind of information that researchers normally tap when studying children's knowledge of gender stereotypes. And this initial categorization of objects and activities clearly affects children's thinking. In one research program, 4- and 5-year-olds were shown unfamiliar gender-neutral toys (for example, spinning bells, a magnet stand), told that these objects were either "for boys" or "for girls," and asked whether they and other boys or girls would like them. Children clearly relied on the labels to guide their thinking. Boys, for example, liked "boy" toys better than girls did, and children assumed that other boys would also like these toys better than other girls would. Just the opposite pattern of reasoning was observed when these same objects were labelled as "for girls." Even highly attractive toys soon lost their lustre if they were labelled as for the other gender (Martin et al., 1995).

In addition, children are said to construct an **own-sex schema**, which consists of detailed plans of action that they will need to perform various gender-consistent behaviours and enact a gender role. So a girl who has a basic gender identity might first learn that sewing is "for girls" and building model airplanes is "for boys." Then, because she is a girl and wants to act consistently with her own self-concept, she will gather a great deal of information about sewing to add to her own-sex schema, while largely ignoring information about building model airplanes (see also Figure 13.6). To test this notion, 4- to 9-year-olds were given boxes of gender-neutral objects (for example, burglar alarms, pizza cutters) and told that these objects were either "boy" items or "girl" items (Bradbard et al., 1986). As predicted, boys subsequently explored "boy" items more than girls did, whereas girls explored them more than boys when the objects were described as "girl" items. One week later, boys recalled much more in-depth information about "boy" items than girls did, whereas girls recalled more than boys about these very same objects if they had been labelled "girl" items. If children's information-gathering efforts are consistently guided by their own-sex schemas in this way, we can easily see how boys and girls might acquire very different stores of knowledge and develop different interests and competencies as they mature.

Once formed, gender schemas serve as scripts for processing social information. Recall from Chapter 8 that preschool children often have a difficult time recalling information that deviates from their scripted knowledge of everyday events. And so it goes with gender-related knowledge: Children are likely to encode and remember information consistent with their gender schemas and to forget schema-inconsistent information or to otherwise distort it so that it becomes more consistent with their stereotypes (Liben & Signorella, 1993; Martin & Halverson, 1983), especially if they have reached age 6 to 7, when their own stereotyped knowledge and preferences have crystallized and are especially strong (Welch-Ross & Schmidt, 1996). Support for this idea was presented in Box 13.2; recall that children who saw pictures in which characters performed gender-atypical behaviours (for example, a girl chopping wood) tended to recall the action but to alter the scene to conform to their gender stereotypes (saying that a boy had been chopping). Surely, these strong tendencies to forget or to distort counterstereotypic information help to explain why unfounded beliefs about males and females are so slow to die.

in-group/out-group schema
one's general knowledge of the mannerisms, roles, activities, and behaviours that characterize males and females

own-sex schema
detailed knowledge of plans of action that enable a person to perform gender-consistent activities and to enact his or her gender role

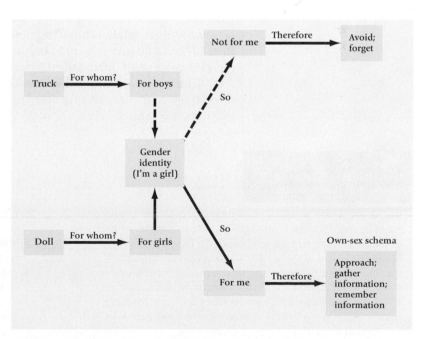

Figure 13.6 *Gender-schema theory in action. A young girl classifies new information according to an in-group/out-group schema as either "for boys" or "for girls." Information about boys' toys and activities is ignored, but information about toys and activities for girls is relevant to the self and so is added to an ever-larger own-sex schema. ADAPTED FROM MARTIN & HALVERSON, 1987.*

In sum, Martin and Halverson's gender schema theory is an interesting new look at the gender-typing process. Not only does this model describe how gender-role stereotypes might originate and persist over time, but it also indicates how these emerging gender schemas might contribute to the development of strong gender-role preferences and gender-typed behaviours long before a child realizes that gender is an unchanging attribute.

An Integrative Theory

Biological, social learning, cognitive-developmental, and gender schema perspectives have each contributed in important ways to our understanding of sex differences and gender-role development (Ruble & Martin, 1998). In fact, the processes that different theories emphasize seem to be especially important at different periods. Biological theories account for the major biological developments that occur before birth that induce people to label the child a boy or a girl and to treat him or her accordingly. The differential reinforcement process that social learning theorists emphasize seems to account rather well for early gender typing: Young children display gender-consistent behaviours largely because other people encourage these activities and often discourage behaviours considered more appropriate for members of the other sex. As a result of this early socialization and the growth of categorization skills, 2½- to 3-year-olds acquire a basic gender identity and begin to form *gender schemas* that tell them (1) what boys and girls are like and (2) how they, as boys and girls, are supposed to think and act. And when they finally understand, at age 6 or 7, that their gender will never change, children begin to focus less exclusively on gender schemas and to pay more and more attention to same-sex models to decide which attitudes, activities, interests, and mannerisms are most appropriate for members of their own sex (Kohlberg's viewpoint). Of course, summarizing developments in an integrative model such as this one (see Table 13.4 for an overview) does not mean that biological forces play no further role after the child is born or that differential reinforcement ceases to affect development once the child acquires a basic gender identity. But an integrative theorist would emphasize that, from age 3 on, children are active *self-socializers* who try very hard to acquire the masculine or feminine attributes that they view as consistent with their male or female self-image. This is why parents who hope to discourage their children from adopting traditional gender roles are often amazed that their sons and daughters seem to become little "sexists" all on their own.

One more point: All theories of gender-role development would agree that what children actually learn about being male or female depends greatly on what their society offers them in the way of a "gender curriculum." In other words, we must view gender-role development through an *ecological* lens and appreciate that there is nothing

---

✔
Concept Check 13.2
Understanding Theories of Gender-Role Development

Check your understanding of theories of gender-role development by matching each descriptive statement below with one of the following concepts or viewpoints: (a) Money and Ehrhardt's biosocial theory, (b) Halpern's psychobiosocial model, (c) Freud's psychoanalytic theory, (d) social learning theory, (e) Kohlberg's cognitive-developmental theory, (f) Martin and Halverson's gender schema theory, (g) basic gender identity, (h) gender consistency. Answers appear in the Appendix.

_____ 1. starting point for self-socialization, according to Kohlberg's theory

_____ 2. claims that there is a critical period for gender typing between 18 months and 3 years

_____ 3. claims that children adopt gender roles by identifying with the same-sex parent

_____ 4. starting point for self-socialization, according to gender schema theory

_____ 5. claims that gender-typed experiences influence development of the brain's neural pathways

_____ 6. claims that early gender typing largely reflects the gender curriculum that parents provide

_____ 7. explains why unfounded beliefs about males and females are likely to persist

_____ 8. cannot easily explain why gender reassignment usually fails with 3- to 5-year-olds

Developmental period	Events and outcomes	Pertinent theory(ies)
Prenatal period	The fetus develops male or female genitalia that others will react to once the child is born.	Biosocial/psychobiosocial
Birth–3 years	Parents and other companions label the child a boy or a girl, frequently remind the child of his or her gender, and begin to encourage gender-consistent behaviour while discouraging cross-sex activities. As a result of these social experiences and the development of very basic classification skills, the young child acquires some gender-typed behavioural preferences and the knowledge that he or she is a boy or a girl (basic gender identity).	Social learning (differential reinforcement)
3–6 years	Once children acquire a basic gender identity, they begin to seek information about sex differences, form gender schemas, and become intrinsically motivated to perform those acts that are viewed as "appropriate" for their own sex. When acquiring gender schemas, children attend to both male and female models. Once their gender schemas are well established, these youngsters are likely to imitate behaviours considered appropriate for their sex, regardless of the gender of the model who displays them.	Gender schema
7–puberty	Children finally acquire a sense of gender consistency—a firm, future-oriented image of themselves as boys who must necessarily become men or girls who will obviously become women. At this point, they begin to rely less exclusively on gender schemas and look to the behaviour of same-sex models to acquire those mannerisms and attributes that are consistent with their firm categorization of self as male or female.	Cognitive-developmental (Kohlberg)
Puberty and beyond	The biological upheavals of adolescence, in conjunction with new social expectations (gender intensification), cause teenagers to reexamine their self-concepts, forming an adult gender identity.	Biosocial/psychobiosocial Social learning Gender schema Cognitive-developmental

TABLE 13.4   An Overview of the Gender-Typing Process from the Perspective of an Integrative Theorist

inevitable about the patterns of male and female development that we see in our society today. (Indeed, recall the gender-role reversals that Mead observed among the Tchambuli tribe of New Guinea.) In another era, in another culture, the gender-typing process can produce very different kinds of boys and girls.

Should we in Western cultures be trying to raise different kinds of boys and girls? As we will see in our next section, some theorists would answer this question with a resounding "Yes!"

PSYCHOLOGICAL ANDROGYNY: A PRESCRIPTION FOR THE FUTURE?

Throughout this chapter, we have used the term *gender-appropriate* to describe the mannerisms and behaviours that societies consider more suitable for members of one sex than the other. Today, many developmentalists believe that these rigidly defined gender-role standards are actually harmful because they constrain the behaviour of both males and females. Sandra Bem (1978), for example, has stated that her major purpose in studying gender roles is "to help free the human personality from the restrictive prison of sex-role stereotyping and to develop a conception of mental health that is free from culturally imposed definitions of masculinity and femininity."

For many years, psychologists assumed that masculinity and femininity were at opposite ends of a single dimension: If one possessed highly masculine traits, one must be very unfeminine; being highly feminine implied being unmasculine. Bem (1974) challenged this assumption by arguing that individuals of either sex can be characterized by psychological **androgyny**—that is, by a balancing or blending of *both* desirable masculine-stereotyped traits (for example, being assertive, analytical, forceful, and independent) and desirable feminine-stereotyped traits (for example, being affectionate, compassionate, gentle, and understanding). In Bem's model, then, masculinity and femininity are *two separate dimensions* of personality. A male or female who has many desirable masculine-stereotyped traits and few feminine ones is defined as a *masculine gender-typed* person. One who has many feminine- and few masculine-stereotyped traits is said to be a *feminine gender-typed* person. The androgynous person possesses both masculine and feminine traits, whereas the *undifferentiated* individual lacks both of these kinds of attributes (see Figure 13.7).

Figure 13.7 *Categories of sex-role orientation based on viewing masculinity and femininity as separate dimensions of personality.*

Do Androgynous People Really Exist?

Bem (1974) and other investigators (Spence & Helmreich, 1978) have developed self-perception inventories that contain both a masculinity (or instrumentality) scale and a femininity (or expressivity) scale. In one large sample of university students (Spence & Helmreich, 1978), roughly 33 percent of the test takers proved to be "masculine" men or "feminine" women, about 30 percent were androgynous, and the remaining individuals were either undifferentiated or "sex-reversed" (masculine gender-typed females or feminine gender-typed males). Janet Boldizar (1991) has developed a similar gender-role inventory for elementary-school children (see Table 13.5 for sample items) and finds that approximately 25 to 30 percent of Grades 3 through 7 children can be classified as androgynous. So androgynous individuals do exist, and in sizable numbers.

Are There Advantages to Being Androgynous?

When we consider the idea that a person can be both assertive and sensitive, both independent and understanding, we can't help but think that being androgynous is psychologically healthy. Is it? Bem (1975, 1978) demonstrated that androgynous men and women behave more flexibly than more traditionally gender-typed individuals. For

androgyny
gender-role orientation in which the individual has incorporated a large number of both masculine and feminine attributes into his or her personality

TABLE 13.5	Sample Items from a Gender-Role Inventory for Elementary-School Children

Personality trait	Item
Masculine	
Dominant	I can control a lot of the kids in my class.
Authoritative	I am a leader among my friends.
Self-sufficient	I can take care of myself.
Ambitious	I am willing to work hard to get what I want.
Masculine	I like to do what boys and men do.
Feminine	
Compassionate	I care about what happens to others.
Cheerful	I am a cheerful person.
Loyal	I am faithful to my friends.
Nurturant	I like babies and small children a lot.
Feminine	I like to do what girls and women do.

Format: The child is asked to respond to each item on a four-point scale, with options ranging from 1 = not at all true of me to 4 = very true of me.

SOURCE: Adapted from Boldizar, 1991.

example, androgynous people, like masculine gender-typed people, can display the "masculine" instrumental trait of *independence* by resisting social pressure to judge very unamusing cartoons as funny just because their companions do. Yet they are as likely as feminine gender-typed individuals to display the "feminine" expressive quality of *nurturance* by interacting positively with a baby. Androgynous people seem to be more highly adaptable, able to adjust their behaviour to the demands of the situation at hand (Harter, Waters, Whitesell, & Kastelic, 1998; Shaffer, Pegalis, & Cornell, 1992). Furthermore, androgynous children and adolescents appear to enjoy higher self-esteem and are perceived as more likable and better adjusted than their traditionally gender-typed peers (Allgood-Merten & Stockard, 1991; Boldizar, 1991; O'Heron & Orlofsky, 1990). It has also become clear that androgynous men can still feel quite masculine and androgynous women can feel quite feminine even though they sometimes express traits traditionally associated with the other sex (Spence, 1993).

But before we conclude that androgyny is a thoroughly desirable attribute, let's note that *children* who strive too hard and express too many of the traits considered more appropriate for members of the other sex are at risk of being rejected by peers and experiencing low self-esteem (Lobel, Stone, & Winch, 1997). What's more, it is the possession of "masculine" traits rather than androgyny per se that is most strongly associated with good adjustment and high self-esteem (Spence & Hall, 1996; Whitley, 1983). This finding should not surprise us, for people in many societies value masculine characteristics more highly than feminine attributes (Turner & Gervai, 1995). But even so, there are signs that the times may be changing. In her study of elementary-school children, Boldizar (1991) found that (1) androgyny was by far the best single predictor of children's impressions of their global self-worth, and (2) femininity predicted some aspects of self-esteem (physical attractiveness; behavioural conduct) just as well as or better than masculinity did. Other research (reviewed by Mayer & Sutton, 1996) finds that androgynous couples are more satisfied with their intimate relationships than traditionally gender-typed couples are and it was the *feminine* component of androgyny that best predicted their relationship satisfaction.

So it may be premature to conclude that one is better off in *all* respects to be androgynous rather than masculine or feminine in orientation. But given the behavioural flexibility that androgynous people display and the strong contribution that androgyny makes to children's global self-worth, we can safely assume that it is probably adaptive and certainly not harmful for girls and women to become a little more "masculine," and for boys and men to become a little more "feminine."

> **?** ──────────────────────── **WHAT DO YOU THINK?**
>
> In some Islamic societies (for example, Iran), gender roles are much more sharply delineated than is true of Western societies such as our own. Do you think that there are any advantages to being psychologically androgynous in such a society? Explain.

Applications: On Changing Gender-Role Attitudes and Behaviour

Today, many people believe that the world would be a better place if sexism were eliminated and boys and girls were no longer steered toward adopting confining "masculine" or "feminine" roles. In a nonsexist culture, women would no longer suffer from a lack of assertiveness and confidence in the world of work, and men would be freer to display their sensitive, nurturant sides that many now suppress in the interest of appearing "masculine." How might we reduce sexism and encourage children to be more flexible about the interests and attributes they might display?

Bem (1983, 1989) believes that parents must take an active role by (1) teaching their young children about genital anatomy as part of a larger lesson that one's biological sex is unimportant outside the domain of reproduction, and (2) delaying children's exposure to gender stereotypes by encouraging cross-sex as well as same-sex play and by dividing household chores more equitably (with fathers cooking and cleaning and mothers cutting the grass or making repairs). If preschoolers come to think of sex as a purely biological attribute and often see themselves and their parents pursuing cross-sex interests and activities, they should be less inclined to construct the rigid gender stereotypes that might otherwise evolve in a highly sexist early environment. Research suggesting that androgynous parents tend to raise androgynous children is consistent with Bem's prescriptions for change (Orlofsky, 1979; see also Weisner & Wilson-Mitchell, 1990). So, too, are findings that children whose parents hold non-traditional attitudes toward gender roles or whose fathers routinely perform "feminine" household and child-care tasks are less aware of gender stereotypes and less likely to display gender-typed interests and ability profiles, compared with youngsters whose parents are more traditional in their gender-role attitudes and behaviours (McHale et al., 1999; Turner & Gervai, 1995).

How might we reach children from more traditional backgrounds, who have already received thousands of gender-stereotyped messages from family members, television, and their peers? Apparently, interventions that simply show children the benefits of cross-gender cooperation or that praise them for playing with other-sex toys and play partners have no lasting effect; children soon retreat to same-sex play and continue to prefer same-sex peers after the interventions are over (Maccoby, 1988). One particularly ambitious program (Guttentag & Bray, 1976) exposed kindergarten and Grades 5 and 9 students to age-appropriate readings and activities designed to teach them about the capabilities of women and the problems created by stereotyping and sexism. This program worked quite well with the younger children, particularly the girls, who often became outraged about what they had learned about sexism. However, it actually had a boomerang effect among Grade 9 boys, who seemed to resist the new ideas they were being taught and actually expressed more stereotyped views after the training than before. And although Grade 9 girls took many of the lessons to heart, they still tended to cling to the idea that women should run the home and that men should be the primary breadwinners.

This study and others (see Katz & Walsh, 1991, for a review) suggest that efforts to change gender-role attitudes are more effective with younger children than with older ones and possibly with girls than with boys. It makes some sense that it is easier to alter children's thinking early on, before their stereotypes have become fully crystallized, and many researchers now favour *cognitive interventions* that either attack the stereotypes directly or remove constraints on children's thinking that permit them to construct these rigid gender schemas. As we see in Box 13.5, these cognitive interventions can be quite effective.

Finally, there is some evidence that programs designed to modify children's gender-stereotyped attitudes and behaviours may be more effective when the adult in charge is a man (Katz & Walsh, 1991). Why? Possibly because men normally make stronger distinctions between "gender-appropriate" and "gender-inappropriate" behaviours than women do; thus, men may be particularly noteworthy as *agents of change*. In other words, children may feel that cross-gender activities and aspirations are legitimate if it is a man who encourages (or fails to discourage) these pursuits.

So new gender-role attitudes can be taught, although it remains to be seen whether such change persists and generalizes to new situations should these attitudes not be reinforced at home or in the culture at large. Sweden is one culture that has made a strong commitment to gender equality: Men and women have the same opportunities to pursue traditionally masculine or traditionally feminine careers, and fathers and mothers are viewed as equally responsible for housework and child care. Swedish adolescents still value masculine attributes more highly than feminine characteristics. However, they are much less adamant about it than American adolescents are, and are much more inclined to view gender roles as acquired domains of expertise rather than biologically programmed duties (Intons-Peterson, 1988).

Although our society has not made the commitment to gender equality that Sweden has, it is slowly becoming more egalitarian, and some people believe that these changes are having an impact on children (Etaugh, Levine, & Mennella, 1984). Judith Lorber (1986) sees

By encouraging and engaging in counterstereotypic activities, parents may deter their children from developing rigid gender stereotypes.

PhotoDisc, Inc.

During the preschool period when children are constructing gender schemas, their thinking tends to be intuitive and one-dimensional. As we have seen, children who encounter a violation of their gender schemas—hearing of a boy who likes to cook, for example—are unlikely to process and retain this information. After all, their one-dimensional, intuitive thinking makes it extremely hard to separate the gender-typed activity (cooking) from the gender category (for girls). So the information doesn't compute and is likely to be distorted or forgotten.

Rebecca Bigler and Lynn Liben (1990, 1992) have devised and compared two cognitive interventions aimed at reducing children's gender schematic thinking about the occupations that men and women might pursue. The 5- to 11-year-olds who participated in this research were assigned to one of three conditions:

1. *Rule training.* Through a series of problem-solving discussions, children were taught that (1) the most important considerations in deciding who would perform well at such traditionally masculine and feminine occupations as construction worker and beautician are the person's interests and willingness to learn, and (2) the person's gender was irrelevant.

2. *Classification training.* Children were given multiple classification tasks that required them to sort objects into two categories at once (for example, men and women engaged in masculine and feminine activities). This training was designed to illustrate that objects can be classified in many ways—knowledge that would hopefully help children to see that occupations can be classified independently of the kinds of people who normally enact these roles.

3. *Control group.* Children were simply given lessons on the contributions of various occupations to the community.

Compared with children in the control group, those who either received rule training or improved in classification skills showed clear declines in occupational stereotyping. Furthermore, later tests of information processing provided further evidence for the weakening of children's stereotypes. Specifically, children who received rule training or who had gained in classification skills after the classification training were much more likely than "control" children to remember counterstereotypic information in stories (for example, recalling that the garbage "man" in a story was actually a woman). It seems, then, that gender stereotypes can be modified by directly attacking their accuracy (rule training) or by promoting the cognitive skills (classification training) that help children to see the fallacies in their own rigid gender schemas.

Unfortunately, teachers may unwittingly foster gender schematic thinking should they group children on the basis of gender and emphasize gender differences during the first few years of school. In a recent experiment, Bigler (1995) randomly assigned some 6- to 11-year-old summer school students to "gender classrooms" in which teachers created separate boy and girl bulletin boards, seated boys with boys and girls with girls, and often made statements that distinguished boys from girls (for example, "All the boys should be sitting down"; "All the girls put their bubble-makers in the air"). Other children were assigned to classrooms in which teachers were instructed to refer to their pupils only by name and to treat the entire class as a unit. After only four weeks, children in the "gender classrooms" endorsed more gender stereotypes than those in control classrooms, particularly if they were one-dimensional thinkers who had trouble understanding that a person can belong to more than one social category at the same time. Recent observations of child-care workers indicated that they too may unwittingly provide opportunities for children to understand gender stereotypes by reinforcing girls and boys for different attributes (e.g., hairstyles versus physical size), allocating more attention to boys, and allowing boys to exert more power (Crick et al., 2002). Early childhood educators, however, also offered opportunities for children to learn how to break these barriers. So it seems that teachers can help to combat gender stereotyping by avoiding grouping pupils on the basis of gender during the early grades and in child-care settings, when young one-dimensional thinkers are prone to construct rigid gender schemas.

Interventions that show men and women participating side by side at traditionally "masculine" or traditionally "feminine" occupations can be highly effective at combatting rigid gender stereotypes.

much hope in her 13-year-old's response to her inquiry about whether a pregnant acquaintance of theirs had delivered a boy or girl: "Why do you want to know?" this child of a new era asked (p. 567).

ADOLESCENT SEXUALITY

Understanding sex and sexual activity is a critical part of life, especially as children move from childhood through puberty and their adolescent years. In Chapter 5 we reviewed many of the biological issues related to sexual maturation. The biological upheaval of puberty brings about major hormonal changes, one of which is increased production of androgens in both boys and girls, which dramatically increases their sex drive (Udry, 1990). Although elementary-school children often play kiss-and-chase games that prepare them for relationships later in life (Thorne, 1993), the new urges they feel make adolescents increasingly aware of their own **sexuality**—an aspect of development that greatly influences their self-concept. One major hurdle adolescents face is figuring out how to properly manage and express their sexual feelings, an issue that is heavily influenced by the social and cultural contexts in which they live. We will explore these contexts in the next sections related to adolescent sexuality.

Cultural Influences on Sexuality

Societies clearly differ in the education they provide children about sexual matters and in their attempts to prepare children for their roles as mature sexual beings (Ford & Beach, 1951). On the island of Ponape, for example, 4- and 5-year-olds receive a thorough "sex education" from adults and are encouraged to experiment with one another. Among the Chewa of Africa, parents believe that practice makes perfect; so, with the blessing of their parents, older boys and girls build huts and play at being husbands and wives in trial marriages. By contrast, *restrictive cultures* view sexuality as a taboo subject and vigorously suppress its expression. In New Guinea, for example, Kwoma children are punished for sex play and are not allowed to touch themselves. In fact, a Kwoma boy caught with an erection is likely to have his penis beaten with a stick!

Where do Canadian and other Western societies fall on this continuum of sexual permissiveness–restrictiveness? Most can be classified as relatively restrictive. If you are like many Western children and adolescents, the "facts of life" may have been related to you, not by your parents, but by an older sibling or peer. In fact, you may have had trouble imagining your parents ever having done what it takes to conceive you (Walters, 1997). In a recent study (2002), Canadian adolescents indicated that peers and teachers served as their primary sources for information about sex and dating. However, these same peers evaluated the information from teachers and parents as more accurate than the information provided by peers. The concern, then, is that one of the two most valued sources of information—parents—is not providing the level of discussion required. It is not a surprising outcome that North American parents generally discourage overt sex play and often find ways to elude the sexually explicit questions their children may ask (Thorne, 1993).

Family physicians provide yet another source of information for youth; however, few young people take advantage of this resource. A study in Nova Scotia indicated that only 8.7 percent of the males and 37.9 percent of the females had talked to their physician about sexual activity (Langille et al., 2001).

sexuality
aspect of self referring to erotic thoughts, actions, and orientation

Concept Check 13.3
On Altering Sexist Attitudes

You are an educator who hopes to modify children's rigid gender stereotypes. Design a program based on the research literature that should help you to achieve this objective. One such program is described in the Appendix.

Adolescents, especially males, appear to have less than ideal exposure to information regarding sexual behaviour. Mainly, adults leave the task of preparing for sexual relations up to children themselves, and children and adolescents end up learning from their peers and through school programs how they should relate to sexual partners (e.g., Whitaker & Miller, 2000).

Sexual Attitudes and Behaviour

How, then, do Western adolescents, who receive so little guidance from adults, ever learn to manage sexual urges and incorporate their sexuality into their self-concepts? These tasks have never been easy and, as we see in Box 13.6, can be especially trying for teenagers who find themselves attracted to members of their own sex. Judging from letters to advice columns, adults seem to think that modern adolescents, driven by raging hormones, are almost obsessed with sex and feel quite free to express their sexuality. How accurate is this portrayal?

Sexual Attitudes

Adolescents have become increasingly liberal in their thinking about sex throughout the 20th century, with recent attitudes reverting only slightly to a more conservative direction due to fears of contracting AIDS (Carroll, 1988; McKenna, 1997). Yet it is clear that today's youth have changed some of their attitudes about sex while retaining many of the same views held by their parents and grandparents.

What has changed? For one thing, adolescents now firmly believe that premarital *sex with affection* is acceptable, although, like teens of earlier eras, they think that casual or exploitive sex is wrong (even if they have had such experiences). Still, only a minority of sexually active adolescents in one American survey (25% of the males and 48% of the females) cited affection for their partner as the reason they first had intercourse (Laumann et al., 1994). Similarly, Canadian data indicate that girls are much more likely than boys to insist that sex and love—physical and emotional intimacy—go together, and they are more likely than boys to have been in a steady relationship with their first sexual partner (Darling, Davidson, & Passarello, 1992). This attitudinal gap between the sexes can sometimes create misunderstandings and hurt feelings, and it may partially explain why girls are less likely than boys to describe their first sexual experience as satisfying (Darling et al., 1992; de Gaston, Jensen, & Weed, 1995).

A second major change in teenage attitudes about sex is the decline of the **double standard**—the idea that many sexual practices viewed as appropriate for males (for example, premarital sex, promiscuity) are less appropriate for females. The double standard hasn't completely disappeared, because American university students of the early 1990s still believed that a woman who has many sexual partners is more immoral than an equally promiscuous man (Robinson et al., 1991). But Western societies are rapidly moving toward a single standard of sexual behaviour for both males and females.

Finally, sexual attitudes today are highly variable and seem to reflect an *increased confusion about sexual norms*. As Philip Dreyer (1982) notes, the "sex with affection" idea is very ambiguous: Must one truly be in love, or is mere liking enough to justify sexual intercourse? It is now up to the individual(s) to decide. Yet these decisions are tough because adolescents receive mixed messages from many sources. On the one hand, they are often told by parents, clergy, and advice columnists to value virginity and to avoid such consequences as pregnancy and sexually transmitted diseases. On the other hand, adolescents are strongly encouraged to be popular and attractive, and the more than 12 000 glamorous sexual innuendos and behaviours that they see annually on television (most of which occur between *unmarried* couples) may convince them that sexual activity is one means to these ends (Associated Press, 1999). Apparently, the behaviour of older siblings adds to the confusion, for younger brothers and sisters of a sexually active sibling tend to be sexually active themselves, often at an earlier age than the older siblings were (East, 1996; East & Jacobson, 2001). In years gone by, the norms of appro-

double standard
view that sexual behaviour that is appropriate for members of one gender is less appropriate for the members of the other gender

13.6

On Sexual Orientation and the Origins of Homosexuality

Part of the task of establishing one's sexual identity is becoming aware of one's sexual orientation—one's preference for sexual partners of the same, other, or both sexes. Sexual orientation exists on a continuum, and not all cultures categorize sexual preferences as ours does (Paul, 1993), but we commonly describe people as having primarily heterosexual, homosexual, or bisexual orientations. Most adolescents establish a heterosexual orientation without much soul-searching. For the 3 to 6 percent of youths who are attracted to members of their own sex, the process of accepting that they have a homosexual orientation and establishing a positive identity in the face of negative societal attitudes can be a long and torturous one (Hershberger & D'Augelli, 1995; Patterson, 1995b). It is not that homosexual youths are especially critical of themselves, because their levels of general self-esteem are comparable with those of heterosexual peers (Savin-Williams, 1995). Yet they may be anxious or even depressed about their gay or lesbian orientation, often because they fear rejection from family members or physical and verbal abuse from peers if their orientation becomes known (Baumrind, 1995; Hershberger & D'Augelli, 1995). Consequently, many gay and lesbian youth do not gather the courage to "come out" until their mid-20s, if they come out at all (Garnets & Kimmel, 1991; Miller, 1995).

How do adolescents become homosexual or heterosexual? In addressing this issue, John Money (1988) emphasizes that sexual orientation is *not* a choice we make but, rather, something that happens to us. In other words, we do not *prefer* to be gay or straight; we simply turn out that way. Not everyone agrees with this viewpoint. As Diana Baumrind (1995) has noted, many bisexual individuals may actively choose to adopt a heterosexual identity even though they have been sexually attracted to members of both sexes. Similarly, Celia Kitzinger and Sue Wilkinson (1995) find that many women with more than 10 years of heterosexual experience, who had always viewed themselves as heterosexuals, make a transition to lesbianism later in adulthood (see also Diamond, 2000), and it now appears that some men become gay later in life after having thought of themselves as (and having lived as) heterosexuals (Savin-Williams, 1998). Clearly, these findings imply that at least *some* homosexual individuals were not predestined to be homosexual and had at least *some* say in the matter.

How, then, might individuals become homosexual? Part of the answer seems to lie in the genetic code. Michael Bailey and his colleagues (Bailey & Pillard, 1991; Bailey et al., 1993, 2000) find that identical twins are more alike in sexual orientation than fraternal twins are. But as we see in the table, only about half of identical twin pairs share the same sexual orientation. This means that *environment contributes at least as much as genes* to the development of sexual orientation.

	Identical twins	Fraternal twins
Both male twins are gay/bisexual if one is	52%	22%
Both female twins are gay/bisexual if one is	48%	16%

SOURCES: Male figures from Bailey & Pillard, 1991; female figures from Bailey et al., 1993.

What environmental factors might help to determine whether a person with a genetic predisposition toward homosexuality comes to be attracted to same-sex companions? We really don't know as yet. The old psychoanalytic view that male homosexuality stems from having a domineering mother and a weak father has received little support (LeVay, 1996). Nor is there any compelling evidence for the long-standing "seduction hypothesis"—the idea that homosexuals have been lured into the lifestyle by an older same-sex companion. Even the once-popular notion that fathers who reject their sons will make them effeminate and push them toward homosexuality has failed to gain much support (Bell, Weinberg, & Hammersmith, 1981; Green, 1987). And growing up with a gay or lesbian parent also seems to have little impact on later sexual orientation (Bailey et al., 1995; Golombok & Tasker, 1996).

A more promising hypothesis is that hormonal influences during the prenatal period may be important. For example, women exposed before birth to diethylstilbestoral (DES) or to heightened levels of androgen are more likely than other women to express a bisexual or lesbian orientation, a finding that suggests that high prenatal doses of sex hormones may predispose at least some females to homosexuality (Dittman et al., 1992; Meyer-Bahlberg et al., 1995). However, the fact is that no one yet knows exactly which factors in the prenatal or postnatal environment contribute, along with genes, to a homosexual orientation (Berenbaum & Snyder, 1995; Paul, 1993).

priate behaviour were much simpler: Sex was fine if you were married (or perhaps engaged), but it should otherwise be avoided. This is not to say that your parents or grandparents always resisted the temptations they faced, but they probably had a lot less difficulty than today's adolescents in deciding whether what they were doing was socially acceptable or unacceptable.

Sexual Behaviour

Not only have sexual attitudes changed over the years, but patterns of sexual behaviour also have. Generally, today's adolescents are involved in more intimate forms of sexual activity (masturbation, petting, and intercourse) at earlier ages than adolescents of earlier eras were (Bingham & Crockett, 1996; Forrest & Singh, 1990). Figure 13.8 shows the percentages of American high-school students from different historical periods who reported ever having experienced premarital intercourse. Notice that the long-term increase in sexual activity at the high-school level may have peaked, because the most recent data available (for 1995) indicate that about half of high-school girls (down from 55 percent in 1990) and 55 percent of high-school boys (down from 60 percent in 1990) have ever had intercourse (McKenna, 1997). The proportion of youth participating in sexual intercourse appears to be somewhat lower in some areas of Canada. For example, data collected on 3862 high-school students in the Niagara region of Ontario indicate that 35.2 percent of the sample had sex by age 18–19 (Youth Lifestyle Choices— Community University Research Alliance, 2001). The data are similar to the American findings in that males and females reported similar sexual intercourse experience (37.4 percent of males and 33.3 percent of females). Other data suggest that the median age of first intercourse among young Canadians ranges from 14 to 16 years. When street youth are studied, the median age drops to between 12 and 15 years of age (Health Canada, Population and Public Health Branch, 2001). Together, these findings suggest that Canadian youth are engaging in less sexual intercourse than their American peers. Notice also from the figure that the sexual behaviour of girls has changed more than that of boys, so that sex differences in adolescent sexual activity have all but disappeared. Finally, it is clearly a myth to assume that today's youth are having sex as early and as often as circumstances permit.

In sum, both the sexual attitudes and the sexual behaviours of adolescents have changed dramatically in this century—so much so that some kind of sexual involvement is now part of the average adolescent's experience (McKenna, 1997). This is true of all major ethnic groups and social classes, and differences in sexual activity among social groups are shrinking dramatically (Forrest & Singh, 1990; Hendrick, 1994).

Personal and Social Consequences of Adolescent Sexual Activity

Who is most inclined to become sexually active early in adolescence, and how risky is this activity? Research has identified a number of factors that contribute to early sexual involvement. Teenagers who have intercourse very early tend to be early maturers from low-income families who are having difficulties at school, whose friends are sexually active, and who are already involved in such delinquent activities as alcohol or substance abuse (Bingham & Crockett, 1996; Fagot et al., 1998; Scaramella et al., 1998).

Sadly, large numbers of sexually active adolescents fail to use contraception, largely because they are (1) uninformed about reproductive issues, (2) too cognitively immature to take seriously the possibility that their behaviour could have serious long-term consequences, and (3) concerned that other people (including their partners) will think negatively of them if they appear prepared and thus "ready" to have sex (Brooks-Gunn & Furstenberg, 1989;

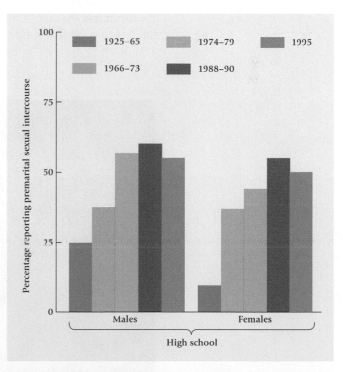

Figure 13.8 *Historical changes in the percentages of American high-school students reporting premarital sexual intercourse.* DATA FOR FIRST THREE TIME PERIODS ADAPTED FROM DREYER, *1982;* DATA FOR MORE RECENT PERIODS FROM BAIER, ROSENZWEIG, & WHIPPLE, *1991;* CENTERS FOR DISEASE CONTROL, *1992;* REINISCH ET AL., *1992;* MCKENNA, *1997.*

Coley & Chase-Lansdale, 1998; Walters, 1997). Of course, such unsafe sex puts them at risk of experiencing two serious consequences: sexually transmitted diseases and teenage pregnancy.

Sexually Transmitted Diseases

In Canada, the rate of some sexually transmitted diseases (STDs) has been decreasing; however, among 15- to 24-year-olds, rates of STDs are above average, especially for gonorrhea and chlamydia (Health Canada, Health Protection Branch, 1998). Other STDs include HIV/AIDS, genital herpes, and syphilis. Collaborators from the University of British Columbia, the University of Ottawa, and Health Canada indicate that the previous rate of decline of new HIV infections has almost levelled off (Patrick, Wong, & Jordan, 2000). The number of reported HIV cases is much higher than the number of AIDS cases. Compared with the 600 AIDS cases reported in 1999, there were 597 cases of HIV among 15- to 19-year-olds and 11 398 cases among 20- to 24-year-olds (Health Canada, Centre for Infectious Disease Prevention and Control, 2000).

The major source of AIDS infection among 10- to 19-year-olds was infected blood or blood products (70 percent), with sexual contact (22 percent) and intravenous drug use (4 percent) as smaller contributors. Among those in the 20- to 24-year-old range, tainted blood accounted for only 8 percent of the infections, while sexual activity (69 percent) and intravenous drug use (13 percent) accounted for the majority of the infections. Unlike the sources of AIDS, the sources of HIV among 10- to 19-year-olds are primarily sexual activity (67 percent) and intravenous drug use (30 percent), with a similar pattern for those in the 20- to 29-year-old group (Health Canada, Centre for Infectious Disease Prevention and Control, 2000).

Among Aboriginal people, the number of HIV/AIDS infections is increasing (Smylie, 2001). For example, in 1989, Aboriginal people accounted for 1.5 percent of the known cases of AIDS infection. By 1996, Aboriginal cases had increased to 5.6 percent, and by 1998, the percentage among some Aboriginal populations was as high as 10.0 percent. If STDs are left untreated, they can cause problems ranging from sterility to death in the infected individual and, as we noted in Chapter 4, birth defects and other complications for his or her children (Cates, 1995). Clearly, the risk of STDs is highest for teenagers who fail to use condoms regularly and for those who have sex with multiple partners. As Box 13.7 highlights, safer sexual practices are a major component in combatting these diseases.

PhotoDisc, Inc.

Some kind of sexual involvement is now part of the average adolescent's experience.

Teenage Pregnancy and Childbearing

Adolescents who are sexually active face another important consequence—pregnancy. In 1997, "an estimated 42 161 Canadian women aged 15 to 19 gave birth, had an abortion or experienced a miscarriage or stillbirth" (Statistics Canada, 2000e, p. 1). The rate of teenage pregnancies in Canada has declined; for example, in 1994 there were an estimated 46 753 pregnancies.

CONSEQUENCES FOR ADOLESCENT MOTHERS. Unfortunately for the adolescent woman who gives birth, the consequences are likely to include an interrupted education, loss of contact with her social network, and a future of low-paying (or no) jobs that perpetuates her economic disadvantage (Bissell, 2001; Furstenberg, Brooks-Gunn, & Chase-Lansdale, 1989). In addition, many adolescent girls, particularly younger ones, are not prepared psychologically to become parents, a fact that can affect their babies' developmental outcomes if supports are not introduced.

CONSEQUENCES FOR BABIES OF ADOLESCENT MOTHERS. As we noted in Chapter 4, teenage mothers, particularly those from economically disadvantaged backgrounds, are more likely than older mothers to be poorly nourished, to use alcohol and drugs while pregnant, and to fail to obtain adequate prenatal care. Consequently, many adolescent mothers experience more prenatal and birth complications than older mothers do and are more likely to deliver premature or small-for-date babies (Chomitz et al., 2000; Seitz & Apfel, 1994a). Compared with teenage mothers in the United States, the consequences of these setbacks for Canadian teenage mothers are not as severe. Although teenage

DEVELOPMENTAL ISSUES

13.7 Combatting Sexually Transmitted Diseases

Although the immediate threat of STDs is not as great for children as for sexually active adolescents, it is important to include younger children, as well as adolescents, in educational programs aimed at combatting the transmission of sexually transmitted diseases. Of the 16 913 cases of AIDS reported in Canada by the end of 1999, 600 (or 3.5 percent) were diagnosed among 10- to 24-year-olds (Health Canada Centre for Infectious Disease Prevention and Control, 2000). This number may underestimate the number of youths at risk. Because the AIDS virus can take 10 or more years to appear, from the point of infection to the onset of the disease, many of the cases reported by older individuals probably occurred when those individuals were adolescents. These prevalence rates demonstrate the importance of educating students both about STDs and how to prevent their transmission.

As the number of cases of AIDS has grown, so too have efforts to educate children and adolescents about how to prevent this deadly disease. Most provinces have initiated AIDS education programs, and there is evidence that these programs can increase children's knowledge about this disease and its prevention (Gill & Beazley, 1993; Maticka-Tyndale, 1997; Osborne, Kistner, & Helgemo, 1993).

One concern that has been highlighted in the recent literature is that youths who are taking oral contraceptives to prevent pregnancy often fail to use condoms to protect against infections from STDs. In a Canadian study involving 1438 participants, only 27 percent of those who used oral contraceptives also used condoms (Boroditsky, Fisher, & Sand, 1996). In addition, survey results from the Canada Youth and AIDS Study conducted through Queen's University show that males report the use of condoms when having sex more often than females (King, Beazley, & Warren, 1988), suggesting greater risk for STDs among females.

Education programs targeting the prevention of STD transmission have resulted in more effective contraceptive use and greater understanding of the importance of condoms (Stanton, Li, & Galbraith, 1996). Canadian programs such as Fisher and Fisher's Information-Motivation-Behaviour Skills, the Skills for Healthy Relationships, and the Guidelines for Sexual Health Education all lead to increases in condom use and reductions in the number of sexual partners (Maticka-Tyndale, 1997). In sum, comprehensive, early STD education programs can produce long-term gains in knowledge that may help children to avoid behaviours that could put them at risk of contracting AIDS later in adolescence.

The incidence of STDs is also higher among injection drug users, especially those who share needles; however, there has been a drop in incidence rates among this group since 1996. Some researchers suggest that this apparent drop simply reflects a saturation point of this high-risk population (Patrick, Wong, & Jordan, 2000), while others point to intervention programs aimed at reducing high-risk behaviours. For example, many communities have set up clinics and outreach programs where needles are made available to users at no cost, reducing the need to share needles. For the most part, research findings suggest that the primary prevention programs that encourage safer sex practices remain the best tool for combatting STDs.

mothers have higher risk rates with respect to diet, drugs, and medical care, the support systems available in Canada reduce the impact of these effects. Recent efforts aimed at enhancing early development have resulted in the development of many accessible intervention programs (e.g., well-baby clinics, prenatal health fairs, hotlines that access public health nurses, etc.) for young pregnant women and young mothers.

Even in Canada, however, income and educational attainment are critical issues facing teenage mothers (Bissell, 2001). Single mothers involved in a long-term study of mothers and their children in Nova Scotia reported low satisfaction with their educational attainment (Nova Scotia Department of Community Services, 2001). Low educational attainment is associated with limited career opportunities and, in turn, results in lower-income jobs (Bissell, 2001). Teenage mothers account for 3 percent of single mothers receiving welfare assistance (Bissell, 2001).

When interventions are not available, not only are their babies at risk for getting off to a rocky start, but so are many adolescent mothers who are ill prepared intellectually for the responsibilities of motherhood and who rarely receive adequate financial or social support from a teenage father (Fagot et al., 1998). Compared with older mothers, adolescent mothers know less about child development, view their infants as more difficult, experience greater parenting stress, and respond to their babies with less sensitivity and affection (Miller, Miceli, et al., 1996; Sommer et al., 1993). It is not completely clear at this point whether the poor parenting practices that characterize many adolescent mothers occur because these mothers are so young or because the adolescent mothers studied come from extremely disadvantaged backgrounds in which parenting (regardless of the parent's age) is generally less sensitive and stimulating (Coley & Chase-Lansdale, 1998). But regardless of how we choose to interpret it, this pattern of parenting can have long-term consequences because children born to teenagers often show intellectual deficits and emotional disturbances during the preschool years, and poor academic achievement, poor peer relations, and delinquent behaviours later in childhood (Hardy et al., 1998; Miller et al., 1996; Spieker et al., 1999). Even with the interventions available to Canadian teenagers, some cognitive decreases (such as lower verbal comprehension) have been noted in children of teenage mothers relative to other children (Nova Scotia Department of Community Services, 2001). A teenage mother's life situation and her child's developmental progress may improve later on, especially if she returns to school and avoids having more children (Bissell, 2001; Hardy et al., 1998).

DEALING WITH THE PROBLEM. How might we reduce the incidence of teenage pregnancy? Earlier, we discussed the importance adolescents place on their parents' information about sexuality. It is clear that early and frank discussions about sexual matters between parents and their teens (or even preteens) can be a helpful preventative strategy—especially *before* teens initiate sex (Miller et al., 1998; Whitaker & Miller, 2000). In Box 13.7 we discuss comprehensive education programs to reduce the incidence of sexually transmitted diseases. These programs include coverage of pregnancy prevention. Sex education that goes beyond the biological facts of reproduction, addressing such topics as contraception and the decision-making skills that teenagers need to resist pressures to have sex, can be very effective. Again, these programs are more effective if presented in late elementary or early high school *before* adolescents become sexually active (R.H. Pollack, personal communication, March 1997; St. Lawrence et al., 1995). And in light of evidence from Western Europe that free distribution of condoms does *not* encourage sexually inactive teenagers to become sexually active, many researchers and educators in this country are calling for similar contraceptive programs (Lowy, 2000; McKay, 1998; R.H. Pollack, personal communication, March 1997).

Finally, adolescent mothers and their babies need lots of help: good prenatal care, daycare (to allow mothers to return to school or to work), job training, and assistance in becoming a more sensitive and responsive parent. Victoria Seitz and Nancy Apfel (1994a) studied pregnant adolescents who had participated in a prenatal intervention where they received good prenatal care, lessons in parenting skills, and counselling to encourage

? WHAT DO YOU THINK?

Suppose that prenatal interventions for pregnant adolescents cost $3000 per participant per year. Some have argued that it is "penny wise and pound foolish" for governments not to fund such programs for all at-risk teens who are likely to benefit from them. What is your position on this issue, and why?

them to complete high school and delay future pregnancies. Compared with other teenage mothers, young women who participated in the intervention had fewer low-birth-weight babies, performed better in school after giving birth, and were less likely to become pregnant again.

SUMMARY

♦ **Gender typing** is the process by which children acquire a gender identity as well as the motives, values, and behaviours considered appropriate in their society for members of their biological sex.

Categorizing Males and Females: Gender-Role Standards

♦ A **gender-role standard** is a motive, value, or behaviour considered more appropriate for members of one sex than the other. Many societies are characterized by a gender-based division of labour in which females are encouraged to adopt an **expressive role** and males an **instrumental role**.

Some Facts and Fictions about Sex Differences

♦ Girls outperform boys in many assessments of verbal ability and are more emotionally expressive, compliant, and timid than boys are. Boys are more active and more physically and verbally aggressive than girls and tend to outperform girls on tests of arithmetic reasoning and **visual/spatial abilities**. In all, however, these sex differences are small, and males and females are far more psychologically similar than they are different.

♦ Of the many traditional gender-role stereotypes that have no basis in fact are the notions that females are more sociable, suggestible, and illogical and less analytical and achievement oriented than males. The persistence of these "cultural myths" can create **self-fulfilling prophecies** that promote sex differences in cognitive performance and steer males and females along different career paths.

Developmental Trends in Gender Typing

♦ By age 2½ to 3, children firmly label themselves as boys or girls, taking their first step in the development of **gender identity**. Between ages 5 and 7, they come to realize that gender is an unchanging aspect of self.

♦ Children begin to learn gender-role stereotypes at about the same age that they display a basic gender identity. By age 10 to 11, children's stereotyping of male and female personality traits rivals that of an adult. At first, stereotypes are viewed as obligatory prescriptions, but children become more flexible in their thinking about gender during middle childhood before becoming somewhat more rigid once again during the adolescent period of **gender intensification**.

♦ Even before reaching basic gender identity, many toddlers display gender-typed toy and activity preferences. By age 3, they display **gender segregation** by preferring to spend time with same-sex associates and developing clear prejudices against members of the other sex. Boys face stronger gender-typing pressures than girls do and are quicker to develop gender-typed toy and activity preferences.

Theories of Gender Typing and Gender-Role Development

♦ Money and Ehrhardt's biosocial theory emphasizes biological developments that occur before birth and influence the way a child is socialized. The behaviour of **androgenized females** implies that prenatal androgen levels may contribute to sex differences in play styles, and males' heightened levels of testosterone may contribute to sex differences in aggression. Yet the development of children raised as members of the other sex (for example, those with **testicular feminization syndrome**) illustrates that social labelling and gender-role socialization play a crucial role in determining one's gender identity and role preferences.

♦ Freud believed that children become gender-typed as they **identify** with the same-sex parent during the **phallic stage** of development in order to resolve their **Oedipus** or **Electra complexes**. However, several lines of research have failed to confirm Freud's theory.

♦ Consistent with social learning theory, children acquire many of their earliest gender-typed toy and activity preferences through **direct tuition** (or differential reinforcement). *Observational learning* also contributes to gender typing as preschool children attend to models of *both sexes* and become increasingly aware of gender stereotypes.

♦ Kohlberg's cognitive-developmental theory claims that children are self-socializers who must pass through **basic gender identity** and **gender stability** before reaching **gender consistency**, the point at which they begin to selectively attend to same-sex models and become gender-typed. However, research consistently reveals that gender typing begins much earlier than Kohlberg thought and that measures of gender consistency do not predict the strength of gender typing.

♦ According to Martin and Halverson's *gender schema* theory, children who have established a basic gender identity construct **in-group/out-group** and **own-sex gender schemas**, which serve as scripts for processing gender-related information and socializing themselves into gender roles. Schema-consistent information is gathered and retained, whereas schema-inconsistent information is ignored or distorted, thus perpetuating gender stereotypes that have no basis in fact.

♦ The best account of gender typing is an eclectic, integrative theory that recognizes that processes emphasized in biosocial, social learning, cognitive-developmental, and gender schema theories all contribute to gender-role development.

Psychological Androgyny: A Prescription for the Future?

♦ The psychological attributes "masculinity" and "femininity" are generally considered opposite ends of a single dimension. However, one new look at gender roles proposes that masculinity *and* femininity are two separate dimensions and that the **androgynous** person is someone who possesses a fair number of masculine and feminine characteristics. Recent research shows that androgynous people do exist, are relatively popular and well adjusted, and may be adaptable to a wider variety of environmental demands than people who are traditionally gender-typed.

♦ Parents and teachers (particularly males) may prevent rigid sex typing by emphasizing that one's sex is largely irrelevant outside the domain of reproduction, by encouraging and modelling other-sex as well as same-sex activities, and by discussing the many exceptions to any unfounded gender stereotypes that children may have acquired.

Adolescent Sexuality

♦ The hormonal changes of puberty bring about an increase in sex drive and the responsibility of managing **sexuality**—a task that may be particularly difficult for teenagers who are sexually attracted to same-sex peers. Sexual attitudes have become increasingly liberal over the years, as a majority of adolescents now think that sex with affection is acceptable and reject the **double standard** for gender differences in sexual behaviour. Teenage sexual activity has also increased, although the sexual behaviour of girls has changed more than that of boys.

♦ Large numbers of sexually active teenagers fail to use contraception regularly, thus putting themselves at risk of contracting sexually transmitted diseases (STDs) or becoming pregnant. Efforts to educate elementary-school children about AIDS have been quite successful.

♦ Adolescent pregnancy and childbearing is an important social issue in Canada. Teenage mothers often drop out of school and experience long-term economic disadvantages. Without intervention, they exhibit poor parenting skills, which contributes to the emotional problems and cognitive deficiencies that their children often display. Canadian support systems reduce the negative impact typically observed in teenage mothers, although their children often show some cognitive deficits. Improved sex education and contraceptive services, coupled with community intervention programs (such as well-baby clinics), can help to reduce the rate of teenage pregnancy and its undesirable consequences.

KEY TERMS

gender typing, 474	gender segregation, 486	identification, 495	gender schemas, 498
gender-role standard, 474	testicular feminization	castration anxiety, 495	in-group/out-group schema,
expressive role, 474	syndrome (TFS), 490	Oedipus complex, 495	499
instrumental role, 474	timing-of-puberty effect, 490	Electra complex, 495	own-sex schema, 499
visual/spatial abilities, 476	congenital adrenal hyperplasia	direct tuition, 495	androgyny, 502
self-fulfilling prophecy, 481	(CAH), 491	basic gender identity, 498	sexuality, 506
gender identity, 482	androgenized females, 491	gender stability, 498	double standard, 507
gender intensification, 485	phallic stage, 495	gender consistency, 498	

 You can find further information on the topics covered in this chapter by visiting:

www.developmentalpsych2e.nelson.com

 For additional reading, go to InfoTrac College Edition, your on-line research library, at:

infotrac.thomsonlearning.com

Aggression, Altruism, and Moral Development

Bob Daemmrich/The Image Works

The Development of Aggression

Altruism: Development of the Prosocial Self

What Is Morality?

Psychoanalytic Explanations of Moral Development

Cognitive-Developmental Theory: The Child as Moral Philosopher

Morality as a Product of Social Learning (and Social Information Processing)

Who Raises Children Who Are Morally Mature?

Summary

What would *you* say is the most important aspect of a child's social development? Surely this is a question that might generate any number of answers. But when one sample of new parents encountered this item in a child-rearing survey conducted by one of the authors' laboratory classes, 74 percent of them indicated that they hoped, above all, that their children would acquire a strong sense of *morality*—right and wrong—to guide their transactions with other people.

When then asked what sort of moral principles they hoped to instill, these new parents provided many answers. However, most of their responses fit into one of the following three categories:

1. *Avoid hurting others.* Parents generally hoped their children could learn to become appropriately autonomous and to serve their needs without harming others. In fact, unprovoked and intentional acts of harmdoing—or *aggression*—was one class of behaviour that most parents said they would try to suppress.

2. *Prosocial concern.* Another value that many parents hoped to instill was a sense of *altruism*—that is, a selfless concern for the welfare of other people and a willingness to act on that concern. In fact, it is not at all unusual for parents to encourage such altruistic acts as sharing, comforting, or helping others while their children are still in diapers.

3. *A personal commitment to abide by rules.* Finally, almost all of the survey respondents mentioned the importance of persuading children to comply with socially condoned rules of conduct and monitoring their behaviour to ensure that these rules are followed. They felt that the ultimate goal of this *moral socialization* is to help the child acquire a set of *personal* values, or ethical principles, that will enable her to distinguish right from wrong and to do the right things, even when there may be no one else present to monitor and evaluate her conduct.

This chapter explores these three interrelated aspects of social development that people often consider when making judgments about one's character. We begin with the topic of aggression, asking how it develops and changes over time and then considering some of the ways that adults might effectively control such conduct. Our focus will then shift from harmdoing to a seemingly incompatible form of social activity—altruism and prosocial behaviour—as we consider how young and reputedly selfish children might learn to make personal sacrifices to benefit others. Finally, we turn to the broader issue of moral development as we trace the child's evolution from a seemingly self-indulgent creature who appears to respect no rules to a moral philosopher of sorts who has internalized certain ethical principles to evaluate his own and others' conduct.

THE DEVELOPMENT OF AGGRESSION

What qualifies as **aggression**? According to the most widely accepted definition, an aggressive act is any form of behaviour designed to harm or injure a living being who is motivated to avoid such treatment (Coie & Dodge, 1998). Notice that it is the actor's *intent* that defines an act as aggressive, not the act's consequences. So this *intentional definition* would classify as aggressive all acts in which harm was intended but not done (for example, a violent kick that misses its target, an undetected snub) while excluding accidental harm or rough-and-tumble play in which participants are enjoying themselves with no harmful intent.

Aggressive acts are often divided into two categories: **hostile aggression** and **instrumental aggression**. If an actor's major goal is to harm a victim, his or her behaviour qualifies as hostile aggression. By contrast, instrumental aggression describes those situations in which one person harms another as a means to some other end. Clearly, the same overt act could be classified as either hostile or instrumental aggression depending on the circumstances. If a young boy clobbered his sister and then teased her for crying, we might consider this hostile aggression. But these same actions could be labelled instrumental aggression (or a mixture of hostile and instrumental aggression) had the boy also grabbed a toy that his sister was using.

Origins of Aggression in Infancy

Although young infants get angry and may occasionally strike people, it is difficult to think of these actions as having an aggressive intent. Piaget (1952) describes an incident in which he frustrated 7-month-old Laurent by placing his hand in front of an interesting object that Laurent was trying to reach. The boy then smacked Piaget's hand, as if it merely represented an obstruction that must be removed.

However, the picture soon changes. Marlene Caplan and her associates (1991) found that 1-year-old infants can be quite forceful with each other when one infant controls a toy that the other wants. Even when duplicate toys were available, 12-month-olds occasionally ignored these unused objects and tried to overpower a peer in order to control *that child's* toy. And the intimidators in these tussles appeared to be treating the other child as an *adversary* rather than an inanimate obstacle, implying that the seeds of instrumental aggression may already have been sown by the end of the first year.

Although 2-year-olds have at least as many **conflicts** over toys as 1-year-olds do, they are more likely than 1-year-olds to resolve these disputes by negotiating and sharing than by fighting, particularly when toys are in short supply (Caplan et al., 1991). According to Michel Perlman of the University of Toronto and Hildy Ross of the University of Waterloo (1997), early conflicts need not be training grounds for aggression and can even be adaptive, serving as a context in which infants, toddlers, and preschool children can learn to negotiate and to achieve their aims without resorting to shows of force—especially when adults intervene and encourage harmonious means of resolving conflicts. Indeed, Japanese mothers are especially intolerant of harmdoing and encourage their children to suppress anger in the interest of promoting social harmony. As a result, Japanese *preschoolers* are already less angered by interpersonal conflicts and less likely to respond aggressively to them than American children are (Zahn-Waxler et al., 1996).

aggression
behaviour performed with the intention of harming a living being who is motivated to avoid this treatment

hostile aggression
aggressive acts for which the perpetrator's major goal is to harm or injure a victim

instrumental aggression
aggressive acts for which the perpetrator's major goal is to gain access to objects, space, or privileges

conflict
circumstances in which two (or more) persons have incompatible needs, desires, or goals

Developmental Trends in Aggression

The character of children's aggression changes dramatically with age. In her classic study of the development of aggression among preschoolers, Florence Goodenough (1931) asked mothers of 2- to 5-year-olds to keep diaries in which they recorded the details of their children's angry outbursts. In examining these data, Goodenough found that unfocused temper tantrums become less and less common between ages 2 and 3 as children began to *physically retaliate* (by hitting or kicking) when playmates frustrate or attack them. However, physical aggression gradually declines between ages 3 and 5, only to be replaced by teasing, tattling, name-calling, and other forms of verbal aggression. What were these preschoolers squabbling about? Goodenough found that they fought most often over toys and other possessions, so that their aggression was usually *instrumental* in character.

Over the course of middle childhood, the overall incidence of physical and verbal aggression declines as children learn to settle most disputes in amicable ways (Loeber & Stouthamer-Loeber, 1998). Yet hostile aggression increases slightly, even as instrumental aggression becomes less common (Hartup, 1974). Why? Probably because older children are acquiring the role-taking skills to better infer others' *harmful intent*, to which they sometimes react by retaliating against the harmdoer (Coie et al., 1991; Hartup, 1974). In fact, elementary-school children are reluctant to condemn this **retaliatory aggression**, often viewing fighting back as a normal (though not necessarily moral) response to provocation (Astor, 1994; Coie et al., 1991).

Sex Differences

Although the trends we've described hold for both boys and girls, data from more than 100 countries around the world reveal that boys and men are more physically and more verbally aggressive, on average, than girls and women are (Harris, 1992; Maccoby & Jacklin, 1974). As we noted in Chapter 13, boys' higher levels of male sex hormones—namely, testosterone—may contribute to sex differences in aggression. However, recent studies reveal that very young boys are *not* more aggressive than girls (Hay, Castle, &

As children mature, an increasing percentage of their aggressive acts qualify as examples of hostile aggression.

Nick Kelsh/Corbis/Magma

retaliatory aggression
aggressive acts elicited by real or
imagined provocations

Davies, 2000). Marlene Caplan and her associates (1991), for example, found that forceful, aggressive resolutions of disputes over toys were actually more numerous among 1-year-olds when the play groups were dominated *by girls*! Even at age 2, groups dominated by boys were more likely than those dominated by girls to negotiate and share when toys were scarce. It is not until age 2½ to 3 that sex differences in aggression are reliable, and this is clearly enough time for gender typing to have steered boys and girls in different directions (Fagot, Leinbach, & O'Boyle, 1992).

What social influences might conspire to make boys more aggressive than girls? For one, parents play rougher with boys than with girls and react more negatively to the aggressive behaviours of daughters than to those of sons, according to Rosemary Mills of the University of Manitoba and Kenneth Rubin of the University of Maryland (1990; see also Parke & Slaby, 1983). Furthermore, the guns, tanks, missile launchers, and other symbolic implements of destruction that boys often receive encourage the enactment of aggressive themes—and actually promote aggressive behaviour (Feshbach, 1956; Watson & Peng, 1992). During the preschool years, children come to view aggression as a male attribute in their gender schemas, and by middle childhood, boys expect aggressive acts to provide them with more tangible benefits and to elicit less disapproval from either parents or peers than girls do (Hertzberger & Hall, 1993; Perry, Perry, & Weiss, 1989). So even though biological factors may contribute, it is clear that sex differences in aggression depend to no small extent on gender typing and gender differences in social learning.

One final point: Some investigators today believe that boys may appear so much more aggressive than girls because researchers have focused on overt aggressive behaviours and have failed to consider *covertly* hostile acts that may be more common among girls than boys. The research in Box 14.1 clearly supports this point of view.

From Aggression to Antisocial Conduct

The incidence of hostile and other overt, easily detectable forms of aggression continue to decline from middle childhood throughout adolescence (Loeber & Stouthamer-Loeber, 1998; Nagin & Tremblay, 1999; Tremblay, 2003). However, this does not necessarily mean that adolescents are becoming any better behaved. **Relational aggression** in girls becomes more subtle and malicious during the adolescent years (Galen & Underwood, 1997), and teenage boys become more inclined to express their anger and frustrations *indirectly*, through such acts as theft, truancy, substance abuse, and sexual misconduct (Loeber & Stouthamer-Loeber, 1998; U.S. Department of Justice, 1995). So it seems that adolescents who are becoming less overtly aggressive may simply turn to other forms of antisocial conduct to express their discontents.

relational aggression
acts such as snubbing, exclusion, withdrawing acceptance, or spreading rumours that are aimed at damaging an adversary's self-esteem, friendships, or social status

Is Aggression a Stable Attribute?

Apparently, aggression is a reasonably stable attribute. Not only are aggressive toddlers likely to become aggressive 5-year-olds (Cummings, Iannotti, & Zahn-Waxler, 1989), but also longitudinal research conducted in Finland, Iceland, New Zealand, and the United States reveals that the amount of moody, ill-tempered, and aggressive behaviour that children display between ages 3 and 10 is a fairly good predictor of their aggressive or other antisocial inclinations later in life (Hart, Hofmann, et al., 1997; Henry et al., 1996; Kokko & Pulkkinen, 2000; Newman et al., 1997). Rowell Huesmann and his associates (1984), for example, tracked one group of 600 participants for 22 years. As we see in Figure 14.1, highly aggressive 8-year-olds often became relatively hostile 30-year-olds who were likely to batter their spouses or children and to be convicted of criminal offences. In fact, Richard Tremblay and colleagues (Brame, Nagain, & Tremblay, 2001) suggest that

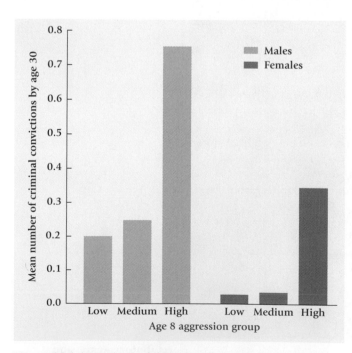

Figure 14.1 *Aggression in childhood predicts criminal behaviour in adulthood for both males and females.* FROM HUESMANN ET AL., *1984.*

Nicki Crick and Jennifer Grotpeter (1995) proposed that both boys and girls can be quite hostile and aggressive, but they display their aggression in very different ways. Boys, who often pursue competitive, instrumental goals, are likely to strike, insult, or display other *overt* forms of aggression toward others who displease them or who interfere with their objectives. Girls, by contrast, are more likely to focus on *expressive* or *relational* goals—on establishing close, intimate connections with others rather than attempting to compete with or dominate their associates. So Crick and Grotpeter proposed that girls' aggressive behaviour would be more consistent with the *social* goals they pursue, consisting largely of covert forms of relational aggression—actions such as withdrawing acceptance from an adversary, excluding her from one's social network, or taking some sort of action (for example, spreading rumours) that might damage her friendships or general status in the peer group.

To test this hypothesis, Grades 3 through 6 students were asked to nominate classmates who often displayed (1) overtly aggressive acts (for example, hitting or insulting others) and (2) *relationally manipulative* acts (for example, withdrawing acceptance, snubbing, or excluding others). As we see in the figure, far more boys than girls were viewed as high in overt aggression, a finding that replicates past research. However, far more girls than boys were perceived to be high in relational aggression. Clearly, such subtle or indirect expressions of hostility may be difficult at times for victims to detect, and may thus allow the perpetrator to behave aggressively while avoiding open conflict. Even 3- to 5-year-old girls are learning this lesson because they are already more inclined than preschool boys are to try to exclude rather than hit a peer who provokes them (Crick, Casas, & Mosher, 1997; Crick et al., 1998) and to victimize certain peers in relationally manipulative ways (Crick, Casas, & Ku, 1999).

Do other children perceive these attempts to undermine a person's status or the quality of his or her personal relationships as clear examples of aggression? Crick and her associates (1996) addressed this issue by asking 9- to 12-year-olds to indicate the ways in which peers of each sex try to get back at or be mean to someone who makes them mad. Overwhelmingly, children said that boys will hit or insult their adversaries, whereas they felt that the most likely response for girls was to try to undermine an adversary's social standing. So children clearly do view these relationally manipulative acts as harmful and aggressive—a viewpoint that grows even stronger among adolescents (Galen & Underwood, 1997). Furthermore, girls who frequently display relational aggression are often lonely and are rejected by their peers in much the same way that boys high in overt aggression are at risk of poor peer relations (McNeilly-Choque et al., 1996; Tomada & Schneider, 1997).

In sum, boys and girls often tend to express their hostilities in very different ways. Because most prior research on children's aggression has focused on physical and verbal assaults and has largely ignored relationally manipulative acts, it clearly underestimates girls' aggressive inclinations.

Percentage of girls and boys nominated by classmates as high in relationally manipulative behaviours and overt aggression (physical or verbal assaults) by a sample of Grades 3 through 6 students. ADAPTED FROM CRICK & GROTPETER, 1995.

there is little evidence for a late onset of high levels of physical aggression. These behaviours most often can be predicted from early childhood, making the detection of problems in preschool an important component of problem prevention strategies.

Clearly, these findings reflect group trends and do not necessarily imply that all highly aggressive children remain highly aggressive over time. In fact, one study by Daniel Nagin from Carnegie Mellon University and Richard Tremblay from Université de Montréal found that only about one of eight highly aggressive kindergarten boys remained highly aggressive as adolescents (Nagin & Tremblay, 1999). (See Box 14.2 for a summary of Tremblay's review of current knowledge of aggressive behaviour.) Yet we should not be surprised to find that aggression is a reasonably stable attribute for many children. Consider that children who are genetically predisposed to be temperamentally irritable may remain relatively aggressive over time because they *regularly* evoke negative reactions from other people, which may foster hostile, aggressive responses (see for example, Eley, Lichtenstein, & Stevenson, 1999; O'Connor et al., 1998). And regardless of their genetic predispositions, other children may remain highly aggressive because they are raised in home environments that *nurture* and *maintain* aggressive habits (Coie & Dodge, 1998). Before examining these "training grounds" for aggression, let's briefly consider the characteristics that aggressive children display.

Richard E. Tremblay

Richard E. Tremblay

Richard Tremblay works in the Department of Psychiatry/Psychology/Pediatrics and is the Director of the Research Unit on Children's Psychosocial Maladjustment at Université de Montréal. For the past 19 years he has conducted longitudinal and experimental studies addressing the physical, cognitive, emotional, and social development of children from conception onward to gain a better understanding of the development and prevention of antisocial and violent behaviour.

A re children born with an aggressive instinct, or do they have to learn to be aggressive? This fundamental question is a critical one for developmental psychologists such as Richard Tremblay at Université de Montréal.

In general, most of the research conducted during the twentieth century concentrated on the development of aggression in adolescents and elementary-school children. Focusing on these age groups implicitly assumes that aggression is learned during these developmental periods. Tremblay and his colleagues, however, argue that aggression starts much earlier and there are developmental changes in how aggression is presented (Tremblay, 2003). For example, children start by physically aggressing during infancy and go on to verbal aggression once they have learned to talk (Tremblay et al., 1996; Tremblay et al., 1999). The form of aggressive behaviour that is generally considered more "serious" or "socially unacceptable" (physical aggression), then, clearly precedes less "serious" forms of aggressive behaviour such as verbal aggression or indirect aggression.

This pattern is supported by observations that the frequency of physical aggression decreases with age. For example, parent reports in a sample of more than 22 000 children (representative of the population of 0- to 11-year-old children in Canada in 1994) indicate that, although the frequency of physical aggression decreases from age 3 to age 11, indirect aggression increases from age 4 to age 8 (Tremblay et al., 1996).

In the past, infants' physical aggression has generally not been considered developmentally significant. This is probably because of the "weakness of their limbs" and the apparent lack of "intentionality." Tremblay's work establishes the importance of examining the development of aggressive behaviour during the first few years after birth, and differentiating among forms of aggressive behaviour. To have a relatively complete description of the life-span developmental trajectories of human aggressive behaviour by the end of the 21st century, Tremblay suggests that we need more longitudinal studies that have collected data on aggressive behaviour from infancy onwards.

Individual Differences in Aggressive Behaviour

Although children vary dramatically in their levels of aggression, only a small percentage can be described as chronically aggressive. In fact, some researchers who have charted aggressive incidents among elementary- and high-school students find that a small minority of youngsters are involved in a large majority of the conflicts. Who is involved? In many groups, the participants are a handful of highly aggressive instigators and the 10 to 15 percent of their classmates who are regularly abused by these bullies (Olweus, 1984; Perry, Kusel, & Perry, 1988).

Recent research points to two kinds of highly aggressive children: *proactive aggressors* and *reactive aggressors*. Compared with nonaggressive youngsters, **proactive aggressors** are quite confident that aggression will "pay off" in tangible benefits (such as control of a disputed toy), and they are inclined to believe that they can enhance their self-esteem by dominating other children, who generally submit to them before any serious harm has been done (Crick & Dodge, 1996; Quiggle et al., 1992). So for proactive aggressors, shows of force are an *instrumental* strategy by which they achieve personal goals.

By contrast, **reactive aggressors** display high levels of hostile, retaliatory aggression. These youngsters are quite suspicious and wary of other people, often viewing them as belligerent adversaries who *deserve* to be dealt with in a forceful manner (Astor, 1994; Crick & Dodge, 1996).

Interestingly, each of these groups of aggressive children display distinct biases in their processing of social information that contribute to their high levels of aggressive behaviour. Let's take a closer look.

proactive aggressors
highly aggressive children who find aggressive acts easy to perform and who rely heavily on aggression as a means of solving social problems or achieving other personal objectives

reactive aggressors
children who display high levels of hostile, retaliatory aggression because they overattribute hostile intent to others and can't control their anger long enough to seek nonaggressive solutions to social problems

Dodge's Social Information-Processing Theory of Aggression

Kenneth Dodge (1986; Crick & Dodge, 1994) has formulated a social information-processing model that seeks to explain how children come to favour aggressive or nonaggressive solutions to social problems. To illustrate, imagine that you are an 8-year-old who is harmed under ambiguous circumstances: A peer walks by, nudges your table with his leg and says "Oops!" as he scatters a nearly completed jigsaw puzzle you have been working on for a long time. How would you respond? Dodge proposes that a child's response will depend on the outcome of six cognitive steps that are illustrated in Figure 14.2. The youngster who is harmed first *encodes* and *interprets* the available social cues (What is the harmdoer's reaction? Did he mean to do it?). After interpreting the meaning of these cues, the child then *formulates a goal* (to resolve the situation), *generates* and *evaluates* possible strategies for achieving this goal, and finally *selects* and *enacts* a response. Notice that the model proposes that a child's *mental state*—that is, his or her past social experiences, social expectancies (especially those involving harmdoing), knowledge of social rules, emotional reactivity, and the ability to regulate emotions—can influence any of the model's six phases of information processing.

According to Dodge, the mental states of *reactive aggressors*, who have a history of bickering with peers, are likely to include an expectancy that "others are hostile to me." So when harmed under ambiguous circumstances (such as having their puzzle scattered by a careless peer), they are much more inclined than nonaggressive children to (1) search for and find cues compatible with this expectancy, (2) attribute hostile intent to the harmdoer, and (3) become very angry and quickly retaliate in a hostile manner without carefully considering other nonaggressive solutions. Not only does research consistently indicate that reactive aggressors overattribute hostile intent to peers (Crick & Dodge, 1996; Dodge, 1980), but by virtue of their own hostile retaliations these children also have many negative experiences with teachers and peers (Trachtenberg & Viken, 1994), who come to dislike them, thereby reinforcing their expectancy that "others are hostile to me" (see Figure 14.3). Interestingly, girls can be as reactively aggressive as boys, displaying the same kind of **hostile attributional bias** and a strong readiness to react aggressively to ambiguous harmdoing (Crick & Dodge, 1996; Guerra & Slaby, 1990).

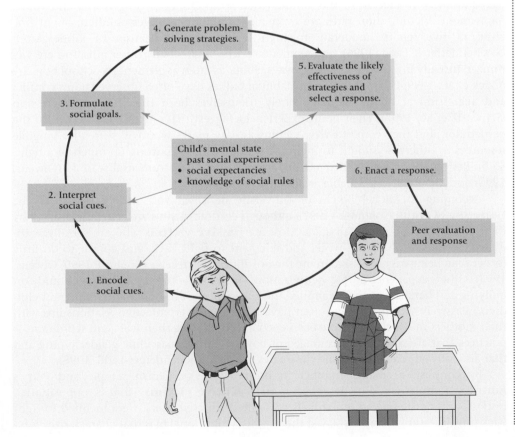

Figure 14.2 *Dodge's social information-processing model of the steps children take when deciding how to respond to harmdoing or other social problems. The boy whose creation is destroyed by the other boy's nudging the table must first encode and interpret the social clues (i.e., did he mean it or was it accidental?) and then proceed through the remaining steps to formulate a response to this harmdoing. Adapted from Crick and Dodge, 1994.*

hostile attributional bias
tendency to view harm done under ambiguous circumstances as having stemmed from a hostile intent on the part of the harmdoer; characterizes reactive aggressors

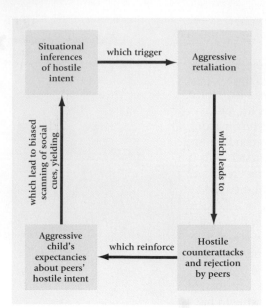

Figure 14.3 *A social-cognitive model of the reactive aggressor's biased attributions about ambiguous harmdoing and their behavioural outcomes.*

Within the figure:

Situational inferences of hostile intent — **which trigger** → Aggressive retaliation

Aggressive retaliation — **which leads to** → Hostile counterattacks and rejection by peers

Hostile counterattacks and rejection by peers — **which reinforce** → Aggressive child's expectancies about peers' hostile intent

Aggressive child's expectancies about peers' hostile intent — **which lead to biased scanning of social cues, yielding** → Situational inferences of hostile intent

Proactive aggressors display a different pattern of social information processing. According to Francois Poulin of Université du Québec à Montréal and Michel Boivin from Université de Laval (2000), because these youngsters do not feel especially disliked (and may even have many friends) (see also Rodkin et al., 2000), they are not so inclined to quickly attribute hostile intent to a harmdoer. But this does not mean that the proactive aggressor is inclined to let the incident pass. In fact, these youngsters are likely to carefully formulate an *instrumental* goal (for example, "I'll teach careless peers to be more careful around me") and to *coolly* and *consciously decide* that an aggressive response is likely to be most effective at achieving this aim. In fact, proactive aggressors are likely to display such positive emotions as happiness during aggressive encounters with peers (Arsenio, Cooperman, & Lover, 2000). Their mental states favour aggressive solutions to conflict because they expect positive outcomes to result from their use of force, and they feel quite capable about the prospect of dominating their adversaries (Crick & Dodge, 1996).

Perpetrators and Victims of Peer Aggression

Bullying in the classroom and school playground is common. In naturalistic observations of playground activity in a Canadian city, Wendy Craig of Queen's University and Debra Pepler of York University (1997; Pepler, Craig, & Roberts, 1998) found that an episode of bullying occurred approximately every seven minutes. In a study of Canadian classrooms, bullying was observed twice every hour (Atlas & Pepler, 1998). Each of us has probably known at least one victimized peer—a youngster who repeatedly serves as a target for other children's hostile acts. Who are these children, and who singles them out for abuse?

Research with Swedish male adolescents (Olweus, 1984, 1993) and American elementary-school children of both sexes (Egan & Perry, 1998; Kochenderfer & Ladd, 1996; Perry et al., 1988) provides some clues. Based on teacher ratings, about 10 percent of Olweus's adolescent sample could be described as habitual bullies who regularly subjected another 10 percent of the sample (their whipping boys) to physical and verbal harassment. Victimization rates are even higher among younger children; about one child in five reports moderate to high levels of victimization in kindergarten (Kochenderfer & Ladd, 1996), and elementary-school girls bully other girls and are victimized (usually in verbally aggressive ways) about as often as elementary-school boys are (Crick et al., 1999; Perry et al., 1988). Habitual bullies have often observed adult conflict and aggression at home but have rarely themselves been the target of aggression (Schwartz et al., 1997). Their home experiences suggest that aggression pays off for the perpetrator, and they come to view victims as easy marks who will surrender tangible resources or otherwise submit to their dominance without putting up much of a fight. So bullies appear to harass their victims for personal or instrumental reasons (Olweus, 1993) and are usually classifiable as *proactive* aggressors.

According to Michel Boivin of Université de Laval and Shelley Hymel of the University of British Columbia (1997), although chronic victims are generally disliked by their peers, they are not at all alike. Most are **passive victims** who are socially withdrawn, sedentary, physically weak, and reluctant to fight back, and appear to do little (other than being easy marks) to invite the hostilities they receive (Boulton, 1999; Olweus, 1993). Others experience ethnic victimization. (See Box 14.3 for a summary of a study on bullying and harassment that examined the experiences of minority and immigrant children.) Passively victimized boys often have had close, overprotective relationships with their mothers in which they have been encouraged to voice their fears and self-doubts—practices that are generally discouraged of boys as part of masculine gender typing and that are not well received by male classmates (Ladd & Kochenderger-Ladd, 1998).

By contrast, a smaller number in both Olweus's Swedish sample and Perry's American samples could be described as **provocative victims**—that is, oppositional, restless, and hot-tempered individuals who often irritated peers, were inclined to fight back (unsuccessfully), and displayed the hostile attributional bias that characterizes reac-

passive victims (of aggression)
socially withdrawn, anxious children with low self-esteem whom bullies torment, even though they appear to have done little to trigger such abuse

provocative victims (of aggression)
restless, hot-tempered, and oppositional children who are victimized because they often irritate their peers

tive aggressors. Provocative victims have often been physically abused or otherwise victimized at home and have learned from their experiences to view other people as hostile adversaries (Schwartz et al., 1997).

Unfortunately, many children and adolescents who become chronic victims continue to be victimized, especially if they blame themselves for their victimization and have no friends to stick up for them and help them acquire social skills (Graham & Juvonen, 1998; Hodges et al., 1997; Schwartz et al., 2000). And victimized children are at risk for a variety of adjustment problems, including loneliness, anxiety, depression, further erosion of self-esteem, and a growing dislike for and avoidance of school (Egan & Perry, 1998; Hodges et al., 1999; Kochenderfer-Ladd & Wardrop, 2001). Clearly there is a pressing need for interventions that not only take strong steps to discourage bullying but also help chronic victims to build self-esteem and develop the social skills and supportive friendships that will improve their social standing and make them less inviting targets for their tormentors (Egan & Perry, 1998; Hodges et al., 1999).

Cultural and Subcultural Influences on Aggression

Cross-cultural and ethnographic studies consistently indicate that some societies and subcultures are more violent and aggressive than others. Groups such as the Arapesh of Papua New Guinea, the Lepchas of Sikkim, and the Pygmies of central Africa all use

---

14.3

THE INSIDE TRACK

Debra Pepler

Debra Pepler works in the Department of Psychology at York University. She is also director of the LaMarsh Centre for Research on Violence and Conflict. She studies risk and protective factors associated with the adjustment of children in violent homes, as well as children's aggressive behaviours, particularly in school and peer contexts.

Concerns about bullying have been growing in Canada as educators and parents have become more aware of it. Schools and parent groups are taking action to reduce bullying problems at school (Pepler & Craig, 1999). Debra Pepler of York University conducts research on children's aggressive behaviours, particularly in the school and peer contexts. The central part of her work comprises naturalistic observations of interactions among school-aged peers using remote microphones and video cameras. This innovative method enables Pepler to examine children's interactions that are normally hidden from adults, such as bullying. In a recent study, Pepler and colleagues found that peers were present during 88% of bullying episodes in a school playground but intervened in only 19% of the episodes (Hawkins, Pepler, & Craig, 2001). Pepler argues that interventions to reduce bullying must focus beyond the aggressive child and the victim to include peers, school staff, parents, and the broader community. The interventions must therefore be systematic and involve all contexts of children's lives (Craig & Pepler, 1997).

Pepler's research demonstrates that bullying and harassment are pervasive among late-elementary and high-school students. Ethnic minority and immigrant youth, in particular, may be targets of bullying. In one study of the experiences of Canadian minority and immigrant children, Pepler, Jennifer Connolly of York University, and Wendy Craig of Queen's University (2001) found that 17 percent of elementary- and high-school students had experienced ethnic victimization. Elementary-school students from ethnic minority groups were more likely to experience ethnic victimization than students from the majority group. The pattern in high school was similar but not statistically significant. A similar pattern was evident for immigration status: High-school students not born in Canada reported more ethnically based victimization than those born in Canada. The trend for elementary-school students was similar but not statistically significant.

These data indicate that we should be concerned about the reception of minority and immigrant students in schools because they may be harassed and excluded by other students. Among the elementary-school students, there were no differences between the minority and majority students in reports of perpetrating bullying. Immigrant high-school students were more likely to report bullying others than the second-generation students were. This pattern suggests that as students mature they may become increasingly frustrated and hostile, particularly if they experience bullying as a function of their family background. The students' reports of behaviour problems indicate significant concern for the students who are engaged as bullies, victims, and bully–victims in experiences associated with ethnically based bullying.

weapons to hunt but rarely show any kind of interpersonal aggression. When these peace-loving societies are invaded by outsiders, their members retreat to inaccessible regions rather than stand and fight (Gorer, 1968).

In marked contrast to these groups are the Gebusi of Papua New Guinea, who teach their children to be combative and emotionally unresponsive to the needs of others and who show a murder rate that is more than 50 times higher than that of any industrialized nation (Scott, 1992). The United States is also an aggressive society. On a percentage basis, the incidence of rape, homicide, and assault is higher in the United States than in any other industrialized nation, and the United States ranks a close second to Spain (and far above third-place Canada) in the incidence of armed robbery (Wolff, Rutten, & Bayer, 1992).

Studies conducted in the United States and in England also point to social class differences in aggression: Children and adolescents from the lower socioeconomic strata (SES), particularly males from larger urban areas, exhibit more aggressive behaviour and higher levels of delinquency than their age-mates from the middle class (Loeber & Stouthamer-Loeber, 1998).

? WHAT DO YOU THINK?

Why do you think that the incidence of violent crimes such as murder and rape is nearly twice as high in the relatively affluent United States as in the countries ranked second for each of these offences—that is, Canada for murder and Sweden for rape (Wolff et al., 1992)? How might you evaluate your hypotheses?

These trends appear to be closely linked to social class differences in child rearing. For example, parents from lower-income families are more likely than middle-class parents to rely on physical punishment to discipline aggression and defiance, thereby *modelling aggression* even as they try to suppress it (Dodge, Pettit, & Bates, 1994). Low-SES parents are also more inclined to endorse aggressive solutions to conflict and to encourage their children to respond forcefully when provoked by peers (Dodge et al., 1994; Jagers, Bingham, & Hans, 1996)—practices that may foster the development of the *hostile attributional bias* that highly aggressive youngsters so often display. Finally, low-SES parents often live complex, stressful lives that may make it difficult for them to manage or monitor their children's whereabouts, activities, and choice of friends. Unfortunately, this lack of parental monitoring is consistently associated with such aggressive or delinquent activities as fighting, sassing teachers, destroying property, drug use, and breaking rules outside the home (Kilgore, Synder, & Lentz, 2000; Pettit et al., 2001).

Antisocial or delinquent conduct is common among teenagers whose parents fail to monitor their activities, whereabouts, and choice of friends.

In sum, a person's aggressive and antisocial inclinations depend, in part, on the extent to which the culture or subculture condones or fails to discourage such behaviour. Yet not all people in pacifistic societies are kind, cooperative, and helpful, and the vast majority of people raised in relatively aggressive societies or subcultures are not especially prone to violence. Why are there such dramatic individual differences in aggression within a given culture or subculture? Gerald Patterson and his associates answer by claiming that highly aggressive children often live in homes that can be described as breeding grounds for hostile, antisocial conduct.

Coercive Home Environments: Breeding Grounds for Aggression and Delinquency

Patterson (1982; Patterson, Reid, & Dishion, 1992) has observed patterns of interaction among children and their parents in families that have at least one highly aggressive child. The aggressive children in Patterson's sample seemed "out of control"; they fought a lot at home and at school and were generally unruly and defiant. These families were then compared with other families of the same size and socioeconomic status that had no problem children.

Families as Social Systems

Patterson soon discovered that he could not explain out of control behaviour by merely focusing on the child-rearing practices that parents used. Instead, it seemed that highly aggressive children lived in atypical family environments that were characterized by a social climate that *they had helped to create*. Unlike most homes, where people frequently display approval and affection, the highly aggressive problem child usually lived in a setting in which family members were constantly bickering with one another: They were reluctant to initiate conversations, and, when they did talk, they tended to needle, threaten, or otherwise irritate other family members rather than conversing amiably. Patterson called these settings **coercive home environments** because a high percentage of interactions centred on one family member's attempts to force another to stop irritating him or her. Patterson also noted that **negative reinforcement** was important in maintaining these coercive interactions: When one family member makes life unpleasant for another, the second learns to whine, yell, tease, or hit because these actions often force the antagonist to stop (and thus are reinforced). Consider the following sequence of events, which may be fairly typical in a coercive home environment:

1. A girl teases her brother, who makes her stop teasing by yelling at her (yelling is negatively reinforced).

2. A few minutes later, the girl calls her brother a nasty name. The boy then chases and hits her.

3. The girl stops calling him names (which negatively reinforces hitting). She then whimpers and hits him back, and he withdraws (negatively reinforcing her hits). The boy then approaches and hits his sister again, and the conflict escalates.

4. At this point, the mother intervenes. However, her children are too emotionally disrupted to listen to reason, so she finds herself applying punitive and coercive tactics to make them stop fighting.

5. The fighting stops (thus reinforcing the mother for using coercive methods). However, the children soon begin to whine, cry, or yell at the mother. These countercoercive techniques are then reinforced if the mother backs off and accepts peace at any price. Unfortunately, backing off is only a temporary solution. The next time the children antagonize each other and become involved in an unbearable conflict, the mother is likely to use even more coercion to get them to stop. The children once again apply their own methods of countercoercion to induce her to "lay off," and the family atmosphere becomes increasingly unpleasant for everyone.

coercive home environment
home in which family members often annoy one another and use aggressive or otherwise antisocial tactics as a method of coping with these aversive experiences

negative reinforcer
stimulus whose removal or termination as the consequence of an act increases the probability that the act will recur

Mothers of problem children rarely use social approval as a means of behaviour control, choosing instead to largely ignore prosocial conduct, to interpret many innocuous acts as antisocial, and rely almost exclusively on coercive tactics to deal with perceived misconduct (Nix et al., 1999; Strassberg, 1995). Perhaps the overwhelmingly negative treatment that these problem children receive at home (including parents' tendency to label ambiguous events as antisocial) helps explain why they generally mistrust other people and display the *hostile attributional bias* so commonly observed among highly aggressive children (Dishion, 1990; Weiss et al., 1992). And, ironically, children from highly coercive home environments eventually become resistant to punishment: They have learned to fight coercion with countercoercion and often do so by defying the parent and *repeating the very act that she or he is trying to suppress*. Why? Because this is one of the few ways that the child can successfully command the attention of an adult who rarely offers praise or shows any signs of affection. No wonder Patterson calls these children out of control! By contrast, children from noncoercive families receive much more positive attention from siblings and parents, so that they don't have to irritate other family members to be noticed (Patterson, 1982).

So we see that the flow of influence in the family setting is *multidirectional:* Coercive *interactions* between parents and their children and the children themselves affect the behaviour of *all* parties and contribute to the development of a hostile family environment—a true breeding ground for aggression (Garcia et al., 2000). Unfortunately, these problem families may never break out of this destructive pattern of attacking and counterattacking one another unless they receive help. In Box 14.4, we consider one particularly effective approach to this problem—a method that necessarily focuses on the family as a social system rather than simply on the aggressive child who has been referred for treatment.

Coercive Home Environments as Contributors to Chronic Delinquency

How serious are the risks faced by out of control children who grow up in a coercive home environment? Patterson and his associates (1989) have addressed this issue by reviewing the literature on problem children and have drawn some strong conclusions. As shown in Figure 14.4, coercive parenting early in childhood contributes to the development of children's hostile attributional biases; defiant, aggressive behaviours; and general lack of self-restraint, which, by middle childhood, can cause these youngsters to be rejected by elementary-school peers, to be criticized by teachers, and to flounder academically (Birch & Ladd, 1998; Coie & Dodge, 1998). These poor outcomes may then cause parents to feel less invested in their children and less inclined to closely monitor their activities (Patterson et al., 1989; Vuchinich et al., 1992).

Furthermore, the rejection that problem children experience from peers, coupled with their likely placement in classes with other academically deficient children, often means that they have ample exposure to other relatively defiant, aggressive, and socially unskilled youngsters like themselves. By age 11 to 14, these youngsters associate mainly with other hostile, antisocial classmates, banding together to form deviant peer cliques—groups that tend to devalue academics, encourage aggression, and promote such dysfunctional activities as sexual misconduct, substance abuse, dropping out of school, and a variety of other antisocial or delinquent behaviours (Dishion et al., 1995; Patterson et al., 1992; Poulin & Boivin, 2000). So, to return to the question raised earlier, Patterson claims that living in a coercive home environment poses serious risks indeed and is often a crucial first step along the road to chronic aggression and delinquency.

Although boys are more likely than girls to take the developmental path described in Figure 14.4 (McFadyen-Ketchum et al., 1996), the delinquency gender gap is narrowing. Male delinquents still dominate violent crime statistics, but females are about as likely as males to be involved in larcenies, sexual misconduct, and substance abuse, and they are more likely than males to be arrested for such offences as running away from home and engaging in prostitution (*Federal Bureau of Investigation*, 1997). It may take a more disordered home environment to push girls along the path to delinquency, but girls can become just as chronically antisocial as boys (Loeber & Stouthamer-Loeber, 1998).

Helping Children (and Parents) Who Are "Out of Control"

How does one treat a problem child who is hostile, defiant, and "out of control"? Rather than focusing on the problem child, Gerald Patterson's (1981, 1982) approach is to work with the entire family. Patterson begins by carefully observing the family's interactions and determining just how family members are reinforcing one another's coercive activities. The next step is to describe the nature of the problem to parents and to teach them a new approach to managing their children's behaviour. Some of the principles, skills, and procedures that Patterson stresses are the following:

- Don't give in to the child's coercive behaviour.
- Don't escalate your own coercion when the child becomes coercive.
- Control the child's coercion with the *time-out* procedure in which the child is sent to her room (or some other location) until she calms down and stops using coercive tactics.
- Identify those of the child's behaviours that are most irritating, and then establish a point system in which the child can earn credits (rewards, privileges) for acceptable conduct or lose them for unacceptable behaviour. Parents with older problem children are taught how to formulate "behavioural contracts" that specify how the child is expected to behave at home and at school, as well as how deviations from this behavioural code will be punished. Whenever possible, children should have a say in negotiating these contracts.

- Be on the lookout for occasions when you can respond to the child's prosocial conduct with warmth and affection. Although this is often difficult for parents who are accustomed to snapping at their children and accentuating the negative, Patterson believes that parental affection and approval reinforce good conduct and eventually elicit displays of affection from the child—a clear sign that the family is on the road to recovery.

A clear majority of problem families respond favourably to these methods. Not only do problem children become less coercive, defiant, and aggressive, but the mother's depression fades as she gradually begins to feel better about herself, her child, and her ability to resolve family crises (Patterson, 1981). Some problem families show an immediate improvement. Others respond more gradually to the treatment and may require periodic "booster shots"— that is, follow-up treatments in which the clinician visits the family, determines why progress has slowed (or broken down), and then retrains the parents or suggests new procedures to correct the problems that are not being resolved. Clearly, this therapy works because it recognizes that "out of control" behaviour stems from a *family system* in which both parents and children influence each other and contribute to the development of a hostile family environment. Therapies that focus exclusively on the problem child are not enough!

Not surprisingly, antisocial male adolescents tend to pair up with antisocial females. Not only are these antisocial couples at risk of experiencing hostile and abusive intimate relationships (Capaldi & Clark, 1998; Murphy & Blumenthal, 2000), they are also inclined to make an early entry into parenthood and to rely on the same unresponsive and coercive child-rearing practices that their parents used with them (Fagot et al., 1998; Serbin et al., 1998), thus exposing their own children to a home environment that fosters coercive child behaviours, hostile attributional biases, and all their concomitants (review Figure 14.4). Here, then, is one way in which hostile, antisocial inclinations are transmitted from generation to generation (Patterson, 1998).

Family interventions of the kind described in Box 14.4 can be quite effective at modifying the antisocial tendencies of preadolescent (and younger) children. However, once antisocial patterns continue into adolescence, so many factors conspire to maintain them that interventions are usually unsuccessful (Kazdin,

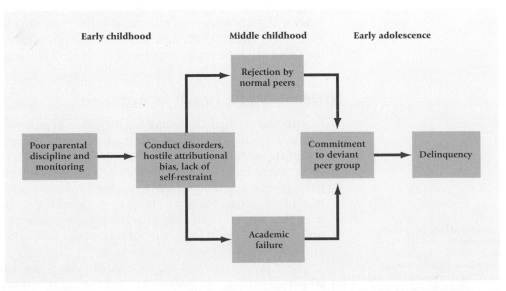

Figure 14.4 *A model of the development of chronic antisocial behaviour.* ADAPTED FROM PATTERSON, DEBARYSHE, & RAMSEY, 1989.

1995) and sometimes even increase the likelihood of delinquent conduct (Dishion, McCord, & Poulin, 1999). Note the implication here: To cope with the problem of chronic delinquency, we must think in terms of *preventive* interventions—ideally, programs that would (1) teach parents more effective child-management techniques, (2) foster children's social skills to prevent them from being rejected by their peers, and (3) provide any academic remediation that may be necessary to keep children on track at school and to lessen the likelihood that they will fall in with deviant peer groups or become high-school dropouts. Of course, any intervention that makes aggressive, antisocial conduct a less viable or attractive option is a step in the right direction. Let's now consider some of the procedures that developmentalists have used in attempting to control children's hostilities.

Methods of Controlling Aggression and Antisocial Conduct

What approaches other than family therapy might assist parents and teachers in suppressing the aggressive antics of children so that antisocial solutions to conflict do not become habitual? Let's look at three general strategies that have achieved some success.

Creating Nonaggressive Environments

One simple but effective approach for reducing children's aggression is to create play areas that minimize the likelihood of conflict. For example, parents and teachers might remove (or refuse to buy) aggressive toys such as guns, tanks, and rubber knives that provoke violent fantasies and aggressive behaviour (Dunn & Hughes, 2001; Watson & Peng, 1992). Providing ample space for vigorous play also helps to eliminate the accidental bumps, shoves, and trips that often escalate into full-blown hostilities (Hartup, 1974). Finally, children are likely to play quite harmoniously if adults provide enough balls, blocks, swings, and other toys to keep them from having to compete for scarce resources (Smith & Connolly, 1980).

Developmentalists now recognize that different forms of aggression require different kinds of intervention (Coie & Koeppl, 1990; Crick & Dodge, 1996). Recall that proactive aggressors rely on forceful strategies because they are easy to enact and often enable these youngsters to achieve personal goals. An effective intervention for these children might teach them that aggression doesn't pay and that alternative prosocial responses, such as cooperation or sharing, are better ways to achieve their objectives. By contrast, hotheaded reactive aggressors may profit more from programs that teach them to control their anger and suppress their tendency to overattribute hostile intentions to companions who displease them. Let's take a closer look at these two kinds of intervention.

Eliminating the Payoffs for Aggression

Parents and teachers can reduce the incidence of proactive aggression by identifying and eliminating its reinforcing consequences and encouraging alternative means of achieving one's objectives. For example, if 4-year-old Lennie were to hit his 3-year-old sister Gail in order to take possession of a toy, Lennie's mother could teach him that this instrumental aggression doesn't pay by simply returning the toy to Gail and denying him his objective. However, this strategy wouldn't work if Lennie is an insecure child who feels neglected and has attacked his sister *in order to attract his mother's attention*; under these circumstances, the mother would be reinforcing Lennie's aggression if she attended to it at all! So what is she to do?

One proven method that she might use is the **incompatible-response technique**—a strategy of *ignoring* all but the most serious of Lennie's aggressive antics (thereby denying him an "attentional" reward) while reinforcing such acts as cooperation and sharing that are incompatible with aggression. Teachers who have tried this

incompatible-response technique
nonpunitive method of behaviour modification in which adults ignore undesirable conduct while reinforcing acts that are incompatible with these responses

strategy find that it quickly produces an increase in children's prosocial conduct and a corresponding decrease in their hostilities (Brown & Elliot, 1965; Slaby & Crowley, 1977). And how might adults handle *serious* acts of aggression without reinforcing them with their attention? One effective approach is the **time-out technique** that Patterson favours, in which the adult removes the offender from the situation in which his aggression is reinforced (for example, by sending him to his room until he is ready to behave appropriately). Although this approach may generate some resentment, the adult in charge is not physically abusing the child or serving as an aggressive model and is not likely to unwittingly reinforce the child who misbehaves as a means of attracting attention. The time-out procedure is most effective at controlling children's hostilities when adults also reinforce cooperative or helpful acts that are incompatible with aggression (Parke & Slaby, 1983).

Social-Cognitive Interventions

Highly aggressive youngsters, particularly those high in reactive aggression, can profit from social-cognitive interventions that help them to (1) regulate their anger and (2) become more skilled at empathizing with and taking others' perspectives so that they will not be so likely to overattribute hostile intentions to their peers (Crick & Dodge, 1996). In one study (Guerra & Slaby, 1990), a group of violent adolescent offenders were coached in such skills as (1) looking for nonhostile cues that might be associated with harmdoing, (2) controlling their anger, and (3) generating nonaggressive solutions to conflict. Not only did these violent offenders show dramatic improvements in their social problem-solving skills, but they also became less inclined to endorse beliefs supporting aggression and became less aggressive in their interactions with authority figures and other inmates. Michael Chandler of the University of British Columbia (1973) found a similar reduction in the hostile social cognitions and aggressive behaviours of a group of 11- to 13-year-old delinquents who had participated in a 10-week program designed specifically to make them more aware of other people's intentions and feelings.

Developmentalists interested in reducing aggression and violence in our schools believe that comprehensive *preventive* interventions aimed at minimizing rewards for aggression, replacing aggression with prosocial responses, and helping children to control their own emotions, to understand others' feelings and intentions, and to seek nonaggressive solutions to conflict are likely to prove highly effective (Conduct Problems Prevention Group, 1999; Henrich, Brown, & Aber, 1999). Recent evaluations of two such pilot programs that targeted elementary-school children in New York City and Seattle found that program participants were significantly less aggressive at school than comparable children who did not participate. And there was more. Program participants also

time-out technique
form of discipline in which children who misbehave are removed from the setting until they are prepared to act more appropriately

Concept Check 14.1
Understanding Aggression and Antisocial Conduct

Check your understanding of the development of aggression and antisocial conduct by matching each descriptive statement below with one of the following concepts or processes: (a) deviant peer cliques, (b) passive victims, (c) provocative victims, (d) relational aggression, (e) coercive home environment, (f) peer rejection, (g) negative reinforcement, (h) proactive aggressors, (i) reactive aggressors, (j) instrumental aggression, (k) hostile aggression. Answers appear in the Appendix.

_____ 1. type of aggression for which girls exceed boys
_____ 2. these individuals think that aggression pays off and are high in instrumental aggression
_____ 3. process by which unpleasant interactions are maintained in coercive home environments
_____ 4. thought to be a strong, direct contributor to chronically antisocial conduct
_____ 5. this kind of aggression is first to appear, often by 12 months
_____ 6. aggression of these individuals often stems from a hostile attributional bias
_____ 7. type of aggression that becomes more common with the growth of role-taking skills
_____ 8. thought to be a strong, direct contributor to one's affiliation with deviant peer cliques
_____ 9. often the first step along the road to chronic delinquency
_____ 10. reactive aggressors may often become the _____ of bullies
_____ 11. overprotected boys are at risk for becoming the _____ of bullies

529
Chapter Fourteen
Aggression, Altruism, and Moral Development

NEL

showed increases in prosocial behaviour and academic achievement, decreases in internalizing disorders such as anxiety and depression, and reductions in racially prejudicial attitudes; and the longer children participated in the programs, the more positive the outcomes (see Henrich et al., 1999, for an overview of these interventions). Similar programs integrated into the *kindergarten* curriculum also appear to help young children to resolve their conflicts amicably (Stevahn et al., 2000). More research will be necessary to fine-tune these programs and properly evaluate their long-term effectiveness. But the early returns are highly encouraging, and, at a cost of $80 to $100 per child per year, these (or other similar) interventions are something that communities may wish to consider as an economical means of helping to optimize the interpersonal competencies of our elementary-school children.

Finally, according to Douglas Cohen and Janet Strayer (1996) of Simon Fraser University, highly aggressive children are often found to be deficient in **empathy**—a social-cognitive attribute that parents can easily foster by modelling empathic concern and by using disciplinary techniques that (1) point out the harmful consequences of their child's aggressive acts while (2) encouraging her to put herself in the victim's place and imagine how the victim feels. In the next section of the chapter, we will see that parents who rely mainly on these rational, nonpunitive disciplinary techniques tend to raise sympathetic children who seem genuinely concerned about the welfare of others.

ALTRUISM: DEVELOPMENT OF THE PROSOCIAL SELF

As we noted in opening this chapter, most parents hope that their children acquire a sense of **altruism**—a genuine concern for the welfare of other people and a willingness to act on that concern. In fact, many parents encourage altruistic acts such as sharing, cooperating, or helping while their children are still in diapers! Experts in child development once would have claimed that these well-intentioned adults were wasting their time, because infants and toddlers were thought to be incapable of considering the needs of anyone other than themselves. But the experts were wrong!

Origins of Altruism

Long before children receive any formal moral or religious training, they may act in ways that resemble the prosocial behaviour of older people. Twelve- to 18-month-olds, for example, occasionally offer toys to companions (Hay et al., 1991) and even attempt to help their parents with such chores as sweeping or dusting or setting the table (Rheingold, 1982). And the prosocial conduct of very young children even has a certain rationality about it. For example, 2-year-olds are more likely to offer toys to a peer when playthings are scarce rather than plentiful (Hay et al., 1991).

Are toddlers capable of expressing sympathy and behaving compassionately toward their companions? Yes, indeed, and these displays of prosocial concern are not all that uncommon (Eisenberg & Fabes, 1998; Zahn-Waxler et al., 1992). Consider the reaction of 21-month-old John to his distressed playmate, Jerry:

> Today Jerry was kind of cranky; he just started ... bawling and he wouldn't stop. John kept coming over and handing Jerry toys, trying to cheer him up.... He'd say things like "Here Jerry," and I said to John "Jerry's sad; he doesn't feel good; he had a shot today." John would look at me with his eyebrows wrinkled

empathy
ability to experience the same emotions that someone else is experiencing

altruism
selfless concern for the welfare of others that is expressed through prosocial acts such as sharing, cooperating, and helping

together like he really understood that Jerry was crying because he was unhappy…. He went over and rubbed Jerry's arm and said "Nice Jerry," and continued to give him toys (Zahn-Waxler, Radke-Yarrow, & King, 1979, pp. 321–2).

Clearly, John was concerned about his little playmate and did what he could to make him feel better.

Although some toddlers often try to comfort distressed companions, others rarely do. These individual variations are due, in part, to temperamental variations. For example, 2-year-olds who are behaviourally inhibited are likely to become highly upset by others' distress and are more likely than uninhibited toddlers to turn away from a distressed acquaintance in an attempt to regulate their arousal (Young, Fox, & Zahn-Waxler, 1999).

Yet individual differences in early compassion also depend quite heavily on parents' reactions to occasions in which their toddler has harmed another child. Carolyn Zahn-Waxler and her associates (1979) found that mothers of less compassionate toddlers typically used coercive tactics such as verbal rebukes or physical punishment to discipline aggression. By contrast, mothers of highly compassionate toddlers frequently disciplined harmdoing with **affective explanations** that may foster sympathy (and perhaps some remorse) by helping children to see the relation between their own acts and the distress they caused (for example, "You made Doug cry; it's not nice to bite!").

Developmental Trends in Altruism

Although many 2- to 3-year-olds show sympathy and compassion toward distressed companions, they are not particularly eager to make truly self-sacrificial responses, such as sharing a treasured toy with a peer. Sharing and other benevolent acts are more likely to occur if adults instruct a toddler to consider others' needs (Levitt et al., 1985) or if a peer actively elicits sharing through a request or a threat of some kind, such as "I won't be your friend if you won't gimme some" (Birch & Billman, 1986). But, on the whole, acts of *spontaneous* self-sacrifice in the interest of others are relatively infrequent among toddlers and young preschool children. Is this because toddlers are largely oblivious to others' needs and to the good they might do by sharing or helping their companions? Probably not, because at least one observational study in a nursery-school setting found that 2½- to 3½-year-olds often took pleasure in performing acts of kindness for others during *pretend play*; by contrast, 4- to 6-year-olds performed more *real* helping acts and rarely play-acted the role of an altruist (Bar-Tal, Raviv, & Goldberg, 1982).

Preschool children must often be coaxed to share.

Many studies conducted in cultures from around the world find that sharing, helping, and most other forms of prosocial conduct become more and more common from the early elementary-school years onward (see, for example, Underwood & Moore, 1982; Whiting & Edwards, 1988). Indeed, much of the research that we will examine seeks to explain why older children and adolescents tend to become more prosocially inclined. Before turning to this research, let's address one other issue that developmentalists have pondered: Are there sex differences in altruism?

Although people commonly assume that girls are (or will become) more helpful, generous, or compassionate than boys (see Shigetomi, Hartmann, & Gelfand, 1981), there is little evidence for this notion in either laboratory experiments or survey studies (Grusec, Goodnow, & Cohen, 1996; Radke-Yarrow et al., 1983). According to Paul Hastings from Concordia University and colleagues (Hastings et al., 2000), girls sometimes emit stronger *facial* expressions of sympathy than boys do; however, the majority of studies find that girls and women do not differ appreciably from boys and men in either the amount of sympathy that they *say* they experience or in their willingness to comfort, help, or share resources with people in need. Nor is there much evidence for the idea that girls are more likely than boys to reliably *seek* assistance. From first through fifth grade, children of both sexes become less and less dependent on others to accomplish tasks for them, and they are equally likely to favour indirect help (such as hints)

affective explanations
discipline that focuses a child's attention on the harm or distress that his or her conduct has caused others

that will enable them to master tasks on their own (Shell & Eisenberg, 1996). So the notions that girls are any more altruistic than boys and any less capable of accomplishing tasks without direct assistance are probably best described as cultural myths that have little basis in fact.

Social-Cognitive and Affective Contributors to Altruism

Children and adolescents with well-developed role-taking skills are often found to be more helpful or compassionate than poor role takers, largely because they are better able to infer a companion's need for assistance or comforting (Eisenberg, Zhou, & Koller, 2001; Shaffer, 2000). In fact, evidence for a causal link between *affective* and *social* perspective taking (recognizing what another person is feeling, thinking, or intending) and altruism is quite clear in studies showing that children and adolescents who receive training to further these role-taking skills subsequently become more charitable, more cooperative, and more concerned about the needs of others when compared with age-mates who receive no training (Chalmers & Townsend, 1990; Iannotti, 1978). However, role taking is only one of several personal attributes that play a part in the development of altruistic behaviour. Two especially important contributors are children's level of **prosocial moral reasoning** and their empathic reactions to the distress of other people.

Prosocial Moral Reasoning

Over the past 25 years, researchers have charted the development of children's reasoning about prosocial issues and its relationship to altruistic behaviour. Nancy Eisenberg and her colleagues, for example, presented children with stories in which the central character has to decide whether or not to help or comfort someone when the prosocial act would be personally costly. Here is one such story (Eisenberg-Berg & Hand, 1979):

WHAT DO YOU THINK?

Despite ample evidence to the contrary, many people simply refuse to believe that girls and women are not any more inclined to seek assistance or to require help than boys and men are. Why might the weight of the research evidence be so hard for so many people to accept?

One day a girl named Mary was going to a friend's birthday party. On her way she saw a girl who had fallen down and hurt her leg. The girl asked Mary to go to her house and get her parents so that [they] could come and take her to a doctor. But if Mary did ... she would be late to the party and miss the ice-cream, cake, and all the games. What should Mary do?

As illustrated in Table 14.1, reasoning about these prosocial dilemmas may progress through as many as five levels between early childhood and adolescence. Notice that preschoolers' responses are frequently *self-serving*: These youngsters often say that Mary should go to the party so as not to miss out on the goodies. But as children mature, they tend to become increasingly responsive to the needs and wishes of others; so much so that some high-school students feel that they could no longer respect themselves were they to ignore the appeal of a person in need in order to pursue their own interests (Eisenberg, 1983; Eisenberg, Miller, et al., 1991).

Does a child's or adolescent's level of prosocial moral reasoning predict his or her altruistic behaviour? Apparently so. Preschoolers who have progressed beyond the hedonistic level of prosocial moral reasoning are more likely to help and to *spontaneously* share valuable commodities with their peers than are those who still reason in a self-serving way (Eisenberg-Berg & Hand, 1979; Miller et al., 1996). Studies of older participants tell a similar story. Mature moral reasoners among a high-school sample often said they would help someone they *disliked* if that person really needed their help, whereas immature moral reasoners were apt to ignore the needs of a person they dislike

prosocial moral reasoning
the thinking that people display when deciding whether to help, share with, or comfort others when these actions could prove costly to themselves

(Eisenberg, 1983; Eisenberg, Miller, et al., 1991). Finally, Eisenberg and her associates (1999) found in a 17-year longitudinal study that the children who showed more spontaneous sharing and were relatively mature in their levels of prosocial moral reasoning at ages 4 to 5 remained more helpful, were more considerate of others, and reasoned more complexly about prosocial issues and social responsibility throughout childhood, adolescence, and into young adulthood. Thus prosocial dispositions can be established early and often remain reasonably stable over time.

Why are mature moral reasoners so sensitive to the needs of others—even *disliked* others? Eisenberg's view is that the child's growing ability to *empathize* with others contributes heavily to mature prosocial reasoning and to the development of a selfless concern for promoting the welfare of *whomever* might require one's assistance (Eisenberg et al., 1999, 2001). Let's now consider what researchers have learned about the relationship between empathy and altruism.

Empathy: An Important Affective Contributor to Altruism

Empathy refers to a person's ability to experience the emotions of other people. According to Martin Hoffman (1981, 1993), empathy is a universal human response that has a neurological basis and can be either fostered or suppressed by environmental influences. Hoffman believes that empathic arousal eventually becomes an important mediator of altruism. Why else, Hoffman asks, would we set aside our own selfish motives to help other people or to avoid harming them unless we had the capacity to share their emotions and experience their distress?

Although infants and toddlers seem to recognize and often react to the distress of their companions (Zahn-Waxler et al., 1979, 1992; see also Box 2.4), their responses are not always helpful ones. In fact, some young children experience *personal* distress on witnessing the distress or misfortunes of others (this may be the predominant response early in life) and may ignore or turn away from a person in need in order to relieve their *own* discomfort (Young, Fox, & Zahn-Waxler, 1999). Yet other children (even some young ones) are more inclined to interpret their empathic arousal as concern for distressed others, and it is this **sympathetic empathic arousal**, rather than **self-oriented distress**, that should eventually come to promote altruism (Batson, 1991; Eisenberg et al., 1999).

SOCIALIZATION OF EMPATHY. As we noted earlier when discussing the origins of compassion in toddlers, parents can help to promote sympathetic empathic arousal by (1) modelling empathic concern and (2) relying on affectively oriented forms of discipline that

sympathetic empathic arousal
feeling of sympathy or compassion that may be elicited when one experiences the emotions of (that is, empathizes with) a distressed other; thought to become an important mediator of altruism

self-oriented distress
feeling of *personal* discomfort or distress that may be elicited when we experience the emotions of (that is, empathize with) a distressed other; thought to inhibit altruism

---

TABLE 14.1   Eisenberg's Levels of Prosocial Moral Reasoning

Level	Approximate age	Brief description and typical response
Hedonistic	Preschool, early elementary school	Concern is for one's own needs. Giving help is most likely if it will benefit the self. Example: "I wouldn't help 'cause I'd miss the party."
Needs oriented	Elementary school and a few preschoolers	Others' needs are recognized as a legitimate basis for helping, but there is little evidence of sympathy or guilt for failing to help. Example: "I'd help because she needs help."
Stereotyped, approval oriented	Elementary school and some high-school students	Concern for approval and stereotyped images of good and bad heavily influence one's thinking. Example: "My mother would hug me for helping."
Empathic orientation	Older elementary-school and high-school students	Judgments now include evidence of sympathetic feelings; vague references are sometimes made to duties and values. Example: "I'd feel good about helping because she was in pain."
Internalized values orientation	Small minority of high-school students; no elementary-school students	Justifications for helping (or not helping) are based on internalized values, norms, convictions, and responsibilities; violating these principles could undermine self-respect. Example: "I refused to make a donation because the [charity] wastes too much money fundraising and gives little to its intended recipients."

SOURCE: Adapted from Eisenberg, Lennon, & Roth, 1983.

help young children to understand the harmful effects of any distress they may have caused others (Eisenberg, Fabes, et al., 1991; Hastings et al., 2000; Zahn-Waxler et al., 1979, 1992). Interestingly, mothers who use more *positive* facial expressions while modelling sympathy and who explicitly verbalize their own sympathetic feelings have children who act more sympathetically—probably because the mother's positivity and her affective explanations help to counteract the negative reactions that young children may have to others' misfortunes, thus making them less inclined to interpret their own arousal as *personal* distress (Fabes et al., 1994).

AGE TRENDS IN THE EMPATHY–ALTRUISM RELATIONSHIP.

So what is the relationship between empathy and altruism? The answer depends, in part, on how empathy is measured and how old the research participants are. In studies that assess empathy by having children report their own feelings about the misfortunes of story characters, researchers have found little association between empathy and altruism. However, teacher ratings of children's empathic sensitivities and children's own *facial* expressions of emotion in response to others' misfortunes are better predictors of prosocial behaviour (Chapman et al., 1987; Eisenberg et al., 1990). Overall, it seems that the evidence for a link between empathy and altruism is modest at best for preschool and young elementary-school children but stronger for preadolescents, adolescents, and adults (Underwood & Moore, 1982).

One possible explanation for these age trends is that it simply takes some time for children to become better at regulating negative emotionality and suppressing personal distress to others' misfortunes so that they can respond more sympathetically (Eisenberg, Fabes, et al., 1998). And it is likely that social-cognitive development plays an important part in this process, because younger children may lack the role-taking skills and insight about their own emotional experiences to fully understand and appreciate (1) *why* others are distressed and, thus, (2) *why* they are feeling aroused (Roberts & Strayer, 1996). For example, when kindergartners see a series of slides showing a boy becoming depressed after his dog runs away, they usually attribute his sadness to an external cause (the dog's disappearance) rather than to a more personal or internal one, such as the boy's longing for his pet (Hughes, Tingle, & Sawin, 1981). And, although kindergartners report that they feel sad after seeing the slides, they usually provide egocentric explanations for their empathic arousal that seem to reflect *personal distress* (for example, "I might lose my dog"). However, 7- to 9-year-olds begin to associate their own empathic emotions with those of the story character as they put themselves in his place and infer the *psycho-*

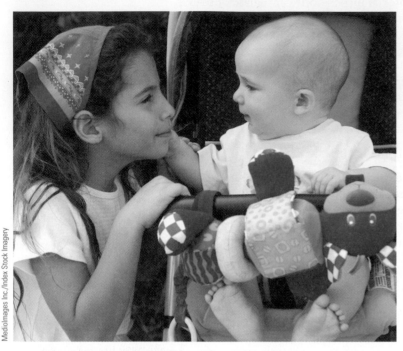

As children mature and develop better role-taking skills, they are more likely to sympathize with distressed companions and to provide them with comfort or assistance.

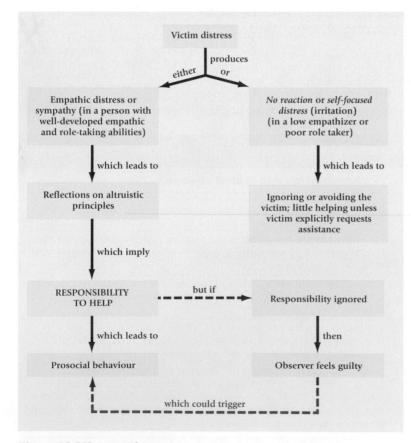

Figure 14.5 *How empathy promotes altruism: A "felt responsibility" interpretation.*

logical basis for his sadness (for example, "I'm sad because he's sad ... because, if he really liked the dog, then.... "). So empathy may become a stronger contributor to altruism once children become better at inferring others' points of view (role taking) and understanding the causes of their own empathic emotions—causes that can help them to feel *sympathy* for distressed or needy companions (Eisenberg et al., 2001; Roberts & Strayer, 1996).

THE "FELT RESPONSIBILITY" HYPOTHESIS. Now an important question: *How* exactly does empathy promote altruism? One possibility is that a child's *sympathetic* empathic arousal causes him to reflect on altruistic lessons that he has learned, such as the Golden Rule, the *norm of social responsibility* (that is, help others who need help), or even the knowledge that other people approve of helping behaviour. As a result of this reflection, the child is likely to assume some personal *responsibility* for helping a victim in distress and would now feel guilty for callously ignoring that obligation (Chapman et al., 1987; Williams & Bybee, 1994) (see Figure 14.5). Notice that this **"felt responsibility" hypothesis** is reflected in Eisenberg's higher levels of prosocial moral reasoning (see Table 14.1) and may help explain why the link between empathy and altruism becomes stronger with age. Because older children are likely to have learned (and internalized) more altruistic principles than younger children, they should have much more to reflect on as they experience empathic arousal. Consequently, they are more likely than younger children to feel responsible for helping a distressed person and to follow through by rendering the necessary assistance.

Cultural and Social Influences on Altruism

Cultural Influences

Cultures clearly differ in their endorsement or encouragement of altruism. In one interesting cross-cultural study, Beatrice and John Whiting (1975) observed the altruistic behaviour of 3- to 10-year-olds in six cultures: Kenya, Mexico, the Philippines, Okinawa, India, and the United States. As we see in Table 14.2, the cultures in which children were most altruistic were the less industrialized societies—cultures in which people live in large families and children *routinely contribute to the family welfare* by processing food, preparing meals, fetching wood and water, or caring for younger brothers and sisters. According to Joan Grusec of the University of Toronto and associates (Grusec et al., 1996), although children in Western industrialized societies are involved in relatively few family-maintenance activities, those who are assigned housework or other tasks that *benefit family members* are more prosocially inclined than age-mates whose responsibilities consist mainly of *self*-care routines, such as cleaning their own rooms.

Another factor contributing to the low altruism scores of children from Western industrialized nations is the tremendous emphasis that these societies place on competition and on individual rather than group goals. Self-sacrificial, other-oriented behaviours are certainly approved of but are generally not obligatory. By contrast, children from *col-*

TABLE 14.2	**Prosocial Behaviour in Six Cultures: Percentage of Children in Each Culture Who Scored above the Median Altruism Score for the Cross-Cultural Sample as a Whole**		
Type of society	**Percentage scoring high in altruism**	**Type of society**	**Percentage scoring high in altruism**
Nonindustrialized		*Industrialized*	
Kenya	100	Okinawa	29
Mexico	73	India	25
Philippines	63	United States	8

SOURCE: Based on Whiting & Whiting, 1975.

"felt responsibility" hypothesis
theory that empathy may promote altruism by causing one to reflect on altruistic norms and thus to feel some obligation to help distressed others

In Western individualistic societies children are taught that prosocial acts are laudable and that they should take credit for their self-sacrificing behaviours. By contrast, children in one collectivist society, the People's Republic of China, not only learn that prosocial conduct is necessary and an obligation, but are also taught to be modest, to avoid self-aggrandizement, and thus not to seek praise or personal recognition for their own good deeds. How might these teachings affect Chinese children's thinking about prosocial issues? Would they truly seek to downplay their acts of kindness?

To address these issues, Kang Lee and his associates (1997) conducted a cross-cultural study in which 7-, 9-, and 11-year-old children from Canada and the People's Republic of China evaluated four brief stories. To compare Canadian and Chinese children's thinking about *prosocial* issues, two stories involved a child who first carried out a good deed (e.g., anonymously donating money to a classmate who otherwise could not go on a field trip) and who then either *truthfully admitted* this prosocial act or *lied* about it (saying "I didn't do it" when the teacher asked, "Do you know who is responsible for this act of kindness?"). For comparative purposes, children's thinking about *antisocial* conduct was also assessed. Each participant heard two stories in which the actor committed a misdeed (e.g., injuring a classmate by knocking him down) and then either *truthfully admitted* or *lied* about this act when questioned by a teacher. After hearing each story, participants evaluated the goodness or naughtiness of both the actor's behaviour and his or her statement about the behaviour.

Interestingly, there were no major cultural differences in evaluations of either the actor's *antisocial* conduct (which was considered very bad) or the actor's statements about it. Both Canadian and Chinese children felt that it was very good for harmdoers to tell the truth about committing transgressions and very bad to lie about them. Similarly, both Canadian and Chinese children evaluated *prosocial* acts quite positively. However, their thinking about lying and telling the truth about prosocial conduct diverged sharply.

As the figure illustrates, Canadian children at all three ages thought that altruists should readily admit (tell the truth and take credit for) their good deeds and that denying responsibility for (lying about) them was bad (or perhaps stupid). By contrast, we see that as Chinese children grow older they increasingly come to view taking credit for prosocial acts in *less* positive terms and denying responsibility for them much *more* positively. In fact, the strong emphasis on self-effacement and modesty in Chinese culture eventually overrides children's reluctance to lie, so that Chinese children come to view acting modest about performing behaviour expected of them to be more praiseworthy than boldly telling the truth and calling undue attention to acts that any good child should perform (Lee et al., 1997).

In sum, Lee's study clearly illustrates that the values that shape people's thinking about prosocial behaviour (as well as the circumstances under which "little white lies" might be appropriate) can vary dramatically from culture to culture.

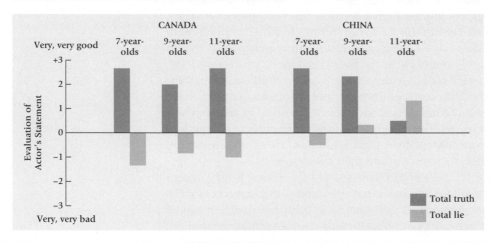

Rating by Canadian and Chinese children of actors who told the truth or lied about committing good deeds. ADAPTED FROM LEE ET AL., 1997.

lectivist societies and subcultures are taught to suppress individualism and to cooperate with others for the greater good of the group (Triandis, 1995). So for children in many of the world's collectivist societies, prosocial behaviour does not have the same "discretionary" quality about it that is true of individualistic societies; instead, giving of oneself for the greater good of the group is as much an *obligation* as resolving not to break moral rules (Chen, 2000; Triandis, 1995). As explained in Box 14.5, Kang Lee and associates (1997) found that children from one collectivist society (People's Republic of China) became so attuned to their culture's prosocial ideals that they thought it highly inappropriate to call attention to their own good deeds and even denied responsibility for them!

Although cultures may differ in the emphasis that they put on altruism, most people in most societies endorse the norm of social responsibility—the rule that one should help others who need help. Let's now consider some of the ways that adults might persuade young children to adopt this important value and become more concerned about the welfare of other people.

Reinforcing Altruism

Many experiments (reviewed in Shaffer, 2000) reveal that likeable and respectable adults can promote children's prosocial behaviour by *verbally reinforcing* their acts of kindness. Children are generally motivated to live up to the standards of people they admire, and praise that accompanies their kindly acts suggests that they are accomplishing that objective. However, youngsters who are "bribed" with tangible rewards for their prosocial acts are not especially altruistic. Why? Because they tend to attribute their kindly behaviours to a desire to earn the incentives rather than to a concern for others' welfare, and they are actually less likely than nonrewarded peers to make sacrifices for others once the rewards stop (Fabes et al., 1989; Grusec, 1991).

Practising and Preaching Altruism

Laboratory experiments consistently indicate that young children who observe charitable or helpful models become more charitable or helpful themselves, especially if the model has established a warm relationship with them, provides a compelling justification (rationale) for performing acts of kindness, and regularly *practises what he preaches* (Rushton, 1980). And it appears that exposure to these altruistic models can have *long-term* effects on children's behaviour—effects that generalize to new situations. For example, children who observe charitable models are more generous than those who observe no models or selfish models, even when they are not tested until two to four months later (Rice & Grusec, 1975; Rushton, 1980). So it seems that encounters with altruistic models help promote the development of prosocial concern—a conclusion that is strongly reinforced in the child-rearing literature.

Children who are committed to performing prosocial acts often have parents who have encouraged altruism and who have practised what they preach.

Who Raises Altruistic Children?

Studies of unusually charitable adults indicate that these "altruists" have enjoyed a warm and affectionate relationship with parents who themselves were highly concerned about the welfare of others. For example, Christians who risked their lives to save Jews from the Nazis during World War II reported that they had had close ties to moralistic parents who always acted in accordance with their ethical principles (London, 1970). And interviews of White "freedom riders" from the U.S. civil rights movement of the 1960s reveal that *"fully committed"* activists (volunteers who gave up their homes or careers to work full time for the cause) differed from *"partially committed" (part-time) activists* in two major ways: They had enjoyed warmer relations with their parents, and they had had parents who advocated altruism and backed up these exhortations by performing many kind and compassionate deeds. By contrast, parents of partially committed activists had often preached but rarely practised altruism (Rosenhan, 1970; see also Clary & Snyder, 1991). Clearly, these findings are consistent with the laboratory evidence we have reviewed, which indicates that warm and compassionate models who practise what they preach are especially effective at eliciting prosocial responses from young children.

Parental reactions to a child's harmdoing also play an important role in the development of altruism. Recall that mothers of less compassionate infants and toddlers react to harmdoing in punitive or forceful ways, whereas mothers of compassionate toddlers rely more heavily on nonpunitive, affective explanations in which they display sympathy as they persuade the child to accept personal responsibility for her harmdoing and urge her to direct some sort of comforting or helpful response toward the victim (Zahn-Waxler et al., 1979, 1992). Research with older children paints a similar picture: Parents who continue to rely on rational, nonpunitive disciplinary techniques in which they regularly display sympathy and concern for others tend to raise children who are sympathetic and self-sacrificing, whereas frequent use of forceful and punitive discipline appears to inhibit altruism and lead to the development of self-centred values (Brody & Shaffer, 1982; Eisenberg et al., 1992; Krevans & Gibbs, 1996).

Now let's look at the broader issue of *moral development*, which encompasses both the growth of prosocial concern and the inhibition of hostile, antisocial impulses.

WHAT IS MORALITY?

As we develop, most of us arrive at a point at which we wish to behave responsibly and to think of ourselves (and be thought of by others) as *moral* individuals (Damon & Hart, 1992). What is **morality**? University students generally agree that morality implies a capacity to (1) *distinguish right from wrong*, (2) *act on this distinction*, and (3) *experience pride in virtuous conduct and guilt or shame over acts that violate one's standards* (Quinn, Houts, & Graesser, 1994; Shaffer, 1994a). When asked by Lawrence Walker and Russell Pitts from the University of British Columbia to indicate the particular attributes that *morally mature* individuals display, adults in Canada generally agreed on six aspects of moral maturity that appear in Table 14.3.

Implicit in this definition is the idea that *morally mature* individuals do not submit to society's dictates because they expect tangible rewards for complying or fear punishments for transgressing. Rather, they eventually *internalize* moral principles that they have learned and conform to these ideals, even when authority figures are not present to enforce them. As we will see, virtually all contemporary theorists consider **internalization**—the shift from externally controlled actions to conduct that is governed by internal standards and principles—to be a most crucial milestone along the road to moral maturity.

morality
set of principles or ideals that help the individual to distinguish right from wrong, to act on this distinction, and to feel pride in virtuous conduct and guilt (or other unpleasant emotions) for conduct that violates one's standards

internalization
process of adopting the attributes or standards of other people; taking these standards as one's own

TABLE 14.3	Six Dimensions of Character that Define Moral Maturity for Canadian Adults	
Character dimension	**Sample traits**
1. Principled–idealistic	Has clear values; concerned about doing right; ethical; highly developed conscience; law abiding
2. Dependable–loyal	Responsible; loyal; reliable; faithful to spouse; honourable
3. Has integrity	Consistent; conscientious; rational; hard working
4. Caring–trustworthy	Honest; trustful; sincere; kind; considerate
5. Fair	Virtuous; fair; just
6. Confident	Strong; self-assured; self-confident

SOURCE: Walker & Pitts, 1998.

Concept Check 14.2
Understanding Cognitive and Social Contributors to Altruism

Check your understanding of cognitive, affective, and social contributors to prosocial conduct by matching each of the descriptive statements following with one of the following concepts or processes: (a) altruistic lessons (or norms), (b) felt responsibility, (c) verbal reinforcement, (d) competitive orientation, (e) self-oriented distress, (f) sympathetic empathic arousal, (g) tangible incentives, (h) role-taking skills. Answers appear in the Appendix.

_____ 1. others' attempts to foster this attribute may undermine prosocial conduct

_____ 2. empathic arousal that is thought to *inhibit* altruism

_____ 3. what altruistic individuals may focus on when experiencing others' distress

_____ 4. may be the most *direct* contributor to an empathizer's prosocial conduct

_____ 5. helps children to interpret empathic arousal as sympathy rather than personal distress

_____ 6. treatment that promotes children's prosocial conduct when given by a respected or admired adult

_____ 7. empathic arousal that is thought to *promote* altruism

_____ 8. treatment that may undermine prosocial conduct

How Developmentalists Look at Morality

Developmental theorizing and research have centred on the same three moral components that university students mention in their consensual definition of morality:

1. An *affective*, or emotional, component that consists of the feelings (guilt, concern for others' feelings, and so on) that surround right or wrong actions and that motivate moral thoughts and actions.

2. A *cognitive* component that centres on the way we conceptualize right and wrong and make decisions about how to behave.

3. A *behavioural* component that reflects how we actually behave when we experience the temptation to lie, cheat, or violate other moral rules.

As it turns out, each of the three major theories of moral development has focused on a different component of morality. Psychoanalytic theorists emphasize the affective component, or powerful **moral affects**. They believe that children are motivated to act in accordance with their ethical principles in order to experience positive affects such as pride and to avoid such negative moral emotions as guilt and shame. Cognitive-developmental theorists have concentrated on the cognitive aspects of morality, or **moral reasoning**, and have found that the ways children think about right and wrong may change dramatically as they mature. Finally, the research of social learning and social information-processing theorists has helped us to understand how children learn to resist temptation and to practise **moral behaviour**, inhibiting actions such as lying, stealing, and cheating that violate moral norms.

In examining each of these theories and the research it has generated, we will look at the relationships among moral affect, moral reasoning, and moral behaviour. This information should help us to decide whether a person really has a unified moral character that is stable over time and across situations. We will then consider how various child-rearing practices may affect a child's moral development, and attempt to integrate much of the information we have reviewed.

PSYCHOANALYTIC EXPLANATIONS OF MORAL DEVELOPMENT

In Chapter 2, we learned that psychoanalysts view the mature personality as having three components: an irrational *id* that seeks the immediate gratification of instinctual needs, a rational *ego* that formulates *realistic* plans for meeting these needs, and a moralistic *superego* (or conscience) that monitors the acceptability of the ego's thoughts and deeds. Freud claimed that infants and toddlers lack a superego and act on their selfish impulses unless parents control their behaviour. But once the superego emerges, it was said to function as an *internal* censor that has the power to make a child feel proud of his virtuous conduct and guilty or shameful about committing moral transgressions. So children who are morally mature should generally resist temptation to violate moral norms in order to maintain self-esteem and avoid experiencing negative moral affects.

Freud's Theory of Oedipal Morality

According to Freud (1935/1960), the superego develops during the phallic stage (ages 3 to 6), when children were said to experience an emotional conflict with the same-sex parent that stemmed from their incestuous desire for the other-sex parent. To resolve his

moral affect
emotional component of morality, including feelings such as guilt, shame, and pride in ethical conduct

moral reasoning
cognitive component of morality; the thinking that people demonstrate when deciding whether various acts are right or wrong

moral behaviour
behavioural component of morality; actions that are consistent with one's moral standards in situations in which one is tempted to violate them

Oedipus complex, a boy was said to *identify* with and pattern himself after his father, particularly if his father was a threatening figure who aroused fear. Not only does he learn his masculine role in this manner, but he also internalizes his father's moral standards. A girl resolves her *Electra complex* by identifying with her mother and internalizing her mother's moral standards. However, Freud claimed that because girls do not experience the intense fear of castration that boys experience, they will develop weaker superegos than boys do.

Evaluating Freud's Theory and Newer Psychoanalytic Ideas about Morality

We might credit Freud for pointing out that moral emotions such as pride, shame, and guilt are potentially important determinants of ethical conduct and that the internalization of moral principles is a crucial step along the way to moral maturity. Yet the specifics of his theory are largely unsupported. For example, threatening and punitive parents do not raise children who are morally mature. Quite the contrary: Parents who rely on harsh forms of discipline tend to have children who often misbehave and rarely express feelings of guilt, remorse, shame, or self-criticism (Brody & Shaffer, 1982; Kochanska, 1997b). Furthermore, there is simply no evidence that boys develop stronger superegos than girls. Finally, Freud's proposed age trends for moral development are actually quite pessimistic. As early as 13 to 15 months some toddlers are already complying with some prohibitions in the absence of external surveillance (Kochanska, Tjebkes, & Forman, 1998). By age 2 more toddlers are beginning to show clear signs of distress when they violate rules (Kochanska et al., 1995), and they sometimes try to correct any mishaps they think they have caused, *even when no one else is present to tell them to* (Cole, Barrett, & Zahn-Waxler, 1992). These observations imply that the process of moral internalization may have already begun long before young children would have even experienced an Oedipus or Electra complex, much less have resolved it. So even though Freud's broader themes about the significance of moral emotions have some merit, perhaps it is time to lay his theory of **oedipal morality** to rest.

This is exactly what modern psychoanalytic theorists have done. They argue that children may begin to form a conscience *as toddlers* if they are *securely attached* to warm and responsive parents who have often cooperated with their wishes during joint play and have shared many positive emotional experiences with them. Within the context of a warm, **mutually responsive relationship** (rather than a fear-provoking one), toddlers are likely to display the kind of **committed compliance**—an orientation in which they are (1) highly motivated to embrace the parent's agenda and to comply with her rules and requests, (2) sensitive to a parent's emotional signals indicating whether they have done right or wrong, and (3) beginning to internalize those parental reactions to their triumphs and transgressions, coming to experience the pride, shame, and (later) guilt that will help them to evaluate and regulate their own conduct (Emde et al., 1991; Kochanska, 1997b; Labile & Thompson, 2000). By contrast, aloof or insensitive parents who have shared few mutually enjoyable activities with a toddler are likely to promote **situational compliance**—generally nonoppositional behaviour that stems more from parents' power to control the child's conduct than from the child's eagerness to cooperate or comply. Although data to evaluate those newer psychoanalytic ideas are not extensive, Grazyna Kochanska and Kathleen Murray (2000) found that preschoolers who had earlier enjoyed warm, mutually responsive emotional relationships with their mothers as 2- to 3½-year-olds show more signs of having a strong internalized conscience (for example, a willingness to comply with rules when adults are not present) at ages 5 to 6 than do age-mates whose earlier mother–toddler relationships had been less warm and mutually responsive.

Unfortunately, psychoanalytic theorists have had less to say about moral development beyond the preschool period or about children's *moral reasoning*—the very issue that cognitive-developmentalists emphasize.

oedipal morality
Freud's theory that moral development occurs during the phallic period (ages 3 to 6), when children internalize the moral standards of the same-sex parent as they resolve their Oedipus or Electra conflict

mutually responsive relationship
parent–child relationship characterized by mutual responsiveness to each other's needs and goals and shared positive affect

committed compliance
compliance based on the child's eagerness to cooperate with a responsive parent who has been willing to cooperate with him or her

situational compliance
compliance based primarily on a parent's power to control the child's conduct

COGNITIVE-DEVELOPMENTAL THEORY: THE CHILD AS MORAL PHILOSOPHER

Cognitive developmentalists study morality by charting the development of *moral reasoning* that children display when deciding whether various acts are right or wrong. According to cognitive theorists, both cognitive growth and social experiences help children to develop progressively richer understandings of the meaning of rules, laws, and interpersonal obligations. As children acquire these new understandings, they are said to progress through an *invariant sequence* of moral stages, each of which evolves from and replaces its predecessor and represents a more advanced or mature perspective on moral issues. In this section, we first examine Jean Piaget's early theory of moral development before turning to Lawrence Kolberg's revision and extension of Piaget's approach.

Piaget's Theory of Moral Development

Piaget's (1932/1965) early work on children's moral judgments focused on two aspects of moral reasoning. He studied developing *respect for rules* by playing marbles with Swiss children between ages 5 and 13. As they played, Piaget asked questions such as "Where do these rules come from? Must everyone obey a rule? Can these rules be changed?" To study children's conceptions of *justice*, Piaget gave them moral-decision stories to ponder. Here is one example (Piaget, 1932/1965, p. 122):

> *Story A.* A little boy who is called John is in his room. He is called to dinner. He goes into the dining room. But behind the door there was a chair, and on the chair there was a tray with 15 cups on it. John couldn't have known that there was all this behind the door. He goes in, the door knocks against the tray, bang go the 15 cups, and they all get broken.

> *Story B.* Once there was a little boy whose name was Henry. One day when his mother was out he tried to reach some jam out of the cupboard. He climbed onto a chair and stretched out his arm. But the jam was too high up, and he couldn't reach it.... While he was trying to get it, he knocked over a cup. The cup fell down and broke.

Having heard the stories, participants were asked such questions as "Which child is naughtier? Why?" and "How should the naughtier child be punished?" Using these research techniques, Piaget formulated a theory of moral development that includes a premoral period and two moral stages.

The Premoral Period

According to Piaget, preschool children show little concern for or awareness of rules. In a game of marbles, these **premoral** children do not play systematically with the intent of winning. Instead, they seem to make up their own rules, and they think the point of the game is to take turns and have fun.

Heteronomous Morality

Between the ages of 5 and 10, children develop a strong respect for rules as they enter Piaget's stage of **heteronomous morality** (heteronomous means "under the rule of another"). Children now believe that rules are laid down by powerful authority figures

premoral period
in Piaget's theory, the first five years of life, when children have little respect for or awareness of socially defined rules

heteronomous morality
Piaget's first stage of moral development, in which children view the rules of authority figures as sacred and unalterable

such as God, the police, or their parents, and they think that these regulations are sacred and unalterable. Try breaking the speed limit with a 6-year-old at your side and you may see what Piaget was talking about. Even if you are rushing to the hospital in a medical emergency, the young child may note that you are breaking a "rule of the road" and consider your behaviour unacceptable conduct that deserves to be punished. Heteronomous children think of rules as *moral absolutes*. They believe that there is a right side and a wrong side to any moral issue, and right always means following the rules.

Heteronomous children are also likely to judge the naughtiness of an act by its objective consequences more so than by the actor's intent. For example, many 5- to 9-year-olds judged John, who broke 15 cups while performing a well-intentioned act, to be naughtier than Henry, who broke one cup while stealing jam.

Heteronomous children also favour *expiatory punishment*—punishment for its own sake, with no concern for its relation to the nature of the forbidden act. So a 6-year-old might favour spanking a boy who had broken a window rather than making the boy pay for the window from his allowance. Furthermore, the heteronomous child believes in **immanent justice**—the idea that violations of social rules will invariably be punished in one way or another. So if a 6-year-old girl were to fall and skin her knee while stealing cookies, she might conclude that this injury was the punishment she deserved for her transgression. Life for the heteronomous child is fair and just.

Autonomous Morality

By age 10 or 11, most children have reached Piaget's second moral stage—**autonomous morality**. Older, autonomous children now realize that social rules are arbitrary agreements that can be challenged and even changed with the consent of the people they govern. They also feel that rules can be violated in the service of human needs. Thus, a driver who speeds during a medical emergency is no longer considered immoral, even though she is breaking the law. Judgments of right and wrong now depend more on the actor's intent to deceive or to violate social rules rather than the objective consequences of the act itself. So 10-year-olds reliably say that Henry, who broke one cup while stealing some jam (bad intent), is naughtier than John, who broke 15 cups while coming to dinner (good or neutral intent).

When deciding how to punish transgressions, the morally autonomous child usually favours *reciprocal punishments*—that is, treatments that tailor punitive consequences to the "crime" so that the rule breaker will understand the implications of a transgression and perhaps be less likely to repeat it. So an autonomous child may decide that the boy who deliberately breaks a window should pay for it out of his allowance (and learn that windows cost money) rather than simply submitting to a spanking. Finally, autonomous youngsters no longer believe in immanent justice, because they have learned from experience that violations of social rules often go undetected and unpunished.

Moving from Heteronomous to Autonomous Morality

According to Piaget, both cognitive maturation and social experience play a role in the transition from heteronomous to autonomous morality. The cognitive advances that are necessary for this shift are a general decline in egocentrism and the development of role-taking skills that enable the child to view moral issues from several perspectives. The kind of social experience that Piaget considers important is *equal-status* contact with peers. As we noted in Chapter 12, peers must learn to take each other's perspectives and resolve their disagreements in mutually beneficial ways, often without any adult intervention, if they are to play cooperatively or accomplish other group goals. So equal-status contacts with peers may lead to a more flexible, autonomous morality because they (1) lessen the child's respect for adult authority, (2) increase his or her self-respect and respect for peers, and (3) illustrate that rules are arbitrary agreements that can be changed with the consent of the people they govern.

And what role do parents play? Interestingly, Piaget claimed that unless parents relinquish some of their power, they may *slow* the progress of moral development by reinforcing the child's respect for rules and authority figures. If, for example, a parent

immanent justice
notion that unacceptable conduct will invariably be punished and that justice is ever present in the world

autonomous morality
Piaget's second state of moral development, in which children realize that rules are arbitrary agreements that can be challenged and changed with the consent of the people they govern

enforces a demand with a threat or a statement such as "Do it because I told you to!" it is easy to see how the young child might conclude that rules are absolutes that derive their "teeth" from the parent's power to enforce them.

An Evaluation of Piaget's Theory

Many researchers in many cultures have replicated Piaget's findings when they rely on his research methods. For example, younger children around the world are more likely than older ones to display such aspects of heteronomous morality as a belief in imminent justice or a tendency to emphasize consequences more than intentions when judging how wrong an act is (Jose, 1990; Lapsley, 1996). In addition, the maturity of children's moral judgments is related to such indications of cognitive development as IQ and role-taking skills (Lapsley, 1996). There is even some support for Piaget's "peer participation" hypothesis: Popular children who often take part in peer-group activities and assume positions of leadership tend to make mature moral judgments (Bear & Rys, 1994; Keasey, 1971).

Nevertheless, there is ample reason to believe that Piaget's theory clearly underestimates the moral capacities of preschool and elementary-school children.

Do Younger Children Ignore an Actor's Intentions?

Consider Piaget's claim that children younger than 9 or 10 judge acts as right or wrong based on the consequences that the acts produce more so than the intentions that guided them. Unfortunately, Piaget's moral-decision stories were flawed in that they (1) confounded intentions and consequences by asking whether a person who caused little harm with a bad intent was naughtier than one who caused more harm while serving good intentions, and (2) made information about the consequences of an act *much clearer* than information about the actor's intentions.

Sharon Nelson (1980) overcame these flaws in an interesting experiment with 3-year-olds. Each child listened to stories in which a character threw a ball to a playmate. The actor's motive was described as *good* (his friend had nothing to play with) or *bad* (the actor was mad at his friend), and the consequences of his act were either *positive* (the friend caught the ball and was happy to play with it) or *negative* (the ball hit the friend in the head and made him cry). To ensure that her 3-year-olds understood the actor's intentions, Nelson showed them drawings such as Figure 14.6, which depicts a negative intent.

Not surprisingly, the 3-year-olds in this study judged acts that had positive consequences more favourably than those that caused harm. However, as Figure 14.7 shows, they also judged the well-intentioned child who had wanted to play much more favourably than the child who intended to hurt his friend, *regardless of the consequences of his actions*. What's more, 3- to 5-year-olds clearly discriminate and react more negatively to blatant *lies*, in which a person presents false information with *intent* to deceive, from honest mistakes on the person's part (Siegal & Peterson, 1998). So even *preschool* children consider an actor's intentions when making moral judgments. In fact, young children often attempt to escape punishment through such *intentional* pleas

Figure 14.6 *Example of drawings used by Nelson to convey an actor's intentions to preschool children.* Adapted from Nelson, 1980.

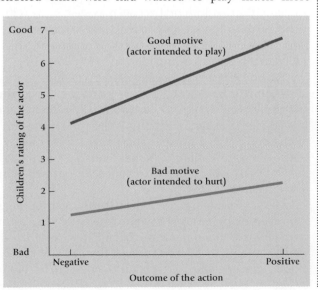

Figure 14.7 *Average ratings of an actor's behaviour for actors who produced positive or negative outcomes while serving either good or bad intentions.* Adapted from Nelson, 1980.

as "I didn't *mean* to, mummy!" But Piaget was right in one respect: Younger children do assign more weight to consequences and less weight to intentions than older children do, even though both younger and older children consider both sources of information when evaluating others' conduct (Lapsley, 1996; Zelazo, Helwig, & Lau, 1996).

Do Younger Children Respect All Rules (and Adult Authority)?

According to Piaget, heteronomous children think of rules as sacred and obligatory prescriptions that are laid down by respected authority figures and are not to be challenged. However, Elliot Turiel (1983) notes that children actually encounter two kinds of rules. **Moral rules** focus on the welfare and basic rights of individuals and include proscriptions against hitting, stealing, lying, cheating, or otherwise harming others or violating their rights. By contrast, **social-conventional rules** are determined by social consensus and regulate conduct in particular social situations. These standards are more like rules of social etiquette and include the rules of games as well as school rules that forbid snacking in class or using the restroom without permission. Do children treat these two kinds of rules as equivalent?

Apparently not. Judith Smetana (1981, 1985; Smetana, Schlagman, & Adams, 1993) finds that even 2½- to 3-year-olds consider moral transgressions such as hitting, stealing, and refusing to share to be much more serious and more deserving of punishment than social-conventional violations such as snacking in class or not saying "please" when requesting a toy. When asked whether a violation would be okay if there were no rule against it, children said that moral transgressions are always wrong but social-conventional violations are okay in the absence of any explicit rule. Clearly, parents view themselves as responsible for enforcing both moral and social-conventional rules. However, they attend more closely to moral violations and put much more emphasis on the harm such violations do to others (Nucci & Smetana, 1996; Nucci & Weber, 1995), perhaps explaining why children understand the need for and importance of *moral* proscriptions by age 2½ to 3—much sooner than Piaget had assumed they would.

Furthermore, Piaget's theory predicts that 6- to 10-year-old heteronomous children are quite capable of questioning adult authority. They believe that parents are justified in enforcing rules against stealing and other *moral* transgressions, but they feel that a parent is clearly abusing authority should he arbitrarily make decisions that affect them or impose rules that restrict their choice of friends or leisure activities—areas that they perceive as either negotiable or under their own *personal* jurisdiction (Helwig & Kim, 1999; Tisak & Tisak, 1990). In addition, they increasingly recognize that adult authority may be limited to certain contexts, acknowledging, for example, that teachers have a right to regulate smoking at school but not in the neighbourhood (Smetana & Bitz, 1996). Even heteronomous children who are very religious insist that not even God can proclaim that an immoral act such as stealing is right and make it so (Nucci & Turiel, 1993). So 6- to 10-year-olds do have ideas about what constitutes *legitimate* authority, and those ideas are not based solely on an unwavering respect for the sanctity or wisdom of adults, as Piaget had assumed.

Finally, Piaget was partially right in claiming that parents and other adults can retard moral growth by exerting authority and relying on their greater power to enforce rules and regulations. Where he was wrong was in implying that most adults operate this way. Indeed recent research by Larry Walker and associates demonstrates that when parents discuss *real-life* moral issues and present their own, more sophisticated reasoning in a gentle, supportive manner (rather than in a lecture-like format as a lesson to be learned), they typically *foster* rather than impede the growth of moral reasoning (Walker, Henning, & Krettenauer, 2000).

Developmentalists are indebted to Piaget for suggesting that children's moral reasoning develops in stages that are closely tied to cognitive growth. Even today, his theory continues to stimulate research and new insights—including the previous findings, which reveal that children younger than 10 are considerably more sophisticated in their moral reasoning than Piaget made them out to be. But is moral reasoning fully developed by age 10 to 11, as Piaget assumed? Lawrence Kohlberg certainly didn't think so.

moral rules
standards of acceptable and unacceptable conduct that focus on the rights and privileges of individuals

social-conventional rules
standards of conduct determined by social consensus that indicate what is appropriate within a particular social context

Kohlberg's Theory of Moral Development

Kohlberg (1963, 1984; Colby & Kohlberg, 1987) refined and extended Piaget's theory of moral development by asking 10-, 13-, and 16-year-old boys to resolve a series of moral dilemmas. Each dilemma challenged the respondent by requiring him to choose between (1) obeying a rule, law, or authority figure and (2) taking some action that conflicted with these rules and commands while serving a human need. The following story is the best known of Kohlberg's moral dilemmas:

> In Europe, a woman was near death from a special kind of cancer. There was one drug that doctors thought might save her. It was a form of radium that a druggist in the same town had recently discovered. The drug was expensive to make, but the druggist was charging $2000, or 10 times the cost of the drug, for a small (possibly life-saving) dose. Heinz, the sick woman's husband, borrowed all the money he could, about $1000, or half of what he needed. He told the druggist that his wife was dying and asked him to sell the drug cheaper or to let him pay later. The druggist replied "No, I discovered the drug, and I'm going to make money from it." Heinz then became desperate and broke into the store to steal the drug for his wife. Should Heinz have done that?

Kohlberg was actually less interested in the respondent's decision (that is, what Heinz should have done) than in the underlying rationale, or "thought structures," that the individual used to justify his decision. So, if a participant says, "Heinz should steal the drug to save his wife's life," it is necessary to determine why her life is so important. Is it because she cooks and irons for Heinz? Because it's a husband's duty to save his wife? Or because the preservation of life is among the highest of human values? To determine the structure of a person's moral reasoning, Kohlberg asked probing questions: Does Heinz have an obligation to steal the drug? If Heinz doesn't love his wife, should he steal it for her? Should Heinz steal the drug for a stranger? Is it important for people to do everything they can to save another life? Is it against the law to steal? Does that make it morally wrong? The purpose of these probes was to clarify how individual participants reasoned about obedience and authority on the one hand and about human needs, rights, and privileges on the other.

Through his use of these elaborate *clinical interviews*, Kohlberg's first discovery was that moral development extends far beyond Piaget's autonomous stage, becoming progressively complex throughout adolescence and into young adulthood. Careful analyses of his participants' responses to several dilemmas led Kohlberg to conclude that moral growth progresses through an *invariant sequence* of three moral levels, each of which is composed of two distinct moral stages. According to Kohlberg, the order of these moral levels and stages is invariant because they depend on the development of certain cognitive abilities that evolve in an invariant sequence. Like Piaget, Kohlberg assumes that each succeeding stage evolves from and replaces its predecessor; once the individual has attained a higher stage of moral reasoning, he or she should never regress to earlier stages.

Before examining Kohlberg's moral stages, it is important to emphasize that each stage represents a particular perspective, or *method of thinking*, about moral dilemmas rather than a particular type of moral decision. As we will see, decisions are not very informative in themselves, because people at each moral stage might well endorse either course of action when resolving one of these ethical dilemmas. (However, participants at Kohlberg's highest moral level generally favour serving human needs over complying with rules or laws that would compromise others' welfare.)

The basic themes and defining characteristics of Kohlberg's three moral levels and six stages are as follows:

Level 1: Preconventional Morality

Rules are truly external to the self rather than internalized. The child conforms to rules imposed by authority figures to avoid punishment or obtain personal rewards. Morality is self-serving: What is right is what one can get away with or what is personally satisfying.

preconventional morality
Kohlberg's term for the first two stages of moral reasoning, in which moral judgments are based on the tangible punitive consequences (Stage 1) or rewarding consequences (Stage 2) of an act for the actor rather than on the relationship of that act to society's rules and customs

Stage 1: Punishment-and-Obedience Orientation. The goodness or badness of an act depends on its consequences. The child obeys authorities to avoid punishment, but may not consider an act wrong if it is not detected and punished. The greater the harm done or the more severe the punishment, the more bad the act is. The following two responses reflect a "punishment-and-obedience" orientation to the Heinz dilemma:

> *Protheft:* It isn't really bad to take the drug—he did ask to pay for it first. He wouldn't do any other damage or take anything else, and the drug he'd take is only worth $200, not $2000.

> *Antitheft:* Heinz doesn't have permission to take the drug. He can't just go and break through a window. He'd be a bad criminal doing all that damage ... and stealing anything so expensive would be a big crime.

Stage 2: Naive Hedonism. A person at this second stage conforms to rules in order to gain rewards or satisfy personal objectives. There is some concern for the perspective of others, but other-oriented behaviours are ultimately motivated by the hope of benefiting in return. "You scratch my back and I'll scratch yours" is the guiding philosophy. Here are two samples of this hedonistic, self-serving morality:

> *Protheft:* Heinz isn't really doing any harm to the druggist, and he can always pay him back. If he doesn't want to lose his wife, he should take the drug.

> *Antitheft:* Hey, the druggist isn't wrong, he just wants to make a profit like everybody else. That's what you're in business for, to make money.

Level 2: Conventional Morality

The individual now strives to obey rules and social norms in order to win others' approval or to maintain social order. Social praise and the avoidance of blame have now replaced tangible rewards and punishments as motivators of ethical conduct. The perspectives of other people are clearly recognized and given careful consideration.

Stage 3: "Good Boy" or "Good Girl" Orientation. Moral behaviour is that which pleases, helps, or is approved of by others. People are often judged by their intentions. "Meaning well" is valued and being nice is important, as we see in the following responses to the Heinz dilemma:

> *Protheft:* Stealing is bad, but Heinz is only doing something that is natural for a good husband to do. You can't blame him for doing something out of love for his wife. You'd blame him if he didn't save her.

> *Antitheft:* If Heinz's wife dies, he can't be blamed. You can't say he is heartless for failing to commit a crime. The druggist is the selfish and heartless one. Heinz tried to do everything he really could.

Stage 4: Social-Order-Maintaining Morality. At this stage, the individual considers the perspectives of the generalized other—that is, the will of society as reflected in law. Now what is right is what conforms to the rules of *legal* authority. The reason for conforming is not a fear of punishment, but a belief that rules and laws maintain a social order that is worth preserving. As we see in the following responses, laws always transcend special interests:

> *Protheft:* The druggist is leading the wrong kind of life if he just lets somebody die; so it's Heinz's duty to save [his wife]. But Heinz just can't go around breaking laws—he must pay the druggist back and take his punishment for stealing.

conventional morality
Kohlberg's term for the third and fourth stages of moral reasoning, in which moral judgments are based on a desire to gain approval (Stage 3) or to uphold laws that maintain social order (Stage 4)

Antitheft: It's natural for Heinz to want to save his wife, but it's still always wrong to steal. You have to follow the rules regardless of your feelings or the special circumstances.

Level 3: Postconventional (or Principled) Morality

A person at this highest level of moral reasoning defines right and wrong in terms of broad principles of justice that could conflict with written laws or with the dictates of authority figures. Morally right and legally proper are not always one and the same.

STAGE 5: THE SOCIAL-CONTRACT ORIENTATION. At Stage 5, the individual views laws as instruments for expressing the will of the majority and furthering human values. Laws that accomplish these ends and are impartially applied are viewed as social contracts that one has an obligation to follow, but imposed laws that compromise human rights or dignity are considered unjust and worthy of challenge. Notice how distinctions between what is legal and what is moral begin to appear in the following Stage 5 responses to Heinz's dilemma:

> *Protheft:* Before you say stealing is morally wrong, you've got to consider this whole situation. Of course, the laws are quite clear about breaking into a store. And ... Heinz would know that there were no *legal* grounds for his actions. Yet it would be reasonable for anybody, in that kind of situation, to steal the drug.

> *Antitheft:* I can see the good that would come from illegally taking the drug. But the ends don't justify the means. The law represents a consensus of how people have agreed to live together, and Heinz has an obligation to respect these agreements. You can't say Heinz would be completely wrong to steal the drug, but even these circumstances don't make it right.

STAGE 6: MORALITY OF INDIVIDUAL PRINCIPLES OF CONSCIENCE. At this highest moral stage, the individual defines right and wrong on the basis of the self-chosen ethical principles of his or her own conscience. These principles are not concrete rules such as the Ten Commandments. They are abstract moral guidelines or principles of universal justice (and respect for the rights of *all* human beings) that *transcend* any law or social contract that may conflict with them. Here are two Stage 6 responses to the Heinz dilemma:

> *Protheft:* When one must choose between disobeying a law and saving a human life, the higher principle of preserving life makes it morally *right* to steal the drug.

> *Antitheft:* With many cases of cancer and the scarcity of the drug, there may not be enough to go around to everybody who needs it. The correct course of action can only be the one that is right by all people concerned. Heinz ought to act not on emotion or the law, but according to what he thinks an ideally just person would do in this case.

Stage 6 is Kohlberg's vision of ideal moral reasoning. But because it is so very rare and virtually no one functions consistently at this level, Kohlberg came to view it as a hypothetical construct—that is, the stage to which people would progress were they to develop beyond Stage 5. In fact, the later versions of Kohlberg's manual for scoring moral judgments no longer attempt to measure Stage 6 reasoning (Colby & Kohlberg, 1987).

Support for Kohlberg's Theory

Although Kohlberg believed that his stages form an invariant and universal sequence of moral growth that is closely tied to cognitive development, he also claimed that cognitive growth, by itself, is not sufficient to guarantee moral development. In order to ever

postconventional morality
Kohlberg's term for the fifth and sixth stages of moral reasoning, in which moral judgments are based on social contracts and democratic law (Stage 5) or on universal principles of ethics and justice (Stage 6)

move beyond the preconventional level of moral reasoning, children must be exposed to people or situations that introduce *cognitive disequilibria*—that is, conflicts between existing moral concepts and new ideas that force them to reevaluate their viewpoints. So, like Piaget, Kohlberg believed that both cognitive development and *relevant social experiences* underlie the growth of moral reasoning.

How much support is there for these ideas? Let's review the evidence, starting with data bearing on Kohlberg's invariant-sequence hypothesis.

Are Kohlberg's Stages an Invariant Sequence?

If Kohlberg's stages represent a true developmental sequence, we should find a strong positive correlation between age and maturity of moral reasoning. This is precisely what researchers have found in studies conducted in the Bahamas, Taiwan, Turkey, Honduras, India, Nigeria, the United States, Mexico, and Kenya (Colby & Kohlberg, 1987). So it seems that Kohlberg's levels and stages of moral reasoning are universal structures that are age-related, just as we would expect them to be if they formed a developmental sequence. But do these studies establish that Kohlberg's stages form a fixed, or *invariant*, sequence?

No, they do not! The problem is that participants at each age level were *different* people, and we cannot be certain that a 25-year-old at Stage 5 has progressed through the various moral levels and stages in the order specified by Kohlberg's theory.

THE LONGITUDINAL EVIDENCE. Clearly, the most compelling evidence for Kohlberg's invariant-sequence hypothesis would be a demonstration that individual children progress through the moral stages in precisely the order that Kohlberg said they should. Ann Colby and her associates (1983) have conducted a 20-year longitudinal study of Kohlberg's original research participants, who were reinterviewed five times at 3- to 4-year intervals. As shown in Figure 14.8, moral reasoning developed very gradually, with use of preconventional reasoning (Stages 1 and 2) declining sharply in adolescence—the same period in which conventional reasoning (Stages 3 and 4) is on the rise. Conventional reasoning remained the dominant form of moral expression in adulthood, with very few participants ever moving beyond it to postconventional morality (Stage 5). But even so, participants proceeded through the stages they did attain in precisely the order Kohlberg predicted and no one ever skipped a stage. Similar results have been reported in a nine-year longitudinal study of adolescents in Israel and a 12-year longitudinal project conducted in Turkey (Colby & Kohlberg, 1987). So Kohlberg's moral stages

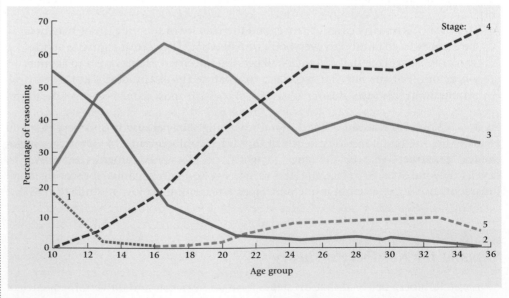

Figure 14.8 *Use of Kohlberg's moral stages at ages 10 through 36 by male participants studied longitudinally over a 20-year period. ADAPTED FROM COLBY ET AL., 1983.*

do seem to represent an invariant sequence (see also Rest, Thoma, & Edwards, 1997). Let's note, however, that people progress in an orderly fashion to *their* highest stage of reasoning and that Stage 3 or 4 is the end of this developmental journey for most individuals worldwide (Snarey, 1985).

Cognitive Prerequisites for Moral Growth

According to Kohlberg (1963), the young, preconventional child reasons about moral issues from an egocentric point of view. At Stage 1, the child thinks that certain acts are bad because they are punished. At Stage 2, the child shows a limited awareness of the needs, thoughts, and intentions of others but still judges *self-serving* acts as appropriate. However, conventional reasoning clearly requires some *role-taking* abilities. A person at Stage 3, for example, must necessarily recognize others' points of view before she will evaluate intentions that would win their approval as good or morally acceptable. Furthermore, Kohlberg proposed that postconventional moral reasoning requires *formal operations*. A Stage 5 individual who bases moral judgments on abstract principles must be able to reason abstractly rather than simply adhering to the rule of law or concrete moral norms.

These hypotheses have received ample support. Lawrence Walker (1980), for example, found that all 10- to 13-year-olds who had reached Kohlberg's Stage 3 ("good boy–good girl" morality) were quite proficient at mutual role taking, although not all proficient role takers had reached Stage 3 in their moral reasoning. Similarly, Carolyn Tomlinson-Keasey and Charles Keasey (1974) and Deanne Kuhn and her associates (1977) found that (1) all participants who showed any evidence of postconventional (Stage 5) moral reasoning had reached formal operations but that (2) most formal operators had not reached Kohlberg's postconventional level of moral reasoning. What these findings imply is that role-taking skills are *necessary but not sufficient* for the development of conventional morality and that formal operations are *necessary but not sufficient* for the emergence of postconventional morality. This pattern is precisely what Kohlberg expected, because he viewed cognitive growth as only one prerequisite for moral development. The other prerequisite is *relevant social experience*—that is, exposure to people or situations that force a person to reevaluate and alter his or her current moral perspectives.

Evidence for Kohlberg's Social-Experience Hypothesis

Does research support the proposition that social experience contributes to moral development? Yes, indeed, and at least three lines of research tell us so.

PEER INTERACTIONS. Like Piaget, Kohlberg felt that interactions with peers probably contribute more to moral growth than one-sided discussions with adult authority figures. And they were right to call attention to the role that peers play as agents of moral socialization. Children do seem to think more actively and deeply about their own and their partners' moral ideas and show more moral growth in discussions with peers than in talks with their parents or other adults (Kruger, 1992; Kruger & Tomasello, 1986).

Interestingly, the participants who seem to benefit most from peer discussions are those whose moral reasoning was least mature before the discussions began. And the changes in moral reasoning that they display are not merely a modelling effect. Berkowitz and Gibbs (1983) report that change is unlikely to occur unless the discussions include **transactive interactions**—exchanges in which each discussant performs mental operations on the reasoning of his or her partner (for example, "Your reasoning misses an important distinction," "Here's an elaboration of your position," "We can combine our positions into a common view"). This is an important finding, because it reinforces Kohlberg's idea that social experiences promote moral growth by introducing cognitive challenges to one's current reasoning that the *less mature* individual will adapt to by assimilating and accommodating to the other person's logic. Why do the more mature discussants not move in the direction of their less mature partners? Because the challenges introduced by their less mature partners are based on reasoning that they have already rejected. In fact, their failure to regress in the face of such logic provides additional support for Kohlberg's invariant-sequence hypothesis.

transactive interactions
verbal exchanges in which individuals perform mental operations on the reasoning of their discussion partners

Discussing weighty ethical issues with peers often promotes the growth of moral reasoning.

ADVANCED EDUCATION. Another kind of social experience that promotes moral growth is receiving an advanced education. Michael Pratt, Bruce Hunsberger, Mark Pancer, and associates from Wilfrid Laurier University (Pratt et al., 1991) found that adults who go on to university and receive many years of education consistently reason with more complexity about moral issues than those who are less educated (see also Speicher, 1994), and differences in the moral reasoning between university students and their nonstudent peers become greater with each successive year of school that the university students complete (Rest & Thoma, 1985). Advanced education may foster moral growth in two ways by (1) contributing to cognitive growth and (2) exposing students to diverse moral perspectives that produce cognitive conflict and soul searching (Kohlberg, 1984; Mason & Gibbs, 1993).

CULTURAL INFLUENCES. Finally, simply living in a complex, diverse, and democratic society can stimulate moral development. Just as we learn the give-and-take of mutual perspective taking by discussing issues with our friends, we learn in a diverse democracy that the opinions of many groups must be weighed and that laws reflect a consensus of the citizens rather than the arbitrary rulings of a dictator. Cross-cultural studies suggest that postconventional moral reasoning emerges primarily in Western democracies and that people in rural villages in many nonindustrialized countries show no signs of it (Harkness, Edwards, & Super, 1981; Snarey & Keljo, 1991). People in these homogeneous communities may have less experience with the kinds of political conflicts and compromises that take place in a more diverse society and so may never have any need to question conventional moral standards. By adopting a contextual perspective on development, we can appreciate that the conventional (mostly Stage 3) reasoning typically displayed by adults in these societies—with its emphasis on cooperation and loyalty to the immediate social group—is adaptive and mature within their own social systems (Harkness et al., 1981).

In sum, Kohlberg described an invariant sequence of moral stages and identified some of the cognitive factors and major environmental influences that determine how far an individual progresses in this sequence. Yet critics have offered many reasons for suspecting that Kohlberg's theory is far from a complete account of moral development.

Criticisms of Kohlberg's Approach

Many of the criticisms of Kohlberg's theory have centred on the possibilities that it is biased against certain groups of people, that it underestimates the moral sophistication of young children, and that it says much about moral reasoning but little about moral affect and moral behaviour.

Is Kohlberg's Theory Biased?

CULTURAL BIAS. Although research indicates that children and adolescents in many cultures proceed through the first three or four of Kohlberg's stages in order, we have seen that postconventional morality as Kohlberg defines it simply does not exist in some societies. Critics have charged that Kohlberg's highest stages reflect a Western ideal of justice and that his stage theory is therefore biased against people who live in non-Western societies or who do not value individualism and individual rights highly enough to want to challenge society's rules (Gibbs & Schnell, 1985; Shweder, Mahapatra, & Miller, 1990). People in collectivist societies that emphasize social harmony and place the good of the group ahead of the good of the individual may be viewed as conventional moral thinkers

*I*s each of the following acts wrong? If so, how serious a violation is it?

1. A young married woman is beaten black and blue by her husband after going to a movie without his permission despite having been warned not to do so again.

2. A brother and sister decide to get married and have children.

3. The day after his father dies, the oldest son in a family gets a haircut and eats chicken.

These are three of 39 acts presented by Richard Shweder, Manamahan Mahapatra, and Joan Miller (1990) to children ages 5 to 13 and adults in India and the United States. You may be surprised to learn that Hindu children and adults rated the son's getting a haircut and eating chicken after his father's death as among the very more morally offensive of the 39 acts they rated, and the husband's beating of his disobedient wife as not wrong at all. American children and adults, of course, viewed wife beating as far more serious than breaking seemingly arbitrary rules about appropriate mourning behaviour. Although Indians and Americans could agree that a few acts (for example, brother–sister incest) were serious moral violations, they did not agree on much else.

Furthermore, Indian children and adults viewed the Hindu ban against behaviour disrespectful of one's dead father as a *universal moral rule*; they thought it would be best if *everyone in the world* followed it and strongly disagreed that it would be acceptable to change the rule if most people in their society wanted to change it. Hindus also believed that it is a serious moral offence for a widow to eat fish or wear brightly coloured clothes or for a woman to cook food for her family during her menstrual period. To orthodox Hindus, rules against such behaviour are required by natural law; they are not just arbitrary social conventions created by members of society. Hindus also regard it as morally necessary for a man to beat his disobedient wife in order to uphold his obligations as head of the family.

What effects do cultural beliefs of this sort have on moral development? The developmental trend in moral thinking that Shweder detected in India was very different from the developmental trend he observed in the United States, as the accompanying figure shows. With age, Indian children saw more and more issues as matters of universal moral principle, whereas American children saw fewer and fewer issues in the same light (and more and more as matters of arbitrary social convention that can legitimately differ from society to society).

Based on these cross-cultural findings, Shweder calls into question Kohlberg's claims that all children everywhere construct similar moral codes at similar ages and that certain universal moral principles exist. Instead, he believes that culture defines exactly what is morally acceptable or unacceptable and then assists the young to adopt that conceptual framework. Indeed, we saw evidence of this very process in Box 14.5: Children from the collectivist People's Republic of China gradually adopt their society's communist-collectivist ideals of behaving prosocially and remaining modest or humble about it—to the point that they think it better to lie and deny personal responsibility for a good deed than to claim responsibility or seek recognition for their acts of kindness.

Interestingly, there are also important *subcultural* influences on moral reasoning. For example, individuals who occupy a subordinate position within the societies (e.g., Arab women and Brazilian children from the socioeconomic strata) are more inclined than age-mates of higher status to view themselves as having relatively few personal choices about how to behave and as under greater moral obligation to submit to authority (Nucci, Camino, & Sapiro, 1996; Turiel & Wainryb, 2000).

Clearly, these findings challenge the cognitive-developmental position that *all* important aspects of moral growth are universal. Instead, they tend to support a *contextual* perspective on moral development by suggesting that children's moral judgments are shaped by the culture and subculture in which they live. In Canada, for example, according to Walker and Pitts (1998), one need not display a strong sense of religiosity or spiritualism to be considered morally mature; whereas a strong sense of spiritualism and adherence to an "ethics of divinity" is of central importance to Hindus—and seems to explain their tendency to view so many cultural prescriptions as universal moral laws (Shweder, 1997). What then should we conclude about culture and moral reasoning? Perhaps children all over the world think in more *cognitively complex* ways about issues of morality and justice as they get older, as Kohlberg claimed, but at the same time adopt different notions about what is right and what is wrong (or a personal choice versus a moral obligation) as Shweder and others claim.

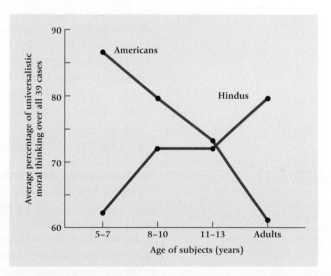

Universalistic moral thinking—the tendency to view rules of behaviour as universally valid and unalterable—increases with age among Hindu children in India but decreases with age in the United States. The course of moral development is likely to be different in different societies. ADAPTED FROM SHWEDER, MAHAPATRA, & MILLER, 1990.

in Kohlberg's system but may actually have very sophisticated concepts of justice (Snarey & Keljo, 1991; Shweder, 1997). Although some aspects of moral development do seem to be common to all cultures, the research presented in Box 14.6 indicates that other aspects of moral growth can vary considerably from society to society.

GENDER BIAS. Critics have also charged that Kohlberg's theory, which was developed from data provided by *male* participants, does not adequately represent female moral reasoning. Carol Gilligan (1982, 1993), for example, has been disturbed by the fact that, in some early studies, women seemed to be the moral inferiors of men, typically reasoning at Kohlberg's Stage 3 while men usually reasoned at Stage 4. Her response was to argue that differential gender typing causes boys and girls to adopt different moral orientations. The strong independence and assertiveness training that boys receive encourages them to view moral dilemmas as inevitable conflicts of interest between *individuals* that laws and other social conventions are designed to resolve. Gilligan calls this orientation the **morality of justice**, a perspective that approximates Stage 4 in Kohlberg's scheme. By contrast, girls are taught to be nurturant, empathic, and concerned about others—in short, to define their sense of goodness in terms of their interpersonal *relationships*. So for females, morality implies a sense of caring or compassionate concern for human welfare—a **morality of care** that may seem to represent Stage 3 in Kohlberg's scheme. However, Gilligan insists that the morality of care that females adopt can become quite abstract or "principled," even though Kohlberg's scheme might place it at Stage 3 because of its focus on interpersonal obligations.

At this point, there is little support for Gilligan's claim that Kohlberg's theory is biased against women. Most studies indicate that women reason just as complexly about moral issues as men do when their answers are scored by Kohlberg's criteria (Jadack et al., 1995; Walker, 1995). Nor is there much evidence for sex differences in moral orientations: According to Lawrence Walker of the University of British Columbia and Gillian Wark and Dennis Krebs of Simon Fraser University, when reasoning about real-life dilemmas they have faced, *both* males and females raise issues of compassion and interpersonal responsibility about as often as or more often than they talk about issues of law, justice, and individual rights (Walker, 1995; Wark & Krebs, 1996). What's more, young men and women view *both* justice-related and care-related attributes as central elements of moral maturity (Walker & Pitts, 1998; and review Table 14.3). So it has become quite clear that the justice and care orientations are *not* sex-specific moralities, as Gilligan claimed.

Nevertheless, Gilligan's theory and the research designed to test it have broadened our view of morality by illustrating that both men and women often think about moral issues—especially real-life as opposed to hypothetical moral issues—in terms of their responsibilities for the welfare of other people. Kohlberg emphasized only one way, a very legalistic way, of thinking about right and wrong. There seems to be merit in tracing the development of *both* a morality of justice and a morality of care in *both* males and females (Brabeck, 1983; Gilligan, 1993).

Is Kohlberg's Theory Incomplete?

Another common criticism of Kohlberg's theory is that it focuses too heavily on moral reasoning and neglects moral affect and behaviour. Yet Kohlberg does largely ignore the role of such powerful emotions as pride, shame, guilt, and remorse that influence our moral thoughts and actions (Haan et al., 1985; Hart & Chmiel, 1992). Yet he did assume that mature moral reasoners should be more inclined to *behave* morally and that the relationship between moral reasoning and moral behaviour would become stronger as individuals progress toward higher levels of moral understanding.

DOES MORAL REASONING PREDICT MORAL CONDUCT? Most of the available data are consistent with Kohlberg's viewpoint. With few exceptions (for example, Kochanska & Murray, 2000), most researchers have found that the moral judgments of young children do *not* predict their behaviour in situations where they are induced to cheat or to violate other moral norms (see Shaffer, 2000 for a review). However, studies of older elementary-

morality of justice
Gilligan's term for what she presumes to be the dominant moral orientation of males, which focuses more on socially defined justice as administered through law than on compassionate concerns for human welfare

morality of care
Gilligan's term for what she presumes to be the dominant moral orientation of females, which focuses more on compassionate concerns for human welfare than on socially defined justice as administered through law

school children, adolescents, and young adults often find that individuals at higher stages of moral reasoning are more likely than those at lower stages to behave altruistically and conscientiously and are less likely to cheat or to take part in delinquent or criminal activity (Colby & Kohlberg, 1987; Rest et al., 1997). Kohlberg (1975), for example, found that only 15 percent of university students who reasoned at the postconventional level actually cheated on a test when given an opportunity, compared with 55 percent of the conventional students and 70 percent of the preconventional students. Yet the relationship between stage of moral reasoning and moral behaviour is only moderate at best (Bruggerman & Hart, 1996). Why? Because personal qualities other than moral reasoning, and many situational factors as well (for example, likelihood that transgressions will be punished or do harm to others), influence moral conduct in daily life. The process of moral growth may even contribute to inconsistencies between moral reasoning and moral behaviour. Stephen Thoma and James Rest (1999), for example, propose that situational factors will have a stronger influence on moral decision making when a person is reexamining (and often rejecting) existing moral principals as she makes the transition from one moral stage to the next higher stage.

KOHLBERG UNDERESTIMATES YOUNG CHILDREN. Finally, Kohlberg's focus on legalistic dilemmas that laws were designed to address caused him to overlook other nonlegalistic forms of moral reasoning that influence the behaviour of elementary-school children. For example, we've seen that young elementary-school children do often consider the needs of others or do whatever they think people will approve of when resolving Eisenberg's *prosocial* moral dilemmas—even though these same youngsters are hopelessly mired in Stage 1 (or Stage 2) when tested on Kohlberg's dilemmas. Furthermore, 8- to 10-year-old Stage 1 reasoners have often developed some sophisticated notions about *distributive justice*—deciding what is a fair and just allocation of limited resources (toys, candies, etc.) among a group of deserving recipients (Damon, 1988; Sigelman & Waitzman, 1991)—reasoning not adequately represented in Kohlberg's theory. Interestingly, fear of punishment, deference to authority, and other legalistic themes that Kohlberg believes characterize the moral judgments of 8- to 10-year-olds do not even appear in children's distributive-justice reasoning. So by focusing so heavily on legalistic concepts, Kohlberg has clearly underestimated the moral sophistication of elementary-school children.

> **?** **WHAT DO YOU THINK?**
>
> Do you think it is acceptable for public schools in a multicultural society such as Canada to provide a moral education to pupils whose own moral beliefs may depend very heavily on their diverse religious, cultural, and familial backgrounds? Why or why not?

Although children this young usually display preconventional moral reasoning on Kohlberg's legalistic dilemmas, they actually have some reasonably sophisticated standards of distributive justice.

PhotoDisc, Inc.

In sum, Kohlberg's theory of moral development has many strengths; yet there is also some merit to the criticisms. His theory does not fully capture the morality of people who live in non-Western societies or who choose to emphasize a morality of care rather than a morality of justice, and it clearly underestimates the moral reasoning of young children. And because Kohlberg concentrates so heavily on moral reasoning, we must rely on other perspectives to help us to understand how moral affect and moral behaviour develop, and how thought, emotions, and behaviour interact to make us the moral beings that most of us ultimately become.

MORALITY AS A PRODUCT OF SOCIAL LEARNING (AND SOCIAL INFORMATION PROCESSING)

doctrine of specificity
viewpoint shared by many social learning theorists that holds that moral affect, reasoning, and behaviour may depend more on the situation that one faces than on an internalized set of moral principles

Social learning theorists such as Albert Bandura (1986, 1991) and Walter Mischel (1974) have been primarily interested in the *behavioural* component of morality—what we actually do when faced with temptation. They claim that moral behaviours are learned in the same way that other social behaviours are—through the operation of reinforcement and punishment and through observational learning. They also consider moral behaviour to be strongly influenced by the specific situations in which people find themselves. It is not at all surprising, they say, to see a person behave morally in one situation but transgress in another situation, or to proclaim that nothing is more important than honesty but then lie or cheat.

How Consistent Are Moral Conduct and Moral Character?

The most extensive study of children's moral conduct is one of the oldest—the Character Education Inquiry reported by Hugh Hartshorne and Mark May (1928–30). This 5-year project investigated the moral character of 10 000 children ages 8 to 16 by repeatedly tempting them to lie, cheat, or steal in a variety of situations. The most noteworthy finding of this massive investigation was that children tended *not* to be consistent in their moral behaviour; a child's willingness to cheat in one situation did not predict his or her willingness to lie, cheat, or steal in other situations. Of particular interest was the finding that children who cheated in a particular setting were just as likely as those who did not to state that cheating is wrong! Hartshorne and May concluded that honesty is largely specific to the situation rather than a stable character trait.

However, more modern and sophisticated analyses of data from the Character Education Inquiry (Burton, 1963) and newer studies (Kochanska & Murray, 2000; Rushton, 1980) have challenged Hartshorne and May's **doctrine of specificity**, finding that moral behaviours of a *particular kind* (for example, a child's willingness to cheat or not cheat on tests or to share or not share toys with playmates) are reasonably consistent over time and across situations. What's more, the correlations among measures of children's moral conduct, moral reasoning, and moral behaviour become progressively stronger with age (Blasi, 1990). So there is some consistency or coherence to moral character after all, especially as we become more morally mature. Yet we should never expect even the most morally mature individuals to be perfectly consistent across *all* situations because one's willingness to lie, cheat, or violate other moral norms (or one's feelings and thoughts about doing so) may always depend to some extent on contextual factors, such as the importance of the goal that might be achieved by transgressing or the amount of encouragement provided by peers for deviant conduct (Burton, 1976).

PhotoDisc, Inc.

Sometimes it is difficult to tell whether children are working together, helping each other, or using each other's work. Although there is some consistency to moral behaviour, a child's conduct in any particular situation is likely to be influenced by factors such as the importance of the goal that might be achieved by breaking a moral rule and the probability of being caught should he or she commit a transgression.

Learning to Resist Temptation

From society's standpoint, one of the more important indexes of morality is the extent to which an individual is able to resist pressures to violate moral norms, *even when the possibility of detection and punishment is remote* (Hoffman, 1970). A person who resists temptation in the absence of external surveillance not only has learned a moral rule but is *internally* motivated to abide by that rule. How do children acquire moral standards, and what motivates them to obey these learned codes of conduct? Social learning theorists have attempted to answer these questions by studying the effects of reinforcement, punishment, and social modelling on children's moral behaviour.

Reinforcement as a Determinant of Moral Conduct

We have seen on several occasions that the frequency of many behaviours can be increased if these acts are reinforced. Moral behaviours are certainly no exception. Grazyna Kochanska from the University of Iowa and Leon Kuczynski from the University of Guelph (Kochanska, 1997b; Kuczynski & Kochanska, 1995) found that when warm, accepting parents set clear and reasonable standards for their children and often *praise* them for behaving well, even toddlers are likely to meet their expectations and display strong evidence of an internalized conscience by age 4 to 5. Children are generally motivated to comply with the wishes of a warm, socially reinforcing adult, and the praise that accompanies their desirable conduct tells them that they are accomplishing that objective.

The Role of Punishment in Establishing Moral Prohibitions

Although reinforcing acceptable behaviours is an effective way to promote desirable conduct, adults often fail to recognize that a child has *resisted* a temptation and is deserving of praise. Yet many adults are quick to *punish* moral transgressions. Is punishment an effective way to foster the development of **inhibitory controls**? The answer depends very critically on the child's *interpretation* of these aversive experiences.

EARLY RESEARCH. Ross Parke (1977) used the *forbidden-toy paradigm* to study the effects of punishment on children's resistance to temptation. During the first phase of a typical experiment, participants are punished (by hearing a noxious buzzer) whenever they touch an attractive toy; however, nothing happens when they play with unattractive toys. Once the child has learned the prohibition, the experimenter leaves and the child is surreptitiously observed to determine whether he or she plays with the forbidden toys.

Recall from our discussion in Chapter 6 (see Box 6.5) that *firm* (rather than mild) punishments administered *immediately* (rather than later) and *consistently* by a *warm* (rather than an aloof) disciplinarian proved most effective at inhibiting a child's undesirable conduct. Yet Parke's most important discovery was that all forms of punishment became more effective if accompanied by a cognitive rationale that provides the transgressor with reasons for not performing a forbidden act.

EXPLAINING THE EFFECTS OF COGNITIVE RATIONALES. Why do rationales increase the effectiveness of punishment, even mild or delayed punishments that produce little moral restraint by themselves? Probably because rationales provide children with information specifying why the punished act is wrong and why *they* should feel guilty or shameful for repeating it. So when these youngsters think about committing the forbidden act in the future, they should experience a general uneasiness (stemming from previous disciplinary encounters), should be inclined to make an *internal attribution* for this arousal (for example, "I'd feel guilty if I caused others harm," "I'd violate my positive self-image"), and should eventually become more likely to inhibit the forbidden act and to feel rather good about their mature and responsible conduct. By contrast, children who receive no rationales or who have heard reasoning that focuses their attention on the negative con-

inhibitory control
ability to display acceptable conduct by resisting the temptation to commit a forbidden act

sequences that *they* can expect for future transgressions (for example, "You'll be spanked again if you do it") will experience just as much uneasiness when they think about committing the forbidden act. However, these youngsters tend to make *external attributions* for their emotional arousal (for example, "I'm worried about getting caught and punished") that might make them comply with moral norms in the presence of authority figures but probably won't inhibit deviant conduct if there is no one around to detect their transgressions.

So fear of detection and punishment is not enough to persuade children to resist temptation in the absence of external surveillance. In order to establish truly internalized *self*-controls, adults must structure disciplinary encounters to include an appropriate rationale—one that informs the child about why the prohibited act is wrong and why *she* should feel guilty or shameful about repeating it (Hoffman, 1988). Clearly, true *self*-restraint is largely under *cognitive* control; it depends more on what's in children's heads rather than on the amount of fear or uneasiness in their guts.

Moral Self-Concept Training. If making internal attributions about one's conduct truly promotes moral self-restraint, we should be able to convince children that they can resist temptations to violate moral norms *because* they are good, honest, or otherwise responsible persons (an internal attribution).

This kind of moral self-concept training really does work. William Casey and Roger Burton (1982) found that 7- to 10-year-olds became much more honest while playing games if honesty was stressed and the players learned to remind themselves to follow the rules. Yet when honesty was *not* stressed, players often cheated. Furthermore, David Perry and his associates (1980) found that 9- to 10-year-olds who had been told that they were especially good at carrying out instructions and following rules (moral self-concept training) behaved very differently after succumbing to a nearly irresistible temptation (leaving a boring task to watch an exciting TV show) than did peers who had not been told they were especially good. Specifically, children who had heard positive attributions about themselves were more inclined than control participants to *punish their own transgressions* by giving back many of the valuable prize tokens they had been paid for working at the boring task. So it seems that labelling children as good or honest may not only increase the likelihood that they will resist temptations, but also contributes to children's feelings of guilt or remorse should they behave inappropriately and violate their positive self-images.

In sum, moral self-concept training, particularly when combined with praise for desirable conduct, can be a most effective alternative to punishment as a means of establishing inhibitory controls—one that should help convince the child that "I'm resisting temptation because I want to" and lead to the development of truly internalized controls rather than a response inhibition based on a fear of detection and punishment. Furthermore, this positive, nonpunitive approach should produce none of the undesirable side effects (for example, resentment) that often accompany punishment.

Effects of Social Models on Children's Moral Behaviour

Might children be influenced by rule-following models who exhibit moral behaviours in a passive way by failing to commit forbidden acts? Indeed they may, as long as they are aware that the passive model is resisting the temptation to violate a rule. Joan Grusec from the University of Toronto and her associates (1979) found that a rule-following model can be particularly effective at inspiring children to behave in kind if he clearly verbalizes that he is following a rule *and* states a rationale for not committing the deviant act. Furthermore, rule-following models whose rationales match the child's customary level of moral reasoning are more influential than models whose rationales are well beyond that level (Toner & Potts, 1981).

Finally, consider what Nace Toner and his associates (1978) found: 6- to 8-year-olds who were persuaded to *serve* as models of moral restraint for other children became more likely than age-mates who had not served as rule-following models to obey other rules during later tests of resistance to temptation. It was almost as if serving as a model produced a change in children's self-concepts, so that they now defined themselves as

"people who follow rules." The implications for child-rearing are clear: Parents can succeed in establishing inhibitory controls in their older children by appealing to their
maturity and persuading them to serve as models of self-restraint for their younger
brothers and sisters.

WHO RAISES CHILDREN WHO ARE MORALLY MATURE?

Many years ago, Martin Hoffman (1970) reviewed the child-rearing literature to see
whether the disciplinary techniques that *parents* actually use have any effect on the
moral development of their children. Three major approaches were compared:

1. **Love withdrawal:** withholding attention, affection, or approval after a child misbehaves or, in other words, creating anxiety over a loss of love.

2. **Power assertion:** use of superior power to control the child's behaviour (including
   techniques such as forceful commands, physical restraint, spankings, and withdrawal of privileges that may generate fear, anger, or resentment).

3. **Induction:** explaining why a behaviour is wrong and should be changed by
   emphasizing how it affects other people, often suggesting how the child might repair
   any harm done.

Suppose that little Suzie has just terrorized the family dog by chasing him with a lit
sparkler during a Canada Day celebration. Using *love withdrawal*, a parent might say,
"How could you? Get away! I can't bear to look at you." Using *power assertion*, a parent
might spank Suzie or say, "That's it! No movie for you this Saturday." Using *induction*, the
parent might say, "Suzie, look how scared Pokey is. You could have set him on fire, and
you know how sad we'd all be if he was burned." Induction, then, is a matter of providing rationales that focus special attention on the consequences of one's wrongdoing
for other people (or dogs, as the case may be).

Although only a limited number of child-rearing studies had been conducted by
1970, their results suggested that (1) neither love withdrawal nor power assertion were
particularly effective at promoting moral maturity, but that (2) induction seemed to
foster the development of all three aspects of morality—moral affect, moral reasoning,
and moral behaviour (Hoffman, 1970). Table 14.4 summarizes the relationships among
the three patterns of parental discipline and various measures of children's moral maturity that emerged from a later review of the literature that included many more studies
(Brody & Shaffer, 1982). Clearly, these data confirm Hoffman's conclusions: Parents
who rely on inductive discipline tend to have children who are morally mature,
whereas frequent use of power assertion is more often associated with moral *immatu-*

love withdrawal
form of discipline in which an
adult withholds attention,
affection, or approval in order to
modify or control a child's
behaviour

power assertion
form of discipline in which an
adult relies on his or her superior
power (for example, by
administering spankings or
withholding privileges) to modify
or control a child's behaviour

induction
nonpunitive form of discipline in
which an adult explains why a
child's behaviour is wrong and
should be changed by
emphasizing its effects on others

| TABLE 14.4 | Relationships between Parents' Use of Three Disciplinary Strategies and Children's Moral Development |

Direction of relationship between parents' use of a disciplinary strategy and children's moral maturity	Type of discipline		
	Power assertion	**Love withdrawal**	**Induction**
+ (positive correlation)	7	8	38
– (negative correlation)	32	11	6

NOTE: Table entries represent the number of occasions on which a particular disciplinary technique was found to be associated (either positively or negatively) with a measure of children's moral affect, reasoning, or behaviour.
SOURCE: Adapted from Brody & Shaffer, 1982.

rity than with moral maturity. The few cases in which induction was *not* associated with moral maturity all involved children under age 4. However, recent research indicates that induction can be highly effective with 2- to 5-year-olds, reliably promoting sympathy and compassion for others as well as a willingness to comply with parental requests. By contrast, use of such high-intensity power-assertive tactics as becoming angry and physically restraining or spanking the child is already associated with and seems to promote noncompliance, defiance, and a lack of concern for others (Crockenberg & Litman, 1990; Kochanska, 1997b; Kochanska & Murray, 2000; Zahn-Waxler et al., 1979).

Why is inductive discipline effective? Hoffman cites several reasons. First, it provides children with *cognitive standards* (or rationales) to evaluate their conduct. Second, this form of discipline helps children to sympathize with others (Krevans & Gibbs, 1996) and allows parents to talk about such *moral affects* as pride, guilt, and shame that are not easily discussed with a child who is made emotionally insecure by love withdrawal techniques or angry by power-assertive techniques (see Labile & Thompson, 2000). Finally, parents who use inductive discipline are likely to explain to the child (1) what he or she *should have done* when tempted to violate a prohibition and (2) what he or she *can now do* to make up for a transgression. So induction may be an effective method of moral socialization because it calls attention to the cognitive, affective, and behavioural aspects of morality and may help the child to integrate them.

Finally, note that few if any parents are totally inductive, love oriented, or power assertive in their approach to discipline; most make at least some use of all three disciplinary techniques. Although parents classified as inductive rely heavily on reasoning, they occasionally take punitive measures whenever punishment is necessary to command the child's attention or to discipline repeated transgressions. So the style of parenting that Hoffman calls induction may be very similar to the "rationale plus firm punishment" treatment that Parke (1977) found most effective in laboratory studies of resistance to temptation.

CRITICISMS OF HOFFMAN'S IDEAS ABOUT DISCIPLINE. Several investigators have wondered whether Hoffman's conclusions about the effectiveness of inductive discipline might be overstated. For example, inductive discipline used by White, middle-class mothers is consistently associated with measures of children's moral maturity; however, the same findings don't always hold for fathers or for parents from other socioeconomic backgrounds (Brody & Shaffer, 1982; Grusec & Goodnow, 1994). Furthermore, the positive association between parents' use of power-assertive discipline and children's aggressive, antisocial conduct seems to hold for European-American but not for African-American children (Deater-Deckard & Dodge, 1997). Clearly, more research is needed to establish how culturally specific Hoffman's ideas may be.

Other critics have raised the *direction-of-effects* issue: Does induction promote moral maturity? Or, rather, do morally mature children elicit more inductive forms of discipline from their parents? Because child-rearing studies are based on correlational data, either of these possibilities can explain Hoffman's findings. Hoffman (1975) responded by claiming that parents exert far more control over their children's behaviour than children exert over parents. In other words, he believes that parental use of inductive discipline promotes moral maturity rather than the other way around. And there is some *experimental* support for Hoffman's claim in that induction is much more effective than other forms of discipline at persuading children to keep their promises and to comply with rules imposed by *unfamiliar* adults (Kuczynski, 1983).

Yet children can influence the discipline they receive. For example, the research presented in Box 14.7 reveals that a child's *temperament* can influence how he or she reacts to different kinds of discipline, which in turn may affect how he or she is treated. A child who acts out or defies his parents, for example, will often elicit more coercive (and less effective) forms of discipline in the future (Patterson, 1998). And although most youngsters may respond favourably to inductive discipline, it is becoming quite clear that there is no one discipline that works best for *all* children and that effective approaches are those that provide a good fit with the child's behaviours and other attributes (Grusec, Goodnow, & Kuczynski, 2000).

Temperament, Discipline, and Moral Internalization

Grazyna Kochanska (1993, 1997a) proposed that the kind of parenting most likely to foster moral internalization depends on a child's temperament. Some children are temperamentally *fearful*—that is, prone to become highly anxious and to burst into tears when they receive a sharp reprimand from their parents. According to Kochanska, fearful children respond much more favourably to gentle, psychological forms of discipline that de-emphasize power assertion—something akin to Hoffman's induction. Other children are highly impulsive and temperamentally *fearless*. Kochanska believes that these emotionally nonreactive youngsters may not be sufficiently aroused by mild psychological forms of discipline to internalize parental rules or even to stop performing the behaviour for which they are being reprimanded! Although their parents may be inclined to become forceful with them when gentle forms of discipline do not work, Kochanska claims that resorting to power assertion proves no more effective with a fearless child than with a fearful one. Instead, she proposes that the route to moral internalization for a fearless child is warm, sensitive parenting of the kind that promotes secure attachments and a mutually cooperative parent–child relationship. Her view is that a secure and mutually positive orientation fosters *committed compliance* from the child, who wants to cooperate with and please his or her parents.

To test her theory, Kochanska (1995, 1997a) classified a sample of 2- to 3-year-olds as temperamentally fearful or fearless. She then observed each of them interacting with their mothers to assess each mother's warmth and responsiveness to social signals and the kinds of discipline that the mother used. Data on the security of the child's attachment to his or her mother were also available. The strength of children's moral internalization was assessed at three times: ages 2 to 3, 4, and 5. Measures of moral internalization included complying with requests and following rules (that is, refusing to touch prohibited toys) at ages 2 to 3, as well as refusing to cheat at games and maturity of moral reasoning at ages 4 and 5.

The results of this longitudinal study provided clear support for Kochanska's theory. For the *fearful* children, use of gentle, inductive discipline that was low in power assertion predicted higher levels of moral internalization at all three ages. Yet this same discipline bore no relationship to the levels of moral internalization that *fearless* participants displayed. Instead, a secure attachment to a mother who was highly responsive to their social signals is what predicted strength of conscience among fearless children.

Here, then, is another example of how "goodness of fit" between parenting practices and children's temperaments foster adaptive outcomes. Judging from the child-rearing literature, most children probably are sufficiently aroused by gentle, inductive disciplinary techniques to learn moral lessons, although this approach may be essential to foster moral internalization among especially fearful youngsters. However, continued reliance on this same discipline constitutes a poor fit for highly fearless children, who are more likely to internalize moral lessons in the context of a secure relationship with a parent whose discipline is firm and reminds the child of the desirability of maintaining the warm, mutually cooperative relationship they have enjoyed. Finally, Kochanska and her associates (Kochanska, Murray, et al., 1996) find that mothers' frequent use of power assertion consistently *inhibits* children's moral internalization and represents a poor fit with all temperaments.

A CHILD'S-EYE VIEW OF DISCIPLINE. What do children think about various disciplinary strategies? Do they feel (as many developmentalists do) that physical punishment and love withdrawal are ineffective methods of promoting moral restraint? Would they favour inductive techniques or perhaps prefer that their parents adopt more permissive attitudes about transgressions?

✔ **Concept Check 14.3**
Understanding Moral Development

Check your understanding of theories and selected aspects of moral development by matching each descriptive statement that follows with one of the following concepts or processes: (a) role-taking skills, (b) formal operations, (c) disequilibrating social experiences, (d) induction, (e) moral rules, (f) morality of care, (g) peer interactions, (h) power assertion, (i) social-conventional rules, (j) mutually responsive parent–child relationship, (k) harsh parenting fosters moral immaturity.
Answers appear in the Appendix.

_____ 1. preschoolers' strong respect for _____ contradicts Piaget's theory

_____ 2. Freud's oedipal morality is discredited by this observation

_____ 3. both Piaget and Kohlberg emphasize this *social* contributor to moral development

_____ 4. according to Gilligan, Kohlberg overlooks the growth of this moral aspect

_____ 5. discipline consistently associated with moral *immaturity*

_____ 6. most children, particularly fearful ones, respond well to this discipline

_____ 7. may be particularly important for successful moral socialization of fearless children

_____ 8. cognitive prerequisite for Kohlberg's postconventional morality

_____ 9. cognitive prerequisite for Kohlberg's conventional morality

_____ 10. prerequisite for all moral growth beyond Kohlberg's preconventional level

_____ 11. become *less* (rather than more) common with age in some societies

Michael Siegal and Jan Cowen (1984) addressed these issues by asking children and adolescents between the ages of 4 and 18 to listen to stories describing different kinds of misdeeds and to evaluate strategies that parents had used to discipline these antics. Five kinds of transgressions were described: (1) simple disobedience (the child refusing to clean his or her room), (2) causing physical harm to others (the child punching a playmate), (3) causing physical harm to oneself (ignoring an order not to touch a hot stove), (4) causing psychological harm to others (making fun of a physically disabled person), and (5) causing physical damage (breaking a lamp while roughhousing). The four disciplinary techniques on which parents were said to have relied were *induction* (reasoning with the culprit by pointing out the harmful consequences of his or her actions), *physical punishment* (striking the child), *love withdrawal* (telling the child to stay away), and *permissive nonintervention* (ignoring the incident and assuming that the child would learn important lessons on his or her own). Each participant heard 20 stories that resulted from pairing each of the four disciplinary strategies with each of the five transgressions. After listening to or reading each story, the participant indicated whether the parent's approach to the problem was "very wrong," "wrong," "half right–half wrong," "right," or "very right."

The results were clear: Induction was the most preferred disciplinary strategy for participants of all ages (even preschoolers), and physical punishment was the next most favourably evaluated technique. So all participants seemed to favour a rational disciplinarian who relies heavily on reasoning that is occasionally backed by power assertion. By contrast, love withdrawal and permissiveness were favourably evaluated by no age group. However, the 4- to 9-year-olds in the sample favoured *any* form of discipline, even love withdrawal, over a permissive attitude on the parent's part (which they viewed as wrong or very wrong). Apparently, young children see the need for adults to step in and restrain their inappropriate conduct, because they were disturbed by stories in which youngsters were completely free to do their own thing.

In sum, the disciplinary style that children favour (induction backed by occasional use of power assertion) is the one most closely associated with measures of moral maturity in child-rearing studies and with resistance to temptation in the laboratory. Perhaps another reason that inductive discipline may promote moral maturity is simply that children view this approach as the right way to deal with transgressions, and they may be highly motivated to accept influence from a disciplinarian whose world view matches their own. By contrast, children who favour induction but are usually disciplined in other ways may see little justification for internalizing the values and exhortations of a disciplinarian whose very methods of inducing compliance seem unwise, unjust, and hardly worthy of their respect.

SUMMARY

♦ Three interrelated aspects of social development are often considered when making judgments about a child's moral character: the emergence and control of aggression, the development of altruism, and the establishment of an internalized sense of morality.

The Development of Aggression

♦ Intentional acts of harmdoing, or **aggression**, are often divided into two categories: **hostile aggression** and **instrumental aggression**. Instrumental aggression appears by the end of the first year as infants have **conflicts** with siblings and peers over toys and other possessions.

♦ During early childhood, aggression becomes less physical and increasingly verbal, and somewhat less instrumental and increasingly hostile or **retaliatory** in nature. Boys are more overtly aggressive than girls, but girls exceed boys in **relational aggression**. Although overt aggression declines with age, more covert forms of antisocial conduct show a corresponding rise. Aggressiveness is a moderately stable attribute for both males and females.

♦ Two types of highly aggressive children have been identified. **Proactive aggressors** rely on aggression to satisfy personal objectives and are quite confident that aggression will pay off for them. By contrast, **reactive aggressors** display a **hostile attributional bias** that causes them to over-

560

attribute hostile intent to others and to retaliate in a hostile manner to imagined provocations. Proactive aggressors may become bullies, whereas reactive aggressors may often become **provocative victims**. However, most victims of abuse are **passive victims** whom bullies find easy to dominate.

♦ A person's aggressive inclinations depend, in part, on the cultural, subcultural, and family settings in which he or she is raised. Due in part to social class differences in parenting, children and adolescents from disadvantaged backgrounds are more aggressive and display higher rates of delinquency than their middle-class peers.

♦ Children from any social background can become highly aggressive and find themselves on a path leading to chronic delinquency if they live in a **coercive home environment** in which hostile behaviours are **negatively reinforced.** In order to help these highly combative children, it is often necessary to treat the entire family.

♦ The incidence of children's aggression can be reduced by taking care to create nonaggressive play environments. *Proactive aggressors* can benefit when adults rely on such control procedures as the **time-out technique** and the **incompatible-response technique**, which teaches them that aggression doesn't pay and that nonaggressive means of problem solving are better ways to achieve their objectives. And all aggressive youngsters, particularly hot-headed *reactive aggressors*, can benefit from social-cognitive interventions that help them to regulate their anger and to become more skilled at taking others' perspectives, thus becoming less inclined to attribute hostile intents to other people.

Altruism: Development of the Prosocial Self

♦ Early indications of **altruism,** such as sharing toys and comforting distressed companions, appear in infancy and toddlerhood, particularly among youngsters whose parents emphasize **affective explanations** as part of their disciplinary strategies.

♦ Sharing, helping, and other forms of prosocial conduct become more and more common from the preschool period onward. Contrary to widely held stereotypes, girls are neither more altruistic than boys nor any less capable than boys of accomplishing tasks without seeking assistance.

♦ The growth of altruistic concern is linked to the development of role-taking skills, **prosocial moral reasoning**, and **sympathetic empathic arousal**. Although young children often interpret empathic arousal as personal, or **self-oriented, distress**, they eventually acquire the role-taking skills to interpret their reactions as sympathy for others, which promotes altruism by making them feel responsible for others' welfare (the **"felt responsibility" hypothesis**).

♦ Like aggression, a person's altruistic tendencies are influenced by his or her cultural and family environments. Parents can promote altruistic behaviour by praising their child's kindly deeds, and by practising themselves the prosocial lessons that they preach. Furthermore, parents who discipline harmdoing with nonpunitive, affective explanations that point out the negative effects of children's misconduct on victims are likely to raise children who become sympathetic, self-sacrificing, and concerned about the welfare of others.

What Is Morality?

♦ **Morality** has been defined in many ways, although almost everyone agrees that it implies a set of **internalized** principles or ideals that help the individual to distinguish right from wrong and to act on this distinction. Morality has three basic components: **moral affect**, **moral reasoning**, and **moral behaviour**.

Psychoanalytic Explanations of Moral Development

♦ According to Freud's theory of **oedipal morality**, children internalize the moral standards of the same-sex parent during the phallic stage as they resolve their Oedipus or Electra complexes and form a conscience or superego.

♦ Research has consistently discredited Freud's theory. However, newer psychoanalytic ideas that the conscience forms earlier in toddlerhood in the context of a warm, **mutually responsive relationship** (rather than a fear-provoking one) has received some support.

Cognitive-Developmental Theory: The Child as Moral Philosopher

♦ Cognitive-developmental theorists have emphasized the cognitive component of morality by studying the development of moral reasoning. Jean Piaget formulated a two-stage model of moral development based on changes that occur in children's conceptions of rules and their sense of social justice. From a **premoral period** in which children allegedly respect no rules, they progress to **heteronomous morality**, in which they view rules as moral absolutes and believe in **immanent justice**, and finally to **autonomous morality**, in which they regard rules as flexible and justice as relative rather than absolute.

♦ Piaget clearly identified some important trends in the development of moral reasoning. However, shortcomings of his research methods and his failure to capture children's distinctions between **moral rules** and **social-conventional rules** caused him to underestimate the moral sophistication of preschool and young elementary-school children.

♦ Lawrence Kohlberg's revision and extension of Piaget's theory views moral reasoning as progressing through an invariant sequence of three levels (**preconventional, conventional**, and **postconventional moralities**), each composed of two distinct stages. According to Kohlberg, the order of progression through the levels and stages is invariant because each of these modes of thinking depends, in part, on the development of cognitive abilities that evolve in a fixed sequence. Yet Kohlberg also claimed that no moral growth occurs in the absence of social experiences that would cause a person to reevaluate her or his existing moral concepts.

♦ Research indicates that Kohlberg's stages do form an invariant sequence. Furthermore, both cognitive development and such relevant social experiences as exposure to divergent moral perspectives in the context of discussions with parents, peers, and other participants in higher education or democratic activities do contribute to the growth of moral reasoning. However, Kohlberg's theory may not adequately describe the morality of people who live in many non-Westernized societies or who emphasize a **morality of** care rather than a **morality of justice**; and, like Piaget, Kohlberg clearly underestimates the moral reasoning of young children. Critics also claim that the theory says too little about moral affect and moral behaviour.

Morality as a Product of Social Learning (and Social Information Processing)

♦ Although their **doctrine of specificity** is clearly an overstatement, social learning theorists have helped to explain how children learn to resist temptation and inhibit acts that violate moral norms. Among the factors that promote the development of **inhibitory controls** are praise given for virtuous conduct, punishments that include appropriate rationales, and exposing children to (or having them

serve as) models of moral restraint. Other nonpunitive techniques such as moral self-concept training are also quite effective at promoting moral behaviour.

Who Raises Children Who Are Morally Mature?

♦ Child-rearing studies consistently imply that use of **induction discipline** promotes moral maturity, whereas **love withdrawal** has little effect, and **power assertion** is associated with moral *immaturity*. The effectiveness of induction may vary, however, depending on the child's temperament. But children generally prefer inductive discipline to other approaches, and most seem highly motivated to accept influence from an inductive adult whose methods they can respect.

KEY TERMS

aggression, 516

hostile aggression, 516

instrumental aggression, 516

conflict, 516

retaliatory aggression, 517

relational aggression, 518

proactive aggressors, 520

reactive aggressors, 520

hostile attributional bias, 521

passive victims (of aggression), 522

provocative victims (of aggression), 522

coercive home environment, 525

negative reinforcer, 525

incompatible-response technique, 528

time-out technique, 529

empathy, 530

altruism, 530

affective explanations, 531

prosocial moral reasoning, 532

sympathetic empathic arousal, 533

self-oriented distress, 533

"felt responsibility" hypothesis, 535

morality, 538

internalization, 538

moral affect, 539

moral reasoning, 539

moral behaviour, 539

oedipal morality, 540

mutually responsive relationship, 540

committed compliance, 540

situational compliance, 540

premoral period, 541

heteronomous morality, 541

immanent justice, 542

autonomous morality, 542

moral rules, 544

social-conventional rules, 544

preconventional morality, 545

conventional morality, 546

postconventional morality, 547

transactive interactions, 549

morality of justice, 552

morality of care, 552

doctrine of specificity, 554

inhibitory control, 555

love withdrawal, 557

power assertion, 557

induction, 557

You can find further information on the topics covered in this chapter by visiting:

www.developmentalpsych2e.nelson.com

For additional reading, go to InfoTrac College Edition, your on-line research library, at:

infotrac.thomsonlearning.com

The Family

When Burnam and Addie Ledford hosted the Ledford family reunion, he was 102, she 93. They had married in 1903 and were nearing their 75th wedding anniversary. They had 13 children, 9 of them still surviving; the oldest was age 69. They also had 32 grandchildren and 39 great-grandchildren—so many that Burnam marveled, "It's like planting seeds.... They just keep coming up." Burnam and Addie clearly valued their bonds to past, present, and future generations of Ledfords.

EGERTON, 1983

The Ledfords' emphasis on family ties is not at all unusual. The vast majority of children in all societies grow up in a home setting with at least one biological parent or other relative. So virtually all of us are bound to families. We are born into them, work our way toward adulthood in them, start our own as adults, and remain connected to them in old age. We are part of our families, and they are part of us.

Our focus in this chapter is on the family—an institution that both influences and is influenced by its children. What functions do families serve? How does the birth of a child affect other family members? Do the existing (or changing) relationships among other members of the family have any effect on the care and training that a child or an adolescent receives? Are some patterns of parenting better than others? Do parents decide how they will raise their children, or do children influence their parents? Does the family's cultural heritage and socioeconomic status affect parenting and parent–child interactions? How important are siblings as socialization agents? How are children affected by the increasing diversity of family life that we see today—by growing up with adoptive or gay or lesbian parents or by having to adjust to maternal employment, divorce, or a return to the two-parent family when a single parent remarries? And why do some parents abuse their children? These are some of the major issues that we will consider as we look at the important roles that families play in the cognitive, social, and emotional development of children and adolescents.

Understanding the Family

Parental Socialization during Childhood and Adolescence

The Influence of Siblings and Sibling Relationships

Diversity in Family Life

When Parenting Breaks Down: The Problem of Child Abuse

Reflections on the Family

Summary

UNDERSTANDING THE FAMILY

From a developmental perspective, the most important function that families serve in all societies is to care for and *socialize* their young. **Socialization** refers to the process by which children acquire the beliefs, values, and behaviours deemed significant and appropriate by the older members of their society.

socialization
process by which children acquire the beliefs, values, and behaviours considered desirable or appropriate by the society to which they belong

Clearly, families are not the only institution involved in this socialization process. Religious institutions, for example, provide important emotional supports and moral socialization that often increase family cohesion and promote healthy developmental outcomes (Brody, Stoneman, & Flor, 1996). And as we will see in Chapter 16, such institutions as schools, the mass media, and children's groups (e.g., Boy Scouts and Girl Guides) frequently supplement the training and emotional support functions served by families. Nevertheless, many children have limited exposure to people outside the family for their first several years, until they are placed in daycare or nursery school or begin their formal schooling. So the family has a clear head start on other institutions when it comes to socializing a child. And because the events of the early years are so very important to the child's social, emotional, and intellectual development, it is appropriate to think of the family as society's primary instrument of socialization.

The Family as a Social System

When developmentalists began to study socialization in the 1940s and 1950s, they focused almost entirely on the mother–child relationship, operating under the assumption that mothers (and, to a lesser extent, fathers) were the agents who moulded children's conduct and character (Ambert, 1992). However, modern family researchers have rejected this simple unidirectional model in favour of a more comprehensive "systems" approach (Minuchin, 1988) that is similar to Urie Bronfenbrenner's (1993, 1995) ecological systems theory that we discussed in Chapter 2. The systems approach recognizes that parents influence their children. But it also stresses that (1) children influence the behaviour and child-rearing practices of their parents, and (2) families are complex **social systems**—that is, networks of *reciprocal* relationships and alliances that are constantly evolving and are greatly affected by community and cultural influences. Now consider some implications of this systems perspective.

family social system
complex network of relationships, interactions, and patterns of influence that characterizes a family with three or more members

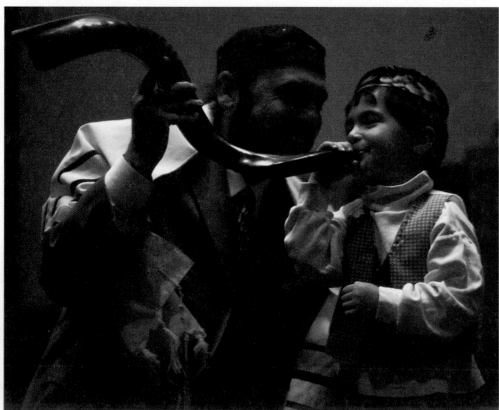

For many families, religious activities provide an important source of social/emotional support that increases family cohesion and helps to promote healthy developmental outcomes.

Direct and Indirect Influences

What does it mean to say that a family is a social system? To Jay Belsky (1981), it means that the family, much like the human body, is a *holistic structure* consisting of interrelated parts, each of which affects and is affected by every other part, and each of which contributes to the functioning of the whole.

To illustrate, consider the simplest of **nuclear families**, consisting of a mother, a father, and a first-born child. According to Belsky (1981), even this man–woman–infant system is quite complex. An infant interacting with his or her mother is already involved in a process of *reciprocal influence*, as is evident when we notice that the infant's smile is likely to be greeted by the mother's smile or that a mother's concerned expression often makes her infant wary. These influences, in which any pair of family member affects and is affected by another's behaviour, are called **direct effects**. And what happens when Dad arrives? As shown in Figure 15.1, the mother–infant dyad is suddenly transformed into a "*family system* [comprising] a husband–wife as well as mother–infant and father–infant relationships" (Belsky, 1981, p. 17).

One implication of viewing the family as a system is that interactions between any two family members are likely to be influenced by the attitudes and behaviours of a third family member—a phenomenon known as an **indirect, or third-party, effect**. To illustrate, fathers clearly influence the mother–infant relationship: Happily married mothers who have close, supportive relationships with their husbands tend to interact much more patiently and sensitively with their infants than mothers who experience marital tension and feel that they are raising their children on their own (Cox et al., 1989, 1992). Meanwhile, mothers indirectly influence the father–infant relationship: Fathers tend to be more involved with their infants when their wives believe that a father should play an important role in a child's life (Palkovitz, 1984) and when the two parents talk frequently about the baby (Belsky, Gilstrap, & Rovine, 1984; Levy-Shiff, 1994). Overall, children fare best when couples **coparent**—that is, mutually support each other's parenting efforts and function as a cooperative (rather than an antagonistic) team. Unfortunately, effective coparenting is difficult for couples experiencing marital discord and other life stresses (Kitzmann, 2000; McHale, 1995), and disputes between parents over child-rearing issues can be particularly harmful, often forecasting increases in childhood and adolescent adjustment problems over and above those attributable to other aspects of marital conflict (Mahoney, Jouriles, & Scavone, 1997). Clearly, both mothers and fathers can influence their children *indirectly* through their interactions with their spouses.

Figure 15.1 *A model of the family as a social system. As implied in the diagram, a family is bigger than the sum of its parts. Parents affect infants, who affect each parent and the marital relationship. Of course, the marital relationship may affect the parenting that the infant receives, the infant's behaviour, and so on. Clearly, families are complex social systems. As an exercise, you may want to rediagram the patterns of influence within a family after adding a sibling or two. FROM BELSKY, 1981.*

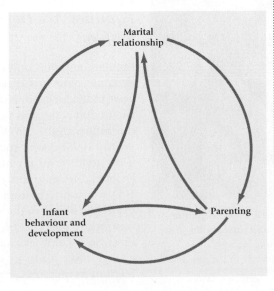

nuclear family
family unit consisting of a wife/mother, a husband/father, and their dependent child(ren)

direct effect
instances in which any pair of family members affects and is affected by each other's behaviour

indirect, or third-party, effect
instances in which the relationship between two individuals in a family is modified by the behaviour or attitudes of a third family member

coparenting
circumstance in which parents mutually support each other and function as a cooperative parenting team

Of course, children also exert direct and indirect effects on their parents. A highly impulsive toddler who shows little inclination to comply with requests may drive some mothers to punitive coercive methods of discipline (direct child-to-mother effect; Donovan, Leavitt, & Walsh, 2000), which, in turn, may make the child more defiant than ever (direct mother-to-child effect) (Crockenberg & Litman, 1990). Alarmed by this state of affairs, the exasperated mother may then criticize her husband for his nonintervention, thereby precipitating an unpleasant discussion about parental obligations and responsibilities (an indirect effect of the child's impulsivity on the husband–wife relationship).

In short, every person and every relationship within the family affects every other person and relationship through pathways of reciprocal influence illustrated in Figure 15.1. Now we begin to see why it was rather naive to think we might understand how families influence children by concentrating exclusively on the mother–child relationship.

Now think about how complex the family system becomes with the birth of a second child and the addition of sibling–sibling and sibling–parent relationships. Or consider the complexity of an **extended family** household, in which parents and their children live with other kin—some combination of grandparents, aunts, uncles, nieces, and nephews. Extended family households are common in many cultures of the world. In Canada, the majority of extended families involve at least one senior, and in most cases a senior woman (Statistics Canada, 2001e). It turns out that living in extended families is also a fairly common arrangement for African Americans—and an adaptive one for economically disadvantaged African-American mothers, who are likely to become more sensitive, responsive parents should they receive much-needed child-rearing assistance and social support from their own mothers or other relatives, or even from their child's father if they are residing elsewhere (Burton, 1990; Coley, 1998; Taylor & Roberts, 1995). Indeed, disadvantaged African-American schoolchildren and adolescents whose families receive ample kinship support typically experience competent parenting at home, which in turn, is associated with such positive outcomes as a strong sense of self-reliance, solid academic performances, and few, if any, behavioural problems (Taylor, 1996; Taylor & Roberts, 1995; Zimmerman, Salem, & Maton, 1995). And in cultures such as the Sudan, where social life is governed by collectivist ideals stressing intergenerational harmony, children routinely display better patterns of psychological adjustment if raised in extended-family households than in Westernized, two-parent nuclear families (Al-Awad & Sonuga-Barke, 1992). Clearly, families come in many configurations, and the healthiest family contexts for development depend heavily on both the needs of individual families and the values that families within particular cultural (and subcultural) contexts are trying to promote.

extended family
group of blood relatives from more than one nuclear family (for example, grandparents, aunts, uncles, nieces, and nephews) who live together, forming a household

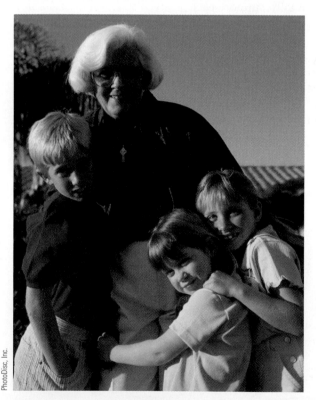

PhotoDisc, Inc.

Older members of extended families serve many useful functions. In addition to providing information and emotional support to young parents, grandmothers and even great-grandmothers may figure prominently in the care and guidance of the family's children.

Families Are Developing Systems

Families are not only complex social systems, they are also dynamic systems. Consider that every family member is a *developing* individual and that relationships between husband and wife, parent and child, and sibling and sibling also change in ways that can influence the development of each family member (Klein & White, 1996). Many such changes are planned, as when parents allow toddlers to do more things on their own as a means of encouraging autonomy and developing individual initiative. However, a host of unplanned or unforeseen changes (such as the death of a sibling or the souring of the mother–father relationship) can greatly affect family interactions and the growth of its children. So a family is not only a system in which developmental change takes place; its dynamics also change with the development of its members.

Families Are Embedded Systems

The social systems perspective also emphasizes that all families are embedded within larger cultural and subcultural contexts and that the ecological niche that a family occupies (for example, the family's socioeconomic status, its religion, and the values that prevail within a subculture, a community, or even a neighbourhood) can affect family interactions and the development of a family's children (Bronfenbrenner, 1995; Greenberg et al., 1999). As we will see later in the chapter, economic hardship exerts a strong influence on parenting: Parents often become depressed over their financial situation, which, in turn, can lead to marital conflict and cause them to become less nurturant toward and involved with their children (McLoyd, 1998). However, economically distressed parents who have close ties to a community—a church group, a volunteer organization, or circle of close friends—experience far less stress and less disruption of their parenting routines (Burchinal, Follmer, & Bryant, 1996; Hashima & Amato, 1994). Clearly, the broader social contexts that families experience can greatly affect the ways that family functions are carried out.

In sum, even the simplest of families is a true social system that is much bigger than the sum of its parts. Not only does each family member influence the behaviour of every other, but also the relationship between any two family members can affect the interactions and relationships of all other family members. And when we consider that family members develop, relationships change, and all family dynamics are influenced by the broader social contexts in which families are embedded, it becomes clear that socialization within the family is best described not as a two-way street between parents and children but as the busy intersection of many, many avenues of influence.

A Changing Family System in a Changing World

Not only is the family a complex, developing system, but it exists and develops in a world that is constantly changing. During the last half of the 20th century, several dramatic social changes affected the makeup of the typical family and the character of family life. Drawing on Canadian census data and other surveys, we highlight the following changes.

More Single Adults

More adults are living as singles today than in the past. Marriage isn't "out," however, because about 90 percent of young adults eventually marry (Chadwick & Heaton, 1992).

Active Postponement of Marriage

Many young singles postpone marriage to pursue educational and career goals. The average age of first marriage has risen to 27.4 years for women and 29.5 years for men (Statistics Canada, 2001a).

Decreased Childbearing

Today's adults not only wait longer after they marry to have children but they also have fewer of them. In addition, more women are choosing not to have children (Statistics Canada, 2004a). In 1999 the birth rate was 1.52 live births among women of childbearing age (Statistics Canada, 2002c). Although there was a brief baby boom in the 1980s, there has generally been a decline in birth rates since the early 1970s (Statistics Canada, Federal, Provincial and Territorial Advisory Committee on Population Health, 2000a). Relative to other countries, Canada has a lower birth rate than the United States, Australia, France, and the United Kingdom and a higher birth rate than countries such as Germany, Spain, and Japan (Statistics Canada, Federal, Provincial and Territorial Advisory Committee on Population Health, 2000a).

More Women Are Employed

In one Canadian survey, approximately 59.5 percent of women reported that they worked full time in the year 2000 (Statistics Canada, 2001b). Forty percent of women who work full time have a child 16 or under at home, and 56 percent of women who work part time have at least one child under 16 at home. Although women still carry the lion's share of child-rearing and housework responsibilities, fewer and fewer children have a mother whose full-time job is that of homemaker.

More Divorces

In 1986, Canada amended the Divorce Act (1985) to allow marriages to be dissolved after one year of separation rather than the three years of separation required prior to the amendment. As a result, a dramatic rise in divorces was reported in 1987 (Statistics Canada, 1999b). After this rise, the divorce rate declined substantially. For example, in 1997 the divorce rate decreased by 5.8 percent from the previous year, resulting in the lowest number of divorces since 1985 (Statistics Canada, 1999b). Then, in 1998, the rate increased again, up 2.5 percent from 1997 and another 3 percent between 1998 and 2000. Based on the 2000 rate, more than a third of marriages are expected to end (Statistics Canada, 2002b).

More Single-Parent Families

In 1996 in Canada, there were nearly 1.1 million lone-parent families (Statistics Canada, 2001a, 2004b), more than twice the number of lone-parent families in 1971. This means that an average of 20 percent of Canadian families are headed by a lone parent, ranging from 17 percent in Newfoundland to 24 percent in the Yukon (Kidder et al., 2000). It is clear from these increases that many children born in the 1990s onward will spend some time in a **single-parent family** (Teegartin, 1994). Most single-parent families are headed by women (83 percent), but the rate for male single parents has been rising. For example, from 1991 to 1996 there was a 16 percent increase in the number of male single parents (Statistics Canada, 2001a).

single-parent family
family system consisting of one parent (either the mother or the father) and the parent's dependent child(ren)

blended, or reconstituted, families
new families resulting from cohabitation or remarriage that include a parent, one or more children, and step-relations

More Children Living in Poverty

Unfortunately, the increase in the number of single-parent families has contributed to an increase in the proportion of children living below the poverty line. Although there is no internationally agreed-upon definition of poverty (Fellegi, 1997), low-income families are at greater risk for failing to meet the necessities of life than other income groups. The majority of low-income families in Canada are headed by a single female parent (Fellegi, 1997). To give you an idea of what poverty looks like in Canadian lone-parent families, consider the number of hours (see Figure 15.2) a lone parent would need to work in each province, if paid the minimum wage, just to meet the income cutoff that would put his or her family above the "poverty line" (as defined by Statistics Canada and the Canadian Institute of Child Health in Kidder et al., 2000).

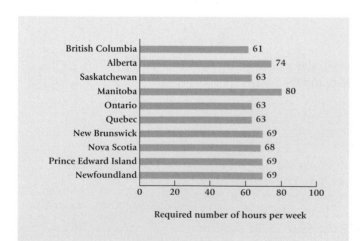

Figure 15.2 Number of hours per week a lone parent, paid minimum wage, would have to work to meet the cutoff for the "poverty line," 1996. (Numbers were not available for the Yukon, the Northwest Territories, and Nunavut.) ADAPTED FROM KIDDER ET AL., 2000.

More Remarriages

Because more married couples are divorcing, more adults (about 72 percent of divorced mothers and 80 percent of divorced fathers) are remarrying, forming **blended (or reconstituted) families** that involve at least one child, his or her biological parent, and a stepparent and that

Jack Hollingsworth/Photodisc

Because divorce and remarriage are so common, many children now live in blended (stepparent) families with stepsiblings.

often blend multiple children from two families into a new family system (Hetherington et al., 1999). About 12 percent of Canadian children spent some time in a stepparent family in 2001 (Statistics Canada, 2002a).

What these changes tell us is that modern families are much more diverse than ever. Our stereotyped image of the model family—the *Leave It to Beaver* nuclear aggregation with a breadwinning father, a homemaking mother, and at least two children—is just that: a stereotype. By one estimate, this "typical" family represented about 50 percent of American households in 1960, but only 12 percent in 1995 (Hernandez, 1997). Although the family is by no means dying, we must broaden our image of it to include the many dual-career, single-parent, and blended families that exist today, which are influencing the development of the *majority* of our children. Bear that in mind as we begin our discussion of family life, seeking to determine how families influence the development of their children.

Concept Check 15.1
Families as Social Systems

Check your understanding of families and family processes by matching each descriptive statement that follows with one of the following principles or concepts: (a) nuclear family, (b) extended family, (c) single-parent family, (d) blended family, (e) direct effect, (f) indirect, or third-party, effect, (g) coparenting; (h) families are "embedded" entities, (i) families are "developing" entities. The answers appear in the Appendix.

_____ 1. child abuse is more common in cultures that sanction the use of physical punishment

_____ 2. a sensitive, responsive father gains his infant's trust and affection

_____ 3. arrangement in which a child lives with a biological parent and a nonbiological parent

_____ 4. still the dominant family model but becoming less common

_____ 5. as soon as he is able, Billy's parents allow him to dress himself

_____ 6. living arrangement experienced at one time or another by nearly 1.1 million or 20 percent of Canadian families

_____ 7. type of family in which children show better psychological adjustment in societies that stress communal interdependence

_____ 8. a husband's aloofness toward his son causes his wife to criticize him, thus precipitating marital discord

_____ 9. process leading to best outcomes for children in nuclear families

PARENTAL SOCIALIZATION DURING CHILDHOOD AND ADOLESCENCE

In previous chapters, we learned that warm and sensitive parents who often talk to their infants and toddlers and try to stimulate their curiosity are contributing in a positive way to the establishment of secure emotional attachments, and to the child's sociability, intellectual development, and willingness to see challenges. Indeed, Jay Belsky (1981, p. 8) has argued that caregiver warmth/sensitivity "is the most influential dimension of [parenting] in infancy. It not only fosters healthy psychological functioning during this developmental epoch, but also ... lays the foundation on which future experiences will build."

As children reach age 2 to 3, parents continue to be caregivers and playmates, but they also become much more concerned with teaching children how to behave (or how not to behave) in a variety of situations (Fagot & Kavanaugh, 1993). According to Erik Erikson (1963), this is the period when socialization begins in earnest. Parents must now manage the child's budding autonomy in the hope of instilling a sense of social propriety and self-control, while taking care not to undermine his or her curiosity, initiative, and feelings of personal competence.

Two Major Dimensions of Parenting

Erikson and others (for example, Maccoby & Martin, 1983) claim that two aspects of parenting are especially important throughout childhood and adolescence: *parental acceptance/responsiveness* and *parental demandingness/control* (sometimes called permissiveness–restrictiveness).

Acceptance/responsiveness refers to the extent to which parents are supportive, sensitive to their children's needs, and willing to provide affection and praise when their children meet their expectations. Accepting, responsive parents often smile at, praise, and encourage their children although they can become quite critical when a child misbehaves. Less accepting and responsive parents, by contrast, are often quick to belittle, criticize, punish, or ignore their children and rarely communicate to children that they are valued or loved.

Demandingness/control refers to the amount of regulation and control that parents undertake with their children. Controlling/demanding parents set rules, expect their children to follow them, and closely monitor their children's activities to ensure that these rules are followed. Less controlling/undemanding parents are much less restrictive; they make fewer demands and allow children considerable freedom to pursue their interests and to make decisions about their own activities.

We assume that you have little difficulty deciding that parental acceptance and responsiveness are preferable to parental rejection and insensitivity. As we have seen throughout this book, warm, responsive parenting is consistently associated with such positive outcomes as secure emotional attachments, a prosocial orientation and good peer relations, high self-esteem, a strong sense of morality, and many other virtues. Children generally want to please loving parents and so are motivated to do what is expected of them and learn what parents would like them to learn (Forman & Kochanska, 2001; Kochanska & Murray, 2000). By contrast, a primary contributor to poor peer relations, clinical depression, and other psychosocial problems later in life is a family setting in which one or both parents have treated the child as if he or she was unworthy of their attention and affection (Ge et al., 1996; MacKinnon-Lewis et al., 1997). Children simply do not thrive when they are often ignored and rejected.

Is it better for parents to be highly controlling, or should they impose few restrictions and grant their children considerable autonomy? To answer this question, we need to be more specific about the kinds of control that parents exercise and to look carefully at patterns of parental acceptance.

Ryan McVay/Photodisc

Warmth and affection are crucial components of effective parenting.

acceptance/responsiveness
dimension of parenting that describes the amount of responsiveness and affection that a parent displays toward a child

demandingness/control
dimension of parenting that describes how restrictive and demanding parents are

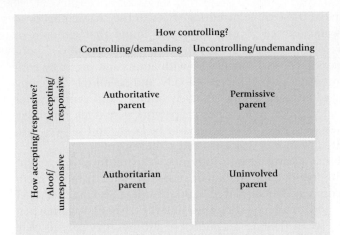

Figure 15.3 *Two major dimensions of parenting. When we cross the two dimensions, we come up with four parenting styles: accepting/controlling (or "authoritative"), accepting/uncontrolling (or "permissive"), aloof/controlling (or "authoritarian"), and aloof/uncontrolling (or "uninvolved"). Which parenting style did your parents use?* BASED ON MACCOBY & MARTIN, 1983.

Four Patterns of Parenting

It turns out that the two major parenting dimensions are reasonably independent, so that we find parents who display each of the four possible combinations of acceptance/responsiveness and control/demandingness shown in Figure 15.3. How are these four parenting styles related to a child's or an adolescent's social, emotional, and intellectual development?

Baumrind's Early Research

Perhaps the best-known research on parenting styles is Diana Baumrind's (1967, 1971) early studies of preschool children and their parents. Each child in Baumrind's sample was observed on several occasions in nursery school and at home. These data were used to rate the child on such behavioural dimensions as sociability, self-reliance, achievement, moodiness, and self-control. Parents were also interviewed and observed while interacting with their children at home. When Baumrind analyzed the parental data, she found that individual parents generally used one of three parenting styles shown in Figure 15.3 (none of her parents could be classified as "uninvolved"). These three patterns of parenting were described as follows:

- **Authoritarian parenting:** A very restrictive pattern of parenting in which adults impose many rules, expect strict obedience, rarely if ever explain to the child why it is necessary to comply with all these regulations, and often rely on punitive, forceful tactics (that is, power assertion or love withdrawal) to gain compliance. Authoritarian parents are not sensitive to a child's conflicting viewpoints, expecting instead for the child to accept their word as law and to respect their authority.

- **Authoritative parenting:** This is a controlling but flexible style in which involved parents make many reasonable demands of their children. They are careful to provide rationales for complying with the limits they set and ensure that their children follow those guidelines. However, they are much more accepting of and responsive to their children's points of view than authoritarian parents are and often seek their children's participation in family decision making. So authoritative parents exercise control in a *rational, democratic* (rather than a domineering) way that recognizes and respects their children's perspectives.

- **Permissive parenting:** An accepting but lax pattern of parenting in which adults make relatively few demands, permit their children to freely express their feelings and impulses, do not closely monitor their children's activities, and rarely exert firm control over their behaviour.

authoritarian parenting
restrictive pattern of parenting in which adults set many rules for their children, expect strict obedience, and rely on power rather than reason to elicit compliance

authoritative parenting
flexible style of parenting in which adults allow their children autonomy but are careful to explain the restrictions they impose and ensure that their children follow these guidelines

permissive parenting
pattern of parenting in which otherwise accepting adults make few demands of their children and rarely attempt to control their behaviour

When Baumrind (1967) linked these three parenting styles to the characteristics of the preschool children who were exposed to each style, she found that children of authoritative parents were developing rather well. They were cheerful, socially responsible, self-reliant, achievement oriented, and cooperative with adults and peers. By contrast, children of authoritarian parents tended to be moody and seemingly unhappy much of the time, easily annoyed and unfriendly, relatively aimless, and generally not very pleasant to be around. Finally, children of permissive parents were often impulsive and aggressive, especially if they were boys. They tended to be bossy and self-centred, lacking in self-control, and quite low in independence and achievement.

Although Baumrind's findings clearly favour authoritative parenting, one might legitimately wonder whether children of authoritarian or permissive parents might eventually outgrow whatever shortcomings they displayed as preschoolers. Seeking to answer this question, Baumrind (1977) observed her participants (and their parents) again when they were 8 to 9 years old. As we see in Table 15.1, children of authoritative parents were still relatively high in both *cognitive competencies* (that is, they showed originality in thinking, had high achievement motivation, liked intellectual challenges) and *social skills* (for example, they were sociable and outgoing, participated actively and showed leadership in group activities); whereas children of authoritarian parents were generally average to below average in cognitive and social skills, and children of permissive parents were relatively unskilled in both areas. Indeed, the strengths of children exposed to authoritative parenting were still evident in adolescence: Compared with teenagers raised by either permissive or authoritarian parents, they were relatively confident, achievement oriented, and socially skilled, and they tended to stay clear of drug abuse and other problem behaviours (Baumrind, 1991). The link between authoritative parenting and positive developmental outcomes seems to hold for all racial and ethnic groups studied to date in the United States (Glasgow et al., 1997; Luster & McAdoo, 1996; Steinberg et al., 1994) and in a variety of different cultures as well (C. Chen et al., 1998; Pinto, Folkers, & Sines, 1991).

Uninvolved Parenting

In recent years, it has become clear that the least successful parenting style is what might be termed **uninvolved parenting**—an extremely lax and undemanding approach displayed by parents who have either *rejected* their children or are so overwhelmed with their own stresses and problems that they haven't much time or energy to devote to child-rearing (Maccoby & Martin, 1983). By age 3, children of uninvolved parents are already relatively high in aggression and such externalizing behaviours as temper tantrums (Miller et al., 1993). Furthermore, they tend to perform very poorly in the classroom and to display conduct disorders later in childhood (Eckenrode, Laird, & Doris,

uninvolved parenting
pattern of parenting that is both aloof (or even hostile) and overpermissive, almost as if parents cared neither about their children nor about what they may become

TABLE 15.1	Relationships between Child-Rearing Patterns and Developmental Outcomes in Middle Childhood and Adolescence	
Child-rearing pattern	**Outcomes**	
	Childhood	**Adolescence**
Authoritative	High cognitive and social competencies	High self-esteem, excellent social skills, strong moral/prosocial concern, high academic achievement
Authoritarian	Average cognitive and social competencies	Average academic performance and social skills, more conforming than adolescents of permissive parents
Permissive	Low cognitive and social competencies	Poor self-control and academic performance, more drug use than adolescents of authoritative or authoritarian parents

SOURCES: Baumrind, 1977, 1991; Steinberg et al., 1994.

1993; Kilgore et al., 2000), and often become hostile, selfish, and rebellious adolescents who lack meaningful long-range goals and are prone to commit such antisocial and delinquent acts as alcohol and drug abuse, sexual misconduct, truancy, and a wide variety of criminal offences (Kurdek & Fine, 1994; Patterson et al., 1992; Weiss & Schwarz, 1996). In effect, these youngsters have neglectful, detached parents whose actions (or lack thereof) seem to be saying, "I don't care about you or about what you do"—a message that undoubtedly breeds resentment and the motivation to strike back at these aloof, uncaring adversaries or other authority figures.

Explaining the Effectiveness of Authoritative Parenting

Why is authoritative parenting so consistently associated with positive social, emotional, and intellectual outcomes? Probably for several reasons. First, authoritative parents are warm and accepting: They communicate a sense of *caring concern* that may motivate their children to comply with the directives they receive in a way that children of more aloof and demanding (authoritarian) parents do not. Then there is the issue of how control is exercised. Unlike the authoritarian parent, who sets *inflexible* standards and *dominates* the child, allowing little if any freedom of expression, the authoritative parent exercises control in a *rational* way, carefully explaining his or her point of view, while also considering the child's viewpoint. Demands that come from a warm, accepting parent and appear to be fair and reasonable rather than arbitrary and dictatorial are likely to elicit committed compliance rather than complaining or defiance (Kochanska & Murray, 2000). Finally, authoritative parents are careful to tailor their demands to the child's ability to regulate his or her own conduct. In other words, they set standards that children can *realistically* achieve and allow children some freedom, or *autonomy*, in deciding how best to comply with these expectations. This kind of treatment carries an important message—something like "You are a capable human being whom I trust to be self-reliant and to accomplish important objectives." Of course, we've seen in earlier chapters that feedback of this sort fosters the growth of self-reliance, achievement motivation, and high self-esteem in childhood, and provides the kind of support that adolescents need to feel comfortable about exploring various roles and ideologies to forge a personal identity.

In sum, it appears that authoritative parenting—warmth combined with *moderate* and *rational* parental control—is the parenting style most consistently associated with positive developmental outcomes. Children apparently need love *and* limits, a set of rules that help them to structure and evaluate their conduct. Without such guidance, they may not learn self-control and may become quite selfish, unruly, and lacking in clear achievement goals, particularly if their parents are also aloof or uncaring (Steinberg et al., 1994). But if they receive too much guidance and are hemmed in by inflexible restrictions, they may have few opportunities to become self-reliant and may lack confidence in their own decision-making abilities (Pettit et al., 2001; Steinberg et al., 1994).

Parent Effects or Child Effects?

The study of human development has long been guided by a simple **parent effects model**, which assumes that influences in families run primarily one way, from parent to child. Proponents of this viewpoint would claim that authoritative parenting fosters (i.e., causes) positive developmental outcomes. By contrast, a **child effects model** of family influences claims that children have a major influence on their parents. Proponents of this viewpoint claim that authoritative parenting looks so adaptive because easygoing, manageable, and competent children persuade their parents to become more authoritative.

Diana Baumrind (1983, 1993) favours the parent effects model. She notes that children of authoritative parents often resist parental demands at first, but they eventually come around because parents are firm in their demands and sufficiently patient to allow their children time to comply without caving in to the children's unreasonable demands or turning to power-assertive tactics. Indeed, longitudinal studies of early parental control strategies used by mothers with their 1½- to 3-year-olds clearly supports Baumrind's parental-influence hypothesis. Specifically, authoritative mothers who insisted that their children perform competent actions (or *do's*) and who dealt firmly but patiently with

parent effects model
model of family influence in which parents are believed to influence their children rather than vice versa

child effects model
model of family influence in which children are believed to influence their parents rather than vice versa

noncompliance had toddlers who became more compliant over time and displayed few problem behaviours. By contrast, authoritarian mothers whose demands emphasized *don'ts* (don't touch, don't yell) and who used arbitrary, power-assertive control strategies had children who were less competent and cooperative and who displayed an increase in problem behaviours over time (Crockenberg & Litman, 1990; Kuczynski & Kochanska, 1995).

Yet it is also true that extremely stubborn and impulsive children who show little self-control tend to elicit more coercive forms of parenting (Kuczynski & Kochanska, 1995; Neiderhiser et al., 1999) and may eventually wear their parents out, causing them to become more lax, less affectionate, and possibly even hostile and uninvolved (Lytton, 1990; Stice & Barrera, 1995). Today, most developmentalists favour a **transactional model** of family influence in which socialization is viewed as a matter of reciprocal influence (Collins et al., 2000). Longitudinal studies generally imply that patterns of parenting influence children more than children influence parenting (Crockenberg & Litman, 1990; Wakshclag & Hans, 1999). Yet the transactional model recognizes that (1) children can and often do affect their parents, for better or worse, and (2) we simply cannot take it for granted, as John Watson (1928) proclaimed, that parents are almost solely responsible for determining whether their children turn out good or bad (for more discussion on this issue, see Current Controversies, Box 3.4).

> **? WHAT DO YOU THINK?**
>
> In view of the data suggesting that parenting styles clearly differ in effectiveness, some developmentalists believe that a course in parenting should become a required part of the high-school curriculum. Do you agree with this proposal? Why or why not?

Social Class and Ethnic Variations in Child-Rearing

Associations between authoritative parenting and healthy psychological development have been found in many cultures and subcultures. Yet people from different social strata and ethnic backgrounds face different kinds of problems, pursue different goals, and adopt different values about what it takes to adapt to their environments, and these ecological considerations often affect their approaches to child-rearing.

Social Class Differences in Child-Rearing

How, then, do parenting styles differ by social class? Compared with middle- and upper-class parents, economically disadvantaged and working-class parents tend to (1) stress obedience and respect for authority; (2) be more restrictive and authoritarian, more frequently using power-assertive discipline; (3) reason with their children less frequently; and (4) show less warmth and affection. (Maccoby, 1980; McLoyd, 1990)

According to Eleanor Maccoby (1980), these class-linked differences in parenting have been observed in many cultures and across racial and ethnic groups in the United States. Clearly, we are talking about *group trends* rather than absolute contrasts. Some middle-class parents are highly restrictive, power-assertive, and aloof in their approach to child-rearing whereas many economically disadvantaged and working-class parents function more like their counterparts in the middle class (Kelley, Power, & Wimbush, 1992; Laosa, 1981). But on average, it appears that lower-socioeconomic-strata and working-class parents are somewhat more critical, punitive, and intolerant of disobedience than are parents from the middle and upper socioeconomic strata.

Explaining Social Class Differences in Child-Rearing

transactional model
model of family influence in which parent and child are believed to influence one another reciprocally

Undoubtedly, many factors contribute to social class differences in child-rearing, and stresses associated with low-income living seem to head the list. Consider that a low income may mean that living quarters are crowded; family members must occasionally make do without adequate food, clothing, or medical care; and parents are constantly tense or anxious about living under these marginal conditions. Eleanor Maccoby (1980) suggests that low-income living is probably much more *stressful* for parents and that stress affects the ways in which parental functions are carried out. Vonnie McLoyd (1989, 1990) agrees. Her reviews of the literature suggest that economic hardship creates a general discomfort or distress about life's conditions that makes lower-income adults more edgy and irritable and more vulnerable to all negative life events (including the daily hassles associated with child-rearing), thereby diminishing their capacity to be warm, supportive parents who are highly involved in their children's lives.

Rand Conger and his associates (1992, 1994, 1995; see also Bolger et al., 1995) offered support for this economic distress hypothesis by finding clear links among family economic hardships, nonnurturant/uninvolved parenting, and poor child-rearing outcomes. The causal sequence, shown in Figure 15.4, goes like this: Parents who experience strong economic pressure tend to become depressed, which often increases marital conflict. Marital conflict, in turn, disrupts each parent's ability to be a supportive, involved parent—largely, perhaps, by undermining feelings of coparenting or spousal support that would help parents to feel efficacious at handling child-rearing problems (Gondoli & Silverberg, 1997). And parents may have reasons for feeling ineffectual because their children and adolescents often react negatively to marital strife and the insensitive parenting they receive, experiencing a loss of *emotional security*, which contributes to such child and adolescent adjustment problems as declining grades, low self-esteem, poor peer relations, depression, and hostility/antisocial conduct (Davies & Cummings, 1998). These child adjustment problems that nonnurturant/coercive parenting helps to create may further exasperate parents, causing them to back away and become even less nurturant and less involved in the lives of their children (Rueter & Conger, 1998; Vuchinich, Bank, & Patterson, 1992). Of course, many, many low-income adults are able to cope with their problems and parent quite effectively, particularly if their economic or marital distresses are not prolonged, they maintain a positive outlook on life and their families, they continue to rely on firm but rational discipline, and they receive emotional and parenting support from friends or relatives (Ackerman et al., 1999b; Jackson et al., 2000; McLoyd, 1998). Nevertheless, it appears that Maccoby was quite correct in assuming that economic hardships are a very important contributor to the relatively aloof and coercive style of parenting often observed in low-income, economically distressed families.

Another explanation for the link between social class and parenting styles focuses on the skills needed by workers in white-collar and blue-collar jobs (Arnett, 1995; Kohn, 1979). A large percentage of lower-socioeconomic-strata and working-class breadwinners are blue-collar workers who must please a supervisor and defer to his or her authority. So many lower-income parents may emphasize obedience and respect for authority because these are precisely the attributes that they view as critical for success in the blue-collar economy. By contrast, middle- and upper-class parents may reason and negotiate more

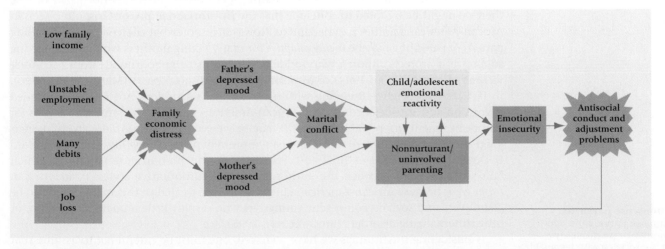

Figure 15.4 *A model of the relationship among family economic distress, patterns of parenting, and child/adolescent adjustment.* ADAPTED FROM CONGER ET AL., 1992.

with their children while emphasizing individual initiative, curiosity, and creativity because these are the skills, attributes, and abilities that matter in their own occupations as business executives, white-collar workers, or professionals (Greenberger, O'Neil, & Nagel, 1994).

Ethnic Variations in Child-Rearing

Parents of different ethnicities may also hold distinct child-rearing beliefs and values that are products of their cultural backgrounds or the ecological niches they occupy in society (MacPhee, Fritz, & Miller-Heyl, 1996). For example, Aboriginal and Hispanic parents, whose cultural backgrounds stress communal rather than individual goals, are more inclined than parents of European ancestry to (1) maintain close ties to a variety of kin and (2) insist that their children display calm, proper, and polite behaviours and a strong respect for others, as opposed to independence, competitiveness, and the pursuit of individual goals (Harwood et al., 1996, 1999; MacPhee et al., 1996). Yet these two groups foster such attributes in different ways; Aboriginal parents are very indulgent and rarely resort to punishment, whereas Hispanic parents are more likely to use scoldings to make their points.

Asian and Asian-American parents also tend to stress self-discipline and interpersonal harmony and appear to be more authoritarian than parents of other ethnicities (Greenberger & Chen, 1996; Uba, 1994). Yet authoritarian parenting may mean something quite different for these children than for European Americans. Ruth Chao (1994, 2001), for example, notes that Chinese children are well behaved and perform very well in school despite the fact that their parents are highly restrictive and controlling. In addition, Canadian researchers such as Xinyin Chen of the University of Western Ontario have demonstrated that child-rearing behaviours may produce different outcomes in different populations. In the case of Chinese children, inhibition in children was most likely when mothers adopted a punishment orientation; exactly the opposite was found in a comparison Canadian group (Chen et al., 1998). In Chinese culture, parents believe that strictness is the best way to express love for children and to train them properly, and children accept longstanding cultural values specifying that they obey elders and honour their families. Thus, an authoritarian style that may be too controlling to work well for European Americans appears highly effective indeed in China (and among recent Asian immigrant families in the United States; see Fuligni, 1997; Huntsinger, Jose, & Larson, 1998).

It is difficult to summarize the diversity of child-rearing practices that characterize African-American families. However, research suggests that urban African-American mothers (particularly if they are single and less educated) are inclined to demand strict obedience from their children and to use coercive forms of discipline to ensure that they get it (Kelley et al., 1992; Ogbu, 1994). Were we to quickly assume (as researchers did for years) that one particular pattern of parenting (authoritative) is superior to all others, then we might be tempted to conclude that the **no-nonsense parenting** often seen in African-American families is maladaptive. However, a somewhat coercive and controlling pattern of parenting may be *highly adaptive* for many young mothers who lack caregiving support if it protects children who reside in dangerous neighbourhoods from becoming victims of crime (Ogbu, 1994) or associating with antisocial peers (Mason et al., 1996). In fact, use of coercive discipline within the normal range does not foster heightened aggression and antisocial conduct in African-American youth in the same way it does for European Americans, possibly because it may be viewed by African-American children as a sign of caring and concern rather than a symptom of parental hostility (Deater-Deckard & Dodge, 1997; Spieker et al., 1999). Furthermore, this no-nonsense parenting, which falls somewhere in between the authoritarian and authoritative styles, is adaptive in other ways because African-American children who are treated in this manner tend to be cognitively and socially competent youngsters who display little anxiety, depression, or other internalizing disorders (Brody & Flor, 1998).

Considering the findings we have reviewed, one must be careful *not* to assume that a middle-class pattern of authoritative parenting that seems to promote favourable outcomes in many contexts is necessarily the most adaptive pattern for all ecological niches.

no-nonsense parenting
mixture of authoritative and authoritarian parenting styles that is associated with favourable outcomes in African-American families

Louis Laosa (1981, p. 159) made this same point more than 20 years ago, noting that "indigenous patterns of child care throughout the world represent largely successful adaptations to conditions of life that have long differed from one people to another. [Adults] are 'good [parents]' by the only relevant standards, those of their own culture."

The Quest for Autonomy: Renegotiating the Parent–Child Relationship during Adolescence

One of the most important developmental tasks that adolescents face is to achieve a mature and healthy sense of **autonomy**—the capacity to make one's own decisions and to manage life tasks without being overly dependent on other people. If adolescents are to make it as adults, they can't be rushing home for loving hugs after every little setback. Nor can they continue to rely on parents to get them to work on time or to remind them of their duties and obligations.

So what happens within the family system as children mature and begin to act more autonomously? Sparks fly! In cultures as diverse as China and the United States, conflicts between parents and children about self-governance issues become much more common early in adolescence and gradually decline in frequency (though not necessarily in intensity) throughout the teenage years (Laursen, Coy, & Collins, 1998; Smetana & Gaines, 1999). These squabbles, which occur about as often in families that have immigrated from collectivist cultures as in European-American homes (Fuligini, 1998), are usually neither prolonged nor severe, often centring around such issues as the adolescent's physical appearance, her choice of friends, or neglect of schoolwork and household chores. And much of the friction stems from the different perspectives that parents and adolescents adopt. Parents view conflicts through a moral or *social-conventional* lens, feeling that they have a responsibility to monitor and regulate their child's conduct, whereas the adolescent, locked in a quest for autonomy, often views his nagging parents as infringing on *personal* rights and choices (Smetana & Gaines, 1999). As teenagers continue to assert themselves and parents slowly loosen the reins, the parent–child relationship gradually evolves from an enterprise in which the parent is dominant to one in which parents and adolescents are on a more equal footing (S. Steinberg, 1996). Yet Chinese and Asian-American parents tend to exert their authority far longer than European-American parents do (Greenberger & Chen, 1996; Yau & Smetana, 1996), a practice that often bothers and may depress Asian-American adolescents (Greenberger & Chen, 1996; Zhou & Bankston, 1998).

Researchers once believed that the most adaptive route to establishing autonomy was for adolescents to separate from parents by cutting the emotional cords. Indeed, young adolescents who perceive their relationships with parents to be very conflictual and nonsupportive appear to be better adjusted if they distance themselves a bit from their families and can gain the support of a teacher, a "Big Brother," or another adult mentor from outside the home (Fuhrman & Holmbeck, 1995; Rhodes, Grossman, & Resch, 2000). Yet adolescents who are warmly received at home would be ill advised to cut the cords because those who gradually achieve more autonomy while maintaining *close attachments* to family members display the best overall pattern of psychosocial adjustment (Lamborn & Steinberg, 1993; Roth & Brooks-Gunn, 2000).

Encouraging Autonomy

Adolescents are most likely to become appropriately autonomous, achievement oriented, and otherwise well adjusted if their parents gradually relinquish control. Parents should consistently enforce a reasonable set of rules while involving their teenagers in discussions and decisions about self-governance issues, monitoring their comings and goings, and continuing to be warm and supportive, even in the face of the inevitable conflicts that arise (Steinberg, 1996). Does this parenting style sound familiar? It should, because this winning combination of parental acceptance and a pattern of flexible control that is neither too lax nor overly restrictive is an *authoritative* approach that is consistently asso-

As adolescents begin their quest for autonomy, conflicts with parents become more commonplace.

autonomy
capacity to make decisions independently, serve as one's own source of emotional strength, and otherwise manage life tasks without depending on others for assistance; an important developmental task of adolescence

ciated with healthy developmental outcomes in many, many contexts. Indeed, adolescents treated this way often interpret parents' questions about their activities and whereabouts as a sign of concern and will volunteer or otherwise disclose this information, thereby preventing parents from having to badger them or to snoop in order to know what they are doing (Kerr & Stattin, 2000). See Box 15.1 for a summary of some current work that Michael Pratt of Wilfrid Laurier University has conducted on parental optimism about adolescent children. It is mainly when parents react negatively to a teenager's push for autonomy and become overly controlling or overly permissive that adolescents are likely to experience personal distress or to rebel and get into trouble (Barber, Olsen, & Shagle, 1994; Pettit et al., 2001; Kerr & Stattin, 2000).[1] Of course, we must remind ourselves that socialization within the family is a matter of reciprocal influence, and that it may be much easier for a parent to respond authoritatively to a responsible, level-headed adolescent than to one who is hostile and defiant.

In sum, conflicts and power struggles are an almost inevitable consequence of an adolescent's quest for autonomy. Yet most teenagers and their parents are able to resolve these differences while maintaining positive feelings for one another as they renegotiate their relationship so that it becomes more equal. As a result, young autonomy seekers become more self-reliant while also developing a more "friendlike" attachment to their parents.

THE INFLUENCE OF SIBLINGS AND SIBLING RELATIONSHIPS

Although families are getting smaller, the majority of Canadian children still grow up with at least one sibling, and there is certainly no shortage of speculation about the roles that brothers and sisters play in a child's life. Many parents, distressed by the fighting and bick-

---

THE INSIDE TRACK

15.1

Michael Pratt

Michael Pratt works in the Department of Psychology at Wilfrid Laurier University. His research interests include moral development, social-cognitive development, identity development, narrative, aging, parenting, and grandparenting.

In recent research, Pratt and his colleagues (e.g., Pratt et al., 2001) have been studying how optimistic parents are about their children, and how this relates to how families behave. In this longitudinal study, the researchers described both mothers' and fathers' levels of optimism about their adolescent children's future lives. To do this, researchers asked parents to tell their 14-year-old adolescent stories about teaching an important value, such as honesty or kindness. The researchers then scored the stories on the basis of

how positive they were. Two years later, the families were interviewed again, and both parents and children were asked about the kinds of parenting practices that were used in the family. The specific focus of interest at this time was on the extent to which parents were now willing to grant opportunities to the adolescents to make more of their own decisions (autonomy granting) and also the extent to which parents were punitive in how they disciplined the adolescents. Both parents and children provided information about these parenting practices at age 16. As expected, the researchers found that when a parent was more optimistic in the kind of story told about the child at 14, he or she was more likely to trust the child to make independent decisions at age 16, and was also less likely to be punitive in disciplining the child. In addition to helping us understand the concept of parent optimism in adults' own words, these findings suggest that family stories can be a useful technique for finding out about family process and relationships.

---

[1] There is one exception to the rule: Adolescents living in dangerous, high-risk, urban neighbourhoods often fare better psychologically when their parents are more controlling and strive to limit their autonomy. Their youngsters are less likely to get into trouble, and they tend to interpret their parents' restrictiveness as a sign of caring and concern about their welfare (Boykin, McElhaney, & Allen, 2001).

Does Part-Time Employment Foster a Healthy Sense of Autonomy (and Positive Developmental Outcomes)?

More than 63 percent of high-school students in Canada have a job outside the home (Human Resources Development Canada, 2001b), and it is reasonable to assume that their work experiences could have any number of effects on their development. On the positive side, Michael Shanahan and his associates (1996) find that the money that teenagers make often fosters a sense of self-efficacy and economic autonomy. Other investigators have reported that working youth feel that they have become more punctual, dependable, responsible, and self-reliant as a result of having held a job (see Mortimer et al., 1996, for a review). However, some potential disadvantages of adolescent employment have been reported as well.

Lawrence Steinberg and his associates have compared working and nonworking youth on such outcome measures as their autonomy from parents, academic performance, psychological adjustment, and involvement in delinquent activities (Greenberger & Steinberg, 1986; Steinberg & Dornbusch, 1991; Steinberg, Fegley, & Dornbusch, 1993). Overall, this research reports far more bad news than good about teenagers who work, particularly about those who work more than 20 hours per week during the school year. Specifically, adolescents who worked such long hours had much more autonomy over day-to-day decisions than age-mates who worked 10 hours a week or less. Yet this greater autonomy seemed to be directed toward "cutting the cords" to parents, because teenagers who were heavily invested in work were much less involved in family activities and were monitored less closely by older family members. And the psychological and behavioural correlates of all this freedom were downright gloomy. Compared with peers who worked 10 hours a week or less, teenagers who worked 20 or more hours a week were lower in self-esteem; made lower grades at school; reported higher levels of anxiety, depression, and somatic complaints (for example, headaches, stomach aches); and reported more frequent involvement in alcohol and drug use and other delinquent activities. So are adolescents better off avoiding employment and concentrating on their schooling?

Not necessarily. Critics have argued that working may look like such a negative influence because the adolescents who worked long hours in the earlier reports often came from nonsupportive home environments or were already experiencing academic (or other) difficulties that may have *caused* them to separate from parents and to seek greater involvement in the world of work. In other words, their pre-existing problems, rather than their heavy work involvement, could have been the primary contributor to their poor psychosocial outcomes. In agreement with earlier reports, Michael Shanahan and his associates (1996) found that younger (Grades 7 to 10) working youth spent less time with their families and were monitored less closely than nonworking peers. Yet, within this rural sample, adolescent employment was associated with more sharing of advice with older family members and with *improved* emotional relationships with them. In another four-year longitu-

dinal study of 1000 high-school students that controlled for such other variables as family background and prior academic performance that might influence developmental outcomes, Jeylen Mortimer and associates (1996) found that working 20 hours or more per week did *not* undermine teenagers' academic achievement, self-esteem, or other aspects of psychological adjustment. In fact, the figure shows that Grade 12 students who worked a moderate number (1 to 20) of hours per week actually made better grades than those who didn't work. The sole cause for concern was that Grade 12 students who worked more than 20 hours a week used alcohol more often than those who were not employed.

Some developmentalists believe that adolescents are much more likely to benefit from challenging jobs that provide opportunities for self-direction and decision making than from menial, repetitive fast-food or manual labour positions that require few academic skills and do little to foster a sense of self-efficacy or self-esteem. Indeed, Michael Shanahan and his associates (1991; Call, Mortimer, & Shanahan, 1995) found that adolescent boys displayed clear increases in mastery motivation and became less depressed when the work they performed offered opportunities for advancement and provided skills that would be useful in the future. By contrast, boys showed declines in mastery motivation and became more depressed while working at menial jobs with demands that conflicted with their involvement in school. So whether working fosters a healthy sense of autonomy and has positive or negative effects on adolescent adjustment may depend far more on the *quality* of adolescents' work experiences than on the quantity of work they perform.

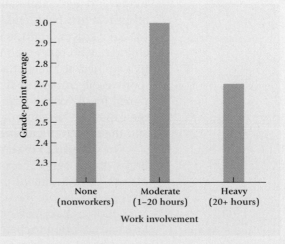

Grade-point averages of Grade 12 students as a function of work involvement. Students who worked a moderate amount made the best grades, and even the students who were heavily invested in work performed just as well as their nonworking peers. ADAPTED FROM MORTIMER ET AL., 1996.

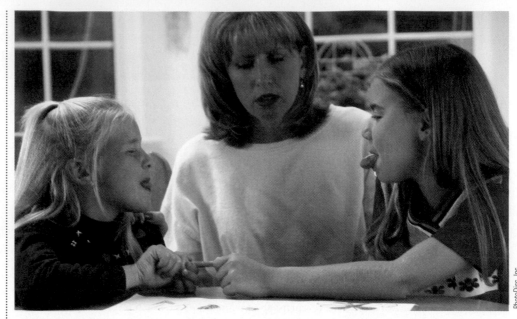

Coercive and rivalrous conduct between siblings is a normal aspect of family life.

ering that their children display, often fear that such rivalrous conduct will undermine the growth of children's prosocial concerns and their ability to get along with others. At the same time, the popular wisdom is that only children are likely to be lonely, overindulged "brats" who would profit both socially and emotionally from having siblings to teach them that they are not nearly as "special" as they think they are (Falbo, 1992).

Although rivalries among siblings are certainly commonplace, we will see that siblings can play some very positive roles in a child's life. And yet, we will also see that only children may not be nearly as disadvantaged by their lack of sibling relationships as people have commonly assumed.

Changes in the Family System When a New Baby Arrives

Judy Dunn and Carol Kendrick (1982; see also Dunn, 1993) have studied how children adapt to a new baby, and the account they provide is not an entirely cheerful one. After the baby arrives, mothers typically devote less warm and playful attention to their older children, who may respond to this perceived neglect by becoming difficult and disruptive and less securely attached, particularly if they are 2 years of age or older and can more readily appreciate that their exclusive relationship with caregivers has been undermined by the baby's birth (Teti et al., 1996). Clearly, older children often resent losing their mothers' attention and may harbour animosities toward the baby for stealing it, and their own difficult behaviour may make matters worse by alienating their parents.

Thus, **sibling rivalry**—a spirit of competition, jealousy, or resentment between siblings—often begins as soon as a younger brother or sister arrives. How can it be minimized? The adjustment process is easier if the first-born had secure relationships with both parents before the baby arrived and continues to enjoy close ties afterward (Dunn & Kendrick, 1982; Volling & Belsky, 1992). Parents are advised to continue to provide love and attention to their older children and to maintain their normal routines as much as possible. It also helps to encourage older children to become aware of the baby's needs and assist in the care of their new brother or sister (Dunn & Kendrick, 1982; Howe & Ross, 1990). Yet Dunn & Kendrick (1982) find that parents may have to walk a thin line between two traps: becoming so attentive to the new baby that they deprive the older child of attention, and becoming so indulgent of the first-born that he or she becomes a "spoiled brat" who resents any competition from the younger sibling.

sibling rivalry
spirit of competition, jealousy, and resentment that may arise between two or more siblings

Sibling Relationships over the Course of Childhood

Fortunately, most older siblings adjust fairly quickly to having a new brother or sister, becoming much less anxious and less inclined to display the problem behaviours that they showed early on. But even in the best of sibling relationships, conflict is normal. Indeed, Judy Dunn (1993) reports that the number of skirmishes between very young siblings can range as high as 56 per hour! Rivalrous conduct typically declines with age and presents few problems, with older siblings often becoming the more domineering parties and younger siblings the more compliant ones (Abramovitch et al., 1986; Berndt & Bulleit, 1985). Yet older siblings also initiate more helpful, playful, and other prosocial behaviours, a finding that may reflect the pressure parents put on them to demonstrate their maturity by caring for a younger brother or sister.

In general, siblings are much more likely to get along if their parents get along (Dunn, 1993). Marital conflict is a very good predictor of antagonistic sibling interactions, especially if the older sibling has a shaky, insecure relationship with a mother who relies heavily on power-assertive discipline (Erel et al., 1998). Marital conflict may put children on edge and contribute directly to emotional insecurity (Davies & Cummings, 1998), whereas parental use of power assertion may communicate to more powerful older siblings that forceful strategies are the way one deals with associates (particularly smaller, less powerful associates) who displease them.

Sibling relationships are also friendlier if parents make an effort to monitor their children's activities. Unfortunately, normal conflicts among young preschool siblings can escalate into serious incidents that become habitual if parents often let them pass without intervening (Kramer, Perozynski, & Chung, 1999). In fact, intense sibling battles that occur against a backdrop of uninvolved parenting are a strong predictor of aggressive, antisocial conduct outside the home (Garcia et al., 2000).

Conflicts need not be perceived as entirely negative experiences. Conflicts provide opportunities for siblings to engage in constructive problem solving to resolve disagreements and competing interests. Recent work by Hildy Ross and Avigail Ram (2001) of the University of Waterloo demonstrates that siblings can negotiate conflicts and come to resolutions without expressing hostility. In particular, they identify the quality of the sibling relationship as an important variable for predicting whether conflicts will be resolved speedily and with minimal hostility. Details about the research findings are presented in Box 15.3.

Finally, sibling relationships tend to be less conflictual if mothers and fathers respond warmly and sensitively to *all* their children and do not consistently favour one child over the other (Brody, 1998; McHale et al., 1995). Perlman and Ross (1997) have found that parents who intervene in sibling fights that are intense and show no signs of de-escalating can produce changes that result in siblings using more sophisticated forms of negotiation. Younger siblings are particularly sensitive to unequal treatment, often reacting negatively and displaying adjustment problems if they perceive that the older sibling is favoured by parents (McHale et al., 1995; Tarullo et al., 1995). It is not that older siblings are unaffected by differential treatment, but because they are older, they are usually better able to understand that siblings may have different needs and that unequal treatment may be justified, even if that means that parents may favour a younger sibling in certain respects (Kowal & Kramer, 1997).

As is true of parent–child relationships, sibling relationships become much more egalitarian during the adolescent years. Siblings now quarrel less frequently and their relationships otherwise become less intense, probably because teenagers spend less time with brothers and sisters who are, after all, part of the family from whom they want to develop some autonomy (Furman & Buhrmester, 1992; Larson et al., 1996). But even though they immerse themselves in close friendships and romantic relationships, adolescents continue to perceive their siblings as important and intimate associates—people to whom they can turn for support and companionship, despite the fact that relations with them have often been stormy (Buhrmester & Furman, 1990; Furman & Buhrmester, 1992). Nina Howe and

Hildy Ross

Hildy Ross works in the Department of Psychology at the University of Waterloo. Her research examines the development of young children's social relationships within the family and among peers. She is particularly interested in issues related to family conflict and conflict resolution.

Not surprisingly, conflicts are a prevalent feature of sibling relationships. After all, siblings spend a considerable amount of time together and are often in situations where they are competing for limited resources (e.g., a single toy, the TV remote control) or have different perspectives. Although it is easy to imagine that these situations would give way to fights, research conducted in Hildy Ross's lab suggests that siblings often engage in constructive problem-solving behaviours to resolve their conflicts.

In a recent investigation, pairs of young siblings (4- and 6-year-olds) and older siblings (6- and 8-year-olds) were placed in a position where they were required to negotiate the division of six toys (Ram & Ross, 2001). Before being placed in this situation, the children independently rated the desirability of each toy and the quality of the sibling relationship. The degree of conflict between siblings was determined by comparing their desirability ratings for the toys—high conflict represented toys that both siblings rated as highly desirable. Both the degree of conflicts of interest and the quality of sibling relationships predicted children's use of problem-solving and contentious negotiation strategies, and was related to the types of resolutions achieved. In cases where conflicts of interest were low, differences were resolved quickly. In cases where conflicts of interest were high and the sibling relationship was rated as positive, negotiations were longer but constructive and creative, and led to agreeable resolutions. In cases where conflicts of interest were high and the sibling relationship was rated as negative, negotiations were more destructive and often resulted in failures to reach agreement.

Two developmental differences were also observed. First, children in the older sibling pairs were more sophisticated in their negotiations and more sensitive to the desires of the other sibling. However, subsequent research by Ross and her colleagues suggests that even young children can provide coherent, goal-based descriptions of conflicts with their siblings, indicating that they understand the other sibling's perspectives (Ross, Siddiqui, Ram, & Ward, 2004). Second, within both the younger and older sibling pairs, the older sibling took the lead in negotiation and benefited slightly more from the resolution. The findings support the development of conflict resolution behaviours and demonstrate that, in general, children use many constructive problem-solving strategies rather than contentious tactics to negotiate conflict situations.

---

her colleagues at Concordia University have demonstrated the importance of the intimate relationship even among preteen siblings (Howe et al., 2000). In their study, sibling disclosure was an important predictor of warmth in sibling relationships.

Perhaps these seemingly paradoxical data make perfectly good sense if we carefully examine the findings on the nature of sibling–sibling interactions. Yes, rivalries and conflicts among siblings are a normal part of family life. Yet the observational record consistently shows that brothers and sisters often do nice things for one another and that these acts of kindness and affection are typically much more common than hateful or rivalrous conduct (Abramovitch et al., 1986; Baskett & Johnson, 1982).

Contributions of Siblings to Development

What positive roles might siblings play in one another's development? One of their most important functions is to provide *emotional support*. Brothers and sisters confide in one another and protect and comfort one another in rough times. For example, children with severe congenital problems and those who have an alcoholic or a mentally ill parent show fewer behavioural problems and more favourable developmental outcomes if they have solid, supportive relationships with siblings (Vandell, 2000). Older children are especially inclined to comfort a distressed infant or toddler sibling, particularly if they are securely attached themselves to their mothers (Teti & Ablard, 1989) and have developed the role-taking skills to understand why their younger brother or sister is distressed (Garner, Jones, & Palmer, 1994; Stewart & Marvin, 1984). And a secure tie to a sibling can help to prevent the anxiety and the other adjustment problems that can result from being ignored or rejected by their peers (East & Rook, 1992; Stormshak et al., 1996).

Older siblings often serve as teachers for their younger brothers and sisters.

Second, older siblings often provide *caretaking* services for younger ones. In one cross-cultural study, older siblings were the *principal* caregivers for infants and toddlers in 57 percent of the 186 cultures surveyed (Weisner & Gallimore, 1977). In our society, older siblings, especially girls, are frequently asked to baby-sit or otherwise tend to their young brothers and sisters (McHale & Gamble, 1989).

Third, older siblings often *teach* new skills to younger brothers and sisters. Abramovitch, Corter, and Pepler (1980) of the University of Toronto found that even infants are quite attentive to older siblings, often choosing to imitate their behaviours or take over toys that they have abandoned. Younger children tend to admire their older siblings, who continue to serve as important models and tutors throughout childhood (Buhrmester & Furman, 1990). Given a problem to master, children are likely to learn more when they have an older sibling available to guide them than when they have access to an equally competent older peer (Azmitia & Hesser, 1993). Why? Because (1) older siblings feel a greater responsibility to teach if the pupil is a younger *sibling*, (2) they provide more detailed instructions and encouragement than older peers do, and (3) younger children are more inclined to seek the older sibling's guidance. This kind of informal instruction clearly pays off: When older siblings play school with younger brothers and sisters, teaching them such lessons as the ABCs, younger siblings have an easier time learning to read (Norman-Jackson, 1982). What's more, older siblings who often tutor younger ones may profit as well, because they score higher on tests of academic aptitude and achievement than peers who have not had these tutoring experiences (Paulhus & Shaffer, 1981; Smith, 1990).

Finally, the sheer frequency and intensity of sibling interactions imply that these contacts may foster the growth of many other competencies. In Chapters 10 and 12, for example, we learned that playful interactions among siblings contribute to the growth of effective communication skills and to children's emerging theory of mind. Furthermore, siblings are not at all shy about communicating their wants, needs, and emotional reactions to conflict, thus providing each other with information that fosters the growth of perspective-taking skills, emotional understanding, a capacity for negotiation and compromise, and more mature forms of moral reasoning (Dunn, Brown, & Maguire, 1995; Herrera & Dunn, 1997; Howe, Petrakos, & Rinaldi, 1998). Clearly, there are many ways in which children may benefit from their experiences with siblings.

Characteristics of Only Children

Are only children who grow up without siblings the spoiled, selfish, overindulged brats that people often presume them to be? Hardly! Two major reviews of hundreds of pertinent studies found that only children are (1) relatively high, on average, in self-esteem and achievement motivation; (2) more obedient and slightly more intellectually competent than children with siblings; and (3) likely to establish good relations with peers (Falbo, 1992; Falbo & Polit, 1986).

Might these findings simply reflect the fact that parents who choose to have only one child differ systematically from those who have more children? Probably not. In 1979, the People's Republic of China implemented a one-child family policy in an attempt to control its burgeoning population. So regardless of the number of children that parents may have wanted, most Chinese couples, in urban areas at least, have been limited to one child. Contrary to the fears of many critics, there is no evidence that China's one-child policy has produced a generation of spoiled, self-centred brats who behave like "little emperors." Only children in China closely resemble only children in Western countries, scoring slightly higher than children with siblings on measures of intelligence and academic achievement and showing few meaningful differences in personality (Falbo & Poston, 1993; Jaio, Ji, & Jing, 1996). In fact, only children in China actually report *less* anxiety and depression than children with siblings do, a finding that may reflect China's social condemnation of multichild families and only children's tendency to taunt children with siblings with such remarks as "You shouldn't be here" or "Your parents should have only one child" (Yang et al., 1995).

So evidence from very different cultural settings suggests that only children are hardly disadvantaged by having no brothers and sisters. Apparently, many singletons are able to gain through their friendships and peer alliances whatever they may miss by not having siblings at home.

DIVERSITY IN FAMILY LIFE

As we noted earlier in the chapter, modern families are so diverse that the *majority* of our children are growing up in dual-career, single-parent, or blended families that may be very different than the two-parent, single-breadwinner aggregation with two or more children that people often think of as the typical family unit. So let's examine some of these variations in family life.

Adoptive Families

Adoption provides a means for many couples and unattached individuals to become parents or to extend their existing family. Among couples, infertility issues often lead to the consideration of adoption. A clear majority of adoptive parents develop strong emotional ties to their adoptees (Levy-Shiff et al., 1991), and it now appears as if an adult's desire to be a parent is much more important to a child's outcome than the adult's genetic ties (or lack thereof) to his or her children (Golombok et al., 1995, 2001). Nevertheless, since adoptive parents and their children share no genes, the rearing environments that adoptive parents provide may not be as closely compatible with an adoptee's own genetic predispositions as they are for a biological child. These environmental incompatibilities, coupled with the fact that many adoptees have been neglected or abused before their adoptions, or have other special needs (Kirchner, 1998), may help to explain why adoptees display more learning difficulties, more emotional problems, and higher rates of conduct disorders and delinquency than do their nonadopted peers later in childhood and adolescence (Deater-Deckard & Plomin, 1999; Miller et al., 2000; Sharma, McGue, & Benson, 1998).

✔
Concept Check 15.2
**Understanding Parental and
Sibling Influences**

Check your understanding of selected influences that parents and siblings may have on developing children by matching each descriptive statement below with one of the following groups or concepts: (a) authoritarian parenting, (b) authoritative parenting, (c) economic distress, (d) emotional support, (e) increased academic aptitude, (f) mastery motivation, (g) no-nonsense parenting, (h) marital conflict, (i) only children, (j) autonomy, (k) uninvolved parenting. The answers appear in the Appendix.

_____ 1. can undermine an adult's ability to be a supportive, involved parent

_____ 2. benefit that older siblings may receive by instructing younger siblings

_____ 3. adolescent goal that can cause family conflict

_____ 4. children exposed to this inflexible, controlling parenting style show average to below-average cognitive and social competencies

_____ 5. contrary to popular belief, children who are not developmentally disadvantaged

_____ 6. very ineffective parenting style that is consistently associated with poor developmental outcomes

_____ 7. benefit that younger siblings often receive from older siblings

_____ 8. often increases among adolescents who work a moderate number of hours in *challenging* jobs

_____ 9. parenting style that illustrates that *rational* exercise of control contributes to positive developmental outcomes

_____ 10. coercive yet concerned parenting style that is adaptive for raising children in dangerous environments

_____ 11. strong predictor of antagonistic sibling interactions

Don't misunderstand. The vast majority of adopted children are quite well adjusted and typically fare much better in adoptive homes than in foster care, where their foster parents may not be very invested in them or their long-range prospects (Brodzinsky, Smith, & Brodzinsky, 1998; Miller et al., 2000). Even *transracially adopted* children from lower socioeconomic backgrounds usually fare quite well intellectually and academically and display healthy patterns of psychosocial adjustment when raised in supportive, relatively affluent middle-class adoptive homes (Brodzinsky et al., 1987; DeBerry et al., 1996; Sharma et al., 1998). So adoption is a highly satisfactory arrangement for most adoptive parents and their adoptees.

In Canada, adoption laws vary from province to province, but there are some general consistencies across the country. In each province, child welfare departments handle adoptions. Some provinces also grant licences to nonprofit societies that act as adoption agencies, and some provinces allow private adoptions. Adoption practices are changing from a confidential system, in which the identities of the birth mother and adoptive parents are withheld from each other, to a more open system that allows for varying amounts of direct or indirect contact between birth mothers and members of adoptive families. For example, see the new adoption amendments in British Columbia (Ministry of Health Services, British Columbia Vital Statistics Agency, 2001). Because adoptees are often curious about their biological origins and may be upset about the prospect of never knowing their birth parents, more open arrangements may prove beneficial to them. Preliminary research with 5- to 13-year-old adoptees reveals that children (particularly older ones) are both more curious and more satisfied with information about their roots when they can share information or even have contact with their birth mothers (Wrobel et al., 1996), yet there was no evidence in this study that providing information about birth mothers had such harmful effects as confusing children about the meaning of adoption or undermining their self-esteem, as some critics of open adoption policies feared.

Gay and Lesbian Families

In North America many gay men and lesbians are parents, most through previous heterosexual marriages, although some have adopted children or conceived through donor insemination (Flaks et al., 1995). Historically, many courts have been so opposed to the prospect of lesbians and gay men raising children that they have denied the petitions of homosexual parents in child custody hearings solely on the basis of these parents' sexual orientation. Among the concerns people have are that gay and lesbian parents may be less mentally healthy or that they will molest their children, who in turn are at risk of being stigmatized by peers because of their parents' sexual orientation. But perhaps the greatest concern is the fear that children raised by gay or lesbian parents are likely to become gay or lesbian themselves (Bailey et al., 1995).

Interestingly, there is virtually no basis for any of these speculations. As shown in Figure 15.5, more than 90 percent of adult children of lesbian mothers or gay fathers develop a heterosexual orientation—a figure that is not significantly different from the percentages of heterosexuals raised by heterosexual parents. Furthermore, children of gay and lesbian parents are just as cognitively, emotionally, and morally mature, on average, and are otherwise as well adjusted as children of heterosexual parents (Chan, Raboy, & Patterson, 1998; Flaks et al., 1995). Finally, gay fathers or lesbian mothers are every bit as knowledgeable about effective child-rearing techniques as heterosexual parents are (Bigner & Jacobsen, 1989; Flaks et al., 1995), and partners of homosexual parents are usually attached to the children and assume some caregiving responsibilities. In fact, lesbian

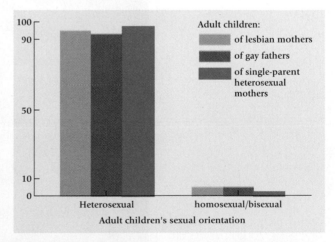

Figure 15.5 *Sexual orientation of adult children raised by lesbian mothers, gay fathers, and single-parent heterosexual mothers. (Notice that children with homosexual parents are just as likely to display a heterosexual orientation as children raised by heterosexuals.)* ADAPTED FROM BAILEY ET AL., 1995; GOLOMBOK & TASKER, 1996.

mothers are happiest and their children somewhat better adjusted when child-care responsibilities are more evenly distributed between the biological parent and her partner (Patterson, 1995a).

So there is no credible scientific evidence that would justify denying a person's rights of parenthood on the basis of his or her sexual orientation. Aside from the possibility of being stigmatized by their parents' lifestyle, children raised by gay and lesbian parents are virtually indistinguishable from those of heterosexual couples.

The Impacts of Family Conflict and Divorce

Earlier, we noted that many children born in the 1990s will spend some time in a single-parent home, usually one headed by the mother (Hetherington, Henderson, & Reiss, 1999). What effects might a divorce have on developing children? As we address this issue, let's first note that divorce is *not* a singular life event; instead, it represents a series of stressful experiences for the entire family that begins with marital conflict before the actual separation and includes a multitude of life changes afterward. As Mavis Hetherington and Kathleen Camara (1984) see it, families must often cope with "the diminution of family resources, changes in residence, assumption of new roles and responsibilities, establishment of new patterns of [family] interaction, reorganization of routines ... and [possibly] the introduction of new relationships [that is, stepparent/child and stepsiblings relationships] into the existing family" (p.398).

Before the Divorce: Exposure to Marital Conflict

The period prior to divorce is often accompanied by a dramatic rise in family conflict that may include many heated verbal arguments and even physical violence between parents. How are children influenced by their exposure to marital conflict? A growing body of evidence indicates that they often become extremely distressed and that continuing conflict at home increases the likelihood that children will have hostile, aggressive interactions with siblings and peers (Cummings & Davies, 1994). Furthermore, regular exposure to marital discord is a contributor to a number of other child and adolescent adjustment problems, including anxiety, depression, and externalizing conduct

The Image Bank/Getty Images

Youngsters who live in conflict-ridden nuclear families often suffer physically and emotionally. In the long run, children of divorce are usually better adjusted than those whose unhappily married parents stay together "for the sake of the children."

disorders (Davies & Cummings, 1998; Harold et al., 1997; Shaw, Winslow, & Flanagan, 1999). Marital discord can have both *direct effects* on children and adolescents, by putting them on edge emotionally and undermining the maturity of their behaviour, and *indirect effects* by undermining parental acceptance or sensitivity and the quality of the parent–child relationship (Erel & Burman, 1995; Harold et al., 1997). So conflict-ridden homes are not healthy contexts for child or adolescent development, and many researchers now believe that children in these settings often fare better in the long run if their parents separate or divorce (Amato, Loomis, & Booth, 1995; Hetherington et al., 1998). Nevertheless, divorce is often a highly unsettling life transition that may have its own effects on the well-being of all family members.

Immediate Effects of Divorce: Crisis and Reorganization

Most families going through a divorce experience a *crisis period* of a year or more in which the lives of all family members are seriously disrupted (Booth & Amato, 1991; Hetherington, 1989; Hetherington, Cox, & Cox, 1982). Typically, both parents experience emotional as well as practical difficulties.

Custodial issues become important. For example, in 1998 about 31 percent of divorces with children had to be resolved through legal interventions—a custody order (Statistics Canada, 2000d). Custody was granted to mothers in 60 percent of these cases, joint custody (both mother and father) was arranged for 30 percent, and custody was given to fathers in 10 percent of the cases (Statistics Canada, 2000d). The mother, who obtains custody of any children in more than 80 percent of divorcing families, may feel angry, depressed, lonely, or otherwise distressed, although often relieved as well. A noncustodial father is also likely to be distressed, particularly if he did not seek the divorce and feels shut off from his children. Having just become single adults, both parents often feel isolated from former married friends and other bases of social support on which they relied as marrieds. Divorced women with children usually face the added problem of getting by with less money—about 50 to 75 percent of the family income they had before, on average (Bianchi, Subaiya, & Kahn, 1997). And life may seem especially difficult if they must move to a lower-income neighbourhood and try to work and raise young children single-handedly (Emery & Forehand; 1994).

As you might suspect, psychologically distressed adults do not make the best parents. Hetherington and her associates (1982, 1998) report that custodial mothers, overwhelmed by responsibilities and by their own emotional reactions to divorce, often become edgy, impatient, and insensitive to their children's needs, and they frequently adopt more restrictive and coercive methods of child-rearing. Noncustodial fathers are likely to change in a different way, becoming more permissive and indulging during visits with their children. Perhaps you can imagine how these changes in parenting are likely to be received. Children of divorce, who are often anxious, angry, or depressed by the family breakup, may react by becoming whiney and argumentative, disobedient, and downright disrespectful. Parent–child relationships during this crisis phase are best described as a vicious cycle in which the child's emotional distress and problem behaviours and the adults' ineffective parenting styles feed on each other and make everyone's life unpleasant (Baldwin & Skinner, 1989). However, children's initial reactions to divorce vary somewhat as a function of their age, temperament, and sex.

CHILDREN'S AGE. Younger, cognitively immature preschool and early-elementary-school children often display the most visible signs of distress as a divorce unfolds. They may not understand why their parents have divorced and are even inclined to feel guilty if they think they are somehow responsible for the breakup of their family (Hetherington, 1989). Older children and adolescents are better able to understand the personality conflicts and lack of caring that may lead distressed parents to divorce and to resolve any loyalty conflicts that may arise; however, they often remain highly distressed over their parents' divorce and may react by withdrawing from family members and becoming more involved in such undesirable peer-sponsored activities as truancy, sexual misconduct, substance abuse, and other forms of delinquent behaviour (Amato, 1993; Hetherington et al., 1998). So even though they are better able to comprehend the reasons for the parents' divorce and to feel less responsible for having caused it, older children and adolescents seem to suffer no less than younger children do (Amato, 1993; Hetherington & Clingempeel, 1992).

Children's Temperament and Sex. The stresses associated with parental conflict and divorce hit particularly hard at temperamentally difficult children, who display more immediate and long-range adjustment problems to these events than easygoing children do (Henry et al., 1996; Hetherington & Clingempeel, 1992). Often, the highly volatile behaviour of a temperamentally difficult child elicits more coercive forms of parenting from his impatient and highly distressed caregiver, which, in turn, represents an extremely poor fit with a difficult child's reactive demeanour and contributes substantially to his or her adjustment difficulties.

Although the finding is by no means universal, many investigators report that the impact of marital strife and divorce is more powerful and enduring for boys than for girls. Even before a divorce, boys already display more overt behavioural problems than girls do (Block, Block, & Gjerde, 1986, 1988). And at least two longitudinal studies found that girls had largely recovered from their social and emotional disturbances two years after a divorce, whereas boys, who improved dramatically over this same period, were nevertheless continuing to show signs of emotional stress and problems in their relationships with parents, siblings, teachers, and peers (Hetherington et al., 1982; Wallerstein & Kelly, 1980).

A word of caution on sex differences, however: Most research concerns mother-headed families and focuses on *overt* behaviour problems that are easy to detect. More recent studies suggest that boys fare better when their fathers are the custodial parent (Amato & Keith, 1991; Clarke-Stewart & Hayward, 1996) and that girls in divorced families experience more *covert* distress than boys do, often becoming depressed or withdrawn rather than acting out their angers, fears, or frustrations (Chase-Lansdale, Cherlin, & Kiernan, 1995; Doherty & Needle, 1991). What's more, a disproportionate number of girls from divorced families show precocious sexual activity early in adolescence and a persistent lack of self-confidence in their relationships with boys and men (Cherlin, Kiernan, & Chase-Lansdale, 1995; Hetherington et al., 1998). So divorce can strike very hard at children of either sex, although it is likely to affect boys and girls in somewhat different ways.

Long-Term Reactions to Divorce

Although many of the emotional and behavioural disturbances that accompany a divorce diminish considerably over the next two years, there may be aftereffects. Compared with children in harmonious, two-parent families, some children of divorce show signs of academic difficulties and psychological distress throughout adolescence and into young adulthood (Chase-Lansdale et al., 1995; Jonsson & Gahler, 1997). Yet it is important to note that the vast majority of children from divorced families improve dramatically over time and display healthy patterns of psychological adjustment (Hetherington et al., 1998).

Nevertheless, even the *well-adjusted children* of divorce may show at least some lingering aftereffects. In one longitudinal study, children from divorced families were still rather negative in their assessments of the impact of divorce on their lives when interviewed more than 20 years after the breakup of their families (Wallerstein & Lewis, as cited by Fernandez, 1997). Another interesting long-term reaction is that adolescents from divorced families are more likely than those from nondivorced families to fear that their own marriages will be unhappy (Franklin, Janoff-Bulman, & Roberts, 1990; Wallerstein & Blakeslee, 1989). There may well be some basis for this concern, because adults whose parents divorced are more likely than adults from intact families to experience an unhappy marriage and a divorce themselves (Amato, 1996).

In sum, divorce tends to be a most unsettling and troubling life event that few children feel very positive about, even after 20 to 25 years have elapsed. But despite the gloomy portrait that we have painted here, there are some more encouraging messages. First, researchers consistently find that children in stable, single-parent (or stepparent) homes are usually better adjusted than those who remain in conflict-ridden two-parent families. Indeed, many of the behaviour problems that children display after a divorce are actually evident well *before* the divorce and may be more closely related to long-standing family conflict than to the divorce itself (Amato & Booth, 1996; Shaw et al., 1999). Take away the marital discord and the breakdown in parenting often associated with divorce, and the experience, while almost always stressful, need not always be damaging. So today's conventional wisdom holds that unhappily married couples who have irreconcilable differences might well *divorce* for the good of the children; that is, children are likely to *benefit* if ending a stormy marriage ultimately reduces the stress they experience and enables either or both parents to be more sensitive and responsive to their needs (Amato et al., 1995; Hetherington et al., 1998).

A second encouraging message is that not all divorcing families experience all the difficulties we have described. In fact, some adults and children manage this transition quite well and may even grow psychologically as a result of it. Who are these survivors? Box 15.4 provides some clues by exploring the factors that seem to promote a positive adjustment to divorce.

Remarriage and Blended Families

Within three to five years of a divorce, about 75 percent of single-parent families experience yet another major change when the custodial parent remarries or *cohabits* (lives with) a partner outside of marriage and the children acquire a stepparent, and perhaps new siblings as well (Hetherington et al., 1998; Messinger, 2001). Remarriage often improves the financial and other life circumstances of custodial parents, and most newly remarried adults report that they are satisfied with their second marriages. Yet these reconstituted families introduce new challenges for children, who must now adjust not only to the parenting of an unfamiliar adult but to the behaviour of stepsiblings (if any) and to the possibility of receiving less attention from both their custodial and noncustodial parents (Hetherington et al., 1998). In fact, the restabilizing of family roles after the custodial parent remarries, often takes considerably longer than was true after divorce (Hetherington et al., 1999) and second marriages are somewhat more likely to end in divorce than first marriages are (Cherlin & Furstenberg, 1994). Imagine, then, the stresses experienced by families that find themselves in a recurring cycle of marriage, marital conflict, divorce, single parenthood, and remarriage. Indeed, recent studies reveal that the more marital transitions that elementary-school children have experienced, the poorer their academic performance and the less well-adjusted they are (Kurdek, Fine, & Sinclair, 1995). (See Figure 15.6.)

So how do children fare in relatively *stable* blended families? The answer depends in part on their age and gender and on whether their mother or father has formed the new family.

Mother–Stepfather Families

In the early years of remarriage, after initial confusions about family roles iron themselves out, boys seem to benefit more than girls by gaining a *stepfather*. Stepfathers who are warm and accepting offer relief from the coercive cycles that boys may have experienced with a custodial mother, so that these stepsons often enjoy a boost in self-esteem and will eventually overcome many of the adjustment problems they displayed before their mother remarried (Hetherington, 1989; Vuchinich et al., 1991). Why do girls not fare as well? Certainly *not* because stepfathers are treating stepdaughters any worse than stepsons; in fact, just the opposite is true during the early stages of remarried life, and no matter how hard stepfathers try, their stepdaughters often remain rather cool and aloof. Girls often view stepfathers as threats to their relationships with their mothers and may even resent their mothers for remarrying and becoming less attentive to their needs (Hetherington, 1989; Vuchinich et al., 1991).

Figure 15.6 *Elementary school boys' risk for poor adjustment outcomes (that is, antisocial behaviour, low self-esteem, peer rejection, drug use, depression, poor academic performance, and deviant peer associations) as a function of number of marital transitions experienced. FROM CAPALDI & PATTERSON, 1991.*

Smoothing the Rocky Road to Recovery from a Divorce

Some individuals adjust well to a divorce, whereas others may suffer negative and long-lasting effects. Who is likely to fare well and what factors make the process of adjustment easier for members of divorcing families?

Adequate financial support

Divorcing families fare much better if they have adequate finances (Hetherington, 1989; Simons et al., 1993). Unfortunately, many mother-headed families experience a precipitous drop in income, which may necessitate a move to a lower-income neighbourhood and a mother's return to work at precisely the time that her children need stability and increased attention. Furthermore, a lack of money for trips, treats, and other amenities to which children may be accustomed can be a significant contributor to family quarrels and bickering. Unfortunately, only about half of noncustodial fathers pay any child support (Sorensen, 1997), and recent efforts to require noncustodial parents to pay their fair share are a step in the right direction.

Adequate parenting by the custodial parent

The custodial parent obviously plays a crucial role in the family's adjustment to divorce. If he or she can continue to respond in a warm, consistent, and authoritative manner, children are much less likely to experience serious problems (Forgatch & DeGarmo, 1999; Hetherington et al., 1998). Of course, it is difficult to be an effective parent when one is highly stressed or depressed. Yet both the custodial parent and the children can benefit immensely from receiving outside social support—not the least important of which is that provided by the noncustodial parent.

Social/emotional support from the noncustodial parent

If divorced parents continue to squabble and are hostile to each other, both are likely to be upset, the custodial parent's parenting is likely to suffer, and the children will likely feel caught in the middle, torn in their loyalties, and will probably have difficulties adjusting (Amato, 1993; Buchanan, Maccoby, & Dornbusch, 1991). The state of Arizona has passed a law requiring couples hoping to divorce to complete a $4^1/_2$-hour seminar to understand the impact of the divorce on their children before their divorce action may proceed (Associated Press, 1996). The purpose of the seminar is to make parents aware of research showing that (1) their children are likely to be more traumatized by the parents' postdivorce wranglings than by the separation itself, and (2) *regular contact* with a noncustodial parent who *supports* the custodial guardian in his or her parenting role is a strong contributor to children's positive adjustment to life in a single-parent home (Coley 1998; Hetherington et al., 1998). Ideally, then, children should be permitted to maintain close, affectionate ties with *both* parents and should be shielded from any continuing conflict between them.

One way of ensuring that children of divorce do not lose contact with a noncustodial parent is to seek *joint physical custody* and have children spend part of the time in each parent's home. This arrangement can work if parents get along; but if their relationship is hostile, their children may feel caught in the middle—an impression associated with high levels of stress and poor adjustment outcomes (Buchanan et al., 1991). It doesn't really matter whether families obtain joint custody as long as children are permitted to maintain close affectionate ties to *both* parents, who are committed to *coparenting* and to shielding their children from any continuing conflict between them (Amato, 1993; Coley, 1998).

Additional social support

Divorcing adults are often less depressed if they participate in support groups such as *Parents without Partners* (an international organization with local chapters that attempts to help single parents cope with their problems) or if they have relatives or close confidants to whom they can turn (Emery, 1988; Hetherington et al., 1998). Children also benefit from the support they receive from close friends (Lustig, Wolchik, & Braver, 1992) and from participating in peer-support programs at school, in which they and other children of divorce are encouraged to share their feelings, correct their misconceptions, and learn positive coping skills (Grych & Fincham, 1992; Pedro-Carroll & Cowen, 1985). In sum, friends, peers, school personnel, and other sources of social support outside the nuclear family can do much to help families adjust to divorce.

Minimizing additional stress

Generally, families respond more positively to divorce if additional disruptions are kept to a minimum—for example, if parents do not have to go through messy divorce trials and custody hearings, seek new jobs or residences, cope with the loss of their children, and so on. One way to accomplish some of these aims is through *divorce mediation*—meetings before the divorce in which a trained professional tries to help divorcing parents reach amiable agreements on disputed issues such as child custody and property settlements. Divorce mediation does appear to be an effective intervention—one that not only increases the likelihood of out-of-court settlements but also promotes better feelings between divorcing adults and increases the likelihood that a noncustodial father will pay child support and remain involved in the lives of his children (Dillon & Emery, 1996).

Here, then, we have some effective first steps on the path toward a positive divorce experience as well as a better understanding of why divorce is more disruptive for some families than for others. This research also serves as yet another excellent example of the family as a social system embedded in larger social systems. Mother, father, and children will all influence one another's adjustment to divorce, and the family's experience will also depend on the supports available within the neighbourhood, the schools, the community, and family members' own social networks.

Father–Stepmother Families

Less is known about children's reactions to stepmothers because stepmother families are still relatively uncommon (recall that fathers currently receive custody of their children in only about 10 percent of all custody hearings). What research there is indicates that introduction of a stepmother into the family system is somewhat more disruptive initially than the introduction of a stepfather, in part because (1) fathers granted custody typically have very close relations with their children that stepmothers may disrupt (Mekos, Hetherington, & Reiss, 1996), and (2) stepmothers play more active roles as behaviour monitors and disciplinarians than stepfathers do (Santrock & Sitterle, 1987). Furthermore, the transition from a father-custody single-parent home to a two-parent stepmother family is once again more disruptive and difficult for girls than for boys, particularly if the biological mother maintains frequent contact with her children (Brand, Clingempeel, & Bowen-Woodward, 1988; Clingempeel & Segal, 1986). Girls are often so closely allied with their mothers that they are bothered by either a stepfather competing for their mother's attention or a stepmother attempting to play a substitute-mother role. However, their adjustment to life in stable stepparent families generally improves over time. In a recent longitudinal study of stepfamilies at 5 or 10 years after remarriage, Mavis Hetherington and her associates (1999) found that girls no longer appeared to be disadvantaged by living in a stepparent home. In fact, they were actually more autonomous and socially responsible (though somewhat lower in self-esteem) than boys.

Family Composition and Age

The composition of a stepparent family often influences how well children adjust to it. Problems of all kinds are more common in **complex stepparent homes**—true blended families in which each parent brings at least one biological child to the new family unit. Both mothers and fathers in these complex aggregations tend to show an **ownness effect,** displaying more warmth, support, and involvement with their biological children than with their stepchildren (Hetherington et al., 1999). And children pick up on this differential treatment, often reacting negatively to it and remaining somewhat more distant and less affectionate over the long run toward their steprelations than toward biological kin (Hetherington et al., 1999; Mekos et al., 1996). Clearly, it is harder for adults to effectively *coparent* if each parent consistently favours his or her biological children. By contrast, coparenting is much more common in **simple stepparent homes,** particularly if family roles stabilize before the children reach adolescence (Hetherington et al., 1999).

Given the many changes that occur early in adolescence (for example, pubertal changes, school transitions, heightened needs for autonomy), it may come as no surprise to learn that early adolescents of both sexes find it more difficult to adjust to a remarriage than younger children or older adolescents do. In fact, Mavis Hetherington and Glenn Clingempeel (1992) reported that children who were early adolescents at the time of their parent's remarriage were significantly less well adjusted than age-mates from nondivorced homes and showed little improvement over the 26-month course of their study. Of course, many early adolescents adapt reasonably well to this family interaction, and authoritative parenting within stepparent families is consistently associated with more favourable adjustment outcomes for stepchildren of *all* ages (Hetherington & Clingempeel, 1992; Maccoby, 1992; Hetherington et al., 1999). Nevertheless, a fair number (perhaps one-third) of adolescents disengage from their reconstituted families, and the incidence of academic problems, sexual misconduct, and many other delinquent activities is higher among adolescents from stepparent homes (particularly complex stepparent homes) than among age-mates from nondivorced families (see Hetherington et al., 1999, for a review).

complex stepparent home
family consisting of two married (or cohabiting) adults, each of whom has at least one biological child living at home

ownness effect
tendency of parents in complex stepparent homes to favour and be more involved with their own biological children than with their stepchildren

simple stepparent home
family consisting of a parent and his or her biological children and a stepparent

❓ WHAT DO YOU THINK?

Recently there have been a number of court cases in which grandparents have petitioned in court for the right to visit their grandchildren after the grandchildren's parents divorce. Do you think grandparents should have the right to petition for these visitation privileges? What limitations might be placed on grandparent visitation to protect the interests of the custodial parent? the children?

But before we get too carried away about the antisocial tendencies of adolescents in blended families, an important truth should be stated here: The vast majority of adolescents who experience this marital transition turn out to be perfectly normal teenagers who may experience some initial problems adjusting but are unlikely to display any prolonged psychopathological tendencies (Emery & Forehand, 1994; Hetherington et al., 1999). In fact, disengagement from a reconstituted family may even be beneficial if a teenager's time away from home is spent at a job or at extracurricular activities that foster constructive, supportive relationships with adult mentors or peers (Hetherington et al., 1998).

Maternal Employment

In Chapter 11, we learned that a majority of Canadian mothers now work outside the home and that this arrangement need not and usually does not undermine the emotional security of their infants, toddlers, and preschool children. And research with older children suggests that maternal employment is unlikely to impede a child's social or intellectual development (Harvey, 1999). In fact, the opposite may be true because children of working mothers (particularly daughters) tend to be more independent, to enjoy higher self-esteem, and to hold higher educational and occupational aspirations and less stereotyped views of men and women than those whose mothers are not employed (Richards & Duckett, 1994; Hoffman, 1989). Indeed, one study of a national sample of *low-income* families linked maternal employment to children's cognitive *competence*: Second-graders whose mothers had worked regularly outperformed those whose mothers had worked less (if at all) in mathematics, reading, and language achievement (Vandell & Ramanan, 1992).

Maternal Employment and Father Involvement

One reason why children of employed mothers often experience favourable outcomes and tend to be socially mature is that maternal employment often causes fathers to play a bigger role in their children's lives. When mothers work long hours, fathers become more heavily involved in child rearing (Lamb, 1997) and know more about their children's activities, whereabouts, and companions (Crouter et al., 1999b). This kind of father involvement (whether inspired by a mother's working or by other factors) can be a very positive factor for children. Elementary school children and adolescents whose fathers are *warm, supportive,* and *emotionally invested* in child rearing are,

---

✔ Concept Check 15.3
Understanding Family Diversity and Family Transitions

Check your understanding of variations and changes in families and their developmental implications by matching each descriptive statement that follows with one of the following responses: (a) coercive parenting; (b) delinquent conduct; (c) increased father involvement; (d) supervised after-school care; (e) gay/lesbian parenting; (f) adoption; (g) noncustodial parental support; (h) unhappy marital relations; (i) complex stepparent home; (j) simple stepparent home; (k) predivorce family conflict. The answers appear in the Appendix.

_____ 1. more common among adolescents in reconstituted families than among those from nuclear families

_____ 2. type of reconstituted family associated with poorest adjustment outcomes

_____ 3. factor that helps children adjust to a divorce

_____ 4. type of reconstituted family in which effective coparenting is unlikely to be undermined by the ownness effect

_____ 5. may contribute as much (or more) to a child's postdivorce adjustment problems as the changes associated with divorce do

_____ 6. can be a positive consequence of maternal employment for developing children

_____ 7. long-term risk of being a child of divorce

_____ 8. significant social support for working parents of school-age children

_____ 9. highly satisfactory family transition for the vast majority who experience it

_____ 10. fears about the possible consequences of _____ have proved to be unfounded

_____ 11. postdivorce change in family dynamics that may contribute to children's adjustment difficulties on average, more academically competent, more socially skilled, and less inclined to display behavioural problems or delinquent conduct compared with age-mates whose fathers are less nurturant and less involved with their lives (Cabrera et al., 2000; Rohner, 2000). Favourable outcomes associated with positive father involvement are *unique* in that they still occur after accounting for the impact of other variables known to influence child development, such as family income and mothers' child-rearing practices (Black et al., 1999; Cabrera et al., 2000). So maternal employment can be beneficial if it prompts sensitive and supportive fathers to play a larger role in their children's lives.

Of course, not all children of working mothers fare so well, especially if their parents experience lots of work pressures and associated stress that spill over to the home setting and compromise the quality of parent–child interactions (Crouter et al., 1999b; Greenberger, O'Neil, & Nagel, 1994). These families often need help if they are to raise children successfully.

The Importance of Good Daycare

Aside from spousal *coparenting,* one of the strongest supports that working parents could hope for is *high-quality* daycare for their children. Recall from Chapter 11 that children who enter high-quality daycare centres early in life tend to display positive social, emotional, and intellectual outcomes from infancy through early adolescence (Andersson, 1989, 1992; Broberg et al., 1997). Much of the research that points to the long-term benefits of excellent daycare comes from Western European countries, where daycare for infants, toddlers, and preschool children is often government subsidized; staffed with trained, well-paid childcare professionals; and widely available to all citizens at a modest fee (usually less than 10 percent of an average woman's wages; Scarr, 1998). By comparison, daycare in Canada is much more variable in quality and often inadequate. For example, in 1998, regulated child care was available for only 10 percent of Canadian children in daycare (Kidder et al., 2000).

Daycare centres and homes are often staffed by poorly compensated caregivers who have little training or experience in early childhood education and who rarely stay in the profession long enough to gain much expertise (Scarr, 1998; Zigler & Gilman, 1993). For example, in 1998 the annual income after taxes for daycare teachers in Newfoundland was only $11 353, and even the higher incomes in Ontario ($20 643) and the Northwest Territories ($22 906) were still very low (University of Toronto, Childcare Resource and Research Unit, 2000). Furthermore, Canadian daycare is expensive. Median rates for providing one child with what is often far less than optimal care can range in cost from $360 a month in Prince Edward Island, New Brunswick, and Newfoundland and Labrador to $541 in Ontario for preschoolers; and can range from $380 a month in New Brunswick to $783 a month in Ontario for infants. These figures represent a considerable part of the annual income of a minimum-wage worker (University of Toronto, Childcare Resource and Research Unit, 2000). Although most provinces have programs in place to offer some tax relief to parents to help offset the cost of daycare, these financial considerations do not ensure the availability of *high-quality* care at a *reasonable cost* to *all* who may need it. This means that many parents have to struggle to find and finance the kind of alternative care that helps them to optimize the development of their children. In most provinces there are subsidies for daycare, but for the most part parents assume the brunt of costs for their children's care. For example, in 1998, on average only 31 percent of children were in subsidized daycare across Canada (Kidder et al., 2000).

Children fare rather well, both socially and academically, if their working parents are authoritative and carefully monitor their activities.

Self-Care

The importance of adequate alternative care raises another employment-related issue: the after-school care of children whose mothers work. "A growing number of the 2.1 million Canadian kids between the ages of 10 and 14 are left on their own before and after school" while their parents are at work (Habib,

2000). These children qualify as **self-care**, **or latchkey**, **children** because they care for themselves with little or no adult supervision (Zigler & Finn-Stevenson, 1993). Are these children at risk of being victimized, led astray by peers, or experiencing other less than desirable outcomes?

Research designed to answer these questions often yields contradictory results. Some studies find that self-care children display higher levels of anxiety, poorer academic performance, and more delinquent or antisocial conduct than supervised youngsters do (Marshall et al., 1997; Pettit et al., 1997), whereas other studies find no such effects (Galambos & Maggs, 1991; Vandell & Corasantini, 1988). Why the inconsistencies? Let's begin by noting that the risks of self-care do seem to be greater for lower-income children in unsafe urban neighbourhoods that may present many opportunities for unsupervised children to associate with deviant peer groups and to take part in antisocial conduct (Pettit et al., 1999; Posner & Vandell, 1994). And regardless of the neighbourhood, the way self-care children spend their time may be crucial. Elementary-school children and adolescents who have received authoritative parenting, who are required to come home after school to complete homework or other chores, and who are monitored at a distance by telephone calls are generally responsible and well-adjusted. By contrast, unmonitored age-mates who are allowed to hang out after school are more inclined to be influenced by antisocial peers and to engage in delinquent conduct (Pettit et al., 1999; Steinberg, 1986).

So it appears that there are steps that working parents can take to minimize some of the potential risks of leaving schoolchildren to care for themselves—namely, by requiring them to go home after school, by supervising them *in absentia* to ensure that they do, and by parenting them in an authoritative manner. Nevertheless, leaving children younger than 8 or 9 to fend for themselves may be asking for trouble (Pettit et al., 1997). Not only is the practice illegal in all provinces (children must be between 10 and 12 years old before being left alone), but 5- to 7-year-olds often lack the cognitive skills to avoid high-risk hazards such as swimming pools or heavy traffic or to cope with such emergencies as personal injuries or fires (Peterson, Ewigman, & Kivlahan, 1993). Younger children in self-care also appear to be more vulnerable to sexual abuse and to harm at the hands of burglars (Zigler & Finn-Stevenson, 1993).

Fortunately, organized after-school care for school-aged children is now becoming more common (Rosenthal & Vandell, 1996). These programs differ in quality, ranging from "social addresses" where children hang out largely unsupervised to well-run programs with trained and responsible staff, reasonable child-to-staff ratios, and curricula that include a variety of age-appropriate activities including sports, games, dance, art projects, music, computer activities, and academic assistance. Not only do children prefer the higher-quality after-school care programs (Rosenthal & Vandell, 1996), but they fare better in them as well. Jill Posner and Deborah Vandell (1994), for example, found that 9-year-olds from high-risk neighbourhoods who attended *closely supervised* after-school care programs providing ample recreational opportunities, academic assistance, or both were more academically competent, were rated as better adjusted by teachers, and were much *less* likely to be involved in antisocial activities than age-mates who were not supervised after school by an adult. A follow-up on these participants revealed that even after controlling for the competencies they displayed in third grade, children who had spent more time between third and fifth grades in program-related enrichment activities such as theatre, music, dance, or other learning projects were rated as better adjusted emotionally by their fifth-grade teachers and were performing better academically than unsupervised age-mates, who spent much of their after-school time hanging out or watching television (Posner & Vandell, 1999). However, the same benefits of after-school care are *not* found if the programs children attend are primarily custodial and provide little positive stimulation or adult guidance (Pierce, Hamm, & Vandell, 1999; Vandell & Corasantini, 1988). So the *quality* of daycare that children receive is important at *all* ages (see also Hustson et al., 2001). Given the success of the publicly funded programs that Posner and Vandell evaluated, we might encourage politicians and community leaders to look carefully at them as a potentially affordable means of (1) optimizing developmental outcomes and (2) preventing more children of working parents from having to face the risks of being alone in the afternoon and early evening.

self-care, or latchkey, children
children who care for themselves after school or in the evenings while their parents are working

WHEN PARENTING BREAKS DOWN: THE PROBLEM OF CHILD ABUSE

Family relationships can be our greatest source of nurturance and support, but they can also be a powerful source of anguish. Nowhere is this more obvious than in cases of **child abuse**. Every day, thousands of infants, children, and adolescents are burned, beaten, starved, suffocated, sexually molested, or otherwise mistreated by their care-givers. Other children are not targets of these physical forms of abuse but are victims of such *psychological abuse* as rejection, ridicule, or even being terrorized by their parents (Wiehe, 1996). Still others are *neglected* and deprived of the basic care and stimulation that they need to develop normally. Although instances of severe battering are the most visible forms of child abuse and are certainly horrible, many investigators now believe that strong and recurrent psychological abuse and neglect may prove to be even more harmful to children in the long run (Erickson & Egeland, 1996; Lowenthal, 2000).

Child abuse is a very serious problem. About *3 million* reports of child maltreatment are filed each year in the United States, and about *1 million* of these are substantiated as abuse cases by child protection agencies (Emery & Laumann-Billings, 1998; Golden, 2000). Although there is some evidence that child neglect is somewhat lower in Canada than in the United States (Statistics Canada, Federal, Provincial and Territorial Advisory Committee on Population Health, 2000a), child abuse in all its forms affects a significant number of Canadian children.

It is difficult to estimate the number of Canadian children who are victims of abuse, especially given estimates that 90 percent of victims never report the abuse (Locke, 2000). Using police reports, assaults on youths and children account for 24 percent of all assaults reported (Locke, 2000). What's more, youths and children account for a dispro-portionately large amount of all sexual assaults—60 percent (Locke, 2000). Sexual and physical violence is most likely to occur against girls and young women (Statistics Canada, Federal, Provincial and Territorial Advisory Committee on Population Health, 2000b). In the United States, surveys of sexual abuse find that more than 400 000 American children a year are coerced into oral, anal, or genital intercourse (Finkelhor & Dziuba-Leatherman, 1994), usually by a father, a stepfather, an older sibling, or another male relative or family friend (Trickett & Putnam, 1993; Wiehe, 1996). It is not a pretty picture is it? Reports of child abuse have increased over the past 20 years, due, in part, to increased awareness of the problem but also to true increases in family violence associ-ated with greater poverty, increased use of illegal drugs, and the disintegration of family-oriented neighbourhoods (Emery & Laumann-Billings, 1998; Garbarino, 1995).

There are many, many factors that contribute to a social problem as widespread as child abuse. Fortunately, researchers are beginning to gain a better understanding of why abuse occurs through a social systems perspective that recognizes why (1) some adults may be more inclined than others to abuse children, (2) some children may be more likely than others to be abused, and (3) abuse may be more likely to occur in some con-texts, communities, and cultures than in others.

Who Are the Abusers?

Researchers have found that there is no single abusive personality syndrome that char-acterizes adults who commit child abuse (Wiehe, 1996). Child abusers come from all races, ethnic groups, and social classes, and many of them even appear on the surface to be normal, loving parents who would never harm their children.

Yet there are at least some differences between parents who abuse their children and those who do not. Let's first note that about 20 to 40 percent of child abusers have an alcohol or drug problem that plays a role in precipitating abuse (Emery & Laumann-

child abuse
term used to describe any extreme maltreatment of children, involving physical batterings; sexual molestations; psychological insults such as persistent ridicule, rejection, and terrorizing; and physical or emotional neglect

Billings, 1998). And about 30 percent of maltreated children will abuse their own children when they become parents, thus implying that abusive parenting practices are often passed from generation to generation (Simons et al., 1991; van IJzendoorn, 1992). In addition, abusive mothers are often battered women—victims of abuse in their own romantic relationships (Coohey & Braun, 1997; McCloskey et al., 1995). They may have learned through their experiences as a child and a romantic partner that violence is a common reaction to frustrations. Abusive mothers are also often young, poverty-stricken, poorly educated, and raising children without a partner to share their burdens (Wiehe, 1996; Wolfner & Gelles, 1993). And many abusive parents are *emotionally insecure* individuals who are likely to interpret children's irritability or normal self-assertive behaviours as signs of *disrespect* or *rejection*. Finally, abusive parents generally favour authoritarian control over authoritative techniques (which they view as largely ineffective), and they rely heavily on severely punitive tactics, such as yanking children's hair, hitting them in the face, or striking them with objects (Trickett & Susman, 1988).

In sum, abusive parents not only tend to have been exposed to harsh punishment and abusive relationships themselves, but they also have little social support, low self-esteem, and a strong belief in the effectiveness of coercive discipline, and they find parenting more unpleasant and ego-threatening than nonabusive parents do. Still, there are many *nonabusive* parents who display all these characteristics, and it has been difficult to predict exactly who will or will not become a child abuser.

Who Is Abused?

Abusive parents often single out only one child in the family as a target, implying that some children may bring out the worst in their parents (Gil, 1970). No one is suggesting that children are to *blame* for this abuse, but some children do appear to be more at risk than others. For example, infants who are emotionally unresponsive, hyperactive, irritable, impulsive, or sickly are far more likely to be abused than quiet, healthy, and responsive babies who are easy to care for (Ammerman & Patz, 1996; Belsky, 1993). Yet it is important to emphasize that many such "difficult" children are never abused, whereas many cheerful and seemingly easygoing children will be mistreated. Just as caregiver characteristics cannot fully predict or explain why abuse occurs, neither can characteristics of children, although it is likely that the combination of a high-risk parent and a high-risk child spells trouble (Bugental, Blue, & Cruzcosa, 1989).

But even the match between high-risk children and caregivers does not invariably result in child abuse. The broader social contexts in which families are embedded matter too.

Social-Contextual Triggers: The Ecology of Child Abuse

Child abuse is much more likely to occur in families under stress. Such significant life changes as a divorce, the death of a family member, the loss of a job, or moving to a new home can disrupt social and emotional relationships within a family and contribute to neglectful or abusive parenting (Emery & Laumann-Billings, 1998; Wolfner & Gelles, 1993). Children are also much more likely to be abused or neglected if their parents are unhappily married (Belsky, 1993).

High-Risk Neighbourhoods

Families are embedded in broader social contexts (that is, a neighbourhood, a community, and a culture) that can affect a child's chances of being abused. Some residential areas can be labelled **high-risk neighbourhoods** because they have much higher rates of child abuse than other neighbourhoods with similar demographic characteristics (Coulton et al., 1995). What are these high-risk areas like? According to James Garbarino

The incidence of child abuse is relatively high in deteriorating neighbourhoods that offer few services and little if any social support to financially troubled families.

Lionel Delevingne/Stock Boston

high-risk neighbourhood residential area in which the incidence of child abuse is much higher than in other neighbourhoods with the same demographic characteristics

(1995; Garbarino & Kostelny, 1992), they tend to be impoverished and deteriorating neighbourhoods that offer struggling parents little in the way of *community services*, such as organized support groups, recreation centres, preschool programs, churches, and parks, or *informal support systems*, such as contact with friends and relatives. Reports from some Aboriginal communities parallel these concerns. Although there are no national data on the levels of violence in Aboriginal communities, several studies suggest that violence is a prevalent feature accompanied by unemployment (Health Canada, 2001a). Consequently, socially isolated parents who live in these neighbourhoods have nowhere to turn for advice and assistance during particularly stressful periods and often end up taking out their frustrations on their children.

Cultural Influences

Finally, the broader cultural contexts in which families live can affect the likelihood that children will be abused. Some developmentalists believe that child abuse is rampant in the United States because that society (1) has a permissive attitude toward violence and (2) generally sanctions the use of physical punishment as a means of controlling children's behaviour (Whipple & Richey, 1997). There may well be some truth to these assertions, because cross-cultural studies reveal that children are less often abused in societies that discourage the use of physical punishment and advocate nonviolent ways of resolving interpersonal conflicts (Belsky, 1993; Gilbert, 1997). In fact, several Scandinavian countries, where children are rarely abused, have *outlawed* the use of corporal punishment (spanking), even by parents (Finkelhor & Dziuba-Leatherman, 1994).

Clearly, child abuse is a very complex phenomenon with many causes and contributing factors (see Table 15.2 for a brief review). It is not always easy to recognize probable abusers, but we know that abuse is most likely to occur when a psychologically vulnerable parent faces overwhelming stress with insufficient social support (Wolfner & Gelles, 1993).

Consequences of Abuse and Neglect

According to David Wolfe and colleagues from London, Ontario (Wolfe, Crooks, Lee, McIntyre-Smith, & Jaffe, 2003), children who are neglected or abused tend to display a number of serious problems, including intellectual deficits, academic difficulties, depression, social anxiety, low self-esteem, and disturbed relationships with teachers and peers (see Bagley, 1995; Bolger, Patterson, & Kupersmidt, 1998; Trickett & McBride-Chang, 1995). (See Box 15.5 for some noteworthy consequences of childhood sexual abuse.) The behavioural correlates of physical abuse differ somewhat from those of neglect.

TABLE 15.2	Factors Contributing to Child Abuse and Neglect
Contributing factor	**Examples**
Parental characteristics	Younger age (under 25), low educational level, depression or other psychological disturbance, history of rejection or abuse, belief in effectiveness of coercive discipline, general insecurity or low ego strength
Child characteristics	Irritable or impulsive temperament, hyperactivity, prematurity, inattentiveness, sickliness or other chronic developmental problems
Family characteristics	Financial strain or poverty, job loss, frequent moves, marital instability, lack of spousal support, many children to care for, divorce
Neighbourhood	High-risk areas characterized by few community services and little opportunity for informal social support from friends or relatives
Culture	Approval of coercive methods of resolving conflicts and use of corporal punishment to discipline children

15.5

Childhood Sexual Abuse

In the 1970s, developmentalists began to discover that the sexual abuse of children was far more common than they had thought. If we count all those individuals who report that they were *ever* molested as children, as David Finkelhor and his associates (1990) did in a national survey, 27 percent of women and 16 percent of men had experienced some form of sexual abuse, ranging from being fondled in ways they considered inappropriate to actually being raped. About 25 percent of the victims were first victimized before age 8, usually by a father, stepfather, grandfather, uncle, teacher, or other male authority figure whom the victim knew well and trusted (Burkhardt & Rotatori, 1995; Wiehe, 1996). In Canada, sexual offences account for 10 percent of all violent crimes reported, with 62 percent of the victims being under 18 years of age and 30 percent being 12 or under (Statistics Canada, 1999a). Women also commit sexual abuse, although female-initiated sex offences are often underreported because boys are less likely than girls to disclose their abuse (Rudin, Zalewski, & Bodmer-Turner, 1995).

Sexual abuse is more common in poverty-stricken families, particularly those in which parents are unhappily married and one or both of them abuse alcohol or drugs and were molested themselves as children (Emery & Laumann-Billings, 1998). Yet sexual abuse can and does occur (and is probably underreported) in middle-class families that display none of these risk factors. In many cases, the perpetrator entices and entraps the victim by implying that the child is special and that their sexual activity will be a mutual secret. This pretext is then reinforced by the offender giving the victim gifts, special favours, or privileges (Wiehe, 1996). And often the victim has little choice but to comply because he or she either does not understand what is happening or is operating under threats of reprisal for noncompliance.

Correlates of abuse

After reviewing 45 studies, Kathleen Kendall-Tackett and her associates (1993) concluded that there is no one distinctive "syndrome" of psychological disorders that characterizes all who experience sexual abuse. Instead, these victims display any number of problems commonly seen in emotionally disturbed individuals, including anxiety, depression, low self-esteem, acting out, aggression, withdrawal, and academic difficulties. Roughly 20 to 30 percent of sexual abuse victims experience each of these problems, and boys seem to display the same types and degrees of disturbance as girls do.

Many of these aftereffects boil down to feelings of shame, a lack of self-worth, and a strong reluctance to trust other people (Bolger et al., 1998; Wiehe, 1996). And there are two problems that seem to be uniquely associated with sexual abuse. First, about a third of the victims engage in "sexualized behaviours"—acting out sexually by placing objects in their vaginas, masturbating in public, behaving seductively, or, if they are older, becoming sexually promiscuous (Kendall-Tackett et al., 1993). Perhaps it is not surprising, then, that adults who were sexually abused as children are more likely than nonabused individuals to be sexually victimized as adults and to report dissatisfaction with their sexual relationships and marriages (Bagley, 1995). Second, about one-third of abuse victims show the symptoms of *posttraumatic stress disorder*, a clinical syndrome that includes nightmares, flashbacks to the traumatizing events, and feelings of helplessness and anxiety in the face of danger (Kendall-Tackett et al., 1993; Saywitz et al., 2000). Victims who are extremely traumatized are also at risk of displaying such self-destructive acts as drug and alcohol abuse, reckless behaviour, and suicide attempts (Wiehe, 1996). And yet, about half of all children and adolescents who are sexually abused display no long-term psychological symptoms as young adults (Bagley, 1995; Kilpatrick, 1992).

Preventing and treating child abuse

Overcoming the harmful effects of sexual abuse can be very difficult, particularly if it occurred frequently over a long period, if the perpetrator was a close relative such as the father or an older sibling, and the child's mother looked the other way, refused to believe the child's story, or was hostile toward the victim for making such accusations (Kendall-Tackett et al., 1993; Trickett et al., 1991). Yet many symptoms fade within a year or two, and recovery may proceed particularly well if the nonabusing parent believes the child's story, puts a stop to the abuse, and provides a stable and loving home environment thereafter (Kendall-Tackett et al., 1993). Psychotherapy aimed at treating the anxiety, depression, and self-blame that many victims experience and teaching them to avoid being victimized again can also contribute to the healing process (O'Donohue & Elliott, 1992; Saywitz et al., 2000).

Perhaps the best way to combat child sexual abuse is to identify it early and prevent it from continuing. Sex education programs at school are one promising strategy: When children learn how to recognize inappropriate "touches" and other sexual advances, they are more inclined to report them to teachers (Bagley, 1995). It is also important that teachers be trained to recognize the signs of sexual abuse and how to report any child disclosures or their own suspicions to the appropriate child protection or law enforcement agencies (Burkhardt & Rotatori, 1995). Early identification of a problem is crucial to limit the victims' suffering and ensure that they get the help they need.

Neglected children are more likely than those who are physically and sexually abused to flounder academically (Eckenrode et al., 1993; Golden, 2000) and are unlikely to have close friends (Bolger et al., 1998). Victims of neglect may receive very little stimulation from nurturing adults that would foster their intellectual, academic, or social competencies (Lowenthal, 2000). By contrast, hostility, aggression, and disordered social relationships are more common among physically abused youngsters, who often create disciplinary problems at school (Eckenrode et al., 1993) and are likely to be rejected by peers (Bolger et al., 1998; Salzinger et al., 1993). Unfortunately, many maltreated children are victims of both abuse and neglect, and any of the previously mentioned consequences may appear in any particular child who is a victim of severe and prolonged maltreatment, regardless of the types of maltreatment he or she has experienced (Bolger & Patterson, 2001; Bolger et al., 1998).

One particularly disturbing correlate of physical abuse is a lack of normal empathy in response to the distress of peers. When Mary Main and Carol George (1985) observed the responses of abused and nonabused toddlers to the fussing and crying of peers, they found that nonabused children typically attended carefully to the distressed child, showed concern, or even attempted to provide comfort. But as shown in Figure 15.7, not one physically abused child showed appropriate concern; instead, abused toddlers were likely to become angry and attack the crying child (see also Klimes-Dougan & Kistner, 1990). So it seems that children who are physically abused are likely to become abusive companions who have apparently learned from their own experiences at home that distress signals are particularly irritating to others and often elicit angry responses rather than displays of sympathy. Other forms of domestic violence (for example, spouse battering) are also common in families that abuse children (McCloskey et al., 1995). Hence, victims of abuse may have few occasions to learn to regulate negative emotions and respond compassionately to others' distress (Shields, Ryan, & Cicchetti, 2001) but many opportunities to learn aggressive solutions to conflict (Bolger & Patterson, 2001). It is no wonder these children are often rejected by their peers.

Unfortunately, the harmful social and emotional consequences of abuse and neglect can be long lasting, and some adolescents try to escape their pain, anxieties, self-doubts, and disordered social lives by attempting to take their own lives (Bagley, 1995; Sternberg et al., 1993). Furthermore, adults who were abused as children are prone to violence, both inside and outside the family, and show higher-than-average rates of criminal activity, substance abuse, depression, and other psychological disturbances (Bagley, 1995; Malinosky-Rummell & Hansen, 1993).

The good news is that many youngsters who are abused or neglected are remarkably resilient, especially if they are able to establish a warm, secure, and supportive relationship with a nonabusive parent, a grandparent, or even a particularly close friend (Bolger et al., 1998; Egeland et al., 1988). And even though abused children are at risk of becoming abusive parents, it is worth emphasizing once again that a sizable majority of abuse victims do *not* abuse their own children. Abused parents who succeed at breaking the cycle of abuse are more likely than those who do not to have (1) received emotional support from a nonabusive parent (or parent substitute), a therapist, and their spouses; and (2) avoided severe stress as adults (Egeland et al., 1988; Vondra & Belsky, 1993).

How Might We Solve the Problem?

It can be discouraging to realize that so many factors contribute to the maltreatment of children. Where do we begin to intervene? How many problems must be corrected before we can prevent or stop the violence and discourage the neglect? Despite the complexity of the problem, progress has been made.

Preventing Abuse and Neglect

Let's first consider the task of preventing child maltreatment before it starts. This requires identifying high-risk families, a task that is greatly aided by the kinds of studies we have reviewed. For example, once neonatal assessment indicates that an infant may be at risk of abuse or neglect because he or she is particularly irritable or unresponsive, it makes sense to help the child's parents to handle the frustrations of dealing with those traits and to appreciate and evoke the baby's positive qualities. These interventions, which are often implemented through *home-visitor programs*, are particularly effective when targeted at high-risk parents who are experiencing high levels of stress or otherwise living

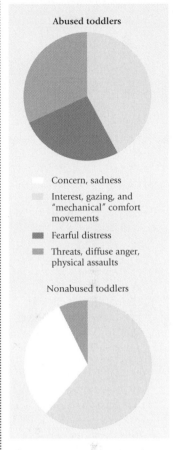

Abused toddlers

- Concern, sadness
- Interest, gazing, and "mechanical" comfort movements
- Fearful distress
- Threats, diffuse anger, physical assaults

Nonabused toddlers

Figure 15.7 *Responses to the distress of peers observed in abused and nonabused toddlers in the daycare setting. (The circles show the mean proportion of responses falling into each category for the nine abused and nine nonabused toddlers.)*
ADAPTED FROM MAIN & GEORGE, 1985.

under very difficult circumstances (for example, in poverty without much social support). Home visitations are aimed at addressing a high-risk parent's *material* needs (for example, cribs, transportation, and child care), *psychological* needs (parenting education; techniques for reducing stress), and *educational* needs (providing job skills), and they do seem both to improve parents' well-being and to reduce the incidence of child abuse (Emery & Laumann-Billings, 1998).

At the community level, steps might be taken to assess the probable impact on children of action undertaken by the government or industry. For example, a local planning board's decision to rezone a stable residential area or to locate a highway there can create a high-risk neighbourhood by causing property values to decline, destroying play areas, and ultimately isolating families from friends, community services (which may no longer exist), or other bases of social support. James Garbarino (1995) is one of many theorists who believe that significant numbers of American children are likely to be mistreated because of political or economic decisions that undermine the health and stability of low-risk, family-oriented neighbourhoods. The demonstrated success of these and similar interventions has led child-welfare agencies to develop family support and education programs designed to prevent child abuse (Zigler & Finn-Stevenson, 1993). For example, funding for programs is provided through many governmental sources, including the *Community Action Program for Children* (see http://www.hc-sc.gc.ca/hppb/childhood-youth/cbp/capc/index.html). This program funds community groups who provide prevention and intervention services for children from birth to 6 years. In addition, Health Canada coordinates the federal *Family Violence Initiative* (see http://www.hc-sc.gc.ca/hppb/familyviolence/initiative_e.html), which involves increasing public awareness of the problem and assisting service providers and community organizations in developing and providing effective interventions. Specific provincial and regional programs and resources have been established in accordance with these federal programs as well as other community programs with private funding sources.

Controlling Abuse

How do we deal with parents who are already abusive? What does seem clear is that a few visits from a social worker are unlikely to solve the problem. Kempe and Kempe (1978) report that a fair percentage of abusive parents stop physically maltreating their children if they are persuaded to use certain services, such as 24-hour hot lines or crisis nurseries, that enable them to discuss their hostile feelings with a volunteer or to get away from their children for a few hours when they are about to lose control. However, these are only stopgap measures that will probably not work for long unless the abuser

Rimer, Pearl (2003). Making A Difference: The Community Responds To Child Abuse, Fourth Edition. Toronto: Toronto Child Abuse Centre.

A number of programs and services have been developed as attempts to prevent or respond to the problem of child abuse.

also takes advantage of other services, such as family therapy, that are designed to help the caregiver to understand his or her problem while providing the friendship and emotional support that an abusive parent so often lacks (Golden, 2000). Ultimately, however, a comprehensive approach is likely to be most effective. Abusive parents need emotional support *and* opportunities to learn more effective parenting and coping skills and the victims of abuse and neglect need stimulating daycare programs *and* specialized training to help them overcome the cognitive, social, and emotional problems associated with abuse (Lowenthal, 2000; Wiehe, 1996). In short, the ultimate goal in attempting to prevent or control child abuse must be to convert a pathological family system into a healthy one. In addition, it is important to provide resources for children. In Canada, the Kids Help Phone is available 24 hours a day, 7 days a week (1-800-668-6868, on-line http://kidshelp.sympatico.ca). The service connects children with counsellors who can also make referrals if necessary. Parents, teachers, and other concerned adults can also call this hot line for referral information.

Yet some abusive family systems are more pathological than others and may not respond to supportive interventions of the kind we've discussed. It may shock you to learn that 35 to 50 percent of all fatalities resulting from child abuse or neglect occur in cases of *severe* and *repeated* maltreatment of which law enforcement and child protection agencies *are already aware* (Lung & Daro, 1996)! Robert Emery and Lisa Laumann-Billings (1998) argue that cases in which a child's physical or psychological welfare is immediately and profoundly compromised require *coercive* rather than supportive interventions. One such control tactic becoming increasingly common involves arresting and prosecuting parents for acts that would qualify as criminal or sexual assault if they occurred between strangers. Yet even severe abuse is often difficult to prove (beyond the reasonable doubt required for criminal conviction), and North American courts are quite hesitant to take children away from their parents, even when there is reason to suspect a child has been repeatedly abused (Gelles, 1996). One reason for this reluctant attitude is that, historically, children have been treated as their parents' possessions (Hart & Brassard, 1987). Another is that abused children and their parents are often attached to each other, so that neither the abusive adult nor the mistreated child wants to be separated. However, developmentalists the world over have argued that no caregiver has the right to abuse a child (Hart, 1991) and that, in cases of severe abuse or neglect, our first priority must be to provide for the health and safety of mistreated children, even if that means terminating the abusers' legal rights of parenthood and placing their children in foster care or adoptive homes (Emery & Laumann-Billings, 1998; Golden, 2000). The challenge that we now face is to become much more successful at preventing and controlling child abuse so that the difficult decision of whether to separate children from their parents needs to be made far less frequently than it is at present.

WHAT DO YOU THINK?

What, in your opinion, are reasonable grounds for severing legal rights of parenthood in cases of neglect or abuse? How do your criteria compare with those currently used in your province?

REFLECTIONS ON THE FAMILY

James Garbarino (1992) characterizes the family as "the basic unit of human experience" (p. 7). To fully appreciate the awesome significance of the family for children and adolescents, think for a moment about how very badly things can go when the family does not fulfil its important functions. Start with a neglected infant who may not only fail to thrive physically (see Chapter 5) but also does not experience anything faintly resembling warm, sensitive, and responsive care. How is this child to form the secure attachments that serve as foundations for later social and intellectual competencies? Or think about the child whose parents are downright hostile and either provide no guidance at all or who control the child with strict rules and punish his every misstep. How is this child to learn how to care about other people, to become appropriately autonomous, and to fit into society?

Regina Campos and her associates (1994) have studied homeless street youths in Brazil whose families have failed them by neglecting, abusing, or otherwise dismissing them as unimportant. Compared with age-mates who worked on the streets but lived at home, homeless youths fared very poorly. They struggle daily to survive, often begging if necessary to get by. What's more, homeless street youth are often victimized by predatory adults or deviant peers, which depresses them severely, and they tend to become heavily involved in such antisocial behaviours as prostitution, drug abuse, thievery, and a host of other criminal activities (Whitbeck, Hoyt, & Bao, 2000). In short, these youngsters who have no family life are pursuing a highly atypical and deviant lifestyle that may place them on the fast track to psychopathology, as we see in one 16-year-old's account of his daily routine:

> When you go to sleep it's about 5 in the morning; we wake up around 2 or 3 in the afternoon ... get up, wash your face, if you have money you have breakfast [then] go out to steal, then you start to sell the stuff and the money all goes on drugs, because in the street it's all drugs!... Then, you get high, you're all set, then you come down and sleep. (Campos et al., 1994, p. 322)

What happens to these homeless street youths when they grow up? Clearly, there is reason to suspect that their outcomes will be grim in view of the fact that 80 percent of the prison population of one major Brazilian city consists of former street youth (Campos et al., 1994).

You get the picture. It is often easier to illustrate the grave importance of families by accentuating the negative. Fortunately, most of us have fared much better than this, even though we do not always acknowledge just how significant our families have been in underwriting our developmental successes. So think about what you have learned in this chapter the next time you gather with the closest members of your own family. Chances are you will understand why children and adults who are asked to reflect on whom or what is most important in their lives almost invariably speak of their families (Furman & Buhrmester, 1992; Whitbourne, 1986). Although we change and our families change as we get older, it seems that most of us never cease to affect, or to be affected by, those folks we call family.

SUMMARY

Understanding the Family

♦ The family is the primary agent of **socialization**, the context in which children begin to acquire the beliefs, attitudes, values, and behaviours considered appropriate in their society.

♦ Both **traditional nuclear families** and **extended families** are best viewed as **social systems** in which each family member has **direct effects** and **indirect, or third-party, effects** on all other family members. Children fare better when adult members of the family can effectively **coparent**, mutually supporting each other's parenting efforts.

♦ Families are also developing social systems embedded in community and cultural contexts that affect family functioning.

♦ Social changes affecting family life today include greater numbers of single adults, later marriages, a decline in childbearing, more female participation in the work force, and more divorces, **single-parent families**, and **blended,** or **reconstituted, families**, and greater numbers of families living in poverty.

Parental Socialization during Childhood and Adolescence

♦ Parents differ along two broad child-rearing dimensions: **acceptance/responsiveness** and **demandingness/control** that, when considered together, yield four patterns of parenting. Generally, accepting and demanding (or **authoritative**) parents who appeal to reason in order to enforce their demands tend to raise highly competent, well-adjusted children. Children of less accepting but more demanding (or **authoritarian**) parents and accepting but undemanding (or **permissive**) parents display somewhat less favourable developmental outcomes, and children of unaccepting, unresponsive, and undemanding (or **unin-**

volved) parents are often deficient in virtually all aspects of psychological functioning.

◆ Developmentalists have traditionally assumed that parenting patterns determine developmental outcomes (**parent effects model**). Yet we now know that children can influence parenting as well (**child effects model**), and that a complete account of family socialization recognizes reciprocal influences between parents and their children (**transactional model**).

◆ Parents from different cultures, subcultures, and social classes have different values, concerns, and outlooks on life that influence their child-rearing practices. Yet parents from all social backgrounds emphasize the characteristics that contribute to *success as they know it* in their own ecological niches, and it is inappropriate to conclude that one particular style of parenting is somehow better or more competent than all others.

◆ Parent–child relationships are renegotiated when adolescents begin to seek **autonomy**. Although family conflict escalates during this period, adolescents are likely to become appropriately autonomous if their parents willingly grant them more freedom, explain the rules and restrictions that they impose, involve their adolescents in family decision making, and continue to be loving and supportive guides.

The Influence of Siblings and Sibling Relationships

◆ **Sibling rivalry** is a normal aspect of family life that may begin as soon as a younger sibling arrives, escalate over time, and sometimes promote later conduct disorders. Yet there is a positive side to having siblings. Siblings are typically viewed as intimate associates who can be counted on for support. Older siblings frequently serve as caregivers, sources of security, models, and teachers for their younger siblings, and they often profit themselves from the instruction and guidance that they provide. Yet sibling relationships are not essential for normal development, because only children are just as socially, emotionally, and intellectually competent (or slightly more so), on average, than are children with siblings.

Diversity in Family Life

◆ Infertile couples and single adults who want to be parents often adopt a child to start a family. Although adoptees display more emotional and learning problems than biological children do, adoption is a highly satisfactory arrangement for the vast majority of adoptive parents and their children. Adopted children are often more satisfied with their family lives in open adoption systems that permit them to learn about their biological roots.

◆ Gay and lesbian parents are just as effective as heterosexual parents are. Their children tend to be well adjusted and are overwhelmingly heterosexual in orientation.

◆ Divorce represents a major transition in family life that is stressful and unsettling for children and their parents. Children's initial reactions often include anger, fear, depression, and guilt, which may last more than a year. The emotional upheaval that follows a divorce often influences the parent–child relationship. Children often become cranky, disobedient, or otherwise difficult, while the custodial parent may suddenly become more punitive and controlling. The stresses resulting from a divorce and this new coercive lifestyle often

affect the child's peer relations and schoolwork. Visible signs of distress may be most apparent in younger children and those with difficult temperaments, and girls seem to adjust better than boys to life in a single-parent, mother-headed home. Although some effects of divorce can be seen even after 10 to 20 years have elapsed, children of divorce are usually better adjusted than those who remain in conflict-ridden two-parent families. Among the factors that help children to make positive adjustments to divorce are adequate financial and emotional support from the noncustodial parent, additional social support (from friends, relatives, and the community) for custodial parents and their children, and a minimum of additional stressors surrounding the divorce itself.

◆ Forming a family after a single parent remarries (or cohabits) is often a stressful transition for all family members. Initially, boys adjust better than girls to having a stepparent, and young children and older adolescents adjust better than early adolescents do. Adjustment outcomes are better in **simple stepparent homes** than in **complex stepparent homes**. Although the incidence of antisocial conduct is higher in reconstituted families than in nondivorced families, the vast majority of children and adolescents successfully negotiate this family transition, displaying no psychopathological tendencies.

◆ Maternal employment is often associated with such favourable child outcomes as self-reliance, sociability, competent intellectual and academic performances, and less stereotyped views of men and women, particularly when a mother's work induces warm, supportive fathers to become more involved in their children's lives. One of the strongest supports that working parents can hope for is stimulating daycare for their children, a support system that is woefully inadequate in Canada, compared with that provided by many other Western industrialized nations. Large numbers of Canadian elementary-school children whose mothers work must care for themselves after school. When monitored from a distance by authoritative parents, these **self-care (or latchkey) children** fare well. After-school daycare programs are becoming more common, and well-managed ones that offer children meaningful activities can help to optimize developmental outcomes and lessen the chances that children of working mothers will engage in antisocial conduct.

When Parenting Breaks Down: The Problem of Child Abuse

◆ **Child abuse** is related to conditions within the family, the community, and the larger culture. Abusers come from all social strata and walks of life, although many of them are young, highly stressed caregivers who favour coercive forms of discipline and were themselves abused as children. Highly impulsive children and those who are irritable, emotionally unresponsive, or sickly are more vulnerable to abuse than are healthy, even-tempered children who are easy to care for. The incidence of child abuse is highest when stressed caregivers live in **high-risk neighbourhoods** where they are isolated from sources of social support and the broader culture approves of force as a means of resolving conflicts. The long-term consequences of abuse are often severe and long lasting. Comprehensive programs designed to assist abused children and their abusive parents have achieved some noteworthy success. However, we are still a long way from solving the problem.

KEY TERMS

socialization, 564

family social system, 564

nuclear family, 565

direct effect, 565

indirect, or third-party, effect, 565

coparenting, 565

extended family, 566

single-parent family, 568

blended (or reconstituted) families, 568

acceptance/responsiveness, 570

demandingness/control, 570

authoritarian parenting, 571

authoritative parenting, 571

permissive parenting, 571

uninvolved parenting, 572

parent effects model, 573

child effects model, 573

transactional model, 574

no-nonsense parenting, 576

autonomy, 577

sibling rivalry, 580

complex stepparent home, 591

ownness effect, 591

simple stepparent home, 591

self-care (or latchkey) children, 594

child abuse, 595

high-risk neighbourhood, 596

 You can find further information on the topics covered in this chapter by visiting:

www.developmentalpsych2e.nelson.com

 For additional reading, go to InfoTrac College Edition, your on-line research library, at:

infotrac.thomsonlearning.com

Extrafamilial Influences: Television, Computers, Schools, and Peers

Photodisc, Inc.

I n Chapter 15, we considered the family as an agent of socialization, looking at the ways that parents and siblings affect developing children. Although families have an enormous impact on children, it is only a
matter of time before other societal institutions begin to exert their influence.
For example, infants, toddlers, and preschool children are often exposed to alternative caregivers and many new playmates when their working parents place
them in some kind of child-care setting. Yet even those toddlers who remain at
home soon begin to learn about a world beyond the family once they develop
an interest in television. And by age 6 or 7, virtually all children in Western societies go to elementary school, a setting that requires them to interact with other
children and adults who may be similar or very different from themselves and
to adjust to rules and practices that may differ greatly from those they follow at
home.

So as they mature, children become increasingly familiar with the outside
world and spend much less time under the watchful eyes of their parents. How
do these experiences affect their lives? This is the issue to which we will now
turn as we consider the impact of four **extrafamilial influences** on development: television, computer technology, schools, and the society of one's peers.

Early Windows: Effects of
Television and Computer
Technologies on Children
and Adolescents

School as a Socialization
Agent

Peers as Agents of
Socialization

Parents and Peers as
Influence Agents

Summary

EARLY WINDOWS: EFFECTS OF TELEVISION AND COMPUTER TECHNOLOGIES ON CHILDREN AND ADOLESCENTS

It seems almost incomprehensible that the average Canadian of only 60 years
ago had never seen a television. Now more than 98 percent of Canadian homes
have one or more TV sets, and children between the ages of 2 and 11 watch an

extrafamilial influences
social agencies other than the
family that influence a child's or
an adolescent's cognitive, social,
and emotional development

average of 15.3 hours of TV a week (Statistics Canada, 2003b). See Table 16.1 for 2002 figures on the average number of hours per week that Canadian children and adolescents spend watching television, by province. By age 18, a child born today will have spent more time watching television than in any other single activity except sleeping (Liebert & Sprafkin, 1988). Boys watch more TV than girls do, and ethnic minority children living in poverty are especially likely to be heavy viewers (Huston et al., 1999; Signorielli, 1991). Is all this time in front of the tube damaging to children's cognitive, social, and emotional development, as many critics have feared?

One way to assess the global impact of television is to see whether children who have access to the medium differ systematically from those who live in remote areas not served by television. One such study of Canadian children gave some cause for concern. Before the introduction of television to the isolated town "Notel," children living there tested higher in creativity and reading proficiency than did age-mates in comparable Canadian towns served by television. Yet two to four years after television was introduced, the children of Notel showed declines in their creativity and reading skills (to levels shown by peers in other towns), less community involvement, and dramatic increases in aggression and gender stereotyping (Corteen & Williams, 1986; Harrison & Williams, 1986).

Although sobering, other investigators report that the biggest impact of the coming of television is that children substituted TV viewing for other leisure activities such as listening to the radio, reading comics, or going to movies (Huston et al., 1999; Liebert & Sprafkin, 1988). And as long as TV viewing is not excessive, children exposed to the medium show no significant cognitive or academic deficiencies and spend no less time playing with peers (Huston et al., 1999; Liebert & Sprafkin, 1988). In fact, one recent longitudinal study found that children may actually learn a great deal of useful information from television, particularly educational programming (Anderson et al., 2001).

So in moderate doses, television neither deadens young minds nor impairs children's social development. Yet we will see that this medium does have the potential to do good or harm depending on *what* children are watching and their ability to understand and interpret what they have seen.

Development of Television Literacy

Television literacy refers to one's ability to understand how information is conveyed on the small screen. It involves the ability to process program *content* to construct a story line from characters' activities and the sequencing of scenes. It also involves an ability to

television literacy
one's ability to understand how information is conveyed in television programming and to properly interpret this information

TABLE 16.1	Television Viewing by Canadian Children and Adolescents, 2002	
Province	**Children aged 2–11** (average hours per week)	**Adolescents aged 12–17** (average hours per week)
Newfoundland and Labrador	17.0	13.7
Prince Edward Island	15.7	15.7
Nova Scotia	16.1	15.9
New Brunswick	16.3	13.4
Quebec	14.7	14.4
Ontario	14.5	13.8
Manitoba	15.0	13.9
Saskatchewan	16.0	12.3
Alberta	14.2	12.4
British Columbia	13.1	12.5

SOURCE: Statistics Canada, 2003b.

interpret the *form* of the message—production features such as zooms, fade-outs, split-screens, and sound effects—that are often essential to understanding a program's content (Fitch, Huston, & Wright, 1993).

Before age 8 or 9, children process program content in a piecemeal fashion. They are likely to be captivated by zooms, fast-paced action, loud music, and children's (or cartoon characters') voices, and often direct their attention elsewhere during slower scenes that contain adults or quiet dialogue (Schmidt, Anderson, & Collins, 1999). Consequently, preschool children are often unable to construct a causal chain of events leading from the beginning to the end of a story. Even 6-year-olds have trouble recalling a coherent story line due, in part, to their tendency to remember the *actions* that characters perform rather than the motives or goals that characters pursue and the events that shaped these goals (McKenna & Ossoff, 1998; van den Broek, Lorch, & Thurlow, 1996). Furthermore, children younger than 7 do not fully grasp the fictional nature of television programming, often believing that characters retain their roles (and scripted characteristics) in real life (Wright et al., 1994). And even though 8-year-olds may know that TV programming is fiction, they may still view it as an *accurate* portrayal of everyday events (Wright et al., 1995).

Comprehension of TV programming increases sharply from middle childhood throughout adolescence. Experience watching TV helps children to properly interpret the zooms, fade-outs, musical scores, and other production features that assist viewers in inferring characters' motives and connecting nonadjacent scenes. Furthermore, older children and adolescents are increasingly able to draw inferences about scenes that are widely separated in time, in much the same way that they integrate semantic information that is separated by intervening paragraphs in a written story (van den Broek, 1997) (see Chapter 10). So if a character were to act nice and gain someone's trust in order to dupe her later, a 10-year-old would eventually recognize the character's deceptive intent and evaluate him negatively. By contrast, a 6-year-old, who focuses more on concrete behaviours than on subtle intentions, will often brand this con artist a "nice guy" and is likely to evaluate his later self-serving acts much more positively (van den Broek et al., 1996).

Does their strong focus on actions and general lack of television literacy increase the likelihood that younger children will imitate the particularly vivid behaviours that TV characters display? Yes, indeed; and whether these imitations are beneficial or harmful depends critically on *what* children happen to be viewing.

Some Potentially Undesirable Effects of Television

Effects of Televised Violence

As early as 1954, parents, teachers, and experts in child development questioned the violence in television programming. Indeed, the National Television Violence Study, a two-year survey of the frequency, nature, and context of TV violence, revealed that American television programming is incredibly violent (Mediascope, 1996; Seppa, 1997b). Fifty-eight percent of programs broadcast between 6 A.M. and 11 P.M. contained *repeated* acts of overt aggression, and 73 percent contained violence in which the perpetrator neither displayed any remorse nor received any penalty or criticism. Canadian research indicates that by the time children graduate from elementary school, they will have witnessed over 8000 murders on television (Campbell, 1993). The violence index for Canadian shows, calculated in 1993, was 23.4 percent lower than for American shows (Paquette & De Guise, 1994), but children in Canada watch a significant amount of American programming. In fact, the most violent TV programs are those intended for children, especially cartoons, and nearly 40 percent of the violence on TV is initiated by heroes or other characters portrayed as attractive role models for children (Seppa, 1997b). Furthermore, nearly two-thirds of the violent incidents in children's programming are couched in humour.

Does TV Violence Instigate Aggression? It has been argued that the often-comical violence portrayed in children's programming is unlikely to affect the behaviour of young viewers. Yet hundreds of experimental studies and correlational surveys suggest otherwise. Simply stated, children and adolescents who watch a lot of televised violence tend to be more hostile and aggressive than their classmates who watch little violence. This positive relationship between exposure to TV violence and aggressive behaviour in naturalistic settings has been documented over and over with elementary-school boys and girls in Canada, Australia, Finland, Great Britain, and Poland and with preschool, elementary-school, high-school, and adult participants in the United States (Bushman & Huesmann, 2001; Geen, 1998). Furthermore, longitudinal studies suggest that the link between TV violence and aggression is *reciprocal:* Watching TV violence increases children's aggressive tendencies, which stimulates interest in violent programming, which promotes further aggression (Eron, 1982; Huesmann, Lagerspitz, & Eron, 1984). The strongest instigating effects of televised violence are seen among children who clearly identify with violent television characters. Preschool boys and (to a lesser extent) girls who identify with television violence become more aggressive over the next 10 to 13 years, and preschool girls who favour violent programming make lower grades later in high school than girls who had watched less violence (Anderson et al., 2001). Although longitudinal surveys are correlational research and do *not* demonstrate causality, their results are at least consistent with the argument that early exposure to a heavy diet of televised violence can lead to the development of hostile, antisocial habits that persist over time. Indeed, when Rowell Huesmann (1986) followed up on boys from an earlier study when they were 30 years old, he found that their earlier preferences for violent television at age 8 predicted not only their aggressiveness as adults but also their involvement in serious criminal activities (see Figure 16.1).

Figure 16.1 Relationship between boys' preference for violent TV programming at age 8 and mean violence of crimes committed by age 30. Adapted from Huesmann, 1986.

Other Effects of Televised Violence. Even if children do not act out the aggression that they observe on television, they may be influenced by it nonetheless. For example, a steady diet of televised violence can instil **mean-world beliefs**—a tendency to view the world as a violent place inhabited by people who typically rely on aggressive solutions to their interpersonal problems (Huston & Wright, 1998; Slaby et al., 1995). In fact, 7- to 9-year-olds who show the strongest preferences for violent television are the ones most likely to believe that violent shows are an accurate portrayal of everyday life.

In a similar vein, prolonged exposure to televised violence can *desensitize* children— that is, make them less emotionally upset by violent acts and more willing to tolerate them in real life. Margaret Thomas and her colleagues (1977; Drabman & Thomas, 1974) tested this **desensitization hypothesis** with 8- to 10-year-olds. Each participant watched either a violent detective show or a nonviolent but exciting sporting event while hooked up to a physiograph that recorded his or her emotional reactions. Then the participant was told to watch over two kindergartners, visible in the next room on a TV monitor, and to come to get the experimenter should *anything* go wrong. A prepared film then showed the two kindergartners getting into an intense battle that escalated until the screen went blank. Participants who had earlier watched the violent program were now less physiologically aroused by the fight they observed and were more inclined to tolerate it (by being much slower to intervene) than their counterparts who had watched an equally arousing but nonviolent sporting event. Apparently, TV violence can desensitize viewers to real-world instances of aggression.

Television as a Source of Social Stereotypes

Another unfortunate effect that television may have on children is to reinforce a variety of potentially harmful social stereotypes (Huston & Wright, 1998). In Chapter 13, for example, we noted that sex-role stereotyping is common on television and that children who watch a lot of commercial TV are likely to hold more traditional views of men and women than their classmates who watch little TV. Yet television might also be employed to counter gender stereotypes. Early attempts to accomplish this aim by showing males performing competently at traditionally feminine activities and females excelling at traditionally masculine pursuits are enjoying some limited success (Johnston & Ettema,

mean-world belief
belief, fostered by televised violence, that the world is a more dangerous and frightening place than is actually the case

desensitization hypothesis
notion that people who watch a lot of media violence will become less aroused by aggression and more tolerant of violent and aggressive acts

1982; Rosenwasser, Lingenfelter, & Harrington, 1989). However, these programs would undoubtedly be more effective if they were combined with the kinds of cognitive training procedures, described in Chapter 13, that undermine the inflexible and erroneous *beliefs* on which gender stereotypes rest (Bigler & Liben, 1990, 1992).

Stereotyped views of minorities are also common on television. While it is true that the representation of Aboriginal populations and visible minorities on television has increased, members of these groups play supporting roles rather than main characters. In a 1992 MediaWatch study of eight made-in-Canada TV shows, White males played 50 percent of the lead character roles, while people from diverse racial and ethnic backgrounds accounted for 16 percent of the actors but were seldom given the central role (cited in Media Awareness Network, 1997). And when non-African- American minorities do appear, they are often portrayed in an unfavourable light, cast as villains or victims (Liebert & Sprafkin, 1988; Staples, 2000).

Although the evidence is limited, it seems that children's ethnic and racial attitudes are influenced by televised portrayals of minority groups. For example, research indicates that earlier depictions of African Americans as comical, inept, or lazy led to negative racial attitudes (Liebert & Sprafkin, 1988), whereas positive portrayals of minorities in cartoons and on such educational programs as *Sesame Street* appear to reduce children's racial and ethnic stereotypes and increase their likelihood of having ethnically diverse friends (Graves, 1993; Gorn, Goldberg, & Kanungo, 1976). Apparently, television has the power to bring people of different racial and ethnic backgrounds closer together or to drive them further apart, depending on the ways in which these social groups are depicted on the small screen.

Children's Reactions to Commercial Messages

In the United States, the average child is exposed to nearly 20 000 television commercials each year, many of which extol the virtues of toys, fast foods, and sugary treats that parents may not wish to buy. Nevertheless, young children continue to ask for products that they have seen on television, and conflicts often ensue when parents refuse to honour their requests (Atkin, 1978; Kunkel & Roberts, 1991). Young children may be so persistent because they rarely understand the manipulative (selling) intent of ads, often regarding them like public service announcements that are intended to be helpful and informative (Liebert & Sprafkin, 1988). By age 9 to 11, most children realize that ads are designed to persuade and sell, and by 13 or 14, they have acquired a healthy skepticism about advertising and product claims (Linn, de Benedictis, & Delucchi, 1982; Robertson & Rossiter, 1974). Nevertheless, even adolescents are often persuaded by the ads they see, particularly if the product endorser is a celebrity or the appeals are deceptive and misleading (Huston et al., 1992).

Is it any wonder, then, that many parents are concerned about the impact of commercials on their children? Not only do children's ads often push products that are unsafe or of poor nutritional value, but also the many ads for over-the-counter drugs and glamorous depictions of alcohol use (think of beer ads) could cause children to underestimate the consequences of such risky behaviours as drinking, self-medication, and drug use (Tinsley, 1992). Policymakers are beginning to respond to the outcries, as evidenced by a recent law limiting the number of commercials on children's programs and requiring broadcasters to offer more educational programming or risk losing their licences (Zigler & Finn-Stevenson, 1993).

Reducing the Harmful Effects of Television Exposure

How might concerned parents limit the potentially harmful effects of commercial television? Table 16.2 lists several effective strategies recommended by experts, including monitoring children's home viewing habits to limit their exposure to highly violent or otherwise offensive fare, while trying to interest them in programs with prosocial or educational themes. Alternatively, the Media Awareness Network/Réseau Éducation-Médias provides information and advice for adults who want to help children become media-

TABLE 16.2	Effective Strategies for Regulating Children's Exposure to Television
Strategy	**Implementation**
Limit TV viewing	Set clear rules that limit when children may watch TV. Don't use the medium as an electronic babysitter or increase its attractiveness by withholding TV privileges as a punishment.
Encourage appropriate viewing	Encourage children to watch child-appropriate informational or prosocial programs. Use lock-out features available on cable or satellite systems to restrict child access to channels with excessive violent or sexual content.
Explain televised information to children	Watch TV with children and point out subtleties that they may miss, such as an aggressor's antisocial motives and the unpleasant consequences that perpetrators may suffer as a result of their violent acts. Critical discussions centring on the violence and negative social stereotypes portrayed on television help children to evaluate what they see and view it as less "real."
Model good viewing habits	Parental viewing practices influence children's viewing practices, so avoid watching too much television, particularly programs that are inappropriate for children.
Parent authoritatively	Warmth coupled with reasonable and rational limit setting make children more responsive to parental control, including restrictions on TV viewing.

SOURCES: Slaby et al., 1995; Seppa, 1997b.

wise. The network provides printed and on-line information for educators, care-providers, and children regarding all types of media. You can contact this organization at 1500 Merivale Road, Third Floor, Ottawa, ON K2E 6Z5 (phone: 613-224-7721 or 1-800-896-3342, fax: 613-224-1958, Web site: http://www.media-awareness.ca, e-mail: info@ media-awareness.ca).

? WHAT DO YOU THINK?

The *Mighty Morphin Power Rangers* was one of the most popular and yet most violent television programs for children and was shown to dramatically increase the incidence of aggressive behaviour among 5- to 11-year-olds (see Boyatzis, Matillo, & Nesbitt, 1995). How would you attempt to combat the influence of a violent show on your own children if you felt incapable of preventing them from watching it away from home?

Television as an Educational Tool

Thus far, we've cast a wary eye at television, talking mostly about its capacity to do harm. Yet this "early window" could be a very effective way of teaching a number of valuable lessons if only its content were altered to convey such information. Let's examine some of the evidence to support this claim.

Educational Television and Children's Prosocial Behaviour

Many TV programs—especially offerings such as *Sesame Street* that are broadcast on public television—are designed, in part, to illustrate the benefits of such prosocial activities as cooperation, sharing, and comforting distressed companions. One major review of the literature found that young children who often watch prosocial programming become more prosocially inclined (Hearold, 1986). However, it is important to emphasize that these programs may have few if any *lasting* benefits unless an adult monitors the broadcasts and encourages children to rehearse and enact the prosocial lessons that they have learned (Friedrich & Stein, 1975; Friedrich-Cofer et al., 1979). Furthermore, young children are more likely to process and enact any prosocial lessons that are broadcast when the programming is free of violent acts that otherwise compete for their attention. But despite these important qualifications, it seems that the positive effects of prosocial programming greatly outweigh the negatives (Hearold, 1986), especially if adults encourage children to pay close attention to episodes that emphasize constructive methods of resolving interpersonal conflicts.

Children learn many valuable lessons from educational TV programs such as Sesame Street.

Television as a Contributor to Cognitive Development

In 1968, the U.S. government and a number of private foundations provided funds to create *Children's Television Workshop* (*CTW*), an organization committed to producing TV programs that would hold children's interest and foster their intellectual development. CTW's first production, *Sesame Street*, became the world's most popular children's series, seen an average of three times a week by about half of America's preschool children and broadcast to nearly 50 other countries around the world (Liebert & Sprafkin, 1988). Starting in 1972, a modified version of the program was aired across Canada that contained some segments exclusively geared to Canadian culture (e.g., French language, Aboriginal cultures) (Lavoie, 1986). Targeted at 3- to 5-year-olds, *Sesame Street* attempts to foster important cognitive skills such as counting, recognizing and discriminating numbers and letters, ordering and classifying objects, and solving simple problems. It was hoped that children from disadvantaged backgrounds would be much better prepared for school after viewing this program regularly.

EVALUATING SESAME STREET. During the first season that *Sesame Street* was broadcast, its impact was assessed by the Educational Testing Service. About 950 children (3- to 5-year-olds) from five areas of the United States took a pretest that measured their cognitive skills and determined what they knew about letters, numbers, and geometric forms. At the end of the season, they took this test again to see what they had learned.

When the data were analyzed, it was clear that *Sesame Street* was achieving its objectives. As shown in Figure 16.2, children who watched *Sesame Street* the most (groups Q3 and Q4, who watched four or more times a week) showed the biggest improvements in their (a) total test scores, (b) scores on the alphabet test, and (c) ability to write their names. The 3-year-olds posted bigger gains than the 5-year-olds, probably because the younger children knew less to begin with (Ball & Bogatz, 1970). The results of a second similar study that included only urban disadvantaged preschoolers parallelled those of the original study (Bogatz & Ball, 1972), and others have found that regular exposure to *Sesame Street* is associated with impressive gains in preschoolers' vocabularies and prereading skills as well (Rice et al., 1990). Finally, disadvantaged children who had been heavy viewers of *Sesame Street* were later rated by their Grade 1 teachers as better prepared for school and more interested in school activities than classmates who had rarely watched the program (Bogatz & Ball, 1972).

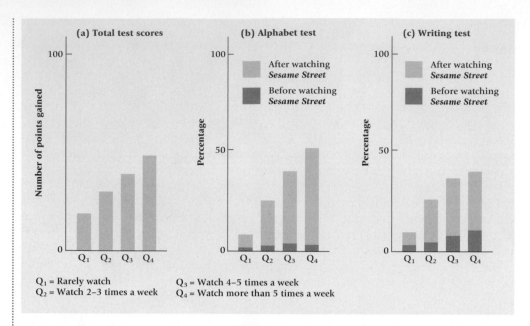

Figure 16.2 *Relationship between amount of viewing of Sesame Street and children's abilities: (a) improvement in total test scores for children grouped into different quartiles according to amount of viewing; (b) percentage of children who recited the alphabet correctly, grouped according to quartiles of amount of viewing; (c) percentage of children who wrote their first names correctly, grouped according to quartiles of amount of viewing. FROM LIEBERT & SPRAFKIN, 1988.*

OTHER EDUCATIONAL PROGRAMS. The success of *Sesame Street* prompted other producers to create programs that teach children subjects such as reading skills (*Reading Rainbow*), problem solving (*Bear in the Big Blue House*), science (*The Magic School Bus, Bill Nye the Science Guy*), as well as shows such as *Barney & Friends* that address a mix of areas (e.g., cognitive, social, emotional, and physical).

CONCERNS ABOUT EDUCATIONAL PROGRAMMING. Critics have argued that viewing educational television is a passive activity that displaces more valuable growth-enhancing pursuits such as reading and active learning under the guidance of an adult (Singer & Singer, 1990). Yet this concern now seems unfounded. More time spent watching general audience programs and cartoons is associated with decreases in children's reading and other educational activities; however, time spent watching *educational* programming is not (Anderson et al., 2001; Huston et al., 1999; Koolstra & van der Voort, 1996). In fact, parents who encourage their children to watch educational programming are also inclined to provide other educational activities as alternatives to TV, which have the effect of limiting their children's exposure to general audience programming (Huston et al., 1999).

It was also once feared that *Sesame Street* might actually widen the intellectual gap between disadvantaged and their middle-class peers if the middle-class children were more inclined to watch the program (Cook et al., 1975). Yet later research revealed that children from disadvantaged backgrounds not only watch *Sesame Street* about as often as their advantaged peers (Pinon, Huston, & Wright, 1989) but learn just as much from it (Rice et al., 1990). And unlike many other educational programs, children benefit from viewing this series even when they watch it alone (Rice et al., 1990).What's more, the impact of this program can be long lasting. Recent longitudinal research reveals that heavy preschool viewing of *Sesame Street* is associated with better academic performances and (to a lesser extent) increased involvement in creative activities 10 to 13 years later in high school (Anderson et al., 2001). So viewing *Sesame Street* appears to be a potentially valuable experience for *all* preschool children—and a true educational bargain that only costs about a penny a day per viewer (Anderson et al., 2001). The formidable task is to convince more parents that *Sesame Street* and other educational programs are valuable resources that they and their children should not be missing (Larson, 2001).

Child Development in the Computer Age

Like television, computer technology has the potential to influence children's learning and lifestyles. But in what ways? Most educators today believe that computer technology is an effective supplement to classroom instruction that helps children to learn more and to have more fun doing so. By 1999, there was one computer for every nine elementary-school students, one for every eight lower-secondary students, and one for every seven upper-secondary students (Statistics Canada, 2000a). Eighty-eight percent of elementary-school and 97 percent of secondary-school students attend a school that has access to the Internet for instruction. In fact, Canada ranks among the highest in the world in terms of computer access at school and at home. In 2000, close to 90 percent of young Canadians reported having a computer at home and 70 percent had access to the Internet (Statistics Canada, 2002d). So computers are now widely accessible, but do they really help children to learn, think, or create? Is there a danger that young "hackers" will become so enamoured of computer technology and so reclusive or socially unskilled that they risk being ostracized by their peers?

Computer Technology in the Classroom

Studies reveal that classroom use of computers produces many benefits. For example, elementary-school students do learn more and report that they enjoy school more when they receive at least some **computer-assisted instruction (CAI)** (Clements & Nastasi, 1992; Collis et al., 1996; Lepper & Gurtner, 1989). Many CAI programs are simply drills that start at a student's current level of mastery and present increasingly difficult problems, often intervening with hints or clues when progress breaks down. Other, more elaborate forms of CAI are guided tutorials that rely less on drill and more on the discovery of important concepts and principles in the context of highly motivating, thought-provoking games. Regular use of drill programs during the early grades does seem to improve children's basic reading and math skills, particularly for disadvantaged students and other low achievers (Clements & Nastasi, 1992; Fletcher-Flinn & Gravatt, 1995; Lepper & Gurtner, 1989). However, the benefits of CAI are greatest when children receive at least some exposure to highly involving guided tutorials as well as simple drills. In addition, having access to computers does not necessarily mean that they are being used effectively. One study of Canadian 15-year-olds revealed that only 39 percent of students reported that they used a computer at school almost every day or a few times a week (Statistics Canada, 2002d).

WORD PROCESSING. Aside from their drill function, computers are also *tools* that can further children's basic writing and communication skills (Clements, 1995). Once children can read and write, using word-processing programs eliminates much of the drudgery of handwriting and increases the likelihood that children will revise, edit, and polish their writing (Clements & Nastasi, 1992). Furthermore, computer-prompted metacognitive strategies help students think about what they want to say and organize their thoughts into more coherent essays (Lepper & Gurtner, 1989).

INTERNET USE. In a study of Internet use in the classroom, about one-third of elementary-school and over half of secondary-school students had used e-mail, and two-thirds had used the World Wide Web for educational purposes (Statistics Canada, 2000a). An increasing number of high-school teachers and university/college professors offer courses and course content on-line, giving students the flexibility to learn at their convenience. These instructors often stimulate discussion of course material on-line, a strategy they believe will reduce concerns about speaking in public while inducing students to ponder course materials more deeply and critically (Hara, Bonk, & Angeli, 2000; Murray, 2000). Although educators and students report many benefits of the Internet for ease of access to information and for communication purposes, research on its benefits, however, is still in its infancy.

computer-assisted instruction (CAI)
use of computers to teach new concepts and give students practice in academic skills

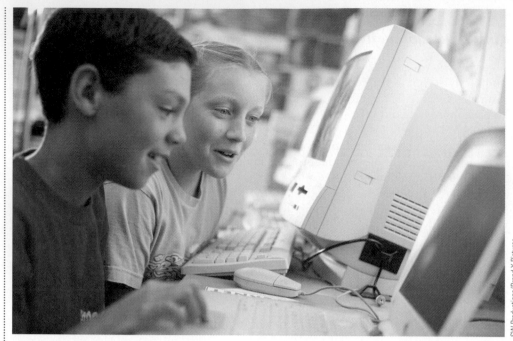

Learning by computer is an effective complement to classroom instruction and an experience that can teach young children to collaborate.

COMPUTER PROGRAMMING AND COGNITIVE GROWTH. Finally, it seems that teaching students to *program* (and thus *control*) a computer can have such important benefits as fostering mastery motivation and self-efficacy as well as promoting novel modes of thinking that are unlikely to emerge from computer-assisted academic drills. In his own research, Douglas Clements (1991, 1995) trained first- and third-graders in Logo, a computer language that allows children to translate their drawings into input statements so that they can reproduce their creations on the computer monitor. Although Clements's "Logo children" performed no better on achievement tests than age-mates who participated in the more usual kinds of computer-assisted academic exercises, Logo users scored higher on tests of Piagetian concrete-operational abilities, mathematical problem-solving strategies, and creativity (Clements, 1995; Nastasi & Clements, 1994). And because children must learn to detect errors and debug their Logo programs to get them to work, programming fosters thinking about one's own thinking and is associated with gains in metacognitive knowledge (Clements, 1990).

Clearly, these findings are important because they suggest that computers are useful not only for teaching children academic lessons but also for helping them to *think* in new ways.

SOCIAL IMPACTS. Are young computer users at risk of becoming reclusive, socially unskilled misfits as some people have feared? Hardly! Children often use home computers as a toy to *attract* playmates (Crook, 1992; Kee, 1986). And research conducted in classrooms reveals that students who are learning to program or solve problems with a computer are (1) likely to *seek* collaborative solutions to the challenges they face and (2) more inclined to persist after experiencing problems when they are collaborating with a peer (Nastasi & Clements, 1993, 1994; Weinstein, 1991). Conflicts may arise should collaborators disagree about how to approach a problem; yet the strong interest that collaborators frequently display when facing a programming challenge often supersedes their differences and encourages amiable methods of resolving conflicts (Nastasi & Clements, 1993). So computer technology seems to promote (rather than impede) peer interactions—contacts that are often lively and challenging and that appear to foster the growth of socially skilled behaviours.

Concerns about Computer Technology

What are the danger signs of exposing children to computer technology? Three concerns are raised most often.

CONCERNS ABOUT VIDEO GAMES. The results of one recent survey in British Columbia revealed that more than 80 percent of adolescents in that province play video games at least occasionally (Media Analysis Laboratory, 1998). Fifty percent of the sample spent less than three hours a week on video games, but 25 percent spent between three and seven hours a week and the remainder over seven hours a week. It is not that this activity necessarily diverts children from schoolwork and peer activities, as many parents have assumed; time spent playing at the computer is usually a substitute for other leisure activities, most notably TV viewing. Nevertheless, critics have feared (and early evidence suggests) that heavy exposure to such popular and incredibly violent video games as *Alien Intruder* and *Mortal Kombat* can instigate aggression and cultivate aggressive habits in the same ways that televised violence does (Fling et al., 1992; Williams, 1998).

The critics' concerns are valid ones. At least three surveys of fourth- to twelfth-graders found moderate positive correlations between the amount of time spent playing video games and real-world aggressive behaviours (Dill & Dill, 1998). The experimental evidence is even more revealing: One study of third- and fourth-graders (Kirsch, 1998) and another study of college students (Anderson & Dill, 2000) found that participants randomly assigned to play violent video games displayed a strong hostile attributional bias toward later ambiguous provocations and significantly more aggressive behaviour than their counterparts who had played nonviolent video games. And because violent game players are *actively* involved in planning and performing aggressive acts and *reinforced* for their successful symbolic violence, it has been argued that the aggression-instigating effects of violent video games is probably far greater than that of violent television programming, in which children are only passively exposed to aggression and violence (Anderson & Dill, 2000; Larson, 2001). Clearly, these early findings suggest that parents should be at least as concerned about what their children are playing on-screen as they are about what their children watch.

CONCERNS ABOUT SOCIAL INEQUALITIES. Other critics are convinced that the computer revolution may leave some groups of children behind, lacking in skills that are required in our increasingly computer-dependent society—commonly referred to as the "digital divide." For example, children from economically disadvantaged families may be exposed to computers at school but are unlikely to have them at home (Rocheleau, 1995). Also, boys are far more likely than girls to take an interest in computers and to sign up for computer camps. Why? Probably because computers are often viewed as involving mathematics, a traditionally masculine subject, and many available computer games are designed to appeal to boys (Lepper, 1985; Ogletree & Williams, 1990). Yet this gender gap is narrowing, largely due to the increasing use of computers to foster *cooperative* classroom learning activities that girls typically enjoy (Collis et al., 1996; Rocheleau, 1995).

CONCERNS ABOUT INTERNET EXPOSURE. The proliferation of home computers and on-line services means that literally millions of children and adolescents around the world may now have unsupervised access to the Internet and the World Wide Web. Clearly, exposure to information available on the Web can be a boon to students researching topics pertinent to their school assignments. Nevertheless, many parents and teachers are alarmed about potentially unsavoury Web influences. For example, children and adolescents chatting with acquaintances on-line have been drawn into cybersexual relationships and, occasionally, to meetings with and exploitation by their adult chat-mates (Curry, 2000; Donnerstein & Smith, 2001; Williams, 1998). Furthermore, the Web is (or has been) a primary recruiting tool for such dangerous cults as Heaven's Gate and hate organizations such as the Ku Klux Klan (Downing, 2001). So there are reasons to suspect that unrestricted Web access could prove harmful to some children and adolescents, and additional research aimed at estimating those risks is sorely needed.

Like television, then, computer technology may prove to be either a positive or a negative force on development, depending on how it is used. Outcomes may be less than positive if a young person's primary uses of the computer are to fritter away study time chatting about undesirable topics on-line, or to hole up alone, zapping mutant aliens from space. But the news may be positive for youngsters who use computer technology to learn, create, and collaborate amicably with siblings and peers.

SCHOOL AS A SOCIALIZATION AGENT

Of all the formal institutions that children encounter away from home, few have as much opportunity to influence their development as the schools they attend. Obviously, students acquire a great deal of knowledge and many academic skills at school. But schooling also promotes cognitive and *metacognitive* growth by teaching children a variety of rules, strategies, and problem-solving skills (including an ability to concentrate and an appreciation for abstraction) that they can apply to many different kinds of information (Ceci, 1991). Consider what Jeffrey Bisanz and Connie Varnhagan from the University of Alberta and Frederick Morrison from Loyola University of Chicago found when comparing the cognitive performance of children who had just made the cutoff for entering Grade 1 with that of youngsters who had just missed the cutoff and had spent the year in kindergarten. When tested at the end of the year, the youngest first-graders clearly outperformed the nearly *identically aged* kindergartners in mental addition accuracy (Bisanz, Morrison, & Dunn, 1995), complexity of storytelling tasks (Varnhagan, Morrison, & Everall, 1994), and in reading, memory, language, and arithmetic skills (Morrison, Griffith, & Alberts, 1997; Morrison, Smith, & Dow-Ehrensberger, 1995). In another study of fourth-, fifth-, and sixth-grade children in Israel (Cahan & Cohen, 1989), children at any given grade performed at higher levels on a variety of intellectual tests than their chronological *age-mates* in the next-lower grade—another indication that intellectual performance is influenced, in part, by the *amount* of schooling one has had.

In addition to the cognitive and academic challenges they provide, schools expose children to an **informal curriculum**: Students are expected to obey rules, cooperate with their classmates, respect authority, and become good citizens. And much of the influence that peers may have on developing children occurs in the context of school-related activities and may depend very critically on the type of school that a child attends and the quality of a child's school experiences. So it is quite proper to think of the school as an agent of socialization that is likely to affect children's social and emotional development as well as to impart knowledge and help to prepare students for a job and economic self-sufficiency.

The vast majority of children in our society now begin their schooling well before age 6, attending junior and then senior kindergarten as 4- and 5-year-olds and, in many cases, going to preschool or daycare before that (Clarke-Stewart, 1993). Is this a healthy trend? As we will see in Box 16.1, advantages as well as some possible disadvantages are associated with early entry into a school-like environment.

informal curriculum
noncurricular objectives of schooling, such as teaching children to cooperate, respect authority, obey rules, and become good citizens

Concept Check 16.1
Understanding Some Effects of Television and Computer Technology

Check your understanding of *selected effects* of television and computer technology by matching each descriptive statement below with one of the following alternatives: (a) ethnic/gender stereotypes, (b) mean-world beliefs, (c) television literacy, (d) aggressive children, (e) disadvantaged children, (f) adult monitoring/encouragement, (g) poor peer relations, (h) advertisements aimed at children, (i) metacognitive development, (j) computer-assisted instruction, (k) violent video games. The answers appear in the Appendix.

_____ 1. display the strongest preference for and effects of exposure to violent programming

_____ 2. often displayed and reinforced in commercial television programs

_____ 3. thought by some critics to be more harmful than televised violence

_____ 4. associated with increases in basic reading and math skills in the primary grades

_____ 5. especially likely to instigate aggression because of the child's active involvement

_____ 6. demonstrated effect of computer programming experience

_____ 7. promotes children's enactment of lessons from prosocial television programming

_____ 8. possible consequence of heavy exposure to televised violence

_____ 9. attribute young children lack that causes them to misinterpret TV programming

_____ 10. their cognitive gains illustrated the benefits of *Sesame Street*

_____ 11. hypothesized negative consequence of computer use that proved to be unfounded

16.1 Should Preschoolers Attend School?

In recent years, children in Canada have begun their schooling at increasingly younger ages. Not only is kindergarten for 5-year-olds common in Canada (95 percent of 5-year-olds attend kindergarten), but also junior kindergarten and preschool programs for 4-year-olds are offered by school boards in some provinces (Council of Ministers of Education, Canada, 2003). And already many preschoolers spend two to eight hours a day in preschool and child-care settings or nursery schools that have a strong academic emphasis and attempt to ready them for the classroom.

Is attending preschool beneficial? Developmentalists such as Edward Zigler (1987) and David Elkind (1981), author of *The Hurried Child*, express some concerns that the current push for earlier and earlier education may be going too far. They feel that many young children today are not given enough time to simply be children—to play and socialize as they choose. Elkind even worries that children may lose their initiative and their enjoyment of learning if their lives are orchestrated by parents who incessantly push them to achieve.

Four studies seem to confirm Elkind's concerns (Hart, Burts, et al., 1998; Hirsh-Pasek, Hyson, & Rescorla, 1989; Marcon, 1999; Stipek et al., 1995). Three- to-6-year-olds in academically oriented preschools or kindergartens displayed an initial advantage in such basic academic competencies as a knowledge of letters and reading skills but had lost it by the end of kindergarten. What's more, students in these highly structured, academically oriented programs proved to be less creative, more stressed, and more anxious about tests, less proud of their successes, less confident about succeeding in the future, and generally less enthused about school than children who attended preschool or kindergarten programs that emphasized child-centred social agendas and flexible, hands-on, discovery-based learning. So there may well be dangers in overemphasizing academics during the preschool period after all.

On the other hand, preschool programs that offer a healthy mix of play and basic skill-building activities can be very beneficial to young children, especially to disadvantaged children. Children who attend high-quality preschools often develop social skills at an earlier age than those who remain at home (Clarke-Stewart, 1993). And, although most children who attend preschool classes are no more or less intellectually advanced than those who remain at home, disadvantaged preschoolers who attend programs designed to prepare them for school display more cognitive growth and achieve more success in school than other disadvantaged youngsters (Burchinal et al., 1997; Ramey & Ramey, 1998). So as long as preschool programs allow plenty of time for play and for skill building in the context of group social interactions, they can help children from all social backgrounds acquire social and communication skills, as well as an appreciation of rules and routines, that will smooth the transition from individual learning at home to group learning in an elementary-school classroom (Zigler & Finn-Stevenson, 1993).

Determinants of Effective (and Ineffective) Schooling

One of the first questions that parents often ask when searching for a home in a new town is "Where should we live so that our children will get the best education?" This concern reflects the common belief that some schools are "better" or "more effective" than others. But are they?

Michael Rutter (1983) certainly thinks so. According to Rutter, **effective schools** are those that promote academic achievement, social skills, polite and attentive behaviour, positive attitudes toward learning, low absenteeism, continuation of education beyond the age at which attendance is mandatory, and acquisition of skills that enable students to find and hold a job. Rutter argues that some schools are more successful than others at accomplishing these objectives regardless of the students' racial, ethnic, or socioeconomic backgrounds. Let's examine the evidence for this claim.

In one study, Rutter and his associates (1979) conducted extensive interviews and observations in 12 high schools serving lower- to lower-middle-income populations in London, England. As adolescents entered these schools, they were given a battery of achievement tests to measure their prior academic accomplishments. At the end of high school, the pupils took another major exam to assess their academic progress. Other information, such as attendance records and teacher ratings of classroom behaviour, was also available. When the data were analyzed, Rutter found that the 12 schools clearly differed in effectiveness: students from the "better" schools exhibited fewer problem behaviours, attended school more regularly, and made more academic progress than students from the less effective schools. We get some idea of the importance of these "schooling effects" from

effective schools
schools that are generally successful at achieving curricular and noncurricular objectives regardless of the racial, ethnic, or socioeconomic backgrounds of the student population

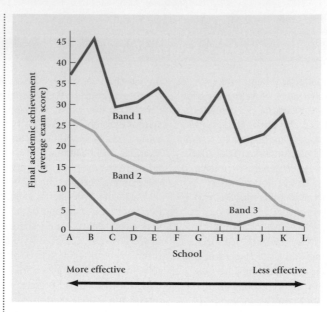

Figure 16.3 *Average level of academic achievement in secondary school as a function of initial achievement at the time of entry (Bands 1–3) and the school that pupils were attending (schools A–L). Note that pupils in all three bands performed at higher levels on this final academic assessment if they attended the more effective schools. Furthermore, students in Band 2 performed like Band 1 students in the more effective schools but like Band 3 students in the least effective schools.* FROM RUTTER ET AL., *1980.*

Figure 16.3. The "bands" on the graph refer to the pupils' academic accomplishments *at the time they entered* high school (Band 1 = high achievers, Band 3 = low achievers). In all three bands, students attending the more effective schools outperformed those in the less effective schools on the final assessment of academic achievement. Even more revealing is the finding that the initially poor students (Band 3) who attended the better schools ended up scoring just as high on this final index of academic progress as the initially good (Band 1) students who attended the least effective schools. Similar findings were obtained in other large studies of elementary and high schools. Even after controlling for important variables such as the racial composition and socioeconomic backgrounds of the student bodies and the types of communities served, some elementary schools were found to be much more effective than others (Brookover et al., 1979; Hill, Foster, & Gendler, 1990).

So the school that children attend can make a difference. And you may be surprised by some of the factors that do and do not have a bearing on how "effective" a school is.

Some Misconceptions about Effective Schooling

MONETARY SUPPORT. Surprising as it may seem, a school's level of *financial* support has little to do with the quality of education that students receive. Seriously inadequate funding *can* undermine the quality of education, but as long as a school has qualified teachers and a reasonable level of support, the precise amount of money spent per pupil, the number of books in the school library, and teachers' salaries and academic credentials play only a minor role in determining student outcomes (Rutter, 1983).

SCHOOL AND CLASS SIZE. Another factor that has relatively little to do with a school's effectiveness is *average class size*. In typical elementary- and secondary-school classes ranging from 20 to 40 students, class size has little or no effect on academic achievement (Odden, 1990; Toch, Streisand, & Butler, 1997). However, classes smaller than 15 to 20 pupils are beneficial in the primary grades (kindergarten through Grade 3) (Finn & Achilles, 1990; Finn, Pannozzo, & Archilles, 2003; Hanusheck, 1997) or for remedial education (Cooper et al., 2000), and primary students in larger classes—especially disadvantaged or low-ability students—do much better in reading and math when they are tutored part of the day in smaller study groups (Odden, 1990; Toch et al., 1997). So if a school district has money available to hire additional instructors, the wisest allocation might be to devote these "personnel resources" to the primary grades—precisely the settings in which smaller classes promote academic achievement.

There is some evidence that the size of one's school affects older students' participation in structured extracurricular activities, where such aspects of the "informal curriculum" as cooperation, fair play, and healthy attitudes toward competition are likely to be stressed. Although larger high schools offer a greater number of extracurricular activities, students in smaller schools tend to be (1) more heavily involved, (2) more likely to hold positions of responsibility and leadership, and (3) more satisfied with extracurricular experiences (Barker & Gump, 1964; Jacobson, Jacobs, & Chase, 1989). Why? One reason is that students in larger schools receive much less encouragement to participate, often becoming lost in the crowd and feeling a sense of alienation and lack of connectedness with peers and the academic culture. This is indeed unfortunate, because one recent longitudinal study that tracked adolescents from Grades 7 through 12 found that high-school students—particularly less competent students with poor social skills—were much less likely to drop out of school if they had maintained a voluntary connection to their school environments by participating in one or more extracurricular activities (Mahoney, 2000; Mahoney & Cairns, 1997). (See Figure 16.4.) The implications of these findings are clear: To better accomplish their mission of educating students and properly preparing them for adult life, middle and secondary schools—large and small—should encourage *all* students to participate in extracurricular activities and avoid denying them those opportunities because of marginal academic performances (Mahoney & Cairns, 1997).

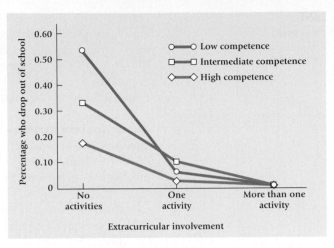

Figure 16.4 *Rates of high-school dropout as a function of student social/academic competencies and participation in extracurricular activities. Clearly, students of low or intermediate competence are more likely to stay in school if they participate in extracurricular activities and maintain a positive and voluntary connection to peers and the school environment.* MAHONEY & CAIRNS, 1997.

ABILITY TRACKING. The merits of **ability tracking**—a procedure in which students are grouped by IQ or academic achievement and then taught in classes made up of students of comparable "ability"—have been debated for years. Some educators believe that students learn more when surrounded by peers of equal ability. Others argue that ability tracking undermines the self-esteem of lower-ability students and contributes to their poor academic achievement and high dropout rate.

In his early review of the literature, Rutter (1983) found that neither ability tracking nor mixed-ability teaching has decisive advantages: Both procedures are common in highly effective and less effective schools. Yet recent research suggests some qualifications. Apparently, ability tracking does widen the gap between high and low achievers (Dornbusch, Glasgow, & Lin, 1996; Slavin, 1987), whereas mixed-ability instruction in elementary and middle schools seems to promote the academic achievement of less capable students without undermining the performance of their more capable peers (Kulik & Kulik, 1992). Ability tracking *can* be beneficial to high-ability students *if* they are exposed to a curriculum tailored to their learning needs (Fuligni, Eccles, & Barber, 1995; Kulik & Kulik, 1992). However, lower-ability students are unlikely to benefit and may well suffer if they are stigmatized as "dummies" and are not challenged academically, or if they are denied access to the more effective instructors who might help them to master such challenges (Fuligni et al., 1995; Kulik & Kulik, 1992; Mehan et al., 1996).

Some schools combine different grade levels or age groups within one classroom (called split-grade or multi-grade), not due to ability tracking, but typically because of declining student enrolment or uneven class size (Veenman, 1995). In this case, classes are combined because there are not enough students to form a single-grade class. In an extensive review of studies examining this issue across 12 countries, including four from Canada, Veenman (1995, 1996) argues that the effect of split-grade classrooms on students' overall academic achievement is negligible.

Factors That Contribute to Effective Schooling

COMPOSITION OF THE STUDENT BODY. To some extent, the "effectiveness" of a school is a function of what it has to work with. On average, academic achievement is lowest in schools with a preponderance of economically disadvantaged students (Lee, Loeb, &

ability tracking
educational practice of grouping students according to ability and then educating them in classes with students of comparable educational or intellectual standing

Lubeck, 1998; Rutter, 1983), and it appears that *any* child is likely to make more academic progress if taught in a school with a higher concentration of highly motivated, intellectually capable peers. However, this *does not* mean that a school is only as good as the students it serves, for many schools that draw heavily from disadvantaged minority populations are highly effective at motivating students and preparing them for jobs or higher education (Reynolds, 1992).

The Scholastic Atmosphere of Successful Schools. So what is it about the learning environment of some schools that allows them to accomplish so much? Reviews of the literature (Phillips, 1997; Reynolds, 1992; Rutter, 1983) point to the following values and practices that characterize effective schools:

1. *Academic emphasis.* Effective schools have a clear focus on academic goals. Children are regularly assigned homework, which is checked, corrected, and discussed with them.

2. *Classroom management.* In effective schools, teachers waste little time getting activities started or dealing with distracting disciplinary problems. Lessons begin and end on time. Pupils are told exactly what is expected of them and receive clear and unambiguous feedback about their academic performance. The classroom atmosphere is comfortable; all students are actively encouraged to work to the best of their abilities, and ample praise acknowledges good work.

3. *Discipline.* In effective schools, the staff is firm in enforcing rules and does so on the spot rather than sending offenders off to the principal's office. Teachers do not resort to physical sanctions (slapping or spanking), which contribute to truancy, defiance, and a tense classroom atmosphere.

4. *Teamwork.* Effective schools have faculties that work as a team, jointly planning curricular objectives and monitoring student progress, under the guidance of a principal who provides active, energetic leadership.

In sum, the effective school environment is a *comfortable* but *businesslike* setting in which academic success is expected and students are *motivated* to learn.

The "Goodness of Fit" between Students and Schools. Characteristics of the student and of the school environment often *interact* to affect student outcomes—a phenomenon that Lee Cronbach and Richard Snow (1977) call **aptitude–treatment interaction (ATI)**. Over the years, much educational research has been based on the assumption that a particular teaching method, philosophy of education, or organizational system will prove superior for all students regardless of their abilities, personalities, and cultural backgrounds. This assumption is often wrong. Instead, many approaches to education are highly effective with *some* kinds of students but quite ineffective with others. The secret to being effective is to find an appropriate fit between learners and educational practices.

> ### ? WHAT DO YOU THINK?
>
> Some Canadian schools require students to wear school uniforms. Proponents believe that this policy improves the educational atmosphere by (among other things) decreasing the incidence of fighting and other misconduct. Critics, however, claim that requiring uniforms imposes economic hardships and restricts students' rights to self-expression. What do you think about requiring students to wear uniforms, and why?

aptitude–treatment interaction (ATI)
phenomenon whereby characteristics of the student and of the school environment interact to affect student outcomes, such that any given educational practice may be effective with some students but not with others

For example, teachers tend to get the most out of *high-ability, middle-class* students by moving at a quick pace and insisting on high standards of performance—that is, by challenging these students. By contrast, *low-ability* and *disadvantaged* students often respond more favourably to a teacher who motivates them by being warm and encouraging rather than intrusive and demanding (Good & Brophy, 1994; Sacks & Mergendoller, 1997).

Sensitivity to students' cultural traditions is also crucial for designing an effective instructional program. European-American students come from cultures that stress individual learning, perhaps making them especially well-suited for the individual mastery expectations that are emphasized in traditional classrooms. By contrast, students from cultures that stress cooperation and collaborative approaches to learning sometimes founder in traditional classrooms. Unfortunately, young adolescents from any social background may begin to lose interest in academics if they experience a mismatch between their school environments and their changing developmental needs—a point well illustrated by the findings presented in Box 16.2.

In sum, the goodness of fit between students and their classroom environments is a crucial aspect of effective schooling. Education that is carefully tailored to students' cultural backgrounds, personal characteristics, and developmental needs is much more likely to succeed.

Do Our Schools Meet the Needs of All of Our Children?

Many of the students educated in our public schools come from non-White social backgrounds. How well are minority students served by our schools? And how well do schools meet the needs of students with developmental disabilities and other special needs?

Educational Experiences of Ethnic Minorities

Aboriginal children in Canada tend to have lower school achievement than children of the dominant non-Native culture (Gotowiec & Beiser, 1993). In the United States, African-American, Latino, and Native-American children tend to earn poorer grades in school and lower scores on standardized achievement tests than their European-American classmates, whereas Asian Americans (particularly recent immigrants) tend to outperform European-American students at school (Chen & Stevenson, 1995; Fuligni, 1997; Slaughter-Defoe et al., 1990). These ethnic differences in academic achievement are still found even after group differences in socioeconomic status are controlled, and they are not merely the product of group differences in intellectual ability (Alexander & Entwisle, 1988; Pungello et al., 1996; Sue & Okazaki, 1990). Why, then, do such differences exist?

Children are more likely to do well in school if their parents value education and are interested and involved in school activities.

PARENTAL ATTITUDES AND INVOLVEMENT. Let's first note that underachieving minority students do not flounder at school because their parents devalue education. However, minority parents are often less knowledgeable about the school system and less involved in many school activities, and this lack of participation may partially counteract their message to children that school is important. Yet, when minority parents *are* highly involved in school activities, their children feel more confident about mastering academic challenges and tend to do well in school (Connell, Spencer, & Aber, 1994; Luster & McAdoo, 1996; Slaughter-Defoe et al., 1990). So active parental involvement can make a big difference.

PATTERNS OF PARENTING AND PEER INFLUENCES. Although minority parents often play an important role in fostering their children's school achievement, we cannot fully appreciate their contribution without also understanding how peers influence academic achievement. For example, in the United States, Lawrence Steinberg and his colleagues (1992) conducted a large-scale study of school achievement among African-, Latino-, Asian-, and European-American high-school students. They found that academic success and good personal adjustment are usually associated with *authoritative parenting*. However, this positive parental influence on academic achievement may be undermined by African-American peers, who often devalue academic achievement and pressure many African-American students to choose between academic success and peer acceptance (see also Ogbu, 1994).

Latino parents tend to be strict and somewhat authoritarian rather than flexible and authoritative. As a result, Latino students may have relatively few opportunities at home to act autonomously and acquire decision-making skills that would serve them well in school (Steinberg et al., 1992). Furthermore, Latino students from low-income areas tend to associate with peers who do not strongly value academics and may undercut their parents' efforts to promote academic achievement. By contrast, European-American stu-

On the Difficult Transition to Secondary School

For some time now, educators have been concerned about a number of undesirable changes that often occur when students make the transition from elementary school to junior high school: loss of self-esteem and interest in school, declining grades, and increased trouble-making, to name a few (Eccles et al., 1993, 1996; Seidman et al., 1994). Why is this a treacherous move?

One reason that the transition is difficult is because young adolescents, particularly girls, are often experiencing major physical and psychological changes at the same time that they are required to change schools. Roberta Simmons and Dale Blyth (1987), for example, found that girls who were reaching puberty as they were making the transition from Grade 6 in an elementary school to Grade 7 in a junior high school were more likely to experience drops in self-esteem and other negative changes than girls who remained in a kindergarten–Grade 8 (K–8) school during this vulnerable period. Adolescents at greatest risk of academic and emotional difficulties are those who must also cope with other life transitions, such as family turmoil or a change in home, at about the time that they change schools (Flanagan & Eccles, 1993). Could it be, then, that more adolescents would remain interested in academics and show better adjustment outcomes if they weren't forced to change schools at the precise time that they are experiencing many other changes often associated with puberty? This has been part of the rationale for the development of middle schools, which serve Grades 6 through 8 (Braddock & McPartland, 1993).

Yet Jacquelynne Eccles and her colleagues (Eccles, Lord, & Midgley, 1991; Eccles et al., 1993) report that students do not necessarily find the transition to middle school any easier than the transition to junior high school. This has led them to suspect that it is not as important when adolescents make a school change as what their new school is like. Specifically, they have proposed a "goodness of fit" hypothesis stating that the transition to a new school is likely to be especially difficult when that school is poorly matched to the adolescents' developmental needs.

What mismatches might be involved? Consider that the transition from elementary to middle or high school often involves going from a small school with close teacher–student ties, a good deal of choice regarding learning activities, and gentle discipline to a larger, more bureaucratized environment where teacher–student relationships are impersonal, good grades are emphasized but harder to come by, opportunities for choice in learning activities are limited, and discipline is rigid—all this at a time when adolescents are seeking more rather than less autonomy (Andermann & Midgely, 1997).

Eccles and others have demonstrated that the "fit" between developmental needs and school environment is indeed an important influence on adolescent adjustment to school. In one study (Mac Iver & Reuman, 1988), the transition to junior high brought about a decline in intrinsic interest in learning mainly among students who wanted more involvement in classroom decisions but ended up with fewer such opportunities than they had had in elementary school. A second study illustrates just how important a good fit between students and school environments can be. Students experienced negative changes in their attitudes toward mathematics if their transition to junior high resulted in less personal and supportive relations with math teachers, but for those few students whose transition to junior high involved gaining more supportive teachers than they had in elementary school, interest in academics actually increased (Midgley, Feldlaufer, & Eccles, 1989). Finally, students in a third study fared better psychologically and academically when they felt that their school encouraged all students to do their best than when competition for grades was emphasized (Roeser & Eccles, 1998).

The message? Declines in academic motivation and performance are not inevitable as students move from elementary to secondary schools. These declines occur primarily when the fit between student and school environment goes from good to poor. How might we improve the fit? Parents can help by recognizing how difficult school transitions can be and communicating this understanding to their teens. Indeed, one study found that adolescents whose parents were in tune with their developmental needs and who fostered autonomy in decision making generally adjusted well to the transition to junior high and posted gains in self-esteem (Lord, Eccles, & McCarthy, 1994). Teachers can also help by setting mastery goals rather than focusing on grades and by seeking parents' opinions about scholastic matters and keeping them involved during this transitional period—a time when collaborative relations between parents and teachers normally decline and adolescents often feel that they are facing the stresses of this new, impersonal academic atmosphere with little social support (Eccles & Harold, 1993). Programs that support adolescents as they make the transition from elementary to secondary school can reduce the odds that young adolescents will drop out of school (Smith, 1997).

Moving from small, close-knit elementary schools to highly bureaucratic and impersonal secondary schools is stressful for adolescents, many of whom lose interest in academics and become more susceptible to peer-group influences.

Bob Daemmrich/The Image Works

dents are more likely than either African-American or Latino students to have *both* authoritative parents and peer support for education working in their favour. Recent research by Gerald Adams of the University of Guelph and his colleagues accentuates how important parental influence can be on school success (see Box 16.3).

Interestingly, high-achieving Asian-American students often experience restrictive, authoritarian parenting at home. However, this highly controlling pattern, coupled with a *very strong* emphasis on education and the *very high* achievement standards that many Asian-American parents set for their children, actually *fosters* academic success. Why? Because Asian-American children are also taught from a very early age to be respectful of and obey their elders, who have a duty to train them to be socially responsible and competent human beings (Chao, 1994; Zhou & Bangston, 1998). Given this kind of socialization in Asian-American homes, it is hardly surprising that the Asian-American peer group strongly endorses education and encourages academic success (Fuligni, 1997). The result? Asian-American students typically spend more hours studying, often with their supportive friends, than other students do, which undoubtedly accounts for much of their academic success (Fuligni, 1997; Steinberg et al., 1992).

TEACHER EXPECTANCIES. Finally, we must consider another hypothesis about ethnic differences in school achievement: the possibility that underachievement by some minority students is rooted in subtle stereotyping on the part of teachers. According to social stereotypes, Asians are expected to be bright and hard-working, whereas Blacks from low-income neighbourhoods are expected to perform poorly in school. And teachers are hardly immune to these stereotypes. Minority students often feel that White teachers do not understand them and that they could do better in school if they were given more respect and understanding (Ford & Harris, 1996). Consistent with this viewpoint, teachers in one study were asked to select from a checklist those attributes that best described their lower-income minority pupils. Teachers consistently chose adjectives such as *lazy*, *fun-loving*, and *rebellious*, thus implying that they did not expect much of these students (Gottlieb, 1966).

THE INSIDE TRACK

16.3

Gerald Adams

Gerald Adams works in the Department of Family Relations and Applied Nutrition at the University of Guelph. His research interests include identity formation, school and family processes that facilitate academic success and adjustment, and problem gambling among adolescents.

The microsystems of the family and school touch as a child comes and goes from the family to school and back again. The influences in one system (like the family) can be transferred in another system (such as the school). Gerald Adams and his colleagues (Adams, Ryans, Ketsetzis, & Keating, 2000) tested this notion (see also Midgett, Ryan, Adams, & Corville-Smith, 2002) by studying the associations among (1) family processes (family cohesion, control, and conflict), (2) school-focused parent–child interactions (parental support and pressure about achievement), (3) the child's own characteristics (assertiveness, frustration, tolerance, intellectual effectiveness, and self-esteem), and (4) correlates of good citizenship (rule compliance and

peer sociability in the classroom). Data were gathered from Canadian parents, children (Grades 4 and 7), and teachers.

Both family climate and school-focused parent–child interactions were associated with children's characteristics that were linked to rule compliance and peer sociability. Most important, the child's level of assertiveness, intellectual effectiveness, and frustration tolerance were substantially correlated with sociability and rule compliance. These three characteristics may have strong genetic links to parents. Further, for the fourth-grade children, parental pressure was associated with less expression of assertiveness or intellectual effectiveness. And the use of parental pressure was higher when families were more controlled and lower when families were more cohesive. In Grade 7, parental pressure was associated with lower frustration tolerance and lower intellectual effectiveness, reducing the positive effects of these two child characteristics on school success. Again, parental control in the family predicted higher use of parental pressure. These and other findings in the study demonstrate that family processes and the child's personal characteristics can have substantial influences on a child's citizenship behaviours in school, demonstrating the importance of recognizing contextual links between the home and the school in understanding children's school success.

Perhaps you can see how teachers who form expectancies based on these stereotypes might unwittingly contribute to ethnic variations in academic achievement. For example, they may subtly communicate to an Asian-American student that she is expected to do well by rephrasing questions the child has missed or by giving helpful hints if she looks indecisive, thus sending the message that failures can be overcome by *persisting* and *trying harder*. By contrast, an Aboriginal or Black student from a low-income neighbourhood might be tagged by teachers as a low-ability student, who is then rarely challenged and is even criticized for errors in ways that cause him to doubt his abilities. Even minority students who are doing well at school are at risk of becoming underachievers if negative stereotypes about their ethnicity are subtly communicated to them and they begin to experience the stereotype threat that we discussed in Box 9.2, which can clearly undermine academic performance (Steele, 1997).

In sum, parents' values and styles of parenting, peers' level of support for academic achievement, and teacher expectancies probably all contribute to ethnic differences in school achievement. Some theorists believe that children from lower-income minority subcultures are at an immediate disadvantage when they enter a middle-class scholastic setting and that schools must change dramatically if they are to motivate and better educate these children. Researchers have known for years that underachieving ethnic minorities fare better at school if the experiences that they have in class or read about in their textbooks include more information about people of their ethnicity (Kagan & Zahn, 1975; Stevenson et al., 1990), and this knowledge is part of the rationale behind recent efforts to make school experiences more culturally relevant for these children. Among the positive changes that we see today are multicultural education programs designed to bring the perspectives of many cultural and subcultural groups into the classroom so that all students feel more welcome there (Banks, 1993; Burnette, 1997).

Educating Students with Special Needs

One major challenge that educators face is successfully educating students with special needs: learning disabilities, mental retardation, physical and sensory handicaps, and other developmental disorders. These youngsters used to be placed in separate schools or classrooms—or in some cases, were rejected as unteachable by public schools—until provincial governments passed legislation requiring school boards to provide all children with special needs with an education comparable to that received by other children. The intent of these laws was to better prepare children with special needs to participate in society by ensuring that their educational experiences were as similar as possible to those of pupils in typical public school classrooms. How might these laws be served? Many school boards have opted for **inclusion** (or *mainstreaming*), the practice of integrating special-needs children into regular classrooms for all or large parts of the day, as opposed to segregating them in special schools or classrooms.

Has inclusion accomplished its objectives? Not very well, unfortunately. Compared with other children with special needs who attend segregated special education classes, mainstreamed students sometimes fare better academically and socially but often do not (Buysse & Bailey, 1993; Hunt & Goetz, 1997; Manset & Semmel, 1997). Furthermore, their self-esteem often declines because classmates tend to ridicule them and are reluctant to choose them as friends or playmates (Guralnick & Groom, 1988; Taylor, Asher, & Williams, 1987), due in part, to their poor social skills (Watson et al., 1999).

Do these findings imply that inclusion has failed? No, they do not! Robert Slavin and his colleagues (1991, 1996; Stevens & Slavin, 1995a, b) argue that inclusion can work quite well if educators emphasize **cooperative learning methods** in which a mainstreamed child and several classmates are assigned to work teams and are reinforced for performing well *as a team*. For example, each member of a math team is given problems to solve that are appropriate to his or her ability level. Yet members of a work team also monitor one another's progress and offer aid when needed. To encourage this cooperation, the teams that complete the most math units are rewarded, for example, with special certificates that designate them as "superteams." Here, then, is a formula for ensuring that children of different social backgrounds and ability levels will interact in a context

inclusion
educational practice of integrating students with special needs into regular classrooms rather than placing them in segregated special education classes (formerly referred to as *mainstreaming*)

cooperative learning methods
educational practice whereby children of different races or ability levels are assigned to teams; each team member works on problems geared to his or her ability level, and all members are reinforced for "pulling together" and performing well as a team

where the efforts of even the least capable team members are important to the *group's* success.

Clearly, these cooperative learning methods work. Mainstreamed second- to sixth-graders in classrooms that stress cooperative learning come to like school better and to outperform mainstreamed peers in traditional classrooms in vocabulary, reading and language skills, and tests of metacognitive knowledge, posting even bigger advantages in the second year of cooperative learning than in the first (Stevens & Slavin, 1995a). What's more, both special-needs children and gifted children thrive in the cooperative learning classrooms, often displaying clear gains in self-esteem and becoming more fully accepted by peers (Stevens & Slavin, 1995b). So inclusion *can* succeed if educators deliberately design learning experiences that encourage students from different backgrounds or ability levels to pool their efforts in order to achieve common goals.

By stressing teamwork to achieve shared goals, cooperative learning activities make inclusion a more fruitful experience for children of all ability levels.

How Well Educated Are Our Children? A Cross-Cultural Comparison

How successful are our schools at imparting academic skills to their pupils? Large surveys of the reading and mathematical achievement of 13- to 16-year-old Canadian students reveal that most of them do learn to read during the elementary-school years and have acquired such mathematical proficiencies as basic computational skills and graph-reading abilities by the time they finish high school (Council of Ministers of Education, Canada, School Achievement Indicators Program, 1997). In a study conducted in 1997, many students demonstrated weaknesses in math and reading comprehension, with only 24 percent of 16-year-olds able to solve math problems (Council of Ministers of Education, Canada, School Achievement Indicators Program, 1997). More recently, however, 15-year-old students in Canada ranked 6th out of 31 countries on mathematics achievement (see Table 16.3), 2nd on reading, and 5th on science, Canada's achievement in comparison to other countries has improved substantially over time (Statistics Canada, 2003a). It is important to note that (a) we do not know whether Canadian students' performance has improved or whether we have just advanced in relation to other countries, and (b) whether Canada's overall performance masks considerable variation in achievement within and among provinces (Statistics Canada, 2003a). Are these findings cause for concern?

Many educators think so (Short & Talley, 1997; Tirozzi & Uro, 1997). For example, the international study of achievement discussed above highlighted the consistently high performance of Korea, Japan, and Finland (Statistics Canada, 2003a) relative to other countries. American students in particular had notably lower scores than these countries. Cross-cultural research conducted by Harold Stevenson and his colleagues (Chen & Stevenson, 1995; Stevenson, Lee, & Stigler, 1986; Stevenson, Chen, & Lee, 1993) leaves no doubt that schoolchildren in Taiwan, the People's Republic of China, and Japan outperform students in the United States in math, reading, and other school subjects. The gap in math performance is especially striking; in recent tests of fifth-grade students, for example, only 4 percent of Chinese children and 10 percent of Japanese students had scores on a math achievement test as low as those of the average American child

TABLE 16.3	Mathematics scores of 15-year-old students from 31 countries in the most recent international study of reading, mathematics, and science achievement

Mathematics Literacy

Japan 557	Denmark 514	Spain 476
S. Korea 547	Iceland 514	Poland 470
New Zealand 537	Liechtenstein 514	Latvia 463
Finland 536	Sweden 510	Italy 457
Australia 533	Ireland 503	Portugal 454
Canada 533	Norway 499	Greece 447
Switzerland 529	Czech Republic 498	Luxembourg 446
United Kingdom 529	United States 493	Mexico 387
Belgium 520	Germany 493	Brazil 334
France 517	Hungary 488	**OECD average 500**
Austria 515	Russia 478	

SOURCE: Statistics Canada, 2003a.

(Stevenson et al., 1993). Achievement differences of this sort are evident from the time children enter school and grow larger each year as children progress from Grades 1 to 5 to 11 (Geary et al., 1996; Stevenson et al., 1993). Why do these differences exist, and what can they tell us about improving education?

The problem is not that American students are any less intelligent, because they enter school performing just as well on IQ tests as their Asian counterparts (Stevenson et al., 1985), and they score at least as well as Japanese and Chinese students on general information tests covering material not typically covered in school (Stevenson et al., 1993). In Chapter 8, we touched on some linguistic and instructional supports that help East Asian children to acquire mathematical knowledge. Yet most of the achievement gap between American and Asian students seems to reflect cultural differences in educational attitudes and practices. For example:

Caroline Penn/Corbis/Magma

Children in traditional Asian classrooms are required to stay in their seats working on assignments or paying close attention to their teacher.

Classroom Instruction

Asian students spend more time being educated than American students do. Elementary-school teachers in Asian countries devote more class time to core academic subjects: for example, two to three times as many hours a week on math instruction. The Asian classroom is a comfortable but businesslike setting where little time is wasted; Asian students spend about 95 percent of their time on "on-task" activities such as listening to the teacher and completing assignments, whereas American students spend only about 80 percent of their time "on task" (Stigler, Lee, & Stevenson, 1987). Asian students also attend school for more hours per day and more days per year (often attending half the day on Saturdays) than American students do (Fuligni & Stevenson, 1995; Stevenson et al., 1986).

Parental Involvement

Asian parents are strongly committed to the educational process. They hold higher achievement expectations for their children than American parents do, and even though their children excel by American standards, Asian parents are much less likely than American parents to be satisfied with their children's current academic performance (Chen & Stevenson, 1995; Stevenson et al., 1993). Asian parents think that homework is more important than American parents do, and they also receive frequent communications from their children's teachers in notebooks that children carry to and from school each day. These communications enable Asian parents to keep close tabs on how their children are progressing and to follow teachers' suggestions about how they can encourage and assist their children at home (Stevenson, Lee, et al., 1990). By contrast, communications between U.S. parents and teachers are often limited to brief annual parent–teacher conferences.

Student Involvement

Not only do Asian students spend more days in class and more class time on academic assignments than American children do, but they are assigned and complete more homework as well (Stevenson et al., 1993). During the high-school years, Asian students continue to devote more time to scholastic activities and spend much less time working, dating, or socializing with friends than American students do (Fuligni & Stevenson, 1995).

A Strong Emphasis on Effort

A major reason that Asian students apply themselves so diligently to academic activities is that their parents, teachers, and they themselves share the strong belief that *all* youngsters have the potential to master their studies if they work hard enough. By contrast, their American counterparts are more inclined to believe that academic success reflects other factors, such as the quality of the child's teachers (see Figure 16.5) or the child's native intelligence (Chen & Stevenson, 1995; Stevenson et al., 1993). Asian students face

Figure 16.5 Percentages of American, Chinese, and Japanese high-school students who picked "studying hard" or having "a good teacher" as the most important factor influencing their performance in mathematics. ADAPTED FROM CHEN & STEVENSON, *1995.*

especially strong pressures to excel in the classroom because their prospects for obtaining a university education largely depend on the results of a competitive exam taken in high school. Yet their strong belief that effort will ultimately pay off in better learning (and higher test scores) helps to explain why Asian youngsters are no more anxious about school or otherwise psychologically maladjusted than American students are (Chen & Stevenson, 1995; Crystal et al., 1994).

So the formula for more effective education may not be so mysterious after all, judging from the success of the Chinese and Japanese educational systems. The secret is to get teachers, students, and parents working together to make education a top priority, to set high achievement goals, and to invest the day-by-day effort required to attain those objectives.

PEERS AS AGENTS OF SOCIALIZATION

Throughout this text we have focused heavily on adults as socializing agents. In their various roles as parents, teachers, and coaches, among others, adults represent the authority, power, and expertise of a society. However, some theorists, Jean Piaget among them, believe that peers may contribute as much (or even more) to a child's or an adolescent's development as adults do (Harris, 1998, 2000; Youniss, McLellan, & Strouse, 1994). In effect, they argue that there are two "social worlds of childhood"—one involving adult–child transactions, and the other involving the society of one's peers—and that these social systems influence development in different ways.

By the time they enter school, most children spend the majority of their leisure time in the company of peers. What roles might peers play in a child's or an adolescent's development? If we allow ourselves to be influenced by such popular novels and films as *Lord of the Flies* and *Dead Poets Society*, we might conclude that peers are subversive agents who often undermine the best-laid plans of adults and lead the child into a life of rebelliousness and antisocial conduct. However, developmentalists now know that this perspective on peer influences is highly distorted and unnecessarily negative (Hartup & Stevens, 1997). Yes, peers are occasionally "bad influences," but they clearly have the potential to affect their playmates in any number of positive ways.

If we assume that peers are important agents of socialization, a number of questions remain to be answered: Who qualifies as a peer? How do peers influence one another? What is it about peer influence that is unique? What are the consequences (if any) of poor peer relations? Is it important to have special peer alliances, or friendships? Do peers eventually become a more potent source of influence than parents or other adults? These are some of the issues that we will explore in the pages that follow.

Concept Check 16.2
Schools as Socialization Agents

Check your understanding of selected effects of schools and educational practices on children by matching each descriptive statement below with one of the following terms, principles, or concepts: (a) academically oriented preschools; (b) parental devaluation of education; (c) cooperative learning methods; (d) group differences in IQ; (e) informal curriculum; (f) inclusion; (g) monetary support; (h) parental involvement; (i) peer influences; (j) extracurricular activities; (k) ability tracking; (l) aptitude-treatment interaction. The answers appear in the Appendix.

_____ 1. may undermine the self-esteem of students with special needs

_____ 2. contributes to ethnic differences in achievement

_____ 3. likely to undermine the academic achievement of low-ability students

_____ 4. aimed at teaching students how to fit into the culture

_____ 5. not a strong contributor to school effectiveness

_____ 6. strong contributor to academic success of students of minority youth and students in Asian cultures

_____ 7. protects against adolescents' dropping out of school

_____ 8. factor that best describes the effectiveness (or ineffectiveness) of particular educational practices

_____ 9. does *not* account for cross-cultural differences in academic achievement

_____ 10. successful method of promoting the objectives of inclusion

_____ 11. may undermine creativity and make children less enthused about school

_____ 12. does *not* explain the poor academic performances of underachieving ethnic minorities

Who or What Is a Peer, and What Functions Do Peers Serve?

The *ITP Nelson Canadian Dictionary* defines a **peer** as "one who has equal standing with another or others." Developmentalists also think of peers as *social equals* or as individuals who, for the moment at least, *are operating at similar levels of behavioural complexity* (Lewis & Rosenblum, 1975). According to this activity-based definition, children who differ somewhat in age could still be considered "peers" as long as they can adjust their behaviours to suit one another's capabilities as they pursue common interests or goals.

Same-Age (or Equal-Status) Contacts

We gain some idea of why peer contacts among age-mates may be important by contrasting them to contacts with parents. A child's interactions with parents are lopsided: Because parents have more power than children do, children are put in a subordinate position and must often defer to adult authority. By contrast, age-mates typically have equal status and power and must learn to appreciate each other's perspectives, to negotiate and compromise, and to cooperate with each other if they hope to get along or achieve joint objectives. Thus, *equal-status* contacts with age-mates likely contribute to the development of social competencies that are difficult to acquire in the nonegalitarian atmosphere of the home.

Mixed-Age Interactions

According to Hartup (1983), interaction among children of *different* ages is also an important context for development. Although cross-age interactions tend to be somewhat *asymmetrical*, with one child (typically the elder) possessing more power than the other, these asymmetries may help children to acquire certain social competencies. One cross-cultural survey revealed that the presence of younger peers fostered the development of compassion, caregiving, prosocial inclinations, assertiveness, and leadership skills in older children (Whiting & Edwards, 1988). At the same time, younger children benefited from mixed-age interactions by acquiring a variety of new skills from older playmates and learning how to seek assistance from and defer gracefully to these more powerful associates. Older children usually took charge of mixed-age interactions and adjusted

Both older and younger children benefit from mixed-age interactions.

peers
two or more people who are operating at similar levels of behavioural complexity

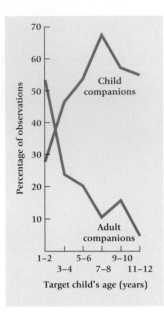

Figure 16.6 *Developmental changes in children's companionship with adults and other children.* ADAPTED FROM ELLIS, ROGOFF, & CROMER, 1981.

their behaviour to the competencies of their younger companions (see also Brody, Graziano, & Musser, 1983; Graziano et al., 1976). Even 2-year-olds show such powers of leadership and accommodation, because they are more inclined to take the initiative and display simpler and more repetitive play routines when paired with an 18-month-old toddler than with an age-mate (Brownell, 1990).

Perhaps you have noticed that mixed-age peer interactions seem to benefit older and younger children in many of the same ways that sibling interactions benefit older and younger siblings (see Chapter 15). But there is a crucial difference between sibling and peer contacts: One's standing as either a younger or an older sibling is *fixed* by order of birth whereas one's position among peers is more *flexible,* depending on the associates one chooses. Thus, mixed-age *peer* interactions may provide children with experiences that they might otherwise miss in their mixed-age sibling interactions and, in fact, may be the primary context in which (1) a habitually domineering elder sibling learns to be more accommodating (when interacting with older peers), (2) an oppressed younger sibling learns to lead and to show compassion (when dealing with even younger children), and (3) an only child (who has no siblings) acquires both sets of social competencies. Viewed in this way, mixed-age peer associations may be important experiences indeed.

Frequency of Peer Contacts

Between the ages of 2 and 12, children spend more and more time with peers and less and less time with adults. This trend is illustrated in Figure 16.6, which summarizes what Sherri Ellis and her colleagues (1981) found while observing 436 children playing in their homes and around the neighbourhood. Interestingly, this same study revealed that youngsters of all ages spent *less* time with age-mates (defined as children whose ages were within a year of their own) than with children who were more than a year older or younger than they were. Apparently, we must take seriously the idea that peers are "social equals" rather than age-mates.

Another finding of this study is a familiar one: Even 1- to 2-year-olds played more often with same-sex companions than with other-sex companions, and this *gender segregation* increased with age. Once in their sex-segregated worlds, boys and girls experience different kinds of social relationships. Boys tend to form "packs," whereas girls form "pairs"; that is, a boy often plays competitive games or team sports in groups, whereas a girl more often establishes a longer and more cooperative relationship with one playmate (Archer, 1992; Benenson, Apostoleris, & Parnass, 1997; Lansford & Parker, 1999).

Overall, then, children spend an increasing amount of time with peers, and those peers are typically *same*-sex children who are only *roughly similar* in age but who enjoy the same kinds of gender-typed activities.

How Important Are Peer Influences?

To this point, we have speculated that peer interactions may foster many social and personal competencies that are not easily acquired within nonegalitarian parent–child or sibling–sibling relationships. Is there truly any basis for such a claim? And if so, just how important are these peer influences? Developmentalists became very interested in these questions once they learned of Harry Harlow's research with rhesus monkeys.

HARLOW'S WORK WITH MONKEYS. If youngsters have little or no contact with peers, will they turn out to be abnormal or maladjusted? To find out, Harlow and his associates (Alexander & Harlow, 1965; Suomi & Harlow, 1978) raised groups of rhesus monkeys with their mothers and denied them the opportunity to play with peers. These **"mother-only" monkeys** failed to develop normal patterns of social behaviour. When finally exposed to age-mates, the peer-deprived youngsters preferred to avoid them. On those occasions when they did approach a peer, these social misfits tended to be highly (and inappropriately) aggressive, and their antisocial tendencies often persisted into adulthood.

Monkeys raised only with peers form strong mutual attachments and often attack other monkeys from outside their peer group.

"mother-only" monkeys
monkeys who are raised with their mothers and denied any contact with peers

Is peer contact, then, the key to normal social development? Not entirely. In later experiments, Harlow and his colleagues separated rhesus monkey infants from their mothers and raised them so that they had continuous exposure to peers. These **"peer-only" monkeys** were observed to cling tenaciously to one another and to form strong mutual attachments. Yet their social development was somewhat atypical in that they became highly agitated over minor stresses or frustrations (see also Higley et al., 1992), and as adults they were unusually aggressive toward monkeys from outside their peer groups.

A HUMAN PARALLEL. In 1951, Anna Freud and Sophie Dann reported a startling human parallel to Harlow's peer-only monkeys. During the summer of 1945, six 3-year-olds were found living by themselves in a Nazi concentration camp. By the time these children were 12 months old, their parents had been put to death. Although they received minimal caregiving from a series of inmates who were periodically executed, these children had, in effect, reared themselves.

When rescued at the war's end, the six orphans were flown to a treatment centre in England, where attempts were made to rehabilitate them. How did these "peer-only" children respond to this treatment? They began by breaking nearly all their toys, damaging their furniture, and displaying cold indifference or open hostility toward the staff at the centre. Like Harlow's peer-only monkeys, these children were strongly attached to one another and often became upset when separated from other members of the group, even for brief periods. They also showed a remarkable prosocial concern for one another (Freud & Dann, 1951, pp. 132–133):

> There was no occasion to urge the children to "take turns"; they did it spontaneously. They were extremely considerate of each other's feelings.... At mealtimes handing food to the neighbor was of greater importance than eating oneself.

Although these youngsters displayed many signs of anxiety and were highly suspicious of outsiders, they eventually established positive relationships with their adult caregivers and acquired a new language during their first year at the centre. The story even has a happy ending, because 35 years later these orphans were leading productive lives as middle-aged adults (Hartup, 1983).

Taken together, Harlow's monkey research and Freud and Dann's observations of their war orphans suggest that parents and peers each contribute something essential but different and perhaps unique to a child's (or monkey's) social development. Regular contacts with sensitive, responsive parents not only permit infants to acquire some basic social interactive skills, but also provide a sense of *security* that enables them to venture out to explore the environment and discover that other people can be interesting companions (Hartup, 1989; Rubin, Bukowski, & Parker, 1998). By contrast, later contacts with peers may allow children to elaborate their basic interactive routines and to develop competent and adaptive patterns of social behaviour with associates who are more or less similar to themselves. Indeed, Harlow's "peer-only" monkeys lacked the security of a mother–infant relationship, perhaps explaining why they clutched at one another, were reluctant to explore, and were terrified by (and aggressive toward) outsiders. But *within their own peer groups*, they developed competent interactive routines and displayed normal patterns of social behaviour (Suomi & Harlow, 1978).

Just how important is it for humans to establish and maintain *harmonious* relations with their peers? Apparently, it is very important. One review of more than 30 studies revealed that youngsters who had been rejected by their peers during elementary school are much more likely than those who had enjoyed good peer relations to drop out of school, become involved in delinquent or criminal activities, and display serious psychological difficulties later in adolescence and young adulthood (Parker & Asher, 1987; Parker et al., 1995; see also Crick, 1996, 1997; Morison & Masten, 1991). So merely having contact with peer associates is not enough to ensure positive developmental outcomes; getting along with peers is important too.

"peer-only" monkeys
monkeys who are separated from their mothers (and other adults) soon after birth and raised with peers

In sum, peers do seem to be meaningful agents of socialization, and the task of becoming *appropriately* sociable with peers is a very important developmental hurdle. In our next section, we will focus on the growth of peer sociability and on some of the factors that influence how appropriately (or inappropriately) sociable a child turns out to be.

The Development of Peer Sociability

Sociability is a term that describes a person's willingness to engage others in social interaction and to seek their attention or approval. In Chapter 11, we learned that even young infants are sociable creatures: Months before forming their first attachments, they are already smiling, cooing, or otherwise trying to attract the attention of caregivers and are likely to protest whenever *any* adult puts them down or walks off and leaves them alone. But would they be so positively disposed to another infant or toddler?

Peer Sociability in Infancy and Toddlerhood

Although babies show an interest in other babies from the first months of life, they do not really *interact* until about the middle of the first year. By then, infants often smile or babble at their tiny companions, vocalize, offer toys, and gesture to one another (Vandell & Mueller, 1995; Vandell, Wilson, & Buchanan, 1980). However, many of these friendly gestures go unnoticed and unreciprocated.

Between 12 and 18 months of age, toddlers begin to react more appropriately to each other's behaviour, often partaking in more complex exchanges in which participants appear to take turns. Here is one example (Mueller & Lucas, 1975, p. 241):

> Larry sits on the floor and Bernie turns and looks toward him. Bernie waves his hand and says "da," still looking at Larry. He repeats the vocalization three more times before Larry laughs, Bernie vocalizes again and Larry laughs again. This same sequence is repeated twelve more times before Bernie … walks off.

Yet there is some question about whether these action/reaction episodes qualify as true social discourse because 12- to 18-month-olds often seem to treat peers as particularly responsive "toys" that they can control by making them look, gesture, smile, and laugh (Brownell, 1986).

By 18 months of age, however, almost all toddlers begin to display *coordinated interactions* with age-mates that are clearly social in character. They now take great delight in *imitating* each other and often gaze and smile at their partners as they turn their imitative sequences into social games (Eckerman & Stein, 1990; Howes & Matheson, 1992). By age 20 to 24 months, toddlers' play has a strong verbal component: Playmates often describe their ongoing play activities to each other ("I fall down!" "Me too, I fall down") or attempt to influence the role that their partner should assume ("You go in playhouse") (Eckerman & Didow, 1996). This coordinated social speech makes it easier for 2- to 2½-year-olds to assume *complementary roles*, such as chaser or chasee in a game of tag, or to cooperate to achieve a shared goal, such as one child operating a handle so the other can retrieve toys from a container (Brownell & Carriger, 1990).

Both social and cognitive developments contribute to the growth of peer sociability over the first two years. In Chapter 11, we learned that toddlers who are securely attached to their caregivers are generally more outgoing and even more "popular" as playmates than those who are insecurely attached, implying that the sensitive, responsive caregiving that securely attached infants receive contributes in a positive way to the development of **social skills**. And 18- to 24-month-olds begin to display truly coordinated, reciprocal interactions at precisely the time that they first recognize themselves in a mirror and can discriminate photographs of themselves from those of peers (see Chapter 12). This may be no accident. Celia Brownell and Michael Carriger (1990) propose that toddlers must first realize that both they and their companions are autonomous causal agents who can make things happen before they are likely to play

sociability
willingness to interact with others and to seek their attention or approval

social skills
thoughts, actions, and emotional regulatory activities that enable children to achieve personal or social goals while maintaining harmony with their social partners

complementary games or try to coordinate their actions to accomplish a goal. Indeed, they found that toddlers who cooperated successfully to achieve a goal scored higher on a test of self–other differentiation than their less cooperative age-mates, thus implying that early interactive skills may depend heavily on social-cognitive development.

Sociability during the Preschool Period

Between the ages of 2 and 5, children not only become more outgoing but also direct their social gestures to a wider audience. Observational studies suggest that 2- to 3-year-olds are more likely than older children to stay near an adult and seek physical affection, whereas the sociable behaviours of 4- to 5-year-olds normally consist of playful bids for attention or approval that are directed at *peers* rather than adults (Harper & Huie, 1985; Hartup, 1983).

As children become more peer oriented, the character of their interactions changes as well. In a classic study, Mildred Parten (1932) observed 2½- to 4-year-olds during free-play periods at nursery school, looking for developmental changes in the *social complexity* of peer interactions. She found that preschoolers' play activities could be divided into four categories, arranged from least to most socially complex:

1. **Nonsocial activity.** Children watch others play or engage in their own solitary play and largely ignore what others are doing.
2. **Parallel play.** Children play side by side but interact very little and do not try to influence the behaviour of other players.
3. **Associative play.** Children now share toys and swap materials, but pursue their own agendas and do not cooperate to achieve shared goals.
4. **Cooperative play.** Children now act out make-believe themes, assume reciprocal roles, and collaborate to achieve shared goals.

As we see in Figure 16.7, solitary and parallel play decline with age, whereas associative and cooperative play become more common. However, all four kinds of play were observed among children of *all* ages, and even a nonsocial activity like solitary play need not be considered "immature" if the child is doing something constructive such as drawing pictures or completing a puzzle (Hartup, 1983). In contrast, Robert Coplan and his colleagues from Carleton University suggest that preschoolers who frequently display

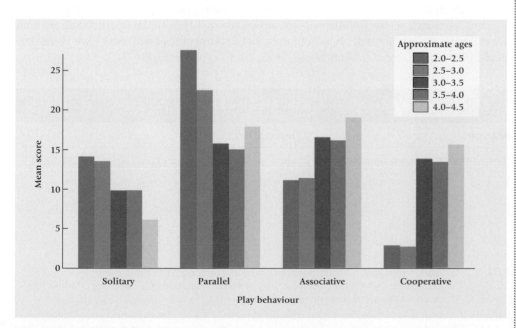

Figure 16.7 *Frequency of activities engaged in by preschool children of different ages. With age, solitary and parallel play occur less frequently, whereas associative and cooperative play occur more frequently.* ADAPTED FROM PARTEN, 1932.

nonsocial activity
onlooker behaviour and solitary play

parallel play
largely noninteractive play in which players are in close proximity but do not often attempt to influence one another

associative play
form of social discourse in which children pursue their own interests but swap toys or comment on one another's activities

cooperative play
true social play in which children cooperate or assume reciprocal roles while pursuing shared goals

PhotoDisc, Inc.

Young adolescents spend more time socializing with their peers than with their parents or siblings. Much time is spent with small numbers of same-sex associates who genuinely like one another and prefer similar activities. These same-sex cliques often evolve into mixed-sex (heterosexual) cliques by mid-adolescence.

a boisterous, physical type of solitary play at preschool may be at risk for academic difficulties and peer rejection even in early childhood (Coplan, Gavinski-Molina, Lagace-Sequin, & Wichman, 2001; Coplan, Wichman, & Lagace-Sequin, 2001).

Could it be, then, that the "maturity" of preschool play depends as much (or more) on its *cognitive complexity* as on its social or nonsocial character? To test this notion, Carolee Howes and Catherine Matheson (1992) conducted a longitudinal study in which the play activities of a group of 1- to 2-year-olds were observed at six-month intervals for three years. They found that play became more and more cognitively complex with age, as described by the six-category sequence in Table 16.4. What's more, there was a clear relationship between the cognitive complexity of a child's play and the child's social competence with peers: Children whose play was more complex at any given age were rated as more outgoing and prosocially inclined and as less aggressive and withdrawn at the next observation period six months later. So it seems that the *cognitive complexity* of a child's play (particularly pretend play) is a reliable predictor of his or her future social competencies with peers (see also Doyle et al., 1992; Rubin, Fein, & Vandenberg, 1983; Rubin et al., 1998).

TABLE 16.4 Changes in Play Activities from Infancy through the Preschool Period		
Play type	**Age of appearance**	**Description**
Parallel play	6–12 months	Two children perform similar activities without paying any attention to each other.
Parallel aware play	By age 1	Children engage in parallel play while occasionally looking at each other or monitoring each other's activities.
Simple pretend play	1–1½ years	Children engage in similar activities while talking, smiling, sharing toys, or otherwise interacting.
Complementary and reciprocal play	1½–2 years	Children display action-based role reversals in social games such as run-and-chase or peekaboo.
Cooperative social pretend play	2½–3 years	Children play complementary *nonliteral*, or "pretend," roles (for example, mummy and baby), but without any planning or discussion about the meaning of these roles or about the form that the play will take.
Complex social pretend play	3½–4 years	Children actively *plan* their pretend play. They name and explicitly assign roles for each player and propose a play script, and may stop playing to modify the script if play breaks down.

SOURCE: Adapted from Howes & Matheson, 1992.

How important are the pretend-play activities of the preschool period? Carolee Howes (1992) claims that they serve at least three crucial developmental functions. First, pretend play helps children master ways of communicating effectively with their social equals. Second, play provides opportunities for younger children to learn to *compromise* as they negotiate the roles they will enact in their play and the rules that guide these pretend episodes. Third, social pretext is a context that permits children to display feelings that may bother them, thereby providing opportunities to better understand their own (or their partner's) emotional crises, to receive social support from (or provide it to) playmates, and to develop a sense of trust and even intimate ties to these associates. So pretend play may be a major contributor to the growth of communication skills, emotional understanding, social perspective taking, and an enhanced capacity for caring. Viewed in this way, it is hardly surprising that preschoolers who are relatively proficient at pretend-play activities tend to be favourably received by their peers (Rubin et al., 1998).

Peer Sociability in Middle Childhood and Adolescence

Peer interactions become increasingly sophisticated throughout the elementary-school years. Not only do cooperative forms of complex pretend play become more commonplace, but by ages 6 to 10 children are becoming enthusiastic participants in games (such as T-ball and *Monopoly*) that are governed by formal sets of rules (Hartup, 1983; Piaget, 1965).

Another very noticeable way that peer interactions change during middle childhood is that contacts among 6- to 10-year-olds more often occur in true **peer groups**. When psychologists talk about peer groups, they are referring not merely to a collection of playmates but, rather, to a true confederation that (1) interacts on a regular basis; (2) defines a sense of belonging; (3) formulates its own *norms* that specify how members are supposed to dress, think, and behave; and (4) develops a structure or hierarchical organization (for example, leader and other roles) that enables group members to work together to accomplish shared goals. Furthermore, elementary-school children clearly *identify* with their groups: being a Brownie, a Scout, or a member of a team is often a source of great personal pride. So between ages 6 and 10, children expose themselves to a potent social context—the *peer group*—in which they are likely to discover the value of teamwork, develop a sense of commitment and loyalty to shared goals, and learn a number of other important lessons about how social organizations pursue their objectives (Hartup, 1983; Sherif et al., 1961).

By early adolescence, youngsters spend more time with peers, particularly with small groups of close friends known as **cliques**, than with parents, siblings, or any other agent of socialization (Berndt, 1996; Larson & Richards, 1991). Early peer cliques usually consist of four to eight *same-sex* members who share similar values and activity preferences, but by mid-adolescence boy cliques and girl cliques begin to interact more frequently, eventually forming *heterosexual cliques* (Dunphy, 1963; Richards et al., 1998). Once formed, cliques often develop distinct and colourful dress codes, dialects, and behaviours that set them apart and help members establish a firm sense of belongingness, or a group identity (Cairns et al., 1995).

Often, several cliques with similar norms and values coalesce into larger, more loosely organized aggregations known as **crowds** (Connolly, Furman, & Konarski, 2000). Crowds do not replace cliques; membership in a crowd is based on reputation, and individual members within a particular clique may even belong to different crowds (Urberg et al., 1995). Crowds are defined by the attitudes and activities their members share, and they come into play mainly as a mechanism for defining an adolescent's niche within the larger social structure of a high school and, occasionally, for organizing such social activities as parties, trips to the football game, and so on. The names may vary, but most schools have crowds of "brains," "populars," "jocks," "partyers," "grungers," and "burnouts," each consisting of a loose aggregation of cliques that are similar to one another in some fundamental way and different from adolescents in other crowds (Brown et al., 1993; Brown & Lohr, 1987). And everyone in the high school seems to recognize these differences: "[The brains] all wear glasses and 'kiss up' to teachers" (Brown et al., 1994, p. 128); "the partyers goof off a lot more than the jocks do, but they don't come to school stoned like the burnouts do" (p. 133).

peer group
confederation of peers that interacts regularly, defines membership in the group, and formulates norms that specify how members are supposed to look, think, and act

clique
small group of friends that interacts frequently

crowd
large, loosely organized peer group made up of several cliques that share similar norms, interests, and values

Not only do cliques and crowds permit adolescents to express their values and try out new roles as they begin their quest to forge an identity apart from their families, but they also pave the way for the establishment of romantic relationships (Brown, 1990; Connolly et al., 2000; Dunphy, 1963). Gender segregation usually breaks down early in adolescence as members of boys' and girls' cliques begin to interact. Same-sex cliques provide what amounts to a secure base for exploring ways to behave with members of the other sex; talking to girls when your buddies are there is far less threatening than doing so on your own. And as heterosexual cliques and crowds take shape, adolescents are likely to have many opportunities to get to know members of the other sex in casual social situations without having to be intimate. Eventually, strong cross-sex friendships develop and couples form, often double-dating or spending time with a small number of other couples (Feiring, 1996). From this point on, crowds often begin to disintegrate, having served their purposes of helping adolescents to establish a social identity and bringing the boys and girls together (Brown, 1990; Dunphy, 1963).

Parental Effects on Peer Sociability

Some children are drawn to peers and seem to thrive on social interaction, whereas others appear rather unsociable or even withdrawn. Although we learned in Chapter 11 that sociability is influenced to some extent by one's genotype, it is also clear that the path to positive or negative peer relations often begins at home and that parents may either foster or inhibit peer sociability.

PROMOTING PEER CONTACTS. There are many ways in which parents influence the sheer amount of contact their children have with peers. Their choice of a residence is one such influence: A decision to live in a neighbourhood with widely spaced homes and few available playgrounds or playmates could seriously restrict access to peers. When young children cannot easily get together on their own, their contact with peers depends heavily on whether their parents serve as "booking agents" for peer interaction—whether parents arrange visits with playmates, enrol their children in daycare or nursery school, or encourage their participation in other organized activities for children (Hart et al., 1997; Parke & Kellum, 1994). As we noted earlier in Box 16.1, children who receive good daycare or attend nursery schools that emphasize a social curriculum tend to develop social skills at an earlier age than those who remain at home. Why? One reason is that children often develop secure attachments to preschool teachers, which foster positive working models of other people that help them to establish close friendships with preschool peers (Howes, Hamilton, & Philipsen, 1998). Children may also become more outgoing with daycare or nursery-school classmates because they have gotten to know them better. Indeed, preschoolers' play is much more cooperative, complex, and socially skilled among familiar companions than among strangers (Brody et al., 1983; Doyle, Connolly, & Rivest, 1980; Harper & Huie, 1985).

MONITORING AND CONTROLLING PLAY ACTIVITIES. Of course, parents who arrange home visits with peer playmates are also in a position to influence their child by monitoring his or her peer interactions to ensure that play proceeds smoothly and amiably, without major conflicts. This brings us to an interesting issue.

Should parents closely monitor or intrude on playful interactions between young children? Gary Ladd and Beckie Golter (1988) attempted to answer this question by asking parents of preschool children how they had supervised any recent interactions that their child had had with peers at home. Some parents reported that they had closely watched over the children or had even participated in their play activities (direct monitoring), whereas others said they had checked occasionally on the children without often intruding or becoming involved as a playmate (indirect monitoring). Which form of monitoring is associated with successful and harmonious peer interactions? Ladd and Golter's findings clearly favour indirect parental monitoring. As we see in Figure 16.8, preschoolers whose parents had indirectly monitored their peer interactions were much better liked (and less often disliked) by their nursery-school classmates than those whose parents closely monitored and often intruded on their play activities.

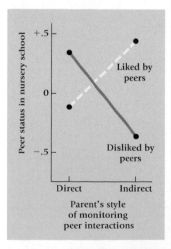

Figure 16.8 Nursery-school children enjoy a more favourable status with peers when parents have indirectly monitored their interactions with playmates.
BASED ON LADD & GOLTER, 1988.

Interestingly, mothers who believe that their children are not very socially skilled are most likely to intrude on their children's play activities—a finding that implies that conflictual peer interactions may promote direct monitoring rather than the other way around (Mize, Pettit, & Brown, 1995). Nevertheless, the quality of monitoring and intervention that parents provide clearly matters. If a parent's coaching is positive, supportive and optimistic, and focuses heavily on prosocial strategies, the child is likely to develop a strong prosocial orientation that fosters positive relationships with peers (Clark & Ladd, 2000; Mize & Pettit, 1997). By contrast, parents who become agitated and angry and who issue commands rather than seek constructive solutions usually elicit negative responses from their children, who continue to display poor social skills and conflictual peer interactions (Carson & Parke, 1996; Isley et al., 1999). Not surprisingly, negative, controlling parents who are constantly barking orders, and failing to suppress their own negative affect tend to have children who are also poor at regulating negative emotions—and poor emotional regulation is a strong correlate of nonharmonious peer interactions (Fabes et al., 1999; Pope & Bierman, 1999). What's more, these parents may also inhibit sociability by teaching their children to be bossy and dictatorial themselves, a style that elicits negative reactions from playmates, which may convince a child that contacts with peers are not all that pleasant (Kochanska, 1992; MacKinnon-Lewis, Rabiner, & Starnes, 1999).

In sum, parents of appropriately sociable preschool children tend to be warm, accepting companions who (1) indirectly monitor their children's interactions with peers to ensure that they comply with rules of social etiquette while (2) allowing children considerable freedom to structure their own play activities and resolve minor disputes on their own (Ladd & Hart, 1992). Clearly, this pattern of warmth, sensitivity, and moderate control sounds very much like the *authoritative* pattern of child-rearing that we have commented on favourably throughout the text—a pattern that is consistently associated with children's socially skilled behaviours and acceptance by peers (Baumrind, 1971; Hinshaw et al., 1997; Mize & Pettit, 1997). By contrast, highly authoritarian (or uninvolved) parents who rely heavily on power assertion as a control tactic tend to raise youngsters who are often aggressive or otherwise socially unskilled when interacting with other children and are likely to be *rejected* by peers (Dekovic & Janssens, 1992; Hart et al., 1998; MacKinnon-Lewis et al., 1994). Clearly, there is ample evidence that the path to positive (or negative) peer interactions often begins at home.

Peer Acceptance and Popularity

Perhaps no other aspect of children's social lives has received more attention than **peer acceptance**: the extent to which a child is viewed by peers as a worthy or likable companion. Typically, researchers assess peer acceptance through self-report instruments called **sociometric techniques**. In a sociometric survey, children might be asked to nominate several classmates whom they like and several whom they dislike, or they may be asked to rate each of their classmates with respect to his or her desirability as a social companion (Terry & Coie, 1991). Even 3- to 5-year-olds can respond appropriately to sociometric surveys (Denham et al., 1990), and according to Shelley Hymel (1983) from the University of British Columbia, the choices (or ratings) that children provide correspond reasonably well to teacher ratings of peer popularity, thus suggesting that sociometric surveys provide *valid* assessments of children's social standing in their peer groups.

When sociometric data are analyzed, it is usually possible to classify each child into one of the following categories: **popular children**, who are liked by many peers and disliked by few; **rejected children**, who are disliked by many peers and liked by a few; **neglected children**, who receive very few nominations as a liked or a disliked companion and who seem almost invisible to their peers; and **controversial children**, who are liked by many peers but disliked by many others. Together, these four types of children make up about two-thirds of the pupils in a typical elementary-school classroom; the remaining one-third are **average-status children**, who are liked or disliked by a moderate number of peers (Coie, Dodge, & Coppotelli, 1982).

peer acceptance
measure of a person's likability (or dislikability) in the eyes of peers

sociometric techniques
procedures that ask children to identify those peers whom they like or dislike or to rate peers for their desirability as companions; used to measure children's peer acceptance (or nonacceptance)

popular children
children who are liked by many peers and disliked by very few

rejected children
children who are disliked by many peers and liked by few

neglected children
children who receive few nominations by peers as either a liked or a disliked individual

controversial children
children who receive many nominations by peers as a liked individual and many as a disliked individual

average-status children
children who receive a moderate number of nominations by peers as a liked or a disliked individual

Notice that both neglected children and rejected children are low in acceptance and are not well received by their peers. Yet it is not nearly so bad to be ignored by other children as to be rejected by them. Neglectees do not feel as lonely as rejectees do (Cassidy & Asher, 1992; Crick & Ladd, 1993), and they are much more likely than rejected children to eventually attain a more favourable sociometric status should they enter a new class at school or a new play group (Coie & Dodge, 1983). Furthermore, rejected children are the ones who face the greater risk of displaying deviant, antisocial behaviour and other serious adjustment problems later in life (Asher & Coie, 1990; Morison & Masten, 1991; Parker & Asher, 1987; Rubin et al., 1998).

Why Are Children Accepted, Neglected, or Rejected by Peers?

At several points throughout the text, we have discussed factors that seem to contribute to children's popularity with peers. By way of brief review:

Parenting styles. Warm, sensitive, and authoritative parents who rely on reasoning rather than power to guide and control children's conduct tend to raise youngsters who are *liked* by adults and peers. By contrast, highly authoritarian or uninvolved parents who rely heavily on power assertion as a control tactic often have youngsters who are surly, uncooperative, and aggressive, and are actively *disliked* by peers.

Temperamental characteristics. Certain aspects of children's temperaments are correlated with and undoubtedly contribute to their sociometric status. For example, we learned in Chapter 11 that difficult children who are often irritable and impulsive are at risk for having nonharmonious interactions with peers that could cause them to become rejected. In addition, relatively passive children who are behaviourally inhibited or slow to warm up are at risk (in Western societies at least) of being neglected or even rejected by peers.

Cognitive skills. Research by Lucy LeMare of Simon Fraser University and Kenneth Rubin of the University of Maryland suggests that popular children tend to have well-developed role-taking skills (LeMare & Rubin, 1987). Popular, average-status, and neglected youngsters also tend to perform better academically and score higher on IQ tests than rejected children and adolescents do, according to William Bukowski of Concordia University (Bukowski et al., 1993), Xinyin Chen of the University of Western Ontario (Chen, Rubin, & Li, 1997), and their associates (see also Wentzel & Asher, 1995).

At least two additional characteristics seem to reliably predict children's standing among their peers: their physical attractiveness (particularly facial attractiveness) and their patterns of interpersonal behaviour.

Facial attractiveness. Despite the maxim that "beauty is only skin deep," many of us seem to think otherwise. Even 6-month-old infants can easily discriminate attractive from unattractive faces (Langlois et al., 1991), and 12-month-old infants already prefer to interact with attractive rather than unattractive strangers (Langlois, Roggman, & Rieser-Danner, 1990). By the preschool period, attractive youngsters are often described in more favourable ways (i.e., friendlier, smarter) than their less attractive classmates by both teachers and peers (Adams & Crane, 1980; Langlois, 1986), and attractive children are generally more popular than unattractive children from elementary school onward (Langlois, 1986). This link between facial attractiveness and peer acceptance even begins to make some sense when we consider how attractive and unattractive children interact with their playmates. Although attractive and unattractive 3-year-olds do not yet differ a great deal in the character of their social behaviours, by age 5, unattractive youngsters are more likely than attractive ones to be active and boisterous during play sessions and to respond aggressively toward peers (Langlois & Downs, 1979). So unattractive children seem to develop patterns of social interaction that could alienate other children.

Why might this happen? Some theorists have argued that parents, teachers, and other children may contribute to a self-fulfilling prophecy by subtly (or not so subtly) communicating their expectations to attractive youngsters, letting them know that they are smart and are supposed to do well in school, behave pleasantly, and be likable. Information of this sort undoubtedly has an effect on children: Attractive youngsters may become progressively more confident, friendly, and outgoing; whereas unattractive children may resent the less favourable feedback that they receive and become more defiant and aggressive. This is precisely how a "beautiful is good" stereotype could become a reality (Langlois & Downs, 1979).

BEHAVIOURAL CONTRIBUTORS. Although one's physical characteristics and cognitive, scholastic, and athletic prowess are all meaningfully related to peer acceptance, even the brightest and most attractive children may be unpopular if peers consider their behaviour inappropriate or antisocial (Dodge, 1983). What behavioural characteristics are most important in influencing a child's standing with peers?

Several studies of preschool, elementary, and middle school (young adolescent) children report pretty much the same findings. *Popular* children are observed to be relatively calm, outgoing, friendly, and supportive companions who can successfully initiate and maintain interactions and resolve disputes amicably (Coie, Dodge, & Kupersmidt, 1990; Denham et al., 1990; Ladd, Price, & Hart, 1988). Stated another way, these "sociometric stars" are warm, cooperative, and compassionate individuals who display many prosocial behaviours and are seldom disruptive or aggressive (Chen et al., 2000; Newcomb, Bukowski, & Pattee, 1993; Rubin et al., 1998).

Neglected children, by contrast, often appear shy or withdrawn. They are not very talkative, they make fewer attempts than children of average status to enter play groups, and they seldom call attention to themselves (Coie et al., 1990; Harrist et al., 1997). Nevertheless, these "neglectees" are no less socially skilled than children of average status, nor are they any more lonely or more distressed about the character of their social relationships (Cassidy & Asher, 1992; Wentzel & Asher, 1995). According to Alastair Younger at the University of Ottawa and Tina Daniels at Carleton University (1992), the withdrawn behaviour of neglected children appears to stem more from their own social anxieties and their belief that they are not socially skilled than from any active ostracism or exclusion by their peer groups (see also Cassidy & Asher, 1992).

There are at least two kinds, or categories, of *rejected* children, each with a distinct behavioural profile. **Rejected-aggressive children** often alienate peers by using forceful *proactive* means to dominate them or their resources. These disruptive braggarts tend to be uncooperative and critical of peer-group activities and display very low levels of prosocial behaviour (Newcomb et al., 1993; Parkhurst & Asher, 1992). Rejected-aggressive children clearly overestimate their social standing, often saying that they are liked just as well as, or better than, most children (Zakriski & Coie, 1996). These are the youngsters who display the greatest risk of becoming chronically hostile and displaying externalizing conduct disorders and even committing criminal acts of violence later in adolescence and adulthood (Crick & Ladd, 1993; Parker & Asher, 1987; Rubin et al., 1998).

Rejected-withdrawn children, on the other hand, are typically socially awkward companions who display many unusual, immature behaviours, are insensitive to peer-group expectations, and may become hostile and *react* aggressively to any criticism by peers. Unlike rejected-aggressive children, they are well aware that other children do not like them and eventually begin to withdraw as peers actively exclude them from their activities (Harrist et al., 1997; Hymel, Bowker, & Woody, 1993; Zakriski & Coie, 1996). These withdrawn rejectees feel especially lonely and are at risk of experiencing low self-esteem, depression, and other internalizing disorders (Hymel et al., 1993; Rabiner, Keane, & MacKinnon-Lewis, 1993). And because of their unusual behaviours, hypersensitivity to criticism, and lack of close friends to stick up for them, they are particularly inviting targets for abuse at the hands of bullies (Hodges, Malone, & Perry, 1997; Parkhurst & Asher, 1992).

Do popular children become popular because they are friendly, cooperative, and nonaggressive? Or is it that children become friendlier, more cooperative, and less aggressive after achieving their popularity? One way to test these competing hypotheses is to

rejected-aggressive children
subgroup of rejected children who display high levels of hostility and aggression in their interactions with peers

rejected-withdrawn children
subgroup of rejected children who are often passive, socially unskilled, and insensitive to peer-group expectations

put children in play groups with *unfamiliar* peers and then see whether the behaviours they display predict their eventual status in the peer group. Several studies of this type have been conducted (Coie & Kupersmidt, 1983; Dodge, 1983; Dodge et al., 1990; Ladd, Price, & Hart, 1988; Ladd, Birch, & Buhs, 1999), and the results are reasonably consistent: The patterns of behaviour that children display predict the statuses they achieve with their peers. Children who are ultimately accepted by unfamiliar peers are effective at initiating social interactions and at responding positively to others' bids for attention. When they want to join a group activity, for example, these socially skilled, *soon-to-be-accepted* children first watch and attempt to understand what is going on, and then comment constructively about the proceedings as they blend smoothly into the group. By contrast, children who are ultimately *rejected* are pushy and self-serving; they often criticize or disrupt group activities and may even threaten reprisals if they are not allowed to join in. Other children who end up being *neglected* by their peers tend to hover around the edges of a group, initiating few interactions and shying away from other children's bids for attention.

In sum, peer popularity is affected by many factors. It may help to have a pleasant temperament, an attractive face and academic skills, but it is even more important to display good social-cognitive skills and to behave in socially competent ways. Definitions of desirable social behaviour, of course, may vary from culture to culture and change over time. In Box 11.1, for example, we learned that a socially reserved demeanour, which may undermine one's popularity in Western societies, actually promotes peer acceptance in China, where being quiet and reserved are more socially desirable traits. The ingredients of popularity also change with age: According to William Bukowski of Concordia University, Lorrie Sippola of the University of Saskatchewan, and Andrew Newcomb of University of Richmond, although aggression is generally associated with unfavourable peer status at any age, during preadolescence and early adolescence at least *some* "tough" boys who view themselves as cool, popular, and antisocial do become popular with male classmates and attractive to girls (Bukowski, Sippola, & Newcomb, 2000; see also Rodkin et al., 2000). See Box 16.4 for more information. What's more, establishing close relationships with members of the opposite sex suddenly enhances popularity during adolescence, whereas frequent consorting with "the enemy" violates norms of gender segregation during childhood and *detracts* from one's popularity (Kovacs, Parker, & Hoffman, 1996; Sroufe et al., 1993). In short, contextual factors influence who is popular and who is not.

THE INSIDE TRACK

16.4

William Bukowski

William Bukowski is a Professor in the Department of Psychology and Centre for Research in Human Development at Concordia University, Montreal. His research interests concern peer relations, especially in ways that peer relations (a) contribute to children's emotional and social development, and (b) affect their adjustment during adolescence.

Is aggression always related to peer rejection? Work by William Bukowski suggests that it is not (see Bukowski, 2003). For example, one study by Bukowski and his colleagues (Bukowski, Sippola, & Newcomb, 2000) examined the features (e.g., sex, age, aggression, emotional sensitivity, school competence) of same and other-sex peers to whom early adolescents were attracted. Early adolescents completed questionnaires over three time periods, in Grades 5, 6, and 7. The most important findings of the study were that as early adolescents grew older and entered middle school (Grades 6 and 7), they tended to be attracted to peers who stood out in the peer group in easily observable ways. Girls in particular were attracted to aggressive boys. In contrast, at all three assessment periods, girls showed little attraction to aggressive girls. Clearly, girls saw aggression as an undesirable feature in other girls but became more tolerant of aggression in boys following the transition to middle school. In fact, attraction to peers who presented features associated with good classroom-based behaviour decreased over time. It may be that the more aggressive boys appear more "adult-like" than other boys their age, and hence, that makes them more attractive to girls who are entering a maturity gap (Moffitt, 1993) in which they begin to evidence biological maturity but have not yet achieved full adult status.

William Bukowski

Unfortunately, children who are rejected by peers are likely to retain their rejected status from grade to grade and are at risk of experiencing some (or all) of the adjustment problems associated with peer rejection (Brendgen et al., 2001; Cillessen et al., 1992; Coie et al., 1990). In Box 16.5, we will examine some of the programs that have helped rejected children to improve their social skills and their prospects for experiencing healthier psychological outcomes.

Children and Their Friends

As young children become more outgoing and are exposed to a wider variety of peers, they typically form close ties to one or more playmates—bonds that we call **friendships**. Recall from Chapter 12 that children have some pretty firm ideas about what qualifies someone as a friend. Before age 8, the principal basis for friendship is *common activity:* Children view a friend as someone who likes them and who enjoys similar kinds of play activities. By contrast, 8- to 10-year-olds, equipped with more sophisticated social perspective-taking skills, begin to see friends as individuals who are *psychologically similar* and who can be trusted to be loyal, kind, cooperative, and sensitive to each other's feelings and needs (Berndt, 1989; Pataki, Shapiro, & Clark, 1994). And although adolescents continue to think that loyalty and shared psychological attributes are characteristics that friends display, their conceptions of friendship now focus more on *reciprocal emotional commitments*. That is, friends are viewed as *intimate* associates who truly understand each other's strengths and accept each other's weaknesses and are willing to share their innermost thoughts and feelings (Hartup, 1996).

Social Interactions among Friends and Acquaintances

As early as age 1 to 2, children may become attached to a preferred play partner and respond very differently to this "friend" than to other playmates. For example, friends display more advanced forms of pretend play, more affection, and more approval than acquaintances do (Howes, Droege, & Matheson, 1994; Whaley & Rubenstein, 1994). Friends often do nice things for each other, and many altruistic behaviours may first appear within these early alliances of the preschool era. Frederick Kanfer and his associates (1981), for example, found that 3- to 6-year-olds were generally willing to give up their own valuable play time to perform a dull task if their efforts would benefit a friend, yet this same kind of self-sacrifice was almost never made for a mere acquaintance. Similarly, Lynne Zarbatany and associates from the University of Western Ontario found that fifth-graders were more likely to sacrifice winning a large prize if it would mean helping a friend rather than helping a nonfriend (Zarbatany et al., 1996). Young children also express more sympathy in response to the distress of a friend than to that of an acquaintance, and they are more inclined to try to relieve the friend's distress (Costin & Jones, 1992; Farver & Branstetter, 1994).

It is often said that there is a "chemistry" to close friendships and that best friends seem to be "in tune with each other." Research clearly supports this notion. Casual conversations among pairs of sixth-graders are much more cheerful, playful, and relaxed when the members of these pairings are good friends rather than mere acquaintances (Field et al., 1992). In fact, a measure of participants' saliva cortisol levels (a physiological correlate of stress) taken after the conversations suggested that casual interactions between acquaintances are more stressful than those between friends. Even when collaborating on school assignments, friends tend to be more "in synch," agreeing more readily with each other and spending more time "on task" than collaborating acquaintances do (Hartup, 1996). One reason why interactions among friends may be so synchronous and productive is that friends are more similar than acquaintances are in personality and their levels of prosocial behaviour (Haselager et al., 1998). So, contacts between friends are often characterized by a sense of mutuality and positive affect and do have a favourable chemistry about them.

friendship
close and often enduring relationship between two individuals that may be characterized by loyalty and mutual affection

On Improving the Social Skills of Unpopular Children

The finding that peer rejection is a strong predictor of current and future psychological difficulties has prompted many investigators to devise interventions aimed at improving the social skills of unpopular children. Here are some of the more effective techniques.

Reinforcement and Modelling Therapies

Many early approaches to social-skills training were based on learning theory and involved (1) reinforcing children (with tokens or praise) for displaying such socially appropriate behaviours as cooperation and sharing, or (2) exposing children to social models who displayed a variety of socially skilled acts. Both approaches have been successful at increasing the frequency of children's socially skilled behaviours. And when teachers and peers participate in the intervention, they are much more likely to notice changes in the rejected child's behaviour and are more inclined to change their opinion of him or her (Bierman & Furman, 1984; White & Kistner, 1992). Similarly, some modelling therapies are more effective than others. Modelling programs work best when the model is similar to the target child and when his socially skillful actions are accompanied by some form of commentary that directs the child's attention to the purposes and benefits of behaving appropriately toward peers (Asher, Renshaw, & Hymel, 1982).

Cognitive Approaches to Social-Skills Training

The fact that modelling strategies work better when accompanied by verbal rationales and explanations implies that interventions that prompt the child to think about or imagine the consequences of various social overtures are likely to be effective. Why? Because the child's active cognitive involvement in the social-skills training may increase her understanding and appreciation of the principles that are taught, thereby persuading her to internalize and then rely on these lessons when interacting with peers.

Coaching is a cognitive social learning technique in which the therapist displays one or more social skills, carefully explains the rationales for using them, allows children to practise such behaviour, and then suggests how the children might improve on their performances. Sherri Oden and Steven Asher (1977) coached third and fourth grade social isolates on four important skills: how to participate in play activities, how to take turns and share, how to communicate effectively, and how to give attention and help to peers. Not only did the children who were coached become more outgoing and positive, but follow-up measures a year later revealed that these former isolates had achieved even further gains in social status (see also Bierman, 1986; Mize & Ladd, 1990; Schneider, 1992).

Other cognitive interventions, firmly grounded in cognitive-developmental theory, include attempts to improve children's role-taking skills and social problem-solving abilities (Chandler, 1973; Rabiner, Lenhart, & Lochman, 1990). These techniques can be especially effective with rejected-aggressive children, who often display a hostile attributional bias (a tendency to overattribute hostile intentions to their companions) that has been acquired at home from coercive parents who mistrust other people and endorse aggression (Keane, Brown, & Crenshaw, 1990; Pettit, Dodge, & Brown, 1988). In order to help these aggressive rejectees, the training must not only emphasize that aggression is inappropriate but also demonstrate ways to generate nonaggressive solutions to conflict. One approach that looks promising is the **social problem-solving training** that Myrna Shure and George Spivack (1978; Shure, 1989) devised to help preschoolers generate and then evaluate amicable solutions to interpersonal problems. Over a 10-week period, children role-played conflict scenarios with puppets and were encouraged to discuss the impact of their solutions on the feelings of all parties involved in a conflict. Shure and Spivack found that fewer aggressive solutions were offered the longer the children had participated in the program. Furthermore, the children's classroom adjustment (as rated by teachers) improved as they became better able to think through the social consequences of their own actions.

Academic-Skills Training

Children who are failing miserably at school are often rejected by their classmates (Dishion, Andrews, & Crosby, 1995). Might we elevate their social status by improving their academic skills and bringing them back into the mainstream of school activities? One research team tried this approach, providing extensive academic-skills training to low-achieving, socially rejected fourth-grade students (Coie & Krehbiel, 1984). This training not only improved the children's reading and math achievement but also their social standing. One year after the intervention ended, these former rejectees enjoyed average status in their peer group.

So adults might rely on a variety of techniques to improve the social skills of unpopular children and help them establish a more favourable standing among their peers. Yet a caution is in order, because the long-term success of any intervention could easily be compromised if the new social skills and problem-solving strategies that children have acquired are likely to be undermined by coercive, mistrusting parents who endorse aggressive solutions to conflict or by highly aggressive friends. For these reasons, Gregory Pettit and his associates (1988) favour preventive therapies that are undertaken (1) as soon as a child's problems with peers become apparent and (2) are not limited solely to groups of problem children. Unfortunately, programs that centre exclusively on groups of 11- to 16-year-old aggressive, antisocial rejectees, with no involvement of parents or more accepted peers, actually seem to backfire: Participants show little change in their peer status and often display increases in problem behaviours and delinquent conduct (Dishion, McCord, & Poulin, 1999). So social-skills training programs are most effective when they are undertaken early, before rejected youngsters band together into deviant peer cliques that encourage antisocial conduct (Dishion et al., 1999; Kazdin, 1995).

How long do children's friendships last? It may surprise you to learn that even preschool friendships can be highly stable. Carollee Howes (1988), for example, found that children who attend the same daycare centre for several years often keep the same close friends for more than a year. Although they may wax and wane in strength, close friendships often remain stable from year to year during middle childhood (Berndt & Hoyle, 1985; Cairns et al., 1995). However, friendship networks (the list of *all* individuals that a child might nominate as "friends") tend to shrink in size as children approach adolescence (Berndt, Hawkins, & Hoyle, 1986; Berndt & Hoyle, 1985). This loss of friends may simply reflect the young adolescent's growing awareness that the obligations of friendship, which now include exchanging intimate information and providing emotional support, are easier to live up to if one selects a smaller circle of very close friends.

Are There Distinct Advantages to Having Friends?

Do friends play a unique role in shaping a child's development? Do children who have established adequate peer relations but no close friends turn out any differently from those who have one or more of these special companions? Although few well-controlled longitudinal studies needed to answer these questions have yet been conducted (Hartup, 1996), we can draw some tentative conclusions about the roles that friends play as socializing agents. In addition, see Box 16.6 for a summary of current research conducted by Xinyin Chen of the University of Western Ontario examining the relationship between friendship and psychosocial adjustment with Chinese adolescents.

FRIENDS AS PROVIDERS OF SECURITY AND SOCIAL SUPPORT. One strong clue that friends play an important role in children's lives is the finding that having at least one supportive friend can go a long way toward reducing the loneliness and victimization of unpopular children who are excluded from the larger peer group (Hodges et al., 1999; Parker & Asher, 1993; Schwartz et al., 2000). A close relationship with one or more friends may provide an emotional safety net, a kind of security that not only helps children to deal more constructively with new challenges but may also make almost any other form of life stress (for example, coping with a divorce or with a rejecting parent) a little easier to bear (Bagwell, Newcomb, & Bukowski, 1998). Indeed, Gary Ladd and his associates (1987, 1997) found that children who enter kindergarten along with their friends seem to like school better and have fewer adjustment problems than those who enter school without many friends. Furthermore, we saw in Chapter 15 that

coaching
method of social-skills training in which an adult displays and explains various socially skilled behaviours, allows the child to practise them, and provides feedback aimed at improving the child's performances

social problem-solving training
method of social-skills training in which an adult helps children (through role playing or role-taking training) to make less hostile attributions about harmdoing and to generate nonaggressive solutions to conflict

---

THE INSIDE TRACK

16.6

Xinyin Chen

Xinyin Chen works in the Department of Psychology at the University of Western Ontario. His research interests include socio-emotional development, children's peer relationships and groups, and family interactions. He also is interested in children's psychopathological functions, including externalizing and internalizing problems such as acting-out and depression.

Xinyin Chen and his colleagues have conducted a series of cross-cultural, longitudinal projects concerning socialization and development in Chinese and Canadian children. The projects have focused mainly on cultural differences in early socio-emotional functioning, such as inhibition and self-regulation, and parenting beliefs and practices (e.g., Chen et al., 1998, 2003). In some recent

multi-cultural projects, Chen and his colleagues (e.g., Chen, Chang, & He, 2003; Chen et al., in press) have investigated the nature, quality, and functions of friendship and peer group networks in Brazilian, Canadian, Chinese, Cuban, and Italian children and adolescents. They have found that Canadian children and adolescents have more mutual friendships than their counterparts in other cultures, a finding consistent with the emphasis on peer relationships in North America. Across cultures, children who have mutual friends appear to be more competent and better adjusted than children who do not. Moreover, children with mutual friends in different cultures are largely similar on social functioning and adjustment. However, children without friends appear to display different characteristics across cultures. Children who are academically poor in China, shy in Brazil and Canada, and emotionally inactive or distressed in Italy tend to have more difficulties with psychological adjustment and in establishing and maintaining social relationships.

children who respond most constructively to their parents' divorce are often those who have the support of friends, particularly those whose parents are also divorced. Close, supportive friendships play an especially important role in promoting the social competencies and self-esteem of children from nonnurturant, noncohesive families, and if youngsters from such nonsupportive family environments lose a particularly close friend, they often experience sizable declines in their feelings of self-worth (Gauze et al., 1996).

So friends are potentially important sources of security and **social support**, and they become increasingly important in fulfilling this role as children grow older. Fourth-graders, for example, say that their parents are their primary sources of social support; however, friends are perceived to be (1) as supportive as parents by seventh-graders and (2) the most frequent providers of social support by tenth-grade adolescents (Furman & Buhrmester, 1992).

FRIENDS AS CONTRIBUTORS TO SOCIAL PROBLEM-SOLVING SKILLS. Because friendships are usually described as pleasant and rewarding relationships that are worth preserving, children should be highly motivated to resolve any conflicts with these special companions (Hartup, 1996). And apparently they are: Even during the preschool period, disagreeing friends are more likely than disagreeing acquaintances to step away before the squabbles become intense, to make concessions by accepting equal outcomes, and to continue playing together after the conflict is over (Hartup et al., 1988; Laursen, Hartup, & Koplas, 1996). By middle childhood, friends are much more inclined than acquaintances are to follow the rules (and not cheat) while playing competitive games and to respect the opinions, needs, and wishes of their partner while negotiating to settle a dispute (Fonzi et al., 1997; Nelson & Aboud, 1985). These experiences at amicably resolving conflicts with a friend are undoubtedly important contributors to the growth of mature social problem-solving skills—one of the strongest predictors of a healthy sociometric status with peers (Rubin et al., 1998).

FRIENDSHIPS AS PREPARATION FOR ADULT LOVE RELATIONSHIPS. We've seen that *close* friendships are characterized by increasing intimacy and mutuality from middle childhood through adolescence. Could these relatively intense and intimate ties to what are overwhelmingly *same-sex* companions be necessary for the development of the deep interpersonal sensitivity and commitment so often observed in stable adult love relationships? Harry Stack Sullivan (1953) thought so. Sullivan reported that many of his lonely, mentally depressed patients had failed to form close friendships when they were young, and he concluded that the close bonds that develop between same-sex friends (or "chums") during preadolescence provide the foundation of caring and compassion that a person needs to establish and maintain intimate love relationships later in life. Consistent with Sullivan's ideas, young adolescents who have established *intimate* same-sex friendships are more likely than their friendless age-mates to have broken through the gender segregation barrier and begun to forge closer ties with members of the opposite sex (Connolly, Furman, & Konarski, 2000; George & Hartmann, 1996).

However, a stronger test of Sullivan's theory would require a longitudinal **prospective study** to determine whether preadolescents who are friendless really do turn out any different as adults from age-mates who have at least one close chum. Bagwell, Newcomb, and Bukowski (1998) recently tested the importance of "chumships" and generated conclusions that support Sullivan's ideas. For more information about this research, see Box 16.7.

social support
tangible and intangible resources provided by other people in times of uncertainty or stress

prospective study
study in which the suspected causes or contributors to a developmental outcome are assessed earlier to see if they accurately forecast the developments they are presumed to influence

PhotoDisc, Inc.

Sometimes nothing is as reassuring as the affection and encouragement of a friend.

Quality of Friendships and Adjustment

There is one more point, and it is an important one. Friendships clearly differ in quality, and the very children who tend to have poor social skills—those who are insecurely attached to their parents, who have highly controlling or uninvolved parents, or who are rejected by peers—also tend to have friendships that are unsupportive and lacking in trust (Dishion et al., 1995, 1999; Kerns, Klepec, & Cole, 1996; Lieberman, Doyle, & Markiewicz, 1999; Parker & Asher, 1993). Does the *quality* of a child's friendships influence his or her adjustment and developmental outcomes?

Apparently so. Studies of both kindergartners (Ladd, Kochenderfer, & Coleman, 1996) and seventh- and eighth-grade preadolescents (Berndt & Keefe, 1995) reveal that children who entered a school year with close, supportive friendships typically showed an increase in their liking for or involvement with school, whereas students whose friendships were more rivalrous and conflictual displayed poorer attitudes toward school, often becoming less engaged in scholastic activities and increasingly disruptive. And it seems that only when friendships *are* close and supportive do they foster the social competencies and self-esteem of children from nonnurturant and disordered families (Gauze et al., 1996). Finally, adolescents who have close, supportive *same-sex* friendships are much more likely than those who do not to establish close, nonconflictual romantic relationships as they begin to date (Connolly et al., 2000). Clearly, these findings have an important practical implication: In view of the crucial roles that intimate, supportive friendships can play in a child's life, perhaps our interventions for at-risk, unpopular children should be broadened to include lessons in how to establish and maintain these intimate ties as well as more general kinds of social-skills training (Murphy & Schneider, 1994; Rose & Asher, 1999).

DEVELOPMENTAL ISSUES

16.7

A Longitudinal Analysis of the Benefits of Chumships

A recent collaborative project by Catherine Bagwell and Andrew Newcomb of Richmond University in Virginia and William Bukowski of Concordia University (1998) involved a prospective longitudinal study to test Sullivan's (1953) hypothesis that children who establish close, intimate friendships as preadolescents will show some strengths as adults (i.e., very positive mental health, a strong sense of self-worth, and solid ties to romantic partners) that their chumless peers are less likely to display. Participants were 15 males and 15 females who, as 11-year-old fifth-grade students, had completed sociometric measures that enabled the researchers to determine (1) their levels of general peer acceptance and (2) whether they had established a close, reciprocal tie with a best friend. Twelve years later, these participants (now age 23) completed an extensive packet of questionnaires that assessed such adjustment indexes as their general self-worth, school and job performance, levels of aspiration for the future, perceived competence in romantic relationships and relationships with family members, and depressive and other measures of psychopathological symptomatology.

The results provided impressive support for Sullivan's theory. Preadolescents who had established close ties to a best friend were found as young adults to feel more competent with one group of intimate associates (family members), to have a stronger sense of self-worth, and to report less depressive symptomatology than their counterparts who had been chumless as preadolescents. What's more, these findings were uniquely attributable to participants' earlier friendship status rather than to their general levels of peer acceptance. Although befriended preadolescents in this study did not view themselves as any more competent 12 years later in their adult romantic relationships than did their chumless age-mates, it is possible that the results may have differed had the assessments of romantic competence come from the romantic partners rather than the participants themselves—after all, who among 23-year-olds would like to admit that they are incompetent romantics?

Interestingly, a person's level of general peer acceptance also predicted later adjustment outcomes, but the outcomes it predicted differed from those forecast by participants' earlier status as a befriended or a chumless preadolescent. Specifically, participants who had been rejected in Grade 5 had lower levels of aspiration 12 years later and viewed themselves as less competent in their school and job performance than their counterparts who had enjoyed more favourable sociometric status. Finally, both earlier peer acceptance and earlier friendship status made important contributions to participants' general mental health, such that young adults who had been rejected and chumless as preadolescents reported the highest levels of psychopathological symptoms.

In sum, this study clearly implies that close, supportive friendships with a preadolescent chum promote many of the very competencies that Sullivan emphasized in his earlier theorizing. And although the study is like many others in suggesting that general peer acceptance is a potent contributor to healthy adult adjustment outcomes, its strength lies in illustrating that close, supportive friendships can have positive effects on social development over and above those stemming from one's general acceptance by peers.

PARENTS AND PEERS AS INFLUENCE AGENTS

Developmentalists now know that peers, especially friends, become more and more important contributors to child development as children mature. In fact, some theorists, most notably Judith Harris (1998, 2000), claim that children are socialized into the ways of their culture primarily by the peer group and would become approximately the same people even if they had lived in a different home with different parents. Indeed, immigrant children readily learn the local culture from peers even though it may be very different from that of their parents (Fuligni, Tseng, & Lam, 1999; Phinney, Ong, & Madden, 2000). Yet, while not denying the importance of peers as socialization agents, other developmentalists think that many apparent peer influences are hidden parental influences because, as we will see, parents can have a major impact on the company their children and adolescents keep.

Increasing Conformity to Peers

A major reason that peers become increasingly important as agents of socialization is that, from middle childhood onward, an increasing percentage of peer interactions occur in true *peer groups*—confederations that influence their members by setting **norms** specifying how group members are supposed to look, dress, think, and act. And children do become increasingly responsive to normative peer pressures as they grow older, although they are hardly the blind conformists that many people believe them to be.

In his classic study of **peer conformity**, Thomas Berndt (1979) asked third-through twelfth-graders to indicate the likelihood that they would bend to peer pressure when peers were advocating various prosocial or antisocial acts. He found that conformity with peer pressure for prosocial behaviours did not change much with age. Instead, the most striking developmental change was a sharp increase in conformity to peers urging *antisocial behaviour*. This receptivity to peer-sponsored misconduct peaked in the ninth grade (or about age 15; see Figure 16.9) and then declined throughout the high-school years (see also Brown, Clasen, & Eicher, 1986; Steinberg & Silverberg, 1986). So parents may have some grounds for worrying that their 13- to 15-year-olds could wind up in trouble by going along with the crowd. Peer pressure of all kinds is especially strong at this age (Gavin & Furman, 1989), and there is nothing worse than being viewed as a "dweeb" who does not fit in (Kinney, 1993).

Why does conformity to peer-sponsored misconduct *decrease* by the end of high school? Perhaps this trend reflects the progress that older adolescents have made in their quest for autonomy: They are now better able to make their own decisions and are less dependent on the opinions of *either* parents or peers. According to Lawrence Steinberg and Susan Silverberg (1986), strong conformity to peer pressure early in adolescence may even be a necessary step in the development of autonomy: Young adolescents who are struggling to become less dependent on their parents may need the security that peer acceptance provides before they develop confidence to take their own stands and stick by them. And they are unlikely to gain such acceptance if they conform too closely to adult rules and values without taking a chance and going along with peers every now and then (Allen, Weissberg, & Hawkins, 1989). Although the parent whose teenager is nabbed with his friends for cherry-bombing mailboxes or deflating tires may not be totally comforted by this thought, it does seem that a period of heavy peer influence may pave the way for later independence.

It is also important to keep in mind that adolescents, even within peer groups, vary greatly in their level of maturity. Nancy Galambos of the University of Alberta identifies the impact of maturity level in relation to both family conflict and social behaviours. See Box 16.8 for more information.

Figure 16.9 *Average scores by grade for conformity to peer pressure for prosocial and antisocial behaviours.* ADAPTED FROM BERNDT, 1979.

norms
group-defined rules or expectations about how the members of that group are to think or behave

peer conformity
tendency to go along with the wishes of peers or to yield to peer-group pressures

Cultural Influences

Do young adolescents in other cultures suddenly become more susceptible *to peer-spon-sored* misconduct as they seek to become more autonomous and experience more hassles with their parents at home?

Apparently not. In their recent study of misconduct reported by early (seventh- and eighth-grade) adolescents in the United States, Taiwan, and the People's Republic of China, Chuansheng Chen and associates (1998) found that participants in all three cultures reported *similar levels* of general misconduct, such as cheating on tests, lying to parents, fighting, destroying property, smoking, drinking alcohol, and so on. This was true even though the Chinese peer groups in this study were found to be much *less* inclined than Chinese-American and European-American peer groups to endorse this kind of behaviour. So it seems that Chinese and Taiwanese adolescents are no better behaved than their American counterparts, even though their peers are less likely than American peers to encourage antisocial conduct. Here, then, is a clue that much of the blame on *peers* for triggering adolescent misconduct may be overstated. Let's consider another body of research that makes this same point in a different way.

? | **WHAT DO YOU THINK?**

Do you think that Steinberg and Silverberg (1986) are correct in arguing that strong peer conformity early in adolescence fosters autonomy later on? Why or why not, and how might you test your hypothesis?

Are Cross-Pressures a Problem?

In years gone by, adolescence was often characterized as a stormy period when all youths experience **cross-pressures**—strong conflicts that stem from differences in the values or practices advocated by parents and those favoured by peers. How accurate is this life por-

cross-pressures
conflicts stemming from differences in the values and practices advocated by parents and those favoured by peers

---

THE INSIDE TRACK

16.8

Nancy Galambos

Nancy Galambos

Nancy Galambos works in the Department of Psychology at the University of Alberta. Her research interests span the areas of adolescents' psychosocial maturity, parent–adolescent relations, the family as a context for adolescent development, gender roles in adolescence, and adolescent problem behaviours.

How can we define maturity in adolescent populations? Clearly, adolescents are diverse in many ways, including level of maturity. The work of Nancy Galambos (Galambos, Barker, & Tilton-Weaver, 2003; Galambos & Tilton-Weaver, 2000) examines maturity in adolescent samples, with one recent study identifying three different types of maturity—*pseudomatures, matures,* and *immatures*—that vary on three dimensions. These dimensions are psychological maturity (self-reliance, identity, and work orientation), level of problem behaviour (for example, frequency of marijuana use), and subjective age (how old an adolescent feels relative to same-age peers). The relation of the variables to type of maturity follows:

1. Pseudomatures (25 percent of the sample) scored well above the mean on subjective age and problem behaviour, and below the mean on two measures of psychological maturity (identity and work orientation), although they scored above the mean on self-reliance.

2. Matures (11 percent of the sample) scored slightly below the mean on subjective age, below the mean on problem behaviour, and above the mean on all three measures of psychological maturity.

3. Immatures scored below the mean on all measures (i.e., low in psychological maturity, low in problem behaviour, and young in subjective age).

These categories provide an important framework for understanding and predicting adolescent behaviour, expectations, and experiences. Galambos found that these maturity groups differed on several important characteristics. For example, pseudomature adolescents exhibited more advanced physical maturity and were more likely to have older brothers and older friends relative to the other two groups. Interestingly, they also found that pseudomature adolescents were more likely than immature and mature adolescents to indicate a desire to be older and to be like their older brothers. These results support Moffitt's (1993) assumption that many adolescents are caught in a maturity gap, where they desire the privileges of being older, and therefore emulate adolescents who are perceived to have those privileges. The findings by Galambos demonstrate that it is the pseudomature and, to a lesser extent, immature adolescents, who appear particularly to be caught in this maturity gap.

trait of the teenage years? According to researchers in Montreal (Vitaro et al., 1997), it may have some merit for some adolescents, especially those "rejected" youth who form deviant peer cliques and endorse antisocial behaviours that are likely to alienate their parents, teachers, and most other peers (see also Dishion et al., 1995, 1999; Fuligni et al., 2001; Poulin & Boivin, 2000). But there are several reasons to believe that the "cross-pressures problem" is not a problem for most adolescents.

One reason that parent–peer conflicts are kept to a minimum is that parents and peers tend to exert their influence in different domains. Hans Sebald (1986), for example, has asked adolescents whether they would seek the advice of their parents or the advice of their peers on a number of different issues. Adolescents claimed that they would depend more on their *parents* when the issue involved scholastic or occupational goals or other future-oriented decisions. *Peers* were likely to be more influential than parents on such issues as what styles to wear and which clubs, social events, hobbies, and other recreational activities to choose. Teenagers are unlikely to be torn between parent and peer pressures as long as parents and peers have different areas of influence.

A second and more important reason why parent–peer warfare is typically kept to a minimum is that parents have a good deal of influence on the company that their adolescents keep (Collins et al., 2000). Authoritative parents who are warm, neither too controlling nor too lax, and consistent in their discipline generally find that their adolescents are closely attached to them and have internalized their values. These adolescents have little need to rebel or to desperately seek acceptance from peers when they are so warmly received at home (Brown et al., 1993; Fuligni & Eccles, 1993). In fact, they tend to associate with friends who share their values, which largely protects them from unhealthy peer influences (Bogenscheider et al., 1998; Fletcher et al., 1995).

Interestingly, problems for youths who *do* "fall in with the wrong crowd" and display antisocial behaviour usually begin at home. One way that parents can go wrong is by being too strict and failing to adjust to an adolescent's needs for greater autonomy. This may cause adolescents to become alienated from parents and overly susceptible to negative peer influences, to the point that they let schoolwork slide or break parental rules to please their friends (Fuligni & Eccles, 1993; Fuligni et al., 2001). Parents can also go wrong by failing to provide enough discipline and by not monitoring their children's activities closely enough (Brown et al., 1993; Dishion et al., 1991, 1995; Pettit et al., 2001). So parents have a good deal of power to influence, through their parenting, whether their adolescents end up in "good" or "bad" crowds and are exposed to healthy or unhealthy peer pressures.

Of course, there are some issues for which parental opinions are likely to conflict with those of many peers (e.g., opinions about acceptable conduct on dates or about the harm involved in experimenting with tobacco, alcohol, or marijuana). But even so, peer-group values are rarely as deviant as adults commonly assume, and the adolescent's

Concept Check 16.3
Understanding Peer Sociability
and Peer Influences

Check your understanding of *selected aspects* of peer sociability and peer influences by matching each descriptive statement below with one of the following concepts or processes: (a) neglected children; (b) rejected-aggressive children; (c) rejected-withdrawn children; (d) perceived self-worth; (e) alcohol use; (f) deviant peer clique; (g) authoritarian/uninvolved parenting; (h) patterns of social behaviour; (i) close friends; (j) play complexity; (k) crowd; (l) same-sex clique. The answers appear in the Appendix.

_____ 1. social contributor to unharmonious peer interactions

_____ 2. personal characteristic that predicts the future social competencies of toddlers and preschool children

_____ 3. important mechanism for promoting cross-sex friendships

_____ 4. at greatest risk of becoming chronically hostile and antisocial

_____ 5. passive youngsters who often improve their sociometric status

_____ 6. perhaps the strongest contributor to sociometric status

_____ 7. cross-pressures are often a problem for members of these aggregations

_____ 8. strongest providers of social support by mid-adolescence

_____ 9. at greatest risk of experiencing depression and low self-esteem

_____ 10. form that the peer group takes in early adolescence

_____ 11. attribute that is a product of both parental and peer influences

_____ 12. attribute that may depend more on the quality of one's friendships than on one's general peer acceptance behaviour is usually a product of both parental and peer influences. Denise Kandel (1973), for example, studied a group of adolescents whose best friends either did or did not smoke marijuana and whose parents either did or did not use psychoactive drugs. Among those teenagers whose parents used drugs but whose friends did not, only 17 percent were marijuana users. When parents did not use drugs but best friends did, 56 percent of the adolescents used marijuana. From these findings, we might conclude that the peer group is more influential than parents over marijuana use (see also Bentler, 1992). However, the highest rate of marijuana smoking (67 percent) occurred among teenagers whose parents and peers both used psychoactive drugs, and a similar pattern emerges when we look at parental and peer influences on use of alcohol, tobacco, and illicit drugs (Bogenschneider et al., 1998; Chassin et al., 1996; Newcomb & Bentler, 1989).

In sum, adolescent socialization is not a continual war of parents *versus* peers; instead, these two important sources of influence are generally complementary rather than contradictory (Collins et al., 2000). Most adolescents have cordial relationships with their parents, accept many of their parents' values, and are reluctant to associate with peers who stray too far from these guidelines. And most parents know how important it is for their children and adolescents to establish close relationships with their social equals. They seem to appreciate what developmentalists of the past quarter century have learned: Many of the social competencies that serve people well are the fruits of their alliances with close friends and peers.

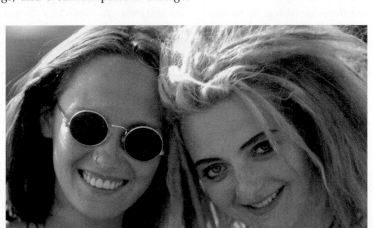

Although teenagers are often characterized as wild or rebellious, many of their norms and values are a reflection of adult society.

SUMMARY

Early Windows: Effects of Television and Computer Technologies on Children and Adolescents

◆ Although children spend more time watching television than in any other waking activity, TV viewing, in moderate doses, is unlikely to impair their cognitive growth, academic achievement, or peer relations. Cognitive development and experience watching television leads to increases in **television literacy** during middle childhood and adolescence.

◆ Televised violence can instigate aggressive behaviour, cultivate aggressive habits and **mean-world beliefs**, and **desensitize** children to aggression. TV also presents stereotypes that influence viewers' beliefs about ethnicity, race, and gender, and children are easily manipulated by TV commercials that push products that parents may be reluctant to purchase.

◆ On the positive side, children are likely to learn prosocial lessons and to put them into practice after watching acts of kindness on television. Parents can help by watching shows such as *Mister Rogers' Neighborhood* with their children and then encouraging them to verbalize or role-play the prosocial lessons that they have observed. Educational programs such as *Sesame Street* have been quite successful at fostering basic

cognitive skills, particularly when children watch with an adult who discusses the material with them and helps them to apply what they have learned.

◆ Children seem to benefit, both intellectually and socially, from their use of computers. **Computer-assisted instruction (CAI)** often improves children's basic academic skills, word-processing programs foster the growth of writing skills, and computer programming facilitates cognitive and metacognitive development. Furthermore, computers promote rather than inhibit social interactions with peers.

◆ Despite the advantages associated with children's use of computers, critics fear that (1) disadvantaged children and girls may reap fewer of these benefits, (2) violent computer games may instigate aggression, and (3) harm may result from youngsters' unrestricted access to the Internet and the World Wide Web.

School as a Socialization Agent

◆ Schools influence many aspects of development. Formal scholastic curricula are intended to impart academic knowledge, and schooling promotes cognitive and metacognitive development by teaching rules and problem-solving strategies that can be applied to many different kinds of information. Schools also pursue an **informal curriculum** that teaches children skills that help them to become good citizens.

♦ Some schools are more effective than others at producing positive outcomes such as low absenteeism, an enthusiastic attitude toward learning, academic achievement, occupational skills, and socially desirable patterns of behaviour. What makes a school effective is not its physical characteristics, whether students experience **ability tracking**, or the amount of money spent per pupil. Instead, **effective schools** are those in which (1) students are motivated to learn; (2) teachers create a classroom environment that is comfortable, engaging, and task-focused; and (3) there are positive **aptitude-treatment interactions**—that is, a good fit between students' personal or cultural characteristics and the kinds of instruction they receive.

♦ Ethnic differences in academic achievement can often be traced to parental and peer influences and to teacher expectancies. At best, **inclusion** has produced modest improvements in the academic performance of students with special needs, while failing to enhance their peer acceptance or self-esteem. Among the steps that might be taken to better meet the educational needs of all of our students are creating stronger bilingual and diversity educational programs and making greater use of **cooperative learning methods** in the classroom.

♦ The achievement gap that exists between North American schoolchildren and those in other industrialized societies centres around cultural differences in educational attitudes, educational practices, and the involvement of both parents and students in the learning process.

Peers as Agents of Socialization

♦ **Peer** contacts represent a second world for children—a world of equal-status interactions that is very different from the nonegalitarian environment of the home. Contacts with peers increase dramatically with age, and during the preschool or early-elementary-school years, children are spending at least as much of their leisure time with peers as with adults. The "peer group" consists mainly of same-sex associates of somewhat different ages.

♦ Research with **"mother-only" monkeys** and **"peer-only" monkeys** and young children indicates that peer contacts are important for the development of competent and adaptive patterns of social behaviour. Children who fail to establish and maintain adequate relations with their peers run the risk of experiencing any number of serious adjustment problems later in life.

♦ **Sociability** between peers emerges by the middle of the first year. By ages 18 to 24 months, toddlers' sociable interactions are becoming much more complex and coordinated as they reliably imitate each other, assume complementary roles in simple social games, and occasionally coordinate their actions to achieve shared goals. During the preschool years, **nonsocial activities** and **parallel play** become less common, whereas the **social skills** that foster **associative play** and **cooperative play** become more common. During middle childhood, more peer interactions occur in true **peer groups**—confederations that associate regularly, define a sense of group membership, and formulate norms that specify how group members are supposed to behave. By early adolescence, youngsters are spending even more time with peers—particularly with their closest friends in small **cliques** and in larger confederations of like-minded cliques known as **crowds**. Cliques and crowds help adolescents to forge an identity apart from their families and pave the way for the establishment of romantic relationships.

♦ Parents influence their children's sociability with peers by virtue of the neighbourhood in which they choose to live, their willingness to serve as "booking agents" for peer contacts, and their monitoring of peer interactions. Warm, sensitive, authoritative parents tend to raise appropriately sociable children who establish good relations with peers; whereas highly authoritarian or uninvolved parents—particularly those who rely on power assertion as a control tactic—tend to raise disruptive, aggressive youngsters whom peers often dislike.

♦ Children clearly differ in **peer acceptance**—the extent to which other youngsters view them as likable (or dislikable) companions. Using **sociometric techniques**, developmentalists find that there are five categories of peer acceptance: (1) **popular children** (liked by many and disliked by few), (2) **rejected children** (disliked by many and liked by few), (3) **controversial children** (liked by many and disliked by many), (4) **neglected children** (seldom nominated by others as likable or dislikable), and (5) **average-status children** (those who are liked or disliked by a moderate number of peers). Neither neglected children nor rejected children are well received by peers; however, it is the rejected child who is typically the lonelier of the two and at greater risk of displaying serious adjustment problems later in life.

♦ Although physical attractiveness, cognitive prowess, and the parenting one has received may contribute to a child's popularity with peers, one's patterns of social behaviour are the strongest predictor of peer acceptance. Popular children are generally warm, cooperative, and compassionate companions who display many prosocial behaviours and are rarely disruptive or aggressive. Neglected children often have adequate social skills, but they experience social anxieties that cause them to appear shy and to hover at the edge of peer-group activities. Rejected children display many unpleasant and annoying behaviours and few prosocial ones. **Rejected-aggressive children** are hostile, impulsive, highly uncooperative, and aggressive, whereas **rejected-withdrawn children** are socially awkward and immature companions who are hypersensitive to criticism and have actively isolated themselves from peers. Programs to improve the social skills of rejectees work better (1) with younger children than with adolescents and (2) when the target children's classmates also participate in the intervention.

♦ Children typically form close ties, or **friendships**, with one or more members of their play groups. Younger children view a friend as a harmonious playmate, whereas older children and adolescents come to think of friends as close companions who share similar interests and values and are willing to provide them with intimate social and emotional support. Interactions among friends are warmer, more cooperative, more compassionate, and more synchronous than those among acquaintances. Close friendships seem to promote positive developmental outcomes by (1) providing security and **social support**, (2) promoting the growth of social problem-solving skills and an ability to compromise, and (3) fostering caring and compassionate feelings that are the foundation of intimate love relationships later in life.

However, friendships differ in quality, and only close, supportive friendships seem to foster adaptive developmental outcomes.

Parents and Peers as Influence Agents

♦ Peers become increasingly important as socialization agents as children mature. **Peer conformity** pressures peak at mid-adolescence, when teenagers are highly susceptible to peer-group **norms**, including those that endorse misconduct.

♦ Strong **cross-pressures** are not a problem for most adolescents who have established warm relations with their parents and have generally internalized many of their parents' values. What's more, peer-group values are often very similar to those of parents, and peers are more likely to discourage than to condone antisocial conduct. So adolescent socialization is not a continual battle between parents and peers; instead, these two important influences interact to affect one's development.

KEY TERMS

extrafamilial influences, 606

television literacy, 606

mean-world belief, 608

desensitization hypothesis, 608

computer-assisted instruction (CAI), 613

informal curriculum, 616

effective schools, 617

ability tracking, 619

aptitude–treatment interaction (ATI), 620

inclusion, 624

cooperative learning methods, 624

peers, 629

"mother-only" monkeys, 630

"peer-only" monkeys, 631

sociability, 632

social skills, 632

nonsocial activity, 633

parallel play, 633

associative play, 633

cooperative play, 633

peer group, 635

clique, 635

crowd, 635

peer acceptance, 637

sociometric techniques, 637

popular children, 637

rejected children, 637

neglected children, 637

controversial children, 637

average-status children, 637

rejected-aggressive children, 639

rejected-withdrawn children, 639

friendship, 643

coaching, 643

social problem-solving training, 643

social support, 644

prospective study, 644

norms, 646

peer conformity, 646

cross-pressures, 647

 You can find further information on the topics covered in this chapter by visiting:

www.developmentalpsych2e.nelson.com
One major influence on early development is mass media— television in particular. By visiting the Media Literacy Online project, at http://interact.uoregon.edu/MediaLit/FA/MLmediaviolence.html, you can access more than 20 on-line articles on the impact of television on children and adolescents. The site includes many links to related sites.

 For additional reading, go to InfoTrac College Edition, your on-line research library, at:

infotrac.thomsonlearning.com

Appendix

Glossary

References

Name Index

Subject Index

Credits

Appendix: Answers to Concept Checks

CHAPTER 1

Concept Check 1.1

1.   *d. structured observation.* Obvious transgressions are events that children may not admit to in an interview, may not be detected by a case study, or may not occur while they are being monitored by an adult observer.

2.   *a. structured interview.* If young children listening to the same vignettes regularly guess that the characters who display the most negative traits are the minority rather than majority group members, we might infer that they have already acquired some negative stereotypes about members of minority groups.

3.   *e. psychophysiological methods.* By recording changes in such physiological responses as heart rate or event-related potentials, even a nonverbal 6-month-old can "tell us" if she can discriminate stimuli that differ only in their colour.

4.   *c. naturalistic observation.* To answer this question, you would probably want to observe boys and girls in the natural environment where conflicts are likely to occur.

5.   *b. ethnography.* Close and enduring contact with members of Sambia culture provides a richer understanding of the impact of cultural traditions than do limited observations or questionnaire methods.

Note: Of course, most of the above research questions can be addressed by a variety of research methods

Concept Check 1.2

1.   *b.* The other conclusions make inappropriate causal inferences from correlational data.

2.   *c.* Chang has failed to control for any potentially confounding variables. For example, the boys may have earned higher grades than the girls because they were smarter to begin with (intelligence is a confounding variable). Moreover, having boys in the treatment group and girls in the control group confounds treatment with gender. Had Chang wanted to see whether increases in self-esteem *cause* increases in academic performance, he should have *randomly assigned* boys and girls to the treatment and control groups, thereby helping to ensure that all potentially confounding variables were roughly equivalent across these two conditions. If children in the treatment group subsequently earned higher grades than their counterparts in the control group, a causal inference would then be warranted.

Concept Check 1.3

1.   *a. cross-sectional design.* Although either the longitudinal or the sequential design could provide similar information, neither of these alternatives is very quick.

2.   *c. sequential design.* The researcher's question concerns the long-term effects of interventions given to children of different ages, thus calling for a sequential design.

3.   *d. cross-cultural design.* The only way to determine whether there are any true "universals" in development is to conduct cross-cultural research to see whether children show the same developmental patterns despite differences in their rearing environments.

4.   *b. longitudinal design.* Because our researcher is interested in the stability of children's intellectual performance relative to their peers between ages 2 and 6, he or she could answer the question by following a group of 2-year-olds over a four-year period in a simple longitudinal

comparison. The cross-sectional design is inappropriate here because each child is observed only once, thus providing no information about the *development* of individuals.

CHAPTER 2

Concept Check 2.1

This person is a *discontinuity theorist*, as evidenced by the claim that all children progress through the same phases (stages) of intellectual development. The spokesperson's claims that intelligence is passed from parents to child and that children will develop their own intellectual potential imply the opinions that intelligence is heavily influenced by *nature* (rather than nurture) and that children are *actively* (rather than passively) involved in their intellectual development.

Concept Check 2.2

1.   *b. Eric Erikson* (1950, p. 32), explaining that humans are biological beings whose development is heavily influenced by the cultural contexts in which they live.

2.   *d. Albert Bandura* (1977, p. 10), criticizing the radical behaviourist views of B.F. Skinner and emphasizing cognitive contributors to social learning.

3.   *c. B.F. Skinner* (1971, p. 17), explaining why he thinks that free will is an illusion and that behaviour is controlled by its external (reinforcing or punitive) consequences.

4.   *a. Sigmund Freud* (1905, p. 78), arguing that it is possible to probe into the unconscious depths of the mind and reveal the conflicts that motivate many behaviours.

Concept Check 2.3

1.   *c. ethology*

2.   *a. Piaget's cognitive-developmental theory*

3.   *d. ecological systems theory*

4.   *b. information-processing theory*

5.   *e. Vygotsky's sociocultural theory*

6.   *All of the previous theories* view developing persons as "active" rather than "passive" agents.

CHAPTER 3

Concept Check 3.1

1.   *a. 100%.* Monozygotic twins have 100 percent of their genes in common and are always the same sex.

2.   *c. 50%.* Your mother cannot curl her tongue and can pass only recessive (non-tongue-curling) genes to her children. And because your sister cannot curl her tongue, she received a recessive gene from each parent. So your father is *heterozygous* for tongue curling. Half of his sperm will carry the dominant tongue-curling gene, thus implying that your odds of being able to curl your tongue are 50 percent.

3.   *a. 100%.* Since both parents cannot curl their tongues, they can pass only recessive genes to their children.

4.   *100% for each child.* If both parents are colour-blind, all their X chromosomes contain a colour-blind allele, and all their children will be colour-blind.

Concept Check 3.2

1. *e. Down syndrome*
2. *f. Tay-Sachs disease*
3. *g. ultrasound*
4. *a. mutation*
5. *b. supermale syndrome*
6. *d. phenylketonuria (PKU)*
7. *c. chorionic villus sampling (CVS)*
8. *h. germline gene theory*

Concept Check 3.3

1. *c. low.* $H = (r_{mz} - r_{dz}) \times 2 = (.61 - .50) \times 2 = $ **.22**

2. *a.* This is a trait for which both SE and NSE contribute more than heredity does. The contribution of NSE (i.e., $1 - r_{mz}$ twins, or **.39**) is about twice as large as the hereditary contribution. And a rough estimate of the contribution of SE (that is, $1 - (NSE + H) = 1 - (.39 + .22)$, or **.39** is comparable in magnitude to that of NSE.

Concept Check 3.4

1. *d. active genotype/environment correlations*
2. *c. evocative genotype/environment correlations*
3. *a. reaction range*
4. *e. passive genotype-environment correlations*
5. *b. canalization*

CHAPTER 4

Concept Check 4.1

Event	Period	Time Span	Term for organism
Implantation	germinal	10–14 days	zygote
Age of viability	fetal	7th month	fetus
First heartbeats	embryonic	4th week	embryo
Kicks first felt by mother	fetal	4th month	fetus
Organs form	embryonic	2 weeks–2 months	embryo
Sexual differentiation (external genitalia)	fetal	3rd month	fetus

Concept Check 4.2

1. *g. syphilis*
2. *c. diethylstilbestrol (DES)*
3. *f. alcohol*
4. *b. toxoplasmosis*
5. *e. folic acid*
6. *d. rubella*
7. *a. severe malnutrition*

Concept Check 4.3

1. *d. NBAS training*
2. *a. cranial bleeding*
3. *c. respiratory distress syndrome*
4. *e. RH incompatibility*
5. *f. natural (and prepared) childbirth*
6. *b. emotional bonding/engrossment*

CHAPTER 5

Concept Check 5.1

1. *c.* Establishment of *lateral preferences* is one consequence of cerebral lateralization.

2. *d.* Many subcortical *reflexes disappear* as the higher cortical centres mature.

3. *f.* The formation of glia and proliferation of synapses early in life are important contributors to the *brain growth spurt*.

4. *a.* With the loss of unused neural pathways, the brain becomes *less plastic.*

5. *b.* Increasing myelinization of the nervous system over the course of childhood is thought to underlie the *increases in attention span* that children display.

6. *e.* Neurons will *degenerate* if not properly stimulated.

Concept Check 5.2

1. *f. sex-role socialization*
2. *d. peak of pubertal changes*
3. *a. early maturation*
4. *a. early maturation*
5. *g. menarche/ejaculation*
6. *e. locomotor skills*
7. *b. late maturation*
8. *b. & c. late maturation; on-time maturation*

Concept Check 5.3

1. *b. malnutrition*
2. *a.* increases in GH production (testosterone plays a secondary role for boys).
3. *d. stress-induced inhibition of GH*
4. *f. sedentary lifestyle*
5. *c. increase in testosterone/estrogen production*
6. *b. & e. malnutrition; insensitive/abusive caregiving*

CHAPTER 6

Concept Check 6.1

1. *c. vision*
2. *h. high-amplitude sucking*
3. *b. & d. audition (hearing); olfaction (smell)*
4. *f. otitis media*
5. *i. innoculation*
6. *g. phoneme discrimination*
7. *a. & e. habituation method; evoked potential method*

Concept Check 6.2

1. *d. kinetic (motion) cues*
2. *b. depth cues*
3. *h. size constancy*
4. *f. pictorial cues*
5. *g. maturation of the brain's visual centres*
6. *i. depth perception*
7. *a. intermodal perception*
8. *c. face perception*
9. *e. phonological awareness*

Concept Check 6.3

Vignette	Kind of learning	Consequence responsible for learning
1. Scumbags learn to stick with old hits.	Operant learning	Positive reinforcement for playing old hits.
2. Dog becomes excited at the sight of a yellow jacket.	Classical conditioning	By pairing the yellow jacket with a UCS (walking) that elicits excitement, the yellow jacket becomes a CS for excitement.
3. Fred distrusts politicians after hearing a group of strangers who are unanimous in questioning their integrity.	Observational learning	None; learning occurs at a symbolic level, without reinforcement or punishment.

4. Jo comes to apply insect repellent before venturing outdoors.	Operant conditioning	Negative reinforcement (applying repellent ends the aversive insect attacks).
5. Jim no longer notices an initially powerful odour.	Habituation	Becoming bored with, or indifferent to, a now-familiar stimulus.

CHAPTER 7

Concept Check 7.1

1. *e. disequilibrium*
2. *d. reversibility*
3. *c. accommodation*
4. *a. organization*
5. *b. assimilation*

Concept Check 7.2

1. *g. Piaget*
2. *h. neo-nativist theorists*
3. *b. secondary circular reaction*
4. *f. A-not-B error*
5. *a. primary circular reaction*
6. *i. "theory" theorists*
7. *e. deferred imitation*
8. *d. inner experimentation*
9. *c. tertiary circular reaction*

Concept Check 7.3

1. *c. seriation (concrete operations)*
2. *e. animism (preoperational stage)*
3. *b. failure to conserve (concrete operations)*
4. *d. dual representation (preoperational stage)*
5. *g. hypothetical reasoning (formal operations)*
6. *f. hypothetico-deductive reasoning (formal operations)*
7. *a. reversibility (concrete operations)*

Concept Check 7.4

1. *b. private speech*
2. *c. zone of proximal development*
3. *e. guided participation*
4. *g. scaffolding*
5. *d. elementary mental functions*
6. *a. tools of intellectual adaptation*
7. *f. cooperative learning exercises*

CHAPTER 8

Concept Check 8.1

1. *b. long-term store*
2. *i. utilization deficiency*
3. *j. span of apprehension*
4. *k. executive control processes*
5. *a. gist*
6. *c. short-term store/working memory*
7. *e. implicit learning/memory*
8. *h. production deficiency*
9. *f. increase in processing speed*
10. *d. adaptive strategy choice model*
11. *g. development of strategies*

Concept Check 8.2

1. *h. sustained attention*
2. *c. elaboration*
3. *f. scripts*
4. *b. knowledge base*
5. *j. autobiographical memory*
6. *i. retrieval*
7. *e. story-like narratives*
8. *d. false memories*
9. *g. metamemory*
10. *a. rehearsal*

CHAPTER 9

Concept Check 9.1

1. *c. J.P. Guilford (structure of intellect model)*
2. *d. Charles Spearman (early factor-analytic model of intelligence)*
3. *b. Howard Gardner (theory of multiple intelligences)*
4. *f. Louis Thurstone (early factor-analytic model of intelligence)*
5. *a. Raymond Cattell/John Horn (modern psychometric view of intelligence)*
6. *e. Robert Sternberg (triarchic theory of intelligence)*

Concept Check 9.2

1. *d. dynamic assessment*
2. *g. developmental quotient (DQ)*
3. *a. Wechsler Intelligence Scale for Children—III (WISC-III)*
4. *c. cumulative deficit*
5. *h. habituation rate*
6. *f. tacit (or practical) intelligence*
7. *b. Stanford-Binet Intelligence Scale*
8. *e. grades previously earned*

CHAPTER 10

Concept Check 10.1

1. *d. sensitive-period hypothesis*
2. *b. recasts*
3. *e. creolizing of pidgins by children*
4. *h. appropriate semantics*
5. *g. conversations with language users*
6. *f. universals in cognitive development*
7. *c. language acquisition device*
8. *a. appropriate grammar*

Concept Check 10.2

1. *c. expressive style*
2. *f. intonational cues*
3. *e. holophrastic speech*
4. *h. referential style*
5. *a. vocal turn-taking*
6. *i. object scope constraint*
7. *d. telegraphic speech*
8. *b. syntactical bootstrapping*
9. *g. overextension*

Concept Check 10.3

1. *d. transformational grammar*
2. *c. metalinguistic awareness*
3. *f. morphological knowledge*
4. *a. referential communication skills*
5. *g. grammatical morphemes*

6. b. overregularization

7. e. phonological awareness

CHAPTER 11

Concept Check 11.1

1. c. self-recognition

2. j. infant emotional expressions

3. h. ability to interpret emotions (emotional understanding)

4. e. social referencing

5. f. disconfirmed expectancies

6. b. emotional self-regulation

7. g. shared environmental influences

8. i. nonshared environmental influences

9. k. shyness/behavioural inhibition

10. a. goodness of fit

11. d. lack of inhibition/uninhibited

Concept Check 11.2

1. e. Mary Ainsworth (ethological viewpoint)

2. c. learning perspective (Robert Sears)

3. f. cognitive-developmental perspective

4. a. Sigmund Freud (psychoanalytic viewpoint)

5. d. John Bowlby (ethological viewpoint)

6. b. Erik Erikson (psychoanalytic viewpoint)

Concept Check 11.3

1. c. Thomas and Chess's goodness-of-fit model

2. b. Kagan's temperament hypothesis

3. g. social stimulation hypothesis

4. a. Ainsworth's caregiving hypothesis

5. e. Bowlby/Bretherton internal working models hypothesis

6. f. maternal deprivation hypothesis

7. d. Kochanska's integrative model

CHAPTER 12

Concept Check 12.1

1. c. self-esteem

2. l. private self

3. e. social/relational attributes

4. d. looking-glass self

5. a. autism

6. j. self-recognition

7. b. categorical self

8. g. belief-desire theory of mind

9. k. friendship quality

10. i. social comparison

11. f. parental warmth/responsiveness

12. h. pretend play

Concept Check 12.2

1. i. identity foreclosure

2. c. negative peer influences

3. f. children with a mastery orientation

4. j. identity diffusion

5. g. children with a learned-helplessness orientation

6. k. identity achievement

7. a. strong parental criticism of failures

8. d. stability of achievement attributions

9. b. process-oriented praise

10. e. person praise

11. h. identity crisis

Concept Check 12.3

1. c. psychological similarities

2. f. behavioural comparisons

3. a. loyalty/sharing of intimacies

4. h. psychological constructs

5. e. role-taking skills

6. b. common activities

7. j. social experiences with peers

8. i. psychological comparisons

9. g. belief-desire theory of mind

10. d. entity perspective on personality

CHAPTER 13

Concept Check 13.1

1. e. reading comprehension

2. b. gender identity

3. i. gender-role standard

4. f. self-fulfilling prophecy

5. h. visual/spatial ability

6. d. gender segregation

7. a. achievement motivation

8. c. gender intensification

9. g. gender-role stereotypes

Concept Check 13.2

1. h. gender consistency

2. a. Money and Ehrhardt's biosocial theory

3. c. Freud's psychoanalytic theory

4. g. basic gender identity

5. b. Halpern's psychobiosocial model

6. d. social learning theory

7. f. Martin and Halverson's gender schema theory

8. e. Kohlberg's cognitive-developmental theory

Concept Check 13.3

The program might target 3- to 6-year-olds whose gender stereotypes are just forming and are not entrenched. The program should encourage cross-sex as well as same-sex play activities, and its adult leaders should model both same- and cross-sex pursuits. Question-and-answer sessions about the gender stereotypes that children already hold should provide opportunities to point out that one's interests and willingness to learn, rather than one's gender, are the most important considerations in determining the activities that people should pursue (rule training). Giving children multiple classification tasks that require them to sort objects into more than one category (and illustrate that men and women often share similar interests and occupational goals) should also help children to break free of rigid gender stereotypes. Finally, at least part of the training might be conducted by an adult male, because it is males who normally make the stronger distinctions between what is "appropriate" for males and females and thus may be more noteworthy as agents of change.

CHAPTER 14

Concept Check 14.1

1. d. relational aggression

2. h. proactive aggressors

3. g. negative reinforcement

4. a. deviant peer cliques

5. j. instrumental aggression

6. i. reactive aggressors

7. *k. hostile aggression*

8. *f. peer rejection*

9. *e. coercive home environment*

10. *c. provocative victims*

11. *b. passive victims*

Concept Check 14.2

1. *d. competitive orientation*

2. *e. self-oriented distress*

3. *a. altruistic norms*

4. *b. felt responsibility*

5. *h. role-taking skills*

6. *c. verbal reinforcement*

7. *f. sympathetic empathic arousal*

8. *g. tangible incentives*

Concept Check 14.3

1. *e. moral rules*

2. *k. harsh parenting fosters moral immaturity*

3. *g. peer interactions*

4. *f. morality of care*

5. *h. power assertion*

6. *d. induction*

7. *j. mutually responsive parent-child relationship*

8. *b. formal operations*

9. *a. role-taking skills*

10. *c. disequilibrating social experiences*

11. *i. social-conventional rules*

CHAPTER 15

Concept Check 15.1

1. *h.* This finding illustrates that families are *embedded* in a larger societal context that influences parenting practices.

2. *e.* In this *direct effect*, the father's parenting influences the father–infant relationship.

3. *d.* Such an arrangement is called a *blended (or reconstituted) family*.

4. *a. nuclear family*

5. *i.* Family dynamics change with the *development* of *family* members.

6. *c.* Due to divorce and out-of-wedlock deliveries, the *single-parent family* is common today.

7. *b.* In communal societies, children in *extended families* seem to fare better.

8. *f.* In this *indirect effect*, the father–son relationship influences the husband–wife relationship.

9. *g. coparenting*

Concept Check 15.2

1. *c. economic distress (marital conflict is also an appropriate answer)*

2. *e. increased academic aptitude*

3. *j. autonomy*

4. *a. authoritarian parenting*

5. *i. only children*

6. *k. uninvolved parenting*

7. *d. emotional support*

8. *f. mastery motivation*

9. *b. authoritative parenting*

10. *g. no nonsense parenting*

11. *h. marital conflict*

Concept Check 15.3

1. *b. delinquent conduct*

2. *i. complex stepparent home*

3. *g. noncustodial parental support*

4. *j. simple stepparent home*

5. *k. predivorce family conflict*

6. *c. increased father involvement*

7. *h. unhappy marital relations*

8. *d. Supervised after school care*

9. *f. adoption*

10. *e. gay/lesbian parenting*

11. *a. coercive parenting*

CHAPTER 16

Concept Check 16.1

1. *d. aggressive children*

2. *a. ethnic/gender stereotypes*

3. *h. advertisements for children; (k. violent video games is also correct)*

4. *j. computer assisted instruction*

5. *k. violent video games*

6. *i. metacognitive development*

7. *f. adult monitoring/encouragement*

8. *b. mean-world beliefs*

9. *c. television literacy*

10. *e. disadvantaged children*

11. *g. poor peer relations*

Concept Check 16.2

1. *f. inclusion (mainstreaming)*

2. *i. peer influences*

3. *k. ability tracking*

4. *e. informal curriculum*

5. *g. monetary support*

6. *h. parental involvement*

7. *j. extracurricular activities*

8. *l. aptitude-treatment interaction*

9. *d. group differences in IQ*

10. *c. cooperative learning methods*

11. *a. academically oriented preschools*

12. *b. parental devaluation of education*

Concept Check 16.3

1. *g. authoritarian/uninvolved parenting (h. patterns of social behaviour is also correct)*

2. *j. play complexity*

3. *k. crowd*

4. *b. rejected-aggressive children*

5. *a. neglected children*

6. *h. patterns of social behaviour*

7. *f. deviant peer cliques*

8. *i. close friends*

9. *c. rejected-withdrawn children*

10. *l. same-sex clique*

11. *e. alcohol use*

12. *d. perceived self-worth*

Glossary

ability tracking: the educational practice of grouping students according to ability and then educating them in classes with students of comparable educational or intellectual standing.

acceptance/responsiveness: a dimension of parenting that describes the amount of responsiveness and affection that a parent displays toward a child.

accommodation: the process of modifying existing schemes in order to incorporate or adapt to new experiences.

achievement attributions: causal explanations that one provides for one's successes and failures.

achievement expectancy: how well (or poorly) one expects to perform should he or she try to achieve a particular objective.

achievement motivation: a willingness to strive to succeed at challenging tasks and to meet high standards of accomplishment.

acquired immune deficiency syndrome (AIDS): a viral disease that can be transmitted from a mother to her fetus or neonate and that results in a weakening of the body's immune system and, ultimately, death.

active genotype/environment correlations: the notion that our genotypes affect the types of environments that we prefer and seek out.

active/passive issue: a debate among developmental theorists about whether children are active contributors to their own development or passive recipients of environmental influence.

adaptation: an inborn tendency to adjust to the demands of the environment.

adaptive strategy choice model: Siegler's model to describe how strategies change over time; the view that multiple strategies exist within a child's cognitive repertoire at any one time, with these strategies competing with one another for use.

adolescent growth spurt: the rapid increase in physical growth that marks the beginning of adolescence.

adoption design: study in which adoptees are compared with their biological relatives and their adoptive relatives to estimate the heritability of an attribute.

affective explanations: discipline that focuses a child's attention on the harm or distress that his or her conduct has caused others.

age of viability: a point between the 22nd and 28th prenatal weeks when survival outside the uterus may be possible.

aggression: behaviour performed with the intention of harming a living being who is motivated to avoid this treatment.

aging-ova hypothesis: the hypothesis that an older mother is more likely to have children with chromosomal abnormalities because her ova are degenerating as she nears the end of her reproductive years.

alleles: alternative forms of a gene that can appear at a particular site on a chromosome.

alternative birth centre: a hospital birthing room or other independent facility that provides a homelike atmosphere for childbirth but still makes medical technology available.

altruism: a selfless concern for the welfare of others that is expressed through such prosocial acts as sharing, cooperating, and helping.

amae: Japanese concept that refers to an infant's feeling of total dependence on his or her mother and the presumption of the mother's love and indulgence.

amniocentesis: a method of extracting amniotic fluid from a pregnant woman so that fetal body cells within the fluid can be tested for chromosomal abnormalities and other genetic defects.

amnion: a watertight membrane that develops from the trophoblast and surrounds the developing embryo, serving to regulate its temperature and to cushion it against injuries.

analogical reasoning: reasoning that involves using something one knows already to help reason about something not known yet.

androgenized females: females who develop male-like external genitalia because of exposure to male sex hormones during the prenatal period.

androgyny: a gender-role orientation in which the individual has incorporated a large number of both masculine and feminine attributes into his or her personality.

animism: attributing life and lifelike qualities to inanimate objects.

anorexia nervosa: a life-threatening eating disorder characterized by self-starvation and a compulsive fear of getting fat.

A-not-B error: the tendency of 8- to 12-month-olds to search for a hidden object where they previously found it, even after they have seen it moved to a new location.

anoxia: a lack of sufficient oxygen to the brain; may result in neurological damage or death.

Apgar test: a quick assessment of the newborn's heart rate, respiration, colour, muscle tone, and reflexes that is used to gauge perinatal stress and to determine whether a neonate requires immediate medical assistance.

appearance/reality distinction: the ability to keep the true properties or characteristics of an object in mind despite the deceptive appearance that the object has assumed; notably lacking among young children during the preconceptual period.

aptitude-treatment interaction (ATI): a phenomenon whereby characteristics of the student and of the school environment interact to affect student outcomes, such that any given educational practice may be effective with some students but not with others.

arousal: feelings of sympathy or compassion that may be elicited when we experience the emotions of (i.e., empathize with) a distressed other; thought to become an important

mediator of altruism.

asocial phase (of attachment): approximately the first six weeks of life, in which infants respond in an equally favourable way to interesting social and nonsocial stimuli.

assimilation: the process of interpreting new experiences by incorporating them into existing schemes.

associative play: form of social discourse in which children pursue their own interests but will swap toys or comment on one another's activities.

attachment: a close emotional relationship between two persons, characterized by mutual affection and a desire to maintain proximity.

attachment Q-set (AQS): alternative method of assessing attachment security that is based on observing the child's attachment-related behaviours at home; can be used with infants, toddlers, and preschool children.

attention deficit-hyperactivity disorder (ADHD): an attentional disorder involving distractibility, hyperactivity, and impulsive behaviour that often leads to academic difficulties, poor self-esteem, and social/emotional problems.

attention span: capacity for sustaining attention to a particular stimulus or activity.

attribution retraining: therapeutic intervention in which "helpless" children are persuaded to attribute failures to their lack of effort rather than a lack of ability.

authoritarian parenting: a restrictive pattern of parenting in which adults set many rules for their children, expect strict obedience, and rely on power rather than reason to elicit compliance.

authoritative parenting: a flexible, democratic style of parenting in which warm, accepting parents provide guidance and control while allowing the child some say in how best to meet challenges and obligations.

autobiographical memory: memory for important experiences or events that have happened to us.

autonomous morality: Piaget's second stage of moral development, in which children realize that rules are arbitrary agreements that can be challenged and changed with the consent of the people they govern.

autonomy: the capacity to make decisions independently, to serve as one's own source of emotional strength, and to otherwise manage one's life tasks without depending on others for assistance; an important developmental task of adolescence.

autosomes: the 22 pairs of human chromosomes that are identical in males and females.

autostimulation theory: a theory proposing that REM sleep in infancy is a form of self-stimulation that helps the central nervous system to develop.

average-status children: children who receive a moderate number of nominations by peers as a liked or a disliked individual.

avoidant attachment: an insecure infant–caregiver bond, characterized by little separation protest and a tendency of the child to avoid or ignore the caregiver.

babbles: vowel–consonant combinations that infants begin to produce at about 4 to 6 months of age.

baby biography: a detailed record of an infant's growth and development over a period of time.

basic gender identity: the stage of gender identity in which the child first labels the self as a boy or a girl.

behavioural comparisons phase: the tendency to form impressions of others by comparing and contrasting their overt behaviours.

behavioural genetics: the scientific study of how genotype interacts with environment to determine behavioural attributes such as intelligence, personality, and mental health.

behavioural inhibition: a temperamental attribute reflecting one's tendency to withdraw from unfamiliar people or situations.

behavioural schemes: organized patterns of behaviour that are used to represent and respond to objects and experiences.

behaviourism: a school of thinking in psychology that holds that conclusions about human development should be based on controlled observations of overt behaviour rather than speculation about unconscious motives or other unobservable phenomena; the philosophical underpinning for the early theories of learning.

belief-desire theory: the theory of mind that develops between ages 3 and 4; the child now realizes that both beliefs and desires may determine behaviour and that people act on their beliefs, even if they are inaccurate.

benefits-to-risks ratio: a comparison of the possible benefits of a study for advancing knowledge and optimizing life conditions versus its costs to participants in terms of inconvenience and possible harm.

bilingual: fluent in two languages.

blended, or reconstituted, families: new families resulting from cohabitation or remarriage that include a parent, one or more children, and step-relations.

bound morphemes: Morphemes that cannot stand alone but that modify the meaning of free morphemes (e.g., the *-ed* attached to English verbs to indicate past tense).

brain growth spurt: the period between the seventh prenatal month and 2 years of age when more than half of the child's eventual brain weight is added.

breech birth: a delivery in which the fetus emerges feet or buttocks first rather than head first.

Broca's area: structure located in the frontal lobe of the left hemisphere of the cerebral cortex that controls language production.

bulimia: a life-threatening eating disorder characterized by recurrent eating binges followed by such purging activities as heavy use of laxatives or vomiting.

canalization: genetic restriction of phenotype to a small number of developmental outcomes; a highly canalized attribute is one for which genes channel development along predetermined pathways, so that the environment has little effect on the phenotype that emerges.

cardinality: the principle specifying that the last number in a counting sequence specifies the number of items in a set.

caregiving hypothesis: Ainsworth's notion that the type of attachment that an infant develops with a particular caregiver depends primarily on the kind of caregiving he or she has received from that person.

carrier: a heterozygous individual who displays no sign of a recessive allele in his or her own phenotype but can pass this gene to offspring.

case study: a research method in which the investigator gathers extensive information about the life of an individual and then tests developmental hypotheses by analyzing the events of the person's life history.

castration anxiety: in Freud's theory, a young boy's fear that his father will castrate him as punishment for his rivalrous conduct.

catch-up growth: a period of accelerated growth in which children who have experienced growth deficits grow very rapidly to "catch up" to the growth trajectory that they are genetically programmed to follow.

categorical self: a person's classification of the self along socially significant dimensions such as age and sex.

centration: in Piaget's theory, the tendency of preoperational children to attend to one aspect of a situation to the exclusion of others; in contrast with *decentration*.

cephalocaudal development: a sequence of physical maturation and growth that proceeds from the head (cephalic region) to the tail (or caudal region).

cerebral cortex: the outer layer of the brain's cerebrum that is involved in voluntary body movements, perception, and higher intellectual functions such as learning, thinking, and speaking.

cerebral lateralization: the specialization of brain functions in the left and right cerebral hemispheres.

cerebrum: the highest brain centre; includes both hemispheres of the brain and the fibres that connect them.

cesarean section: surgical delivery of a baby through an incision made in the mother's abdomen and uterus.

child abuse: any extreme maltreatment of children, involving physical batterings; sexual molestations, psychological insults such as persistent ridicule, rejection, and terrorization; and physical or emotional neglect.

child effects model: model of family influence in which children are believed to influence their parents rather than vice versa.

chorion: a membrane that develops from the trophoblast and becomes attached to the uterine tissues to gather nourishment for the embryo.

chorionic villus sampling (CVS): a method of extracting fetal cells from the chorion for prenatal tests; can be performed earlier in pregnancy than is possible with amniocentesis.

chromosome: a threadlike structure made up of genes; in humans, there are 46 chromosomes in the nucleus of each body cell.

chronosystem: in ecological systems theory, changes in the individual or the environment that occur over time and influence the direction of development.

classical conditioning: a type of learning in which an initially neutral stimulus is repeatedly paired with a meaningful nonneutral stimulus so that the neutral stimulus comes to elicit the response originally made only to the nonneutral stimulus.

clinical method: a type of interview in which a participant's response to each successive question (or problem) determines what the investigator will ask next.

clique: a small group of friends that interacts frequently.

coaching: method of social-skills training in which an adult displays and explains various socially skilled behaviours, allows the child to practise them, and provides feedback aimed at improving the child's performances.

codominance: a condition in which two heterozygous but equally powerful alleles produce a phenotype in which genes are both fully and equally expressed.

coercive home environment: a home in which family members often annoy one another and use aggressive or otherwise antisocial tactics as a method of coping with these aversive experiences.

cognition: the activity of knowing and the processes through which knowledge is acquired.

cognitive development: changes that occur in mental activities such as attending, perceiving, learning, thinking, and remembering.

cognitive equilibrium: Piaget's term for the state of affairs in which there is a balanced, or harmonious, relationship between one's thought processes and the environment.

cognitive operation: an internal mental activity that one performs on objects of thought.

cognitive self-guidance system: in Vygotsky's theory, the use of private speech to guide problem-solving behaviour.

cohort effect: age-related difference among cohorts that is attributable to cultural and historical differences in cohorts' growing-up experiences rather than to true developmental change.

collectivist (or communal) society: society that values cooperative interdependence, social harmony, and adherence to group norms. These societies generally hold that the group's well-being is more important than that of the individual.

committed compliance: compliance based on the child's eagerness to cooperate with a responsive parent who has been willing to cooperate with him or her.

communication: the process by which one organism transmits information to and influences another.

compensatory interventions: special educational programs designed to further the cognitive growth and scholastic achievements of disadvantaged children.

complex stepparent home: family consisting of two married (or cohabiting) adults, each of whom has at least one biological child living at home.

computer-assisted instruction (CAI): use of computers to teach new concepts and give students practice in academic skills.

conception: the moment of fertilization, when a sperm penetrates an ovum, forming a zygote.

concordance rate: the percentage of cases in which a particular attribute is present for one member of a twin pair if it is present for the other.

concrete operations: Piaget's third stage of cognitive development, lasting from about age 7 to age 11, when children acquire cognitive operations and think more logically about real objects and experiences.

conditioned response (CR): a learned response to a stimulus that was not originally capable of producing the response.

conditioned stimulus (CS): an initially neutral stimulus that comes to elicit a particular response after being paired with a UCS that always elicits the response.

confidentiality: the right of participants to concealment of their identity with respect to the data that they provide.

conflict: circumstances in which two (or more) persons have incompatible needs, desires, or goals.

confluence hypothesis: Zajonc's notion that a child's intellectual development depends on the average intellectual level of all family members.

confounding variable: some factor other than the independent variable that, if not controlled by the experimenter, could explain any differences across treatment conditions in participants' performance on the dependent variable.

congenital adrenal hyperplasia (CAH): a genetic anomaly that causes one's adrenal glands to produce unusually high levels of androgen from the prenatal period onward; often has masculinizing effects on female fetuses.

congenital defect: a problem that is present (though not necessarily apparent) at birth; may stem from genetic and prenatal influences or from complications of the birth process.

connectionism: the field of cognitive science that seeks to understand mental processes as resulting from assemblies (or groups) of real or artificial neurons.

conservation: the recognition that the properties of an object or substance do not change when its appearance is altered in some superficial way.

constructivist: one who gains knowledge by acting or otherwise operating on objects and events to discover their properties.

context-independent learning: learning that has no immediate relevance to the present context, as is done in modern schools; acquiring knowledge for knowledge's sake.

contextual model: view of children as active entities whose developmental paths represent a continuous, dynamic interplay between internal forces (nature) and external influences (nurture).

continuity/discontinuity issue: a debate among theorists about whether developmental changes are quantitative and continuous or qualitative and discontinuous (i.e., stagelike).

controversial children: children who receive many nominations by peers as a liked individual and many as a disliked individual.

conventional morality: Kohlberg's term for the third and fourth stages of moral reasoning, in which moral judgments are based on a desire to gain approval (Stage 3) or to uphold laws that maintain social order (Stage 4).

convergent thinking: thinking that requires one to come up with a single correct answer to a problem; what IQ tests measure.

cooperative learning methods: an educational practice whereby children of different races or ability levels are assigned to teams; each team member works on problems geared to his or her ability level, and all members are reinforced for "pulling together" and performing well as a team.

cooperative play: true social play in which children cooperate or assume reciprocal roles while pursuing shared goals.

coordination of secondary circular reactions: fourth substage of Piaget's sensorimotor stage; infants begin to coordinate two or more actions to achieve simple objectives.

coos: vowel-like sounds that young infants repeat over and over during periods of contentment.

coparenting: circumstance in which parents mutually support each other and function as a cooperative parenting team.

core language: involves explicit instruction in a second language, usually through a specific language course (e.g., French class); occasionally the explicit instruction is embedded within a particular curriculum area.

corpus callosum: the bundle of neural fibres that connects the two hemispheres of the brain and transmits information from one hemisphere to the other.

correlational design: a type of research design that indicates the strength of associations among variables; though correlated variables are systematically related, these relationships are not necessarily causal.

correlation coefficient: a numerical index (symbolized by an *r* and ranging from −1.00 to +1.00) of the strength and direction of the relationship between two variables.

counterconditioning: a treatment based on classical conditioning in which the goal is to extinguish an undesirable response and replace it with a new and more adaptive one.

creativity: the ability to generate novel ideas or works that are useful and valued by others.

creoles: languages that develop when pidgins are transformed into grammatically complex "true" languages.

cross-cultural comparison: a study that compares the behaviour and/or development of people from different cultural or subcultural backgrounds.

cross-generational problem: the fact that long-term changes in the environment may limit conclusions of a longitudinal project to that generation of children who were growing up while the study was in progress.

crossing over: a process in which genetic material is exchanged between pairs of chromosomes during meiosis.

cross-pressures: conflicts stemming from differences in the values and practices advocated by parents and those favoured by peers.

cross-sectional design: a research design in which subjects from different age groups are studied at the same point in time.

crowd: a large, loosely organized peer group made up of several cliques that share similar norms, interests, and values.

crystallized intelligence: the ability to understand relations or solve problems that depend on knowledge acquired from schooling and other cultural influences.

cued recall: a recollection that is prompted by a cue associated with the setting in which the recalled event originally occurred.

cultural bias: the situation that arises when one cultural or subcultural group is more familiar with test items than another group and therefore has an unfair advantage.

cultural test bias hypothesis: the notion that IQ tests and testing procedures have a built-in, middle-class bias that explains the substandard performance of children from lower-class and minority subcultures.

culture-fair IQ tests: intelligence tests constructed to minimize any irrelevant cultural biases in test content that could influence test performance.

cumulative-deficit hypothesis: the notion that impoverished environments inhibit intellectual growth and that these inhibiting effects accumulate over time.

decentration: in Piaget's theory, the ability of concrete-operational children to consider multiple aspects of a stimulus or situation; contrasts with *centration*.

deferred imitation: the ability to reproduce a modelled activity that has been witnessed at some point in the past.

demandingness/control: a dimension of parenting that describes how restrictive and demanding parents are.

deoxyribonucleic acid (DNA): long, double-stranded molecules that make up chromosomes.

dependent variable: the aspect of behaviour that is measured in an experiment and assumed to be under the control of the independent variable.

deprivation dwarfism: a childhood growth disorder that is triggered by emotional deprivation and characterized by decreased production of GH, slow growth, and small stature.

desensitization hypothesis: the notion that people who watch a lot of media violence will become less aroused by aggression and more tolerant of violent and aggressive acts.

desire theory: early theory of mind in which a person's actions are thought to be a reflection of her or his desires rather than other mental states such as belief.

development: systematic continuities and changes in the individual over the course of life.

developmental continuities: ways in which we remain stable over time or continue to reflect our past.

developmental psychology: branch of psychology devoted to identifying and explaining the continuities and changes that individuals display over time.

developmental quotient (DQ): a numerical measure of an infant's performance on a developmental schedule relative to the performance of other infants of the same age.

developmental stage: a distinct phase within a larger sequence of development; a period characterized by a particular set of abilities, motives, behaviours, or emotions that occur together and form a coherent pattern.

diethylstilbestrol (DES): a synthetic hormone, formerly prescribed to prevent miscarriage, that can produce cervical cancer in adolescent female offspring and genital-tract abnormalities in males.

differentiation theory: a theory specifying that perception involves detecting distinctive features or cues that are contained in the sensory stimulation we receive.

difficult temperament: temperamental profile in which the child is irregular in daily routines and adapts slowly to new experiences, often responding negatively and intensely.

direct effect: instances in which any pair of family members affects and is affected by each other's behaviour.

direct tuition: teaching young children how to behave by reinforcing "appropriate" behaviours and by punishing or otherwise discouraging inappropriate conduct.

disequilibriums: imbalances or contradictions between one's thought processes and environmental events; by contrast, *equilibrium* refers to a balanced, harmonious relationship between one's cognitive structures and the environment.

dishabituation: increase in responsiveness that occurs when stimulation changes.

disorganized/disoriented attachment: an insecure infant–caregiver bond, characterized by the infant's dazed appearance on reunion or a tendency to first seek and then abruptly avoid the caregiver.

distinctive features: characteristics of a stimulus that remain constant; dimensions on which two or more objects differ and can be discriminated (sometimes called *invariances* or *invariant features*).

divergent thinking: thinking that requires a variety of ideas or solutions to a problem when there is no one correct answer.

dizygotic (or fraternal) twins: twins that result when a mother releases two ova at roughly the same time and each is fertilized by a different sperm, producing two zygotes that are genetically different.

doctrine of specificity: a viewpoint shared by many social-learning theorists that holds that moral affect, reasoning, and behaviour may depend as much or more on the situation that one faces than on an internalized set of moral principles.

dominant allele: a relatively powerful gene that is expressed phenotypically and masks the effect of a less powerful gene.

double standard: the view that sexual behaviour that is appropriate for members of one gender is less appropriate for the members of the other gender.

Down syndrome: a chromosomal abnormality (also known as trisomy-21) caused by the presence of an extra 21st chromosome; people with this syndrome have a distinctive physical appearance and are moderately to severely retarded.

dual representation (dual encoding; dual orientation): the ability to represent an object simultaneously as an object itself and as a representation of something else.

dynamic assessment: an approach to assessing intelligence that evaluates how well individuals learn new material when an examiner provides them with competent instruction.

dynamical systems theory: a theory that views motor skills as active reorganizations of previously mastered capabilities that are undertaken to find more effective ways of exploring the environment or satisfying other objectives.

easy temperament: temperamental profile in which the child quickly establishes regular routines, is generally good-natured, and adapts easily to novelty.

eclectics: those who borrow from many theories in their attempts to predict and explain human development.

ecological systems theory: Bronfenbrenner's model emphasizing that the developing person is embedded in a series of environmental systems that interact with one another and with the person to influence development.

ecological validity: state of affairs in which the findings of one's research are an accurate representation of processes that occur in the natural environment.

effective schools: schools that are generally successful at achieving curricular and noncurricular objectives regardless of the racial, ethnic, or socioeconomic background of the student population.

ego: psychoanalytic term for the rational component of the personality.

egocentric speech: Piaget's term for the subset of a young child's utterances that are nonsocial—that is, neither directed to others nor expressed in ways that listeners might understand.

egocentrism: the tendency to view the world from one's own perspective while failing to recognize that others may have different points of view.

elaboration: a strategy for remembering that involves adding something to (or creating meaningful links between) the bits of information one is trying to retain.

Electra complex: female version of the Oedipus complex, in which a 3- to 6-year-old girl was thought to envy her father for possessing a penis and would choose him as a sex object in the hope that he would share with her this valuable organ that she lacked.

embryo: name given to the prenatal organism from the third through the eighth week after conception.

emergent literacy: skills, knowledge, and attitudes that precede and seem to promote conventional forms of reading and writing.

emotional bonding: term used to describe the strong affectionate ties that parents may feel toward their infant; some theorists believe that the strongest bonding occurs shortly after birth, during a sensitive period.

emotional display rules: culturally defined rules specifying which emotions should or should not be expressed under which circumstances.

emotional self-regulation: strategies for managing emotions or adjusting emotional arousal to a comfortable level of intensity.

empathic concern: a measure of the extent to which an individual recognizes the needs of others and is concerned about their welfare.

empathy: the ability to experience the same emotions that others display.

encoding: the process by which external stimulation is converted to a mental representation.

engrossment: paternal analogue of maternal emotional bonding; term used to describe fathers' fascination with their neonates, including their desire to touch, hold, caress, and talk to the newborn baby.

enrichment theory: a theory specifying that we must "add to" sensory stimulation by drawing on stored knowledge in order to perceive a meaningful world.

entity view of ability: belief that one's ability is a highly stable trait that is little influenced by effort or practice.

environmental determinism: the notion that children are passive creatures who are moulded by their environments.

environmental hypothesis: the notion that groups differ in IQ because the environments in which they are raised are not equally conducive to intellectual growth.

estrogen: female sex hormone, produced by the ovaries, that is responsible for female sexual maturation.

ethnography: a method in which the researcher seeks to understand the unique values, traditions, and social processes of a culture or subculture by living with its members and making extensive observations and notes.

ethology: the study of the bioevolutionary bases of behaviour and development.

event memory: long-term memory for events.

evocative genotype/environment correlations: the notion that our heritable attributes will affect others' behaviour toward us and thus influence the social environment in which development takes place.

evoked potential: a change in patterning of the brain waves that indicates that an individual detects (senses) a stimulus.

executive control processes: the processes involved in regulating attention and determining what to do with the information just gathered or retrieved from long-term memory.

exosystem: social systems that children and adolescents do not directly experience but that may nonetheless influence their development; the third of Bronfenbrenner's environmental layers or contexts.

expansions: responding to a child's ungrammatical utterance with a grammatically improved form of that statement.

experimental control: steps taken by an experimenter to ensure that all extraneous factors that could influence the dependent variable are roughly equivalent in each experimental condition; these precautions must be taken before an experimenter can be reasonably certain that observed changes in the dependent variable were caused by manipulating the independent variable.

experimental design: a research design in which the investigator introduces some change in the participant's environment and then measures the effect of that change on the participant's behaviour.

expressive role: a social prescription, usually directed toward females, that one should be cooperative, kind, nurturant, and sensitive to the needs of others.

expressive style: early linguistic style in which toddlers use language mainly to call attention to their own and others' feelings and to regulate social interactions.

extended family: a group of blood relatives from more than one nuclear family (for example, grandparents, aunts, uncles, nieces, and nephews) who live together, forming a household.

extended self: more mature self-representation, emerging between ages 3½ and 5 years, in which children are able to integrate past, current, and unknown future self-representations into a notion of a self that endures over time.

extinction: gradual weakening and disappearance of a learned response that occurs because the CS is no longer paired with the UCS (in classical conditioning) or the response is no longer reinforced (in operant conditioning).

extrafamilial influences: social agencies other than the family that influence a child's or an adolescent's cognitive, social, and emotional development.

factor analysis: a statistical procedure for identifying clusters of tests or test items (called *factors*) that are highly correlated with one another and unrelated to other test items.

false-belief task: method of assessing one's understanding that people can hold inaccurate beliefs that can influence their conduct, wrong as these beliefs may be.

false-self behaviour: acting in ways that do not reflect one's true self or the "true me."

falsifiability: a criterion for evaluating the scientific merit of theories; a theory is falsifiable when it is capable of generating predictions that could be disconfirmed.

family social system: the complex network of relationships, interactions, and patterns of influence that characterizes a family with three or more members.

fast-mapping: process of linking a word with its referent after hearing the word once or twice.

"felt responsibility" hypothesis: the theory that empathy may promote altruism by causing one to reflect on altruistic norms and, thus, to feel some obligation to help distressed others.

fetal alcohol effects (FAE): a group of mild congenital problems that are sometimes observed in children of mothers who drink sparingly to moderately during pregnancy.

fetal alcohol syndrome (FAS): a group of serious congenital problems commonly observed in the children of mothers who abuse alcohol during pregnancy.

fetus: the prenatal organism from the ninth week of pregnancy until birth.

field experiment: an experiment that takes place in a naturalistic setting such as a home, school, or playground.

first stage of labour: the period of the birth process lasting from the first regular uterine contractions until the cervix is fully dilated.

fixation: arrested development at a particular psychosexual stage that can prevent movement to higher stages.

fluid intelligence: the ability to perceive relationships and solve relational problems of the type that are not taught and are relatively free of cultural influences.

Flynn effect: systematic increase in IQ scores observed over the 20th century.

folic acid: B-complex vitamin that helps to prevent defects of the central nervous system.

foreclosure: identity status characterizing individuals who have prematurely committed themselves to occupations or ideologies without really thinking about these commitments.

formal operations: Piaget's fourth and final stage of cognitive development, from age 11 or 12 and beyond, when the individual begins to think more rationally and systematically about abstract concepts and hypothetical events.

Fragile-X syndrome: abnormality of the X chromosome caused by a defective gene and associated with mild to severe mental retardation, particularly when the defective gene is passed from mother to child.

free morphemes: morphemes that can stand alone as a word (e.g., *cat, go, yellow*)

free recall: a recollection that is not prompted by specific cues or prompts.

friendship: a close and often enduring relationship between two individuals that may be characterized by loyalty and mutual affection.

fuzzy-trace theory: theory proposed by Brainerd and Reyna that postulates that people encode experiences on a continuum from literal, verbatim traces to fuzzy, gistlike traces.

g: Spearman's abbreviation for *neogenesis*, which, roughly translated, means one's ability to understand relations (or general mental ability).

gender consistency: the stage of gender identity in which the child recognizes that a person's gender is invariant despite changes in the person's activities or appearance (also known as *gender constancy*).

gender identity: one's awareness of one's gender and its implications.

gender intensification: a magnification of sex differences early in adolescence; associated with increased pressure to conform to traditional gender roles.

gender-role standard: a behaviour, value, or motive that members of a society consider more typical or appropriate for members of one sex.

gender schemas: organized sets of beliefs and expectations about males and females that guide information processing.

gender segregation: children's tendency to associate with same-sex playmates and to think of the other sex as an out-group.

gender stability: the stage of gender identity in which the child recognizes that gender is stable over time.

gender typing: the process by which a child becomes aware of his or her gender and acquires motives, values, and behaviours considered appropriate for members of that sex.

genes: hereditary blueprints for development that are transmitted unchanged from generation to generation.

genetic counselling: a service designed to inform prospective parents about genetic diseases and to help them determine the likelihood that they would transmit such disorders to their children.

genetic epistemology: the experimental study of the development of knowledge, developed by Piaget.

genetic hypothesis: the notion that group differences in IQ are hereditary.

genetic imprinting: pattern of inheritance in which a pair of alleles is biochemically marked so that only one parent's allele is expressed, regardless of its composition.

genital herpes: a sexually transmitted disease that can infect infants at birth, causing blindness, brain damage, or even death.

genotype: the genetic endowment that an individual inherits.

germinal period: first phase of prenatal development, lasting from conception until the developing organism becomes firmly attached to the wall of the uterus (also called *period of the zygote*).

germline gene therapy: a procedure, not yet perfected or approved for use with humans, in which harmful genes would be repaired or replaced with healthy ones, thereby permanently correcting a genetic defect.

giftedness: the possession of unusually high intellectual potential or other special talents.

gist: a fuzzy representation of information that preserves the central content but few precise details.

glia: nerve cells that nourish neurons and encase them in insulating sheaths of myelin.

"goodness-of-fit" model: Thomas and Chess's notion that development is likely to be optimized when parents' child-rearing practices are sensitively adapted to the child's temperamental characteristics.

grammatical morphemes: prefixes, suffixes, prepositions, and auxiliary verbs that modify the meaning of words and sentences.

growth hormone (GH): the pituitary hormone that stimulates the rapid growth and development of body cells; primarily responsible for the adolescent growth spurt.

guided participation: adult–child interactions in which children's cognitions and modes of thinking are shaped as they participate with or observe adults engaged in culturally relevant activities.

habits: well-learned associations between stimuli and responses that represent the stable aspects of one's personality.

habituation: a decrease in one's response to a stimulus that has become familiar through repetition.

Head Start: a large-scale preschool educational program designed to provide children from low-income families with a variety of social and intellectual experiences that might better prepare them for school.

heritability: the amount of variability in a trait that is attributable to hereditary factors.

heritability coefficient: a numerical estimate, ranging from .00 to +1.00, of the amount of variation in an attribute that is due to hereditary factors.

heteronomous morality: Piaget's first stage of moral development, in which children view the rules of authority figures as sacred and unalterable.

heterozygous: having inherited two alleles for an attribute that have different effects.

heuristic value: a criterion for evaluating the scientific merit of theories; a heuristic theory is one that continues to stimulate new research and discoveries.

hierarchical model of intelligence: model of the structure of intelligence in which a broad, general ability factor is at the top of the hierarchy, with a number of specialized ability factors nested underneath.

high-amplitude sucking method: a method of assessing infants' perceptual capabilities that capitalizes on their ability to make interesting events last by varying the rate at which they suck on a special pacifier.

high-risk neighbourhood: a residential area in which the incidence of child abuse is much higher than in other neighbourhoods with the same demographic characteristics.

holistic perspective: a unified view of the developmental process that emphasizes the important interrelationships among the physical, mental, social, and emotional aspects of human development.

holophrase: a single-word utterance that represents an entire sentence's worth of meaning.

holophrastic period: the period when the child's speech consists of one-word utterances, some of which are thought to be holophrases.

HOME inventory: a measure of the amount and type of intellectual stimulation provided by a child's home environment.

homozygous: having inherited two alleles for an attribute that are identical in their effects.

horizontal décalage: Piaget's term for a child's uneven cognitive performance; an inability to solve certain problems even though one can solve similar problems requiring the same mental operations.

hostile aggression: aggressive acts for which the perpetrator's major goal is to harm or injure a victim.

hostile attributional bias: tendency to view harm done under ambiguous circumstances as having stemmed from a hostile intent on the part of the harmdoer; characterizes reactive aggressors.

Huntington's disease: a genetic disease caused by a dominant allele that typically appears later in life and causes the nervous system to degenerate.

hypothesis: a theoretical prediction about some aspect of experience.

hypothetico-deductive reasoning: in Piaget's theory, a formal operational ability to think hypothetically.

id: psychoanalytic term for the inborn component of the personality that is driven by the instincts.

identification: Freud's term for the child's tendency to emulate another person, usually the same-sex parent.

identity: a mature self-definition; a sense of who one is, where one is going in life, and how one fits into society.

identity achievement: identity status characterizing individuals who have carefully considered identity issues and have made firm commitments to an occupation and ideologies.

identity crisis: Erikson's term for the uncertainty and discomfort that adolescents experience when they become confused about their present and future roles in life.

identity diffusion: identity status characterizing individuals who are not questioning who they are and have not yet committed themselves to an identity.

identity training: an attempt to promote conservation by teaching nonconservers to recognize that a transformed object or substance is the same object or substance, regardless of its new appearance.

ideographic development: individual variations in the rate, extent, or direction of development.

immanent justice: the notion that unacceptable conduct will invariably be punished and that justice is ever present in the world.

immersion: involves instruction in a second language where all or most of the curriculum is provided in the second language.

implantation: the burrowing of the blastocyst into the lining of the uterus.

imprinting: an innate or instinctual form of learning in which the young of certain species follow and become attached to moving objects (usually their mothers).

inclusion: educational practice of integrating students with special needs into regular classrooms rather than placing them in segregated special education classes (formerly referred to as *mainstreaming*).

incompatible-response technique: a nonpunitive method of behaviour modification in which adults ignore undesirable conduct, while reinforcing acts that are incompatible with these responses.

incremental view of ability: the belief that one's ability can be improved through increased effort and practice.

independent assortment: the principle stating that each pair of chromosomes segregates independently of all other chromosome pairs during meiosis.

independent variable: the aspect of the environment that an experimenter modifies or manipulates in order to measure its impact on behaviour.

indirect, or third-party, effect: instances in which the relationship between two individuals in a family is modified by the behaviour or attitudes of a third family member.

individualistic society: society that values personalism and individual accomplishments, which often take precedence over group goals. These societies tend to emphasize ways in which individuals differ from each other.

induction: a nonpunitive form of discipline in which an adult explains why a child's behaviour is wrong and should be changed by emphasizing its effects on others.

infantile amnesia: a lack of memory for the early years of one's life.

infant states: levels of sleep and wakefulness that young infants display.

informal curriculum: non-curricular objectives of schooling such as teaching children to cooperate, respect authority, obey rules, and become good citizens.

information-processing theory: a perspective that views the human mind as a continuously developing symbol-manipulating system, similar to a computer, into which information flows, is operated on, and is converted to output (answers, inferences, or solutions to problems).

informed consent: the right of research participants to receive an explanation, in language they can understand, of all aspects of research that may affect their willingness to participate.

in-group/out-group schema: one's general knowledge of the mannerisms, roles, activities, and behaviours that characterize males and females.

inhibition: the ability to prevent ourselves from executing some cognitive or behavioural response.

inhibitory control: an ability to display acceptable conduct by resisting the temptation to commit a forbidden act.

innate purity: the idea that infants are born with an intuitive sense of right and wrong that is often misdirected by the demands and restrictions of society.

inner experimentation: the sixth substage of Piaget's sensorimotor stage; the ability to solve simple problems on a mental, or symbolic, level without having to rely on trial-and-error experimentation.

instinct: inborn biological force that motivates a particular response or class of responses.

instrumental aggression: aggressive acts for which the perpetrator's major goal is to gain access to objects, space, or privileges.

intelligence: in Piaget's theory, a basic life function that enables an organism to adapt to its environment.

intelligence quotient (IQ): a numerical measure of a person's performance on an intelligence test relative to the performance of other examinees.

interactionist theory: the notion that biological factors and environmental influences interact to determine the course of language development.

internalization: the process of adopting the attributes or standards of other people; taking these standards as one's own.

internal working models: cognitive representations of self, others, and relationships that infants construct from their interactions with caregivers.

intrinsic achievement orientation: a desire to achieve in order to satisfy one's *personal* needs for competence or mastery (as opposed to achieving for external incentives such as grades).

introversion/extroversion: the opposite poles of a personality dimension: Introverts are shy, anxious around others, and tend to withdraw from social situations; extroverts are highly sociable and enjoy being with others.

intuitive period: the later substage of preoperations, from age 4 to age 7, when the child's thinking about objects and events is dominated by salient perceptual features.

invariant developmental sequence: a series of developments that occur in one particular order because each development in the sequence is a prerequisite for those appearing later.

investment theory of creativity: recent theory specifying that the ability to invest in innovative projects and to generate creative solutions depends on a convergence of creative resources—namely, background knowledge, intellectual abilities, personality characteristics, motivation, and environmental support/encouragement.

iron deficiency anemia: a listlessness caused by too little iron in the diet that makes children inattentive and may retard physical and intellectual development.

Kaufman Assessment Battery for Children (K-ABC): an individual intelligence test for children; grounded heavily in information-processing theory.

kewpie-doll effect: the notion that infantile facial features are perceived as cute and lovable and elicit favourable responses from others.

kinetic cues: cues created by movements of objects or movements of the body; provide important information for the perception of forms and spatial relations.

kinship: the extent to which two individuals have genes in common.

knowledge base: one's existing information about a topic or content area.

kwashiorkor: a growth-retarding disease that affects children who receive enough calories but little if any protein.

language: a small number of individually meaningless symbols (sounds, letters, gestures) that can be combined according to agreed-on rules to produce an infinite number of messages.

language acquisition device (LAD): Chomsky's term for the innate knowledge of grammar that humans were said to possess, which might enable young children to infer the rules governing others' speech and to use these rules to produce language.

language-making capacity (LMC): a hypothesized set of specialized linguistic processing skills that enable children to analyze speech and to detect phonological, semantic, and syntactical relationships.

lanugo: the fine hair that covers the fetus's body; helps vernix stick to the skin.

learned helplessness: the failure to learn how to respond appropriately in a situation because of previous exposures to uncontrollable events in the same or similar situations.

learned helplessness orientation: a tendency to give up or to stop trying after failing because these failures have been attributed to a lack of ability that one can do little about.

learning: a relatively permanent change in behaviour (or behavioural potential) that results from one's experiences or practice.

learning goal: state of affairs in which one's primary objective in an achievement context is to increase one's skills or abilities.

learning to learn: improvements in performance on novel problems as a result of acquiring a new rule or strategy from the earlier solution of similar problems.

Level I abilities: Jensen's term for lower-level intellectual abilities (such as attention and short-term memory) that are important for simple association learning.

Level II abilities: Jensen's term for higher-level cognitive skills that are involved in abstract reasoning and problem solving.

lexical contrast constraint: notion that young children make inferences about word meanings by contrasting new words with words they already know.

linguistic universal: an aspect of language development that all children share.

longitudinal design: a research design in which one group of subjects is studied repeatedly over a period of months or years.

long-term store (LTS): third information-processing store, in which information that has been examined and interpreted is permanently stored for future use.

looking-glass self: the idea that a child's self-concept is largely determined by the ways that other people respond to him or her.

love withdrawal: a form of discipline in which an adult withholds attention, affection, or approval in order to modify or control a child's behaviour.

macrosystem: the larger cultural or subcultural context in which development occurs; Bronfenbrenner's outermost environmental layer or context.

manic depression: a psychotic disorder characterized by extreme fluctuations in mood.

marasmus: a growth-retarding disease that affects infants who receive insufficient protein and too few calories.

mastery motivation: an inborn motive to explore, understand, and control one's environment.

mastery orientation: a tendency to persist at challenging tasks because of a belief that one has high ability and that earlier failures can be overcome by trying harder.

maternal deprivation hypothesis: the notion that socially deprived infants develop abnormally because they have failed to establish attachments to a primary caregiver.

maturation: developmental changes in the body or behaviour that result from the aging process rather than from learning, injury, illness, or some other life experience.

mean-world belief: a belief, fostered by televised violence, that the world is a more dangerous and frightening place than is actually the case.

mechanistic model: view of children as passive entities whose developmental paths are primarily determined by external (environmental) influences.

meiosis: the process in which a germ cell divides, producing gametes (sperm or ova) that each contain half of the parent cell's original complement of chromosomes; in humans, the products of meiosis contain 23 chromosomes.

memory span: a measure of the amount of information that can be held in the short-term store.

menarche: the first occurrence of menstruation.

mental age (MA): a measure of intellectual development that reflects the level of age-graded problems a child is able to solve.

mental retardation: significant below-average intellectual functioning associated with impairments in adaptive behaviour in everyday life.

mental seriation: a cognitive operation that allows one to mentally order a set of stimuli along a quantifiable dimension such as height or weight.

mesosystem: the interconnections among an individual's immediate settings or microsystems; the second of Bronfenbrenner's environmental layers or contexts.

metacognition: one's knowledge about cognition and about the regulation of cognitive activities.

metalinguistic awareness: a knowledge of language and its properties; an understanding that language can be used for purposes other than communicating.

metamemory: one's knowledge about memory and memory processes.

microgenetic development: changes that occur over relatively brief periods of time—in seconds, minutes, or days—as opposed to larger-scale changes, as conventionally studied in ontogenetic development.

microsystem: the immediate settings (including role relationships and activities) that the person actually encounters; the innermost of Bronfenbrenner's environmental layers or contexts.

mitosis: the process in which a cell duplicates its chromosomes and then divides into two genetically identical daughter cells.

mnemonics (memory strategies): effortful techniques used to improve memory, including rehearsal, organization, and elaboration.

monozygotic (or identical) twins: twins that result when a single zygote divides into two separate but identical cells that each develop independently; each member of a monozygotic twin pair inherits exactly the same set of genes.

moral affect: the emotional component of morality, including feelings such as guilt, shame, and pride in ethical conduct.

moral behaviour: the behavioural component of morality; actions that are consistent with one's moral standards in situations in which one is tempted to violate them.

morality: a set of principles or ideals that help the individual to distinguish right from wrong, to act on this distinction, and to feel

pride in virtuous conduct and guilt (or shame) for conduct that violates one's standards.

morality of care: Gilligan's term for what she presumes to be the dominant moral orientation of females, which focuses more on compassionate concerns for human welfare than on socially defined justice as administered through law.

morality of justice: Gilligan's term for what she presumes to be the dominant moral orientation of males, which focuses more on socially defined justice as administered through law than on compassionate concerns for human welfare.

moral reasoning: the cognitive component of morality; the thinking that people demonstrate when deciding whether various acts are right or wrong.

moral rules: standards of acceptable and unacceptable conduct that focus on the rights and privileges of individuals.

moratorium: identity status characterizing individuals who are currently experiencing an identity crisis and are actively exploring occupational and ideological positions in which to invest themselves.

morphemes: the smallest meaningful units of language; these include words and grammatical markers such as prefixes, suffixes, and verb-tense modifiers (for example, *-ed, -ing*).

morphological knowledge: one's knowledge of the meaning of morphemes that make up words.

morphology: rules governing the formation of meaningful words from sounds.

motherese: the short, simple, high-pitched (and often repetitive) sentences that adults use when talking with young children (also called *child-directed speech*).

"mother-only" monkeys: monkeys who are raised with their mothers and denied any contact with peers.

multimodal motherese: older companion's use of information that is exaggerated and synchronized across two or more senses to call an infant's attention to the referent of a spoken word.

mutation: a change in the chemical structure or arrangement of one or more genes that has the effect of producing a new phenotype.

mutual exclusivity constraint: notion that young children assume that each object has only one label and that different words refer to separate and not overlapping categories.

mutually responsive relationship: parent–child relationship characterized by mutual responsiveness to each other's needs and goals and shared positive affect

myelinization: the process by which neurons are enclosed in waxy myelin sheaths that facilitate the transmission of neural impulses.

naming explosion: the dramatic increase in the pace at which infants acquire new words in the latter half of the second year; so named because many of the new words acquired are the names of objects.

naturalistic observation: a method in which the scientist tests hypotheses by observing people as they engage in everyday activities in their natural habitats (for example, at home, at school, or on the playground).

natural, and prepared, childbirth: a delivery in which physical and psychological preparations for the birth are stressed and medical assistance is minimized.

natural (or quasi-) experiment: a study in which the investigator measures the impact of some naturally occurring event that is assumed to affect people's lives.

natural selection: an evolutionary process, proposed by Charles Darwin, stating that individuals with characteristics that promote adaptation to the environment will survive, reproduce, and pass these adaptive character-istics to offspring; those lacking these adaptive characteristics will eventually die out.

nature/nurture issue: the debate among developmental theorists about the relative importance of biological predispositions (nature) and environmental influences (nurture) as determinants of human development.

negative punishment: a punishing consequence that involves the removal of something pleasant following a behaviour.

negative reinforcer: any stimulus whose removal or termination as the consequence of an act increases the probability that the act will recur.

neglected children: children who receive few nominations as either a liked or a disliked individual.

Neonatal Behaviour Assessment Scale (NBAS): a test that assesses a neonate's neurological integrity and responsiveness to environmental stimuli.

neonate: a newborn infant from birth to approximately 1 month of age.

neo-nativism: the idea that much cognitive knowledge, such as the object concept, is innate, requiring little in the way of specific experiences to be expressed, and that there are biological constraints in that the mind/body is designed to process certain types of information in certain ways.

neural tube: the primitive spinal cord that develops from the ectoderm and becomes the central nervous system.

neurons: nerve cells that receive and transmit neural impulses.

neurotic disorder: an irrational pattern of thinking or behaviour that a person may use to contend with stress or to avoid anxiety.

no-nonsense parenting: mixture of authoritative and authoritarian parenting styles that is associated with favourable outcomes in African-American families.

nonorganic failure to thrive: an infant growth disorder, caused by lack of attention and affection, that causes growth to slow dramatically or stop.

nonrepresentative sample: a subgroup that differs in important ways from the larger group (or population) to which it belongs.

nonshared environmental influence (NSE): an environmental influence that people living together do not share that should make these individuals different from one another.

nonsocial activity: onlooker behaviour and solitary play.

normal distribution: a symmetrical, bell-shaped curve that describes the variability of certain characteristics within a population; most people fall at or near the average score, with relatively few at the extremes of the distribution.

normative development: developmental changes that characterize most or all members of a species; typical patterns of development.

norms: group-defined rules or expectations about how the members of that group are to think or behave.

nuclear family: a family unit consisting of a wife/mother, a husband/father, and their dependent child(ren).

obese: a medical term describing individuals who are at least 20 percent above the ideal weight for their height, age, and sex.

object permanence: the realization that objects continue to exist when they are no longer visible or detectable through the other senses.

object scope constraint: the notion that young children assume that a new word applied to an object refers to the whole object rather than to parts of the object or to object attributes (for example, its colour).

observational learning: learning that results from observing the behaviour of others.

observer influence: tendency of participants to react to an observer's presence by behaving in unusual ways.

oedipal morality: Freud's theory that moral development occurs during the phallic period (ages 3 to 6) when children internalize the moral standards of the same-sex parent as they resolve their Oedipus or Electra conflicts.

Oedipus complex: Freud's term for the conflict that 3- to 6-year-old boys were said to experience when they develop an incestuous desire for their mothers and a jealous and hostile rivalry with their fathers.

ontogenetic development: development of the individual over his or her lifetime.

open classroom: a less structured classroom arrangement in which there is a separate area for each educational activity and children distribute themselves around the room, working individually or in small groups.

operant conditioning: a form of learning in which freely emitted acts (or operants) become either more or less probable depending on the consequences they produce.

operant learning: a form of learning in which voluntary acts (or operants) become either more or less probable, depending on the consequences they produce.

operating efficiency hypothesis: in Case's theory, the notion that operating space in working memory increases with age because we come to process information faster or more efficiently.

organismic model: view of children as active entities whose developmental paths are primarily determined by forces from within themselves.

organization: an inborn tendency to combine and integrate available schemes into coherent systems or bodies of knowledge.

original sin: the idea that children are inherently negative creatures who must be taught to rechannel their selfish interests into socially acceptable outlets.

otitis media: a common bacterial infection of the middle ear that produces mild to moderate hearing loss.

overextension: the young child's tendency to use relatively specific words to refer to a broader set of objects, actions, or events than adults do (for example, using the word *car* to refer to all motor vehicles).

overregularization: the overgeneralization of grammatical rules to irregular cases where the rules do not apply (for example, saying *mouses* rather than *mice*).

owness effect: tendency of parents in complex stepparent homes to favour and be more involved with their own biological children than with their stepchildren.

own-sex schema: detailed knowledge or plans of action that enable a person to perform gender-consistent activities and to enact his or her gender role.

parallel play: largely noninteractive play in which players are in close proximity but do not often attempt to influence one another.

parent effects model: model of family influence in which parents are believed to influence their children rather than vice versa.

Parents Anonymous: an organization of reformed child abusers (modelled after Alcoholics Anonymous).

parsimony: a criterion for evaluating the scientific merit of theories: a parsimonious theory is one that uses relatively few explanatory principles to explain a broad set of observations.

passive genotype/environment correlations: the notion that the rearing environments that biological parents provide are influenced by the parents' own genes, and hence are correlated with the child's own genotype.

passive victims (of aggression): socially withdrawn, anxious children with low self-esteem whom bullies torment, even though they appear to have done little to trigger such abuse.

peer acceptance: a measure of a person's likability (or dislikability) in the eyes of peers.

peer conformity: the tendency to go along with the wishes of peers or to yield to peer-group pressures.

peer group: a confederation of peers that interacts regularly, defines membership in the group, and formulates norms that specify how members are supposed to look, think, and act.

peers: two or more persons who are operating at similar levels of behavioural complexity.

perception: the process by which we categorize and interpret sensory input.

perceptual learning: changes in one's ability to extract information from sensory stimulation that occur as a result of experience.

performance goal: state of affairs in which one's primary objective in an achievement context is to display one's competencies (or to avoid looking incompetent).

period of the embryo: second phase of prenatal development, lasting from the third through the eighth prenatal week, during which the major organs and anatomical structures take shape.

period of the fetus: third phase of prenatal development, lasting from the ninth prenatal week until birth; during this period, all major organ systems begin to function and the fetus grows rapidly.

permissive parenting: a pattern of parenting in which otherwise accepting adults make few demands of their children and rarely attempt to control their behaviour.

person praise: praise focusing on desirable personality traits such as intelligence; this praise fosters performance goals in achievement contexts.

personal agency: recognition that one can be the cause of an event.

phallic stage: Freud's third stage of psychosexual development (from 3 to 6 years of age), in which children gratify the sex instinct by fondling their genitals and developing an incestuous desire for the parent of the other sex.

phase of indiscriminate attachments: period between 6 weeks and 6 to 7 months of age in which infants prefer social to nonsocial stimulation and are likely to protest whenever any adult puts them down or leaves them alone.

phase of multiple attachments: period when infants form attachments to companions other than their primary attachment object.

phase of specific attachment: period between 7 and 9 months of age when infants are attached to one close companion (usually the mother).

phenotype: the ways in which a person's genotype is expressed in observable or measurable characteristics.

phenylketonuria (PKU): a genetic disease in which the child is unable to metabolize phenylalanine; if left untreated, it soon causes hyperactivity and mental retardation.

phlyogenetic development: development over evolutionary time.

phonemes: the smallest meaningful units of sound that make up a spoken language.

phonology: the sound system of a language and the rules for combining these sounds to produce meaningful units of speech.

physical activity play: moderate to vigorous play activities such as running, jumping, climbing, play fighting, or game playing that raise a child's metabolic rate far above resting levels.

pictorial (perspective) cues: depth and distance cues (including linear perspective, texture gradients, sizing, interposition, and shading) that are monocular—that is, detectable with only one eye.

pidgins: structurally simple communication systems that arise when people who share no common language come into constant contact.

pincer grasp: a grasp in which the thumb is used in opposition to the fingers, enabling an infant to become more dexterous at lifting and fondling objects.

pituitary: a "master gland" located at the base of the brain that regulates the endocrine glands and produces growth hormone.

placenta: an organ, formed from the lining of the uterus and the chorion, that provides for respiration and nourishment and the elimination of metabolic wastes in the embryo and fetus.

plasticity: capacity for change; a developmental state that has the potential to be shaped by experience.

polygenic trait: a characteristic that is influenced by the action of many genes rather than a single pair.

popular children: children who are liked by many members of their peer group and disliked by very few.

positive punishment: a punishing consequence that involves the presentation of something unpleasant following a behaviour.

positive reinforcer: any stimulus whose presentation, as the consequence of an act, increases the probability that the act will recur.

postconventional morality: Kohlberg's term for the fifth and sixth stages of moral reasoning, in which moral judgments are based on social contracts and democratic law (Stage 5) or on universal principles of ethics and justice (Stage 6).

postpartum depression: strong feelings of sadness, resentment, and despair that may affect the mother shortly after childbirth and that can linger for months.

power assertion: a form of discipline in which an adult relies on his or her superior power (for example, by administering spankings or withholding privileges) to modify or control a child's behaviour.

practice effect: changes in participants' natural responses as a result of repeated testing.

pragmatics: principles that underlie the effective and appropriate use of language in social contexts.

preadapted characteristic: an innate attribute that is a product of evolution and serves some function that increases the chances of survival for the individual and the species.

preconceptual period: the early substage of preoperations, from age 2 to age 4, characterized by the appearance of primitive ideas, concepts, and methods of reasoning.

preconventional morality: Kohlberg's term for the first two stages of moral reasoning, in which moral judgments are based on the tangible punitive consequences (Stage 1) or rewarding consequences (Stage 2) of an act for the actor rather than on the relationship of that act to society's rules and customs.

preference method: a method used to gain information about infants' perceptual abilities by presenting two (or more) stimuli and observing which stimulus the infant prefers.

prelinguistic phase: the period before children utter their first meaningful words.

premoral period: in Piaget's theory, the first five years of life, when children have little respect for or awareness of socially defined rules.

prenatal development: development that occurs between the moment of conception and the beginning of the birth process.

preoperational stage: Piaget's second stage of cognitive development, lasting from about age 2 to age 7, when children think at a symbolic level but do not yet use cognitive operations.

present self: early self-representation in which 2- and 3-year-olds recognize current representations of self but are unaware that past self-representations or self-relevant events have implications for the present.

preterm infants: infants born more than three weeks before their normal due dates.

primary circular reactions: second substage of Piaget's sensorimotor stage; a pleasurable response, centred on the infant's own body, that is discovered by chance and performed over and over.

primary mental abilities: seven mental abilities, identified by factor analysis, that Thurstone believed to represent the structure of intelligence.

primary (or basic) emotions: the set of emotions present at birth or emerging early in the first year that some theorists believe to be biologically programmed.

primitive reflexes: reflexes controlled by subcortical areas of the brain that gradually disappear over the first year of life.

private self (or I): those inner, or subjective, aspects of self that are known only to the individual and are not available for public scrutiny.

private speech: Vygotsky's term for the subset of a child's verbal utterances that serve a self-communicative function and guide the child's thinking.

proactive aggressors: highly aggressive children who find aggressive acts easy to perform and who rely heavily on aggression as a means of solving social problems or achieving other personal objectives.

process-oriented praise: praise of effort expended to formulate good ideas and effective problem-solving strategies; this praise fosters learning goals in achievement contexts.

processing constraints: cognitive biases or tendencies that lead infants and toddlers to favour certain interpretations of the meaning of new words over other interpretations.

production deficiency: a failure to spontaneously generate and use known strategies that could improve learning and memory.

productive language: that which the individual is capable of expressing (producing) in his or her own speech.

proprioceptive feedback: sensory information from the muscles, tendons, and joints that help one to locate the position of one's body (or body parts) in space.

prosocial moral reasoning: the thinking that people demonstrate when deciding whether to help, share with, or comfort others when these actions could prove costly to themselves.

prospective study: study in which the suspected causes or contributors to a developmental outcome are assessed earlier to see if they accurately forecast the developments they are presumed to influence.

protection from harm: the right of research participants to be protected from physical or psychological harm.

provocative victims (of aggression): Restless, hot-tempered, and oppositional children who are victimized because they often irritate their peers.

proximodistal development: a sequence of physical maturation and growth that proceeds from the centre of the body (the proximal region) to the extremities (distal regions).

psycholinguists: those who study the structure and development of children's language.

psychological comparisons phase: tendency to form impressions of others by comparing and contrasting these individuals on abstract psychological dimensions.

psychological constructs phase: tendency to base one's impressions of others on the stable traits that these individuals are presumed to have.

psychometric approach: a theoretical perspective that portrays intelligence as a trait (or set of traits) on which individuals differ; psychometric theorists are responsible for the development of standardized intelligence tests.

psychophysiological methods: methods that measure the relationships between physiological processes and aspects of children's physical, cognitive, or emotional behaviour/development.

psychosexual theory: Freud's theory that states that maturation of the sex instinct underlies stages of personality development, and that the manner in which parents manage children's instinctual impulses determines the traits that children display.

psychosocial theory: Erikson's revision of Freud's theory that emphasizes sociocultural (rather than sexual) determinants of development and posits a series of eight psychosocial conflicts that people must resolve successfully to display healthy psychological adjustment.

puberty: the point at which a person reaches sexual maturity and is physically capable of fathering or conceiving a child.

public self (or me): those aspects of self that others can see or infer.

punisher: any consequence of an act that suppresses the response and decreases the probability that it will recur.

Pygmalion effect: the tendency of teacher expectations to become self-fulfilling prophecies, causing students to perform better or worse depending on their teacher's estimation of their potential.

qualitative change: changes in kind that make individuals fundamentally different than they were before; for example, the transformation of a prelinguistic infant into a language user is a qualitative change in communication skills.

quantitative change: incremental change in degree without sudden transformations; for example, the small yearly increases in height and weight that 2- to 11-year-olds display.

random assignment: a control technique in which participants are assigned to experimental conditions through an unbiased procedure so that the members of the groups are not systematically different from one another.

range-of-reaction principle: the idea that genotype sets limits on the range of possible phenotypes that a person might display in response to different environments.

reactive aggressors: children who display high levels of hostile, retaliatory aggression because they overattribute hostile intents to others and can't control their anger long enough to seek nonaggressive solutions to social problems.

reactive attachment disorder: inability to form secure attachment bonds with other people; characterizes many victims of early social deprivation and/or abuse.

reasoning: a particular type of problem solving that involves making inferences.

recasts: responding to a child's ungrammatical utterance with a nonrepetitive statement that is grammatically correct.

receptive language: that which the individual comprehends when listening to others' speech.

recessive allele: a less powerful gene that is not expressed phenotypically when paired with a dominant allele.

reciprocal determinism: the notion that the flow of influence between children and their environments is a two-way street; the environment may affect the child, but the child's behaviour also influences the environment.

referential communication skills: abilities to generate clear verbal messages, to recognize when others' messages are unclear, and to clarify any unclear messages one transmits or receives.

referential style: early linguistic style in which toddlers use language mainly to label objects.

reflex: an unlearned and automatic response to a stimulus or class of stimuli.

reflex activity: first substage of Piaget's sensorimotor stage; infants' actions are confined to exercising innate reflexes, assimilating new objects into these reflexive schemes, and accommodating their reflexes to these novel objects.

rehearsal: a strategy for remembering that involves repeating the items one is trying to retain.

reinforcer: a desirable consequence of an act that increases the probability that the act will recur.

rejected-aggressive children: a subgroup of rejected children who display high levels of hostility and aggression in their interactions with peers.

rejected children: children who are disliked by many peers and liked by few.

rejected-withdrawn children: a subgroup of rejected children who are often passive, socially unskilled, and insensitive to peer-group expectations.

relational aggression: acts such as snubbing, exclusion, withdrawing acceptance, or spreading rumours that are aimed at damaging an adversary's self-esteem, friendships, or social status.

relational primacy hypothesis: the hypothesis that analogical reasoning is available in infancy.

relational self-worth: feelings of self-esteem within a particular relationship context (e.g., with parents, with classmates); may differ across relationship contexts.

reliability: the extent to which a measuring instrument yields consistent results, both over time and across observers.

REM sleep: a state of active or irregular sleep in which the eyes move rapidly beneath the eyelids and brain wave activity is similar to the pattern displayed when awake.

representational insight: the knowledge that an entity can stand for (represent) something other than itself.

repression: a type of motivated forgetting in which anxiety-provoking thoughts and conflicts are forced out of conscious awareness.

resistant attachment: an insecure infant–caregiver bond, characterized by strong separation protest and a tendency of the child to remain near but resist contact initiated by the caregiver, particularly after a separation.

respiratory distress syndrome: a serious condition in which a preterm infant breathes very irregularly and is at risk of dying (also called *hyaline membrane disease*).

retaliatory aggression: aggressive acts elicited by real or imagined provocations.

reticular formation: area of the brain that activates the organism and is thought to be important in regulating attention.

retrieval: the class of strategies aimed at getting information out of the long-term store.

reversibility: the ability to reverse or negate an action by mentally performing the opposite action (negation).

RH factor: a blood protein that, when present in a fetus but not the mother, can cause the mother to produce antibodies; these antibodies may then attack the red blood cells of subsequent fetuses who have the protein in their blood.

rites of passage: rituals that signify the passage from one period of life to another (for example, puberty rites).

role taking: the ability to assume another person's perspective and understand his or her thoughts, feelings, and behaviours.

rubella (German measles): a disease that has little effect on a mother but may cause a number of serious birth defects in unborn children who are exposed in the first three to four months of pregnancy.

s: Spearman's term for mental abilities that are specific to particular tests.

scaffolding: the process by which an expert, when instructing a novice, responds contingently to the novice's behaviour in a learning situation, so that the novice gradually increases his or her understanding of a problem.

scheme: an organized pattern of thought or action that one constructs to interpret some aspect of one's experience; Piaget sometimes used the term *cognitive structures* as a synonym for schemes.

schizophrenia: a serious form of mental illness characterized by disturbances in logical thinking, emotional expression, and interpersonal behaviour.

scientific method: an attitude or value about the pursuit of knowledge that dictates that investigators be objective and allow their data to determine the merits of their theorizing.

script: a general representation of the typical sequencing of events (that is, what occurs and when) in some familiar context.

secondary circular reactions: the third substage of Piaget's sensorimotor stage; a pleasurable response, centred on an external object, that is discovered by chance and performed over and over.

secondary (or complex) emotions: self-conscious or self-evaluative emotions that emerge in the second year and depend, in part, on cognitive development.

secondary reinforcer: an initially neutral stimulus that acquires reinforcement value by virtue of its repeated association with other reinforcing stimuli.

second stage of labour: the period of the birth process during which the fetus moves through the birth canal and emerges from the mother's body (also called *delivery*).

secular trend: a trend in industrialized societies toward earlier maturation and greater body size now than in the past.

secure attachment: an infant–caregiver bond in which the child welcomes contact with a close companion and uses this person as a secure base from which to explore the environment.

secure base: an infant's use of a caregiver as a base from which to explore the environment and to which to return for emotional support.

selective attention: capacity to focus on task-relevant aspects of experience while ignoring irrelevant or distracting information.

selective attrition: nonrandom loss of participants during a study that results in a nonrepresentative sample.

selective breeding experiment: a method of studying genetic influences by determining whether traits can be bred in animals through selective mating.

self: the combination of physical and psychological attributes that is unique to each individual.

self-care, or latchkey, children: children who care for themselves after school or in the evenings while their parents are working.

self-concept: one's perceptions of one's unique attributes or traits.

self-esteem: one's evaluation of one's worth as a person based on an assessment of the qualities that make up the self-concept.

self-fulfilling prophecy: phenomenon whereby people cause others to act in accordance with the expectations they have about those others.

self-oriented distress: feeling of *personal* discomfort or distress that may be elicited when we experience the emotions of (that is, empathize with) a distressed other; thought to inhibit altruism.

self-recognition: the ability to recognize oneself in a mirror or a photograph.

semantic organization: a strategy for remembering that involves grouping or classifying stimuli into meaningful (or manageable) clusters that are easier to retain.

semantics: the expressed meaning of words and sentences.

sensation: detection of stimuli by the sensory receptors and transmission of this information to the brain.

sensitive period: period of time that is optimal for the development of particular capacities or behaviours and in which the individual is particularly sensitive to environmental influences that would foster these attributes; outside this period, the same environmental influences must be much stronger to produce comparable effects.

sensitive-period hypothesis (of language acquisition): the notion that human beings are most proficient at language learning before they reach puberty.

sensorimotor stage: Piaget's first intellectual stage, from birth to 2 years, when infants are relying on behavioural schemes as a means of exploring and understanding the environment.

sensory store (or sensory register): first information-processing store, in which stimuli are noticed and are briefly available for further processing.

separation anxiety: a wary or fretful reaction that infants and toddlers often display when separated from the people to whom they are attached.

sequential design: a research design in which subjects from different age groups are studied repeatedly over a period of months or years.

sex-linked characteristic: an attribute determined by a recessive gene that appears on the X chromosome; more likely to characterize males.

sexuality: aspect of self referring to erotic thoughts, actions, and orientation.

shared environmental influence (SE): an environmental influence that people living together share that should make these individuals similar to one another.

short-term store (STS): second information-processing store, in which stimuli are retained for several seconds and operated upon (also called *working memory*).

sibling rivalry: the spirit of competition, jealousy, and resentment that may arise between two or more siblings.

sickle-cell anemia: a genetic blood disease that causes red blood cells to assume an unusual sickled shape and to become inefficient at distributing oxygen.

simple dominant-recessive inheritance: a pattern of inheritance in which one allele dominates another so that only its phenotype is expressed.

simple stepparent home: family consisting of a parent and his or her biological children and a stepparent.

single-parent family: a family system consisting of one parent (either the mother or the father) and the parent's dependent child(ren).

situational compliance: compliance based primarily on a parent's power to control the child's conduct.

size constancy: the tendency to perceive an object as the same size from different distances despite changes in the size of its retinal image.

skeletal age: a measure of physical maturation based on the child's level of skeletal development.

slow-to-warm-up temperament: temperamental profile in which the child is inactive and moody and displays mild passive resistance to new routines and experiences.

small-for-date, or small-for-gestational-age, babies: infants whose birth weight is far below normal, including those born close to their normal due dates.

sociability: willingness to interact with others and to seek their attention or approval.

social cognition: thinking people display about the thoughts, feelings, motives, and behaviours of themselves and other people.

social comparison: the process of defining and evaluating the self by comparing oneself with other people.

social-conventional rules: standards of conduct determined by social consensus that indicate what is appropriate within a particular social context.

socialization: the process by which children acquire the beliefs, values, and behaviours considered desirable or appropriate by the society to which they belong.

social problem-solving training: method of social-skills training in which an adult helps children (through role playing or role-taking training) to make less hostile attributions about harmdoing and to generate nonaggressive solutions to conflict.

social referencing: the use of others' emotional expressions to infer the meaning of otherwise ambiguous situations.

social stimulation hypothesis: the notion that socially deprived infants develop abnormally because they have had little contact with companions who respond contingently to their social overtures.

social support: tangible and intangible resources provided by other people in times of uncertainty or stress.

sociocultural theory: Vygotsky's perspective on cognitive development, in which children acquire their culture's values, beliefs, and problem-solving strategies through collaborative dialogues with more knowledgeable members of society.

sociohistorical development: changes that have occurred in one's culture and the values, norms, and technologies such a history has generated.

sociolinguistic knowledge: culturally specific rules specifying how language should be structured and used in particular social contexts.

sociometric techniques: procedures that ask children to identify those peers whom they like or dislike or to rate peers for their desirability as companions; used to measure children's peer acceptance (or nonacceptance).

span of apprehension: the number of items that people can keep in mind at any one time, or the amount of information that people can attend to at a single time without operating mentally to store this information.

spina bifida: a bulging of the spinal cord through a gap in the spinal column.

Stanford-Binet Intelligence Scale: the modern descendent of the first successful intelligence test; measures general intelligence and four factors: verbal reasoning, quantitative reasoning, spatial reasoning, and short-term memory.

stereopsis: the fusion of two flat images to produce a single image that has depth.

stereotype threat: a fear that one will be judged to have traits associated with negative social stereotypes about his or her racial or ethnic group.

store model: information-processing model that depicts information as flowing through three processing units (or stores): the sensory store, the short-term store (STS), and the long-term store (LTS).

stranger anxiety: a wary or fretful reaction that infants and toddlers often display when approached by an unfamiliar person.

strange situation: a series of eight separation and reunion episodes to which infants are exposed in order to determine the quality of their attachments.

strategic memory: processes involved as one consciously attempts to retain or retrieve information.

strategies: goal-directed and deliberately implemented mental operations used to facilitate task performance.

strategy choice model: Siegler's model to describe how strategies change over time; the view that multiple strategies exist within a child's cognitive repertoire at any one time, with these strategies competing with one another for use.

structured interview or structured questionnaire: a technique in which all participants are asked the same questions in precisely the same order so that the responses of different participants can be compared.

structured observation: a method in which the investigator cues the behaviour of interest and observes participants' responses in a laboratory.

structure-of-intellect model: Guilford's factor-analytic model of intelligence, which proposes that there are 180 distinct mental abilities.

sudden infant death syndrome (SIDS): the unexplained death of a sleeping infant who suddenly stops breathing (also called *crib death*).

superego: psychoanalytic term for the component of the personality that consists of one's internalized moral standards.

survival reflexes: inborn responses such as breathing, sucking, and swallowing that enable the newborn to adapt to the environment.

symbolic function: the ability to use symbols (for example, images and words) to represent objects and experiences.

symbolic (or pretend) play: play in which one object, action, or actor symbolizes or stands for another.

symbolic schemes: internal mental symbols (such as images or verbal codes) that one uses to represent aspects of experience.

sympathetic empathic arousal: the feeling of sympathy or compassion that may be elicited when one experiences the emotions of (that is, empathizes with) a distressed other; thought to become an important mediator of altruism.

synapse: the connective space (juncture) between one nerve cell (neuron) and another.

synaptogenesis: the formation of connections (synapses) among neurons.

synchronized routines: generally harmonious interactions between two people in which participants adjust their behaviour in response to each other's actions.

syntactical bootstrapping: the notion that young children make inferences about the meaning of words by analyzing the way words are used in sentences and inferring whether they refer to objects (nouns), actions (verbs), or attributes (adjectives).

syntax: the structure of a language; the rules specifying how words and grammatical markers are to be combined to produce meaningful sentences.

syphilis: a common sexually transmitted disease that may cross the placental barrier in the middle and later stages of pregnancy, causing miscarriage or serious birth defects.

tabula rasa: the idea that the mind of an infant is a "blank slate" and that all knowledge, abilities, behaviours, and motives are acquired through experience.

tacit (or practical) intelligence: ability to size up everyday problems and solve them; only modestly related to IQ.

telegraphic speech: early sentences that consist of content words and omit the less meaningful parts of speech, such as articles, prepositions, pronouns, and auxiliary verbs.

television literacy: one's ability to understand and interpret how information is conveyed in television programming.

temperament: a person's characteristic modes of responding emotionally and behaviourally to environmental events, including such attributes as activity level, irritability, fearfulness, and sociability.

temperament hypothesis: Kagan's view that the strange-situation test measures individual differences in infants' temperaments rather than the quality of their attachments.

teratogens: external agents such as viruses, drugs, chemicals, and radiation that can harm a developing embryo or fetus.

tertiary circular reactions: the fifth substage of Piaget's sensorimotor stage; an exploratory scheme in which the infant devises a new method of acting on objects to reproduce interesting results.

testicular feminization syndrome (TFS): a genetic anomaly in which a male fetus is insensitive to the effects of male sex hormones and develops female-like external genitalia.

test norms: standards of normal performance on psychometric instruments that are based on the average scores and the range of scores obtained by a large, representative sample of test takers.

testosterone: male sex hormone, produced by the testes, that is responsible for male sexual maturation.

thalidomide: a mild tranquilizer that, taken early in pregnancy, produced a variety of malformations of the limbs, eyes, ears, and heart.

theory: a set of concepts and propositions designed to organize, describe, and explain an existing set of observations.

theory of mind: the understanding that people are cognitive beings with mental states (beliefs, motives, feelings, and intentions) that are not always accessible to others and that often guide their behaviour.

theory of multiple intelligences: Gardner's theory that humans display at least seven distinct kinds of intelligence, each linked to a particular area of the brain, several of which are not measured by IQ tests.

"theory" theories: theories of cognitive development that combine neo-nativism and constructivism, proposing that cognitive development progresses by children generating, testing, and changing theories about the physical and social world.

third stage of labour: expulsion of the placenta (afterbirth).

three-stratum theory of intelligence: Carroll's hierarchical model of intelligence with *g* at the top of the hierarchy, eight broad abilities at the second level, or stratum, and narrower domains of each second-stratum ability at the third stratum.

thyroxine: a hormone produced by the thyroid gland; essential for normal growth of the brain and the body.

time-out technique: a form of discipline in which children who misbehave are removed from the setting until they are prepared to act more appropriately.

time-sampling: procedure in which the investigator records the frequencies with which individuals display particular behaviours during the brief time intervals that each participant is observed.

timing-of-puberty effect: the finding that people who reach puberty late perform better on visual/spatial tasks than those who mature early.

tools of intellectual adaptation: Vygotsky's term for methods of thinking and problem-solving strategies that children internalize from their interactions with more competent members of society.

toxoplasmosis: a disease caused by a parasite found in raw meat and cat feces; can cause birth defects if transmitted to an embryo in the first trimester; can cause miscarriage later in pregnancy.

traditional classroom: a classroom arrangement in which all pupils sit facing the teacher, who normally teaches one subject at a time by lecturing or giving demonstrations.

transactional model: model of family influence in which parent and child are believed to influence one another reciprocally.

transactive interactions: verbal exchanges in which individuals perform mental operations on the reasoning of their discussion partners.

transformational grammar: rules of syntax that allow one to transform declarative statements into questions, negatives, imperatives, and other kinds of sentences.

transitivity: the ability to recognize relations among elements in a serial order (for example, if A is greater than B, and if B is greater than C, then A is greater than C).

triarchic theory: a recent information-processing theory of intelligence that emphasizes three aspects of intelligent behaviour not normally tapped by IQ tests: the context of the action; the person's *experience* with the task (or situation); and the *information-processing strategies* the person applies to the task (or situation).

twin design: study in which sets of twins that differ in zygosity (kinship) are compared to determine the heritability of an attribute.

two-generation intervention: interventions with goals to both stimulate children's intellectual development through preschool daycare/education and to assist parents to move out of poverty.

ulnar grasp: an early manipulative skill in which an infant grasps objects by pressing the fingers against the palm.

ultrasound: method of detecting gross physical abnormalities by scanning the womb with sound waves, thereby producing a visual outline of the fetus.

umbilical cord: a soft tube containing blood vessels that connects the embryo to the placenta.

unconditioned response (UCR): the unlearned response elicited by an unconditioned stimulus.

unconditioned stimulus (UCS): a stimulus that elicits a particular response without any prior learning.

unconscious motives: Freud's term for feelings, experiences, and conflicts that influence a person's thinking and behaviour, but lie outside the person's awareness.

underextension: the young child's tendency to use general words to refer to a smaller set of objects, actions, or events than adults do (for example, using *candy* to refer only to mints).

uninvolved parenting: a pattern of parenting that is both aloof (or even hostile) and overpermissive, almost as if parents neither cared about their children nor about what they may become.

utilization deficiency: a failure to benefit from effective strategies that one has spontaneously produced; thought to occur in the early phases of strategy acquisition when executing the strategy requires much mental effort.

validity: the extent to which a measuring instrument accurately reflects what the researchers intended to measure.

vernix: the white cheesy substance that covers the fetus to protect the skin from chapping.

visual acuity: a person's ability to see small objects and fine detail.

visual cliff: an elevated platform that creates an illusion of depth, used to test the depth perception of infants.

visual contrast: the amount of light/dark transition in a visual stimulus.

visual looming: the expansion of the image of an object to take up the entire visual field as it gets very close to the face.

visual/spatial abilities: the ability to mentally manipulate or otherwise draw inferences about pictorial information.

vitamin/mineral deficiency: a form of malnutrition in which the diet provides sufficient protein and calories but is lacking in one or more substances that promote normal growth.

vocables: unique patterns of sound that a prelinguistic infant uses to represent objects, actions, or events.

Wechsler Intelligence Scale for Children—III (WISC-III): widely used individual intelligence test that includes a measure of general intelligence and both verbal and performance intelligence.

Wernicke's area: structure located in the temporal lobe of the left hemisphere of the cerebral cortex that is responsible for interpreting speech.

working memory: the capacity to store and operate on information being held in the short-term store.

X chromosome: the longer of the two sex chromosomes; normal females have two X chromosomes, whereas normal males have only one.

Y chromosome: the shorter of the two sex chromosomes; normal males have one Y chromosome, whereas females have none.

zone of proximal development: Vygotsky's term for the range of tasks that are too complex to be mastered alone but that can be accomplished with guidance and encouragement from a more skillful partner.

zygote: a single cell formed at conception from the union of a sperm and an ovum.

Abel, E.L. (1981). Behavioral teratology of alcohol. *Psychological Bulletin, 90,* 564–81.

Abma, J.C., & Mott, F.L. (1991). Substance use and prenatal care during pregnancy among young women. *Family Planning Perspectives, 23* (3), 117–22, 128.

Aboud, F.E. (1988). *Children and prejudice.* New York: Blackwell.

Abramovitch, R., Corter, C., & Pepler, D.J. (1980). Observations of mixed-sex sibling dyads. *Child Development, 51,* 1268–71.

Abramovitch, R., Corter, C., Pepler, D.J., & Stanhope, L. (1986). Sibling and peer interaction: A final follow-up and a comparison. *Child Development, 57,* 217–29.

Abramovitch, R., Freedman, J.L., Henry, K., & Van Brunschot, M. (1995). Children's capacity to agree to psychological research: Knowledge of risks and benefits and voluntariness. *Ethics & Behavior, 5,* 25–48.

Abravanel, E., & Sigafoos, A.D. (1984). Exploring the presence of imitation during early infancy. *Child Development, 55,* 381–92.

Achenbach, T.M., Phares, V., Howell, C.T., Rauh, V.A., & Nurcombe, B. (1990). Seven-year outcome of the Vermont Intervention Program for low-birthweight infants. *Child Development, 61,* 1672–81.

Ackerman, B.P. (1993). Children's understanding of the speaker's meaning in referential communication. *Journal of Experimental Child Psychology, 55,* 56–86.

Ackerman, B.P., Schoff, K., Levinson, K., Youngstrom, E., & Izard, C.E. (1999b). The relations between cluster indexes of risk and promotion and the problem behaviors of 6- and 7-year-old children from economically disadvantaged families. *Developmental Psychology, 35,* 1355–66.

Ackerman, B.P., Szymanski, J., & Silver, D. (1990). Children's use of common ground in interpreting ambiguous referential utterances. *Developmental Psychology, 26,* 234–45.

Ackermann-Liebrich, U., Voegeli, T., Gunter-Witt, K., Kunz, I., Zullig, M., Schlindler, C., & Maurer, M. (1996). Home versus hospital deliveries: Follow up study of matched pairs for procedures and outcome. *British Medical Journal, 313,* 1313–8.

Acredolo, L.P., & Goodwyn, S.W. (1990). Sign language in babies: The significance of symbolic gesturing for understanding language development. In R. Vasta (Ed.), *Annals of child development* (Vol. 7, pp. 1–42). Greenwich, CT: JAI Press.

Adams, G.R., Abraham, K.G., & Markstrom, C.A. (1987). The relations among identity development, self-consciousness, and self-focusing during middle and late adolescence. *Developmental Psychology, 23,* 292–7.

Adams, G.R., & Crane, P. (1980). An assessment of parents' and teachers' expectations of preschool children's social preference for attractive or unattractive children and adults. *Child Development, 51,* 224–31.

Adams, G.R., Ryan, B.A., Ketsetzis, M., & Keating, L. (2000). Rule compliance and peer sociability: A study of family process, school-focused parent–child interactions, and children's classroom behavior. *Journal of Family Psychology, 14* (2), 237–50.

Adams, M.J., Treiman, R., & Pressley, M. (1998). Reading, writing and literacy. In W. Damon (Series Ed.) & I.E. Sigel & K.A. Renninger (Vol. Eds.), *Handbook of child psychology: Vol. 4. Child psychology in practice* (5th ed., pp. 275–357). New York: Wiley.

Adams, R., & Courage, M. (1998). Human newborn colour vision: Measurement with chromatic stimuli varying in excitation purity. *Journal of Experimental Child Psychology, 68* (1), 22–34.

Adey, P.S., & Shayer, M. (1992). Accelerating the development of formal thinking in middle and high school students: II. Postproject effects on science achievement. *Journal of Research in Science Teaching, 29,* 81–92.

Adler, A. (1964). *Problems of neurosis.* New York: Harper & Row. (Original work published 1929.)

Adolph, K.E., Eppler, M.A., & Gibson, E.J. (1993). Crawling versus walking infants' perception of affordances for locomotion over sloping surfaces. *Child Development, 64,* 1158–74.

Aguiar, A., & Baillargeon, R. (1998). Eight-and-a-half-month-old infants' reasoning about containment events. *Child Development, 69,* 636–53.

Ainsworth, M.D.S. (1967). *Infancy in Uganda: Infant care and the growth of love.* Baltimore, MD: Johns Hopkins University Press.

Ainsworth, M.D.S. (1979). Attachment as related to mother–infant interaction. In J.S. Rosenblatt, R.A. Hinde, C. Beer, & M. Busnel (Eds.), *Advances in the study of behavior* (Vol. 9). New York: Academic Press.

Ainsworth, M.D.S. (1989). Attachments beyond infancy. *American Psychologist, 44,* 709–16.

Ainsworth, M.D.S., Bell, S.M., & Stayton, D.J. (1972). Individual differences in the development of some attachment behaviors. *Merrill-Palmer Quarterly, 18,* 123–43.

Ainsworth, M.D.S., Blehar, M., Waters, E., & Wall, S. (1978). *Patterns of attachment.* Hillsdale, NJ: Erlbaum.

Akhtar, N., Carpenter, M., & Tomasello, M. (1996). The role of discourse novelty in early word learning. *Child Development, 67,* 635–45.

Akhtar, N., Jipson, J., & Callanan, M.A. (2001). Learning words through overhearing. *Child Development, 72,* 416–30.

Al-Awad, A.M., & Sonuga-Barke, E.J. (1992). Childhood problems in a Sudanese city: A comparison of extended and nuclear families. *Child Development, 63,* 906–14.

Albert, R.S. (1994). The achievement of eminence: A longitudinal study of exceptionally gifted boys and their families. In R.F. Subotnik & K.D. Arnold (Eds.), *Beyond Terman: Contemporary studies of giftedness and talent* (pp. 282–315). Norwood, NJ: Ablex.

Alessandri, S.M., Bendersky, M., & Lewis, M. (1998). Cognitive functioning in 8- to 18-month-old drug-exposed infants. *Developmental Psychology, 34,* 565–73.

Alessandri, S.M., & Lewis, M. (1996). Differences in pride and shame in maltreated and nonmaltreated toddlers. *Child Development, 67,* 1857–69.

Alessandri, S.M., & Sullivan, M.W., Imaizumi, S., & Lewis, M. (1993). Learning and emotional responsivity in cocaine-exposed infants. *Developmental Psychology, 29,* 989–97.

Alexander, B.K., & Harlow, H.F. (1965). Social behavior in juvenile rhesus monkeys subjected to different rearing conditions during the first 6 months of life. *Zoologische Jarbucher Physiologie, 60,* 167–74.

Alexander, G.M., & Hines, M. (1994). Gender labels and play styles: Their relative contribution to children's selection of playmates. *Child Development, 65,* 869–79.

Alexander, K.L., & Entwisle, D.R. (1988). Achievement in the first two years of school: Patterns and processes. *Monographs of the Society for Research in Child Development, 53* (2, Serial No. 218).

Alfieri, T., Ruble, D.N., & Higgins, E.T. (1996). Gender stereotypes during adolescence: Developmental changes and the transition to junior high school. *Developmental Psychology, 32,* 1129–37.

Alibali, M.W. (1999). How children change their minds: Strategy choice can be gradual or abrupt. *Developmental Psychology, 35,* 127-145.

Allen, J.P., Moore, C., Kuperminc, G., & Bell, K. (1998). Attachment and adolescent psychosocial functioning. *Child Development, 69,* 1406–19.

Allen, J.P., Weissberg, R.P., & Hawkins, J.A. (1989). The relation between values and social competence in early adolescence. *Developmental Psychology, 25,* 458–64.

Allen, M.C., & Capute, A.J. (1986). Assessment of early auditory and visual abilities of extremely premature infants. *Developmental Medicine and Child Neurology, 28,* 458–66.

Allen, S.E.M., & Crego, M.B. (1996). Early passive acquisition in Inuktitut. *Journal of Child Language, 23,* 129-156.

Alley, T.R. (1981). Head shape and the perception of cuteness. *Developmental Psychology, 17,* 650–4.

Allgood-Merten, B., & Stockard, J. (1991). Sex role identity and self-esteem: A comparison of children and adolescents. *Sex Roles, 25,* 129–39.

Amabile, T.M. (1983). *The social psychology of creativity.* New York: Springer-Verlag.

Amato, P.R. (1993). Children's adjustment to divorce: Theories, hypotheses, and empirical support. *Journal of Marriage and the Family, 55,* 23–38.

Amato, P.R. (1996). Explaining the intergenerational transmission of divorce. *Journal of Marriage and the Family, 58,* 628–40.

Amato, P.R., & Booth, A. (1996). A prospective study of divorce and parent–child relationships. *Journal of Marriage and the Family, 58,* 356–65.

Amato, P.R., & Keith, B. (1991). Parental divorce and the well-being of children: A meta-analysis. *Psychological Bulletin, 110,* 26–46

Amato, P.R., Loomis, L.S., & Booth, A. (1995). Parental divorce, marital conflict, and offspring well-being during early childhood. *Social Forces, 73,* 895–915.

Ambert, A. (1992). *The effect of children on parents.* New York: Haworth.

American Academy of Pediatrics (2000). Changing concepts of sudden infant death syndrome: Implications for infant sleeping environment and sleep position (RE8946). *Pediatrics, 105,* 650-656.

American Psychiatric Association. (1994). *Diagnostic and statistical manual of mental disorders* (4th ed.). Washington, DC: Author.

American Psychological Association. (1992). Ethical principles of psychologists and code of conduct. *American Psychologist, 47,* 1597–611.

Amini, S. B., Cataloano, P.M., Dierker, L.J., & Mann, L.I. (1996). Births to teenagers: Trends and obstetric outcomes. *Obstetrics and Genecology, 87,* 668–674.

Ammerman, R.T., & Patz, R.J. (1996). Determinants of child abuse potential: Parent and child factors. *Journal of Clinical Child Psychology, 25,* 300–7.

Andermann, E.M., & Midgley, C. (1997). Changes in achievement goal orientation, perceived academic competence, and grades across the transition to middle level schools. *Contemporary Educational Psychology, 22,* 269–98.

Anderson, C.A., & Dill, K.E. (2000). Video games and aggressive thoughts, feelings, and behavior in the laboratory and in life. *Journal of Personality and Social Psychology, 78,* 772–90.

Anderson, D.R., Huston, A.C., Schmitt, K.L., Linebarger, D.L., & Wright, J.C. (2001). Early childhood television viewing and adolescent behavior. *Monographs of the Society for Research in Child Development, 66* (1, serial No. 264).

Anderson, J. (1996). Gynecological and obstetrical issues for HIV-infected women. In R.R. Faden & N.E. Kass (Eds.), *HIV, AIDS, and childbearing* (pp. 31–62). New York: Oxford University Press.

Andersson, B. (1989). Effects of public day-care: A longitudinal study. *Child Development, 60,* 857–66.

Andersson, B. (1992). Effects of day-care on cognitive and socioemotional competence of thirteen-year-old Swedish schoolchildren. *Child Development, 63,* 20–36.

Anglin, J.M. (1993). Vocabulary development: a morphological analysis. *Monographs of the Society for Research in Child Development, 58* (10, Serial No. 238).

Anisfield, M. (1996). Only tongue protrusion modeling is matched by neonates. *Developmental Review, 16,* 149–161.

Apgar, V., & Beck, J. (1974). *Is my baby all right?* New York: Pocket Books.

Archer, J. (1991). The influence of testosterone on human aggression. *British Journal of Psychology, 82,* 1–28.

Archer, J. (1992a). Childhood gender roles: Social context and organisation. In H. McGurk (Ed.), *Childhood social development: Contemporary perspectives* (pp. 31–61). Hove, England: Erlbaum.

Archer, J. (1992b). *Ethology and human development.* Hertfordshire, England: Harvester Wheatsheaf.

Archer, J. (1996). Sex differences in social behavior: Are the social role and evolutionary explanations compatible? *American Psychologist, 51,* 909–17.

Archer, S.L. (1982). The lower age boundaries of identity development. *Child Development, 53,* 1551–6.

Archer, S.L. (1992). A feminist's approach to identity research. In G.R. Adams, T.P. Gullotta, & R. Montemayor (Eds.), *Advances in adolescent development: Vol. 4. Adolescent identity formation* (pp. 25–49). Newbury Park, CA: Sage.

Archer, S.L. (1994). *Interventions for adolescent identity development.* Thousand Oaks, CA: Sage.

Aries, P. (1962). *Centuries of childhood.* New York: Knopf.

Arnett, J.J. (1995). Broad and narrow socialization: The family in the context of a cultural theory. *Journal of Marriage and the Family, 57,* 617–28.

Aro, H., & Taipale, V. (1987). The impact of timing of puberty on psychosomatic symptoms among fourteen- to sixteen-year-old Finnish girls. *Child Development, 58,* 261–8.

Aronson, J., Fried, C. B., & Good, C. (2002). Reducing the effects of stereotype threat on African American college students by shaping theories of intelligence. *Journal of Experimental Social Psychology.*

Aronson, E., & Rosenbloom, S. (1971). Space perception within a common auditory-visual space. *Science, 172,* 1161–3.

Arsenio, W.F., Cooperman, S., & Lover, A. (2000). Affective predictors of preschoolers' aggression and peer acceptance: Direct and indirect effects. *Developmental Psychology, 36,* 438–48.

Arsenio, W.F., & Kramer, R. (1992). Victimizers and their victims: Children's conceptions of mixed emotional consequences of moral transgressions. *Child Development, 63,* 915–27.

Arterberry, M., Yonas, A., & Bensen, A.S. (1989). Self-produced locomotion and the development of responsiveness to linear perspective and texture gradients. *Developmental Psychology, 25,* 976–82.

Asendorpf, J.B., & Baudonniere, P. (1993). Self-awareness and other-awareness: Mirror self-recognition and synchronic imitation among unfamiliar peers. *Developmental Psychology, 29,* 88–95.

Asendorpf, J.B., Warkentin, V., & Baudonniere, P. (1996). Self-awareness and other awareness II: Mirror self-recognition, social contingency awareness, and synchronic imitation. *Developmental Psychology, 32* (2), 313–21.

Asher, S.R., & Coie, J.D. (1990). *Peer rejection in childhood.* Cambridge, England: Cambridge University Press.

Asher, S.R., Renshaw, P.D., & Hymel, S. (1982). Peer relations and the development of social skills. In S.G. Moore & C.R. Cooper (Eds.), *The young child: Reviews of research* (Vol. 3, pp. 137–58). Washington, DC: National Association for the Education of Young Children.

Aslin, R.N. (1987). Visual and auditory development in infancy. In J.D. Osofsky (Ed.), *Handbook of infant development* (2nd ed.). New York: Wiley.

Aslin, R.N., Pisoni, D.B., & Jusczyk, P.W. (1983). Auditory development and speech perception in infancy. In M.M. Haith & J.J. Campos (Eds.), *Handbook of child psychology: Vol. 2. Infancy and developmental psychobiology.* New York: Wiley.

Associated Press. (1994a, July 30). Science: A man's domain. *Atlanta Constitution,* p. A6.

Associated Press. (1996, December 30). Arizona to require divorcing parents to study impact on children. *Dallas Morning News,* p. 18a.

Associated Press. (1999, January 10). TV sex rampant, critics say. *Atlanta Constitution,* pp. D1, D3.

Astington, J.W., & Jenkins, J.M. (1995). Theory of mind development and social understanding. *Cognition and Emotion, 9,* 151–65.

Astor, R. A. (1994). Children's moral reasoning about family and peer violence: The role of provocation and retribution. *Child Development, 65,* 1054-1067.

Atkin, C. (1978). Observation of parent–child interaction in supermarket decision-making. *Journal of Marketing, 42,* 41–5.

Atkinson, L., Scott, B., Chisholm, V., Blackwell, J., Dickens, S., Tam, F., & Goldberg, S. (1995). Cognitive coping, affective stress, and material sensitivity: Mothers of children with Down Syndrome. *Developmental Psychology, 31,* 668–76.

Atkinson, R.C., & Shiffrin, R.M. (1968). Human memory: A proposed system and its control processes. In K.W. Spence & J.T. Spence (Eds.), *The psychology of learning and motivation: Advances in research and theory* (Vol. 2, pp. 90–195). Orlando, FL: Academic Press.

Atlas, R.S., & Pepler, D.J. (1998). Observations of bullying in the classroom. *Journal of Educational Research, 92* (2), 86–99.

Ausley, J.A., & Guttentag, R.E. (1993). Direct and indirect assessments of memory: Implications for the study of memory development. In M.L. Howe & R. Pasnak (Eds.), *Emerging themes in cognitive development: Vol. 1. Foundations.* New York: Springer-Verlag.

Austin, R.J., & Moawad, A.H. (1993). The very low birth weight fetus. In C. Lin, M.S. Verp, & R.E. Sabbagha (Eds.), *The high-risk fetus: Pathophysiology, diagnosis, management.* New York: Springer-Verlag.

Aviezer, D., Sagi, A., Joels, T., & Ziv, Y. (1999). Emotional availability and attachment representations in kibbutz infants and their mothers. *Developmental Psychology, 35,* 811–21.

Axia, G., Bonichini, S., & Benini, F. (1999). Attention and reaction to distress in infancy: A longitudinal study. *Developmental Psychology, 35,* 500–504.

Azmitia, M. (1988). Peer interaction and problem-solving: When are two heads better than one? *Child Development, 59,* 87–96.

Azmitia, M. (1992). Expertise, private speech, and the development of self-regulation. In R.M. Diaz & L.E. Berk (Eds.), *Private speech: From social interaction to self-regulation.* Hillsdale, NJ: Erlbaum.

Azmitia, M., & Hesser, J. (1993). Why siblings are important agents of cognitive development: A comparison of siblings and peers. *Child Development, 64,* 430–44.

Backschneider, A.G., Shatz, M., & Gelman, S.A. (1993). Preschoolers' ability to distinguish living kinds as a function of regrowth. *Child Development, 64,* 1242–57.

Bagley, C. (1995). *Child sexual abuse and mental health in adolescents and adults.* Aldershot, England: Ashgate.

Bagwell, C.L., Newcomb, A.F., & Bukowski, W.M. (1998). Preadolescent friendship and peer rejection as predictors of adult adjustment. *Child Development, 69,* 140–53.

Bahrick, L.E. (1988). Intermodal learning in infancy: Learning on the basis of two kinds of invariant relations in audible and visible events. *Child Development, 59,* 197–209.

Bahrick, L.E., & Lickliter, R. (2000). Intersensory redundancy guides attentional selectivity and perceptual learning in infancy. *Developmental Psychology, 36,* 190–201.

Bahrick, L.E., Netto, D., & Hernandez-Reif, M. (1998). Intermodal perception of adult and child faces and voices by infants. *Child Development, 69,* 1263–75.

Bai, D.L., & Bertenthal, B.I. (1992). Locomotor status and the development of spatial search skills. *Child Development, 63,* 215–26.

Baier, J.L., Rosenzweig, M.G., & Whipple, E. (1991). Patterns of sexual behavior, coercion, and victimization of university students. *Journal of College Student Development, 32,* 310–22.

Bailey, J.M., Brobow, D., Wolfe, M., & Mikach, S. (1995). Sexual orientation of adult sons of gay fathers. *Developmental Psychology, 31,* 124–9.

Bailey, J. M., Dunne, M. P., & Martin, N. G. (2000). Genetic and environmental influences on sexual orientation and its correlates in an Australian twin sample. *Journal of Personality and Social Psychology, 78,* 524–36.

Bailey, J.M., & Pillard, R.C. (1991). A genetic study of the male sexual orientation. *Archives of General Psychiatry, 48,* 1089–96.

Bailey, J.M., Pillard, R.C., Neale, M.C., & Agyei, Y. (1993). Heritable factors influence sexual orientation in women. *Archives of General Psychiatry, 50,* 217–23.

Baillargeon, R. (1987). Object permanence in 3½- and 4½-month-old infants. *Developmental Psychology, 23,* 655–64.

Baillargeon, R., & De Vos, J. (1991). Object permanence in young infants: Further evidence. *Child Development, 62,* 1227–46.

Baillargeon, R., & Graber, M. (1988). Evidence of location memory in 8-month-old infants in a nonsearch AB task. *Developmental Psychology, 24,* 502–11.

Baillargeon, R., Kotovsky, L., & Needham, A. (1995). The acquisition of physical knowledge in infancy. In G. Lewis, D. Premack, & D. Sperber (Eds.), *Casual understandings in cognition and culture.* Oxford: Oxford University Press.

Baird, P., Yee, I, & Sadovnick, A. (1994). Population based study of long-term outcomes after amniocentesis. *Lancet, 344,* 1134–6.

Baker, D.P. (1992). Compared to Japan the U.S. is a low achiever—really. *Educational Research, 22,* 18-20.

Baker, D.P., & Jones, D.P. (1992). Opportunity and performance: A sociological explanation for gender differences in academic mathematics. In J. Wrigley (Ed.), *Education and gender equality* (pp. 193– 201). London, England: Falmer Press.

Baker, R.L., & Mednick, B.R. (1984). *Influences on human development: A longitudinal perspective.* Boston: Kluwer Nijhoff.

Baker-Ward, L., Ornstein, P.A., & Holden, D. (1984). The expression of memorization in early childhood. *Journal of Experimental Child Psychology, 37,* 555–75.

Baldwin, D.A., Markman, E.M., Bill, B., Desjardins, R.N., Irwin, J.M., & Tidball, G. (1996). Infants' reliance on social criteria for establishing word–object relations. *Child Development, 67,* 3135–53.

Baldwin, D.A., & Moses, L.J. (1996). The ontogeny of social information gathering. *Child Development, 67,* 1915–39.

Baldwin, D.V., & Skinner, M.L. (1989). Structural model for antisocial behavior: Generalization to single-mother families. *Developmental Psychology, 25,* 45–50.

Ball, S., & Bogatz, C. (1970). *The first year of Sesame Street: An evaluation.* Princeton, NJ: Educational Testing Service.

Baltes, P.B., Reese, H.W., & Lipsitt, L.P. (1980). Lifespan developmental psychology. *Annual Review of Psychology, 31,* 65–110.

Bandura, A. (1965). Influence of models' reinforcement contingencies on the acquisition of imitative responses. *Journal of Personality and Social Psychology, 1,* 589–95.

Bandura, A. (1971). *Psychological modeling.* New York: Lieber-Atherton.

Bandura, A. (1977). *Social learning theory.* Englewood Cliffs, NJ: Prentice-Hall.

Bandura, A. (1986). *Social foundations of thought and action. A social cognitive theory.* Englewood Cliffs, NJ: Prentice-Hall.

Bandura, A. (1989). Social cognitive theory. In R. Vasta (Ed.), *Annals of child development: Vol. 6. Theories of child development: Revised formulations and current issues* (pp. 1–60). Greenwich, CT: JAI Press.

Bandura, A. (1991). Social cognitive theory of moral thought and action. In W.M. Kurtines & J.L. Gewirtz (Eds.), *Handbook of moral behavior and development* (Vol. 1, pp. 45–103). Hillsdale, NJ: Erlbaum.

Bandura, A. (1992). Perceived self-efficacy in cognitive development and functioning. *Educational Psychologist, 28,* 117–48.

Banks, J.A. (1993). Multicultural education: Historical development, dimensions,and practice. *Review of Educational Research, 19,* 3–49.

Banks, M.S., & Ginsburg, A.P. (1985). Infant visual preferences: A review and new theoretical treatment. In H.W. Reese (Ed.), *Advances in child development and behavior* (Vol. 19, pp. 207–46). Orlando, FL: Academic Press.

Banks, M.S., & Salapatek, P. (1983). Infant visual perception. In P.H. Mussen (Series Ed.) & M.M. Haith & J.J. Campos (Vol. Eds.), *Handbook of child psychology: Vol. 2. Infancy and developmental psychobiology* (4th ed., pp. 436–571). New York: Wiley.

Barber, B.K., Olsen, J.E., & Shagle, S.C. (1994). Associations between parental psychological and behavioral control and youth internalized and externalized behaviors. *Child Development, 65,* 1120–36.

Barden, R.C., Ford, M.E., Jensen, A.G., Rogers-Salyer, M., & Salyer, K.E. (1989). Effects of craniofacial deformity in infancy on the quality of mother–infant interactions. *Child Development, 60,* 819–24.

Barenboim, C. (1981). The development of person perception in childhood and adolescence: From behavioral comparisons to psychological constructs to psychological comparisons. *Child Development, 52,* 129–44.

Barker, E., & Galambos, N. (2003). Body dissatisfaction of adolescent girls and boys: Risk and resource factors. *Journal of Early Adolescence, 23* (2), 141-165.

Barker, R.G., & Gump, P.V. (1964). *Big school, small school.* Stanford, CA: Stanford University Press.

Barnard, K.E., & Bee, H.L. (1983). The impact of temporally patterned stimulation on the development of preterm infants. *Child Development, 54,* 1156–67.

Barnett, W.S. (1995, Winter). Long-term effects of early childhood programs on cognitive and school outcomes. *The Future of Children, 5* (3), 25–50.

Baron, N.S. (1992). *Growing up with language: How children learn to talk.* Reading, MA: Addison-Wesley.

Baron-Cohen, S. (1995). *Mindblindness: An essay on autism and theory of mind.* Cambridge, MA: MIT Press.

Baroni, M.R., & Axia, G. (1989). Children's meta-pragmatic abilities and the identification of polite and impolite requests. *First Language, 9,* 285–97.

Barr, H.M., Streissguth, A.P., Darby, B.L., & Sampson, P.D. (1990). Prenatal exposure to alcohol, caffeine, tobacco, and aspirin: Effects in three gross and gross motor performance in 4-year-old children. *Developmental Psychology, 26,* 339–48.

Barr, R., & Haynes, H. (1999). Developmental changes in imitation from television during infancy. *Child Development, 70,* 1067–1084.

Barrera, M.E., & Maurer, D. (1981). Recognition of mother's photographed face by the three-month-old infant. *Child Development, 52,* 714–6.

Barrett, D.E., & Frank, D.A. (1987). *The effects of undernutrition on children's behavior.* New York: Gordon and Breach.

Barrow, R. (1995). Keep them bells a-tolling. *Alberta Journal of Educational Research. Special Issue: Canadian perspectives on The Bell Curve, 41* (3), 289–96.

Barry, H., III, Bacon, M.K., & Child, I.L. (1957). A cross-cultural survey of some sex differences in socialization. *Journal of Abnormal and Social Psychology, 55,* 327–32.

Bar-Tal, D., Raviv, A., & Goldberg, M. (1982). Helping behavior among preschool children: An observational study. *Child Development, 53,* 396–402.

Bartholomew, K., & Horowitz, L.M. (1991). Attachment styles among young adults: A test of a four-category model. *Journal of Personality and Social Psychology, 61,* 226–44.

Barton, M.E., & Tomasello, M. (1991). Joint attention and conversation in mother-infant-sibling triads. *Child Development, 62,* 517–29.

Bartsch, K., & London, K. (2000). Children's use of mental state information in selecting persuasive arguments. *Developmental Psychology, 36,* 352–65.

Baskett, L.M., & Johnson, S.M. (1982). The young child's interaction with parents versus siblings: A behavioral analysis. *Child Development, 53,* 643–50.

Bates, E. (1993, March). *Nature, nurture, and language.* Invited address presented at the biennial meeting of the Society for Research in Child Development, New Orleans, LA.

Bates, E. (1999). On the nature of language. In R. Levi-Montalcini, D. Baltimore, R. Dulbecco, & F. Jacob (Series Eds.), & E. Bizzi, P. Calissano, & V. Volterra (Vol. Eds.), *Frontiere della biologia [Frontiers of biology]: The brain of homo sapiens.* Rome: Giovanni Trecanni.

Bates, E., O'Connell, B., & Shore, C. (1987). Language and communication in infancy. In J.D. Osofsky (Ed.), *Handbook of infant development* (2nd ed., pp. 149–203). New York: Wiley.

Bates, E., Thal, D., Whitsell, K., Fenson, L., & Oakes, L. (1989). Integrating language and gesture in infancy. *Developmental Psychology, 25,* 1004–19.

Bates, J.E., Pettit, G.S., Dodge, K.A., & Ridge, B. (1998). Interaction of temperamental resistance to control and restrictive parenting in the development of externalizing behavior. *Developmental Psychology, 34,* 982–95.

Bateson, D. (1995). How can the Bell Curve be taken seriously? *Alberta Journal of Educational Research. Special Issue: Canadian perspectives on The Bell Curve, 41* (3), 271–3.

Batson, C.D. (1991). *The altruism question: Toward a social-psychological answer.* Hillsdale, NJ: Erlbaum.

Bauer, P.J. (1997). Development of memory in early childhood. In N. Cowan (Ed.), *The development of memory in childhood* (pp. 83–111). London, England: London University College Press.

Bauer, P.J., & Wewerka, S.S. (1995). One- and two-year-olds recall events: Factors facilitating immediate and long-term memory in 13.5 and 16.5-month-old children. *Child Development, 64,* 1204–23.

Baumrind, D. (1967). Child care practices anteceding three patterns of preschool behavior. *Genetic Psychology Monographs, 75,* 43–88.

Baumrind, D. (1971). Current patterns of parental authority. *Developmental Psychology Monographs, 4* (1, Pt. 2), 1–103.

Baumrind, D. (1977, March). *Socialization determinants of personal agency.* Paper presented at the biennial meeting of the Society for Research in Child Development, New Orleans, LA.

Baumrind, D. (1983). Rejoinder to Lewis's reinterpretation of parental firm control effects: Are authoritative families really harmonious? *Psychological Bulletin, 94,* 132–42.

Baumrind, D. (1991). Effective parenting during the early adolescent transition. In P.A. Cowan & M. Hetherington (Eds.), *Family transitions.* Hillsdale, NJ: Erlbaum.

Baumrind, D. (1993). The average expectable environment is not good enough: A response to Scarr. *Child Development, 64,* 1299–317.

Baumrind, D. (1995). Commentary on sexual orientation: Research and social policy implications. *Developmental Psychology, 31,* 130–6.

Bayley, N. (1969). *Bayley Scales of Infant Development.* New York: Psychological Corporation.

Bayley, N. (1993). *Bayley Scales of Infant Development* (2nd ed.). San Antonio, TX: Psychological Corporation.

Beal, C.R. (1990). Development of knowledge about the role of inference in text comprehension. *Child Development, 61,* 1011–23.

Beal, C.R. (1994). *Boys and girls: The development of gender roles.* New York: McGraw-Hill.

Beal, C.R., & Belgrad, S.L. (1990). The development of message evaluation skills in young children. *Child Development, 61,* 705–12.

Bear, G.G., & Rys, G.S. (1994). Moral reasoning, classroom behavior, and sociometric status among elementary school children. *Developmental Psychology, 30,* 633–8.

Beard, R., & Chapple, J. (1995). An evaluation of maternity services. In B.P. Sachs, R. Beard, E. Papiernik, & C. Russell (Eds.), *Reproductive health care for women and babies* (pp. 246–62). New York: Oxford University Press.

Begley, S. (2000). Designer babies. In K.L. Freiberg (Ed.), *Human development 01/02* (29th ed., pp. 8–12). Guilford, CT: McGraw-Hill/Dushkin.

Begley, S. (2001). Decoding the human body. In K. H. Freiberg (Ed.), *Human Development 01/02* (29th ed., pp. 8–12). Guilford, CT: McGraw-Hill/Duskin.

Behnke, M., Davis Eyler, F., Wilson Garvan, C., Wobie, K., & Hou, W. (2002). Cocaine exposure and developmental outcome from birth to 6 months. *Neurotoxicology and Teratology, 24,* 283–295.

Behrend, D.A., Rosengren, K., & Perlmutter, M. (1989). A new look at children's private speech: The effects of age, task difficulty, and parent presence. *International Journal of Behavioral Development, 12,* 305–20.

Beidelman, T.O. (1971). *The Kaguru: A matrilineal people of East Africa.* New York: Holt, Rinehart & Winston.

Beilin, H. (1992). Piaget's enduring contribution to developmental psychology. *Developmental Psychology, 28,* 191–204.

Bell, A.P., Weinberg, M.S., & Hammersmith, S.K. (1981). *Sexual preference: Its development in men and women.* Bloomington, IN: Indiana University Press.

Bell, M.A., & Fox, N.A. (1992). The relations between frontal brain electrical activity and cognitive development during infancy. *Child Development, 63,* 1142–63.

Bell, R.Q. (1979). Parent, child, and reciprocal influences. *American Psychologist, 34,* 821–6.

Bellugi, U. (1988). The acquisition of a spatial language. In F.S. Kessel (Ed.), *The development of language and language researchers: Essays in honor of Roger Brown* (pp. 153–85). Hillsdale, NJ: Erlbaum.

Belsky, J. (1981). Early human experience: A family perspective. *Developmental Psychology, 17,* 3–23.

Belsky, J. (1993). Etiology of child maltreatment: A developmental ecological analysis. *Psychological Bulletin, 114,* 413–34.

Belsky, J. (1996). Parent, infant, and social-contextual antecedents of father–son attachment security. *Developmental Psychology, 32,* 905–13.

Belsky, J., Friedman, S.L., & Hsieh, K. (2001). Testing a core emotion-regulation prediction: Does early attentional persistence moderate the effect of infant negative emotionality on later development? *Child Development, 72,* 123–33.

Belsky, J., Garduque, L., & Hrncir, E. (1984). Assessing performance, competence, and executive capacity in infant play: Relations to home environment and security of attachment. *Developmental Psychology, 20,* 406–11.

Belsky, J., Gilstrap, B., & Rovine, M. (1984). The Pennsylvania infant and family development project: I. Stability and change in mother–infant and father–infant interaction in a family setting at one, three, and nine months. *Child Development, 55,* 692–705.

Belsky, J., Rosenberger, K., & Crnic, K. (1995). Maternal personality, marital quality, social support, and infant temperament: Their significance for mother–infant attachment in human families. In C. Pryce, R. Martin, & D. Skuse (Eds.), *Motherhood in human and nonhuman primates* (pp. 115–24). Basel, Switzerland: Kruger.

Belsky, J., & Rovine, M. (1988). Nonmaternal care in the first year of life and the security of infant–parent attachment. *Child Development, 59,* 157–67.

Belsky, J., Rovine, M., & Taylor, D.G. (1984). The Pennsylvania Infant and Family Development Project III: The origins of individual differences in infant–mother attachment—maternal and infant contributions. *Child Development, 55,* 718–28.

Belsky, J., Spritz, B., & Crnic, K. (1996). Infant attachment security and affective-cognitive information processing at age 3. *Psychology Science, 7,* 111–4.

Bem, S.L. (1974). The measurement of psychological androgyny. *Journal of Consulting and Clinical Psychology, 42,* 155–62.

Bem, S.L. (1975). Sex-role adaptability: One consequence of psychological androgyny. *Journal of Personality and Social Psychology, 31,* 63–43.

Bem, S.L. (1978). Beyond androgyny: Some presumptuous prescriptions for a liberated sexual identity. In J.A. Sherman & F.L. Denmark (Eds.), *The psychology of women: Future directions in research* (pp. 1–22). New York: Psychological Dimensions.

Bem, S.L. (1983). Gender schema theory and its implications for child development: Raising gender aschematic children in a gender-schematic society. *Signs: Journal of Women in Culture and Society, 8,* 598–616.

Bem, S.L. (1989). Genital knowledge and gender constancy in preschool children. *Child Development, 60,* 649–62.

Benasich, A.A., & Brooks-Gunn, J. (1996). Maternal attitudes and knowledge of child-rearing: Associations with family and child outcomes. *Child Development, 67,* 1186–205.

Benbow, C.P., & Arjimand, O. (1990). Predictors of high academic achievement in mathematics and science by mathematically talented students: A longitudinal study. *Journal of Educational Psychology, 82,* 430–41.

Bendersky, M., & Lewis, M. (1994). Environmental risk, biological risk, and developmental outcome. *Developmental Psychology, 30,* 484-494.

Benedict, H. (1979). Early lexical development: Comprehension and production. *Journal of Child Language, 6,* 183–200.

Benenson, J.F., Apostoleris, N.H., & Parnass, J. (1997). Age and sex differences in dyadic and group interaction. *Developmental Psychology, 33,* 538–43.

Benoit, D., & Parker, K.C.H. (1994). Stability and transmission of attachment across three generations. *Child Development, 65,* 1444–56.

Bentler, P.M. (1992). Etiologies and consequences of adolescent drug use: Implications for prevention. *Journal of Addictive Diseases, 11,* 47–61.

Berenbaum, S.A., & Snyder, E. (1995). Early hormonal influences on childhood sex-typed activity and playmate preferences: Implications for the development of sexual orientation. *Developmental Psychology, 31,* 31–42.

Berg, W.K., & Berg, K.M. (1987). Psychophysiologic development in infancy: State, startle, and attention. In J. Osofsky (Ed.), *Handbook of infant development* (2nd ed.). New York: Wiley.

Bergen, D.J., & Williams, J.E. (1991). Sex stereotypes in the United States revisited: 1972–1988. *Sex Roles, 24,* 413–24.

Berk, L.E. (1992). Children's private speech: An overview of theory and the status of research. In R.M. Diaz & L.E. Berk (Eds.), *Private speech: From social interaction to self-regulation* (pp. 17–53). Hillsdale, NJ: Erlbaum.

Berk, L.E., & Landau, S. (1993). Private speech of learning disabled and normally achieving children in classroom academic and laboratory contexts. *Child Development, 64,* 556–71.

Berk, L.E., & Spuhl, S.T. (1995). Maternal intervention, private speech, and task performance in preschool children. *Early Childhood Research Quarterly, 10,* 145–69.

Berkey, C.S., Wang, X., Dockery, D.W., & Ferris, B.G. (1994). Adolescent height growth of U.S. children. *Annals of Human Biology, 21,* 435–42.

Berko, J. (1958). The child's learning of English morphology. *Word, 14,* 150–77.

Berkowitz, M.W., & Gibbs, J.C. (1983). Measuring the developmental features of moral discussion. *Merrill-Palmer Quarterly, 29,* 399–410.

Berman, A.L., & Jobes, D.A. (1991). *Adolescent suicide: Assessment and intervention.* Washington, DC: American Psychological Association.

Bermejo, V. (1996). Cardinality development and counting. *Developmental Psychology, 22,* 263-268.

Berndt, T.J. (1979). Developmental changes in conformity to peers and parents. *Developmental Psychology, 15,* 608–16.

Berndt, T.J. (1989). Friendships in childhood and adolescence. In W. Damon (Ed.), *Child development today and tomorrow.* San Francisco: Jossey-Bass.

Berndt, T.J. (1996). Friendship quality affects adolescents' self-esteem and social behavior. In W.M. Bukowski, A.F. Newcombe, & W.W. Hartup (Eds.), *The company they keep: Friendship during childhood and adolescence* (pp. 346–65). New York: Cambridge University Press.

Berndt, T.J., & Bulleit, T.N. (1985). Effects of sibling relationships on preschoolers' behavior at home and at school. *Developmental Psychology, 21,* 761–7.

Berndt, T.J., Hawkins, J.A., & Hoyle, S.G. (1986). Changes in friendship during a school year: Effects on children's and adolescents' impressions of friendship and sharing with friends. *Child Development, 57,* 1284–97.

Berndt, T.J., & Hoyle, S.G. (1985). Stability and change in childhood and adolescent friendships. *Developmental Psychology, 21,* 1007–15.

Berndt, T.J., & Keefe, K. (1995). Friends' influence on adolescents' adjustment to school. *Child Development, 66,* 1312–29.

Berndt, T.J., & Perry, T.B. (1990). Distinctive features and effects of early adolescent friendships. In R. Montemayor, G.R. Adams, & T.P. Gulotta (Eds.), *From childhood to adolescence: A transitional period* (pp. 269–87). Newbury Park, CA: Sage.

Berrueta-Clement, J.R., Schweinhart, L.J., Barnett, S.W., Epstein, A.S., & Weikart, D.P. (1984). *Changed lives: The effects of the Perry Preschool Program on youths through age 19.* Ypsilanti, MI: High/Scope Press.

Berry, J.W., Poortinga, Y.H., Segall, M., & Dasen, P.R. (1992). *Cross-cultural psychology: Research and applications.* Cambridge, England: Cambridge University Press.

Bertenthal, B.I. (1993, March). *Emerging trends in perceptual development.* Paper presented at the biennial meeting of the Society for Research in Child Development, New Orleans, LA.

Bertenthal, B.I., & Campos, J.J. (1987). New directions in the study of early experience. *Child Development, 58,* 560–7.

Bertenthal, B.I., Campos, J.J., Haith, M.M. (1980). Development of visual organization: The perception of subjective contours. *Child Development, 51,* 1077–80.

Bertenthal, B.I., Proffitt, D.R., & Cutting, J.E. (1984). Infant sensitivity to figural coherence in biomechanical motions. *Journal of Experimental Child Psychology, 37,* 213–30.

Best, C.T., McRoberts, G.W., LaFleur, R., & Silver-Isenstadt, J. (1995). Divergent developmental patterns for infants' perception of two non-native consonant contrasts. *Infant Behavior and Development, 18* (3), 339–50.

Best, D. L., Williams, J. E., Cloud, J. M., Davis, S. W., Robertson, L. S., Edwards, J. R., Giles, H., & Fowlkes, J. (1977). Development of sex-trait stereotypes among young children in the United States, England, and Ireland. *Child Development, 48,* 1375-1384.

Best Start. (2002, February). Low birth weight & preterm multiple births: A Canadian profile for health professionals. Retrieved from www.opc.on.ca/beststart/pract_prod/low_aware/newsltr.pdf on October 1, 2003.

Bewley, S., & Cockburn, J. (2002). Responding to fear of childbirth. *The Lancet, 359,* 2128-29.

Bialystok, E. (1986). Factors in the growth of linguistic awareness. *Child Development, 57,* 498–510.

Bialystok, E. (1988). Levels of bilingualism and levels of metalinguistic awareness. *Developmental Psychology, 24,* 560–7.

Bialystok, E. (1997). Effects of bilingualism and biliteracy on children's emerging concepts of print. *Developmental Psychology, 33,* 429–40.

Bialystok, E. (1999). Cognitive complexity and attentional control in the bilingual mind. *Child Development, 70,* 636-44.

Bialystok, E., Majumder, S., & Martin, M. (2003). Developing phonological awareness: Is there a bilingual advantage? *Applied Psycholinguistics, 24,* 27-44.

Bialystok, E., Shenfield, T., & Codd, J. (2000). Languages, scripts and the environment: Factors in developing concepts of print. *Developmental Psychology, 36* (1), 66–76.

Bianchi, S.M., Subaiya, L., & Kahn, J. (1997, March). *Economic well-being of husbands and wives after marital disruption.* Paper

presented at the annual meeting of the Population Association of America, Washington, DC.

Bickerton, D. (1983). Creole languages. *Scientific American, 249,* 116–22.

Bickerton, D. (1984). The language bioprogram hypothesis. *Behavioral and Brain Sciences, 7,* 173–221.

Bierman, K.L. (1986). Process of change during social skills training with preadolescents and its relation to treatment outcome. *Child Development, 57,* 230–40.

Bierman, K.L., & Furman, W. (1984). The effects of social skills training and peer involvement on the social adjustment of preadolescents. *Child Development, 55,* 157–62.

Biernat, M. (1991). Gender stereotypes and the relationship between masculinity and feminity: A developmental analysis. *Journal of Personality and Social Psychology, 61,* 351–65.

Bigelow, A.E. (1999). Infants' sensitivity to impart contingency in social interaction. In P. Rochat (Ed.), *Early social cognition: Understanding others in the first months of life* (pp. 137–54). Hillsdale, NJ: Erlbaum.

Bigler, R.S. (1995). The role of classification skill in moderating environmental influences on children's gender stereotyping: A study of the functional use of gender in the classroom. *Child Development, 66,* 1072–87.

Bigler, R.S., & Liben, L.S. (1990). The role of attitudes and interventions in gender-schematic processing. *Child Development, 61,* 1440–52.

Bigler, R.S., & Liben, L.S. (1992). Cognitive mechanisms in children's gender stereotyping: Theoretical and educational implications of a cognitive-based intervention. *Child Development, 63,* 1351–63.

Bigler, R.S., & Liben, L.S. (1993). A cognitive-developmental approach to racial stereotyping and reconstructive memory in Euro-American children. *Child Development, 64,* 1507–18.

Bigner, J.J., & Jacobsen, R.B. (1989). Parenting behaviors of homosexual and heterosexual fathers. *Journal of Homosexuality, 18,* 173–86.

Bijeljac-Babic, R., Bertoncini, J., & Mehler, J. (1993). How do 4-day-old infants categorize multisyllabic utterances? *Developmental Psychology, 29,* 711–21.

Bingham, C.R., & Crockett, L.J. (1996). Longitudinal adjustment patterns of boys and girls experiencing early, middle, and later sexual intercourse. *Developmental Psychology, 32,* 647–58.

Birch, E.E. (1993). Stereopsis in infants and its developmental relation to visual acuity. In K. Simons (Ed.), *Early visual developmental: Normal and Abnormal* (pp. 224–36). New York: Oxford University Press.

Birch, L.L. (1990). Development of food acceptance patterns. *Developmental Psychology, 26,* 515–9.

Birch, L.L., & Billman, J. (1986). Preschool children's food sharing with friends and acquaintances. *Child Development, 57,* 387–95.

Birch, L.L., & Ladd, G.W. (1998). Children's interpersonal behaviors and the teacher-child relationship. *Developmental Psychology, 34,* 934–46.

Birch, L.L., Marlin, D.W., & Rotter, J. (1984). Eating as the "means" activity in a contingency: Effects on young children's food preference. *Child Development, 55,* 431–9.

Biringen, Z. (1990). Direct observation of maternal sensitivity and dyadic interactions in the home: Relations to maternal thinking. *Developmental Psychology, 26,* 278–84.

Biringen, Z., Emde, R.N., Campos, J.J., & Appelbaum, M.I. (1995). Affective reorganization in the infant, the mother, and the dyad: The role of upright locomotion and its timing. *Child Development, 66,* 499–514.

Bisanz, J., & LeFevre, J. (1990). Strategic and nonstrategic processing in the development of mathematical cognition. In D. Bjorklund (Ed.), *Children's strategies: Contemporary views of cognitive development* (pp. 213–44). Hillsdale, NJ: Erlbaum .

Bisanz, J., & LeFevre, J. (1992). Understanding elementary mathematics. In J. Campbell (Ed.), *The nature and origins of mathematical skills* (pp. 113–36). Amsterdam: Elsevier Science Publishers.

Bisanz, J., Morrison, F.J., & Dunn, M. (1995). Effects of age and schooling on the aquisition of elementary quantitative skills. *Developmental Psychology, 31* (2), 221–36.

Bissell, M. (2001, Fall). Socio-economic outcomes of teen pregnancy and parenthood: A review of the literature. *Canadian Journal of Human Sexuality, 9* (3), 191–204.

Bivens, J.A., & Berk, L.E. (1990). A longitudinal study of the development of elementary school children's private speech. *Merrill-Palmer Quarterly, 36,* 443–63.

Bjorklund, D.F. (1987). How age changes in knowledge base contribute to the development of children's memory: An interpretive review. *Developmental Review, 7,* 93–130.

Bjorklund, D.F. (2000). *Children's thinking: Developmental function and individual differences* (3rd ed.). Belmont, CA: Wadsworth.

Bjorklund, D.F., & Bjorklund, B.R. (1985). Organization versus item effects of an elaborated knowledge base on children's memory. *Developmental Psychology, 21,* 1120–31.

Bjorklund, D.F., & Bjorklund, B.R. (1992). *Looking at children: An introduction to child development.* Pacific Grove, CA: Brooks/Cole.

Bjorklund, D.F., Bjorklund, B.R., Brown, R.D., & Cassel, W.S. (1998). Children's susceptibility to repeated questions: How misinformation changes children's answers and their minds. *Applied Developmental Science, 2,* 99–111.

Bjorklund, D.F., Brown, R.D., & Bjorklund, B.R. (2001). Children's eyewitness memory: Changing reports and changing representations. In P. Graff & N. Ohta (Eds.), *Lifespan memory development.* Cambridge, MA: MIT Press.

Bjorklund, D.F., & Douglas, R.N. (1997). The development of memory strategies. In N. Cowan (Ed.), *The development of memory in childhood* (pp. 201–46). London, England: London University College Press.

Bjorklund, D.F., & Harnishfeger, K.K. (1990). Children's strategies: Their definition and origins. In D.F. Bjorklund (Ed.), *Children's strategies: Contemporary views of cognitive development* (pp. 309–23). Hillsdale, NJ: Erlbaum.

Bjorklund, D.F., Miller, P.H., Coyle, T.R., & Slawinski, J.L. (1997). Instructing children to use memory strategies: Evidence of utilization deficiencies in memory training studies. *Developmental Review, 17,* 411–42.

Bjorklund, D.F., & Pellegrini, A.D. (2000). Child development and evolutionary psychology. *Child Development, 71,* 1687–708.

Bjorklund, D.F., & Rosenblum, K.E. (2001). Children's use of multiple and variable addition strategies in a game context. *Developmental Science, 4,* 183-193.

Bjorklund, D.F., & Schwartz, R. (1996). The adaptive nature of developmental immaturity: Implications for language acquisition and language disabilities. In M. Smith & J. Damico (Eds.), *Childhood language disorders.* New York: Thieme Medical.

Black, M.M., Dubowitz, H., & Starr, R.H., Jr. (1999). African-American fathers in low income urban families: Development, behavior, and home environment of their three-year-old children. *Child Development, 70,* 967–78.

Black-Gutman, D., & Hickson, F. (1996). The relationship between racial attitudes and social-cognitive development in children: An Australian study. *Developmental Psychology, 32,* 448–56.

Blake, J., & Boysson-Bardies, B. de (1992). Patterns in babbling: a cross-linguistic study. *Journal of Child Language, 19,* 51–74.

Blakemore, J. E. O., LaRue, A. A., & Olejnik, A. B. (1979). Sex-appropriate toy preference and the ability to conceptualize toys as sex-role related. *Developmental Psychology, 15,* 339-340.

Blasi, A. (1990). Kohlberg's theory and moral motivation. In D. Schrader (Ed.), *New directions for child development* (No. 47, pp. 51–7). San Francisco: Jossey-Bass.

Blass, E. M. (1997). Infant formula quiets crying human newborns. *Developmental and Behavioral Pediatrics, 18,* 162–5.

Blass, E.M., & Ciaramitaro, V. (1994). A new look at some old mechanisms in human newborns: Taste and tactile determinants of state, affect, and action. *Monographs of the Society for Research in Child Development, 59* (l, Serial No. 239).

Block, J., & Robins, R.W. (1993). A longitudinal study of consistency and change in self-esteem from early adolescence to early adulthood. *Child Development, 64,* 909–23.

Block, J.H. (1976). Issues, problems, and pitfalls in assessing sex differences: A critical review of *The psychology of sex differences. Merrill-Palmer Quarterly, 27,* 283–308.

Block, J.H., Block, J., & Gjerde, P.F. (1986). The personality of children prior to divorce: A prospective study. *Child Development, 57,* 827–40.

Block, J.H., Block, J., & Gjerde, P.F. (1988). Parental functioning and the home environment of families of divorce: Prospective and current analyses. *Journal of the American Academy of Child and Adolescent Psychiatry, 27,* 207–13.

Bloom, L. (1970). *Language development: Form and function in emerging grammars.* Cambridge, MA: MIT Press.

Bloom, L. (1973). *One word at a time: The use of single word utterances before syntax.* The Hague: Mouton.

Bloom, L., Hood, L., & Lightbown, P. (1974). Imitation in language development: If, when and why. *Cognitive Psychology, 6,* 380–420.

Bloom, L., Margulis, C., Tinker, E., & Fujita, N. (1996). Early conversations and word learning: Contributions from child and adult. *Child Development, 67,* 3154–75.

Blöte, A. W., Resing, W. C. M., Mazer, P., & Van Noort, D. A. (1999). Young children's organizational strategies on a same-different task: A microgenetic study and a training study. *Journal of Experimental Child Psychology, 74,* 21-43.

Blount, R. (1986, May 4). "I'm about five years ahead of my age." *Atlanta Journal and Constitution,* pp. C17–C20.

Bogartz, R. S., Shinskey, J. L., & Schilling, T. H. (2000). Object permanence in five-and-a-half-month-old infants? *Infancy, 1* (4), 403–428.

Bogatz, G.A., & Ball, S. (1972). *The second year of Sesame Street: A continuing evaluation.* Princeton, NJ: Educational Testing Service.

Bogenschneider, K., Wu, M., Raffaelli, M., & Tsay, J.C. (1998). Parental influences on adolescent peer orientation and substance use: The interface of parenting practices and values. *Child Development, 69,* 1672–88.

Bohannon, J.N., III, & Bonvillian, J.D. (1997). Theoretical approaches to language acquisition. In J.K. Gleason (Ed.), *The development of language* (4th ed.). Boston: Allyn & Bacon.

Bohannon, J.N., III, MacWhinney, B., & Snow, C. (1990). No negative evidence

revisee: Beyond learnability on who has to prove what to whom. *Developmental Psychology, 26*(2), 221–6.

Bohannon, J.N., III, Padgett, R.J., Nelson, K.E., & Mark, M. (1996). Useful evidence on negative evidence. *Developmental Psychology, 32,* 551–5.

Bohannon, J.N., III, & Stanowicz, L. (1988). The issue of negative evidence: Adult responses to children's language errors. *Developmental Psychology, 24* (5), 684–9.

Bohlin, G., & Hagekull, B. (1993). Stranger wariness and sociability in the early years. *Infant Behavior and Development, 16,* 53–67.

Boismier, J.D. (1977). Visual stimulation and the wake-sleep behavior in human neonates. *Developmental Psychobiology, 10,* 219-227.

Boivin, M., & Hymel, S. (1997). Peer experiences and social self-perceptions: A sequential model. *Developmental Psychology, 33,* 135–45.

Boldizar, J.P. (1991). Assessing sex-typing and androgyny in children: The children's sex-role inventory. *Developmental Psychology, 27,* 505–15.

Bolger, K.E., & Patterson, C.J. (2001). Developmental pathways from child maltreatment to peer rejection. *Child Development, 72,* 549–68.

Bolger, K.E., Patterson, C.J., & Kupersmidt, J.B. (1998). Peer relationships and self-esteem among children who have been maltreated. *Child Development, 69,* 1171–97.

Bolger, K.E., Patterson, C.J., Thompson, W.W., & Kupersmidt, J.B. (1995). Psychosocial adjustment among children experiencing persistent intermittent family economic hardship. *Child Development, 66,* 1107–29.

Boloh, Y., & Champaud, C. (1993). The past conditional verb form in French children: The role of semantics in late grammatical development. *Journal of Child Language, 20,* 169–89.

Boone, R. T., & Cunningham, J. G. (1998). Children's decoding of emotion in expressive body movement: The development of cue attunement. *Developmental Psychology, 34,* 1007–1016.

Booth, A., & Amato, P. (1991). Divorce and psychological stress. *Journal of Health and Social Behavior, 32,* 396-407.

Booth, A., Johnson, D., Granger, D., Crouter, A., & McHale, S. (2003). Testosterone and child adolescent adjustment: The moderating role of parent-child relationships. *Developmental Psychology, 39* (1), 85-98.

Bornstein, M.H. (1992). Perception across the lifespan. In M.H. Bornstein & M.E. Lamb (Eds.), *Developmental psychology. An advanced textbook* (3rd ed., pp. 155–209). Hillsdale, NJ: Erlbaum.

Bornstein, M.H., Haynes, O.M., O'Reilly, A.W., & Painter, K.M. (1996). Solitary and collaborative pretense play in early childhood: Sources of individual variation in the development of representational competence. *Child Development, 67,* 2910–29.

Bornstein, M.H., Haynes, O.M., Pascual, L., Painter, K.M., & Galperin, C. (1999). Play in two societies: Pervasiveness of process, specificity of structure. *Child Development, 70,* 317–31.

Bornstein, M.H., Kessen, W., & Weiskopf, S. (1976). Color vision and hue categorization in young human infants. *Journal of Experimental Psychology: Human Perception and Performance, 2,* 115–29.

Boroditsky, R., Fisher, W., & Sand, M. (1996, December). Condoms: Attitudes and practices of Canadian women. The 1995 Canadian contraception study. *Journal of the Society of Obstetricians and Gynaecologists of Canada, 18* (Special suppl.), 1–29.

Borstelmann, L.J. (1983). Children before psychology: Ideas about children from antiquity to the late 1800s. In P.H. Mussen (Ed.), *Handbook of child psychology* (Vol. 1, pp. 1–40). New York: Wiley.

Bouchard, T.J., Jr., Lykken, D.T., McGue, M., Segal, N.L., & Tellegen, A. (1990). Sources of human psychological differences: The Minnesota study of twins reared apart. *Science, 250,* 223–8.

Bouchard, T.J., Jr., & McGue, M. (1981). Family studies of intelligence: A review. *Science, 212,* 1055–9.

Boulton, M.H. (1999). Concurrent and longitudinal relations between children's playground behavior and social preferences, victimization, and bullying. *Child Development, 70,* 944–54.

Bower, T.G.R. (1982). *Development in infancy.* New York: W.H. Freeman.

Bower, T.G.R., Broughton, J.M., & Moore, M.K. (1970). The coordination of vision and tactile input in infancy. *Perception and Psychophysics, 8,* 51–3.

Bowlby, J. (1969). *Attachment and loss: Vol. 1. Attachment.* New York: Basic Books.

Bowlby, J. (1973). *Attachment and loss: Vol. 2. Separation, anxiety and anger.* New York: Basic Books.

Bowlby, J. (1980). *Attachment and loss: Vol. 3. Loss, sadness, and depression.* New York: Basic Books.

Bowlby, J. (1988). *A secure base: Clinical applications of attachment theory.* London, England: Routledge.

Boyatzis, C.J., Matillo, G.M., & Nesbitt, K.M. (1995). Effects of the "Mighty Morphin Power Rangers" on children's aggression with peers. *Child Study Journal, 25,* 44–55.

Boyes, M.C., & Chandler, M. (1992). Cognitive development, epistemic doubt, and identity formation in adolescence. *Journal of Youth and Adolescence, 21,* 277–304.

Boykin, A.W. (1994). Harvesting talent and culture: African-American children and educational reform. In R. Rossi (Ed.), *Schools and students at risk* (pp. 116–38). New York: Teachers College Press.

Boykin, A.W., McElhaney, K., & Allen, J.P. (2001). Autonomy and adolescent social functioning: The moderating effect of work. *Child Development, 72,* 220–35.

Brabeck, M. (1983). Moral judgment: Theory and research on differences between males and females. *Developmental Review, 3,* 274–91.

Brackbill, Y., McManus, K., & Woodward, L. (1985). *Medication in maternity: Infant exposure and maternal information.* Ann Arbor, MI: University of Michigan Press.

Bradbard, M.R., Martin, C.L., Endsley, R.C., & Halverson, C.F. (1986). Influence of sex stereotypes on children's exploration and memory: A competence versus performance distinction. *Developmental Psychology, 22,* 481–6.

Braddock, J.H., II, & McPartland, J.M. (1993). Education of early adolescents. *Review of Educational Research, 19,* 135–70.

Bradley, E.A., Thompson, A., & Bryson, S.E. (2002). Mental retardation in teenagers: Prevalence data from the Niagara region, Ontario. *Canadian Journal of Psychiatry, 47,* 652–659.

Bradley, R.H., & Caldwell, B.M. (1982). The consistency of the home environment and its relationship to child development. *International Journal of Behavioral Development, 5,* 445–65.

Bradley, R.H., Caldwell, B.M., & Rock, S.L. (1988). Home environment and school performance: A ten-year follow-up and examination of three models of environmental action. *Child Development, 59,* 852–67.

Bradley, R.H., Caldwell, B.M., Rock, S.L., Ramey, C.T., Barnard, K.E., Gray, C.,

Hammond, M. A., Mitchell, S., Gottfried, A.W., Siegel, L., & Johnson, D.L. (1989). Home environment and cognitive development in the first 3 years of life: A collaborative study involving six sites and three ethnic groups in North America. *Developmental Psychology, 25,* 217–35.

Bradley, R.H., Whiteside, L., Mundfrom, D.J., Casey, P.H., Kelleher, K.J., & Pope, S.K. (1994). Contribution of early intervention and early caregiving experiences to resilience of low-birthweight premature children living in poverty. *Journal of Clinical Child Psychology, 23,* 425–34.

Brainerd, C.J. (1996). Piaget: A centennial celebration. *Psychological Science, 7,* 191–5.

Brainerd, C.J., & Gordon, L.L. (1994). Development of verbatim and gist memory for numbers. *Developmental Psychology, 30,* 163–77.

Brainerd, C.J., & Kingma, J. (1985). On the independence of short-term memory and working memory in cognitive development. *Cognitive Psychology, 17,* 210–47.

Brainerd, C.J., & Poole, D.A. (1997). Long-term survival of children's false memories: A review. *Learning and Individual Differences, 9,* 125–52.

Brainerd, C.J., & Reyna, V.F. (2001). Fuzzy-trace theory: Dual processes in memory, reasoning, and cognitive neuroscience. *Advances in Child development and Behavior, 6,* 359–64. San Diego: Academic Press.

Brainerd, C.J., Reyna, V.F., & Poole, D.A. (2000). Fuzzy-trace theory and false memory: Memory theory in the courtroom. In D.F. Bjorklund (Ed.), *Research and theory in false-memory creation in children and adults* (pp. 93–127). Hillsdale, NJ: Erlbaum.

Brame, B., Nagain, D.S., & Tremblay, R.E. (2001). Developmental trajectories of physical aggression from school entry to late adolescence. *Journal of Child Psychology and Psychiatry and Allied Disciplines, Special Issue 42* (4), 503–12.

Brand, E., Clingempeel, W.G., & Bowen-Woodward, K. (1988). Family relationships and children's psychological adjustment in stepmother and stepfather families: Findings and conclusions from the Philadelphia Stepfamily Research Project. In E.M. Hetherington & J.D. Arasteh (Eds.), *Impact of divorce, single-parenting, and stepparenting on children* (pp. 299–324). Hillsdale, NJ: Erlbaum.

Braungart, J.M., Fulker, D.W., & Plomin, R. (1992). Genetic mediation of the home environment during infancy: A sibling adoption study of the HOME. *Developmental Psychology, 28,* 1048–55.

Braungart, J.M., Plomin, R., DeFries, J.C., & Fulker, D.W. (1992). Genetic influence on tester-rated infant temperament as assessed by Bayley's Infant Behavior Record: Nonadoptive and adoptive siblings and twins. *Developmental Psychology, 28,* 40–7.

Brazelton, T.B. (1979). Behavioral competence of the newborn infant. *Seminars in Perinatology, 3,* 35–44.

Brendgen, M., Vitaro, F., Bukowski, W.M., Doyle, A.B., & Markiewicz, D. (2001). Developmental profiles of peer social preference over the course of elementary school: Associations with trajectories of externalizing and internalizing behavior. *Developmental Psychology, 37,* 308–20.

Bretherton, I. (1985). Attachment theory: Retrospect and prospect. In I. Bretherton & E. Waters (Eds.), *Growing points of attachment theory and research. Monographs of the Society for Research in Child Development, 50* (1–2, Serial No. 209).

Bretherton, I. (1990). Open communication and internal working models: Their role in the development of attachment relationships. In R.A. Thompson (Ed.), *Nebraska Symposium on Motivation: Vol. 36. Socioemotional development* (pp. 57–113). Lincoln: University of Nebraska Press.

Bretherton, I., Stolberg, U., & Kreye, M. (1981). Engaging strangers in proximal interaction: Infants' social initiative. *Developmental Psychology, 17,* 746–55.

Bridges, L.J., & Grolnick, W.S. (1995). The development of emotional self-regulation in infancy and early childhood. In N. Eisenberg (Ed.), *Social development: Vol. 15. Review of personality and social psychology.* Thousand Oaks, CA: Sage.

Britt, G.C., & Myers, B.J. (1994). The effects of the Brazelton intervention. *Infant Mental Health Journal, 15,* 278–92.

Broberg, A.G., Wessels, H., Lamb, M.E., & Hwang, C.P. (1997). Effects of day care on the cognitive development of 8-year-olds: A longitudinal study. *Developmental Psychology, 33,* 62–9.

Brockington, I. (1996). *Motherhood and mental health.* Oxford: Oxford University Press.

Brody, G.H. (1998). Sibling relationship quality: Its causes and consequences. *Annual Review of Psychology, 49,* 1–24.

Brody, G.H., & Flor, D.L. (1998). Maternal resources, parenting practices, and child competence in rural single-parent African American families. *Child Development, 69,* 803-816.

Brody, G.H., Graziano, W.G., & Musser, L.M. (1983). Familiarity and children's behavior in same-age and mixed-age peer groups. *Developmental Psychology, 19,* 568–76.

Brody, G.H., & Shaffer, D.R. (1982). Contributions of parents and peers to children's moral socialization. *Developmental Review, 2,* 31–75.

Brody, G.H., Stoneman, Z., & Flor, D. (1996). Parental religiosity, family processes, and youth competence in rural, two-parent African-American families. *Developmental Psychology, 32,* 696–706.

Brody, N. (1992). *Intelligence* (2nd ed.). San Diego: Academic Press.

Brody, N. (1997). Intelligence, schooling, and society. *American Psychologist, 52,* 1046–50.

Brodzinsky, D.M., Radice, C., Huffman, I., & Merkler, K. (1987). Prevalence of clinically significant symptomatology in nonclinical samples of adopted and nonadopted children. *Journal of Clinical Child Psychology, 16,* 350–6.

Brodzinsky, D.M., Smith, D.W., & Brodzinsky, A.B. (1998). *Children's adjustment to adoption: Developmental and clinical issues.* London, England: Sage.

Bronfenbrenner, U. (1970). *Two worlds of childhood: US and USSR.* New York: Russell Sage Foundation.

Bronfenbrenner, U. (1977). Toward an experimental ecology of human development. *American Psychologist, 32,* 513–31.

Bronfenbrenner, U. (1979). *The ecology of human development.* Cambridge, MA: Harvard University Press.

Bronfenbrenner, U. (1989). Ecological systems theory. In R. Vasta (Ed.) *Annals of child development: Theories of child development: Revised formulations and current issues* (Vol. 6, pp. 187–251). Greenwich, CT: JAI Press.

Bronfenbrenner, U. (1993). The ecology of cognitive development: Research models and fugitive findings. In R.H. Wozniak & K.W. Fischer (Eds.), *Development in context* (pp. 3–44). Hillsdale, NJ: Erlbaum.

Bronfenbrenner, U. (1995). The bioecological model from a life course perspective: Reflections of a participant observer. In P. Moen, G.H. Elder, Jr., & K. Luscher (Eds.), *Examining lives in context* (pp. 599–618). Washington, DC: American Psychological Association.

Bronfenbrenner, U., & Ceci, S.J. (1994). Nature–nurture reconceptualized in developmental perspective: A bioecological model. *Psychological Review, 101,* 568–86.

Bronfenbrenner, U., & Neville, P.R. (1995). America's children and families: An international perspective. In S.L. Kagan & B. Weissbourd (Eds.), *Putting families first* (pp. 3–27). San Francisco: Jossey-Bass.

Bronson, G.W. (1991). Infant differences in rate of visual encoding. *Child Development, 62,* 44–54.

Brookover, W., Beady, C., Flood, P., Schweitzer, J., & Wisenbaker, J. (1979). *School social systems and student achievement: Schools can make a difference.* New York: Praeger.

Brooks, P.J., & Tomasello, M. (1999). Young children learn to produce passives with nonce verbs. *Developmental Psychology, 35,* 29-44.

Brooks-Gunn, J. (1988). Antecedents and consequences of variation in girls' maturational timing. *Journal of Adolescent Health Care, 9,* 365–73.

Brooks-Gunn, J., & Furstenberg, F.F., Jr. (1989). Adolescent sexual behavior. *American Psychologist, 44,* 249–57.

Brooks-Gunn, J., Klebanov, P.K., Liaw, F., & Spiker, D. (1993). Enhancing the development of low birthweight, premature infants: Changes in cognition and behavior over the first three years. *Child Development, 64,* 736–53.

Brooks-Gunn, J., & Warren, M.P. (1988). The psychological significance of secondary sexual characteristics in nine- to eleven-year-old girls. *Child Development, 59,* 1061–9.

Broverman, I.K., Vogel, S.R., Clarkson, F.E., & Rosenkrantz, P.S. (1972). Sex-role stereotypes: A current appraisal. *Journal of Social Issues, 28,* 59–78.

Brown, A.L., & Campione, J.C. (1990). Communities of learning and thinking, or a context by any other name. In D. Kuhn (Ed.), *Developmental perspectives on teaching and learning thinking skills: Vol. 21. Contributions to human development* (pp. 108–26). Basel, Switzerland: Karger.

Brown, A.L., & Kane, M.J. (1988). Preschool children can learn to transfer: Learning to learn and learning by example. *Cognitive Psychology, 20,* 493–523.

Brown, A. L., Kane, M. J., & Long, C. (1989). Analogical transfer in young children: Analogies as tools for communication and exposition. *Applied Cognitive Psychology, 3,* 275–93.

Brown, A.M. (1990). Development of visual sensitivity to light and color vision in human infants: A critical review. *Vision Research, 30,* 1159–88.

Brown, B.B. (1990). Peer groups and peer cultures. In S.S. Feldman & G.R. Elliott (Eds.), *At the threshold: The developing adolescent* (171–96). Cambridge, MA: Cambridge University Press.

Brown, B.B., Clasen, D.R., & Eicher, S.A. (1986). Perceptions of peer pressure, peer conformity dispositions, and self-reported behavior among adolescents. *Developmental Psychology, 22,* 521–30.

Brown, B.B., & Lohr, M.J. (1987). Peer-group affiliation and adolescent self-esteem: An integration of ego-identity and symbolic-interaction theories. *Journal of Personality and Social Psychology, 52,* 47–55.

Brown, B. B., Mory, M. S., & Kinney, D. (1994). Casting adolescent crowds in a relational perspective: Caricature, channel, and context. In R. Montemayor, G.R. Adams, & T.P. Gulotta (Eds.), *Personal relationships during adolescence.* Thousand Oaks, CA: Sage.

Brown, B.B., Mounts, N., Lamborn, S.D., & Steinberg, L. (1993). Parenting practices and peer group affiliation in adolescence. *Child Development, 64,* 467–82.

Brown, J.D. (1998). *The self.* New York: McGraw-Hill.

Brown, J.L. (1964). States in newborn infants. *Merrill-Palmer Quarterly, 10,* 313–27.

Brown, J.R., & Dunn, J. (1996). Continuities in emotion understanding from three to six years. *Child Development, 67,* 789–802.

Brown, P., & Elliot, R. (1965). Control of aggression in a nursery school class. *Journal of Experimental Child Psychology, 2,* 103–7.

Brown, R. (1973). *A first language: The early stages.* Cambridge, MA: Harvard University Press.

Brown, R., Cazden, C., & Bellugi, U. (1969). The child's grammar from I to III. In J.P. Hill (Ed.), *Minnesota Symposia on Child Psychology* (Vol. 2, pp. 28–73). Minneapolis: University of Minnesota Press.

Brownell, C.A. (1986). Convergent developments: Cognitive-developmental correlates of growth in infant/toddler peer skills. *Child Development, 57,* 275–86.

Brownell, C.A. (1990). Peer social skills in toddlers: Competencies and constraints illustrated by same-age and mixed-age interaction. *Child Development, 61,* 838–48.

Brownell, C.A., & Carriger, M.S. (1990). Changes in cooperation and self/other differentiation during the second year. *Child Development, 61,* 1164–74.

Brownlee, S. (2001). Baby talk. In K.L. Frieberg (Ed.), *Human Development 01/02* (29th ed., pp. 49-55). Guilford, CT: McGraw-Hill/Duskin.

Bruck, M., Ceci, S.J., Francoeur, E., & Renick, A. (1995b). Anatomically detailed dolls do not facilitate preschoolers' reports of a pediatric examination involving genital touching. *Journal of Experimental Psychology: Applied, 1,* 95–109.

Bruck, M., Ceci, S.J., & Hembrooke, H. (1998). Reliability and credibility of young children's reports: From research to policy and practice. *American Psychologist, 53,* 136–51.

Bruggerman, E.L., & Hart, K.J. (1996). Cheating, lying, and moral reasoning by religious and secular high school students. *Journal of Educational Research, 89,* 340–4.

Bruner, J.S. (1983). *Child's talk: Learning to use language.* New York: Norton.

Buchanan, C.M., Eccles, J.S., & Becker, J.B. (1992). Are adolescents the victims of raging hormones: Evidence for activational effects of hormones on moods and behavior at adolescence. *Psychological Bulletin, 111,* 62–107.

Buchanan, C.M., Maccoby, E.E., & Dornbusch, S.M. (1991). Caught between parents: Adolescents' experiences in divorced homes. *Child Development, 62,* 1008–29.

Bugental, D.B., Blue, J., & Cruzcosa, M. (1989). Perceived control over caregiving outcomes: Implications for child abuse. *Developmental Psychology, 25,* 532–9.

Buhrmester, D. (1990). Intimacy of friendship, interpersonal competence, and adjustment during preadolescence and adolescence. *Child Development, 61,* 1101–11.

Buhrmester, D., & Furman, W. (1990). Perceptions of sibling relationships during middle childhood and adolescence. *Child Development, 61,* 1387–98.

Bukowski, W. M. (2003). What does it mean to say that aggressive children are competent or incompetent? *Merrill-Palmer Quarterly, 48* (3), 390-400.

Bukowski, W.M., Gauze, C., Hoza, B., & Newcomb, A.F. (1993). Differences and consistency between same-sex and other-sex peer relationships during early adolescence. *Developmental Psychology, 29,* 253–63.

Bukowski, W.M., Sippola, L.K., & Newcomb, A.F. (2000). Variations in patterns of attraction to same- and other-sex peers during early adolescence. *Developmental Psychology, 36,* 147–54.

Bullock, M. (1985). Animism in childhood thinking: A new look at an old question. *Developmental Psychology, 21,* 217–25.

Bullock, M., & Lutkenhaus, P. (1990). Who am I? Self-understanding in toddlers. *Merrill-Palmer Quarterly, 36,* 217–38.

Burchinal, M.R., Campbell, F.A., Bryant, D.M., Wasik, B.H., & Ramey, C.T. (1997). Early intervention and mediating processes in the cognitive performance of low-income African American families. *Child Development, 68,* 933–54.

Burchinal, M.R., Follmer, A., & Bryant, D.M. (1996). The relations of maternal social support and family structure with maternal responsiveness and child outcomes among African-American families. *Developmental Psychology, 32,* 1073–83.

Burchinal, M.R., Roberts, J.E., Hooper, S., & Zeisel, S.A. (2000). Cumulative risk and early cognitive development: A comparison of statistical risk models. *Developmental Psychology, 36,* 793–807.

Burchinal, M.R., Roberts, J.E., Nabors, L.A., & Bryant, D.M. (1996). Quality of center child care and infant cognitive and language development. *Child Development, 67,* 606–20.

Burhans, K.K., & Dweck, C.S. (1995). Helplessness in early childhood: The role of contingent worth. *Child Development, 66,* 1719–38.

Burkhardt, S.A., & Rotatori, A.F. (1995). *Treatment and prevention of childhood sexual abuse: A child-generated model.* Washington, DC: Taylor & Francis.

Burn, S., O'Neil, A.K., & Nederend, S. (1996). Childhood tomboyishness and adult androgyny. *Sex Roles, 34,* 419–28.

Burnette, E. (1997). Talking openly about race thwarts racism in children. *Monitor of the American Psychological Association, 28* (6), 33.

Burnham, D.K., & Harris, M.B. (1992). Effects of real gender and labeled gender on adults' perceptions of infants. *Journal of Genetic Psychology, 153,* 165–83.

Burns, G.W., & Bottino, P.J. (1989). *The science of genetics* (6th ed.). New York: Macmillan.

Burton, L.M. (1990). Teenage childrearing as an alternative life-course strategy in multigenerational black families. *Human Nature, 1,* 123–43.

Burton, R.V. (1963). The generality of honesty reconsidered. *Psychological Review, 70,* 481–99.

Burton, R.V. (1976). Honesty and dishonesty. In T. Lickona (Ed.), *Moral development and behavior* (pp. 173–97). New York: Holt, Rinehart & Winston.

Bushman, B., & Huesmann, L.R. (2001). Effects of televised violence on aggression. In D. Singer & J. Singer (Eds.), *Handbook of children and the media* (pp. 223–54). Thousand Oaks, CA: Sage.

Bushnell, E.W., & Boudreau, J.P. (1993). Motor development and the mind: The potential role of motor abilities as a determinant of aspects of perceptual development. *Child Development, 64,* 1005–21.

Buss, A.H., & Plomin, R. (1984). *Temperament: Early developing personality traits.* Hillsdale, NJ: Erlbaum.

Buss, K.A., & Goldsmith, H.H. (1998). Fear and anger regulation in infancy: Effects on temporal dynamics of affective expression. *Child Development, 69,* 359–74.

Bussell, D.A., Neiderhiser, J.M., Pike, A., Plomin, R., Simmons, S., Howe, G.W., Hetherington, E.M., Carroll, E., & Reiss, D. (1999). Adolescents' relationships to siblings and mothers: A multivariate genetic analysis. *Developmental Psychology, 35,* 1248–59.

Bussey, K. (1992). Lying and truthfulness: Children's definitions, standards, and evaluative reactions. *Child Development, 63,* 129–37.

Bussey, K., & Bandura, A. (1992). Self-regulatory mechanisms governing gender development. *Child Development, 63,* 1236–50.

Bussey, K., & Bandura, A. (1999). Social cognitive theory of gender development and differentiation. *Psychological Review, 106,* 676-713.

Butcher, C., & Goldin-Meadow, S. (2000). Gesture and the transition from one- to two-word speech: When hand and mouth come together. In D. McNeill (Ed.), *Language and gesture: Window into thought and action.* Cambridge, England: Cambridge University Press.

Butler, R. (1998). Age trends in the use of social and temporal comparison for self-evaluation: Examination of a novel developmental hypothesis. *Child Development, 69,* 1054–73.

Butler, R. (1999). Information seeking and achievement motivation in middle childhood and adolescence: The role of conceptions of ability. *Developmental Psychology, 35,* 146-163.

Butler, R., & Ruzany, N. (1993). Age and socialization effects on the development of social comparison motives and normative ability assessment in kibbutz and urban children. *Child Development, 64,* 532–43.

Butterfield, E.C., & Siperstein, G.N. (1972). Influence of contingent auditory stimulation on non-nutritional suckle. In J.F. Bosma (Ed.), *Third symposium on oral sensation and perception: The mouth of the infant.* Springfield, IL: Charles C. Thomas.

Buysse, V., & Bailey, D.B. (1993). Behavioral and developmental outcomes in young children with disabilities in integrated and segregated settings: A review of comparative studies. *Journal of Special Education, 26,* 434–61.

Byrnes, J. P., & Fox, N.A. (1998). The educational relevance of research in cognitive neuroscience. *Educational Psychology Review, 10,* 297-342.

Byrnes, J.P., & Takahira, S. (1993). Explaining gender differences on SAT-math items. *Developmental Psychology, 29,* 805–10.

Cabaniss, M.L. (1996). Amniocentesis. In J.A. Kuller, N.C. Cheschier, & R.C. Cefalo (Eds.), *Prenatal diagnosis and reproductive genetics* (pp. 136–44). St. Louis, MO: Mosby.

Cabrera, N.J., Tamis-LeMonda, C.S., Bradley, R.H., Hofferth, S., & Lamb, M.E. (2000). Fatherhood in the twenty-first century. *Child Development, 71,* 127–36.

Cahan, S., & Cohen, N. (1989). Age versus schooling effects on intelligence development. *Child Development, 60,* 1239–49.

Cairns, R.B., Leung, M., Buchanan, L., & Cairns, B.D. (1995). Friendships and social networks in childhood and adolescence: Fluidity, reliability, and interrelations. *Child Development, 66,* 1330–45.

Caldera, Y. M., Huston, A. C., & O'Brien, M. (1989). Social interactions and play patterns of parents and toddlers with feminine, masculine, and neutral toys. *Child Development, 60,* 70-76.

Caldwell, B.M., & Bradley, R.H. (1984). *Manual for the Home Observation for Measurement of the Environment.* Little Rock: University of Arkansas Press.

Call, J., & Tomasello, M. (1999). A nonverbal false belief task: The performance of children and great apes. *Child Development, 70,* 381–95.

Call, K.T., Mortimer, J.T., & Shanahan, M. (1995). Helpfulness and the development of competence in adolescence. *Child Development, 66,* 129–38.

Callaghan, T., & Rankin, M.P. (2002). Emergence of graphic symbol functioning and the question of domain specificity: A longitudinal training study. *Child Development, 73(2).* 359-376.

Calman, R., & Daniel, I. (1998). A board's-eye view of core French: The North York

Board of Education. In S. Lapkin (Ed.), *French second-language education in Canada* (chap. 12). Toronto: University of Toronto Press.

Campbell, F.A., Pungello, E.P., Miller-Johnson, S., Burchinal, M., & Ramey, C.T. (2001). The development of cognitive and academic abilities: Growth curves from an early childhood educational experiment. *Developmental Psychology, 37,* 231–42.

Campbell, F.A., & Ramey, C.T. (1994). Effects of early intervention on intellectual and academic achievement: A follow-up study of children from low-income families. *Child Development, 65,* 684–98.

Campbell, F.A., & Ramey, C.T. (1995). Cognitive and school outcomes for high-risk African-American students at middle adolescence: Positive effects of early intervention. *American Educational Research Journal, 32,* 743–72.

Campbell, S. (1993, November). Media violence and children. *The Bulletin,* 12–6.

Campbell, S.B., Cohn, J.F., Flanagan, C., Popper, S., & Meyers, T. (1992). Course and correlates of postpartum depression during the transition to parenthood. *Development and Psychopathology, 4,* 29–47.

Campbell, S.B., Cohn, J.F., & Myers, T. (1995). Depression in first-time mothers: Mother–infant interaction and depression chronicity. *Developmental Psychology, 31,* 349–57.

Campione, J.C., Brown, A.L., Ferrara, R.A., & Bryant, N.R. (1984). The zone of proximal development: Implications for individual differences and learning. In B. Rogoff & J.V. Wertsch (Eds.), *Children's learning in the "zone of proximal development"* (*New Directions for Child Development,* No. 23). San Francisco: Jossey-Bass.

Camp Jumoke. (2001). Sickle cell anemia: What is SCA? Retrieved August 14, 2001 from http://www.jumoke.org/SCA/sca.htm.

Campos, J.J., Bertenthal, B.I., & Kermoian, R. (1992). Early experience and emotional development: The emergence of wariness of heights. *Psychological Science, 3,* 61–4.

Campos, J.J., Langer, A., & Krowitz, A. (1970). Cardiac responses on the visual cliff in prelocomotor human infants. *Science, 170,* 196–7.

Campos, R., Raffaelli, M., Ude, W., Greco, M., Ruff, A., Rolf, J., Antunes, C.M., Halsley, N., Greco, D., & the Street Youth Study Group. (1994). Social networks and daily activities of street youth in Belo Horizonte, Brazil. *Child Development, 65,* 319–30.

Campos, R.G. (1989). Soothing pain-elicited distress in infants with swaddling and pacifiers. *Child Development, 60,* 781–92.

Camras, L.A., Oster, H., Campos, J.J., Miyake, K., & Bradshaw, D. (1992). Japanese and American infants' responses to arm restraint. *Developmental Psychology, 28,* 578–83.

Canadian Association of Midwives. (2001, January 31). The Canadian Association of Midwives. Retrieved August 14, 2001 from http://members.home.net/midwives.canada/about/index.html.

Canadian Association of Midwives. (2003). The Canadian Association of Midwives. Retrieved December 2003 from http://members.home.net/midwives.canada/about/index.html.

Canadian Heritage. (1999). *Canadian Heritage annual report 1999–2000.* Retrieved June 24, 2001 from http://www.pch.gc.ca/progs/native.htm.

Canadian Paediatric Society. (1996). Neonatal circumcision revisited. *Canadian Medical Association Journal, 154* (6), 769–80.

Canadian Paediatric Society. (1998; reaffirmed January 2001). Eating disorders in adolescents: Principles of diagnosis and

treatment. *Paediatrics and Child Health, 3* (3), 189–92. Retrieved February 26, 2001 from http://www.cps.ca/english/statements/AM/am96-04.htm.

Canadian Psychological Association. (2000). *Canadian code of ethics for psychologists* (3rd ed.). Ottawa: Author.

Canfield, R.L., & Smith, E.G. (1996). Number-based expectations and sequential enumeration by 5-month-old infants. *Developmental Psychology, 32,* 269–79.

Cantwell, D.P. (1996). Attention deficit disorder: A review of the past 10 years. *Journal of the American Academy of Child and Adolescent Psychiatry, 35,* 978–87.

Capaldi, D.M., & Clark, S. (1998). Prospective family predictors of aggression toward female partners for at-risk young men. *Developmental Psychology, 34,* 1175–88.

Capaldi, D.M., & Patterson, G.R. (1991). Relation of parental transitions to boys' adjustment problems: I. A linear hypothesis. II. Mothers at risk for transition and unskilled parenting. *Developmental Psychology, 27,* 489–504.

Caplan, M., Vespo, J., Pedersen, J., & Hay, D.F. (1991). Conflict and its resolution in small groups of one- and two-year-olds. *Child Development, 62,* 1513–24.

Caputo, D.V., & Mandell, W. (1970). Consequences of low birth weight. *Developmental Psychology, 3,* 363–83.

Carey, S., Diamond, R., & Woods, B. (1980). Development of face recognition: A maturational component? *Developmental Psychology, 16,* 257–69.

Carlson, E.A. (1998). A prospective longitudinal study of attachment disorganization/disorientation. *Child Development, 69,* 1107–28.

Carlson, S.M., Moses, L.J., & Hix, H.R. (1998). The role of inhibitory processes in young children's difficulties with deception and false belief. *Child Development, 69,* 672–91.

Carlson, V., Cicchetti, D., Barnett, D., & Braunwald, K. (1989). Disorganized/disoriented attachment relationships in maltreated infants. *Developmental Psychology, 25,* 525–31.

Carpenter, T.P., & Moser, J.M. (1982). The development of addition and subtraction problem-solving skills. In T.P. Carpenter, J.M. Moser, & T.A. Romberg (Eds.), *Addition and subtraction: A cognitive perspective* (pp. 9–24). Hillsdale, NJ: Erlbaum.

Carr, J. (1995). *Down syndrome: Children growing up.* Cambridge, England: Cambridge University Press.

Carr, M., Kurtz, B.E., Schneider, W., Turner, L.A., & Borkowski, J.G. (1989). Strategy acquisition and transfer among American and German children: Environmental influences on metacognitive development. *Developmental Psychology, 25,* 765–71.

Carraher, T.N., Carraher, D., & Schliemann, A.D. (1985). Mathematics in the streets and in the schools. *British Journal of Developmental Psychology, 3,* 21–29.

Carrington, D. (1995). Infections. In M.J. Whittle & J.M. Connor (Eds.), *Prenatal diagnosis in obstetric practice* (2nd ed., pp. 100–13). Oxford: Blackwell.

Carroll, J.B. (1993). *Human cognitive abilities: A survey of factor-analytic studies.* Cambridge, England: University of Cambridge Press.

Carroll, L. (1988). Concern with AIDS and the sexual behavior of college students. *Journal of Marriage and the Family, 50,* 405–11.

Carson, J.L., & Parke, R.D. (1996). Reciprocal negative affect on parent–child interactions and children's peer competency. *Child Development, 67,* 2217–26.

Carson, S.A. (1993). Nongenetic causes of pregnancy loss. In C. Lin, M.S. Verp, & R.E.

Sabbagha (Eds.), *The high-risk fetus: Pathophysiology, diagnosis, management.* New York: Springer-Verlag.

Carver, L.J., & Bauer, P.J. (1999). When the event is more than the sum of its parts: Individual differences in 9-month-olds' long-term ordered recall. *Memory, 7,* 147–74.

Casasola, M., & Cohen, L.B. (2000). Infants' association of linguistic labels with causal actions. *Developmental Psychology, 36,* 155–68.

Case, R. (1985). *Intellectual development: Birth to adulthood.* Orlando, FL: Academic Press.

Case, R. (1992). *The mind's staircase: Exploring the conceptual underpinnings of children's thought and knowledge.* Hillsdale, NJ: Erlbaum.

Case, R. (1998). The development of conceptual structures. In W. Damon (Series Ed.) & D. Kuhn & R.S. Siegler (Vol. Eds.), *Handbook of child psychology: Vol. 2. Cognition, perception, and language* (5th ed.). New York: Wiley.

Case, R., & Griffin, S. (1990). Child cognitive development: The role of central conceptual structures in the development of scientific and social thought. In C.A. Hauert (Ed.), *Developmental psychology: cognitive, perceptual-motor, and psychological perspectives* (pp. 193–230). Amsterdam: Elsevier.

Case, R., Griffin, S., McKeough, A., & Okamoto, Y. (1992). Parallels in the development of children's social, numerical, and spatial thought. In R. Case (Ed.), *The mind's staircase: Stages in the development of human intelligence* (pp. 269–84). Hillsdale, NJ: Erlbaum.

Case, R., & McKeough, A. (1990). Schooling and the development of central conceptual structures: An example from the domain of children's narrative. *International Journal of Educational Psychology, 8,* 835–55.

Case, R., & Okamoto, Y. (1996). The role of central conceptual structures in the development of children's thought. *Monographs of the Society for Research in Child Development, 61* (1–2, Serial No. 246).

Case, R., Okamoto, Y., Henderson, B., & McKeough, A. (1993). Individual variability and consistency in cognitive development: New evidence of the existence of central conceptual structures. In R. Case & W. Edelstein (Eds.), *The new structuralism in developmental theory and research: Analysis of individual developmental pathways* (pp. 71–100). Basel, Switzerland: Karger.

Case, R., & Sandieson, R. (1988). A developmental approach to the identification and teaching of central conceptual structures in mathematics and science in the middle grades. In J. Hiebert & M. Behr (Eds.), *Number concepts and operations in the middle grades* (pp. 236–59). Reston, VA: National Council of Teachers of Mathematics.

Casey, M.B. (1996). Understanding individual differences in spatial ability within females: A nature/nurture interactions framework. *Developmental Review, 16,* 241–60.

Casey, M.B., Nuttall, R.L., & Pezaris, E. (1997). Mediators of gender differences in mathematics college entrance test scores: A comparison of spatial skills with internalized beliefs and anxieties. *Developmental Psychology, 33,* 669–80.

Casey, W.M., & Burton, R.V. (1982). Training children to be consistently honest through verbal self-instructions. *Child Development, 53,* 911–9.

Cashon, C.H., & Cohen, L.B. (2000). Eight-month-old infants' perceptions of possible and impossible events. *Infancy, 1* (4), 429–46.

Caspi, A., Elder, G.H., Jr., & Bem, D.J. (1988). Moving away from the world: Life-course patterns of shy children. *Developmental Psychology, 24,* 824–31.

Caspi, A., Lynam, D., Moffitt, T.E., & Silva, P.A. (1993). Unraveling girls' delinquency: Biological, dispositional, and contextual contributors to adolescent misbehavior. *Developmental Psychology, 29,* 19–30.

Caspi, A., & Silva, P.A. (1995). Temperamental qualities at age three predict personality traits in young adulthood: Longitudinal evidence from a birth cohort. *Child Development, 66,* 486–98.

Cassel, W.S., & Bjorklund, D.F. (1995). Developmental patterns of eyewitness memory and suggestibility: An ecologically based short-term longitudinal study. *Law & Human Behavior, 19,* 507–32.

Cassidy, J., & Asher, S.R. (1992). Loneliness and peer relations in young children. *Child Development, 63,* 350–65.

Cassidy, J., & Berlin, L.J. (1994). The insecure/ambivalent pattern of attachment: Theory and research. *Child Development, 65,* 971–91.

Cassidy, J., Kirsh, S.J., Scolton, K.L., & Parke, R.D. (1996). Attachment and representations of peer relationships. *Developmental Psychology, 32,* 892–904.

Cassidy, J., Parke, R.D., Butkovsky, L., Braungart, J.M. (1992). Family–peer connections: The roles of emotional expressiveness within the family and children's understanding of emotions. *Child Development, 63,* 603–18.

Cassidy, K.W. (1998). Preschoolers' use of desires to solve theory of mind problems in a pretense context. *Developmental Psychology, 34,* 503–11.

Casteel, M.A. (1993). Effects of inference necessity and reading goal on children's inferential generation. *Developmental Psychology, 29,* 346–57.

Cates, W., Jr. (1995). Sexually transmitted diseases. In B.P. Sachs, R. Beard, E. Papiernik, & C. Russell (Eds.), *Reproductive health care for women and babies* (pp. 57–84). New York: Oxford University Press.

Cattell, R.B. (1963). Theory of fluid and crystallized intelligence: A critical experiment. *Journal of Educational Psychology, 54,* 1–22.

Cauffman, E., & Steinberg, L. (1996). Interactive effects of menarcheal status and dating on dieting and disordered eating among adolescent girls. *Developmental Psychology, 32,* 631–5.

Caughy, M.O. (1996). Health and environmental effects on the academic readiness of school-age children. *Developmental Psychology, 32,* 515–22.

Cavanaugh, J.C., & Perlmutter, M. (1982). Metamemory: A critical examination. *Child Development, 53,* 11–28.

Ceci, S.J. (1991). How much does schooling influence general intelligence and its cognitive components? A reassessment of the evidence. *Developmental Psychology, 27,* 703–22.

Ceci, S.J., & Bruck, M. (1993). Suggestibility of the child witness: A historical review and synthesis. *Psychological Bulletin, 113,* 403–39.

Ceci, S.J., & Bruck, M. (1998). Children's testimony: Applied and basic issues. In W. Damon (Series Ed.) & I.E. Sigel & K.A. Renninger (Vol. Eds.), *Handbook of child psychology: Vol. 4. Child psychology in practice* (5th ed., pp. 713–74). New York: Wiley.

Ceci, S.J., Loftus, E.F., Leichtman, M., & Bruck, M. (1994). The role of source misattributions in the creation of false beliefs among preschoolers. *International Journal of Clinical and Experimental Hypnosis, 62,* 304–20.

Ceci, S.J., & Williams, W.W. (1997). Schooling, intelligence, and income. *American Psychologist, 52,* 1051–8.

Cefalo, R.C. (1996). Prevention of neural tube defects. In J.A. Kuller, N.C. Cheschier, & R.C. Cefalo (Eds.), *Prenatal diagnosis and reproductive genetics* (pp. 2–9). St. Louis, MO: Mosby.

Centers for Disease Control. (1992). Sexual behavior among high-school students— United States, 1990. *Morbidity and Mortality Weekly Reports, 40,* 885–8.

Cernoch, J.M., & Porter, R.H. (1985). Recognition of maternal axillary odors by infants. *Child Development, 56,* 1593–8.

Cervantes, C.A., & Callanan, M.A. (1998). Labels and explanations in mother–child emotion talk: Age and gender differentiation. *Developmental Psychology, 34,* 88–98.

Chadwick, B.A., & Heaton, T.B. (1992). *Statistical handbook on the American family.* Phoenix, AZ: Onyx Press.

Chall, J.S. (1983). *Stages of reading development.* New York: McGraw-Hill.

Chalmers, J.B., & Townsend, M.A.R. (1990). The effects of training in social perspective taking on socially maladjusted girls. *Child Development, 61,* 178–90.

Chan, R.W., Raboy, B., & Patterson, C.J. (1998). Psychosocial adjustment among children conceived via donor insemination by lesbian and heterosexual mothers. *Child Development, 69,* 443–57.

Chandler, M.J. (1973). Egocentrism and antisocial behavior: The assessment and training of social perspective taking skills. *Developmental Psychology, 9,* 326–32.

Chandler, M.J., & Lalonde, C. (1998). Cultural continuity as a hedge against suicide in Canada's First Nations. *Transcultural Psychiatry, 35,* 191–219.

Chandler, M.J., Lalonde, C.E., Sokol, B.W., & Hallett, D. (2003). Personal persistence, identity development, and suicide. *Monographs of the Society for Research in Child Development.* Boston, MA: Blackwell Publishing.

Chandler, S., & Field, P.A. (1997). Becoming a father: First-time fathers' experience of labor and delivery. *Journal of Nurse-Midwifery, 42,* 17–24.

Chao, R. (1994). Beyond parental control and authoritarian parenting style: Understanding Chinese parenting through the cultural notion of training. *Child Development, 65,* 1111–9.

Chao, R. (2001). Extending research on the consequences of parenting style for Chinese Americans and European Americans. *Child Development, 72* (6), 1832–43.

Chapman, M., & Lindenberger, U. (1988). Functions, operations, and decalage in the development of transitivity. *Developmental Psychology, 24,* 542–51.

Chapman, M., Zahn-Waxler, C., Cooperman, G., & Iannotti, R.J. (1987). Empathy and responsibility in the motivation of children's helping. *Developmental Psychology, 23,* 140–5.

Charlesworth, W.R. (1992). Darwin and developmental psychology: Past and present. *Developmental Psychology, 28,* 5–16.

Chase-Lansdale, P.L., Cherlin, A.J., & Kiernan, K.E. (1995). The long-term effects of parental divorce on the mental health of young adults: A developmental perspective. *Child Development, 66,* 1614–34.

Chassin, L., Curran, P.J., Hussong, A.M., & Colder, C.R. (1996). The relation of parent alcoholism to adolescent substance use: A longitudinal follow-up study. *Journal of Abnormal Psychology, 105,* 70–80.

Chavkin, W. (1995). Substance abuse in pregnancy. In B.P. Sachs, R. Beard, E. Papiernik, & C. Russell (Eds.), *Reproductive health care for women and babies* (pp. 305–21). New York: Oxford University Press.

Chen, C., Greenberger, E., Lester, J., Dong, Q., & Guo, M. (1998). A cross-cultural study of family and peer correlates of adolescent misconduct. *Developmental Psychology, 34,* 770–81.

Chen, C., Li, D., Li, Z., Li, B., & Liu, M. (2000). Sociable and prosocial dimensions of social competence in Chinese children: Unique contributions to social, academic, and psychological adjustment. *Developmental Psychology, 36,* 302–14.

Chen, C., & Stevenson, H.W. (1995). Motivation and mathematics achievement: a comparative study of Asian-American, Caucasian-American, and East Asian high school students. *Child Development, 66,* 1215–34.

Chen, X. (2000). Growing up in a collectivistic culture: Socialization and socioemotional development in Chinese children. In A.L. Comunian & U.P. Gielen (Eds.), *International perspectives on human development* (pp. 331–53). Lengerich, Germany: Pabst.

Chen, X., Chang, L., & He, Y. (2003). The peer group as a context: Mediating and moderating effects on the relations between academic achievement and social functioning in Chinese children. *Child Development, 27,* 710–727.

Chen, X., Hastings, P., Rubin, K.H., Chen, H., Chen, G., & Shannon, S.L. (1998). Child-rearing attitudes and behavioral inhibition in Chinese and Canadian toddlers: A cross-cultural study. *Developmental Psychology, 34* (4), 677–86.

Chen, X., He, Y., De Oliveira, A.M., Lo Coco, A., Zappulla, C., Kaspar, V., Schneider, B., Valdivia, I.A., Chi-Hang Tse, H., & DeSouza, A. (in press). Loneliness and social adaptation in Brazilian, Canadian, Chinese and Italian children: A multi-national comparative study. *Journal of Child Psychology and Psychiatry.*

Chen, X., Rubin, K.H., & Li, D. (1997). Relation between academic achievement and social adjustment: Evidence from Chinese children. *Developmental Psychology, 33,* 518–25.

Chen, X., Rubin, K.H., & Li, Z. (1995). Social functioning and adjustment in Chinese children: A longitudinal study. *Developmental Psychology, 31,* 531–9.

Chen, X., Rubin, K.H., Liu, M., Chen, H., Wang, L., Li, D., Gao, X., Cen, G., Gu, H., & Li, B. (2003). Compliance in Chinese and Canadian toddlers: A cross-cultural study. *International Journal of Behavioral Development, 27,* 428–436.

Chen, X., Rubin, K.H., & Sun, Y. (1992). Social reputation in Chinese and Canadian children: A cross-cultural study. *Child Development, 63,* 1336–43.

Chen, Z., & Daehler, M. (1989). Positive and negative transfer in analogical reasoning problem-solving. *Cognitive Development, 4,* 327–44.

Chen, Z., & Klahr, D. (1999). All other things being equal: Acquisition and transfer of the control of variables strategy. *Child Development, 70,* 1098–1120.

Chen, Z., Sanchez, R.P., & Campbell, T. (1997). From beyond to within their grasp: The rudiments of analogical problem solving in 10- and 13-month olds. *Developmental Psychology, 33,* 790–801.

Cherlin, A.J., & Furstenberg, F.F. (1994). Stepfamilies in the United States: A reconsideration. In J. Blake & J. Hagen (Eds.), *Annual review of sociology* (pp. 359–81). Palo Alto, CA: Annual Reviews.

Cherlin, A.J., Kiernan, K.E., & Chase-Lansdale, P.L. (1995). Parental divorce in childhood and demographic outcomes in young adulthood. *Demography, 32,* 299–318.

Cheschier, N.C. (1996). Overview of obstetric sonography. In J.A. Kuller, N.C. Cheschier, & R.C. Cefalo (Eds.), *Prenatal diagnosis and reproductive genetics.* St. Louis, MO: Mosby.

Chess, S., & Thomas, R. (1984). *Origins and evolution of behavior disorders.* New York: Brunner/Mazel.

Chi, M.H.T. (1978). Knowledge structures and memory development. In R.S. Siegler (Ed.), *Children's thinking: What develops?* (pp. 73–96). Hillsdale, NJ: Erlbaum.

Chick, K., Heilman-Houser, R., & Hunter, M. (2002). The impact of child care on gender roles development and gender stereotypes. *Early Childhood Education Journal, 29* (3), 149–54.

Child and Family Services Act. RSO 1990, c. C.12, as amended.

Chisholm, K. (1998). A three-year follow up of attachment and indiscriminate friendliness in children adopted from Romanian orphanages. *Child Development, 69,* 1092–1106.

Chomitz, V.R., Chung, L.W.Y., & Lieberman, E. (2000). The role of lifestyle in preventing low birth weight. In K.L. Freiberg (Ed.), *Human development 00/01* (28th ed., pp. 18–28). Guilford, CT: McGraw-Hill/Dushkin.

Chomsky, N. (1959). A review of B.F. Skinner's *Verbal Behavior. Language, 35* (1), 26–58.

Chomsky, N. (1968). *Language and mind.* San Diego, CA: Harcourt Brace Jovanovich.

Christopherson, E.R. (1989). Injury control. *American Psychologist, 44,* 237–41.

Chuah, Y.M.L., & Maybery, M.T. (1999). Verbal and spatial short-term memory: Common sources of developmental change? *Journal of Experimental Child Psychology, 73,* 7–44.

Cillessen, A.H.N., van IJzendoorn, H.W., van Lieshout, C.F.M., & Hartup, W.W. (1992). Heterogeneity among peer-rejected boys: Subtypes and stabilities. *Child Development, 63,* 893–905.

Clark, E.V. (1973). What's in a word? On the child's acquisition of semantics in his first language. In T.E. Moore (Ed.), *Cognitive development and the acquisition of language* (pp. 65–110). New York: Academic Press.

Clark, H.H., & Clark, E.V. (1977). *Psychology and language: An introduction to psycholinguistics.* San Diego, CA: Harcourt Brace Jovanovich.

Clark, K.E., & Ladd, G.W. (2000). Connectedness and autonomy support in parent–child relationships: Links to children's socioemotional orientation and peer relationships. *Developmental Psychology, 36,* 485–98.

Clark, R., Guilmain, J., Saucier, P., & Tavarez, J. (2003). Two steps forward, one step back: The presence of female characters and gender stereotyping in award winning picture books between the 1930's and the 1960's. *Sex Roles, 48* (9/10), 439–49.

Clark, R., Hyde, J.S., Essex, M.J., & Klein, M.H. (1997). Length of maternity leave and quality of mother-infant interactions. *Child Development, 68,* 364–83.

Clarke, A.M., & Clarke, A.D.B. (1976). *Early experience: Myth and evidence.* New York: Free Press.

Clarke-Stewart, A. (1989). Infant day care: Maligned or malignant. *American Psychologist, 44,* 266–73.

Clarke-Stewart, A. (1993). *Daycare.* Cambridge, MA: Harvard University Press.

Clarke-Stewart, K.A., & Hayward, C. (1996). Advantages of father custody and contact for the psychological well-being of school-age children. *Journal of Applied Developmental Psychology, 17,* 239–70.

Clarkson, M.G., & Berg, W.K. (1983). Cardiac orienting and vowel discrimination in newborns: Crucial stimulus parameters. *Child Development, 54,* 162–71.

Clary, E.G., & Snyder, M. (1991). A functional analysis of altruism and prosocial behavior: The case of volunteerism. *Review of Personality and Social Psychology, 12,* 119–48.

Clausen, J.A. (1975). The social meaning of differential physical and sexual maturation. In S.E. Dragastin & G.H. Elder (Eds.), *Adolescence in the life cycle* (pp. 25–47). New York: Halsted Press.

Clements, D.H. (1990). Metacomponential development in a Logo programming environment. *Journal of Educational Psychology, 82,* 141–9.

Clements, D.H. (1991). Enhancement of creativity in computer environments. *American Educational Research Journal, 28,* 173–87.

Clements, D.H. (1995). Teaching creativity with computers. *Educational Psychology Review, 7,* 141–61.

Clements, D.H., & Nastasi, B.K. (1992). Computers and early childhood education. In M. Gettinger, S.N. Elliott, & T.R. Kratochwill (Eds.), *Advances in school psychology: Preschool and early childhood treatment directions.* Hillsdale, NJ: Erlbaum.

Clifton, R.K., Muir, D.W., Ashmead, D.H., & Clarkson, M.G. (1993). Is visually guided reaching in early infancy a myth? *Child Development, 64,* 1099–110.

Clingempeel, W.G., & Segal, S. (1986). Stepparent–stepchild relationships and the psychological adjustment of children in stepmother and stepfather families. *Child Development, 57,* 474–84.

Coates, B., & Hartup, W.W. (1969). Age and verbalization in observational learning. *Developmental Psychology, 1,* 556–62.

Cohen, D., & Strayer, J. (1996). Empathy in conduct-disordered and comparison youth. *Developmental Psychology, 32,* 988–98.

Cohen, L.B. & Cashon, C.H. (2003). Infant perception and cognition. In R.M. Lerner, M.A. Easterbrooks, et al. (Eds.), *Handbook of Psychology: Developmental Psychology (6)* (pp. 65-89). New York, NY: John Wiley & Sons, Inc.

Cohen, M. (1996). Preschooler's practical thinking and problem solving: The acquisition of an optimal solution. *Cognitive Development, 11,* 357–73.

Cohen, S., & Williamson, G.M. (1991). Stress and infectious disease in humans. *Psychological Bulletin, 109,* 5–24.

Coie, J.D., & Dodge, K.A. (1983). Continuities and changes in children's social status: A five-year longitudinal study. *Merrill-Palmer Quarterly, 19,* 261–82.

Coie, J.D., & Dodge, K.A. (1998). Aggression and antisocial behavior. In W. Damon (Series Ed.) & N. Eisenberg (Vol. Ed.), *Handbook of child psychology: Vol. 3. Social, emotional, and personality development* (pp. 779–862). New York: Wiley.

Coie, J.D., Dodge, K.A., & Coppotelli, H. (1982). Dimensions and types of social status: A cross-age perspective. *Developmental Psychology, 18,* 557–70.

Coie, J.D., Dodge, K.A., & Kupersmidt, J.B. (1990). Peer group behavior and social status. In S.R. Asher & J.D. Coie (Eds.), *Peer rejection in childhood.* Cambridge, England: Cambridge University Press.

Coie, J.D., Dodge, K.A., Terry, R., & Wright, V. (1991). The role of aggression in peer relations: An analysis of aggression episodes in boys' play groups. *Child Development, 62,* 812–26.

Coie, J.D., & Koeppl, G.K. (1990). Adapting intervention to the problems of aggressive and disruptive rejected children. In S.R. Asher & J.D. Coie (Eds.), *Peer rejection in childhood.* New York: Cambridge University Press.

Coie, J.D., & Krehbiel, G. (1984). Effects of academic tutoring on the social status of low-achieving, socially rejected children. *Child Development, 55,* 1465–78.

Coie, J.D., & Kupersmidt, J.B. (1983). A behavioral analysis of emerging social status in boys' groups. *Child Development, 54,* 1400–16.

Colapinto, J. (2000). *As nature made him: The boy who was raised as a girl.* Toronto: HarperCollins.

Colburn, D. (1996, September 24). Fetal alcohol babies face life of problems. *Washington Post,* p. Z5.

Colby, A., & Kohlberg, L. (1987). *The measurement of moral judgment: Vol. 1. Theoretical foundations and research validation.* Cambridge, England: Cambridge University Press.

Colby, A., Kohlberg, L., Gibbs, J., & Lieberman, M. (1983). A longitudinal study of moral judgment. *Monographs of the Society for Research in Child Development, 48* (1–2, Serial No. 200).

Cole, D.A., Martin, J.M., Peeke, L.A., Seroczynski, A.D., & Fier, J. (1999). Children's over- and underestimation of academic competence: A longitudinal study of gender differences, depression, and anxiety. *Child Development, 70,* 459–73.

Cole, M. (1990). Cognitive development and formal schooling: The evidence from cross-cultural research. In L.C. Moll (Ed.), *Vygotsky and education* (pp. 89–110). New York: Cambridge University Press.

Cole, M., & Scribner, S. (1977). Cross-cultural studies of memory and cognition. In R.V. Kail & J.W. Hagen (Eds.), *Perspectives on the development of memory and cognition* (pp. 239–71). Hillsdale, NJ: Erlbaum.

Cole, P.M., Barrett, K.C., & Zahn-Waxler, C. (1992). Emotion displays in two-year-olds during mishaps. *Child Development, 63,* 314–24.

Cole, P.M., & Tamang, B.L. (1998). Nepali children's ideas about emotional displays in hypothetical challenges. *Developmental Psychology, 34,* 640–6.

Coley, R.L. (1998). Children's socialization experiences and functioning in single-mother households: The importance of fathers and other men. *Child Development, 69,* 219–30.

Coley, R.L., & Chase-Lansdale, P.L. (1998). Adolescent pregnancy and parenthood: Recent evidence and future directions. *American Psychologist, 53,* 152–66.

College of Physicians and Surgeons of Manitoba. (2001). Sickle cell disease: Early diagnosis and treatment of children. *College on the Web, 920.* Retrieved August 14, 2001 from http://www.umanitoba.ca/colleges/ physicians_and_surgeons/_Guide/920. html.

Collins, W.A., Maccoby, E.E., Steinberg, L., Hetherington, E.M., & Bornstein, M.H. (2000). Contemporary research on parenting: The case for nature and nurture. *American Psychologist, 55,* 218–32.

Collis, B.A., Knezek, G.A., Lai, K., Miyashita, K.T., Pelgrum, W.J., Plump, T., & Sakamoto, T. (1996). *Children and computers in school.* Mahwah, NJ: Erlbaum.

Coltheart, M. (1978). Lexical access in simple reading tasks. In G. Underwood (Ed.), *Strategies of information processing* (pp. 151–216). New York: Academic Press.

Columbo, J. (1993). *Infant cognition: Predicting later intellectual functioning.* Newbury Park, CA: Sage.

Columbo, J., & Horowitz, F.D. (1987). Behavioral state as a lead variable in neonatal research. *Merrill-Palmer Quarterly, 33,* 423–37.

Committee on Nutritional Status during Pregnancy and Lactation, Institute of Medicine. (1990). *Nutrition during pregnancy. Part I: Weight gain. Part II: Nutrient supplements.* Retrieved August 14, 2001 from http://books.nap.edu/books/0309041384/htm l/index.html.

Condry, J., & Condry, S. (1976). Sex differences: A study in the eye of the beholder. *Child Development, 47,* 812–9.

Conduct Problems Prevention Research Group. (1999). Initial impact of the Fast Track Prevention Trial for Conduct Problems: II. Classroom effects. *Journal of Consulting and Clinical Psychology, 67,* 648–57.

Conger, R.D., Conger, K.J., Elder, G.J., Jr., Lorenz, F.O., Simons, R.L., & Whitbeck, L.B. (1992). A family process model of economic hardship and adjustment of early adolescent boys. *Child Development, 63,* 527–41.

Conger, R.D., Ge, X., Elder, G.H., Jr., Lorenz, F.O., & Simons, R.L. (1994). Economic stress, coercive family processes, and developmental problems of adolescents. *Child Development, 65,* 541–61.

Conger, R.D., Patterson, G.R., & Ge, X. (1995). It takes two to replicate: A mediational model for the impact of parents' stress on adolescent adjustment. *Child Development, 66,* 80–97.

Connell, J.P., Spencer, M.B., & Aber, J.L. (1994). Educational risk and resilience in African-American youth: Context, self, action, and outcomes in school. *Child Development, 65,* 493–506.

Connolly, D. & Lindsay, D.S. (2001). The influence of suggestions on children's reports of a unique experience versus an instance of a repeated experience. *Applied Cognitive Psychology, 15,* 205–23.

Connolly, J., Furman, W., & Konarski, R. (2000). The role of peers in the emergence of heterosexual romantic relationships in adolescence. *Child Development, 71,* 1395–1408.

Connolly, J.A., & Doyle, A. (1984). Relation of social fantasy play to social competence in preschoolers. *Developmental Psychology, 20,* 797–806.

Connor, J.M. (1995). Prenatal diagnosis of single-gene disorders by DNA analysis. In M.J. Whittle & J.M. Connor (Eds.), *Prenatal diagnosis in obstetric practice* (2nd ed., pp. 86–99). Oxford: Blackwell.

Coohey, C., & Braun, N. (1997). Toward an integrated framework for understanding child physical abuse. *Child Abuse and Neglect, 21,* 1081–94.

Cook, T.D., Appleton, H., Conner, R.F., Shaffer, A., Tabkin, G., & Weber, J.S. (1975). *Sesame Street revisited.* New York: Russell Sage Foundation.

Cooley, C. H. (1902). *Human nature and the social order.* New York: Scribner's.

Coon, H., Fulker, D.W., DeFries, J.C., & Plomin, R. (1990). Home environment and cognitive ability of 7-year-old children in the Colorado Adoption Project: Genetic and environmental etiologies. *Developmental Psychology, 26,* 459–68.

Cooper, H., Charlton, K., Valentine, J.C., & Muhlenbruck, L. (2000). Making the most of summer school: A meta-analytic and narrative review. *Monographs of the Society for Research in Child Development, 65* (1, Serial No. 260).

Cooper, R.P., & Aslin, R.N. (1990). Preference for infant-directed speech in the first month after birth. *Child Development, 61,* 1585–95.

Coopersmith, S. (1967). *The antecedents of self-esteem.* New York: W.H. Freeman.

Coplan, R.J., Gavinski-Molina, M., Lagace-Sequin, D.G., & Wichman, C. (2001). When girls versus boys play alone: Nonsocial play and adjustment in kindergarten. *Developmental Psychology, 37* (4), 464–74.

Coplan, R.J., Wichman, C., & Lagace-Sequin, D. (2001). Solitary-active play: A marker variable for maladjustment in the preschool? *Journal of Research in Childhood Education, 15* (2), 164–72.

Corah, N.L., Anthony, E.J., Painter, P., Stern, J.A., & Thurston, D. (1965). Effects of perinatal anoxia after seven years. *Psychological Monographs, 79* (3, No. 596), 1–34.

Corbin, C. (1973). *A textbook of motor development.* Dubuque, IA: William C. Brown.

Coren, S., Porac, C., & Duncan, P. (1981). Lateral preference behaviors in preschool children and young adults. *Child Development, 52,* 443–50.

Corenblum, B., & Annis, R.C. (1987). Racial identity and preference in Native and White

Canadian children. *Canadian Journal of Behavioural Science, 19* (3), 254–65.

Correctional Service of Canada. (1995, February). The patterns of violent crime by women. In M. Shaw & S. Dubois (Eds.), *Understanding violence by women: A review of the literature.* FSW No. 23. Retrieved May 21, 2001 from http://www.csc-scc.gc.ca/text/ prgrm/fsw23/fsw23e01.shtml.

Corteen, R.S., & Williams, T. (1986). Television and reading skills. In T. Williams (Ed.), *The impact of television: A natural experiment in three communities.* Orlando, FL: Academic Press.

Corter, C.M., Zucker, K.J., & Galligan, R.F. (1980). Patterns in the infant's search for mother during brief separation. *Developmental Psychology, 16,* 62–9.

Costin, S.E., & Jones, D.C. (1992). Friendship as a facilitator of emotional responsiveness and prosocial interventions among young children. *Developmental Psychology, 28,* 941–7.

Cote, J.E., & Levine, C. (1988). A critical examination of the ego identity status paradigm. *Developmental Review, 8,* 147–84.

Coulton, C.J., Korbin, J.E., Su, M., & Chow, J. (1995). Community level factors and child maltreatment rates. *Child Development, 66,* 1262–76.

Council of Ministers of Education, Canada, Education Indicators in Canada. (2003). *Report of the Pan-Canadian Education Indicators Program 2003.* Retrieved December 18, 2003 from http://www.cesc.ca/pceip/PCEIP2003en.pdf.

Council of Ministers of Education, Canada, School Achievement Indicators Program. (1997). *Report on mathematics assessment 1997.* Retrieved November 3, 2001 from http://www.cmec.ca/saip/math97/index.stm.

Courage, M., & Adams, R. (1996). Infant peripheral vision: The development of monocular acuity in the first 3 months of post-natal life. *Vision Research, 36* (8), 1207–15.

Cousins, S.D. (1989). Culture and self-perception in Japan and the United States. *Journal of Personality and Social Psychology, 56,* 124–131.

Cowan, N., Nugent, L.D., Elliott, E.M., Ponomarev, I., & Saults, J.S. (1999). The role of attention in the development of short-term memory: Age differences in the verbal span of apprehension. *Child Development, 70,* 1082–97.

Cowan, P.A. (1978). *Piaget: With feeling.* New York: Holt, Rinehart and Winston.

Cowley, G. (2001). Generation XXL. In K.L. Frieberg (Ed.), *Human development 01/02* (29th ed., pp. 120–121). Guilford, CT: McGraw-Hill/Duskin.

Cox, C.M. (1926). *Genetic studies of genius: Vol. 2. The early mental traits of three hundred geniuses.* Stanford, CA: Stanford University Press.

Cox, M.J., Owen, M.T., Henderson, V.K., & Margand, N.A. (1992). Prediction of infant–father and infant–mother attachment. *Developmental Psychology, 28,* 474–83.

Cox, M.J., Owen, M.T., Lewis, J.M., & Henderson, V.K. (1989). Marriage, adult adjustment, and early parenting. *Child Development, 60,* 1015–24.

Coyle, T.R. (2001). Factor analysis of variability measures in eight independent samples of children and adults. *Journal of Experimental Child Psychology, 78,* 330–58.

Coyle, T.R., & Bjorklund, D.F. (1996). The development of strategic memory: A modified microgenetic assessment of utilization deficiencies. *Cognitive Development, 11,* 295–314.

Coyle, T.R., & Bjorklund, D.F. (1997). Age differences in, and consequences of, multiple-and variable-strategy use on a multitrial sort-

recall task. *Developmental Psychology, 33,* 372–80.

Coyle, T.R., Read, L.E., Gaultney, J.F., & Bjorklund, D.F. (1999). Giftedness and variability in strategic processing on a multitrial memory task: Evidence for stability in gifted cognition. *Learning and Individual Differences, 10,* 273–90.

Craig, W.M., & Pepler, D.J. (1997). Observations of bullying and victimization on the schoolyard. *Canadian Journal of School Psychology, 13* (2), 41–59.

Crain-Thoreson, C., & Dale, P.S. (1992). Do early talkers become early readers? Linguistic precocity, preschool language, and emergent literacy. *Developmental Psychology, 28,* 421–9.

Craton, L.G. (1996). The development of perceptual completion abilities: Infants' perception of stationary partially occluded objects. *Child Development, 67,* 890–904.

Craton, L.G., Elicker, J., Plumert, J.M., & Pick, H.L., Jr. (1990). Children's use of frames of reference in communication of spatial location. *Child Development, 61,* 1528–43.

Crews, F. (1996). The verdict on Freud [Review of *Freud evaluated: The completed arc*]. *Psychological Science, 7,* 63–8.

Crick, K., Heilman-Houser, R., & Hunter, M. (2002). The impact of childcare on gender role development and gender stereotypes. *Early Childhood Education Journal, 29*(3), 149–154.

Crick, N.R. (1996). The role of overt aggression, relational aggression, and prosocial behavior in the prediction of children's future social adjustment. *Child Development, 67,* 2317–27.

Crick, N.R. (1997). Engagement in gender normative versus nonnormative forms of aggression: Links to social-psychological adjustment. *Developmental Psychology, 33,* 610–7.

Crick, N.R., Bigbee, M.A., & Howes, C. (1996). Gender differences in children's normative beliefs about aggression: How do I hurt thee? Let me count the ways. *Child Development, 67,* 1003–14.

Crick, N.R., Casas, J.F., & Ku, H. (1999). Relational and physical forms of peer victimization in preschool. *Developmental Psychology, 35,* 376–85.

Crick, N.R., Casas, J.F., & Mosher, M. (1997). Relational and overt aggression in preschool. *Developmental Psychology, 33,* 579–88.

Crick, N.R., & Dodge, K.A. (1994). A review and reformulation of social information processing mechanisms in children's social adjustment. *Psychological Bulletin, 115,* 74–101.

Crick, N.R., & Dodge, K.A. (1996). Social information-processing mechanisms in reactive and proactive aggression. *Child Development, 67,* 993–1002.

Crick, N.R., & Grotpeter, J.K. (1995). Relational aggression, gender, and social-psychological adjustment. *Child Development, 66,* 710–22.

Crick, N.R., & Ladd, G.W. (1993). Children's perceptions of their peer experiences: Attributions, loneliness, social anxiety, and social avoidance. *Developmental Psychology, 29,* 244–54.

Crick, N.R., Wellman, N.E., Casas, J.F., O'Brien, K.M., Nelson, D.A., Grotpeter, J.K., & Markon, K. (1998). Childhood aggression and gender: A new look at an old problem. In D. Bernstein (Ed.), *Nebraska Symposium on Motivation: Vol. 44. Gender and motivation* (pp. 75–141). Lincoln: University of Nebraska Press.

Crockenberg, S., & Litman, C. (1990). Autonomy as competence in 2-year-olds: Maternal correlates of child defiance, compliance, and self-assertion. *Developmental Psychology, 26,* 961–71.

Crockenberg, S., & Litman, C. (1991). Effects of maternal employment on maternal and two-year-old child behavior. *Child Development, 62,* 930–53.

Cronbach, L.J., & Snow, R.E. (1977). *Aptitude and instructional methods: A handbook for research on interactions.* New York: Irvington.

Crook, C.K. (1978). Taste perception in the newborn infant. *Infant Behavior and Development, 1,* 52–69.

Crook, C. K. (1992). Cultural artefacts in social development: The case of computers. In H. McGurk (Ed.), *Childhood social development: Contemporary perspectives.* Hove, England: Erlbaum.

Cross, W.E. (1985). Black identity: Rediscovering the distinction between personal identity and reference group orientation. In M.B. Spencer, G.K. Brookins, & W.R. Allen (Eds.), *Beginnings: The social and affective development of black children.* Hillsdale, NJ: Erlbaum.

Crouter, A.C., Helms-Erikson, H., Updegraff, K., & McHale, S.M. (1999b). Conditions underlying parents's knowledge about children's daily lives in middle childhood: Between- and within-family comparisons. *Child Development, 70,* 246–59.

Crouter, A.C., Manke, B.A., & McHale, S.M. (1995). The family context of gender intensification in early adolescence. *Child Development, 66,* 317–29.

Crowell, J.A., & Feldman, S.S. (1991). Mothers' working models of attachment relationships and mother and child behavior during separation and reunion. *Developmental Psychology, 27,* 597–605.

Crowley, K., Shrager, J., & Siegler, R.S. (1997). Strategy discovery as a complete negotiation between metacognitive and associative mechanisms. *Developmental Review, 17,* 462–89.

Crowley, K., & Siegler, R.S. (1993). Flexible strategy use in young children's tic-tac-toe. *Cognitive Science, 17,* 531–61.

Crystal, D.S., Chen, C., Fuligni, A.J., Stevenson, H.W., Hsu, C., Ko, H., Kitamura, S., & Kimura, S. (1994). Psychological maladjustment and academic achievement: A cross-cultural study of Japanese, Chinese, and American high school students. *Child Development, 65,* 738–53.

Crystal, D.S., Watanabe, H., Weinfert, K., & Wu, C. (1998). Concepts of human differences: A comparison of American, Japanese, and Chinese children and adolescents. *Developmental Psychology, 34,* 714–22.

Cummings, E.M., & Davies, P.T. (1994). *Children and marital conflict: The impact of family dispute and resolution.* New York: Guilford Press.

Cummings, E.M., Iannotti, R.J., & Zahn-Waxler, C. (1989). Aggression between peers in early childhood: Individual continuity and developmental change. *Child Development, 60,* 887–95.

Cunningham, H. (1996). The history of childhood. In C.P. Hwang, M.E. Lam, & I.E. Sigel (Eds.), *Images of childhood.* Mahwah, NJ: Erlbaum.

Curry, L.M. (2000). Net provides new expression for sexual offenders. *Monitor on Psychology, 31,* 21.

Curtiss, S. (1977). *Genie: A psycholinguistic study of a modern-day "wild child."* New York: Academic Press.

Curtiss, S. (1988). *The case of Chelsea: a new test case of the critical period for language acquisition.* Unpublished manuscript. University of California, Los Angeles.

Dabbs, J.M., Jr., Carr, T.S., Frady, F.L., & Riad, J.K. (1995). Testosterone, crime, and misbehavior among 692 prison inmates. *Personality and Individual Differences, 18,* 627–33.

Dabbs, J.M., & Morris, R. (1990). Testosterone, social class, and antisocial behavior in a sample of 4462 men. *Psychological Science, 1,* 209–11.

Dale, P.S. (1976). *Language development: Structure and function.* New York: Holt, Rinehart & Winston.

Damast, A.M., Tamis-LeMonda, C.S., & Bornstein, M.H. (1996). Mother–child play: Sequential interactions and the relation between maternal beliefs and behaviors. *Child Development, 67,* 1752–66.

Damon, W. (1977). *The social world of the child.* San Francisco: Jossey-Bass.

Damon, W. (1988). *The moral child.* New York: Free Press.

Damon, W., & Hart, D. (1988). *Self-understanding in childhood and adolescence.* New York: Cambridge University Press.

Damon, W., & Hart, D. (1992). Self-understanding and its role in social and moral development. In M.H. Bornstein & M.E. Lamb (Eds.), *Developmental psychology: An advanced textbook.* Hillsdale, NJ: Erlbaum.

Daniels, D. (1986). Differential experiences of siblings in the same family as predictors of adolescent sibling personality differences. *Journal of Personality and Social Psychology, 51,* 339–46.

Daniels, D., & Plomin, R. (1985). Differential experience of siblings in the same family. *Developmental Psychology, 21,* 747–60.

Dapretto, M., & Bjork, E.L. (2000). The development of word retrieval abilities in the second year and its relation to early vocabulary growth. *Child Development, 71,* 635–48.

Darling, C.A., Davidson, J.K., & Passarello, L.C. (1992). The mystique of first intercourse among college youth: The role of partners, contraceptive practices, and psychological reactions. *Journal of Youth and Adolescence, 21,* 97–117.

Darlington, R.B. (1991). The long-term effects of model preschool programs. In L. Okagaki & R.J. Sternberg (Eds.), *Directors of development: Influences on the development of children's thinking.* Hillsdale, NJ: Erlbaum.

Darwin, C.A. (1877). A biographical sketch of an infant. *Mind, 2,* 285–94.

Das Eiden, R., Teti, D.M., & Corns, K.M. (1995). Maternal working models of attachment, marital adjustment, and the parent–child relationship. *Child Development, 66,* 1504–18.

Dasen, P.R. (1977). *Piagetian psychology: Cross-cultural contributions.* New York: Gardner Press.

da Silva, O.P. (1994). Prevention of low birth weight/preterm birth. In Canadian Task Force on the Periodic Health Examination, *The Canadian guide to clinical preventive health care* (pp. 38–50). Ottawa: Health Canada. Retrieved October 23, 2001 from http://www.hc-sc.gc.ca/hppb/healthcare/pubs/clinical_preventive/sec1e.htm.

David, H.P. (1992). Born unwanted: Long-term developmental effects of denied abortion. *Journal of Social Issues, 48,* 163–81.

David, H.P. (1994). Reproductive rights and reproductive behavior: Clash or convergence of private values and public policies. *American Psychologist, 49,* 343–9.

Davies, P.T., & Cummings, E.M. (1998). Exploring children's emotional security as a mediator of the link between marital relations and child adjustment. *Child Development, 69,* 124–39.

Davis, B.L., MacNeilage, P.F., Matyear, C.L., & Powell, J.K. (2000). Prosodic correlates of stress in babbling: An acoustical study. *Child Development, 71,* 1258-1270.

Davis, T.L. (1995). Gender differences in masking negative emotions: Ability or motivation. *Developmental Psychology, 31,* 660–7.

Day, R.H. (1987). Visual size constancy in infancy. In B.E. McKenzie & R.H. Day (Eds.), *Perceptual development in early infancy: Problems and issues.* Hillsdale, NJ: Erlbaum.

Day, R.H., & McKenzie, B.E. (1981). Infant perception of the invariant size of approaching and receding objects. *Developmental Psychology, 17,* 670–7.

DeAngelis, T. (1997b). When children don't bond with parents. *Monitor of the American Psychological Association, 28* (6), 10–2.

Deater-Deckard, K., & Dodge, K.A. (1997). Externalizing behavior problems and discipline revisited: Nonlinear effects and variation by culture, context, and gender. *Psychological Inquiry, 8,* 161–75.

Deater-Deckard, K., & O'Connor, T.G. (2000). Parent–child mutuality in early childhood: Two behavioral genetic studies. *Developmental Psychology, 36,* 561–70.

Deater-Deckard, K., & Plomin, R. (1999). An adoption study of the etiology of teacher and parent reports of externalizing behavior problems in middle childhood. *Child Development, 70,* 144–54.

DeBerry, K.M., Scarr, S., & Weinberg, R. (1996). Family racial socialization and ecological competence: Longitudinal assessments of African-American transracial adoptees. *Child Development, 67,* 2375–99.

DeCasper, A.J., & Fifer, W.P. (1980). Of human bonding: Newborns prefer their mother's voices. *Science, 208,* 1174–6.

DeCasper, A.J., & Spence, M.J. (1986). Prenatal maternal speech influences newborns' perception of speech sounds. *Infant Behavior and Development, 9,* 133–50.

DeCasper, A.J., & Spence, M.J. (1991). Auditorially mediated behavior during the perinatal period: A cognitive view. In M.J.S. Weiss & P.R. Zelazo (Eds.), *Newborn attention: Biological constraints and the influence of experience* (pp. 142–76). Norwood, NJ: Ablex.

de Gaston, J.P., Jensen, L., & Weed, S. (1995). A closer look at adolescent sexual activity. *Journal of Youth and Adolescence, 24,* 465–79.

de Haan, M., & Nelson, C.A. (1999). Brain activity differentiates face and object processing in 6-month-old infants. *Developmental Psychology, 35,* 1113–21.

Dekovic, M., & Janssens, J.M.A.M. (1992). Parents' child-rearing style and children's sociometric status. *Developmental Psychology, 28,* 925–32.

Delcampo, D.S., & Delcampo, R.L. (1998). *Taking sides: Clashing views on controversial issues in childhood and society* (2nd ed.). Guilford, CT: Dushkin/McGraw-Hill.

De Lisi, R., & Staudt, J. (1980). Individual differences in college students' performance on formal operations tasks. *Journal of Applied Developmental Psychology, 1,* 163–74.

DeLoache, J.S. (1986). Memory in very young children: Exploitation of cues to the location of a hidden object. *Cognitive Development, 1,* 123–38.

DeLoache, J.S. (1987). Rapid change in the symbolic functioning of very young children. *Science, 238,* 1556–7.

DeLoache, J.S. (1991). Symbolic functioning in very young children: Understanding of pictures and models. *Child Development, 62,* 736–52.

DeLoache, J.S. (2000). Dual representation and young children's use of scale models. *Child Development, 71,* 329–38.

DeLoache, J.S., Miller, K.F., & Pierroutsakos, S.L. (1998). Reasoning and problem solving. In W. Damon (Series Ed.) & D. Kuhn & R.S. Siegler (Vol. Eds.), *Handbook of child psychology: Vol. 2. Cognitive, language, and perceptual development* (pp. 801–850). New York: Wiley.

DeLoache, J.S., Perralta de Mendoza, O.A., & Anderson, K.N. (1999). Multiple factors in early symbol use: Instructions, similarity, and age in understanding a symbol–referent relation. *Cognitive Development, 14,* 299–312.

DeLuccie, M.F. (1995). Mothers as gatekeepers: A model of maternal mediators of father involvement. *Journal of Genetic Psychology, 156,* 115–31.

deMause, L. (1974). The evolution of childhood. In L. deMause (Ed.), *The history of childhood* (pp. 1–54). New York: Psychohistory Press.

Dempster, F.N. (1981). Memory span: Sources of individual and developmental differences. *Psychological Bulletin, 89,* 63–100.

Dempster, F.N. (1993). Resistance to interference: Developmental changes in a basic processing mechanism. In M.L. Howe & R. Pasnak (Eds.), *Emerging themes in cognitive development: Vol. 1. Foundations* (pp. 1–27). New York: Springer-Verlag.

DeMulder, E.K., Denham, S., Schmidt, M., & Mitchell, J. (2000). Q-sort assessment of attachment security during the preschool years: Links from home to school. *Developmental Psychology, 36,* 274–82.

Denham, S.A., McKinley, M., Couchoud, E.A., & Holt, R. (1990). Emotional and behavioral predictors of preschool peer ratings. *Child Development, 61,* 1145–52.

Denning, C.R., Kagan, B.M., Mueller, D.H., & Neu, H.C. (1991). The CF gene—one year later. *Cystic Fibrosis Currents, 6,* 1–19.

Dennis, W. (1960). Causes of retardation among institutional children: Iran. *Journal of Genetic Psychology, 96,* 47–59.

D'Entremont, B., & Muir, D. (1999). Infant responses to adult happy and sad vocal and facial expressions during face-to-face interactions. *Infant Behavior & Development, Special Issue, 22* (4), 527–39.

Descartes, R. (1965). La dioptrique. In R.J. Herrnstein & E.G. Boring (Eds.), *A sourcebook in the history of psychology.* Cambridge, MA: Harvard University Press. (Original work published 1638.)

Despert, J.L. (1965). *The emotionally disturbed child: Then and now.* New York: Brunner/ Mazel.

de Villiers, J.G., & de Villiers, P.A. (1973). A cross-sectional study of the acquisition of grammatical morphemes in child speech. *Journal of Psycholinguistic Research, 2,* 267–78.

de Villiers, P.A., & de Villiers, J.G. (1979). *Early language.* Cambridge, MA: Harvard University Press.

de Villiers, P.A., & de Villiers, J.G. (1992). Language development. In M.H. Bornstein & M.E. Lamb (Eds.), *Developmental psychology: An advanced textbook* (3rd ed., pp. 337–418). Hillsdale, NJ: Erlbaum.

DeVries, R. (1969). Constancy of generic identity in the years three to six. *Monographs of the Society for Research in Child Development, 34* (Serial No. 127).

De Wolff, M.S., & van IJzendoorn, M.H. (1997). Sensitivity and attachment: A meta-analysis on parental antecedents of infant attachment. *Child Development, 68,* 571–91.

Dews, S., Winner, E., Kaplan, J., Rosenblatt, E., Hunt, M., Lim, K., McGovern, A., Qualter, A., & Smarsh, B. (1996). Children's understanding of the meaning and functions of verbal irony. *Child Development, 67,* 3071–85.

Dewsbury, D.A. (1992). Comparative psychology and ethology: A reassessment. *American Psychologist, 47,* 208–15.

Diagnostic and Statistical Manual of Mental Disorders, Fourth Edition (DSM-IV). (1994). Washington, DC: American Psychiatric Association.

Diamond, A. (1985). Development of the ability to use recall to guide action, as indicated by the infant's performance on AB. *Child Development, 56,* 868–83.

Diamond, A. (1991). Frontal lobe involvement in cognitive changes during the first year of life. In K.R. Gibson & A.C. Petersen (Eds.), *Brain maturation and cognitive development: Comparative and cross-cultural perspectives* (pp. 127–60). New York: Aldine de Gruyter.

Diamond, A. (1995). Evidence of robust recognition memory in early life even when assessed by reaching behavior. *Journal of Experimental Child Psychology, 59,* 419–56.

Diamond, A., & Taylor, C. (1996). Development of an aspect of executive control: Development of the abilities to remember what I said and to "Do as I say, not as I do." *Developmental Psychobiology, 29,* 315–24.

Diamond, L.M. (2000). Sexual identity, attractions, and behavior among young sexual-minority women over a 2-year period. *Developmental Psychology, 36,* 241–50.

Diamond, M., & Sigmundson, H.K. (1997). Sex reassignment at birth: Long-term review and clinical implications. *Archives of Pediatric and Adolescent Medicine, 151,* 298–304.

Diaz, J. (1997). *How drugs influence behavior: A neuro-behavioral approach.* Upper Saddle River, NJ: Prentice-Hall.

Diaz, R.M. (1983). Thought and two languages: The impact of bilingualism on cognitive development. In E.W. Gordon (Ed.), *Review of research in education* (Vol. 10, pp. 23–54). Washington, DC: American Educational Research Association.

Diaz, R.M. (1985). Bilingual cognitive development: Addressing three gaps in recent research. *Child Development, 56,* 1376–88.

Diaz, R.M., Neal, C.J., & Vachio, A. (1991). Maternal teaching in the zone of proximal development: A comparison of low- and high-risk dyads. *Merrill-Palmer Quarterly, 37,* 83–108.

Dick, D.M., Rose, R.J., Viken, R.J., & Kaprio, J. (2000). Pubertal timing and substance use between and within families across late adolescence. *Developmental Psychology, 36,* 180–9.

Dick-Read, G. (1972). *Childbirth without fear: The original approach to natural childbirth.* New York: Harper & Row. (Original work published 1933.)

Diener, E., Sandvik, E., & Larsen, R.J. (1985). Age and sex effects for emotional intensity. *Developmental Psychology, 21,* 542–6.

DiLalla, L.F., Kagan, J., & Reznick, J.S. (1994). Genetic etiology of behavioral inhibition among 2-year-old children. *Infant Behavior and Development, 17,* 405–12.

Dill, K.E., & Dill, J.C. (1998). Video game violence: A review of the empirical literature. *Aggression and Violent Behavior: A Review Journal, 3,* 407–28.

Dillon, P.A., & Emery, R.E. (1996). Divorce mediation and resolution of child custody disputes: Long-term effects. *American Journal of Orthopsychiatry, 66,* 131–40.

DiPietro, J.A., Hodgson, D.M., Costigan, K.A., Hilton, S.C., & Johnston, T.R.B. (1996). Fetal neurobehavioral development. *Child Development, 67,* 2553–67.

Dishion, T.J. (1990). The family ecology of boys' peer relations in middle childhood. *Child Development, 61,* 874–92.

Dishion, T.J., Andrews, D.W., & Crosby, L. (1995). Antisocial boys and their friends in early adolescence: Relationship characteristics, quality, and interactional process. *Child Development, 66,* 139–51.

Dishion, T.J., McCord, J., & Poulin, F. (1999). When interventions harm: Peer groups and problem behavior. *American Psychologist, 54,* 755–64.

Dishion, T.J., Patterson, G.R., Stoolmiller, M., & Skinner, M.L. (1991). Family, school, and behavioral antecedents to early adolescent involvement with antisocial peers. *Developmental Psychology, 27,* 172–80.

Dittman, R.W., Kappes, M.E., & Kappes, M.H. (1992). Sexual behavior in adolescent and adult females with congenital adrenal hyperplasia. *Psychoneuroendocrinology, 17,* 153–70.

Dixon, R.A., & Lerner, R.M. (1992). A history of systems in developmental psychology. In M.H. Bornstein & M.E. Lamb (Eds.), *Developmental psychology: An advanced textbook.* Hillsdale, NJ: Erlbaum.

Dodge, K.A. (1980). Social cognition and children's aggressive behavior. *Child Development, 51,* 162–70.

Dodge, K.A. (1983). Behavioral antecedents of peer social status. *Child Development, 54,* 1386–99.

Dodge, K.A. (1986). A social information processing model of social competence in children. In M. Perlmutter (Ed.), *Minnesota Symposia on Child Psychology* (Vol. 18, pp. 77–125). Hillsdale, NJ: Erlbaum.

Dodge, K.A., Coie, J.D., Pettit, G.S., & Price, J.M. (1990). Peer status and aggression in boys' groups: Developmental and contextual analyses. *Child Development, 61,* 1289–1309.

Dodge, K.A., Pettit, G.S., & Bates, J.E. (1994). Socialization mediators of the relation between socioeconomic status and child conduct problems. *Child Development, 65,* 649–65.

Doherty, G., Lero, D.S., Goelman, H., Tougas, J., & LaGrange, A. (2000). *You bet I care! Caring and learning environments: Quality in regulated family child care across Canada.* Guelph, ON: University of Guelph, Centre for Families, Work and Well-Being. Retrieved November 12, 2001 from http://action.web.ca/home/cfwwb/attach/ybic _report_3.pdf.

Doherty, W.J., & Needle, R.H. (1991). Psychological adjustment and substance abuse among adolescents before and after a parental divorce. *Child Development, 62,* 328–37.

Dolan, B. (1999). From the field: Cognitive profiles of First Nations and Caucasian children referred for psychoeducational assessment. *Canadian Journal of School Psychology, 15* (1), 63–71.

Dolgin, K.G., & Behrend, D.A. (1984). Children's knowledge about animates and inanimates. *Child Development, 55,* 1646–50.

Dollberg, S., Seidman, D.S., Armon, Y., Stevenson, D.K., & Gale, R. (1996). Adverse perinatal outcome in the older primipara. *Journal of Perinatology, 16,* 93–7.

Domjan, M. (1993). *Principles of learning and behavior* (3rd ed.). Pacific Grove, CA: Brooks/Cole.

Dondi, M., Simion, F., & Caltran, G. (1999). Can newborns discriminate between their own cry and the cry of another newborn infant? *Developmental Psychology, 35,* 418–426.

Donnerstein, E., & Smith, S. (2001). Sex in the media: Theory, influences, and solutions. In D. Singer & J. Singer (Eds.), *Handbook of children and the media* (pp. 287–307). Thousand Oaks, CA: Sage.

Donovan, W.L., Leavitt, L.A., & Walsh, R.O. (2000). Maternal illusory control predicts socialization strategies and toddler compliance. *Developmental Psychology, 36,* 402–11.

Dornbusch, S.M., Glasgow, K.L., & Lin, I. (1996). The social structure of schooling. *Annual Review of Psychology, 47,* 401–29.

Dougherty, T.M., & Haith, M.M. (1997). Infant expectations and reaction time as predictors of childhood speed of processing and IQ. *Developmental Psychology, 33,* 146–55.

Downing, L.L. (2001). *Fragile realities: Conversion and commitment in cults and other powerful groups.* Oneonta, NY: State University of New York at Oneonta.

Doyle, A.B., & Aboud, F.E. (1995). A longitudinal study of white children's racial prejudice as a social-cognitive development. *Merrill-Palmer Quarterly, 41* (2), 209–28.

Doyle, A.B., Connolly, J., & Rivest, L. (1980). The effects of playmate familiarity on the social interaction of very young children. *Child Development, 51,* 217–23.

Doyle, A.B., Doehring, P., Tessier, O., de Lorimier, S., & Shapiro, S. (1992). Transitions in children's play: A sequential analysis of states preceding and following social pretense. *Developmental Psychology, 28,* 137–44.

Drabman, R.S., & Thomas, M.H. (1974). Does media violence increase children's toleration of real-life aggression? *Developmental Psychology, 10,* 418–21.

Dreyer, P.H. (1982). Sexuality during adolescence. In B.B. Wolman (Ed.), *Handbook of developmental psychology.* New York: Wiley.

Drillien, C.M. (1969). School disposal and performance for children of different birthweight born 1953–1960. *Archives of Diseases in Childhood, 44,* 562–70.

Droege, K.L., & Stipek, D.J. (1993). Children's use of dispositions to predict classmates' behavior. *Developmental Psychology, 29,* 646–54.

Drotar, D. (1992). Personality development, problem solving, and behavior problems among preschool children with early histories of nonorganic failure-to-thrive. *Developmental and Behavioral Pediatrics, 13,* 266–73.

Drummey, A.B., & Newcombe, N. (1995). Remembering versus knowing the past: Children's explicit and implicit memory. *Journal of Experimental Child Psychology, 59,* 549–65.

Dubas, J.S., Graber, J.A., & Petersen, A.C. (1991). The effects of pubertal development on achievement during adolescence. *American Journal of Education, 99,* 444–60.

Dube, E. F. (1982). Literacy, cultural familiarity, and "intelligence" as determinants of story recall. In U. Neisser (Ed.), *Memory observed: Remembering in natural contexts.* San Francisco: W. H. Freeman.

Duffy, J., Gunther, G., & Walters, L. (1997). Gender and mathematical problem solving. *Sex Roles: A Journal of Research, 37* (7–8), 477–94.

Duke, P.M., Carlsmith, J.M., Jennings, D., Martin, J.A., Dornbusch, S.M., Gross, R.T., & Siegel-Gorelick, B. (1982). Educational correlates of early and late sexual maturation in adolescence. *Journal of Pediatrics, 100,* 633–7.

Duncan, G.J., & Brooks-Gunn, J. (1997). *Growing up poor: Consequences across the life span.* New York: Russell Sage Foundation.

Duncan, G.J., & Brooks-Gunn, J. (2000). Family poverty, welfare reform, and child development. *Child Development, 71,* 188–96.

Duncan, R.M. (1995). Piaget and Vygotsky revisited: Dialogue or assimilation? *Developmental Review, 15,* 458–72.

Duncan, R.M. (2000). Experimental studies of the forms and functions of private speech in young adults (talking to oneself). *Dissertation Abstracts International: B. The Physical Sciences and Engineering, 60* (7-B), 3552.

Duncan, R.M., & Pratt, M.W. (1997). Microgenetic change in the quantity and quality of preschoolers' private speech. *International Journal of Behavioral Development, 20* (2), 367–83.

Dunham, P., Hurshman, A., Litwin, E., Gusella, J., Ellsworth, C., & Dodd, P. (1998). Computer-mediated social support: Single young mothers as a model system. *American Journal of Community Psychology, 26* (2), 281–306.

Dunn, J. (1993). *Young children's close relationships. Beyond attachment.* Newbury Park, CA: Sage.

Dunn, J. (1994). Changing minds and changing relationships. In C. Lewis & P. Mitchel (Eds.), *Children's early understanding of mind: Origins and development* (pp. 297–310). Hove, England: Erlbaum.

Dunn, J., Brown, J., & Beardsall, L. (1991). Family talk about feeling states and children's later understanding of children's emotions. *Developmental Psychology, 27,* 448–55.

Dunn, J., Brown, J.R., & Maguire, M. (1995). The development of children's moral sensibility: Individual differences and emotional understanding. *Developmental Psychology, 31,* 649–59.

Dunn, J., & Hughes, C. (2001). "I got some swords and you're dead!" Violent fantasy, antisocial behavior, friendship, and moral sensibility in young children. *Child Development, 72,* 491–505.

Dunn, J., & Kendrick, C. (1982). *Siblings: Love, envy, and understanding.* Cambridge, MA: Harvard University Press.

Dunn, J., & Plomin, R. (1990). *Separate lives: Why siblings are so different.* New York: Basic Books.

Dunphy, D.C. (1963). The social structure of urban adolescent peer groups. *Sociometry, 26,* 230–46.

Durrant, J., Broberg, A., & Rose-Krasnor, L. (1999). Predicting use of physical punishment during mother–child conflicts in Sweden and Canada. In P. Hastings & C. Piotrowski (Eds.), *Maternal beliefs about child rearing. New Directions for Child and Adolescent Development, 86,* 25–42.

Durrant, J., & Rose-Krasnor, L. (1995). *Parental beliefs and practice in Canada: Implications for reducing rates of corporal punishment.* Report for the Family Violence Prevention Division, Health Canada. Ottawa: Health Canada.

Dweck, C.S. (1975). The role of expectations and attributions in the alleviation of learned helplessness. *Journal of Personality and Social Psychology, 31,* 674–85.

Dweck, C.S. (1978). Achievement. In M.E. Lamb (Ed.), *Social and personality development* (pp. 114–30). New York: Holt, Rinehart, and Winston.

Dweck, C.S. (2001). Caution—praise can be dangerous. In K.L. Freiberg (Ed.), *Human development 01/02* (29th ed., pp. 105–109). Guilford, CT: Duskin/McGraw-Hill.

Dweck, C.S., Davidson, W., Nelson, S., & Enna, B. (1978). Sex differences in learned helplessness. II. The contingencies of evaluative feedback in the classroom. III. An experimental analysis. *Developmental Psychology, 14,* 268–76.

Dweck, C.S., & Elliott, E.S. (1983). Achievement motivation. In P.H. Mussen (Series Ed.) & E.M. Hetherington (Vol. Ed.), *Handbook of child psychology: Vol. 4. Socialization, personality, and social development* (4th ed.). New York: Wiley.

Dweck, C.S., & Leggett, E.L. (1988). A social-cognitive approach to motivation and personality. *Psychological Review, 95,* 256–73.

Dwyer, T., Ponsonby, A.L.B., Newman, N.M., & Gibbons, L.E. (1991). Prospective cohort study of prone sleeping position and sudden infant death syndrome. *Lancet, 337,* 1244–7.

Dyer, K.F. (1977). The trend of male–female performance differential in athletics, swimming, and cycling 1948–1976. *Journal of Biosocial Science, 9,* 325–38.

Eagly, A.H. (1995). The science and politics of comparing men and women. *American Psychologist, 50,* 145–58.

East, P.L. (1996). The younger sisters of childbearing adolescents: Their attitudes, expectations, and behaviors. *Child Development, 67,* 267–82.

East, P.L., & Jacobson, L.J. (2001). The younger siblings of teenage mothers: A follow-up of their pregnancy risk. *Developmental Psychology, 37,* 254–64.

East, P.L., & Rook, K.S. (1992). Compensatory patterns of support among children's peer relationships: A test using

school friends, nonschool friends, and siblings. *Developmental Psychology, 28,* 163–72.

Eaton, W.O., & Enns, L.R. (1986). Sex differences in human motor activity level. *Psychological Bulletin, 100,* 19–28.

Eaton, W.O., & Ritchot, K.F.M. (1995). Physical maturation and information-processing speed in middle childhood. *Development Psychology, 31* (6), 967–72.

Eaton, W.O., & Yu, A.P. (1989). Are sex differences in child motor activity level a function of sex differences in maturational status? *Child Development, 60,* 1005–11.

Ebeling, K.S., & Gelman, S.A. (1988). Coordination of size standards by young children. *Child Development, 59,* 888–96.

Ebeling, K.S., & Gelman, S.A. (1994). Children's use of context in interpreting "big" and "little." *Child Development, 65,* 1178–92.

Eccles, J.S., Flanagan, C., Lord, S., & Midgley, C. (1996). Schools, families, and early adolescents: What are we doing wrong and what can we do instead? *Journal of Developmental and Behavioral Pediatrics, 17,* 267–76.

Eccles, J.S., & Harold, R.D. (1993). Parent–school involvement during the early adolescent years. *Teachers College Record, 94,* 568–87.

Eccles, J.S., Jacobs, J.E., & Harold, R.D. (1990). Gender role stereotypes, expectancy effects, and parents' socialization of gender differences. *Journal of Social Issues, 46,* 183–201.

Eccles, J.S., Lord, S., & Midgley, C. (1991). What are we doing to early adolescents? The impact of educational contexts on early adolescents. *American Journal of Education, 99,* 521–42.

Eccles, J.S., Midgley, C., Wigfield, A., Buchanan, C.M., Reuman, D., Flanagan, C., & Mac Iver, D. (1993). Development during adolescence: The impact of stage-environment fit on young adolescents' experiences in schools and in families. *American Psychologist, 48,* 90–101.

Eckenrode, J., Laird, M., & Doris, J. (1993). School performance and disciplinary problems among abused and neglected children. *Developmental Psychology, 29,* 53–62.

Eckerman, C.O., & Didow, S.M. (1996). Nonverbal imitation and toddlers' mastery of verbal means of achieving coordinated action. *Developmental Psychology, 32,* 141–52.

Eckerman, C.O., & Stein, M.R. (1990). How imitation begets imitation and toddlers' generation of games. *Developmental Psychology, 26,* 370–8.

Eder, R.A. (1989). The emergent personalogist: The structure and content of 3 1/2-, 5 1/2-, and 7 1/2-year olds' concepts of themselves and other persons. *Child Development, 60,* 1218–28.

Eder, R.A. (1990). Uncovering young children's psychological selves: Individual and developmental differences. *Child Development, 61,* 849–63.

Egan, S.K., & Perry, D.G. (1998). Does low self-regard invite victimization? *Developmental Psychology, 34,* 299–309.

Egeland, B., Jacobvitz, D., & Sroufe, L.A. (1988). Breaking the cycle of abuse. *Child Development, 59,* 1080–8.

Egerton, J. (1983). *Generations: An American family.* Lexington, KY: University Press of Kentucky.

Ehrhardt, A.A. (1985). The psychobiology of gender. In A.S. Rossi (Ed.), *Gender and the life course.* New York: Aldine.

Ehrhardt, A.A., & Baker, S.W. (1974). Fetal androgens, human central nervous system differentiation, and behavioral sex differences. In R.C. Friedman, R.M. Rickard, & R.L. Van de Wiele (Eds.), *Sex differences in behavior* (pp. 33–51). New York: Wiley.

Eichorn, D.H. (1979). Physical development: Current foci of research. In J.D. Osofsky (Ed.), *Handbook of infant development* (pp. 253–82). New York: Wiley.

Eilers, R.E., & Oller, D.K. (1994). Infant vocalizations and the early diagnosis of severe hearing impairment. *Journal of Pediatrics, 124*, 199–203.

Eimas, P.D. (1975a). Auditory and phonetic cues for speech: Discrimination of the (r-l) distinction by young infants. *Perception and Psychophysics, 18*, 341–7.

Eimas, P.D. (1975b). Speech perception in early infancy. In L.B. Cohen & P. Salapatek (Eds.), *Infant perception: From sensation to cognition.* Orlando, FL: Academic Press.

Eimas, P.D. (1985). The perception of speech in early infancy. *Scientific American, 252*, 46–52.

Eisele, J., & Lust, B. (1996). Knowledge about pronouns: A developmental study using a truth-value judgment task. *Child Development, 67*, 3086–100.

Eisenberg, N. (1983). Children's differentiations among potential recipients of aid. *Child Development, 54*, 594–602.

Eisenberg, N., & Fabes, R.A. (1998). Prosocial development. In W. Damon (Series Ed.) & N. Eisenberg (Vol. Ed.), *Handbook of child psychology: Vol. 3. Social, emotional, and personality development* (5th ed., pp. 701–78). New York: Wiley.

Eisenberg, N., Fabes, R.A., Carlo, G., Troyer, D., Speer, A.L., Karbon, M., & Switzer, G. (1992). The relations of maternal practices and characteristics to children's vicarious emotional responsiveness. *Child Development, 63*, 583–602.

Eisenberg, N., Fabes, R.A., Miller, P.A., Shell, R., Shea, C., & May-Plumlee, T. (1990). Preschoolers' vicarious emotional responding and their situational and dispositional prosocial behavior. *Merrill-Palmer Quarterly, 36*, 507–29.

Eisenberg, N., Fabes, R.A., Murphy, B., Maszk, P., Smith, M., & Karbon, M. (1995). The role of emotionality and regulation in children's social functioning: A longitudinal study. *Child Development, 66*, 1360–84.

Eisenberg, N., Fabes, R.A., Schaller, M., Carlo, G., & Miller, P.A. (1991). The relations of parental characteristics and practices in children's vicarious emotional responding. *Child Development, 62*, 1393–1408.

Eisenberg, N., Guthrie, I.K., Fabes, R.A., Reiser, M., Murphy, B.C., Holgren, R., Maszk, P., & Losoya, S. (1997). The relations of regulation and emotionality to resiliency and competent social functioning in elementary school children. *Child Development, 68*, 295–311.

Eisenberg, N., Guthrie, I.K., Murphy, B.C., Shepard, S.A., Cumberland, A., & Carlo, G. (1999). Consistency and development of prosocial dispositions. *Child Development, 70*, 1360–72.

Eisenberg, N., Lennon, R., & Roth, K. (1983). Prosocial development: A longitudinal study. *Developmental Psychology, 19*, 846–55.

Eisenberg, N., Miller, P.A., Shell, R., McNalley, S., & Shea, C. (1991). Prosocial development in adolescence: A longitudinal study. *Developmental Psychology, 27*, 849–57.

Eisenberg, N., Murray, E., & Hite, T. (1982). Children's reasoning regarding sex-typed toy choices. *Child Development, 53*, 81–6.

Eisenberg, N., Zhou, Q., & Koller, S. (2001). Brazilian adolescents' prosocial moral judgement and behavior: Relations to sympathy, perspective-taking, gender-role orientation, and demographic characteristics. *Child Development, 72*, 518–534.

Eisenberg-Berg, N., & Hand, M. (1979). The relationship of preschoolers' reasoning about prosocial moral conflicts to prosocial behavior. *Child Development, 50*, 356–63.

Elder, G.H., Liker, J.K., & Cross, C.E. (1984). Parent–child behavior in the Great Depression: Life course and intergenerational influences. In P.B. Baltes & O.G. Brim (Eds.), *Life-span development and behavior* (Vol. 6, pp. 109–58). New York: Academic Press.

Eldred, L., & Chaisson, R. (1996). The clinical course of HIV infection in women. In R.R. Faden & N.E. Kass (Eds.), *HIV, AIDS, and childbearing* (pp. 15–30). New York: Oxford University Press.

Eley, T.C., Lichtenstein, P., & Stevenson, J. (1999). Sex differences in the etiology of aggressive and nonaggressive antisocial behavior: Results from two twin studies. *Child Development, 70*, 155–68.

Elicker, J., Englund, M., & Sroufe, L.A. (1992). Predicting peer competence and peer relationships in childhood from early parent–child relationships. In R.D. Parke & G.W. Ladd (Eds.), *Family–peer relationships: Modes of linkage* (pp. 77–106). Hillsdale, NJ: Erlbaum.

Elkind, D. (1977). Giant in the nursery—Jean Piaget. In E.M. Hetherington & R.D. Parke (Eds.), *Contemporary readings in child psychology.* New York: McGraw-Hill.

Elkind, D. (1981). *The hurried child: Growing up too fast too soon.* Reading, MA: Addison-Wesley.

Elkind, D. (1996). Inhelder and Piaget on adolescence and adulthood: A postmodern appraisal. *Psychological Science, 7*, 216–20.

Ellis, S., Rogoff, B., & Cromer, C.C. (1981). Age segregation in children's social interactions. *Developmental Psychology, 17*, 399–407.

Ellsworth, C.P., Muir, D.W., & Hains, S.M.J. (1993). Social competence and person–object differentiation: An analysis of the still-face effect. *Developmental Psychology, 29*, 63–73.

Elman, J.L., Bates, E.A., Johnson, M.H., Karmiloff-Smith, A., Parisi, D., & Plunket, K. (1996). *Rethinking innateness: A connectionist perspective on development.* Cambridge, MA: MIT Press.

Emde, R.N., Biringen, Z., Clyman, R.B., & Oppenheim, D. (1991). The moral self of infancy: Affective core and procedural knowledge. *Developmental Review, 11*, 251–70.

Emde, R.N., Plomin, R., Robinson, J., Corley, R., DeFries, J., Fulker, D.W., Reznick, J.S., Campos, J., Kagan, J., & Zahn-Waxler, C. (1992). Temperament, emotion, and cognition at fourteen months: The MacArthur longitudinal twin study. *Child Development, 63*, 1437–55.

Emery, R.E. (1988). *Marriage, divorce, and children's adjustment.* Beverly Hills, CA: Sage.

Emery, R.E., & Forehand, R. (1994). Parental divorce and children's well-being: A focus on resilience. In R.J. Haggerty, L.R. Sherrod, N. Garmezy, & M. Rutter (Eds.), *Stress, risk, and resilience in children and adolescents* (pp. 64–99). New York: Cambridge University Press.

Emery, R.E., & Laumann-Billings, L. (1998). An overview of the nature, causes, and consequences of abusive family relationships: Toward differentiating maltreatment and violence. *American Psychologist, 53*, 121–35.

Englund, M.M., Levy, A.K., Hyson, D.M., & Sroufe, L.A. (2000). Adolescent social competence: Effectiveness in a group setting. *Child Development, 71*, 1049–60.

Entwisle, D.R., & Baker, D.P. (1983). Gender and young children's expectations for performance in arithmetic. *Developmental Psychology, 19*, 200–9.

Environment Canada. Women, Environment, Science & Technology (WEST). (1999, June). *Environment Canada WEST Committee final report.* Retrieved May 4, 2001 from http://www.ec.gc.ca/scitech/west/ec_west/documents/june1999report.pdf.

Epstein, L.H., McCurley, J., Wing, R.R., & Valoski, A. (1990). Five-year follow-up of family-based treatments for childhood obesity. *Journal of Consulting and Clinical Psychology, 58*, 661–4.

Epstein, L.H., Wing, R.R., Koeske, R., & Valoski, A. (1987). Long-term effects of family-based treatment of childhood obesity. *Journal of Consulting and Clinical Psychology, 55*, 91–5.

Erel, O., & Burman, B. (1995). Interrelatedness of marital relations and parent-child relations: A meta-analytic review. *Psychological Bulletin, 118*, 108–32.

Erel, O., Margolin, G., & John, R.S. (1998). Observed sibling interaction: Links with the marital and the mother-child relationship. *Developmental Psychology, 34*, 288–98.

Erickson, M.F., & Egeland, B.J. (1996). Child neglect. In J. Biere, L. Berliner, J. Bulkey, C. Jenny, & T. Reid (Eds.), *The APSAC handbook on child maltreatment* (pp. 4–20). Thousand Oaks, CA: Sage.

Erikson, E.H. (1963). *Childhood and society* (2nd ed.). New York: Norton.

Erikson, E.H. (1982). *The life cycle completed. A review.* New York: Norton.

Eron, L.D. (1982). Parent–child interaction, television violence, and aggression of children. *American Psychologist, 37*, 197–211.

Etaugh, C., Levine, D., & Mennella, A. (1984). Development of sex biases in children: 40 years later. *Sex Roles, 10*, 911–22.

Evans, D.W., & Gray, F.L. (2000). Compulsive-like behavior in individuals with Down syndrome: Its relation to mental age level, adaptive and maladaptive behavior. *Child Development, 71*, 288–300.

Evans, M., Shaw, D., & Bell, M. (2000). Home literacy activities and their influence on early literacy skills. *Canadian Journal of Experimental Psychology, 2*, 65–75.

Eyer, D.E. (1992). *Mother–infant bonding. A scientific fiction.* New Haven, CT: Yale University Press.

Fabes, R.A., Eisenberg, N., Jones, S., Smith, M., Guthrie, I., Poulin R., Shepard, S., & Friedman, J. (1999). Regulation, emotionality, and preschoolers' socially competent peer interactions. *Child Development, 70*, 432–42.

Fabes, R.A., Eisenberg, N., Karbon, M., Bernzweig, J., Speer, A.L., & Carlo, G. (1994). Socialization of children's vicarious emotional responding and prosocial behavior: Relations with mothers' perceptions of children's emotional reactivity. *Developmental Psychology, 30*, 44–55.

Fabes, R.A., Eisenberg, N., & Miller, P.A. (1990). Maternal correlates of children's vicarious emotional responsiveness. *Developmental Psychology, 26*, 639–48.

Fabes, R.A., Fultz, J., Eisenberg, N., May-Plumlee, T., & Christopher, F.S. (1989). Effects of rewards on children's prosocial motivation: A socialization study. *Developmental Psychology, 25*, 509–15.

Fabes, R.A., Martin, C.L., Hanish, L.D., & Updegraff, K.A. (2000). Criteria for evaluating the significance of developmental research in the twenty-first century: Force and counterforce. *Child Development, 71*, 212–21.

Facon, B., & Facon-Bollengier, T. (1999). Chronological age and performance of persons with mental retardation on verbal subtests of the Wechsler Intelligence Scale for Children—Revised, French Version. *Psychological Reports, 85* (3, Pt. 1), 857–62.

Faden, R.R., & Kass, N.E. (1996). *HIV, AIDS, and childbearing.* New York: Oxford University Press.

Fagan, J.F., III. (1984). Infant memory: History, current trends, and relations to cognitive psychology. In M. Moscovitch (Ed.), *Infant memory: Its relation to normal and pathological memory in humans and other animals.* New York: Plenum.

Fagot, B.I. (1978). The influence of sex of child on parental reactions to toddler children. *Child Development, 49,* 459–65.

Fagot, B. I. (1985a). Beyond the reinforcement principle: Another step toward understanding sex-role development. *Developmental Psychology, 21,* 1097-1104.

Fagot, B.I. (1985b). Changes in thinking about early sex-role development. *Developmental Review, 5,* 83–98.

Fagot, B.I. (1997). Attachment, parenting, and peer interactions of toddler children. *Developmental Psychology, 33,* 489–99.

Fagot, B.I., & Gauvain, M. (1997). Mother–child problem solving: Continuity through the early childhood years. *Developmental Psychology, 33,* 480–8.

Fagot, B.I., & Hagan, R.I. (1991). Observations of parent reactions to sex-stereotyped behaviors: Age and sex effects. *Child Development, 62,* 617–28.

Fagot, B. I., & Kavanagh, K. (1990). The prediction of antisocial behavior from avoidant attachment classifications. *Child Development, 61,* 864–73.

Fagot, B.I., & Kavanagh, K. (1993). Parenting during the second year: Effects of children's age, sex, and attachment classification. *Child Development, 64,* 258–71.

Fagot, B.I., & Leinbach, M.D. (1989). The young child's gender schema: Environmental input, internal organization. *Child Development, 60,* 663–72.

Fagot, B.I., Leinbach, M.D., & Hagan, R. (1986). Gender labeling and the adoption of sex-typed behaviors. *Developmental Psychology, 22,* 440–3.

Fagot, B.I., Leinbach, M.D., & O'Boyle, C. (1992). Gender labeling, gender stereotyping, and parenting behaviors. *Developmental Psychology, 28,* 225–30.

Fagot, B.I., Pears, K.C., Capaldi, D.M., Crosby, L., & Leve, C.S. (1998). Becoming an adolescent father: Precursors and parenting. *Developmental Psychology, 34,* 1209–19.

Fairburn, C.G., Cooper, Z., Doll, H.A., & Welch, S.L. (1999). Risk factors for anorexia nervosa: Three integrated case-control comparisons. *Archives of General Psychology, 56,* 468–76.

Falbo, T. (1992). Social norms and the one-child family: Clinical and policy implications. In F. Boer & J. Dunn (Eds.), *Children's sibling relationships* (pp. 71–82). Hillsdale, NJ: Erlbaum.

Falbo, T., & Polit, D.F. (1986). Quantitative review of the only child literature: Research evidence and theory development. *Psychological Bulletin, 100,* 176–89.

Falbo, T., & Poston, D.L., Jr. (1993). The academic, personality, and physical outcomes of only children in China. *Child Development, 64,* 18–35.

Fantz, R.L. (1961). The origin of form perception. *Scientific American, 204,* 66-72.

Fantz, R.L. (1963). Pattern vision in newborn infants. *Science, 140,* 296–7.

Farrant, K., & Reese, E. (2000). Maternal style and children's participation in reminiscing: Stepping stones in children's autobiographical memory development. *Journal of Cognition and Development, 1,* 193–225.

Farver, J.M., & Branstetter, W.H. (1994). Preschoolers' prosocial responses to their peers' distress. *Developmental Psychology, 30,* 334–41.

Faust, M.S. (1960). Developmental maturity as a determinant of prestige in adolescent girls. *Child Development, 31,* 173–84.

Fearon, I., Kisilevsky, B., Hains, S., Muir, D., Tranmer, J. (1997). Swaddling after heel lance: Age-specific effects on behavioral recovery in preterm infants. *Journal of Developmental and Behavioral Pediatrics, 18* (4), 222–32.

Federal Bureau of Investigation. *Uniform Crime Reports for the United States, 1997.* Washington, DC: U.S. Government Printing Office.

Fein, G.G. (1986). The affective psychology of play. In A.W. Gottfried & C.C. Brown (Eds.), *Play interactions. The contributions of play material and parental involvement in children's development.* Lexington, MA: Lexington Books.

Feingold, A. (1994). Gender differences in personality: A meta-analysis. *Psychological Bulletin, 116,* 429–56.

Feinman, S. (1992). *Social referencing and the social construction of reality in infancy.* New York: Plenum.

Feiring, C. (1996). Concepts of romance in 15-year-old adolescents. *Journal of Research on Adolescence, 6,* 181–200.

Feldhusen, J.F., & Goh, B.E. (1995). Assessing and accessing creativity: An interpretive review of theory, research, and development. *Creativity Research Journal, 8,* 231–47.

Feldman, D.H. (1982). A developmental framework for research with gifted children. In D.H. Feldman (Ed.), *New directions for child development: No. 17. Developmental approaches to giftedness and creativity* (pp. 31–45). San Francisco: Jossey-Bass.

Feldman, D.H., & Goldsmith, L.T. (1991). *Nature's gambit.* New York: Teacher's College Press.

Fellegi, I.P. (1997, September). *On poverty and low income.* Statistics Canada Catalogue No. 13F00027XIE. Retrieved May 20, 2001 from http://www.statcan.ca/english/concepts/poverty/pauv.htm.

Fentress, J.C. & McLeod, P.J. (1986). Motor patterns in development. In E.M. Blass (Ed.), *Handbook of behavioral neurobiology: Vol. 8. Developmental psychology and developmental neurobiology.* New York: Plenum.

Ferguson, C.A. (1977). Learning to produce: The earliest stages of phonological development in the child. In F.D. Minifie & L.L. Lloyd (Eds.), *Communication and cognitive abilities: Early behavioral assessment.* Baltimore: University Park Press.

Fernald, A. (1989). Intonation and communicative intent in mothers' speech to infants: Is the melody the message? *Child Development, 60,* 1497–1510.

Fernald, A. (1993). Approval and disapproval: Infant responsiveness to vocal affect in familiar and unfamiliar languages. *Child Development, 64,* 657–74.

Fernald, A., & Morikawa, H. (1993). Common themes and cultural variations in Japanese and American mothers' speech to infants. *Child Development, 64,* 637–56.

Fernandez, E. (1997, June 3). The grim legacy of divorce. *The Atlanta Constitution,* p. F5.

Ferreira, F., & Morrison, F.J. (1994). Children's metalinguistic knowledge of syntactical constituents: Effects of age and schooling. *Developmental Psychology, 30,* 663–78.

Feshbach, S. (1956). The catharsis hypothesis and some consequences of interaction with aggressive and neutral play objects. *Journal of Personality, 24,* 449–61.

Feuerstein, R., Feuerstein, R., & Gross, S. (1997). The learning potential assessment device. In D.P. Flanagan, J. Genshaft, & P.L. Harrison (Eds.), *Contemporary intellectual assessment: Theories, tests, and issues.* New York: Guilford Press.

Field, D. (1981). Can preschool children really learn to conserve? *Child Development, 52,* 326–34.

Field, T.M, Greenwald, P., Morrow, C., Healy, B., Foster, T., Guthertz, M., & Frost, P. (1992). Behavior state matching during interactions of preadolescent friends versus acquaintances. *Developmental Psychology, 28,* 242–50.

Field, T.M., Healy, B., Goldstein, S., Perry, S., Bendell, D., Schanberg, S., Zimmerman, E.A., & Kuhn, C. (1988). Infants of depressed mothers show "depressed" behavior even with nondepressed adults. *Child Development, 59,* 1569–79.

Field, T.M., Sandberg, D., Garcia, R., Nitza, V., Goldstein, S. & Guy, L. (1985). Pregnancy problems, postpartum depression, and early mother–infant interactions. *Developmental Psychology, 21,* 1152–6.

Field, T.M., Schanberg, S.M., Scafidi, F., Bauer, C.R., Vega-Lahr, N., Garcia, R., Nystrom, J., & Kuhn, C.M. (1986). Effects of tactile/kinesthetic stimulation on preterm neonates. *Pediatrics, 77,* 654–8.

Field, T.M., Woodson, R., Greenberg, R., & Cohen, D. (1982). Discrimination and imitation of facial expressions by neonates. *Science, 218,* 179–81.

Fincham, F.D., Hokoda, A., & Sanders, R., Jr. (1989). Learned helplessness, test anxiety, and academic achievement: A longitudinal analysis. *Child Development, 60,* 138–45.

Finegan, J.A.K., Sitarenios, G., Bolan, P., & Farabura, A.D. (1996). Children whose mothers had second trimester amniocentesis: Follow-up at school age. *British Journal of Obstetrics and Gynaecology, 103,* 214–8.

Finkelhor, D., & Dziuba-Leatherman, J. (1994). Victimization of children. *American Psychologist, 49,* 173–83.

Finkelhor, D., Hotaling, G.T., Lewis, I., & Smith, C. (1990). Sexual abuse in a national survey of adult men and women: Prevalence, characteristics, and risk factors. *Child Abuse & Neglect, 14,* 14–28.

Finkelstein, N.W., & Ramey, C.T. (1977). Learning to control the environment in infancy. *Child Development, 48,* 806–19.

Finn, J.D., & Achilles, C.M. (1990). Answers and questions about class size: A statewide experiment. *Educational Research Journal, 27,* 557–77.

Finn, J.D., Pannozzo, G.M., & Achilles, C.M. (2003). The "why's" of class size: student behavior in small classes. *Review of Educational Research, 73* (3), 321–68.

Fischer, K.W. (1980). A theory of cognitive development: The control and construction of hierarchies of skills. *Psychological Review, 87,* 477–531.

Fischer, K.W., & Bidell, T. (1998). Dynamic development of psychological structures in action and thought. In W. Damon (Series Ed.) & R.M. Lerner (Vol. Ed.), *Handbook of child psychology: Vol. 1. Theoretical models of human development* (5th ed., pp. 467–561). New York: Wiley.

Fischer, K.W., & Hencke, R.W. (1996). Infants' construction of actions in context: Piaget's contribution to research on early development. *Psychological Science, 7,* 204–11.

Fischer, K.W., Kenny, S.L., & Pipp, S.L. (1990). How cognitive processes and environmental conditions organize discontinuities in the development of abstractions. In C.N. Alexander & E.J. Langer (Eds.), *Higher stages of human development. Perspectives on adult growth* (pp. 162–87). New York: Oxford University Press.

Fischer, K.W., & Rose, S.P. (1995, Fall). Concurrent cycles in the dynamic development of the brain and behavior. *SRCD Newsletter,* pp. 3–4, 15–6.

Fisher, C., & Tokura, H. (1996). Acoustic cues to grammatical structure in infant-directed speech: Cross-linguistic evidence. *Child Development, 67,* 3192–218.

Fisher, C.B., Higgins-D'Alessandro, A., Rau, J.B., Kuther, T.L., & Belanger, S. (1996). Referring and reporting research participants at risk: Views from urban adolescents. *Child Development, 67,* 2086–100.

Fisher, E.P. (1992). The impact of play on development: A meta-analysis. *Play and Culture, 5,* 159–81.

Fisher, J.A., & Birch, L.L. (1995). 3–5-year-old children's fat preferences and fat consumption are related to parental adiposity. *Journal of the American Dietetic Association, 95,* 759–64.

Fisher, L., Ames, E.W., Chisholm, K., & Savoie, L. (1997). Problems reported by parents of Romanian orphans adopted to British Columbia. *International Journal of Behavioral Development, 20,* 67–82.

Fitch, M., Huston, A.C., & Wright, J.C. (1993). From television forms to gender schemata: Children's perceptions of television reality. In G.L. Berry & J.K. Asamen (Eds.), *Children and television: Images in a changing sociocultural world* (pp. 38–52). Newbury Park, CA: Sage.

Fivush, R. (1997). Event memory in childhood. In N. Cowan (Ed.), *The development of memory in childhood* (pp. 139–61). Hove, England: Psychology Press.

Fivush, R., & Hamond, N.R. (1990). Autobiographical memory across the preschool years: Toward reconceptualizing childhood amnesia. In R. Fivush & J.A. Hudson (Eds.), *Knowing and remembering in young children* (pp. 223–48). New York: Cambridge University Press.

Fivush, R., Kuebli, J., & Clubb, P.A. (1992). The structure of events and event representations: A developmental analysis. *Child Development, 63,* 188–201.

Flaks, D.K., Ficher, I., Masterpasqua, F., & Joseph, G. (1995). Lesbians choosing motherhood: A comparative study of lesbian and heterosexual parents and their children. *Developmental Psychology, 31,* 105–14.

Flanagan, C. A., & Eccles, J. S. (1993). Changes in parents' work status and adolescents' adjustment to school. *Child Development, 64,* 246-257.

Flavell, J.H. (1963). *The developmental psychology of Jean Piaget.* New York: Van Nostrand Reinhold.

Flavell, J.H. (1996). Piaget's legacy. *Psychological Science, 7,* 200–3.

Flavell, J. H. (1999). Cognitive development: Children's knowledge about the mind. In J. T. Spence, J. M. Darley, & D. J. Foss (Eds.), *Annual Review of Psychology* (pp. 21-45). Palo Alto, CA: Annual Reviews.

Flavell, J.H., Beach, D.R., & Chinsky, J.H. (1966). Spontaneous verbal rehearsal in a memory task as a function of age. *Child Development, 37,* 283–99.

Flavell, J.H., Everett, B.H., Croft, K., & Flavell, E.R. (1981). Young children's knowledge about visual perception: Further evidence for the level 1-level 2 distinction. *Developmental Psychology, 17,* 99–103.

Flavell, J.H., Flavell, E.R., & Green, F.L. (1983). Development of the appearance– reality distinction. *Cognitive Psychology, 15,* 95–120.

Flavell, J.H., Flavell, E.R., & Green, F.L. (1987). Young children's knowledge about apparent-real and pretend-real distinctions. *Developmental Psychology, 23,* 816–22.

Flavell, J. H., & Green, F. L. (1999). Development of intuitions about the controllability of different mental states. *Cognitive Development, 14,* 133-146.

Flavell, J.H., Green, F.L., & Flavell, E.R. (1986). Development of knowledge about the appearance–reality distinction. *Monographs of the Society for Research in Child Development, 51* (1, Serial No. 212), 1–89.

Flavell, J.H., Green, F.L., & Flavell, E.R. (1989). Young children's ability to differentiate appearance-reality and level 2 perspectives in the tactile modality. *Child Development, 60,* 201–13.

Flavell, J. H., Green, F.L., & Flavell, E.R. (1995). Young children's knowledge about thinking. Monographs of the Society for Research in Child Development, 60 (1 Serial No. 243).

Flavell, J. H., Green, F. L., & Flavell, E. R. (1998). The mind has a mind of its own: Developing knowledge about mental uncontrollability. *Cognitive Development, 13,* 127-138.

Flavell, J.H., Green, F.L., & Flavell, E.R. (2000). Development of children's awareness of their own thoughts. *Journal of Cognition and Development, 1,* 97–122.

Flavell, J.H., Green, F.L., Flavell, E.R., & Lin, N.T. (1999). Development of children's knowledge about unconsciousness. *Child Development, 70,* 396–412.

Flavell, J.H., & Miller, P.H. (1998). Social cognition. In W. Damon (Series Ed.) & D. Kuhn & R. Siegler (Vol. Eds.), *Handbook of child psychology: Vol. 2. Cognition, perception, and language* (5th ed., pp. 851–98). New York: Wiley.

Flavell, J.H., Miller, P.H., & Miller, S.A. (1993). *Cognitive development* (3rd ed.). Englewood Cliffs, NJ: Prentice Hall.

Fletcher, A.C., Darling, N.E., Steinberg, L., & Dornbusch, S.M. (1995). The company they keep: Relation of adolescents' adjustment and behavior to their friends' perceptions of authoritative parenting in the social network. *Developmental Psychology, 31,* 300–10.

Fletcher-Flinn, C.M., & Gravatt, B. (1995). The efficacy of computer-assisted instruction (CAI): A meta-analysis. *Journal of Educational Computing Research, 12,* 219–42.

Flieller, A. (1999). Comparison of the development of formal thought in adolescent cohorts ages 10 to 15 (1967–1996 and 1972–1993). *Developmental Psychology, 35,* 1048–58.

Fling, S., Smith, L., Rodriguez, T., Thornton, D., Atkins, E., & Nixon, K. (1992). Video games, aggression, and self-esteem: A survey. *Social Behavior and Personality, 20,* 39–46.

Flynn, J.R. (1987). Massive IQ gains in 14 nations: What IQ tests really measure. *Psychological Bulletin, 101,* 171–91.

Flynn, J.R. (1991). *Asian-Americans: Achievement beyond IQ.* Hillsdale, NJ: Erlbaum.

Flynn, J.R. (1996). What environmental factors affect intelligence: The relevance of IQ gains over time. In D.K. Detterman (Ed.), *Current topics in human intelligence: Vol. 5. The environment.* Norwood, NJ: Ablex.

Fogel, A. (1995). Relational narratives of the prelinguistic self. In P. Rochat (Ed.), *The self in infancy: Theory and research* (pp. 117–139). Amsterdam: North Holland-Elsevier.

Folven, R.J., & Bonvillian, J.D. (1991). The transition for nonreferential to referential language in children acquiring American Sign Language. *Developmental Psychology, 27,* 806–16.

Fonagy, P., Steele, H., & Steele, M. (1991). Maternal representations of attachment during pregnancy predict the organization of infant-mother attachment at one year of age. *Child Development, 62,* 891-905.

Fonzi, A., Schneider, B.H., Tani, F., & Tomada, G. (1997). Predicting children's friendship status from their dyadic interaction in structured situations of potential conflict. *Child Development, 68,* 496–506.

Ford, C.S., & Beach, F.A. (1951). *Patterns of sexual behavior.* New York: Harper & Row.

Ford, D.Y., & Harris, J.J., III. (1996). Perceptions and attitudes of black students toward school, achievement, and other educational variables. *Child Development, 67,* 1141–52.

Fordham, S., & Ogbu, J. (1986). Black students' school success: Coping with the "burden of 'acting white.'" *Urban Review, 18,* 176–206.

Forgatch, M.S., & DeGarmo, D.S. (1999). Parenting through change: An effective prevention program for single mothers. *Journal of Consulting and Clinical Psychology, 67,* 711–24.

Forman, D.R., & Kochanska, G. (2001). Viewing imitation as child responsiveness: A link between teaching and discipline domains of socialization. *Developmental Psychology, 37,* 198–206.

Forrest, J.D., & Singh, S. (1990). The sexual and reproductive behavior of American women, 1982–1988. *Family Planning Perspectives, 22,* 206–14.

Fox, N.A., Bell, M.A., & Jones, N.A. (1992). Individual differences in response to stress and cerebral asymmetry. *Developmental Neuropsychology, 8,* 161–84.

Fox, N.A., & Fitzgerald, H.E. (1990). Autonomic function in infancy. *Merrill-Palmer Quarterly, 36,* 27–51.

Fox, N.A., Henderson, H.A., Rubin, K.H., Calkins, S.D., & Schmidt, L.A. (2001). Continuity and discontinuity of behavioral inhibition and exuberance: Psychophysiological and behavioral influences across the first four years of life. *Child Development, 72,* 1–21.

Fox, N.A., Kimmerly, N.L., & Schafer, W.D. (1991). Attachment to mother/attachment to father: A meta-analysis. *Child Development, 62,* 210–25.

Fox, N.A., Rubin, K.H., Calkins, S.D., Marshall, T.R., Coplan, R.J., Porges, S.W., Long, J.M., & Stewart, S. (1995). Frontal activation asymmetry and social competence at four years of age. *Child Development, 66,* 1770–84.

Franco, P., Schliwowski, H., Dramaix, M., & Kuhn, A. (1998). Polysomnographic study of the autonomic nervous system in potential victims of sudden infant death syndrome. *Clinical Autonomic Research, 8,* 243–49.

Frank, D., Brown, J., Johnson, S., & Cabral, H. (2002). Forgotten fathers: An exploratory study of mothers' report of drug and alcohol problems among fathers of urban newborns. *Neurotoxicology and Teratology, 24,* 339–47.

Frankel, K.A., & Bates, J.E. (1990). Mother-toddler problem-solving: Antecedents in attachment, home behavior, and temperament. *Child Development, 61,* 810–9.

Frankenberg, W.K., & Dodds, J.B. (1967). The Denver development screening test. *Journal of Pediatrics, 71,* 181–91.

Franklin, K.M., Janoff-Bulman, R., & Roberts, J.E. (1990). Long-term impact of parental divorce on optimism and trust: Changes in general assumptions or narrow beliefs? *Journal of Personality and Social Personality, 59,* 743–55.

Fredriks, A.M., Van Buuren, S., Burgmeijer, R., Meulmeester, J., Beuker, R., Brugman, E., Roede, M., Verloove-VanHorick, S., & Wit, J.M. (2000). Continuing Positive Secular Growth Change in the Netherlands 1955–1997. Pediatric Research, 47, 316–23.

Freedman, D.G. (1979). Ethnic differences in babies. *Human Nature, 2,* 36–43.

Freeman, M. (1978). *Life among the Qallunaat.* Edmonton, AB: Hurtig.

French, C., French, F., & Rutherford, P. (1999). Applications of the WPPSI-R with a Canadian sample. *Canadian Journal of School Psychology, 15* (1), 1–10.

Freud, A., & Dann, S. (1951). An experiment in group upbringing. *The Psychoanalytic Study of the Child, 6,* 127–68.

Freud, S. (1905). Fragment of an analysis of a case of hysteria. In J. Strachey (Ed. and Trans.), *The standard edition of the complete psychological works of Sigmund Freud* (Vol. 7). London, England: Hogarth Press.

Freud, S. (1930). *Three contributions to the theory of sex.* New York: Nervous and Mental Disease. (Original work published 1905.)

Freud, S. (1933). *New introductory lectures in psychoanalysis.* New York: Norton.

Freud, S. (1960). *A general introduction to psychoanalysis.* New York: Washington Square Press. (Original work published 1935.)

Freud, S. (1961). The dissolution of the Oedipus complex. In J. Strachey (Ed. and Trans.), *The standard edition of the complete psychological works of Sigmund Freud* (Vol. 19). London, England: Hogarth Press. (Original work published 1924.)

Freud, S. (1964). An outline of psychoanalysis. In J. Strachey (Ed. and Trans.), *The standard edition of the complete psychological works of Sigmund Freud* (Vol. 23). London, England: Hogarth Press. (Original work published 1940.)

Freund, L.S. (1990). Maternal regulation of children's problem-solving behavior and its impact on children's performance. *Child Development, 61,* 113–26.

Frey, K.S., & Ruble, D.N. (1985). What children say when the teacher is not around: Conflicting goals in social comparison and performance assessment in the classroom. *Journal of Personality and Social Psychology, 48,* 550–62.

Frey, K.S., & Ruble, D.N. (1992). Gender constancy and the cost of sex-typed behavior: A test of the conflict hypothesis. *Developmental Psychology, 28,* 714–21.

Frick, J.E. (1999, July). *Reducing the risk of sudden infant death syndrome.* Paper presented at the Athens, Georgia Maternity Fair.

Fried, P.A. (1993). Prenatal exposure to tobacco and marijuana: Effects during pregnancy, infancy, and early childhood. *Clinical Obstetrics and Gynecology, 36,* 319–37.

Fried, P.A., & Watkinson, B. (2001). Differential effects on facets of attention in adolescents prenatally exposed to cigarettes and marihuana. *Neurotoxicology and Teratology, 23,* 421–30.

Fried, P.A., Watkinson, B., & Gray, R. (2003). Differential effects on cognitive functioning in 13 to 16-year-olds prenatally exposed to cigarettes and marihuana. *Neurotoxicology and Teratology, 25,* 427–36.

Friedman, H.S., Tucker, J.S., Schwartz, J.E., Tomlinson-Keasey, C., Martin, L.R., Wingard, D.L., & Criqui, M.H. (1995). Psychosocial and behavioral predictors of longevity: The aging and death of the "termites." *American Psychologist, 50,* 69–78.

Friedman, J.M., & Polifka, J.E. (1996). *The effects of drugs on the fetus and nursing infant.* Baltimore, MD: Johns Hopkins University Press.

Friedrich, L.K., & Stein, A.H. (1973). Aggressive and prosocial television programs and the natural behavior of preschool children. *Monographs of the Society for Research in Child Development, 38* (4, Serial No. 51), 1–64.

Friedrich, L.K., & Stein, A.H. (1975). Prosocial television and young children: The effects of verbal labeling and role-playing on learning and behavior. *Child Development, 46,* 27–38.

Friedrich-Cofer, L.K., Huston-Stein, A., Kipnis, D.M., Susman, E.J., & Clewett, A.S. (1979). Environmental enhancement of prosocial television content: Effects on interpersonal behavior. *Developmental Psychology, 15,* 637–46.

Friel-Patti, S., & Finitzo, T. (1990). Language learning in a prospective study of otitis media with effusion in the first two years of life. *Journal of Speech and Hearing Research, 33,* 188–94.

Friendly, M. (2000). *Child care and Canadian federalism in the 1990s: Canary in a coal mine.* (Occasional Paper No. 11). Toronto: University of Toronto, Childcare Resource and Research Unit.

Frodi, A. (1985). When empathy fails: Aversive infant crying and child abuse. In B.M. Lester & C.F.Z. Boukydis (Eds.), *Infant crying: Theoretical and research perspectives* (pp. 263–77). New York: Plenum.

Fry, C.L. (1996). Age, aging, and culture. In R.H. Binstock & L.K. George (Eds.), *Handbook of aging and the social sciences* (4th ed., pp. 117–36). San Diego: Academic Press.

Frye, D., Zelazo, P.D., Brooks, P.J., & Samuels, M.C. (1996). Inference and action in early causal reasoning. *Developmental Psychology, 32,* 120–31.

Fuchs, D., & Thelen, M.H. (1988). Children's expected interpersonal consequences of communicating their affective state and reported likelihood of expression. *Child Development, 59,* 1314–22.

Fuhrman, T., & Holmbeck, G.N. (1995). A contextual-moderator analysis of emotional anatomy and adjustment in adolescence. *Child Development, 66,* 793–811.

Fuligni, A.J. (1997). The academic achievement of adolescents from immigrant families: The roles of family background, attitudes, and behavior. *Child Development, 68,* 351–63.

Fuligni, A.J. (1998). Authority, autonomy, and parent-adolescent conflict and cohesion: A study of adolescents from Mexican, Chinese, Filipion, and European backgrounds. *Developmental Psychology, 34,* 782–92.

Fuligni, A.J., & Eccles, J.S. (1993). Perceived parent-child relationships and early adolescents' orientation toward peers. *Developmental Psychology, 29,* 622–32.

Fuligni, A.J., Eccles, J.S., & Barber, B.K. (1995). The long-term effects of seventh-grade ability grouping in mathematics. *Journal of Early Adolescence, 15,* 58–69.

Fuligni, A.J., Eccles, J.S., Barber, B.L., & Clements, P. (2001). Early adolescent peer orientation and adjustment during high school. *Developmental Psychology, 37,* 28–36.

Fuligni, A.J., & Stevenson, H.W. (1995). Time use and mathematics achievement among American, Chinese, and Japanese high school students. *Child Development, 66,* 830–42.

Fuligni, A.J., Tseng, V., & Lam, M. (1999). Attitudes toward family obligations among American adolescents with Asian, Latin-American, and Euro-American backgrounds. *Child Development, 70,* 1030–44.

Fuller, B., Holloway, S.D., & Liang, X. (1996). Family selection of child-care centers: The influence of household support, ethnicity, and parental practices. *Child Development, 67,* 3320–37.

Fullerton, J.T., & Severino, R. (1992). In-hospital care for low-risk childbirth. Comparison with results from the National Birth Center Study. *Journal of Nurse Midwifery, 37,* 331–40.

Furman, W., & Buhrmester, D. (1985). Children's perceptions of the qualities of sibling relationships. *Child Development, 56,* 448–61.

Furman, W., & Buhrmester, D. (1992). Age and sex differences in perceptions of networks of personal relationships. *Child Development, 63,* 103–15.

Furstenberg, F.F., Jr., Brooks-Gunn, J., & Chase-Lansdale, L. (1989). Teenaged pregnancy and childbearing. *American Psychologist, 44,* 313–20.

Fuson, K.C. (1988). *Children's counting and concepts of number.* New York: Springer-Verlag.

Fuson, K.C. (1992). Research on learning and teaching addition and subtraction of whole numbers. In G. Leinhardt, R.T. Putnam, & R.A. Hattrup (Eds.), *The analysis of arithmetic for mathematics teaching* (pp. 53–187). Hillsdale, NJ: Erlbaum.

Fuson, K.C., & Kwon, Y. (1992). Korean children's understanding of multidigit addition and subtraction. *Child Development, 63,* 491–506.

Fyans, L.J., Jr., Salili, F., Maehr, M.L., & Desai, K.A. (1983). A cross-cultural exploration into the meaning of achievement. *Journal of Personality and Social Psychology, 44,* 1000–13.

Gaddis, A., & Brooks-Gunn, J. (1985). The male experience of pubertal change. *Journal of Youth and Adolescence, 14,* 61–9.

Galambos, N.L., Almeida, D.M., & Petersen, A.C. (1990). Maculinity, femininity, and sex role attitudes in early adolescence: Exploring gender intensification. *Child Development, 61,* 1905–14.

Galambos, N.L., Barker, E.T., & Tilton-Weaver, L.C. (2003). Canadian adolescents' implicit theories of immaturity: What does "childish" mean? In J.J. Arnett & N.L. Galambos (Eds.), *New directions for child and adolescent development: Exploring cultural conceptions of the transition to adulthood* (No.100, pp. 77–89). San Francisco: Jossey-Bass.

Galambos, N.L., Barker, E.T., & Tilton-Weaver, L.C. (2003). Who gets caught at maturity gap? A study of pseudomature, immature, and mature adolescents. *International Journal of Behavioral Development, 27* (3), 253–63.

Galambos, N.L. & Goldin-Meadow, S. (1990). The effects of learning two languages on levels of metalinguistic awareness. *Cognition, 34,* 1–56.

Galambos, N.L., & Maggs, J.L. (1991). Out-of-school care of young adolescents and self-reported behavior. *Developmental Psychology, 27,* 644–55.

Galambos, N.L., & Tilton-Weaver, L.C. (2000). Adolescents' psychosocial maturity, problem behavior, and subjective age: In search of the adultoid. *Applied Developmental Science, 4,* 178–92.

Galen, B.R., & Underwood, M.K. (1997). A developmental investigation of social aggression among children. *Developmental Psychology, 33,* 589–600.

Gallagher, J.M., & Easley, J.A., Jr. (1978). *Knowledge and development: Vol. 2. Piaget and education.* New York: Plenum.

Gallahue, D.L. (1989). *Understanding motor development* (2nd ed.). Carmel, ID: Benchmark Press.

Gallant, N., & Terisse, B. (2001). The adolescent mother: A developmental or social concept. In *Children & Youth at Risk.* Toronto, ON: Canadian Education Statistics Council. Available online November 27, 2003 at www.statcan.ca/english/freepub/81-589 XIE/81-589 XIE01001.pdf.

Gallistel, C.R., & Gelman, R. (1992). Preverbal and verbal counting and computation. *Cognition, 44,* 43–74.

Gallup, G.G., Jr. (1979). Self-recognition in chimpanzees and man: A developmental and comparative perspective. In M. Lewis & L.A. Rosenblum (Eds.), *Genesis of behavior: Vol. 2. The child and its family* (pp. 107–26). New York: Plenum.

Galuska, D.A., Serdula, M., Pamuck, E., Siegel, P.Z., & Byers, T. (1996). Trends in overweight among U.S. adults from 1987 to 1993: A multistate telephone survey. *American Journal of Public Health, 86,* 1729–35.

Ganchrow, J.R., Steiner, J.E., & Daher, M. (1983). Neonatal facial expressions to different qualities and intensities of gustatory stimuli. *Infant Behavior and Development, 6,* 189–200.

Gandelman, R. (1992). *Psychobiology of behavioral development.* New York: Oxford University Press.

Garbarino, J. (1995). Growing up in a socially toxic environment: Life for children and families in the 1990s. In G.B. Melton (Ed.),

Nebraska Symposium on Motivation: Vol. 42. The individual, the family and the social good: Personal fulfillment in times of change (pp. 1–20). Lincoln: University of Nebraska Press.

Garbarino, J., & Kostelny, K. (1992). Child maltreatment as a community problem. *Child Abuse and Neglect, 16,* 455–64.

Garcia, M.M., Shaw, D.S., Winslow, E.B., & Yaggi, K.E. (2000). Destructive sibling conflict and the development of conduct problems in young boys. *Developmental Psychology, 36,* 44–53.

Gardner, H. (1983). *Frames of mind: The theory of multiple intelligences.* New York: Basic Books.

Gardner, H. (1993). *Creating minds.* New York: Basic Books.

Gardner, H. (1999). Are there additional intelligences? The case for naturalist, spiritual, and existential intelligences. In J. Kane (Ed.), *Education, information, and transformation* (pp. 111–31). Englewood Cliffs, NJ: Prentice-Hall.

Gardner, L.J. (1972). Deprivation dwarfism. *Scientific American, 227,* 76–82.

Garner, P.W., Jones, D.C., & Miner, J.L. (1994). Social competence among low-income preschoolers: Emotion socialization practices and social cognitive correlates. *Child Development, 65,* 622–37.

Garner, P.W., Jones, D.C., & Palmer, D.J. (1994). Social-cognitive correlates of preschool children's sibling caregiving behavior. *Developmental Psychology, 30,* 905–11.

Garner, P.W., & Power, T.G. (1996). Preschoolers' emotional control in the disappointment paradigm and its relation to temperament, emotional knowledge, and family expressiveness. *Child Development, 67,* 1406–19.

Garnets, L., & Kimmel, D. (1991). Lesbian and gay male dimensions of the psychological study of human diversity. In J.D. Goodchilds (Ed.), *Psychological perspectives on human diversity in America* (pp. 143–92). Washington, DC: American Psychological Association.

Garrett, P., Ng'andu, N., & Ferron, J. (1994). Poverty experiences of young children and the quality of their home environments. *Child Development, 65,* 331–45.

Garton, A.F., & Pratt, C. (1990). Children's pragmatic judgments of direct and indirect requests. *First Language, 10,* 51–9.

Gaultney, J.F. (1995). The effect of prior knowledge and metacognition on the acquisition of a reading comprehension strategy. *Journal of Experimental Child Psychology, 59,* 142–63.

Gauvain, M., & Rogoff, B. (1989). Collaborative problem solving and children's planning skills. *Developmental Psychology, 25,* 139–51.

Gauze, C., Bukowski, W.M., Aquan-Assee, J., & Sippola, L.K. (1996). Interactions between family environment and friendship and associations with well-being during early adolescence. *Child Development, 67,* 2201–16.

Gavin, L.A., & Furman, W. (1989). Age differences in adolescents' perceptions of their peer groups. *Developmental Psychology, 25,* 827–34.

Ge, X., Best, K.M., Conger, R.D., & Simons, R.L. (1996). Parenting behaviors and the occurrence and co-occurrence of adolescent depressive symptoms and conduct problems. *Developmental Psychology, 32,* 717–31.

Ge, X., Conger, R.D., & Elder, G.H., Jr. (1996). Coming of age too early: Pubertal influences on girls' vulnerability to psychological distress. *Child Development, 67,* 3386–400.

Geary, D.C. (1995). Reflections on evolution and culture in children's cognition. *American Psychologist, 50,* 24–37.

Geary, D.C., & Bjorklund, D.F. (2000). Evolutionary developmental psychology. *Child Development, 71,* 57–65.

Geary, D.C., Bow-Thomas, C.C., Fan, L., & Siegler, R.S. (1993). Even before formal instruction, Chinese children outperform American children in mental arithmetic. *Cognitive Development, 8,* 517–29.

Geary, D.C., Bow-Thomas, C.C., Liu, F., & Siegler, R.S. (1996). Development of arithmetical competencies in Chinese and American children: Influence of age, language, and schooling. *Child Development, 67,* 2022–44.

Geary, D.C., & Burlingham-Dubre, M. (1989). External validation of the strategy choice model for addition. *Journal of Experimental Child Psychology, 47,* 175–92.

Geary, D.C., Fan, L., & Bow-Thomas, C.C. (1992). Numerical cognition: Loci of ability differences comparing children from China and the United States. *Psychological Science, 3,* 180–5.

Geary, D.C., Salthouse, T.A., Chen, P., & Fan, L. (1996). Are East Asian versus American differences in arithmetical ability a recent phenomenon? *Developmental Psychology, 32,* 254–62.

Geary, D.C., & Widaman, K.F. (1992). Numerical cognition: On convergence of componential and psychometric models. *Intelligence, 16,* 47–80.

Geen, R.G. (1998). Aggression and antisocial behavior. In D.T. Gilbert, S.T. Fiske, & G. Lindzey (Eds.), *Handbook of social psychology* (Vol. 2, pp. 317–56). New York: McGraw-Hill.

Geldart, S., Mondloch, C.J., Maurer, D., de Schonen, S., & Brent, H.P. (2002). The effect of early visual deprivation on the development of face processing. *Developmental Science, 5* (4), 490–501.

Gelles, R.J. (1996). *The book of David: How preserving families can cost children's lives.* New York: Basic Books.

Gelman, R. (1969). Conservation acquisition: A problem of learning to attend to relevant attributes. *Journal of Experimental Child Psychology, 7,* 167–87.

Gelman, R. (1978). Cognitive development. *Annual Review of Psychology, 29,* 297–322.

Gelman, R., & Baillargeon, R. (1983). A review of Piagetian concepts. In P.H. Mussen (Series Ed.) & J.H. Flavell & E.M. Markman (Vol. Eds.), *Handbook of child psychology: Vol. 3. Cognitive development* (4th ed., pp. 167–230). New York: Wiley.

Gelman, R., & Shatz, M. (1977). Appropriate speech adjustments: The operation of conversational constraints on talk to two-year-olds. In M. Lewis & L.A. Rosenblum (Eds.), *Interaction, conversation, and the development of language* (pp. 27–61). New York: Wiley.

Gelman, R., & Williams, E.M. (1998). Enabling constraints for cognitive development and learning: Domain-specificity and epigenesis. In W. Damon (Series Ed.) & D. Kuhn & R.S. Siegler (Vol. Eds.), *Handbook of child psychology: Vol. 2. Cognition, perception, and language* (5th ed., pp. 575–620). New York: Wiley.

Gelman, S.A., & Ebeling, K.S. (1989). Children's use of nonegocentric standards in judgments of functional size. *Child Development, 60,* 920–32.

Gelman, S.A., & Gottfried, G.M. (1996). Children's causal explanations of animate and inanimate motion. *Child Development, 67,* 1970–87.

Genesee, F. (2001). Portrait of the bilingual child. In V. Cook (Ed.), *Portraits of the second language user.* Clevedon, England: Multilingual Matters.

Genesee, F., Boivin, I., & Nicoladis, E. (1996). Talking with strangers: A study of bilingual children's communicative competence. *Applied Psycholinguistics, 17,* 427–42.

Genesee, F., Nicoladis, E., & Paradis, J. (1995). Language differentiation in preschool bilingual children. *Journal of Child Language, 22,* 611–31.

Georgas, J., Weiss, L., Van De Vijver, F., & Saklofske, D. (2003). *Culture and Children's Intelligence: Cross Cultural Analysis of the WISC-III.* Academic Press London.

George, T.P., & Hartmann, D.P. (1996). Friendship networks of unpopular, average, and popular children. *Child Development, 67,* 2301–16.

Gerken, L., Landau, B., & Remez, R.E. (1990). Function morphemes in young children's speech perception and production. *Developmental Psychology, 26,* 204–16.

Gerken, L., & McIntosh, B.J. (1993). Interplay of function morphemes and prosody in early language. *Developmental Psychology, 24,* 448–57.

Gesell, A. (1933). Maturation and the patterning of behavior. In C. Murchison (Ed.), *A handbook of child psychology.* Worcester, MA: Clark University Press.

Gesell, A., & Thompson, H. (1929). Learning and growth in identical twins: An experimental study by the method of co-twin control. *Genetic Psychology Monographs, 6,* 1–123.

Getzels, J.W., & Jackson, P.W. (1962). *Creativity and intelligence: Explorations with gifted children.* New York: Wiley.

Gewirtz, J.L., & Pelaez-Nogueras, M. (1992). Skinner, B.F.: Legacy to human infant behavior and development. *American Psychologist, 47,* 1411–22.

Gewirtz, J.L., & Petrovich, S.B. (1982). Early social and attachment learning in the frame of organic and cultural evolution. In T.M. Field, A. Huston, H.C. Quay, L. Troll, & G.E. Finley (Eds.), *Review of human development.* New York: Wiley.

Ghatala, E.S., Levin, J.R., Pressley, M., & Goodwin, D. (1986). A componential analysis of the effects of derived and supplied strategy-utility information on children's strategy selections. *Journal of Experimental Child Psychology, 41,* 76–92.

Ghim, H. (1990). Evidence for perceptual organization in infants: Perception of subjective contours by young infants. *Infant Behavior and Development, 13,* 221–48.

Gibbs, J.C., & Schnell, S.V. (1985). Moral development "versus" socialization. A critique. *American Psychologist, 40,* 1071–80.

Gibson, D., & Harris, A. (1988). Aggregated early information effects for Down's syndrome persons: Patterning and longevity of benefits. *Journal of Mental Deficiency Research, 32,* 1–7.

Gibson, E.J. (1969). *Principles of perceptual learning and development.* East Norwalk, CT: Appleton-Century-Crofts.

Gibson, E.J. (1987). Introductory essay: What does infant perception tell us about theories of perception? *Journal of Experimental Psychology: Human Perception and Performance, 13,* 515–23.

Gibson, E.J. (1992). How to think about perceptual learning: Twenty-five years later. In H.L. Pick, P. van den Brock, & D.C. Knill (Eds.), *Cognition: Conceptual and methodological issues* (pp. 215–337). Washington, DC: American Psychological Association.

Gibson, E.J., Gibson, J.J., Pick, A.D., & Osser, H.A. (1962). A developmental study of the discrimination of letter like forms. *Journal of Comparative and Physiological Psychology, 55,* 897–906.

Gibson, E.J., & Walk, R.D. (1960). The "visual cliff." *Scientific American, 202,* 64–71.

Gibson, E.J., & Walker, A.S. (1984). Development of knowledge of visual–tactile affordances of substance. *Child Development, 55*, 453–60.

Gil, D.G. (1970). *Violence against children.* Cambridge, MA: Harvard University Press.

Gilbert, N. (1997). *Combating child abuse: International perspectives and trends.* New York: Oxford University Press.

Gill, N.J., & Beazley, R.P. (1993). Grade 6 students benefit from learning about AIDS. *Canadian Journal of Public Health, 84* (Suppl. 1), S24–7.

Gillberg, C., Melander, H., von Knorring, A-L., Janols, L-O., Thernlund, G., Hagglof, B., Eidevall-Wallin, L. Gustafsson, P., & Kopp, S. (1997). Long-term stimulant treatment of children with attention-deficit hyperactivity disorder symptoms: A randomized, double-blind, placebo-controlled trial. *Archives of General Psychiatry, 54*, 857–64.

Gilligan, C. (1982). *In a different voice: Psychological theory and women's development.* Cambridge, MA: Harvard University Press.

Gilligan, C. (1993). Adolescent development reconsidered. In A. Garrod (Ed.), *Approaches to moral development: New research and emerging themes.* New York: Teachers College Press.

Ginsburg, G.S., & Bronstein, P. (1993). Family factors related to children's intrinsic/extrinsic motivational orientation and academic performance. *Child Development, 64*, 1461–74.

Ginsburg, H.J., & McCoy, I.H. (1982). An empirical rationale for foreign languages in elementary schools. *Modern Language Journal, 65*, 36-42.

Ginsberg, H.J., & Opper, S. (1988). *Piaget's theory of intellectual development* (3rd ed.). Englewood Cliffs, NJ: Prentice-Hall.

Girard, C. (1993). Age, gender, and suicide: A cross-national analysis. *American Sociological Review, 58*, 553–74.

Glasgow, K.L., Dornbusch, S.M., Troyer, L., Steinberg, L., & Ritter, P.L. (1997). Parenting style, adolescents' attributions, and educational outcomes in nine heterogeneous high schools. *Child Development, 68*, 507–29.

Gleason, T.R., Sebanc, A.M., & Hartup, W.W. (2000). Imaginary companions of preschool children. *Developmental Psychology, 36*, 419–28.

Gleitman, H. (1991). *Psychology* (3rd ed.). New York: Norton.

Gleitman, L.R. (1990). The structural sources of verb meanings. *Language Acquisition, 1*, 3–55.

Gnepp, J. (1989). Personalized inferences of emotions and appraisals: Component processes and correlates. *Developmental Psychology, 25*, 277–88.

Gnepp, J., & Klayman, J. (1992). Recognition of uncertainty in emotional inferences: Reasoning about emotionally equivocal situations. *Developmental Psychology, 28*, 145–58.

Goelman, H., Doherty, G., Lero, D.S., LaGrange, A., & Tougas, J. (2000) *You bet I care! Caring and learning environments: Quality in child care centres across Canada.* Guelph, ON: University of Guelph, Centre for Families, Work and Well-Being.

Gogate, L.J., Bahrick, L.E., & Watson, J. D. (2000). A study of multimodal motherese: The role of temporal synchrony between verbal labels and gestures. *Child Development, 71*, 878–94.

Golbus, M.S., & Fries, M.M. (1993). Surgical fetal therapy. In C. Lin, M.S. Verp, & R.E. Sabbagha (Eds.), *The high-risk fetus: Pathophysiology, diagnosis, management.* New York: Springer-Verlag.

Goldberg, S. (1983). Parent–infant bonding: Another look. *Child Development, 54*, 1355–82.

Golden, M., Birns, B., Bridger, W., & Moss, A. (1971). Social class differentiation in cognitive development among black preschool children. *Child Development, 42*, 37–46.

Golden, O. (2000). The federal response to child abuse and neglect. *American Psychologist, 55*, 1050–53.

Goldenberg, R.L. (1995). Small for gestational age infants. In B.P. Sachs, R. Beard, E. Papiernik, & C. Russell (Eds.), *Reproductive health care for women and babies* (pp. 391–9). New York: Oxford University Press.

Goldfarb, W. (1943). The effects of early institutional care on adolescent personality. *Journal of Experimental Education, 12*, 107–29.

Goldfarb, W. (1947). Variations in adolescent adjustment in institutionally reared children. *Journal of Orthopsychiatry, 17*, 449-457.

Goldfield, E.C. (1989). Transition from rocking to crawling: Postural constraints on infant movement. *Developmental Psychology, 25*, 913–9.

Goldin-Meadow, S. (2000). Beyond words: The importance of gestures to researchers and learners. *Child Development, 71*, 231–39.

Goldin-Meadow, S., & Mylander, C. (1984). Gestural communication in deaf children: The effects and noneffects of parental input on early language development. *Monographs of the Society for Research in Child Development, 49* (3–4, Serial No. 207), 11–56.

Goldsmith, H.H., & Alansky, J.A. (1987). Maternal and infant temperamental predictors of attachment: A meta-analytic review. *Journal of Consulting and Clinical Psychology, 55*, 805–16.

Goldsmith, H.H., Buss, A.H., Plomin, R., Rothbart, M.K., Thomas, A., Chess, S., Hinde, R.A., & McCall, R.B. (1987). Roundtable: What is temperament? Four approaches. *Child Development, 58*, 505–29.

Goldsmith, H.H., Buss, K.A., & Lemery, K.S. (1997). Toddler and childhood temperament: Expanded content, stronger genetic evidence, new evidence for the importance of environment. *Developmental Psychology, 33*, 891–905.

Goldsmith, H.H., Lemery, K.S., Buss, K.A., & Campos, J.J. (1999). Genetic analysis of focal aspects of infant temperament. *Developmental Psychology, 35*, 972–85.

Golinkoff, R.M., Jacquet, R.C., Hirsh-Pasek, K., & Nandakumer, R. (1996). Lexical principles may underlie the learning of verbs. *Child Development, 67*, 3101–19.

Gollin, E.S. (1962). Further studies of visual recognition of incomplete objects. *Perceptual and Motor Skills, 13*, 307–314.

Golomb, C., & Galasso, L. (1995). Make believe and reality: Explorations of the imaginary realm. *Developmental Psychology, 31*, 800–10.

Golombok, S., Cook, R., Bish, A., & Murray, C. (1995). Families created by new reproductive technologies: Quality of parenting and social and emotional development of the children. *Child Development, 66*, 285–98.

Golombok, S., MacCallum, F., & Goodman, E. (2001). The "test-tube" generation: Parent–child relationships and the psychological well-being of in vitro fertilization children at adolescence. *Child Development, 72*, 599–608.

Golombok, S., & Tasker, F. (1996). Do parents influence the sexual orientation of their children: Findings from a longitudinal study of lesbian families. *Developmental Psychology, 32*, 3–11.

Gondoli, D.M., & Silverberg, S.B. (1997). Maternal emotional distress and diminished responsiveness: The mediating role of parenting efficacy and parental perspective taking. *Developmental Psychology, 33*, 861–68.

Good, T.L., & Brophy, J.E. (1994). *Looking in classrooms* (6th ed.). New York: HarperCollins.

Goodenough, F.L. (1931). *Anger in young children.* Minneapolis: University of Minnesota Press.

Goodman, G.S., Quas, J.A., Batterman-Faunce, J.M., Riddlesberger, & Kuhn, J. (1994). Predictors of accurate and inaccurate memories of traumatic events experiences in childhood. *Consciousness and Cognition, 3*, 269–94.

Goodman, J.C., McDonough, L., & Brown, N.B. (1998). The role of semantic context and memory in the acquisition of novel nouns. *Child Development, 69*, 1330–44.

Goodwyn, S.W., & Acredolo, L.P. (1993). Symbolic gesture versus word: Is there a modality advantage for onset of symbol use? *Child Development, 64*, 688–701.

Goossens, F.A., & van IJzendoorn, M.H. (1990). Quality of infants' attachments to professional caregivers: Relation to infant–parent attachment and day-care characteristics. *Child Development, 61*, 832–7.

Gopnik, A. (1996). The post-Piaget era. *Psychological Science, 7*, 221–5.

Gopnik, A., & Choi, S. (1995). *Beyond names for things: Children's acquisition of verbs.* Hillsdale, NJ: Erlbaum.

Gopnik, A., & Meltzoff, A.N. (1987). Language and thought in the young child: Early semantic developments and their relationships to object permanence, means–ends understanding, and categorization. In K. Nelson & A. Van Kleeck (Eds.), *Children's language* (Vol. 6). Hillsdale, NJ: Erlbaum.

Gopnik, A., & Meltzoff, A.N. (1997). *Words, thought, and theories.* Cambridge, MA: MIT Press.

Gordon, P. (1990). Learnability and feedback. *Developmental Psychology, 26*, 217–20.

Gorer, G. (1968). Man has no "killer" instinct. In M.F.A. Montague (Ed.), *Man and aggression.* New York: Oxford University Press.

Gorn, G.J., Goldberg, M.E., & Kanungo, R.N. (1976). The role of educational television in changing the intergroup attitudes of children. *Child Development, 47*, 277–80.

Gosden, C., Nicolaides, K., & Whitting, V. (1994). *Is my baby all right?: A guide for expectant parents.* Oxford: Oxford University Press.

Goswami, U. (1995). Transitive relational mapping in three- and four-year-olds: The analogy of Goldilocks and the Three Bears. *Child Development, 66*, 877–92.

Goswami, U. (1996). Analogical reasoning and cognitive development. In H.W. Reese (Ed.), *Advances in child development and behavior* (Vol. 26, pp. 92–138). San Diego: Academic.

Goswami, U., & Brown, A.L. (1990). Higher-order structure and relational reasoning: Contrasting analogical and thematic relations. *Cognition, 36*, 207–26.

Gotlib, I.H., Whiffen, V.E., Wallace, P.M., & Mount, J. (1991). Prospective investigation of postpartum depression: Factors involved in onset and recovery. *Journal of Abnormal Psychology, 100*, 122–32.

Gotowiec, A., & Beiser, M. (1993). Aboriginal children's mental health: Unique challenges. *Canada's Mental Health, 41* (4), 7–11.

Gottesman, I.I. (1963). Genetic aspects of intelligent behavior. In N. Ellis (Ed.), *Handbook of mental deficiency.* New York: McGraw-Hill.

Gottesman, I.I. (1991). *Schizophrenia genesis: The origins of madness.* New York: W.H. Freeman.

Gottfried, A.E., Fleming, J.S., & Gottfried, A.W. (1998). Role of cognitively stimulating home environment in children's academic intrinsic motivation: A longitudinal study. *Child Development, 69*, 1148–60.

Gottfried, A.W., Gottfried, A.E., Bathurst, K., & Guerin, D.W. (1994). *Gifted IQ: Early* developmental aspects: *The Fullerton Longitudinal Study.* New York: Plenum.

Gottlieb, D. (1966). Teaching and students: The views of Negro and white teachers. *Sociology of Education, 37,* 344–53.

Gottlieb, G. (1991a). Experiential canalization of behavioral development: Results. *Developmental Psychology, 27,* 35–9.

Gottlieb, G. (1996). Commentary: A systems view of psychobiological development. In D. Magnusson (Ed.), *The lifespan development of individuals: Behavioral, neurobiological, and psychosocial perspectives. A synthesis.* Cambridge, England: Cambridge University Press.

Gottlieb, G. (2003). On making behavioral genetics truly developmental. *Human Development, 46* (6), 337–55.

Graber, J.A., Brooks-Gunn, J., Paikoff, R.L., & Warren, M.P. (1994). Prediction of eating problems: An 8-year study of adolescent girls. *Developmental Psychology, 30,* 823–34.

Graham, S., & Juvonen, J. (1998). Self-blame and peer victimization in middle school: An attributional analysis. *Developmental Psychology, 34,* 587–99.

Granrud, C.E. (1987). Size constancy in newborn human infants. *Investigative Ophthalmology and Visual Science, 28,* 5.

Granrud, C.E., & Yonas, A. (1984). Infants' perceptions of pictorally specified interposition. *Journal of Experimental Child Psychology, 37,* 500–11.

Grantham-McGregor, S., Powell, C., Walker, S., Chang, S., & Fletcher, P. (1994). The long-term follow-up of severely malnourished children who participated in an intervention program. *Child Development, 65,* 428–39.

Graves, S.B. (1993). Television, the portrayal of African Americans, and the development of children's attitudes. In G.L. Berry & J.K. Asamen (Eds.), *Children and television: Images in a changing sociocultural world* (pp. 179–90). Newbury Park, CA: Sage.

Gray, S.W., & Klaus, R.A. (1970). The early training project: A seventh-year report. *Child Development, 41,* 909–24.

Graziano, W.G., French, D., Brownell, C.A., & Hartup, W.W. (1976). Peer interaction in same- and mixed-age triads in relation to chronological age and incentive condition. *Child Development, 47,* 707–14.

Green, R. (1987). *The "sissy boy syndrome" and the development of homosexuality.* New Haven, CT: Yale University Press.

Green, R.W., Biederman, J., Faraone, S.V., Sienna, M., & Garcia-Jetton, J. (1997). Adolescent outcome of boys with attention-deficit/hyperactivity disorder and social disability: Results from a 4-year longitudinal follow-up study. *Journal of Consulting and Clinical Psychology, 65,* 758–67.

Greenberg, M., & Morris, N. (1974). Engrossment: The newborn's impact upon the father. *American Journal of Orthopsychiatry, 44,* 520–31.

Greenberg, M.T., Lengua, L.J., Coie, J.D., Pinderhughes, E.E., & The Conduct Problems Prevention Research Group. (1999). Predicting developmental outcomes at school entry using a multiple-risk model: Four American communities. *Developmental Psychology, 35,* 403–17.

Greenberger, E., & Chen, C. (1996). Perceived family relationships and depressed mood in early and late adolescence: A comparison of European and Asian Americans. *Developmental Psychology, 32,* 707–16.

Greenberger, E., O'Neil, R., & Nagel, S.K. (1994). Linking workplace and homeplace: Relations between the nature of adult work and their parenting behavior. *Developmental Psychology, 30,* 990–1002.

Greenberger, E., & Steinberg, L. (1986). *When teenagers work: The psychological and social costs of adolescent employment.* New York: Basic Books.

Greenfield, P.M., & Smith, J.H. (1976). *The structure of communication in early language development.* New York: Academic.

Greenhoot, A.F., Ornstein, P.A., Gordon, B.N., & Baker-Ward, L. (1999). Acting out the details of a pediatric check-up: The impact of interview condition and behavioral style on children's memory reports. *Child Development, 70,* 363–80.

Greenough, W.T., & Black, J.E. (1992). Induction of brain structure by experience: Substrates for cognitive development. In M.R. Gunnar & C.A. Nelson (Eds.), *Minnesota Symposia on Child Psychology: Vol. 24. Developmental neuroscience* (pp. 155–200). Hillsdale, NJ: Erlbaum.

Greenough, W.T., Black, J.E., & Wallace, C.S. (1987). Experience and brain development. *Child Development, 58,* 539–59.

Gregoire, J., Penhouet, C., & Boy, T. (1996). The French adaptation of the Wechsler Intelligence Scale for Children, version III. *Orientation Scolaire et Professionelle, 25* (4), 489–506.

Greif, E.B., & Ulman, K.J. (1982). The psychological impact of menarche on early adolescent females: A review of the literature. *Child Development, 53,* 1413–30.

Grolnick, W.S., Bridges, L.J., & Connell, J.P. (1996). Emotion regulation in two-year-olds: Strategies and emotional expression in four contexts. *Child Development, 67,* 928–41.

Grolnick, W.S., & Ryan, R.M. (1989). Parents' styles associated with children's self-regulation and competence in school. *Journal of Educational Psychology, 81,* 143–54.

Groome, L.J., Swiber, M.J., Atterbury, J.L., Bentz, L.S., & Holland, S.B. (1997). Similarities and differences in behavioral state organization during sleep periods in the perinatal infant before and after birth. *Child Development, 68,* 1–11.

Gross, A.L., & Ballif, B. (1991). Children's understanding of emotion from facial expressions and situations: A review. *Developmental Review, 11,* 368–98.

Grossman, F.K., Eichler, L.S., Winickoff, S.A., & Associates. (1980). *Pregnancy, birth, and parenthood: Adaptations of mothers, fathers, and infants.* San Francisco: Jossey-Bass.

Grossmann, K., Grossmann, K.E., Spangler, S., Suess, G., & Unzner, L. (1985). Maternal sensitivity and newborn responses as related to quality of attachment in Northern Germany. In I. Bretherton & E. Waters (Eds.), Growing points of attachment theory and research. *Monographs of the Society for Research in Child Development, 50* (1–2, Serial No. 209).

Grotevant, H.D., & Cooper, C.R. (1986). Individuation in family relations: A perspective on individual differences in the development of identity and role-taking skills in adolescence. *Human Development, 29,* 82–100.

Group for the Advancement of Psychiatry, Committee on Adolescence. (1996). *Adolescent suicide.* (GAP Report 140). Washington, DC: American Psychiatric Press.

Growing Healthy Kids. (2001). *Growing healthy Canadians: A guide for positive child development.* Retrieved November 19, 2001 from http://www.growinghealthykids.com/home.htm.

Gruber, H. (1982). On the hypothesized relation between giftedness and creativity. In D.H. Feldman (Ed.), *New directions for child development: No. 17. Developmental approaches to giftedness and creativity* (pp. 7–30). San Francisco: Jossey-Bass.

Grusec, J.E. (1991). Socializing concern for others in the home. *Developmental Psychology, 27,* 338–42.

Grusec, J.E. (1992). Social learning theory and developmental psychology: The legacies of Robert Sears and Albert Bandura. *Developmental Psychology, 28,* 776–86.

Grusec, J.E., & Goodnow, J.J. (1994). Impact of parental discipline methods on the child's internalization of values: A reconceptualization of current points of view. *Developmental Psychology, 30,* 4–19.

Grusec, J.E., Goodnow, J.J., & Cohen, L. (1996). Household work and the development of concern for others. *Developmental Psychology, 32,* 999–1007.

Grusec, J.E., Goodnow, J.J., & Kuczynski, L. (2000). New directions in analyses of parenting contributions to children's acquisition of values. *Child Development, 71,* 205–11.

Grusec, J.E., Kuczynski, L., Rushton, J.P., & Simutis, Z. (1979). Learning resistance to temptation through observation. *Developmental Psychology, 15,* 233–40.

Grych, J.H., & Clark, R. (1999). Maternal employment and development of the father-infant relationship in the first year. *Developmental Psychology, 35,* 893–903.

Grych, J.H., & Fincham, F.D. (1992). Interventions for children of divorce: Toward greater integration of research and action. *Psychological Bulletin, 111,* 434–54.

Guberman, S.R. (1996). The development of everyday mathematics in Brazilian children with limited formal education. *Child Development, 67,* 1609–23.

Guerra, N.G., & Slaby, R.G. (1990). Cognitive mediators of aggression in adolescent offenders: 2. Intervention. *Developmental Psychology, 26,* 269–77.

Guilford, J.P. (1967). *The nature of human intelligence.* New York: McGraw-Hill.

Guilford, J.P. (1988). Some changes in the structure-of-the-intellect model. *Educational and Psychological Measurement, 40,* 1–4.

Gunderson, V., & Sackett, G.P. (1982). Paternal effects on reproductive outcome and developmental risk. In M.E. Lamb & A.L. Brown (Eds.), *Advances in developmental psychology* (Vol. 2). Hillsdale, NJ: Erlbaum.

Gunnar, M.R., Malone, S., Vance, G., & Fisch, R.O. (1985). Coping with aversive stimulation in the neonatal period: Quiet sleep and plasma cortisol levels during recovery from circumcision. *Child Development, 56,* 824–34.

Guralnick, M.J., & Groom, J.M. (1988). Friendships of preschool children in mainstreamed playgroups. *Developmental Psychology, 24,* 595–604.

Gurucharri, C., & Selman, R.L. (1982). The development of interpersonal understanding during childhood, preadolescence, and adolescence: A longitudinal follow-up study. *Child Development, 53,* 924–7.

Gustafson, G.E., & Harris, K.L. (1990). Women's responses to young infants' cries. *Developmental Psychology, 26,* 144–52.

Guttentag, M., & Bray, H. (1976). *Undoing sex stereotypes. Research and resources for educators.* New York: McGraw-Hill.

Guttentag, R.E., Ornstein, P.A., & Seimans, L. (1987). Children's spontaneous rehearsal: Transitions in strategy acquisition. *Cognitive Development, 2,* 307–26.

Gzesh, S.M., & Surber, C.F. (1985). Visual perspective-taking skills in children. *Child Development, 56,* 1204–13.

Haan, N., Aerts, E., & Cooper, B.A.B. (1985). *On moral grounds. The search for practical morality.* New York: New York University Press.

Habib, M. (2000). Safety officials warn against leaving kids alone without a plan of action. *Canadian Press.* Retrieved May 14, 2001 from http://www.canoe.ca/LifewiseFamilyTuesday00/1219_homealone_cp.html.

Hagerman, R.J. (1996). Biomedical advances in developmental psychology: The case of

Fragile X syndrome. *Developmental Psychology, 32,* 416–24.

Hagerman, R.J., & Cronister, A. (1996). *Fragile X syndrome: Diagnosis, treatment, and research* (2nd ed.). Baltimore, MD: Johns Hopkins University.

Haight, W.L., Wang, X.-L., Fung, H. H.-T., Williams, K., & Mintz, J. (1999). Universal, developmental, and variable aspects of young children's play: A cross-cultural comparison of pretending at home. *Child Development, 70,* 1477–88.

Hakuta, K. (1988). Why bilinguals? In F.S. Kessel (Ed.), *The development of language and language researchers: Essays in honor of Roger Brown* (pp. 299–318). Hillsdale, NJ: Erlbaum.

Hakuta, K., & Garcia, E.E. (1989). Bilingualism and education. *American Psychologist, 44,* 374–9.

Hala, S., & Chandler, M. (1996). The role of strategic planning in accessing false-belief understanding. *Child Development, 67* (6), 2948–66.

Halford, G.S. (2002). Information-processing models of cognitive development. In U. Goswami (Ed.), *Blackwell Handbook of Cognitive Development.* Oxford: Blackwell Publishers Inc.

Hall, D.G., Quantz, D.H., & Persoage, K.A. (2000). Preschoolers' use of form class cues in word learning. *Developmental Psychology, 36,* 449–62.

Hall, D.G., & Waxman, S.R. (1993). Assumptions about word meaning: Individuation and basic-level kinds. *Child Development, 64,* 1550–70.

Hall, E. (1970, May). A conversation with Jean Piaget and Bärbel Inhelder. *Psychology Today, 3,* 25–56.

Hall, G.S. (1891). The contents of children's minds on entering school. *Pedagogical Seminary, 1,* 139–73.

Hall, G.S. (1904). *Adolescence.* New York: Appleton-Century-Crofts.

Halpern, D. F. (1997). Sex differences in intelligence: Implications for education. *American Psychologist, 52,* 1091-1102.

Halpern, L.F., MacLean, W.E., Jr., & Baumeister, A.A. (1995). Infant sleep–wake characteristics: Relation to neurological status and prediction of developmental outcome. *Developmental Review, 15,* 255–91.

Halverson, H.M. (1931). An experimental study of prehension in infants by means of systematic cinema records. *Genetic Psychology Monographs, 10,* 107–286.

Hamers, J., & Blanc, M. (2000). *Bilinguality and bilingualism* (2nd ed.). Cambridge, England: Cambridge University Press.

Hamilton, C.E. (2000). Continuity and discontinuity of attachment from infancy through adolescence. *Child Development, 71,* 690–4.

Hamond, N.R., & Fivush, R. (1991). Memories of Mickey Mouse: Young children recount their trip to Disney world. *Cognitive Development, 6,* 433–48.

Hans, S. (2002). Studies of prenatal exposure to drugs: Focusing on parental care of children. *Neurotoxicology and Teratology, 24,* 329–37.

Hanushek, E.A. (1997). Assessing the effects of school resources on student performance: An update. *Educational Evaluation and Policy Analysis, 19,* 141–64.

Hara, N., Bonk, C.J., & Angeli, C. (2000). Content analyses of online discussion in an applied educational psychology course. *Instructional Science, 28,* 115–52.

Hardy, J.B., Astone, N.M., Brooks-Gunn, J., Shapiro, S., & Miller, T.L. (1998). Like mother, like child: Intergenerational patterns of age at first birth and associations with childhood and adolescent characteristics and outcomes in the second generation. *Developmental Psychology, 34,* 1220–32.

Harkness, S., Edwards, C.P., & Super, C.M. (1981). Social roles and moral reasoning: A case study in a rural African community. *Developmental Psychology, 17,* 595–603.

Harley, K., & Reese, E. (1999). Origins of autobiographical memory. *Developmental Psychology, 35,* 1338–48.

Harnishfeger, K.K. (1995). The development of cognitive inhibition: Theories, definitions, and research evidence. In F. Dempster & C. Brainerd (Eds.), *New perspectives on interference and inhibition in cognition* (pp. 176–204). New York: Academic Press.

Harnishfeger, K.K., & Bjorklund, D.F. (1990). Children's strategies: A brief history. In D.F. Bjorklund (Ed.), *Children's strategies: Contemporary views of cognitive development* (pp. 1–22). Hillsdale, NJ: Erlbaum.

Harnishfeger, K.K., & Bjorklund, D.F. (1994). The development of inhibition mechanisms and their relation to individual differences in children's cognitions. *Learning and Individual Differences, 6,* 331–55.

Harold, G.T., Fincham, F.D., Osborne, L.M., & Conger, R.D. (1997). Mom and dad are at it again: Adolescent perceptions of marital conflict and adolescent psychological distress. *Developmental Psychology, 33,* 333–50.

Harper, L.V., & Huie, K.S. (1985). The effects of prior group experience, age, and familiarity on the quality and organization of preschoolers' social relationships. *Child Development, 56,* 704–17.

Harrington, D.M., Block, J.H., & Block, J. (1987). Testing aspects of Carl Rogers's theory of creative environments in young adolescents. *Journal of Personality and Social Psychology, 52,* 851–6.

Harris, J.R. (1998). *The nurture assumption: Why children turn out the way they do.* New York: Free Press.

Harris, J.R. (2000). Socialization, personality development, and the child's environments: Comment on Vandell (2000). *Developmental Psychology, 36,* 711–823.

Harris, M. (1992). *Language experience and early language development: From input to uptake.* Hove, England: Erlbaum.

Harris, M. & Pexman, P. (2003). Children's perceptions of the social functions of verbal irony. *Discourse Processes, 36(3),* 147–165.

Harris, N.B. (1992). Sex, race, and the experience of aggression. *Aggressive Behavior, 18,* 201–17.

Harris, P.L. (1989). Developmental changes in children's understanding of simple, multiple, and blended emotion concepts. In C. Saarni & P. Harris (Eds.), *Children's understanding of emotion.* Cambridge, England: Cambridge University Press.

Harris, P.L., Kavanaugh, R.D., & Meredith, M.C. (1994). Young children's comprehension of pretend episodes: The integration of successive actions. *Child Development, 65,* 16–30.

Harrison, L.F., & Williams, T. (1986). Television and cognitive development. In T. Williams (Ed.), *The impact of television: A natural experiment in three communities.* Orlando, FL: Academic Press.

Harrist, A.W., Zaia, A.F., Bates, J.E., Dodge, K.A., & Pettit, G.S. (1997). Subtypes of social withdrawal in early childhood: Sociometric status and social-cognitive differences across four years. *Child Development, 68,* 278–94.

Hart, B., & Risley, T.R. (1995). *Meaningful differences in the everyday experiences of young American children.* Baltimore, MD: Paul H. Brooks.

Hart, C.H., Burts, D.C., Durland, M.A., Charlesworth, R., DeWolf, M., & Fleege, P.O. (1998). Stress behaviors and activity type participation of preschoolers in more and less developmentally appropriate classrooms: SES

and sex differences. *Journal of Research in Childhood Education, 12,* 176–96.

Hart, C.H., Nelson, D., Robinson, C.C., Olsen, S.F., & McNeilly-Choque, M.K. (1998). Overt and relational aggression in Russian nursery-school-age children: Parenting style and marital linkages. *Developmental Psychology, 34,* 687–97.

Hart, C.H., Olsen, S.F., Robinson, C.C., & Mandleco, B.L. (1997). The development of social and communicative competence in childhood: Review and a model of personal, familial, and extrafamilial processes. *Communication Yearbook, 20,* 305–73.

Hart, D., & Chmiel, S. (1992). Influence of defense mechanisms on moral judgment development: A longitudinal study. *Developmental Psychology, 28,* 722–30.

Hart, D., Hofmann, V., Edelstein, W., & Keller, M. (1997). The relation of childhood personality types to adolescent behavior and development: A longitudinal study of Icelandic children. *Developmental Psychology, 33,* 195–205.

Hart, E.L., Lahey, B.B., Loeber, R., Applegate, B., & Frick, P.J. (1995). Developmental change in attention-deficit hyperactivity disorder in boys: A four-year longitudinal study. *Journal of Abnormal Child Psychology, 23,* 729–49.

Hart, S.N. (1991). From property to person status: Historical perspective on children's rights. *American Psychologist, 46,* 53–9.

Hart, S.N., & Brassard, M.R. (1987). A major threat to children's mental health. Psychological maltreatment. *American Psychologist, 42,* 160–5.

Harter, S. (1982). The perceived competence scale for children. *Child Development, 53,* 87-97.

Harter, S. (1983). Developmental perspectives on the self-system. In P.H. Mussen (Series Ed.) & E.M. Hetherington (Vol. Ed.), *Handbook of child psychology: Vol. 4. Socialization, personality and social development* (4th ed., 275–385). New York: Wiley.

Harter, S. (1996). Historial roots in contemporary issues involving self-concept. In B.A. Bracken (Ed.), *Handbook of self-concept: Developmental, social, and clinical considerations.* New York: Wiley.

Harter, S. (1999). *The construction of the self: A developmental perspective. Distinguished contributions in psychology.* New York, NY: Guilford Press, xv, 413.

Harter, S., Marold, D.B., Whitesell, N.R., & Cobbs, G. (1996). A model of the effects of perceived parent and peer support on adolescent false self behavior. *Child Development, 67,* 360–74.

Harter, S., & Monsour, A. (1992). Developmental analysis of conflict caused by opposing attributes in the adolescent self-portrait. *Developmental Psychology, 28,* 251–60.

Harter, S. & Pike, R. (1984). The pictorial scale of perceived competence and social acceptance for young children. *Child Development, 55,* 1969–1982.

Harter, S., Waters, P.L., Whitesell, N.R., & Kastelic, D. (1998). Level of voice among female and male high school students: Relational context, support, and gender orientation. *Developmental Psychology, 34,* 892–901.

Harter, S., & Whitesell, N. (1989). Developmental changes in children's understanding of simple, multiple, and blended emotion concepts. In C. Saarni & P. Harris (Eds.), *Children's understanding of emotion.* Cambridge, England: Cambridge University Press.

Hartshorne, H., & May, M.S. (1928–1930). *Studies in the nature of character* (Vols. 1–3). New York: Macmillan.

Hartung, B., & Sweeney, K. (1991). Why adult children return home. *Social Science Journal, 28,* 467–80.

Hartup, W.W. (1974). Aggression in childhood: Developmental perspectives. *American Psychologist, 29,* 336–41.

Hartup, W.W. (1983). Peer relations. In P.H. Mussen (Series Ed.) & E.M. Hetherington (Vol. Ed.), *Handbook of child psychology: Vol. 4. Socialization, personality and social development* (4th ed., pp. 103–96). New York: Wiley.

Hartup, W.W. (1989). Social relationships and their developmental significance. *American Psychologist, 44,* 120–6.

Hartup, W.W. (1992). Friendships and their developmental significance. In H. McGurk (Ed.), *Childhood social development: Contemporary perspectives* (pp. 175–205). Hove, England: Erlbaum.

Hartup, W.W. (1996). The company they keep: Friendships and their developmental significance. *Child Development, 67,* 1–13.

Hartup, W.W., Laursen, B., Stewart, M.I., & Eastenson, A. (1988). Conflict and friendship relations of young children. *Child Development, 59,* 1590–600.

Hartup, W.W., & Stevens, N. (1997). Friendships and adaptation in the life course. *Psychological Bulletin, 121,* 355–70.

Harvey, E. (1999). Short-term and long-term effects of early parental employment on children of the National Longitudinal Survey of Youth. *Developmental Psychology, 35,* 445–59.

Harvey, J. & Robinson, J.D. (2003). Eating disorders in men: Current considerations. *Journal of Clinical Psychology in Medical Settings, 10* (4), 297–306.

Harvey, S., Jarrell, J., Brant, R., Stainton, C., & Rach, D. (1996). A randomized, controlled trial of nurse-midwifery care. *Birth, 23,* 128–35.

Harwood, R.L., Schoelmerich, A., Ventura-Cook, E., Schulze, P.A., & Wilson, S.P. (1996). Culture and class influences on Anglo and Puerto Rican mothers' beliefs regarding long-term socialization goals and child behavior. *Child Development, 67,* 2446–61.

Haselager, G.J.T., Hartup, W.W., van Lieshout, C.F.M., & Riksen-Walraven, J.M.A. (1998). Similarities between friends and nonfriends in middle childhood. *Child Development, 69,* 1198–1208.

Hashima, P.Y., & Amato, P.R. (1994). Poverty, social support, and parental behavior. *Child Development, 65,* 394–403.

Haskett, M.E., & Kistner, J.A. (1991). Social interactions and peer perceptions of young physically abused children. *Child Development, 62,* 979–90.

Hasselhorn, M. (1992). Task dependency and the role of category typicality and metamemory in the development of an organizational strategy. *Child Development, 63,* 202–14.

Hasselhorn, M. (1995). Beyond production deficiency and utilization inefficiency: Mechanisms of the emergence of strategic categorization in episodic memory tasks. In F.E. Weinert & W. Schneider (Eds.), *Memory performance and competencies: Issues in growth and development* (pp. 141–59). Hillsdale, NJ: Erlbaum.

Hastings, P.D., Zahn-Waxler, C.Z., Robinson, J., Usher, B., & Bridges, D. (2000). The development of concern for others in children with behavior problems. *Developmental Psychology, 36,* 531–46.

Hauser-Cram, P. (1996). Mastery motivation in toddlers with developmental disabilities. *Child Development, 67,* 236–48.

Hauser-Cram, P., Warfield, M.E., Shonkoff, J.P., Krauss, M.W., Upshur, C.C., & Sayer, A. (1999). Family influences on adaptive development in young children with Down syndrome. *Child Development, 70,* 979-89.

Hawkins, D.L., Pepler, D.J., & Craig, W.M. (2001). Naturalistic observations of peer interventions in bullying. *Social Development, 10* (4), 512–27.

Hay, D.F., Caplan, M., Castle, J., & Stimson, C.A. (1991). Does sharing become increasingly "rational" in the second year of life? *Developmental Psychology, 27,* 987–93.

Hay, D.F., Castle, J., & Davies, L. (2000). Toddlers' use of force against familiar peers: A precursor of serious aggression? *Child Development, 71,* 457–67.

Hayden, C.A., Haine, R.R., & Fivush, R. (1997). Developing narrative structure in parent–child reminiscing across the preschool years. *Developmental Psychology, 33,* 295–307.

Hayes, B.K., & Hennessy, R. (1996). The nature and development of nonverbal implicit memory. *Journal of Experimental Child Psychology, 63,* 22–43.

Hayne, H., & Rovee-Collier, C. (1995). The organization of reactivated memory in infancy. *Child Development, 66,* 893–906.

Hayward, C., Killen, J.D., Wilson, D.M., Hammer, L.D., Litt, I.F., Kraemer, H.C., Haydel, F., Varady, M., & Taylor, C.B. (1997). Psychiatric risk associated with puberty in adolescent girls. *Journal of the American Academy of Child and Adolescent Psychiatry, 36,* 255–62.

Health Canada. (2000). Make the world safe for your little ones. *Health! Canada.* Retrieved August 14, 2001, from http://www.hc-sc.gc.ca/english/magazine/2000_11/kids.htm.

Health Canada. (2001b, January 31). *Family-centered maternity and newborn care: National guidelines* (4th ed., chap. 5). Retrieved August 14, 2001 from http://www.hc-sc.gc.ca/hppb/childhood-youth/cyfh/pdf/fcmc/fcmc05.pdf.

Health Canada. (2003). *Folic Acid: Why all women who could become pregnant should be taking Folic Acid.* Available online November 27, 2003 at http://www.hc-sc.gc.ca/english/folicacid/index.html.

Health Canada. (2001a). Canadian National Health Eating Disorder Information Centre. For leaders: Positive self and body image: A crucial link. *Vitality leader's kit.* Retrieved February 26, 2001 from http://www.hc-sc.gc.ca/hppb/nutrition/pube/vtlk/e_vitlk07.htm.

Health Canada, Canadian Perinatal Surveillance System. (2001a). Alcohol and pregnancy. Retrieved August 14, 2001 from http://www.hc-sc.gc.ca/hpb/lcdc/brch/factshts /alcprg_e.html.

Health Canada, Canadian Perinatal Surveillance System. (2001b, January 31). *Canadian perinatal health report 2000.* Retrieved August 14, 2001 from http://www.hc-sc.gc.ca/hpb/lcdc/publicat/cphr-rspc00/pdf/cphr00e.pdf.

Health Canada, Canadian Perinatal Surveillance System. (2001c, February 19). Sudden infant death syndrome. Retrieved August 14, 2001 from http://www.hc-sc.gc.ca/hpb/lcdc/brch/factshts/sids_e.html.

Health Canada, Centre for Infectious Disease Prevention and Control. (2000). HIV and AIDS in Canada. Surveillance Report to June 30, 2000. Retrieved January 15, 2002 from http://www.hc-sc-gc.ca/hpb/lcdc/ publicat/aids/hiv-aic11-00/index.html.

Health Canada, Childhood and Youth Division. (1998, October). Aboriginal Head Start Urban and Northern Initiative: Principles and guidelines. Retrieved January 1, 2001 from http://www.hc-sc.gc.ca/hppb/childhod-youth/acy/pdf/PrincGuideE.pdf.

Health Canada, Childhood and Youth Division. (2001). Aboriginal Head Start Initiative. Retrieved January 1, 2001 from http://www.hc-sc.gc.ca/hppb/childhod-youth/acy.html.

Health Canada, Health Protection Branch. (1998, April). Oral contraceptive and condom use. *STD Epi Update: Sexually Transmitted Disease (STD).* Series #5. Retrieved November 26, 2001 from http://www.hc-sc.gc.ca/hpb/lcdc/bah/epi/std511_e.html.

Health Canada, Laboratory Centre for Disease Control. (1996, June 16). *Measuring up: A health surveillance update on Canadian children and youth.* Retrieved October 24, 2001 from http://www.hc-sc.gc.ca/hpb/lcdc/brch/measuring/index.html.

Health Canada, Population and Public Health Branch. (2001, May). HIV and AIDS among youth in Canada. *HIV/AIDS Epi Update.* Retrieved November 26, 2001 from http://www.hc-sc.gc.ca/hpb/lcdc/bah/epi/youth_e.html.

Hearold, S. (1986). A synthesis of 1043 effects of television on social behavior. In G. Comstock (Ed.), *Public communications and behavior* (Vol. 1, pp. 65–133). New York: Academic Press.

Heath, S.B. (1989). Oral and literate traditions among black Americans living in poverty. *American Psychologist, 44,* 367–73.

Hebb, D.O. (1980). *Essay on mind.* Hillsdale, NJ: Erlbaum.

Hedges, L.V., & Nowell, A. (1995, July 7). Sex differences in mental test scores, variability, and numbers of high-scoring individuals. *Science, 269,* 41–5.

Heimann, M., & Ullstadius, E. (1999). Neonatal imitation and imitation among children with autism and Down's syndrome. In J. Nadel & G. Butterworth (Eds.), *Imitation in Infancy* (pp. 235–53). Cambridge University Press.

Heinonen, O.P., Slone, D., & Shapiro, S. (1977). *Birth defects and drugs in pregnancy.* Littleton, MA: Publishing Sciences Group.

Helms, J.E. (1992). Why is there no study of cultural equivalence in standardized cognitive-ability testing? *American Psychologist, 47,* 1083–101.

Helms, J.E. (1997). The triple quandary of race, culture, and social class in standardized cognitive ability testing. In D.P. Flanagan, J. Genshaft, & P.L. Harrison (Eds.), *Contemporary intellectual assessment: Theories, tests, and issues* (pp. 517–32). New York: Guilford Press.

Helwig, C.C., & Kim, S. (1999). Children's evaluations of decision-making procedures in peer, family, and school contexts. *Child Development, 70,* 502–12.

Hendler, M., & Weisberg, P. (1992). Conservation acquisition, maintenance, and generalization by mentally retarded children using equality-rule training. *Journal of Experimental Child Psychology, 54,* 258–76.

Hendrick, B. (1994, June 7). Teen sexual activity increases, as does kids' use of condoms. *Atlanta Constitution,* pp. A1, A6.

Hendrick, V., & Altshuler, L.L. (1999). Biological determinants of postpartum depression. In L.J. Miller (Ed.), *Postpartum mood disorders* (pp. 65–82). Washington, DC: American Psychiatric Press.

Henker, B., & Whalen, C.K. (1989). Hyperactivity and attention deficits. *American Psychologist, 44,* 216–23.

Hennessey, B.A., & Amabile, T.M. (1988). The conditions of creativity. In R.J. Sternberg (Ed.), *The nature of creativity. Contemporary psychological perspectives* (pp. 11–38). Cambridge, England: Cambridge University Press.

Henrich, C.C., Brown, J.L., & Aber, J.L. (1999). Evaluating the effectiveness of school-based violence prevention: Developmental approaches. *Society for Research in Child Development Social Policy Report, 13,* Number 3.

Henry, B., Caspi, A., Moffitt, T.E., & Silva, P.A. (1996). Temperamental and familial predictors of violent and nonviolent criminal convictions: Age 3 to age 18. *Developmental Psychology, 32*, 614–23.

Herbert, J., & Hayne, H. (2000). Memory retrieval by 18-30-month-olds: Age related changes in representational flexibility. *Developmental Psychology, 36*, 473–84.

Herdt, G.H., & Davidson, J. (1988). The Sambia "turnim-man": Sociocultural and clinical aspects of gender formation in male pseudohermaphrodites with 5-alpha-reductase deficiency in Papua New Guinea. *Archives of Sexual Behavior, 17*, 33–56.

Herkowitz, J. (1978). Sex-role expectations and motor behavior of the young child. In M.V. Ridenour (Ed.), *Motor development: Issues and applications* (pp. 83–98). Princeton, NJ: Princeton Book Company.

Herman-Giddens, M.E., Slora, E.J., Wasserman, R.C., Bourdony, C.J., Bhapkar, M.V., Koch, G.G., & Hasemeier, C.M. (1997). Secondary sexual characteristics and menses in young girls seen in office practice: A study from the Pediatric Research in Office Settings Network. *Pediatrics, 99*, 505–12.

Hernandez, D.J. (1997). Child development and the social demography of childhood. *Child Development, 68*, 149–69.

Herrera, C., & Dunn, J. (1997). Early experiences with family conflict: Implications for arguments with a close friend. *Developmental Psychology, 33*, 869–81.

Herrnstein, R.J., & Murray, C. (1994). *The bell curve: Intelligence and class structure in American life.* New York: Free Press.

Hershberger, S.L., & D'Augelli, A.R. (1995). The impact of victimization on the mental health and suicidality of lesbian, gay, and bisexual youths. *Developmental Psychology, 31*, 65–74.

Hertsgaard, L., Gunnar, M., Erickson, M.F., & Nachmias, M. (1995). Adrenocortical responses to the Strange Situation in infants with disorganized/disoriented attachment relationships. *Child Development, 66*, 1100–6.

Hertzberger, S.D., & Hall, J.A. (1993). Consequences of retaliatory aggression against siblings and peers: Urban minority children's expectations. *Child Development, 64*, 1773–85.

Hetherington, E.M. (1989). Coping with family transitions: Winners, losers, and survivors. *Child Development, 60*, 1–14.

Hetherington, E.M., Bridges, M., & Insabella, G.M. (1998). What matters? What does not? Five perspectives on the association between marital transitions and children's adjustment. *American Psychologist, 53*, 167–84.

Hetherington, E.M., & Camara, K.A. (1984). Families in transition: The processes of dissolution and reconstitution. In R.D. Parke (Ed.), *Review of child development research. Vol. 7: The family* (pp. 398–431). Chicago: University of Chicago Press.

Hetherington, E.M. & Clingempeel, W.G. (1992). Coping with marital transitions. *Monographs of the Society for Research in Child Development, 57* (2–3, Serial No. 227).

Hetherington, E.M., Cox, M., & Cox, R. (1982). Effects of divorce on parents and children. In M.E. Lamb (Ed.), *Nontraditional families* (pp. 233–88). Hillsdale, NJ: Erlbaum.

Hetherington, E.M., & Frankie, G. (1967). Effect of parental dominance, warmth, and conflict on imitation in children. *Journal of Personality and Social Psychology, 6*, 119–25.

Hetherington, E.M., Henderson, S.H., & Reiss, D. (1999). Adolescent siblings in stepfamilies: Family functioning and adolescent adjustment. *Monographs of the Society for Research in Child Development, 64* (4, Serial No. 259).

Hetherington, E.M., & Parke, R.D. (1975). *Child psychology: A contemporary viewpoint.* New York: McGraw-Hill.

Hewlett, B.S., Lamb, M.E., Shannon, D., Leyendecker, B., & Scholmerich, A. (1998). Culture and early infancy among central African foragers and farmers. *Developmental Psychology, 34*, 653–61.

Heyes, C. (2001). Causes and consequences of imitation. *Trends in Cognitive Sciences, 5* (6), 253–61.

Heyman, G.D. & Dweck, C.S. (1998). Children's thinking about traits: Implications for judgments of the self and others. *Child Development, 69*(2), 391–403.

Heyman, G.D., & Gelman, S.A. (1999). Young children use motive information to make trait inferences. *Developmental Psychology, 34*, 310–21.

Higgins, C.I., Campos, J.J., & Kermoian, R. (1996). Effect of self-produced locomotion on infant postural compensation to optic flow. *Developmental Psychology, 32*, 836–41.

Higgins, E.T., & Parsons, J.E. (1983). Stages as subcultures: Social-cognitive development and the social life of the child. In E.T. Higgins, W.W. Hartup, & D.N. Ruble (Eds.), *Social cognition and social development: A sociocultural perspective.* New York: Cambridge University Press.

Higley, J.D., Hopkins, W.D., Thompson, W.W., Byrne, E.A., Hirsh, R.M., & Suomi, S.J. (1992). Peers as primary attachment sources in yearling rhesus monkeys. *Developmental Psychology, 28*, 1163–71.

Hildebrand, D.K., & Saklofske, D. H. (1996). The Wechsler Adult Intelligence Scale—Third Edition: A Canadian standardized study. *Canadian Journal of School Psychology, 12*(1), 75–6.

Hill, A.E. (1997, May 13). Doctors debate circumcision for infants. *Atlanta Constitution*, p. B3.

Hill, J.P., & Lynch, M.E. (1983). The intensification of gender-related role expectations during early adolescence. In J. Brooks-Gunn & A.C. Petersen (Eds.), *Girls at puberty: Biological and psychosocial perspectives.* New York: Plenum.

Hill, M. (2003). Musculoskeletal bone development. University of New South Wales, Sydney, Australia. Available online December 2, 2003 at http://anatomy.med.unsw.edu.au/cbl/embryo/Notes/skmus9.htm.

Hill, P.T., Foster, G.E., & Gendler, T. (1990). *High schools with character: Alternatives to bureaucracy.* Santa Monica, CA: Rand Corporation.

Hill, S.D., & Tomlin, C. (1981). Self-recognition in retarded children. *Child Development, 53*, 1320–9.

Hincks-Dellcrest Centre. (2001). About the Treatment Centre: Mission, services and philosophy. Retrieved October 23, 2001 from http://www.hincksdellcrest.org/treatment-centre/index.html.

Hinde, R.A. (1989). Ethological and relationship approaches. In R. Vasta (Ed.), *Annals of child development: Vol. 6. Theories of child development: Revised formulations and current issues* (pp. 251–85). Greenwich, CT: JAI Press.

Hines, M., & Kaufman, F.R. (1994). Androgen and the development of human sex-typical behavior: Rough-and-tumble play and sex of preferred playmates in children with congenital adrenal hyperplasia. *Child Development, 65*, 1042–53.

Hinshaw, S.P., & Melnick, S.M. (1995). Peer relationships in boys with attention-deficit hyperactivity disorder with and without comorbid aggression. *Development and Psychopathology, 7*, 627–47.

Hinshaw, S.P., Zupan, B.A., Simmel, C., Nigg, J.T., & Melnick, S. (1997). Peer status in boys with attention-deficit hyperactivity disorder: Predictions from overt and covert

antisocial behavior, social isolation, and authoritative parenting beliefs. *Child Development, 68*, 880–96.

Hirsh-Pasek, K., Hyson, M.C., & Rescorla, L. (1989). *Academic environments in early childhood: Challenge or pressure?* Chicago: Spencer Foundation.

Hirsh-Pasek, K., Kemler Nelson, D.G., Jusczyk, P.W., Cassidy, K.W., Druss, B., & Kennedy, L. (1987). Clauses are perceptual units for young infants. *Cognition, 26*, 269–86.

Hobbes, T. (1904). *Leviathan.* Cambridge, England: Cambridge University Press. (Original work published 1651.)

Hock, E., & DeMeis, D.K. (1990). Depression in mothers of infants: The role of maternal employment. *Developmental Psychology, 26*, 285–91.

Hodges, E.V.E., Boivin, M., Vitaro, F., & Bukowski, W.M. (1999). The power of friendship: Protection against an escalating cycle of peer victimization. *Developmental Psychology, 35*, 94–104.

Hodges, E.V.E., Finnegan, R.A., & Perry, D.G. (1999). Skewed autonomy-relatedness in preadolescents' conceptions of their relationships with mother, father, and best friend. *Child Development, 70*, 737–48.

Hodges, E.V.E., Malone, M.J., & Perry, D.G. (1997). Individual risk and social risk as interacting determinants of victimization in the peer group. *Developmental Psychology, 33*, 1032–9.

Hodges, J., & Tizard, B. (1989). IQ and behavioral adjustment of ex-institutional adolescents. *Journal of Child Psychology and Psychiatry, 30*, 53–75.

Hoff-Ginsberg, E. (1997). *Language development.* Pacific Grove, CA: Brooks/Cole.

Hoffman, L.W. (1989). Effects of maternal employment in the two-parent family. *American Psychologist, 44*, 283–92.

Hoffman, L.W. (1991). The influence of family environment on personality: Accounting for sibling differences. *Psychological Bulletin, 108*, 187–203.

Hoffman, L.W. (1994). Commentary on Plomin, R. (1994): A proof and a disproof questioned. *Social Development, 3*, 60–3.

Hoffman, M.L. (1970). Moral development. In P.H. Mussen (Ed.), *Carmichael's manual of child psychology* (Vol. 2, pp. 261–300). New York: Wiley.

Hoffman, M.L. (1975). Moral internalization, parental power, and the nature of parent–child interaction. *Developmental Psychology, 11*, 228–39.

Hoffman, M.L. (1981). Is altruism part of human nature? *Journal of Personality and Social Psychology, 40*, 121–37.

Hoffman, M.L. (1988). Moral development. In M.H. Bornstein & M.E. Lamb (Eds.), *Developmental psychology: An advanced textbook* (2nd ed., pp. 497–548). Hillsdale, NJ: Erlbaum.

Hoffman, M.L. (1993). Empathy, social cognition, and moral education. In A. Garrod (Ed.), *Approaches to moral development: New research and emerging themes* (pp. 157–79). New York: Teachers College Press.

Hoffner, C., & Badzinski, D.M. (1989). Children's integration of facial and situational cues to emotion. *Child Development, 60*, 411–22.

Hofsten, C. von. (1984). Developmental changes in the organization of prereaching movements. *Developmental Psychology, 20*, 378–88.

Holden, G.W. (1988). Adults' thinking about a child rearing problem: Effects of experience, parental status, and gender. *Child Development, 59*, 1623–32.

Holden, G.W., & Miller, P.C. (1999). Enduring and different: A meta-analysis of the similarity in parents' child rearing. *Psychological Bulletin, 125*, 223–54.

Hollich, G.J., Hirsh-Pasek, K., & Golinkiff, R. (2000). Breaking the language barrier: An emergentist coalition model for the origins of word learning. *Monographs of the Society for Research in Child Development, 65* (3, Serial no. 262).

Honzik, M.P. (1983). Measuring mental abilities in infancy. The value and limitations. In M. Lewis (Ed.), *Origins of intelligence. Infancy and early childhood* (2nd ed.). New York: Plenum.

Honzik, M.P., Macfarlane, J.W., & Allen, L. (1948). The stability of mental test performance between two and eighteen years. *Journal of Experimental Education, 17,* 309–24.

Hopkins, B. (1991). Facilitating early motor development: An intracultural study of West Indian mothers and their infants living in Britain. In J.K. Nugent, B.M. Lester, & T.B. Brazelton (Eds.), *The cultural context of infancy: Vol. 2. Multicultural and interdisciplinary approaches to parent–infant relations.* Norwood, NJ: Ablex.

Hopwood, N.J., Kelch, R.P., Hale, P.M., Mendes, T.M., Foster, C.M., & Beitins, I.Z. (1990). The onset of human puberty: Biological and environmental factors. In J. Bancroft & J.M. Reinisch (Eds.), *Adolescence and puberty* (pp. 29–49). New York: Oxford University Press.

Horn, J.L., & Noll, J. (1997). Human cognitive capabilities: G_f-G_c theory. In D.P. Flanagan, J. Genshaft, & P.L. Harrison (Eds.), *Contemporary intellectual assessment: Theories, tests, and issues* (pp. 53–81). New York: Guilford.

Horney, K. (1967). *Feminine psychology.* New York: Norton. (Original work published 1923–37.)

Hornik, R., & Gunnar, M.R. (1988). A descriptive analysis of social referencing. *Child Development, 59,* 626–34.

Horowitz, F.D. (1992). John B. Watson's legacy: Learning and environment. *Developmental Psychology, 28,* 360–7.

Howe, M., & Courage, M. (1997). The emergence and early development of autobiographical memory. *Psychological Review, 104* (3), 499–523.

Howe, M.L., & Courage, M.L. (1993). On resolving the enigma of infantile amnesia. *Psychological Bulletin, 113,* 305–26.

Howe, N., Aquan-Assee, J., Bukowski, W., Rinaldi, C., & Lehoux, P. (2000). Sibling self-disclosure in early adolescence. *Merrill-Palmer Quarterly, 46* (6), 653–71.

Howe, N., & Jacobs, E. (1995). Child care research: A case for Canadian national standards. *Canadian Psychology, 36* (2), 131–48.

Howe, N., Petrakos, H., & Rinaldi, C.M. (1998). "All the sheeps are dead. He murdered them": Sibling pretense negotiation, internal state language, and relationship quality. *Child Development, 69,* 182–91.

Howe, N., & Ross, H.S. (1990). Socialization, perspective-taking and the sibling relationship. *Developmental Psychology, 26,* 160–5.

Howe, R.B. (1995). Evolving policy on children's rights in Canada. In K. Covell (Ed.), *Readings in child development* (pp. 3–27). Scarborough, ON: Nelson.

Howes, C. (1988). Peer interaction of young children. *Monographs of the Society for Research in Child Development, 53* (1, Serial No. 217).

Howes, C. (1990). Can the age of entry into child care and the quality of child care predict adjustment in kindergarten? *Developmental Psychology, 26,* 292–303.

Howes, C. (1997). Children's experiences in center-based child care as a function of teacher background and adult:child ratio. *Merrill-Palmer Quarterly, 43,* 404–25.

Howes, C., Droege, K., & Matheson, C.C. (1994). Play and communicative processes within long-term and short-term friendship dyads. *Journal of Social and Personal Relationships, 11,* 401–10.

Howes, C., Hamilton, C.E., & Philpsen, L.C. (1998). Stability and continuity of child-caregiver and child-peer relationships. *Child Development, 69,* 418–26.

Howes, C., & Matheson, C.C. (1992). Sequences in the development of competent play with peers: Social and social pretend play. *Developmental Psychology, 28,* 961–74.

Howes, C., Phillips, D.A., & Whitebrook, M. (1992). Thresholds of quality: Implications for the social development of children in center-based child care. *Child Development, 63,* 449–60.

Howes, C., Unger, O.A. & Matheson, C.C. (1992). The collaborative construction of pretend: Social pretend play functions. SUNY series, *Children's Play in Society.* Albany, NY: State University of New York Press, vi, 162.

Howes, P., & Markman, H.J. (1989). Marital quality and child functioning: A longitudinal investigation. *Child Development, 60,* 1044–51.

Hsu, L.K.G. (1990). *Eating disorders.* New York: Guilford Press.

Hudson, J.A. (1990). Constructive processing in children's event memory. *Developmental Psychology, 26,* 180–7.

Huesmann, L.R. (1986). Psychological processes promoting the relation between exposure to media violence and aggressive behavior by the viewer. *Journal of Social Issues, 42,* 125–39.

Huesmann, L.R., Lagerspitz, K., & Eron, L.D. (1984). Intervening variables in the TV violence–aggression relation: Evidence from two countries. *Developmental Psychology, 20,* 746–75.

Hughes, C., & Dunn, J. (1998). Understanding of mind and emotion: Longitudinal associations with mental-state talk between young friends. *Developmental Psychology, 34,* 1026–37.

Hughes, R., Jr., Tingle, B.A., & Sawin, D.B. (1981). Development of empathic understanding in children. *Child Development, 52,* 122–8.

Human Resources Development Canada, Applied Research Branch. (2001b). *Profile of Canadian youth in the labour market.* Second annual report to the Forum of Labour Market Ministers 2000. Retrieved May 20, 2001 from http://www.hrdc-drhc.gc.ca/arb/publications/books/youth_prof.shtml.

Human Resources Development Canada. (2003). *National Longitudinal Survey of Children and Youth.* Retrieved from http://www.hrdc-drhc.gc.ca/sp-ps/arb-dgra/nlscy-elnej/home.shtml.

Humphreys, L.G., Rich, S.A., & Davey, T.C. (1985). A Piagetian test of general intelligence. *Developmental Psychology, 21,* 872–7.

Hunt, P., & Goetz, L. (1997). Research on inclusive educational programs, practices, and outcomes for students with severe disabilities. *Journal of Special Education, 31,* 3–29.

Hunter, J.E., & Hunter, R.F. (1984). Validity and utility of alternative predictors of job performance. *Psychological Bulletin, 96,* 72–98.

Hunter, S.K., & Yankowitz, J. (1996). Medical fetal therapy. In J.A. Kuller, N.C. Cheschier, & R.C. Cefalo (Eds.), *Prenatal diagnosis and reproductive genetics.* St. Louis, MO: Mosby.

Huntsinger, C.S., Jose, P.E., & Larson, S.L. (1998). Do parent practices to encourage academic competence influence the social adjustment of young European American and Chinese American children? *Developmental Psychology, 34,* 747–56.

Huq, M., & Hayden, M.R. (1998, September 30). Huntington disease. Seattle, WA: GeneTests-GeneClinics, University of Washington. Retrieved November 19, 2001 from http://www.geneclinics.org/profiles/huntington/details.html.

Hura, S.L., & Echols, C.H. (1996). The role of stress and articulatory difficulty in childrens' early productions. *Developmental Psychology, 32,* 165–76.

Huston, A.C. (1983). Sex-typing. In P.H. Mussen (Series Ed.) & E.M. Hetherington (Vol. Ed.), *Handbook of child psychology: Vol. 4. Socialization, personality, and social development* (4th ed., pp. 387–467). New York: Wiley.

Huston, A.C., Donnerstein, E., Fairchild, H., Feshbach, N.D., Katz, P.A., Murray, J.P., Rubinstein, E.A., Wilcox, B.L., & Zuckerman, D. (1992). *Big world, small screen.* Lincoln: University of Nebraska Press.

Huston, A.C., Duncan, G.J., Granger, R., Bos, J., McLoyd, V., Mistry, R., Crosby, D., Gibson, C., Magnuson, K., Romich, J., & Venture, A. (2001). Work-based antipoverty programs for parents can enhance the school performance and social behavior of children. *Child Development, 72,* 318–36.

Huston, A.C., & Wright, J.C. (1998). Mass media and children's development. In W. Damon (Series Ed.) & I.E. Sigel & K.A. Renninger (Vol. Eds.), *Handbook of child psychology: Vol. 4. Child psychology in practice* (5th ed., pp. 999–1058). New York: Wiley.

Huston, A.C., Wright, J.C., Marquis, J., & Green S.B. (1999). How children spend their time: Television and other activities. *Developmental Psychology, 35,* 912–25.

Hutt, C. (1972). *Males and females.* Baltimore, MD: Penguin Books.

Huttenlocher, J., Levine, S., & Vevea, J. (1998). Environmental input and cognitive growth: A study using time-period comparisons. *Child Development, 69,* 1012–98.

Huttenlocher, P.R. (1994). Synaptogenesis, synapse elimination, and neural plasticity in the human cerebral cortex. In C.A. Nelson (Ed.), *Threats to optimal development: Integrating biological, psychological, and social risk factors: Minnesota symposia on child psychology* (Vol. 27, pp. 35–54). Hillsdale, NJ: Erlbaum.

Hutton, N. (1996). Health prospects for children born to HIV-infected women. In R.R. Faden & N.E. Kass (Eds.), *HIV, AIDS, and childbearing* (pp. 63–77). New York: Oxford University Press.

Hwang, C.P. (1986). Behavior of Swedish primary and secondary caretaking fathers in relation to mother's presence. *Developmental Psychology, 22,* 749–51.

Hyde, J.S. (1984). How large are sex differences in aggression? A developmental meta-analysis. *Developmental Psychology, 20,* 722–36.

Hyde, J.S., Fennema, E., & Lamon, S.J. (1990). Gender differences in mathematics performance: A meta-analysis. *Psychological Bulletin, 107,* 139–55.

Hyde, J.S., & Plant, E.A. (1995). Magnitude of psychological gender differences: Another side to the story. *American Psychologist, 50,* 159–61.

Hymel, S. (1983). Preschool children's peer relations: Issues in sociometric assessment. *Merrill-Palmer Quarterly, 19,* 237–60.

Hymel, S., Bowker, A., & Woody, E. (1993). Aggressive versus withdrawn unpopular children: Variations in peer and self-perceptions in multiple domains. *Child Development, 64,* 879–96.

Hymes, J.L. (1990). *The year in review: A look at 1989.* Washington DC: National Association for the Education of Young Children.

Iannotti, R.J. (1978). Effect of role-taking experiences on role-taking, empathy, altruism, and aggression. *Developmental Psychology, 14,* 119–24.

Ignace, M.B. (1998, April). *Handbook for Aboriginal language program planning in British*

Columbia. Report prepared for the First Nations Steering Committee. Retrieved June 24, 2001 from http://www.schoolnet.ca/aboriginal/fnesc/index-e.html.

Imperato-McGinley, J., Peterson, R.E., Gautier, T., & Sturla, E. (1979). Androgyns and the evolution of male gender identity among male pseudohermaphrodites with 5a-reducase deficiency. *New England Journal of Medicine, 300,* 1233–7.

Ingram, D. (1986). Phonological development: Production. In P. Fletcher & M. Garman (Eds.), *Language acquisition* (2nd ed., pp. 223–39). Cambridge: Cambridge University Press.

Ingram, D. (1989). *First language acquisition: Method, description, and explanation.* Cambridge, England: Cambridge University Press.

Inhelder, B., & Piaget, J. (1958). *The growth of logical thinking from childhood to adolescence.* New York: Basic Books.

Institute of Medicine. (1999). *Reducing the odds.* Washington, DC: National Academy of Sciences.

Intons-Peterson, M.J. (1988). *Gender concepts of Swedish and American youth.* Hillsdale, NJ: Erlbaum.

Intons-Peterson, M.J., & Reddel, M. (1984). What do people ask about a neonate? *Developmental Psychology, 20,* 358–9.

Isabella, R.A. (1993). Origins of attachment: Maternal interactive behavior across the first year. *Child Development, 64,* 605–21.

Isabella, R.A., & Belsky, J. (1991). Interactional synchrony and the origins of infant-mother attachment. *Child Development, 62,* 373–84.

Isberg, R.S., Hauser, S.T., Jacobson, A.M., Powers, S.I., Noam, G., Weiss-Perry, B., & Follansbee, D. (1989). Parental contexts of adolescent self-esteem: A developmental perspective. *Journal of Youth and Adolescence, 18,* 1–23.

Isley, S.L., O'Neil, R.O., Clatfelter, D., & Parke, R.D. (1999). Parent and child expressed affect and children's social competence: Modeling direct and indirect pathways. *Developmental Psychology, 35,* 547–60.

Ismail, M.A. (1993). Maternal–fetal infections. In C. Lin, M.S. Verp, & R.E. Sabbagha (Eds.), *The high-risk fetus: Pathophysiology, diagnosis, management.* New York: Springer-Verlag.

Izard, C.E. (1982). *Measuring emotions in infants and children.* New York: Cambridge University Press.

Izard, C.E. (1993). Four systems for emotion activation: Cognitive and noncognitive processes. *Psychological Review, 100,* 68–90.

Izard, C.E., Fantauzzo, C.A., Castle, J.M., Haynes, O.M., Rayias, M.F., & Putnam, P.H. (1995). The ontogeny and significance of infants' facial expressions in the first 9 months of life. *Developmental Psychology, 31,* 997–1013.

Jacklin, C. N., & Maccoby, E. E. (1978). Social behavior at 33 months in same-sex and mixed-sex dyads. *Child Development, 49,* 557-569.

Jackson, A.P., Brooks-Gunn, J., Hwang, C., & Glassman, M. (2000). Single mothers in low-wage jobs: Financial strain, parenting, and preschoolers' outcomes. *Child Development, 71,* 1409–23.

Jackson, J.F. (1993). Human behavioral genetics, Scarr's theory, and her views on interventions: A critical review and commentary on their implications for African-American children. *Child Development, 63,* 1318–32.

Jacobs, E. (2000). A national picture of child care options. In L. Prochner & N. Howe, *Early childhood care and education in Canada* (pp. 133–60). Vancouver: University of British Columbia Press.

Jacobs, J.E., & Eccles, J.S. (1992). The impact of mothers' gender-role stereotypic beliefs on mothers' and children's ability perceptions. *Journal of Personality and Social Psychology, 63,* 932–44.

Jacobsen, T., & Hofmann, V. (1997). Children's attachment representations: Longitudinal relations to school behavior and academic competency in middle childhood and adolescence. *Developmental Psychology, 33,* 703–10.

Jacobson, J.L., Jacobs, L.C., & Chase, C.I. (1989). Student participation in and attitudes toward high school activities. *The High School Journal, 22,* 175–81.

Jacobson, J.L., & Jacobson, S.W. (1996). Methodological considerations in behavioral toxicology in infants and children. *Developmental Psychology, 32,* 390–403.

Jacobson, J.L., Jacobson, S.W., Fein, G.G., Schwartz, P.M., & Dowler, J.K. (1984). Prenatal exposure to an environmental toxin: A test of the multiple effects model. *Developmental Psychology, 20,* 523–32.

Jacobson, J.L., Jacobson, S.W., & Humphrey, H.E. (1990). Effects of in utero exposure to polychlorinated biphenyls and related contaminants on cognitive functioning in young children. *Journal of Pediatrics, 116,* 38–45.

Jacobson, J.L., Jacobson, S.W., Padgett, R., Brumitt, G.A., & Billings, R.L. (1992). Effects of PCB exposure and infant information processing ability. *Developmental Psychology, 28,* 297–306.

Jacobson, J.L., Jacobson, S.W., Sokol, R.J., Martier, S.S., Ager, J.W., & Kaplan-Estrin, M.G. (1993). Teratogenic effects of alcohol on infant development. *Alcoholism: Clinical and Experimental Research, 17,* 174–83.

Jacobson, J.L., & Wille, D.E. (1986). The influence of attachment pattern on developmental changes in peer interaction from the toddler to the preschool period. *Child Development, 57,* 338–47.

Jacobvitz, D., & Sroufe, L.A. (1987). The early caregiver-child relationship and attention-deficit disorder with hyperactivity in kindergarten: A prospective study. *Child Development, 58,* 1496–1504.

Jadack, R. A., Hyde, J. S., Moore, C. F., & Keller, M. L. (1995). Moral reasoning about sexually transmitted diseases. *Child Development, 66,* 167-177.

Jagers, R.J., Bingham, K., & Hans, S.L. (1996). Socialization and social judgments among inner-city African-American kindergarteners. *Child Development, 67,* 140–50.

Jaio, S., Ji, G., & Jing, Q. (1996). Cognitive development of Chinese urban only children and children with siblings. *Child Development, 67,* 387–95.

James, S.J., Pogribna, M., Pogribna, I.P., Melnyk, S., Hine, R.J., Gibson, J.B., Vi, P., Tafoya, D.L., Swenson, D.H., Wilson, V.L., & Gaylor, D.W. (1999). Abnormal folate metabolism and mutation in the methylene tetrahyrofolate reductase gene may be maternal risk factors for Down Syndrome. *American Journal of Clinical Nutrition, 70,* 495–501.

James, W. (1890). *Principles of psychology* (2 vols.). New York: Holt.

Janowsky, J. S., & Carper, R. (1996). Is there a neural basis for cognitive transitions in school-age children? In A. J. Sameroff & M. M. Haith (Eds.), *The five to seven year shift: The age of reason and responsibility.* Chicago: University of Chicago Press.

Janowsky, J.S., & Finlay, B.L. (1986). The outcome of perinatal brain damage: The role of normal neuron loss and axon retraction. *Developmental Medicine and Child Neurology, 28,* 375–89.

Jarrold, C., Butler, D.W., Cottingham, E.M., & Jimenez, F. (2000). Linking theory of mind and central coherence bias in autism and in the general population. *Developmental Psychology, 36,* 126–38.

Jeffery, R., & Jeffery, P.M. (1993). Traditional birth attendants in rural northern India: The social organization of childbearing. In S. Lindenbaum & M. Lock (Eds.), *Knowledge, power, and practice: The anthropology of medicine and everyday life* (pp. 7–31). Berkeley, CA: University of California Press.

Jenkins, J.M., & Astington, J.W. (1996). Cognitive factors and family structure associated with theory of mind development in young children. *Developmental Psychology, 32,* 70–8.

Jensen, A.R. (1969). How much can we boost IQ and scholastic achievement? *Harvard Educational Review, 39,* 1–123.

Jensen, A.R. (1980). *Bias in mental testing.* New York: Free Press.

Jensen, A.R. (1985). The nature of black–white difference on various psychometric tests: Spearman's hypothesis. *Behavioral and Brain Sciences, 8,* 193–263.

Jensen, A.R. (1998). *The g factor: The science of mental ability.* Westport, CT: Praeger.

Joffe, R.T., Offord, D.R. & Boyle, M.H. (1988). Ontario Child Health Study: Suicidal behavior in youth age 12–16 years. *American Journal of Psychiatry, 145* (11), 1420–3.

Johnsen, E.P. (1991). Searching for the social and cognitive outcomes of children's play: A selective second look. *Play and Culture, 4,* 201–13.

Johnson, C.J., Pick, H.L., Siegel, G.M., Cicciarelli, A.W., & Garber, S.R. (1981). Effects of interpersonal distance on children's vocal intensity. *Child Development, 52,* 721–3.

Johnson, C.N., & Wellman, H.M. (1980). Children's developing understanding of mental verbs: Remember, know, and guess. *Child Development, 51,* 1095–1102.

Johnson, D.W., & Johnson, R.T. (1987). *Learning together and alone: Cooperative, competitive, and individualistic learning* (2nd ed.). Englewood Cliffs, NJ: Prentice Hall.

Johnson, D.W., & Johnson, R.T. (1989). *Cooperation and competition: Theory and research.* Edina, MN: Interaction.

Johnson, H., & Smith, L.B. (1981). Children's inferential abilities in the context of reading to understand. *Child Development, 52,* 1216–23.

Johnson, J., & Newport, E. (1989). Critical period effects in second language learning: The influence of maturational state on the acquisition of English as a second language. *Cognitive Psychology, 21,* 60–99.

Johnson, J., Wilson, R., Singer, J., Winsor, E., Harman, C., Armson, B., Benzie, R., Dansereau, J., Ho, M., Mohide, P., Natale, R., & Okun, N. (1999). Technical factors in early amniocentesis predict adverse outcome. Results of the Canadian Early versus Mid-Trimester Amniocentesis Trial. *Prenatal Diagnosis, 19* (8), 732–8.

Johnson, M. (2000). Functional brain development in infants: Elements of an interactive specialization framework. *Child Development, 71* (1), 75–81.

Johnson, M.H. (1997). *Developmental cognitive neuroscience: An introduction.* Cambridge, MA: Blackwell.

Johnson, M.H. (1998). The neural basis of cognitive development. In W. Damon (Series Ed.) & D. Kuhn & R.S. Siegler (Vol Eds.), *Handbook of child psychology: Vol. 2. Cognition, perception, and language* (5th ed). New York: Wiley.

Johnson, M.H., Dziurawiec, S., Ellis, H., & Morton, J. (1991). Newborns' preferential tracking of face-like stimuli and its subsequent decline. *Cognition, 40,* 1–19.

Johnson, M.H., & Gilmore, R.O. (1996). Developmental cognitive neuroscience: A biological perspective on cognitive change. In R. Gelman & T.K. Au (Eds.), *Handbook of perception and cognition: Vol. 13. Perceptual and cognitive development* (pp. 333–72). San Diego, CA: Academic Press.

Johnson, N., & Cremo, E. (1995). Socialization and the Native family. In K.Covell (Ed.), *Readings in child development* (pp. 159–71). Scarborough, ON: Nelson.

Johnson, R., & Swain, M. (1997). *Immersion education: International perspectives.* Cambridge, England: Cambridge University Press.

Johnson, S.P., & Aslin, R.N. (1995). Perception of object unity in 2-month-old infants. *Developmental Psychology, 31,* 739–45.

Johnson, W., Emde, R.N., Pannabecker, B., Stenberg, C., & Davis, M. (1982). Maternal perception of infant emotion from birth through 18 months. *Infant Behavior and Development, 5,* 313–22.

Johnston, J., & Ettema, J.S. (1982). *Positive images.* Newbury Park, CA: Sage.

Jones, D.C., Abbey, B.B., & Cumberland, A. (1998). The development of display role knowledge: Linkage with family expressiveness and social competence. *Child Development, 69,* 1209–22.

Jones, D.S., Byers, R.H., Bush, T.J., Oxtoby, M.J., & Rogers, M.F. (1992). Epidemiology of transfusion-associated acquired immunodeficiency syndrome in children in the United States, 1981 through 1989. *Pediatrics, 89,* 123–7.

Jones, K.L., Smith, D.W., Ulleland, C.N., & Streissguth, A.P. (1973). Pattern of malformation in offspring of chronic alcoholic mothers. *Lancet, 1,* 1267–71.

Jones, M.C. (1924). A laboratory study of fear: The case of Peter. *Pedagogical Seminary, 31,* 308–15.

Jones, M.C. (1965). Psychological correlates of somatic development. *Child Development, 36,* 899–911.

Jones, M.C., & Bayley, N. (1950). Physical maturing among boys as related to behavior. *Journal of Educational Psychology, 41,* 129–48.

Jonsson, J.O., & Gahler, M. (1997). Family dissolution, family reconstitution, and children's educational careers: Recent evidence for Sweden. *Demography, 34,* 277–93.

Jose, P.M. (1990). Just world reasoning in children's immanent justice arguments. *Child Development, 61,* 1024–33.

Juszcyk, P.W. (1995). Language acquisition: Speech sounds and phonological development. In J.L. Miller & P.D. Eimas (Eds.), *Handbook of perception and cognition: Vol. 11. Speech, language, and communication* (pp. 263–301). Orlando, FL: Academic Press.

Juszcyk, P.W. (1999). How infants begin to extract words from speech. *Trends in Cognitive Sciences, 3,* 323–8.

Juszcyk, P.W., Cutler, A., & Redanz, N.J. (1993). Infants' preference for the predominant stress patterns of English words. *Child Development, 64,* 675–87.

Jussim, L., & Eccles, J.S. (1992). Teacher expectations II: Construction and reflection of student achievement. *Journal of Personality and Social Psychology, 63,* 947–61.

Justice, E.M., Baker-Ward, L., Gupta, S., & Jannings, L.R. (1997). Means to the goal of remembering: Developmental changes in awareness of strategy use–performance relations. *Journal of Experimental Child Psychology, 65,* 293–314.

Kagan, J. (1972). Do infants think? *Scientific American, 226,* 74–82.

Kagan, J. (1976). Emergent themes in human development. *American Scientist, 64,* 186–96.

Kagan, J. (1984). *The nature of the child.* New York: Basic Books.

Kagan, J. (1989). *Unstable ideas: Temperament, cognition, and self.* Cambridge, MA: Cambridge University Press.

Kagan, J. (1991). Continuity and discontinuity. In S.E. Brauth, W.S. Hall, & R.J. Dooling (Eds.), *Plasticity of development.* Cambridge, MA: Bradford Books, MIT Press.

Kagan, J. (1992). Behavior, biology, and the meaning of temperamental constructs. *Pediatrics, 90,* 510–3.

Kagan, J., Kearsley, R.B., & Zelazo, P.R. (1978). *Infancy: Its place in human development.* Cambridge, MA: Harvard University Press.

Kagan, J., & Moss, H.A. (1962). *Birth to maturity.* New York: Wiley.

Kagan, J., Snidman, N., & Areus, D. (1998). Childhood derivatives of high and low reactivity in infancy. *Child Development, 69,* 1483–93.

Kagan, S. & Zahn, G.L. (1975). Field dependence and the school achievement gap between Anglo-American and Mexican-American children. *Journal of Educational Psychology, 67,* 643–50.

Kahana-Kalman, R., & Walker-Andrews, A.S. (2001). The role of person familiarity in young infants' perception of emotional expression. *Child Development, 72,* 352–69.

Kail, R. (1991). Processing time declines exponentially during childhood and adolescence. *Developmental Psychology, 27,* 259–66.

Kail, R. (1992). Processing speed, speech rate, and memory. *Developmental Psychology, 28,* 899–904.

Kail, R. (1997). Processing time, imagery, and spatial memory. *Journal of Experimental Child Psychology, 64,* 67–78.

Kail, R.V., & Salthouse, T.A. (1994). Processing speed as a mental capacity. *Acta Psychologica, 86,* 199–225.

Kaitz, M., Meschulach-Sarfaty, O., Auerbach, J., & Eidelman, A. (1988). A reexamination of newborns' ability to imitate facial expressions. *Developmental Psychology, 24,* 3–7.

Kamerman, S.B. (2000). Parental leave policies: An essential ingredient in early childhood education and care policies. *Social policy report* (Vol. 14, No. 2). Ann Arbor, MI: Society for Research in Child Development.

Kamins, M.L., & Dweck, C.S. (1999). Person versus process praise and criticism: Implications for contingent self-worth and coping. *Developmental Psychology, 35,* 835–47.

Kandel, D. (1973). Adolescent marijuana use: Role of parents and peers. *Science, 181,* 1067–70.

Kanfer, F.H., Stifter, E., & Morris, S.J. (1981). Self-control and altruism: Delay of gratification for another. *Child Development, 52,* 674–82.

Kant, I. (1958). *Critique of pure reason.* New York: Modern Library. (Original work published 1781.)

Kaplan, P.S., Jung, P.C., Ryther, J.S., & Zarlengo-Strouse, P. (1996). Infant-directed versus adult-directed speech as signals for faces. *Developmental Psychology, 32,* 880–91.

Karmiloff-Smith, A. (1992). *Beyond modularity: A developmental perspective on cognitive science.* Cambridge, MA: MIT Press.

Karoly, L.A., Greenwood, P.W., Everingham, S.S., Houbé, J., Kilburn, M.R., Rydell, C.P., Sanders, M., & Chiesa, J. (1998). *Investing in our children: What we know and don't know about the costs and benefits of early childhood interventions.* RAND Distribution Services.

Katcher, A. (1955). The discrimination of sex differences by young children. *Journal of Genetic Psychology, 87,* 131–43.

Katz, G.S., Cohn, J.F., & Moore, C.A. (1996). A combination of vocal, dynamic and summary features discriminates between three pragmatic categories of infant-directed speech. *Child Development, 67,* 205–17.

Katz, P.A. (1979). The development of female identity. *Sex Roles, 5,* 155–78.

Katz, P.A., & Walsh, P.V. (1991). Modification of children's gender-stereotyped behavior. *Child Development, 62,* 338–51.

Kaufman, A.S., Kamphaus, R.W., & Kaufman, N.L. (1985). New directions in intelligence testing: The Kaufman Assessment Battery for Children (K-ABC). In B.B. Wolman (Ed.), *Handbook of intelligence.* New York: Wiley.

Kaufman, A.S., & Kaufman, N.L. (1983). *Kaufman Assessment Battery for Children: Interpretive manual.* Circle Pines, MN: American Guidance Service.

Kaye, K., & Marcus, J. (1981). Infant imitation: The sensory-motor agenda. *Developmental Psychology, 17,* 258–65.

Kazdin, A.E. (1995). *Conduct disorders in childhood and adolescence* (2nd ed.). Thousand Oaks, CA: Sage.

Kean, A.W.G. (1937). The history of the criminal liability of children. *Law Quarterly Review, 3,* 364–70.

Keane, S.P., Brown, K.P., & Crenshaw, T.M. (1990). Children's intention-cue detection as a function of maternal social behavior: Pathways to social rejection. *Developmental Psychology, 26,* 1004–9.

Kearins, J.M. (1981). Visual-spatial memory in Australian aboriginal children of desert regions. *Cognitive Psychology, 13,* 434–60.

Keasey, C.B. (1971). Social participation as a factor in the moral development of preadolescents. *Developmental Psychology, 5,* 216–20.

Keating, D., & Clark, L.V. (1980). Development of physical and social reasoning in adolescence. *Developmental Psychology, 16,* 23–30.

Kee, D. W. (1986). Computer play. In A. W. Gottfried & C. C. Brown (Eds.), *Play interactions: The contribution of play materials and parental involvement to children's development.* Lexington, MA: Lexington Books.

Kee, D.W. (1994). Developmental differences in associative memory: Strategy use, mental effort, and knowledge-access interactions. In H.W. Reese (Ed.), *Advances in child development and behavior* (Vol. 25, pp. 7–32). New York: Academic Press.

Keith, J. (1985). Age in anthropological research. In R.H. Binstock & E. Shanus (Eds.), *Handbook of aging and the social sciences* (2nd ed.). New York: Van Nostrand Reinhold.

Keller, A., Ford, L.H., Jr., & Meachum, J.A. (1978). Dimensions of self-concept in preschool children. *Developmental Psychology, 14,* 483–9.

Keller, H., Lohaus, A., Volker, S., Cappenberg, M., & Chasiotis, A. (1999). Temporal contingency as an independent component of parenting behavior. *Child Development, 70,* 474–85.

Keller, H., & Scholmerich, A. (1987). Infant vocalizations and parental reactions during the first four months of life. *Developmental Psychology, 23,* 62–7.

Kelley, M.L., Power, T.G., & Wimbush, D.D. (1992). Determinants of disciplinary practices in low-income Black mothers. *Child Development, 63,* 573–82.

Kelley, S.A., Brownell, C.A., & Campbell, S.B. (2000). Mastery motivation and self-evaluative affect in toddlers: Longitudinal relations with maternal behavior. *Child Development, 71,* 1061–71.

Kelley-Buchanan, C. (1988). *Peace of mind during pregnancy: An A–Z guide to the substances that could affect your unborn baby.* New York: Facts on File.

Kellman, P.J., & Banks, M.S. (1998). Infant visual perception. In W. Damon (Series Ed.) &

D. Kuhn & R.S. Siegler (Vol. Eds.), Handbook of child psychology: Vol. 2. *Cognitive, language, and perceptual development*. New York: Wiley.

Kellman, P.J., & Spelke, E.S. (1983). Perception of partly occluded objects in infancy. *Cognitive Psychology, 15*, 483–524.

Kellman, P.J., Spelke, E.S., & Short, K.R. (1986). Infant perception of object unity from translatory motion in depth and vertical translation. *Child Development, 57*, 72–86.

Kempe, R.S., & Kempe, C.H. (1978). *Child abuse*. Cambridge, MA: Harvard University Press.

Kendall-Tackett, K.A., Williams, L.M., & Finkelhor, D. (1993). Impact of sexual abuse on children: A review and synthesis of recent empirical studies. *Psychological Bulletin, 113*, 164–80.

Kennell, J.H., Voos, D.K., & Klaus, M.H. (1979). Parent–infant bonding. In J.D. Osofsky (Ed.), *Handbook of infant development*. New York: Wiley.

Keough, J., & Sugden, D. (1985). *Movement skill development*. New York: MacMillan.

Kermoian, R., & Campos, J.J. (1988). Locomotor experience: A facilitator of spatial cognitive development. *Child Development, 59*, 908–17.

Kerns, K.A., & Berenbaum, S.A. (1991). Sex differences in spatial ability in children. *Behavior Genetics, 21*, 383–96.

Kerns, K.A., Klepec, L., & Cole, A. (1996). Peer relationships and preadolescents' perceptions of security in the child–mother relationship. *Developmental Psychology, 32*, 457–66.

Kerr, M., Lambert, W.W., & Bem, D.J. (1996). Life course sequelae of childhood shyness in Sweden: Comparison with the United States. *Developmental Psychology, 32*, 1100–5.

Kerr, M., Lambert, W.W., Stattin, H., & Klackbengerg-Larsson, I. (1994). Stability of inhibition in a Swedish longitudinal sample. *Child Development, 65*, 138–46.

Kerr, M., & Stattin, H. (2000). What parents know, how they know it, and several forms of adolescent adjustment: Further support for a reinterpretation of monitoring. *Developmental Psychology, 36*, 366–80.

Kessel, B. (1995). Reproductive cycles in women: Quality of life impact. In B.P. Sachs, R. Beard, E. Papiernik, & C. Russell (Eds.), *Reproductive health care for women and babies* (pp. 18–39). New York: Oxford University Press.

Kessen, W. (1965). *The child*. New York: Wiley.

Kessen, W. (1975). *Childhood in China*. New Haven, CT: Yale University Press.

Kessen, W. (1996). American psychology just before Piaget. *Psychological Science, 7*, 196–9.

Kessner, D.M. (1973). *Infant death: An analysis by maternal risk and health care*. Washington, DC: National Academy of Sciences.

Kett, J.F. (1977). *Rites of passage. Adolescence in America, 1790 to the present*. New York: Basic Books.

Kidder, K., Avard, D., Fraser, J., Stein, J., & Canadian Institute of Child Health. (2000). *The health of Canada's children: A CICH profile* (3rd ed.). Ottawa: Canadian Institute of Child Health.

Kilgore, K., Snyder, J., & Lentz, C. (2000). The contribution of parental discipline, parental monitoring, and school risk to early-onset conduct problems in African American boys and girls. *Developmental Psychology, 36*, 835–45.

Kilpatrick, A. (1992). *Long-range effects of child and adolescent sexual experiences: Myths, mores, and menaces*. Hillsdale, NJ: Erlbaum.

Kim, K.H.S., Relkin, N.R., Lee, K., Hirsch, J., et al. (1997). Distinct cortical areas associated with native and second languages. *Nature, 388*, 171–74.

Kimura, D. (1992). Sex differences in the brain. *Scientific American, 267*, 119–25.

King, A., Beazley, R., & Warren, W. (1988). *Canada youth and AIDS study*. Kingston, ON: Queen's University Press.

Kinney, D.A. (1993). From nerds to normals: The recovery of identity among adolescents from middle school to high school. *Sociology of Education, 44*, 21–40.

Kinney, H.C., Filiano, J.J., Sleeper, L.A., Mandell, F., Valdes-Dapena, M., & White, W.F. (1995). Decreased muscarinic receptor binding in the arcuate nucleus in sudden infant death syndrome. *Science, 269*, 1446-50.

Kinsbourne, M. (1989). Mechanisms and development of hemisphere specialization in children. In C.R. Reynolds & E. Fletcher-Janzen (Eds.), *Handbook of clinical child neuropsychology*. New York: Plenum Press.

Kirby, J.R. (1995). Intelligence and social policy. Special Issue: Canadian perspectives on the Bell Curve. *Alberta Journal of Educational Research, 41(3)*, 322–34.

Kirsh, S.J. (1998). Seeing the world through Mortal Kombat-colored glasses: Violent video games and the development of a short-term hostile attribution bias. *Childhood, 5*, 177–84.

Kisilevsky, B.S., & Muir, D.W. (1984). Neonatal habituation and dishabituation to tactile stimulation during sleep. *Developmental Psychology, 20*, 367–73.

Kitzinger, C., & Wilkinson, S. (1995). Transitions from heterosexuality to lesbianism: The discursive production of lesbian identities. *Developmental Psychology, 31*, 95–104.

Kitzmann, K.M. (2000). Effects of marital conflict on subsequent triadic family interactions and parenting. *Developmental Psychology, 36*, 3–13.

Klahr, D. (1992). Information-processing approaches to cognitive development. In M.H. Bernstein & M.E. Lamb (Eds.), *Developmental psychology: An advanced textbook* (3rd ed., pp. 273–335). Hillsdale, NJ: Erlbaum.

Klahr, D., & MacWhinney, B. (1998). Information processing. In W. Damon (Series Ed.) & D. Kuhn & R.S. Siegler (Vol. Eds.), *Handbook of child psychology: Vol. 2. Cognition, perception, and language* (5th ed., pp. 631–78). New York: Wiley.

Klaus, M.H., & Kennell, J.H. (1976). *Maternal–infant bonding*. St. Louis, MO: Mosby.

Klaus, M.H., & Kennell, J.H. (1982). *Parent–infant bonding*. St. Louis, MO: Mosby.

Klebanov, P.K., Brooks-Gunn, J., McCarton, C., & McCormick, M.C. (1998). The contribution of neighborhood and family income to developmental test scores over the first three years of life. *Child Development, 69*, 1420–36.

Klein, D.M., & White, J.M. (1996). *Family theories: An introduction*. Thousand Oaks, CA: Sage.

Klein, J., & Bisanz, J. (2000). Preschoolers doing arithmetic: The concepts are willing but the working memory is weak. *Canadian Journal of Experimental Psychology, 4*, 105–15.

Klimes-Dougan, B., & Kistner, J. (1990). Physically abused preschoolers' responses to peers' distress. *Developmental Psychology, 26*, 599–602.

Klineberg, O. (1963). Negro–white differences in intelligence test performance: A new look at an old problem. *American Psychologist, 18*, 198–203.

Klinnert, M.D., Emde, R.N., Butterfield, P., & Campos, J.J. (1986). Social referencing: The infant's use of emotional signals from a friendly adult with mother present. *Developmental Psychology, 22*, 427–32.

Klump, K., McGue, M., & Iacono, W.G. (2000). Age differences in genetic and environmental influences on eating attitudes and behaviours in preadolescent and adolescent female twins. *Journal of Abnormal Psychology, 109*, 239–51.

Kochanska, G. (1991). Socialization and temperament in the development of guilt and conscience. *Child Development, 62*, 1379-1392.

Kochanska, G. (1992). Children's interpersonal influence with mothers and peers. *Developmental Psychology, 28*, 491–9.

Kochanska, G. (1993). Toward a synthesis of parental socialization and child temperament in early development of conscience. *Child Development, 64*, 325–47.

Kochanska, G. (1995). Children's temperament, mother's discipline, and security of attachment: Multiple pathways to emerging internalization. *Child Development, 66*, 597–615.

Kochanska, G. (1997a). Multiple pathways to conscience for children with different temperaments: From toddlerhood to age 5. *Developmental Psychology, 33*, 228–40.

Kochanska, G. (1997b). Mutually responsive orientation between mothers and their young: Implications for early socialization. *Child Development, 68*, 94–112.

Kochanska, G. (1998). Mother–child relationships, child fearfulness, and emerging attachment: A short-term longitudinal study. *Developmental Psychology, 34*, 480–90.

Kochanska, G. (2001). Emotional development in children with different attachment histories: The first three years. *Child Development, 72*, 474–90.

Kochanska, G., Casey, R.J., & Fukumoto, A. (1995). Toddlers' sensitivity to standard violations. *Child Development, 66*, 643–56.

Kochanska, G., Murray, K., Jacques, T.Y., Koenig, A.L., & Vandegeest, K.A. (1996). Inhibitory control in young children and its role in emerging internalization. *Child Development, 67*, 490–507.

Kochanska, G., & Murray, K.T. (2000). Mother-child mutually responsive orientation and conscience development: From toddler to early school age. *Child Development, 71*, 417–31.

Kochanska, G., Tjebkes, T. L., & Forman, D. R. (1998). Children's emerging regulation of conduct: Restraint, compliance, and internalization from infancy to the second year. *Child Development, 69*, 1378–89.

Kochenderfer, B.J., & Ladd, G.W. (1996). Peer victimization: Cause or consequence of school maladjustment? *Child Development, 67*, 1305–17.

Kochenderfer-Ladd, B., & Wardrop, J.L. (2001). Chronicity and instability of children's peer victimization experiences as predictors of loneliness and social satisfaction trajectories. *Child Development, 72*, 134–51.

Kodituwakku, P.W., Kalberg, W., & May, P. (2001). The effects of prenatal alcohol exposure on executive functioning. *Alcohol Research and Health, 25*, 192–8.

Koepke, J., & Bigelow, A. (1997). Observations of newborn suckling behavior. *Infant Behavior and Development, 20 (1)*, 93–8.

Koff, E., & Rierdan, J. (1995). Early adolescent girls' understanding of menstruation. *Women and Health, 22*, 1–19.

Kohlberg, L. (1963). The development of children's orientations toward a moral order: I. Sequence in the development of moral thought. *Vita Humana, 6*, 11–33.

Kohlberg, L. (1966). A cognitive-developmental analysis of children's sex-role concepts and attitudes. In E.E. Maccoby (Ed.), *The development of sex differences* (pp. 82–172). Stanford, CA: Stanford University Press.

Kohlberg, L. (1975, June). The cognitive-developmental approach to moral education. *Phi Delta Kappan*, 670–7.

Kohlberg, L. (1984). *Essays on moral development: Vol. 2. The psychology of moral development*. San Francisco: Harper & Row.

Kohlberg, L., Yaeger, J., & Hjertholm, E. (1968). Private speech: Four studies and a review of theories. *Child Development, 39,* 691–736.

Kohn, M.L. (1979). The effects of social class on parental values and practices. In D. Reiss & H.A. Hoffman (Eds.), *The American family: Dying or developing?* (pp. 49–68). New York: Plenum.

Kokko, K., & Pulkkinen, L. (2000). Aggression in childhood and long-term unemployment in adulthood: A cycle of maladaptation and some protective factors. *Developmental Psychology, 36,* 463–72.

Kolata, G.B. (1986). Obese children: A growing problem. *Science, 232,* 20–1.

Kolb, B., & Fantie, B. (1989). Development of the child's brain and behavior. In C.R. Reynolds & E. Fletcher-Janzen (Eds.), *Handbook of clinical child neuropsychology* (pp. 17–41). New York: Plenum Press.

Kolb, B., Gibb, R., & Gorny, G. (2003). Experience-dependent changes in dendritic arbor and spine density in neocortex vary with age and sex. *Neurobiology of Learning and Memory, 79,* 1–10.

Kolb, B., Gibb, R., & Robinson, T. (2003). Brain Plasticity and behaviour. *Current Directions in Psychological Science, 12* (1), 1–5.

Koolstra, C.M., & van der Voort, T.H. (1996). Longitudinal effects of television on children's leisure time reading. *Human Communication Research, 23,* 4–35.

Kopp, C.B. (1989). Regulation of distress and negative emotions: A developmental view. *Developmental Psychology, 25,* 343–54.

Kopp, C.B., & Kaler, S.R. (1989). Risk in infancy. *American Psychologist, 44,* 224–30.

Korner, A.F. (1972). State as a variable, as obstacle and as mediator of stimulation in infant research. *Merrill-Palmer Quarterly, 18,* 77–94.

Korner, A.F. (1996). Reliable individual differences in preterm infants' excitation management. *Child Development, 67,* 1793–1805.

Kortenhaus, C.M., & Demarest, J. (1993). Gender role stereotyping in children's literature: An update. *Sex Roles, 28,* 219–32.

Kovacs, D.M., Parker, J.G., & Hoffman, L.W. (1996). Behavioral, affective, and social correlates of involvement in cross-sex friendships in elementary school. *Child Development, 67,* 2269–86.

Kowal, A., & Kramer, L. (1997). Children's understanding of parental differential treatment. *Child Development, 68,* 113–26.

Kowaleski-Jones, L., & Duncan, G.J. (1999). The structure of achievement and behavior across middle childhood. *Child Development, 70,* 930–43.

Kramer, L., Perozynski, L.A., & Chung, T. (1999). Parental responses to sibling conflict: The effects of development and parent gender. *Child Development, 70,* 1401–14.

Krauss, R.M., & Glucksberg, S. (1977). Social and nonsocial speech. *Scientific American, 236,* 100–5.

Kreutzer, M.A., Leonard, C., & Flavell, J.H. (1975). An interview study of children's knowledge about memory. *Monographs of the Society for Research in Child Development, 40* (1, Serial No. 159).

Krevans, J., & Gibbs, J.C. (1996). Parents' use of inductive discipline: Relations to children's empathy and prosocial behavior. *Child Development, 67,* 3263–77.

Krishnan, P. (1995). The Bell Curve: Some statistical concerns. *Alberta Journal of Educational Research. Special Issue: Canadian perspectives on The Bell Curve, 41* (3), 274–6.

Kroger, J. (1995). The differentiation of "firm" and "developmental" foreclosure identity statuses: A longitudinal study. *Journal of Adolescent Research, 10,* 317–37.

Kroger, J. (1996). Identity, regression, and development. *Journal of Adolescence, 19,* 203–22.

Kroll, J. (1977). The concept of childhood in the Middle Ages. *Journal of the History of the Behavioral Sciences, 13,* 384–93.

Kruger, A.C. (1992). The effect of peer and adult-child transductive discussions on moral reasoning. *Merrill-Palmer Quarterly, 38,* 191–211.

Kruger, A.C., & Tomasello, M. (1986). Transactive discussions with peers and adults. *Developmental Psychology, 22,* 681–5.

Kuczynski, L. (1983). Reasoning, prohibitions, and motivations for compliance. *Developmental Psychology, 19,* 126–34.

Kuczynski, L., & Kochanska, G. (1995). Function and content of maternal demands: Developmental significance of early demands for competent action. *Child Development, 66,* 616–28.

Kuczynski, L., Zahn-Waxler, C., & Radke-Yarrow, M. (1987). Development and content of imitation in the second and third years of life: A socialization perspective. *Developmental Psychology, 23,* 276–82.

Kuebli, J., Butler, S., & Fivush, R. (1995). Mother–child talk about past emotions: Relations of maternal language and child gender over time. *Cognition and Emotion, 9,* 265–83.

Kuhl, P.K., Andruski, J.E., Christovich, I.A., Christovich, L.A., Kozhevnikova, E.V., Ryskina, V.L., Stolyarova, E.I., Sundberg, U., & Lacerda, F. (1997). Cross-language analysis of phonetic units in language addressed to infants. *Science, 277,* 684–86.

Kuhn, D. (1992). Cognitive development. In M.H. Bornstein & M.E. Lamb (Eds.), *Developmental psychology. An advanced textbook* (3rd ed., pp. 211–72). Hillsdale, NJ: Erlbaum.

Kuhn, D., Amsel, E., & O'Loughlin, M. (1988). *The development of scientific thinking skills.* San Diego: Academic.

Kuhn, D., Kohlberg, L., Langer, J., & Haan, N. (1977). The development of formal operations in logical and moral judgment. *Genetic Psychology Monographs, 95,* 97–188.

Kuhn, D., Nash, S. C., & Brucken, L. (1978). Sex-role concepts of two- and three-year-olds. *Child Development, 49,* 445-451.

Kulik, J.A., & Kulik, C.C. (1992). Meta-analytic findings on grouping programs. *Gifted Child Quarterly, 36,* 73–7.

Kulin, H., Frontera, M., Demers, I., et al. (1989). The onset of sperm production in pubertal boys—the relationship to gonadotropin excretion. *American Journal of Disabled Children, 143* (2), 190–93.

Kuller, J.A. (1996). Chorionic villus sampling. In J.A. Kuller, N.C. Cheschier, & R.C. Cefalo (Eds.), *Prenatal diagnosis and reproductive genetics* (pp. 145–58). St. Louis, MO: Mosby.

Kuller, J.A., Cheschier, N.C., & Cefalo, R.C. (1996). *Prenatal diagnosis and reproductive genetics.* St. Louis, MO: Mosby.

Kunkel, D., & Roberts, D. (1991). Young minds and marketplace value: Issues in children's advertising. *Journal of Social Issues, 47* (1), 57–72.

Kurdek, L.A., & Fine, M.A. (1994). Family acceptance and family control as predictors of adjustment in young adolescents: Linear, curvilinear, or interactive effects? *Child Development, 65,* 1137–46.

Kurdek, L.A., Fine, M.A., & Sinclair, R.J. (1995). School adjustment in sixth graders: Parenting transitions, peer climate, and peer norm effects. *Child Development, 66,* 430–45.

Kurtz, B.E. (1990). Cultural influences on children's cognitive and meta-cognitive development. In W. Schneider & F.E. Wienert (Eds.), *Interactions among aptitude, strategies, and knowledge in cognitive performance* (pp. 177–99). Hillsdale, NJ: Erlbaum.

Labile, D.J., & Thompson, R.A. (2000). Mother-child discourse, attachment security, shared positive affect, and early conscience development. *Child Development, 71,* 1424–40.

Laboratory of Comparative Human Cognition. (1983). Culture and cognitive development. In P.H. Mussen (Series Ed.) & W. Kessen (Vol. Ed.), *Handbook of child psychology: Vol. 1. History, theory, and methods* (4th ed., pp. 294–356). New York: Wiley.

Ladd, G. W. (1990). Having friends, keeping friends, making friends, and being liked by peers in the classroom: Predictors of children's early school adjustment. *Child Development, 61,* 1081–1100.

Ladd, G.W., Birch, S.H., & Buhs, E.S. (1999). Children's social and scholastic lives in kindergarten: Related spheres of influence? *Child Development, 70,* 1373–1400.

Ladd, G.W., & Golter, B.S. (1988). Parents' management of preschoolers' peer relations: Is it related to children's social competence? *Developmental Psychology, 24,* 109–17.

Ladd, G.W., & Hart, C.H. (1992). Creating informal play opportunities: Are parents' and preschoolers' initiations related to children's competence with peers? *Developmental Psychology, 28,* 1179–87.

Ladd, G.W., Kochenderfer, B.J., & Coleman, C.C. (1996). Friendship quality as a predictor of young children's early school adjustment. *Child Development, 67,* 1103–18.

Ladd, G.W., Kochenderfer, B.J., & Coleman, C.C. (1997). Classroom peer acceptance, friendship, and victimization: Distinct relational systems that contribute uniquely to children's school adjustment. *Child Development, 68,* 1181–97.

Ladd, G.W., & Kochenderfer-Ladd, B. (1998). Parenting behaviors and parent-child relationships: Correlates of peer victimization in kindergarten. *Developmental Psychology 34,* 1450-1458.

Ladd, G.W., & Price, J.M. (1987). Predicting children's social and school adjustment following the transition from preschool to kindergarten. *Child Development, 58,* 1168–89.

Ladd, G.W., Price, J.M., & Hart, C.H. (1988). Predicting preschoolers' play status from their playground behaviors. *Child Development, 59,* 986–92.

La Freniere, P., Strayer, F.F., & Gauthier, R. (1984). The emergence of same-sex affiliative preferences among preschool peers: A developmental ethological perspective. *Child Development, 55,* 1958–65.

Lagattuta, K.H., & Wellman, H.M. (2001). Thinking about the past: Early knowledge about links between prior experience, thinking, and emotion. *Child Development, 72,* 82–102.

Lamaze, F. (1958). *Painless childbirth: Psychoprophylactic method.* London, England: Burke.

Lamb, M.E. (1997). *The role of the father in child development* (3rd ed.). New York: Wiley.

Lamborn, S.D., Mounts, N.S., Steinberg, L., & Dornbusch, S.M. (1991). Patterns of competence and adjustment among adolescents from authoritative, authoritarian, indulgent, and neglectful families. *Child Development, 62,* 1049–65.

Lamborn, S.D., & Steinberg, L. (1993). Emotional autonomy redux: Revising Ryan and Lynch. *Child Development, 64,* 483–99.

Landau, S., Milich, S., & Lorch, E.P. (1992). Visual attention to and comprehension of television in attention-deficit hyperactivity disordered and normal boys. *Child Development, 63,* 928–37.

Langille, D.B., Tomblin Murphy, G., Hughes, J., & Rigby, J.A. (2001). Nova Scotia high school students' interactions with physicians for sexual health information and services. *Canadian Journal of Public Health, 92,* 219–22.

Langlois, J.H. (1986). From the eye of the beholder to behavioral reality: Development of social behaviors and social relations as a function of physical attractiveness. In C.P. Herman, M.P. Zanna, & E.T. Higgins (Eds.), *Physical appearance, stigma, and social behavior: The Ontario Symposium on Personality and Social Psychology* (Vol. 3). Hillsdale, NJ: Erlbaum.

Langlois, J.H., & Downs, A.C. (1979). Peer relations as a function of physical attractiveness: The eye of the beholder or behavioral reality. *Child Development, 50,* 409–18.

Langlois, J.H., Ritter, J.M., Casey, R.J., & Sawin, D.B. (1995). Infant attractiveness predicts maternal behaviors and attitudes. *Developmental Psychology, 31,* 464–72.

Langlois, J.H., Ritter, J.M., Roggman, L.A., & Vaughn, L.S. (1991). Facial diversity and infant preferences for attractive faces. *Developmental Psychology, 27,* 79–84.

Langlois, J.H., Roggman, L.A., Casey, R.J., Ritter, J.M., Reiser-Danner, L.A., & Jenkins, V.Y. (1987). Infant preferences for attractive faces: Rudiments of a stereotype? *Developmental Psychology, 23,* 363–9.

Langlois, J.H., Roggman, L.A., & Rieser-Danner, L.A. (1990). Infants' differential social responses to attractive and unattractive faces. *Developmental Psychology, 26,* 153–9.

Langlois, S., & Morrison, P. (2002). Suicide deaths and suicide attempts. *Health Reports, 13* (2), Statistics Canada Catalogue 82-003. Accessed February 2, 2004 at http://www.statcan.ca/english/studies/82-003/feature/hrar2002013002s0a01.pdf.

Lansford, J.E., & Parker, J.G. (1999). Children's interactions in triads: Behavioral profiles and effects of gender and patterns of friendship among members. *Developmental Psychology, 35,* 80–93.

Lantzouni, E., Frank, G., Golden, N., & Shenker, R. (2002). Reversibility of growth stunting in early onset anorexia nervosa: A prospective study. *Journal of Adolescent Health, 31,* 162–65.

Lanza, E. (1992). Can bilingual 2-year-olds code-switch? *Journal of Child Language, 19,* 633–58.

Laosa, L.M. (1981). Maternal behavior: Sociocultural diversity in modes of family interaction. In R.W. Henderson (Ed.), *Parent–child interaction: Theory, research, and prospects* (pp. 125–67). Orlando, FL: Academic Press.

Lapkin, S. (Ed.). (1998). *French second language education in Canada: Empirical studies.* Toronto: University of Toronto Press.

Lapsley, D.K. (1996). *Moral psychology.* Boulder, CO: Westview.

Larivèe, S., Normandeau, S., & Parent, S. (2000). The French Connection: Some contributions of French-language research in the post-Piagetian era. *Child Development, 71,* 823–39.

Larroque, B., Kaminski, M., & Lelong, N. (1993). Effects on birth weight of alcohol and caffeine consumption during pregnancy. *American Journal of Epidemiology, 137,* 941–50.

Larson, R. (2001). Commentary. In D.R. Anderson, A.C. Huston, K.L. Schmitt, D.L. Linebarger, & J.C. Wright, *Early childhood television viewing and adolescent behavior. Monographs of the Society for Research in Child Development, 66* (1, Serial No. 264).

Larson, R., & Ham, M. (1993). Stress and "storm and stress" in early adolescence: The relationship of negative events with dysphoric affect. *Developmental Psychology, 29,* 130–40.

Larson, R.W., & Richards, M.H. (1991). Daily companionship in late childhood and early adolescence: Changing developmental contexts. *Child Development, 62,* 284–300.

Larson, R.W., Richards, M.H., Moneta, G., Holmbeck, G., & Duckett, E. (1996).

Changes in adolescents' daily interactions with their families from ages 10 to 18: Disengagement and transformation. *Developmental Psychology, 32,* 744–54.

Laumann, E.O., Gagnon, J.H., Michael, R.T., & Michaels, S. (1994). *The social organization of sexuality: Sexual practices in the United States.* Chicago: University of Chicago Press.

Laursen, B., Coy, K.C., & Collins, W.A. (1998). Reconsidering changes in parent-child conflict across adolescence: A meta-analysis. *Child Development, 69,* 817–32.

Laursen, B., Hartup, W.W., & Koplas, A.L. (1996). Towards understanding peer conflict. *Merrill-Palmer Quarterly, 42,* 76–102.

Lavoie, M. (1986). CBC *Sesame Street* at 15. *CBC Sesame Street Newsletter, 5* (1), 2–3.

Leadbeater, B.J., Kuperminc, G.P., Blatt, S.J., & Herzog, C. (1999). A multivariate model of gender differences in adolescents' internalizing and externalizing problems. *Developmental Psychology, 35,* 1268–82.

Leaper, C. (1994). *New directions for child development: Vol. 65. Childhood gender segregation: Causes and consequences.* San Francisco: Jossey-Bass.

Leaper, C. (2000). Gender, affiliation, assertion, and the interactive context of parent-child play. *Developmental Psychology, 36,* 381–93.

Leaper, C., Anderson, K.J., & Sanders, P. (1998). Moderators of gender effects on parents' talk to their children. *Developmental Psychology, 34,* 3–27.

Leaper, C., Tennenbaum, H.R., & Shaffer, T.G. (1999). Communication patterns in African American girls and boys from low-income urban backgrounds. *Child Development, 70,* 1489–503.

Leboyer, F. (1975). *Birth without violence.* New York: Knopf.

Lederberg, A.R., Prezbindowski, A.K., & Spencer, P.E. (2000). Word-learning skills of deaf preschoolers: The development of novel mapping and rapid word-learning strategies. *Child Development, 71,* 1571–85.

Lee, K., Cameron, C.A., Xu, F., Fu, G., & Board, J. (1997). Chinese and Canadian children's evaluations of lying and truth telling: Similarities and differences in the context of pro- and antisocial behaviors. *Child Development, 68* (5), 924–35.

Lee, V.E., Loeb, S., & Lubeck, S. (1998). Contextual effects of pre-kindergarten classrooms for disadvantaged children on cognitive development: The case of Chapter 1. *Child Development, 69,* 479–94.

Leekam, S.R., Lopez, B., & Moore, C. (2000). Attention and joint attention in preschool children with autism. *Developmental Psychology, 36,* 261–73.

LeFevre, J., Sadesky, G., & Bisanz, J. (1996). Selection of procedures in mental addition: Reassessing the problem-size effect in adults. *Journal of Experimental Psychology: Learning, Memory and Cognition, 22,* 216–30.

Lefkowitz, M.M. (1981). Smoking during pregnancy: Long-term effects on offspring. *Developmental Psychology, 17,* 192–4.

Legerstee, M. (1991). The role of people and objects in early imitation. *Journal of Experimental Child Psychology, 51,* 423–33.

Legerstee, M., Anderson, D., & Schaffer, A. (1998). Five- and eight-month-olds recognize their faces and voices as familiar social stimuli. *Child Development, 69,* 37–50.

Legerstee, M., Barna, J., & DiAdamo, C. (2000). Precursors to the development of intention at 6 months: Understanding people and their actions. *Developmental Psychology, 36,* 627–34.

Le Grand, R., Mondloch, C.J., Maurer, D., & Brent, H.P. (2001). Early visual experience and face processing. *Nature, 410* (6831), 890.

Lehman, E.B., McKinley-Pace, M.J., Wilson, J.A., Savsky, M.D., & Woodson, M.E. (1997). Direct and indirect measures of intentional forgetting in children and adults: Evidence for retrieval inhibition and reinstatement. *Journal of Experimental Child Psychology, 64,* 295–316.

Leinbach, M.D., & Fagot, B.I. (1986). Acquisition of gender labeling: A test for toddlers. *Sex Roles, 15,* 655–66.

Leinbach, M.D., & Fagot, B.I. (1993). Categorical habituation to male and female faces: Gender schematic processing in infancy. *Infant Behavior and Development, 16,* 317–22.

LeMare, L.J., & Rubin, K.H. (1987). Perspective taking and peer interaction: Structural and developmental analyses. *Child Development, 58,* 306–15.

LeMare, L.J., Warford, L., & Fernyhough, L. (2001, April 19–22). Peer relationships of Romanian orphans 10 years after being adopted to Canada. Poster presented at the Biennial Meeting of the Society for Research in Child Development, Minneapolis, MN.

Lemery, K.S., Goldsmith, H.H., Klinnert, M.D., & Mrazek, D.A. (1999). Developmental models of infant and childhood temperament. *Developmental Psychology, 35,* 189–204.

Lemonick, M.D. (2001). The genome is mapped. Now what? In K.L. Frieberg (Ed.), *Human development 01/02* (29th ed., pp. 13–7). Guilford, CT: McGraw-Hill/Dushkin.

Lenneberg, E.H. (1967). *Biological foundations of language.* New York: Wiley.

Lepper, M.R. (1985). Microcomputers in education: Motivation and social issues. *American Psychologist, 40,* 1–18.

Lepper, M.R., & Gurtner, J. (1989). Children and computers: Approaching the twenty-first century. *American Psychologist, 44,* 170–8.

Lerner, R.M. (1991). Changing organism–context relations as the basic process of development: A developmental contextual perspective. *Developmental Psychology, 27,* 27–32.

Lerner, R.M. (1996). Relative plasticity, integration, temporality, and diversity in human development: A developmental contextual perspective about theory, process, and method. *Developmental Psychology, 32,* 781–86.

Lerner, R.M., Fisher, C.B., & Weinberg, R.A. (2000). Toward a science of and for the people: Promoting civil society through the application of developmental science. *Child Development, 71,* 11–20.

Lerner, R.M., & von Eye, A. (1992). Sociobiology and human development: Arguments and evidence. *Human Development, 35,* 12–33.

Lester, B.M. (1984). A biosocial model of infant crying. In L.P. Lipsitt (Eds.), *Advances in infancy research* (pp. 167–212). Norwood, NJ: Ablex.

Lester, B.M., Corwin, M.J., Sepkoski, C., Seifer, R., Peucker, M., McLaughlin, S., & Golub, H.L. (1991). Neurobehavioral syndromes in cocaine-exposed newborn infants. *Child Development, 62,* 694–705.

Lester, B.M., Hoffman, J., & Brazelton, T.B. (1985). The rhythmic structure of mother–infant interactions in term and preterm infants. *Child Development, 56,* 15–27.

Lester, B.M., Kotelchuck, M., Spelke, E., Sellers, M.J., & Klein, R.E. (1974). Separation protest in Guatemalan infants: Cross-cultural and cognitive findings. *Developmental Psychology, 10,* 79–85.

LeVay, S. (1996). *Queer science: The use and abuse of research into homosexuality.* Cambridge, MA: MIT Press.

Leve, L.D., & Fagot, B.I. (1997). Gender-role socialization and discipline processes in one- and two-point families. *Sex Roles, 36,* 1–21.

Levin, I., & Druyan, S. (1993). When sociocognitive transaction among peers fails: The case of misconceptions in science. *Child Development, 64*, 1571–91.

LeVine, R.A., Dixon, S., LeVine, S., Richman, A., Liederman, P.H., Keefer, C.H., & Brazelton, T.B. (1994). *Child care and culture: Lessons from Africa.* New York: Cambridge University Press.

Levine, S.C., Huttenlocher, J., Taylor, A., & Langrock, A. (1999). Early sex differences in spatial skill. *Developmental Psychology, 35*, 940–49.

Levinson, D. (1989). *Family violence in cross-cultural perspective.* Newbury Park, CA: Sage.

Leviton, A. (1993). Coffee, caffeine, and reproductive hazards in humans. In S. Garattini (Ed.), *Monographs of the Mario Negri Institute for Pharmacological Research, Milan: Caffeine, Coffee, and Health* (pp. 348–58). New York: Raven Press.

Levitt, M.J., Weber, R.A., Clark, M.C., & McDonnell, P. (1985). Reciprocity of exchange in toddler sharing behavior. *Developmental Psychology, 21*, 122–3.

Levy, F., Hay, D.A., Mcstephen, M., Wood, C., & Waldman, I. (1997). Attention-deficit hyperactivity disorder: A category or a continuum? Genetic analysis of a large-scale twin study. *Journal of the American Academy of Child and Adolescent Psychiatry, 36*, 737–44.

Levy, G.D., Taylor, M.G., & Gelman, S.A. (1995). Traditional and evaluative aspects of flexibility in gender roles, social conventions, moral rules, and physical laws. *Child Development, 66*, 515–31.

Levy, S.R., & Dweck, C.S. (1999). The impact of children's static versus dynamic conceptions of people on stereotype formation. *Child Development, 70*, 1163–80.

Levy-Shiff, R. (1994). Individual and contextual correlates of marital change across the transition to parenthood. *Developmental Psychology, 30*, 591–601.

Levy-Shiff, R., Goldschmidt, I., & Har-Even, D. (1991). Transition to parenthood in adoptive families. *Developmental Psychology, 27*, 131–40.

Levy, Y. (1999). Early metalinguistic competence: Speech monitoring and repair behavior. *Developmental Psychology, 35*, 822–34.

Lewin, L.M., Hops, H., Davis, B., & Dishion, T.J. (1993). Multimethod comparison of similarity in school adjustment of siblings and unrelated children. *Developmental Psychology, 24*, 963–9.

Lewis, C. Freeman, N.H., Kyriakidou, C., Maridaki-Kassotaki, K., & Berridge, D.M. (1996). Social influences on false belief access: Specific sibling influences or general apprenticeship? *Child Development, 67*, 2930–47.

Lewis, M., Alessandri, S.M., & Sullivan, M.W. (1990). Violation of expectancy, loss of control and anger expressions in young infants. *Developmental Psychology, 26*, 745–51.

Lewis, M., Alessandri, S.M., & Sullivan, M.W. (1992). Differences in shame and pride as a function of children's gender and task difficulty. *Child Development, 63*, 630–8.

Lewis, M., & Brooks-Gunn, J. (1979). *Social cognition and the acquisition of self.* New York: Plenum.

Lewis, M., & Ramsay, D.S. (1999). Effect of maternal soothing on infant stress response. *Child Development, 20*, 11–20.

Lewis, M., & Rosenblum, M.A. (1975). *Friendship and peer relations.* New York: Wiley.

Lewis, M., Stanger, C., & Sullivan, M.W. (1989). Deception in 3-year-olds. *Developmental Psychology, 24*, 434–40.

Lewis, M., Sullivan, M.W., Stanger, C., & Weiss, M. (1989). Self-development and self-conscious emotions. *Child Development, 60*, 146–56.

Lewontin, R.C. (1976). Race and intelligence. In N.J. Block & G. Dworkin (Eds.), *The IQ controversy: A critical reader* (pp. 78–92). New York: Pantheon.

Leyens, J.P., Parke, R.D., Camino, L., & Berkowitz, L. (1975). Effects of movie violence on aggression in a field setting as a function of group dominance and cohesion. *Journal of Personality and Social Psychology, 32*, 346–60.

Liben, L.S., & Signorella, M.L. (1993). Gender-schematic processing in children: The role of initial interpretations of stimuli. *Developmental Psychology, 29*, 141–9.

Lidz, C.S. (1997). Dynamic assessment approaches. In D.P. Flanagan, J. Genshaft, & P.L. Harrison (Eds.), *Contemporary intellectual assessment: Theories, tests, and issues* (pp. 281–96). New York: Guilford.

Lieberman, M., Doyle, A.B., & Markiewicz, D. (1999). Developmental patterns of security of attachment to mother and father in late childhood and early adolescence: Association with peer relations. *Child Development, 70*, 202–13.

Liebert, R.M., & Baron, R.A. (1972). Some immediate effects of televised violence on children's behavior. *Developmental Psychology, 6*, 469–75.

Liebert, R.M., & Sprafkin, J. (1988). *The early window: Effects of television on children and youth* (3rd ed.). New York: Pergamon Press.

Lieven, E.V.M. (1994). Crosslinguistic and crosscultural aspects of language addressed to children. In C. Gallaway & B.J. Richards (Eds.), *Input and interaction in language acquisition.* Cambridge, England: Cambridge University Press.

Lillard, A.S. (1993). Pretend play skills and the child's theory of mind. *Child Development, 64*, 348–71.

Lin, C. (1993a). Breech presentation. In C. Lin, M.S. Verp, & R.E. Sabbagha (Eds.), *The high-risk fetus: pathophysiology, diagnosis, management.* New York: Springer-Verlag.

Lin, C. (1993b). Fetal growth retardation. In C. Lin, M.S. Verp, & R.E. Sabbagha (Eds.), *The high-risk fetus: Pathophysiology, diagnosis, management.* New York: Springer-Verlag.

Lin, C. C., & Fu, V. R. (1990). A comparison of child-rearing practices among Chinese, immigrant Chinese, and Caucasian-American parents. *Child Development, 61*, 429-433.

Lindberg, M.A., Keiffer, J., & Thomas, S.W. (1999). Eyewitness testimony for physical abuse as a function of personal experience, development, and focus of study. *Journal of Applied Developmental Psychology, 21*, 555–91.

Linn, M.C., de Benedictis, T., & Delucchi, K. (1982). Adolescent reasoning about advertisements: Preliminary investigations. *Child Development, 53*, 1599–1613.

Linn, M.C., & Petersen, A.C. (1985). Emergence and characterization of sex differences in spatial ability: A meta-analysis. *Child Development, 56*, 1479–98.

Lipsitt, L.P., & Kaye, H. (1964). Conditioned sucking in the human newborn. *Psychonomic Science, 1*, 29–30.

Littenberg, R., Tulkin, S., & Kagan, J. (1971). Cognitive components of separation anxiety. *Developmental Psychology, 4*, 387–8.

Little, A.H., Lipsitt, L.P., & Rovee-Collier, C.K. (1984). Classical conditioning and retention of the infant's eyelid response: Effects of age and interstimulus interval. *Journal of Experimental Child Psychology, 37*, 512–24.

Littschwager, J.C., & Markman, E.M. (1994). Sixteen- and 24-month-olds' use of mutual exclusivity as a default assumption in second-label learning. *Developmental Psychology, 30*, 955–68.

Liu, J., & Chen, Y. (2003). Friendship networks and social, school and psychological adjustment in Chinese junior high school students. *Psychology in the Schools, 40* (1), 5–17.

Livesley, W.J., & Bromley, D.B. (1973). Person perception in childhood and adolescence. London, England: Wiley.

Livson, N., & Peskin, H. (1980). Perspectives on adolescence from longitudinal research. In J. Adelson (Ed.), *Handbook of adolescent psychology* (pp. 47–98). New York: Wiley.

Lobel, M. (1994). Conceptualizations, measurement, and effects of prenatal maternal stress on birth outcomes. *Journal of Behavioral Medicine, 17*, 225–72.

Lobel, T., & Menashri, J. (1993). Relations of conceptions of gender-role transgressions and gender constancy to gender-typed toy preferences. *Developmental Psychology, 29*, 150–5.

Lobel, T., Slone, M., & Winch, G. (1997). Masculinity, popularity, and self-esteem among Israeli preadolescent girls. *Sex Roles, 36*, 395–408.

Locke, D. (2000). Violence against children and youth by family members. In Statistics Canada, Canadian Centre for Justice Statistics, *Family violence in Canada: A statistical profile 2000* (pp. 31–8). Catalogue No. 85-224-XIE. Retrieved November 1, 2001 from http://www.statcan.ca:80/english/freepub/85-224-XIE/0000085-224-XIE.pdf.

Locke, J.L. (1913). *Some thoughts concerning education* (sections 38 & 40). London, England: Cambridge University Press. (Original work published 1690.)

Locke, J.L. (1997). A theory of neurolinguistic development. *Brain and Language, 58*, 265–326.

Loeber, R., & Stouthamer-Loeber, M. (1998). Development of juvenile aggression and violence: Some common misconceptions and controversies. *American Psychologist, 53*, 242–59.

Loehlin, J.C. (1985). Fitting heredity–environment models jointly to twin and adoption data from the California Psychological Inventory. *Behavior Genetics, 15*, 199–221.

Loehlin, J.C. (1992). *Genes and environment in personality development.* Newbury Park, CA: Sage.

Loehlin, J.C., Lindzey, G., & Spuhler, J.N. (1975). *Race differences in intelligence.* New York: W.H. Freeman.

Loehlin, J.C., & Nichols, R.C. (1976). *Heredity, environment, and personality.* Austin: University of Texas Press.

Loftus, E.F., & Pickrell, J.E. (1995). The formation of false memories. *Psychiatric Annals, 25*, 720–5.

London, P. (1970). The rescuers: Motivational hypotheses about Christians who saved Jews from the Nazis. In J. Macaulay & L. Berkowitz (Eds.), *Altruism and helping behavior* (pp. 241–50). Orlando, FL: Academic Press.

Lonigan, C.J., Burgess, S.R., & Anthony, J.L. (2000). Development of emergent literacy and early reading skills in preschool children: Evidence from a latent-variable longitudinal study. *Developmental Psychology, 36*, 596–613.

Lorber, J. (1986). Dismantling Noah's ark. *Sex Roles, 14*, 567–80.

Lord, S. E., Eccles, J. S., & McCarthy, K. A. (1994). Surviving the junior high school transition: Family processes and self-perceptions as protective and risk factors. *Journal of Early Adolescence, 14*, 162-199.

Lore, D. (2000, December 19). Choices grow for treating attention deficit. *Atlanta Constitution*, p. F4.

Lorenz, K.Z. (1937). The companion in the bird's world. *Auk, 54*, 245–73.

Lorenz, K.Z. (1943). The innate forms of possible experience. *Zeitschrift fur Tierpsychologie, 5*, 233–409.

Lorsbach, T.C., Katz, G.A., & Cupak, A.J. (1998). Developmental differences in the ability to inhibit the initial misinterpretation of garden path passages. *Journal of Experimental Child Psychology, 71,* 275–96.

Loupe, D. (1997, May 8). No consensus on best way to teach reading. *Atlanta Constitution,* p. C5.

Lowenthal, B. (2000). Effects of maltreatment and ways to promote children's resiliency. In K.L. Freiberg (Ed.), *Human development 00/01* (28th ed., pp. 151–4). Guilford, CT: Dushkin/McGraw-Hill.

Lowy, J. (2000, February 24). U.S. teen pregnancy rate still high. *Atlanta Constitution,* p. E2.

Lozoff, B. (1989). Nutrition and behavior. *American Psychologist, 44,* 231–6.

Lozoff, B., Park, A., Radan, A., & Wolf, A. (1995). Using the HOME Inventory with infants in Costa Rica. *International Journal of Behavioral Development, 18* (2), 277–95.

Lubart, T.I., & Sternberg, R.J. (1995). An investment approach to creativity: Theory and data. In S.M. Smith, T.B. Ward, & R.A. Finke (Eds.), *The creative cognition approach* (pp. 269–302). Cambridge, MA: MIT Press.

Luecke-Aleksa, D., Anderson, D.R., Collins, P.A., & Schmitt, K.L. (1995). Gender constancy and television viewing. *Developmental Psychology, 31,* 773–80.

Lummis, M., & Stevenson, H.W. (1990). Gender differences in beliefs and achievement: A cross-cultural study. *Developmental Psychology, 26,* 254–63.

Lung, C.T., & Daro, D. (1996). *Current trends in child abuse reporting and fatalities: The results of the 1995 annual fifty state survey.* Chicago: National Committee to Prevent Child Abuse.

Luria, A.R. (1961). *The role of speech in the regulation of normal and abnormal behavior.* New York: Liveright.

Luster, T., & Dubow, E. (1992). Home environment and maternal intelligence as predictors of verbal intelligence: A comparison of preschool and school-age children. *Merrill-Palmer Quarterly, 38,* 151–75.

Luster, T., & McAdoo, H. (1996). Family and child influences on educational attainment: A secondary analysis of the High/Scope Perry preschool data. *Developmental Psychology, 32,* 26–39.

Lustig, J.L., Wolchik, S.A., & Braver, S.L. (1992). Social support in chumships and adjustment in children of divorce. *American Journal of Community Psychology, 20,* 393–9.

Lynch, M.P., Eilers, R.E., Oller, D.K., & Urbano, R.C. (1990). Innateness, experience, and music perception. *Psychological Science, 1,* 272–6.

Lynn, R. (1997). Direct evidence for a genetic basis for black-white differences in IQ. *American Psychologist, 52,* 73–4.

Lyon, T.D., & Flavell, J.H. (1993). Young children's understanding of forgetting over time. *Child Development, 64,* 789–800.

Lyons-Ruth, K., Alpern, L., & Repacholi, B. (1993). Disorganized infant attachment classification and maternal psychosocial problems as predictors of hostile-aggressive behavior in the preschool classroom. *Child Development, 64,* 572–85.

Lyons-Ruth, K., Connell, D.B., Grunebaum, H., & Botein, S. (1990). Infants at social risk: Maternal depression and family support services as mediators of infant development and security of attachment. *Child Development, 61,* 85–98.

Lyons-Ruth, K., Easterbrooks, M.A., & Cibelli, C.D. (1997). Infant attachment strategies, infant mental lag, and maternal depressive symptoms: Predictors of internalizing and externalizing problems at age 7. *Developmental Psychology, 33,* 681–92.

Lytton, H. (1990). Child and parent effects in boys' conduct disorder. A reinterpretation. *Developmental Psychology, 26,* 683–97.

Lytton, H., & Romney, D.M. (1991). Parents' differential socialization of boys and girls: A meta-analysis. *Psychological Bulletin, 109,* 267–96.

Mabbott, D. & Bisanz, J. (2003). Developmental change and individual differences in children's multiplication. *Child Development, 74* (4), 1091–107.

Maccoby, E.E. (1980). *Social development.* San Diego, CA: Harcourt Brace Jovanovich.

Maccoby, E.E. (1988). Gender as a social category. *Developmental Psychology, 24,* 755–65.

Maccoby, E.E. (1992). Family structure and children's adjustment: Is quality of parenting the major mediator? In E.M. Hetherington & W.G. Clingempeel, with E. Anderson, J. Deal, M. Hagan, A. Hollier, & M. Lindner (Eds.), *Coping with marital transitions: A family systems perspective. Monographs of the Society for Research in Child Development, 57* (2–3, Serial No. 227).

Maccoby, E.E. (1998). *The two sexes: Growing up apart, coming together.* Cambridge, MA: Harvard University Press.

Maccoby, E.E. (2002). Gender and group process: A developmental perspective. *Current Directions in Psychological Science, 11* (2), 54–58.

Maccoby, E.E., & Jacklin, C.N. (1974). *The psychology of sex differences.* Stanford, CA: Stanford University Press.

Maccoby, E.E., & Martin, J.A. (1983). Socialization in the context of the family: Parent–child interaction. In P.H. Mussen (Series Ed.) & E.M. Hetherington (Vol. Ed.), *Handbook of child psychology: Vol. 4. Socialization, personality, and social development* (4th ed., pp. 1–101). New York: Wiley.

Macfarlane, A. (1977). *The psychology of childbirth.* Cambridge, MA: Harvard University Press.

MacGregor, S.N., & Chasnoff, I.J. (1993). Substance abuse in pregnancy. In C. Lin, M.S. Verp, & R.E. Sabbagha (Eds.), *The high-risk fetus: Pathophysiology, diagnosis, management.* New York: Springer-Verlag.

Mac Iver, D., & Reuman, D.A. (1988, April). *Decision-making in the classroom and early adolescents' valuing of mathematics.* Paper presented at the annual meeting of the American Educational Research Association, New Orleans, LA.

MacKinnon-Lewis, C., Rabiner, D., & Starnes, R. (1999). Predicting boys' social acceptance and rejection: Role of mother–child interactions and boys' beliefs about peers. *Developmental Psychology, 35,* 632–9.

MacKinnon-Lewis, C., Starnes, R., Volling, B., & Johnson, S. (1997). Perceptions of parenting as predictors of boys' sibling and peer relations. *Developmental Psychology, 33,* 1024–31.

MacKinnon-Lewis, C., Volling, B.L., Lamb, M.E., Dechman, K., Rabiner, D., & Curtner, M.E. (1994). A cross-contextual analysis of boys' social competence: From family to school. *Developmental Psychology, 30,* 325–33.

MacPhee, D., Fritz, J., & Miller-Heyl, J. (1996). Ethnic variations in personal social networks and parenting. *Child Development, 67,* 3278–95.

MacPhee, D., Ramey, C.T., & Yeates, K.O. (1984). Home environment and early cognitive development: Implications for intervention. In A.W. Gottfried (Ed.), *Home environment and early cognition development. Longitudinal research* (pp. 343–69). Orlando, FL: Academic Press.

Madison, L.S., Madison, J.K., & Adubato, S.A. (1986). Infant behavior and development in relation to fetal movement and habituation. *Child Development, 57,* 1475–82.

Magenis, R.E., Overton, K.M., Chamberlin, J., Brady, T., & Lorrien, E. (1977). Parental origin of the extra chromosome in Down's syndrome. *Human Genetics, 37,* 7–16.

Magnusson, D. (1995). Individual development: A holistic, integrated model. In P. Moen, G.H. Elder, Jr., & K. Luscher (Eds.), *Examining lives in context: Perspectives on the ecology of human development* (pp. 19–60). Washington, DC: American Psychological Association.

Mahler, M.S., Pine, F., & Bergman, A. (1975). *The psychological birth of the infant.* New York: Basic Books.

Mahoney, A., Jouriles, E.N., & Scavone, J. (1997). Marital adjustment, marital discord over childrearing, and child behavior problems: Moderating effects of child age. *Journal of Clinical Child Psychology, 26,* 415–23.

Mahoney, J.L. (2000). School extracurricular activity participation as a moderator in the development of antisocial patterns. *Child Development, 71,* 502–16.

Mahoney, J.L., & Cairns, R.B. (1997). Do extracurricular activities protect against early school dropout? *Developmental Psychology, 33,* 241–53.

Main, M., & Cassidy, J. (1988). Categories of response to reunion with the parent at age 6: Predictable from infant attachment classifications and stable over a 1-month period. *Developmental Psychology, 24,* 415–26.

Main, M., & George, C. (1985). Responses of abused and disadvantaged toddlers to distress in age mates: A study in the day-care setting. *Developmental Psychology, 21,* 407–12.

Main, M., & Goldwyn, R. (1994). *Interview-based adult attachment classifications: Related to infant–mother and infant–father attachment.* Unpublished manuscript, University of California, Berkeley.

Main, M., & Solomon, J. (1990). Procedures for identifying infants as disorganized/disoriented during the Ainsworth Strange Situation. In M.T. Greenberg, D. Cicchetti, & E.M. Cummings (Eds.), *Attachment in the preschool years: Theory, research, and intervention* (pp. 21–60). Chicago: University of Chicago Press.

Main, M., & Weston, D.R. (1981). The quality of the toddler's relationship to mother and to father: Related to conflict and the readiness to establish new relationships. *Child Development, 52,* 932–40.

Major, B., & Schmader, T. (1998). Coping with stigma through psychological disengagement. In J. Swim & C. Stangor (Eds.), *Stigma: The target's perspective.* New York: Academic Press.

Malatesta, C.Z., Culver, C., Tesman, J.R., & Shepard, B. (1989). The development of emotion expression during the first two years of life. *Monographs of the Society for Research in Child Development, 54* (1–2, Serial No. 219), 1–104.

Malatesta, C.Z., Grigoryev, P., Lamb, C., Albin, M., & Culver, C. (1986). Emotional socialization and expressive development in preterm and full-term infants. *Child Development, 57,* 316–30.

Malatesta, C.Z., & Haviland, J.M. (1982). Learning display rules: The socialization of emotion expression in infancy. *Child Development, 53,* 991–1003.

Malina, R.M. (1990). Physical growth and performance during the transitional years (9–16). In R. Montemayer, G.R. Adams, & T.P. Gullotta (Eds.), *From childhood to adolescence: A transitional period?* (pp. 41–62). Newbury Park, CA: Sage.

Malinosky-Rummell, R., & Hansen, D.J. (1993). Long-term consequences of childhood physical abuse. *Psychological Bulletin, 114,* 68–79.

Mandel, D.R., Jusczyk, P.W., & Pisoni, D.B. (1995). Infants' recognition of sound patterns of their own names. *Psychological Science, 5,* 314–317.

Mandler, J. (1998). Representation. In W. Damon (Series Ed.) & D. Kuhn & R.S. Siegler (Vol. Eds.), *Handbook of child psychology: Vol. 2. Cognition, perception, and language* (5th ed.). New York: Wiley.

Mandler, J. & McDonough, L. (1995). Long-term recall of event sequences in infancy. *Journal of Experimental Child Psychology, 59,* 457–74.

Mangelsdorf, S.C. (1992). Developmental changes in infant–stranger interaction. *Infant Behavior and Development, 15,* 191–208.

Mangelsdorf, S.C., Plunkett, J.W., Dedrick, C.F., Berlin, M., Meisels, S.J., McHale, J.L., & Dichtellmiller, M. (1996). Attachment security in very low birth weight infants. *Developmental Psychology, 32,* 914–20.

Mangelsdorf, S.C., Shapiro, J.R., & Marzolf, D. (1995). Developmental and temperamental differences in emotion regulation in infancy. *Child Development, 66,* 1817–28.

Mannuzza, S., Klein, R.G., Bessler, A., Malloy, P., & LaPadula, M. (1993). Adult outcome of hyperactive boys: Educational achievement, occupational rank, and psychiatric status. *Archives of General Psychiatry, 50,* 565–76.

Manset, G., & Semmel, M.I. (1997). Are inclusive programs for students with mild disabilities effective? A comparative review of model programs. *Journal of Special Education, 31,* 155–80.

Mao, Y., Moloughney, B.W., Semenciw, R.M., & Morrison, H.I. (1992). Indian reserve and registered Indian mortality in Canada. *Canadian Journal of Public Health, 83* (5), 350–3.

Marcia, J.E. (1980). Identity in adolescence. In J. Adelson (Ed.), *Handbook of adolescent psychology* (pp. 159–81). New York: Wiley.

Marcia, J.E., Waterman, A.S., Matteson, D., Archer, S.C., & Orlofsky, J. (1993). *Ego identity: A handbook for psychosocial research.* New York: Springer-Verlag.

Marcon, R.A. (1999). Differential impact of preschool models on developmental and early learning of inner-city children: A three-cohort study. *Developmental Psychology, 35,* 358–75.

Marcovitch, S., Goldberg, S., Gold, A., Washington, J., Wasson C., Krekwich, K., & Handley-Derry, M. (1997). Determinents of behavioral problems in Romanian children adopted in Ontario. *International Journal of Behavioral Development, 20,* 17–31.

Marcovitch, S., & Zelazo, P.D. (1999). The A-not-B error: Results from a logistic meta-analysis. *Child Development, 70,* 1297–1313.

Marcus, H.R. & Kitayama, S. (1994). A collective fear of the collective: Implications for selves and theories of selves. Special issue: The Self and the Collective. *Personality and Social Psychology Bulletin, 20*(5), 568–79.

Marcus, D.E., & Overton, W.F. (1978). The development of cognitive gender constancy and sex-role preferences. *Child Development, 49,* 434–44.

Marcus, G.F., Pinker, S., Ullman, M., Hollander, M., Rosen, T.J., & Xu, F. (1992). Overregularization in language acquisition. *Monographs of the Society for Research in Child Development, 57* (4, Serial No. 228).

Marean, G.C., Werner, L.A., & Kuhl, P.K. (1992). Vowel categorization by very young infants. *Developmental Psychology, 28,* 396–405.

Marini, Z., & Case, R. (1994). The development of abstract reasoning about the physical and social world. *Child Development, 65,* 147–59.

Markovits, H., & Dumas, C. (1999). Developmental patterns in the understanding of social and physical transitivity. *Journal of Experimental Child Psychology, 73* (2), 95–114.

Markstrom-Adams, C. (1992). A consideration of intervening factors in adolescent identity formation. In G. R. Adams, T. P. Gullotta, & R. Montemayer (Eds.), *Adolescent identity formation* (Advances in Adolescent Development, Vol. 4). Newbury Park, CA: Sage.

Marlier, L., Schall, B., & Soussignan, R. (1998). Neonatal responsiveness to the odor of amniotic and lacteal fluids: A test of perinatal chemosensory continuity. *Child Development, 69,* 611–23.

Marsh, H.W., Craven, R., & Debus, R. (1998). Structure, stability, and development of children's self-concepts: A multicohort-multioccasion study. *Child Development, 69,* 1030–52.

Marshall, N.L., Coll, C.G., Marx, F., McCartney, K., Keefe, N., & Ruh, J. (1997). After-school time and children's behavioral adjustment. *Merrill-Palmer Quarterly, 43,* 497–514.

Marshall, W.A. (1977). *Human growth and its disorders.* Orlando, FL: Academic Press.

Martin, C.L. (1990). Attitudes and expectations about children with non-traditional gender roles. *Sex Roles, 22,* 151–65.

Martin, C.L. (1994). Cognitive influences on the development and maintenance of gender segregation. *New Directions for Child Development, 65,* 35–51.

Martin, C.L., Eisenbud, L., & Rose, H. (1995). Children's gender-based reasoning about toys. *Child Development, 66,* 1453–71.

Martin, C.L., & Fabes, R.A. (2001). The stability and consequences of young children's same-sex peer interactions. *Developmental Psychology, 37,* 431–46.

Martin, C.L., & Halverson, C.F., Jr. (1981). A schematic processing model of sex typing and stereotyping in children. *Child Development, 52,* 1119–34.

Martin, C.L., & Halverson, C.F., Jr. (1983). The effects of sex-typing schemas on young children's memory. *Child Development, 54,* 563–74.

Martin, C.L., & Halverson, C.F., Jr. (1987). The roles of cognition in sex role acquisition. In D.B. Carter (Ed.), *Current conceptions of sex roles and sex typing: Theory and research.* New York: Praeger.

Martin, G.B., & Clark, R.D., III. (1982). Distress crying in neonates: Species and peer specificity. *Developmental Psychology, 18,* 3–9.

Martorell, R. (1980). Interrelationships between diet, infectious disease, and nutritional status. In L.S. Green & F.E. Johnston (Eds.), *Social and biological predictors of nutritional status, physical growth, and neurological development* (pp. 81–106). New York: Academic Press.

Marx, M.H., & Henderson, B.B. (1996). A fuzzy trace analysis of categorical inferences and instantial associations as a function of retention interval. *Cognitive Development, 11,* 551–69.

Marzolf, D.P., & DeLoache, J.S. (1994). Transfer in young children's understanding of spatial representation. *Child Development, 65,* 7–15.

Masataka, N. (1992). Early ontogeny of vocal behavior of Japanese infants in response to maternal speech. *Child Development, 63,* 1177–85.

Masataka, N. (1996). Perception of motherese in a signed language by 6-month-old deaf infants. *Developmental Psychology, 32,* 874–9.

Masden, A.S., Coatsworth, J.D., Neeman, J., Gest, J.D., Tellegen, A., & Garmezy, N. (1995). The structure and coherence of competence from childhood through adolescence. *Child Development, 66,* 1635–59.

Mason, C.A., Cauce, A.M., Gonzales, N., & Hiraga, Y. (1996). Neither too sweet nor too sour: Problem peers, maternal control, and problem behavior in African-American adolescents. *Child Development, 67,* 2115–30.

Mason, M.G., & Gibbs, J.C. (1993). Social perspective taking and moral judgment among college students. *Journal of Adolescent Research, 8,* 109–23.

Masters, J.C., Ford, M.E., Arend, R., Grotevant, H.D., & Clark, L.V. (1979). Modeling and labeling as integrated determinants of children's sex-typed imitative behavior. *Child Development, 50,* 364–71.

Matejcek, Z., Dytrych, Z., & Schuller, V. (1979). The Prague study of children born from unwanted pregnancies. *International Journal of Mental Health, 7,* 63–74.

Matias, R., & Cohn, J.F. (1993). Are Max-specified infant facial expressions during face-to-face interaction consistent with differential emotions theory? *Developmental Psychology, 29,* 524–31.

Maticka-Tyndale, E. (1997). Reducing the incidence of sexually transmitted disease through behavioural and social change. *Canadian Journal of Human Sexuality, 6* (2), 89–104.

Matlin, M.W., & Foley, H.J. (1997). *Sensational and perception* (4th ed.). Boston: Allyn & Bacon.

Matsumoto, D. (1990). Cultural similarities and differences in display rules. *Motivation and Emotion, 14,* 195–214.

Matthews, K.A., Batson, C.D., Horn, J., & Rosenman, R.H. (1981). "Principles in his nature which interest him in the fortune of others": The heritability of empathic concern for others. *Journal of Personality, 49,* 237–47.

Maurer, D., Stager, C.L., & Mondloch, C.J. (1999). Cross-modal transfer of shape is difficult to demonstrate in one-month-olds. *Child Development, 70* (5), 1047–57.

Mayberry, R.I. (1994). The importance of childhood to language acquisition: Evidence from American Sign Language. In J.C. Goodman & H.C. Nusbalm (Eds.), *The development of speech perception: The transition from speech sounds to spoken words* (pp. 57–90). Cambridge, MA: MIT Press.

Maye, J., Werker, J. Gerken, L. (2002). Infant sensitivity to distributional information can affect phonetic discrimination. *Cognition, 82,* 101–11.

Mayer, F.S., & Sutton, K. (1996). *Personality: An integrative approach.* Saddle River, NJ: Prentice-Hall.

Mayes, L. (2002). A behavioural teratogenic model of the impact of prenatal cocaine exposure on arousal regulatory systems. *Neurotoxicology and Teratology, 24,* 385-395.

Mayes, L.C., & Zigler, E. (1992). An observational study of the affective concomitants of mastery in infants. *Journal of Psychology and Psychiatry, 4,* 659–67.

McCall, R.B. (1977). Challenges to a science of developmental psychology. *Child Development, 48,* 333–44.

McCall, R.B., Applebaum, M.I., & Hogarty, P.S. (1973). Developmental changes in mental performance. *Monographs of the Society for Research in Child Development, 38* (3, Serial No. 150).

McCall, R.B., & Carriger, M.S. (1993). A meta-analysis of infant habituation and recognition memory performance as predictors of later IQ. *Child Development, 64,* 57–79.

McCall, R.B., & Groark, C.J. (2000). The future of applied developmental research and public policy. *Child Development, 71,* 197–204.

McCartney, K., Harris, M.J., & Bernieri, F. (1990). Growing up and growing apart: A developmental meta-analysis of twin studies. *Psychological Bulletin, 107,* 226–37.

McCarton, C.M., Brooks-Gunn, J.,

Wallace, I.F., Bauer, C.R., Bennett, F.C., Bernbaum, J.C., Broyles, S., Casey, P.H., McCormick, M.C., Scott, D.T., Tyson, J., Tonascia, J., & Meinhart, C.L. (1997). Results at age 8 years of early intervention for low-birth-weight premature infants. *Journal of the American Medical Association, 277*, 126–32.

McCarty, M.E., & Ashmead, D.H. (1999). Visual control of reaching and grasping in infants. *Developmental Psychology, 35*, 620–31.

McClelland, D.C., Atkinson, J.W., Clark, R.A., & Lowell, E.L. (1953). *The achievement motive.* East Norwalk, CT: Appleton-Century-Crofts.

McClelland, J.L., & Rumelhart, D.E. (1986). *Parallel distributed processing* (Vols. 1 & 2). Cambridge, MA: MIT Press.

McCloskey, L.A., Figueredo, A.J., & Koss, M.P. (1995). The effects of systematic family violence on children's mental health. *Child Development, 66*, 1239–61.

McCubbin, J.A., Lawson, E.J., Cox, S., Shermin, J.J., Norton, J.A., & Read, J.A. (1996). Prenatal maternal blood pressure response to stress predicts birth weight and gestational age: A preliminary study. *American Journal of Obstetrics and Gynecology, 175*, 706–12.

McFadyen-Ketchum, S.A., Bates, J.E., Dodge, K.A., & Pettit, G.S. (1996). Patterns of change in early childhood aggressive-disruptive behavior: Gender differences in predictions from early coercive and affectionate mother–child interactions. *Child Development, 67*, 2417–33.

McGhee, P.E., & Frueh, T. (1980). Television viewing and the learning of sex-role stereotypes. *Sex Roles, 6*, 179–88.

McGhee-Bidlack, B. (1991). The development of noun definitions: a metalinguistic analysis. *Journal of Child Languages, 18*, 417–34.

McGilley, B.M., & Pryor, T.L. (1998). Assessment and treatment of bulimia nervosa. *American Family Physician, 69*, 113–19.

McGilly, K., & Siegler, R.S. (1990). The influence of encoding strategic knowledge on children's choices among serial recall strategies. *Developmental Psychology, 26*, 931–41.

McGraw, M.B. (1935). *Growth: A study of Johnny and Jimmy.* East Norwalk, CT: Appleton-Century-Crofts.

McGue, M., Sharma, A., & Benson, P. (1996). The effect of common rearing on adolescent adjustment: Evidence from a U.S. adoption cohort. *Developmental Psychology, 32*, 604–13.

McHale, J.P. (1995). Coparenting and triadic interactions during infancy: The roles of marital distress and child gender. *Developmental Psychology, 31*, 985–96.

McHale, S.M., Crouter, A.C., McGuire, S.A., & Updegraff, K.A. (1995). Congruence between mothers' and fathers' differential treatment of siblings: Links with family relations and children's well-being. *Child Development, 66*, 116–28.

McHale, S.M., Crouter, A.C., & Tucker, C.J. (1999). Family context and gender role socialization in middle childhood: Comparing girls to boys and sisters to brothers. *Child Development, 70*, 990–1004.

McHale, S.M., & Gamble, W.C. (1989). Sibling relationships of children with disabled and nondisabled brothers and sisters. *Developmental Psychology, 25*, 421–9.

McHale, S.M., Updegruff, K.A., Helms-Erikson, H., & Crouter, A.C. (2001). Sibling influences on gender development in middle childhood and early adolescence: A longitudinal study. *Developmental Psychology, 37*, 115–25.

McKay, A. (1998). *Sexual ideology and schooling: Towards democratic sexuality education.* London, ON: Althouse Press.

McKenna, M. A. J. (1997, May 2). U.S., Georgia get welcome news on teenagers and sex. *Atlanta Constitution*, p. D1.

McKenna, M.W., & Ossoff, E.P. (1998). Age differences in children's comprehension of a popular television program. *Child Study Journal, 28*, 53–68.

McKeough, A. (1992). Testing for the presence of a central social structure: Use of the transfer paradigm. In R. Case (Ed.), *The mind's staircase: Stages in the development of human intelligence* (pp. 207–25). Hillsdale, NJ: Erlbaum.

McKeough, A. (2000, October). *Central social structures in childhood and adolescence: Mapping the development of narrative thought.* Paper presented at A Design for Development: The Legacy of Robbie Case. Conference of the Department of Human Development and Applied Psychology, Ontario Institute for Studies in Education, Toronto, ON.

McKeough, A. & Genereux, R. (2003). Transformation in narrative thought during adolescence: The Structure and content of story compositions. *Journal of Educational Psychology, 95* (3), 537–52.

McKeough, A., Misfeldt, D., Hubley, K., Deprey, L., Foulkes, E., Malcolm, J., & Fung, T. (2000). *The development of narrative thought in late childhood and early adolescence.* Paper presented at the annual meeting of the Canadian Society for the Study of Education, Edmonton, AB.

McKusick, V.A. (1995). *Mendelian inheritance in man* (10th ed.). Baltimore, MD: Johns Hopkins University Press.

McLoyd, V.C. (1989). Socialization and development in a changing economy: The effects of paternal job and income loss on children. *American Psychologist, 44*, 293–302.

McLoyd, V.C. (1990). The impact of economic hardship on Black families and children: Psychological distress, parenting, and socioemotional development. *Child Development, 61*, 311–46.

McLoyd, V.C. (1998). Socioeconomic disadvantage and child development. *American Psychologist, 53*, 185–204.

McMahon, M.J., & Katz, V.L. (1996). Clinical teratology. In J.A. Kuller, N.C. Cheschier, & R.C. Cefalo (Eds.), *Prenatal diagnosis and reproductive genetics* (pp. 207–17). St. Louis, MO: Mosby.

McNeill, D. (1970). *The acquisition of language.* New York: Harper & Row.

McNeilly-Choque, M.K., Hart, C.H., Robinson, C.C., Nelson, L.J., & Olsen, S.F. (1996). Overt and relational aggression on the playground: Correspondence among different informants. *Journal of Research in Childhood Education, 11*, 47–67.

Mead, G.H. (1934). *Mind, self, and society.* Chicago: University of Chicago Press.

Mead, M. (1935). *Sex and temperament in three primitive societies.* New York: William Morrow.

Mead, M., & Newton, N. (1967). Cultural patterning of perinatal behavior. In S.A. Richardson & A.F. Guttmacher (Eds.), *Childbearing: Its social and psychological aspects* (pp. 142–244). Baltimore, MD: Williams & Wilkins.

Measelle, J.R., Albow, J.C., Cowan, P., & Cowan, C.P. (1998). Assessing young children's views of their academic, social, and emotional lives: An evaluation of the self-perception scales of the Berkeley Puppet Interview. *Child Development, 69*, 1556–76.

Media Analysis Laboratory. (1998, October). Video game culture: Leisure and play preferences of B.C. teens. Retrieved November 3, 2001 from http://www.media-awareness.ca/eng/issues/violence/resource/reports/vgames.htm.

Media Awareness Network. (1997). The white screen. Retrieved November 3, 2001 from http://www.media-awareness.ca/eng/med/class/teamedia/invisble.htm.

Mediascope. (1996). *National Television Violence Study: Executive summary 1994–1995.* Studio City, CA: Author.

Mehan, H., Villaneueva, I., Hubbard, L., & Lintz, A. (1996). *Constructing school success: The consequences of untracking low-achievement students.* New York: Cambridge University Press.

Mehlman, M.J., & Botkin, J.R. (1998). *Access to the genome: The challenge to equality.* Washington, DC: Georgetown University Press.

Meier, R.P. (1991). Language acquisition by deaf children. *American Scientist, 79*, 69–70.

Meilman, P.W. (1979). Cross-sectional age changes in ego identity status during adolescence. *Developmental Psychology, 15*, 230–1.

Mekos, D., Hetherington, E.M., & Reiss, D. (1996). Sibling differences in problem behavior and parental treatment in nondivorced and remarried families. *Child Development, 67*, 2148–65.

Melot, A.M. (1998). The relationship between metacognitive knowledge and metacognitive experiences: Acquisition and re-elaboration. *European Journal of Psychology of Education, 13*, 75–89.

Melson, G.F., Peet, S., & Sparks, C. (1991). Children's attachments to their pets: Links to socioemotional development. *Children's Environmental Quarterly, 8*, 55–65.

Meltzoff, A.N. (1988a). Imitation of televised models by infants. *Child Development, 59*, 1221–9.

Meltzoff, A.N. (1988b). Infant imitation after a 1-week delay: Long-term memory for novel acts and multiple stimuli. *Developmental Psychology, 24*, 470–6.

Meltzoff, A.N. (1988c). Infant imitation and memory: Nine-month-olds in immediate and deferred tests. *Child Development, 59*, 217–25.

Meltzoff, A.N. (1990a). Foundations for developing a concept of self: The role of imitation in relating self to other and the value of social mirroring, social modeling, and self-practice in infancy. In D. Cicchetti & M. Beeghly (Eds.), *The self in transition: Infancy to childhood* (pp. 139–164). Chicago: University of Chicago Press.

Meltzoff, A.N. (1990b). Towards a developmental cognitive science: The implications of cross-modal matching and imitation for the development of memory in infancy. *Annals of the New York Academy of Sciences, 608*, 1–37.

Meltzoff, A.N. (1995a). Understanding the intentions of others: Re-enactment of intended acts by 18-month-old children. *Developmental Psychology, 31*, 838–50.

Meltzoff, A.N. (1995b). What infant memory tells us about infantile amnesia: Long-term recall and deferred imitation. *Journal of Experimental Child Psychology, 59*, 497–515.

Meltzoff, A.N., & Moore, M.K. (1977). Imitation of facial and manual gestures by human neonates. *Science, 198*, 75–8.

Meltzoff, A.N., & Moore, M.K. (1992). Early imitation within a functional framework: The importance of person, identity, movement, and development. *Infant Behavior and Development, 15*, 479–505.

Mendelson, M., Mendelson, B., & Andrews, J. (2000). Self-esteem, body esteem, and body-mass in late adolescence. Is a competence x importance model needed? *Journal of Applied Development Psychology, 21*, 249–66.

Mendelson, M., Mendelson, B., & White, D. (2001). Body-esteem scale for adolescents and adults. *Journal of Personality Assessment, 76*, 90–106.

Merewood, A. (2000). Sperm under siege. In K.L. Freiberg (Ed.), *Human development 00/01* (28th ed., pp. 41–5). Guilford, CT: McGraw-Hill/Dushkin.

Mervis, C.B., Golinkoff, R.M., & Bertrand, J. (1994). Two-year-olds readily learn multiple labels for the same basic-level category. *Child Development, 65,* 1163–77.

Mervis, C.B., & Johnson, K.E. (1991). Acquisition of the plural morpheme: A case study. *Developmental Psychology, 27,* 222–35.

Messinger, L. (2001). Transitional marriage stages from divorce to remarriage. *DivorceMagazine.Com.* Retrieved September 4, 2001 from http://www.DivorceMagazine.com/proforum/articles/marriagestages.html.

Meulemans, T., Van der Linden, M., & Perruchet, P. (1998). Implicit sequence learning in children. *Journal of Experimental Child Psychology, 69,* 199–21.

Meyer-Bahlberg, H.F.L., Ehrhardt, A.A., Rosen, L.R., Gruen, R.S., Veridiano, N.P., Vann, F.H., & Neuwalder, H.F. (1995). Prenatal estrogens and the development of homosexual orientation. *Developmental Psychology, 31,* 12–21.

Midgett, J., Ryan, B.A., Adams, G.R., & Corville-Smith, J. (2002). Complicating achievement and self-esteem: Considering the joint effects of child characteristics and parent-child interactions. *Contemporary Educational Psychology, 27* (1), 132–43.

Midgley, C., Feldlaufer, H., & Eccles, J.S. (1989). Student/teacher relations and attitudes toward mathematics before and after the transition to junior high school. *Child Development, 60,* 981–92.

Millberger, S., Biederman, J., Faraone, S.V., Chen, L., & Jones, J. (1996). Is maternal smoking during pregnancy a risk factor for attention deficit hyperactivity disorder in children? *American Journal of Psychiatry, 153,* 1138–42.

Miller, B.C., Fan, X., Christensen, M., Grotevant, H.D., & Van Dulmen, M. (2000). Comparisons of adopted and nonadopted adolescents in a large, nationally representative sample. *Child Development, 71,* 1458–73.

Miller, C.L. (1983). Developmental changes in male/female voice classification by infants. *Infant Behavior and Development, 6,* 313–30.

Miller, C.L., Miceli, P.J., Whitman, T.L., & Borkowski, J.G. (1996). Cognitive readiness to parent and intellectual-emotional development in children of adolescent mothers. *Developmental Psychology, 32,* 533–41.

Miller, G.V. (1995). *The gay male's odyssey in the corporate world.* Binghamton, NY: Haworth Press.

Miller, J.L., & Eimas, P.D. (1996). Internal structure of voicing categories in early infancy. *Perception and Psychophysics, 58,* 1157–67.

Miller, K.F., Smith, C.M., Zhu, J., & Zhang, H. (1995). Preschool origins of cross-national differences in mathematical competence. *Psychological Science, 6,* 56–60.

Miller, K.S., Levin, M.L., Whitaker, D.J., & Xu, X. (1998). Patterns of condom use among adolescents: The impact of mother-adolescent communication. *American Journal of Public Health, 88,* 1542–44.

Miller, L.T., & Vernon, P.A. (1997). Developmental changes in speed of information processing in young children. *Developmental Psychology, 33,* 549–54.

Miller, N.B., Cowan, P.A., Cowan, C.P., Hetherington, E.M., & Clingempeel, W.G. (1993). Externalizing in preschoolers and early adolescents: A cross-study replication of a family model. *Developmental Psychology, 29,* 3–18.

Miller, P.A., Eisenberg, N., Fabes, R.A., & Shell, R. (1996). Relations of moral reasoning and vicarious emotion to young children's prosocial behavior toward peers and adults. *Developmental Psychology, 32,* 210–9.

Miller, P.H. (1990). The development of strategies of selective attention. In D.F. Bjorklund (Ed.), *Children's strategies: Contemporary views of cognitive development* (pp. 157–84). Hillsdale, NJ: Erlbaum.

Miller, P.H. (2000). How best to utilize a deficiency. *Child Development, 71,* 1013–7.

Miller, P.H., & Seier, W.L. (1994). Strategy utilization deficiencies in children. In H.W. Reese (Ed.), *Advances in child development and behavior* (Vol. 25, pp. 107–56). New York: Academic Press.

Miller, P.H., & Weiss, M.G. (1981). Children's attention allocation, understanding of attention, and performance on the incidental learning task. *Child Development, 52,* 1183–90.

Miller, P.H., & Weiss, M.G. (1982). Children's and adults' knowledge about what variables affect selective attention. *Child Development, 53,* 543–9.

Miller, P.H., Woody-Ramsey, J., & Aloise, P.A. (1991). The role of strategy effortfulness in strategy effectiveness. *Developmental Psychology, 27,* 738–45.

Miller, S.A. (1997). *Developmental research methods* (2nd ed.). Englewood Cliffs, NJ: Prentice-Hall.

Mills, R.S.L., & Rubin, K.H. (1990). Parental beliefs about problematic social behaviors in early childhood. *Child Development, 61,* 138–51.

Milunsky, A. (1992). *Genetic disorders and the fetus: Diagnosis, prevention, and treatment* (3rd ed.). Baltimore, MD: Johns Hopkins University Press.

Ministry of Health Services, British Columbia Vital Statistics Agency. (2001). *British Columbia Vital Statistics Agency new Adoption Act.* Retrieved May 20, 2001 from http://www.vs.gov.bc.ca/adoption.

Minton, H.L., & Schneider, F.W. (1980). *Differential psychology.* Pacific Grove, CA: Brooks/Cole.

Minuchin, P.P. (1988). Relationships within the family: A systems perspective on development. In R.A. Hinde & J. Stevenson-Hinde (Eds.), *Relationships within families: Mutual influences* (pp. 7–26). New York: Oxford University Press.

Minuchin, S., Rosman, B.L., & Baker, L. (1978). *Psychomatic families: Anorexia nervosa in context.* Cambridge, MA: Harvard University Press.

Mischel, W. (1974). Processes in delay of gratification. In L. Berkowitz (Ed.), *Advances in experimental social psychology* (Vol. 7, pp. 249–92). New York: Academic Press.

Mistry, J. (1997). The development of remembering in cultural context. In N. Cowan (Ed.), *The development of memory in childhood* (pp. 343–68). Hove, England: Psychology Press.

Mitchell, J.E., Baker, L.A., & Jacklin, C.N. (1989). Masculinity and femininity in twin children: Genetic and environmental factors. *Child Development, 60,* 1475–85.

Mitchell, P. (1997). *Introduction to theory of mind: Children, autism, and apes.* London, England: Arnold.

Miura, I.T., Okamoto, Y., Vlahovic-Stetic, V., Kim, C.C., & Han, J.H. (1999). Language supports for children's understanding of numerical fractions: A cross-national comparison. *Journal of Experimental Child Psychology, 74,* 356–65.

Miyawaki, K., Strange, W., Verbrugge, R., Liberman, A.M., Jenkins, J.J., & Fujimura, D. (1975). An effect of linguistic experience: The discrimination of [r] and [l] by native speakers of Japanese and English. *Perception and Psychophysics, 18,* 331–40.

Mize, J., & Ladd, G.W. (1990). A cognitive–social learning approach to social skill training with low-status preschool children. *Developmental Psychology, 26,* 388–97.

Mize, J. & Pettit, G.S. (1997). Mother's social coaching, mother–child relationship style, and children's peer competence: Is the medium the message? *Child Development, 68,* 312–22.

Mize, J., Pettit, G.S., & Brown, E.G. (1995). Mothers' supervision of their children's peer play: Relations with beliefs, perceptions, and knowledge. *Developmental Psychology, 31,* 311–21.

Moely, B.E., Santulli, K.A., & Obach, M.S. (1995). Strategy instruction, metacognition, and motivation in the elementary school classroom. In F.E. Weinert & W. Schneider (Eds.), *Memory performance and competencies: Issues in growth and development* (pp. 301–21). Hillsdale, NJ: Erlbaum.

Moerk, E.L. (1989). The LAD was a lady and the tasks were ill-defined. *Developmental Review, 9,* 21–57.

Moffitt, T. (1993). Adolescence-limited and life-course persistent antisocial behavior: A developmental taxonomy. *Psychological Review, 100,* 674–701.

Molfese, D.L. (1977). Infant cerebral asymmetry. In S.J. Segalowitz & F.A. Gruber (Eds.), *Language development and neurological theory.* New York: Academic Press.

Molina, B.S.G., & Chassin, L. (1996). The parent–adolescent relationship at puberty: Hispanic ethnicity and parental alcoholism as moderators. *Developmental Psychology, 32,* 675–86.

Moller, L.C., & Serbin, L.A. (1996). Antecedents of toddler gender segregation: Cognitive consonance, gender-typed toy preferences and behavioral compatibility. *Sex Roles, 35,* 445–60.

Monass, J.A., & Engelhard, J.A., Jr. (1990). Home environment and the competitiveness of accomplished individuals in four talent fields. *Developmental Psychology, 26,* 264–8.

Mondloch, C.J., Geldart, S., Maurer, D., & Le Grand, R. (2003). Developmental changes in face processing skills. *Journal of Experimental Child Psychology, 86* (1), 67–84.

Mondloch, C.J., Le Grand, R., & Maurer, D. (2002). Configural face processing develops more slowly than featural face processing. *Perception, 31* (5), 553–66.

Money, J. (1985). Pediatric sexology and hermaphrodism. *Journal of Sex and Marital Therapy, 11,* 139–56.

Money, J. (1988). *Gay, straight, and in-between: The sexology of erotic orientation.* New York: Oxford University Press.

Money, J., & Ehrhardt, A. (1972). *Man and woman, boy and girl.* Baltimore, MD: Johns Hopkins University Press.

Montemayor, R., & Eisen, M. (1977). The development of self-conceptions from childhood to adolescence. *Developmental Psychology, 13,* 314–9.

Moon, C., Cooper, R.P., & Fifer, W.P. (1993). Two-day-olds prefer their native language. *Infant Behavior and Development, 16,* 495–500.

Moore, C., Angelopoulos, M., & Bennett, P. (1999). Word learning in the context of referential and salience cues. *Developmental Psychology, 35,* 60–68.

Moore, E.G.J. (1986). Family socialization and the IQ test performance of traditionally and transracially adopted black children. *Developmental Psychology, 22,* 317–26.

Moore, K.L., & Persaud, T.V.N. (1993). *Before we are born: Essentials of embryology and birth defects* (4th ed.). Philadelphia, PA: Saunders.

Moore, S.M. (1995). Girls' understanding and social constructions of menarche. *Journal of Adolescence, 18,* 87–104.

Morgan, G.A., & Ricciuti, H.N. (1969). Infants' responses to strangers during the first year. In B.M. Foss (Ed.), *Determinants of infant behavior* (Vol. 4, pp. 253–72). London, England: Methuen.

Morgan, J.L., & Saffran, J.R. (1995). Emerging integration of sequential and suprasegmental information in preverbal speech segmentation. *Child Development, 66,* 911–36.

Morison, P., & Masten, A.S. (1991). Peer reputation in middle childhood as a predictor of adaptation in adolescence: A seven-year follow-up. *Child Development, 62,* 991–1007.

Morison, S.J., Ames, E.W., & Chisholm, K. (1995). The development of children adopted from Romanian orphanages. *Merrill-Palmer Quarterly, 41* (4), 411–30.

Morison, S.J., & Ellwood, A. (2000). Resiliency in the aftermath of deprivation. A second look at the development of Romanian orphanage children. *Merrill-Palmer Quarterly, 46* (4), 717–37.

Morris, M. (2000, May 29). *Women, poverty and Canadian public policy in an era of globalization.* Paper presented to the International Colloquium: Globalization, Societies, Cultures. Congress of the Social Sciences and Humanities, Edmonton, AB. Retrieved August 14, 2001 from http://www.criaw-icref.ca/Poverty_and_globalization.htm.

Morrison, F.J., Griffith, E.M., & Alberts, D.M. (1997). Native-nurture in the classroom: Entrance age, school readiness, and learning in children. *Developmental Psychology, 33,* 254–62.

Morrison, F.J., Smith, L., & Dow-Ehrensberger, M. (1995). Education and cognitive development: A natural experiment. *Developmental Psychology, 31,* 789–99.

Mortimer, J.T., Finch, M.D., Ryu, S., Shanahan, M.J., & Call, K.T. (1996). The effects of work intensity on adolescent mental health, achievement, and behavioral adjustment: New evidence from a prospective study. *Child Development, 67,* 1243–61.

Moses, L.J., Coon, J.A., & Wusinich, N. (2000). Young children's understanding of desire information. *Developmental Psychology, 36,* 77–90.

Moshman, D. (1998). Cognitive development beyond childhood. In W. Damon (Series Ed.) & D. Kuhn & R.S. Siegler (Vol. Eds.), *Handbook of child psychology: Vol. 2. Cognitive, language, and perceptual development.* New York: Wiley.

Mueller, C.M., & Dweck, C.S. (1998). Praise for intelligence can undermine children's motivation and performance. *Journal of Personality and Social Psychology, 75,* 33–52.

Mueller, E., & Lucas, T. (1975). A developmental analysis of peer interactions among toddlers. In M. Lewis & L. Rosenblum (Eds.), *Friendship and peer relations.* New York: Wiley.

Muir, D., & Hains, S. (1999). Young infants' perception of adult intentionality: Adult contingency and eye direction. In P. Rochat (Ed.), *Early social cognition: Understanding others in the first months of life* (pp. 155–87). Hillsdale, NJ: Erlbaum.

Muir-Broaddus, J.E. (1995). Gifted underachievers: Insights from the characteristics of strategic functioning associated with giftedness and achievement. *Learning and Individual Differences, 7,* 189–206.

Mullis, A.K., Mullis, R.L., & Normandin, D. (1992). Cross-sectional and longitudinal comparisons of adolescent self-esteem. *Adolescence, 27,* 51–61.

Mumford, M.D., & Gustafson, S.B. (1988). Creativity syndrome: Integration, application, and innovation. *Psychological Bulletin, 103,* 27–43.

Mumme, D.L., Fernald, A., & Herrera, C. (1996). Infants' responses to facial and vocal emotional signals in a social referencing paradigm. *Child Development, 67,* 3219–37.

Munro, G., & Adams, G.R. (1977). Ego-identity formation in college students and working youth. *Developmental Psychology, 13,* 523–4.

Munroe, R.H., Shimmin, H.S., & Munroe, R.L. (1984). Gender understanding and sex-role preferences in four cultures. *Developmental Psychology, 20,* 673–82.

Murphy, C.M., & Blumenthal, D.R. (2000). The mediating influence of interpersonal problems on the integenerational transmission of relationship aggression. *Personal Relationships, 7,* 203–18.

Murphy, K., & Schneider, B. (1994). Coaching socially rejected early adolescents regarding behaviors used by peers to infer liking: A dyad-specific intervention. *Journal of Early Adolescence, 14,* 82–94.

Murray, A.D., Dolby, R.M., Nation, R.L., & Thomas, D.B. (1981). Effects of epidural anesthesia on newborns and their mothers. *Child Development, 52,* 71–82.

Murray, B. (2000). Reinventing class discussion online. *Monitor on Psychology, 31,* 54–6.

Murray, L., Fiori-Cowley, A., & Hooper, R. (1996). The impact of postnatal depression and associated adversity on early mother–infant interactions and later infant outcome. *Child Development, 67,* 2512–26.

Mussen, P.H., & Rutherford, E. (1963). Parent–child relations and parental personality in relation to young children's sex-role preferences. *Child Development, 34,* 589–607.

Mustard, J.F., McCain, M.N., & Bertrand, J. (2000, Autumn). Changing beliefs to change policy: The early years study. *Isuma, 1* (2). Retrieved November 19, 2001 from http://www.isuma.net/v01n02/mustard/mustard_e.shtml.

Muter, V., Hulme, C., Snowling, M., & Taylor, S. (1998). Segmentation, not rhyming, predicts early progress in learning to read. *Journal of Experimental Child Psychology, 71,* 3–27.

Nagin, D., & Tremblay, R.E. (1999). Trajectories of boys' physical aggression, opposition, and hyperactivity on the path to physically violent and nonviolent juvenile delinquency. *Child Development, 70,* 1181–96.

Naigles, L.G. (1990). Children use syntax to learn verb meanings. *Journal of Child Language, 17,* 357–74.

Naigles, L.G., & Gelman, S.A. (1995). Overextensions in comprehension and production revisited: Preferential looking in a study of dog, cat, and cow. *Journal of Child Language, 22,* 19–46.

Naigles, L.G., & Hoff-Ginsberg, E. (1995). Input to verb learning: Evidence for the plausibility of syntactic bootstrapping. *Developmental Psychology, 31,* 827–37.

Nanez, J., & Yonas, A. (1994). Effects of luminance and texture motion on infant defensive reactions to optical collision. *Infant Behavior and Development, 17,* 165–74.

Nastasi, B.K., & Clements, D.H. (1993). Motivational and social outcomes of cooperative computer education environments. *Journal of Computing in Childhood Education, 4,* 15–43.

Nastasi, B.K., & Clements, D.H. (1994). Effectance motivation, perceived scholastic competence, and higher-order thinking in two cooperative computer environments. *Journal of Educational Computing Research, 10,* 249–75.

Needlman, R., Stevenson, J., & Zuckerman, B. (1991). Psychosocial correlates of severe temper tantrums. *Journal of Developmental and Behavioral Pediatrics, 12,* 77–83.

Neiderhiser, J.M., Reiss, D., Hetherington, E.M., & Plomin, R. (1999). Relationships between parenting and adolescent adjustment over time: Genetic and environmental contributions. *Developmental Psychology, 35,* 680–92.

Neimark, E.D. (1979). Current status of formal operations research. *Human Development, 22,* 60–7.

Neimark, J. (2000). Nature's clones. In K.L. Freiberg (Ed.), *Human development 00/01* (28th ed., pp. 10–7). Guilford, CT: McGraw-Hill/Dushkin.

Neisser, U. (1997). Never a dull moment. *American Psychologist, 52,* 79–81.

Neisser, U., Boodoo, G., Bouchard, T.J., Jr., Boykin, A.W., Brody, N., Ceci, S.J., Halpern, D.F., Loehlin. J.C., Perloff, R., Sternberg, R.J., & Urbina, S. (1996). Intelligence: Knowns and unknowns. *American Psychologist, 51,* 77–101.

Nelson, C., Bloom, F., Cameron, J., Amaral, D., Dahl, R., & Pine, D. (2002). An integrative, multidisciplinary approach to the study of brain-behaviour relations in the context of typical and atypical development. *Development and Psychopathology, 14,* 499–520.

Nelson, C.A. (1987). The recognition of facial expressions in the first two years of life: Mechanisms of development. *Child Development, 58,* 889–909.

Nelson, C.A. (1995). The ontogeny of human memory: A cognitive neuroscience perspective. *Developmental Psychology, 31,* 723–38.

Nelson, C.A., & Bloom, F.E. (1997). Child development and neuroscience. *Child Development, 68,* 970–87.

Nelson, J., & Aboud, F.E. (1985). The resolution of social conflict among friends. *Child Development, 56,* 1009–17.

Nelson, K. (1973). Structure and strategy in learning to talk. *Monographs of the Society for Research in Child Development, 38* (1–2, Serial No. 149), 1–136.

Nelson, K. (1981). Individual differences in language development: Implications for development and language. *Developmental Psychology, 17,* 170–87.

Nelson, K. (1993). The psychological and social origins of autobiographical memory. *Psychological Science, 4,* 1–8.

Nelson, K. (1996). *Language in cognitive development: The emergence of the mediated mind.* New York: Cambridge University Press.

Nelson, K., Hampson, J., & Shaw, L.K. (1993). Nouns in early lexicons: Evidence, explanations, and implications. *Journal of Child Language, 20,* 61–4.

Nelson, S.A. (1980). Factors influencing young children's use of motives and outcomes as moral criteria. *Child Development, 51,* 823–29.

Nesmith, J., & McKenna, M.A.J. (2000, June 27). Genetic code map a milestone: But hurdles remain to conquer disease. *Atlanta Constitution,* pp. A1, A5.

Neville, H.J., Coffey, S.A., Lawson, D.S., Fischer, A., Emmorey, K., & Bellugi, U. (1997). Neural systems mediating American Sign Language: Effects of sensory experience and age of acquisition. *Brain and Language, 57,* 285–308.

Newcomb, A.F., Bukowski, W.M., & Pattee, L. (1993). Children's peer relations: A meta-analytic review of popular, rejected, neglected, controversial, and average sociometric status. *Psychological Bulletin, 113,* 99–128.

Newcomb, M.D., & Bentler, P.M. (1989). Substance use and abuse among children and teenagers. *American Psychologist, 44,* 242–8.

Newcombe, N., & Dubas, J.S. (1987). Individual differences in cognitive ability: Are they related to timing of puberty? In R.M. Lerner & T.T. Foch (Eds.), *Biological–psychosocial interactions in early adolescence: A life-span perspective.* Hillsdale, NJ: Erlbaum.

Newcombe, N., & Dubas, J.S. (1992). A longitudinal study of predictors of spatial ability in adolescent females. *Child Development, 63,* 37–46.

Newcombe, N., & Fox, N.A. (1994). Infantile amnesia: Through a glass darkly. *Child Development, 65,* 31–40.

Newcombe, N., & Huttenlocher, J. (1992). Children's early ability to solve perspective-taking problems. *Developmental Psychology, 28,* 635–43.

Newell, A., & Simon, H.A. (1961). Computer simulation of human thinking. *Science, 134,* 2011–17.

Newman, D.L., Caspi, A., Moffitt, T.E., & Silva, P.A. (1997). Antecedents of adult interpersonal functioning: Effects of individual differences in age 3 temperament. *Developmental Psychology, 33,* 206–17.

Newport, E.L. (1991). Contrasting conceptions of the critical period for language. In S. Carey & R. Gelman (Eds.), *The epigenesis of mind: Essays on biology and cognition* (pp. 111–30). Hillsdale, NJ: Erlbaum.

NICHD Early Child Care Research Network. (1997). The effects of infant child care on mother–infant attachment security: Results of the NICHD study of early child care. *Child Development, 68,* 860–79.

NICHD Early Child Care Research Network. (1998a.) Early child care and self-control, compliance, and problem behavior at twenty-four and thirty-six months. *Child Development, 69,* 1145–70.

NICHD Early Child Care Research Network. (1998b). Relations between family predictors and child outcomes: Are they weaker for children in child care? *Developmental Psychology, 34,* 1119–28.

NICHD Early Child Care Research Network. (1999). Child care and mother–child interaction in the first 3 years of life. *Developmental Psychology, 35,* 1399–1413.

NICHD Early Child Care Research Network. (2000). The relation of child care to cognitive and language development. *Child Development, 71,* 960-980.

Nicholls, J.G., & Miller, A.T. (1984). Reasoning about the ability of self and others: A developmental study. *Child Development, 55,* 1990–9.

Nichols, M.R. (1993). Parental perspectives on the childbirth experience. *Maternal-Child Nursing Journal, 21,* 99–108.

Nicoladis, E. (2002). Some gestures develop in conjunction with spoken language development and others don't: Evidence from bilingual preschoolers. *Journal of Nonverbal Behavior, 26 (4),* 241–66

Nicoladis, E., Mayberry, R.I., & Genesee, F. (1999). Gesture and early bilingual development. *Developmental Psychology, 35,* 514–26.

Nielson, C.T., Skakkebaek, N., Richardson, D., Darling, J., Hunter, W., Jorgensen, M., Nielson, A., Ingerslev, O., Keidling, N., & Muller, J. (1986). Onset of the release of spermatozoa (spermarche) in boys in relation to age, testicular growth, pubic hair, and height. *Journal of Clinical Endocrinology and Metabolism, 62,* 532–35.

Nielson, C.T., Skakkebaek, N., Richardson, D., Darling, J., Hunter, W., Jorgensen, M., Nielson, A., Ingerslev, O., Keidling, N., & Muller, J. (2003). Onset of the release of spermatozoa (spermarche) in boys in relation to age, testicular growth, pubic hair, and height. *Journal of Clinical Endocrinology and Metabolism, 62,* 532–35. Available online December 6, 2003 at http://jcem.endojournals.org/cgi/content/abstract/62/3/532.

Ninio, A., & Rinott, N. (1988). Fathers' involvement in the care of their infants and their attributions of cognitive competence to infants. *Child Development, 59,* 652–63.

Nix, R.L., Pinderhughes, E.E., Dodge, K.A., Bates, J.E., Pettit, G.S., & McFadyen-Ketchum, S.A. (1999). The relation between mothers' hostile attribution tendencies and children's externalizing behavior problems: The mediating role of mothers' harsh discipline practices. *Child Development, 70,* 896–909.

Norman-Jackson, J. (1982). Family interactions, language development, and primary reading achievement of Black children in families of low income. *Child Development, 53,* 349–58.

Nottelmann, E.D. (1987). Competence and self-esteem during transition from childhood to adolescence. *Developmental Psychology, 23,* 441–50.

Nova Scotia Department of Community Services. (2001). *The family mosaic. Educational profiles of mothers: A longitudinal study of lone-parent and two-parent families.* Halifax: Author.

Nucci, L., Camino, C., & Sapiro, C.M. (1996). Social class effects on northeastern Brazilian children's conceptions of areas of personal choice and social regulation. *Child Development, 67,* 1223–42.

Nucci, L., & Smetana, J.G. (1996). Mothers' concepts of young children's areas of personal freedom. *Child Development, 67,* 1870–86.

Nucci, L., & Turiel, E. (1993). God's word, religious rules, and their relation to Christian and Jewish children's concepts of morality. *Child Development, 64,* 1475–91.

Nucci, L., & Weber, E.K. (1995). Social interactions in the home and the development of young children's conceptions within the personal domain. *Child Development, 66,* 1438–52.

Nugent, J.K., Lester, B.M., & Brazelton, T.B. (1989). *Biology, culture, and development* (Vol. 1). Norwood, NJ: Erlbaum.

Oakes, M.A., & Hyman, I.E., Jr. (2000). The changing face of memory and self. In D.F. Bjorklund (Ed.), *Research and theory in false-memory creation in children and adults* (pp. 45–67). Mahwah, NJ: Erlbaum.

Ochs, E. (1982). Talking to children in western Samoa. *Language in Society, 11,* 77–104.

O'Connor, B.P. (1995). Identity development and perceived parental behavior as sources of adolescent egocentrism. *Journal of Youth and Adolescence, 24,* 205–27.

O'Connor, N., & Hermelin, B. (1991). Talents and preoccupations in idiot-savants. *Psychological Medicine, 21,* 959–64.

O'Connor, T.G., Deater-Deckard, K., Fulker, D., Rutter, M., & Plomin, R. (1998). Genotype-environment correlations in late childhood and early adolescence: Antisocial behavior problems and coercive parenting. *Developmental Psychology, 34,* 970–81.

O'Connor, T.G., Rutter, M., Beckett, C., Keaveney, L., Kreppner, J.M., & the English and Romanian Adoptees Study Team (2000). The effects of global severe privation on cognitive competence: Extension and longitudinal follow-up. *Child Development, 71,* 376–90.

Odden, A. (1990). Class size and student achievement: Research-based policy alternatives. *Educational Evaluation and Policy Analysis, 12,* 213–27.

O'Dempsey, T.J.D. (1988). Traditional belief and practice among the Pokot people of Kenya with particular reference to mother and child health: 2. Mother and child health. *Annals of Tropical Paediatrics, 8,* 125.

Oden, S., & Asher, S.R. (1977). Coaching children in social skills for friendship making. *Child Development, 48,* 495–506.

O'Donohue, W.T., & Elliott, A.N. (1992). Treatment of the sexually abused child: A review. *Journal of Clinical Child Psychology, 21,* 218–28.

Ogbu, J.U. (1994). From cultural differences to differences in cultural frames of reference. In P.M. Greenfield & R.R. Cocking (Eds.), *Cross-cultural roots of minority child development* (pp. 365–91). Hillsdale, NJ: Erlbaum.

Ogletree, S.M., & Williams, S.W. (1990). Sex and sex-typing effects on computer attitudes and aptitude. *Sex Roles, 23,* 703–12.

O'Heron, C.A., & Orlofsky, J.L. (1990). Stereotypic and nonstereotypic sex role trait and behavior orientations, gender identity, and psychological adjustment. *Journal of Personality and Social Psychology, 58,* 134–43.

Oller, D.K., & Eilers, R.E. (1988). The role of audition in infant babbling. *Child Development, 59,* 441–9.

Olvera-Ezzell, N., Power, T.G., & Cousins, J.H. (1990). Maternal socialization of children's eating habits: Strategies used by obese Mexican-American mothers. *Child Development, 61,* 395–400.

Olweus, D. (1984). Aggressors and their victims: Bullying at school. In H. Frude & H. Gault (Eds.), *Disruptive behaviors in schools* (pp. 57–76). New York: Wiley.

Olweus, D. (1993). *Bullying at school.* Oxford: Blackwell.

Olweus, D., Mattsson, A., Schalling, D., & Low, H. (1980). Testosterone, aggression, physical and personality dimensions in normal adolescent males. *Psychosomatic Medicine, 42,* 253–69.

O'Mahoney, J.F. (1989). Development of thinking about things and people: Social and nonsocial cognition during adolescence. *Journal of Genetic Psychology, 150,* 217–24.

O'Neill, D.K. (1996). Two-year-old children's sensitivity to a parent's knowledge state when making requests. *Child Development, 67,* 659–67.

Ontario Children's Secretariat. (2001, March). *The early years guidelines for community coordinators and steering committees (revised).* Retrieved November 19, 2001 from http://www.childsec.gov.on.ca/3_resources/early_years_study/steering_guidlines.html.

Oppenheim, D., Nir, A., Warren, S., & Emde, R.N. (1997). Emotion regulation in mother–child narrative co-construction: Associations with children's narratives and adaptation. *Developmental Psychology, 33,* 284–94.

Oppenheim, D., Sagi, A., & Lamb, M.E. (1988). Infant–adult attachments on the kibbutz and their relation to socioemotional development 4 years later. *Developmental Psychology, 24,* 427–33.

O'Reilly, A.W., & Bornstein, M.H. (1993). Caregiver–child interaction in play. In M.H. Bornstein & A.W. O'Reilly (Eds.), *The role of play in the development of thought.* San Francisco: Jossey-Bass.

Orlofsky, J.L. (1979). Parental antecedents of sex-role orientation in college men and women. *Sex Roles, 5,* 495–512.

Ornstein, P.A., Gordon, B.N., & Larus, D.M. (1992). Children's memory for a personally experienced event: Implications for testimony. *Applied Developmental Psychology, 6,* 49–60.

Ornstein, P.A., Medlin, R.G., Stone, B.P., & Naus, M.J. (1985). Retrieving for rehearsal: An analysis of active rehearsal in children's memory. *Developmental Psychology, 21,* 633–41.

Ornstein, P.A., Naus, M.J., & Liberty, C. (1975). Rehearsal and organizational processes in children's memory. *Child Development, 46,* 818–30.

Osborne, M.L., Kistner, J.A., & Helgemo, B. (1993). Developmental progression in children's knowledge of AIDS: Implications for educational and attitudinal change. *Journal of Pediatric Psychology, 18,* 177–92.

Oshimo-Takane, Y., Goodz, E., & Derevensky, J. (1996). Birth order effects on early language development: Do secondborn children learn from overheard speech? *Child Development, 67,* 621–34.

O'Sullivan, J.T. (1996). Children's metamemory about the influence of conceptual relations on recall. *Journal of Experimental Child Psychology, 62*, 1–29.

O'Sullivan, J.T. (1997). Effort, interest, & recall: Beliefs and behaviors of preschoolers. *Journal of Experimental Child Psychology, 65*, 43–67.

Overman, W., Bachevalier, J., Miller, M., & Moore, K. (1996). Children's performance on "animal tests" of oddity: Implications for cognitive processes required for tests of oddity and delayed nonmatch to sample. *Journal of Experimental Child Psychology, 62*, 223–42.

Overton, W.F. (1984). World views and their influence on psychological theory and research: Kuhn-Lakatos-Laudan. In H.W. Reese (Ed.), *Advances in child development and behavior* (Vol. 18, pp. 191–226). New York: Academic Press.

Overton, W.F., Ward, S.L., Noveck, I.A., Black, J., & O'Brien, D.P. (1987). Form and content in the development of deductive reasoning. *Developmental Psychology, 23*, 22–30.

Oviatt, S.L. (1980). The emerging ability to comprehend language: An experimental approach. *Child Development, 51*, 97–106.

Oyen, A-S., & Bebko, J.M. (1996). The effects of computer games and lesson context on children's mnemonic strategies. *Journal of Experimental Child Psychology, 62*, 173–89.

Paarlberg, K.M., Vingerhoets, A.J.J.M., Passchier, J., Dekker, G.A., & van Geijn, H.P. (1995). Psychosocial factors and pregnancy outcome: A review with emphasis on methodological issues. *Journal of Psychosomatic Research, 39*, 563–95.

Paikoff, R.L., & Brooks-Gunn, J. (1991). Do parent–child relationships change at puberty? *Psychological Bulletin, 110*, 47–66.

Palinscar, A.S., Brown, A.L., & Campione, J.C. (1993). First-grade dialogues for knowledge acquisition and use. In E.A. Forman, N. Minilk, & C.A. Stone (Eds.), *Contexts for learning* (pp. 43–57). New York: Oxford University Press.

Palkovitz, R. (1984). Parental attitudes and fathers' interactions with their 5-month-old infants. *Developmental Psychology, 20*, 1054–60.

Palkovitz, R. (1985). Fathers' birth attendance, early contact, and extended contact with their newborns: A critical review. *Child Development, 56*, 392–406.

Palmer, C.F. (1989). The discriminating nature of infants' exploratory actions. *Developmental Psychology, 25*, 885–93.

Pan, B.A., & Gleason, J.K. (1997). Semantic development: Learning the meaning of words. In J.K. Gleason (Ed.), *The development of language* (4th ed., chap. 4). Boston: Allyn & Bacon.

Panigrahy, A., Filiano, J.J., & Sleeper, L.A., et al. (1997). Decreased karinate binding in the arcuate nucleus of the sudden infant death syndrome. *Journal of Neuropathological Experimental Neurology, 56*, 1253-61.

Panksepp, J. (1998). Attention deficit hyperactivity disorders, psychostimulants, and intolerance of childhood playfulness: A tragedy in the making? *Current Directions in Psychological Science, 7*, 91–98.

Papiernik, E. (1995). Prevention of preterm birth in France. In B.P. Sachs, R. Beard, E. Papiernik, & C. Russell (Eds.), *Reproductive health care for women and babies* (pp. 322–47). New York: Oxford University Press.

Papousek, H. (1967). Experimental studies of appetitional behavior in human newborns and infants. In H.W. Stevenson, E.H. Hess, & H.L. Rheingold (Eds.), *Early behavior: Comparative and developmental approaches* (pp. 249–77). New York: Wiley.

Paquette, G., & De Guise, J. (1994, March). *An index of violence on Canadian television: Final report.* Quebec City, PQ: Université Laval.

Paris, S.G. (1988). Models and metaphors of learning strategies. In C.E. Weinstein, E.T. Goetz, & P.A. Alexander (Eds.), *Learning and study strategies: Issues in assessment, instruction, and evaluation.* San Diego, CA: Academic Press.

Park, S., Belsky, J., Putnam, S., & Cynic, K. (1997). Infant emotionality, parenting, and 3-year inhibition: Exploring stability and lawful discontinuity in a male sample. *Developmental Psychology, 33*, 218–27.

Parke, R.D. (1972). Some effects of punishment on children's behavior. In W.W. Hartup (Ed.), *The young child* (Vol. 2). Washington, DC: National Association for the Education of Young Children.

Parke, R.D. (1977). Some effects of punishment on children's behavior—revisited. In E.M. Hetherington & R.D. Parke (Eds.), *Contemporary readings in child psychology.* New York: McGraw-Hill.

Parke, R.D., & Kellum, S.G. (1994). *Exploring family relationships with other social contexts.* Hillsdale, NJ. Erlbaum.

Parke, R.D., & Slaby, R.G. (1983). The development of aggression. In P.H. Mussen (Series Ed.) & E.M. Hetherington (Vol. Ed.), *Handbook of child psychology: Vol. 4. Socialization, personality, and social development* (4th ed., pp. 547–641). New York: Wiley.

Parker, J.G., & Asher, S.R. (1987). Peer relations and later adjustment: Are low-accepted children "at risk"? *Psychological Bulletin, 102*, 357–89.

Parker, J.G., & Asher, S.R. (1993). Friendship and friendship quality in middle childhood: Links with peer group acceptance and feelings of loneliness and social dissatisfaction. *Developmental Psychology, 29*, 611–21.

Parker, J.G., Rubin, K.H., Price, J., & DeRosier, E. (1995). Peer relationships, child development, and adjustment. A developmental psychopathology perspective. In D. Cicchetti & E. Cohen (Eds.), *Developmental Psychopathology: Vol. 2. Risk, disorder, and adaptation* (pp. 96–161). New York: Wiley.

Parkhurst, J.T., & Asher, S.R. (1992). Peer rejection in middle school: Subgroup differences in behavior, loneliness, and interpersonal concerns. *Developmental Psychology, 28*, 231–41.

Parsons, J.E., Adler, T.F., & Kaczala, C.M. (1982). Socialization of achievement attitudes and beliefs: Parental influences. *Child Development, 53*, 310–21.

Parsons, T. (1955). Family structure and the socialization of the child. In T. Parsons & R.F. Bales (Eds.), *Family socialization and interaction processes* (pp. 35–62). New York: Free Press.

Parten, M. (1932). Social participation among preschool children. *Journal of Abnormal and Social Psychology, 27*, 243–69.

Pascual-Leone, J. (1987). Organismic processes for neo-Piagetian theories: A dialectical causal account of cognitive development. *International Journal of Psychology, 22*, 531–70.

Passingham, R.E. (1982). *The human primate.* Oxford: W.H. Freeman.

Pataki, S.P., Shapiro, C., & Clark, M.S. (1994). Children's acquisition of appropriate norms for friendships and acquaintances. *Journal of Social and Personal Relationships, 11*, 427–42.

Patel, N., Power, T.G., & Bhavnagri, N.P. (1996). Socialization values and practices of Indian immigrant parents: Correlates of modernity and acculturation. *Child Development, 67*, 303–13.

Patrick, D.M., Wong, T., & Jordan, R.A. (2000). Sexually transmitted infections in Canada: Recent resurgence threatens national goals. *The Canadian Journal of Human Sexuality, 9* (3), 149–66.

Patterson, C.J. (1995a). Families of the lesbian baby boom: Parents' division of labor and children's adjustment. *Developmental Psychology, 31*, 115–23.

Patterson, C.J. (1995b). Sexual orientation and human development: An overview. *Developmental Psychology, 31*, 3–11.

Patterson, C.J., Kupersmidt, J.B., & Vaden, N.A. (1990). Income level, gender, ethnicity, and household compositions as predictors of children's school-based competence. *Child Development, 61*, 485–94.

Patterson, G.R. (1981). Mothers: The unacknowledged victims. *Monographs of the Society for Research in Child Development, 45* (5, Serial No. 186).

Patterson, G.R. (1982). *Coercive family processes.* Eugene, OR: Castalia.

Patterson, G.R. (1998). Continuities—A search for causal mechanisms: Comment on the special section. *Developmental Psychology, 34*, 1263–68.

Patterson, G.R., DeBaryshe, B.D., & Ramsey, E. (1989). A developmental perspective on antisocial behavior. *American Psychologist, 44*, 329–35.

Patterson, G.R., Littman, R.A., & Bricker, W. (1967). Assertive behavior in children: A step toward a theory of aggression. *Monographs of the Society for Research in Child Development, 32* (5, Serial No. 113).

Patterson, G.R., Reid, J.B., & Dishion, T. (1992). *Antisocial boys.* Eugene, OR: Castalia.

Patterson, S.J., Sochting, I., & Marcia, J.E. (1992). The inner space and beyond: Women and identity. In G.R. Adams, T.P. Gullotta, & R. Montemayor (Eds.), *Adolescent identity formation: Vol. 4. Advances in adolescent development* (pp. 9–24). Newbury Park, CA: Sage.

Paul, J.P. (1993). Childhood cross-gender behavior and adult homosexuality: The resurgence of biological models of sexuality. *Journal of Homosexuality, 24*, 41–54.

Paulhus, D., & Shaffer, D.R. (1981). Sex differences in the impact of number of older and number of younger siblings on scholastic aptitude. *Social Psychology Quarterly, 44*, 363–8.

Pederson, D.R., Gleason, K., Moran, G., & Bento, S. (1998). Maternal attachment representations, maternal sensitivity, and the infant–mother attachment relationship. *Developmental Psychology, 34* (4), 925–33.

Pederson, D.R., & Moran, G. (1996). Expressions of the attachment relationship outside of the Strange Situation. *Child Development, 67*, 915–29.

Pedlow, R., Sanson, A., Prior, M., & Oberklaid, F. (1993). Stability of maternally reported temperament from infancy to 8 years. *Developmental Psychology, 29*, 998–1007.

Pedro-Carroll, J.L., & Cowen, E.L. (1985). The children of divorce intervention program: An investigation of the efficacy of a school-based prevention program. *Journal of Consulting and Clinical Psychology, 53*, 603–11.

Pegg, J.E., & Werker, J.F. (1997). Adult and infant perception of two English phones. *Journal of the Acoustical Society of America, 102*, 3742–53.

Pegg, J.E., Werker, J.F., & McLeod, P.J. (1992). Preference for infant-directed over adult-directed speech: Evidence from 7-week-old infants. *Infant Behavior and Development, 15*, 325–45.

Pelham, W.E., Jr., Carlson, C., Sams, S.E., Vallano, G., Dixon, M.J., & Hoza, B. (1993). Separate and combined effects of methylphenidate and behavior modification on boys with attention deficit-hyperactivity disorder in the classroom. *Journal of Consulting and Clinical Psychology, 61*, 506–15.

Pellegrini, A.D. (1996). *Observing children in their natural worlds: A methodological primer.* Mahwah, NJ: Erlbaum.

Pellegrini, A.D. (2002). Rough-and-tumble play from childhood through adolescence: Development and possible functions. In P.K. Smith & C.H. Hart (Eds.), *Blackwell Handbook of Childhood Social Development* (pp. 437-453). Blackwell Handbooks of Developmental Psychology. Malden, MA: Blackwell Publishers.

Pellegrini, A.D., & Smith, P.K. (1998). Physical activity play: The nature and function of a neglected aspect of play. *Child Development, 69*, 577–98.

Pellegrini, D.S. (1985). Social cognition and competence in middle childhood. *Child Development, 56*, 253–64.

Pence, A.R., & Benner, A. (2000). Child care research in Canada, 1965–99. In L. Prochner & N. Howe (Eds.), *Early childhood care and education in Canada* (pp. 133–60). Vancouver: University of British Columbia Press.

Penner, S.G. (1987). Parental responses to grammatical and ungrammatical child utterances. *Child Development, 58*, 376–84.

Pepler, D., Connolly, J., & Craig, W. (2001). *Bullying and harassment: Experiences of minority and immigrant youth.* CERIS research report. Retrieved October 31, 2001 from http://ceris.metropolis.net/Virtual%20Library/education/pepler1.html.

Pepler, D.J., & Craig, W.M. (1999). Understanding bullying and victimization from a dynamic systems perspective. In A. Slater and D. Muir (Eds.), *Developmental psychology: An advanced reader* (pp. 441–51). London, England: Blackwell.

Pepler, D.J., Craig, W.M., & Roberts, W.L. (1998). Observations of aggressive and nonaggressive children on the school playground. *Merrill-Palmer Quarterly, 44* (1), 55–76.

Perez, L.A., Peynircioglu, Z.F., & Blaxton, T.A. (1998). Developmental differences in implicit and explicit memory performance. *Journal of Experimental Child Psychology, 70*, 167–85.

Perez-Granados, D.R., & Callanan, M.A. (1997). Conversations with mothers and siblings: Young children's semantic and conceptual development. *Developmental Psychology, 33*, 120–34.

Perlman, M., & Ross, H.S. (1997). The benefits of parent intervention in children's disputes: An examination of concurrent changes in children's fighting styles. *Child Development, 68* (4), 690–700.

Perner, J. Ruffman, T., & Leekam, S.R. (1994). Theory of mind is contagious: You can catch it from your sibs. *Child Development, 65*, 1228–38.

Perry, D.G., Kusel, S.J., & Perry, L.C. (1988). Victims of peer aggression. *Developmental Psychology, 24*, 807–14.

Perry, D. G., Perry, L. C., Bussey, K., English, D., & Arnold, G. (1980). Processes of attribution and children's self-punishment following misbehavior. *Child Development, 51*, 545-551.

Perry, D.G., Perry, L.C., & Weiss, R.J. (1989). Sex differences in the consequences that children anticipate for aggression. *Developmental Psychology, 25*, 312–9.

Peskin, J. (1992). Ruse and representations: On children's ability to conceal information. *Developmental Psychology, 28*, 84–9.

Peterson, C. (1999). Children's memory for traumatic injury: Two years later. *Developmental Psychology, 35*, 1493–1506.

Peterson, C. (2002). Children's long-term memory for autobiographical events. *Developmental Review, 22*, 370-402.

Peterson, C., & Whalen, N. (2001). Five years later: Children's memory for medical emergencies. *Applied Cognitive Psychology, 15*, s7–s24.

Peterson, G.H., Mehl, L.E., & Liederman, P.H. (1979). The role of some birth-related variables in father attachment. *American Journal of Orthopsychiatry, 49*, 330–8.

Peterson, L., Ewigman, B., & Kivlahan, C. (1993). Judgments regarding appropriate child supervision to prevent injury: The role of environmental risk and child age. *Child Development, 64*, 934–50.

Petitto, L.A., Holowka, S., Sergio, L.E., & Ostry, D. (2001, September 6). Language rhythms in babies' hand movements. *Nature, 413*, 35–6.

Petitto, L.A., & Marentette, P.F. (1991). Babbling in the manual mode: Evidence for the ontogeny of language. *Science, 251*, 1493–6.

Petretic, P.A., & Tweney, R.D. (1977). Does comprehension precede production? The development of children's responses to telegraphic sentences of varying grammatical adequacy. *Journal of Child Language, 4*, 201–9.

Pettit, G.S., Bates, J.E., & Dodge, K.A. (1997). Supportive parenting, ecological context, and children's adjustment: A seven-year longitudinal study. *Child Development, 68*, 908–23.

Pettit, G.S., Bates, J.E., Dodge, K.A., & Meese, D.W. (1999). The impact of after-school peer contact on early adolescent externalizing problems is moderated by parental monitoring, perceived neighborhood safety, and prior adjustment. *Child Development, 70*, 768–78.

Pettit, G.S., Dodge, K.A., & Brown, M.M. (1988). Early family experience, social problem-solving patterns, and children's social competence. *Child Development, 59*, 107–20.

Pettit, G.S., Laird, R.D., Dodge, K.A., Bates, J.E., & Criss, M.M. (2001). Antecedents and behavior-problem outcomes of parental monitoring and psychological control in early adolescence. *Child Development, 72*, 583–98.

Pezdek, K., & Hodge, D. (1999). Planting false childhood memories in children: The role of event plausibility. *Child Development, 70*, 887–95.

Pezdek, K. & Taylor, J. (2000). Discriminating between accounts of true and false events. In D.F. Bjorklund (Ed.), *Research and theory in false-memory creation in children and adults* (pp. 69–91). Mahwah, NJ: Erlbaum.

Phillips, D. (1984). The illusion of incompetence among academically competent children. *Child Development, 55*, 2000–16.

Phillips, M. (1997). What makes schools effective? A comparison of the relationships of communitarian climate and academic climate to mathematics achievement and attendance during middle school. *American Educational Research Journal, 34*, 633–62.

Philpott, R.H. (1995). Maternal health care in the developing world. In B.P. Sachs, R. Beard, E. Papiernik, & C. Russell (Eds.), *Reproductive health care for women and babies* (pp. 226–45). New York: Oxford University Press.

Phinney, J.S., Ong, A., & Madden, T. (2000). Cultural values and intergenerational value discrepancies in immigrant and nonimmigrant families. *Child Development, 71*, 528–39.

Piaget, J. (1926). *The language and thought of the child.* New York: Harcourt, Brace & World.

Piaget, J. (1950). *The psychology of intelligence.* San Diego, CA: Harcourt Brace Jovanovich.

Piaget, J. (1951). *Play, dreams, and imitation in childhood.* New York: Norton.

Piaget, J. (1952). *The origins of intelligence in children.* New York: International Universities Press.

Piaget, J. (1954). *The construction of reality in the child.* New York: Basic Books.

Piaget, J. (1960). *Psychology of intelligence.* Paterson, NJ: Littlefield, Adams.

Piaget, J. (1965). *The moral judgment of the child.* New York: Free Press. (Original work published 1932.)

Piaget, J. (1970). Piaget's theory. In P.H. Mussen (Ed.), *Carmichael's manual of child psychology* (3rd ed., Vol. 1, pp. 703–32). New York: Wiley.

Piaget, J. (1971). *Science of education and the psychology of the child.* New York: Viking Press.

Piaget, J. (1972). Intellectual evolution from adolescence to adulthood. *Human Development, 15*, 1–12.

Piaget, J. (1976). *To understand is to invent: The future of education.* New York: Penguin.

Piaget, J. (1977). The role of action in the development of thinking. In W.F. Overton & J.M. Gallagher (Eds.), *Knowledge and development* (Vol. 1, pp. 17–42). New York: Plenum.

Piaget, J., & Inhelder, B. (1969). *The psychology of the child.* New York: Basic Books.

Pickens, J. (1994). Perception of auditory-visual distance relations by 5-month-old infants. *Developmental Psychology, 30*, 537–44.

Pickens, J., & Field, T. (1993). Facial expressivity in infants of depressed mothers. *Developmental Psychology, 29*, 986–8.

Pierce, K.M., Hamm, J.V., & Vandell, D.L. (1999). Experiences in after-school programs and children's adjustment in first-grade classrooms. *Child Development, 70*, 756–67.

Pike, A., McGuire, S., Hetherington, E.M., Reiss, D., & Plomin, R. (1996). Family environment and adolescent depressive symptoms and antisocial behavior: A multivariate genetic analysis. *Developmental Psychology, 32*, 590–603.

Pike, K.M., & Rodin, J. (1991). Mothers, daughters, and disordered eating. *Journal of Abnormal Psychology, 100*, 198–204.

Pillow, B.H. (1988). Young children's understanding of attentional limits. *Child Development, 59*, 31–46.

Pine, J.M. (1994). The language of primary caregivers. In C. Gallaway & B.J. Richards (Eds.), *Input and interaction in language acquisition* (pp. 15–37). Cambridge, England: Cambridge University Press.

Pine, J.M. (1995). Variation in vocabulary development as a function of birth order. *Child Development, 66*, 272–81.

Pinker, S. (1991). Rules of language. *Science, 253*, 530–35.

Pinker, S. (1994). *The language instinct.* New York: William Morrow.

Pinon, M., Huston, A.C., & Wright, J.C. (1989). Family ecology and child characteristics that predict young children's educational television viewing. *Child Development, 60*, 846–56.

Pinto, A., Folkers, E., & Sines, J.O. (1991). Dimensions of behavior and home environment in school-age children: India and the United States. *Journal of Cross-Cultural Psychology, 22*, 491–508.

Pipp, S., Easterbrooks, M.A., & Harmon, R.J. (1992). The relation between attachment and knowledge of self and mother in one-year-old infants to three-year-old infants. *Child Development, 63*, 738–50.

Pipp-Siegel, S., & Foltz, C. (1997). Toddlers' acquisition of self/other knowledge: Ecological and interpersonal aspects of self and other. *Child Development, 68*, 69–79.

Plomin, R. (1990). *Nature and nurture: An introduction to behavior genetics.* Pacific Grove, CA: Brooks/Cole.

Plomin, R. (1994). *Genetics and experience: The interplay between nature and nurture.* Thousand Oaks, CA: Sage.

Plomin, R., DeFries, J.C., & Loehlin, J.C. (1977). Genotype–environment interaction and correlation in the analysis of human behavior. *Psychological Bulletin, 84*, 309–22.

Plomin, R., DeFries, J.C., McClearn, G.E., & Rutter, M. (1997). *Behavioral genetics: A primer* (3rd ed.). New York: W.H. Freeman.

Plomin, R., Reiss, D., Hetherington, E.M., & Howe, G.W. (1994). Nature and nurture: Genetic contributions to measures of the family environment. *Developmental Psychology, 30,* 32–43.

Plomin, R., & Rende, R. (1991). Human behavioral genetics. *Annual Review of Psychology, 42,* 161–90.

Plomin, R., & Rutter, M. (1998). Child development, molecular genetics, and what to do with genes once they are found. *Child Development, 69,* 1223–42.

Plumert, J.M., Ewert, K., & Spear, S.J. (1995). The early development of children's communication about nested spatial relations. *Child Development, 66,* 959–69.

Plumert, J.M., & Nichols-Whitehead, P. (1996). Parental scaffolding of young children's spatial communication. *Developmental Psychology, 32,* 523–32.

Plunkett, K. (2000). Development in a connectionist framework: Rethinking the nature-nurture debate. In K. Lee (Ed.), *Childhood Cognitive Development: Essential Readings.* Oxford: Blackwell Publishers Inc.

Polak, A., & Harris, P.L. (1999). Deception by young children following noncompliance. *Developmental Psychology, 35,* 561–68.

Polivy, J., & Herman, P. (2002). Causes of eating disorders. *Annual Review of Psychology, 53* (1), 187-213.

Pollack, R.H. (1997, March). Personal communication.

Pollitt, E. (1994). Poverty and child development: Relevance of research in developing countries to the United States. *Child Development, 65,* 283–95.

Pollitt, E., Golub, M., Gorman, K., Grantham-McGregor, S., Levitsky, D., Schurch, B., Strupp, B., & Wachs, T. (1996). A reconceptualization of the effects of undernutrition on children's biological, psychological, and behavioral development. *SRCD Social Policy Report (*Vol. 10, No. 5). Ann Arbor, MI: Society for Research in Child Development.

Pomerantz, E.M., & Ruble, D.N. (1997). Distinguishing multiple dimensions and conceptions of ability: Implications for self-evaluation. *Child Development, 68,* 1165–80.

Pomerantz, E.M., Ruble, D.N., Frey, K.S., & Grenlich, F. (1995). Meeting goals and confronting conflict: Children's changing perceptions of social comparison. *Child Development, 66,* 723–38.

Pomerleau, A., Bolduc, D., Malcuit, G., & Cossette, L. (1990). Pink or blue: Environmental gender stereotypes in the first two years of life. *Sex Roles, 22,* 359–67.

Poole, D.A., & Lindsay, D.S. (1995). Interviewing preschoolers: Effects of nonsuggestive techniques, parental coaching and leading questions on reports of nonexperienced events. *Journal of Experimental Child Psychology, 60,* 129–54.

Poole, D., & White, L. (1995). Tell me again and again: Stability and change in the repeated testimonies of children and adults. In M.S. Zaragoza, J.R. Graham, C.N. Gordon, R. Hirschman, & Y.S. Ben Porath (Eds.), *Memory and testimony in the child witness* (pp. 24–43). Newbury Park, CA: Sage.

Pope, A.W., & Bierman, K.L. (1999).Predicting adolescent peer problems and antisocial activities: The relative roles of aggression and dysregulation. *Developmental Psychology, 35,* 335–46.

Pope, S., & Kipp, K.K. (1998). The development of efficient forgetting: Evidence from directed-forgetting tasks. *Developmental Review, 18,* 86–123.

Porter, F.L., Porges, S.W., & Marshall, R.E. (1988). Newborn pain cries and vagal tone: Parallel changes in response to circumcision. *Child Development, 59,* 495–505.

Porter, R.H., Makin, J.W., Davis, L.B., & Christensen, K.M. (1992). Breast-fed infants respond to olfactory clues from their own mother and unfamiliar lactating females. *Infant Behavior and Development, 15,* 85–93.

Posada, G., Gao, Y., Wu, F., Posada, R., Tascon, M., Schoelmerich, A., Sagi, A., Kondo-Ikemura, K., Haaland, W., & Synnevang, B. (1995). The secure-base phenomenon across cultures: Children's behavior, mothers' preferences, and experts' concepts. In E. Waters, B.E. Vaughn, G. Posada, & K. Kondo-Ikemura (Eds.), *Caregiving, cultural, and cognitive perspectives on secure-base behavior and working models: New growing points of attachment theory and research. Monographs of the Society for Research in Child Development, 60* (2–3, Serial No. 244), 27–48.

Posada, G., Jacobs, A., Carbonell, O. A., Alzate, G., Bustamante, M. R., & Arenas, A. (1999). Maternal care and attachment security in ordinary and emergency contexts. *Developmental Psychology, 35,* 1379-1388.

Posner, J.K., & Vandell, D.L. (1994). Low-income children's after-school care: Are there beneficial effects of after-school programs? *Child Development, 65,* 440–56.

Posner, J.K., & Vandell, D.L. (1999). After-school activities and the development of low-income urban children: A longitudinal study. *Developmental Psychology, 35,* 868–79.

Poulin, F., & Boivin, M. (2000). The role of proactive and reactive aggression in the formation and development of boys' friendships. *Developmental Psychology, 36,* 233–40.

Poulin-DuBois, D., Serbin, L., & Derbyshire, A. (1998). Toddlers' intermodal and verbal knowledge about gender. *Merrill-Palmer Quarterly, 44* (3), 338–54.

Poulin-Dubois, D., Serbin, L.A., Kenyon, B., & Derbyshire, A. (1994). Infants' intermodal knowledge about gender. *Developmental Psychology, 30,* 436–42.

Povinelli, D.J., Landau, K.R., & Perilloux, H.K. (1996). Self-recognition in young children using delayed versus live feedback: Evidence of a developmental asynchrony. *Child Development, 67,* 1540–54.

Povinelli, D.J., Landry, A.M., Theall, L.A., Clark, B.R., & Castile, C.M. (1999). Development of young children's understanding that the recent past is causally bound to the present. *Developmental Psychology, 35,* 1426–39.

Povinelli, D.J., & Simon, B.B. (1998). Young children's reactions to briefly versus extremely delayed images of the self: Emergence of the autobiographical stance. *Developmental Psychology, 34,* 188–94.

Power, T.G., and Chapieski, M.L. (1986). Childrearing and impulse control in toddlers: A naturalistic investigation. *Developmental Psychology, 22* (2), 271–5.

Powlishta, K.K. (1995). Intergroup processes in childhood: Social categorization and sex role development. *Developmental Psychology, 31,* 781–8.

Pratt, K.C. (1954). The neonate. In L. Carmichael (Ed.), *Manual of child psychology* (pp. 190–254). New York: Wiley.

Pratt, M.W., Diessner, R., Hunsberger, B., Pancer, S.M., & Savoy, K. (1991). Four pathways in the analysis of adult development and aging: Comparing analyses of reasoning about personal life dilemmas. *Psychology and Aging, 4,* 666–75.

Pratt, M.W., Green, D., MacVicar, J., & Bountrogianni, M. (1992). The mathematical parent: Parental scaffolding, parenting style, and learning outcomes in long-division mathematics homework. *Journal of Applied Developmental Psychology, 13,* 17–34.

Pratt, M.W., Norris, J.E., van de Hoef, S., & Arnold, M.L. (2001). Stories of hope: Parental optimism in narratives about adolescent children. *Journal of Social and Personal Relationships, 18,* 603–23.

Pratt, M.W., & Savoy-Levine, K.M. (1998). Contingent tutoring of long-division skills in fourth and fifth graders: Experimental tests of some hypotheses about scaffolding. *Journal of Applied Developmental Psychology, 19,* 287–304.

Previc, F.H. (1991). A general theory concerning the prenatal origins of cerebral lateralization in humans. *Psychological Review, 98,* 299–334.

Priel, B., & deSchonen, S. (1986). Self-recognition: A study of a population without mirrors. *Journal of Experimental Child Psychology, 41,* 237–50.

Provence, J., & Lipton, R.C. (1962). *Infants in institutions.* New York: International Universities Press.

Psychological Corporation. (2001). *WAIS-III Canadian Technical Manual.* Toronto: Psychological Corporation.

Pungello, E.P., Kupersmidt, J.B., Burchinal, M.R., & Patterson, C.J. (1996). Environmental risk factors and children's achievement from middle childhood to early adolescence. *Developmental Psychology, 32,* 755–67.

Quas, J.A., Goodman, G.S., Bidrose, S., Pipe, M.-E., & Craw, S. (1999). Emotion and memory: Children's long-term remembering, forgetting, and suggestibility. *Journal of Experimental Child Psychology, 72,* 235–70.

Quay, L.C. (1971). Language dialect, reinforcement, and the intelligence-test performance of Negro children. *Child Development, 42,* 5–15.

Quiggle, N.L., Garber, J., Panak, W.F., & Dodge, K.A. (1992). Social information processing in aggressive and depressed children. *Child Development, 63,* 1305–20.

Quinn, R.A., Houts, A.C., & Graesser, A.C. (1994). Naturalistic conceptions of morality: A question-answering approach. *Journal of Personality, 62,* 260–7.

Rabiner, D.L., Keane, S.P., & MacKinnon-Lewis, C. (1993). Children's beliefs about familiar and unfamiliar peers in relation to their sociometric status. *Developmental Psychology, 29,* 236–43.

Rabiner, D.L., Lenhart, L., & Lochman, J.E. (1990). Automatic versus reflective social problem solving in relation to children's sociometric status. *Developmental Psychology, 26,* 1010–6.

Radke-Yarrow, M., Cummings, E.M., Kuczynski, L., & Chapman, M. (1985). Patterns of attachment in two- and three-year-olds in normal families and families with parental depression. *Child Development, 56,* 884–93.

Radke-Yarrow, M., Zahn-Waxler, C., & Chapman, M. (1983). Children's prosocial dispositions and behavior. In P.H. Mussen (Series Ed.) & E.M. Hetherington (Vol. Ed.), *Handbook of child psychology: Vol. 4. Socialization, personality, and social development* (4th ed., pp. 469–545). New York: Wiley.

Rakic, P. (1991). Plasticity of cortical development. In S.E. Brauth, W.S. Hall, & R.J. Dooling (Eds.), *Plasticity of development.* Cambridge, MA: Bradford/MIT Press.

Ram, A., & Ross, H. (2001). Problem-solving, contention, and struggle: How siblings resolve a conflict of interest. *Child Development, 72* (6).

Ramey, C.T., & Ramey, S.L. (1998). Early intervention and early experience. *American Psychologist, 53,* 296–309.

Ramos-Ford, V., & Gardner, H. (1997). Giftedness from a multiple intelligences perspective. In N. Conangelo & G.A. Davis (Eds.), *Handbook of gifted education* (2nd ed., pp. 54–66). Boston: Allyn & Bacon.

Rasmussen, C., Ho, E., & Bisanz, J. (2003). Use of the mathematical principle of inversion in young children. *Journal of Experimental Child Psychology, 85,* 89–102.

Raz, S., Goldstein, R., Hopkins, T.L., Lauterbach, M.D., Shah, F., Porter, C.L., Riggs, W.W., Magill, L.H., & Sander, C.J. (1994). Sex differences in early vulnerability to cerebral injury and their neurobehavioral implications. *Psychobiology, 22,* 244–53.

Raz, S., Lauterbach, M. D., Hopkins, T. L., Glogowski, B. K., Porter, C. L., Riggs, W. W., & Sander, C. J. (1995). A female advantage in cognitive recovery from early cerebral insult. *Developmental Psychology, 31,* 958-966.

Reed, T.E. (1997). "The genetic hypothesis": It was not tested but it could have been. American Psychologist, 52, 77–8.

Reeder, K. (1981). How young children learn to do things with words. In P.S. Dale & D. Ingram (Eds.), *Child language—an international perspective*. Baltimore, MD: University Park Press.

Reese, E., & Cox, A. (1999). Quality of adult book reading affects children's emergent literacy. *Developmental Psychology, 35,* 20–28.

Reese, E., & Fivush, R. (1993). Parental styles of talking about the past. *Developmental Psychology, 29,* 546–606.

Reese, E., Hayden, C., & Fivush, R. (1993). Mother–child conversations about the past: Relationships of style and memory over time. *Cognitive Development, 8,* 403–30.

Reese, H.A. (1963). Perceptual set in young children. *Child Development, 34,* 151–9.

Reich, P.A. (1986). *Language development.* Englewood Cliffs, NJ: Prentice-Hall.

Reijonen, J., Pratt, H., Patel, D., & Greydanus, D. (2003). Eating disorders in the adolescent population: An overview. *Journal of Adolescent Research, 18* (3), 209–22.

Reikehof, L. (1963). *Talk to the deaf.* Springfield, MO: Gospel Publishing House.

Reinisch, J.M., Sanders, S.A., Hill, C.A., & Ziemba-Davis, M. (1992). High-risk sexual behavior among heterosexual undergraduates at a midwestern university. *Family Planning Perspectives, 24,* 116.

Remley, A. (1988, October). The great parental value shift: From obedience to independence. *Psychology Today,* 56–9.

Repacholi, B.M. (1998). Infants' use of attentional cues to identify the referent of another person's emotional expression. *Developmental Psychology, 34,* 1017–25.

Repacholi, B.M., & Gopnik, A. (1997). Early reasoning about desires: Evidence from 14- and 18-month-olds. *Developmental Psychology, 33,* 12–21.

Resnick, S.M., Berenbaum, S.A., Gottesman, I.I., & Bouchard, T.J. (1986). Early hormonal influences on cognitive functioning in congenital adrenal hyperplasia. *Developmental Psychology, 22,* 191–8.

Rest, J.R., & Thoma, S.J. (1985). Relation of moral judgment development to formal education. *Developmental Psychology, 21,* 709–14.

Rest, J.R., Thoma, S.J., & Edwards, L. (1997). Designing and validating a measure of moral judgment: Stage preference and stage consistency approaches. *Journal of Educational Psychology, 89,* 5–28.

Revelle, G.L., Wellman, H.M., & Karabenick, J.D. (1985). Comprehension monitoring in preschool children. *Child Development, 56,* 654–63.

Reyna, V.F., & Brainerd, C.J. (1995). Fuzzy-trace theory: An interim synthesis. *Learning and Individual Differences, 7,* 1–75.

Reynolds, D. (1992). School effectiveness and school improvement: An updated review of the British literature. In D. Reynolds & P. Cuttance (Eds.), *School effectiveness: Research, policy, and practice.* London, England: Cassell.

Reznick, J.S., & Goldfield, B.A. (1992). Rapid change in lexical development in comprehension and production. *Developmental Psychology, 28,* 406–13.

Rheingold, H.L. (1982). Little children's participation in the work of adults, a nascent prosocial behavior. *Child Development, 53,* 114–25.

Rheingold, H.L., & Adams, J.L. (1980). The significance of speech to newborns. *Developmental Psychology, 16,* 397–403.

Rhodes, J.E., Grossman, J.B., & Resch, N.L. (2000). Agents of change: Pathways through which mentoring relationships influence adolescents' academic adjustment. *Child Development, 71,* 1662–71.

Rholes, W.S., & Ruble, D.N. (1984). Children's understanding of dispositional characteristics of others. *Child Development, 55,* 550–60.

Ribble, M. (1943). *The rights of infants.* New York: Columbia University Press.

Rice, C., Koinis, D., Sullivan, K., Tager-Flusberg, H. & Winner, E. (1997). When 3-year olds pass the appearance-reality test. *Developmental Psychology, 33,* 54–61.

Rice, M.E., & Grusec, J.E. (1975). Saying and doing: Effects on observer performance. *Journal of Personality and Social Psychology, 32,* 584–93.

Rice, M.L., Huston, A.C., Truglio, R., & Wright, J. (1990). Words from "Sesame Street": Learning vocabulary while viewing. *Developmental Psychology, 26,* 421–8.

Richards, J.E. (1997). Effects of attention on infant's preference for briefly exposed visual stimuli in the paired-comparison recognition-memory paradigm. *Developmental Psychology, 32,* 22–31.

Richards, M.H., Boxer, A.M., Petersen, A.C., & Albrecht, R. (1990). Relation of weight to body image in pubertal girls and boys from two communities. *Developmental Psychology, 26,* 313–21.

Richards, M.H., Crowe, P.A., Larson, R., & Swarr, A. (1998). Developmental patterns and gender differences in the experience of peer companionship during adolescence. *Child Development, 69,* 154–63.

Richards, M.H., & Duckett, E. (1994). The relationship of maternal employment to early adolescent daily experience with and without parents. *Child Development, 65,* 225–36.

Richardson, J.G., & Simpson, C.H. (1982). Children, gender, and social structure: An analysis of the contents of letters to Santa Claus. *Child Development, 53,* 429–36.

Richardson, K. (2002). What IQ tests test. *Theory and Psychology, 12* (3), 283-314.

Richman, E.L., & Shaffer, D.R. (2000). "If you let me play sports": How might sport participation influence the self-esteem of adolescent females? *Psychology of Women Quarterly, 24,* 189–99.

Ridderinkhoff, K.R., & van der Molen, M.W. (1995). A psychophysiological analysis of developmental differences in the ability to resist interference. *Child Development, 66,* 1040–56.

Riesen, A. H. (1947). The development of visual perception in man and chimpanzee. *Science, 106,* 107–08.

Riesen, A.H., Chow, K.L., Semmes, J., & Nissen, H.W. (1951). Chimpanzee vision after four conditions of light deprivation. *American Psychologist, 6,* 282.

Rieser, J., Yonas, A., & Wilkner, K. (1976). Radial localization of odors by human newborns. *Child Development, 47,* 856–9.

Roberts, K. (2002). Children's ability to distinguish between memories from multiple sources: Implications for the quality and accuracy of eyewitness statements. *Developmental Review, 22,* 403–35.

Roberts, K., & Powell, M. (2001). Describing individual incidents of sexual abuse: A review of research on the effects of multiple sources of information on children's reports. *Child Abuse and Neglect, 25,* 1643–59.

Roberts, L.R., Sarigiani, P.A., Petersen, A.C., & Newman, J.L. (1990). Gender differences in the relationship between achievement and self-image during early adolescence. *Journal of Early Adolescence, 10,* 159–75.

Roberts, W., & Strayer, J. (1996). Empathy, emotional expressiveness, and prosocial behavior. *Child Development, 67* (2), 449–70.

Robertson, T.S., & Rossiter, J.R. (1974). Children and commercial persuasion: An attribution theory analysis. *Journal of Consumer Research, 1,* 13–20.

Robin, D.J., Berthier, N.E., & Clifton, R.K. (1996). Infants' predictive reaching for moving objects in the dark. *Developmental Psychology, 32,* 824–35.

Robinson, B.F., & Mervis, C.B. (1998). Disentangling early language development: Modeling lexical and grammatical acquisition using an extension of case-study methodology. *Developmental Psychology, 34,* 363–75.

Robinson, C.C., & Morris, J.T. (1986). The gender-stereotyped nature of Christmas toys received by 36-, 48-, and 60-month-old children: A comparison between nonrequested vs. requested toys. *Sex Roles, 15,* 21–32.

Robinson, I., Ziss, K., Ganza, B., Katz, S., & Robinson, E. (1991). Twenty years of sexual revolution, 1965–1985: An update. *Journal of Marriage and the Family, 53,* 216–20.

Robinson, J.L., Kagan, J., Reznick, J.S., & Corley, R. (1992). The heritability of inhibited and uninhibited behavior. A twin study. *Developmental Psychology, 28,* 1030–7.

Rochat, P. (1989). Object manipulation and exploration in 2- to 5-month-old infants. *Developmental Psychology, 25,* 871–84.

Rochat, P., & Goubet, N. (1995). Development of sitting and reaching in 5- to 6-month-old infants. *Infant Behavior and Development, 18,* 53–68.

Rochat, P., Querido, J.G., & Striano, T. (1999). Emerging sensitivity to the timing and structure of protoconversation in early infancy. *Developmental Psychology, 35,* 950–57.

Roche, A.F. (1981). The adipocyte-number hypothesis. *Child Development, 52,* 31–43.

Rocheleau, B. (1995). Computer use by school-age children: Trends, patterns, and predictors. *Journal of Educational Computing Research, 12,* 1–17.

Rock, A.M.L., Trainor, L.J., & Addison, T.L. (1999). Distinctive messages in infant-directed lullabies and play songs. *Developmental Psychology, 35,* 527–34.

Rodkin, P.C., Farmer, T.W., Pearl, R., & Van Aker, R. (2000). Heterogeneity of popular boys: Antisocial and prosocial configurations. *Developmental Psychology, 36,* 14–24.

Rodning, C., Beckwith, L., & Howard, J. (1991). Quality of attachment and home environments in children prenatally exposed to PCP and cocaine. *Development and Psychopathology, 3,* 351–66.

Roeleveld, N., Zielhuis, G.A., & Gabreels, F. (1997). The prevalence of mental retardation: A critical review of present literature. *Developmental Medicine and Child Neurology, 39,* 125–32.

Roeser, R.W., & Eccles, J.S. (1998). Adolescents' perceptions of middle school: Relation to longitudinal changes in academic and psychological adjustment. *Journal of Research in Adolescence, 8,* 123–58.

Rogoff, B. (1990). *Apprenticeship in thinking: Cognitive development in social context.* New York: Oxford University Press.

Rogoff, B. (1998). Cognition as a collaborative process. In W. Damon (Series Ed.) & D. Kuhn

& R.S. Siegler (Vol. Eds.), *Handbook of child psychology: Vol. 2. Cognition, perception, and language* (5th ed., pp. 679–744). New York: Wiley.

Rogoff, B., Mistry, J., Göncü, A., & Mosier, C. (1993). Guided participation in cultural activity by toddlers and caregivers. *Monographs of the Society for Research in Child Development, 58* (8, Serial No. 236), 1–174.

Rogoff, B., & Waddell, K.J. (1982). Memory for information organized in a scene by children from two cultures. *Child Development, 53,* 1224–8.

Rohner, R.P. (2000). Father love and child development: History and current evidence. In K.L. Frieberg (Ed.), *Human development 00/01* (28th ed., pp. 124–128). Guilford, CT: Dushkin/McGraw-Hill.

Roid, G., & Worrall, W. (1997). Replication of the Wechsler Intelligence Scale for Children—Third edition four-factor model in the Canadian normative sample. *Psychological Assessment, 9*(4), 512–5.

Roithmaier, A., Kiess, W., Kopecky, M., Fuhrmann, G., & Butenandt, O. (1988). Psychosozialer Minderwuchs. *Monatschift fur Kinderheilkunde, 133,* 760–3.

Roland, M.G.M., Cole, T.J., & Whitehead, R.G. (1977). A quantitative study into the role of infection in determining nutritional status in Gambian village children. *British Journal of Nutrition, 37,* 441–50.

Rose, A.J., & Asher, S.R. (1999). Children's goals and strategies in response to conflicts within a friendship. *Developmental Psychology, 35,* 69–79.

Rose, R.M., Bernstein, I.S., & Gordon, T.P. (1975). Consequences of social conflict on plasma testosterone levels in rhesus monkeys. *Psychosomatic Medicine, 37,* 50–61.

Rose, S.A. (1988). Shape recognition in infancy: Visual integration of sequential information. *Child Development, 59,* 1161–76.

Rose, S.A., & Feldman, J.F. (1995). Prediction of IQ and specific cognitive abilities from infancy measures. *Developmental Psychology, 31,* 685–96.

Rose, S.A., & Feldman, J.F. (1996). Memory and processing speed in preterm children at eleven years: A comparison with full-terms. *Child Development, 67,* 2005–21.

Rose, S.A., Feldman, J.F., & Jankowski, J.J. (2001). Attention and recognition memory in the 1st year of life: A longitudinal study of preterm and full-term infants. *Developmental Psychology, 37,* 135–51.

Rose, S.A., Feldman, J.F., Wallace, I.F., & McCarton, C. (1989). Infant visual attention: Relation to birth status and developmental outcome during the first 5 years. *Developmental Psychology, 25,* 560–76.

Rose, S.A., Gottfried, A.W., & Bridger, W.H. (1981). Cross-modal transfer in 6-month-old infants. *Developmental Psychology, 17,* 661–9.

Rosen, B.C., & D'Andrade, R. (1959). The psychosocial origins of achievement motivation. *Sociometry, 22,* 185–218.

Rosen, J.C., Tracey, B., & Howell, D. (1990). Life stress, psychological symptoms, and weight reducing behavior in adolescent girls: A prospective analysis. *International Journal of Eating Disorders, 9,* 17–26.

Rosen, W.D., Adamson, L.B., & Bakeman, R. (1992). An experimental investigation of infant social referencing: Mothers' messages and gender differences. *Developmental Psychology, 28,* 1172–8.

Rosenblum, G.D., & Lewis, M. (1999). The relations among body image, physical attractiveness, and body mass in adolescents. *Child Development, 70,* 50–64.

Rosenhan, D.L. (1970). The natural socialization of altruistic autonomy. In J.L. Macaulay & L. Berkowitz (Eds.), *Altruism and helping behavior.* New York: Academic Press.

Rosenholtz, S.J., & Simpson, C. (1984). The formation of ability conceptions: Developmental trend or social construction? *Review of Educational Research, 54,* 31–63.

Rosenthal, M.K. (1982). Vocal dialogues in the neonatal period. *Developmental Psychology, 18,* 17–21.

Rosenthal, R., & Vandell, D.L. (1996). Quality of care at school-aged child-care programs: Regulatable features, observed experiences, child perspectives, and parent perspectives. *Child Development, 67,* 2434–45.

Rosenwasser, S.M., Lingenfelter, M., & Harrington, A.F. (1989). Nontraditional gender role portrayals on television and children's gender role perceptions. *Journal of Applied Developmental Psychology, 10,* 97–105.

Rosenzweig, M.R. (1984). Experience, memory, and the brain. *American Psychologist, 39,* 365–76.

Ross, D.P., Scott, K., & Kelly, M.A. (1996, November 20). Overview: Children in Canada in the 1990s. In Statistics Canada, National Longitudinal Survey of Children and Youth, *Growing up in Canada: A detailed portrait of children and young people* (chap. 1). Catalogue No. 89-550-MPE. Ottawa: Statistics Canada.

Ross, H.S., & Lollis, S.P. (1987). Communication within infant social games. *Developmental Psychology, 23,* 241–8.

Ross, H.S., Siddiqui, A., Ram, A., & Ward, L. (2004). Perspectives on self and other in children's representations of sibling conflict. *International Journal of Behavioral Development, 28* (1), 37–47.

Ross, R.T., Begab, M.J., Dondis, E.H., Giampiccolo, J.S., Jr., & Meyers, C.E. (1985). *Lives of the mentally retarded. A forty-year follow-up study.* Stanford, CA: Stanford University Press.

Roth, J., & Brooks-Gunn, J. (2000). What do adolescents need for healthier development? Implications for youth policy. *Social policy report* (Vol. 14, No. 1). Chicago: Society for Research in Child Development.

Rothbart, M.K. (1981). Measurement of temperament in infancy. *Child Development, 52,* 569–78.

Rothbaum, F., Pott, M., Azuma, H., Miyake, K., & Weisz, J. (2000). The development of close relationships in Japan and the United States: Paths of symbiotic harmony and generative tension. *Child Development, 71,* 1121–42.

Rothbaum, F., Weisz, J., Pott, M., Miyake, K., & Morelli, G. (2000). Attachment and culture: Security in the United States and Japan. *American Psychologist, 35,* 1093–104.

Rothberg, A.D., & Lits, B. (1991). Psychosocial support for maternal stress during pregnancy: Effect on birth weight. *American Journal of Obstetrics and Gynecology, 165,* 403–7.

Rousseau, J.J. (1955). *Émile.* New York: Dutton. (Original work published 1762.)

Rovee-Collier, C.K. (1987). Learning and memory in infancy. In J.D. Osofsky (Ed.), *Handbook of infant development* (2nd ed., pp. 98–148). New York: Wiley.

Rovee-Collier, C.K. (1995). Time windows in cognitive development. *Developmental Psychology, 31,* 147–69.

Rovee-Collier, C.K. (1997). Dissociations in infant memory: Retention without remembering. In J.D. Osofsky (Ed.), *Handbook of infant development* (2nd ed.). New York: Wiley.

Rowe, D.C. (1994). *The limits of family influence: Genes, experience, and behavior.* New York: Guilford.

Rowe, D.C. (1999). Genetic and environmental influences on vocabulary IQ: Parental education level as a moderator. *Child Development, 70,* 1157–62.

Rowe, D.C., & Plomin, R. (1981). The importance of nonshared (E_1) environmental

influences in behavioral development. *Developmental Psychology, 17,* 517–31.

Rubenstein, A.J., Kalakanis, L., & Langlois, J.H. (1999). Infant preferences for attractive faces: A cognitive explanation. *Developmental Psychology, 35,* 848–55.

Rubenstein, J.L., Heeren, T., Housman, D., Rubin, C., & Stechler, G. (1989). Suicidal behavior in normal adolescents: Risks and protective factors. *American Journal of Orthopsychiatry, 59,* 59–71.

Rubin, K.H., Bukowski, W.M., & Parker, J.G. (1998). Peer interactions, relationships, and groups. In W. Damon (Series Ed.) & N. Eisenberg (Vol. Ed.), *Handbook of child psychology: Vol. 3. Social, emotional, and personality development* (5th ed., pp. 619–700). New York: Wiley.

Rubin, K.H., Fein, G., & Vandenberg, B. (1983). Play. In P.H. Mussen (Series Ed.) & E.M. Hetherington (Vol. Ed.), *Handbook of child psychology: Vol. 4. Socialization, personality and social development* (4th ed., pp. 693–744). New York: Wiley.

Ruble, D.N., Balaban, T., & Cooper, J. (1981). Gender constancy and the effects of sex-typed televised toy commercials. *Child Development, 52,* 667–73.

Ruble, D.N., & Dweck, C.S. (1995). Self-conceptions, person conceptions, and their development. In N. Eisenberg (Ed.), *Social development.* Thousand Oaks, CA: Sage.

Ruble, D.N., & Martin, C.L. (1998). Gender development. In W. Damon (Series Ed.) & N. Eisenberg (Vol. Ed.), *Handbook of child psychology: Vol. 3. Social, emotional, and personality development* (5th ed., pp. 933–1016). New York: Wiley.

Ruble, T.L. (1983). Sex stereotypes: Issues of change in the 1970s. *Sex Roles, 9,* 397–402.

Rudin, M., Zalewski, C., & Bodmer-Turner, J. (1995). Characteristics of child sexual abusive victims according to perpetrator gender. *Child Abuse & Neglect, 19,* 963–73.

Rueter, M.A., & Conger, R.D. (1998). Reciprocal influences between parenting and adolescent problem-solving behavior. *Developmental Psychology, 34,* 1470–82.

Ruff, H.A., Capozzoli, M., & Weisberg, R. (1998). Age, individuality, and context as factors in sustained visual attention during the preschool years. *Developmental Psychology, 34,* 454–64.

Ruffman, T., Perner, J., Naito, M., Parkin, L., & Clements, W.A. (1998). Older (but not younger) siblings facilitate false belief understanding. *Developmental Psychology, 34,* 161–74.

Ruffman, T.K., & Olson, D.R. (1989). Children's ascriptions of knowledge to others. *Developmental Psychology, 25,* 601–6.

Ruffman, T.K., Olson, D.R., Ash, T., & Keenan, T. (1993). The ABCs of deception: Do young children understand deception in the same way as adults? *Developmental Psychology, 29,* 74–87.

Rumelhart, D., & McClelland, J. (Eds.). (1986). *Parallel distributed processing: Explorations in the microstructure of cognition.* Cambridge MA: MIT Press/Bradford Books.

Runco, M.A. (1992). Children's divergent thinking and creative ideation. *Developmental Review, 12,* 233–64.

Rushton, J.P. (1980). *Altruism, socialization, and society.* Englewood Cliffs, NJ: Prentice-Hall.

Rushton, J.P. (1992). Contributions to the history of psychology: XC. Evolutionary biology and heritable traits (with reference to Oriental–white–black differences). *Psychological Reports, 71,* 811–21.

Ruston, J.P. (1999). *Race, evolution, and behavior.* New Brunswick, NH: Transaction.

Russell, G.F.M., Szmukler, G.I., Dare, C., & Eisler, I. (1987). An evaluation of family therapy in anorexia nervosa and bulimia nervosa. *Archives of General Psychiatry, 44*, 1047–56.

Rutter, D.R., & Durkin, K. (1987). Turn-taking in mother–infant interaction: An examination of vocalizations and gaze. *Developmental Psychology, 23*, 54–61.

Rutter, M. (1979). Protective factors in children's responses to stress and disadvantage. In M.W. Kent & J.E. Rolf (Eds.), *Primary prevention of psychopathology: Vol. 3. Social competence in children* (pp. 49–74). Hanover, NH: University Press of New England.

Rutter, M. (1981). *Maternal deprivation revisited* (2nd ed.). New York: Penguin Books.

Rutter, M. (1983). School effects on pupil progress: Research findings and policy implications. *Child Development, 54*, 1–29.

Rutter, M., Maughan, B., Mortimore, P., Ouston, J., & Smith, A. (1980). *Fifteen thousand hours: Secondary schools and their effects on children.* Cambridge, MA: Harvard University Press.

Rvachew, S., Slawinski, E., Williams, M., & Green, C. (1999). The impact of early onset Otitis-Media on babbling and early language development. *Journal of The Acoustic Society of America, 105*, 467–75.

Saarni, C. (1990). Emotional competence: How emotions and relationships become integrated. In R.A. Thompson (Ed.), Socioemotional development. *Nebraska Symposium on Motivation: Vol. 36* (pp. 115–82). Lincoln: University of Nebraska Press.

Saarni, C. (1999). *The development of emotional competence.* New York: Guilford.

Sabbagh, M.A., & Callanan, M.A. (1998). Metarepresentation in action: 3-, 4- and 5-year-olds' developing theories of mind in parent-child conversations. *Developmental Psychology, 34*, 491–502.

Sacks, C.H., & Mergendoller, J.R. (1997). The relationship between teachers' theoretical orientation toward reading and student outcomes in kindergarten children with different initial reading abilities. *American Educational Research Journal, 34*, 721–39.

Sacks, O. (1993, December 27). A neurologist's notebook: An anthropologist on Mars. *New Yorker*, pp. 106–25.

Sadler, T.W. (1996). Embryology and experimental teratology. In J.A. Kuller, N.C. Cheschier, & R.C. Cefalo (Eds.), *Prenatal diagnosis and reproductive genetics* (pp. 218–26). St. Louis, MO: Mosby.

Sagi, A., & Hoffman, M.L. (1976). Empathic distress in newborns. *Developmental Psychology, 12*, 175–6.

Sagi, A., van IJzendoorn, M.H., Aviezer, O., Donnell, F., & Mayseless, O. (1994). Sleeping out of home in a kibbutz communal arrangement: It makes a difference for mother–infant attachment. *Child Development, 65*, 992–1004.

Sahni, R., Schulze, K.F., Stefanski, M., Myers, M.M., & Fifer, W.P. (1995). Methodological issues in coding sleep states in immature infants. *Developmental Psychobiology, 28*, 85–101.

Saigal, S., Hoult, L.A., Streiner, D.L., Stoskopf, F.L., & Rosenbaum, P.L. (2000). School difficulties at adolescence in a regional cohort of children who were extremely low birth weight. *Pediatrics, 105*, 325–31.

Saklofske, D.H. (2003). In J. Georgas, L. Weiss, F. VanDe Vijver, & D. Saklofske, *Culture and Children's Intelligence: Cross Cultural Analysis of the WISC-III.* Academic Press London.

Saklofske, D.H., Austin, E., & Minski, P. (2003). Factor structure and validity of a trait emotional intelligence measure. *Personality and Individual Differences, 34*, 707–21.

Saklofske, D.H., Caravan, G., & Schwartz, C. (2000). Concurrent validity of the Wechsler Abbreviated Scale of Intelligence (WASI) with a sample of Canadian children. *Canadian Journal of School Psychology, 16*(1), 87–94.

Saklofske, D.H., Hildebrand, D.K., & Gorsuch, R.L. (2000). Replication of the factor structure of the Wechsler Adult Intelligence Scale—Third edition with a Canadian sample. *Psychological Assessment. Special issue, 12* (4), 436–9.

Salapatek, P. (1975). Pattern perception in early infancy. In L.B. Cohen & P. Salapatek (Eds.), *Infant perception: From sensation to cognition* (Vol. 1, pp. 133–248). New York: Academic Press.

Salzinger, S., Feldman, R.S., Hammer, M., & Rosario, M. (1993). The effects of physical abuse on children's social relationships. *Child Development, 64*, 169–87.

Sameroff, A.J., & Chandler, M.J. (1975). Reproductive risk and the continuum of caretaking casualty. In F.D. Horowitz, M. Hetherington, S. Scarr-Salapatek, & G. Siegel (Eds.), *Review of child development research* (Vol. 4, pp. 187–244). Chicago: University of Chicago Press.

Sameroff, A.J., Seifer, R., Baldwin, A., & Baldwin, C. (1993). Stability of intelligence from preschool to adolescence: The influence of social and family risk factors. *Child Development, 64*, 80–97.

Samuels, C. (1986). Bases for the infant's development of self-awareness. *Human Development, 29*, 36–48.

Samuelson, L.K., & Smith, L.B. (2000). Grounding development in cognitive processes. *Child Development, 71*, 98–106.

Sansavini, A., Bertoncini, J., & Giovanelli, G. (1997). Newborns discriminate the rhythm of multisyllabic stressed words. *Developmental Psychology, 33*, 3–11.

Santrock, J.W., & Sitterle, K.A. (1987). Parent–child relationships in stepmother families. In K. Pasley & M. Ihinger-Tallman (Eds.), *Remarriage and stepparenting: Current research and theory* (pp. 273–99). New York: Guilford Press.

Sapp, F., Lee, K., & Muir, D. (2000). Three-year-olds' difficulty with the appearance-reality distinction: Is it real or is it apparent? *Developmental Psychology, 36*, 547–60.

Sattler, J.M. (2001). *Assessment of Children* (4th. ed.). San Diego, CA: J.M. Sattler.

Savage-Rumbaugh, E.S., Murphy, J., Sevcik, R.A., Brakke, K.E., Williams, S.L., & Rumbaugh, D.M. (1993). Language comprehension in ape and child. *Monographs of the Society for Research in Child Development, 58* (3–4, Serial No. 233).

Savelsbergh, G., van der Kamp, J., & Rosengren, K. (2002). Walking through history: Changing constraints in developmental thinking. *Infant Behaviour and Development, 25*, 94-97.

Savin-Williams, R.C. (1995). An exploratory study of pubertal maturation timing and self-esteem among gay and bisexual male youths. *Developmental Psychology, 31*, 56–64.

Savin-Williams, R.C. (1998). *And Then I Became Gay: Young Men's Stories.* New York: Routledge.

Savin-Williams, R.C., & Demo, D.H. (1984). Developmental change and stability in adolescent self-concept. *Developmental Psychology, 20*, 1100–10.

Savin-Williams, R.C., & Small, S.A. (1986). The timing of puberty and its relationship to adolescent and parent perceptions of family interactions. *Developmental Psychology, 32*, 342–7.

Saxton, M. (1997). The contrast theory of negative input. *Journal of Child Language, 24*, 139–61.

Saywitz, K.J., Mannarino, A.P., Berliner, L., & Cohen, J.A. (2000). Treatment for sexually abused children and adolescents. *American Psychologist, 55*, 1040–9.

Scafidi, F.A., Field, T.M., Schanberg, S.M., Bauer, C.R., Vega-Lahr, N., Garcia, R., Poirier, J., Nystrom, G., & Kuhn, C.M. (1986). Effects of tactile/kinesthetic stimulation on the clinical course and sleep/wake behavior pattern of preterm neonates. *Infant Behavior and Development, 9*, 91–105.

Scafidi, F.A., Field, T.M., Schanberg, S.M., Bauer, C.R., Vega-Lahr, N., Garcia, R., Poirier, J., Nystrom, G., & Kuhn, C.M. (1990). Massage stimulates growth in preterm infants: A replication. *Infant Behavior and Development, 13*, 167–88.

Scaramella, L.V., Conger, R.D., Simons, R.L., & Whitbeck, L.B. (1998). Predicting risk for pregnancy by late adolescence: A social-contextual perspective. *Developmental Psychology, 34*, 1233–45.

Scarr, S. (1992). Developmental theories for the 1990s: Development and individual differences. *Child Development, 63*, 1–19.

Scarr, S. (1998). American child care today. *American Psychologist, 53*, 95–108.

Scarr, S., & McCartney, K. (1983). How people make their own environments: A theory of genotype/ environment effects. *Child Development, 54*, 424–35.

Scarr, S., Pakstis, A.J., Katz, S.H., & Barker, W. (1977). The absence of a relationship between degree of white ancestry and intellectual skills within a black population. *Human Genetics, 39*, 69–86.

Scarr, S., & Weinberg, R.A. (1978). The influence of family background on intellectual attainment. *American Sociological Review, 43*, 674–92.

Scarr, S., & Weinberg, R.A. (1983). The Minnesota adoption studies: Genetic differences and malleability. *Child Development, 54*, 260–7.

Schachar, R.J., Tannock, R., Cunningham, C., & Corkum, P.V. (1997). Behavioral, situational, and temporal effects of treatment of ADHD with methylphenidate. *Journal of the American Academy of Child and Adolescent Psychiatry, 36*, 754–63.

Schaefer, G., & Plummert, K. (1998). Rapid word learning by 15-month-olds under tightly controlled conditions. *Child Development, 69*, 309–20.

Schaffer, H.R. (1971). *The growth of sociability.* Baltimore, MD: Penguin Books.

Schaffer, H.R., & Emerson, P.E. (1964). The development of social attachments in infancy. *Monographs of the Society for Research in Child Development, 29* (3, Serial No. 94).

Schaie, K.W. (1990). Intellectual development in adulthood. In E.J. Birren & K.W. Schaie (Eds.). *The handbook of the psychology of aging* (3rd ed., pp. 291–309). San Diego, CA: Academic Press.

Schalock, R.L., Holl, C., Elliott, B., & Ross, I. (1992). A longitudinal follow-up of graduates from a rural special education program. *Learning Disability Quarterly, 15*, 29–38.

Schauble, L. (1990). Belief revision in children: The role of prior knowledge and strategies for generating evidence. *Journal of Experimental Child Psychology, 49*, 31–57.

Schieffelin, B.B. (1986). *How Kaluli children learn what to say, what to do, and how to feel.* New York: Cambridge University Press.

Schiff-Myers, N. (1988). Hearing children of deaf parents. In D. Bishop & K. Mogford (Eds.), *Language development in exceptional circumstances* (pp. 47–61). Edinburgh, Scotland: Churchill Livingstone.

Schlegel, A., & Barry, H., III. (1991). *Adolescence: An anthropological inquiry.* New York: Free Press.

Schliemann, A.D. (1992). Mathematical concepts in and out of school in Brazil: From developmental psychology to better teaching. *Newsletter of the International Society for the*

Study of Behavioural Development (2, Serial No. 22), 1–3.

Schmidt, K. L., Anderson, D. R., & Collins, P. A. (1999). Form and content: Looking at visual features of television. *Developmental Psychology, 35*, 1156-1167.

Schmucker, M.A., & Tsang-Tong, H.Y. (2000). The role of visual and body movement information in infant search. *Developmental Psychology, 36*, 499–510.

Schneider, B.H. (1992). Didactic methods for enhancing children's peer relations: A quantitative review. *Clinical Psychology Review, 12*, 363–82.

Schneider, B.H., Atkinson, L., & Tardiff, C. (2001). Child–parent atttachment and children's peer relations: A quantitative review. *Developmental Psychology, 37*, 86–100.

Schneider, M.L., Roughton, E.C., Koehler, A.J., & Lubach, G.R. (1999). Growth and development following prenatal stress exposure in primates: An examination of ontogenetic vulnerability. *Child Development, 70*, 263–74.

Schneider, W., & Bjorklund, D.F. (1998). Memory. In W. Damon (Series Ed.) & D. Kuhn & R.S. Siegler (Vol. Eds.), *Handbook of child psychology: Vol. 2. Cognition, perception, and language* (5th ed., pp. 467–521). New York: Wiley.

Schneider, W., & Bjorklund, D.F. (2001). Memory and knowledge development. In J. Valsiner & K. Connolly (Eds.), *Handbook of developmental psychology*. London, England: Sage.

Schneider, W., Bjorklund, D.F., & Maier-Bruckner, W. (1996). The effects of expertise and IQ on children's memory: When knowledge is, and when it is not enough. *International Journal of Behavioral Development, 19*, 773–96.

Schneider, W., Gruber, H., Gold, A., & Opwis, K. (1993). Chess expertise and memory for chess positions in children and adults. *Journal of Experimental Child Psychology, 56*, 328–49.

Schneider, W., Körkel, J., & Weinert, F.E. (1989). Domain-specific knowledge and memory performance: A comparison of high- and low-aptitude children. *Journal of Educational Psychology, 81*, 306–12.

Schneider, W., Kuspert, P., Roth, E., & Visé, M. (1997). Short- and long-term effects of training phonological awareness in kindergarten: Evidence from two German studies. *Journal of Experimental Child Psychology, 66*, 311-340.

Schneider, W., & Naslund, J.C. (1999). The impact of early phonological processing skills on reading and spelling in school: Evidence from the Munich longitudinal study. In F.E. Weinert & W. Schneider (Eds.), *The Munich longitudinal study on the genesis of individual competencies (LOGIC)*. Cambridge: Cambridge University Press.

Schneider, W., & Pressley, M. (1997). *Memory development between 2 and 20* (2nd ed.). Mahwah, NJ: Erlbaum.

Scholl, T.O., Hediger, M.L., & Belsky, D.H. (1994). Prenatal care and maternal health during adolescent pregnancy: A review and meta-analysis. *Journal of Adolescent Health, 15*, 444–56.

Schulman, J.D., & Black, S.H. (1993). Genetics of some common inherited diseases. In R.G. Edwards (Ed.), *Preconception and preimplantation diagnosis of human genetic disease* (pp. 101–25). Cambridge, England: Cambridge University Press.

Schuster, D.T. (1990). Fulfillment of potential, life satisfaction, and competence: Comparing four cohorts of gifted women at midlife. *Journal of Educational Psychology, 82*, 471–8.

Schwanenflugel, P.J., Henderson, R.L., & Fabricius, W.V. (1998). Developing organization of mental verbs and theory of mind in middle childhood: Evidence from extension. *Developmental Psychology, 34*, 512–24.

Schwartz, D., Dodge, K.A., Pettit, G.S., & Bates, J.E. (1997). The early socialization of aggressive victims of bullying. *Child Development, 68*, 665–75.

Schwartz, D., Dodge, K.A., Pettit, G.S., Bates, J.E., & the Conduct Problems Prevention Research Group. (2000). Friendship as a moderating factor in the pathway between early harsh home environment and later victimization in the peer group. *Developmental Psychology, 36*, 646–62.

Schwebel, D.C., & Plumert, J.M. (1999). Longitudinal and concurrent relations among termperament, ability estimation, and accident proneness. *Child Development, 70*, 700–12.

Schwebel, D.C., Plumert, J.M., & Pick, H.L. (2000). Integrating basic and applied developmental research: A new model for the twenty-first century. *Child Development, 71*, 222–30.

Scott, J.P. (1992). Aggression: Functions and control in social systems. *Aggressive Behavior, 18*, 1–20.

Scott, W.A., Scott, R., & McCabe, M. (1991). Family relationships and children's personality: A cross-cultural, cross-source comparison. *British Journal of Social Psychology, 30*, 1–20.

Seabrook, C. (1997, February 12). Eating disorders can be overcome. *Atlanta Constitution*, C1.

Sears, R.R. (1963). Dependency motivation. In M. Jones (Ed.), *Nebraska Symposium on Motivation: Vol. 11* (pp. 25–64). Lincoln: University of Nebraska Press.

Sebald, H. (1986). Adolescents' shifting orientation toward parents and peers: A curvilinear trend over recent decades. *Journal of Marriage and the Family, 48*, 5–13.

Segal, U.A. (1991). Cultural variables in Asian Indian families. *Families in society: The Journal of Contemporary Human Services, 72*, 233–42.

Seidenberg, M.S., & McClelland, J.L. (1989). A distributed, developmental model of word recognition and naming. *Psychological Review, 96*, 523–68.

Seidman, E., Allen, L., Aber, J.L., Mitchell, C., & Feinman, J. (1994). The impact of school transitions in early adolescence on the self-system and perceived social context of poor urban youth. *Child Development, 65*, 507–22.

Seifer, R., Schiller, M., Sameroff, A.J., Resnick, S., & Riordan, K. (1996). Attachment, maternal sensitivity, and infant temperament during the first year of life. *Developmental Psychology, 32*, 12–25.

Seitz, V., & Apfel, N.H. (1994a). Effects of a school for pregnant students on the incidence of low-birthweight deliveries. *Child Development, 65*, 666–76.

Seitz, V., & Apfel, N.H. (1994b). Parent-focused intervention: Diffusion effects on siblings. *Child Development, 65*, 677–83.

Seitz, V., Rosenbaum, L.K., & Apfel, N.H. (1985). Effects of family support intervention: A ten-year follow-up. *Child Development, 56*, 376–91.

Selman, R.L. (1976). Social-cognitive understanding: A guide to educational and clinical practice. In T. Lickona (Ed.), *Moral development and behavior: Theory, research, and social issues*. New York: Holt, Rinehart and Winston.

Selman, R.L. (1980). *The growth of interpersonal understanding*. Orlando, FL: Academic Press.

Senechal, M. & Lefevre, J. (2002). Parental involvement in the development of children's reading skill: A five year longitudinal study. *Child Development, 73*(2), 445–60.

Sénéchal, M., LeFevre, J., Thomas, E.M., & Daley, K.E. (1998). Differential effects of home literacy experiences on the development of oral and written language. *Reading Research Quarterly, 33*, 96–116.

Seppa, N. (1997b). Children's TV remains steeped in violence. *Monitor of the American Psychological Association, 28* (6), 36.

Serbin, L., Peters, P., & Schwartzman, A. (1996). Longitudinal study of early childhood injuries and acute illnesses in the offspring of adolescent mothers who were aggressive, withdrawn, or aggressive-withdrawn in childhood. *Journal of Abnormal Psychology, 105* (4), 500–7.

Serbin, L., Poulin-Dubois, D., & Eichstedt, J.A. (2002). Infant's response to gender-inconsistent events. *Infancy, 3* (4), 531–42.

Serbin, L.A., Cooperman, J.M., Peters, P.L., Lehoux, P.M., Stack, D.M., & Schwartzman, A.E. (1998). Intergenerational transfer of psychosocial risk in women with childhood histories of aggression, withdrawal, or aggression and withdrawal. *Developmental Psychology, 34*, 1246–62.

Serbin, L.A., Powlishta, K.K., & Gulko, J. (1993). The development of sex typing in middle childhood. *Monographs of the Society for Research in Child Development, 58* (2, Serial No. 232).

Shafer, H.H., & Kuller, J.A. (1996). Increased maternal age and prior anenploid conception. In J.A. Kuller, N.C. Cheschier, & R.C. Cefalo (Eds.), *Prenatal diagnosis and reproductive genetics* (pp. 23–8). St. Louis, MO: Mosby.

Shaffer, D.R. (1973). *Children's responses to a hypothetical proposition*. Unpublished manuscript. Kent, OH: Kent State University.

Shaffer, D.R. (1994a). Do naturalistic conceptions of morality provide any [novel] answers? *Journal of Personality, 62*, 263–8.

Shaffer, D.R. (2000). *Social and personality development* (4th ed.). Belmont, CA: Wadsworth.

Shaffer, D.R., Pegalis, L.J., & Cornell, D.P. (1992). Gender and self-disclosure revisited: Personal and contextual variations in self-disclosure to same-sex acquaintants. *Journal of Social Psychology, 132*, 307–15.

Shanahan, M.J., Elder, G.H., Jr., Burchinal, M., & Conger, R.D. (1996). Adolescent paid labor and relationships with parents: Early work–family linkages. *Child Development, 67*, 2183–200.

Shanahan, M.J., Finch, M.D., Mortimer, J.T., & Ryu, S. (1991). Adolescent work experience and depressive affect. *Social Psychology Quarterly, 54*, 299–317.

Shantz, C.U. (1983). Social cognition. In P.H. Mussen (Series Ed.) & J.H. Flavell & E.M. Markman (Vol. Ed.), *Handbook of child psychology: Vol. 3. Cognitive development* (4th ed., pp. 495–555). New York: Wiley.

Sharma, A.R., McGue, M.K., & Benson, P.L. (1998). The psychological adjustment of United States adopted adolescents and their nonadopted siblings. *Child Development, 69*, 791–802.

Shatz, M. (1983). Communication. In P.H. Mussen (Series Ed.) & J.H. Flavell & E.M. Markman (Vol. Eds.), *Handbook of child psychology: Vol 3. Cognitive development* (4th ed., pp. 841–89). New York: Wiley.

Shatz, M. (1994). Theory of mind and the development of sociolinguistic intelligence in early childhood. In C. Lewis & P. Mitchell (Eds.), *Children's early understanding of the mind* (pp. 311–29). Hillsdale, NJ: Erlbaum.

Shatz, M., & Gelman, R. (1973). The development of communication skills: Modifications in the speech of young children as a function of listener. *Monographs of the Society for Research in Child Development, 38* (5, Serial No. 152), 1–37.

Shaw, D.S., Winslow, E.E., & Flanagan, C. (1999). A prospective study of the effects of marital status and family relations on young children's adjustment among African American and European American families. *Child Development, 70,* 742–55.

Shearer, L. (1994, April 2). U.Ga. symposium speaker raps "crack babies" research. *Athens Banner-Herald,* pp. 1A, 10A.

Sheingold, K., & Tenney, Y.J. (1982). Memory for a salient childhood event. In U. Neisser (Ed.), *Memory observed: Remembering in natural contexts* (pp. 201–12). San Francisco: W.H. Freeman.

Shell, R.M., & Eisenberg, N. (1996). Children's reactions to the receipt of direct and indirect help. *Child Development, 67,* 1391–1405.

Sherif, M., Harvey, O.J., White, B.J., Hood, W.R., & Sherif, C.W. (1961). *Intergroup conflict and cooperation: The Robber's Cave experiment.* Norman: University of Oklahoma Press.

Shields, A., Ryan, R.M., & Cicchetti, D. (2001). Narrative representations of caregivers and emotional dysregulation as predictors of maltreated children's rejection by peers. *Developmental Psychology, 37,* 321–37.

Shigetomi, C.C., Hartmann, D.P., & Gelfand, D.M. (1981). Sex differences in children's altruistic behavior and reputations for helpfulness. *Developmental Psychology, 17,* 434–7.

Shirley, M.M. (1933). *The first two years: A study of 25 babies: Vol. 1. Postural and locomotor development.* Minneapolis: University of Minnesota Press.

Short, R.J., & Talley, R.C. (1997). Rethinking psychology and the schools: Implications of recent national policy. *American Psychologist, 52,* 234–40.

Shulman, S., Elicker, J., & Sroufe, A. (1994). Stages of friendship growth in preadolescence as related to attachment history. *Journal of Social and Personal Relationships, 11,* 341–61.

Shultz, T.R. (1998). A computational analysis of conservation. *Developmental Science, 1,* 103–26.

Shultz, T.R. (2003). *Computational Developmental Psychology.* Cambridge: The MIT Press.

Shure, M.B. (1989). Interpersonal competence training. In W. Damon (Ed.), *Child development today and tomorrow.* San Francisco: Jossey-Bass.

Shure, M.B., & Spivack, G. (1978). Problem-solving techniques in childrearing. San Francisco: Jossey-Bass.

Shurkin, J.N. (1992). *Terman's kids. The groundbreaking study of how the gifted grow up.* Boston: Little, Brown.

Shwe, H.I., & Markman, E.M. (1997). Young children's appreciation of the mental impact of their communicative signals. *Developmental Psychology, 33,* 630–6.

Shweder, R.A. (1997, April). Varieties of moral intelligence: Autonomy, community, divinity. In L.A. Jensen (Chair), *Shweder's ethics of autonomy, community, and divinity: Theory and research.* Symposium presented at the biennial meeting of the Society for Research in Child Development, Washington, DC.

Shweder, R.A., Mahapatra, M., & Miller, J.G. (1990). Culture and moral development. In J.W. Stigler, R.A. Shweder, & G. Herdt (Eds.), *Cultural psychology. Essays on comparative human development* (pp. 130–204). Cambridge, England: Cambridge University Press.

Siegal, M., & Cowen, J. (1984). Appraisals of intervention: The mother's versus the culprit's behavior as determinants of children's evaluations of discipline techniques. *Child Development, 55,* 1760–6.

Siegal, M., & Peterson, C.C. (1998). Preschoolers' understanding of lies and innocent and negligent mistakes. *Developmental Psychology, 34,* 332–41.

Siegel, L.S. (1995). Does the IQ god exist? *Alberta Journal of Education Research. Special Issue: Canadian Perspectives on the Bell Curve, 41* (3), 283–8.

Siegler, R.S. (1976). Three aspects of cognitive development. *Cognitive Psychology, 8,* 481–520.

Siegler, R.S. (1991). *Children's thinking* (2nd ed.). Englewood Cliffs, NJ: Prentice Hall.

Siegler, R.S. (1996a). A grand theory of development. In R. Case, Y. Okamoto, & Associates (Eds.), *The role of central conceptual structures in the development of children's thought. Monographs of the Society for Research in Child Development, 61* (1–2, Serial No. 246), 266–75.

Siegler, R.S. (1996b). *Beyond the immaculate transition: Change processes in children's thinking.* New York: Oxford University Press.

Siegler, R.S. (1996c). *Emerging minds: The process of change in children's thinking.* New York: Oxford University Press.

Siegler, R.S., & Crowley, K. (1992). Microgenetic methods revisited. *American Psychologist, 47,* 1241–3.

Siegler, R.S., & Ellis, S. (1996). Piaget on childhood. *Psychological Science, 7,* 211–5.

Siegler, R.S., & Jenkins, E. (1989). *How children discover strategies.* Hillsdale, NJ: Erlbaum.

Siegler, R.S., & Munakata, Y. (1993, Winter). Beyond the immaculate transition: Advances in the understanding of change. *Newsletter of the Society for Research in Child Development.*

Sigelman, C.K. (1999). *Life-span human development* (3rd ed.). Pacific Grove, CA: Brooks/Cole.

Sigelman, C.K., Carr, M.B., & Begley, N.L. (1986). Developmental changes in the influence of sex-role stereotypes on person perception. *Child Study Journal, 16,* 191–205.

Sigelman, C.K., Miller, T.E., & Whitworth, L.A. (1986). The early development of stigmatizing reactions to physical differences. *Journal of Applied Developmental Psychology, 7,* 17–32.

Sigelman, C.K., & Waitzman, K.A. (1991). The development of distributive justice orientations: Contextual influences on children's resource allocations. *Child Development, 62,* 1367–78.

Sigman, M., & Sena, R. (1993). Pretend play in high-risk and developmentally delayed children. In M.H. Bornstein & A.W. O'Reilly (Eds.), *The role of play in the development of thought. New directions for child development, No. 59.* San Francisco: Jossey-Bass.

Signorella, M.L., Bigler, R.S., & Liben, L.S. (1993). Developmental differences in children's gender schemata about others: A meta-analytic review. *Developmental Review, 13,* 147–83.

Signorella, M.L., Jamison, W., & Krupa, M.H. (1989). Predicting spatial performance from gender stereotyping in activity preferences and in self-concept. *Developmental Psychology, 25,* 89–95.

Signorielli, N. (1991). *A sourcebook on children and television.* Westport, CT: Greenwood Press.

Signorielli, N., & Lears, M. (1992). Children, television, and conceptions about chores: Attitudes and behaviors. *Sex Roles, 27,* 157–70.

Silver, L.B. (1992). *Attention-deficit hyperactivity disorder: A clinical guide to diagnosis and treatment.* Washington, DC: American Psychiatric Press.

Simmons, R.G., & Blyth, D.A. (1987). *Moving into adolescence: The impact of pubertal change in school context.* New York: Aldine de Gruyter.

Simmons, R.G., Burgeson, R., Carlton-Ford, S., & Blyth, D.A. (1987). The impact of cumulative change in early adolescence. *Child Development, 58,* 1220–34.

Simon, T.J., Hespos, S.J., & Rochat, P. (1995). Do infants understand simple arithmetic? A replication of Wynn (1992). *Cognitive Development, 10,* 253–69.

Simonoff, E., Bolton, P., & Rutter, M. (1996). Mental retardation: Genetic findings, clinical implications, and research agenda. *Journal of Child Psychology and Psychiatry and Allied Disciplines, 37,* 259–80.

Simons, R.L., Beaman, J., Conger, R.D., & Chao, W. (1993). Stress, support, and antisocial behavior trait as determinants of emotional well-being and parenting practices among single mothers. *Journal of Marriage and the Family, 55,* 385–98.

Simons, R.L., Whitbeck, L.B., Conger, R.D., & Wu, C. (1991). Intergenerational transmission of harsh parenting. *Developmental Psychology, 27,* 159–71.

Simonton, D.K. (1994). Individual differences, developmental changes, and social context. *Behavioral and Brain Sciences, 17,* 552–3.

Simonton, D.K. (2000). Creativity: Cognitive, personal, developmental, and social aspects. *American Psychologist, 55,* 151–8.

Simpson, J.L. (1993). Genetic causes of spontaneous abortion. In C. Lin, M.S. Verp, & R.E. Sabbagha (Eds.), *The high-risk fetus: Pathophysiology, diagnosis, management* (pp. 98–111). New York: Springer-Verlag.

Simpson, K.R., & Creehan, P.A. (1996). *Perinatal nursing.* Philadelphia, PA: Lippincott-Raven.

Simpson, M., Carone, D., Burns, W., Seidman, T., Montgomery, D., & Sellers, A. (2002). Assessing giftedness with the WISC-II and the SB-IV. *Psychology in the Schools, 39* (5), 515–24.

Singer, L., Salvator, A., Arendt, R., Minnes, S., Farkas, K., & Kliegman, R. (2002). Effects of cocaine/polydrug exposure and maternal psychological distress on infant birth outcomes. *Neurotoxicology and Teratology, 24,* 127–135.

Singer, D. G., & Singer, J. L. (1990). *The house of make-believe: Children's play and the developing imagination.* Cambridge, MA: Harvard University Press.

Singer, L.M., Brodzinsky, D.M., Ramsay, D., Steir, M., & Waters, E. (1985). Mother–infant attachments in adoptive families. *Child Development, 56,* 1543–51.

Skinner, B.F. (1953). *Science and human behavior.* New York: Macmillan.

Skodak, M., & Skeels, H.M. (1949). A final follow-up study of one hundred adopted children. *Journal of Genetic Psychology, 75,* 85–125.

Skouteris, H., McKenzie, B.E., & Day, R.H. (1992). Integration of sequential information for shape perception by infants: A developmental study. *Child Development, 63,* 1164–76.

Slaby, R.G., & Crowley, C.G. (1977). Modification of cooperation and aggression through teacher attention to children's speech. *Journal of Experimental Child Psychology, 23,* 442–58.

Slaby, R.G., Roedell, W.C., Arezzo, D., & Hendrix, K. (1995). *Early violence prevention.* Washington, DC: National Association for the Education of Young Children.

Slade, A. (1987). A longitudinal study of maternal involvement and symbolic play during the toddler period. *Child Development, 58,* 367–75.

Slade, A., Belsky, J., Aber, J.L., & Phelps, J.L. (1999). Mothers' representation of their relationships with their toddlers: Links to adult attachment and observed mothering. *Developmental Psychology, 35,* 611–9.

Slater, A., Mattock, A., & Brown, E. (1990). Size constancy at birth: Newborn infants' responses to retinal and real size. *Journal of Experimental Child Psychology, 49,* 314–22.

Slater, A., Morrison, V., Somers, M., Mattock, A., Brown, E., & Taylor, D. (1990b). Newborn and older infants' perception of partly occluded objects. *Infant Behavior and Development, 13,* 33–49.

Slaughter-Defoe, D.T., Nakagawa, K., Takanishi, R., & Johnson, D.J. (1990). Toward cultural/ecological perspectives on schooling and achievement in African- and Asian-American children. *Child Development, 61,* 363 83.

Slavin, R.E. (1987). Ability grouping and student achievement in elementary schools: A best evidence synthesis. *Review of Educational Research, 57,* 293–336.

Slavin, R.E. (1991). Cooperative learning and group contingencies. *Journal of Behavioral Education, 1,* 105–15.

Slavin, R.E. (1996). Research on cooperative learning and achievement: What we know, what we need to know. *Contemporary Educational Psychology, 21,* 43–69.

Sleek, S. (1994). Bilingualism enhances student growth. *Monitor of the American Psychological Association, 25* (4), 48–9.

Slobin, D.I. (1979). *Psycholinguistics.* Glenview, IL: Scott, Foresman.

Slobin, D.I. (1985). Crosslinguistic evidence for the language making capacity. In D.I. Slobin (Ed.), *The crosslinguistic study of language acquisition: Vol. 2. Theoretical issues* (pp. 1157–256). Hillsdale, NJ: Erlbaum.

Smetana, J.G. (1981). Preschool children's conceptions of moral and social rules. *Child Development, 52,* 1333–6.

Smetana, J.G. (1985). Preschool children's conceptions of transgressions: Effects of varying moral and conventional domain-related attributes. *Developmental Psychology, 21,* 18–29.

Smetana, J.G., & Bitz, B. (1996). Adolescents' conceptions of teachers' authority and their relations to rule violations at school. *Child Development, 67,* 1153–72.

Smetana, J.G., & Gaines, C. (1999). Adolescent-parent conflict in middle-class African American families. *Child Development, 70,* 1447–63.

Smetana, J.G., Schlagman, N., & Adams, P.W. (1993). Preschool children's judgments about hypothetical and actual transgressions. *Child Development, 64,* 202–14.

Smith, B.A., & Blass, E.M. (1996). Taste-mediated calming in premature, preterm, and full-term human infants. *Developmental Psychology, 32,* 1084–89.

Smith, D. (2000). Women and minorities make gains in science and engineering education. *Monitor on Psychology, 31* (10), 32.

Smith, F.T. (1997). *Obesity in childhood.* New York: Basic Books.

Smith, L.B., & Katz, D.B. (1996). Activity-dependent processes in perceptual and cognitive development. In R. Gelman & T.K. Au (Eds.), *Perceptual and cognitive development* (pp. 413–45). San Diego, CA: Academic Press.

Smith, P.K., & Connolly, K.J. (1980). *The ecology of preschool behavior.* New York: Cambridge University Press.

Smith, P.K., & Daglish, L. (1977). Sex differences in parent and infant behavior in the home. *Child Development, 48,* 1250–4.

Smith, T.W. (1990). Academic achievement and teaching younger siblings. *Social Psychology Quarterly, 53,* 352–63.

Smolak, L., & Levine, M.P. (1993). Separation-individuation difficulties and the distinction between bulimia nervosa and anorexia nervosa in college women. *International Journal of Eating Disorders, 14,* 33–41.

Smoll, F.L., & Schutz, R.W. (1990). Quantifying gender differences in physical performance: A developmental perspective. *Developmental Psychology, 26,* 360–9.

Smylie, J. (2001, January). A guide for health professionals working with Aboriginal peoples: Health issues affecting Aboriginal peoples. *Journal of the Society of Obstetricians and Gynaecologists of Canada, 100,* 1–15.

Snarey, J.R. (1985). Cross-cultural universality of social-moral development: A critical review of Kohlbergian research. *Psychological Bulletin, 97,* 202–32.

Snarey, J.R., & Keljo, K. (1991). In a gemeinschaft voice: The cross-cultural expansion of moral development theory. In W.M. Kurtines & J.L. Gewirtz (Eds.), *Handbook of moral behavior and development* (Vol. 1, pp. 395–424). Hillsdale, NJ: Erlbaum.

Snidman, N., Kagan, J., Riordan, L., & Shannon, D.C. (1995). Cardiac function and behavioral reactivity. *Psychophysiology, 32,* 199–207.

Snow, C.E., Arlman-Rupp, A., Hassing, Y., Jobse, J., Joosken, J., & Vorster, J. (1976). Mother's speech in three social classes. *Journal of Psycholinguistic Research, 5,* 1–20.

Snow, C.E., & Ferguson, C.A. (Eds.). (1977). *Talking to children.* Cambridge, England: Cambridge University Press.

Snow, M.E., Jacklin, C.N., & Maccoby, E.E. (1983). Sex-of-child differences in father-child interaction at one year of age. *Child Development, 54,* 227–32.

Sobesky, W.E. (1983). The effects of situational factors on moral judgments. *Child Development, 54,* 575–84.

Socha, T.J., & Socha, D.M. (1994). Children's task-group communication. In L.R. Frey (Ed.), *Group communication in context: Studies of natural groups.* Hillsdale, NJ: Erlbaum.

Society of Obstetricians and Gynaecologists of Canada. (2000). Multiple birth: Facts. Retrieved November 28, 2001 from http://www.sogc.org/multiple/facts_e.shtml.

Society for Research in Child Development. (1993). Ethical standards for research with children. In *Directory of members* (pp. 337–9). Ann Arbor, MI: Author.

Sodian, B., Taylor, C., Harris, P.L., & Perner, J. (1991). Early deception and the child's theory of mind: False trails and genuine markers. *Child Development, 62,* 468–83.

Soken, N.H., & Pick, A.D. (1999). Infants' perception of dynamic affective expressions: Do infants distinguish specific expressions? *Child Development, 70,* 1275–82.

Sokolov, J.L. (1993). A local contingency analysis of the fine-tuning hypothesis. *Developmental Psychology, 29,* 1008–23.

Sommer, K., Whitman, T.L., Borkowski, J.G., Schellenbach, C., Maxwell, S., & Kerugh, D. (1993). Cognitive readiness and adolescent parenting. *Developmental Psychology, 29,* 389–98.

Somsen, R.J.M., van't Klooster, B.J., van der Molen, M.W., van Leeuwen, H.M.P., & Licht, R. (1997). Growth spurts in brain maturation during middle childhood as indexed by EEG power spectra. *Biological Psychology, 44,* 187–209.

Sonnenschein, S. (1986). Development of referential communication skills: How familiarity with a listener affects a speaker's production of redundant messages. *Developmental Psychology, 22,* 549–55.

Sonnenschein, S. (1988). The development of referential communication: Speaking to different listeners. *Child Development, 59,* 694–702.

Sorensen, E. (1997). A national profile of nonresident fathers and their ability to pay child support. *Journal of Marriage and the Family, 59,* 785–97.

Spearman, C. (1927). *The abilities of man.* New York: Macmillan.

Speicher, B. (1994). Family patterns of moral judgment during adolescence and early adulthood. *Developmental Psychology, 30,* 624–32.

Spelke, E.S. (1991). Physical knowledge in infancy: Reflections on Piaget's theory. In S. Carey & R. Gelman (eds.), *Epigenesis of Mind: Essays in Biology and Knowledge.* Hillsdale, NJ: Erlbaum.

Spelke, E.S., Breinlinger, K., Macomber, J., & Jacobson, K. (1992). Origins of knowledge. *Psychological Review, 99,* 605–32.

Spelke, E.S., & Newport, E.L. (1998). Nativism, empiricism, and the development of knowledge. In W. Damon (Series Ed.) & R.M. Lerner (Vol. Ed.), *Handbook of child psychology: Vol. 1. Theoretical models of human development* (5th ed.). New York: Wiley.

Speltz, M. L., Endriga, M. C., Fisher, P. A., & Mason, C. A. (1997). Early predictors of attachment in infants with cleft lip/or palate. *Child Development, 68,* 12-25.

Spence, J.T. (1993). Gender-related traits and gender ideology: Evidence for a multifactorial theory. *Journal of Personality and Social Psychology, 64,* 624–35.

Spence, J.T., & Hall, S.K. (1996). Children's gender-related self-perceptions, activity preferences, and occupational stereotypes: A test of three models of gender constructs. *Sex Roles, 35,* 659–91.

Spence, J.T., & Helmreich, R.L. (1978). *Masculinity and femininity: Their psychological dimensions, correlates, and antecedents.* Austin: TX: University of Texas Press.

Spencer, M.B. (1988). Self-concept development. In D.T. Slaughter (Ed.), *Black children in poverty: Developmental perspectives.* San Francisco: Jossey-Bass.

Spencer, M.B., & Markstrom-Adams, C. (1990). Identity processes among racial and ethnic minority children in America. *Child Development, 61,* 290–310.

Spencer, P.E. (1996). The association between language and symbolic play at two years: Evidence from deaf toddlers. *Child Development, 67,* 867–76.

Spieker, S.J., Larson, N.C., Lewis, S.M., Keller, T.E., & Gilchrist, L. (1999). Developmental trajectories of disruptive behavior problems in preschool children of adolescent mothers. *Child Development, 70,* 443–58.

Spiker, D., Ferguson, J., & Brooks-Gunn, J. (1993). Enhancing maternal interactive behavior and child social competence in low birthweight, premature infants. *Child Development, 64,* 754–68.

Spitz, R.A. (1945). Hospitalism: An inquiry into the genesis of psychiatric conditions in early childhood. In A. Freud (Ed.), *The psychoanalytic study of the child* (Vol. 1, pp. 53–74). New York: International Universities Press.

Spitz, R.A. (1965). *The first year of life: A psychoanalytic study of normal and deviant object relations.* New York: International Universities Press.

Spreen, O., Risser, A.H., & Edgell, D. (1995). *Developmental neuropsychology.* New York: Oxford University Press.

Sprigle, J.E., & Schaefer, L. (1985). Longitudinal evaluation of the effects of two compensatory preschool programs on fourth- through sixth-grade students. *Developmental Psychology, 21,* 702–8.

Springen, K. (2001). The state of the art pregnancy. In K.L. Freiberg (Ed.), *Human development 01/02* (29th ed., pp. 18–20). Guilford, CT: Dushkin/McGraw-Hill.

Sroufe, L.A. (1977). Wariness of strangers and the study of infant development. *Child Development, 48,* 1184–99.

Sroufe, L.A. (1985). Attachment classification from the perspective of infant–caregiver relationships and infant temperament. *Child Development, 56,* 1–14.

Sroufe, L.A. (1997). Psychopathology as an outcome of development. *Development of Psychopathology, 9,* 251–68.

Sroufe, L.A., Bennett, C., Englund, M., Urban, J., & Shulman, S. (1993). The significance of gender boundaries in preadolescence: Contemporary correlates and antecedents of boundary violation and maintenance. *Child Development, 64,* 455–66.

Sroufe, L.A., Egeland, B., & Kreutzer, T. (1990). The fate of early experience following developmental change: Longitudinal approaches to individual adaptation in childhood. *Child Development, 61,* 1363–73.

Sroufe, L.A., Waters, E., & Matas, L. (1974). Contextual determinants of affective expression in infancy. In M. Lewis & L.A. Rosenblum (Eds.), *The origins of fear.* New York: Wiley.

Staats, A. (1975). *Social behaviorism.* Homewood, IL: Dorsey Press.

Stack, D.M., & Muir, D.W. (1992). Adult tactile stimulation during face-to-face interactions modulates five-month-olds' affect and attention. *Child Development, 63,* 1509–25.

Staffieri, J.R. (1967). A study of social stereotype of body image in children. *Journal of Personality and Social Psychology, 7,* 101–4.

Stager, C., & Werker, J.F. (1997). Infants listen for more phonetic detail in speech perception than in word-learning tasks. *Nature, 388,* 381–2.

Stanton, B., Li, X., & Galbraith, J. (1996). Sexually transmitted diseases, human immunodeficiency virus, and pregnancy prevention: Combined contraceptive practices among urban African-American adolescents. *Archives of Pediatric and Adolescent Medicine, 150* (1), 17–24.

Staples, G.B. (2000, November 15). Television in black and white: Report on the Children Now survey of ethnic representation in television programming. *Atlanta Constitution,* pp. D1–2.

Statistics Canada. (1993, January 12). *Knowledge of languages. 1991 Census of population.* Catalogue No. 93-318, pp. 24–30.

Statistics Canada. (1997). *Suicide, and suicide rate, by sex, by age group.* Catalogue No. 82F0075XCB. Retrieved October 24, 2001 from http://www.statcan.ca/english/Pgdb/People/Health/health01.htm.

Statistics Canada. (1999a, March 29). *Juristat: Sex offenders, 1997.* Catalogue No. 85-002-XPE. Retrieved May 20, 2001 from http://www.statcan.ca/english/indepth/85-002/feature/jurl1999003029sda.htm.

Statistics Canada. (1999b, May 18). Divorces, 1997. *The Daily.* Retrieved May 20, 2001 from http://www.statcan.ca/Daily/English/990518/d990518b.htm.

Statistics Canada. (1999c, October 14). National Longitudinal Survey of Children and Youth: School component. *The Daily.* Retrieved October 2, 2001 from http://www.statcan.ca/Daily/English/991014/d991014a.htm.

Statistics Canada. (1999f, December 21). Youth violent crimes. *Juristat, 19* (13). Catalogue No. 85-002-XPE99013. Retrieved May 1, 2001 from http://www.statcan.ca/english/indepth/85-002/feature/jurl1999012021sda.htm.

Statistics Canada. (2000a). *Education indicators in Canada: Report of the Pan-Canadian Education Indicators Program 1999.* Catalogue No. 81-582-XIE. Retrieved November 3, 2001 from http://www.statcan.ca/english/freepub/81-582-XIE/free.htm.

Statistics Canada. (2000c, September 14). Women in Canada. *The Daily.* Retrieved May 4, 2001 from http://www.statcan.ca/Daily/English/000914/d000914c.htm.

Statistics Canada. (2000d, September 28). Divorces, 1998. *The Daily.* Retrieved May 20, 2001 from http://www.statcan.ca/Daily/English/000928/d000928b.htm.

Statistics Canada. (2000e, October 20). Teenage pregnancy. *The Daily.* Retrieved November 26, 2001 from http://www.statcan.ca/Daily/English/001020/d001020b.htm.

Statistics Canada. (2001a). Census families in private households by family structure, 1991 and 1996. In *Family studies kit* (chap. 1, chart 5). Retrieved May 20, 2001 from http://www.statcan.ca/english/kits/Family/HTML/fam1_5.htm.

Statistics Canada. (2001b, Autumn). *Perspectives on labour and income.* Catalogue No. 75-001-XPE.

Statistics Canada. (2001d, April 17). *Population by knowledge of official languages. 1996 Census.* Catalogue No. 93F0024XDB96005. Retrieved June 24, 2001 from http://www.statcan.ca/english/census96/dec2/off.htm.

Statistics Canada. (2001e, May 13). Chapter 1, Did you know…. In *Family Studies Kit.* Retrieved May 20, 2001 from http://www.statcan.ca/english/kits/Family/HTML/Fam1_12.htm.

Statistics Canada. (2002a, July 11). Changing conjugal life in Canada. *The Daily.* Retrieved from www.statcan.ca/daily/English/020711/d020711a.htm.

Statistics Canada. (2002b, December 2). Divorces. *The Daily.* Retrieved from http://www.statcan.ca/Daily/English/021202/d021202f.htm.

Statistics Canada. (2002c, July 3). Trends in Canadian and American Fertility. *The Daily.* Retrieved from www.statcan.ca/daily/english/020703/d020703a.htm.

Statistics Canada. (2002d, October 29). Computer access at school and at home. *The Daily.* Retrieved from http://www.statcan.ca/english/edu/feature/computer.htm.

Statistics Canada. (2003a). Measuring up: the performance of Canada's youth in reading, mathematics and science. *OECD PISA study.* Retrieved November 20, 2003 from http://www.pisa.gc.ca/pisa/81-590-xpe.pdf.

Statistics Canada. (2003b, November 21). *Average hours per week of television viewing.* Catalogue No. 87F006XPE. Retrieved December 16, 2003 from http://www.statcan.ca/english/Pgdb/arts23.htm.

Statistics Canada. (2003c) National longitudinal survey of children and youth: Challenges of late adolescence. Available on-line at www.statcan.ca/Daily/English/030616/d030616a.htm.

Statistics Canada. (2004a). *2001 Census Consultation Guide: Fertility Recent Trends.* Available on-line at www.statcan.ca/english/freepub/92-125-GIE/htm/FER.htm.

Statistics Canada. (2004b). The people: Lone parenthood. Retrieved from http://142.206.72.67/02/02d/02d_0013_e.htm.

Statistics Canada, Federal, Provincial and Territorial Advisory Committee on Population Health. (2000a, March). Births and fertility. In *Statistical report on the health of Canadians 1999* (pp. 23–5). Catalogue No. 82-570-XIE. Retrieved May 20, 2001 from http://www.statcan.ca:80/english/freepub/82-570-XIE/01_11.pdf.

Statistics Canada, Federal, Provincial and Territorial Advisory Committee on Population Health. (2000b, March). Family violence. In *Statistical report on the health of Canadians 1999* (pp. 54–7). Catalogue No. 82-570-XIE. Retrieved May 20, 2001 from http://www.statcan.ca:80/english/freepub/82-570-XIE/01_11.pdf.

Statistics Canada, National Longitudinal Survey of Children and Youth. (1996, November 20). *Growing up in Canada: A detailed portrait of children and young people.* Catalogue No. 89-550-MPE.

Statistics Sweden. (1996). Spanking and other forms of physical punishment: A study of adults' and middle school students' opinions, experience, and knowledge. *Demographic Report No. 1.2.* Stockholm: Statistics Sweden.

Stattin, H., & Magnusson, D. (1990). *Paths through life: Vol. 2. Pubertal maturation in female development.* Hillsdale, NJ: Erlbaum.

Steele, B.F., & Pollock, C.B. (1974). A psychiatric study of parents who abuse infants and small children. In R.E. Helfer & C.H. Kempe (Eds.), *The battered child* (2nd ed.). Chicago: University of Chicago Press.

Steele, C.M. (1997). A threat in the air: How stereotypes shape intellectual identity and performance. *American Psychologist, 52,* 613–29.

Steele, C.M., & Aronson, J. (1995). Stereotype threat and the intellectual test performance of African Americans. *Journal of Personality and Social Psychology, 69,* 797–811.

Steele, H., Steele, M., & Fonagy, P. (1996). Associations among attachment classifications of mothers, fathers, and their infants. *Child Development, 67,* 541–55.

Stein, J.H., & Reiser, L.W. (1994). A study of white middle-class adolescent boys' responses to "semenarche" (the first ejaculation). *Journal of Youth and Adolescence, 23,* 373–84.

Stein, Z.A., & Susser, M.W. (1976). Prenatal nutrition and mental competence. In J.D. Lloyd-Still (Ed.), *Malnutrition and intellectual development.* Littleton, MA: Publishing Sciences Group.

Steinberg, L. (1981). Transformatoins in family relations at puberty. *Developmental Psychology, 17,* 833–40.

Steinberg, L. (1986). Latchkey children and susceptibility to peer pressure: An ecological analysis. *Developmental Psychology, 22,* 433–9.

Steinberg, L. (1988). Reciprocal relation between parent–child distance and pubertal maturation. *Developmental Psychology, 24,* 122–8.

Steinberg, L. (1996). *Adolescence* (4th ed.). New York: McGraw-Hill.

Steinberg, L., & Dornbusch, S.M. (1991). Negative correlates of part-time employment during adolescence: Replication and elaboration. *Developmental Psychology, 27,* 304–13.

Steinberg, L., Dornbusch, S.M., & Brown, B.B. (1992). Ethnic differences in adolescent achievement: An ecological perspective. *American Psychologist, 47,* 723–9.

Steinberg, L., Elmen, J.D., & Mounts, N.S. (1989). Authoritative parenting, psychosocial maturity, and academic success among adolescents. *Child Development, 60,* 1424–36.

Steinberg, L., Fegley, S., & Dornbusch, S.M. (1993). Negative impact of part-time work on adolescent adjustment: Evidence from a longitudinal study. *Developmental Psychology, 29,* 171–80.

Steinberg, L., Lamborn, S.D., Darling, N., Mounts, N.S., & Dornbusch, S.M. (1994). Over-time changes in adjustment and competence among adolescents from authoritative, authoritarian, indulgent, and neglectful families. *Child Development, 65,* 754–70.

Steinberg, L., & Silverberg, S.B. (1986). The vicissitudes of autonomy in early adolescence. *Child Development, 57,* 841–51.

Steiner, J.E. (1979). Human facial expressions in response to taste and smell stimulation. In H.W. Reese & L.P. Lipsitt (Eds.), *Advances in child development and behavior* (Vol. 13, pp. 257–95). Orlando, FL: Academic Press.

Stern, D. (1977). *The first relationship: Infant and mother.* Cambridge, MA: Harvard University Press.

Stern, D.N. (1995). Self/other differentiation in the domain of intimate socio-affective interaction: Some considerations. In P. Rochat (Ed.), *The self in infancy: Theory and research* (pp. 419–429). Amsterdam: North Holland-Elsevier.

Stern, H.H. (1998). The languages of Canada. In *The Canadian Encyclopedia* (2nd ed.). Edmonton: Hurtig.

Stern, W. (1912). *Die psychologischen methoden der intelligenzprufung.* Liepzig, Germany: Barth.

Sternberg, J. & Grigorenko, E. (2002). *Dynamic Testing.* Cambridge: Cambridge University Press.

Sternberg, K.J., Lamb, M.E., Greenbaum, C., Cicchetti, D., Dawud, S., Cortes, R.M., Krispin, O., & Lorey, F. (1993). Effects of domestic violence on children's behavior problems and depression. *Developmental Psychology, 29,* 44–52.

Sternberg, R.J. (1985). *Beyond IQ. A triarchic theory of human intelligence.* Cambridge, England: Cambridge University Press.

Sternberg, R.J. (1991). Theory-based testing of intellectual abilities: Rationale for the triarchic abilities test. In H.A.H. Rowe (Ed.), *Intelligence: Reconceptualization and measurement* (pp. 183–202). Hillsdale, NJ: Erlbaum.

Sternberg, R.J. (1995). Investing in creativity: Many happy returns. *Educational Leadership, 53,* 80–4.

Sternberg, R.J. (1997). The concept of intelligence and its role in lifelong learning and success. *American Psychologist, 52,* 1030–7.

Sternberg, R.J., & Lubart, T.I. (1996). Investing in creativity. *American Psychologist, 51,* 677–88.

Sternberg, R.J., Wagner, R.K., Williams, W.M., & Horvath, J.A. (1995). Testing common sense. *American Psychologist, 50,* 912–27.

Stetsenko, A., Little, T.D., Gordeeva, T., Grasshof, M., & Oettingen, G. (2000). Gender effects in children's beliefs about school performance: A cross-cultural study. *Child Development, 71,* 517–27.

Stevahn, L., Johnson, D.W., Johnson, R.T., Oberle, K., & Wahl, L. (2000). Effects of conflict resolution training integrated into a kindergarten curriculum. *Child Development, 71,* 772–84.

Stevens, R.J., & Slavin, R.E. (1995a). Effects of a cooperative learning approach in reading and writing on academically handicapped and nonhandicapped students. *Elementary School Journal, 95,* 241–62.

Stevens, R.J., & Slavin, R.E. (1995b). The cooperative elementary school: Effects on students' achievement, attitudes, and social relations. *American Educational Research Journal, 32,* 321–51.

Stevenson, H.W., Chen, C., & Lee, S. (1993). Mathematics achievement of Chinese, Japanese, and American children: Ten years later. *Science, 259,* 53–58.

Stevenson, H.W., & Lee, S.Y. (1990). Contexts of achievement: A study of American, Chinese, and Japanese children. *Monographs of the Society for Research in Child Development, 55* (1-2, Serial No. 221).

Stevenson, H.W., Lee, S.Y., Chen, C., Stigler, J.W., Hsu, C., & Kitamura, S. (1990). Contexts of achievement: A study of American, Chinese, and Japanese children. *Monographs of the Society for Research in Child Development, 55* (1–2, Serial No. 221).

Stevenson, H.W., Lee, S.Y., & Stigler, J.W. (1986). Mathematics achievement of Chinese, Japanese, and American children. *Science, 231,* 693–9.

Stevenson, H.W., Stigler, J.W., Lee, S.Y., Lucker, G.W., Kitamura, S., & Hsu, C. (1985). Cognitive performance and academic achievement of Japanese, Chinese, and American children. *Child Development, 56,* 718–34.

Stewart, R.B., & Marvin, R.S. (1984). Sibling relations: The role of conceptual perspective-taking in the ontogeny of sibling caregiving. *Child Development, 55,* 1322–32.

Stice, E., & Barrera, M., Jr. (1995). A longitudinal examination of the reciprocal relations between perceived parenting and adolescents' substance use and externalizing behaviors. *Developmental Psychology, 31,* 322–34.

Stigler, J.W., Lee, S.Y., & Stevenson, H.W. (1987). Mathematics classrooms in Japan, Taiwan, and the United States. *Child Development, 58,* 1272–85.

Stipek, D., Feiler, R., Daniels, D., & Milburn, S. (1995). Effects of different instructional approaches on young children's achievement and motivation. *Child Development, 66,* 209–33.

Stipek, D., Gralinski, H., & Kopp, C. (1990). Self-concept development in the toddler years. *Developmental Psychology, 26,* 972–7.

Stipek, D., & Mac Iver, D. (1989). Developmental change in children's assessment of intellectual competence. *Child Development, 60,* 521–38.

Stipek, D.J., Recchia, S., & McClintic, S. (1992). Self-evaluation in young children. *Monographs of the Society for Research in Child Development, 57* (1, Serial No. 226).

St. James-Roberts, I., & Plewis, I. (1996). Individual differences, daily fluctuations, and developmental changes in amounts of infant waking, fussing, crying, feeding, and sleeping. *Child Development, 67,* 2527–40.

St. Lawrence, J.S., Jefferson, K.W., Alleyne, E., & Brasfield, T.L. (1995). Comparison of education versus behavioral skills training interventions in lowering sexual HIV risk behavior of substance dependent adolescents. *Journal of Consulting and Clinical Psychology, 63,* 221–37.

Stockman, A.F., & Altmaier, E. (2001). Relation of self-efficacy to reported pain and pain medication usage during labour. *Journal of Clinical Psychology in Medical Settings, 8* (3), 161–66.

Stoddart, T., & Turiel, E. (1985). Children's concepts of cross-gender activities. *Child Development, 56,* 1241–52.

Stormshak, E.A., Bellanti, C.J., Bierman, K.L., and the Conduct Problems Prevention Research Group. (1996). The quality of sibling relationships and the development of social competence and behavioral control in aggressive children. *Developmental Psychology, 32,* 79–89.

Strachan, T., & Read, A.P. (1996). *Human molecular genetics.* New York: Wiley.

Strassberg, Z. (1995). Social information processing in compliance situations by mothers of behavior-problem boys. *Child Development, 66,* 376–89.

Strassberg, Z., Dodge, K.A., Pettit, G.S., and Bates, J.E. (1994). Spanking in the home and children's subsequent aggression toward kindergarten peers. *Development and Psychopathology, 6,* 445–61.

Stratton, K., Howe, C., & Battaglia, F. (1996). *Fetal alcohol syndrome: Diagnosis, epidemiology, prevention, and treatment.* Washington, DC: National Academy Press.

Strauss, M.A., Sugarman, D.B., and Giles-Sims, J. (1997). Spanking by parents and subsequent antisocial behavior of children. *Archives of Pediatric Adolescent Medicine, 151,* 761–7.

Strauss, M.S., & Curtis, L.E. (1981). Infant perception of numerosity. *Child Development, 52,* 1146–52.

Streissguth, A.P., Bookstein, F.L., Sampson, P.D., & Barr, H.M. (1993). *The enduring effects of prenatal alcohol exposure on child development.* Ann Arbor, MI: University of Michigan Press.

Streitmatter, J. (1993). Gender differences in identity development: An examination of longitudinal data. *Adolescence, 28,* 55–66.

Streri, A., & Spelke, E.S. (1988). Haptic perception of objects in infancy. *Cognitive Psychology, 20,* 1–23.

Strigini, P., Sanone, R., Carobbi, S., & Pierluigi, M. (1990). Radiation and Down's syndrome. *Nature, 347,* 717.

Strough, J., & Berg, C.A. (2000). Goals as a mediator of high-affiliation dyadic conversations. *Developmental Psychology, 36,* 117–25.

Stumpf, H., & Stanley, J.C. (1996). Gender-related differences on the College Board's Advanced Placement and Achievement Tests, 1982–1992. *Journal of Educational Psychology, 88,* 353–64.

Stunkard, A.J., Harris, J.R., Pedersen, N., & McClearn, G.E. (1990). The body-mass index of twins who have been reared apart. *New England Journal of Medicine, 322,* 1483–7.

Stuss, D.T. (1992). Biological and psychological development of executive functions. *Brain & Cognition, 20,* 8–23.

Subotnik. R.F., Karp, D.E., & Morgan, E.R. (1989). High IQ children at midlife: An investigation into the generalizability of Terman's genetic studies of genius. *Roeper Review, 11,* 139–44.

Sudhalter, V., & Braine, M.D.S. (1985). How does comprehension of passives develop? A comparison of actional and experiential verbs. *Journal of Child Language, 12,* 455–70.

Sue, S., & Okazaki, S. (1990). Asian-American educational achievements: A phenomenon in search of explanation. *American Psychologist, 45,* 913–20.

Sullivan, H.S. (1953). *The interpersonal theory of psychiatry.* New York: Norton.

Sullivan, M.W., Lewis, M., & Alessandri, S.M. (1992). Cross-age stability in emotional expressions during learning and extinction. *Developmental Psychology, 28,* 58–63.

Suomi, S.J., & Harlow, H.F. (1978). Early experience and social development in rhesus monkeys. In M.E. Lamb (Ed.), *Social and personality development* (pp. 252–71). New York: Holt, Rinehart and Winston.

Super, C.M., Herrera, M.G., & Mora, J.O. (1990). Long-term effects of food supplementation and psychosocial intervention on the physical growth of Columbian infants at risk of malnutrition. *Child Development, 61,* 29–49.

Susser, M., & Stein, Z. (1994). Timing in prenatal nutrition: A reprise of the Dutch Famine Study. *Nutrition Reviews, 52,* 84–94.

Suzuki, L.A., & Valencia, R.R. (1997). Race-ethnicity and measured intelligence: Educational implications. *American Psychologist, 52,* 1103–14.

Swarr, A.E., & Richards, M.H. (1996). Longitudinal effects of adolescent girls' pubertal development, perceptions of pubertal timing, and parental relations on eating problems. *Developmental Psychology, 32,* 636–46.

Symons, D., & Carr, T. (1995). Maternal employment and early infant social development: Process and policy. In K. Covell (Ed.), *Readings in child development: A Canadian perspective* (pp. 109–28). Toronto: Nelson.

Symons, D., Clark, S., Isaksen, G., & Marshall, J. (1998). Stability of Q-sort attachment security from age two to five. *Infant Behavior & Development, 21* (4), 785–91.

Szkrybalo, J., & Ruble, D.N. (1999). "God made me a girl": Sex-category constancy judgements and explanations revisited. *Developmental Psychology, 35,* 392–402.

Tamis-LeMonda, C.S., & Bornstein, M.H. (1989). Habituation and maternal encouragement of attention as predictors of toddler language, play, and representational competence. *Child Development, 60,* 738–51.

Tanner, J.M. (1962). *Growth at adolescence* (2nd ed.). Oxford: Blackwell.

Tanner, J. M. (1978). *Education and physical growth* (2nd ed.). London: Hodder & Stroughton.

Tanner, J.M. (1981). Growth and maturation during adolescence. *Nutrition Review, 39,* 43–55.

Tanner, J.M. (1990). *Foetus into man: Physical growth from conception to maturity* (2nd ed.). Cambridge, MA: Harvard University Press.

Tanner, J.M., Whitehouse, R.H., & Takahishi, A. (1966). Standards from birth to maturity for height, weight, height velocity, weight velocity: British children, 1965, part II. *Archives of Diseases in Childhood, 41,* 613–35.

Tardif, T., Gelman, S.A., & Xu, F. (1999). Putting the "noun bias" in context: A comparison of English and Mandarin. *Child Development, 70,* 620–35.

Tarullo, L.B., DeMudler, E.K., Ronsaville, D.S., Brown, E., & Radke-Yarrow, M. (1995). Maternal depression and maternal treatment of siblings as predictors of child psychopathology. *Developmental Psychology, 31,* 395–405.

Taylor, A.R., Asher, S.R., & Williams, G.A. (1987). The social adaptation of mainstreamed mildly retarded children. *Child Development, 58,* 1321–34.

Taylor, H.G., Klein, N., Minich, N.M., & Hack, M. (2000). Middle-school-age outcomes in children with very low birth weight. *Child Development, 71,* 1495–1511.

Taylor, M., & Carlson, S.M. (1997). The relation between individual differences in fantasy and theory of mind. *Child Development, 68,* 436–55.

Taylor, M., & Gelman, S.A. (1988). Adjectives and nouns: Children's strategies for learning new words. *Child Development, 59,* 411–9.

Taylor, M., & Gelman, S.A. (1989). Incoporating new words into the lexicon: Preliminary evidence for language hierarchies in two-year-old children. *Child Development, 60,* 625–36.

Taylor, M.G. (1996). The development of children's beliefs about social and biological aspects of gender differences. *Child Development, 67,* 1555–71.

Taylor, R.D. (1996). Adolescents' perceptions of kinship support and family management practices: Association with adolescent adjustment in African-American families. *Developmental Psychology, 32,* 687–95.

Taylor, R.D., & Roberts, D. (1995). Kinship support and maternal and adolescent well-being in economically disadvantaged African-American families. *Child Development, 66,* 1585–97.

Teegartin, C. (1994, July 25). Never-marrieds soar among single parents. *Atlanta Constitution,* pp. A1, A7.

Teele, D.W., Klein, J.O., Chase, C., et al., and the Greater Boston Otitis Media Study Group. (1990). Otitis media in infancy and intellectual ability, school achievement, speech, and language at age 7 years. *Journal of Infectious Disease, 162,* 685–94.

Teeven, R.C., & McGhee, P.E. (1972). Childhood development of fear of failure motivation. *Journal of Personality and Social Psychology, 21,* 345–8.

Templeton, L.M., & Wilcox, S.A. (2000). A tale of two representations: The misinformation effect and children's developing theory of mind. *Child Development, 71,* 402–16.

Terman, L.M. (1954). The discovery and encouragement of exceptional talent. *American Psychologist, 9,* 221–38.

Terry, R., & Coie, J.D. (1991). A comparison of methods for defining sociometric status among children. *Developmental Psychology, 27,* 867–80.

Tessier, R., Cristo, M., Velez, S., Giron, M., Nadeau, L., Figueroa de Calume, Z., Ruiz-Palaez, J., & Charpak, N. (2003). Kangaroo Mother Care: A method for protecting high-risk low-birth-weight and premature infants against developmental delay. *Infant Behaviour and Development, 26,* 384-397.

Tessier, R., Nadeau, L., Boivin, M., & Tremblay, R. (1997). The social behaviour of 11- to 12-year-old children born as low birthweight and/or premature infants. *International Journal of Behavioral Development, 21* (4), 795–811.

Teti, D.M., & Ablard, K.E. (1989). Security of attachment and infant–sibling relationships: A laboratory study. *Child Development, 60,* 1519–28.

Teti, D.M., Gelfand, D.M., Messinger, D.S., & Isabella, R. (1995). Maternal depression and the quality of early attachment: An examination of infants, preschoolers, and their mothers. *Developmental Psychology, 31,* 364–76.

Teti, D.M., Sakin, J.W., Kucera, E., Corns, K.M., & Das Eiden, R. (1996). And baby makes four: Predictors of attachment security among preschool-age firstborns during the transition to siblinghood. *Child Development, 67,* 579–96.

Tharp, R.G. (1989). Psychocultural variables and constants: Effects on teaching and learning in schools. *American Psychologist, 44,* 349–59.

Tharp, R.G. (1994). Intergroup differences among Native Americans in socialization and child cognition: An ethnographic analysis. In P.M. Greenfield and R. Cocking (Eds.), *Cross-cultural roots of minority child development* (pp. 87–105). Hillsdale, NJ: Erlbaum.

Thelen, E. (1984). Learning to walk: Ecological demands and phylogenetic constraints. In L.P. Lipsitt & C. Rovee-Collier (Eds.), *Advances in infancy research* (Vol. 3, pp. 213–50). Norwood, NJ: Ablex.

Thelen, E. (1986). Treadmill-elicited stepping in seven-month-old-infants. *Child Development, 57,* 1498–1506.

Thelen, E. (1995). Motor development: a new synthesis. *American Psychologist, 50,* 79–95.

Thelen, E., Corbetta, D., Kamm, K., Spencer, J.P., Schneider, K., & Zernicke, R.F. (1993). The transition to reaching: Mapping intention and intrinsic dynamics. *Child Development, 64,* 1058–98.

Thelen, E., & Fisher, D.M. (1982). Newborn stepping: An explanation for a disappearing reflex. *Developmental Psychology, 18,* 760–75.

Thelen, E., Fisher, D., & Ridley-Johnson, R. (2002). The relationship between physical growth and a newborn reflex. *Infant Behaviour and Development, 25,* 72-85.

Thoma, S.J., & Rest, J.R. (1999). The relationship between moral decision making and patterns of consolidation and transition in moral judgement development. *Developmental Psychology, 35,* 323–34.

Thoman, E.B. (1990). Sleeping and waking states in infants: A functional perspective. *Neuroscience and Behavioral Review, 14,* 93–107.

Thoman, E.B., & Ingersoll, E.W. (1993). Learning in premature infants. *Developmental Psychology, 28,* 692–700.

Thoman, E.B., & Whitney, M.P. (1989). Sleep states of infants monitored in the home: Individual differences, developmental trends, and origins of diurnal cyclicity. *Infant Behavior and Development, 12,* 59–75.

Thomas, A., & Chess, S. (1977). *Temperament and development.* New York: Brunner/Mazel.

Thomas, A., & Chess, S. (1986). The New York longitudinal study: From infancy to early adult life. In R. Plomin & J. Dunn (Eds.), *The study of temperament: Changes, continuities, and challenges.* Hillsdale, NJ: Erlbaum.

Thomas, A., Chess, S., & Birch, H.G. (1970). The origin of personality. *Scientific American, 223,* 102–9.

Thomas, A., Chess, S., & Korn, S. (1982). The reality of difficult temperament. *Merrill-Palmer Quarterly, 28,* 1–20.

Thomas, D., Campos, J.J., Shucard, D.W., Ramsay, D.S., & Shucard, J. (1981). Semantic comprehension in infancy: a signal detection approach. *Child Development, 52,* 798–803.

Thomas, J.R., & French, K.E. (1985). Gender differences across age in motor performance: A meta-analysis. *Psychological Bulletin, 98,* 260–82.

Thomas, M.H., Horton, R.W., Lippincott, E.C., & Drabman, R.S. (1977). Desensitization to portrayals of real-life aggression as a function of exposure to television violence. *Journal of Personality and Social Psychology, 35,* 450–8.

Thomas, M.S.C., & Karmiloff-Smith, A. (2002). Modeling typical and atypical cognitive development: Computational constraints on mechanisms of change. In U. Goswami (Ed.), *Blackwell Handbook of Childhood Cognitive Development.* Oxford: Blackwell Publishers Inc.

Thompson, R., & Nelson, C. (2001). Developmental science and the media. *American Psychologist, 56* (1), 5–15.

Thompson, R.A. (1990). Vulnerability in research: A developmental perspective on research risk. *Child Development, 61,* 1–16.

Thompson, R.A. (1994). Emotion regulation: A theme in search of definition. In N.A. Fox (Ed.), *The development of emotion regulation: Biological and behavioral considerations. Monographs of the Society for Research in Child Development, 59* (2–3, Serial No. 240).

Thompson, R.A. (1998). Early sociopersonality development. In W. Damon (Series Ed.) & N. Eisenberg (Vol. Ed.), *Handbook of child psychology: Vol. 3. Social, emotional, and personality development* (5th ed., pp. 25–104). New York: Wiley.

Thompson, R.F. (1993). *The brain: A neuroscience primer* (2nd ed.). New York: W.H. Freeman.

Thompson, S.K. (1975). Gender labels and early sex-role development. *Child Development, 46,* 339–47.

Thorndike, R.L., Hagen, E.P., & Sattler, J.M. (1986). *The Stanford-Binet Intelligence Scale* (4th ed.). Chicago: Riverside Publishing.

Thorndike, R.M. (1997). The early history of intelligence testing. In D.P. Flanagan, J.L. Genshaft, & P.L. Morrison (Eds.), *Contemporary intellectual assessment: Theories, tests, and issues* (pp. 3–16). New York: Guilford.

Thorne, A., & Michaelieu, Q. (1996). Situating adolescent gender and self-esteem with personal memories. *Child Development, 67,* 1374–90.

Thorne, B. (1993). *Gender play. Girls and boys in school.* New Brunswick, NJ: Rutgers University Press.

Thurber, C.A. (1995). The experience and expression of homesickness in preadolescent and adolescent boys. *Child Development, 66,* 1162–78.

Thurstone, L.L. (1938). *Primary mental abilities.* Chicago: University of Chicago Press.

Tinsley, B.J. (1992). Multiple influences on the acquisition and socialization of children's health attitudes and behavior: An integrative review. *Child Development, 63,* 1043–69.

Tirozzi, G.N., & Uro, G. (1997). Education reform in the United States: National policy in support of local efforts for school improvement. *American Psychologist, 52,* 241–9.

Tisak, M.S., & Tisak, J. (1990). Children's conceptions of parental authority, friendship, and sibling relations. *Merrill-Palmer Quarterly, 36,* 347–68.

Toch, T., Streisand, B., & Butler, S. (1997, October 13). Does class size matter? *U.S. News & World Report, 123,* 22–9.

Tolmie, J.L. (1995). Chromosome disorders. In M.J. Whittle & J.M. Connor (Eds.), *Prenatal diagnosis in obstetric practice* (2nd ed., pp. 34–57). Oxford: Blackwell.

Tomada, G., & Schneider, B.H. (1997). Relational aggression, gender, and peer acceptance: Invariance across culture, stability over time, and concordance among informants. *Developmental Psychology, 33,* 601–9.

Tomasello, M. (1995). Language is not an instinct. *Cognitive Development, 10,* 131–56.

Tomasello, M. (1999). Having intentions, understanding intentions, and understanding communicative intentions. In P.D. Zelazo, J.W. Astington, & D.R. Olson (Eds.), *Developing theories of intention: Social understanding and self-control* (pp. 63–75). Mahwah, NJ: Erlbaum.

Tomasello, M., & Camaioni, L. (1997). A comparison of the gestural communication of apes and human infants. *Human Development, 40,* 7–24.

Tomasello, M., Conti-Ramsden, G., & Ewert, B. (1990). Young children's conversations with their mothers and fathers: Differences in breakdown and repair. *Journal of Child Language, 17,* 115–30.

Tomlinson-Keasey, C., & Keasey, C.B. (1974). The mediating role of cognitive development in moral judgment. *Child Development, 45,* 291–8.

Tomlinson-Keasey, C., & Little, T.D. (1990). Predicting educational attainment, occupational achievement, intellectual skill, and personal adjustment among gifted men and women. *Journal of Educational Psychology, 82,* 442–55.

Toner, I. J., Moore, L. P., & Ashley, P. K. (1978). The effect of serving as a model of self-control on subsequent resistance to deviation in children. *Journal of Experimental Child Psychology, 26,* 85-91.

Toner, I.J., & Potts, R. (1981). Effect of modeled rationales on moral behavior, moral choice, and level of moral judgment in children. *Journal of Psychology, 107,* 153–62.

Torrance, E.P. (1988). The nature of creativity as manifest in its testing. In R.J. Sternberg (Ed.), *The nature of creativity: Contemporary psychological perspectives* (pp. 43–75). Cambridge, England: Cambridge University Press.

Trabasso, T. (1975). Representation, memory, and reasoning: How do we make transitive inferences? In A.D. Pick (Ed.), *Minnesota Symposia on Child Psychology* (Vol. 9, pp. 135–72). Minneapolis: University of Minnesota Press.

Trachtenberg, S., & Viken, R.J. (1994). Aggressive boys in the classroom: Biased attributions or shared perceptions. *Child Development, 65,* 829–35.

Trehub, S.E., Schneider, B.A., Thorpe, L.A., & Judge, P. (1991). Observational measures of auditory sensitivity in early infancy. *Developmental Psychology, 27,* 40–9.

Tremblay, M., & Willms, D. (2000). Secular trends in the body mass index of Canadian children. *Canadian Medical Association Journal, 163* (11), 1429–33.

Tremblay, R.E. (2003). Why socialization fails?: The case of chronic physical aggression. In B.B. Lahey, T.E. Moffitt, & A. Caspi (Eds.), *The Causes of Conduct Disorder and Juvenile Delinquency* (pp. 182-224). Guilford Press.

Tremblay, R.E., Boulerice, B., Harden, P.W., McDuff, P., Perusse, D., Pihl, R.O., & Zoccolillo, M. (1996). Do children in Canada become more aggressive as they approach adolescence? In Statistics Canada, National Longitudinal Survey of Children and Youth, *Growing up in Canada: A detailed portrait of children and young people* (pp. 127–37). Catalogue No. 89-550-MPE. Ottawa: Statistics Canada.

Tremblay, R.E., Japel, C., Perusse, D., McDuff, P., Boivin, M., Zoccolillo, M., & Montplaisir, J. (1999). The search for the age of "onset" of physical aggression: Rousseau and Bandura revisited. *Criminal Behaviour & Mental Health, 9* (1), 8–23.

Triandis, H.C. (1995). *Individualism and collectivism.* Boulder, Co: Westview Press.

Trickett, P.K., Aber, J.L., Carlson, V., & Cicchetti, D. (1991). Relationship of socioeconomic status to the etiology and developmental sequelae of physical child abuse. *Developmental Psychology, 27,* 148–58.

Trickett, P.K., & McBride-Chang, C. (1995). The developmental impact of different forms of child abuse and neglect. *Developmental Review, 15,* 311–37.

Trickett, P.K., & Putnam, F.W. (1993). Impact of child sexual abuse on females: Toward a developmental, psychobiological integration. *Psychological Science, 4,* 81–7.

Trickett, P.K., & Susman, E.J. (1988). Parental perceptions of child-rearing practices in physically abusive and nonabusive families. *Developmental Psychology, 24,* 270–6.

Tronick, E.Z. (1989). Emotions and emotional communications in infants. *American Psychologist, 44,* 112–9.

Tronick, E.Z., Morelli, G.A., & Ivey, P.K. (1992). The Efe forager infant and toddler's pattern of social relationships: Multiple and simultaneous. *Developmental Psychology, 28,* 568–77.

Tronick, E.Z., Thomas, R.B., & Daltabuit, M. (1994). The Quecha Manta pouch: A caregiving practice for buffering the Peruvian infant against multiple stresses of high altitude. *Child Development, 65,* 1005–13.

Tryon, R.C. (1940). Genetic differences in maze learning in rats. *Yearbook of the National Society for Studies in Education, 39,* 111–9.

Tucker, G. (1998). A global perspective on multilingualism and multilingual education. In J. Cenoz and F. Genesee (Eds.), *Beyond bilingualism: Multilingualism and multilingual education* (pp. 3–15). Clevedon, England: Multilingual Matters.

Tudge, J.R.H. (1992). Processes and consequences of peer collaboration: A Vygotskian analysis. *Child Development, 63,* 1364–79.

Tulkin, S.R., & Konner, M.J. (1973). Alternative conceptions of intellectual functioning. *Human Development, 16,* 33–52.

Tulsky, D., Saklofske, D.H., Chelvne, R. K., Ivnik, R.J., Bornstein, R., Prifitera, A. & Ledbetter, M.F. (Eds.). (2003). *Clinical Interpretation of the WAIS-III and MMS-III.* San Diego: Academic Press.

Turiel, E. (1983). *The development of social knowledge: Morality and convention.* Cambridge, England: Cambridge University Press.

Turiel, E., & Wainryb, C. (2000). Social life in culture: Judgements, conflict, and subversion. *Child Development, 71,* 250–6.

Turkheimer, E. (1991). Individual and group differences in adoption studies of IQ. *Psychological Bulletin, 110,* 392–405.

Turnbull, M., Lapkin, S., Hart, D., & Swain, M. (1998). Time on task and immersion graduates' French proficiency. In S. Lapkin (Ed.), *French as a second language education in Canada: Recent empirical studies.* Toronto: University of Toronto Press.

Turner, P.J., & Gervai, J. (1995). A multidimensional study of gender typing in preschool children and their parents: Personality, attitudes, preferences, behavior, and cultural differences. *Developmental Psychology, 31,* 759–72.

Turner-Bowker, D.M. (1996). Gender stereotyped descriptions in children's picture books: Does "curious Jane" exist in the literature? *Sex Roles, 35,* 461–88.

Twenge, J.M. (1997). Changes in masculine and feminine traits over time: A meta-analysis. *Sex Roles, 36,* 305–25.

Tyson, P., & Tyson, R.L. (1990). *Psychoanalytic theories of development: An integration.* New Haven, CT: Yale University Press.

Uba, L. (1994). *Asian Americans: Personality patterns, identity, and mental health.* New York: The Guilford Press.

Udry, J.R. (1990). Hormonal and social determinants of adolescent sexual initiation. In J. Bancroft & J.M. Reinisch (Eds.), *Adolescence and puberty* (pp. 70–87). New York: Oxford University Press.

Uller, C., Carey, S., Huntley-Fenner, G., & Klatt, L. (1999). What representations might underlie infant numerical knowledge? *Cognitive Development, 14,* 1–36.

Underwood, B., & Moore, B. (1982). Perspective-taking and altruism. *Psychological Bulletin, 91,* 143-173.

Underwood, M.K., Coie, J.D., & Herbsman, C.R. (1992). Display rules for anger and aggression in school-age children. *Child Development, 63,* 366–80.

Underwood, M.K., Hurley, J.C., Johnson, C.A., & Mosley, J.E. (1999). An experimental observational study of children's responses to peer provocation: Developmental and gender differences in middle childhood. *Child Development, 70,* 1428–46.

Underwood, M.K., Schockner, A.E., & Hurley, J.C. (2001). Children's responses to same- and other-gender peers: An experimental investigation with 8-, 10-, and 12-year-olds. *Developmental Psychology, 37,* 362–72.

University of British Columbia, Public Affairs. (1996, November 14). Global warming will take toll on Canada's North. Media release. Retrieved May 4, 2001 from http://www.publicaffairs.ubc.ca/mr/mr96/mr-96-78.html.

University of Toronto, Childcare Resource and Research Unit. (2000). *Early childhood care and education in Canada: Provinces and territories 1998* (4th ed.). Toronto: Author.

Updegraff, K., McHale, S.M., & Crouter, A.C. (1996). Gender roles in marriage: What do they mean for girls' and boys' school achievement? *Journal of Youth and Adolescence, 25,* 73-88.

Urberg, K. A. (1979). Sex-role conceptualization in adolescents and adults. *Developmental Psychology, 15,* 90-92.

Urberg, K.A., Degirmencioglu, S.M., Tolson, J.M., & Halliday-Scher, K. (1995). The structure of adolescent peer networks. *Developmental Psychology, 31,* 540–7.

U.S. Bureau of the Census. (1997). *Statistical abstract of the United States: 1997* (117th ed.). Washington, DC: U.S. Government Printing Office.

U.S. Department of Health and Human Services. (1999, December). Summary. In *Treatment of attention-deficit/hyperactivity disorder.* Evidence Report/Technology Assessment: Number 11. (AHCPR Publication No. 99-E017). Rockville, MD: Author. Retrieved October 18, 2001 from http://www.ahrq.gov/clinic/adhdsum.htm.

U.S. Department of Justice. (1995). *Crime in the United States.* Washington, DC: U.S. Government Printing Office.

Usher, J.A., & Neisser, U. (1993). Childhood amnesia and the beginnings of memory for four early life events. *Journal of Experimental Psychology: General, 122,* 155–65.

Uttal, D., Schreiber, J.C., & DeLoache, J.S. (1995). Waiting to use a symbol: The effects of delay on children's use of models. *Child Development, 66,* 1875–89.

Valdez-Menchaca, M.C., & Whitehurst, G.J. (1992). Accelerating language development through picture book reading: A systematic extension to Mexican day care. *Developmental Psychology, 28,* 1106–14.

Valenza, E., Simion, F., Cassia, V.M., & Umilta, C. (1996). Face perception at birth. *Journal of Experimental Psychology: Human Perception and Performance, 22,* 892–903.

Valenzuela, M. (1990). Attachment in chronically underweight young children. *Child Development, 61,* 1984–96.

Valenzuela, M. (1997). Maternal sensitivity in a developing society: The context of urban poverty and infant chronic undernutrition. *Developmental Psychology, 33,* 845–55.

Valian, V., Hoeffner, J., & Aubry, S. (1996). Young children's imitation of sentence subjects: Evidence of processing limitations. *Developmental Psychology, 32,* 153–64.

Vandell, D.L. (2000). Parents, peer groups, and other socializing influences. *Developmental Psychology, 36,* 699–710.

Vandell, D.L., & Corasantini, M.A. (1988). The relation between third graders' after-school care and social, academic, and emotional functioning. *Child Development, 59,* 868–75.

Vandell, D.L., & Mueller, E.C. (1995). Peer play and friendships during the first two years. In H.C. Smith, A.J. Chapman, & J.R. Smith (Eds.), *Friendship and social relations in children* (pp. 181–208). New Brunswick, NJ: Transaction.

Vandell, D.L., & Ramanan, J. (1992). Effects of early and recent maternal employment on children from low-income families. *Child Development, 63,* 938–49.

Vandell, D.L., Wilson, K.S., & Buchanan, N.R. (1980). Peer interaction in the first year of life: An examination of its structure, content, and sensitivity to toys. *Child Development, 51,* 481–8.

van den Boom, D.C. (1995). Do first-year intervention efforts endure? Follow-up during toddlerhood of a sample of Dutch irritable infants. *Child Development, 66,* 1798–1816.

van den Broek, P. (1989). Causal reasoning and inference making in judging the importance of story statements. *Child Development, 60,* 286–97.

van den Broek, P., Lorch, E.P., & Thurlow, R. (1996). Children's and adults' memory for television stories: The role of causal factors, story-grammar categories, and hierarchical level. *Child Development, 67,* 3010–28.

van den Broek, P.W. (1997). Discovering the element of the universe: The development of event comprehension from childhood to adulthood. In P. van den Broek, P. Bauer, & T. Bourg (Eds.), *Developmental spans in event comprehension: Bridging fictional and actual events* (pp. 321–42). Mahwah, NJ: Erlbaum.

Van De Vijver, F. (2003). Principles of adaptation of intelligence tests to other cultures. In J. Georgas, L. Weiss, F. Van De Vijver, & D. Saklofske, *Culture and Children's Intelligence: Cross Cultural Analysis of the WISC-III.* Academic Press London.

van Doorninck, W.J., Caldwell, B.M., Wright, C., & Frankenberg, W.K. (1981). The relationship between twelve-month home stimulation and school achievement. *Child Development, 52,* 1080–3.

van IJzendoorn, M.H. (1992). Intergenerational transmission of parenting: A review of studies in nonclinical populations. *Developmental Review, 12,* 76–99.

van IJzendoorn, M.H. (1995). Adult attachment representations, parental responsiveness, and infant attachment: A meta-analysis on the predictive validity of the Adult Attachment Interview. *Psychological Bulletin, 117,* 387–403.

van IJzendoorn, M. H., & De Wolff, M. S. (1997). In search of the absent father—meta-analysis of infant-father attachment: A rejoinder to our discussants. *Child Development, 68,* 604–609.

van IJzendoorn, M.H., Goldberg, S., Kroonenberg, P.M., & Frenkel, O.J. (1992). The relative effects of maternal and child problems on the quality of attachment: A meta-analysis of attachment in clinical samples. *Child Development, 63,* 840–58.

van IJzendoorn, M.H., & Sagi, A. (1999). Cross-cultural patterns of attachment: Universal and contextual dimensions. In J. Cassidy & P.R. Shaver (Eds.), *Handbook of attachment: Theory, research, and clinical applications* (pp. 713–34). New York: Guilford Press.

Vannatta, R.A. (1996). Risk factors related to suicidal behavior among male and female adolescents. *Journal of Youth and Adolescence, 25,* 149–60.

Varnhagen, C.K., Morrison, F.J., & Everall, R. (1994). Age and schooling effects in story recall and story production. *Developmental Psychology, 30* (6), 969–79.

Vaughn, B.E., Bradley, C.F., Joffe, L.S., Seifer, R., & Barglow, P. (1987). Maternal characteristics measured prenatally are predictive of ratings of temperamental "difficulty" on the Carey Infant Temperament Questionnaire. *Developmental Psychology, 23,* 152–61.

Vaughn, B.E., Kopp, C.B., & Krakow, J.B. (1984). The emergence and consolidation of self-control from eighteen to thirty months of age: Normative trends and individual differences. *Child Development, 55,* 990–1004.

Vaughn, B.E., Stevenson-Hinde, J., Waters, E., Kotsaftis, A., Lefever, G.B., Shouldice, A., Trudel, M., & Belsky, J. (1992). Attachment security and temperament in infancy and early childhood: Some conceptual clarification. *Developmental Psychology, 28,* 463–73.

Vaughn, B.E., & Waters, E. (1990). Attachment behavior at home and in the lab: Q-sort observations and Strange Situation classifications of 1-year-olds. *Child Development, 61,* 1965–73.

Veenman, S. (1995). Cognitive and non-cognitive effect of multigrade and multi-age classes: A best-evidence synthesis. *Review of Educational Research, 65* (4), 319–81.

Veenman, S. (1996). Effects of multigrade and multi-age classes reconsidered. *Review of Educational Research, 66* (3), 323–340.

Vellutino, F. (1991). Introduction to three studies on reading acquisition: Convergent findings on theoretical foundations of code-oriented versus whole language approaches to reading instruction. *Journal of Educational Psychology, 83,* 437–43.

Vernon-Feagans, L., Manlove, E.E., & Volling, B.L. (1996). Otitis media and the social behavior of day-care-attending children. *Child Development, 67,* 1528–39.

Verp, M.S. (1993a). Environmental causes of pregnancy loss and malformations. In C. Lin, M.S. Verp, & R.E. Sabbagha (Eds.), *The high-risk fetus: Pathophysiology, diagnosis, management.* New York: Springer-Verlag.

Verp, M.S. (1993b). Genetic counseling and screening. In C. Lin, M.S. Verp, & R.E. Sabbagha (Eds.), *The high-risk fetus: Pathophysiology, diagnosis, management.* New York: Springer-Verlag.

Verschueren, K., Buyck, P., & Marcoen, A. (2001). Self-representations and socioemotional competence in young children: A 3-year longitudinal study. *Developmental Psychology, 37,* 126–34.

Verschueren, K., & Marcoen, A. (1999). Representation of self and socioemotional competence in kindergarten: Combined and differential effects of attachment to mother and to father. *Child Development, 70,* 183–201.

Verschueren, K., Marcoen, A., & Schoefs, V. (1996). The internal working model of self, attachment, and competence in five-year-olds. *Child Development, 67,* 2493–511.

Vihman, M.M., Kay, E., Boysson-Bardies, B. de., Durand, C., & Sundberg, U. (1994). External sources of individual differences? A cross-linguistic analysis of the phonetics of mothers' speech to 1-year-old children. *Developmental Psychology, 30,* 651–62.

Vinden, P.G. (1996). Junin Quechua children's understanding of mind. *Child Development, 67,* 1707–16.

Vinter, A. (1986). The role of movement in eliciting early imitation. *Child Development, 57,* 66–71.

Vinter, A., & Perruchet, P. (2000). Implicit learning in children is not related to age: Evidence from drawing behavior. *Child Development, 71,* 1223–40.

Vitaro, F., Tremblay, R.E., Kerr, M., Pagani, L., & Bukowski, W.M. (1997). Disruptiveness, friends' characteristics, and delinquency in early adolescence: A test of two competing models of development. *Child Development, 68,* 676–89.

Vobejda, B. (1991, September 15). The future deferred. Longer road from adolescence to adulthood often leads back through parents' home. *The Washington Post,* pp. A1, A29.

Volling, B.L., & Belsky, J. (1992). The contribution of mother–child and father–child relationships to the quality of sibling interaction: A longitudinal study. *Child Development, 63,* 1209–22.

Vondra, J., & Belsky, J. (1993). Developmental origins of parenting: Personality and relationship factors. In T. Luster & L. Okagaki (Eds.), *Parenting. An ecological perspective* (pp. 1–33). Hillsdale, NJ: Erlbaum.

Von Wright, M.R. (1989). Body image satisfaction in adolescent boys and girls: A longitudinal study. *Journal of Youth and Adolescence, 18,* 71–83.

Vorhees, C.V., & Mollnow, E. (1987). Behavioral teratogenesis: Long-term influences on behavior from early exposure to environmental agents. In J.D. Osofsky (Ed.), *Handbook of infant development* (2nd ed., pp. 913–71). New York: Wiley.

Voyer, D., Voyer, S., & Bryden, M.P. (1995). Magnitude of sex differences in spatial abilities: a meta-analysis and consideration of critical variables. *Psychological Bulletin, 117,* 250–70.

Vuchinich, S., Bank, L., & Patterson, G.R. (1992). Parenting, peers, and the stability of antisocial behavior in preadolescent boys. *Developmental Psychology, 28,* 510–21.

Vuchinich, S., Hetherington, E.M., Vuchinich, R.A., & Clingempeel, W.G. (1991). Parent-child interaction and gender differences in early adolescents' adaptation to stepfamilies. *Developmental Psychology, 27,* 618–26.

Vurpillot, E. (1968). The development of scanning strategies and their relation to visual differentiation. *Journal of Experimental Child Psychology, 6,* 632–50.

Vurpillot, E. & Ball, W.A. (1979). The concept of identity and children's selective attention. In G. Hale and M. Lewis (Eds.), *Attention and cognitive development.* New York: Plenum.

Vygotsky, L.S. (1962). *Thought and language.* Cambridge, MA: MIT Press. (Original work published 1934.)

Vygotsky, L.S. (1978). *Mind in society: The development of higher mental processes.* M. Cole, V. John-Steiner, S. Scribner, & E. Souberman (Eds.). Cambridge, MA: Harvard University Press. (Original work published 1930, 1933, 1935.)

Wachs, T.D. (1992). *The nature of nurture.* Newbury Park, CA: Sage.

Waddington, C.H. (1966). *Principles of development and differentiation.* New York: Macmillan.

Wagner, B.M. (1997). Family risk factors for child and adolescent suicidal behavior. *Psychological Bulletin, 121,* 246–98.

Wagner, M. (1998, November). Midwifery in the industrialized world. *Society of Obstetricians and Gynaecologists of Canada, 20* (13), 1225–34.

Wagner, R.K., Torgesen, J.K., & Rashotte, C.A., Hecht, S.A., Barker, T.A., Burgess, S.R., Donahue, J., & Garon, T. (1997). Changing relations between phonological processing abilities and word-level reading as children develop from beginning to skilled readers: A 5-year longitudinal study. *Developmental Psychology, 33,* 468–79.

Wakschlag, L.S., & Hans, S.L. (1999). Relation of maternal responsiveness during infancy to the development of behavior problems in high-risk youths. *Developmental Psychology, 35,* 569–79.

Walden, T.A., & Baxter, A. (1989). The effect of context and age on social referencing. *Child Development, 60,* 1511–8.

Waldman, I.D., Weinberg, K.A., & Scarr, S. (1994). Racial-group differences in IQ in the Minnesota Transracial Adoption Study: A reply to Levin and Lynn. *Intelligence, 19,* 29–44.

Walker, L.J. (1980). Cognitive and perspective-taking prerequisites for moral development. *Child Development, 51,* 131–9.

Walker, L.J. (1995). Sexism in Kohlberg's moral psychology? In W.M. Kurtines & J.L. Gewirtz (Eds.), *Moral development: An introduction* (pp. 83–107). Boston: Allyn & Bacon.

Walker, L.J., Henning, K.H., & Krettenauer, T. (2000). Parent and peer contexts for children's moral reasoning development. *Child Development, 71,* 1033–48.

Walker, L.J., & Pitts, R.C. (1998). Naturalistic conceptions of moral maturity. *Developmental Psychology, 34,* 403–19.

Walker-Andrews, A.S., & Lennon, E.M. (1985). Auditory-visual perception of changing distance by human infants. *Child Development, 56,* 544–8.

Wallach, M.A. (1985). Creativity testing and giftedness. In F.D. Horowitz & M. O'Brien (Eds.), *The gifted and talented: Developmental perspectives* (pp. 99–123). Washington, DC: American Psychological Association.

Wallach, M.A., & Kogan, N. (1965). *Modes of thinking in young children.* New York: Holt, Rinehart & Winston.

Wallen, K. (1996). Nature needs nurture: The interaction of hormonal and social influences on the development of behavioral sex differences in rhesus monkeys. *Hormones and Behavior, 30,* 364–78.

Wallerstein, J.S., & Blakeslee, S. (1989). *Second chances: Men, women, and children a decade after divorce.* New York: Ticknor and Fields.

Wallerstein, J.S., & Kelly, J.B. (1980). *Surviving the breakup: How children and parents cope with divorce.* New York: Basic Books.

Walsh, M., Hickey, C., & Duffy, J. (1999). Influence of item content and stereotype situation on gender differences in mathematical problem solving. *Sex Roles: A Journal of Research, 41* (3–4), 219–40.

Walters, A.S. (1997). Survey of 500 adolescents' discoveries about the facts of life. Unpublished data, University of Georgia.

Want, S.C., & Harris, P.L. (2001). Learning from other people's mistakes: Causal understanding in learning to use a tool. *Child Development, 72,* 431–43.

Ward, S.L., & Overton, W.F. (1990). Semantic familiarity, relevance, and the development of deductive reasoning. *Developmental Psychology, 26,* 488–93.

Wark, G.R., & Krebs, D.L. (1996). Gender and dilemma differences in real-life moral judgments. *Developmental Psychology, 32,* 220–30.

Wartner, U.G., Grossmann, K., Fremmer-Bombik, E., & Suess, G. (1994). Attachment patterns at age six in south Germany: Predictability from infancy and implications for preschool behavior. *Child Development, 65,* 1014–27.

Waterman, A.S. (1982). Identity development from adolescence to adulthood: An extension of theory and a review of research. *Developmental Psychology, 18,* 341–58.

Waterman, A.S. (1992). Identity as an aspect of optimal psychological functioning. In G.R. Adams, T.P. Gullotta, & R. Montemayor (Eds.), *Adolescent identity formation: Vol. 4. Advances in adolescent development* (pp. 50–72). Newbury Park, CA: Sage.

Waterman, A.S., & Archer, S.L. (1990). A life-span perspective on identity formation: Developments in form, function, and process. In P.B. Baltes, D.L. Featterman, & R.M. Lerner (Eds.), *Life-span development and behavior* (Vol. 10, pp. 29–57). Hillsdale, NJ: Erlbaum.

Waters, E., & Cummings, E.M. (2000). A secure base from which to explore close relationships. *Child Development, 71,* 164–72.

Waters, E., Merrick, S., Treboux, D., Crowell, J., & Albersheim, L. (2000). Attachment security in infancy and early adulthood: A twenty-year longitudinal study. *Child Development, 71,* 684–9.

Waters, E., Vaughn, B.E., & Egeland, B.R. (1980). Individual differences in mother–infant attachment relationships at age one: Antecedents in neonatal behavior in an urban, economically disadvantaged sample. *Child Development, 51,* 208–16.

Waters, E., Vaughn, B.E., Posada, G., & Kondo-Ikemura, K. (1995). Caregiving, cultural, and cognitive perspectives on secure-base behavior and working models: New growing points of attachment theory and research. *Monographs of the Society for Research in Child Development, 60* (2–3, Serial No. 244).

Waters, E., Wippman, J., & Sroufe, L.A. (1979). Attachment, positive affect, and competence in the peer group: Two studies in construct validation. *Child Development, 50,* 821–9.

Watkins, W.E., & Pollitt, E. (1999). Iron deficiency and cognition among school-age children. In S. Grantham McGregor (Ed.), *Recent Advances in Research on the Effects of Health and Nutrition on Children's Development an School Achievement in the Third World.* Pan American Health Organization.

Watson, A.C., Nixon, C.L., Wilson, A., & Capage, L. (1999). Social interaction skills and theory of mind in young children. *Developmental Psychology, 35,* 386–91.

Watson, J.B. (1913). Psychology as the behaviorist views it. *Psychological Review, 20,* 158–77.

Watson, J.B. (1925). *Behaviorism.* New York: Norton.

Watson, J.B. (1928). *Psychological care of infant and child.* New York: Norton.

Watson, J.B., & Raynor, R. (1920). Conditioned emotional reactions. *Journal of Experimental Psychology, 3,* 1–14.

Watson, J.S., Hayes, L.A., Vietze, P., & Becker, J. (1979). Discriminative infant smiling to orientations of talking faces of mother and stranger. *Journal of Experimental Child Psychology, 28,* 92–9.

Watson, M.W., & Peng, Y. (1992). The relation between toy gun play and children's aggressive behavior. *Early Education and Development, 3,* 370–89.

Waxman, S.R., & Hatch, T. (1992). Beyond the basics: Preschool children label objects flexibly at multiple hierarchical levels. *Journal of Child Language, 19,* 153–66.

Waxman, S.R., & Markow, D.B. (1998). Object properties and object kind: Twenty-one-month-old infants' extension of novel adjectives. *Child Development, 69,* 1313–29.

Waxman, S.R., & Senghas, A. (1992). Relations among word meanings in early lexical development. *Developmental Psychology, 28,* 862–73.

Weakliem, D., McQuillan, J., & Schauer, T. (1995). Toward meritocracy? Changing social-class differences in intellectual ability. *Sociology of Education, 68,* 271–86.

Wechsler, D. (1989). *Manual for the Wechsler Preschool and Primary Scale of Intelligence—Revised.* New York: Psychological Corporation.

Wechsler, D. (1991). *Manual, WISC-III: Wechsler Intelligence Scale for Children—Third Edition.* San Antonio, TX: Psychological Corporation.

Weinberg, M. K., Tronick, E. A., Cohn, J. F., & Olson, K. L. (1999). Gender differences in emotional expressivity and self-regulation during early infancy. *Developmental Psychology, 35,* 175–88.

Weinberg, R.A., Scarr, S., & Waldman, I.D. (1992). The Minnesota transracial adoption study: A follow-up of IQ test performance at adolescence. *Intelligence, 16,* 117–35.

Weiner, B. (1974). *Achievement and attribution theory.* Morristown, NJ: General Learning Press.

Weiner, B. (1986). *An attributional theory of motivation and emotion.* New York: Springer-Verlag.

Weinfield, N.S., Sroufe, L.A., & Egeland, B. (2000). Attachment from infancy to early adulthood in a high-risk sample: Continuity, discontinuity, and their correlates. *Child Development, 71,* 695–702.

Weinraub, M., Clemens, L.P., Sockloff, A., Ethridge, T., Gracely, E., & Myers, B. (1984). The development of sex-role stereotypes in the third year: Relationships to gender labeling, gender identity, sex-typed toy preferences, and family characteristics. *Child Development, 55,* 1493–1503.

Weinraub, M., & Lewis, M. (1977). The determinants of children's responses to separation. *Monographs of the Society for Research in Child Development, 42* (4, Serial No. 172).

Weinstein, C.S. (1991). The classroom as a social context for learning. *Annual Review of Psychology, 42,* 493–525.

Weisner, T.S., & Gallimore, R. (1977). My brother's keeper: Child and sibling caretaking. *Current Anthropology, 18,* 169–90.

Weisner, T.S., & Wilson-Mitchell, J.E. (1990). Nonconventional family lifestyles and sex typing in six-year-olds. *Child Development, 61,* 1915–33.

Weiss, B., Dodge, K.A., Bates, J.E., & Pettit, G.S. (1992). Some consequences of early harsh discipline: Child aggression and a maladaptive social information processing style. *Child Development, 63,* 1321–35.

Weiss, L.G., Saklofske, D.H., Prifitera, A., Chen, H.Y., & Hildebrand, D. (1999). The calculation of the WISC-III General Ability Index using Canadian norms. *Canadian Journal of School Psychology, 14* (2), 1–10.

Weiss, L.H., & Schwarz, J.C. (1996). The relationship between parenting types and older adolescents' personality, academic achievement, adjustment, and substance use. *Child Development, 67,* 2101–14.

Weisz, J.R., Chaiyasit, W., Weiss, B., Eastman, K.L., & Jackson, E.W. (1995). A multimethod study of problem behavior among Thai and American children in school: Teacher reports versus direct observations. *Child Development, 66,* 402–15.

Weizman, Z.O. & Snow, C.E. (2001). Lexical input as related to children's vocabulary acquisition: effects of sophisticated exposure and support for meaning. *Developmental Psychology, 28,* 862–73.

Welch-Ross, M.K., & Schmidt, C.R. (1996). Gender-schema development and children's constructive story memory: Evidence for a developmental model. *Child Development, 67,* 820–35.

Wellman, H.M. (1985). *Children's searching: The development of search skill and spatial representation.* Hillsdale, NJ: Erlbaum.

Wellman, H.M. (1990). *The child's theory of mind.* Cambridge, MA: MIT Press.

Wellman, H.M., Hollander, M., & Schult, C.A. (1996). Young children's understanding of thought bubbles and of thoughts. *Child Development, 67,* 768–88.

Wellman, H.M., & Lempers, J.D. (1977). The naturalistic communicative abilities of two-year-olds. *Child Development, 48,* 1052–7.

Wellman, H.M., Phillips, A.T., & Rodriquez, T. (2000). Young children's understanding of perception, desire, and emotion. *Child Development, 71,* 895–912.

Wellman, H.M., & Woolley, J. (1990). From simple desires to ordinary beliefs: The early development of everyday psychology. *Cognition, 35,* 245–75.

Wells, L.E. (1989). Self-enhancement through delinquency: A conditional test of self-derogation theory. *Journal of Research in Crime and Delinquency, 26,* 226–52.

Wender, P.H. (1995). *Attention-deficit hyperactivity disorder in adults.* New York: Oxford University Press.

Wendland-Carro, J., Piccinini, C.A., & Millar, W.S. (1999). The role of early intervention in enhancing the quality of mother–infant interaction. *Child Development, 70,* 713–21.

Wentzel, K.R., & Asher, S.R. (1995). The academic lives of neglected, rejected, popular, and controversial children. *Child Development, 66,* 754–63.

Werker, J.F., Cohen, L.B., Lloyd, V.L. Casasola, M., & Stager, C. (1998). Acquisition of word–object associations by 14-month-old infants. *Developmental Psychology, 34,* 1289–1309.

Werker, J.F., & Desjardins, R.N. (1995). Listening to speech in the first year of life: Experiential influences on phoneme perception. *Current Directions in Psychological Science, 4,* 76–81.

Werker, J.F., Fennell, C.T., Corcoran, K.M., & Stager, C. (2002). Infants' ability to learn phonetically similar words: Effects of age and vocabulary size. *Infancy, 3*(1), 1–30.

Werker, J., & Tees, R. (2003). Cross-language speech perception: Evidence for perceptual reorganization during the first year of life. *Infant Behavior and Development, 25,* 121–33.

Werner, E.E., & Smith, R.S. (1992). *Overcoming the odds. High risk children from birth to adulthood.* Ithaca, NY: Cornell University Press.

Wertsch, J.V., & Tulviste, P. (1992). L.S. Vygotsky and contemporary developmental psychology. *Developmental Psychology, 28,* 548–57.

Whaley, K.L., & Rubenstein, T.S. (1994). How toddlers "do" friendship: A descriptive analysis of naturally occurring friendships in a group child care setting. *Journal of Social and Personal Relationships, 11,* 383–400.

Whiffen, V.E. (1992). Is postpartum depression a distinct diagnosis? *Clinical Psychology Review, 12,* 485–508.

Whipp, B.J., & Ward, S.A. (1992). Will women soon outrun men? *Nature, 355,* 25.

Whipple, E.E., & Richey, C.A. (1997). Crossing the line between physical discipline and child abuse: How much is too much. *Child Abuse and Neglect, 21,* 431–44.

Whitaker, D.J., & Miller, K.S. (2000). Parent-adolescent discussion about sex and condoms: Input of peer influences on sexual risk behavior. *Journal of Adolescent Research, 15,* 251–72.

Whitall, J., & Getchell, N. (1995). From walking to running: Applying a dynamical systems approach to the development of locomotor skills. *Child Development, 66,* 1541–53.

Whitbeck, L.B., Hoyt, D.R., & Bao, W. (2000). Depressive symptoms and co-occurring depressive symptoms, substance abuse, and conduct problems among runaway and homeless adolescents. *Child Development, 71,* 721–32.

Whitbourne, S.K. (1986). *The me I know: A study of adult identity.* New York: Springer-Verlag.

White, K.J., & Kistner, J. (1992). The influence of teacher feedback on young children's peer preferences and perceptions. *Developmental Psychology, 28,* 933–40.

White, R.W. (1959). Motivation reconsidered: The concept of competence. *Psychological Review, 66,* 297–333.

White, S.H. (1992). G. Stanley Hall: From philosophy to developmental psychology. *Developmental Psychology, 28,* 25–34.

Whitehurst, G.J., & Lonigan, C.J. (1998). Child development and emergent literacy. *Child Development, 69,* 848–72.

Whitehurst, G.J., & Valdez-Menchaca, M.C. (1988). What is the role of reinforcement in early language acquisition? *Child Development, 59,* 430–40.

Whitehurst, G.J., & Vasta, R. (1975). Is language acquired through imitation. *Journal of Psycholinguistic Research, 4,* 37–59.

Whiting, B.B., & Edwards, C.P. (1988). *Children of different worlds: The formation of social behavior.* Cambridge, MA: Harvard University Press.

Whiting, B.B., & Whiting, J.W.M. (1975). *Children of six cultures.* Cambridge, MA: Harvard University Press.

Whitley, B.E., Jr. (1983). Sex-role orientation and self-esteem: A critical meta-analytic review. *Journal of Personality and Social Psychology, 44,* 765–78.

Whittle, M.J., & Connor, J.M. (1995). *Prenatal diagnosis in obstetric practice* (2nd ed.). Oxford: Blackwell.

Wichstrom, L. (1999). The emergence of gender difference in depressed mood during adolescence: The role of intensified gender socialization. *Developmental Psychology, 35,* 232–45.

Wiehe, V.R. (1996). *Working with child abuse and neglect.* Thousand Oaks, CA: Sage.

Wiggam, A.E. (1923). *The new decalogue of science.* Indianapolis, MN: Bobbs-Merrill.

Wilcock, A., Kobayashi, L., & Murray, I. (1997). Twenty-five years of obstetric patient satisfaction in North America: A review of the literature. *Journal of Perinatal and Neonatal Nursing, 10,* 36–47.

Wilcox, A.J., Baird, D.D., Weinberg, C.R., & Associates. (1995). Fertility in men exposed prenatally to diethylstilbestrol. *New England Journal of Medicine, 332,* 1411–16.

Wile, J., & Arechiga, M. (1999). Sociocultural aspects of postpartum depression. In L.J. Miller (Ed.), *Postpartum mood disorders* (pp. 83–98). Washington, DC: American Psychiatric Press.

Wilens, T.E., & Biederman, J. (1992). The stimulants. *Psychiatric Clinics of North America, 15,* 191–222.

Wille, D. (1991). Relation of preterm birth with quality of infant–mother attachment at one year. *Infant Behavior and Development, 14,* 227–40.

Willems, E.P., & Alexander, J.L. (1982). The naturalistic perspective in research. In B.B. Wolman (Ed.), *Handbook of developmental psychology.* Englewood Cliffs, NJ: Prentice Hall.

Williams, B. (1998, January 19). Stricter controls on internet access sorely needed, parents fear. *Atlanta Constitution,* pp. A1, A15.

Williams, B.R., Ponesse, J.S., Schachar, R.J., Loyan, G.D., & Tannock, R. (1999). Development of inhibitory control across the life span. *Developmental Psychology, 35,* 205–13.

Williams, C., & Bybee, J. (1994). What do children feel guilty about? Developmental and gender differences. *Developmental Psychology, 30,* 617–23.

Williams, J.E., Bennett, S.M., & Best, D.L. (1975). Awareness and expression of sex stereotypes in young children. *Developmental Psychology, 11,* 635–42.

Williams, J.E., & Best, D.L. (1990). *Measuring sex stereotypes: A multination study* (rev. ed.). Newbury Park, CA: Sage.

Williams-Murphy, M., Hoff, C., Thorneycroft, I., & Little, F. (1998, December 7–16). *Pregnancy outcomes in sickle cell disesase (SCD).* Paper presented at INABIS '98—5th Internet World Congress on Biomedical Sciences, McMaster University, Hamilton, ON. Retrieved August 14, 2001 from http://www.mcmaster.ca/inabis98/medicine/williams-murphy0753/two.html.

Willoughby, T., Wood, E., & Khan, M. (1994). Isolating variables that impact on or detract from the effectiveness of elaboration strategies. *Journal of Educational Psychology, 86,* 279–89.

Wilson, R.S. (1978). Synchronies in mental development: An epigenetic perspective. *Science, 202,* 939–48.

Wilson, R.S. (1983). The Louisville twin study: Developmental synchronies in behavior. *Child Development, 54,* 298–316.

Wilson, R.S. (1985). Risk and resilience in early mental development. *Developmental Psychology, 21,* 795–805.

Winick, M. (1976). *Malnutrition and brain development.* New York: Oxford University Press.

Winner, E. (1997). Exceptionally high intelligence and schooling. *American Psychologist, 52,* 1070–81.

Winner, E. (2000). The origins and ends of giftedness. *American Psychologist, 55,* 159–69.

Winterbottom, M. (1958). The relation of need for achievement to learning experiences in independence and mastery. In J. Atkinson (Ed.), *Motives in fantasy, action, and society.* Princeton, NJ: Van Nostrand.

Wintre, M.G. & Vallance, D. (1994). A developmental sequence in the comprehension of emotions: Intensity, multiple emotions, and valence. *Developmental Psychology, 30*(4), 509–14.

Wissow, L., Hutton, N., & McGraw, D.C. (1996). Psychosocial issues for children born to HIV-infected mothers. In R.R. Faden & N.E. Kass (Eds.), *HIV, AIDS, and childbearing* (pp. 78–95). New York: Oxford University Press.

Witelson, S.F. (1987). Neurobiological aspects of language in children. *Child Development, 58,* 653–88.

Wolfe, D.A., Crooks, C.V., Lee, V., McIntyre-Smith, A., & Jaffe, P.G. (2003). The effects of children's violence: A meta-analysis and critique. *Clinical Child and Family Psychology Review, 6* (3), 171–87.

Wolff, M., Rutten, P., & Bayer, A.F., III. (1992). *Where we stand: Can America make it in the race for health, wealth, and happiness?* New York: Bantam Books.

Wolff, P.H. (1966). The causes, controls, and organization of behavior in the neonate. *Psychological Issues, 5* (1, Whole No. 17).

Wolff, P.H. (1969). The natural history of crying and other vocalizations in early infancy. In B.M. Foss (Ed.), *Determinants of infant behavior* (Vol.4). London: Methuen.

Wolfner, G.D., & Gelles, R.J. (1993). A profile of violence toward children: A national study. *Child Abuse and Neglect, 17,* 197–212.

Woo, E. (1995, December 11). Can racial stereotypes psych out students? *Los Angeles Times,* p. D1.

Wood, D., Bruner, J.S., & Ross, G. (1976). The role of tutoring in problem-solving. *Journal of Child Psychology and Psychiatry, 17,* 89–100.

Wood, E., Pressley, M., & Winne, P. (1990). Elaborative interrogation effects on children's learning of factual information. *Journal of Educational Psychology, 82,* 741–8.

Woodward, A.L., Markman, E.M., & Fitzsimmons, C.M. (1994). Rapid word learning in 13- and 18-month-olds. *Developmental Psychology, 30,* 553–66.

Wright, J.C., Huston, A.C., Reitz, A.L., & Piemyat, S. (1994). Young children's perception of television reality: Determinants and developmental differences. *Developmental Psychology, 30,* 229–39.

Wright, J.C., Huston, A.C., Truglio, R., Fitch, M., Smith, E., & Piemyat, S. (1995). Occupational portrayals on television: Children's role schemata, career aspirations, and perceptions of reality. *Child Development, 66,* 1706–18.

Wright, S., & Taylor, D. (2001). Identity and the language of the classroom: Investigating the impact of heritage versus second language instruction on personal and collective self-esteem. *Journal of Educational Psychology, 87* (2), 242–52.

Wrobel, G.M., Ayers-Lopez, S., Grotevant, H.D., McRoy, R.G., & Friedrick, M. (1996). Openness in adoption and level of child participation. *Child Development, 67,* 2358–74.

Wyatt, P. (2000). New Down syndrome statistics: Cytogenetic specimens with trisomy 21 and translocation 21—Canada. *Canadian Down Syndrome Society Quarterly, 13* (1), 8.

Wyman, P.A., Cowen, E.L., Work, W.C., Hoyt-Myers, L., Magnus, K.B., & Fagen, D.B. (1999). Caregiving and developmental factors differentiating young, at-risk urban children showing resilient versus stress-affected outcomes: A replication and extension. *Child Development, 70,* 645–59.

Wynn, K. (1992). Addition and subtraction by human infants. *Nature, 358,* 749–50.

Yang, B., Ollendick, T.H., Dong, Q., Xia, Y., & Lin, L. (1995). Only children and children with siblings in the People's Republic of China: Levels of fear, anxiety, and depression. *Child Development, 66,* 1301–11.

Yankowitz, J. (1996). Surgical fetal therapy. In J.A. Kuller, N.C. Cheschier, & R.C. Cefalo (Eds.), *Prenatal diagnosis and reproductive genetics* (pp. 181–7). St. Louis, MO: Mosby.

Yau, J., & Smetana, J.G. (1996). Adolescent–parent conflict among Chinese adolescents in Hong Kong. *Child Development, 67,* 1262–75.

Yazigi, R.A., Odem, R.R., & Polakoski, K.L. (1991). Demonstration of specific binding of cocaine to human spermatoza. *Journal of the American Medical Association, 266,* 1956–9.

Yeates, K.O., MacPhee, D., Campbell, F.A., & Ramey, C.T. (1983). Maternal IQ and home environment as determinants of early childhood intellectual competence: A developmental analysis. *Developmental Psychology, 19,* 731–9.

Yeates, K.O., & Selman, R.L. (1989). Social competence in the schools: Toward an integrative developmental model for intervention. *Developmental Review, 9,* 64–100.

Yonas, A., Arterberry, M., & Granrud, C.E. (1987). Space perception in infancy. In R.A. Vasta (Ed.) *Annals of child development* (pp. 1–34). Greenwich, CT: JAI Press.

Young, S.K., Fox, N.A., & Zahn-Waxler, C. (1999). The relations between temperament and empathy in 2-year-olds. *Developmental Psychology, 35,* 1189–97.

Young, W.C., Goy, R.W., & Phoenix, C.H. (1964). Hormones and sexual behavior. *Science, 143,* 212–8.

Yonas, A., Cleaves, W., & Pettersen, L. (1978). Development of sesnsitivity to pictorial depth. *Science, 200,* 77–9.

Youngblade, L.M., & Dunn, J. (1995). Individual differences in young children's pretend play with mother and sibling: Links to relationships and understanding other people's feelings and beliefs. *Child Development, 66,* 1472–92.

Younger, A.J., & Daniels, T.M. (1992). Children's reasons for nominating their peers as withdrawn: Passive withdrawal versus active isolation. *Developmental Psychology, 28,* 955–60.

Youniss, J., McLellan, J.A., & Strouse, D. (1994). "We're popular, but we're not snobs": Adolescents describe their crowds. In R. Montemayor, G.R. Adams, & T.P. Gullotta (Eds.), *Personal relationships in adolescence: Vol. 6. Advances in adolescent development.* Thousand Oaks, CA: Sage.

Youth Lifestyle Choices—Community University Research Alliance. (2001). [Survey of youth behaviors]. Unpublished raw data.

Yuill, N., & Pearson, A. (1998). The development of bases for trait attribution: Children's understanding of traits as causal mechanisms based on desires. *Developmental Psychology, 34,* 574–86.

Yussen, S.R., & Bird, J.E. (1979). The development of metacognitive awareness in memory, communication, and attention. *Journal of Experimental Child Psychology, 28,* 300–13.

Zahn-Waxler, C., Friedman, R.J., Cole, P.M., Mizuta, I., & Himura, N. (1996). Japanese and United States preschool children's responses to conflict and distress. *Child Development, 67,* 2462–77.

Zahn-Waxler, C., Radke-Yarrow, M., & King, R.A. (1979). Child rearing and children's prosocial initiations toward victims of distress. *Child Development, 50,* 319–30.

Zahn-Waxler, C., Radke-Yarrow, M., Wagner, E., & Chapman, M. (1992). Development of concern for others. *Developmental Psychology, 28,* 126–36.

Zahn-Waxler, C., Robinson, J.L., & Emde, R.N. (1992). The development of empathy in twins. *Developmental Psychology, 28,* 1038–47.

Zakriski, A.L., & Coie, J.D. (1996). A comparison of aggressive-rejected and nonaggressive-rejected children's interpretations of self-directed and other-directed rejection. *Child Development, 67,* 1048–70.

Zani, B. (1991). Male and female patterns in the discovery of sexuality during adolescence. *Journal of Adolescence, 14,* 163–78.

Zarbatany, L., Brunschot, M.V., Meadows, K., & Pepper, S. (1996). Effects of friendship and gender on peer group entry. *Child Development, 67,* 2287–300.

Zelazo, D. Z., & Jacques, S. (1997). Children's rule use: Representation, reflection and cognitive control. *Annals of Child Development, 12,* 119–76.

Zelazo, N.A., Zelazo, P.R., Cohen, K.M., & Zelazo, P.D. (1993). Specificity of practice effects in elementary neuromotor patterns. *Developmental Psychology, 29,* 686–91.

Zelazo, P.D. & Frye, D. (1997). Cognitive complexity and control: A theory of the development of deliberate reasoning and intentional action. In M. Stamenov (Ed.), *Language structure, discourse, and the access to consciousness* (pp. 113–153). Amsterdam & Philadelphia: John Benjamins.

Zelazo, P.D., Frye, D., & Rapus, T. (1996). An age-related dissociation between knowing rules and using them. *Cognitive Development, 11,* 37-63.

Zelazo, P.D., Helwig, C.C., & Lau, A. (1996). Intention, act, and outcome in behavioral prediction and moral judgment. *Child Development, 67,* 2478–92.

Zelazo, P.R., Kearsley, R.B., & Stack, D.M. (1995). Mental representation for visual sequences: Increased speed of central processing from 22 to 32 months. *Intelligence, 20,* 41–63.

Zelazo, P.R., Zelazo, N.A., & Kolb, S. (1972). "Walking" in the newborn. *Science, 176,* 314–5.

Zeman, J., & Garber, J. (1996). Display rules for anger, sadness, and pain: It depends on who is watching. *Child Development, 67,* 957–73.

Zeman, J., & Shipman, K. (1997). Social-contextual influences on expectancies for managing anger and sadness: The transition from middle childhood to adolescence. *Developmental Psychology, 33,* 917–24.

Zerbe, K.J. (1993). *The body betrayed: Women, eating disorders, and treatment.* Washington, DC: American Psychiatric Press.

Zern, D.S. (1984). Relationships among selected child-rearing variables in a cross-cultural sample of 110 societies. *Developmental Psychology, 20,* 683–90.

Zeskind, P.S. (1980). Adult responses to the cries of low and high risk infants. *Infant Behavior and Development, 3,* 167–77.

Zeskind, P. S., Klein, L., & Marshall, T. R. (1992). Adults' perceptions of experimental modifications of durations of pauses and expiratory sounds in infant crying. *Developmental Psychology, 28,* 1153–62.

Zeskind, P.S., & Ramey, C.T. (1981). Preventing intellectual and interactional sequelae of fetal malnutrition: A longitudinal, transactional, and synergistic approach to development. *Child Development, 52,* 213–8.

Zeskind, P.S., Sale, J., Maio, M.L., Huntington, L., & Weiseman, J.R. (1985). Adult perceptions of pain and hunger cries: A synchrony of arousal. *Child Development, 56,* 549–54.

Zhou, M., & Bankston, C.I. (1998). *Growing up American: How Vietnamese children adapt to life in the United States.* New York: Russell Sage Foundation.

Ziegert, D.I., Kistner, J.A., Castro, R., & Robertson, B. (2001). Longitudinal study of young children's responses to challenging achievement situations. *Child Development, 72,* 609–24.

Zigler, E., & Finn-Stevenson, M.F. (1993). *Children in a changing world: Developmental and social issues.* Pacific Grove, CA: Brooks/Cole.

Zigler, E.F. (1987). Formal schooling for four-year-olds? No. *American Psychologist, 42,* 254–60.

Zigler, E.F., Abelson, W.D., Trickett, P.K., & Seitz, V. (1982). Is an intervention program necessary to improve economically disadvantaged children's IQ scores? *Child Development, 53,* 340–8.

Zigler, E.F., & Gilman, E. (1993). Day care in America: What is needed? *Pediatrics, 91,* 175–8.

Zimmerman, M.A., Salem, D.A., & Maton, K.I. (1995). Family structure and psychosocial correlates among urban African-American adolescent males. *Child Development, 66,* 1598–613.

Abbey, B.B., 395
Abel, E.L., 117
Abelson, W.D., 337
Aber, J.L., 423, 448, 454, 529, 530, 598, 621, 622
Ablard, K.E., 582
Abma, J.C., 126
Aboud, F.E., 464, 469, 470, 644
Abraham, K.G., 461
Abramovitch, R., 581, 582, 583
Abravanel, E., 216
Achenbach, T.M., 137
Achilles, C.M., 618
Ackerman, B.P., 379, 575
Ackermann-Liebrich, U., 132
Acredolo, L.P., 364, 373
Adams, G.R., 461, 462, 623, 638
Adams, J.L., 361
Adams, M.J., 205
Adams, P.W., 544
Adams, R., 187, 188
Adamson, L.B., 398
Addison, T.L., 145
Adey, P.S., 246
Adler, A., 46
Adler, T.F., 481
Adolph, K.E., 165
Aerts, E., 552
Ager, J.W., 119, 120
Ainsworth, M.D.S., 59, 145, 164, 405, 408, 411, 412, 415, 416, 418
Akhtar, N., 367, 368
Alansky, J.A., 418
Al-Awad, A.M., 566
Albersheim, L., 421
Albert, R.S., 346
Alberts, D.M., 616
Albin, M., 137, 394
Albrecht, R., 170
Alessandri, S.M., 122, 393, 436
Alexander, B.K., 630
Alexander, G.M., 487
Alexander, J.L., 14
Alexander, K.L., 621
Alfieri, T., 485
Alibali, M.W., 270
Allen, J.P., 421, 646
Allen, L., 324, 325, 448, 622
Allen, M.C., 113
Allen, S.E.M., 378
Alley, T.R., 408
Alleyne, E., 512
Allgood-Merten, B., 503
Almeida, D.M., 486
Aloise, P.A., 284
Alpern, L., 421
Altmaier, E., 131
Altshuler, L.L., 134
Amabile, T.M., 345, 346

Amaral, D., 158
Amato, P.R., 567, 587, 588, 589, 590
Ambert, A., 564
American Academy of Pediatrics, 144
American Psychiatric Association, 278
American Psychological Association, 32
Ames, E.W., 425, 426, 427
Amini, S. B., 125
Ammerman, R.T., 596
Amsel, E., 246
Andermann, E.M., 622
Anderson, C.A., 615
Anderson, D.R., 178, 436, 498, 606, 608, 612
Anderson, J., 118
Anderson, K.J., 496
Andersson, B., 429, 593
Andrews, D.W., 526, 642, 645, 648
Andrews, J., 170
Andruski, J. E., 359
Angeli, C., 613
Angelopoulos, M., 367
Anglin, J.M., 380
Anisfield, M., 216
Annis, R.C., 439
Anthony, E.J., 135
Anthony, J.L., 205, 381
Antunes, C.M., 602
Apfel, N.H., 126, 342, 343, 511, 512
Apgar, V., 111, 118, 122, 126, 129
Apostoleris, N.H., 630
Applebaum, M.I., 164, 325
Appleton, H., 612
Aquan-Assee, J., 581–582, 644, 645
Archer, J., 58, 460, 492, 493
Archer, S.C., 461
Archer, S.L., 460, 461, 630
Arechiga, M., 134
Arend, R., 496
Arendt, R., 121, 122
Areus, D., 400
Arezzo, D., 610
Aries, P., 7
Aristotle, 117
Arjimand, O., 481, 482
Arlman-Rupp, A., 360
Armon, Y., 125, 126
Armson, B., 86
Arnett, J.J., 575
Arnold, M.L., 578
Aro, H., 172
Aronson, E., 201
Aronson, J., 338
Arsenio, W.F., 397, 522
Arterberry, M., 197
Asendorpf, J.B., 437, 438
Ash, T., 240, 395
Asher, S.R., 397, 624, 631, 638, 639, 642, 643, 645
Ashmead, D.H., 163
Aslin, R.N., 188, 195, 197, 359

Associated Press, 482, 507, 590
Astington, J.W., 356, 443
Astone, N.M., 512
Astor, 517, 520
Atkin, C., 609
Atkins, E., 615
Atkinson, J.W., 452, 453
Atkinson, L., 82, 421
Atkinson, R.C., 265
Atlas, R.S., 522
Atterbury, J.L., 113
Auerbach, J., 216
Ausley, J.A., 272
Austin, E., 321
Austin, R.J., 136
Avard, D., 568, 593
Aviezer, D., 414, 423
Axia, G., 191, 374
Azmitia, M., 258, 583
Azuma, H., 414, 415

Bachevalier, J., 292, 293
Backschneider, A.G., 240
Bacon, M.K., 474, 475
Badzinski, D.M., 397
Bagley, 597, 598, 599
Bagwell, C.L., 643, 644, 645
Bahrick, L.E., 202, 203, 367
Bai, D.L., 199
Baier, J.L., 509
Bailey, D.B., 624
Bailey, J.M., 91, 508, 585
Baillargeon, R., 229, 230, 231, 232, 250
Baird, D.D., 119
Baird, P., 86
Bakeman, R., 398
Baker, D.P., 301, 479, 481
Baker, L.A., 491
Baker, R.L., 126, 138
Baker, S.W., 491
Baker-Ward, L., 279, 282, 291
Balaban, T., 497
Baldwin, A., 324, 332, 335
Baldwin, C., 324, 332, 335
Baldwin, D.A., 367, 396
Baldwin, D.V., 587
Ball, S., 611
Ball, W.A., 275
Ballif, B., 393
Baltes, P.B., 3
Bandura, A., 48, 49, 50, 62, 65, 215, 217, 353, 487, 495, 496, 554
Bank, L., 526, 575
Banks, J.A., 624
Banks, M.S., 187, 188, 192, 193
Bankston, C.I., 577, 623
Bao, W., 602
Barber, B.K., 578, 648
Barber, B.L., 648

Barden, R.C., 408
Barenboim, C., 465
Barglow, P., 125
Barker, E.T., 177, 647
Barker, R.G., 619
Barker, W., 339
Barna, J., 440
Barnard, K.E., 137, 333, 339
Barnett, D., 416
Barnett, W.S., 341
Baron, N.S., 354, 370
Baron, R.A., 21, 22
Baron-Cohen, S., 442
Baroni, M.R., 374
Barr, H.M., 118, 119
Barr, R., 216
Barrera, M., Jr., 574
Barrera, M.E., 194
Barrett, D.E., 175, 176
Barrett, K.C., 540
Barrow, R., 337
Barry, H., III, 171, 474, 475
Bar-Tal, D., 531
Bartholomew, K., 422, 423
Barton, M.E., 382
Bartsch, K., 463
Baskett, L.M., 582
Bates, E., 358, 359, 360, 363, 364
Bates, J.E., 214, 401, 421, 522, 523, 524, 526,
  573, 578, 594, 639, 643, 648
Bateson, D., 337
Bathurst, K., 325, 333
Batson, C.D. 95, 533
Battaglia, F., 119
Batterman-Faunce, J.M., 289
Baudonniere, P., 437, 438
Bauer, C.R., 137, 158, 190
Bauer, P.J., 228, 286, 287
Baumeister, A.A., 145
Baumrind, D., 104, 214, 454, 508, 571, 572,
  573, 637
Baxter, A., 396
Bayer, A.F., III, 524
Bayley, N., 171, 160, 323
Beach, D.R., 279
Beach, F.A., 506
Beady, C., 618
Beal, C.R., 379, 380, 496
Beaman, J., 590
Bear, G.G., 543
Beard, R., 132
Beardsall, L., 396
Beazley, R., 511
Bebko, J.M., 279
Beck, J., 111, 118, 122, 126, 129
Becker, J., 405
Becker, J.B., 171
Beckett, C., 325, 326, 427
Beckwith, L., 122
Bee, H.L., 137
Begab, M.J., 329
Begley, N.L., 485
Begley, S., 89
Behnke, M., 121
Behrend, D.A., 240, 260
Beidelman, T.O., 171
Beilin, H., 54, 55, 248
Beiser, M., 621
Beitins, I.Z., 169
Belanger, S., 33
Belgrad, S.L., 379
Bell, A.P., 508
Bell, K., 421
Bell, M.A., 205, 400
Bell, R.Q., 50
Bell, S.M., 145
Bellanti, C.J., 582

Bellugi, U., 354, 373
Belsky, D.H., 126
Belsky, J., 62, 64, 394, 399, 404, 416, 418, 419,
  422, 423, 430, 453, 565, 570, 580, 596, 597,
  599
Bem, D.J., 403
Bem, S.L., 495, 500, 501, 502, 503
Benasich, A.A., 138
Benbow, C.P., 481, 482
Bendell, D., 416
Bendersky, M., 122, 139
Benedict, H., 365
Benenson, J.F., 630
Benini, F., 191
Benner, A., 428
Bennett, C., 486, 640
Bennett, F.C., 138
Bennett, P., 367
Bennett, S.M., 13
Benoit, D., 423
Bensen, A.S., 197
Benson, P.L., 97, 584, 585
Bentler, P.M., 649
Bento, S., 423
Bentz, L.S., 113
Benzie, R., 86
Berenbaum, S.A., 476, 491, 492, 508
Berg, C.A., 479
Berg, K.M., 142, 143
Berg, W.K., 142, 143, 189
Bergen, D.J., 475
Berk, L.E., 260
Berkey, C.S., 153
Berko, J., 376
Berkowitz, L., 22
Berkowitz, M.W., 549
Berlin, L.J., 415
Berlin, M., 137
Berliner, L., 598
Berman, 449
Bermejo, V., 298
Bernbaum, J.C., 138
Berndt, T.J., 468, 581, 635, 641, 643, 645,
  646
Bernieri, F., 102, 330
Bernstein, I.S., 492
Bernzweig, J., 534
Berridge, D.M., 443
Berrueta-Clement, J.R., 341
Berry, J.W., 206
Bertenthal, B.I., 17, 165, 195, 199, 200
Berthier, N.E., 163
Bertoncini, J., 189, 362
Bertrand, J. 104, 369
Bessler, A., 278
Best Start, 76
Best, C.T., 365
Best, D.L., 13, 474, 475
Best, K.M., 570
Beuker, R., 169
Bewley, S., 131
Bhapkar, M.V., 153, 167, 169
Bhavnagri, N.P., 17
Bialystok, E., 381, 385, 386, 387
Bianchi, S.M., 587
Bickerton, D., 171
Bidell, T. 248, 305
Bidrose, S., 289
Biederman, J., 278
Bierman, K.L., 582, 642
Biernat, M., 484
Bigbee, M.A., 519
Bigelow, A., 140, 440
Bigler, R.S., 439, 464, 485, 505, 609
Bigner, J.J., 585
Bijeljac-Babic, R., 189
Billings, R.L., 123

Binet, A., 52, 312, 313, 320
Bingham, C.R., 509
Birch, E.E., 197
Birch, H.G., 400
Birch, L.L., 178, 526, 531
Birch, S.H., 640
Bird, J.E., 281
Biringen, Z., 164, 416, 540
Birns, B., 335
Bisanz, J., 299, 616
Bish, A., 584
Bissell, M., 511, 512
Bitz, B., 544
Bivens, J.A., 260
Bjork, E.L., 368
Bjorklund, B.R., 6, 282, 285, 289
Bjorklund, D.F., 6, 55, 205, 216, 221, 229, 232,
  233, 240, 249, 250, 253, 264, 268, 269, 270,
  274, 277, 280, 281, 282, 283, 284, 285, 289,
  299, 304, 319, 335, 359, 441
Black, J., 247
Black, J.E., 154, 155
Black, M.M., 419, 593
Black, S.H., 78, 80
Black-Gutman, D., 464
Blackwell, J., 82
Blake, J., 363
Blakemore, 486, 487
Blakeslee, S., 588
Blanc, M., 386
Blasi, A., 554
Blass, E.M., 145, 190
Blatt, S. J., 448, 450
Blaxton, T.A., 272
Blehar, M., 408, 412
Block, J., 344, 450, 588
Block, J.H., 344, 470, 588
Bloom, F.E., 158, 356
Bloom, L., 354, 361, 365, 372, 377
Blote, A.E., 270
Blount, R., 434
Blue, J., 596
Blumenthal, D.R., 527
Blyth, D.A., 170, 172, 448, 622
Board, J., 536
Bodmer-Turner, J., 598
Bogartz, R.S., 232
Bogatz, C., 611
Bogenschneider, K., 648, 649
Bohannon, J.N., 354, 357, 359, 360
Bohlin, G., 410
Boivin, I., 385
Boivin, M., 136, 520, 522, 523, 526, 648
Bolan, P., 86
Boldizar, J.P., 486, 502, 503
Bolduc, D., 473
Bolger, K.E., 575, 597, 598, 599
Boloh, Y., 380
Bolton, P., 329
Bonichini, S., 191
Bonk, C.J., 613
Bonvillian, J.D., 354, 359, 360, 373
Boodoo, G., 312, 315, 322, 326, 327, 335, 337,
  339
Bookstein, F.L., 119
Boone, R.T., 397
Booth, A., 171, 587, 589
Borkowski, J.G., 280, 512
Bornstein, M.H., 17, 104, 188, 203, 208, 235,
  256, 493, 648, 649
Bornstein, R., 321
Boroditsky, R., 511
Borstelmann, L.J., 7
Bos, J., 594
Botein, S., 65, 416, 417
Botkin, J.R., 75, 88, 89
Bottino, P.J., 79, 84

Bouchard, T.J., Jr., 91, 102, 312, 315, 322, 326, 327, 335, 337, 339 492
Boudreau, J.P., 200, 201
Boulerice, B., 520
Boulton, M.H., 522
Bountrogianni, M., 255
Bourdony, C.J., 153, 167, 169
Bowen-Woodward, K., 591
Bower, T.G.R., 162, 188, 201
Bowker, A., 639
Bowlby, J., 59, 60, 140, 402, 407, 408, 411, 420, 422, 423, 425, 446
Bow-Thomas, C.C., 301, 302, 626
Boxer, A.M., 170
Boyatzis, C.J., 610
Boyes, M.C., 461
Boykin, A.W., 312, 315, 322, 326, 327, 335, 337, 339, 578
Boyle, M.H., 449
Boysson-Bardies, B. de., 365
Brackbill, Y., 130, 132
Bradbard, M.R., 449
Braddock, J.H., II, 622
Bradley, C.F., 125
Bradley, E.A., 329
Bradley, R.H., 138, 332, 333, 339, 419, 430, 453 593
Bradshaw, D., 392, 393
Brady, T., 83
Braine, M.D.S., 378, 380
Brainerd, C.J., 248, 272, 273, 289, 291, 305
Brakke, K.E., 355
Brame, B., 518
Brand, E., 591
Branstetter, W.H., 641
Brant, R., 133
Brasfield, T.L., 512
Brassard, M.R., 601
Braun, N., 596
Braungart, J.M., 334, 399
Braunwald, K., 416
Braver, S.L., 590
Bray, H., 504
Brazelton, T.B., 16, 129, 137, 140, 146, 394
Breinlinger, K., 230
Brendgen, M., 641
Brent, H.P., 195, 196
Bretherton, I., 410, 422
Bricker, W., 50
Bridger, W., 335
Bridger, W.H., 201
Bridges, D., 531, 534
Bridges, L.J., 394
Bridges, M., 587, 588, 589, 590, 592
Britt, G.C., 129
Broberg, A.G., 214, 429, 430, 593
Brobow, D., 508, 585
Brockington, I., 76, 120, 121, 125, 126, 130, 131, 132, 134, 137, 144, 178, 180, 403
Brody, G.H., 538, 540, 557, 558, 564, 576, 581, 630, 636
Brody, N., 312, 314, 315, 322, 326, 327, 335, 337, 339
Brodzinsky, A.B., 585
Brodzinsky, D.M., 134, 585
Bromley, D.B., 443, 463
Bronfenbrenner, U., 22, 62, 64, 65, 66, 105, 425, 564, 567
Bronson, G.W., 194
Bronstein, P., 454
Brookover, W., 618
Brooks, P.J., 378, 441
Brooks-Gunn, J., 64, 138, 169, 170, 172, 177, 179, 171, 172, 325, 333, 437, 509, 511, 512, 575, 577
Brophy, J.E., 620
Broughton, J.M., 201

Broverman, I.K., 475
Brown, A.L., 258, 282, 295, 297, 304, 323
Brown, A.M., 188
Brown, B.B., 63, 454, 621, 623, 635, 636, 646, 648
Brown, E., 195, 198, 581
Brown, E.G., 637
Brown, J., 122, 396
Brown, J.D., 435, 445, 446, 450
Brown, J.L., 142, 529, 530
Brown, J.R., 395, 397, 583
Brown, K.P., 642
Brown, M.M., 642
Brown, N.B., 370
Brown, P., 529
Brown, R., 354. 376
Brown, R.D., 289
Brownell, C.A., 235, 438, 454, 630, 632
Brownlee, S., 357, 362
Broyles, S., 138
Bruck, M., 289, 290, 291, 292
Bruggerman, E.L., 553
Brugman, E., 169
Brumitt, G.A., 123
Bruner, J.S., 255, 359
Brunschot, M.V., 641
Bryant, D.M., 428, 567, 617
Bryant, N.R., 323
Bryden, M.P., 476
Bryson, S.E., 329
Buchanan, C.M., 171, 447, 457, 481, 590, 622
Buchanan, L., 635, 643
Buchanan, N.R., 632
Bugental, D.B., 596
Buhrmester, D., 468, 581, 583, 602, 644
Buhs, E.S., 640
Bukowski, W.M., 402, 486, 523, 581–582 631, 634, 635, 638, 639, 640, 641, 643, 644, 645, 648
Bulleit, T.N., 581
Bullock, M., 241, 452, 579
Burchinal, M.R., 343, 428, 429, 430, 567, 617, 621
Burgeson, R., 172
Burgess, S.R., 205, 381
Burgmeijer, R., 169
Burhans, K.K., 454, 458
Burkhardt, S.A., 598
Burlingham-Dubre, M., 301
Burman, B., 587
Burn, S., 486, 487
Burnette, E., 464, 624
Burnham, D.K., 480
Burns, G.W., 79, 84
Burns, W., 325
Burton, L.M., 566
Burton, R.V., 554, 556
Burts, D.C., 617, 637
Bush, T.J., 118
Bushman, B., 608
Bushnell, E.W., 200, 201
Buss, A.H., 398
Buss, D.M., 493
Buss, K.A., 394, 399
Bussell, D.A., 97
Bussey, K., 393, 487, 495
Butcher, C., 364
Butenandt, O., 180
Butler, D.W., 442
Butler, R., 450, 457, 459
Butler, S., 478, 618
Butterfield, E.C., 361
Butterfield, P., 396
Buyck, P., 447
Buysse, V., 624
Bybee, J., 535
Byers, R.H., 118

Byers, T., 178
Byrne, E.A., 631
Byrnes, J.P., 304, 477

Cabaniss, M.L., 85
Cabral, H., 122
Cabrera, N. J., 419, 430, 593
Cahan, S., 616
Cairns, B.D., 635, 643
Cairns, R.B., 619, 635, 643
Caldwell, B.M., 332, 333, 339, 453, 454
Caldera, 473, 486
Calkins, S.D., 156, 400
Call, J., 442, 579
Call, K.T., 579
Callaghan, T., 255
Callanan, M.A., 367, 383, 442, 478
Calman, R., 386
Caltran, G., 435
Camaioni, L., 350
Camara, K.A., 586
Cameron, C.A., 536
Cameron, J., 158
Camino, C., 551
Camino, L., 22
Camp Jumoke, 78, 84
Campbell, F.A., 334, 343, 428, 617
Campbell, S.B., 134, 416, 454
Campbell, T., 294
Campione, J.C., 258, 282, 304, 323
Campos, J.J., 17, 164, 165, 195, 199, 200, 364, 392, 393, 396, 399
Campos, R., 602
Campos, R.G., 145
Camras, L.A., 392, 393
Canadian Association of Midwives, 131, 133
Canadian Heritage, 386
Canadian Institute of Child Health, 568, 593
Canadian Paediatric Society, 177, 191
Canadian Psychological Association, 32
Canfield, R.L., 297
Cantwell, D.P., 278
Capage, L., 624
Capaldi, D.M., 509, 512, 527, 589
Caplan, M., 516, 518, 530
Capozzoli, M., 275
Cappenberg, M., 404
Capute, A.J., 113
Caputo, D.V., 138
Caravan, G., 321
Carey, S., 196, 231
Carlo, G., 533, 534, 538
Carlsmith, J.M., 171, 172
Carlson, C., 278
Carlson, E.A., 416, 421
Carlson, S.M., 240, 442
Carlson, V., 416, 598
Carlton-Ford, S., 172
Carobbi, S., 83, 123
Carone, D., 325
Carpenter, M., 368
Carpenter, T.P., 298
Carper, R., 154
Carr, J., 81
Carr, M., 280
Carr, M.B., 485
Carr, T., 429
Carr, T.S., 492
Carraher, D., 300
Carraher, T. N., 300
Carriger, M.S., 208, 235, 324, 335, 438, 632
Carrington, D., 116, 117, 118
Carroll, J.B., 315
Carroll, L., 507
Carson, J.L., 637

Carson, S.A., 120
Carver, L.J., 228
Casas, J.F., 477, 519, 522
Casasola, M., 366, 367
Case, R., 40, 157, 248, 249, 250, 251, 252, 268, 284, 304
Casey, M.B., 477
Casey, P.H., 138
Casey, R.J., 194, 408, 540
Casey, W.M., 556
Cashon, C.H., 232
Caspi, A., 27, 173, 398, 399, 400, 403, 518, 588
Cassel, W.S., 289
Cassia, V.M., 194
Cassidy, J., 397, 415, 421, 422, 638, 639
Cassidy, K.W., 362, 440, 441
Casteel, M.A., 380
Castile, C.M., 437
Castle, J., 517, 518, 530
Castle, J.M., 392, 393
Castro, R., 458
Cataloano, P.M., 125
Cates, W., 117, 118, 510
Cattell, R.B., 315, 323
Cauce, A.M., 576
Cauffman, E., 169
Caughy, M.O., 138
Cavanaugh, J.C., 282
Cazden, C., 354
Ceci, S.J., 105, 289, 290, 291, 292, 312, 315, 322, 326, 327, 335, 337, 339, 616
Cefalo, R.C., 84, 124, 125
Cen, G., 643
Center for Disease Control, 509
Cernoch, J.M., 190
Cervantes, C.A., 478
Chadwick, B.A., 567
Chaisson, R., 118
Chaiyasit, W., 403
Chall, J.S., 204
Chalmers, J.B., 532
Chamberlin, J., 83
Champaud, C., 380
Chan, R.W., 585
Chandler, M.J., 125, 135, 239, 441, 449, 461, 529, 642
Chandler, S., 134
Chang, L., 643
Chang, S., 124. 176
Chao, R., 576, 623
Chao, W., 590
Chapieski, M.L., 214
Chapman, M., 61, 242, 416, 530, 531, 533, 534, 535, 537
Chapple, J., 132
Charlesworth, R., 617, 637
Charlton, K., 618
Charpak, N., 137
Chase, C., 190
Chase, C.I., 619
Chase-Lansdale, L., 511
Chase-Lansdale, P.L., 510, 512, 588
Chasiotis, A., 404
Chasnoff, I.J., 121, 144
Chassin, L., 171, 649
Chavkin, W., 120, 121, 123
Chelvne, R.K., 321
Chen, C., 171, 301, 302, 481, 572, 576, 577, 621, 624, 625, 626, 627, 628, 639, 647
Chen, G., 576, 643
Chen, H., 576, 643
Chen, H.Y., 320
Chen, L., 278
Chen, P., 303
Chen, X., 296, 403, 455, 536, 576, 638, 643
Chen, Z., 246, 294, 297

Cherlin, A.J., 588, 589
Cheschier, N.C., 84, 86
Chess, S., 398, 400, 401, 402, 418, 420
Chi, M.H.T., 267, 282
Chi-Hang Tse, H., 643
Child, I.L., 474, 475
Chinsky, J.H., 279
Chisholm, K., 425, 427
Chisholm, V., 82
Chmiel, S., 552
Choi, S., 367
Chomitz, V.R., 119, 120, 124, 511
Chomsky, N., 354
Chow, J., 596
Chow, K.L., 154
Christensen, K.M., 190
Christensen, M., 585
Christopher, F.S., 537
Christopherson, E.R., 478
Christovich, I.A., 359
Chuah, Y.M.L., 267
Chung, L.W.Y., 119, 120, 124, 511
Chung, T., 581
Ciaramitaro, V., 190
Cibelli, C.D., 421
Cicchetti, D., 416, 598, 599
Cicciarelli, A.W., 374
Cillessen, A.H.N., 641
Clark, B. R., 437
Clark, E.V., 368, 375, 380
Clark, H.H., 375, 380
Clark, K.E., 63, 637
Clark, L.V., 467, 496
Clark, M.C., 531
Clark, M.S., 641
Clark, R., 65, 419, 430, 497
Clark, R.A., 452, 453
Clark, R.D., 61
Clark, S., 414, 527
Clarke, A.D.B., 427
Clarke, A.M., 427
Clarke-Stewart, A., 423, 428, 616, 617
Clarke-Stewart, K. A., 588
Clarkson, F.E., 475
Clarkson, M.G., 163, 189
Clary, E.G., 537
Clasen, D.R., 646
Clatfelter, D., 637
Clausen, J.A., 172
Cleaves, 197
Clemens, L.P., 486
Clements, D.H., 613, 614
Clements, P., 648
Clements, W.A., 443
Clewett, A.S., 610
Clifton, R.K., 163
Clingempeel, W.G., 64, 572, 588, 589, 591
Clubb, P.A., 287
Clyman, R.B., 540
Coates, B., 24, 25, 26, 217
Coatsworth, J.D., 448
Cobbs, G., 444
Cockburn, J., 131
Codd, J., 385, 386
Coffey, S.A., 373
Cohen, D., 215, 478, 530
Cohen, J.A., 598
Cohen, K.M., 161
Cohen, L., 531, 535
Cohen, L.B., 232, 366, 367
Cohen, M., 269
Cohen, N., 616
Cohen, S., 125
Cohn, J.F., 134, 362, 392, 394, 416
Coie, J.D., 340, 395, 516, 517, 519, 526, 528, 567, 637, 638, 639, 640, 641, 642

Colapinto, J., 494
Colburn, D., 119
Colby, A., 545, 547, 548, 553
Colder, C.R., 649
Cole, A., 645
Cole, D. A., 481
Cole, M., 247, 283
Cole, P.M., 395, 516, 540
Cole, T.J., 179
Coleman, C.C., 645
Coley, R. L., 419, 510, 512, 566, 590
Coll, C.G., 594
College of Physicians and Surgeons of Manitoba, 78
Collins, P.A., 498
Collins, W.A., 104, 577, 648, 649
Collis, B.A., 613, 615
Coltheart, M., 306
Columbo, J., 142, 324
Committee on Nutritional Status during Pregnancy and Lactation, 129
Condry, J., 480
Condry, S., 480
Conduct Problems Prevention Research Group, 340, 523, 529, 567, 582, 643
Conger, K.J., 575, 590, 596
Conger, R.D., 172, 173, 509, 570, 575, 579, 587
Connell, D.B., 65, 416, 417
Connell, J.P., 394, 454, 621
Connolly, D., 291
Connolly, J., 523, 635, 636,644, 645
Connolly, J.A., 235
Connolly, K.J., 528
Connor, J.M., 77, 85, 612
Conti-Ramsden, G., 383
Coohey, C., 596
Cook, R., 584
Cook, T.D., 612
Cooley, G., 434, 447, 470
Coon, H., 334
Coon, J.A., 440
Cooper, B.A.B., 552
Cooper, C.R., 461
Cooper, H., 618
Cooper, J., 497
Cooper, R.P., 359, 362
Cooper, Z., 177
Cooperman, G., 534, 535
Cooperman, J.M., 527
Cooperman, S., 522
Coopersmith, S., 450
Coplan, R.J., 156, 633–634
Coppotelli, H., 637
Corah, N.L., 135
Corasantini, M.A., 594
Corbetta, D., 161, 162, 163
Corbin, C., 157
Corcoran, K.M., 366
Coren, S., 157
Corenblum, B., 439
Corkum, P.V., 278
Corley, R., 82, 399, 400
Cornell, D.P., 503
Corns, K.M., 423, 580
Correctional Service of Canada, 477
Corteen, R.S., 606
Corter, C.M., 411, 581, 582, 583
Cortes, R.M., 599
Corville-Smith, J., 623
Corwin, M.J., 121
Cossette, L., 473
Costigan, K.A., 113, 477
Costin, S.E., 641
Cote, J.E., 462
Cottingham, E.M., 442
Couchoud, E.A., 637, 639

Coulton, C.J., 596
Council of Ministers of Education, 617, 625
Courage, M., 187, 188
Courage, M.L., 213, 285
Cousins, J.H., 178
Cousins, S.D., 445
Cowan, C.P., 572
Cowan, N., 266
Cowan, P.A., 222, 572
Cowen, E.L., 139
Cowen, J., 560
Cowley, G., 178
Cox, A., 381
Cox, C.M., 311
Cox, M., 587, 588
Cox, M.J., 62, 417, 419, 565
Cox, R., 587, 588
Cox, S., 125
Coy, K. C., 577
Coyle, T.R., 253, 269, 270, 277
Craig, W.M., 522, 523
Crain-Thoreson, C., 205
Crane, P., 638
Craton, L.G., 195, 382
Craven, R., 447
Craw, S., 289
Creehan, P.A., 130
Crego, M.B., 378
Cremo, E., 30
Crenshaw, T.M., 642
Crews, F., 44
Crick, K., 505
Crick, N.R., 19, 477, 519, 520, 521, 522, 528,
    529, 631, 638, 639
Criqui, M.H., 328
Criss, M.M., 524, 573, 578, 648
Cristo, M., 137
Crnic, K., 62, 422
Crockenberg, S., 430, 558, 566, 574
Crockett, L.J., 509
Croft, K., 239
Cromer, C.C., 630
Cronbach, L.J., 620
Cronister, A., 81
Crook, C.K., 190, 614
Crooks, C.V., 597
Crosby, D., 594
Crosby, L., 509, 512, 526, 527, 642, 645, 648
Cross, C.E., 8
Cross, W.E., 439
Crouter, A.C., 171, 485, 486, 496, 504, 581,
    592, 593
Crowe, P.A., 448, 635
Crowell, J., 416, 421
Crowley, C.G., 529
Crowley, K., 57, 270
Cruzcosa, M., 596
Crystal, D.S., 445, 628
Culver, C., 137, 394
Cumberland, A., 395, 533
Cummings, E.M., 414, 416, 422, 423, 518, 575,
    581, 586, 587
Cunningham, C., 278
Cunningham, H., 7
Cunningham, J.G., 397
Cupak, A.J., 274
Curran, P.J., 649
Curry, L.M., 615
Curtis, L.E., 297
Curtiss, S., 356
Cutler, A., 362, 365
Cutting, J.E., 195
Cynic, K., 399

da Silva, O.P., 124, 136
Dabbs, J.M., 492

Daehler, M., 297
Daglish, L., 486
Daher, M., 190
Dahl, R., 158
Dale, P.S., 205, 380
Daley, K.E., 205
Daltabuit, M., 146
Damast, A.M., 256
Damon, W., 439, 467, 485, 538, 552
D'Andrade, R., 454
Daniel, I., 386
Daniels, D., 96, 617
Daniels, T.M., 639
Dann, S., 631
Dansereau, J., 86
Dapretto, M., 368
Darby, B.L., 118
Dare, C., 177
Darling, C.A., 507
Darling, J., 168
Darling, N., 572, 573, 648
Darlington, R.B., 341
Daro, D., 601
Darwin, C.A., 58, 61
Das Eiden, R., 423, 580
Dasen, P.R., 206, 247
D'Augelli, A.R., 508
Davey, T.C., 323
David, H.P., 417
Davidson, J.K.,, 507
Davidson, W., 458
Davies, L., 517, 518
Davis Eyler, F., 121
Davis, B.L., 363
Davis, B., 93
Davis, L.B., 190
Davis, M., 392
Davis, T.L., 395
Dawud, S., 599
Day, R.H., 197
de Benedictis, T., 609
de Gaston, J.P., 507
De Guise, J., 607
de Haan, M., 194
De Lisi, R., 247
de Lorimier, S., 634
De Oliveira, A.M., 643
de Villiers, J.G., 369, 372, 376, 377, 378, 381
de Villiers, P.A., 369, 372, 376, 377, 378, 381
De Vos, J., 230
De Wolff, M.S., 419
DeAngelis, T., 424, 425, 427, 428
Deater-Deckard, K., 100, 519, 558, 576, 584
DeBaryshe, B.D., 526, 527
DeBerry, K.M., 585
Debus, R., 447
DeCasper, A.J., 188, 361
Dedrick, C.F., 137
DeFries, J.C., 70, 75, 79, 80, 81, 82, 84, 90, 93,
    94, 97, 100, 103, 334, 399
DeGarmo, D.S., 590
Dekker, G.A., 125
Dekovic, M., 637
Delcampo, D.S., 386
Delcampo, R.L., 386
DeLoache, J.S., 233, 234, 236, 237, 269, 294
DeLuccie, M.F., 419, 609
Demarest, J., 497
deMause, L., 6
DeMeis, D.K., 430
Demers, I., 168
Demo, D.H., 448
Dempster, F.N., 267, 274, 275
DeMulder, E.K., 421, 581
Denham, S.A., 421, 637, 639
Denning, C.R., 87
Dennis, W., 159

D'Entremont, B., 188
Deprey, L., 290
Derbyshire, A., 483
Derevensky, J., 383
DeRosier, E., 631
Desai, K.A., 451
Descartes, R., 184
deSchonen, S., 196, 437
Desjardins, R.N., 189, 206, 362
DeSouza, A., 643
Despert, J.L., 6, 7
DeVries, R., 237
DeWolf, M., 415
Dews, S., 380
Dewsbury, D.A., 58
DiAdamo, C., 440
Diagnostic and Statistical Manual of Mental
    Disorders, Fourth, 329
Diamond, A., 230, 274
Diamond, L.M., 508
Diamond, M., 494
Diamond, R., 196
Diaz, J., 120
Diaz, R.M., 258, 385
Dichtellmiller, M., 137
Dick, D.M., 173
Dickens, S., 82
Dick-Read, G., 131
Didow, S.M., 632
Diener, E., 478
Dierker, L.J., 125
Diessner, R., 550
DiLalla, L.F., 400
Dill, J.C., 615
Dill, K.E., 615
Dillon, P.A., 590
DiPietro, J.A., 113, 477
Dishion, T.J., 93, 525, 526, 528, 642, 645, 648
Dittman, R.W., 491, 508
Dixon, M.J., 278
Dixon, R.A., 65
Dixon, S., 16, 394
Dockery, D.W., 153
Dodd, P., 134
Dodds, J.B., 160
Dodge, K.A., 214, 401, 516, 519, 520, 521, 522,
    523, 524, 526, 528, 529, 558, 573, 576, 578,
    594, 637, 638, 639, 640, 642, 643, 648
Doehring, P., 634
Doherty, G., 429
Doherty, W.J., 588
Dolan, B., 335
Dolby, R.M., 130
Dolgin, K.G., 240
Doll, H.A., 177
Dollberg, S., 125, 126
Domjan, M., 207
Dondi, M., 435
Dondis, E.H., 329
Dong, Q., 572, 583, 647
Donnell, F., 414
Donnerstein, E., 609, 615
Donovan, W.L., 566
Doris, J., 572–573, 598, 599
Dornbusch, S.M., 63, 171, 172, 450, 454, 572,
    573, 579, 590, 619, 621, 623 648
Dougherty, T.M., 324
Douglas, R.N., 269, 281
Dow-Ehrensberger, M., 616
Dowler, J.K., 122
Downing, L.L., 615
Downs, A.C., 638, 639
Doyle, A., 235
Doyle, A.B., 419, 464, 634, 636, 641, 645
Drabman, R.S., 608
Dramaix, M., 144
Dreyer, P.H., 507, 509

Drillien, C.M., 138
Droege, K.L., 456, 463, 641
Drotar, D., 180
Drummey, A.B., 272
Druss, B., 362
Druyan, S., 261
Dubas, J.S., 171, 172, 490, 491
Dube, E.F., 283
Dubow, E., 333, 334, 335
Dubowitz, H., 419, 593
Duckett, E., 171, 581, 592
Duffy, J., 477
Duke, P.M., 171, 172
Dumas, C., 242
Duncan, G.J., 325, 339, 482, 594
Duncan, P., 157
Duncan, R.M., 260, 261
Dunham, P., 134
Dunn, J., 96, 256, 395, 396, 397, 442, 443, 528, 580, 581, 583
Dunn, M., 616
Dunne, M.P., 508
Dunphy, D.C., 635, 636
Durand, C., 365
Durkin, K., 374
Durland, M.A., 617, 637
Durrant, J., 214
Dweck, C.S., 374, 454, 457, 458, 459, 463, 464
Dwyer, T., 144
Dyer, K.F., 166
Dytrych, Z., 416
Dziuba-Leatherman, J., 595, 598
Dziurawiec, S., 187, 194

Eagly, A.H., 479
Easley, J.A., 243
East, P.L., 507
Easterbrooks, M.A., 421, 438
Eastman, K.L., 403
Eaton, W.O., 153, 477
Ebeling, K.S., 378
Eccles, J.S., 171, 447, 457, 481, 482, 619, 622, 648
Echols, C.H., 365
Eckenrode, J., 572–573, 598, 599
Eckerman, C.O., 632
Edelstein, W., 518
Eder, R.A., 439, 463
Edgell, D., 158
Edwards, C.P., 486, 493, 531, 550, 629
Edwards, L., 549, 553
Egan, S.K., 522, 523
Egeland, B., 423, 599
Egeland, B.J., 595
Egeland, B.R., 415
Egerton, 563
Ehrhardt, A.A., 490, 491, 492, 494, 508
Eicher, S.A., 646
Eichler, L.S., 403
Eichorn, D.H., 150, 151
Eichstedt, J.A., 484
Eidelman, A., 216
Eidevall-Wallin, L., 278
Eilers, R.E., 206, 363
Eimas, P.D., 189, 206, 355
Eisele, J., 380
Eisen, M., 443
Eisenberg, N., 394, 479, 487, 530, 532, 533, 534, 535, 537, 538, 637
Eisenberg-Berg, N., 532
Eisenbud, L., 496, 499
Eisler, I., 177
Elder, G.H., 8, 172, 173, 403
Elder, G.J., Jr., 575, 579
Eldred, L., 118
Eley, T. C., 519

Elicker, J., 382, 421
Elkind, D., 243, 248, 488, 617
Elliot, R., 529
Elliott, A.N., 598
Elliott, B., 329
Elliott, E. M., 266
Elliott, E.S., 457
Ellis, H., 187, 194
Ellis, S., 248, 630
Ellsworth, C., 134
Ellwood, A., 427
Elmen, J.D., 454
Elman, J.L., 357
Emde, R.N., 95, 164, 392, 296, 397, 399, 534, 540
Emerson, P.E., 404, 407, 409
Emery, R.E., 587, 590, 592, 595–596, 598, 600, 601
Emmorey, K., 373
Endsley, R.C., 499
Engelhard, J.A., 346
English and Romanian Adoptees Study Team, 325, 326, 427
Englund, M., 421, 486, 640
Enna, B., 458
Enns, L.R., 477
Entwisle, D.R., 481, 621
Environment Canada, 481, 482
Eppler, M.A., 165
Epstein, A.S., 341
Epstein, L.H., 179
Erel, O., 581, 587
Erickson, M.F., 413, 595
Erikson, E.H., 41, 44, 45, 46, 65, 406, 409, 420, 422, 448, 459, 460, 461, 462, 570
Eron, L.D., 518, 608
Essex, M.J., 65, 430
Etaugh, C., 504
Ethridge, T., 486
Ettema, J.S., 608–609
Evans, D. W., 81
Evans, M., 205
Everall, R., 616
Everett, B. H., 239
Everingham, S. S., 343
Ewert, B., 383
Ewert, K., 382
Ewigman, B., 594
Eyer, D.E., 133, 403

Fabes, R.A., 3, 394, 487, 479, 496, 530, 532, 534, 538, 637
Fabricius, W. V., 271
Facon, B., 320
Facon-Bollengier, T., 320
Faden, R.R., 117, 118
Fagan, J.F., 207
Fagen, D.B., 139
Fagot, B.I., 334, 421, 423, 483, 484, 486, 496, 509, 512, 518, 527, 570
Fairburn, C.G., 177
Fairchild, H., 609
Falbo, T., 580, 583
Fan, L., 301, 302, 303
Fan, X., 585
Fantauzzo, C.A., 392, 393
Fantie, B. 154, 157
Fantz, R.L., 185, 192
Farabura, A.D., 86
Faraone, S.V., 278
Farkas, K., 121, 122
Farmer, T.W., 522, 640
Farrant, K., 287, 288
Farver, J.M., 641
Faust, M.S., 172, 173
Fearon, I., 145

Federal Bureau of Investigation, 526
Fegley, S., 579
Feiler, R., 617
Fein, G.G., 122, 235, 634
Feingold, A. 478, 479
Feinman, J., 448, 622
Feinman, S., 194, 396, 410
Feiring, C., 636
Feldhusen, J.F., 345
Feldlaufer, H., 622
Feldman, D.H., 346
Feldman, J.F., 138, 203, 208, 324
Feldman, R.S., 599
Feldman, S.S., 416
Fellegi, I.P., 568
Fennell, C.T., 366
Fennema, E., 477
Fenson, L., 364
Fentress, J.C., 140, 164
Ferguson, C.A., 363
Ferguson, J., 138
Fernald, A., 359, 360, 362, 367, 396
Fernandez, E., 588
Fernyhough, L., 427
Ferrara, R.A., 323
Ferreira, F., 381
Ferris, B.G., 153
Ferron, J., 339
Feshbach, N.D., 609
Feshbach, S., 518
Feuerstein, R., 323
Ficher, I., 585
Field, D., 240
Field, P.A., 134
Field, T.M., 134, 137, 190, 215, 416, 641
Fier, J., 481
Fifer, W.P., 113, 188, 361, 362
Figueredo, A.J., 596, 599
Figueroa de Calume, Z., 137
Filiano, J.J., 144
Finch, M.D., 579
Fincham, F.D., 458, 587, 590
Fine, M.A., 573, 589
Finegan, J.A.K., 86
Finitzo, T., 190
Finkelhor, D., 595, 597, 598
Finkelstein, N.W., 427
Finlay, B.L., 154
Finn, J.D., 618
Finnegan, R.A., 63, 643
Finn-Stevenson, M.F., 594, 600, 609, 617
Fiori-Cowley, A., 134, 416, 417
Fisch, R.O., 191
Fischer, A., 373
Fischer, K.W., 156, 248, 250, 305
Fisher, C., 362
Fisher, C.B., 3, 33
Fisher, D., 159
Fisher, E.P., 235
Fisher, J.A., 178
Fisher, L., 425
Fisher, W., 511
Fitch, M., 607
Fitzgerald, H.E.
Fitzsimmons, C.M., 367
Fivush, R., 58, 287, 288, 289, 478
Flaks, D.K., 585
Flanagan, C., 134, 447, 457, 481, 587, 589, 622
Flavell, E.R., 237, 239, 271, 277
Flavell, J.H., 237, 238, 239, 241, 248, 271, 277, 279, 281, 355, 374, 379, 439, 440, 463
Fleege, P.O., 617, 637
Fleming, J.S., 63, 333, 353
Fletcher, A.C., 648
Fletcher, P., 124, 176
Fletcher-Flinn, C.M., 613
Flieller, A., 248, 331

Fling, S., 615
Flood, P., 618
Flor, D.L., 564, 576
Flynn, J.R., 248, 331, 335
Fogel, A., 436
Foley, H.J., 188
Folkers, E., 572
Follansbee, D., 450
Follmer, A., 567
Foltz, C., 438
Folven, R.J., 373
Fonagy, P., 423
Fonzi, A., 644
Ford, C.S., 506
Ford, D.Y., 455, 623
Ford, L.H., 439
Ford, M.E., 408, 496
Fordham, S., 455
Forehand, R., 587, 592
Forgatch, M.S., 590
Forman, D. R., 540, 570
Forrest, J.D., 509
Foster, C.M., 169
Foster, G.E., 618
Foster, T., 641
Foulkes, E., 290
Fox, N.A., 17, 156, 230, 285, 304, 400, 419, 531, 533
Frady, F.L., 492
Franco, P., 144
Francoeur, E., 291
Frank, D., 122
Frank, D.A., 175, 176
Frank, G., 169
Frankel, K.A., 421
Frankenberg, W.K., 160, 453, 454
Frankie, G., 495
Franklin, K.M., 588
Fraser, J., 568, 593
Fredriks, A.M., 169
Freedman, D.G., 146
Freeman, M., 387
Freeman, N.H., 443
Fremmer-Bombik, E., 421
French, C., 320
French, F., 320
French, D., 630
French, K.E. 165
Frenkel, O.J., 420
Freud, A., 631
Freud, S., 10, 16, 41–46, 54, 59, 65, 285, 420, 495, 539, 540
Freund, L.S., 258
Frey, K.S., 450, 456, 487, 497, 498
Frick, J.E., 144
Fried, C.B., 338
Fried, P.A., 120, 121
Friedman, H.S., 328
Friedman, J., 637
Friedman, J.M., 114, 118, 119, 120, 121, 123, 124, 125, 130
Friedman, R.J., 516
Friedman, S.L., 394
Friedrich, L.K., 22, 610
Friedrich-Cofer, L.K., 610
Friel-Patti, S., 190
Friendly, M., 429
Fries, M.M., 87
Fritz, J., 576
Frodi, A., 145
Frontera, M., 168
Frost, P., 641
Frueh, T., 497
Fry, C.L., 8, 30
Frye, D., 293, 441
Fu, G., 536
Fuchs, D., 478

Fuhrman, T., 577
Fuhrmann, G., 180
Fujimura, D., 206
Fujita, N., 361
Fukumoto, A., 540
Fuligni, A.J., 455, 576, 577, 619, 621, 623, 627, 628, 646, 648
Fulker, D.W., 334, 399, 519
Fuller, B., 429
Fullerton, J.T., 133
Fultz, J., 537
Fung, H. H.-T., 256
Fung, T., 290
Furman, W., 468, 581, 583, 602, 635, 636, 642, 644, 645, 646
Furstenberg, F.F., 509, 511, 589
Fuson, K.C., 298, 302
Fyans, L.J., 451

Gabreels, F., 329
Gaddis, A., 170
Gagnon, J.H., 507
Gahler, M., 588
Gaines, C., 577
Galambos, N.L., 177, 385, 486, 594, 646, 647
Galasso, L., 238
Galbraith, J., 511
Gale, R., 125, 126
Galen, B.R., 518, 519
Gallagher, J.M., 243
Gallahue, D.L., 165
Gallant, N., 126
Galligan, R.F., 411
Gallimore, R., 583
Gallistel, C.R., 298
Gallup, G.G., 438
Galperin, C., 256, 493
Galuska, D.A., 178
Gamble, W.C., 583
Ganchrow, J.R., 190
Gandelman, R., 491, 601
Ganza, B., 507
Gao, X., 643
Gao, Y., 411, 415
Garbarino, J., 595, 596, 597, 600
Garber, J., 395
Garber, S.R., 374, 520
Garcia, E.E., 387
Garcia, M.M., 526, 581
Garcia, R., 134, 137, 190
Garcia-Jetton, J., 278
Gardner, H., 318, 347
Gardner, L.J., 180
Garduque, L., 453
Garmezy, N., 448
Garner, P.W., 395, 397, 582
Garnets, L., 508
Garrett, P., 339
Garton, A.F., 374
Gaultney, J.F., 269, 277
Gauthier, R., 486
Gautier, T., 494
Gauvain, M., 258, 334
Gauze, C., 638, 644, 645
Gavin, L.A., 646
Gavinski-Molina, M., 633–634
Gaylor, D.W., 83, 124
Ge, X., 172, 173, 570, 575
Geary, D.C., 253, 297, 301, 302, 303, 626
Geen, R.G., 492
Geldart, S., 196
Gelfand, D.M., 416, 531
Gelles, R.J., 596, 597, 601
Gelman, R., 229, 240, 242, 250, 298, 359, 379, 381

Gelman, S.A., 58, 240, 367, 369, 370, 378, 463, 485, 486
Gendler, T., 618
Genereux, R., 289, 290
Genesee, F., 364, 385, 386
Georgas, J., 321
George, C., 599
George, T.P., 644
Gerken, L., 362, 372
Gervai, J., 487, 503, 504
Gesell, A., 58, 159
Gest, J.D., 448
Getchell, N., 159
Getzels, J.W., 344
Gewirtz, J.L., 48, 51, 407, 408
Ghatala, E.S., 282
Ghim, H., 195
Giampiccolo, J.S., Jr., 329
Gibb, R., 155
Gibbons, L.E., 144
Gibbs, J.C., 538, 549, 550, 558
Gibson, C., 594
Gibson, D., 81
Gibson, E.J., 165, 184, 198, 199, 201, 203, 204
Gibson, J.B., 83, 124
Gibson, J.J., 204
Gil, D.G., 596
Gilbert, N., 597
Gilchrist, L., 512, 576
Giles-Sims, J., 214
Gill, N.J., 511
Gillberg, C., 278
Gilligan, C., 552
Gilman, E., 428, 593
Gilmore, R.O., 194
Gilstrap, B., 565
Ginsberg, H.J.,
Ginsburg, A.P., 192
Ginsburg, G.S., 454
Ginsburg, H.J., 243, 385
Giovanelli, G., 362
Girard, C., 449
Giron, M., 137
Gjerde, P.F., 588
Glasgow, K.L., 454, 572, 619
Glassman, M., 333, 575
Gleason, J.K., 358, 368
Gleason, K., 423
Gleason, T.R., 234, 235
Gleitman, H., 339
Gleitman, L.R., 369
Glucksberg, S., 381, 382
Gnepp, J., 397, 470
Goelman, H., 429
Goetz, L., 624
Gogate, L.J., 367
Goh, B.E., 345
Golbus, M.S., 87
Gold, A., 267, 425
Goldberg, M., 481, 531
Goldberg, M.E., 609
Goldberg, S., 82, 133, 420, 425
Golden, M., 335
Golden, N., 169
Golden, O., 595, 598, 601
Goldenberg, R.L., 124, 136
Goldfarb, W., 424, 425
Goldfield, B.A., 365
Goldfield, E.C., 161
Goldin-Meadow, S., 357, 364, 385
Goldschmidt, I., 134, 584
Goldsmith, H.H., 394, 398, 399, 418
Goldsmith, L.T., 346
Goldstein, R., 478
Goldstein, S., 134, 416
Goldwyn, R., 423
Golinkiff, R., 370

Golinkoff, R.M., 369
Gollin, E.S., 272
Golomb, C., 238
Golombok, S., 508, 584, 585
Golter, B.S., 636
Golub, H.L., 121
Goncu, A., 255, 257, 261, 305
Gondoli, D.M., 575
Gonzales, N., 576
Good, C., 338
Good, T.L., 620
Goodenough, F.L., 517
Goodman, E., 584
Goodman, G.S., 289
Goodman, J.C., 370
Goodnow, J.J., 531, 535, 558
Goodwin, D., 282
Goodwyn, S.W., 364, 373
Goodz, E., 383
Goossens, F.A., 418
Gopnik, A., 232, 248, 358, 367, 440
Gordeeva, T., 479, 481
Gordon, B.N., 289, 291
Gordon, L.L., 273
Gordon, P., 360
Gordon, T.P., 492
Gorer, G., 524
Gorn, G.J., 609
Gorny, G., 155
Gorsuch, R.L., 321
Gosden, C., 114, 118, 119, 126
Goswami, U., 294, 295, 296, 304
Gotlib, I.H., 134
Gotowiec, A., 621
Gottesman, I.I., 97, 99, 492
Gottfried, A.E., 63, 325, 333, 453
Gottfried, A.W., 63, 201, 333, 339, 453
Gottfried, G.M., 240
Gottlieb, D., 59, 75, 623
Gottlieb, G., 60, 99, 103, 105
Goubet, N., 163
Goy, R.W., 492
Graber, J.A., 169, 171, 172, 177
Graber, M., 230
Gracely, E., 486
Graesser, A.C., 538
Graham, S., 523
Gralinski, H., 438
Granger, D., 171
Granger, R., 594
Granrud, C.E., 197, 198
Grantham-McGregor, S., 124, 176
Grasshof, M., 479, 481
Gravatt, B., 613
Graves, S.B., 609
Gray, C., 333, 339
Gray, F.L., 81
Gray, R., 120, 121
Gray, S.W., 341
Graziano, W.G., 630, 636
Greater Boston Otitis Media Study Group, 190
Greco, D., 602
Greco, M., 602
Green, C., 189
Green, D., 255
Green, F.L., 237, 271, 277
Green, R., 508
Green, R.W., 278
Green, S.B., 606, 612
Greenbaum, C., 599
Greenberg, M., 134, 135
Greenberg, M.T., 340, 567
Greenberg, R., 215
Greenberger, E., 64, 171, 572, 576, 577, 579, 593, 647
Greenfield, P.M., 371
Greenhoot, A.F., 291

Greenough, W.T., 154, 155
Greenwald, P., 641
Greenwood, P.W., 343
Greif, E.B., 169, 170
Grenlich, F., 450, 456
Greydanus, D., 177
Griffin, S., 251, 252
Griffith, E.M., 616
Grigorenko, E., 323
Grigoryev, P., 137, 394
Groark, C.J., 3
Grolnick, W.S., 394, 453
Groom, J.M., 624
Groome, L.J., 113
Gross, A.L., 393
Gross, R.T., 171, 172
Grossman, F.K., 403
Grossman, J.B., 577
Grossmann, K.E., 414, 421
Grotevant, H.D., 461, 496, 585
Grotpeter, J.K., 477, 519
Group for the Advancement of Psychiatry, 49
Growing Healthy Kids, 104
Gruber, H., 267, 346
Gruen, R.S., 508
Grunebaum, H., 65, 416, 417
Grusec, J.E., 51, 531, 535, 537, 556, 558
Grych, J.H., 419, 590
Gu, H., 643
Guberman, S.R., 301
Guerin, D.W., 325, 333
Guerra, N.G., 521, 529
Guilford, J.P., 313, 314, 315, 344
Guilmain, J., 497
Gulko, J., 484, 486
Gump, P.V., 619
Gunderson, V., 123
Gunnar, M., 413
Gunnar, M.R., 191, 396
Gunter-Witt, K., 132
Gunther, G., 477
Guo, M., 572, 647
Gupta, S., 282
Guralnick, M.J., 624
Gurtner, J., 613
Gurucharri, C., 467
Gusella, J., 134
Gustafson, G.E., 145
Gustafson, S.B., 344
Gustafsson, P., 278
Guthertz, M., 641
Guthrie, I.K., 394, 533, 637
Guttentag, M., 504
Guttentag, R.E., 272, 279
Guy, L., 134
Gzesh, S.M., 238

Haaland, W., 411, 415
Haan, N., 549, 552
Habib, M., 593–594
Hack, M., 138
Hagan, R.I., 486, 496
Hagekull, B., 410
Hagen, E.P., 320
Hagerman, R.J., 81
Hagglof, B., 278
Haight, W. L., 256
Haine, R.R., 58, 288, 289
Hains, S., 145, 439
Haith, M.M., 195, 324
Hakuta, K., 385, 387
Hala, S., 239, 441
Hale, P.M., 169
Halford, G.S., 251
Hall, D.G., 369, 370
Hall, E., 244

Hall, G.S., 8, 10
Hall, J.A., 518
Hall, S.K., 503
Hallett, D., 449
Halpern, D.F., 312, 315, 322, 326, 327, 335, 337, 339, 493, 494
Halpern, L.F., 145, 476, 477, 478, 479
Halsley, N., 602
Halverson, C.F., 480, 498, 499, 500
Halverson, H.M., 163
Ham, M., 448
Hamers, J., 386
Hamilton, C.E., 421, 636
Hamm, J.V., 594
Hammer, L.D., 172
Hammer, M., 599
Hammersmith, S.K., 508
Hammond, M.A., 333, 339
Hamond, N.R., 287
Hampson, J., 366
Han, J.H., 302
Hand, M., 532
Handley-Derry, M., 425
Hanish, L.D., 3
Hans, S., 122
Hans, S.L., 574
Hansen, D.J., 599
Hanushek, E.A., 618
Hara, N., 613
Harden, P.W., 520
Hardy, J.B., 512
Har-Even, D., 134, 584
Harkness, S., 550
Harley, K., 285, 287, 288
Harlow, H.F., 406, 630, 631
Harman, C., 86
Harmon, R.J., 421, 438
Harnishfeger, K.K., 268, 269, 274, 275, 293
Harold, G.T., 587
Harold, R.D., 481, 482, 622
Harper, L.V., 633, 636
Harrington, A.F., 609
Harrington, D.M., 344
Harris, A., 81
Harris, J.J., III, 455, 623
Harris, J.R., 178, 628, 646
Harris, K.L., 145
Harris, M., 380, 517
Harris, M.B., 480
Harris, M.J., 102, 330
Harris, N.B., 359
Harris, P.L., 217, 235, 393, 395, 441
Harrison, L.F., 606
Harrist, A.W., 639
Hart, B., 278, 334
Hart, C.H., 519, 617, 636, 637, 639, 640
Hart, D., 386, 439, 443, 518, 538, 552
Hart, K.J., 553
Hart, S.N., 6, 601
Harter, S., 393, 444, 447, 448, 503
Hartmann, D.P., 531, 644
Hartshorne, H., 554
Hartung, B., 8
Hartup, W.W., 24, 25, 26, 217, 234, 235, 468, 517, 528, 628, 629, 630, 631, 633, 635, 641, 642, 644
Harvey, E., 592
Harvey, J., 177
Harvey, O.J., 635
Harvey, S., 133
Harwood, R.L., 576
Haselager, G.J.T., 641
Hasemeier, C.M., 153, 167, 169
Hashima, P.Y., 567
Haskett, M.E., 15
Hasselhorn, M., 280, 282
Hassing, Y., 360

Hastings, P.D., 531, 534, 576, 643
Hatch, T., 241, 369
Hauser, S.T., 450
Hauser-Cram, P., 82, 451
Haviland, J.M., 394
Hawkins, D.L., 523
Hawkins, J.A., 643, 646
Hay, D.A., 278
Hay, D.F., 516, 517, 518, 530
Haydel, F., 172
Hayden, C.A., 58, 288, 289
Hayden, M.R., 80
Hayes, B.K., 272
Hayes, L.A., 405
Hayne, H., 212, 213, 216
Haynes, H., 216
Haynes, O.M., 256, 392, 393, 493
Hayward, C., 172, 588
He, Y., 643
Health Canada, 104, 119, 120, 125, 130, 131, 144, 164, 177, 340, 449, 509, 510, 511, 597
Healy, B., 416, 641
Hearold, S., 610
Heath, S.B., 336
Heaton, T.B., 567
Hebb, D.O., 103
Hedges, L.V., 476
Hediger, M.L., 126
Heeren, T., 449
Heilman-Houser, R., 505
Heimann, M., 216
Heinonen, O.P., 114, 116, 119
Helgemo, B., 511
Helmreich, R.L., 502
Helms, J.E., 335, 336
Helms-Erikson, H., 485, 486, 592, 593
Helwig, C.C., 544
Hembrooke, H., 292
Hencke, R.W., 248
Henderson, B., 252
Henderson, B.B., 273
Henderson, H.A., 400
Henderson, R. L., 271
Henderson, S.H., 569, 586, 589, 591, 592
Henderson, V.K., 62, 417, 419, 565
Hendler, M., 240
Hendrick, B., 509
Hendrick, V., 134
Henker, B., 278, 478
Hennessey, B.A., 346
Hennessy, R., 272
Henning, K.H., 544
Henrich, C.C., 529, 530
Henry, B., 400, 518, 588
Herbert, J., 216
Herbsman, C.R., 395
Herkowitz, J., 165
Herman, P., 177
Herman-Giddens, M.E., 153, 167, 169
Hermelin, B., 319
Hernandez, D.J., 569
Hernandez-Reif, M., 202
Herrera, C., 396, 583
Herrera, M.G., 124, 176
Herrnstein, R.J., 337
Hershberger, S.L., 508
Hertsgaard, L., 413
Hertzberger, S.D., 508
Herzog, C., 448, 450
Hespos, S.J., 231
Hesser, J., 583
Hetherington, E.M., 64, 97, 104, 473, 495, 569, 572, 574, 586, 587, 588, 589, 590, 591, 592, 648, 649
Hewlett, B.S., 394
Heyes, C., 216
Heyman, G.D., 463, 464

Hickey, C., 477
Hickson, F., 464
Higgins, C.I., 164, 200
Higgins, E.T., 470, 485
Higgins-D'Alessandro, A., 33
Higley, J.D., 631
Hildebrand, D.K., 320, 321
Hill, A.E., 191
Hill, C.A., 509
Hill, J.P., 486
Hill, M., 151
Hill, P.T., 618
Hill, S.D., 438
Hilton, S.C., 113, 477
Himura, N., 516
Hincks-Dellcrest Centre, 428
Hinde, R.A., 59, 398
Hine, R.J., 83, 124
Hines, M., 487, 491
Hinshaw, S.P , 278, 637
Hiraga, Y., 576
Hirsch, J., 356
Hirsh, R.M., 631
Hirsh-Pasek, K., 362, 269, 370, 617
Hite, T., 487
Hix, H.R., 240
Hjertholm, E., 260
Ho, E., 299
Ho, M., 86
Hobbes, T., 8, 11
Hock, E., 430
Hodge, D., 291
Hodges, E.V.E., 63, 523, 643
Hodges, J., 427
Hodgson, D.M., 113, 477
Hoeffner, J., 372
Hoff, C., 78
Hofferth, S., 419, 430, 593
Hoffman, J., 137
Hoffman, L.W., 93, 97, 430, 486, 487, 592, 640
Hoffman, M.L., 61, 213, 215, 533, 555, 556, 557, 558
Hoffner, C., 397
Hofmann, V., 422, 453, 518
Hofsten, C. von., 162
Hogarty, P.S., 325
Hokoda, A., 458
Holden, D., 279
Holden, G.W., 144, 423
Holgren, R., 394
Holl, C., 329
Holland, S.B., 113
Hollander, M., 307, 376, 441
Hollich, G.J., 370
Holloway, S.D., 429
Holmbeck, G., 171, 577, 581
Holowka, S., 363
Holt, R., 637, 639
Honzik, M.P., 324, 325
Hood, L., 354
Hood, W.R., 635
Hooper, R., 134, 416, 417
Hooper, S., 429, 430
Hopkins, B., 161
Hopkins, T.L., 478
Hopkins, W.D., 631
Hops, H., 93
Hopwood, N.J., 169
Horn, J., 95
Horn, J.L., 315
Horney, K., 46
Hornik, R., 396
Horowitz, F.D., 47, 50, 142
Horowitz, L.M., 422, 423
Horton, R.W., 608
Horvath, J.A., 327

Hotaling, G.T., 597
Hoube, J., 343
Hoult, L.A., 138, 139
Housman, D., 449
Houts, A.C., 538
Howard, J., 122
Howe, C., 119
Howe, G.W., 97
Howe, M.L., 213, 285
Howe, N., 428, 443, 580, 581–582, 583
Howe, R.B., 10
Howell, C.T., 137
Howell, D., 170
Howes, C., 34, 235, 428, 429, 519, 632, 634, 635, 636, 641, 643
Howes, P., 64, 417
Hoyle, S.G., 468, 643
Hoyt, D.R., 602
Hoyt-Myers, L., 139
Hoza, B., 278, 638
Hrncir, E., 453
Hsieh, K., 394
Hsu, C., 301, 302, 624, 627, 626, 628
Hsu, L.K.G., 177
Hubbard, L., 619
Hubley, K., 290
Hudson, J.A., 287
Huesmann, L.R., 518, 608
Huffman, L., 585
Hughes, C., 442
Hughes, J., 506
Hughes, R., 534
Huie, K.S., 633, 636
Hulme, C., 205
Human Resources Development Canada, 28, 579
Humphrey, H.E., 123
Humphreys, L.G., 323
Hunsberger, B., 550
Hunt, M., 280
Hunt, P., 624
Hunter, J.E., 327
Hunter, M., 505
Hunter, R.F., 327
Hunter, S.K., 87
Hunter, W., 168
Huntington, L., 144
Huntley-Fenner, G., 231
Huntsinger, C.S., 576
Huq, M., 80
Hura, S.L., 365
Hurley, J. C., 395, 486
Hurshman, A., 134
Hussong, A.M., 649
Huston, A.C., 178, 473, 477, 487, 594, 606, 607, 608, 609, 611, 612
Huston-Stein, A., 610
Hutt, C., 490
Huttenlocher, J., 239, 326, 491
Huttenlocher, P.R., 154
Hutton, N., 118
Hwang, C., 333
Hwang, C.P., 419, 429, 430, 575, 593
Hyde, J.S., 65, 430, 477, 479
Hyman, I.E., Jr., 290
Hymel, S., 522, 637, 639, 642
Hyson, D.M., 421
Hyson, M.C., 617

Iacono, W.G., 177
Iannotti, R.J., 518, 532, 534, 535
Ignace, M.B., 386
Imperato-McGinley, J., 494
Ingerslev, O., 168
Ingersoll, E.W., 211
Ingram, D., 364, 365, 371

Inhelder, B., 235, 243, 245, 294
Insabella, G.M., 587, 588, 589, 590, 592
Institute of Medicine, 77, 118
Intons-Peterson, M.J., 473, 504
Isabella, R.A., 404, 416
Isaksen, G., 414
Isberg, R.S., 450
Isley, S.L., 637
Ismail, M.A., 118
Ivey, P.K., 425
Ivnik, R.J., 321
Izard, C.E., 392, 393, 575

Jacklin, C.N., 476, 479, 480, 485, 487, 491, 495, 517
Jackson, A. P., 333, 575
Jackson, E.W., 403
Jackson, J.F., 104
Jackson, P.W., 344
Jacobs, E., 428, 429
Jacobs, J.E., 481, 482
Jacobs, L.C., 619
Jacobsen, R.B., 585
Jacobsen, T., 422, 453
Jacobson, A.M., 450
Jacobson, J.L., 116, 119, 120, 122, 123, 421, 619
Jacobson, K., 230
Jacobson, L.J., 507
Jacobson, S.W., 116, 119, 122, 123
Jacobvitz, D., 278, 599
Jacques, S., 292
Jacques, T.Y., 274, 559
Jacquet, R.C., 369
Jadack, 552
Jaffe, P.G., 597
Jaio, S., 588
James, S.J., 83, 124
James, W., 184
Jamison, W., 491
Jankowski, J.J., 324
Jannings, L.R., 282
Janoff-Bulman, R., 588
Janols, L-O., 278
Janowsky, J.S., 154
Janssens, J.M.A.M., 637
Japel, C., 520
Jarrell, J., 133
Jarrold, C., 442
Jefferson, K.W., 512
Jeffery, P.M., 131
Jeffery, R., 131
Jenkins, E., 253, 270
Jenkins, J.J., 206
Jenkins, J.M., 256, 443
Jenkins, V.Y., 194
Jennings, D., 171, 172
Jensen, A.G., 408
Jensen, A.R., 319, 326, 336, 337, 341
Jensen, L., 507
Ji, G., 583
Jimenez, F., 442
Jing, Q., 583
Jipson, J., 367
Joannisse, M., 305
Jobse, J., 360
Joels, T., 414, 423
Joffe, L.S., 125
Joffe, R.T., 449
John, R. S., 581
Johnsen, E.P., 374
Johnson, C.A., 395
Johnson, C.J., 374
Johnson, C.N., 271
Johnson, D., 171
Johnson, D.J., 454, 621
Johnson, D.L., 333, 339

Johnson, D.W., 258, 530
Johnson, H., 380
Johnson, J., 86, 356, 608–609
Johnson, K.E., 376
Johnson, M., 194, 304
Johnson, M.H., 154, 187, 194, 357, 494
Johnson, N., 30
Johnson, R., 386
Johnson, R.T., 258, 503
Johnson, S., 122, 570
Johnson, S.M., 582
Johnson, S.P., 195
Johnson, W., 392
Johnston, T.R.B., 113, 477
Jones, D.C., 395, 397, 582, 641
Jones, D.P., 479
Jones, D.S., 118
Jones, J., 278
Jones, K.L., 119
Jones, M.C., 171, 172, 209
Jones, N.A., 400
Jones, S., 637
Jonsson, J.O., 588
Jooksen, J., 360
Jordan, R.A., 510, 511
Jorgensen, M., 168
Jose, P.E., 576
Jose, P.M., 543
Joseph, G., 585
Jouriles, E.N., 565
Judge, P., 189
Jung, P.C., 359
Jusczyk, P.W., 188, 189, 362, 365
Jussim, L., 482
Justice, E.M., 282
Juvonen, J., 523

Kaczala, C.M., 481
Kagan, B.M., 87
Kagan, J., 27, 41, 82, 400, 410, 411, 418, 429
Kagan, S., 624
Kahana-Kalman, R., 396
Kahn, J., 587
Kail, R.V., 56, 157, 267, 268
Kaitz, M., 216
Kalakanis, L., 194
Kalberg, W., 116
Kaler, S.R., 136, 138
Kamerman, S.B., 431
Kamins, M.L., 459
Kaminski, M., 119
Kamm, K., 161, 162, 163
Kamphaus, R.W., 337
Kandel, D., 649
Kane, M.J., 297
Kanfer, F.H., 641
Kant, I., 184
Kanungo, R.N., 609
Kaplan, J., 380
Kaplan, P.S., 359
Kaplan-Estrin, M.G., 119, 120
Kappes, M.E., 491, 508
Kappes, M.H., 491, 508
Karabenick, J.D., 379
Karbon, M., 394, 538
Karmiloff-Smith, A., 232, 271, 307, 357
Karoly, L.A., 343
Karp, D.E., 328
Kass, N.E., 117, 118
Kastelic, D., 448, 503
Katcher, A., 495
Katz, D.B., 184
Katz, G.A., 274
Katz, G.S., 362
Katz, P.A., 486, 487, 504, 609

Katz, S., 507
Katz, S.H., 339
Katz, V.L., 119
Kaufman, A.S., 323, 337
Kaufman, F.R., 491
Kaufman, N.L., 323, 337
Kavanagh, K., 423, 570
Kavanaugh, R.D., 235
Kay, E., 365
Kaye, H., 209
Kaye, K., 228
Kazdin, A.E., 527, 642
Kean, A.W.G., 7
Keane, S.P., 639, 642
Kearins, J.M., 283
Kearsley, R.B., 293, 411, 429
Keasey, C.B., 543, 549
Keating, D., 467
Keating, L., 623
Keaveney, L., 325, 326, 427
Kee, D.W., 280, 284, 614
Keefe, K., 645
Keefe, N., 594
Keefer, C.H., 16, 394
Keenan, T., 240, 395
Keidling, N., 168
Keiffer, J., 289, 290
Keith, B., 588
Keith, J., 8
Kelch, R.P., 169
Keljo, K., 550, 552
Kelleher, K.J., 138
Keller, A., 439
Keller, H., 404, 408
Keller, M., 518
Keller, T.E., 512, 576
Kelley, M.L., 574, 576
Kelley, S.A., 454
Kelley-Buchanan, C., 116, 117, 118, 123
Kellman, P.J., 188, 192, 193, 194
Kellum, S.G., 636
Kelly, J.B., 588
Kelly, M.A., 428
Kemler Nelson, D.G., 362
Kempe, C.H., 600
Kempe, R.S., 600
Kendall-Tackett, K.A., 598
Kendrick, C., 580
Kennedy, L., 165
Kennell, J.H., 17, 164, 165, 199, 200
Kenny, S.L., 248, 250
Kenyon, B., 483
Keough, J., 165
Kermoian, R., 17, 164, 165, 199, 200
Kerns, K.A., 476, 645
Kerr, M., 400, 403, 578, 648
Kerugh, D., 512
Kessel, B., 134
Kessen, W., 188, 248, 425
Ketsetzis, M., 623
Kett, J.F., 8
Khan, M., 283
Kidder, K., 568, 593
Kiernan, K.E., 588
Kiess, W., 180
Kilburn, M.R., 343
Kilgore, K., 524, 573
Killen, J.D., 172
Kilpatrick, 598
Kim, C.C., 302
Kim, K.H.S., 356
Kim, S., 544
Kimmel, D., 508
Kimmerly, N.L., 419
Kimura, D., 492
Kimura, S., 628
King, A., 511

King, R.A., 531, 533, 534, 537, 558
Kingma, J., 305
Kinney, D.A., 635, 646
Kinney, H. C., 144
Kinsbourne, M., 157
Kipnis, D.M., 610
Kirby, J.R., 337
Kirchner, 584
Kirsh, S.J., 422, 615
Kisilevsky, B.S., 145, 190
Kistner, J.A., 15, 458, 511, 599, 642
Kitamura, S., 301, 302, 624, 626, 627, 628
Kitayama, S., 445
Kitzinger, C., 508
Kitzmann, K.M., 565
Kivlahan, C., 594
Klackbengerg-Larsson, I., 400
Klahr, D., 565, 246, 256
Klatt, L., 231
Klaus, M.H., 133, 403
Klaus, R.A., 341
Klayman, J., 397
Klebanov, P.K., 339
Klein, D. M., 566
Klein, J., 299
Klein, J.O., 190
Klein, L., 145
Klein, M.H., 65, 430
Klein, N., 138
Klein, R.E., 407
Klein, R.G., 278
Klepec, L., 645
Kliegman, R., 121, 122
Klimes-Dougan, B., 599
Klineberg, O., 325
Klinnert, M.D., 396, 399
Klump, K., 177
Knezek, G.A., 613, 615
Ko, H., 628
Kobayashi, L., 132
Koch, G.G., 153, 167, 169
Kochanska, G., 274, 395, 420, 421, 540, 552, 554, 555, 558, 559, 570, 573, 574, 637
Kochenderfer, B.J., 645
Kochenderfer-Ladd, B., 522, 523
Kodituwakku, P.W., 116
Koehler, A.J., 125
Koenig, A.L., 274, 559
Koepke, J., 140
Koeppl, G.K., 528
Koff, E., 170
Kohlberg, L., 260, 497, 498, 541, 544, 545, 547, 548, 549, 550, 553
Kohn, M.L., 575
Kokko, K., 518
Kolata, G.B., 179
Kolb, B., 154, 155, 157
Kolb, S., 161
Koller, S., 532, 533, 535
Konarski, R., 635, 636, 644, 645
Kondo-Ikemura, K., 411, 414, 415
Konner, M.J., 247
Koolstra, C.M., 612
Kopecky, M., 180
Koplas, A.L., 644
Kopp, C., 438
Kopp, C.B., 135, 136, 138, 394
Kopp, S., 278
Korbin, J.E., 596
Korkel, J., 283
Korn, S., 401
Korner, A.F., 145, 146
Kortenhaus, C.M., 497
Koss, M.P., 596, 599
Kostelny, K., 595, 596, 597
Kotelchuck, M., 407

Kotovsky, L., 230
Kotsaftis, A., 418
Kovacs, D.M., 486, 487, 640
Kowal, A., 581
Kowaleski-Jones, L., 482
Kozhevnikova, E.V., 359
Kraemer, H.C., 172
Krakow, J.B., 135
Kramer, L., 581
Kramer, R. 397
Krauss, M.W., 82
Krauss, R.M., 381, 382
Krebs, D.L., 552
Krehbiel, G., 642
Krekwich, K., 425
Kreppner, J.M., 325, 326, 427
Krettenauer, T., 544
Kreutzer, M.A., 281
Kreutzer, T., 423
Krevans, J., 538, 558
Kreye, M., 410
Krishnan, P., 337
Krispin, O., 599
Kroger, J., 460, 461, 462
Kroll, J., 7
Kroonenberg, P.M., 420
Krowitz, A., 199
Kruger, A.C., 549
Krupa, M.H., 491
Ku, H., 519, 522
Kucera, E., 580
Kuczynski, L., 15, 216, 416, 555, 556, 558, 574
Kuebli, J., 287, 478
Kuhl, P.K., 359, 362
Kuhn, A., 144
Kuhn, C.M., 137, 190
Kuhn, D., 246, 249, 250, 450
Kulik, C.C., 619
Kulik, J.A., 619
Kulin, H., 168
Kuller, J.A., 82, 83, 84, 86
Kunkel, D., 609
Kunz, I., 132
Kuperminc, G.P., 421, 448, 450
Kupersmidt, J.B., 340, 575, 597, 598, 599, 621, 639, 641
Kurdek, L.A., 573, 589
Kurtz, B.E., 280, 283
Kusel, S.J., 520, 522
Kuspert, P., 205, 381
Kuther, T.L., 33
Kwon, Y., 302
Kyriakidou, C., 443

La Freniere, P., 486
Labile, D. J., 540, 558
Laboratory of Comparative Human Cognition, 6
Lacerda, F., 359
Ladd, G.W., 5, 63, 522, 526, 636, 637, 638, 639, 640, 642, 645
LaFleur, R., 365
Lagace-Sequin, D.G., 633–634
Lagattuta, K.H., 397
Lagerspitz, K., 518, 608
LaGrange, A., 429
Lai, K., 613, 615
Laird, M., 572–573, 598, 599
Laird, R.D., 524, 573, 578, 648
Lalonde, C.E., 449
Lam, M., 646
Lamaze, F., 131
Lamb, C., 137, 394
Lamb, M.E., 394, 419, 425, 429, 430, 592, 593, 599
Lambert, W.W., 400, 403

Lamborn, S.D., 450, 454, 572, 573, 577, 635, 648
Lamon, S.J., 477
Landau, B., 372
Landau, K.R., 437, 438
Landau, S., 260, 278
Landry, A.M., 437
Langer, A., 199
Langer, J., 549
Langille, D.B., 506
Langlois, J.H., 194, 408, 638, 639
Langlois, S., 449
Langrock, A., 491
Lansford, J.E., 630
Lantzouni, E., 169
Lanza, E., 385
Laosa, L.M., 574, 577
LaPadula, M., 278
Lapkin, S., 386
Lapsley, D.K., 543, 544
Larivee, S., 249
Larroque, B., 119
Larsen, R.J., 478
Larson, N.C., 512, 576
Larson, R., 448, 612, 615, 635
Larson, R.W., 171, 581, 635
Larson, S.L., 576
Larue, 496
Larus, D.M., 289
Lau, A., 544
Laumann, E.O., 507
Laumann-Billings, L., 595–596, 598, 600, 601
Laursen, B., 577, 644
Lauterbach, M.D., 478
Lavoie, M., 611
Lawson, D.S., 373
Lawson, E.J., 125
Lazar, I., 341
Le Grand, R., 195, 196
Leadbeater, B.J., 448, 450
Leaper, C., 479, 486, 496
Lears, M., 497
Leavitt, L.A., 566
Leboyer, F., 128
Ledbetter, M.F., 321
Lederberg, A.R., 373
Lee, K., 238
Lee, S.Y., 254, 301, 302, 481, 624, 625, 626, 627
Lee, V., 597
Lee, V.E., 619–620
Leekam, S.R., 442, 443
Lefever, G.B., 418
LeFevre, J., 205, 299, 381
Lefkowitz, M.M., 120
Legerstee, M., 436, 439, 440
Leggett, E.L., 456, 457
Lehman, E.B.,
Lehoux, P.M., 527, 581–582
Leichtman, M., 290
Leinbach, M.D., 483, 484, 486, 496, 518
Lelong, N., 119
LeMare, L.J., 426, 427, 470, 638
Lemery, K.S., 399
Lemonick, M.D., 75, 88
Lempers, J.D., 374
Lengua, L.J., 340, 567
Lenhart, L., 642
Lenneberg, E.H., 156, 356
Lennon, R., 202, 533
Lentz, C., 524, 573
Leonard, C., 281
Lepper, M.R., 613, 616
Lerner, R.M., 3, 29, 60, 65
Lero, D.S., 429
Lester, B.M., 121, 137, 145, 146, 407
Lester, J., 572, 647

Leung, M., 635, 643
LeVay, S., 508
Leve, C.S., 509, 512, 527
Leve, L.D., 496
Levin, I., 261
Levin, J.R., 282
Levin, M.L., 512
Levine, C., 462
Levine, D., 504
Levine, M.P., 177
LeVine, R.A., 16, 394
Levine, S.C., 16, 394, 491
LeVine, S., 326
Levinson, D., 64
Levinson, K., 575
Leviton, A., 119
Levitt, M.J., 531
Levy, A.K., 421
Levy, F., 278
Levy, G.D., 485, 486
Levy, S.R., 374, 464
Levy-Shiff, R., 134, 565, 584
Lewin, L.M., 93
Lewis, C., 443
Lewis, I., 597
Lewis, J.M., 62, 417, 565
Lewis, M., 122, 139, 145, 170, 393, 395, 411,
    436, 437, 450, 629
Lewis, S.M., 512, 576
Lewontin, R.C., 337
Leyendecker, B., 394
Leyens, J.P., 22
Li, B., 639, 643
Li, D., 296, 455, 638, 639, 643
Li, X., 511
Li, Z., 403, 639
Liang, X., 429
Liben, L.S., 439, 464, 485, 499, 505, 609
Liberman, A.M., 206
Liberty, C., 279
Licht, R., 157
Lichtenstein, P., 519
Lickliter, R., 203
Lidz, C.S., 323
Lieberman, E., 119, 129, 124, 511
Lieberman, M., 419, 645
Liebert, R.M., 20, 21, 22, 497, 606, 609, 610,
    612
Liederman, P.H., 16, 134, 394
Lieven, E.V.M., 360
Lightbown, P., 354
Liker, J.K., 8
Lillard, A.S., 235
Lin, C., 135, 136
Lin, I., 619
Lin, L., 583
Lin, N.T., 271
Lindberg, M.A., 289, 290
Lindenberger, U., 242
Lindsay, D.S., 289, 291
Lindzey, G., 339
Linebarger, D.L., 178, 606, 608, 612
Lingenfelter, M., 609
Linn, M.C., 477, 609
Lintz, A., 619
Lippincott, E.C., 608
Lipsitt, L.P., 3, 209, 210
Lipton, R.C., 424, 425
Litman, C., 430, 558, 566, 574
Lits, B., 125
Litt, I.F., 172
Littenberg, R., 411
Little, A.H., 210
Little, F., 78
Little, T.D., 328, 479, 481
Littman, R.A., 50
Littschwager, J.C., 369

Litwin, E., 134
Liu, F., 626
Liu, M., 639, 643
Livesley, W.J., 443, 463
Livson, N., 5, 171
Lloyd, V.L. 366
Lo Coco, A., 643
Lobel, M., 125
Lobel, T., 487, 503
Lochman, J.E., 642
Locke, D., 595
Locke, J., 11, 47
Locke, J.L., 360, 373
Loeb, S., 619–620
Loeber, R., 461, 517, 518, 524, 526
Loehlin. J.C., 97, 100, 312, 315, 322, 326, 327,
    335, 337, 339, 491
Loftus, E.F., 290
Lohaus, A., 404
Lohr, M.J., 635
Lollis, S.P., 363
London, K., 463
London, P., 537
Long, C., 297
Long, J.M., 156
Lonigan, C.J., 205, 381
Loomis, L.S., 587, 589
Lopez, B., 442
Lorber, J., 504
Lorch, E.P., 278
Lord, S., 622
Lore, D., 278
Lorenz, F.O., 575
Lorenz, K.Z., 58, 408
Lorey, F., 599
Lorrien, E., 83
Lorsbach, T.C., 274
Loupe, D., 205
Lover, A., 522
Low, H., 492
Lowell, E.L., 452, 453
Lowenthal, B., 595, 598, 601
Lowy, J., 512
Loyan, G.D., 165
Lozoff, B., 176, 179, 180
Lubach, G.R., 125
Lubart, T.I., 344, 345, 346
Lubeck, S., 619–620
Lucas, T., 632
Lucker, G.W., 301, 626
Luecke-Aleksa, D., 498
Lummis, M., 481
Lung, C.T., 601
Lust, B., 380
Luster, T., 63, 333, 334, 335, 572, 621
Lustig, J.L., 590
Lutkenhaus, P., 452
Lykken, D.T., 102
Lynam, D., 173
Lynch, M.E., 486
Lynch, M.P., 206
Lynn, R., 339
Lyon, T.D., 421
Lyons-Ruth, K., 65, 421, 416, 417
Lytton, H., 401, 475, 496, 574

Mabbott, D., 299
Mac Iver, D., 447, 456, 457, 459, 481, 622
MacCallum, F., 584
Maccoby, E.E., 104, 473, 476, 479, 480, 485,
    486, 487, 495, 504, 517, 570, 571, 572, 574,
    575, 576, 590, 591, 648, 649
Macfarlane, A., 128, 473
Macfarlane, J.W., 324, 325
MacGregor, S.N., 121, 473
MacKinnon-Lewis, C., 570, 637, 639

MacLean, W.E., 145
MacNeilage, P.F., 363
Macomber, J., 230
MacPhee, D., 334, 576
MacVicar, J., 255
MacWhinney, B., 264
Madden, T., 646
Madison, J.K.,
Madison, L.S., 207
Maehr, M.L., 451
Magenis, R.E., 83
Maggs, J.L., 594
Magill, L.H., 478
Magnus, K.B., 139
Magnuson, K., 594
Magnusson, D., 171, 173
Maguire, M., 395, 583
Mahapatra, M., 550, 551
Mahler, M.S., 435
Mahoney, A., 565
Mahoney, J.L., 619
Maier-Bruckner, W., 283
Main, M., 413, 416, 419, 421, 423, 599
Maio, M.L., 144
Major, B., 338
Majumder, S., 385, 387
Makin, J.W., 190
Malatesta, C.Z., 137, 394
Malcolm, J., 290
Malcuit, G., 473
Malinosky-Rummell, R., 599
Malloy, P., 278
Malone, M.J., 523
Malone, S., 191
Mandel, D.R., 189
Mandell, F., 144
Mandell, W., 138
Mandleco, B.L., 636
Mandler, J., 228, 229
Mangelsdorf, S.C., 137, 394, 410
Manke, B.A., 486
Mann, L.I., 125
Mannarino, A.P., 598
Mannuzza, S., 278
Manset, G., 624
Mao, Y., 449
Marcia, J.E., 459, 460, 461, 573
Marcoen, A., 419, 422, 447
Marcon, R.A., 617
Marcovitch, S., 229, 425
Marcus, D.E., 498
Marcus, G.F., 307, 376
Marcus, H.R., 445
Marcus, J., 228
Marean, G.C., 362
Marentette, P.F., 363
Margand, N.A., 62, 419, 565
Margolin, G., 581
Margulis, C., 361
Maridaki-Kassotaki, K., 443
Marini, Z., 248, 251
Mark, M., 360
Markiewicz, D., 419, 641, 645
Markman, E.M., 367, 369, 374
Markman, H.J., 64, 417
Markon, K., 519
Markovits, H., 242
Markow, D.B., 369
Markstrom, C.A., 461
Markstrom-Adams, C., 439, 461
Marlier, L., 190
Marlin, D.W., 178
Marold, D.B., 444
Marquis, J., 606, 612
Marsh, H.W., 447
Marshall, J., 414
Marshall, N.L., 594

Marshall, R.E., 191
Marshall, T.R., 145, 156
Marshall, W.A., 152
Martier, S.S., 119, 120
Martin, C.L., 3, 480, 484, 487, 488, 496, 498, 499, 500
Martin, G.B., 61
Martin, J.M., 481
Martin, J.A., 171, 172, 570, 571, 572
Martin, L.R., 328
Martin, M., 385, 387
Martin, N.G., 508
Martorell, R., 179
Marvin, R.S., 582
Marx, F., 594
Marx, M.H., 273
Marzolf, D., 394
Marzolf, D.P., 236
Masataka, N., 362, 373
Masden, A.S., 448
Mason, C.A., 576
Mason, M.G., 550
Masten, A.S., 631, 638
Masterpasqua, F., 585
Masters, J.C., 496
Maszk, P., 394
Matas, L., 410
Matejcek, Z., 416
Matheson, C.C., 27, 235, 632, 634, 635, 641
Matias, R., 392
Maticka-Tyndale, E., 511
Matillo, G.M., 610
Matlin, M.W., 188
Maton, K.I., 566
Matsumoto, D., 395
Matteson, D., 461
Matthews, K.A., 95
Mattock, A., 195, 198
Mattsson, A., 492
Matyear, C.L., 363
Maughan, B., 617, 618
Maurer, D., 194, 195, 196, 201
Maurer, M., 196
Maxwell, S., 512
May, M.S., 554
May, P., 116
Mayberry, R.I., 364, 373
Maybery, M.T., 267
Maye, J., 362
Mayer, F.S., 503
Mayes, L., 121
Mayes, L.C., 451
May-Plumlee, T., 534, 537
Mayseless, O., 414
Mazer, P., 270
McAdoo, H., 63, 572, 621
McBride-Chang, C., 597
McCabe, M., 450
McCain, M.N., 104
McCall, R.B., 3, 22, 208, 324, 325, 335
McCarthy, 622
McCartney, K., 100, 101, 102, 103, 330, 594
McCarton, C., 324. 339
McCarton, C.M., 138
McCarty, M.E., 163
McClearn, G.E., 70, 75, 79, 80, 81, 82, 84, 90, 93, 94, 97, 103, 178
McClelland, D.C., 452, 453
McClelland, J.L., 306, 307
McClintic, S., 393, 451
McCloskey, L.A., 596, 599
McCord, J., 528, 642, 645, 648
McCormick, M.C., 138, 339
McCoy, I.H., 385
McCubbin, J.A., 125
McCurley, J., 179
McDonnell, P., 531

McDonough, L., 228, 370
McDuff, P., 520
McElhaney, K., 578
McFadyen-Ketchum, S.A., 526
McGhee, P.E., 454, 497
McGhee-Bidlack, B., 380
McGilley, B.M., 177
McGovern, A., 380
McGraw, D.C., 118
McGraw, M.B., 159
McGue, M., 91, 97, 102, 177
McGue, M.K., 584, 585
McGuire, S., 97
McGuire, S.A., 581
McHale, J.L., 137
McHale, S.M., 171, 485, 486, 496, 504, 581, 583, 592, 593
McIntosh, B.J., 372
McIntyre-Smith, A., 587
McKay, A., 512
McKenna, 507, 509
McKenna, M.A.J., 88, 89
McKenna, M.W., 607
McKenzie, B.E., 195, 197
McKeough, A., 251, 252, 289, 290
McKinley, M., 637, 639
McKusick, V.A., 77
McLaughlin, S., 121
McLellan, J. A., 628
McLeod, P.J., 140, 164, 359
McLoyd, V.C., 339, 464, 567, 574, 575, 594
McMahon, M.J., 119
McManus, K., 130, 132
McNalley, S., 532, 533
McNeill, D., 375
McNeilly-Choque, M.K., 519
McPartland, J.M., 622
McQuillan, J., 327
McRoberts, G.W., 365
Mcstephen, M., 278
Meachum, J.A., 439
Mead, G.H., 434, 435, 470
Mead, M., 30, 130–131, 493
Meadows, K., 641
Measelle, J.R., 447
Media Analysis Laboratory, 615
Media Awareness Network, 609
Mediascope, 607
Medlin, R.G., 279
Mednick, B.R., 126, 138
Meese, D.W., 594
Mehan, H., 619
Mehl, L.E., 134
Mehler, J., 189
Mehlman, M.J., 75, 88, 89
Meier, R.P., 373
Meilman, P.W., 460
Meinhart, C.L., 138
Meisels, S.J., 137
Mekos, D., 591
Melander, H., 278
Melnick, S.M., 278, 637
Melnyk, S., 83, 124
Melot, A.M., 282
Melson, G.F., 479
Meltzoff, A.N., 215, 216, 228, 231, 232, 286, 358, 435, 436, 442, 463
Menashri, J., 487
Mendel, G., 76, 77
Mendelson, B., 170
Mendelson, M., 170
Mendes, T.M., 169
Mennella, A., 504
Meredith, M.C., 235
Merewood, A., 83, 123
Mergendoller, J.R., 620
Merkler, K., 585

Merrick, S., 421
Mervis, C.B., 359, 369, 376
Meschulach-Sarfaty, O., 216
Messinger, D.S., 416
Messinger, L., 589
Meulemans, T., 272
Meulmeester, J., 169
Meyer-Bahlberg, H.F.L., 508
Meyers, C.E., 329
Meyers, T., 134
Miceli, P.J., 512
Michael, R.T., 507
Michaelieu, Q., 448, 450
Michaels, S., 507
Midgett, J., 623
Midgley, C., 447, 457, 481, 622
Mikach, S., 508, 585
Milbern, S., 617
Milich, S., 278
Mill, J.S., 311
Millar, W.S., 129, 130
Millberger, S., 278
Miller, A.T., 456
Miller, B.C., 585
Miller, C.L., 483, 512
Miller, G.V., 508
Miller, J.G., 550, 551
Miller, J.L., 189, 355
Miller, K.F., 254, 294
Miller, K S., 507, 512
Miller, L.T., 267
Miller, M., 292, 293
Miller, N.B., 572
Miller, P.A., 532, 533, 534
Miller, P.C., 423
Miller, P.H., 241, 269, 276, 277, 284, 355, 374, 379, 439, 440, 463, 584
Miller, S.A., 12, 241, 355, 374, 379, 439, 440
Miller, T.L., 512
Miller, T.E., 178
Miller-Heyl, J., 576
Miller-Johnson, S., 343
Mills, R.S.L., 518
Milton, J., 4
Milunsky, A., 74
Miner, J.L., 397
Minich, N.M., 138
Ministry of Health Services, British Columbia Vital Statistics, 585
Minnes, S., 121, 122
Minski, P., 321
Minton, H.L., 327
Mintz, J., 256
Mischel, W., 554
Misfeldt, D., 290
Mistry, J., 255, 257, 261, 283, 305
Mistry, R., 594
Mitchell, C., 448, 622
Mitchell, J., 421
Mitchell, J.E., 491
Mitchell, S., 333, 339
Miura, I.T., 302
Miyake, K., 392, 393, 414, 415
Miyashita, K.T., 613, 615
Miyawaki, K., 206
Mize, J., 5, 462, 637
Mizuta, I., 516
Moawad, A.H., 136
Moely, B.E., 268, 280
Moerk, E.L., 357
Moffitt, T.E., 27, 173, 400, 518, 588, 640, 647
Mohide, P., 86
Molfese, D.L., 157, 355
Molina, B.S.G., 171
Moller, L.C., 487
Mollnow, E., 122
Moloughney, B.W., 449

Monass, J.A., 346
Mondloch, C.J., 195, 196, 201
Moneta, G., 171, 581
Money, J., 490, 491, 492, 494, 508
Monsour, A., 444
Montemayor, R., 443
Montgomery, D., 325
Montplaisir, J., 520
Moon, C., 362
Moore, C., 367, 421, 440, 442
Moore, C.A., 362
Moore, E.G.J., 86, 110, 112, 113, 115
Moore, K., 292, 293
Moore, M.K., 210, 215, 216
Moore, S.M., 170
Mora, J.O., 124, 176
Moran, G., 414, 423
Morelli, G., 414, 415
Morelli, G.A., 425
Morgan, E.R., 328
Morgan, G.A., 410
Morgan, J.L., 362
Morikawa, H., 360, 367
Morison, P., 631, 638
Morison, S.J., 427, 616
Morris, J.T., 497
Morris, M., 136, 246
Morris, N., 134, 135
Morris, R., 492
Morris, S.J., 641
Morrison, F.J., 381, 616
Morrison, H.I., 449
Morrison, P., 449
Morrison, V., 195
Morrow, C., 641
Mortimer, J.T., 579
Mortimore, P., 617, 618
Morton, J., 187, 194
Mory, M. S., 635
Moser, J.M., 298
Moses, L.J., 240, 367, 396, 440
Mosher, M., 477, 519
Moshman, D., 246
Mosier, C., 255, 257, 261, 305
Mosley, J.E., 395
Moss, A., 335
Moss, H.A., 27
Mott, F.L., 126
Mount, J., 134
Mounts, N.S., 450, 454, 572, 573, 635, 648
Mrazek, D.A., 399
Mueller, C.M., 458
Mueller, D.H., 87
Mueller, E.C., 632
Muhlenbruck, L., 618
Muir, D.W., 145, 163, 188, 190, 238, 439
Muir-Broaddus, J.E., 369, 294
Muller, J., 168
Mullis, A.K., 448
Mullis, R.L., 448
Mumford, M.D., 344
Mumme, D.L., 396
Munakata, Y., 56, 57
Mundfrom, D.J., 138
Munro, G., 462
Munroe, R.H., 498
Munroe, R.L., 498
Murphy, B.C., 394, 533
Murphy, C.M., 527
Murphy, J., 355
Murphy, K., 645
Murray, A.D., 130
Murray, B., 613
Murray, C., 339, 584
Murray, E., 487
Murray, I., 132
Murray, J.P., 609

Murray, K.T., 274, 540, 552, 554, 558, 559, 570, 573
Murray, K., 274, 559
Murray, L., 134, 416, 417
Mussen, P.H., 495
Musser, L.M., 630, 636
Mustard, J.F., 104
Muter, V., 205
Myers, B., 486
Myers, B.J., 129
Myers, M.M., 113
Myers, T., 134, 416
Mylander, C., 357

Nachmias, M., 413
Nadeau, L., 136, 137
Nagain, D.S., 518
Nagel, S.K., 64, 576, 593
Nagin, D., 518, 519
Naigles, L.G., 370
Naito, M., 443
Nakagawa, K., 454, 621
Nandakumer, R., 369
Nanez, J., 197
Nanis, J., 486
Naslund, J.C., 205
Nastasi, B.K., 613, 614
Natale, R., 86
Nation, R.L., 130
Naus, M.J., 279
Neal, C.J., 258
Neale, M.C., 508
Nederend, S., 486, 487
Needham, A., 230
Needle, R.H., 588
Needlman, R., 214
Neeman, J., 448
Neiderhiser, J.M., 97, 574
Neimark, E.D., 246
Neimark, J., 102
Neisser, U., 285, 312, 315, 322, 326, 327, 335, 337, 339
Nelson, C.A., 128, 135, 154, 155, 158, 194, 195, 356, 396
Nelson, D.A., 519
Nelson, J., 469, 470, 644
Nelson, K., 248, 284, 285, 286, 287, 365, 366, 367, 438
Nelson, K.E., 360
Nelson, L.J., 519
Nelson, S.A., 543
Nelson, S., 458
Nesbitt, K.M., 610
Nesmith, J., 88, 89
Netto, D., 202
Neu, H.C., 87
Neuwalder, H.F., 508
Neville, H.J., 373
Neville, P.R., 65
Newcomb, A.F., 486, 638, 639, 640, 643, 644, 645
Newcomb, M.D., 649
Newcombe, N., 239, 272, 285, 490, 491
Newell, A., 264
Newman, D.L., 27, 400, 518
Newman, J.L., 486
Newman, N.M., 144
Newport, E.L., 229, 356
Newton, N., 130–131
Ngandu, N., 339
NICHD Early Child Care Research Network, 417, 428, 429, 430
Nicholls, J.G., 456
Nichols, M.R., 419
Nichols, R.C.
Nichols-Whitehead, P., 255
Nicoladis, E., 364, 385

Nicolaides, K., 114, 118, 119, 126
Nielson, A., 168
Nielson, C.T., 168
Nigg, J.T., 278, 637
Ninio, A., 419
Nir, A., 397
Nissen, H.W., 154
Nitza, V., 134
Nix, R. L., 526
Nixon, C.L., 624
Nixon, K., 615
Noam, G., 450
Noll, J., 315
Normandeau, S., 249
Normandin, D., 448
Norman-Jackson, J., 583
Norris, J.E., 578
Norton, J.A., 125
Nottelmann, E.D., 448
Nova Scotia Department of Community Services, 512
Noveck, I.A., 247
Nowell, A., 476
Nucci, L., 544, 551
Nugent, J.K., 146
Nugent, L.D., 266
Nurcombe, B., 137
Nuttall, R.L., 477
Nystrom, G., 137
Nystrom, J., 190

Oakes, L., 364
Oakes, M.A., 290
Obach, M.S., 268, 280
Oberklaid, F., 399
Oberle, K., 530
O'Boyle, C., 484, 512, 527
O'Brien, D.P., 247
O'Brien, K.M., 473, 519
Ochs, E., 360
O'Connell, B., 363
O'Connor, B.P., 461
O'Connor, N., 319
O'Connor, T.G., 100, 325, 326, 427, 519
Odden, A., 618
Odem, R.R., 123
O'Dempsey, T.J.D., 131
Oden, S., 642
O'Donohue, W.T., 598
Oettingen, G., 479, 481
Offord, D.R., 449
Ogbu, J., 337, 455, 576, 621
O'Heron, C.A., 503
Okamoto, Y., 250, 251, 252, 302
Okun, N., 86
Olejnik, 486
Ollendick, T.H., 583
Oller, D.K., 206, 363
O'Loughlin, M., 246
Olsen, J.E., 578
Olsen, S.F., 519, 636
Olson, D.R., 240, 395
Olson, K. L., 394
Olvera-Ezzell, N., 178
Olweus, D., 492, 520, 522
O'Mahoney, J.F., 466
O'Neil, A.K., 486, 487
O'Neil, R., 64, 576, 593
O'Neil, R.O., 637
O'Neill, D.K., 372, 374, 440
Ong, A., 646
Ontario Children's Secretariat, 104
Oppenheim, D., 397, 425
Opper, S., 243
Opwis, K., 267
O'Reilly, A.W., 235, 256

Orlofsky, J.L., 461, 503, 504
Ornstein, P.A., 279, 289, 291
Osborne, L.M., 587
Osborne, M.L., 511
Oshimo-Takane, Y., 383
Osser, H.A., 204
Ossoff, E.P., 607
Oster, H., 392, 393
Ostry, D., 363
O'Sullivan, J.T., 281, 282
Ouston, J., 617, 618
Overman, W., 292, 293
Overton, K.M., 83
Overton, W.F., 65, 247, 498
Oviatt, S.L., 364
Owen, M.T., 62, 417, 419, 565
Oxtoby, M.J., 118
Oyen, A-S., 279

Paarlberg, K.M., 125
Padgett, R., 123
Padgett, R.J., 360
Pagani, L., 648
Paikoff, R.L., 64, 169, 171, 177
Painter, K.M., 256, 493
Painter, P., 135
Pakstis, A.J., 339
Palinscar, A.S., 258
Palkovitz, R., 135, 419, 565
Palmer, C.F., 163
Palmer, D.J., 582
Pamuck, E., 178
Pan, B.A., 358, 368
Panak, W.F., 520
Pancer, S.M., 550
Panigrahy, A., 144
Panksepp, J., 278
Pannabecker, B., 392
Pannozzo, G.M., 618
Papiernik, E., 136
Papousek, H., 211
Paquette, G., 607
Paradis, J., 385
Parent, S., 249
Paris, S.G., 282
Parisi, D., 357
Park, A., 333
Park, S., 399
Parke, R.D., 22, 213, 215, 422, 473, 518, 529, 555, 558, 636, 637
Parker, J.G., 402, 486, 487, 630, 631, 634, 635, 638, 639, 640, 643, 644, 645
Parker, K.C.H., 423
Parkhurst, J.T., 639
Parkin, L., 443
Parnass, J. 630
Parsons, J.E., 470, 481
Parsons, T., 474
Parten, M., 633
Pascual, L., 256, 493
Pascual-Leone, J., 248, 251
Passarello, L.C., 507
Passchier, J., 125
Passingham, R.E., 356
Pataki, S.P., 641
Patel, D., 177
Patel, N., 17
Patrick, D.M., 510, 511
Pattee, L., 639
Patterson, C.J., 304, 508, 575, 585, 586, 597, 598, 599, 621
Patterson, G.R., 50, 525, 526, 527, 558, 575, 589, 648
Patterson, S.J., 460, 573
Patz, R.J., 596
Paul, J.P., 508

Paulhus, D., 583
Pavlov, I., 208
Pearl, R., 522, 640
Pears, K.C., 509, 512, 527
Pearson, A., 463
Pedersen, J., 516, 518
Pedersen, N., 178
Pederson, D.R., 414, 423
Pedlow, R., 399
Pedro-Carroll, J.L.,
Peeke, L.A., 481
Peet, S., 479
Pegalis, L.J., 503
Pegg, J.E., 359, 365
Pelaez-Nogueras, M., 48, 51
Pelgrum, W.J., 613, 615
Pelham, W.E., Jr., 278
Pellegrini, A.D., 14, 167, 235, 253, 478
Pellegrini, D.S., 468
Pence, A.R., 428
Peng, Y., 518, 528
Penner, S.G., 360
Pepler, D.J., 522, 523, 581, 582, 583
Pepper, S., 641
Perez, L.A., 272
Perez-Granados, D.R., 383
Perilloux, H.K., 437, 438
Perlman, M., 516, 581
Perlmutter, M., 260, 282
Perloff, R., 312, 315, 322, 326, 327, 335, 337, 339
Perner, J., 441, 443
Perozynski, L. A., 581
Perruchet, P., 272
Perry, D.G., 63, 518, 520, 522, 523, 556, 643
Perry, L.C., 518, 520, 522
Perry, S., 416
Perry, T.B., 468
Persaud, T.V.N., 86, 110, 112, 113, 115
Persoage, K.A., 370
Perusse, D., 520
Peskin, H., 5, 171
Peskin, J., 395
Peters, P.L., 527
Petersen, A.C., 170, 171, 172, 477, 486
Peterson, C., 285, 286
Peterson, C.C., 543
Peterson, G.H.,,, 134
Peterson, L., 594
Peterson, R.E., 494
Petitto, L.A., 363
Petrakos, H., 443, 583
Petretic, P.A., 372
Petrovich, S.B., 407, 408
Pettersen, 197
Pettit, G.S., 214, 401, 522, 523, 524, 526, 573, 578, 594, 637, 639, 640, 642, 643, 648
Peucker, M., 121
Peynircioglu, Z.F., 272
Pexman, P., 380
Pezaris, E., 477
Pezdek, K., 291
Phares, V., 137
Phelps, J.L., 423
Phillips, A.T., 440
Phillips, D., 458
Phillips, D.A., 428, 481
Phillips, M., 620
Philpott, R.H., 130
Philpsen, L.C., 636
Phinney, J.S., 646
Phoenix, C.H., 492
Piaget, J., 14, 52–56, 60, 65, 67, 68, 184, 185, 191, 215, 216, 217, 222, 223, 224, 225, 226, 227, 228, 229, 230, 231, 232, 233, 234, 235, 236, 238, 240, 241, 242, 243, 244, 245, 246, 247, 248, 249, 250, 258, 259, 264, 269,

294, 296, 303, 304, 305, 312, 468, 469, 516, 541, 542, 544, 545, 635
Piccinini, C.A., 129, 130
Pick, A.D., 204, 396
Pick, H.L., 3, 374, 382
Pickens, J., 202
Pickrell, J.E., 290
Piemyat, S., 607
Pierce, K.M., 594
Pierluigi, M., 83, 123
Pierroutsakos, S.L., 294
Pihl, R.O., 520
Pike, A., 97
Pike, K.M., 177
Pike, R., 447
Pillard, R.C., 91, 508
Pillow, B.H., 276
Pinderhughes, E.E., 340, 526, 567
Pine, D., 158
Pine, J.M., 359, 367
Pinker, S., 307, 355, 376
Pinon, M., 612
Pinto, A., 572
Pipe, M.-E., 289
Pipp, S.L., 248, 250, 421, 438
Pipp-Siegel, S., 438
Pisoni, D.B., 188, 189
Pitts, R.C., 538, 552
Plant, E.A., 479
Plewis, I., 143, 145
Plomin, R., 39, 70, 73, 75, 79, 80, 81, 82, 84, 88, 90, 92, 93, 94, 95, 96. 97. 98, 100, 103, 105, 334, 344, 398, 399, 519, 574, 584
Plumert, J.M., 3, 165, 255, 382
Plummert, K., 367
Plump, T., 613, 615
Plunket, K., 307, 357
Plunkett, J.W., 137
Pogribna, I.P., 83, 124
Pogribna, M., 83, 124
Poirier, J., 137
Polak, A., 375
Polakoski, K.L.. 123
Politka, J.E., 114, 118, 119, 120, 121, 123, 124, 125, 130
Polit, D.F., 583
Polivy, J., 177
Pollack, R.H., 512
Pollitt, E., 176, 179, 339
Pollock, C.B., 416
Pomerantz, E.M., 450, 456, 458
Pomerleau, A., 473
Ponesse, J.S., 165
Ponomarev, I., 266
Ponsonby, A.L.B., 144
Poole, D.A., 289, 291
Poortinga, Y.H., 206
Pope, S.K., 138
Popper, S., 134
Porac, C., 157
Porges, S.W., 156, 191
Porter, C.L., 478
Porter, F.L., 191
Porter, R.H., 190
Posada, G., 411, 414, 415
Posada, R., 411, 415
Posner, J. K., 594
Poston, D.L., Jr., 583
Pott, M., 414, 415
Potts, R., 556
Poulin, F., 522, 526, 528, 642, 645, 648
Poulin, R., 637
Poulin-DuBois, D., 483, 484
Povinelli, D.J., 437, 438
Powell, C., 124, 176
Powell, J.K., 363
Powell, M., 291

Power, T.G., 17, 178, 214, 395, 574, 576
Powers, S.I., 450
Powlishta, K.K., 484, 486, 487
Pratt, C., 374
Pratt, H., 177
Pratt, K.C., 187, 191
Pratt, M.W., 255, 260, 550, 578
Pressley, M., 205, 268, 280, 282, 283
Previc, F.H., 157
Prezbindowski, A.K., 373
Price, J.M., 531, 639, 640, 643
Priel, B., 437
Prifitera, A., 320, 321
Prior, M., 399
Proffitt, D.R., 195
Provence, J., 424, 425
Pryor, T.L., 177
Psychological Corporation, 321
Pulkkinen, L., 518
Pungello, E.P., 343, 621
Putnam, F.W., 595
Putnam, P.H., 392, 393
Putnam, S., 399

Qualter, A., 380
Quantz, D.H., 370
Quas, J.A., 289
Quay, L.C., 336
Querido, J.G., 363
Quiggle, N.L., 520
Quinn, R.A., 538

Rabiner, D.L., 637, 639, 642
Raboy, B., 585
Rach, D., 133
Radan, A., 333
Radice, C., 585
Radke-Yarrow, M., 61, 216, 416, 530, 531, 533, 534, 537, 558, 581
Raffaelli, M., 602, 648, 649
Rakic, P., 154, 157
Ram, A., 581, 582
Ramanan, J., 592
Ramey, C.T., 124, 176, 333, 334, 339, 341, 342, 343, 427, 428, 617
Ramey, S.L., 341, 342, 428, 617
Ramos-Ford, V., 347
Ramsay, D., 134
Ramsay, D.S., 145, 364
Ramsey, E., 526, 527
Rankin, M.P., 255
Rapus, T., 293
Rashotte, C.A.,
Rasmussen, C., 299
Rau, J.B., 33
Rauh, V.A., 137
Raviv, A., 531
Rayias, M.F., 392, 393
Raynor, R., 47, 209
Raz, S., 478
Read, A.P., 73, 77, 79, 84, 85, 88, 89
Read, J.A., 125
Read, L.E., 277
Recchia, S., 393, 451
Redanz, N.J., 362, 365
Reddel, M., 473
Reed, T.E., 339
Reeder, K., 378
Reese, E., 285, 287, 288, 381, 478
Reese, H.W., 3
Reich, P.A., 385
Reid, J.B., 525, 526
Reijonen, J., 177
Reikehof, L., 373
Reinisch, J.M., 509

Reiser, L.W., 170
Reiser, M., 394
Reiser-Danner, L.A., 194, 638
Reiss, D., 97, 569, 574, 586, 589, 591, 592
Relkin, N.R., 356
Remez, R.E., 372
Remley, A., 8
Rende, R., 98
Renick, A., 291
Renshaw, P.D., 642
Repacholi, B.M., 396, 421, 440
Resch, N.L., 577
Rescorla, L., 617
Resing, W.C.M., 270
Resnick, S., 418
Resnick, S.M., 492
Rest, J.R., 549, 550, 553
Reuman, D., 622
Revelle, G.L., 379
Reyna, V.F., 272, 289, 291
Reynolds, D., 620
Reznick, J.S., 82, 365, 399, 400
Rheingold, H.L., 361, 530
Rhodes, J. E., 577
Rholes, W.S., 463
Riad, J.K., 492
Ribble, M., 424
Ricciuti, H.N., 410
Rice, C., 238
Rice, M.E., 537
Rice, M.L., 611, 612
Rich, S.A., 323
Richards, J.E., 207
Richards, M.H., 170, 171, 177, 448, 581, 592, 635
Richardson, D., 168
Richardson, J.G., 487, 488
Richardson, K., 312
Richey, C.A., 597
Richman, A., 16, 394
Richman, E.L., 167
Ridderinkhoff, K.R., 275
Riddlesberger, 289
Ridge, B. 401
Ridley-Johnson, R., 159
Rierdan, J., 170
Riesen, A.H., 154
Rieser, J., 190
Rigby, J.A., 506
Riggs, W.W., 478
Riksen-Walraven, J.M.A., 641
Rinaldi, C.M., 443, 581–582, 583
Rinott, N., 419
Riordan, K., 418
Riordan, L., 400
Risley, T.R., 278, 334
Risser, A.H., 158
Ritchot, K.F.M., 153
Ritter, J.M., 194, 408, 638
Ritter, P.L., 454, 572
Rivest, L., 636
Roberts, D., 566, 609
Roberts, J.E., 429, 430, 588
Roberts, K., 291
Roberts, L.R., 486
Roberts, W.L., 479, 522, 534, 535
Robertson, B., 458
Robertson, T.S., 609
Robin, D.J., 163
Robins, R.W., 450
Robinson, B.F., 359
Robinson, C.C., 497, 519, 636
Robinson, E., 507
Robinson, I., 507
Robinson, J., 399, 531, 534
Robinson, J.D., 177

Robinson, J.L., 82, 95, 400, 534
Robinson, T., 155
Rochat, P., 163, 231, 363
Roche, A.F., 178
Rocheleau, B., 615
Rock, A.M.L., 145
Rock, S.L., 333, 339, 453
Rodin, J., 177
Rodkin, P.C., 522, 640
Rodning, C., 122
Rodriguez, T., 440, 615
Roede, M., 169
Roedell, W.C., 610
Roeleveld, N., 329
Roeser, R.W., 622
Rogers, M.F., 118
Rogers-Salyer, M., 408
Roggman, L.A., 194, 638
Rogoff, B., 55, 250, 252, 255, 258, 258, 260, 261, 283, 305, 630
Rohner, R.P., 593
Roid, G., 320
Roithmaier, A., 180
Roland, M.G.M., 179
Rolf, J., 602
Romich, J., 594
Romney, D.M., 475, 496
Ronsaville, D.S., 581
Rosario, M., 599
Rose, A.J., 645
Rose, H., 496, 499
Rose, R.J., 173
Rose, R.M., 492
Rose, S.A., 138, 195, 201, 203, 208, 324
Rose, S.P., 156
Rose-Krasnor, L., 214
Rosen, B.C., 454
Rosen, J.C., 170
Rosen, L.R., 508
Rosen, T.J., 307, 376
Rosen, W.D., 398
Rosenbaum, L.K., 342, 343
Rosenbaum, P.L., 138, 139
Rosenberger, K., 62
Rosenblatt, E., 380
Rosenbloom, S., 201
Rosenblum, G.D., 170, 450
Rosenblum, K.E., 270, 299
Rosenblum, M.A., 629
Rosengren, K., 159, 260
Rosenhan, D.L., 537
Rosenholtz, S.J., 456
Rosenkrantz, P.S., 475
Rosenman, R.H., 95
Rosenthal, M.K., 361, 363
Rosenthal, R., 594
Rosenwasser, S.M., 609
Rosenzweig, M.G., 509
Rosenzweig, M.R., 155
Ross, D.P., 428
Ross, G., 255
Ross, H.S., 363, 516, 580, 581, 582
Ross, I., 329
Ross, R.T., 329
Rossiter, J.R., 609
Rotatori, A.F., 598
Roth, E., 205, 381
Roth, J., 577
Roth, K., 533
Rothbart, M.K., 398
Rothbaum, F., 414, 415
Rothberg, A.D., 125
Rotter, J., 178
Roughton, E.C., 125
Rousseau, J.J., 8, 11
Rovee-Collier, C.K., 207, 210, 211, 212, 213, 436

Rovine, M., 416, 430, 565
Rowe, D.C., 92, 95, 96, 97
Rubenstein, A. J., 194
Rubenstein, J.L., 449
Rubenstein, T.S., 641
Rubin, C., 449
Rubin, K.H., 156, 235, 296, 400, 403, 404, 455, 470, 518, 576, 631, 534, 638, 639, 643, 644
Rubinstein, E.A., 609
Ruble, D.N., 450, 456, 458, 463, 483, 484, 487, 488, 496, 497, 498, 500
Rudin, M., 598
Rueter, M.A., 575
Ruff, A., 602
Ruff, H.A., 275
Ruffman, T.K., 240, 395, 443
Ruh, J., 594
Ruiz-Palaez, J., 137
Rumbaugh, D.M., 355
Rumelhart, D.E., 306, 307
Runco, M.A., 344, 345, 346
Rushton, J.P., 335, 339, 537, 554, 556
Russell, G.F.M., 177
Rutherford, E., 495
Rutherford, P., 320
Rutten, P., 524
Rutter, D.R., 374
Rutter, M., 5, 70, 75, 79, 80, 81, 82, 84, 90, 93, 94, 97, 98, 103, 105, 325, 326, 329, 427, 519, 617, 618, 619, 620
Ruzany, N., 450
Rvachew, S., 189
Ryan, B.A., 623
Ryan, R.M., 453, 599
Rydell, C.P., 343
Rys, G.S., 543
Ryskina, V.L., 359
Ryther, J.S., 359
Ryu, S., 579

Saarni, C., 375, 478
Sabbagh, M.A., 442
Sackett, G.P., 123
Sacks, C.H., 620
Sacks, O., 442
Sadesky, G., 299
Sadler, T.W., 110
Saffran, J.R., 362
Sagi, A., 61, 411, 414, 415, 423, 425
Sahni, R., 113
Saigal, S., 138, 139
Sakamoto, T., 613, 615
Sakin, J.W., 580
Saklofske, D.H., 320, 321
Salapatek, P., 197, 192, 193
Sale, J., 144
Salem, D.A., 566
Salili, F., 451
Salthouse, T.A., 268, 303
Salvator, A., 121, 122
Salyer, K.E., 408
Salzinger, S., 599
Sameroff, A.J., 125, 135, 324, 332, 335, 418
Sampson, P.D., 118, 119
Sams, S.E., 278
Samuels, C., 436
Samuels, M.C., 441
Samuelson, L.K., 368
Sanchez, R.P., 294
Sand, M., 511
Sandberg, D., 134
Sander, C.J., 478
Sanders, M., 343
Sanders, P., 496
Sanders, R., 458

Sanders, S.A., 509
Sandieson, R., 252
Sandvik, E., 478
Sanone, R., 83, 123
Sansavini, A., 362
Sanson, A., 399
Santrock, J.W., 591
Santulli, K.A., 268, 280
Sapiro, C.M., 551
Sapp, F., 238
Sarigiani, P.A., 486
Sattler, J.M., 320, 322
Saucier, P., 497
Saults, J. S., 266
Savage-Rumbaugh, E.S., 355
Savelsbergh, G., 159
Savin-Williams, R.C., 172, 448, 508
Savoie, L., 425
Savoy, K., 550
Savoy-Levine, K.M., 255
Sawin, D.B., 408, 534
Saxton, M., 360
Sayer, A., 82
Saywitz, K.J., 598
Scafidi, F.A., 137, 190
Scaramella, L.V., 509
Scarr, S., 95, 100, 101, 102, 103, 104, 330, 331, 339, 340, 430, 585, 593
Scavone, J., 565
Schachar, R.J., 165, 278
Schaefer, G., 367
Schaefer, L., 341
Schafer, W.D., 419
Schaffer, A., 436
Schaffer, H.R., 404, 407, 409
Schaie, K.W., 26
Schall, B., 109, 190
Schaller, M., 534
Schalling, D., 492
Schalock, R.L., 329
Schanberg, S.M., 137, 190, 416
Schauble, L., 270
Schauer, T., 327
Schellenbach, C., 512
Schieffelin, B.B., 360
Schiff-Myers, N., 360
Schiller, M., 418
Schilling, T.H., 232
Schlagman, N., 544
Schlegel, A., 171
Schliemann, A.D., 300
Schlindler, C., 132
Schliwowski, H., 144
Schmader, T., 338
Schmidt, C.R., 484, 499
Schmidt, L.A., 400
Schmidt, M., 421
Schmitt, K.L., 178, 498, 606, 608, 612
Schmucker, M.A., 200
Schneider, B.A., 189
Schneider, B.H., 421, 519, 642, 643, 644, 645
Schneider, F.W., 327
Schneider, K., 161, 162, 163
Schneider, M.L., 125
Schneider, W., 205, 228, 267, 268, 280, 281, 282, 283, 381
Schnell, S.V., 550
Schockner, A. E., 486
Schoefs, V., 447
Schoelmerich, A., 411, 415, 576
Schoff, K., 575
Scholl, T.O., 126
Scholmerich, A., 394, 408
Schreiber, J.C., 234, 236
Schuller, V., 416
Schulman, J.D., 78, 80

Schult, C.A., 441
Schulze, K.F., 113
Schulze, P.A., 576
Schuster, D.T., 328
Schutz, R.W., 165
Schwanenflugel, P. J., 271
Schwartz, C., 321
Schwartz, D., 522, 523, 643
Schwartz, J.E., 328
Schwartz, P.M., 122
Schwartz, R., 359
Schwartzman, A.E., 103, 527
Schwarz, J.C., 573
Schwebel, D.C., 3, 165
Schweinhart, L.J., 341
Schweitzer, J., 618
Scolton, K.L., 422
Scott, B., 82
Scott, D.T., 138
Scott, J.P., 524
Scott, K., 428
Scott, R., 450
Scott, W.A., 450
Scribner, S., 283
Seabrook, C., 177
Sears, R.R., 406
Sebald, H., 648
Sebanc, A.M., 234, 235
Segal, N.L., 102
Segal, S., 591
Segal, U.A., 17
Segall, M., 206
Seidenberg, M.S., 306
Seidman, D.S., 125, 126
Seidman, E., 448, 622
Seidman, T., 325
Seier, W.L., 269
Seifer, R., 121, 125, 324, 332, 335, 418
Seimans, L., 279
Seitz, V., 126, 337, 342, 343, 511, 512
Sellers, A., 325
Sellers, M.J., 407
Selman, R.L., 54, 381, 466, 467
Semenciw, R.M., 449
Semmel, M.I., 624
Semmes, J., 154
Sena, R., 235
Senechal, M., 205, 381
Senghas, A., 369
Sepkoski, C., 121
Seppa, N., 607, 610
Serbin, L., 103, 483, 484, 486, 527
Serbin, L.A., 487
Serdula, M., 178
Sergio, L.E., 363
Seroczynski, A.D., 481
Sevcik, R.A., 355
Severino, R., 133
Shafer, H.H., 82, 83
Shaffer, A., 612
Shaffer, D.R., 167, 244, 503, 532, 537, 538, 540, 552, 557, 558, 583
Shaffer, T.G., 479
Shagle, S.C., 578
Shah, F., 478
Shanahan, M.J., 579
Shannon, D., 394
Shannon, D.C., 400
Shannon, S.L., 576, 643
Shantz, C.U., 359, 468
Shapiro, C., 641
Shapiro, J.R., 394
Shapiro, S., 114, 116, 1119, 512, 634
Sharma, A.R., 97, 584, 585
Shatz, M., 240, 359, 374, 379, 381
Shaw, D., 205
Shaw, D.S., 526, 581, 587, 589

Shaw, L.K., 366
Shayer, M., 246
Shea, C., 532, 533, 534
Shearer, L. 120
Sheingold, K., 285
Shell, R., 532, 533, 534
Shenfield, T., 385, 386
Shenker, R., 169
Shepard, B., 394
Shepard, S.A., 533, 637
Sherif, C.W., 635
Sherif, M., 635
Shermin, J.J., 125
Shields, A., 599
Shiffrin, R.M., 265
Shigetomi, C.C., 531
Shimmin, H.S., 498
Shinskey, J.L., 232
Shirley, M.M., 159
Shonkoff, J.P., 82
Shore, C., 363
Short, K.R., 193
Short, R.J., 625
Shouldice, A., 418
Shrager, J.,
Shucard, D.W., 364
Shucard, J., 364
Shulman, S., 421, 486, 640
Shultz, T. R., 307, 308
Shure, M.B., 5, 642
Shurkin, J.N., 328
Shwe, H.I., 374
Shweder, R.A., 550, 551, 552
Siddiqui, A., 581, 582
Siegal, M., 543, 560
Siegel, G.M., 374
Siegel, L.S., 333, 337, 339
Siegel, P.Z., 178
Siegel-Gorelick, B., 171, 172
Siegler, R.S., 56, 57, 248, 249, 250, 253, 269, 270, 292, 299, 301, 626
Sienna, M., 278
Sigafoos, A.D., 216
Sigelman, C.K., 46, 178, 485, 553
Sigman, M., 235
Sigmundson, H.K., 494
Signorella, M.L., 485, 491, 499
Signorielli, N., 497, 606
Silva, P.A., 27, 173, 398, 399, 400, 500, 518, 588
Silver, D., 379
Silver, L.B., 278
Silverberg, S.B., 575, 646, 647
Silver-Isenstadt, J., 365
Simion, F., 194, 435
Simmel, C., 278, 637
Simmons, R.G., 170, 172, 448, 622
Simmons, S., 97
Simon, B.B., 437
Simon, H.A., 264
Simon, T.J., 231
Simonoff, E., 329
Simons, R.L., 509, 570, 575, 590, 596
Simonton, D.K., 344, 345, 346
Simpson, C., 456
Simpson, C.H., 487, 488
Simpson, J.L., 110
Simpson, K.R., 130
Simpson, M., 325
Simutis, Z., 556
Sinclair, R.J., 589
Sines, J.O., 572
Singer, J., 86, 612
Singer, L., 121, 122, 612
Singer, L.M., 134
Singh, S., 509
Siperstein, G.N., 361

Sippola, L.K., 486, 640, 644, 645
Sitarenios, G., 86
Sitterle, K.A., 591
Skakkebaek, N., 168
Skeels, H.M., 331
Skinner, B.F., 47, 48, 49, 50, 62, 65, 210, 353
Skinner, M.L., 587, 648
Skodak, M., 331
Skouteris, H., 195
Slaby, R.G., 518, 521, 529, 610
Slade, A., 235, 423
Slater, A., 195, 198
Slaughter-Defoe, D.T., 454, 621
Slavin, R.E., 619, 624, 625
Slawinski, E., 189
Sleek, S., 387
Sleeper, L.A., 144
Slobin, D.I., 354, 355, 371, 372
Slone, D., 114, 116, 119
Slone, M., 503
Slora, E.J., 153, 167, 169
Small, S.A., 172
Smetana, J.G., 544, 555, 577
Smith, A., 617, 618
Smith, B.A., 145, 190
Smith, C., 597
Smith, C.M., 254
Smith, D., 481
Smith, D.W., 119, 585
Smith, E., 607
Smith, E.G., 197
Smith, F.T., 178, 622
Smith, J.H., 371
Smith, L., 616, 615
Smith, L.B., 184, 368, 380
Smith, M., 394, 616, 637
Smith, P.K., 167, 235, 478, 486, 528
Smith, R.S., 139
Smith, S., 615
Smith, T.W., 583
Smolak, L., 177
Smoll, F.L., 165
Smylie, J., 144, 510
Snarey, J.R., 549, 550, 552
Snidman, N., 400
Snow, C.E., 354, 360, 363
Snow, M.E., 487
Snow, R.E., 620
Snowling, M., 205
Snyder, E., 491, 508
Snyder, J., 524, 573
Snyder, M., 537
Sobesky, W.E.,
Socha, D.M., 258
Socha, T.J., 258
Sochting, I., 460, 573
Society for Research in Child Development, 32
Society of Obstetricians and Gynaecologists of Canada, 74
Sockloff, A., 486
Sodian, B., 441
Soken, N.H., 396
Sokol, B.W., 449
Sokol, R.J., 119, 120
Sokolov, J.L., 359, 360
Solomon, J., 413, 416
Somers, M., 195
Sommer, K., 512
Somsen, R.J.M., 157
Sonnenschein, S., 382
Sonuga-Barke, E.J., 566
Sorensen, E., 590
Soussignan, R., 190
Spangler, S., 414
Sparks, C., 479
Spear, S.J., 382
Spearman, C., 313, 315

Speer, A.L., 538
Speicher, B., 550
Spelke, E., 407
Spelke, E.S., 193, 194, 201, 229, 230
Speltze, 408
Spence, J.T., 502, 503
Spence, M.J., 188
Spencer, J.P., 161, 162, 163
Spencer, M.B., 439, 454, 621
Spencer, P.E., 373
Spieker, S.J., 512, 576
Spiker, D., 138
Spitz, R.A., 424, 425
Spivack, G., 642
Sprafkin, J., 20, 497, 606, 609, 610, 612
Spreen, O., 158
Sprigle, J.E., 341
Springen, K., 86
Spritz, B., 422
Spuhl, S.T., 260
Spuhler, J.N., 339
Sroufe, A., 421
Sroufe, L.A., 278, 409, 410, 418, 421, 423, 486, 599
St. James-Roberts, I., 143, 145
St. Lawrence, J.S., 512
Staats, A., 209
Stack, D.M., 190, 293, 527
Staffieri, J.R., 178
Stager, C., 366
Stager, C.L., 195, 201
Stainton, C., 133
Stanger, C., 393, 395
Stanhope, L., 581, 582
Stanley, J.C., 477
Stanowicz, L., 360
Stanton, B., 511
Staples, G. B.,
Starnes, R., 570, 637
Starr, R. H., Jr., 419, 593
Statistics Canada, 384, 428, 449, 477, 482, 511, 566, 567, 568, 569, 587, 595, 598, 606, 613, 625, 626
Statistics Sweden, 214
Stattin, H., 173, 400, 578
Staudt, J., 247
Stayton, D.J., 145
Stechler, G., 449
Steele, B.F., 416
Steele, C.M., 337, 338, 624
Steele, H., 423
Steele, M., 423
Stefanski, M., 113
Stein, A.H., 22, 610
Stein, J., 568, 593
Stein, J.H., 170
Stein, M.R., 632
Stein, Z., 124
Stein, Z.A., 124
Steinberg, L., 63, 64, 104, 130, 169, 171, 450, 454, 572, 573, 577, 579, 594, 621, 623, 646, 647, 648, 649
Steinberg, S., 577
Steiner, J.E., 190
Steir, M., 134
Stenberg, C., 392
Stern, D.N., 403, 406, 436
Stern, H.H., 386
Stern, J.A., 135
Stern, W., 320
Sternberg, J., 323
Sternberg, K.J., 599
Sternberg, R.J., 312, 315, 316, 322, 323, 326, 327, 329, 335, 337, 339, 344, 345, 346, 347
Stetsenko, A., 479, 481
Stevahn, L., 530
Stevens, N., 628

Stevens, R.J., 624, 625
Stevenson, D.K., 125, 126
Stevenson, H.W., 254, 301, 302, 481, 621,624, 625, 626, 627, 628
Stevenson, J., 214, 519
Stevenson-Hinde, J., 418
Stewart, R.B., 582
Stewart, S., 156
Stice, E., 574
Stifter, E., 641
Stigler, J.W., 301, 302, 624, 625, 627
Stimson, C.A., 530
Stipek, D.J., 393, 438, 451, 456, 459, 463, 617
Stockard, J., 503
Stockman , A.F., 131
Stoddart, T., 485
Stolberg, U., 410
Stolyarova, E.I., 359
Stone, B.P., 279
Stoneman, Z., 564
Stoolmiller, M., 648
Stormshak, E.A., 582
Stoskopf, F.L., 138, 139
Stouthamer-Loeber, M., 461, 517, 518, 524, 526
Strachan, T., 73, 77, 79, 84, 85, 88, 89
Strange, W., 206
Strassberg, Z., 214, 526
Stratton, K., 119
Strauss, M.A., 214
Strauss, M.S., 297
Strayer, F.F., 486
Strayer, J., 478, 479, 530, 534, 535
Street Youth Study Group, 602
Streiner, D.L., 138, 139
Streisand, B., 618
Streissguth, A.P., 118, 119
Streitmatter, J., 460
Streri, A., 201
Striano, T., 363
Strigini, P., 83, 123
Strough, J., 479
Strouse, D., 628
Stumpf, H., 477
Stunkard, A.J., 178
Sturla, E., 494
Stuss, D.T., 158
Su, M., 596
Subaiya, L., 587
Subotnik. R.F., 328
Sudhalter, V., 378, 380
Sue, S., 621
Suess, G., 414, 421
Sugarman, D.B., 214
Sugden, D., 165
Sullivan, K., 46, 238, 644, 645
Sullivan, M.W., 393, 395, 436
Sun, Y., 403
Sundberg, U., 359, 365
Suomi, S.J., 630, 631
Super, C.M., 124, 176, 550
Surber, C.F., 238
Susman, E.J., 596, 610
Susser, M.W., 124
Sutton, K., 503
Suzuki, L.A., 335
Swain, M., 386
Swarr, A.E., 170, 171, 177, 448, 635
Sweeney, K., 8
Swenson, D.H., 83, 124
Swiber, M.J., 113
Switzer, G., 538
Symons, D., 414, 429
Synnevang, B., 411, 415
Szkrybalo, J., 483
Szmukler, G.I., 177
Szymanski, J., 379

Tabkin, G., 612
Tafoya, D.L., 83, 124
Tager-Flusberg, H., 238
Taipale, V., 172
Takahira, S., 477
Takahishi, A., 150
Takanishi, R., 454, 621
Talley, R.C., 625
Tam, F., 82
Tamang, B.L., 395
Tamis-LeMonda, C.S., 208, 256, 419, 430, 593
Tani, F., 644
Tanner, J.M., 19, 150, 151, 152, 154, 156, 165, 167, 168, 173, 174, 175, 179
Tannock, R., 165, 278
Tardif, R., 367
Tardif, C., 421
Tarullo, L.B., 581
Tascon, M., 411, 415
Tasker, F., 508, 585
Tavarez, J., 497
Taylor, A., 491
Taylor, A.R., 624
Taylor, C., 274, 441
Taylor, C.B., 172
Taylor, D., 195, 387
Taylor, D.G., 416
Taylor, H.G., 138
Taylor, J., 291
Taylor, M.G., 369, 442, 485, 486, 489
Taylor, R.D., 566
Taylor, S., 205
Teegartin, C., 568
Teele, D.W., 190
Tees, R., 362
Teeven, R.C., 454
Tellegen, A., 102, 448
Templeton, L.M., 289
Tennenbaum, H.R., 479
Tenney, Y.J., 285
Terisse, B., 126
Terman, L.M., 319, 320, 328, 344
Terry, R., 517, 637
Tesman, J.R., 394
Tessier, O., 634
Tessier, R., 136, 137
Teti, D.M., 416, 423, 580, 582
Thal, D., 364
Tharp, R.G., 205, 454
Theall, L.A., 437
Thelen, E., 140, 159, 160. 1612, 162, 163. 365
Thelen, M.H., 478
Thernlund, G., 278
Thoma, S.J., 549, 550, 553
Thoman, E.B., 142, 211
Thomas, A., 398, 400, 401, 418, 420
Thomas, D., 364
Thomas, D.B., 130
Thomas, E.M., 205
Thomas, J.R., 165
Thomas, M.H., 608
Thomas, M.S.C., 307
Thomas, R.B., 146, 401, 402
Thomas, S.W., 289, 290
Thompson, A., 329
Thompson, H., 159
Thompson, R., 154, 155
Thompson, R.A., 32, 33, 394, 395, 540, 558
Thompson, R.F., 155
Thompson, S.K.
Thompson, W.W., 631, 575
Thorndike, R.L., 320
Thorndike, R.M., 312
Thorne, A., 448, 450
Thorne, B., 506
Thorneycroft, I., 78
Thornton, D., 615

Thorpe, L.A., 189
Thurber, C.A., 411
Thurston, D., 135
Thurstone, L.L., 313, 315
Tilton-Weaver, L.C., 647
Tinberngen, N., 58
Tingle, B.A., 534
Tinker, E., 361
Tinsley, B.J., 178, 609
Tirozzi, G.N., 625
Tisak, J., 544
Tisak, M.S., 544
Tizard, B., 427
Tjebkes, T.L., 540
Toch, T., 618
Tokura, H., 362
Tolmie, J.L., 83
Tomada, G., 519, 644
Tomasello, M., 350, 357, 358, 359, 360, 368, 378, 382, 383, 440, 442, 549
Tomblin Murphy, G., 506
Tomlin, C., 438
Tomlinson-Keasey, C., 328, 549
Tonascia, J., 138
Toner, I.J., 556
Torrance, E.P., 344
Tougas, J., 429
Townsend, M.A.R., 532
Trabasso, T., 242
Tracey, B., 170
Trachtenberg, S., 521
Trainor, L.J., 145
Tranmer, J., 145
Treboux, D., 421
Trehub, S.E., 189
Treiman, R., 205
Tremblay, M., 178
Tremblay, R., 136
Tremblay, R.E., 518, 519, 520, 648
Triandis, H.C., 445, 536
Trickett, P.K., 337, 595, 596, 597, 598
Tronick, E.A., 394
Tronick, E.Z., 146, 397, 403, 425
Troyer, D., 538
Troyer, L., 454, 572
Trudel, M., 418
Truglio, R., 607, 611, 612
Tryon, R.C., 90
Tsang-Tong, H.Y., 200
Tsay, J.C., 648, 649
Tseng, V., 646
Tucker, C.J., 496, 504
Tucker, G., 384
Tucker, J.S., 328
Tudge, J.R.H., 258, 261
Tulkin, S., 411
Tulkin, S.R., 247
Tulsky, D., 321
Tulviste, P., 221, 252, 261
Turiel, E., 485, 544, 551
Turkheimer, E., 334
Turnbull, M., 386
Turner, L.A., 280
Turner, P.J., 487, 503, 504
Turner-Bowker, D.M., 497
Tweney, R.D., 372
Twenge, J.M., 475
Tyson, J., 138
Tyson, P., 46
Tyson, R.L., 46

U.S. Bureau of the Census, 481
U.S. Department of Health and Human Services, 278
U.S. Department of Justice, 518
Uba, L., 576

Ude, W., 602
Udry, J.R., 506
Ulleland, C.N., 119
Uller, C., 231
Ullman, M., 307, 376
Ullstadius, E., 216
Ulman, K.J., 169, 170
Umilta, C., 194
Underwood, M.K., 395, 486, 518, 519, 531, 534
Unger, O.A.
University of British Columbia, Public Affairs, 482
University of Toronto, Childcare Resource and Research Unit, 593
Unzner, L., 414
Updegruff, K.A., 3, 485, 486, 581, 592, 593
Upshur, C.C., 82
Urban, J., 486, 640
Urbano, R.C., 206
Urberg, K.A., 486
Urbina, S., 312, 315, 322, 326, 327, 335, 337, 339
Uro, G., 625
Usher, B., 531, 534
Usher, J.A., 285
Uttal, D., 234, 236

Vachio, A., 258
Vaden, N.A., 340
Valdes-Dapena, M., 144
Valdez-Menchaca, M.C., 354, 360
Valdivia, I.A., 643
Valencia, R.R., 335
Valentine, J.C., 618
Valenza, E., 194
Valenzuela, M., 176
Valian, V., 372
Vallance, D., 397
Vallano, G., 278
Valoski, A., 179
Van Aker, R., 522, 640
Van Buuren, S., 169
van de Hoef, S., 578
Van De Vijver, F., 321
van den Boom, D.C., 401, 418, 420
van den Broek, P., 380, 607
van der Kamp, J., 159
Van der Linden, M., 272
van der Molen, M.W., 157, 275
van der Voort, T.H., 612
van Doorninck, W.J., 453, 454
Van Dulmen, M., 585
van Geign, H.P., 125
van IJzendoorn, H.W., 641
van IJzendoorn, M.H., 414, 415, 418, 419, 420, 423, 596
van, Leeuwen, H.M.P., 157
van Lieshout, C.F.M., 641
Van Noort, D.A., 270
Vance, G., 191
Vandegeest, K.A., 274, 559
Vandell, D.L., 582, 592, 594, 632
Vandenberg, B., 235, 634
Vann, F.H., 508
Vannatta, R.A., 449
van't Klooster, B.J., 157
Varady, M., 172
Varnhagen, C.K., 616
Vasta, R., 353
Vaughn, B.E., 125, 135, 414, 415, 418
Vaughn, L.S., 638
Veenman, S., 619
Vega-Lahr, N., 137
Velez, S., 137
Ventura-Cook, E., 576

Venture, A., 594
Verbrugge, R., 206
Veridiano, N.P., 508
Verloove-VanHorick, S., 169
Vernon, P.A. 267
Vernon-Feagans, L., 189, 190
Verp, M.S., 87, 114, 120, 122, 126
Verschueren, K., 419, 422, 447
Vespo, J., 516, 518
Vevea, J., 326
Vi, P., 83, 124
Vietze, P., 405
Vihman, M.M., 365
Viken, R.J., 173, 521
Villaneueva, I., 619
Vinden, P.G., 443
Vingerhoets, A.J.J.M., 125
Vinter, A., 216, 272
Vise, M., 205, 381
Vitaro, F., 523, 641, 648
Vlahovic-Stetic, V., 302
Voegeli, T., 132
Volker, S., 404
Volling, B., 570
Volling, B.L., 580
von Eye, A., 60
von Knorring, A-L., 278
Von Wright, M.R., 488
Vondra, J., 599
Voos, D.K., 133
Vorhees, C.V., 122
Vorster, J., 360
Voyer, D., 476
Voyer, S., 476
Vuchinich, R.A., 589
Vuchinich, S., 526, 575, 589
Vurpillot, E., 275, 276
Vygotsky, L.S., 55, 66, 67, 221, 234, 252, 253, 254, 256, 258, 259, 260, 261, 264, 280, 284, 300, 301, 302, 304, 305, 360

Wachs, T.D., 103
Waddell, K.J., 283
Waddington, C.H., 98
Wagner, B.M., 381, 449
Wagner, E., 61, 530, 533, 537
Wagner, M., 131
Wagner, R.K., 327
Wahl, L., 530
Wainryb, C., 551
Waitzman, K.A., 553
Wakschlag, L.S., 574
Walden, T.A., 396
Waldman, I., 278
Waldman, I.D., 331, 340
Walk, R.D., 198, 199
Walker, A.S., 201
Walker, L.J., 538, 544, 549, 552
Walker, S., 124, 176
Walker-Andrews, A.S., 202, 396
Wall, S., 408, 412
Wallace, C.S., 154
Wallace, I.F., 138, 324
Wallace, P.M., 134
Wallach, M.A., 344
Wallen, K., 492
Wallerstein, J.S., 588
Walsh, M., 477
Walsh, P.V., 504
Walsh, R.O., 566
Walters, A.S., 506, 510
Walters, L., 477
Wang, L., 643
Wang, X., 153
Wang, X.-L., 256
Want, S.C., 217

Ward, L., 581, 582
Ward, S.A., 166
Ward, S.L., 247
Wardrop, J.L., 523
Warfield, M.E., 82
Warford, L., 427
Wark, G.R., 552
Warkentin, V., 437, 438
Warren, M.P., 169, 170, 172, 177
Warren, S., 397
Warren, W., 511
Wartner, U.G., 421
Washington, J., 425
Wasik, B.H., 617
Wasserman, R.C., 153, 167, 169
Wasson C., 425
Watanabe, H., 445
Waterman, A.S., 460, 461, 463
Waters, E., 134, 408, 410, 412, 414, 415, 418, 421, 422, 423
Waters, P.L., 448, 503
Watkins, W.E., 176
Watkinson, B., 120, 121
Watson, A.C., 624
Watson, J.D., 367
Watson, J.B., 39, 47, 50, 54, 58, 62, 65, 104, 574
Watson, J.S., 405
Watson, M.W., 518, 528
Waxman, S.R., 241, 369
Weakliem, D., 327
Weber, E.K., 544
Weber, J.S., 612
Weber, R.A., 531
Wechsler, D., 321
Weed, S., 507
Weikart, D.P., 341
Weinberg, C.R., 119
Weinberg, K.A., 331, 340
Weinberg, M.K., 394
Weinberg, M.S., 508
Weinberg, R.A., 3, 95, 101, 331, 340, 585
Weiner, B., 455
Weinert, F.E., 283
Weinfert, K., 445
Weinfield, N.S., 423
Weinraub, M., 411, 486
Weinstein, C.S., 614
Weisberg, P., 240
Weisberg, R., 275
Weiseman, J.R., 144
Weiskopf, S., 188
Weisner, T.S., 504, 583
Weiss, B., 214, 403, 526
Weiss, L.G., 320, 321
Weiss, L.H., 573
Weiss, M., 393
Weiss, M.G., 276, 277
Weiss, R.J., 518
Weissberg, R.P., 646
Weiss-Perry, B., 450
Weisz, J.R., 403, 414, 415
Weizman, Z.O., 354
Welch, S.L., 177
Welch-Ross, M.K., 484, 499
Wellman, H.M., 271, 275, 374, 379, 397, 440, 441
Wellman, N.E., 519
Wells, L.E., 461
Wender, P.H., 278
Wendland-Carro, J., 129, 130
Wentzel, K.R., 638, 639
Werker, J.F., 189, 206, 359, 362, 365, 366
Werner, E.E., 139
Werner, L.A., 362
Wertsch, J.V., 221, 252, 261
Wessels, H., 429, 430, 593

Weston, D.R.,   419
Wewerka, S.S.,   228
Whalen, C.K.,   278, 478
Whalen, N.,   285, 286
Whaley, K.L.,   641
Whiffen, V.E.,   134
Whipp, B.J.,   166
Whipple, E.,   509
Whipple, E.E.,   597
Whitaker, D.J.,   507, 512
Whitall, J.,   159
Whitbeck, L.B.,   509, 575, 596, 602
Whitbourne, S.K.,   602
White, B.J.,   635
White, D.,   170
White, J. M.,   566
White, K.J.,   642
White, L.,   289
White, R.W.,   451, 452
White, S.H.,   10
White, W.F.,   144
Whitebrook, M.,   428
Whitehead, R.G.,   179
Whitehouse, R.H.,   150
Whitehurst, G.J.,   205, 353, 354, 360, 381
Whitesell, N.R.,   383, 444, 448, 503
Whiteside, L.,   138
Whiting, B.B.,   486, 493, 531, 535, 629
Whiting, J.W.M.,   535
Whitley, B.E., Jr.,   503
Whitman, T.L.,   512
Whitney, M.P.,   142
Whitsell, K.,   364
Whitting, V.,   114, 118, 119, 126
Whittle, M.J.,   85
Whitworth, L.A.,   178
Wichman, C.,   633–634
Wichstrom, L.,   170, 172
Widaman, K.F.,   301
Wiehe, V.R.,   595. 596, 598, 601
Wigfield, A.,,   447, 457, 481, 622
Wiggam, A.E.,   39
Wilcock, A.,   132
Wilcox, A.J.,   119
Wilcox, B.L.,   609
Wilcox, S.A.,   289
Wile, J.,   134
Wilens, T.E.,   278
Wilkinson, S.,   508
Wilkner, K.,   190
Wille, D.,   137
Wille, D.E.,   421
Willems, E.P.,   14
Williams, B.,   615
Williams, B.R.,   165
Williams, C.,   535
Williams, E.M.,   229
Williams, G.A.,   624
Williams, J.E.,   13, 474, 475
Williams, K.,   256
Williams, L.M.,   598
Williams, M.,   189
Williams, S.L.,   355
Williams, T.,   606
Williams, W.M.,   327
Williams-Murphy, M.,   78
Williamson, G.M.,   125

Willms, D.,   178
Willoughby, T.,   37, 283
Wilson Garvan, C.,   121
Wilson, A.,   624
Wilson, D.M.,   172
Wilson, K.S.,   632
Wilson, R.,   86
Wilson, R.S.,   93, 95, 138
Wilson, S.P.,   576
Wilson, V.L.,   83, 124
Wilson-Mitchell, J.E.,   504
Wimbush, D.D.,   574, 576
Winch, G.,   503
Wing, R.R.,   179
Wingard, D.L.,   328
Winick, M.,   124
Winickoff, S.A.,   403
Winne, P.,   283
Winner, E.,   238, 319, 328, 344, 345, 346, 347, 380
Winslow, E.B.,   526, 581
Winslow, E.E.,   587, 589
Winsor, E.,   86
Winterbottom, M.,   453
Wintre, M.G.,   397
Wippman, J.,   421
Wisenbaker, J.,   618
Wissow, L.,   118
Wit, J.M.,   169
Wobie, K.,   121
Wolchik, S.A.,   590
Wolf, A.,   333
Wolfe, D.A.,   597
Wolfe, M.,   508, 524, 585
Wolff, P.H.,   143, 144
Wolfner, G.D.,   596, 597
Wong, T.,   510, 511
Woo, E.,   338
Wood, C.,   278
Wood, D.,   255
Wood, E.,   283
Woods, B.,   196
Woodson, R.,   215
Woodward, A.L.,   367
Woodward, L.,   130, 132
Woody, E.,   37, 639
Woody-Ramsey, J.,   269, 284
Woolley, J.,   440, 441
Work, W. C.,   139
Worrall, W.,   320
Wright, C.,   453, 454
Wright, J.,   611, 612
Wright, J.C.,   178, 606, 607, 608, 612
Wright, S.,   387
Wright, V.,   517
Wu, C.,   445, 596
Wu, F.,   411, 415
Wu, M.,   648, 649
Wusinich, N.,   440
Wyatt, P.,   81
Wyman, P.A.,   139
Wynn, K.,   231

Xia, Y.,   583
Xu, F.,   307, 367, 376, 536
Xu, X.,   512

Yaeger, J.,   260
Yaggi, K.E.,   526, 581
Yang, B.,   583
Yankowitz, J.,   87, 89
Yau, J.,   577
Yazigi, R.A.,   123
Yeates, K.O.,   334, 466
Yee, I.,   197
Yonas, A.,   190, 197
Young, S.K.,   531, 533
Young, W.C.,   492
Youngblade, L.M.,   256
Youngstrom, E.,   575
Younger, A.J.,   639
Youniss, J.,   628
Youth Lifestyle Choices—Community
   University Research Alliance, 509
Yu, A.P.,   477
Yuill, N.,   463
Yussen, S.R.,   281

Zahn, G.L.,   624
Zahn-Waxler, C.,   61, 95, 216, 399, 516, 518, 530, 531, 533, 534, 535, 537, 540, 558
Zaia, A.F.,   639
Zakriski, A.L.,   639
Zalewski, C.,   598
Zani, B.,   170
Zappulla, C.,   643
Zarbatany, L.,   641
Zarlengo-Strouse, P.,   359
Zeisel, S.A.,   429, 430
Zelazo, D.Z.,   292
Zelazo, N.A.,   161
Zelazo, P.D.,   161, 229, 293, 441, 544
Zelazo, P.R.,   161, 293, 411, 429
Zelizer,   8
Zeman, J.,   395
Zerbe, K.J.,   177
Zern, D.S.,   475
Zernicke, R.F.,   161, 162, 163
Zeskind, P.S.,   124, 144, 145, 176
Zhang, H.,   254
Zhou, M.,   577, 623
Zhou, Q.,   532, 533, 535
Zhu, J.,   254
Ziegert, D.I.,   458
Zielhuis, G.A.,   329
Ziemba-Davis, M.,   509
Zigler, E.,   451, 594, 600, 609, 617
Zigler, E.F.,   337, 428, 593, 617
Zimmerman, E.A.,   416
Zimmerman, M.A.,   566
Zimmerman, R.,   406
Ziss, K.,   507
Ziv, Y.,   414, 423
Zoccolillo, M.,   520
Zucker, K.J.,   411
Zuckerman, B.,   214
Zuckerman, D.,   609
Zullig, M.,   132
Zupan, B.A.,   278, 637

Subject Index

ability
  theories of, 456–459
  tracking, 619
abnormalities
  chromosomes and, 80–84
  drugs and, 117–122, 123
  heredity and, 80–88
  prevention of, 126
  teratogens and, 114–124
abuse. *See* child abuse
acceptance/responsiveness, 570
accommodation, 53, 225
achievement
  goals and, 458–459
  scholastic, IQ as predictor of, 326–327
achievement motivation, 451–459
  achievement attributions and, 455–459
  learned helplessness theory of, 457–459
  peer-group influences on, 454
achievement-related attributes, 456–457
active genotype/environment correlations, 101
  active/passive issue, 44
  defined, 40
adaptation, 224
adaptive strategy choice model, 270, 292
ADHD (attention deficit-hyperactivity disorder), 277–278
adolescence, 6, 579. *See also* puberty
  autonomy and, 577–579
  brain development during, 157–158
  cultural differences/influences and, 8
  employment and, 579
  formal operational stage and, 243–249
  Hall and, 10
  intelligence quotient and, 324–326
  life span and, 10
  maturity in, 647
  motor development in, 165–166
  parental socialization and, 570–578
  peers in, 635–637, 647–649
  sexuality and, 505–513
  siblings' experience in, 96–97
  suicide and, 449
adolescent growth spurt, 166
adopted children, 425–426
  bonding and, 134
  environment and, 101, 331
  intelligence and, 94, 330–331, 425–426
adoption design, 90
adrenal glands, 174
affective explanations, 531
age
  achievement motivation and, 451–459
  achievement-related attributes and, 456–457
  altruism and, 531, 534–535
  attention and, 275–277
  blended families and, 591–592
  children's, divorce and, 588
  concepts of self and, 443–444, 468
  counting and, 298

development and, 5
differences, information processing and, 268
differences, memory and, 289–291
information-processing capacity and, 266–267
inhibition and, 274
intelligence tests and, 312–313
maturation, of, 167–169, 171–173
memory and, 279–283
morality and, 543–544
mother's, and pregnancy, 125–126
normal for motor development, 160
person perception and, 463–465
same, interactions, 629
school and, 616–622
self-esteem and, 446–447
television viewing and, 607
age of viability, 113
aggression, 49, 515, 528–530
  controlling, 527
  cultural differences/influences on, 523–525
  development of, 516–530
  home environment and, 525–527
  individual differences in, 520–523
  infants', 516, 520
aging-ova hypothesis, 83
AIDS, 118, 119
alcohol, pregnancy and, 119–120
alleles, 76, 77
  genetic imprinting and, 79
alternative birth centre, 132
altruism, 515, 530–538
  age and, 531, 534–535, 536
  contributors to, 531–535
  cultural differences/influences, 535–538
  defined, 60
  empathy and, 533–535
  "felt responsibility" hypothesis and, 535
  human nature and, 61
  prosocial moral reasoning and, 532–533
  sex differences and, 531
amae, 414
American Sign Language, 356, 373
amniocentesis, 80, 85
amnion, 110
analogical reasoning, 292, 294
androgen, 174
androgenized females, 491–492
androgeny, 501–505
Angelman syndrome, 79
animism, 236
anorexia nervosa, 177, 178
A-not-B error, 229–230
anoxia, 135
Apgar test, 129
aphasia, 355, 356
appearance/reality distinction, 237
arithmetic
  complex computations in, 300, 306
  cultural differences/influences and, 300–303

infants and, 231
mental, 298–300
reasoning and, 298–301
unschooled children and, 300–301
assimilation, 53, 224
associative play, 633
ATI (aptitude-treatment interaction), 620–621
Attachment Q-set (AQS), 412
attachments, 391, 402. *See also* emotional attachments
  multiple, 405
attention, 275–277, 304
  development of, 275–27
  disorders, 277–278
  educational strategies and, 297
  selective, 276
attention span, 275
attribution retraining, 458
authoritative parenting, 454
autobiographical memory, 277–278, 284
automatization, 251, 317
autonomous morality, 542
autonomy, 577–579
autosomes, 74, 81
autostimulation theory, 143
average-status children, 637
avoidant, 412, 420, 422

babbling, 363
babies. *See* newborns
baby biographies, 9–10, 16
Bayley Scales of Infant Development, 323
behaviour
  antisocial, 518, 528–530
  disorders, 277–278
  false-self, 444
  gender-typed, 486–488, 503–505
  heredity and, 88–98, 103–105
  infants', 185–187, 213–215
  intelligent, cultural differences/influences and, 316–317
  moral reasoning and, 552
  morality. *See* morality
  peer acceptance and, 639–640
  sexual, 509
  social, 515–516, 610
behaviour disorders, heredity and, 97–98
behavioural genetics, 88
behavioural inhibition, 400
behavioural responses, 185–187, 210–211
behavioural schemes, 223
behaviourism, 47–48
belief-desire theory, 440–441
benefits-to-risk ratio, 32
bilingualism, 356, 383–387
bioecological theory, 62. *See also* ecological systems theory
biosocial theory, 489–495
birth labour

delivery medication and, 130
stages of, 127
birth(s)
    bonding and, 130, 133–134
    complications, 135–139
    cultural attitudes to, 130–133
    defects in. *See* abnormalities
    delivery medication and, 130
    father's experience and, 134–135
    home, 132–133
    labour. *See* birth labour
    mother's experience and, 133–134
    multiple, 73–74
    natural or prepared, 131
    newborn's risk and recovery, 139
    order, IQ and, 334
    postpartum depression and, 130, 134
    process, 127–135
    rates of, 567
    social environment and, 133–135
    weight, 136–137
blastocyst, 109, 110
blended families, 591–592
blood types, 77
body image, 169–170
Body-Esteem scale, 170
bonding. *See* emotional attachments
bound morphenes, 352
brain
    computers and, 264, 305–306
    developing mind and, 249, 267
    development of, 153–158
    differentiation and growth, 155–158
    hemispheres, 156–157
    injuries, infant, 157–158
    language and, 355
    neural development and plasticity of, 153–155
brain growth spurt, 153
breech birth, 135
Broca's area, 355
bulimia, 177, 178
bullying, 51, 523

CAH (congenital adrenal hyperplasia), 491
Canadian Cognitive Abilities Test, 322
canalization, 98–99
cancer, cervical, 119
cardinality, 298
caregiving
    maternal employment and, 428–431, 592–594
    parenting fathers and, 419
    quality of, 415–418
    sensitivity and, 416–417
    temperament and, 420
carrier, 76
case study, 16
Case's theory. *See* neo-Piagetian theory
castration anxiety, 495
catch-up growth, 175, 179
categorical self, 438
cells
    body, 71
    differentiation and synaptogenesis, 154
    germ/sex, 71–72
    sperm, 71
centred thinking, 238
cephalocaudal development, 150–151
cerebral cortex, 156
cerebral lateralization, 156
cerebrum, 156
cesarean section, 118, 119
chemicals and pollutants. *See* environmental hazards
child abuse, 15, 356, 595–601
    consequences of, 597–599
    cultural differences/influences on, 597

child effects model, 573
child-directed speech, 359
childbirth. *See* birth(s)
childhood, 6
    intelligence quotient and, 324–326
    modern-day perspective on, 7–9
children. *See also* adolescence; newborns; siblings; twins
    abused. *See* child abuse
    adopted. *See* adopted children
    aggression and, 49
    information processing and, 57
    motor development in, 165–166
    personality/environment and, 96–102
    popularity and, 637–641
    rights of, 9, 32
    single, 583
    socialization of, 563–564, 628–649
    subjects, as, 9–10
    temperament, 401
    witnesses, as, 289–291
chorion, 110
chorionic villus sampling, 80, 86
chromosomes, 71, 72, 73, 79
    abnormalities and, 80–84
    X and Y, 74–75, 78–79, 81, 111, 473–474
chronosystem, 64
circular reactions, 226–227
circumcision, 190
class. *See* social class school; schools
class inclusion, 237–238
classical conditioning, 208–210
classification, 237–238, 241
clinical method, 12, 13–14, 222
cliques, 635
code mixing, 385, 386
code switching, 385, 386
codominance, 77–78
coercive home environment, 525–526
cognition, 221
cognitive competencies, social origins of, 254–258
cognitive development, 65
    computers and, 613–614
    concrete-operational stage, 241–244
    connectionism and, 305–308
    defined, 51, 221
    explaining, 250
    formal operational stage, 243–249
    identity formation, 461
    infants', 203
    information-processing theory and, 303–305
    intuitive period, 238
    language and, 259–260
    Piaget's stages of, 53, 54, 226–250
    preoperational stage, 233–241
    sensorimotor stage, 226, 229–232
    social and cultural influences, 250
    television and, 610–612
cognitive equilibrium, 222
cognitive operation, 224
cognitive process, 224–225
    control of, 266
    strategies and, 268–272
cognitive schemes, 223–224
cognitive self-guidance system, 259
cognitive structure, 52
cognitive tasks, 313–314
cognitive-developmental theory, 52–58
    attachment, of, 407
    comparing Vygotsky's and Piaget's, 260
    knowing about others and, 465–466
    moral development and, 541–554
    neo-Piagetian, 251
    Piaget's, 52–55, 221–252
    stranger anxiety and, 411–412
cohort effect, 26

colour blindness, 77, 78–79, 84
committed compliance, 559
communal society, 445
communication, 350. *See also* language
    defined, 350
    skills, 378–379, 381–383
compensatory interventions, 340
competence vs. performance, 249
computer-assisted instruction (CAI), 613
computers, 613–615
    cognitive development and, 613–614
    human mind and, 264, 305–306
    Internet use and, 613, 615
    social impacts of, 614, 615
computers video games and, 615
conception, 70, 71
concepts of self, 443–444, 469
conceptual similarity, 292
concordance rate, 91
concrete operations, 241
concrete-operational stage, 53, 241–244
conditioning, 208–215
    viewpoint, 213
conduct disorders, 403
confidentiality, 33
configural processing, 196
conflict, effects of, 586–589
    extended, 566
    gay/lesbian, 585–586
    single-parent, 567
confluence hypothesis, 334
confounding variable, 21
congenital defects, 80
connectionism, 305–308
connectionist theory, 305–308
conservation, 241
    defined, 238
consolidation, 251
constructivism, 233
constructivist, 222
contact comfort, 406
context-independent learning, 255–257
contexts, 58
contextual model, 65
continuity, 2, 26
continuity/discontinuity issue, 40–41
controversial children, 637
convergent thinking, 344
cooing, 362
cooperative learning methods, 624
cooperative play, 633
coordination, children's, 165
coparenting, 565, 590, 593
corpus callosum, 156
correlation coefficient, 19
correlational design, 19–20
counterconditioning, 209
counting, 298
CR (conditioned response), 209
creativity, 344–347
    education and, 347
    investment theory and, 345–347
    multicomponent perspective, 345–347
    psychometric perspective and, 344
    viewing television and, 615
creole, 357
critical period, 60. *See also* sensitive period
cross-cultural comparison, 29–31
    defined, 30
    gender roles and, 30
cross-generational problem, 28
cross-pressures, 647
cross-sectional design, 24–26
    defined, 24
    strengths and limitations, 29
crossing-over, 72, 73
crowds, 635

crying, infants', 59, 143–145
CS (conditioned stimulus), 209
cued recall, 280
cultural bias, 317
  moral development and, 551–552
cultural differences/influences
  adolescence and, 8
  arithmetic and, 300–303
  child abuse and, 597
  emotional attachments and, 414–415
  formal operations and, 246–250
  gender roles and, 30
  information processing and, 267
  intellectual performance and, 255,
    336–340
  intelligence tests and, 320
  intelligent behaviour and, 316–317
  language and, 301–302, 367
  memory and, 283–284
  motor development and, 161
  perception and, 206
  physical growth and, 153
  punishment and, 214
  schools and, 625–628
  soothing of newborns and, 146
  zone of proximal development and, 257
cultural test bias hypothesis, 336
culture, 16, 29, 44, 55
  development, 5
  identity formation, 462
culture-fair IQ tests, 336
cumulative-deficit hypothesis, 325
cystic fibrosis, 84, 87

data gathering. See gathering data
day care, 593
deafness, 189, 356, 357, 373
  infants and, 363
decentration, 238
deductive reasoning, 243, 245
deferred imitation, 216, 228, 286
delinquency
  chronic, 527–528
  home environment and, 525–528
demandingness/control, 570
dependent variable, 20, 21
deprivation dwarfism, 179–180
depth perception, 198–199
DES (diethylstibestrol), 119
description, 3
desensitization hypothesis, 608
desire theory, 440
development, 5. See also brain; cognitive
    development; growth; individual theories;
    learning
  Bronfenbrenner's contexts for, 62–64
  character of, 4–6
  culture, 5
  cumulative, 4
  defined, 2, 3
  designs for studying, 24–29
  hereditary influences on. See heredity
  historical perspective, 6–11
  measures of, 10
  origins of science of, 9–11
  philosophies, summary of, 67
  physical growth, 5
  prenatal, environment and, 114–126
  psychosocial, 5
  sex differences and, 476
  social class, 5
  stages of, 43, 44–46
  subculture, 5
  systematic change, 2
  theories of, 10–11
developmental continuities, 2

developmental psychology
  defined, 2
  research methods in. See research/design
    methods
developmental quotients, 323, 335
developmental stage, 41
developmentalist, 2
  goals of, 3
diabetes, 84, 85
differences, information processing and, 268
differences, memory and, 289–291
differentiating information, 382
differentiation theory, 184, 202, 203–206
diffusion effect, 342
direct tuition, 495
discipline. See punishment
discovery-based education, 243
discovery-based educational programs, 54
diseases
  pregnancy and, 116–117
  sexually transmitted, 118, 510
disequilibriums, 53
dishabituation, 186, 207
distinctive features, 184
divergent thinking, 344
divorce, 568, 586–589
divorce mediation, 590
DNA, 71
  testing, 80, 85
doctrine of specificity, 554
domain specific, 442
  processing efficiency, 267
dominant allele, 76
dominant-recessive inheritance, 76–77
double standard, 507
Down syndrome, 81–83, 85
drugs
  illicit, 120–121
  pharmaceutical/prescription, 118–119
  pregnancy and, 117–122, 123
dual encoding, 237
dual representation, 234
Duchenne-type muscular dystrophy, 84, 85
dynamic assessment, 323
dynamical systems theory, 159

eating behaviours, 175–180
eclectics, 66
ecological systems theory, 51, 58, 62–65
  contributions, 64–65
  criticisms, 64–65
  defined, 62
ecological validity, 22
ectoderm, 110
education
  compensatory, 340–344
  computers and, 613–614
  creativity and, 347
  memory and, 297–303
  moral growth and, 550
  Piaget on, 243
  schools and. See schools
  sociocultural, theory and, 258
  television and, 606–607, 610–612
  Vygotsky's theory and, 258
ego, 44
  defined, 42
egocentric speech, 259
egocentrism, 236, 238–240, 246–247
elaboration, 280
elaborative interrogation, 283
Electra complex, 43, 495
electroencephalogram, 17
embryo, 109, 110–111
embryonic disk, 109
emergent learning, 205

emotional attachments, 59, 402–412, 420–423
  cultural differences/influences, 414–415
  deprivation of, 421–423, 425–426
  friendships and. See friendships
  individual differences in, 412–415
  infant characteristics and, 418–420
  newborns and, 133–134, 404–412
  quality and outcome of, 421–423
  reciprocal, 402–403
  role taking and, 467–468
  security and, 412–420, 421
  synchronized routines and, 403–404
  theories of, 405–409
emotional bonding, 133
emotional development, 391–398
  caregiving and, 428–431
  early, 397–398
  expressions and, 392–395
  maternal employment and, 428–431
  primary attachments and, 404–405
  temperament and. See temperament
emotional reactivity, 391
emotions, 393
  classical conditioning of, 209
  conversations about, 396–397
  display rules of, 393–395
  displaying, 392–395
  moral, 552–554
  physical development and, 179–180
  pregnancy and, 125
  primary, 393
  recognizing/interpreting, 396–398
  regulating, 394–395
  secondary, 393
  self-conscious, 393
  self-evaluative, 393
  sex differences and, 478–479
  shyness. See shyness
  socialization of, 393–395
empathic concern, 94
empathy, 397, 530
  altruism and, 533–535
  defined, 61
empiricist, 184
employment
  adolescence and, 579
  maternal, caregiving and, 428–431,
    592–594
  women and, 568
encoding, 215
endocrine, 174
endocrinology, 174–175
endoderm, 110
engrossment, 134
enrichment theory, 184, 202
  perception, 205
enrichment vs. differentiation, 184–185, 202
environment
  child abuse and, 596–598
  genotype and, 100–102
  heredity and, 98–102
  home. See home environment
  intelligence and, 99–100
  intelligence tests, 91, 331
  perinatal, 127–135
  personality and, 96–97
  physical development and, 174–180
environmental determinism, 50
environmental hazards, pregnancy and,
    122–123
environmental hypothesis, 339–340
environmental layers, 62–64
environments, 3
epistemology, 52
equilibration, 222
Erikson's psychosocial theory, 44–46
estrogen, 174

ethical issues, 31–33
  hereditary disorders and, 88–89
ethical theory of attachment, 407–408
  stranger anxiety and, 411
ethnography, 16
ethology, 58
ethology theory, 58–61
event memory, 277, 284, 286
event-related potentials, 17
evocative genotype/environment correlations, 100
evoked potential, 186, 188
evolutionary theory. See ethology theory
executive control process, 266
exosystem, 64
expansions, 360
experiences, 2
experimental control, 21
experimental design, 20–22
explanation, 3
explicit cognition, 271
exploratory play, 256
expressive role, 474
expressive style, 367
extended self, 437
extinction, 209
extrafamilial influences, 605
eyewitnesses, 289–291

face perception, infants', 194
facial attractiveness, 638–639
facial gestures, newborns', 215–216
fact finding. See gathering data
factor analysis, 313
FAE (fetal alcohol effects), 119
false memories, 289–292
false-belief task, 239, 441
falsifiability, 38
family, 601–602. See also home environment; parenting
  adoptions and, 584–585
  blended, 568–569, 589, 591–592
family study, 89–91
FAS (fetal alcohol syndrome), 119
fast-mapping, 367
fear, 392, 409–412
  sex differences and, 478
"felt responsibility" hypothesis, 535
fertilization, 71
fetal DNA testing, 80
fetal surgery, 87–89
fetus, 109, 111–113
  handedness and, 157
  immune system of, 116
  weight of, 136–137
field experiment, 22
first stage of labour, 127
fixation, 43
Flynn effect, 248, 331
folic acid, 83, 124–125
forbidden-toy paradigm, 555
foreclosure, 459
forgetting, 281–282
form perception, 193–196
formal operational stage, 53, 243–249
  cultural differences/influences, 246–250
formal operations, 243
Fragile-X syndrome, 81, 85
free morphenes, 352
free recall, 280
Freud's psychosexual theory, 41–44
friendships, 458, 641–654
  quality of, 645
frontal cortex, 156
functional MRI, 17

functional play, 235
fuzzy-trace theory, 272–274

gametes, 72
gathering data, 12–18
  case studies, 16
  clinical method, 13–14
  ethnography, 16–17
  interviews and questionnaires, 13
  observational methodologies, 14–16
  psychophysiological methods, 17–18
  reliability and validity, 12
  self-report methods, 12–14
gender. See also sex
  androgynous. See androgeny
  cultural differences/influences on, 30
  skills and, 165–166
gender concept, 482–484
gender identity, 482, 498
gender intensification, 485
gender role development, 490–492
gender role socialization, 165–166
gender role standard, 474
gender roles, 473–475, 479–481, 506
  changing attitudes to, 503–505
  cultural influences and, 30
  stereotypes of, 484–486
gender schemas, 498
gender segregation, 486–488
gender stereotype, 13, 480
gender typing, 474, 482–488
  biosocial theory of, 489–495
  cognitive-developmental theory and, 497–498
  cultural differences/influences on, 493–494
  gender schema theory and, 498–500
  integrative theory and, 500–501
  psychoanalytic theory and, 495
  social-labelling influences on, 492–495
  social learning theory and, 495–497
gene replacement therapy, 87–89
general mental factor (g), 313
generalizability, 16
genes, 2, 70. See also genotype; heredity
  abnormalities and, 80–85
  dominant/recessive, 76–78
  function of, 75
  intelligence and, 91–94
  mutation of, 84
  patterns of expression of, 76–80
  RH factor and, 135
  siblings' experience and, 96–97
genetic code, 71
genetic counselling, 85
genetic engineering, 88
genetic epistemology, 222
genetic hypothesis, 337–339
genetic imprinting, 79
genital herpes, 118, 119
genitals, 111
  growth of, 152
genotype, 70, 71, 76, 77, 88, 99
  environment and, 100–102
  physical development and, 173
germinal period, 109–110
germline gene therapy, 88–89
gestures
  facial, and newborns, 215–216
  language and, 357, 364, 373
  newborns', 364
GH (growth hormone), 174, 180
giftedness, 344. See also creativity
gist, 272
glia, 154
goal-directed behaviour, 227
goals, achievement and, 458–459

gonads, 111
goodness of fit, 401, 420
grammar, 360, 374–378
  transformational, 376–377
  universal, 354
grammatical morphenes, 375
grasping, 163
growth. See also motor development; physical development
  body proportions and, 150–151
  brain, of, 153–158
  disorders, 179–180
  height and weight, in, 150, 166
  maturation and, 150–153
  muscular development and, 152
  physical, individual differences in, 168
  skeletal development and, 151–152
  variations in physical development and, 152–153
guided participation, 255–258

habits, 47
habituation, 185, 187, 207–208
  developmental trends and, 207
  individual differences, and, 207–208
handedness, fetuses and, 157
Head Start, 340, 342
hearing, 188–190
  loss of, 189
hemophilia, 84, 85, 87
hereditary disorders, 80–88
  treating, 87–89
heredity, 93–94. See also genes; inheritance
  abnormalities and, 80–88
  behaviour and, 88–98, 103–105
  behaviour disorders and, 97–98
  environment and, 98–102
  gender roles and, 490–491
  group differences in IQ and, 337–339
  hierarchical model of, 315
  infant, assessing, 323–324
  information-processing theory and, 316–318
  intellectual performance and, 93–94
  intelligence tests, 93–94, 329–331
  kinds of, 315, 318–319
  measuring, 319–326
  mental illness and, 97–98
  misconceptions about, 95
  multiple, 318–319
  personality and, 94–97
  principles of, 70–80
  psychometric view of, 312–315
  structure of, 223–224
  uniqueness and, 72–73
heritability, 89
  estimates, misconceptions about, 95
heritability coefficient, 92
herpes simplex, 118
heteronomous morality, 541
heterozygous, 76
heuristic value, 38
high-amplitude sucking method, 186
high-risk neighbourhood, 596
HIV, 118
holistic, 5
holistic perspective, 3
home environment, 332–335. See also family; parenting
  achievement motivation and, 453–454
  intelligence tests and, 332–335
HOME inventory, 332–335, 453
home-visitor program, 599
homosexuality, 508. See also sexual orientation
homozygous, 76
horizontal décalage, 242

hormone(s)
    contraceptives and, 119
    gender roles and, 491
    physical development and, 173–175
    sex, 111
hostile aggression, 516
hostile attributional bias, 521
Human Genome Project, 88
Huntington's disease, 77, 80, 85, 87
hypothalmus, 174
hypotheses, 243–246
hypothesis, defined, 11
hypothetical propositions, children's responses
    to, 244
hypothetico-deductive reasoning, 243–245

id, 42
identity, 459–462. See also self-concept
identity achievement, 460
identity crisis, 459
identity diffusion, 459
identity formation, 460–462
identity training, 240
ideographic development, 3
illnesses, physical development and, 179
imaginary audience, 246
imitation
    development of, 228
    newborns', 215–217
immanent justice, 542, 544
immersion, 386
immune system
    fetus, of, 116
    maturation and, 152, 179
    pregnancy and, 124–125
implantation, 109–110
implicit cognition, 271
imprinting, 58, 408
in-group/out-group schema, 499
inclusion, 624
incompatible-response technique, 528
independent assortment, 72
independent variable, 20, 21, 23
induction, 551–560
inefficient inhibition, 274
infant states, 142–146
infanticide, 6–7
infantile amnesia, 285, 286
infantile autism, 81
infants. See also newborns
    aggression, 516
inferences, 380
informal curriculum, 616
information processing, 56–58, 207–217,
    264–265
    academic skills and, 297–303
    capacity, age and, 266–267
    Case's theory and, 251
    correcting mistakes and, 57
    efficiency and age differences, 268
    fuzzy-trace theory and, 272–274
    memory and, 297–303
    social influences on, 267–268
    speed changes in, 267–268
    strategy development and, 268–272
    triarchic theory and, 317–318
information-processing capacity, 266–267
information-processing model, 213
information-processing theory, 56–58, 207–217
    cognitive development and, 303–305
    computers and, 264
    defined, 56
    intelligence and, 316–318
    limited-capacity assumption, 264
    Piaget's cognitive development theory and,
        266–268

informed consent, 32
inheritance. See also heredity
    dominant-recessive, 76–77
    parent-specific patterns of, 79
    polygenic, 79–80
    sex-linked, 78–79
inhibition, 274
    moral conduct and, 555
inhibitory controls, 555
innate purity, 8
inner experimentation, 227
instincts, 59
    defined, 42
instrumental aggression, 516
instrumental role, 474
intellectual development. See also cognitive
    development
    culture and, 253–254
intellectual performance. See also intelligence
    tests
    compensatory education and, 340–344
    continuity in, 324–325
    cultural test bias hypothesis and, 336
    environmental hypothesis, 339–340
    genetic hypothesis and, 337–339
    group differences in, 336–340
intelligence, 222–223, 311–347. See also
    cognitive development
    defined, 222
    defining, 312, 316
    environment and, 99–100
    factor analysis and, 313–315
    growth of, 52–53, 139
intelligence quotient, 319
intelligence tests, 91–94, 312–313, 319–326
    ability tracking and, 619
    birth order, family size and, 334
    cultural bias and, 336–337
    cultural differences/influences, 320,
        336–339
    developmental quotient and, 323
    environment, 91, 331
    group, 322
    heredity, 93–94, 329–331
    home environment and, 332
    infants' integrated senses and, 202
    new approaches to, 323
    norms, 320
    origins of, 312–315
    Piaget and, 52
    predictor, as, 326–329
    race/ethnicity and, 335
    scores, distribution of, 322
    scores, factors the influence, 329–331
    social class and, 335
    stability of, 324–326
    twins and, 91
interactionist model, 222
interactionist theory, 358–361
intermodal perception, 200–203
    development of, 201–202
    theories of, 202
internal working models, 422
internalization, 538
internet. See under computers
intervention. See compensatory
    interventions
interviews, 12, 13
intrinsic orientation to achievement, 453
introverion-extroversion, 94
intuitive period, 238
invariant development sequence, 226
    defined, 53
investment theory, 345–347
invisible displacements, 229
IQ, 248, 319. See also intelligence tests
iron deficiency anemia, 176

kangaroo mother care, 138
karyotypes, 74–75
Kaufman Assessment Battery for Children, 323
kewpie-doll effect, 408
kinetic cues, 197–198
kinship, 90
Klinefelter's syndrome, 82, 87
knowledge base, 282–283
kwashiorkor, 176

LAD (language acquisition device), 354
language, 350–351. See also language learning;
    speech
    arithmetic and, 301–302
    brain and, 355
    children's "invention" of, 357
    cognitive development and, 259–260
    cultural differences/influences, 301–302, 367
    deafness and. See deafness
    defined, 350
    deprivation, 356, 357
    gestures and. See gestures
    infants' habituation and, 208
    intelligence tests and, 320
    metalinguistic awareness and, 380–381
    newborns and, 189–190, 361–364
    nonverbal, 353, 364
    Piaget's theory of, 259
    symbolism, 234
    Vygotsky's theory and, 259
language development, 384
    factors influencing, 358–361
    theories of, 353–361
language learning, 233, 307, 360
    adolescence and, 379–383
    cognitive development and, 259–260
    components of. See phonology; pragmatics;
        semantics; syntax
    constraints and, 369–370
    conversation and, 361–361
    cultural differences/influences, 367
    grammar and. See grammar
    holophrastic period, 365–370
    holophrastic phase of, 365–370
    multi-, 356, 383–387
    prelinguistic period and, 361–364
    preschool period, 374–379
    productive, 364
    receptive, 364
    speech and. See speech
    telegraphic period, 371–374
    vocabulary building and, 365–367
    Vygotsky's theory of, 259
    word meanings and, 367–371
lanugo, 113
latchkey children, 593–594
learned helplessness, 425–426, 427
    theory, 457–459
learning, 183. See also development
    classical conditioning and, 208–210
    context-independent, 255–257
    defined, 2, 207
    habituation and, 207–208
    language. See language learning
    observational, 49, 215–217
    operant conditioning and, 210–215
    perception and, 203–218
    perceptual, 203–206
    read, to, 208
    schools and. See schools
    sociocultural, theory and, 258
learning goals, 459
learning processes, 207–217
learning theories, 353–354
    attachment, of, 406–407
    contributions and criticisms, 50–51

learning theorists, 65
lexical contrast constraint, 369
life crises, 44–45
life outcomes, IQ as predictor of, 327–329
linguistic universals, 353, 355
LMC (language-making capacity), 354
locomotor development, 158–166
longitudinal design
  defined, 26
  strengths and limitations, 29
looking-glass self, 434, 438
loom, 197
Lorge-Thorndike Test, 322

macrosystem, 64
magnetic imaging resonance, 17
malnutrition. *See* nutrition
manic depression, 97
marasmus, 176
marriage
  postponement of, 567
  re-, 568–569, 589, 591–592
mastery motive, 451
maternal deprivation hypothesis, 425
maternity blues, 134
mathematical ability, 477
mathematics. *See* arithmetic
maturation, 2, 150–158, 166–169, 171–173
  defined, 2
  growth and, 150–153, 166–169
  individual differences in, 168
mean-world beliefs, 608
mechanistic model, 65
media. *See also* television
  gender typing and, 497
  violence and aggression, 21, 22
media violence, 21, 22, 608
  peer, perpetrators and victims of, 522–523
  sex differences and, 477
  social information-processing theory of, 521–522
meiosis, 72–73
memory, 277–292
  autobiographical, 277–278
  cultural differences/influences, 283–284
  education, 304
  educational strategies and, 297
  eyewitnesses and, 289–291
  false, 289–292
  fuzzy-trace theory and, 272–274
  infants', 207–217
  infants' learning and, 212–213
  information retention/retrieval and, 277–292
  knowledge base and, 282–283
  knowledge of, 281
  legal testimony and, 291–292
  organization and, 279–280
  performance and, 281–282
  retrieval, 280–281
  scripted, 286–287
  short/long term, 265, 266
  social construction of, 287–289
  strategies, 277–283
  working, 265
memory span, 266
menarche, 168
menstruation, first, 168
mental abilities, 313–314
mental age, 313, 319
mental illness, heredity and, 97–98
mental retardation, 328, 329
mental seriation, 242
mental states, 439–441
mesoderm, 110
mesosystem, 63

metacognition, 266, 271, 281, 296
metalinguistic awareness, 381
metamemory, 281–282
microgenetic development, 253
microsystem, 62
midwifery, 132–133
mind
  biology and, 442
  brain and, 249, 267
  capacity/performance relationship, 264, 312
  computers and, 264, 305–306
  cultural differences/influences on, 445
  theory of, 439–443
mitosis, 71
mnemonics, 277
moral behaviour, 539
moral conduct
  moral character and, 554
  moral reasoning and, 552
  punishment and, 555–556, 557–560
  reinforcement and, 555
  social models and, 556–557
moral development
  cognitive-developmental theory of, 541–554
  cultural differences/influences and, 551–552
  gender bias and, 552, 553
  Kohlberg's theory of, 545–554
  parents and, 557–560
  Piaget's theory of, 541–544
  psychoanalytic theory and, 539–540
  temperament and, 559
moral reasoning, 539
moral relativism, 542
moral rules, 544
morality, 515, 538–539
  age and, 543–544
  altruism and, 532–533
  conscience and, 547–548
  conventional, 546
  Oedipal, 539–540
  parents and, 544
  peer, 549
  punishment and, 546
  social learning and, 554–557
  temptation and, 555–557
morality of care, 552
morality of justice, 552
moratorium, 460
morphemes, 352, 374–376
morphene, 307
morphological knowledge, 380
morphology, 352
mortality, 543–544
motherese, 359
motion, infants' perception of, 193–195, 197–198
motivation, 205
motor development
  childhood and adolescence, in, 165–166
  cultural variations in, 161
  depth perception and, 199–200
  dynamic, goal-directed systems, as, 159–162
  early, psychological implications of, 164–165
  experiential (practice) hypothesis and, 159
  "laws" of, 158
  maturational viewpoint on, 159
  skills and, 159–162
  voluntary reaching and, 162–163
muscles, development of, 152
muscular dystrophy, 84, 85
music, infants and, 206
mutations, 84
mutual exclusivity, 369
myelin, 154, 156
myelinization, 156, 251, 268

nativist, 184
nativist theory, 354–358, 442
natural (quasi-) experiment, 23
natural environment, 62
natural selection, 58
natural setting, 22
naturalistic observation, 14
nature/nurture issue, 70, 184
  defined, 39
NBAS (Neonatal Behavioural Assessment Scale), 129
negative punishment, 210
negative reinforcement, 525
negative reinforcer, 210
neo-nativism, 229–232
neo-Piagetian theory, 251
neonate, 125–126. *See also* newborns
networks, 306–307
neural tube, 110
neurons, 154
neurotic disorder, 97–98
newborns
  adopted, bonding of, 134
  aggression and, 520
  appearance of, 128–129
  assessing condition of, 129
  birth process of, 127–135
  bonding, 130, 424–428
  crawling, and, 164–165
  Darwin and, 9
  experience of, 127–128
  family system and, 580, 581
  fathers and, 419
  fussy, 145
  gestures and nonverbal responses, 364
  growth of. *See* growth
  infant states of, 142–146
  language and, 189–190, 361–364
  operant conditioning and, 211–213
  parents and, 130
  preterm, 136–138
  readiness for life, 140–146
  reflexes of, 140–141
  soothing, 145
  sucking and, 186–187
no-nonsense parenting, 576
nonorganic failure to thrive, 179–180
nonrepresentative sample, 27
nonsocial activity, 633
normal distribution, 322
normative development, 3
norms for motor development, 160
NSE (nonshared environmental influence), 92, 96
nutrition
  physical development and, 175–179
  pregnancy and, 124–125
  problems, 175–179

obesity, 178–179
object permanence, 228–229, 230, 358
object scope constraint, 369
observational learning, 48–49, 215–217
  defined, 48, 215
  imitation and, 215–217
  without reinforcement, 49
observational methodologies, 14–16
observer influence, 15
odours. *See* taste and smell
Oedipal morality, 539–540
Oedipus complex, 43, 495
ontogenetic development, 253
operant, 47
operant (instrumental) conditioning, consequence of responses, and, 210–211, 212

defined, 210
  infancy, in, 211–212
operant learning, 48
operating efficiency hypothesis, 268
operational schemes, 224
operational thought, 241–242
optical flow, 164, 200
organismic model, 65
organization, 224
original sin, 8
orphans. *See* adopted children
otitis media, 189
ovaries, 111
overextension, 368
overregularization, 376
ovum, 109
own-sex schema, 499

pain, infants', 143–145, 190–191
parallel play, 633
parent effects model, 573
parenting. *See also* caregiving; family; home
    environment
  achievement motivation and, 453–454
  altruism and, 537–538
  attachment and, 423
  authoritative, 571–574
  child-rearing and, 570–578
  compensatory education and, 341, 342
  dimensions of, 570
  education and, 341, 621, 623, 627
  employment, caregiving and, 430–431,
    592–594
  identity formation, 461
  influence of, 104, 646–649
  moral development and, 557–560
  morality and, 544
  newborns and, 130
  patterns of, 570–574
  peer sociability and, 636–637, 638
  permissive, 571–572
  single, 567
  style, self-esteem and, 450
  uninvolved, 572–573
parenting fathers, 419
parsimony, 38
participant observation. *See* observational
    methodologies
passive genotype/environment correlations,
    100
passive victims, 522
pattern perception, 192–196
peer groups, 635
peers
  acceptance/popularity and, 637–641
  achievement motivation and, 454
  aggression and, 522–523
  behavioural attributes and, 639–640
  cultural differences/influences on, 647
  facial attractiveness and, 638–639
  frequency of contacts of, 630
  influence of, 630–632, 646–649
  schools and, 621
  sociability development of, 632–637
  socialization agents, as, 628–649
perception, 183
  cultural influences on, 206
  defined, 184
  depth, 198–199
  infants' experiences and, 185–187,
    203–206
  intermodal, 200–203
  three-dimensional space, of, 196–200
  visual, 191–200
perceptual learning, 203–206
perceptual similarity, 296

performance goals, 458
performance vs. competence, 249
perinatal environment, 127
period of fetus, 109, 111–113
period of the embryo, 109, 110–111
period of the zygote, 109
permissive non-intervention, 551–560
person perception, 463–465
person praise, 458
personal agency, 436
personality
  components of, 42–43
  environment and, 96–97
  heredity and, 94–97
  resemblances among family members, 95–96
perspective-taking, 239
phallic stage, 495
phenotype, 70, 71, 77, 88
phonemes, 189–190, 205, 351
phonics, 205
phonology, 351, 384
phylogenetic, development, 253
physical activity play, 167
physical development. *See also* growth
  biological mechanisms and, 173–175
  causes and correlates of, 173–180
  cultural differences and, 153
  environmental influences and, 174–180
  illnesses and, 179
  individual differences, and, 168
  puberty, 169–170
  variations in, 152–153
physiological responses, 185–187
Piaget's cognitive development theory, 52–55,
    221–252
  evaluation of, 248–250
  information-processing theory and, 266–268
pictorial cues, 197, 197–198
pidgin, 357
pincer grasp, 163
pituitary gland, 174
PKU (phenylketonuria), 84, 87
placenta, 110
plasticity, 5, 154
play, 235, 633–635, 636–637
  development and, 235
  pretend, 234
Poly-X (superfemale) syndrome, 82
polygenic trait, 79–80
popular children, 637
positive punishment, 210
positive reinforcer, 210
post-traumatic stress disorder, 598
postnatal environment, 138
postpartum depression, 130, 134
poverty, 332, 342, 578
power assertion, 551–560
practice effects, 27
pragmatics, 352, 363, 371, 372–374, 378–379
preadapted characteristic, 408
precausal reasoning, 236
preconceptual period, 233–238
preconeptual reasoning, 236–238
preference method, 185
pregnancy, 108–146
  diseases and, 116–117
  drugs and, 117–122, 123
  environmental hazards and, 122–123
  genetic imprinting and, 79
  hereditary disorders and, 85
  mother's age and, 125–126
  mother's emotional state and, 125
  mother's nutrition and, 124–125
  smoking and, 120
  teenage, 511–513
prelinguistic phase, 361
premodern perspective on childhood, 6–7

premoral, 541
prenatal classes, 130
prenatal development, 108–146
  defined, 108
prenatal experiences, 61
preoperational, 53
  stage, 233–241
present self, 437
preterm infants, 136–138
primary circular reactions, 226
primary mental abilities, 313
primary motor area, 156
primary sensory area, 156
primitive reflexes, 141
private speech, 259–260
proactive aggression, 520–522
problem solving, 292
  skills, 226–228
process-oriented praise, 459
processing constraints, 369
production deficiencies, 268–269
productive language, 364
proprioceptive feedback, 436
proprioceptive information, 163
prospective study, 644
protection from harm, 33
provocative victims, 522
proximodistal development, 151
psychoanalytic theory, 10–11, 41–46, 65
  attachment, of, 406
  Erikson's psychosocial theory, 44–46
  Freud's psychosexual theory, 41–44
  gender typing and, 495
  moral development and, 539–540
psycholinguists, 351
psychological abuse, 595
psychological tests, 12
psychometric theory, intelligence and,
    312–315
psychophysiological methods, 17–18
psychosexual theory, 41–44
psychosocial theory, 44–46
  gender typing and, 495
puberty, 166–173. *See also* adolescence
  defined, 166
  physical changes, reactions to, 169–170
  psychological effects of, 169–173
  social effects of, 170–171
  timing of, 171–173, 491
punisher, 210
  defined, 48
punishment, 210–211
  controlling behaviour, for, 213–215
  moral conduct and, 555–556, 557–560
  morality and, 546
  negative, 210
  positive, 210
pupillary reflex, 187
Pygmalion effect, 623–624

qualitative change, 40
quantitative change, 40
questionnaire, 10, 12
  structured, 13

race/ethnicity, 576–577
  IQ and, 335
  schools and, 621, 623
racism, 464
radiation, pregnancy and, 122
random assignment, 21
randomization, 21
range-of-reaction principle, 99
Raven Progressive Matrices Test, 336
reaction range. *See* range-of-reaction principle

reactive aggression, 520–522
reactive attachment disorder, 425
reading. *See under* learning
reasoning, 233–250, 292, 294
  arithmetic skills and, 298–301
  casual, 240
  deductive/inductive, 245–246
  formal, 246–250
  giftedness and. *See* creativity
  guidcd participation and, 255–257
  hypothetico-deductive, 243–245
  moral, moral conduct and, 552
  moral, prosocial, 532–533
  Piaget's theory of, 259
  preconceptual, 236–238
  Vygotsky's theory of, 259
recasts, 360
receptive language, 364
receptive vocabulary, 380
recessive allelle, 76
reciprocal determinism, 50
referential communication, 379
referential style, 367
reflex activity, 226
reflexes, newborns', 140–141, 190, 226
rehearsal, 278
reinforcement, 407
reinforcer, 210
  defined, 48
  secondary, 406
rejected aggressive children, 639
rejected children, 637
rejected withdrawn children, 639
relational aggression, 518
relational logic, 242
relational primary hypothesis, 294
relational self-worth, 448
relational similarity, 296
relationships. *See* caregiving; emotional
  attachments; friendships; peers
reliability, 12
REM sleep, 143
representational insight, 233–236
repression, 42
research/design methods, 11–33
  case studies and, 16
  clinical, 13–14
  correlational, 19–20
  cross-sectional, 24–26
  ethical considerations, 31–33
  ethnography and, 16–17
  experimental, 20–22
  fact finding and, 12–18
  interviews/questionnaires and, 13
  longitudinal, 26–28
  observational, 14–16
  psychophysiological, 17–18
  scientific, 11–12
  self-report, 12–13
  sequential, 28–29
  strengths, 18
  strengths and limitations, 24
  weaknesses, 18
resistant, 412, 420, 422
respiratory distress syndrome, 137
retaliatory aggression, 517
reticular formation, 156, 275
retrieval, 280
reverse anorexia, 177
reversibility, 238, 241
reversible activity, 224
RH factor, 135
rites of passage, 170–171
role taking, 466–460
roles, gender, 474–475
rubella (German measles), 116
rules, 292, 293

same, interactions, 629
savant syndrome, 318–319
scaffolding, 255
scheme, 52, 223
schizophrenia, 97–98
schools, 616–622
  class size and, 618–619
  classroom organization in, 619–620
  cultural differences/influences in, 625–628
  effectiveness of, 617–621
  socialization agent, as, 616–628
  special-needs students and, 624–625
  teacher expectancies and, 623–624
  transition to secondary, 622
scientific method, 11
script, 286
SE (shared environmental influence), 93
second stage of labour, 127
secondary circular reactions, 226–227
secular trend, 169, 331
secure base, 405
securely attached, 412
seduction hypothesis, 508
selective attention, 276
selective attrition, 27
selective breeding, 89–90
self
  conceptions of. *See* self-concept
  defined, 434
  destruction of, 449
  differentiation and recognition of, 435–438
  private/public, 439
  prosocial, development of, 530–538
self-care, 593–594
self-concept, 443–444
  achievement as motivation and, 451–459
  age and, 436, 469
  defined, 435
  development of, 434–443, 469
  morality and, 556
self-confidence, 172
self-esteem, 169–173, 446–450
  changes, 448–450
  components, 447–448
  peer, 450
  social comparison, 450
  social contributors to, 450
self-fulfilling prophecy, 481
self-oriented distress, 533
self-recognition, 436, 437
self-report methodologies, 12–14
semantic integration, 380
semantic organization, 280
semantics, 352, 365–371, 377–378, 380–381
sensation, 183
  and infant's experiences, 201–202
  defined, 184
  infant's experiences, and, 185–187
senses, 140–141, 188–191
  integration of, 201–202
sensimotor, 53
sensimotor play, 235
sensitive period, 115–116, 133
  defined, 60
sensitive-period hypothesis, 356
sensorimotor stage, 226, 229–232
sensory and perceptual development, 184–206
sensory capabilities, infants', 187–195
sensory store, 265
separation anxiety, 409–412
sequential design, 28–29
sex. *See also* gender
  chromosomes and. *See* chromosomes
  skill differences and, 165–166
sex differences, 473–482
  abilities and, 476–477, 478
  aggression and, 477, 517–518, 519

altruism and, 531
cultural myths and, 479–482
gender-typed behaviour and, 486, 487–488
home influence and, 481–482
psychological, 476
scholastic influence and, 482
socialization and, 476
sex-linked characteristics, 78–79
sex-role development, 490
sexual abuse, 598
sexual attitudes, 507–509
sexual development
  boys, in, 168
  girls, in, 167–168
  individual differences in, 168
sexual maturation, 167–169
sexual orientation, 508
  cliques and, 635
  families and, 585–586
  twin study and, 91
sexuality. *See also* sexual orientation
  adolescent, 505–513
  cultural differences/influences, 505–507
sexually transmitted diseases, 117
shared-attention mechanism, 442
shyness, cultural differences/influences and,
  403
sibling rivalry, 580
siblings, 46, 578–584
  communication skills and, 382–383
  environment and, 101
  experiences as, 96–97
sickle-cell anemia, 77–78, 84, 85, 87
SIDS (sudden infant death syndrome), 143–144
similarity relations, 294
size constancy, 197, 198
skeletal age, 152
skills
  academic, information processing and,
    297–303
  achievement motivation and, 451–459
  cognitive. *See* cognitive development
  communication, 378–379, 381–383
  gender and, 165–166
  language. *See* language
  manipulatory, 163–164
  mathematical. *See* arithmetic
  motor development and, 159–162
  problem-solving, 226–228
  sex and differences in, 165–166
  social, 642, 644
sleep, infants', 143
small for gestational age, 136
smell. *See* taste and smell
smoking, pregnancy and, 120
sociability, 632
social, 44
social class, 574–576, 578
  development, 5
  IQ and, 335
social cognition, 54
  cognitive-developmental theory of, 465
  role-taking theory of, 466–468
social cognitive development, 435
  aggression and, 529
  altruism and, 531–535
  knowing about others and, 463–470
  racism and, 464
  social influences on, 468–470
  theories of, 465–470
social conventional rules, 544
social deprivation, 23
social learning
  cognitive, theory, 48–49
  peers and, 628–649
  reciprocal determinism, as, 50
  schools and, 616–628

social learning theory, 65
social problem-solving training, 642
social referencing, 194, 396, 397
social skills, 632
social speech, 260
social stereotype, 13
social stimulation hypothesis, 426
social support, 644
social system, 564
socially mediated activity, 55
sociocultural theory
    arithmetic and, 300–301
    defined, 55, 252
    Vygotsky's, 55, 252–261
sociohistorical development, 253
sociolinguistic knowledge, 352
sociolinguistic understanding, 382
sociometric technique, 637
span of apprehension, 266
species heredity, 2
speech. See also language
    early, 371–374
    egocentric, 259
    fetal development and, 157
    infants and, 361–371
    learning, 233
    private, 259–260
    single-word, 371
    telegraphic, 371
    two-word, 372–373
spina bifida, 124–125
stability, 26
Stanford-Binet Intelligence Scale, 319–320
STDs (sexually transmitted diseases), 118, 510
stereopsis, 197
stereotype threat, 338
stereotyping. See also gender roles
    children and, 13
    television and, 608–609
stimulus, 143, 209–213
store model, 264–265
strange situation, 412
stranger anxiety, 409–412
strategic memory, 277
strategies, 268. See also research
        design/methods
    arithmetic, 298–301
    attentional, 275–276
    fact-finding, 12–18
    memory, 277–283
    multiple, 269–270
    variable, 269–270
strategy choice model, 270
stress, 191
structure-of-intellect model, 314
structured interview/questionnaire, 13
structured observation, 15
subculture, 16
sucking, 186–187, 210–213
suicide, 449
superego, 42
supermale syndrome, 82, 83
surfactin, 136
survival reflexes, 140–141
switch trials, 293
symbol, 237
symbolic function, 233
symbolic play, 235

symbolic schemes, 223–224
symbolism, 233, 234
    language, 234
sympathetic empathetic arousal, 533
synapse, 154
synaptic pruning, 154
synaptogensis, 154
synchronized routines, 403
syntactical bootstrapping, 369
syntax, 352, 369–370, 380
syphillis, 118, 119
systematic change, development, 2

tabula rasa, 47, 60, 184
    defined, 9
tacit intelligence, 327
taste and smell, infants', 190
Tay-Sachs disease, 84, 85, 87
television
    commercials, 609
    educational tool, as, 610–612
    effects of, 605–612
    literacy, development of, 606–607
    stereotyping and, 608–609
    viewing hours of, 605–606
temperament, 391, 398–402
    caregiving and, 420
    children, 401
    children's, divorce and, 588
    hereditary/environmental influences on,
        399
    moral development and, 559
    profiles, 400–402
    security and, 418–420
    stability of, 399–400
temperature, infants', 190–191
teratogens, 114–124
tertiary circular reactions, 227
test norms, 320
testes, 111
testicular feminization syndrome, 490
testosterone, 111, 174
thalidomide, 117–118, 119
theory of mind, 256, 439
theory of multiple intelligences, 318–319
"theory" theories, 232
theory/theories, 37–39. See also individual
        theories
    defined, 10, 37
    development of, 9–11
    language development, 353–361
    learning, 46–51
    philosophies underlying, 67
    scientific, 37–39
    world views and, 65–67
thinking. See reasoning
third stage of labour, 127
three-stratus theory of intelligence, 315
thyroxine, 174
time out, 214
time-out technique, 529
time-sampling, 15
timing-of-puberty effect, 490
tools of intellectual adaptation, 253–254, 302
touching, infants', 140–141, 190–191
toxoplasmosis, 116–117
transactional model, 574

transactive interactions, 549
transitivity, 242
triarchic theory, 316–318
trisomy, 21, 81
Turner's syndrome, 82, 83, 87
twin design (study), 90
twins
    dizygotic (fraternal), 74
    environment and, 101–103
    gender typing and, 494
    intelligence tests and, 91–94, 330
    low birth weight and, 138
    mental disorders and, 98
    monozgotic (identical), 73–74
    sexual orientation and, 91
    temperament and, 399
two-generation interventions, 342

UCR (unconditional response), 208
UCS (unconditional stimulus), 208
ulnar grasp, 163
ultrasound, 86, 111
umbilical cord, 110
unconscious motives, 42
unitary language system hypothesis, 385
utilization deficiencies, 268–269

validity, 12
verbal ability, 476
vernix, 113
video games. See under computers
violence. See also child abuse
    media, aggression and, 21, 22
    televised, 607–608
vision
    binocular, 197
    colour blindness, and, 77, 78–79
    infants', 187–200
    infants' colour, 187–188
visual acuity, 188
visual cliff, 198–200
visual contrast, 188, 197
visual looming, 197
visual/spatial abilities, 476
visually directed teaching, 224
vitamin/mineral deficiency, 276
vocables, 363

Wechsler Intelligence Scale for Children, 321
Wernicke's area, 355
whole language, 205
whole/part relations, 238
women
    employment and, 568, 592–594
    psychology of, 46
words. See language
working memory, 265

zone of proximal development, 254–255
    cultural differences/influences, 257
    defined, 55
zygote, 71, 108, 109, 114

Credits

Chapter 1

p. 22: Figure in Box 1.2 adapted from "Effects of Movie Violence on Aggression in a Field Setting as a Function of Group Dominance and Cohesion," by J.P. Leyens, R.D. Parke, L. Camino, & L. Berkowitz, 1975, *Journal of Personality and Social Psychology, 1*, pp. 346–60. Copyright ©1975 by the American Psychological Association. Adapted with permission.
p. 25: Figure 1.3 adapted from "Age and Verbalization in Observational Learning," by B. Coates and W.W. Hartup, 1969, *Developmental Psychology, 1*, pp. 556–62. Copyright © 1969 by the American Psychological Association. Adapted with permission.

Chapter 2

p. 49: Figure in Box 2.2 adapted from "Influence of Models' Reinforcement Contingencies on the Acquisition of Imitative Responses," by A. Bandura, 1965, *Journal of Personality and Social Psychology, 1*, pp. 589–95. Copyright © 1965 by the American Psychological Association.
p. 50: Figure 2.3 adapted from "The Self System in Reciprocal Determinism," by A. Bandura, 1978, *American Psychologist, 33*, p. 335. Copyright © 1978 by the American Psychological Association.
p. 63: Figure 2.4 based on *The Ecology of Human Development*, by U. Bronfenbrenner, 1979. Reprinted by permission of the author.

Chapter 3

p. 82: Table 3.1: Robinson et al., 1992; Plomin et al., 1997; Shaffer & Kuller, 1996.
p. 83: Table 3.2 adapted from "Increased Maternal Age and Prior Anenploid Conception," by H.H. Shafer & J.A. Kuller, 1996, in J.A. Kuller, N.C. Cheschier, & R.R. Cefalo (Eds.), *Prenatal Diagnosis and Reproductive Genetics*, pp. 23–28. St. Louis: CV Mosby Co.
p. 84: Table 3.3: Camp Jumoke, 2001; Kuller, Cheschier, & Cefalo, 1996; Strachan & Read, 1996.
p. 86: Figure 3.10 adapted from *Before We Are Born, 4th Ed.* by K.L. Moore & T.V.N. Persaud, 1993, p. 89. Philadelphia: Saunders. Adapted by permission of the author and publisher.
p. 90: Figure 3.11 from *Behavioral Genetics: A Primer, 3rd Ed.*, by R. Plomin, J.C. DeFries, & G.E. McClearn, 1997. Copyright © W.H. Freeman and Company.
p. 91: Figure 3.12 based on "A Genetic Study of the Male Sexual Orientation," by J.M. Bailey & R.C. Pillard, 1991, *Archives of General Psychiatry, 48*, pp. 1089–96. Copyright © 1991 by the Archives of General Psychiatry.

p. 91: Table 3.4 reprinted with permission from "Family Studies of Intelligence: A Review," by T.J. Bouchard, Jr., & M. McGue, 1981, *Science, 212*, pp. 1055–59. Copyright 1981 American Association for the Advancement of Science.
p. 94: Figure 3.13 from "The Louisville Twin Study: Developmental Sychronies in Behavior," by R.S. Wilson, 1983, *Child Development, 54*, pp. 298–316. Copyright © 1983 by The Society for Research in Child Development, Inc.
p. 96: Table 3.5: Loehlin, 1985; Loehlin and Nichols, 1976.
p. 99: Figure 3.14 adapted from "Heritability of Personality: A Demonstration," by I. Gottesman, 1963, *Psychological Monographs, 11* (Whole No. 572). Copyright © 1963 by the American Psychological Association.

Chapter 4

p. 112: Figure 4.4 adapted from *Before We Are Born*, 4th Ed., by K.L. Moore & T.V.N. Persauld, 1993. Philadelphia: Saunders. Adapted by permission from Elsevier.
p. 115: Figure 4.5 adapted from *Before We Are Born*, 4th Ed., by K.L. Moore & T.V.N. Persauld, 1993. Philadelphia: Saunders. Adapted by permission from Elsevier.
p. 117: Table 4.2: Carrington, 1995; Cates, 1995; Faden & Kass, 1996; Kelley-Buchanan, 1988.
p. 123: Table 4.3: Chavkin, 1995; Friedman & Polifka, 1996; Kelley-Buchanan, 1988.
p. 124: Figure 4.6 adapted from Stein & Susser, 1976.
p. 126: Figure 4.7 from Kessner, 1973.
p. 136: Figure 4.9 from Statistics Canada, Canadian Vital Statistics System, 1997, in Health Canada, *Canadian Perinatal Surveillance System* (2001B, Figure 4.7).
p. 138: Figure 4.10 adapted from "Risk and Resilience in Early Mental Development," by R.S. Wilson, 1985, *Developmental Psychology, 21*, pp. 795–805. Copyright © 1985 by the American Psychological Association. Reprinted with permission.
p. 143: Table 4.6: Wolff, 1966.

Chapter 5

p. 150: Figure 5.1 based on a figure in *Archives of the Diseases in Childhood, 41*, by J.M. Tanner, R.H. Whitehouse, & A. Takaishi, 1966, pp. 454–71. Copyright © 1966 by Tanner & Whitehouse (BMJ Publishing Group).
p. 152: Figure 5.4 from *Growth at Adolescence*, 2nd Ed., by J.M. Tanner, 1962. Oxford, England: Blackwell. Copyright © 1962 by Blackwell Scientific Publications, Inc. Reprinted by permission of Blackwell Science Ltd.
p. 154: Figure 5.5 from Janowsky & Carper, 1996.

p. 160: Table 5.1: Bayley, 1969; Frankenberg & Dodds, 1967.
p. 168: Figure 5.8 reprinted by permission of the publishers, from *Foetus into Man: Physical Growth from Conception to Maturity*, 2nd Ed., by J.M. Tanner, 1990. Cambridge, Mass.: Harvard University Press. Copyright © 1978, 1990 by J.M. Tanner.
p. 175: Figure 5.10 reprinted by permission of the publishers from *Foetus into Man: Physical Growth from Conception to Maturity*, 2nd Ed., by J.M. Tanner, 1990. Cambridge, Mass.: Harvard University Press. Copyright © 1978, 1990 by J.M. Tanner.
p. 178: Figure 5.11 adapted from "Long-Term Effects of Family-Based Treatment of Childhood Obesity," by L.H. Epstein, R.R. Wing, R. Koeske, & A. Valoski, 1987, *Journal of Consulting and Clinical Psychology, 55*, pp. 91–95. Copyright © 1987 by the American Psychological Association. Adapted with permission.

Chapter 6

p. 185: Figure 6.1 adapted from "'Perceptual Set' in Young Children," by H. W. Reese, 1963, *Child Development, 34*, pp. 151–59. Copyright © 1963 by the Society for Research in Child Development.
p. 192: Figure 6.3 adapted from "The Origin of Form Perception," by R.l. Fantz, May 1961, *Scientific American, 204*, p. 72 (top). Copyright ©1961 by Scientific American, Inc. Adapted by permission of the artist, Alex Semenoick.
p. 193: Figure 6.4 adapted from "Infant Visual Perception," by M.S. Banks, in collaboration with P. Salapatek, 1983, in *Handbook of Child Psychology, Vol. 2: Infancy and Developmental Psychobiology*, by M.M. Haith & J.J. Campos (Eds.). Copyright © 1983 by John Wiley & Sons. Adapted by permission of John Wiley & Sons, Inc.
p. 193: Figure 6.5 adapted from "Pattern Perception in Infancy," by P. Salapatek, 1975, in *Infant Perception: From Sensation to Cognition*, by L.B. Cohen & P. Salapatek (Eds.). Copyright © 1975 by Academic Press, Inc. Adapted by permission.
p. 194: Figure 6.6 adapted from "Perception of Partly Occluded Objects in Infancy," by P.J. Kellman & E.S. Spelke, 1983, *Cognitive Psychology, 15*, pp. 483–524. Copyright © 1983 by Academic Press, Inc. Adapted by permission.
p. 195: Figure 6.7 adapted from "Development of Visual Organization: The Perception of Subjective Contours," by B.I. Bertenthal, J.J. Campos, & M.M. Haith, 1980, *Child Development, 51*, pp. 1077–80. Copyright © 1980 by the Society for Research in Child Development, Inc. Adapted by permission.

p. 195: Figure 6.8 from "Infant Sensitivity to Figural Coherence in Biomechanical Motions," by B.I. Bertenthal, D.R. Proffitt, & J.E. Cutting, 1984, *Journal of Experimental Child Psychology*, 37, pp. 213–30. Copyright © 1984 by Academic Press, Inc.

p. 197: Figure 6.9 adapted with permission from "Development of Sensitivity of Pivtorial Depth," by A. Yonus, W. Cleaves, & L. Peterson, 1978, *Science*, 200, pp. 77–79. Copyright © 1978 by the American Association for the Advancement of Science.

p. 197: Figure 6.10 from "Infants' Perceptions of Pictorially Specified Interposition," by C.E. Granrud & A. Yonus, 1984, *Journal of Experimental Child Psychology*, 377, pp. 500-11. Copyright © 1984 by Academic Press, Inc. Reprinted by permission.

p. 199: Figure 6.12 adapted from "Locomotor Status and the Development of Spatial Search Skills," by D.L. Bai & B.J. Bertenthal, 1992, *Child Development*, 63, pp. 215–26. Copyright 1992 by The Society for Research in Child Development, Inc.

p. 204: Figure 6.14 adapted from "A Developmental Study of the Discrimination of Letter-like Forms," by E.J. Gibson, J.J. Gibson, A.D. Pick, & H.A. Osser, 1962, *Journal of Comparative and Physiological Psychology*, 55, pp. 897–906.

Chapter 7

p. 230: Figure in Box 7.1 based on "Object Permanence in 3 1/2- and 4 1/2-Month-Old Infants," by R. Baillargeon, 1987, *Developmental Psychology*, 23, pp. 655–64. Copyright © 1987 by the American Psychological Association. Adapted by permission.

p. 232: Figure 7.2 from Bjorklund, 2000.

p. 234: Figure 7.3 from "Rapid Change in the Symbolic Functioning of Very Young Children," by J.S. DeLoache, 1987, *Science, 238*, pp. 1556–57. Copyright © 1987 by the American Association for the Advancement of Science. Reprinted by permission.

p. 247: Figure 7.8 adapted from "Individual Differences in College Students' Performance on Operational Tasks," by R. DeLisi & J. Staudt, 1980, *Journal of Applied Developmental Psychology, 1*, pp. 163–74. Reprinted with the permission of Ablex Publishing Company.

Chapter 8

p. 265: Figure 8.1 adapted from "Human Memory: A Proposed System and Its Control Processes," by R.C. Atkinson & R.M. Shiffrin, 1968, in K.W. Spence & J.T. Spence (Eds.), *The Psychology of Learning and Motivation: Advances in Research and Theory (Vol. 2).* Copyright © 1968 by Academic Press, Inc. Adapted by permission.

p. 267: Figure 8.2 adapted from "Memory Span: Sources of Individual and Developmental Differences," by F.N. Dempster, 1981, *Psychological Bulletin, 89*, pp. 63–100. Copyright © 1981 by the American Psychological Association.

p. 267: Figure 8.3 from "Knowledge Structures and Memory Development," by M.H.T. Chi, 1978, in R.S. Siegler (Ed.), *Children's Thinking: What Develops?* Copyright © 1978 by Lawrence Erlbaum Associates, Inc. Reprinted with permission.

p. 270: Figure 8.4 from Siegler, 1996c.

p. 272: Figure 8.5 reproduced with permission of author and published from Gollin, E.S. "Factors affecting the visual recognition of incomplete objects: A comparative investigation of children and adults." *Perceptual and Motor Skills, 15,* 583–590. © Southern Universities Press 1962.

p. 276: Figure 8.6 based on "The Development of Scanning Strategies and Their Relation to Visual Differentiation," by E. Vurpillot, 1968, *Journal of Experimental Child Psychology, 6*, pp. 632–50.

p. 283: Figure 8.8 adapted from data presented in "Domain-Specific Knowledge and Memory Performance: A Comparison of High- and Low-Aptitude Children," by W. Schneider, J. Korkel, & F.E. Weinert, 1989, *Journal of Educational Psychology, 81*, pp. 306–12.

p. 285: Figure in Box 8.3 from "Childhood Amnesia and the Beginnings of Memory of Four Life Events," by J.A. Usher & U. Neisser, 1993, *Journal of Experimental Psychology: General, 122*, pp. 155–65. Copyright © 1993 by the American Psychological Association. Reprinted with permission.

p. 286: Figure in Box 8.4 adapted from Peterson & Whalen.

p. 293: Figure 8.9 from P.D. Zelazo, D. Frye, & T. Raptus (1996). An age related dissociation between knowing rules and using them. *Cognitive Development, 11,* 37–63. Reprinted with permission from Elsevier.

p. 295: Figure 8.10 from Z. Chen, R.P. Sanchez, & T. Campbell (1997), Beyond to within their grasp: The rudiment of analogical problem solving in 10- and 13-month-olds. *Developmental Psychology, 33*, 790–801. Copyright © 1997 by the American Psychological Association.

p. 295: Figure 8.11 from U. Goswami & A.L. Brown (1990). Higher order structure and relational reasoning: Contrasting analogical and thematic relations. *Cognition, 36*, 207–226. Reprinted with permission of Elsevier Science.

p. 302: From "Contents of Achievement; A Study of American, Chinese, and Japanese Children," by H.W. Stevenson & S.Y. Lee, *Monographs of the Society for Research in Child Development*, 55 (1-2, Serial No. 221). Copyright ©1990 by the Society for Research in Child Development, Inc. Reprinted by permission.

Chapter 9

p. 315: Figure 9.2 adapted from a table in *The Nature of Human Intelligence*, by J.P. Guilford, 1967. Copyright © 1967 by McGraw-Hill, Inc. Adapted by permission.

p. 316: Figure 9.3 from *Human Cognitive Abilities: A Survey of Factor-Analytic Studies*, by J.B. Carroll, 1993. Copyright 1993 by Cambridge University Press. Reprinted by permission.

p. 318: Table 9.1 adapted from *Frames of Mind: The Theory of Multiple Intelligences*, by Howard Gardner, 1983. Copyright © 1983 by Howard Gardner. Reprinted by permission of BasicBooks, a division of Perseus Books Group, LLC.

p. 322: Figure 9.5: Reprinted with permission of the publisher, from *Assessment of Children: Cognitive Applications*, Fourth Edition (2001) by Jerome M. Sattler and published by Jerome M. Sattler, Publisher, Inc.

p. 325: Table 9.2 adapted from Honzik, Macfarlane, & Allen, 1948.

p. 326: Figure 9.6 from "The Effects of Global Severe Privation on Cognitive Competence: Extension and Longitudinal Follow-up," by T.G. O'Connor, M. Rutter, C. Beckett, L. Keaveney, J.M. Kreppner, & the English and Romanian Adoptees Study Team, 2000, *Child Development, 71,* 376–390.

p. 327: Figure 9.7 from "Toward Meritocracy? Changing Social-Class Differences in Intellectual Ability," by D. Weakliem, J. McQuillan, & T. Schauer, 1995, *Sociology of Education, 68*, pp. 271–86 (Fig. 1, p. 276). Reprinted by permission.

p. 329: Table in Box 9.3 adapted from Ross et al., 1985.

p. 332: Table 9.3: Data and descriptions compiled from Sameroff et al., 1993.

p. 333: Table 9.4 adapted from Caldwell & Bardley, 1984.

p. 335: Figure 9.8 based on Brody, 1992; Neisser et al., 1996.

p. 338: Figure in Box 9.4 adapted from "Stereotype Threat and the Intellectual Test Performance of African Americans," by C.M. Steele & J. Aronson, 1995, *Journal of Personality and Social Psychology, 69*, pp. 797–811 (Fig. 2, p. 802). Copyright © 1995 by the American Psychological Association. Adapted by permission.

p. 339: Figure 9.10 adapted from *Psychology*, 3rd Ed., by Henry Gleitman, p. 699. Copyright © 1991, 1986, 1981 by W.W. Norton & Company, Inc. Reprinted by permission of W.W. Norton & Company, Inc.

p. 343: Figure 9.11 adapted from "Effects of Early Intervention on Intellectual and Academic Achievement," by F.A. Campbell & C.T. Ramey, 1994, *Child Development, 65*, pp. 684–98. Copyright © 1994 by the Society for Research in Child Development, Inc. Adapted by permission of the author.

p. 344: Figure 9.12 adapted from *Modes Thinking in Young Children of the Creativity-Intelligence Distinction*, 1st Edition by Michael A. Wallach & Nathan Kogan. Copyright © 1965. Reprinted with permission of Wadsworth, a division of Thomson Learning: www.thomson-rights.com. Fax 800-730-2215.

Chapter 10

p. 356: Figure 10.2 adapted from "Critical Period Effects in Second Language Learning: The Influence of Maturational State on the Acquisition of English as a Second Language," by J.S. Johnson & E.L. Newport, 1989, *Cognitive Psychology, 21*, pp. 60–99. Copyright © 1989 by Academic Press, Inc. Adapted by permission.

p. 366: Table 10.1 adapted from Nelson, 1973.

p. 371: Table 10.3 adapted from *Psycholinguistics*, 2nd Ed., by Dan Isaac Slobin, 1979, pp. 86–87. Copyright © 1979, 1974, 1971 by Scott, Foresman and Company. Adapted by permission of Addison Wesley Educational Publishers Inc.

p. 373: Figure in Box 10.3 from *Talk to the Deaf*, by Lottie Reikehof, 1963. Springfield, MO: Gospel Publishing House. Reprinted by permission.

p. 375: Table 10.4 adapted from McNeill, 1970.

p. 375: Table 10.5 adapted from *Psychology and Language: An Introduction to Psycholinguistics*, by H.H. Clark & E.V. Clark, p. 345. Copyright © 1977 by Harcourt Brace & Company.

p. 376: Figure 10.5 from "A Child's Learning of English Morphology," by J. Berko, 1958, *Word, 14*, pp. 150–77.

p. 382: Table 10.6 adapted from "Social and Non-Social Speech," by R.M. Krauss & S. Glucksberg, *Scientific American*, February 1977, *236*, p. 104. Copyright © 1977 by Scientific American, Inc. Adapted by permission of the artist, Jerome Kuhl.

Chapter 11

p. 395: Figure 11.2 adapted from "An Observational Study of Children's Attempts to

Monitor Their Expressive Behavior," C. Saarni, 1984, *Child Development, 55*, 1504–13. Copyright © 1984 by The Society for Research in Child Development, Inc. Adapted by permission.

p. 399: Figure 11.3 based on Braungart et al., 1992; Emde et al., 1992.

p. 408: Figure 11.4 adapted from "The Innate Forms of Possible Experience," by K.Z. Lorenz, 1943, *Zeitschrift fur Tierpsychologie, 5*, pp. 233–409.

p. 412: Table 11.2 based on *Patterns of Attachment*, by M.D.S. Ainsworth, M. Blehar, E. Waters, & S. Wall, 1978. Copyright © 1978 by Lawrence Erlbaum Associates, Inc.

p. 415: Table 11.3 based on "Sensitivity and Attachment: A Meta-Analysis on Parental Antecedents on Infant Attachment," by M.S. De Wolff & M.H. van Ijzendoorn, 1997, *Child Development, 68*, pp. 571–91.

p. 418: Table 11.4: Ainsworth et al., 1978; Thomas & Chess, 1977.

p. 419: Table in Box 11.3 adapted from "The Quality of the Toddler's Relationship to Mother and to Father: Related to Conflict and the Readiness to Establish New Relationships," by M. Main & D.R. Weston, 1981, *Child Development, 52*, pp. 932–40. Copyright © 1981 by the Society for Research in Child Development, Inc.

p. 420: Figure 11.5 based on "The Relative Effects of Maternal and Child Problems on the Quality of Attachment in Clinical Samples," by M.H. van Ijzendoorn, S. Goldberg, P.M. Kroonenberg, & O.J. Frenkel, 1992, *Child Development, 63*, pp. 840–58. Copyright © 1992 by the Society for Research in Child Development, Inc.

p. 422: Figure 11.6 adapted from "Attachment Styles Among Young Adults: A Test of a Four Category Model," by K. Bartholomew & L.M. Horowitz, 1991, *Journal of Personality and Social Psychology, 61*, pp. 226–44. Copyright © 1991 by the American Psychological Association. Adapted by permission.

p. 422: Figure 11.7 based on Belsky, Spritz, & Crnic, 1996.

p. 431: Table 11.6: Kamerman, 2000.

Chapter 12

p. 438: Figure 12.1 based on "The Relation between Attachment and Knowledge of Self and Mother in One- to Three-Year-Old Infants," by S. Pipp, M.A Easterbrooks, & R.J. Harmon, 1992, *Child Development, 63*, pp. 738–50. Copyright © 1992 by the Society for Research in Child Development, Inc.

p. 444: Figure 12.2 adapted from "Developmental Analysis of Conflict Caused by Opposing Attributes in the Adolescent Self-Portrait," by S. Harter & A. Monsour, 1992, *Developmental Psychology, 28*, pp. 251–260. Copyright © 1992 by the American Psychological Association. Adapted by permission.

p. 445: Figure in Box 12.3 adapted from Cousins, 1989.

p. 447: Figure 12.3 adapted from "Historical Roots in Contemporary Issues Involving Self Concept," by S. Harter, 1996, in *Handbook of self-concept: Developmental, social, and clinical considerations*, B.A. Braken (Ed.) New York: Wiley.

p. 449: Figure in Box 12.4 from Statistics Canada, 1997.

p. 454: Table 12.1 adapted from "The Relationship Between Twelve-Month Home Stimulation and School Achievement," by W.J. van Doorninck, B.M. Caldwell, C. Wright, & W.K. Frankenberg, 1981, *Child Development, 52*,

pp. 1080–83. Copyright © 1981 by The Society for the Research in Child Development, Inc. Adapted by permission.

p. 460: Figure 12.7 from "Cross-Sectional Age Changes in Ego Identity Status During Adolescence," by P.W. Meilman, 1979, *Developmental Psychology, 15*, pp. 230–231. Copyright © 1979 by the American Psychological Association. Reprinted with permission.

p. 465: Figure 12.8 from "The Development of Person Perception in Childhood and Adolescence: From Behavioural Comparisons to Psychological Constructs to Psychological Comparisons," by C. Barenboim, 1981, *Child Development, 52*, pp. 129–44. Copyright © 1981 by Society for Research in Child Development, Inc. Reprinted by permission.

p. 467: Table 12.3 adapted from "Social Cognitive Understanding: A Guide to Educational and Clinical Experience," by R.L. Selman, 1976, in T. Lickona (Ed.), *Moral Development and Behavior: Theory, Research, and Social Issues*. Copyright © 1976 by Holt, Rinehart & Winston. Adapted by permission of the editor.

Chapter 13

p. 475: Table 13.1 adapted from Barry, Bacon & Child, 1957.

p. 477: Figure 13.1 from "Emergence and Characteristics of Sex Differences in Spatial Ability: A Meta-Analysis," by M.C. Linn & A.C. Petersen, 1985, *Child Development, 56*, pp. 1479–98. Copyright © 1985 by the Society for Research in Child Development, Inc. Reprinted with permission.

p. 477: Figure 13.2 adapted from "Gender Differences in Mathematics Performance: A Meta-Analysis," by J. S. Hyde, E. Fennema, & S.J. Lamon, 1990, *Psychological Bulletin, 107*, pp. 139–55. Copyright © 1990 by the American Psychological Association. Adapted by permission.

p. 485: Figure 13.3 adapted from "Children's Concepts of Cross-Gender Activities," by T. Stoddart & E. Turiel, 1985, *Child Development, 59*, pp. 793–814. Copyright © 1985 by the Society for Research in Child Development, Inc. Adapted by permission.

p. 487: Figure 13.4 adapted from "Social Behavior at 33 Months in Same-Sex and Mixed-Sex Dyads," by C.N. Jacklin & E.E. Maccoby, 1978, *Child Development, 49*, pp. 557–69. Copyright © 1978 by the Society for Research in Child Development, Inc. Adapted by permission.

p. 488: Table 13.2 adapted from Richardson & Simpson, 1982.

p. 491: Figure 13.5 from *Man and Woman, Boy and Girl*, by J. Money & A. Ehrhardt, 1972. Copyright © 1972 by Johns Hopkins University Press. Reprinted by permission.

p. 499: Figure 13.6 adapted from "The Roles of Cognition in Sex Roles and Sex-Typing," 1987, in D.B. Carter (Ed.), *Current Conceptions of Sex Roles and Sex-Typing: Theory and Research*. Copyright © 1987 by Praeger Publishers.

p. 502: Table 13.5 adapted from "Assessing Sex-Typing and Androgyny in Children: The Children's Sex-Role Inventory," by J.P. Boldizar, 1991, *Developmental Psychology, 27*, pp. 505–15. Copyright © 1991 by the American Psychological Association. Adapted with permission. Items from BEM Sex Role Inventory reproduced by special permission of the Publisher, Mind Garden, Inc., 1690 Woodside Road #202, Redwood City, CA 94061 USA www.mindgarden.com from the *BEM Sex Role Inventory* by Sandra Bem. Copyright 1978 by Consulting Psychologists Press, Inc. All rights

reserved. Further reproduction is prohibited without the Publisher's written consent.

p. 509: Figure 13.8: Data for first three time periods adapted from Dreyer, 1982; data for more recent periods from Baier, Rosenzweig, & Whipple, 1991; Centers for Disease Control, 1992; Reinisch et al., 1992; McKenna, 1997.

Chapter 14

p. 518: Figure 14.1 from "Stability of Aggression over Time and Generations," by L.R. Huesmann, L.D. Eron, M.M. Lefkowitz, & L.O. Walder, 1984, *Developmental Psychology, 20*, p. 1125. Copyright © 1984 by the American Psychological Association. Reprinted by permission.

p. 519: Figure in Box 14.1 adapted from "Relational Aggression, Gender, and Social-Psychological Adjustment," by N.A. Crick & J.K. Grotpeter, 1995, *Child Development, 66*, pp. 710–22. Copyright © 1995 by the Society for Research in Child Development, Inc.

p. 521: Figure 14.2 adapted from "A Review and Reformation of Social Information Processing Machanisms in Children's Social Adjustment," by N.R. Crick & K.A. Dodge, *Psychological Bulletin, 115*, pp. 74–101. Copyright © 1994 by the American Psychological Association.

p. 527: Figure 14.4 adapted from "A Developmental Perspective on Antisocial Behavior," by G.R. Patterson, B.D. DeBaryshe, & E. Ramsey, 1989, *American Psychologist, 44*, pp. 329–35. Copyright © 1989 by the American Psychological Association. Adapted by permission.

p. 533: Table 14.1 adapted from "Prosocial Development: A Longitudinal Study," by N. Eisenberg, R. Lennon, & K. Roth, 1983, *Developmental Psychology, 19*, pp. 846–55. Copyright © 1983 by the American Psychological Association. Adapted by permission.

p. 535: Table 14.2 based on data from *Children of Six Cultures*, by B.B. Whiting & J.W.M. Whiting. Cambridge, Mass.: Harvard University Press. Copyright © 1975 by the President and Fellows of Harvard College.

p. 536: Figure in Box 14.5 adapted from Lee et al., 1997.

p. 538: Table 14.3 from L.J. Walker and R.C. Pitts, "Naturalistic Conceptions of Moral Maturity," *Developmental Psychology* (1998), No. 34, p. 403–419. Copyright © 1998 by the American Psychological Association. Reprinted with permission.

p. 543: Figure 14.6 adapted from "Factors Influencing Young Children's Use of Motives and Outcomes as Moral Criteria," by S.A. Nelson, 1980, *Child Development, 51*, pp. 823–29. Copyright © 1980 by the Society for Research in Child Development, Inc. Adapted by permission

p. 543: Figure 14.7 adapted from "Factors Influencing Young Children's Use of Motives and Outcomes as Moral Criteria," by S.A. Nelson, 1980, *Child Development, 51*, pp. 823–29. Copyright © 1980 by the Society for Research in Child Development, Inc. Adapted by permission.

p. 548: Figure 14.8 adapted from "A Longitudinal Study of Moral Judgement," by A. Colby, L. Kohlberg, J. Gibbs, & M. Lieberman, 1983, *Monographs of the Society for Research in Child Development, 48*, (Nos. 1–2, Serial No. 200). Copyright © 1983 by the Society for Research in Child Development, Inc. Adapted by permission.

p. 551: Figure in Box 14.6 adapted from "Culture and Moral Development," by R.

Shweder, M. Mahapatra, & J.G. Miller, 1987, in J. Kagan & S. Lamb (Eds.), *The Emergence of Morality in Young Children*. Copyright © 1987 University of Chicago Press. Adapted by permission.

p. 557: Table 14.4 adapted from "Contributions of Parents and Peers to Children's Moral Socialization," by G.H. Brody & D.R. Shaffer, 1982, *Developmental Review, 2*, pp. 31–75. Copyright © 1982 by Academic Press, Inc. Adapted by permission.

Chapter 15

p. 565: Figure 15.1 from "Early Human Experience: A Family Perspective," by J. Belsky, 1981, *Developmental Psychology, 17*, pp. 3–23. Copyright © 1981 by the American Psychological Association. Reprinted by permission.

p. 568: Figure 15.2 adapted from Kidder et al., 2000.

p. 571: Figure 15.3 based on data from "Socialization in the Context of the Family: Parent-Child Interaction," by E.E. Maccoby & J.A. Martin, 1983, in E.M. Hetherington (Ed.: P.H. Mussen, General Ed.), *Handbook of Child Psychology, Vol. 4: Socialization, Personality, and Social Development*, 4th Ed. New York: John Wiley and Sons.

p. 572: Table 15.1: Baumrind, 1977, 1991; Steinberg et al., 1994.

p. 575: Figure 15.4 adapted from "A Family Process Model of Economic Hardship and Adjustment of Early Adolescent Boys," by R.D. Conger, G.H. Elder, Jr., F.O. Lorenz, R.L. Simons, & L.B. Whitbeck, 1992, *Child Development, 63*, pp. 526–41. Copyright © 1992 by the Society for Research in Child Development, Inc.

p. 579: Figure in Box 15.2 adapted from "The Effects of Work Intensity on Adolescent Mental Health, Achievement, and Behavioral Adjustment: New Evidence from a Prospective Study," by J.T. Mortimer, M.D. Finch, S. Ryu, M.J. Shanahan, & K.T. Call, 1996, *Child Development, 67*, pp. 1243–61. Copyright ©

1996 by the Society for Research in Child Development, Inc. Adapted by permission.

p. 585: Figure 15.5 adapted from Bailey et al., 1995; Golombok & Tasker, 1996.

p. 589: Figure 15.6 adapted from "Relation of Parental Transitions to Boys' Adjustment Problems: I. A Linear Hypothesis. II. Mothers at Risk for Transition and Unskilled Parenting," by D.M. Capaldi & G.R. Patterson, 1991 by American Psychological Association.

p. 599: Figure 15.7 adapted from "Responses of Abused and Disadvantaged Toddlers to Distress in Agemates: A Study in Day-Care Setting," by M. Main & C. George, 1985, *Developmental Psychology, 21*, pp. 407–12. Copyright © 1985 by the American Psychological Association. Adapted by permission.

Chapter 16

p. 606: Table 16.1: Statistics Canada, 2003.

p. 608: Figure 16.1 adapted from "Psychological Processes Promoting the Relation between Exposure to Media Violence and Aggressive Behavior by the Viewer," by L.R. Huesmann, 1986, *Journal of Social Issues, 42*, No. 3, pp. 125–39. Copyright © 1986 by the Journal of Social Issues. Adapted by permission.

p. 610: Table 16.2: Slaby et al., 1995; Seppa, 1997b.

p. 612: Figure 16.2 from *The Early Window: Effects of Television on Children and Youth*, 3rd. Ed., by R.M. Liebert & J. Sprafkin, 1988. Copyright © 1988. Reprinted by permission of Allyn & Bacon.

p. 618: Figure 16.3 reprinted by permission of the publisher from *Fifteen Thousand Hours* by Michael Rutter, Barbara Maughan, Peter Mortimore and Janet Ouston, p. 166, Cambridge, Mass.: Harvard University Press, Copyright © 1980 by Nuffield Provincial Hospitals Trust.

p. 619: Figure 16.4 from "Do Extracurricular Activities Protect Against Early School Dropout?"

by J.L. Mahoney & R.B. Cairns, 1997, *Developmental Psychology, 33*, pp. 241–52. Copyright © 1997 by the American Psychological Association. Reprinted by permission.

p. 626: Table 16.3: Statistics Canada, 2003.

p. 627: Figure 16.5 adapted from "Motivation and Mathematical Achievement: A Comparative Study of Asian-American, and East-Asian High School Students," by C. Chen & H.W. Stevenson, 1995, *Child Development, 66*, pp. 1215–34. Copyright © 1995 by the Society for Research in Child Development, Inc. Adapted by permission.

p. 630: Figure 16.6 adapted from "Age Segregation in Children's Social Interactions," by S. Ellis, B. Rogoff, & C.C. Cromer, 1981, *Developmental Psychology, 17*, pp. 399–407. Copyright © 1981 by the American Psychological Association. Adapted by permission.

p. 633: Figure 16.7 adapted from "Social Participation among Preschool Children," by M. Parten, 1932, *Journal of Abnormal and Social Psychology, 27*, pp. 243–69.

p. 634: Table 16.4 adapted from "Sequences in the Development of Competent Play with Peers: Social and Social Pretend Play," by C. Howes & C.C. Matheson, 1992, *Developmental Psychology, 28*, pp. 961–74. Copyright © 1992 by the American Psychological Association. Adapted by permission.

p. 636: Figure 16.8 based on "Parents' Management for Preschoolers' Peer Relations: Is It Related to Children's Social Competence?" by G.W, Ladd & B.S. Golter, 1988, *Developmental Psychology, 24*, pp. 109–17. Copyright © 1988 by the American Psychological Association.

p. 646: Figure 16.9 adapted from "Developmental Changes in Conformity to Peers and Parents," by T.J. Berndt, 1979, *Developmental Psychology, 15*, pp. 608–16. Copyright © 1979 by the American Psychological Association. Adapted by permission.